W. B. YEATS : A LIFE

W. B. YEATS : A LIFE

I : THE APPRENTICE MAGE
1865–1914

R. F. FOSTER

Oxford   New York

OXFORD UNIVERSITY PRESS

1997

Oxford University Press, Great Clarendon Street, Oxford OX2 6DP

Oxford New York
Athens Auckland Bangkok Bogota Bombay
Buenos Aires Calcutta Cape Town Dar es Salaam
Delhi Florence Hong Kong Istanbul Karachi
Kuala Lumpur Madras Madrid Melbourne
Mexico City Nairobi Paris Singapore
Taipei Tokyo Toronto
and associated companies in
Berlin Ibadan

Oxford is a trade mark of Oxford University Press

Published in the United States by
Oxford University Press Inc., New York

British Library Cataloguing in Publication Data
Data available

Library of Congress Cataloging in Publication Data
Foster, R. F. (Robert Fitzroy), 1949–
W. B. Yeats : a life / R. F. Foster.
p. cm.
Includes bibliographical references and index.
Contents: 1. The apprentice mage, 1865–1914
1. Yeats, W. B. (William Butler), 1865–1939—Biography. 2. Poets,
Irish—19th century—Biography. 3. Poets, Irish—20th century—
Biography. 4. Ireland—Intellectual life. I. Title.
PR5906.F66 1997 821'.8—dc20 96–31671
ISBN 0–19–211735–1

1 3 5 7 9 10 8 6 4 2

Typeset in 11/13 pt. Adobe Caslon
by Graphicraft Typesetters Ltd, Hong Kong
Printed in Great Britain by
The Bath Press, Bath

In memory of Francis Stewart Leland Lyons

Supposing the mage to stand outside the All, his evocations and invocations would no longer avail to draw up or to call down; but as things are he operates from no outside standground, he pulls, knowing the pull of everything towards anything in the living system.

Plotinus, *Enneads* (IV, 4, 40),
translated by Stephen MacKenna

A poet is by the very nature of things a man who lives with entire sincerity, or rather the better his poetry the more sincere his life; his life is an experiment in living and those that come after have a right to know it. Above all it is necessary that the lyric poet's life be known that we should understand that his poetry is no rootless flower but the speech of a man. To achieve anything in any art, to stand alone perhaps for many years, to go a path no other man has gone, to accept one's own thought when the thought of others has the authority of the world behind it, that it should seem but a little thing to give one's life as well as one's words which are so much nearer one's soul, to the criticism of the world.

W. B. Yeats, draft of lecture 'Friends of my Youth',
delivered 9 March 1910

CONTENTS

LIST OF ILLUSTRATIONS   xi

SOURCES OF ILLUSTRATIONS   xiv

ACKNOWLEDGEMENTS   xv

FOREWORD   xix

FAMILY TREES   xx

INTRODUCTION   xxv

PROLOGUE   Yeatses and Pollexfens   1

Chapter   1   The Artist's Children: Sligo 1865–1881   6

2   Explorations: Dublin 1881–1887   28

3   Two Years: Bedford Park 1887–1889   59

4   Secret Societies 1889–1891   89

5   The Battles of the Books 1891–1893   112

6   Lands of Heart's Desire 1894–1896   135

7   Waiting for the Millennium 1896–1898   162

8   Shadowy Waters 1898–1900   201

9   Occult Politics 1900–1901   225

10   National Dramas 1901–1902   257

11   The Taste of Salt 1902–1903   282

12   From America to Abbey Street 1903–1904   304

13   Delighting in Enemies 1905–1906   330

14   Synge and the Ireland of His Time 1907–1909   359

15   Severances 1909–1910   402

16   True and False Irelands 1910–1911   433

17   Ghosts 1911–1913   453

18   Memory Harbour 1913–1914   492

CONTENTS

APPENDIX: 'The Poet Yeats Talks Drama with Ashton Stevens',
          from the *San Francisco Examiner*, 30 January 1904   533

ABBREVIATIONS   539

NOTES   542

INDEX   626

ILLUSTRATIONS

Jack B. Yeats, detail from *Memory Harbour*, 1900   *front endpaper*

LIST OF PLATES

Between pages 160 *and* 161

1. John Butler Yeats, 1863
   Susan Pollexfen Yeats as a young married woman
   WBY as a baby, 1865

2. WBY as a child, Sligo, *c.* 1873

3. Sandymount Castle, Dublin, with Corbets and Yeatses
   Merville, Sligo

4. Sligo Harbour in the late nineteenth century
   The Middleton & Pollexfen mills, Ballisodare

5. John Butler Yeats, *c.* 1875
   George Pollexfen, *c.* 1906

6. Sketches by the Yeats children of Branscombe, Devon
   WBY aged about nine

7. WBY, late 1880s
   Jack Yeats, 1900
   George Russell ('AE'), 1890

8. 3 Blenheim Road, Bedford Park

9. Lily and Lolly, early 1890s
   WBY as 'King Goll' by JBY, 1887

10. Maud Gonne, 1889
    Maud Gonne, early 1890s

11. WBY, probably with John Todhunter, early 1890s

12. WBY at Blenheim Road
    MacGregor Mathers

13. *The Land of Heart's Desire*, April 1894
    Florence Farr

14. Constance and Eva Gore-Booth
    Arthur Symons, 1896

15. WBY in his study, 1904
    Woburn Buildings

16. Olivia Shakespear, 1897

ILLUSTRATIONS

Between pages 352 and 353

17. Augusta Gregory, *c.* 1912

18. Tillyra Castle
     Coole Park

19. WBY and George Moore at Coole, 1902

20. Robert Gregory, 1902
     Margaret Gregory with Richard, 1909
     Willie Fay
     Frank Fay as Cuchulain, 1904

21. *Cathleen ni Houlihan*, 1902
     Riders to the Sea, 1906

22. Annie Horniman's costumes for *The King's Threshold*, 1903
     Charles Ricketts's costumes for *On Baile's Strand*, 1915

23. The foyer of the Abbey Theatre
     The stage of the Abbey Theatre

24. The Abbey Theatre, embroidered by Lily Yeats

25. Maud Gonne MacBride, John MacBride and their baby Seaghan (Seán), 1904
     John Quinn
     WBY arrives in New York, 1903

26. Printing at Dun Emer, 1903

27. John Butler Yeats, 1906
     WBY as seen by Augustus John, 1907

28. WBY, Jack and Cottie Yeats and Sara Allgood at Ruth Pollexfen's wedding, 1911

29. Ezra Pound, *c.* 1913
     George Hyde-Lees, *c.* 1910
     Stone Cottage

30. Rabindranath Tagore

31. A spirit photograph of WBY
     'Julia's Bureau'
     Etta Wriedt

32. Iseult Gonne, *c.* 1906
     Maud Gonne, *c.* 1906
     WBY, *c.* 1910

LIST OF TEXT ILLUSTRATIONS

Binding design for *The Wind Among the Reeds*   xxiv

1. Susan Pollexfen Yeats and Lily Yeats, 13 February 1870   22

2. WBY drawn by JBY for the frontispiece of *Mosada*, 1886   40

3. John O'Leary by JBY 42

4. Katharine Tynan by William Strang 54

5. 'A Legend' in the *Vegetarian*, 22 December 1888 66

6. Frontispiece of *Poems* (1895) 151

7. Edward Martyn by Grace Plunkett 166

8. George Russell sketching at Coole 183

9. WBY and the Black Pig, by Russell 192

10. Synge, WBY and Russell fishing at Coole 248

11. Killeeneen *feis* programme, 31 August 1902 271

12. Annie Horniman by JBY 297

13. WBY lecturing in America, as seen by Jack Yeats 310

14. Robert Gregory on 'Sarsfield', 25 September 1906 351

15. Synge at a *Playboy* rehearsal, 25 January 1907 361

16. *The Abbey Row*, a Dublin pamphlet immortalizing the *Playboy* controversy 362

17. 'The Gift' as printed in the *Irish Times*, 11 January 1913 480

18. 'The "Playboy" and the Gallery' as seen by the *Leader*, 5 April 1913 484

Robert Gregory, detail from *Lake at Coole*, n.d. *back endpaper*

SOURCES OF ILLUSTRATIONS

ALL illustrations are reproduced by courtesy of Michael B. Yeats and Anne Yeats, photography by Rex Roberts, with the following exceptions.

PLATES

1 (*top left*) Courtesy of William M. Murphy
4 (*both*) Author's collection
7 (*bottom*) From John Eglinton, *Memoir of A. E.*, 1937
8 Department of English, University of Reading
9 (*bottom*) Author's collection
10 (*insert*) From Lucien Gillain, *Heures de Guérite. Poésies d'un Dragon*, 1893
12 (*bottom*) Department of English, University of Reading
13 (*top*) Mander and Mitchenson Collection
13 (*bottom*) *The Sketch*, 25 April 1894
14 (*top*) Department of English, University of Reading
15 (*top*) *The Tatler*, 157, 29 June 1904
17 Mansell Collection, London
18 (*top*) Irish Tourist Board, Dublin
18 (*bottom*); 19; 20 (*top left and top right*) Courtesy of Colin Smythe
20 (*bottom left*) From W. B. Yeats, *Samhain*, 1904
20 (*bottom right*) Mander and Mitchenson Collection
21 (*top*) *Illustrated London News*
21 (*bottom*) Abbey Theatre Collection, National Library of Ireland
23 (*top*) The National Theatre Society, Abbey Theatre, Dublin. Photo: Rex Roberts
23 (*bottom*) Abbey Theatre Collection, National Library of Ireland
25 (*top*) *The Tatler*, February 1904
25 (*bottom left*) Department of English, University of Reading
27 Courtesy of William M. Murphy
27 (*insert*) Manchester City Art Galleries
29 (*top right*) Courtesy of Dr Grace M. Jaffé
29 (*bottom*) Yale University, Beinecke Rare Book and Manuscript Library
30 Manchester City Art Galleries
31 (*top left*) Courtesy of Professor George Mills Harper
31 (*top right and bottom*) Mary Evans Picture Library

TEXT ILLUSTRATIONS

p. xxiv British Museum
2 Sotheby's, New York 17/12/92
5 British Library Newspaper Library, Colindale
6 From W. B. Yeats, *Poems*, 1895
7 From Grace Plunkett, *To Hold as Twere*, 1920
8 Courtesy of Colin Smythe
9 Robert W. Woodruff Library, Emory University, Atlanta
10 Courtesy of Colin Smythe
11 Berg Collection, New York Public Library
13 Foster-Murphy Collection, New York Public Library
14 Courtesy of Colin Smythe
15 National Library of Ireland, Henderson scrapbook, MS 1730, p. 93
16, 17 British Library Newspaper Library, Colindale
18 Mander and Mitchenson Collection

Back endpaper Hugh Lane Municipal Gallery of Modern Art, Dublin

xiv

ACKNOWLEDGEMENTS

IN the course of writing this book I incurred outstanding debts to many people. The first, to Leland Lyons, is recorded in the foreword and dedication, as is my gratitude to Jennifer Lyons for her unfailing friendship and helpfulness. And I owe an immeasurable amount to Michael and Anne Yeats. Scholars have long been indebted to their authoritative knowledge and discerning care of the unique collection of material to do with their father, and the generosity with which they have entertained never-ending inquiries and visits from all over the world. My own importunities have been met with unfailing good humour and helpfulness, and I am deeply grateful to them both, and to Gráinne Yeats, for many kindnesses: perhaps most of all, for understanding so well the task of the biographer.

Elsewhere too the world of Yeats scholarship has been, all things considered, remarkably generous and friendly to an interloping historian, and I have incurred special obligations to several Yeatsians. John Kelly, whose great edition of the *Collected Letters* was transforming the subject of Yeats's biography even as I wrote, was endlessly helpful and supportive throughout. William Murphy not only cleared an important part of the path with his classic biography of John Butler Yeats but shared many insights, generously gave me access to his archive of transcriptions, and – with his wife Harriet – provided hospitality and encouragement. Warwick Gould and Deirdre Toomey, who have also blazed new trails through the indispensable *Yeats Annual*, were sterling guides, critics and friends from the outset. Their close reading of the text steered me out of several errors and provided many pointers to where I might go. And I am extremely grateful to Colin Smythe – another figure whose intellectual enterprise has extended the boundaries of Yeats studies – for his kindness in answering queries and making material available to me.

I should also like to thank the custodians and librarians at many institutions for helping me find material and answering inquiries, in particular Cathy Henderson at the Harry Ransom Humanities Research Center, Austin, Texas; Anthony Bliss, Bancroft Library, University of California at Berkeley; Steve Crook and the late Lola Szladits at the Berg Collection, New York Public Library; Nicole Laillet at the Bibliothèque Nationale, Paris; Robert O'Neill at the Burns Library, Boston College; Nancy Weyant at the Ellen Clarke Bertrand Library, Bucknell University; Paula Lee at the University of Chicago Library; Kathy Knox and Stephen Enniss at the Robert R. Woodruff Library, Emory University; the staff at the Houghton Library, Harvard; Alexandra Mason at the Kenneth Spencer Research Library, University of Kansas at

Lawrence; Christopher Sheppard at the Brotherton Library, Leeds; Catherine Fahy at the National Library of Ireland; the staff at the Firestone Library, Princeton University; Margaret Kimball at Stanford; Bernard Meehan at Trinity College, Dublin; John McTernan at the Sligo County Library; and the staff at the Beinecke Rare Book and MS Library, Yale University. Many others provided insights, answered queries, and helped to make the life of the wandering scholar a more pleasant one than it might otherwise have been. They include Douglas Archibald, George Bornstein, Liz Cullingford Butler, Wayne Chapman, David R. Clark, Eamon Duffy, Tom Dunne, Stephen Fay, Richard Finneran, Adrian Frazier, Michael Gilsenan, Victoria Glendinning, Robert Greacen, George Mills Harper, Ruth Harris, Elizabeth Heine, Fritz and Leslie Hoffecker, Michael Holroyd, Sam Hynes, Declan Kiberd, Peter Kuch, Gifford Lewis, Walton Litz, Edna Longley, Lucy McDiarmid, James McFadden, Gerald MacMahon, John Maddicott, Robert Mahony, Christina Hunt Mahony, Clare O'Halloran, Tom Paulin, James Pethica, David Pierce, Omar Pound, Ann Saddlemyer, Linda Satchwell, Ron and Keith Schuchard, Bob Spoo, Tom Staley, Tom Steele, Colm Tóibín, Jay Tolson and Mary Bradshaw, Marina Warner and George Watson.

Other assistance was provided by those who helped in the search for material and the checking of references: Mary-Lou Legg most of all, but also Ben Levitas, Gerard Keown, and Sarah Foster. I am grateful to those who granted me access to privately held material: Maureen Rosenhaupt for her collection of JBY letters and sketches, Nicholas Boyle for William Boyle's correspondence, and Edward Plunkett for his grandmother's diary. Anna MacBride White allowed me to consult the correspondence between Maud Gonne and W. B. Yeats well before its publication. Owen and Ruth Dudley Edwards generously gave me unrestricted access to the research notes and library of their mother, the late Síle Ní Shúilleabháin. And I enjoyed enlightening interviews with Molly Adams (Mary Manning), the late Sir Frederick Ashton, R. J. Gluckstein, Dame Ninette de Valois, the late A. S. O'Connor, Kathleen Raine, Francis Stuart and the late George White.

I am extremely grateful to the British Academy for electing me to a Research Readership at an early stage of my research; to Birkbeck College, the University of London, Hertford College and the University of Oxford for periods of research leave; and to the Institute of Advanced Study, Princeton, and the Department of English, Princeton University, for providing such stimulating and agreeable circumstances in which to work when my research was getting under way in 1988 and 1989. On more recent visits I am indebted to Robert Scally, Eliza O'Grady and the staff at Glucksman Ireland House, New York University.

The actual process of producing this book also owes much to others. Sheila

Sheehan in Kerry provided a safe haven where much of it was written. Valerie Kemp put enormous effort and dedication into preparing the manuscript. At Oxford University Press, the original arrangements were much facilitated by Ivon Asquith and Will Sulkin; Judith Luna's commitment and helpfulness have been constant throughout; and I have depended heavily upon the dedication, good humour and astute advice of Kim Scott Walwyn. In New York, Laura Brown and Amy Roberts were immensely encouraging. I should also like to record my appreciation of the design and pictorial skills of Paul Luna, Sue Tipping and Suzanne Williams. I am grateful to my agent at the time the project was initiated, Giles Gordon, and to my present agent, Gill Coleridge, who has helped me immeasurably in many ways. Andrew Motion and Selina Hastings read the first draft and provided many perceptive and valuable suggestions. And Donna Poppy edited the final version with skill, commitment and flair far transcending the bounds of duty.

A large proportion of the debts recorded here will be carried forward to the second volume. So will the pressures on my children Phineas and Nora, who have put up with a father periodically absent and permanently distracted; and on my wife, Aisling, who has read, discussed and advised on the project for the past eight years. Neither they nor any of those listed above are responsible for the shortcomings in this book, but it could not have been written without them.

Poetry, prose, and unpublished writings by W. B. Yeats and other members of the family appear by permission of Anne Yeats and Michael Yeats. The extract from Canto LXXXIII of *The Pisan Cantos* is quoted with the permission of the estate of Ezra Pound, Faber and Faber Ltd and New Directions. For other permissions I am grateful to Anne de Winton and Catherine Kennedy (unpublished letters of Augusta Gregory and Robert Gregory); the estate of Diarmuid Russell (unpublished letters of George Russell); the estate of J. C. Medley (unpublished letters of George Moore). I am also grateful to the following holders of copyright material who have granted access and permission for quotation: Amherst College Library; Harry Ransom Humanities Research Center, University of Texas at Austin; Bancroft Library, University of California, Berkeley; Henry W. and Albert A. Berg Collection, the New York Public Library (Astor, Lenox and Tilden Foundations); Bibliothèque Nationale de France, Département des Arts du Spectacle; Bodleian Library, Oxford; Burns Library, Boston College; University of Delaware Library, Newark, Delaware; Robert W. Woodruff Library, Emory University, Atlanta; Houghton Library, Harvard University; the Department of Special Collections, Stanford University Libraries, Stanford, California; Huntington

ACKNOWLEDGEMENTS

Library, San Marino, California; University of Illinois at Urbana–Champaign Library; Kenneth Spencer Research Library, University of Kansas, Lawrence, Kansas; Brotherton Collection, Leeds University Library; University of London Library; William M. Murphy; National Library of Ireland; Charles Deering McCormick Library of Special Collections, Northwestern University Library, Evanston, Illinois; Plunkett Foundation, Oxford; Princeton University Libraries; University of Reading Library; Colin Smythe, Ltd; Morris Library, Southern Illinois University at Carbondale; Trinity College, Dublin; Beinecke Rare Book and Manuscript Library, Yale University. Every effort has been made to establish contact with the holders of original copyrights; in cases where this has not been possible I hope this general acknowledgement will be taken as sufficient.

FOREWORD

THIS book is in no sense a work of joint authorship, but the contribution of the late F. S. L. Lyons should be recorded at the outset. For nearly ten years he worked on a biography of W. B. Yeats, amassing a great deal of material before his untimely death in September 1983. A small portion of text had been written, and remains unseen. Both his widow, Jennifer, and I felt that, when I began my own project, it must remain so; nor has any overall plan been found in his papers. Jennifer Lyons, however, has made his archive of transcripts and notes unconditionally available to me, and they immeasurably eased my initial entry into a vast and unfamiliar subject. I owe a great deal to her generosity and friendship, as I do to his. My interpretation and emphasis may inevitably be at variance with what Leland Lyons would have written; when I worked through manuscript collections in his footsteps I often found that we were looking from different angles, and this will be a different book from the one denied to us by his death. But his influence is great and continuing. *The Apprentice Mage* is dedicated to his memory, with gratitude, affection and admiration.

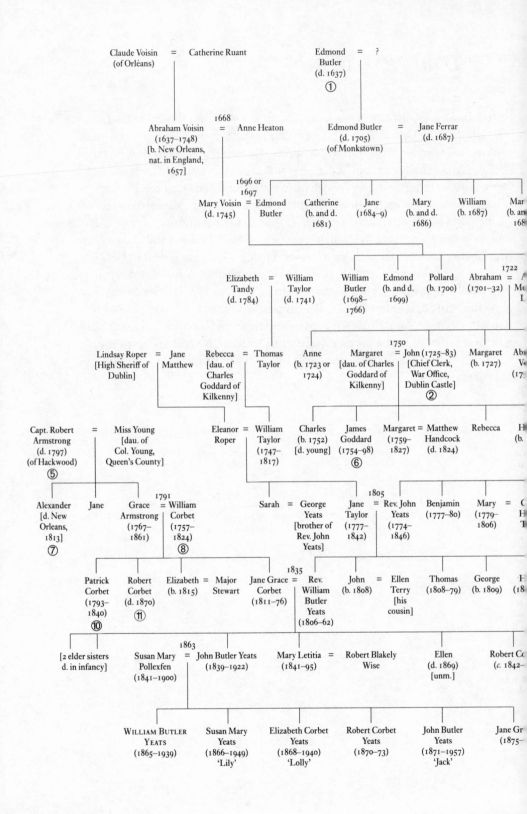

Claude Voisin (of Orléans) = Catherine Ruant

Edmond Butler (d. 1637) ①

1668
Abraham Voisin (1637–1748) [b. New Orleans, nat. in England, 1657] = Anne Heaton

Edmond Butler (d. 1705) (of Monkstown) = Jane Ferrar (d. 1687)

1696 or 1697
Mary Voisin (d. 1745) = Edmond Butler

Catherine (b. and d. 1681)

Jane (1684–9)

Mary (b. and d. 1686)

William (b. 1687)

Mar (b. an 168

Elizabeth Tandy (d. 1784) = William Taylor (d. 1741)

William Butler (1698–1766)

Edmond (b. and d. 1699)

Pollard (b. 1700)

1722
Abraham (1701–32) = A Me L

Lindsay Roper [High Sheriff of Dublin] = Jane Matthew

Rebecca [dau. of Charles Goddard of Kilkenny] = Thomas Taylor

Anne (b. 1723 or 1724)

1750
Margaret [dau. of Charles Goddard of Kilkenny] = John (1725–83) [Chief Clerk, War Office, Dublin Castle] ②

Margaret (b. 1727)

Ab V (17

Capt. Robert Armstrong (d. 1797) (of Hackwood) ⑤ = Miss Young [dau. of Col. Young, Queen's County]

Eleanor Roper = William Taylor (1747–1817)

Charles (b. 1752) [d. young]

James Goddard (1754–98) ⑥

Margaret (1759–1827) = Matthew Handcock (d. 1824)

Rebecca

H (b.

Alexander [d. New Orleans, 1813] ⑦

Jane

1791
Grace Armstrong (1767–1861) = William Corbet (1757–1824) ⑧

Sarah = George Yeats [brother of Rev. John Yeats]

1805
Jane Taylor (1777–1842) = Rev. John Yeats (1774–1846)

Benjamin (1777–80)

Mary (1779–1806) = C H T

Patrick Corbet (1793–1840) ⑩

Robert Corbet (d. 1870) ⑪

Elizabeth (b. 1815) = Major Stewart

1835
Jane Grace Corbet (1811–76) = Rev. William Butler Yeats (1806–62)

John (b. 1808) = Ellen Terry [his cousin]

Thomas (1808–79)

George (b. 1809)

H (18

[2 elder sisters d. in infancy]

1863
Susan Mary Pollexfen (1841–1900) = John Butler Yeats (1839–1922)

Mary Letitia (1841–95) = Robert Blakely Wise

Ellen (d. 1869) [unm.]

Robert Co (c. 1842–

WILLIAM BUTLER YEATS (1865–1939)

Susan Mary Yeats (1866–1949) 'Lily'

Elizabeth Corbet Yeats (1868–1940) 'Lolly'

Robert Corbet Yeats (1870–73)

John Butler Yeats (1871–1957) 'Jack'

Jane Gr (1875–

WBY'S DESCENT THROUGH THE YEATS FAMILY TREE

1 Appears in 'Inquisition' of 20 December 1666 as tenant of premises in Co. Dublin. Will dated 1637.
2 Owned Thomastown, Co. Kildare.
3 Shot by assassins when returning to Bishop of Meath's seat, in revenge for his 'activity in suppressing the late disturbances in the County Meath' – *Dublin Evening Post*, 26 November 1793. See *Autobiographies*, 21.
4 Hannah Wickens m. (2) Thomas Brewer in 1751.
5 According to Lily, his 'brother' was Major-General John Armstrong (1674–1742), ADC to the Duke of Marlborough at Malplaquet and

Oudenarde, appointed Chief Engineer in 1714, Colonel of Royal Irish Regiment of Footsoldiers, 1735–42; buried in Tower of London. But this must have been the previous generation. He was son of Robert Armstrong and Lydia, dau. of Michael Harward, Ballyard, King's County. See *Autobiographies*, 20.
6 Killed in 1798 Rising; a clergyman. See *Autobiographies*, 21.
7 See *Autobiographies*, 21.
8 Son of Patrick Corbet, who came to Ireland from Shropshire as Registrar to the Irish Lord Chancellor.
9 Lived with her nephew Thomas Yeats at Seaview, Ballina, Sligo.

10 Lieut., 8th Madras Infantry, commission dated 12 May 1812; served in Burmese war, notably at taking of Rangoon; created Major on field of battle; governor of Penang; died on voyage home, buried Madras. See *Autobiographies*, 21.
11 Master of 'Sandymount Castle'.
12 'Uncle Matt', Celbridge, agent of Thomastown estate.
13 'Aunt Mickey', Sligo.

The earlier branches of this tree are based on family records and historical notes gathered by Lily Yeats.

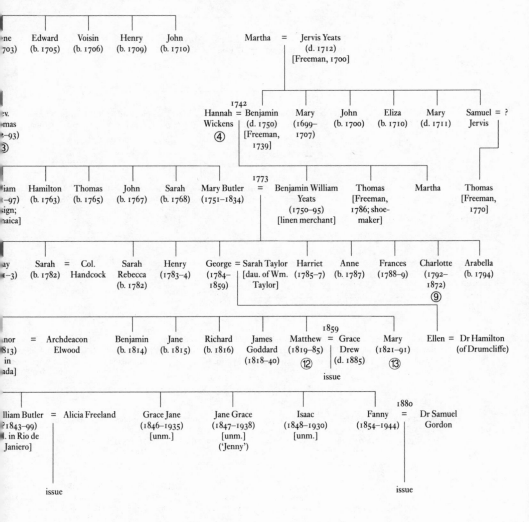

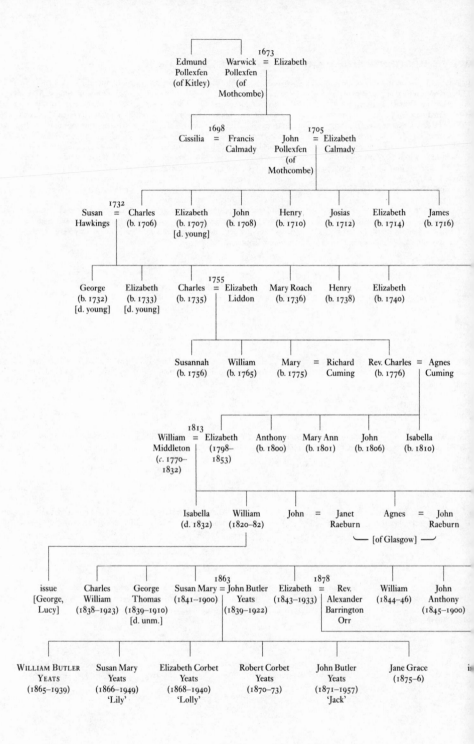

Edmund
Pollexfen
(of Kitley)

1673
Warwick = Elizabeth
Pollexfen
(of
Mothcombe)

1698
Cissilia = Francis
Calmady

1705
John = Elizabeth
Pollexfen   Calmady
(of
Mothcombe)

1732
Susan = Charles   Elizabeth   John   Henry   Josias   Elizabeth   James
Hawkings (b. 1706) (b. 1707)   (b. 1708)   (b. 1710)   (b. 1712)   (b. 1714)   (b. 1716)
                     [d. young]

George   Elizabeth   1755   Mary Roach   Henry   Elizabeth
(b. 1732)   (b. 1733)   Charles = Elizabeth (b. 1736)   (b. 1738)   (b. 1740)
[d. young]   [d. young]   (b. 1735) Liddon

Susannah   William   Mary   = Richard   Rev. Charles = Agnes
(b. 1756)   (b. 1765)   (b. 1775) Cuming   (b. 1776)   Cuming

1813
William = Elizabeth   Anthony   Mary Ann   John   Isabella
Middleton (1798–   (b. 1800)   (b. 1801)   (b. 1806)   (b. 1810)
(c. 1770– 1853)
1832)

Isabella   William   John = Janet   Agnes = John
(d. 1832)   (1820–82)   Raeburn   Raeburn
                            └── [of Glasgow] ──┘

issue   Charles   George   1863   1878
[George,   William   Thomas   Susan Mary = John Butler   Elizabeth = Rev.   William   John
Lucy]   (1838–1923) (1839–1910) (1841–1900) | Yeats   (1843–1933) Alexander   (1844–46)   Anthony
                          [d. unm.] | (1839–1922)   Barrington   (1845–1900)
                                                                              Orr

WILLIAM BUTLER   Susan Mary   Elizabeth Corbet   Robert Corbet   John Butler   Jane Grace   is
YEATS   Yeats   Yeats   Yeats   Yeats   (1875–6)
(1865–1939)   (1866–1949)   (1868–1940)   (1870–73)   (1871–1957)
                  'Lily'   'Lolly'   'Jack'

The earlier branches of this tree are based on information gathered by Gifford Lewis for her book
The Yeats Sisters and the Cuala (Dublin, 1994).

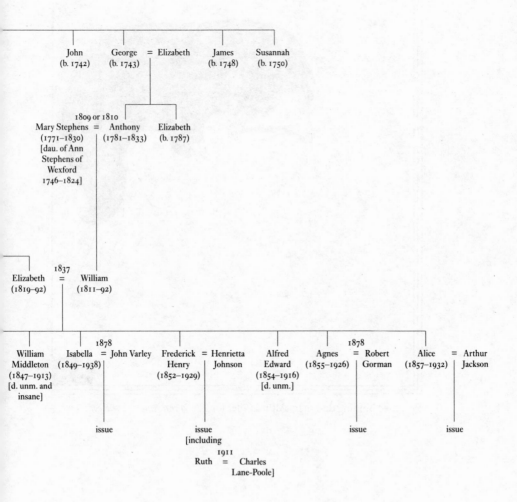

Proposed binding design by Althea Giles for *The Wind Among the Reeds*.

INTRODUCTION

THIS volume of Yeats's biography, the first of two, ends with his memories of childhood and youth. Approaching fifty and looking to the expected future, he sat down to make sense of his early life – and produced a disingenuous masterpiece which said far more about him in 1914 than it did about his life from 1865 to 1886. But when he gave this interim report to the world, it was not universally well received; and the reactions of old friends and enemies tell us much about that preceding fifty years. 'The most vacant things man ever wrote,' remarked George Russell (AE), who had known him since art school days. 'The boy in the book might have become a grocer as well as a poet. Nobody could be astonished if this had been issued as a novel, part one, to find in part two the hero had for some reason given up thinking of literature and become a merchant. Why does he do it?'[1]

Russell's critique, which seems strangely off-beam, was conditioned by his disapproval of his old friend's adoption of a mask, an artistic persona, a preoccupation with style: 'the present WBY is the result'. There is something in this, and the years this book covers are the years of making 'WBY': hence I have adopted this acronym to refer to a man who hated his first name, 'Willie', and whose surname is somehow even more forbiddingly hieratic than his initials. Even his family referred to him as 'WB', and still do. By differentiation, his father remains JBY, and appears thus throughout this book. This is not only a matter of convenience. They were both, in their ways, achieved and astonishing personalities – as William M. Murphy has so eloquently shown. In his own heroic self-construction, as in his continuing reworking of poems, WBY painted many layers over the portrait of himself as a young man. 'Such a delightful creature he was when young!' added Russell. 'And at rare moments when he forgets himself he is still interesting as ever almost.'

This condescension amuses us, because WBY from 1914 was to become incrementally more and more 'interesting' until he died a quarter of a century later. Russell, along with George Moore and many others, assumed that WBY had finished his important work and become an impresario of his own image and the work of others: a 'schoolmaster', as Moore put it, who had instructed a whole generation in poetry, much as Sickert's teaching had trained 'a tribe of little female Sickerts [who] go forth all over Europe, bringing back endless gable ends, every one of which may be hung in an exhibition'. Still, he admitted, 'all begins in Yeats and all ends in Yeats . . . It is easier to write about Yeats now [in 1914] than it was ten years ago, and he is better worth writing about, for as he ceased to write he became literature, or at least the material out of which literature is fashioned.'² As usual, Moore is at once impressively astute and sublimely wrong. By 1914 WBY had become a literary 'subject', but he was very far from ceasing to write. In many ways the poet would have the last laugh; enabled by that faculty which always amazed his wife, of knowing how things would look to people afterwards.

There is a final point concerning that early autobiography – final, that is, until the reader reaches the last chapter of *this* book. Dismissing WBY's *Reveries*, Russell went on to grumble: 'We are interested in Yeats's inner mind, whatever it is, but not in anecdotes of things he saw and whose effect on his own mind is not clear.' Like Moore, he is only half right. We are interested in his inner mind; but the things he saw, and the things he did, are of surpassing interest because of his alchemical capacity to transmute the events of a crowded life, lived on many levels, into art. We are confronting a poetic genius who was also, both serially and simultaneously, a playwright, journalist, occultist, apprentice politician, revolutionary, stage-manager, diner-out, dedicated friend, confidant and lover of some of the most interesting people of his day. To approach his 'inner life' we have to see these 'outer' experiences impacting upon each other, and to reassemble them both chronologically and circumstantially. What is needed is this kind of biography: not another exegesis of the poetry from a biographical angle, not an analysis of the development of his aesthetic theories, and especially not a study that ranges at will across the work of nearly sixty years, relating – as one critic has done – the poetry of the early 1890s to the enterprise of state-building in the 1920s. It is also worth bearing in mind the injunction of Michel Serres: that one can read from the work of art to its conditions, but not – or not entirely – from the conditions to the work of art.³

Here lies the justification for this long book; and for the fact that it is a historian who has written it. WBY's life has been approached over and over again, for the purposes of relating it to his art: a process that began before the end of the period dealt with in the following pages. Shortly after he died, Joseph Hone produced his official life; a literary biography followed from A. Norman Jeffares, and then the luminous works by Richard Ellmann, which still hold the critical field. Many other one-volume biographical studies were still to come, and more are being written at this moment; but they all tend to follow Ellmann's dazzling structure. Faced with the multifarious activities, the feints and turns, the wildly differing worlds which WBY embraced, Ellmann followed his subject's example in dealing with his life thematically. WBY's own *Autobiographies* dictate an arrangement for his life, and it is a thematic one; this is hard not to follow, even if it looks like the way of the chameleon. The natural reaction is to shadow him from young Celtic Revivalist to theatrical manager to witness of revolution to smiling public man; to accept his *Autobiographies* as straightforward records rather than to see them in terms of the time they were composed; and to deal with periods of frantic and diverse involvements, as in the early 1900s, by separating out the strands of occultism, drama and love, and addressing them individually. The result, in Ellmann's work, was a masterpiece of intellectual analysis and psychological penetration, to which all Yeatsians are for ever indebted. However, we do not, alas, live our lives in themes, but day by day; and wby, giant though he was, is no exception.

Most biographical studies of wby are principally about what he wrote; this one is principally about what he did. The marvellously annotated volumes of his *Collected Letters*, as they appear, reconstruct how intensely he combined different preoccupations, involvements, lives, personae, circles of friends; so do the detailed studies of certain episodes in his life by a phalanx of brilliant scholars in the last generation. But in his own memories, the themes were sorted out under various headings, and his personality, in these apprentice years, was presented accordingly. Most of all, an apprenticeship in magical and occult studies required solitude and a rejection of the world. 'When [a mortal] goes his way to supreme Adeptship,' he wrote in 1901, 'he will go absolutely alone, for men attain to the supreme wisdom in a loneliness that is like the loneliness of death.'[4] He meant this. But it was said by someone simultaneously capable of tremendous social gregariousness, who wrote endless letters, who had a connoisseur's taste for psychological quirks and gossip about his friends, who ruefully accepted his own propensity for indiscretion. (Like Marx, the only novelist whose work he read consistently was Balzac, and he was a committed admirer.) And the conjunctions of his life show that he was never more authoritarian, uncompromising, esoteric than after a reversal in one of the parallel 'external' worlds of politics or love. This could work two ways: his obsessive plunge into theatrical activity followed a reverse in the world of occult organizations, and met the needs to which occultism had ministered. At the point this volume ends, at the very time Russell was dismissing him as no longer 'interesting' and mummified beneath his mask, his newer friend Ezra Pound explained to Harriet Monroe (with characteristic certainty) why wby was still the best living poet. 'Yeats knows life, despite his chiaroscuro, and his lack of a certain sort of observation – He learns by emotion, and is one of the few people who have ever had any, who know what violent emotion really is like; who see from the centre of it – instead of trying to look in from the rim.'[5]

What this volume attempts to do is restore the sense of a man involved in life, and in history: notably in the history of his country, at a time of exceptional flux and achievement. His extraordinary life deserves to be studied for its relationship to his work; it also needs to be studied for its influence on his country's biography. This is true in several unexpected ways. His best-known poetry defines for many people the Irish identity which was forged in revolution. But he represented, in the intersections and traditions of his own life, a complex tangle of historical allegiances as well as personal relationships. A historically grounded biography can attempt to survey this, without necessarily adopting the nineteenth-century framework of the 'exemplary life' and merely rearing up what Yeats called an 'image for the affections'. The idealized portraits of national heroes, he once remarked, destroyed 'that delight in what is unforeseen . . . the mere drifting hither and thither that must come before all true thought and emotion'.[6] The delight in what is unforeseen is a theme throughout this book. Moreover, many of the problems which currently exercise Irish historians are woven directly into the interpretation of WBY's life. The marginalization of the Protestant Ascendancy from the 1870s, the chronology of nationalist revival in the 1890s, the importance (or otherwise) of Fenianism around the turn of the century, the impact of the Boer War on Irish politics, the rise and nature of Sinn Féin, the constitutional crisis before the First World War, the effects of deferring Home Rule – all these subjects occur here and in all of them his personal life is deeply implicated. His life also illuminates the large historical theme of the change in Ireland's relation to Britain. The challenge to the authority of the class and caste from which WBY came – the Protestant Ascendancy and middle class – was followed by a challenge to the very idea of a link between the two countries. And the cultural as well as political implications of this lay close to his own preoccupations.

Napoleon's dictum that to understand a man you have to know what was happening in the world when he was twenty is manifestly true of WBY. He came to fame as the poet of the new Ireland, asserting its identity; his own discovery of his voice is often neatly paralleled with his country's discovery of independence. But he was also a product of the *ancien régime*: Victorian, Protestant, Ascendancy Ireland. And his childhood and youth were punctuated by the events which charted its decline. Born in 1865, he was four years old when Gladstone disestablished the Church of Ireland, which provided livings for many of his ancestors. He was five when the 1870 Land Act interfered with landlords' control over their property, and Isaac Butt founded the Home Rule movement. He was seven when the Secret Ballot Act liberated tenant voters and dealt a major blow to landlord political power. He was twelve when Parnell took control of the Irish Parliamentary Party, fourteen when the Land War broke out and tenants began witholding their rents in the long campaign towards a peasant proprietorship, seventeen when Parnell and Gladstone began the *rapprochement* between the Liberal Party and the Irish nationalists which would produce a (failed) Home Rule bill in WBY's twenty-first year. So his youth spanned the exact period of crisis which inaugurated the decline of the Irish Protestant Ascendancy. It was a process of which he and his immediate family – who had become *déclassé* bohemians, living in London – approved, though their relations did not. However, strong Home Rulers though JBY and his children were, it disadvantaged them objectively, and they remained slightly uncomfortable with the successor class who were poised to take over by the eve of the First World War. And WBY's quarrels with himself and others over the shape-changing phenomenon of Irish nationalism fit into this framework with compelling interest.

This background illuminates his creative and mutually dependent friendship with Augusta Gregory, no less than his stormy relationships with his colleagues in the Abbey Theatre; it helps explain the way the dramatic movement's leaders tried to build a nationalist enterprise that would be somehow non-political; and it pervades those memories of childhood which flooded and possessed him in middle age, when this volume ends. At that point he thought he had reached a plateau where he would look back as well as forward, believing that his continual questioning of Irish nationalism and Irish cultural identity had reached some kind of resolution. The mentors of his childhood and youth were to be fixed into a heroic frieze as he relived his past. The irony, marvellous and immense, lies in the fact that so much was yet to come. But he was not wrong in believing that the years up to 1914 fixed the patterns by which he lived his astonishing life. 'Ireland is being made,' he wrote towards the end of the period covered here, '& this gives the few who have clear sight the determination to shape it.'[7] By then his claim to shaping it had been lodged, and these pages chronicle the process.

The themes of an independent mind and a national commitment, continually explored in his writing, are linked closely to WBY's family background and his own political involvements, as well as to the question of contested Irishness which preoccupied him all his life. To examine that life should bring into view a whole range of identifications, backgrounds, experiences, epitomized by himself, his family, his collaborators, his friends: a palimpsest of Irishness, which he never stopped interrogating, and which developed and changed with the conditions of his time. Hence the importance of chronology: of restoring, for instance, the order of his political involvements from 1895 to 1900, strategically jumbled in his *Autobiographies*, and of relating them to his relationships with the important women in his life, Augusta Gregory nearly as much as Maud Gonne. Throughout, it is necessary to hold in the frame his relationships with other people, and how they saw him: to capture them before immobilization into that frieze. The process should recover Gregory's attitude towards Synge's work, or the resentment felt by her son for WBY, as well as his relationship with Dublin opinion, with contemporary Ireland at large, and with the worlds of English literature and (increasingly high) society.

Hence the importance of letters and ephemeral journalism, written before hindsight. In some cases I have quoted a manifesto or a letter with the excisions and cancellations which indicate a thought in the process of formation (with Yeats's erratic spelling and punctuation preserved whenever possible). Similarly, I have tried to see those poems that are discussed here in their immediate historical context. Simple-minded as it may seem, the conjunctions of chronology cast light on the gestation not only of public poems like 'To Ireland in the Coming Times' and 'September 1913' but of 'private' ones like 'The Cold Heaven' and 'Adam's Curse'. In an effort to recapture immediacy, I have often quoted a poem in the first version WBY released to the world – or to a friend, embedded in or alongside a letter. The high polish of the canonical version may be lost, but a more vivid colour sometimes comes through, with a rougher texture. At the same time this volume may contain less about poetry and its making than might be expected. Without endorsing Russell's comment that the boy portrayed in WBY's first autobiography could as easily have become a grocer, it remains true that in his early life numerous commitments and interests competed for his attention, and writing poetry was not always at the forefront. Indeed, during his apprenticeship there were junctures when other forms of writing took nearly all his thought; not only plays (with which he began his writing career) but also fiction and critical commentary. This too is a contemporary emphasis which is reasserted in this volume.

Seamus Heaney has described a poem's construction as building a trellis – the structure – and then training a vine across it. For WBY's life, a strict chronological ordering must form the basic grid; integrating themes then grow across the lattice. But even in building that grid, there is room for reconstruction: for one thing, at least two of the most important encounters of WBY's young life (with Mohini Chatterjee and with Maud Gonne) may have been consistently misdated. And, crucially, the interactions between events in his life, such as the wars over the National Literary Society in Dublin in the early 1890s, the underlying political agenda, and the theoretical principles he laid down in critical manifestos, need to be drawn out. Many of the ambiguities and apparent inconsistencies in WBY's aesthetic and literary pronouncements can be clarified by relating them to events in the 'real' (or at least day-to-day) world.

WBY, like all of us, lived out his life constantly expecting various kinds of future: perhaps more so than many, because he was a practised and committed astrologer. But, as with everyone, the expected future never happened. Unlike most of us, he possessed a protean ability to shift his ground, repossess the advantage, and lay a claim to authority – always with an eye to how people would see things afterwards. Perhaps above all, this biography tries to explain the basis for his expectations, and the reasons why things turned out differently.

Prologue : YEATSES AND POLLEXFENS

> I watched him as the mousing cat, fearful lest some trait, some
> inclination which I had deplored in my own family or in his
> mother's, might develop to his undoing . . . There are no rules
> for the breeding of poets.
>
> John Butler Yeats, unpublished memoirs

A MARRIAGE is not only the union of two people but the confluence of two families. When John Butler Yeats (born 16 March 1839, barrister at law) married Susan Mary Pollexfen (born 13 July 1841), the conjunction brought uneasily together on 10 September 1863 two clans quintessentially of the Irish Protestant middle class. But the strains which they represented were so different, and their individual cultures so contrasting, that it became a commonplace for JBY and his children to ascribe character and fate to the clash of two tribal constellations. Above all, in the view of the father, this produced the poet. 'By marriage with a Pollexfen I have given a tongue to the sea cliffs.'[1]

This determinism curiously anticipated the part that astrology would play in that poet's own attempts to make sense of his life. For the social historian, however, what is interesting is the way that the Yeatses and Pollexfens together spanned the variety of backgrounds, preoccupations and cultural identifications associated with the Victorian Irish Protestant bourgeoisie. This nearly forgotten class was part of the structure of Protestant Ascendancy in Ireland, still in place when JBY married Susan Pollexfen, but about to enter its long decline.

That decline too was typified by the Yeats–Pollexfen marriage. The Yeatses had had money, social influence and a history in Ireland. By the later nineteenth century all they were left with was the history. The aristocratic 'Butler' connection was inserted into most male Yeats names; its link back to the great Norman dynasty of the Dukes of Ormonde was an important part of family lore, though official genealogy did not bear them out.[2] And when Mary Butler married Benjamin William Yeats, son of Benjamin Yeats, a wholesale linen merchant of William Street, Dublin,[3] on 22 August 1773, she allegedly brought with her another thread of romance from the armorial banner of Irish Protestant folk-history: through her great-grandmother, born Mary Voisin, she was supposed to be of Huguenot descent. The Voisins, a family of bankers and goldsmiths, had, however, arrived in Ireland from New Orleans, via London, not as part of the Huguenot diaspora from France to Ireland. Even this romantic association was not all that it might seem.[4]

Benjamin and Mary Yeats's eldest son, John, was born on 13 November 1774; he went to Trinity, took his degree (winning a Berkeley medal) in 1797 and, like many of the family, entered the Church of Ireland. From 1811 to 1846 he was Rector of Drumcliffe, County Sligo, a part of Ireland which his great-grandson would immortalize. He married Jane Taylor, eldest daughter of William Taylor of Dublin Castle, at St Werbergh's on 7 September 1805. By the early nineteenth century the Yeatses appear firmly located in the world of the Protestant middle classes: Trinity College, the Church of Ireland, professional occupations. John's son William Butler Yeats, the poet's grandfather, was even born (on 19 July 1806) in the impeccable surroundings of Dublin Castle, where his maternal grandfather, William Taylor, was Chief Clerk in the Chief Secretary's office – a post held by five generations of his family.[5] William Butler Yeats attended Trinity, married (in November 1835) Jane Grace Corbet,[6] and became a clergyman. After a brief period in the parish of Moira, County Down, he became Rector of Tullylish in the same county. The previous incumbent, Dr Beatty, retired in his favour – possibly because he was a relative by marriage.[7] But the Reverend Yeats left his living inexplicably early in 1853, and did not take up another. Though he remained technically Rector, he stayed away from the parish.[8] Possibly he left under a cloud or after a breakdown; his son JBY remembered him as charming but unrealistic ('he made castles even in Ireland, as others did in Spain'). His daughters, the poet's aunts, never spoke of him.[9] Nine years later he died suddenly at the home of his brother-in-law Robert Corbet, Sandymount Castle, Dublin. This was a castellated house in the Dublin suburbs whose name, like the Yeatses' Huguenot connection and Butler ancestry, could not quite deliver the promise of its associations.[10]

JBY was born in the Old Vicarage, Tullylish, on 16 March 1839; two elder sisters had died of scarlet fever.[11] He grew up in a family 'dyed', he remarked later, 'in a sort of well-mannered evangelicalism'.[12] He remembered life at Tullylish during the Famine, when the clergyman's family were watched through their windows by starving skeletons of people.[13] They were essentially a professional and clerical family, but some farms remained to them at Thomastown, near Enfield, County Kildare, providing rough shooting and bringing in a diminishing rent (£600 gross, £220 net); this had come through Mary Butler, wife of the younger Benjamin Yeats. The atmosphere of Protestant gentility chafed on JBY; with time he turned to free thought, bohemianism and nationalism. The family's friends were clerical, Trinity and Unionist; but an important influence from early on was Isaac Butt, in the 1830s a young Trinity intellectual preoccupied with ideas of Protestant 'nationality'. He would become the founder of the movement for Irish Home Rule in the 1870s, subsequently to be displaced by Parnell. Butt was a close family friend of the Yeatses: another of William Butler Yeats's sons was named after him; Butt's daughter, Rosa, became the great unattainable love of JBY's life. Her father's ghost remained a haunting presence, representing Irish Protestant nationalism as it might have been. 'The career of Butt and its disasters,' JBY wrote to his eldest son, 'is enough to prove the necessity of the Irish poetical movement.'[14] Also characteristic of this culture was a certain contempt for English obviousness – their 'elephantine naivete', in JBY's mordant phrase.[15] This antipathy was shared by many Irish people who would not describe themselves as nationalist.

Heterodox opinions, however, developed against a background of Irish gentility. The concept of an Irish gentleman was central:[16] often defined in contradistinction to Anglo-Saxon unsubtlety and insularity. (When JBY in old age discovered America, he was struck by the liberation of not being seen as a Protestant in Ireland, or as an Irishman in England. 'In London and in Dublin I am arguing on the *defensive*. Here I feel valiantly on the *offensive*.'[17]) Equally important was a graceful style of life, which would be symbolized for JBY's children by their grandmother, his mother – 'a big woman high above her rather petty surroundings. She had a most progressive mind up to the very last. I see her so clearly with her pale colour and handsome nose and mouth and chin, her small very dark eyes, upright figure and dignified dainty clothes. They were both handsome, as her age and position called for, and dainty as a girl's as her habit and character required.'[18] At Sandymount Castle, Lily Yeats remembered, they drank out of silver cups, not glasses;[19] late in life she was still meeting connections on the Yeats side, like the Armstrongs, who clung to the notion of lost Ascendancy. (An Armstrong relation encountered in 1921 'had a most impressive way of dropping his voice and saying sadly, "so very sad that so and so had to be sold". By this I gather the clan owned large estates, all of which he thought was known to me'.[20]) By then, the folk-memory of banishment from a lost Eden was part of the Irish Ascendancy mind: vanished demesnes loomed larger and larger in the mythology. But the asperity of Lily Yeats's tone indicates that she came from a less nostalgic tradition as well: the Pollexfen strain.

The Pollexfens were Irish Protestants too, but much more recently arrived. By origin, they were Devon gentry with branches at Woodbury, Mothcombe and Kitley in the early eighteenth century. The Sligo Pollexfens were descended from the Kitley branch, who by the early nineteenth century were established in Brixham, Devon, where they had shipping interests; through an unprotected entail their fortunes had declined.[21] There was a slender Irish connection through Mary Stephens of Wexford, the wife of Anthony Pollexfen, barrack-master[22] and Keeper of Forts at Torquay, who died in 1833, aged fifty-two. The way their son William came to Ireland has itself an aura of seafaring romance. In the early 1830s William, who was born in 1811, arrived almost by chance into the rainwashed western Irish seaport of Sligo on his ship. Here he found his widowed cousin Elizabeth Middleton in difficulties with the milling and shipping business she had inherited from her late husband, William Middleton, who had died of cholera in 1832. (She came from a Channel Islands branch of the Pollexfen family, where they had become Wesleyans.[23]) William Pollexfen stayed, helped out, entered the firm with her son William Middleton, and eventually married her daughter, Elizabeth (b. 1819) on 4 May 1837.[24] He became a formidable patriarch, raising and terrifying a large family; his eldest daughter, Susan, married JBY and was the mother of the poet.[25]

The Middletons were country businessmen, comfortably off members of the local Protestant bourgeoisie with odd squireen offshoots; the Pollexfens fitted this mould. But, according to JBY, they brought into this world an intense and sardonic flavour all their own. 'Curiously the Pollexfens are entirely without the sentiments of reverence, and so religion never touches them. *Law* they understand, definite rules and laws, but not religion, unless perhaps the kind of religion the Jews practise, a religion of ceremony and fixed law.'[26] With this, JBY always maintained, 'they had all the marks of imagination, the continual absorption in an idea – and that idea never one of the intellectual and reasoning faculty but of the affections and the desires and the senses'. Pollexfens were drawn to mysticism and morbidity; at the same time JBY used the word 'puritan' to distinguish their disapproval of the life of the mind, as much as their Low Church Protestantism. But they had reserves of repressed passion, which altered their world-view: 'a Pollexfen in a rage is like a dog gone mad, everything is blotted out in a general blackness'.[27] And he often repeated that, though the Pollexfens were the most truthful people he ever met, he would not believe a word they said.[28]

Two things should be pointed out regarding JBY's testimony about the Pollexfens. First, it is mostly retrospective, constructed both to answer the question of how he had produced artistic genius in his own family and to explain, self-absolvingly, the shortcomings of his own marriage. And second, most of his Pollexfen generalizations appear to be based on the behaviour and psychology of his brother-in-law George Pollexfen, a figure who obsessed him from their schooldays together at Atholl Academy in the Isle of Man.[29] By no means all the Pollexfens fit into JBY's decisive dichotomies: not only were they descended from gentry at least as well-bred as the Yeatses, but the majority of them settled comfortably into provincial bourgeois lives. However, there was certainly a strain of mental instability, taking the form of manic depression in JBY's sister-in-law Agnes Pollexfen Gorman,[30] and also affecting her daughter Elma and another sister Elizabeth Pollexfen Orr;

a brother, William Middleton Pollexfen, actually died in an insane asylum. Privately, JBY made much of this – particularly when discussing the behaviour of his daughter Elizabeth (Lolly). And his wife's withdrawal into her own abstracted world towards the end of her life was fitted into this pattern too.

All this was far in advance in 1862, when JBY visited his schoolfriend George Pollexfen in Sligo, and ended by proposing marriage to his sister. But it led to the union of two original and distinctive families, which together embrace the ethos of mid-Victorian Protestant Ireland. The Yeatses had their past aristocratic associations, Trinity College culture, remnants of landed property and well-bred fastidiousness; the Pollexfens seem more reminiscent of the 'New English' settlers of an earlier period, tough-minded townsmen, impatient with the pretensions of the Yeats connection. When JBY's son Jack remarked dismissively that 'we had no gate lodges and no carriage drives', he spoke as a Pollexfen, deliberately trying to puncture the Yeats pretensions of his brother Willie.[31] But both clans were, in their own way, peculiarly Irish – as Lily Yeats sharply remarked, long after separation from Britain had redefined 'Irishness' for families like hers. 'We are far more Irish than all the Saints and Martyrs – Parnell – Pearse – Madam Markiewicz – Maud Gonne – De Valera – and no-one ever thinks of speaking of them as Anglo-Irish. Our nearest English blood is a 100 years ago – and Grandfather William Pollexfen's mother Ann Stephens came from Wexford.'[32] The cultural roots of Irishness would strike a problematic note for JBY's children: descended as they were from Irish Protestant stock, living much of their early life in England, but deeply rooted in Ireland in general and Sligo in particular. Moreover, from the 1860s on, a sense of cultural and social marginalization and insecurity haunted the Irish Protestant universe, as the new world of self-confident Catholic democracy took over Irish public life.[33] Behind this, the Yeats–Pollexfen marriage stands as the enduring cornerstone of the family's cultural, as well as their actual, existence. JBY's belief that it made artists of them all may have more truth in it than seems likely at first sight.

Chapter 1 : THE ARTIST'S CHILDREN
SLIGO 1865–1881

> Children live a fantastic life, in which there is everything except
> human love and human pity and human regret. They weep, like
> geniuses, tears upon tears for some dead Orpheus of whom they
> have dreamt and pass with wondering indifference, like geni-
> uses, among the sorrows of their own household.
>
> Cancelled passage from *The Speckled Bird*

I

'EVERYONE's life is a long series of miraculous escapes,' wrote JBY with char-
acteristic insouciance.[1] His own career was certainly a series of determined
attempts to avoid entrapment of one sort or another. The clergyman's son,
with his romantic good looks, graceful manner and myriad talents, grew up
determined to fly by the nets of Irish Protestant respectability. He succeed-
ed in this through a determined *culte de moi*; in many ways sweet-natured,
formidably articulate and relentlessly charming, he was also fundamentally
self-centred and prone to storms of petulance. Like many such people, he was
a great dilettante; although unlike many, he possessed a real artistic talent.
But there was a determined addiction to failure in his character; and he was
often inconsistent, even in his brilliantly articulated opinions.

The career that was marked out for him was one of the preordained
paths for his caste: school in England, Trinity College, Dublin, the Irish
Bar. But early on he was determined to deviate. Symbolically, he described
himself as having an 'incapacity for arithmetic . . . a genius for ignoring
and denying facts'.[2] Long before he met his wife, the patterns which would
infuriate her had been fixed: his refusal to 'settle', his mockery of the world
of 'getting on', his need to be the centre of a sociable circle. And equally early
his simultaneous fascination with and repulsion towards her family had
been awakened. If it is true that in all human relationships a third person
is silently present, that presence in the Yeats marriage was Susan Pollexfen's
brother George.

JBY's obsession with George Pollexfen is important, not least because it
was inherited by his eldest son. Both Yeatses needed to fascinate, and George
Pollexfen was determined not to be fascinated. 'He was a genuine Pollexfen,
and regarded affection as something *contraband*.'[3] Nor, for his part, did he
have any interest in fascinating other people. 'George looks at you with the
face of a horse, which effectively prevents his being a social success.'[4] But what

6

excited JBY about the morose fellow-Irishman he first encountered at his Isle of Man school in 1851 was the original and implicitly poetic nature banked beneath. 'That was the light within him that lured our affection.'[5] He told spellbinding stories to the other boys at night; he was, and remained, a devout believer in astrology and occultism. And he remained unmoved by opinions. To JBY, formed by reading Mill, Comte and other positivists,[6] and plagued by opinions, George presented an infuriating conundrum. JBY's annoyance did not decrease as George retreated into hypochondria and occult invest-igations, and was exacerbated when his friendship, so earnestly desired, was removed from JBY and extended instead to his eldest son. George and JBY fell out, eventually, over an unpaid debt of £20 – a matter in which George's attitude genuinely dumbfounded JBY. 'That in his estimate outweighed all my qualities and, as it were, nullified all the claims of friendship which began at school where we were inseparable companions.'[7] Similarly, he found it incredible that George refused him a 'loan' when JBY was emigrating to the USA – 'to me his school friend who married his sister.'[8] And, a Pollexfen would have added, a man who never paid his debts.

From Atholl Academy JBY proceeded to Trinity College in 1857; never really happy there, he graduated (with an unclassified degree, due to illness) in 1862 and proceeded to read law at the King's Inns. George Pollexfen had returned to Sligo and the family business. And here JBY came to visit in Sep-tember 1862. The Yeatses themselves had Sligo connections through JBY's grandfather John, Rector of Drumcliffe; his courtship of George's sister Susan began, and he returned there to marry her on 10 September 1863. Thus Sligo would be the basis of their marriage; both their addresses were given as the Pollexfen home on Union Place, though JBY stayed at the Imperial Hotel. The wedding at St John's, Sligo, was witnessed by JBY's uncle Thomas Yeats and Susan's uncle William Middleton; the bridesmaids were two Yeatses, a Pollexfen, an Armstrong, a Dawson and a Middleton.[9] A story of their honey-moon was retailed long afterwards by their daughter Lily:

It was here [the Railway Hotel, Galway] Papa and Mama came over 60 years ago on their honeymoon. Mama had never stayed in an hotel, and Papa got ill, and she tried to light a fire and failed, and Papa got cross and said it would take a coach and four to wait on her, and then she went out for help and stood on the landing and looked down the great well to the hall, and heard some children on the top floor saying their prayers, and she felt homesick. They had a sitting room and Papa had to go to bed. She sat alone for dinner and they brought her a shoulder of mutton. She cut it once, and then, aghast at the way it opened out, looking as if she had eaten quite a pound of meat, she had not the courage to cut off even one slice, and so took just the ve-getables. Next day Papa sent for his mother, who came and took him to Dublin in an invalid carriage, and his illness proved to be Diphtheria![10]

This not only indicates the kind of stories their mother told her children, as full of artistic and circumstantial detail as any Irish *seanchaí*; it also symbolizes much about the relationship that was to develop. 'I became engaged on two or three days acquaintance, and it was not first love or love at all,' wrote JBY over fifty years later to Rosa Butt, '(this really *entre nous* – I have never confessed it to anyone) – but just destiny.'[11] Elsewhere he complained that he could never talk to his wife: 'If I showed her my real thoughts she became quite silent and silent for days, though inwardly furious.'[12]

This may be less surprising to us than to him. Susan Pollexfen Yeats was notably pretty; her eldest son was told later that she had been 'the most beautiful woman in Sligo', and her husband's early sketches show a pensive face, large-eyed and delicate. He liked to write of his wife as withdrawn and unsure of herself, but their correspondence before marriage gives a very different impression. It also shows that JBY had a strong intuition of the kind of difficulties that marrying him might involve:

. . . I love you so much that I would like to share every mood with you. And to have nothing secret from your quick strength and common sense – you are more a man than a woman. Only I hope you won't henpeck me. And make me withdraw from the intimacy of all people who are not acceptable to your ladyship. You are fond of the Exercise of power and authority in which I quite agree & which bodes ill to my freedom. I shall be afraid to ask anybody to the house without first asking your permission and if I do how cross you'll be with your head thrown back. Your utterance short and abrupt, your dress rustling angrily. The storeroom key grating harshly and sharply in the lock. How my spirits will sink. And how uncomfortable the unfortunate guest will be. And what a milksop I'll be thought and what a tyrant you'll be thought and how you'll be dreaded accordingly. How my poor sisters will tremble at your frown and how we shall make common cause together.[13]

But it was not Susan who turned out the tyrant; her husband's facility for a *fait accompli* outflanked her. Having married a law student with good connections and a solid background in the Protestant clerical establishment, she had no reason to anticipate being carried off to bohemia, and never reconciled herself to the abduction. Sligo remained her emotional base; reticent and occasionally caustic in the Pollexfen mode, she hated what she construed as the pretensions and social frivolity of 'artistic' life. Nor did she share the Yeats fascination with how people behaved: like her brother George, she put up barriers. 'All the time they were longing for affection,' JBY thought, 'and their longing was like a deep unsunned well. And never having learned the language of affection they did not know how to win it. It is a language which, like good manners, must be learned in childhood. I more than once said to my wife that I never saw her show affection to me or to anyone, and yet it was there all the time.'[14]

8

The Pollexfens' lack of amusement may have been to do with money. At the time of their marriage, the young couple were probably expecting the bride's family to help out. JBY's father died on 24 November 1862; while his capital was valued at about £10,000, it was subject to mortgages and claims, and his eventual estate was registered as 'effects under £300'.[15] The Registry of Deeds in Dublin records a long list of charges on Yeats property arranged by JBY's father – some of them involving deals with the Royal Exchange Assurance Company, which his brother-in-law Robert Corbet represented;[16] in 1861 a case was brought against the Reverend Yeats by a creditor who tried to claim the Thomastown lands, but they stayed in the family's hands and were repeatedly remortgaged.[17] His son's only income came from some Dublin house property (sold for £600 in early 1877, which was all swallowed by debts), and the farms at Thomastown, which had come down from his Butler great-grandmother.[18] Family lore supposed this income to be £500 to £600 a year, a good income for an era when a hundred a year could keep hunters and servants.[19] Actually in 1863 it brought in £379. 6s. 0d. net and that declined with agrarian crisis. It was remortgaged before the end of 1867; in 1873 net receipts were £206; in 1874, £72; and by 1880 it was bringing in practically nothing at all.[20] The Corbet relationship, for all the apparent grandeur of 'Sandymount Castle', ran more spectacularly into insolvency. Uncle Robert Corbet was a stockbroker and agent for the Royal Exchange Assurance Company, working for the Encumbered Estates Court, which sold off bankrupt estates after the Famine; he should have made a comfortable fortune. But he became embroiled in difficulties, and in 1870 committed suicide by jumping off the Holyhead mailboat.[21] The Corbet–Yeats family history brings together all the emblems signifying the decline of an Ascendancy elite.

The Pollexfens, on the other hand, were apparently rich. The milling and shipping interests had prospered and expanded; grandfather Pollexfen reputedly had £4,000 a year. But he gave none of his daughters marriage portions, nor allowances to his unmarried daughters, even though he took over the property they inherited from the Middleton side.[22] George Pollexfen made a good deal of money for his part, according to JBY, through the exertions of an alcoholic clerk possessed by financial genius, called Doyle.[23] Though George was a nominal partner from 1884, in practice the firm was increasingly taken over by Arthur Jackson, who had married Alice Pollexfen. There were subsidiary elements of the business, like the Sligo Steam Navigation Company (founded by Susan's father, William Pollexfen, and his brother-in-law William Middleton), whose Liverpool office was at one point managed by George (and also employed another brother, Alfred). Both Middleton and Pollexfen were directors of the Sligo Gas, Light & Coke Company, and prominent members of the Butter Market.

Middleton & Pollexfen were a not uncontroversial firm. Bitter battles had to be fought on the Town and Harbour Commission Board (a spectacularly unreformed body), and unfortunately for the public image of the brothers-in-law a fellow-member who opposed them, Alexander Gillmor, was also the proprietor of the *Sligo Independent*. William Pollexfen failed to be elected to the town council in November 1863, and again in 1867, running on a stout anti-reform platform. The firm's vested commercial interests were thrown against the Board's efforts to reform regulations concerning pilots. Middleton's immortality may be ensured through a mention on the first page of WBY's *Autobiographies*, expressing gratitude to his great-uncle for the reflection that 'we should not make light of the troubles of children'. But in contemporary local history he emerges as the voice of hard-headed and belligerent business interests,[24] frequently accused of exploitation and monopoly. He was particularly notorious for 'the grasping spirit displayed by him in the salvage courts', through whose activities the firm made much of its money – since they owned the only steam-tug in the port. This explains why William Falconer's *Shipwreck* was the only book WBY remembered upon his grandfather's table, except for the Bible.[25] The *Sligo Independent*'s description of the firm's attitude to rival local interests oddly echoes JBY's description of the Pollexfens: 'uniform bitterness, implacable hostility, and morose discontent'.[26] Later, they were equally unpopular when they blocked the water-run to a local salmon-weir[27] and opposed efforts to reform the harbour administration. They also argued against the preferred scheme for a clean water supply – again, in order to protect family interests.[28] The firm stood 'alone in obstruction and opposition', according to the *Sligo Independent*: 'just the old story over again'.[29] Middleton's effrontery, attempted 'dictatorship' and nepotism in local affairs dominated the Sligo press in the 1870s; his influence in local elections was exerted on the Tory and Protestant side, though the firm employed Catholics and Protestants equally.[30] William Pollexfen was among those found guilty of bribing voters in 1860: Sligo, until its disenfranchisement in 1870, was supposed to be 'the most rotten borough in the kingdom'.

This was the basis on which local prominence was built. Oddly, WBY's childhood vision saw Pollexfen as a passionate Lear-figure, and Middleton as quiet, civil and withdrawn – images reversed in local lore. To their grandchildren's generation, however, Middleton and Pollexfen stood as the elders of the tribe, respected and feared. Lily Yeats remembered returning to the town after a long English visit, aged seven or eight, and being greeted by blazing tar-barrels all along the road from the station.[31] The family's move from Union Place to Merville, a large house outside the town with extensive outbuildings and a fine view of Ben Bulben, signified an advance in status. But they expected respectability of their relations: and JBY did not conform. In January

1866 he was called to the Bar, but in 1867 he abandoned law and went to art school in London: first Heatherley's, then the Slade. He was already a talented draughtsman, and his sketches of scenes in Dublin's law courts had become celebrated – too celebrated to do his career much good.[32] On the strength of encouragement from a London magazine editor (Tom Hood of *Fun*) he took a drastic plunge. His first commission did not come until 1871, by which time he had four children and a discontented wife – all of whom spent much of their time with the Pollexfens in Sligo, for reasons of financial necessity.

Under such circumstances the marriage could not prosper. Susan Yeats, increasingly withdrawn and resentful, left her husband in no doubt about her feelings. 'At first when Susan insulted me and my friends I used to mind a great deal, but afterwards I did not mind at all. I would say laughingly to her that if she drove me away there would not be a friend left to her.'[33] (Such a fate was, of course, far less of a hardship to a Pollexfen than to a Yeats.) Her withdrawal eventually became depressive: Lily Yeats described her habit of lapsing into sleep. '[Her] illness was mental. She used to fall asleep as a young woman any time she sat quiet for a while or read out to us children. We just rattled her up again, poor woman.'[34] Some local opinion thought that Susan was 'always very odd',[35] but JBY too readily stressed the Pollexfen propensity to 'depressive mania'.[36] He endlessly categorized and analysed her character, especially when writing after her death to his great love, Rosa Butt, trying to explain the low-key tragedy of Susan's life. Under the circumstances, he needed to be defensive: it is probable that he unduly emphasized his wife's propensity to lash out at him.[37] Similarly, he stressed her hatred of his relentless sociability with like-minded artistic and literary friends.

She always had a poor opinion of her neighbours. This was her puritanism. Of the cleverest people she would always mutter, '*They had no sense.*' Her ill opinion was most undeviating and impartially unfair. But she never could see any difference between a lord and a labourer. Not that she had any kind of spite against the lord. Simply, distinctions of class did not exist for her, and the labourer she knew a great deal about. She was selfcentred and did not notice any person outside the few people she liked. *They were very few.*[38]

There were, of course, two sides to this story, and hers is silence. JBY was, he told Rosa Butt, 'always chaste . . . I was faithful to my dear wife except for that one transitory passion which was to me a *source of misery* at the time.' Elsewhere he dates this lapse as soon after the marriage, in the 1860s.[39] But there are other forms of infidelity. Susan Yeats, her background dominated by a powerful and taciturn father, entered marriage to be dominated by an equally self-willed, though talkative husband. His letters to her convey exasperation at her anxiety, and her health worries ('You tell me your weight but

I don't know in the least whether it was good or bad – as I don't know what your weight was when last weighed.' 'All your family's ailments begin in the mind a sort of nightmare takes possession of them and they lose their appetite and get ill.'⁴⁰) But she had good reasons to feel uneasy.

From the beginning, it was a peripatetic life. JBY had lived with his widowed mother at 21 Morehampton Road, Dublin, before his marriage; the young couple rented 18 Madeley Terrace, Sandymount, after their wedding, and subsequently (in 1865) 1 George's Ville (now 5 Sandymount Avenue) near the Corbet home at Sandymount Castle. In late February or early March 1867, with JBY's decision to leave the Bar and study art in London, they moved to 10 Gloucester Street, Regent's Park; from 1 July 1867 until July 1873 they occupied 23 Fitzroy Road near by. From October 1874 the whole family, reunited after an interim in Sligo, lived at 14 Edith Villas, North End, in Fulham. There were also studios at Newman Street (from October 1868) and subsequently Holland Park Road and Bedford Gardens: all this before the move to 8 Woodstock Road, Bedford Park, in the spring of 1879. Meanwhile there were the long summers in Sligo, often prolonged for the children into autumn. In 1868 they visited with their grandparents until Christmas; in 1872 Susan and her children stayed there for nearly two years, while Fitzroy Road was being given up. From the summer of 1879, a particularly low point for the Yeats family's morale, finances and parental relationship, the youngest child Jack lived with his grandparents for eight years.

'You must be a good wife,' JBY wrote to Susan in February 1873, '& heroic & not vex yourself about having to stop in Sligo till June or May. I know Merville is not a very pleasant house but I think it is pleasanter to be there than to be here with no money & not enough servants & a husband unsuccessful (you would perhaps put up with the husband but the anxiety and the work would simply kill you).'⁴¹ Alone in London, JBY could exercise unhampered his genius for demanding and intense friendship. He was stimulated by younger companions at Heatherley's, like John Trivett Nettleship and Edwin Ellis, both as interested in literature as in painting:⁴² both would become fixtures in the Yeats circle, resented by Susan Yeats (whom Ellis in turn particularly disliked). They were later joined, from Dublin, by the doctor-turned-poet John Todhunter, lured to London by JBY. From 1869 JBY shared a studio at 74 Newman Street with Ellis. This group of painters and writers, known loosely as 'the Brotherhood', provided him with the kind of circle he craved, and in which he shone. And he had begun what would be a life's course of artistic procrastination, permanently plagued by an inability to finish a picture to his liking, whatever the circumstances. As time passed and poverty encroached, the Pollexfen world (which underwrote his family's precarious finances) maddened JBY: his accusations mounted up, wildly and entertainingly. The

Pollexfens lived only for bad news; they refused to show affection, on principle; on their excruciating Sundays they sat all over the house in different rooms, refusing either to go out or to run the risk of meeting each other.[43] Much of his Pollexfen obsession was rooted in guilt at being supported by them. Forty years later he still dreamt about his father-in-law, 'who asked me how long I expected him to support me. I thought I was staying at Merville. I awoke miserable, and remained so for a long time.'[44] In this uncertain, shifting world, with detached parents and constantly critical finances, the four children[45] of John and Susan Yeats were reared, their only constant point of reference the Pollexfen world of Sligo.

II

One of JBY's more inexplicable remarks comes in a letter of 1903 to Rosa Butt. 'It is often an astonishment to me that I have not a son or daughter of some extraordinary distinction. Had my poor wife a little more intellect she would have been something very remarkable.'[46] By then all four surviving children were in their thirties, and had given ample proof of distinction. Between 1865 and 1871 JBY and Susan had five children (a later child, Jane Grace, was born on 29 August 1875, but died less than a year later of bronchial pneumonia). William Butler was born at George's Ville on 13 June 1865; Susan Mary, always called Lily, on 25 August 1866 at Enniscrone, in Sligo; Elizabeth Corbet, called Lolly, on 11 March 1868, at Fitzroy Road, London; Robert Corbet on 27 March 1870; and John Butler, called Jack, on 29 August 1871. Robert also died in childhood, of croup, at Merville on 3 March 1873. The four who survived grew up as a clan: good-looking, with dark hair and high colouring. (In later years WBY's friend Edward Martyn rather sourly believed there was a Romany strain in the Yeatses; his English schoolfellows, less romantically, speculated that he was liverish.[47]) They were doted upon in Sligo, where they were often deposited; but their young uncles and aunts made harsh remarks, which alarmed WBY as a child and probably reflected a general irritation with the feckless brother-in-law who had condemned Susan to a life of uncertainty. The children were accordingly precocious, talented and knowledgeable about insecurity, both social and psychological. 'Grandmother Yeats thought we were such sad children we quite depressed her.'[48] As children their relationships were intense, close and often quarrelsome. The two eldest, WBY and Lily, would make a 'pair'. Lily was affectionate, funny, strong-minded, and sustained a deep bond (through many mutual exasperations) with her elder brother: 'I always felt so happy and at ease with him.'[49] Deeply attached to her irrepressible father, she could also – occasionally – discipline him. 'No one has a chance once Lillie [sic] abuses them. If Lilly [*sic*] turns on me I always feel ashamed of myself even though I know I am right. The only one who is not afraid of Lilly is Jack, and that is only because he was the youngest and Lilly's unsatisfied maternal heart makes her weak with him.'[50] Her sister Lolly was a less straightforward proposition: angry, talented, handsome and seen by the family as bearer of the hereditary Pollexfen neurosis. JBY dreaded her 'losing her wits'; her elder brother remarked, near the end of his life, 'My sister Elizabeth and I quarrelled at the edge of the cradle and are keeping it up to the graveyard's edge.'[51]

Eventually, as WBY grew away from the family into adulthood, the two girls left behind were necessarily forced to make common cause: their relationship, and joint artistic ventures, would always be fraught with tension and resentment. Jack, on the other hand, sustained ostensibly sunny relationships all around him. But his sweetness, humour and independence were backed by an odd childlike obduracy. Already slow in school, his childhood was disrupted by his removal for eight years to Sligo, where he was brought up in close proximity to his grandparents. This probably conditioned his artistic developments; it also conferred a certain distance from the rest of the family, particularly his brother. But he would make the best of things, and early on showed his gift for enhancing life. His comparatively stable childhood in Sligo may have contributed to this. JBY liked to quote a frequent reflection of his youngest son's: 'I spent seven years looking over the bridge in Sligo, and I'm sorry I didn't spend longer.'[52] His siblings appreciated this gift for transformation too. Lily remembered when she and Lolly arrived first at a particularly hated London house that JBY had rented in Eardley Crescent during 1887 – gloomy, with a dismal back yard. Jack met them at the door. 'He then led us to a window at the back. "Now", he said, "look, and as the Americans say when they show Niagara to strangers, "how do you feel?" and so the back garden became to us a joke.'[53]

In London or at Sligo, life for the children followed a fairly standard Victorian regime (rice pudding, boiled mutton, two jam nights a week, plain bread and butter other days[54]). But it was dominated by poverty, except in Sligo – middle-class poverty, which allowed keeping a servant. 'We were always paupers,' recalled Lily, 'but always had a nurse till Jack, the youngest, was six and then we had Miss Jowitt and a schoolroom. And in Merville we had our nursery. One nurse, Emma, I remember well, an English countrywoman full of country knowledge and ways. She brought up a motherless lamb on the bottle in the Merville nursery and taught us to make cowslip balls.'[55] Martha Jowitt, their Yorkshire governess from 1878 to 1881, was a great favourite, though 'a demon of tidiness' by Yeats standards. Later she told Lily and Lolly that 'she had laughed more in the three years she was with us than in all the rest of her life'.[56]

But entertainment in the London years of childhood had to be cheap and self-starting, like shadow plays: 'Willy was serious about it. We others just romped about.'[57] 'We were there for two Jubilees, several Royal weddings, funerals and one coronation, but not having a penny saw nothing but the local decorations.'[58] In any case, the children were taught by their father that entertainment could always be created through observation and rearrangement. 'When I was a girl,' Lily recalled,

and went even to the letterbox at the end of the road, Papa expected to hear descriptions, adventures. When I felt lazy and said I had seen and heard nothing, he would say, 'Go on now, you saw something, don't be lazy.' Then I used to go ahead and make him laugh. It was not deliberate on his part, he was not training me to observe and recount, he just wanted to hear what I had seen and done, and knew I had eyes and ears and some brains and a tongue.[59]

The traditional Yeats imperatives of disciplined, imaginative, merciless observation and good conversation were imposed by JBY on the household, wherever they were.

He was an unVictorian father. 'Working and caring for children makes me anxious and careful of them, but amusing them makes me fond of them,' he wrote to his wife when they were apart. 'The first week I was here every perambulator passing along the pavement used to make me start fancying it was the children and several times in the night I woke up thinking I heard them crying.'[60] From the beginning JBY devoted a special and intense attention to his eldest son. William Butler, named for his paternal grandfather, the Rector of Tullylish, was a healthy child, delivered at 10.40 p.m. on 13 June 1865. The family was resident in 1 George's Ville, a medium-sized house near the suburban Corbet 'castle'.[61] The doctor, Thomas Beatty (a Corbet relation), 'looked at the baby and said "fine os frontal and so strong you could leave him out all night on the window sill and it could do him no harm".'[62] JBY (still, for the purpose of the birth certificate, a 'law student') was surprised to find himself powerfully possessive about the child. 'I think your birth was the first *great* event in my life,' he wrote to WBY fifty-four years later, when his first grandchild was born. 'I was as surprised as if I had seen a house built up in the nighttime by magic. I developed an instantaneous [   ] for the professional nurse. I could not bear to see you lying on her knees. I was for the first time – I suppose – pure animal. I never felt like that afterwards at the birth of the others.'[63] Something of this is conveyed in a sketch he made of WBY as a baby, and in the close observation he devoted to the child, whom he identified from the outset as an original. 'All little children when they begin to think and talk are like strangers suddenly arrived in our dusty old world, and come from another planet which, though like ours, is by no means identical – hence a certain quaintness in what they say or do. If this quaintness lasts into adult life and continues on to the end, they are men of genius.'[64]

The child grew up lanky, untidy, slightly myopic and painfully thin; he was possibly tubercular. At least one medical friend always suspected so, and later X-rays showed much scar tissue and healed-up spots, which may date from a major but undefined illness when he was four or five years old.[65] Psychologically, he developed marked characteristics which would stay with him in later life – notably a hatred of being ridiculed and (according to his father) an irritatingly deliberate vagueness. 'Willie's sensitiveness to being laughed at is with him an old story. When he was a baby boy, if you laughed at him he would cry oh! so sorrowfully, not with anger but in sorrow that it was pitiful to see.'[66] JBY wrote obsessively about him, not only in after years to journalists but at the time in a letter to his wife, subsequently much quoted.

I am continually anxious about Willy – he is almost never out of my thoughts.

I believe him to be intensely affectionate but from shyness, sensitiveness and nervousness very difficult to win and yet he is worth winning. I should of course like to see him made do what was right but he will only develop by kindness and affection and gentleness. Bobby is robust and hardy and does not mind rebuffs – but Willy is sensitive, intellectual and emotional – very easily rebuffed and continually afraid of being rebuffed – so that with him one has to use great sensitiveness – sensitiveness which is so rare in Merville. Above all keep him from that termagant Agnes who is by no means as indulgent to other people's whims and oddities as she has been to her own. Bobby being very active in nature will always resent a rebuff – and so a rebuff will do him no harm – but Willy is only made timid and unhappy and he would in time lose frankness.

I think he was greatly disimproved by Merville – he was coming on again from being so much with his mother and away from his Grandfather and dictatorial young Aunts.

From his resemblance to Elizabeth he derives his nervous sensitiveness.

I wish greatly Willy could be made more robust – by riding or other means – *not by going to school.* I was very sorry he could not have the pony more but perhaps he might ride that donkey of which he used to tell me . . . Tell Willy not to forget me.[67]

JBY's ideas on education were not typical for his time, with his dislike of boarding-school, flogging and other accepted educational practices. As an under-employed artist, living at home, he saw far more of his children than was normal for the time; when the Sligo summers stopped, and they were strong-willed adolescents, this proximity would lead to much tension. In their early youth it meant that he concerned himself closely with shaping their minds. In his unpublished memoirs he reverts again and again to the efforts he made at imparting knowledge to his eldest son: 'he was a joy to anyone who would tell him things out of ancient philosophy or modern science'.[68] There is a retrospective flavour about this; and while JBY's conversation was first class, it may be doubted if his dilettante genius was best adapted to instructing the young. He did see his son as a potential ally against what he conceived to be the confining trivia of domesticity, since WBY 'was an exasperation in everyday matters over which the women preside'.[69] The development of his son's mind was a preoccupation, at least in retrospect; notably the boy's liking for an appealing or resonant phrase, which, once heard, he would repeat over and over again.[70] Though he had chosen to be a painter, JBY's friends were writers; he read widely and critically, and all his life nurtured literary ambitions of his own, though they were most nearly achieved in his marvellously assertive and entertaining letters. The father also claimed to have dictated his son's interests by reading aloud Balzac's *Le Peau de chagrin* in the summer of 1874, and *David Copperfield, Old Mortality* and *The Antiquary* in the summer of 1879, on a family holiday at Branscombe in Devon.

This last episode (possibly enabled, like the move to Woodstock Road, by a small legacy from JBY's mother[71]) was often and warmly remembered by the family, probably because of its uniqueness.[72] Here and elsewhere, reading aloud from Scott and Macaulay figured largely, particularly *The Lays of Ancient Rome* and *The Lay of the Last Minstrel*. WBY recalled that the reading that interested him most as a boy was 'Scott first, and then Macaulay'; and, instructed to amuse his own children a half-century later, he turned automatically to the *Last Minstrel*, rather to their surprise.[73] In 1872 JBY tried to teach his son, then living with his grandparents in Sligo and being taught erratically by Eliza Armstrong (no relation), who had been his mother's bridesmaid.[74] He also claimed to have taught his son geography and chemistry, on a sketching holiday at Burnham Beeches when he was eleven; WBY would later describe him as 'a tyrant' of a teacher, but insufficiently so. A Sligo neighbour thought JBY was cruel to his son, pushing him around the room. As JBY remembered it, the whole family tried to teach him to read, and became convinced he would never master it; all his life WBY would admit his blindness to grammar, spelling and the appearance of 'my lines upon paper'.[75] Dyslexia has been retrospectively alleged, but is not borne out by the ease and fluency with which WBY devoured books when he finally learnt to read. During that long sojourn in Sligo, from 1870 to 1874, he had lessons from a much loved nursemaid, Ellie Connolly; later he received coaching in spelling and dictation from Esther Merrick, a neighbour who lived in the Sexton's house by St John's, and who read him quantities of verse. 'We always said she made a poet out of Willy.'[76]

III

What stability there was in the children's life was rooted in Sligo, lyrically conjured up years later by Jack.

I remember a small town where no one ever spoke the truth but all thought it. It was a seaport town, like all the best towns. But there was a lake very near to it. The cold brown bosom of the fresh water, and the blue steel verdigris green corsage of the salt water, and between the two the town . . . The weather in this town was ever of the bland and sweet, and the air always smelling sweet. It should have been a rainy place, for it was in a cup of hills. But a rock island, a mountain island, in the sea, off the mouth of the bay before the town, collected all the heavier clouds and caused them to break and run foaming down the mountain side all among the green trees and the moss-covered rocks.[77]

Far from this watery paradise, the Thomastown farms in Kildare remained; and JBY and his children occasionally went there to shoot, staying with the bailiff, John Doran. But the land was remortgaged as early as 1857 for £850, and again in 1868 for £300. The seventeen tenants paid less and less rent. One particular malefactor, Mrs Flanagan, inspired the name of a doll regularly abused by the Yeats children in bouts of primitive magic, since her defection was the constant excuse for their being denied a treat.[78] But Sligo provided security – of more kinds than one, as JBY indicated in a wistful letter from London in April 1870 to his friend John Todhunter.

The worry of living over here beyond our income with the chance of some day being left moneyless is fearful to me and wife – destroying health & spirits & happiness and retarding greatly artistic progress – in Sligo I could live within my means and there are many pictures I could paint there – Since this cold and cough and blood spitting I've been thinking about going to Sligo if I could manage to get the house [Fitzroy Road] off my hands – what do you think? . . . I would there take a small house live within my income and do my work. I would have John Dowden [then a curate in Sligo] for my companion, an occasional sight of you, Edward Dowden and the great family the Pollexfens to give me home love and warmth.

But, he concluded, 'it is after all only a castle in the air'.[79] Certainly, his relationship with the Pollexfens was fantasized in this picture, with heavy irony. For his children, however, the castle in the air bore some semblance to reality. Most of 1870 to 1874 was spent with their grandparents.[80] The summers there, the romantic journeys by steamer from Liverpool Basin to Sligo Harbour,[81] the large house with its bedrooms over the stableyard and the view of the mountains, were all touched with magic. Lily described Merville with the acute memory of old age for long-ago childhood:

In our day it was a solid house, big rooms – about 14 bedrooms, stone kitchen offices & a glorious laundry smelling of soap full of white steam & a clean coke fire with rows of irons heating at it. Our grandmother's store-room like a village shop – a place with windows and fireplace – shelves & drawers & a delicious smell of coffee – the house was of blue grey limestone – the local stone – 60 acres of land round it – a very fine view of Ben Bulben from the front of the house.[82]

Sligo gave the Yeats children confirmation of something their father continually adverted to: the superiority of the Irish ethos not only in scenery and climate but in manners, conversation, artistic sensibility and gentlemanly behaviour. This compensated for distance both from London's bohemia and from the Dublin bourgeois world. For the children, the magical quality of Sligo was enhanced by the family's romantic shipping tradition – colourfully illustrated by the Merville gardens, dotted with ships' figureheads.

They ran a fleet of fast sailing vessels between Sligo – Portugal and Spain. What they traded in I don't know. Salt was, I think, the cargo they brought back from Portugal. In our day these gay little ships' lives were over, and they as old black hulls were used as lighters and clustered round the great corn steamers from America and the Black Sea, yellow corn being poured into them with a delicious rushing sound as the steamers lay out in the deep water anchorage at the Rosses Point. Uncle George used to name them for us and tell of his one adventure when as a young man he had gone in 'The Baccaloo' [*recte* 'Bacalieu'] to Portugal.

In time the sailing ships were replaced by steamers, and the Ballysodare and Sligo mills were bought, and when we were children the firm was big and rich and proud.[83]

It is the world Jack Yeats drew upon for his art, and it formed the imagination of all his siblings too. Years later, Jack's painting of Rosses Point as *Memory Harbour* still filled WBY with 'disquiet and excitement . . . houses and anchored ship and distant lighthouse all set together as in some old map'.[84]

The particular social level of Sligo society occupied by the Pollexfens deserves attention: the provincial Protestant bourgeoisie, with connections through the Middletons to 'squireen' Ireland. They subscribed to the local Protestant charities (though Elizabeth Pollexfen had, unusually, been educated at the convent and retained friends among the nuns).[85] But while their wives attended the meetings of the Sligo Protestant Orphans' Society, they were not on the committee, which was dominated by aristocratic names like Gore-Booth, Wynne and Cooper. Middleton and Pollexfen were not members of the Sligo Board of Guardians, nor the Grand Jury, nor were they even on the 'long list' of those eligible to be called to the latter body until William Pollexfen joined it in 1869. In a word, they were not 'county' – in a society where such things were closely noted. Sligo class distinctions were mordantly explored by the local press, recording how the social claims of 'the mercantile class' were ignored, and mulling over issues like the composition of the Royal Agricultural Society Committee, where 'the county or aristocratic element do things much in the same manner as their forefathers did when Geroge the Third was king and, notwithstanding the shock of time, the idiocy of the class appears to be much the same as in the days of the Plantagenets'.[86] The Pollexfens' well-connected son-in-law also noted this bitterly. 'One reason why I am so incensed against class distinctions is because these very small gentry round Sligo always excluded the Pollexfens from their friendship. Because they were engaged in business they were not fit company.'[87]

None the less, the move from Union Place to Merville was socially important. The Pollexfen houses were substantial dwellings: George's 'Thornhill', a gloomy square block on the Strandhill Road west of Sligo; 'Rathedmond', where Susan Pollexfen's parents moved before their deaths in 1892, 'a good house spoiled by the railway'; the haunted 'Elsinore' at Rosses Point, set low by the sea and lived in during the summer by Henry Middleton, their mother's first cousin. (Dark and eccentric, the family later assumed he was the model for WBY's *John Sherman*.) But these were not 'Big Houses' in the Anglo-Irish sense. And Rosses Point, where the Pollexfens and Middletons built summer villas, had been bought as recently as 1867 by William Middleton from the Cooper family as a land speculation: he paid just under £9,000.[88] By 1879 it was a favoured summer resort, with a Middleton & Pollexfen steamer taking bathers out there from the town. Middleton was building villas, and a hotel had been established.[89] To the young WBY, however, this was not the poetic reality of Sligo. Rather, it featured glimpses of 'grey country houses'[90] over walls and among trees, their names a litany (the Wynnes' Hazelwood, the Gore-Booths' Lissadell, the Coopers' Markree), their life a world apart from haphazard London and bourgeois Merville. When the youthful Jack went to Lissadell for a cricket match, he referred to it as a day 'all among the nobs-oh'.[91] His more precocious brother noted that the Merville avenue was not long enough for social significance.[92] If the intensity of the memory is Proustian, so is the sense of social and psychological apartness.

In another way too the Sligo world was apart: for both family and servants at Merville were, like many mid-Victorian households, preoccupied with the supernatural. The 1832 cholera epidemic had affected Sligo more than any other Irish town, and a Middleton great-grandfather had died with his four-year-old daughter Mary; they were 'seen after death walking hand in hand in the garden . . . a pet dog saw them also and ran to meet them'.[93] The Merville servants 'knew so intimately angels, saints, banshees, and fairies. Our English nurse and English servant in London knew none of these but knew a great deal too much of murders and suicides'.[94] Once more, Irish sensitivity contrasted with English vulgarity. WBY's own early memories featured prescient visions, ghost stories and haunted houses out at Rosses Point: a cousin, Lucy Middleton, was credited with special powers and engaged in experiments with him.[95] The background to all this should be remembered: the context of childhood. The Yeatses were the only children in this family fiefdom until the arrival of their cousin Geraldine Orr, ten years younger than WBY. Everyone in Sligo, it seemed to them, talked of fairies, and so they did – to children. In some ways, WBY required them to project this approach into later life as well.

Family relationships took the Pollexfen form: dinner (at four in the afternoon) was dominated by fear of Grandfather Pollexfen, who stopped his habitual grumbling and glared in silence at the children if they helped themselves to sugar: 'a sigh of relief went up all through Merville when he went to bed'.[96] The young WBY did not respond well to the sardonic Pollexfen manner: JBY worried that his son's aunts, especially the neurotic Agnes, persecuted him for his vagueness and untidiness. When the children's father visited Sligo in the summer of 1873, there was a good deal of tension. For one thing, he refused to go to church; WBY temporarily followed his example until he found it meant reading lessons instead. Not all memories of Merville were happy ones. It was there too that little Robert Yeats died of croup, aged three. Lily and WBY woke to hear their mother cry 'My little son, my little son' and horses' hoofs galloping for the doctor. After the death, the children sat drawing pictures of the ships along Sligo quay, with flags at half-mast. Susan Yeats, who thought she heard the banshee cry before her child died, was probably precipitated by the loss into the depression from which she never really returned.[97]

Not unusually for the times, the children were as close to the servants as to the family. Reading Kate O'Brien's novel *The Ante-Room* in old age, Lily was struck by the similarity between its depiction of late nineteenth-century Irish bourgeois provincial life and her own Merville childhood, 'although there the atmosphere was very Protestant. But we lived much among the servants and men in the stable and gardens and got a good deal of the Catholic side, and Grandmama was very tolerant in all things'.[98] Ellie Connolly, until she emigrated to America, took a great interest in WBY, and was endlessly patient with him. Johnny Healy, the stable boy, was another intimate: WBY and Lily picked up his accent, to the pleasure of their father's London friends,[99] and the two boys read Orange doggerel-poetry together in the hay-loft, creating in WBY's mind a continuing fantasy of commanding a ship's company of young athletes and of dying fighting the Fenians.[100] Outside the walls of Merville, there were relations who provided additional excitements.

1. A pensive and withdrawn Susan Pollexfen Yeats with the three-year-old Lily, drawn by her husband on 13 February 1870 – six weeks before the birth of her short-lived son Robert Corbet Yeats.

There was the glamour of George Pollexfen's horses, racing under his colours of primrose and violet: the children went to Lissadell races with four horses and postilions, nosegays of primroses and violets pinned to their coats.[101] The scene they viewed is preserved in a contemporary description which also makes some critical innuendoes about Middleton & Pollexfen, and surveys the topography of what would one day be commercialized as 'Yeats country'.

As a spectator dragged himself away – especially a youthful one – from the contemplation of the fair beauties in the cars and in the carriages – on horseback and walking – the eye had much to gaze upon in the surrounding beauties of the picturesque scenery that surrounded him on all sides . . . Immediately in his front – taking the line parallel with the starting ground for the first race – was to be seen 'the beautiful city of Sligo', which could be plainly seen with the unaided eye as it lay quietly in the distance, enjoying a repose caused by the desertion of a large proportion of its adult population. No one would suppose by looking at it that anything like an agitation could ever happen in it, or that persons would be found rude enough to disturb the solitude and repose by opposition to its improvement! To the right and to the left of it, behind and before it, nature seemed bountiful of its gifts. Knocknarea stood boldly to the westward of it, like a huge breakwater raised to prevent an inroad of old Neptune; its various slopes and undulations looking 'green far away', and presenting a pretty foreground to the more distant mountains that behind it looked blue in the horizon. The proud Atlantic rolled at its base and from thence, across to Rosses Point, lay Sligo Bay, where the dark blue sea calmly reflected the rays of a mild sun. The neat little sea-side village of Rosses Point appeared on this occasion to the best advantage. Its light house and whitewashed cottages, with the well tilled lands adjoining, gave it a look of peace and comfort, with which we hope soon to see elegance combined, as we know of no place more favourably situated for the purpose of being made a fashionable sea-side resort. We are confident that its new and enterprising proprietor, William Middleton Esq., will take advantage of its highly picturesque situation by making it what it ought to be, the Brighton of the West. The view inland from the Point was exceedingly bold and picturesque – in the distance the woods that surround the handsome residence of our worthy county member, Sir Robert Gore-Booth, Bart., through whose kindness and liberality we are enabled to enjoy each year these sports. Rising from Lissadell, the village of Drumcliffe was to be seen, and its church, and ancient cross was plainly discernible. Behind the many great slopes of land surrounding Drumcliffe, Benbulben raised its mighty overhanging cliffs, and stretched back its slopes like an enormous monster that lay down to sleep. Looking more inward, the hill of Glencar came into view, whose slopes meeting those of Benbulben form a picturesque valley from whence Sligo, it is to be hoped, will be supplied with that desideration which it so much needs – 'pure water'. Gazing more inland, the eye rests on the spot wherein lay 'our own Lough Gill' beyond which the mountains gracefully rise, and are lost in the distance by interminable folds.[102]

There were Yeats connections in the area too: an independent farming 'Aunt Mickey' (Mary, sister of their grandfather William Butler Yeats) lived with one manservant, treasured small pieces of silver, and preserved the traditions and memories of Drumcliffe. At church on Sunday the handsome family were noted: 'the Yeats children are worth getting wet to see'.[103] WBY's *Autobiographies* stressed the respectability and rootedness of his family background in Sligo: possessive love of the landscape conferred a claim on the land, free of politics and suffused with a sense of belonging.[104] In 1891 he wrote that William Allingham 'will always, however, be best loved by those who, like the present writer, have spent their childhood in some small western seaboard town and who remember how it was for years the centre of their world, and how its enclosing mountains and its quiet rivers became a portion of their life for ever'.[105] By then, the links with the Pollexfen world were loosening and his own life was set on a path which would distance him from that enveloping background. But the sense of a lost Eden remained. 'No one will ever see Sligo as we saw it,' he told his sister shortly before his death.[106] This vanished dream stood for more than the lost domain of childhood: it was the world of the Protestant Irish bourgeoisie, integrated into the life of their native place, still (in the 1870s) calmly conscious of a social and economic ascendancy which appeared theirs by right.

But if Sligo seemed the eternal moment, the farms at Thomastown, with their seventeen bickering tenants, recalcitrant income and occasional violent incidents, represented a closer augury of the future. In 1879 the rents received amounted to barely £50. That very year the dislocations of Land War, economic decline and the rise of militant nationalism were about to change the Yeats family world beyond recognition.

IV

'Here you are somebody. There you will be nobody at all.'[107] This cutting remark from a Pollexfen aunt, inevitably Agnes, summed up for WBY the difference between Sligo and London. For JBY's family, London was the background of reality. Their poverty there, the long walks in the dusty streets, painfully missing Sligo, are recalled evocatively in his son's *Autobiographies*; sailing model boats in Kensington's Round Pond was poignantly different from the real seafaring world of Sligo quays. There were intervals out of town: in the autumn of 1876, leaving his family in Sligo, JBY rented lodgings at Farnham Common, near Slough, in order to paint landscape at Burnham Beeches. There he imported his eleven-year-old eldest son, reading to him aloud, educating him erratically in geography and chemistry, and allowing him free range for his natural-history explorations in the surrounding countryside. WBY's first known letter, from Farnham, breathless and semi-literate, recounts adventures with frogs and lizards, as well as his father reading *Redgauntlet*.[108]

A more conventional encounter with education was shortly to follow. On 26 January 1877, aged eleven and a half, WBY started at the Godolphin School, Hammersmith, an old-fashioned and not very distinguished foundation, with a traditional curriculum devoting much time to Latin and 'Arithmetick', and rather less to geography, history and French; science was one period a week.[109] Family lore preserved his prowess at science; he was 'deep in chemistry', according to Lily,[110] and his father recorded that when aged thirteen he won a prize for scientific knowledge, competing against eighteen-year-olds 'whose subject it was, while his knowledge was simply the result of private reading'. Other achievements, according to his father, included a facility for classics. Though he despised Latin and Greek 'under the influence of Huxley', he had a brilliant success translating Catullus into English verse for a visiting examiner.[111] His first school report, which survives, gives a less high-flown impression. In a class of thirty-one boys he was sixth in classics, twenty-seventh in mathematics, eighteenth in modern languages and nineteenth in English. His general work was 'only fair. Perhaps better in Latin than in any other subject. Very poor in spelling.' His writing difficulties obviously held him back. The next two terms saw some modest improvement but nothing spectacular ('Mathematics: still very backward, progress very slow'). Absences were complained of, and black marks accumulated for idleness. In the Lent term of 1878 he was bottom, or next to it, in every subject. He had improved by the summer of 1878 ('seems to like Latin') but was bottom of the class in mathematics and 'very indifferent' in modern languages. The next year, after a long break in Sligo, things were even worse: in a class of thirteen boys he was twelfth in classics, twelfth in modern languages, and bottom of the class in maths and English. By Christmas 1878 his placing had drifted up to twentieth out of thirty-one, with his best work in Latin. His form master, W. G. Harris, generally reported favourably on his behaviour ('Very good boy. Tries to do as well as he can'), but the theme of 'idleness' recurred: though JBY wrote to the headmaster three years later and 'told him you were not naturally at all idle but had a dislike to *dull task* work. In fact your will wants a little being hardened.'[112] As WBY himself recalled it, 'I spent longer than most schoolboys preparing for the next day's work and yet learnt nothing, and would always have been at the bottom of my class but for one or two subjects that I hardly had to learn at all'; he put it down to 'psychological weakness' rather than to 'poetic temperament'. However, his friends were at the top of the class because 'then, as now, I hated fools'.[113] And he was fascinated by biology and zoology, or what was then called 'natural history'. The story his wife heard long afterwards took a typically off-beat form: 'He decided to eat his way through the animal kingdom – but couldn't get beyond the sea gull.'[114]

Outside the classroom a similarly eccentric quality attached to him, as well as the inescapable taint of the shabby-genteel. He remembered his induction into playground cruelty, insults about Irishness, and saying the wrong thing without knowing why: tutored by his father, he 'did not think English people intelligent or well-behaved unless they were artists'.[115] At thirteen he won a cup for running the mile, but did so by 'ambling along, looking behind to see where his great friend was – and the Mothers standing about saying "look at that boy. Did you ever see any boy so thin? I would like to have the feeding of him." '[116] The great friend was Charles Cyril Veasey, a son of Hammersmith neighbours, who had entered Godolphin at the same time: Veasey fought battles on behalf of the unpugilistic WBY, and tried to teach him how to box. Though the Yeatses 'with difficulty paid for Willy to have dinner at school', he tended to go home with Veasey, and wait for him in the garden, sometimes joining the family for pudding through the window.[117] They were not happy years. A certain conventionality was sustained (WBY was confirmed by the Lord Bishop of London at Christ Church, Ealing, on 13 June 1880[118]); but, as he later remembered his childhood, he was indoctrinated with the consciousness that he was an artist's son who necessarily held different opinions from the norm, and 'must take some work as the whole end of my life'. He was elaborately kind to another boy because he knew there was a disgrace in the family; later he discovered that the boy's father's shame consisted in making 'certain popular statues, many of which are now in public places'.[119]

In the spring of 1879 the family moved to yet another address: 8 Woodstock Road, in the district still called Hammersmith, but rapidly identified as the artists' colony of Bedford Park . Though this was a temporary sojourn, JBY came as near to putting down roots as he could: the conscious aestheticism of the architecture, the artistic neighbours, 'the newness of everything' delighted both children and father. In WBY's memories of this period, nearly everything is 'peacock-blue', and Pre-Raphaelitism rules. But 1880 was a particularly low point for the Yeatses: money was scarcer than ever, JBY's debts to his friends accumulated, and the lease on Woodstock Road was due to run out in mid-1881. JBY became possessed with the idea that portrait commissions would arrive more easily in Dublin: the little work that had been commissioned had come largely from Irish sources. He spent more and more time in Dublin, occupying his friend Edward Dowden's rooms in Trinity College for some tense weeks in the spring of 1880, and finally in February 1881 taking lodgings at 90 Lower Gardiner Street as well as studios at 44 York Street, and subsequently at 7 St Stephen's Green. The family stayed in Bedford Park for the moment; but WBY left Godolphin School that summer.[120] The whole family moved to Dublin, taking lodgings in Leeson Street and then moving for the winter to Howth, a fishing village outside the city. Here they first occupied Balscadden Cottage, by the courtesy of friends (probably the Jameson family). They then rented another 'horrible little' Howth house, called Island View, where they stayed for two years.[121] The poverty remained but circumstances were happier, particularly for Susan Yeats, who felt at home by the sea and liked to exchange stories with the local people. JBY managed to escape to convivial company, including the fabled parties given in Howth by Lord Justice FitzGibbon for Lord Randolph Churchill, Father Healy of Little Bray, and other stars of the Dublin social firmament.[122] WBY began to attend the High School, Dublin, a long-established, no-nonsense Protestant establishment on Harcourt Street, travelling in by train from Howth and breakfasting with his father in the St Stephen's Green studio – where he also lunched, for economy's sake, on tea, bread and butter.[123]

He was now fifteen. Much in his life had been miserable, and his later memories of his youth shocked some of his family by what they saw as embittered distortion: 'I remember little of childhood but its pain.'[124] There was certainly more tension and barely repressed anger than JBY could allow himself to remember; but a reflection in his unpublished memoirs stirs an uneasy echo. 'If it is deeply enquired into, I think it will be recognised that the foundation of the artistic nature is affectionateness which, denied its satisfaction, as it always is, in real life, turns to the invention of art and poetry.'[125] He was probably thinking, as usual, principally of himself; but the inclusion of 'poetry' hints that the theory is also applied to his eldest son. WBY himself later remarked that he was constrained in his published memories of this period by the fact that his father was still alive: 'he could not do his father justice by doing him injustice'. 'I could not tell little things about him that would have made him clearer.' He was influenced, almost overshadowed, by JBY's love of intensity. But 'I developed late. For a long time I had trouble in selecting the ideas that belonged to me.'[126]

None the less, it was about this time – between fifteen and sixteen – that he began writing. Lily remembered him composing poems at Howth; and a friend at High School, Frederick Gregg, 'first tempted Willie' away from science by asking him when they were schoolboys to join with him in writing a verse play.[127] At this point his father (watching him as closely as ever) believed WBY discovered in himself the ability to write verse by the ream. 'But an artist must have facility and then not use it. He knew that. He has never made use of it.'[128]

Chapter 2 : EXPLORATIONS
DUBLIN 1881–1887

> At any rate if I had not been an unsuccessful & struggling
> man Willie & Jack would not have been so strenuous – & Lily
> & Lollie? Perhaps they'd have been married like your daughter
> – a successful father is good for the daughters. For the sons it
> is another matter.
>
> JBY to Mrs Hart, 25 May 1916

I

WHEN the family came to live in Dublin in late 1881, WBY remembered
his father's intellectual influence on him as paramount: 'He no longer read
me anything for its story, and all our discussion was of style.'[1] But from this
point too a necessary tension began to develop. While the York Street studio
became a concourse for Dublin's bohemia, JBY's portraits remained unfinished,
and his debts accumulated.[2] And WBY began to note his father's weaknesses,
ruefully delineated by JBY himself. 'At the [Trinity College] entrance examina-
tions . . . the examiner said that my explanation of the rules was without a mis-
take but that all my sums were wrong. It has been so with me all my life. I can
always tell what should be done, but the performance is inadequate.'[3]

Precept and practice continued to diverge in family life as well. Susan Yeats
lived an isolated life out at Kilrock Road in Howth, happy – so her son later
believed – in exchanging stories with fishermen's wives in the kitchen; he would
transpose such a scene into his essay 'Village Ghosts' seven years later.[4] For
the children, the seaside surroundings, marine life on the shore, and rowing
expeditions into Dublin Bay added excitement; but the stimulation of Howth
was not intellectual, though they knew the poet Sir Samuel Ferguson lived
near by at Strand Lodge, and Lily used to present fish at his door in homage.
(He died a few years later, and furnished WBY with the subject of his first review
article.[5])

To WBY, however, Ferguson alive pointed up a certain moral: the fate of
artists who were received into the embrace of the Dublin establishment. In
his poetic youth a romantic Tory nationalist, and an associate of Isaac Butt
and JBY's father in the *Dublin University Magazine* circle, Ferguson had
married a Guinness and immured himself behind the stockade of Protestant
respectability. This was the world the Yeats family had left. The Dublin they
had returned to was possessed by small-scale metropolitan pretensions, and

28

mingled contempt and envy for the attractions of London. City life was compartmentalized: the middle classes knew little of the Stygian slums north of the Liffey, and operated on a closed circuit which took in the professional squares, south-side suburbs like Ballsbridge, Rathgar and (still) Rathmines, and outlying seaside villages such as Blackrock and Dalkey. Social life revolved about a tightly knit nucleus of institutions: the Royal Dublin Society, Trinity College, the National Library, and the clubs around St Stephen's Green. Walking between them, or down Grafton Street, or around the Green, people constantly met one another. Society was small enough to know 'everybody', or at least one of their relations; family links and dynasties counted for much in the structures of career and marriage, though in some professional areas a Catholic elite was becoming prominent (notably medicine and law). The Yeatses, poor as they were, inhabited Protestant Dublin, safely removed from the *petit bourgeois* north-side suburbs anatomized in Joyce's *Dubliners*; the heart of their city was not the plebeian landmark of Nelson's Pillar (hub of the tramway system) but Stephen's Green. The leisured, intimate, comfortably idiosyncratic nature of middle-class life in Dublin created a unique atmosphere; it also imposed limitations. To be of a once distinguished Protestant middle-class family still conferred a sense of caste. But it was a caste whose assumptions were increasingly threatened, and whose perilous superiority had been challenged and, in objective terms, defeated – though full recognition of this came only slowly to the generation after 1881.

The Yeats household derided those who restricted their lives to the complacently introverted world of the Protestant establishment, much like the popular sculptor whose son WBY had befriended in Hammersmith. Ferguson, however, was a less immediate target than a writer of JBY's own generation: Edward Dowden. Dowden, part-time poet, influential critic and Professor of English Literature at Trinity, conveniently represented to JBY the fate of men who subordinated artistic genius to the bourgeois embrace. Their relationship was fraught with half-spoken resentments. JBY needed his respectable friend as an unconscious demonstration of his own moral probity; he was also a convenient source of small loans and occasional favours. Dowden appears to have sustained a genuine affection for the charismatic companion of his youth, and would dispense advice and encouragement to his friend's precocious son – as WBY gratefully remembered much later.[6] His early and enduring reverence for Shelley's poetry, while instituted by his father, also owed something to the influence of Dowden – perhaps the foremost Shelleyan of his time. WBY inherited his father's view of respectable Dublin and of Dowden, who was cast as the symbol of all the city's shortcomings.

The date of the Yeatses' return to Ireland is significant. Since the 1870s the language of constitutional nationalism had changed beyond recognition.

Their family friend Isaac Butt, now dead, had been displaced as leader of the Home Rule party by Charles Stewart Parnell, just entering the zenith of his notoriety as an aggressive nationalist leader apparently prepared to take confrontational politics to the edge of revolution; he was simultaneously President of the Land League, which co-ordinated tenant resistance to land-lords all over Ireland, using violence both explicitly and as a threat. During the autumn of 1881 social and political instability were at their height. In the countryside the writ of the League apparently ran unchecked; landlords and agents lived in a state of siege that was often literal as well as psychological. Parnell was arrested in October, and agitation moved into a new phase of extremism. It was no solution to Unionist fears to have the leader of consti-tutional Irish nationalism incarcerated in Kilmainham Jail, while for the rentier classes landed income had declined to critical levels. In 1881 Gladstone's new Land Act redefined the relationships of landlord and tenant in a manner which both carried enormous implications for the sacrosanct rights of prop-erty, and indicated that Irish Ascendancy interests could not automatically expect the acquiescent protection of British governments.

The Yeatses knew about rent difficulties, incoming and outgoing. The Thomastown tenants lived up to the best Land League precepts, and stopped paying; Uncle Matthew Yeats was now agent, having moved from Fort Louis, Sligo, to Celbridge outside Dublin, and he was continually pestered by JBY for small advances. Though the bailiff from the Thomastown farms appeared on a state visit to Dublin at least once, speaking firmly to the Yeats girls but deferring respectfully to their brother 'the heir', this was an embarrassing and irrelevant reminder of a fading and unprofitable connection.[7] In the real world, rent was due not only on the family's domestic accommodation, but also (from late 1883) on JBY's new studio at 7 St Stephen's Green. In the autumn of 1883[8] they had moved to 10 Ashfield Terrace (now 418 Harold's Cross Road), a cramped terrace house in the dreary red-brick suburb of Terenure. Though geographically close to Dowden's villa on Temple Road, Rathmines, it occupied a distinctly lower rung on Dublin's social ladder. WBY slightly altered its location when writing long afterwards to Augusta Gregory, but the shudder is palpable: 'that Rathgar villa where we all lived when I went to school, a time of crowding and indignity'.[9] Indignity took a financial form: credit was stopped at the butcher's; JBY scrounged from his old TCD acquaintances; the family huddled around a single lamp at night for economy's sake.[10] Yet WBY's schoolfriend Charles Johnston remembered that 'the happiest atmosphere filled his home life, gay, artistic, disinterested, full of generous impracticability . . . The artistic spirit radiated out from everything in the house, sketches, pictures, books, and the perpetual themes of conversation.' But he added that Susan Yeats slept through much of the talking and reading aloud: 'Called on suddenly to tell the subject, she invariably repeated the last sentence, with a quaint little smile.'[11]

Perhaps she was dreaming of Sligo. Escape there was still possible; in the winter of 1881 all four children were staying with their grandparents when Lough Gill froze over, and rapidly learnt to skate. Lily remembered 'Willy's long legs whirling in the air, and seeing that he had red socks', while on the frozen shore fires were kept burning and tea was dispensed from Cottage Island.[12] But their Sligo world was changing too: William Middleton died in January 1882, and seven ships were sold off over the next two years.[13] The firm became W. & G. T. Pollexfen & Co., eventually to be taken over by Alice Pollexfen's Northern husband, Arthur Jackson – whom the disdainful Yeatses considered pushy.

In the Unionist world, land agitation and aggressive Parnellism raised a more ancient spectre: the revolutionary movement for Irish separatism known as the Irish Revolutionary Brotherhood (IRB), or the Fenians. Ostensibly quiescent, the organization was thought, not always fancifully, to pull many of the strings behind the Land League and even sections of the Irish Parliamentary Party. What the Yeats family felt about the political upheavals around them is hard to trace. Surviving correspondence from the early 1880s is innocent of political commentary, which is in itself significant. JBY was a follower of Isaac Butt, for reasons of family affiliation and gentlemanliness, and distrusted Parnell. While disliking the English, he was not inclined towards separatist nationalism – though according to Lily he concealed a gun when asked to do so by the wife of his caretaker at York Street. In May 1882 the Invincibles, an extremist splinter-group from Fenianism, murdered the Chief Secretary and Under-Secretary in Phoenix Park, an outrage which convulsed 'respectable' society. Everyone always remembered what they were doing when the news came. Lily and Lolly were spending the weekend with Uncle Matthew at Celbridge. 'The Rector before he gave his text said that a very terrible thing had happened in Dublin the evening before. He said no more, went on to his sermon. Nearly all the men in the church tip-toed out and vanished to find out more.'[14] But JBY's attitude towards the contemporary crisis remained detached. Symbolically, during the trial of the Invincibles, he sat in court and made sketches.

II

Through these stirring times WBY was still at the High School, Harcourt Street, where he made a distinct impression. A contemporary, W. K. Magee, who later wrote under the name 'John Eglinton', remembered him as 'a yellow-skinned, lank, loose-coated figure, for he was several years older than any of us, and even had the beginnings of a beard': but he may have been influenced by WBY's own later *Autobiographies* as well as by their uneasy personal relationship.[15] The Headmaster, William Wilkins, found 'something quietly repellent [meaning distant] in his manner'. According to Magee, he also betrayed what JBY no doubt would have seen as a Pollexfen streak. 'There was a certain malicious strain in his nature and . . . his worst personal fault was a lack of ordinary good nature. No-one could say that he was without humour, but it was a saturnine humour, and he was certainly not one who suffered gladly the numerous people whom he considered fools. And he was not above a liking for malicious gossip.'[16] The later WBY is so clearly delineated here that one infers a certain retrospection: moreover, he and Magee had had their differences. Another schoolfellow thought WBY floundered in mathematics (though this was denied both by Magee and Johnston) and was undistinguished except by absent-mindedness.[17] While this may just reflect the memory of a complacent philistine (the High School nurtured them in droves), it is a more contemporary recollection than Magee's. Yet another schoolfellow remembered Yeats as 'lackadaisical', uninterested in games, prepared to argue with teachers, and known for an ability to churn out verse.[18]

But he was already claiming his own intellectual niche. He stunned some schoolfellows by relaying JBY's opinions, proclaiming himself an 'evolutionist', and remarking dismissively that 'no-one could write an essay now except Herbert Spencer and Matthew Arnold'. Authoritative intellectual name-dropping came easily to him. 'Brimful of the Descent of Man', he produced a scandalous essay on 'Evolutionary Botany', starting a long-running controversy with a literalist schoolfellow.[19] He was still a keen natural scientist, and wanted to start a field club: though weak on classics and grammar, he liked geometry and algebra. And Magee's claims that his teachers did not much like him may be balanced with a private recollection from John McNeill, who, unlike Magee, had no axe to grind. McNeill

had few remembrances . . . but very pleasant. He was for a year in the class (the upper fourth) which I taught in the High School. He was tall for his age, dark and good-looking and a thoroughly good boy. Of course some of his work – essays for example – was widely different from that of other pupils, showing at every turn signs of unusual genius. In one point, and that was an important one from the point of view of a schoolboy, he was very deficient – his spelling was remarkably bad. He took no interest in school games but was entirely literary. He was very popular with his school fellows and the general verdict was that he was 'a decent fellow'.[20]

WBY's popularity was also stressed by F. R. Montgomery Hitchcock:

a charming fellow, rather fond of attitudinizing, careless rather of his appearance, wore a large hat – I remember his red socks (with holes in the heels) and his longish hair and the far away look in his dark dreamy eyes – a kindly soul that could not hurt a fly . . . His father was an artist and the boy was not properly looked after. The boy had a great manner and looked a Spaniard. It was something to see him salute a lady. It was in the Spanish style, hat lifted high and waved, very wonderful.[21]

Much here presaged the future. Under its Headmaster, Wilkins, the High School was a utilitarian institution, patronized by the middle class of Protestant Dublin; the 'Anglo-Irish' went to St Columba's, Rathfarnham, or to school in England. But 'respectability' marked WBY's schoolfellows, most of whom went on to assured places in the worlds of business, the Church of Ireland, the Civil Service, and other circles where their caste still dominated, often via Trinity College. WBY was not destined for this path; he was, in the eyes of his peers, *déclassé* and disadvantaged, though his father had taught him differently. Harold's Cross required compensation. He approached the situation characteristically: to his more stupid companions, insecurity was masked by hauteur and intellectual pretensions, while to those who could understand him, a much more original (and likeable) side was discernible. Shaky foundations could be concealed by a high style. With a few like-minded friends he formed a self-conscious elite, interested in intellectual fashion: his intimates Frederick Gregg and Charles Johnston drew a facetious tree of evolution which showed 'WBY' as the summit of organic development.[22] He was also displaying a quality which would remain dominant: the need to form organizations, and to assert his authority within them. The attempted natural history society was the first of many. Indeed, what attracted him to the idea may have been the organizational rather than the scientific aspect. His father already suspected that for all his apparent enthusiasm for science, he was 'playing at it'; his son would 'return to his trespasses and sins' and be a poet or an artist.[23]

Magee, again, bore this out. WBY's final results were not spectacular – 'ruined', his headmaster thought, by taking up French and German simultaneously with Latin and Greek. (What he learnt of these modern languages was not of much use to him in later life.) His best mark was in mathematics (76); English (69), classics (28). But Magee saw further. By the time WBY left the High School in 1883, he was 'really an unusually well-read young man of about nineteen [actually eighteen] with a conscious literary ambition'. This, at least, was borne out by the last memory of the sympathetic McNeill. 'My clearest recollection of him is a long talk we had in the [Trinity] College Park shortly after he left school. He confided to me all the plans he had for the future as to writing and reciting poetry – plans which he stuck to firmly and carried out fully.'

Adolescent insecurities and poses were exacerbated by the underlying tension of sex. Later in life WBY recalled his first conscious experience of sexual desire at Bowmore Strand, Sligo, during 1882; some years earlier he had been (incredulously) instructed in the mechanics of sexual reproduction by a well-versed Sligo boy. The experience of sexual desire came upon him like 'the bursting of a shell' – or so he wrote in his fifties, when he had assumed a hard-won (and rather brittle) sexual confidence, and cast himself as an unshockable seer who could say anything. In 1882 it had all been very different. Intellectual knowledge and psychological consciousness remained divorced from experience, and would continue so for many years. Classically, this incongruence was overcome by idealizing unattainable and uninterested women, while remaining resolutely unconscious of the interest indicated by those closer to hand.

The first such ideal was represented by a cousin, Laura Armstrong, red-haired daughter of a Yeats connection and three years older than WBY: pretty, impetuous, unstable and already spoken for (she married shortly afterwards, in September 1884).[24] He first noticed her in 1882, flying past in a pony-carriage at Howth, and after meeting they corresponded in a high-falutin and 'literary' way. Lily, deflating as ever, 'always denied that WBY had been in love with L.A. and said he hardly knew her'.[25] WBY's own later memory of her was intertwined with his first burst of literary creativity. He recalled her 'wild dash of half insane genius. Laura is to me always a pleasent memory she woke me from the metallic sleep of science and set me writing my first play. Do not mistake me she is only as a myth and a symbol.'[26] This confirms that he used her for the scheming *belles dames sans merci* in his early work: the witch Vivien, Margaret Leland in *John Sherman* and the enchantress in *The Island of Statues*. But a myth and symbol she remained.

Part of the reason lay in a lack of confidence in his own attractiveness. His unusual good looks – a thatch of black hair, high cheek-bones, olive skin, and slanting eyes to which myopia contributed a faraway look – were emphasized by all who knew him in his youth. These attributes would shortly be noted by girls like Katharine Tynan. 'I write for boys and girls of twenty,' he remarked forty years later, 'but I am always thinking of myself at that age – the age I was when my father painted me as King Goll, tearing the strings out [of] a harp, being insane with youth, but looking very desirable – alas no woman noticed it at the time – with dreamy eyes and a great mass of black hair. It hangs in our drawingroom now – a pathetic memory of a really dreadful time.'[27]

III

It was the time, none the less, when he began to write, and to be published. By 1882 he was already writing about poetry, and sending verses, to a literary-minded acquaintance encountered at the house of his father's landlord.[28] From this time his family grew used to the 'humming' sound of WBY composing in his room: achieving rhyme and rhythm through articulation, in default of an acquired technique and anticipating the importance of chanting and invocation in his later work.[29] On two occasions JBY recalled that his son composed a verse play with a fellow-pupil at the High School (Frederick Gregg) when aged sixteen, which would have been in 1881.[30] He read verses to Johnston, who persisted in admiring them more than anything he subsequently wrote. Another family memory involved WBY producing screeds of nonsense verse for an importunate neighbour, who respectfully concealed his bewilderment; this suggests a local reputation as well. Certainly, he had cast himself as a writer by the time he left school, and was ready to pursue the literary world with determination. On 20 November 1883 he managed to hear Oscar Wilde lecture in Dublin, despite a transient illness and a detour to Uncle Matt at Celbridge (JBY was begging for rescue from overdue butcher's bills that had pursued them from London). Not everyone took him at his own estimation: the formidable Sarah Purser (herself a fine painter) queried the utility of WBY's literary pretensions, remarking that he could study medicine quite as cheaply and more effectively. JBY claimed he silenced her by reading her WBY's 'The Priest and the Fairy'.[31] This was a long narrative in rhyming couplets, in which a Catholic priest banishes his fairy interrogator by telling him that the souls of his kin are condemned. Adroit though uninspired, it evokes themes which would recur – notably the unimaginative quiescence enjoined by conventional religion, and its blindness to the existence of parallel supernatural worlds.

In the real world, JBY's belief in his son's literary future did not entail following the family tradition at Trinity College.

I still saw that he learned his lessons, and he was still head of the school in science. When he entered the VI form its master, who is now a classical fellow in TCD [George Wilkins, the Headmaster's brother], told me that he could be as good in classics as in science if it were not that, having read Huxley, he despised them. When the other boys of the form entered Trinity he on his own responsibility decided to remain outside, and he entered the art school, where he studied for two years.[32]

Or so the father subsequently convinced himself; the son, more realistically, remembered that JBY wanted him to go to Trinity, but 'neither my classics nor my mathematics were good enough for any examination', and another family tradition remembers his father railing him about 'his various inabilities – his not going to Trinity'.[33] The family's attitude towards the central institution of the Dublin Protestant world was always ambivalent; its intellectual regimen, according to JBY, was uncongenial to 'the vagrant mind' of the artist. 'Always at the back of Trinity College, drawing it on, are hungry parents and the hungry offspring of a poor country.'[34]

The Yeats parents were probably too 'hungry' to commit their offspring to several years of higher education: plans to send Lily to Alexandra College had already been torpedoed by debts, and she had enrolled (with Lolly) at the undistinguished Metropolitan School of Art in Kildare Street in May 1883, where fees were only £1. 2s. 6d. per session. WBY followed them there in May 1884, having left the High School the previous year.[35] Oddly, he spelt his name differently to theirs (Yeates) and appears under a different address. Yet more bizarrely, while their father is entered as 'Artist', WBY's is 'ecclesiastical sculptor'. Possibly some concealment was necessary because of a difficulty with fees: Lily remembered having to walk from Terenure to college because they had no money for trams. Nor was the journey worth it, since they were deeply bored by being 'expected to spend a month making a careful drawing of the Apollo or the Dancing Faun'.[36] They were artist's children; WBY had the highly developed aesthetic sense of all the family (and continued to paint adequate water-colours); colour and its significance were always important to his symbolism, especially in drama. Though his contemporaries included future acquaintances like the poet Dora Sigerson and the sculptor Oliver Sheppard, there was not much colour at Kildare Street in the 1880s. 'We had no scholarship, no critical knowledge of the history of painting, and no settled standards';[37] long afterwards, he still remembered his anger at being told to 'copy from Nature' by drawing a ginger-beer bottle and an apple.[38] Dublin had its avant-garde, but they were not encouraged; their eyes were opened elsewhere. When the new French painting filtered through to Dublin, WBY found it vaguely upsetting; a Manet vision of two cocottes sitting outside a café made him 'miserable for days. I found no desirable place, no man I could have wished to be, no woman I could have loved, no Golden Age, no lure for secret hope, no adventure with myself for theme out of that endless tale I told myself all day long.'[39] This reveals the expectations which he cherished about art, and the inadequacies he perceived in realism; his later aesthetic quarrels with contemporaries like George Moore were inevitable. Attendance at the Metropolitan School of Art petered out in the summer of 1885, followed by classes at the Royal Hibernian Academy;[40] but it was clear to him that the tapestry-like pictures he dreamt of were beyond his teachers' imagination and his own ability. Twenty years later he gave damning evidence to a parliamentary committee on education in Ireland, describing his artistic training as 'destructive of enthusiasm . . . I was bored to death by that routine, and in consequence I have left Art, and have taken to Literature.'[41]

This was tongue-in-cheek; there was, of course, more to it than that. Several of his High School generation saw themselves as writers; heavily influenced by the English Romantics and already widely read in the more obscure reaches of Shelley's *œuvre*, WBY's initial inclination was towards plays rather than lyrics. In 1883 he was still working on verse drama and narrative, and his own recollection of 1892 bears out his father's later memory. 'The first attempt at serious poetry I made was when I was about seventeen and much under the influence of Shelley. It was a dramatic poem, about a magician who set up his throne in Central Asia, and who expressed himself with Queen Mab-like heterodoxy. It was written in rivalry with G— [Gregg]. I forget what he wrote.'[42] There was also a play called at first 'Vivien and Time', dated 8 January 1884, and shown to various friends. Other fragments from this period include a draft play involving a bishop, a monk and a woman accused by shepherds of witchcraft: pagan 'fierceness' is posited against Christian charity. The witch rides in the sky by night, knows the 'language of the sidhe' (fairies, in Irish), and casts aside her shrouds to reveal a robe of peacock feathers and gold ornaments.[43] There are also short, highly conventional love-poems, occasionally in the dialogue form he would later develop so strikingly.[44] Other unpublished attempts included a long narrative poem about a medieval knight set in a German forest: a voyage-poem concerning the search for a visionary lady, incorporating Norse saga-elements as well as the inspiration of Spenser, 'The Poet' in Shelley's *Alastor*, and possibly some images from visionary Gaelic *aisling* poetry.[45] 'I was humiliated,' he recalled later, 'and wrote always of proud, confident men and women.'[46] At least one play nearly reached completion, under the probable title 'The Crater of Olives';[47] a section of it turned up in *The Island of Statues*. One draft of the latter work is dated August 1884, but an earlier version exists in a notebook, where it follows *Time and the Witch Vivien* and *Mosada*.[48] But publication (at least under his full name) eluded him until in March 1885 a new 'monthly magazine of literature, art and university intelligence', the *Dublin University Review*, printed two lyrics: 'Song of the Faeries' and 'Voices'. They were followed in the April–July issue by 'Love and Death' and *The Island of Statues*.

All this work was deeply conventional. It was also, as Johnston noted, utterly unIrish, coming out of 'a vast murmurous gloom of dreams' and dealing with Princesses of Sweden, Moorish magicians or Indian sages. It reflected his absorption of JBY's inexhaustible commentary, the conversation at Dowden's house, and the taste of his High School contemporaries for romance; but it also reproduced echoes from the London circles which his father had frequented. Shelleyan or Spenserian effects were overlaid with Pre-Raphaelite dressing, though JBY noted 'a wild and strange music'[49] which may have been contributed by some specifically Irish influences. When the first instalment of *The Island of Statues* appeared, the proud father wrote excitedly to John Todhunter (who had published *Rienzi* in 1881 and was building a reputation):

I have been wanting to tell you that Willie on his side watches with an almost breathless interest your course as dramatic poet & has been doing so for a long time – he has read carefully everything you have written, most carefully. He finished when at Howth your Rienzi at a single sitting – the sitting ending at 2 o clock in the morning. Your book on Shelley he has already read.

That Willie is a poet I have long known. What I am really interested in is seeing the dramatic idea emerge & I think before this present drama (College Review) of his has been finished, you will see evidence of the dramatic instinct. That he is a poet I know because he has such store of what I may call formative thought – his head is full of plots of drama. He has a Spanish play on hand brilliant in dialogue & so full of music. He is an intense worker with an inbred love for complicated detail & has the patience of youth.[50]

WBY himself described *The Island of Statues* as 'an Arcadian play in imitation of Edmund Spenser',[51] involving a witch, a shepherdess and a lovers' quest that leads to enchantment into stone. The Epilogue, however ('Spoken by a Satyr, carrying a sea-shell'), contained beneath its archaisms a hard philosophical question about the reality of the world and the utility of 'dreaming'. And this fragment (retitled 'The Song of the Happy Shepherd') would be retained by WBY in the canon of his work, conscious though he was of the need for pruning ('my great aim is directness and extreme simplicity').[52]

He had been working on *The Island of Statues* before April 1884, helped by the sympathetic librarian T. W. Lyster and reading it to interested people like Dowden, who liked it – possibly because of the models behind it. JBY responded enthusiastically:

I am glad you are so pleased with Willie. It is curious that long ago I was struck by finding in his mother's people all the marks of imagination – the continual absorption in an idea – and that idea never one of the intellectual or reasoning faculty, but of the affections and desires and the senses . . . To give them a voice is like giving a voice to the sea-cliffs, when what wild babblings must break forth.[53]

Dowden, congenitally equivocal, wrote to John Todhunter that WBY was 'an interesting boy whether he turn out much of a poet or not. The sap in him is all so green and young that I cannot guess what his fibre may afterwards be. So I shall only prophesy that he is to be a great poet after the event.' (That was quintessential Dowden.) Later he added, 'He hangs in the balance between genius & (to speak rudely) fool.'[54]

Thus the voice of the Dublin establishment, in the face of WBY's late-adolescent preoccupation with islands, apple-blossom enchantment, exoticism and impotent yearnings. These climaxed in *Mosada*, a play he may have started even earlier than *The Island of Statues*, but which appeared in the June 1886 issue of the *Dublin University Review*. A Moorish girl, magic-obsessed, is delivered to the Inquisitor, who turns out to be her lost love – though she kills herself too early to find out. WBY would subsequently, and correctly, decide it was 'feeble', but with Dowden's help it was reprinted as a twelve-page pamphlet by the Dublin firm of Sealy, Bryers & Walker in October 1886. Subscriptions were drummed up (particularly from Dowden's episcopal brother in Edinburgh) and copies were pressed on anyone who might be of use – including Gerard Manley Hopkins (then unhappily based at Monasterevin, County Kildare), who visited the St Stephen's Green studio. He was not well disposed to this, nor to another early publication called 'The Two Titans', 'a strained and unworkable allegory about a young man and a sphinx on a rock in the sea (how did they get there? What did they eat? and so on)'.[55]

More striking than the content of this early work is the commitment behind it. The pamphlet edition of *Mosada* carried a portrait of the writer as frontispiece, rather than an illustration from the play: a new author announces his arrival. Obscure though the production was, it received at least one review, from his new friend Katharine Tynan. Long afterwards he would recall, 'I had about me from the first a little group whose admiration for work that had no merit justified my immense self-confidence.'[56] He also had the *Dublin University Review*. This journal was founded in February 1885 by Charles Hubert Oldham, then attached to Trinity College, and T. W. Rolleston, in deliberate emulation of Isaac Butt's *Dublin University Magazine* of the 1830s. Like the *DUM*, it was intended to reflect a pluralist approach to national themes, and, as its first editorial explicitly declared, would be unprovincial and hold aloof from current politics. Around it gathered a group of people who would help launch WBY on his chosen career. Oldham's Contemporary Club acted as a magnet for those self-consciously determined to be raffish and to cross boundaries, against the background of Dublin's intimate and censorious provincialism; 'Contemporary' meant that members need only have in common the fact that they were alive at the same time. Such people wanted more stimulus than Dowden's Sunday-afternoon salon at Temple Road. They could express nationalist leanings by supporting the Young Ireland Society in York Street, which WBY joined in October 1885. And the Contemporary Club met his needs even more precisely.

Oldham was a 25-year-old Trinity star: though he trained as a barrister he eventually became Professor of Commerce and then Economics at the new National University. That institution was more hospitable to his Home Rule politics than his *alma mater*. Though Trinity had its nationally minded element, their ambivalence was defined acutely by JBY. 'Some of them hate England and it is a sign of grace. Hatred itself is a sort of religion that prompts to deeds of self-denial. There are others professing a sort of Olympian superiority who

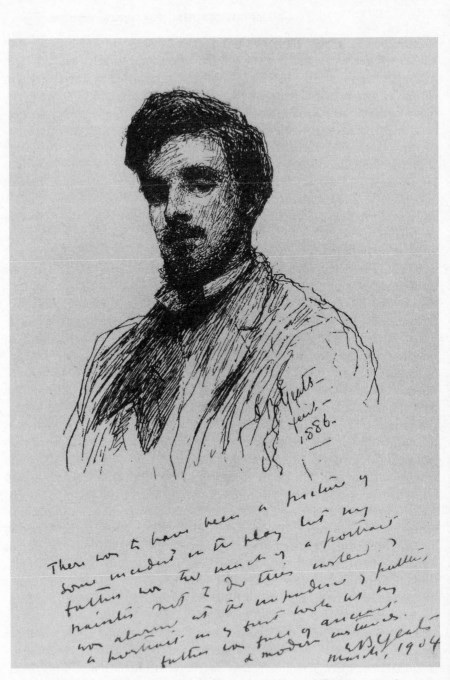

2. WBY drawn by his father for the frontispiece of *Mosada*, 1886. Eighteen years later WBY wrote on John Quinn's copy: 'There was to have been a picture of some incident in the play but my father was too much of a portrait painter not to do this instead. I was alarmed at the imprudence of putting a portrait in my first book but my father was full of ancient & modern instances.'

think that they admire and love England, finding idealism in "an empire on which the sun never sets".[57] Oldham was not of this persuasion. On 2 June 1885, some months after he founded the *DUR*, there was a long discussion in his TCD rooms about 'how to introduce an Irish national spirit into the revue [*sic*]'.[58] One result was the changed tone of the July issue, with a declaration that the *Review*'s columns were to be opened 'to a temperate discussion of certain public questions by representatives of the different parties or social movements in Ireland'. This was inaugurated by the romantic historian and polemicist Standish James O'Grady, writing on conservatism, followed by an attack from Michael Davitt, and an article by the Home Rule politician and littérateur Justin Huntly McCarthy on Irish language and literature.

The next initiative was the Contemporary Club, which first met on 21 November 1885, and continued for about thirty years. In the 1880s gatherings took place outside College walls, at 116 Grafton Street, above Ponsonby's Bookshop. Here on Saturday evenings a curious cross-section of literary and artistic people met to discuss 'the social, political and literary questions of the day'. Declamatory speeches were not allowed; conversation was the preferred mode, conducted sitting down. Drink was not served, but meetings sometimes went on until three or four in the morning.[59] 'Harsh argument which had gone out of fashion in England,' WBY remembered, 'was still the manner of our conversation.'[60] The Club was a broad church: Oldham ironically described to Sarah Purser the never-ending search for subjects acceptable to both religious camps. Unionist and nationalist arguments sometimes clashed head-on, startling those used to the more oblique and inferential nature of Dublin dialogue. But the Club's membership indicates that the political tone was generally nationalist. While Oldham began a short-lived Protestant Home Rule Association in 1886 (again, echoing the ethos of Butt and the young Ferguson), he also grandly referred to 1886 as 'the year of achievement of the Irish Republic'.[61] Fenian rhetoric was, for Club members, an acceptable if half-mocking trope: reflecting the fact that in 1885 Fenianism seemed the heroic past, and Parnellite constitutionalism the hopeful future. This is an important point. In later years WBY was to launch the myth that an attempt to create a national literary culture arose after the shattering fall of Parnell in 1891, and thus led inevitably to political separatism. But the chronology of the *DUR*, the Young Ireland Societies and the Contemporary Club shows that the effort was being made from 1885 – stimulated by the apparent imminence of Home Rule and a triumphant constitutional nationalism. The agenda was not about creating an alternative to politics; it concerned what to do when politics had delivered national autonomy.

3. John O'Leary drawn by JBY: a frequent subject, culminating in the 1904 oil-painting now in the National Gallery of Ireland. With WBY's autobiographies and poetry, these images fixed O'Leary as the type of heroic – and ancient – republican.

WBY may not have been an official 'member' of the Contemporary Club from 1885 to 1887, but he attended. His father was a regular; so were the young Gaelic scholar Douglas Hyde, the nationalist MP, Land War hero (and ex-Fenian) Michael Davitt, the Trinity don and journalist T. W. Rolleston (who may have introduced WBY to Whitman's poetry, as he had translated it into German), the authority on Norse sagas George Sigerson, the Quaker nationalist Alfred Webb, the aggressive barrister J. F. Taylor, WBY's mystically minded student friend George Russell – and the older Fenian journalist returned from exile, John O'Leary.

To Irish Protestants and Unionists, Fenianism was an atavistic bogey: a conspiratorial tradition which had fomented armed rebellion against the British connection in 1867 and might at any time break out once more. But it also carried an indefinable aura of romance, nobility and selfless commitment – once it seemed to be safely dormant. This was apparently the case by the mid-eighties, and the Fenian tradition as discussed in the Contemporary

Club was seen as something honourable if, to some minds, misguided. WBY would later memorialize O'Leary as the inspiration of his own youthful patriotism. By 1885, though at fifty-five hardly ancient, he was certainly a voice from the heroic past: when an observer watched him 'sitting among us muttering of strange old things, I felt as when one suddenly comes on a cromlech standing in a grouse-moor'.[62] The point was that the things of which O'Leary spoke were 'strange' and 'old': his kind of *ci-devant* republicanism, involving desperate and high-flown acts of resistance twenty years before, had an archaic ring, and even WBY found a certain mechanical note in his rhetoric. 'His once passionate mind, in the isolation of prison and banishment, had as it were dried and hardened into certain constantly repeated formulas, unwieldy as pieces of lava, but these formulas were invariably his own, the result of the experiences of his life.'[63] For O'Leary, his life was his art; this was not the least of his attractions for WBY. By contrast, the old rebel's conservatism appalled the young Douglas Hyde: 'He did not think that the masses have a right to the franchise, it was not expedient he said, forgetting that he constituted himself the judge of the expediency.'[64] More brutally, a detective from Dublin Castle, who still kept the ex-revolutionary under desultory supervision, described him as 'an old crank full of whims and honesty'.[65]

O'Leary's importance to the Yeatses (father and son) transcended his political credentials; he was an introduction not only to the acceptable face of the extremist Fenian tradition, but also to a kind of free-thinking Catholic intelligentsia of whose existence Sligo Unionists were blissfully ignorant. Therefore, he indicated ways in which father and son could 'belong' to the new Ireland: a world where like-minded people of both religious traditions could share a pride in an ancient culture, rather than remember the conflicts and dispossessions of the past. Protestant privilege, symbolized by the Trinity College world, had rested on those dispossessions; but by the mid-eighties its foundations were looking shaky. The Yeatses had already sidestepped the world of the Unionist establishment, in search of something more interesting. 'If you will allow me to say so,' JBY wrote to O'Leary later, 'when I met you & your friends I for the first time met people in Dublin who were not entirely absorbed in the temporal & eternal welfare of themselves . . . It was meeting you all that has left an impression on my young people that will never be quite lost'.[66]

It was at O'Leary's urging that WBY joined the Young Ireland Society in late 1885, whose ethos was distinctly armchair-Fenian. Papers entitled 'Means to Freedom', 'Nationalism and Internationalism' and 'Emmet's Legacy to Ireland' were read. Members included Rolleston and the barrister J. F. Taylor, whose paths continually intersected with WBY's over the following years:

Taylor would become a particular enemy, partly because of his own obsession with a glamorous visitor to the Contemporary Club, the young and lovely Maud Gonne. The new names listed in the minute-book of 30 October, along with WBY, constituted a roll-call of the Trinity clique who were also prominent in the Contemporary Club.[67] By early 1886 he was attending eventful Young Ireland Society meetings, punctuated by aggressive debates and threatened expulsions. He may, at this time, have taken the Fenian oath (Maud Gonne thought so, though WBY never admitted to it, and no record remains). Once in this circle he rapidly became a favourite of O'Leary's sister, Ellen, who lived with her brother, and of Sigerson's wife, Hester. Charles Johnston believed that O'Leary pressed Samuel Ferguson's work on his new acolyte, who then discovered the repositories of legends in volumes produced by the Royal Irish Academy and the Irish Texts Society.[68] And it was probably from O'Leary that WBY borrowed the books of the Young Ireland tradition – Thomas Davis's poems, John Mitchel's polemic – which led him to reconsider the canons of national literature, as well as the acceptability of a nationalist stance. From his side O'Leary, while always ready to offer breezy criticism of false notes in WBY's poetry, from the first recognized something remarkable, and expressed his opinion with none of Dowden's equivocation: WBY, he declared, was the only member of the Contemporary Club who would ever be reckoned a genius. (He was not wrong.) It was O'Leary who helped WBY through his influence with the short-lived journal of the new Gaelic Athletic Association, the *Gael* (which started publication in April 1887 and actually paid for contributions), as well as Irish American periodicals like the *Boston Pilot* and the *Providence Sunday Journal*. All published WBY's early poems and reviews. It was important that the outlets for WBY's first work were nationalist in their politics; very possibly this helped shape the nature of the work that saw the light of day.[69] He was certainly more prepared to meet O'Leary's strictures and criticisms than those of many others (including JBY). And in any case, he was tentatively stepping towards more radical politics, in contrast to all he had known in Sligo: not only endorsing Parnell and Home Rule, but admiring the separatist Fenian tradition that stretched back to the romantic nationalism of the early nineteenth century and the memory of the 1798 Rising. Thus he could find a place among people whose interests he shared and whose achievements he admired.

He owed this to the Contemporary Club, though not every acquaintance made through the rooms on Grafton Street was as well disposed as O'Leary. Stephen Gwynn, a thoughtful Protestant nationalist born and bred at the centre of Dublin's professional establishment, remembered that in those years 'every one of us was convinced that Yeats was going to be a better poet than we had yet seen in Ireland; and the significant fact is that this was not out of personal liking'.[70] Douglas Hyde, from the more marginalized background of an eccentric Roscommon rectory, recorded disparaging comments about WBY's verbosity, though they met and talked often at the Club or the Young Ireland Society (on 18 December 1885 they talked for three hours after a Young Ireland meeting ended). At a surprisingly early stage WBY realized the importance of this milieu, and its effect on him: in a few years' time he was already seeing the Contemporary Club as the stuff of future memoirs, suggesting that it be memorialized in an account by Oldham, with sketches by JBY.[71] Thus early, he was preternaturally conscious of the need to impose a shape on his life, and able to anticipate the way it would look in retrospect.

IV

While he was discovering the world of the nationalist intelligentsia, he was serving another apprenticeship – spiritual rather than political. Like his literary explorations, it began as he finished at the High School, and some of the inspiration came from family example. In late 1884 WBY's aunt Isabella Pollexfen Varley, married to an artist in London and more intellectually modish than her sisters, sent WBY a copy of A. P. Sinnett's *Esoteric Buddhism*. This was a founding text of the fashionable New Age religion, Theosophy, blending East and West in a spiritual synthesis readily absorbed by its devotees. WBY probably first heard about it at one of Dowden's Sundays: Dowden had ordered Sinnett's work for the National Library. After obtaining it, WBY lent the book to his friend Charles Johnston, still at the High School. Johnston, handsome and enterprising all his life, had been considering a career in the Church; instead he went to London to interview the founders of the movement, and on his return introduced Theosophy to Dublin.[72] A craze began, to the chagrin of the Headmaster, who saw 'his most promising students [touched] with the indifference of the Orient to such things as college distinction and mundane success'.[73] For some of them, notably Johnston and WBY, the 'craze' continued into the time spent at art school and far beyond.

Johnston was an established friend of WBY since the days at Howth from 1881 to 1882. Here they had gone on rowing expeditions, terrifying JBY on one occasion by becoming marooned on the islet of Ireland's Eye; a search-party found them unconcerned, having become absorbed in a game of chess. This was in keeping with Johnston's other-worldly persona: vegetarian, total-abstainer and ready embracer of the latest fads. His background makes these idiosyncrasies at once surprising and comprehensible: Johnston was an Ulsterman, and his father, William Johnston 'of Ballykilbeg', was the most celebrated Orange firebrand of his day, a founder of newspapers, Member of Parliament and rhetorical scourge of Popery, who hated 'reasonableness' above all things. In the early 1880s the Johnstons were living on Leinster Road, Rathmines, opposite John O'Leary and round the corner from the Yeatses; later they returned to Ballykilbeg, where, WBY noted, everything was made a matter of belief. He visited the Johnstons there, and experimented with eating fungi – probably, at this stage, seeking sustenance rather than hallucination. Charles was, in a sense, ready for WBY. Their paths would intersect through life, with Johnston turning up in the pose of a 'world worn man of society' at Madame Blavatsky's in London later in the 1880s[74] and again as a New York journalist in 1903 (when he remarked, 'There is nothing I cannot learn and nothing that I want to learn' – the blasé schoolboy still[75]). During their art school days they visited the nearby museum in order to search for 'odic force' emanating from sacred objects, a pastime encouraged by the recently founded Society for Psychical Research;[76] more influentially, it was probably Johnston, together with Sinnett's *Esoteric Buddhism*, who encouraged WBY in the new fad of Theosophy.

It was at this stage of his life, looking for a role in the world of art, and trying to define himself against the declamatory certitudes of his father and the easy cynicism of middle-class Dublin, that WBY embarked upon a course of spiritual exploration. Sinnett began it; current intellectual fashion, and his art school companions, carried him further. By the late 1890s he could deliberately distance himself from this early apprenticeship, in lofty recollections:

A little body of young men hired a room in York Street, some dozen years ago, and began to read papers to one another on the Vedas, and the Upanishads, and the Neoplatonists, and on modern mystics and spiritualists. They had no scholarship, and they spoke and wrote badly, but they discussed great problems ardently and simply and unconventionally as men, perhaps, discussed great problems in the medieval universities.[77]

The comparison is not accidental: this Theosophist involvement,[78] and others like it, would be WBY's university. He had begun a long career of forming clubs, of organizing speculative conversations, of interrogating a widely assorted range of spiritual disciplines and secret knowledge. The organization described here, which called itself the Dublin Hermetic Society, dates from 16 June 1885. According to WBY, it was a peripatetic group of discussants, moving 'from back street to back street' and nurturing the voices of a literary renaissance: Charles Johnston, Claude Falls Wright, Charles Weekes, W. K. Magee, occasionally George Russell and, inevitably as Chairman, himself.[79] But it also included the more exotic and experienced figure of Mir Alaud Ali, Professor of Persian, Arabic and Hindustani at Trinity; and in several ways it represented a local reflection of the fashion for Indian things which infused intellectual avant-garde circles in the 1880s.[80] WBY himself returned again and again to the images and parables of Indian philosophy; and, judging by the Indian names that turn up in his poetry from this time, he was probably already reading Kalidasa's lyrical play *Sakuntala*.

Always theosophically bent, the Hermetic Society became in April 1886 the Dublin Theosophical Society – a limitation which disappointed WBY, though he was impressed by the envoy sent by the Theosophist leader Madame Blavatsky. The charter members were almost entirely recent High School products, but Oldham's influence was important. 'Can you manage to come and join one of the circle who are to meet Mr *Mohini* the Theosophist in my rooms on Wednesday afternoon 4 o'clock?' he wrote to Sarah Purser. 'Mohini very like the pictures one sees of Christ. Very gentle. Talks, talks, talks: much like a stream on hillside under the grass: – you listen tho' you don't understand – yet it is pleasant afterwards to remember that you *did* listen awhile. Yes! very pleasant. So "drop in" to the stream!'[81]

WBY dropped in too, and was deeply affected by his first experience of an Eastern holy man: the exoticism, the simplicity, the gnomic utterance all appealed, and were recapitulated in a number of poems. Mohini Chatterjee in his youth was a genuinely impressive presence, preaching the Vedantic way of meditation, asceticism and renunciation. Described by Blavatsky as 'a nutmeg Hindoo with buck eyes', he shortly proved unable to resist the sexual opportunities offered by his English disciples. At least four of them, according to Blavatsky, 'burned with a scandalous, ferocious passion for Mohini – with that craving of old *gourmands* for *unnatural* food'.[82] His own letters to smitten disciples sharpened their appetite, and eventually he was dispatched back to India. By 1900 he had become, according to Russell, 'a very corpulent Brahmin who has a good practice as a lawyer at Bombay', but he still produced a widely read book on Indian spirituality in 1907, as well as his translation of Sankaracharya into German.[83] He supplied Madame Blavatsky with the tenets of Hindu mystical thought, which she fed into the mysteriously derived 'Mahatma' letters to her disciple Sinnett. From 1884 Mohini Chatterjee acted as Theosophy's roving ambassador in Europe. Rather than expounding Sinnett's ideas (which owed more to Western occultism), he broadcast the more existentialist principles of Samkara, a mystical approach which queried much accepted religion and stressed the need to extinguish 'action': the end of Samkara philosophy was to express the supreme in the individual self.[84] Souls, moreover, were emanations from four divine spirits, endlessly incarnated and endlessly returning to their source. Thus in Dublin, during April 1886, he preached the necessity to realize one's individual soul by contemplation and the illusory nature of the material world. To WBY (not yet exposed to Blake, Pater or the French Symbolists, and forty-odd years before his discovery of Berkeley's metaphysics), Theosophy could not have been presented more attractively, although some of the other doctrines, such as the abjuration of all worldly ambition, were probably not so appealing. Mohini's visit was still vivid when WBY recalled it in an important essay fourteen years later; and by then he was able to link the message with esoteric reading from other sources.[85] His friend George Russell, who was also there, was eventually less impressed; like WBY, he preferred not to join the reconstituted Dublin Theosophical Society, but – like WBY – he found his way to Madame Blavatsky some time later.

WBY's own version of the Society's origins is over-simplified, and, as always in his relations with Russell, contrives to suggest a certain number of false directions. Unlike Johnston, Gregg and Magee, inherited from High School, Russell, who left Rathmines College in 1884, was a friend first encountered by WBY at the art school. Russell had been attending it part time since 1880, possibly to escape from his uncomprehending family. Like Johnston, he was by origin an Ulsterman (born in 1867 at Lurgan and therefore two years younger than WBY). Like WBY, he was possessed by the sense of being a solitary, and drawn to the idea of life as a spiritual journey through many incarnations. To the outside world he appeared a scruffy dreamer, wrapped in mysticism: the Yeatses' maid Rose described him as 'a strayed angel'. Periods of withdrawal alternated with euphoric surges of spiritual well-being. He became a painter and poet, but was also a journalist, polemicist and administrator of surprising energy and decisiveness. Quite soon he would become known by the pen-name of 'AE' – derived from 'Aeon', a Gnostic term for the first created beings, which Russell came upon in an inspired trance.

Russell introduced his friend to mysticism as Johnston had interested him in Theosophy. But he felt WBY was already half-way there. 'I first noticed Yeats' interest in life and its shadow,' he remembered, 'when he got excited over a drawing I had made of a man on a mountain startled by his own gigantic shadow in the mist. I was almost sixteen or seventeen [actually, it must have been in 1884] when I did that drawing so the dualist consciousness was already wakened in him.'[86] Their ideas coincided in the rejection of apparent empirical 'realities' in favour of visionary truth. The alliance soon took the form of a secret society, with a uniform of flowing neckties borrowed from the Romantic period. Russell, particularly, was possessed by a sense that the visible world was 'like a tapestry blown and stirred by winds behind it: if it would but raise for an instant I know I would be in Paradise'.[87] The dream of lifting that tapestry bound the two students together. Russell, living near by in Rathmines, was a frequent visitor to Ashfield Terrace, where they 'sat up to all hours talking about everything in heaven and earth'.[88] This was, in a sense, where the Hermetic Society had begun, though Russell refused to join it formally.

Russell's approach to magical investigations was ambivalent. The two friends soon began experimenting in spiritism, notably with a seance inspired by Dowden's account of Shelley trying to evoke the Devil while at Eton. Accounts come filtered through Russell's mild acidity, twenty years after the event. WBY insisted that

all must be done according to ancient formula. The Gods must be evoked with dignity and dismissed with thanks and a high courtesy, or in their anger they might make the rash magician insane. Then he took the most likely of our group, told her to mutter certain words of power making them mentally vibrate within her, and himself walked round the room with a sword pointed solemnly to the four quarters one after another, muttering words of power. Just as the divinity was evoked a rap came at the door. 'Oh', said Yeats cheerfully, 'here is the tea', and went off leaving the dread deity undismissed.[89]

By the time of retrospection[90] Russell had his reasons for distancing himself from WBY and magic; but his correspondence at this time indicates a more indiscriminate enthusiasm for both. Early on, he later recollected, WBY's urge to dominate had alarmed him: he had feared that 'a nature more formidable and powerful' than his own would absorb his own 'will and centre', artistic and spiritual.[91] For his part, WBY disagreed early on with Russell about the correct approach to visions. Russell beatifically accepted them; WBY wanted to interrogate them, as Swedenborg had done.[92] Later, Russell would remark waspishly, 'When I knew him most intimately he was not clairvoyant and had to use other peoples spiritual eyes to see for him but this did not prevent him dogmatizing about what they saw but he did not see. Naturally his mind when unloaded with theory was idealistic. He made a mistake in supposing that symbolism was mysticism.'[93] But both young men, as Peter Kuch has pointed out, were at this stage plunging themselves into the traditionally separate spheres of mysticism and magic. Thought transference, astral travel, the 'Odic force' associated with objects reposing in the National Museum – all were grist to this particular mill. But Russell's course would be set towards mysticism, while WBY was increasingly drawn to the hierarchies, experiments and secret knowledge of the magical tradition.[94]

In this, WBY and Russell were representative of their times. The late 1880s saw a revival of interest in the supernatural and the occult, not paralleled until the 1920s or the 1960s. Key texts came back into circulation, such as Eliphas Lévi's *Mysteries of Magic* and Cornelius Agrippa's *Occult Philosophy*. Sinnett popularized the vogue for Eastern synthesis, and Madame Blavatsky's Theosophy arrived on the bohemian scene, a spiritual experience for all seasons.[95] This doctrine, originating in America during the 1870s,[96] concentrated upon gaining insight into the Divine nature as a way of deducing phenomenal essence; it related readily to esoteric links with the creative process, reflecting many of Russell's and WBY's beliefs in cyclical history, art as transfiguration, and existence as an eternal conflict of opposites. In philosophical terms Theosophy looked to Neo-Platonism, the symbolism of the Cabbala, the mysticism of Swedenborg, and, later, the insights of Indian religion. It was popularized by Blavatsky's *Isis Unveiled* (1875), which posited a sort of occult evolutionism, underpinned by a wide-ranging treatment of comparative religion, and later by her *The Secret Doctrine* (1888). John O'Leary lent the young aspirants Thomas Taylor's translations of Plotinus and the Neo-Platonists. Thus WBY acquired a ready-made agenda for esoteric study. And since Theosophy also reconciled Darwinian evolutionary theory, discoveries in physics and electromagnetism, it did not require – in the short term – an immediate break with nineteenth-century science: evolution was possible on a spiritual level too. This, in fact, was the central thesis of Sinnett's *Esoteric Buddhism*.

More specifically, WBY (and, indeed, Russell and Johnston) might be located in a particular tradition of Irish Protestant interest in the occult, which stretched back through Sheridan Le Fanu and Charles Maturin, took in WBY's contemporary Bram Stoker, and carried forward to Elizabeth Bowen: all figures from the increasingly marginalized Irish Protestant middle class, from families with strong clerical connections, declining fortunes and a tenuous hold on landed authority. An interest in the occult might be seen on one level as a strategy for coping with contemporary threats (Catholicism plays a strong part in all their fantasies), and on another as a search for psychic control. The Irish Protestant sense of displacement, their loss of social and psychological integration towards the end of the nineteenth century, was particularly acute in the Yeatses' case: the family experience had anticipated the decline of a whole subculture. Lily, like her brother, was a believer in second sight and familiar ghosts; Sligo family lore was rich in stories of hauntings. WBY was prepared for belief. And over and above all, far more consciously, he was ready to assert a different allegiance from his father's over-articulate positivism. Yet it was not simple faith, nor ever would be. In occult matters, from very early on, he was conscious of two kinds of truth, essential and factual.[97] The spiritual and real worlds, in WBY's mind, interpenetrated each other, allowing for belief as a metaphorical rather than a literal truth. In this, of course, he was not far from the apologetics of conventional Christian religious faith; but, in terms of his early relationship with Russell, this approach was more sceptical than his fellow-seeker's. Russell saw visions as actualizations; WBY interpreted them as symbols, to be analysed further. And this enabled him, usefully, to come down on two sides of the visionary question at once.

The two friends' differences over mysticism and magic would be lifelong. Spiritualist experiments became the rage in Dublin from 1886 to 1887, and WBY's friends hilariously recalled his enthusiasm for them. On one famous occasion a marvellous vision resolved itself into a glass-reflection of someone polishing the shopfront opposite the seance room; another time 'an athletic youth' in a trance saw a pair of skulls. ' "Skulls! Describe them!" Willie said in a solemn voice. "They are just ordinary rowing sculls." '[98] But much worse happened at a disastrous seance in January 1888, organized by a Dublin spiritualist; Russell refused to go but WBY did. What happened shocked him violently.

Presently my shoulders began to twitch and my hands. I could easily have stopped them, but I had never heard of such a thing and I was curious. After a few minutes the movement became violent and I stopped it. I sat motionless for a while and then my whole body moved like a suddenly unrolled watch-spring, and I was thrown backward on the wall. I again stilled the movement and sat at the table. Everybody began to say I was a medium, and that if I would not resist some wonderful thing would happen.

So it did, but in the frightening form of further convulsive movements, and a wave of group hysteria. His friend Katharine Tynan took to saying Paternosters, while all that WBY could remember as a mantra was the opening of *Paradise Lost*. Equilibrium was slowly regained. But 'for years afterwards', he recalled, 'I would not go to a seance or turn a table and would often ask myself what was that violent impulse that had run through my nerves. Was it a part of myself – something always to be a danger perhaps; or had it come from without, as it seemed?'[99]

That question remained open all his life. None the less, his magical preoccupation continued; fuelled, as Russell nervously saw it, by the obsession that Knowledge is Power. (Here, his father's rational positivism overcame the metaphors of faith.) By December 1888 Russell was already distancing himself from their joint experiments of a few years before; and he had begun to fear the appetite of his friend's ambitious demon. He wrote him a coded warning in the form of a letter to the Theosophical Society's journal *Lucifer* on the subject of the Society's recent decision to form an Esoteric Section for the study of arcane philosophy. Inevitably, WBY joined it, and in an open letter Russell seems to be addressing him rather than Madame Blavatsky:

A young man, whose intellect is of the keenest, and with great power of assimilating and applying knowledge . . . feels there may be something beyond the facts of material science, beyond the anthropomorphic religions of the day. Drifting into that mysterious current which is now flowing through the century, he becomes attracted by Theosophy. For a while he studies it with avidity, strives to live 'the life', to permeate himself with its teaching.

His intellect is satisfied for the time.

But, alas! he commits the fatal fault of forgetting that he has a soul . . . Mystic Union with the Higher Self becomes more and more phantasmal. He recognises its necessity, but postpones the ordeal.

'First let me prove the lower realms of Nature' he cries, and plunges into the phenomena of spiritualism, table rapping, and the evocation of spooks. He declares that

Knowledge is Power . . .

He is remonstrated with. He replies that it is necessary to test all experience, and construes that axiom into a law that Karma is to be moulded and shaped by the conscious Ego. Carried to a logical conclusion, his rendering of the axiom would lead him into the lowest depths of vice to the hurt of his higher nature. He would seek in this transient incarnation to gratify every lust, passion and ideal of his personality.[100]

V

From Russell, we know WBY's working routine – disciplining himself to write for two hours a day, whatever the outcome.[101] By 1886, that year of experiments, he had begun to publish regularly. *Mosada* was followed by a long essay on Samuel Ferguson, who died on 9 August; WBY wrote about him in *Irish Fireside* on 19 October, and the *Dublin University Review* carried a longer version in November.[102] This provided the opportunity for an explicit attack on Dowden and the spirit of West-Britonism in Ireland. 'The Poetry of Samuel Ferguson' charts WBY's awakening interest in Irish legend-cycles (which Ferguson plumbed for inspiration and made accessible) as repositories of national tradition and spiritual truth; it also develops, despite some mistakes,[103] the lofty and authoritative tone with which he had surprised his contemporaries at the High School, and concealed his own insecurity. It came entirely from his own resources; his claim twenty-five years later to have been in the habit of dining with Ferguson seems to have been pure invention.[104] But the assured, direct voice which sounds through his later poetry was already audible in his earliest critical prose.

The content of the Ferguson essay also set guidelines for future development. Though jeering at Matthew Arnold, he still apparently subscribed to the Arnoldian view of the Celt as dreamy, sensitive and doom-laden; but references to 'Fatherland and song' and 'heroic deeds' suggest the different kind of idealization current in the Young Ireland Society, derived from Thomas Davis via O'Leary. And George Eliot, a subject Dowden took seriously, was superbly scorned. WBY returned to this theme in letters at the time and later critical essays: he complained to Gregg that she understood nothing of instinct, beauty, accumulated wisdom and passion. Worst of all, 'she is too reasonable. I hate reasonable people the activity of their brains sucks up all the blood out of their hearts.

'I was once afraid of turning out reasonable myself. The only buisness of the head in the world is to bow a ceaseless obeisance to the heart.'[105]

In more formalized language, the Ferguson essay called for a distinctively Irish passion and imagination against the imposition of bloodless (and self-interested) English rationalism. The arguments probably recapitulate debates current in the Contemporary Club, as well as appealing to the constituency targeted by O'Leary, the Young Ireland Societies and the *Gael*.

I do not appeal to the professorial classes, who, in Ireland, at least, appear at no time to have thought of the affairs of their country till they first feared for their emolument – nor do I appeal to the shoddy society of 'West Britonism' – but to those young men clustered here and there throughout our land, whom the emotion of Patriotism has lifted into that world of selfless passion in which heroic deeds are possible and heroic poetry credible.[106]

This thumbed the nose both at Sligo and Dowden. But if it looks in retrospect like neo-Fenianism, the voice and language are equally reminiscent of the Protestant patriots on the *Dublin University Magazine* a generation before. They also reflect the ideas of a growing circle of literary-minded friends. To Russell and Johnston had now been added a more formidable literary operator, the recently published poet Katharine Tynan.

WBY had met Tynan through the ubiquitous Oldham in the summer of 1885; she remembered him saying, ' "I've got a queer youth named Yeats" – much as one might announce the capture of a rare moth.'[107] She wrote excitedly to a friend on 30 June that Oldham had 'brought a young poet, Mr Yeats, with him. I found him very interesting, he has the saddest, most poetical face I ever saw; he looks a poet much more than Mr [Charles] Fagan though he was poetical-looking also.'[108] (Fagan eventually proved his poetical credentials in another way, by dying young.)

Tynan, four years older than WBY, was the adored daughter of a literary-minded farmer at Clondalkin who had enabled her to publish a book of poetry, *Louise de la Vallière*, in June 1885. Its success had given her a purchase on the literary market which she worked assiduously; the book had been pushed hard by well-connected literary and political acquaintances like Wilfrid Meynell, T. M. Healy, Henry Labouchère, and Justin McCarthy. She cultivated the condescending Gerard Manley Hopkins, who found her 'a simple brightlooking Biddy with glossy very pretty red hair' and a literary persona like 'a sparkling townfountain in public gardens [that] draws her water from other sources'.[109] She soon frequented JBY's studio, bringing along visiting journalists like Mrs Alexander Sullivan, the wife of a well-known American Fenian; JBY painted Tynan in the summer of 1886, during the first flush of her literary celebrity. WBY saw in her not only a friend to discuss poetry with, but also a link to the world of literary editors.

What she saw in him may have been more elemental. He was 'beautiful to look at, with his dark face, its touch of vivid colouring, the night-black hair, the eager dark eyes'. Plain and intense, she was doomed to disappointment.

· KATHARINE · TYNAN · HINKSON ·

4. Katharine Tynan, a woodcut by William Strang for a series which included Arthur Symons and other prominent 'names'. Literary careerism and accomplished 'log-rolling' sustained her long writing life, and helped the young WBY at the outset of his.

Her memoirs of him, written with hindsight, stress how unaffected, gentle and unspoilt he was in the mid-eighties; 'the combative tendencies came to him later'. This does not convince. WBY's egocentricity and aggressiveness were not a late development; they had preserved him through an unstable childhood. But Tynan had been attracted to him, nurtured his talent, helped publicize his early work, possibly received a nervous proposal from him,[110] and then seen him outstrip her. Her later reminiscences must be read in this light.

In 1885, however, her own future career as a high-class hack-writer of relentless facility was as far in the future as WBY's ascent to Olympus. He loved staying at her father's farmhouse, walking the five miles from the red-brick terraces of Harold's Cross to the fields of Clondalkin. (Sometimes he took a lift with the driver of a milk-cart who was, inevitably, 'a mine of information about fairies and spirits'.) Tynan gathered friends here to discuss books and read poetry; WBY became an enthusiastic attender. Their association was mutually supportive (in 1887 WBY reviewed Tynan's new collection *Shamrocks* no less than three times),[111] while she indefatigably reviewed his work (starting with *Mosada*) and profiled his personality as he emerged into celebrity, often emphasizing his good looks.[112] She was a strong nationalist, had worked for the Ladies' Land League, and adhered passionately to Parnell's side after the Irish Parliamentary Party split in 1890: a line also followed by WBY. An intellectual influence is less easy to discern. She probably introduced him to Irish stories like 'The Pursuit of Diarmuid and Graine', which she had written about before the motif occurred in WBY's early novella *Dhoya*; he later remembered that Tynan was 'the first person who ever urged me to write a play about Ireland – I had shown you some wild thing I had called Spanish'.[113] But her prosiness increasingly annoyed him; they drifted apart in the 1890s, and by 1898 he would write that her poetry was 'uninteresting' because 'uncritical and unspeculative'; only the work that reflected her 'impassioned and instinctive Catholicism' was a permanent part of Irish literature.[114]

This said much about the route he had travelled by then. But in 1885 they were young, and mutually animated by literature. Tynan remembered later

the tirelessness of his talk about poetry was often something of a trial to more ordinary mortals. Many a time, when he formed one of a circle in my dear dainty little workroom at my Irish home, have I taken a book out of his hand, replaced it on the shelf, and locked the book-case, to the visible relief of the company, who were usually lovers of poetry, but less possessed than he.[115]

She catalogued his celebrated vagueness, unworldliness and inability to look after himself: once he absently ate a whole packet of opiated cough-lozenges and slept for thirty hours. Years later, less cloyingly, she would sum up what that same obsessive, discriminating approach meant for her generation of Irish poets: 'he swept away the rubbish and cleared the ground'.[116]

This was not yet obvious. The poetry he was beginning to plant out in less and less obscure magazines could be as derivative as 'A Dawn-Song' in the *Irish Fireside* of 5 February 1887 – though it is interesting for introducing references to fairy raths, and awkward Irishisms like *ma cushla*. Equally calculated for its audience was 'How Ferencz Renyi Kept Silent', a patriotic piece for the respected *Boston Pilot* which implicitly paralleled Hungarian and Irish nationalism, and echoed Davis as well as Browning.[117] But a different note was already coming through as well. In December 1886 the *Irish Monthly* published 'The Stolen Child'. Here, the echoes were of Ferguson's subtler translations, the language fresher, the close observation of natural detail a revelation: the most mundane place-names were transformed into magical incantations.

> Away with us he's going,
> The solemn-eyed –
> He'll hear no more the lowing
> Of the calves on the warm hill side,
> Or the kettle on the hob
> Sing peace into his breast,
> Or see the brown mice bob
> Round and round the oatmeal chest.
> *For he comes, the human child,*
> *To the waters and the wild*
> *With a fairy, hand in hand,*
> *For the world's more full of weeping than he can understand.*

WBY, always a good critic of his own work, would see this poem (unlike the work for the *Gael* and the *Pilot*) as canonical: and so it came to be. For inspiration he was already trawling through back numbers of the *Transactions of the Ossianic Society*, where in 1886 he found not only the story 'Oisin in the Land of Youth' but an account of the legendary Irish chieftain Fionn MacCumhail; this provided material for a long article published in the *Gael* on 23 April 1887.[118] The same theme inspired the narrative poem that took shape as *The Wanderings of Oisin*.

He was also working out larger patterns. Walking home to Terenure along Leinster Road with Russell, probably in 1885, he sketched out the plan of what would become his constantly revised verse play *The Shadowy Waters*. 'His hero was a world wanderer trying to *escape from himself*, through a journey to eternity.'[119] There were echoes of *Alastor*, and also, possibly, Maturin's *Melmoth the Wanderer* – as well as the search for an elusive and witch-like lover. But the wanderer, in this version, left his love and travelled on alone. 'He changed this plot which was logical when later he fell in love and did not like the notion of going alone to the world of the immortals.'

Though he had not realized it, he may have already met his fate. Maud Gonne, the daughter of a British army colonel stationed at the Curragh in the mid-1800s, was eighteen months younger than WBY in 1886, and already experimenting with the less hidebound side of Irish life. She remained convinced that she first met WBY as a paint-stained art student at John O'Leary's, when his father was working on O'Leary's portrait; as she remembered it, she was twenty, he twenty-one, and he carried some books home for her.[120] WBY himself thought they met in London three years later. Gonne was notoriously unreliable on dates or places,[121] and, absent-minded though he was, it seems unlikely that WBY would have forgotten such an encounter. But she certainly lived in Dublin from at least January 1885 until November 1886, and frequented some of the same circles. She was not yet a nationalist icon, but would become one; and, unlike Tynan, she was a Shelleyan *princesse lointaine*, equipped with great height, tragic beauty and secret sorrows.

Unknowingly, in these Dublin years, WBY encountered many of the influences which would shape his future. 'I had as many ideas as I have now', he wrote much later, 'but I did not know how to choose from among them those that belonged to my life.'[122] One reason he admired O'Leary was because, constrained though he was by certain strict formulas, 'these formulas were invariably his own, the result of the experiences of his life'[123] – unlike the counter-image of Dowden, who (according to JBY) 'would not trust his nature'.[124] JBY's own nature was unchanged, and so were his prospects. Uncle Matt had died in August 1885: the new agent for the family farms was more businesslike and less amenable to extending 'advances' on an income which had effectively ceased. (In the accounts for October 1886 less than £100 had been received.) The new Ashbourne Act in 1885 allowed tenants to purchase their holdings, and the Thomastown incumbents, active at last, commenced this procedure before the end of the year. Though the pay-off to JBY would be swallowed by debts, the prospect galvanized yet another move: by late 1886 he was back in London.

WBY was less anxious to move. Though no longer on the art school register after the 1885/6 session, he remained in Dublin, spending some of the summer of 1886 at Rosses Point. He was at Dowden's Sunday soirée on 2 January 1887, where Hyde was 'bored to death with his blather'.[125] He was still at Harold's Cross in early March 1887. But by late April he had followed the rest of the family to London. Though at twenty-one he was rejoining his father, and had been intellectually influenced by him for life, he had embraced a psychological and personal course leading in an opposite direction. By now WBY was deliberately drawn to the mystic and irrational; capable of astounding mental energy, while castigating his own propensity to dream; careful with money; calculating where reputation-building was concerned; prepared to act life as a pose; and already constructing a mythology for himself, his past, and the circles with whom he intersected. Just before leaving Dublin, he copied an epigraph on to one of his poetic manuscripts:

> Talent perceives Difference
> Genius unity[126]

This summed up the difference between JBY and himself. He was also ambitious for recognition by the world, and prepared to work towards this single-mindedly. In one important saving characteristic, however, he remained his father's son: he would not compromise his art.

Chapter 3 : Two Years
Bedford Park 1887–1889

> People will forgive a publisher for having an eye to business but
> they certainly will not forgive a poet.
>
> WBY to Charles Elkin Mathews, 16 May [?1910]

I

THE Yeats family arrived back in London piecemeal, WBY initially mov-
ing in with William Giles in Berkley Road, Regent's Park; they slowly con-
verged on a temporary residence rented by JBY in Earls Court. 'The girls seem
well satisfied to be in London,' he wrote airily to O'Leary in May, 'and are
full of cheerful anticipation which I hope will be realised – Willie has I think
been very homesick and has many *uneasy* thoughts – he has not at all settled
down – and looks not at all strong.'[1] This at least was accurate; and by January
1888 even JBY admitted that his daughters saw Dublin as a 'lost Eden'.[2] By
then, however, WBY was finding his feet. Shortly after his arrival he had
excoriated 'this hateful London where you cannot go five paces without
seeing some wretched object broken either by wealth or poverty' – though
this was to Katharine Tynan, who probably required such anathemas.[3] But
much of his initial depression was to do with an unsatisfactory sense of *déjà
vu*, and the hated conditions of the temporary house at 58 Eardley Crescent,
where the family stayed until March 1888: stuffy, cramped and racked by
noise from the neighbouring Earls Court Exhibition Hall. Then they returned
to an earlier lost Eden, Bedford Park. And by that stage WBY had begun to
establish himself as a freelance critic and editor. In his *Autobiographies*, devoted
to asserting personality through gesture, and identifying development by
strictly defined epiphanies, the period from 1887 to 1891 was entitled 'Four
Years': constructed to end with the death of Parnell, seen in retrospect as a water-
shed. But at the time Parnell figured little in WBY's universe: his idea of a
heroic leader was William Morris. It was the first two years that counted,
from early 1887 to the beginning of 1889. And the climax is not the public
upheaval of a politician's death, but a more personal apotheosis: the publica-
tion of WBY's first book.

It was vital too that he had arrived back in London during the mid-1880s:
perhaps the high point of socialist revivalism, anarchist experimentation
and philosophical conjurings amid the debris of conventional religion. In
WBY's exposure to this heady atmosphere, the surroundings and contacts of

Bedford Park were essential. The area around Turnham Green, near Chiswick in west London, had been made accessible by the District Railway from the 1870s; during the Yeatses' previous sojourn there, much of it had been a building-site. By the late 1880s it was established as an affordable location with artistic pretensions; vernacularly styled houses by Norman Shaw, Ernest Godwin and their associates, set in winding, tree-lined streets, gave it the air of a garden suburb. It was not smart. By the eighties, aesthetic arbiters considered Bedford Park an imitation of essential architectural principles 'by cheap builders possessed by the idea that red brick, a blue pot, and a fat sunflower in the window are all that is necessary to be fashionably aesthetic and *Queen Anne*';[4] it was considered rather *passé*. Bedford Park demonstrated that by the 1880s aestheticism, long a butt for satire, was established enough to have moved to the suburbs: a word rejected by the inhabitants, who preferred the idea of a village or colony.[5]

This, of course, was not the least of its attractions for the Yeatses. A milieu where respectable bohemianism met popular aestheticism suited both JBY and his eldest son. The population of Bedford Park included artists, journalists, academics, poets, playwrights, a celebrated pet anarchist (Sergius Stepniak) and an oddly high proportion of retired military men, attracted by the low house prices. Bargain-basement aestheticism existed within convenient range of William Morris's enterprises at Hammersmith, and even Leighton House in Kensington, amid houses characterized by De Morgan tiles, lattice windows, red brick and gables. Activities included artistic bookbinding, societies with large names and small memberships, experiments in drama (there was a local theatre, as well as a Co-operative store and an 'inn' archaically named 'The Tabard') and Utopian socialism. G. K. Chesterton, who was at this time courting the Yeatses' neighbour Frances Bloggs, constantly alluded to 1880s Bedford Park in his fiction and autobiography: its eager fashions for agnosticism, socialism and occultism, its resolute aestheticism, its indefinable pleasantness.[6]

In this atmosphere JBY's house became an extension of his studio circle – much to his wife's annoyance. His prophecy made before their marriage, that his relentless sociability would conflict with her predilections, had come true, and she was unable to stop it. The Yeatses were quickly a Bedford Park fixture. Neighbours like the family of the painter Henry Paget soon began to collect anecdotes about WBY's absent-mindedness (Paget once met him in the street in a downpour and remarked that his mackintosh was inside-out: WBY obediently removed it and put it on with the wet side inside[7]). As in Ireland, people dropped by unannounced for conversation. The people who came in and out included Frederick York Powell, the Icelandic scholar, John Todhunter, stray members of the Morris circle including his despised

son-in-law H. H. Sparling, editor of the journal *Commonweal* and a col-
lection of *Irish Minstrelsy*.[8] From 1893 their next-door neighbour was the pub-
lisher Elkin Mathews, surrounded by sisters. All helped play a part in WBY's
continuing establishment of himself as hard-working littérateur and appren-
tice poet.

The move from Earls Court had been precipitated by Susan Yeats's health.
Shortly after moving into Eardley Crescent she suffered a mild stroke; a
worse one followed on a winter visit to her sister Elizabeth Orr in Derbyshire,
and she was more and more incapacitated, eventually becoming restricted
to her room. By January 1888 JBY had found a more manageable house in
Bedford Park, at 3 Blenheim Road, and set himself to negotiating the rent,
eventually agreeing £50 – 'very cheep', as WBY remarked.[9] (The price-range
for Bedford Park houses in 1880 ran from £35 to £120, partly kept low because
of the notoriously unreliable drains.) It was an attractive house, in the local
Shaw–Godwin style: a pleasant jumble, with a balcony on the kitchen roof
(unfortunately facing north), draped with creeper, and a garden with trees
where the young Yeatses carefully planted aesthetically correct flowers like
sunflowers and love-lies-bleeding. There was even a 'study' for WBY. This
had a ceiling painted with the signs of the zodiac by the ex-art student him-
self; later it was embellished by the resourceful Jack with a map of Sligo, a
ship at each corner.[10]

Thus the Yeats version of the current 'House Beautiful' aesthetic. But
it did not stretch to buying rush matting, art rugs or black furniture, for
reasons of simple poverty. There are constant references in Lolly's diary to
getting groceries 'on tick' with 'only 2 pence in the house';[11] on 25 September
1888 'the only penny in the house went on the Pall Mall [*Gazette*], but I think
it was worth it'. Clothes were cast-offs, socks had holes in them, butter was
always in short supply, and the butcher's bills a recurrent plague. Sometimes
the children resorted to cheap vegetarian concoctions for dinner; often they
were hungry. JBY had long abandoned any compunction about asking vis-
itors for small loans, and at times of desperation was quite capable of divert-
ing minor sums intended for other purposes. Entertainment had to be cheap,
such as visits to the House of Commons (where on 6 May 1887 WBY was
impressed by the 'good earth power' of the Irish nationalist T. M. Healy, a
future enemy). Jack recorded occasional visits to the theatre with his brother,
but WBY's more common routine was to spend mornings in the art library of
the V & A, and the afternoons writing. The Yeats girls, with their friends,
produced for a time an elaborate home-grown magazine, *Ye Pleiades*, in the
best Bedford Park tradition. In the evenings someone often called in for
conversation, no longer inhibited by Susan Yeats's understandably baleful
presence; she had withdrawn almost permanently to her room upstairs.

JBY, irrepressible, obtuse and generous-minded as ever, produced occasional unexpected diversions. In February 1888 he insisted on taking WBY to visit Alexander Middleton, a ruined cousin who had taken refuge in a London hotel after embezzling family money; he may have taken some innocent pleasure in demonstrating that his wife's side of the family had its own Robert Corbet. After sitting in the hotel room with his loquacious father and disgraced relative, WBY clinically noted his own indifference: he put it down to 'the web' which his life had become, rather than to the pure egoism of the artist. Though his quarrels with his father over metaphysics and politics are recorded in his siblings' diaries as well as in his own *Autobiographies*, and according to one source 'they quarrelled more and more as they grew older',[12] there were calmer interludes too; on 19 November 1888 Lolly recorded an evening gathering of J. G. Legge, W. M. Crook, JBY and WBY. 'They are all Home Rulers so they got on well together.'[13] WBY's own politics seem to have continued as those of a fairly unquestioning Home Ruler, though the patronizing approval of English fellow-travellers annoyed him ('as if we were some new sort of deserving poor for whom bazars and such like should be got u p'[14]). He knew about poverty, deserving or otherwise; Lolly also records Susan Yeats intermittently emerging from her upstairs exile, wandering around 'half clothed', bad-tempered, erratically reading out random scraps from whatever book was in her hand; WBY 'sometimes was left to watch his mother, for which he was totally incompetent. He would make her stay in the armchair and not let her get out of it.'[15]

Literary obsessions were one refuge from domestic despair.[16] Another was provided by the occult interests which he had developed in Ireland. As early as the summer of 1887 WBY had found his way to the Theosophist Madame Blavatsky, recently arrived in England; the introduction was effected by Charles Johnston, currently in London working for his Indian Civil Service exams. Madame Blavatsky, now a stock figure in memories of late Victorian spiritualist bohemia, was at a low point in 1887; her mediumistic claims had been exposed by the Society for Psychical Research in June 1885. However, set up in Holland Park by her faithful disciples, she provided an alternative circle as well as a spiritual guru for WBY, who enjoyed her mixture of sardonic Russian wit and all-embracing mysticism, though he complained that one met mostly 'the penitent frivolous there. Still frivolous only dull as well.'[17] Odd exotics were imported to Bedford Park, like ' "beautiful Edmund Russell", the new apostle of aestheticism', who, dressed in Grecian robes, gave lectures in which he destroyed ugly objects with a small hammer. And further entertainment was provided when Charles Johnston, observed showing off to 'the before mentioned penitent frivolous', fell from the designated path of celibacy and eloped with Madame Blavatsky's niece. 'If you only heard Madame

Blavatsky trying to pronounce Ballykilbeg.'[18] Thus one Irish involvement was translated to the fringe world of 1880s Kensington. And on 21 March 1888, four days before moving in to Blenheim Road, WBY made his first visit to the Southwark Irish Literary Club, one of several Irish *émigré* cultural societies in that part of London. Here too was an area where he could establish himself, and build his own following.

II

But the fulcrum of his London life was work, not leisure. Ambition apart, money had to be made. The Thomastown farms had finally been sold, realizing £7,032, which was less than expected; after charges, £1,004. 4s. 8d. materialized, and vanished at once to meet immediate debts. By 10 October 1888, Lolly recorded in her diary, a tax summons had to be met out of WBY's money.[19] These earnings had come about through the web of literary contacts in Bedford Park. As early as May 1887, at one of William Morris's Sunday gatherings, WBY had met Ernest Rhys, editor of the Camelot Classics series for the publisher Walter Scott (and subsequently to become the power behind the great Everyman Library). WBY liked him because, unlike most literary men, he 'had no "bon mots" and several convictions';[20] but he would also be a useful contact.

Rhys was the first in a long line of serious-minded, slightly hero-worshipping British literary men whom WBY set out to dazzle, as an incarnation of unworldly literary genius.[21] He was duly struck by WBY's presence: 'a very pale, exceedingly thin, young man with a raven lock over his forehead, his face so narrow that there was hardly room in it for his luminous black eyes'.[22] They walked home together, WBY missing his train ('he did not mind that at all, and seemed to regard trains as things that came and went at random'). To Rhys, a born-again Welshman starry-eyed about all things 'Celtic', WBY held forth on Irish stories and folklore, bringing him Thomas Crofton Croker's *Fairy Legends and Traditions of the South of Ireland* (1825) a couple of days later. Staying for supper, he ate ravenously, and as recompense invited Rhys to dine in Bedford Park. (Like Katharine Tynan, Rhys was mesmerized by WBY's ability to consume vast quantities of food without appearing to notice it.) WBY pressed the inevitable Tynan on his new acquaintance; while through Rhys he met London writers like Katherine Harris Bradley and Edith Cooper, who wrote plays together as 'Michael Field', as well as being introduced to established literary people and fringe societies like the Fellowship of the New Life. His letters to Tynan record his fledgeling judgements on London literary life: self-consciously blasé, gauged to please his hungry listener in Clondalkin, but betraying a certain excitement at being part of it all. By 1 July

1887 he was dining with William Morris (whom he had probably met in Dublin when Morris visited the Contemporary Club, where he had been sketched by JBY).

Morris's ideas of creative brotherhood, a crusade against the mass-produced values of Victorian capitalism, and promoting the overriding claims of art upon life, were as compelling to WBY as to his father; and Morris, unlike JBY, had made his ideals work in constructing a successful life for himself. WBY was determined to learn from him. Through the Morris circle too he met (on 11 February 1888) the then obscure George Bernard Shaw, a Jaeger-clad Fabian, for whom Morris was also a hero, but who was dedicated to iconoclasm in a way WBY found incomprehensible.[23] 'Like most people who have wit rather than humour, his mind is maybe somewhat wanting in depth.' Shaw was nine years older, and known only in advanced socialist circles, though the Yeatses had been reading his pseudonymous literary criticism in the *Pall Mall Gazette* since their arrival in London. There were odd par-allels between the two young *déclassé* Irish Protestant bohemians, on the make in literary London; a certain mutual respect, prickled with rivalry and dislike, would evolve over the years. For the moment, however, Morris was the focus of WBY's attention. He was asked to contribute to *Commonweal* ('though I think socialism good work I am not sure that it is my work'), and revelled in the surroundings of Rossetti paintings, elaborately beautiful fabrics and Morris's wonderful talk booming down the trestle table. He adopted Morrisite communism, as he later remembered it, and gave it up quite suddenly because of the Morris circle's attitude to religion – mounting an attack in a post-lecture discussion which probably surprised those not trained in the uninhibited school of the Contemporary Club and the Young Ireland Societies.

They attacked religion, I said, or some such words, and yet there must be a change of heart and only religion could make it. What was the use of talking about some new revolution putting all things right, when the change must come, if come it did, with astronomical slowness, like the cooling of the sun, or it may have been like the drying of the moon? Morris rang his chairman's bell, but I was too angry to listen, and he had to ring it a second time before I sat down. He said that night at supper, 'Of course I know there must be a change of heart, but it will not come as slowly as all that. I rang my bell because you were not being understood.' He did not show any vexation, but I never returned after that night; and yet I did not always believe what I had said, and only gradually gave up thinking of and planning for some near sud-den change for the better.[24]

But he was launched, and the new contacts of his London life brought op-portunities for work. By 12 July 1887 Rhys had asked him to edit an 'Irish or

other volume' for the Camelot series; by the following February it was de-
fined as the collection which would become *Fairy and Folk Tales of the Irish
Peasantry*.

Other efforts to earn money were less notable. As the family's debts mul-
tiplied all over Bedford Park and JBY's artistic approach remained resolutely
uncommercial apart from some ill-paid illustrations, WBY and his siblings
placed work where they could. Gnomic references to 'the veg man' in diaries
kept by Lolly and Jack refer to the editor of the *Vegetarian*, who took draw-
ings of Jack's and (on 4 November 1888) a poem of WBY's. 'And now I am going
to begin a story about animals for the vegetarian *if I can*,' wrote Lolly res-
olutely on the same day. 'I wish I knew more about animals.'[25] The *Vegetarian*
printed a story of hers in December. However, she chose instead to concen-
trate on her artistic training, working for a certificate from the Froebel
Institute and then developing a successful 'brushwork' method for teaching
art to children, which she popularized through effective booklets. Lily, from
December 1888, worked on embroidery with the Morrises, bringing in a regu-
lar salary and suffering under Morris's beautiful but termagant daughter,
May (herself being tortured by the denials of a Shavian love-affair). Both Lily
and Lolly were, however, developing the skills which would enable them to
found their own arts-and-crafts enterprise in Dublin a decade later.

In the Blenheim Road study WBY continued to produce what he gloomily
described as 'my ever multiplying boxes of unsaleable MSS – work to[o]
strange at one moment and to[o] incoherent the next for any first class
Magazine and too ambitious for local papers.'[26] But he was able to lower his
sights when necessary. He attempted to find work compiling entries for the
Dictionary of National Biography and Chambers, though hardly qualified by
his erratic spelling and his cavalier approach to factual matters of record.
Employment was, however, offered by the folklorist Alfred Nutt.[27] (This had
probably come his way by yet another Bedford Park contact; Nutt had worked
with York Powell.) By September 1888 WBY recorded that the preceding
months had brought in 'as much work as I could do – only badly paid'.

It was certainly needed. JBY was now living on the precarious proceeds of
stray drawings, and dependent on his children's enterprise. Unrealistic as
ever, he was 'made quite mad' by his eldest son's desire for regular work, sus-
pecting that his facility would lead him into hack writing: WBY was quite aware
of the danger, and thought of his transcriptions for Nutt as less deleterious
to the artistic imagination than indiscriminate book-reviewing. Yet even in
a severe financial crisis during the early spring of 1888, with WBY himself
in debt for small sums to Katharine Tynan's father and probably to O'Leary,
JBY was still prolific with suggestions 'in the vain hope that in the eleventh
hour this regular employment he thinks such an evil might be unnecessary'.[28]

A Legend

W.B. Yeats

The Maker of the Stars and Worlds
Sat underneath the Market Cross
And the old men were walking, walking
And little boys played Pitch and Toss

"The Props" said he "of Stars and Worlds
Are prayers of patient men and good"
The boys, the women and old men
Listening, upon their shadows stood

The gray professor passing cried
"How few the mind's intemperance rule!
What shallow thoughts about deep things
The world grows old and plays the fool"

The mayor came leaning his deaf ear
There was some talking of the poor
And to himself cried "Communist"
And hurried to the guard house door

The bishop came with open book
Whispering along the sunny path
There was some talking of man's God
His god of stupor and of wrath

hat BISHOP MURMURED "ATHEIST!
ow SINfully THE WICKED SCOff
nd SENT THE old MEN ON THEIR WAY
nd DROVE THE BOYS & WOMEN Off

THE PLACE WAS EMPTY NOW Of PEOPLE
A COCK CAME by UPON his TOES
An OLD hORSE LOOKED ACROSS A fENCE
And rubbed Along THE RAIL his NOSE

THE MAKER of THE STARS AND WORLDS.
o his own house did him betake
And on THAT CITY dROPPED A TEAR
And nOW THAT CITY iS A LAKE

5. 'A Legend' as printed in the *Vegetarian*, 22 December 1888, with drawings by Jack Yeats: a product of the youthful domestic industry at Blenheim Road.

Unlike his father, however, WBY wanted to pay his debts, and did so: while his letters, particularly those to Tynan, reflected a pressing sense that he should be at work. Here at least, Pollexfen won out over Yeats.

Against this background, he wrote continually. Influenced by the material he was already collecting for his fairy and folk tale collection, WBY worked on a prose tale in the summer of 1887; it was finished in September, under the title of *Dhoya*, and told the story of a lonely giant and his fairy love, probably inspired by a story from O'Grady.[29] This disappointed JBY, who had encouraged his son to write something which would reflect real life. The result of this advice would become WBY's only published novel, *John Sherman*, which he worked on through 1888. It was a difficult gestation, reflecting his unease with the form dictated by his father. WBY had originally set the book in the eighteenth century (once again reflecting the reading undertaken in his search for anthology material), but he advanced its setting to contemporary provincial Ireland. A first draft was finished by October 1888, although problems of coherence remained and the author's voice was still uncertain: ironic social and psychological observation alternates uneasily with romantic introspection. WBY realized that he was confining himself in an uncongenial framework. 'The difficulty is to keep the characters from turning into eastern symbolic monsters of some sort which would be a curious thing to happen to a curate and a young man from the country.'[30]

None the less, *John Sherman* retains considerable biographical interest: it reflects WBY's reactions to Ireland and the wider world, and the obsession with shaping his life which began to preoccupy him in the late 1880s. Ballah, the setting for much of the novel, is recognizably Sligo, which represents a known, familiar, beloved world; the London scenes are placed in an accurately realized Hammersmith. The Sherman family, 'a deep people', are clearly inspired by Pollexfen–Middletons. Conversely – and strikingly – there is nowhere in this otherwise autobiographical construction for the character, opinions or world of JBY. The indecisive hero, John Sherman, owes something to WBY's reclusive cousin (and occasional host) Henry Middleton, but his dilemmas are those of his creator. Uncertain what to do with his life, he is worried about the opinions of others, and insecurely conscious of his good looks. Provincial Ireland is balanced against metropolitan London; a capricious and challenging woman of the world or a homespun local girl, 'everybody's adviser', with whom an equal friendship negates sexual attraction. This sets a figure reminiscent of Katharine Tynan against a seductive ideal as yet imagined but unknown, unless in the memory of Laura Armstrong. The book's hasty but striking finale suggests an inability to transmute real experience into fictional form: Sherman chooses the maternal world of Ballah, and is chosen by the conventional Mary Carton, who looks on him with 'a reverberation of the feeling of the mother for the child at her breast'. The novel evokes a sense of place, and a passion for a homeland, which at certain key points conveys homesickness and alienation both powerfully and precisely:

Ballah was being constantly suggested to him . . . A certain street-corner made him remember an angle of the Ballah fish-market. At night a lantern, marking where the road was fenced off for mending, made him think of a tinker's swing-can of burning coals . . . Delayed by a crush in the Strand, he heard a faint trickling of water near by; it came from a shop window where a little water-jet balanced a wooden ball upon its point. The sound suggested a cataract with a long Gaelic name, that leaped crying into the Gate of the Winds at Ballah.

Both *John Sherman* and *Dhoya*, written from 1887 to 1888 and pseudonymously published together in 1891,[31] lack artistic confidence: only in the poetry which WBY was writing over the same period does a unique voice begin to claim attention. But his approach here was no less businesslike. In 1887 he was still quarrying local tradition for ballads in a conventional mode. 'Moll Magee', based on a Howth story, was sent to O'Leary (who did not like it much) for publication in the *Gael*, as was a far more awkward piece called 'Lug na Gall', inspired by a story in W. G. Wood-Martin's history of Sligo. As with *Dhoya*, and very much in the current vogue, WBY continued to search for subjects in Irish mythology and 'Old Celtic romance', as he still called it. He was conscious that his, Todhunter's and Tynan's raiding of Irish legends would draw attention not only to the subject but to each other.[32] 'You will find it a good thing to make verses on Irish legends and places and so forth,' he wrote to one of the apprentice poets who asked him for advice as early as January 1889. 'It helps origonality and makes one's verses sincere, and gives one less numerous compeditors. Besides one should love best what is nearest and most interwoven with ones life.'[33] The order of priorities is significant.

While he concentrated on this hard-headed marketing, and tried to persuade newspapers like *United Ireland* to pay on time, his lyrics were none the less gaining in power. In late September 1888 he sent Katharine Tynan a poem called 'An Old Song Re-sung', called in a later incarnation 'Down by the Salley Gardens' and destined to be one of his most popular and enduring early lyrics. Though inspired by a fragment heard in Sligo, it owed much to Ferguson's translations from the Irish;[34] much less rewritten than most of the other early poems which WBY retained in his canon, it rings with a concentrated music.

> Down by the salley gardens my love and I did meet;
> She passed the salley gardens with little snow-white feet.
> She bid me take love easy as the leaves grow on the tree;
> But I, being young and foolish, with her would not agree.

More remarkably, he knew that this hard edge must be striven for, against a natural inclination to the ethereal and unreal. His poetry, he told Tynan in March 1888, was 'the cry of the heart against neccesity. I hope some day to alter that and write poetry of insight and knowledge.'[35] (This was another way of expressing his father's preference for *John Sherman* over *Dhoya*.) In language too a harder edge had to be sought: 'I hate the soft modern manner.'[36] 'Clouds' had to be eliminated, restoring Pre-Raphaelite clarity. However, his vocabulary and imagery remained enmeshed in romanticism, and, though preoccupied by certain philosophical themes (notably the reconciliation of opposites), he was still capable of turning out portentous patriotic verses for Irish American papers like the *Boston Pilot*: on 6 August 1887 it published 'How Ferencz Renyi Kept Silent'. The poem's dedication paralleled the cases of Hungary and Ireland, a concept which would be given wider and influential currency a decade later when Arthur Griffith wrote *The Resurrection of Hungary: A Parallel for Ireland*, and began the movement known as Sinn Féin.[37]

III

Ireland and Irish concerns continued to provide both an emotional refuge and a literary *raison d'être*. In August 1887 WBY set off to stay with relations in Sligo; later in the autumn he moved on to Dublin, and stayed there until January 1888. Here, Katharine Tynan and her father offered hospitality. She had just published *Shamrocks* and was assiduously planting out reviews; WBY's correspondence with her remained intense, and he had stressed from London their literary comradeship. 'I feel more and more that we shall have a school of Irish poetry – founded on Irish myth and History – a neo-romantic movement.'[38] But there was another tone too: random, funny, light in hand, sometimes flippant. 'I see every thing through the coloured glass of my own moods, not being I supose very sympathetic.'[39] He indulged in introspection to her, as to no other surviving correspondent, describing the 'web' he was trapped in: 'You used to say I had no heart – that is all the web.'[40] He was, he would later say, breaking 'my life in a morter', and had to give it shape and purpose.[41]

This was dangerous territory. A few years later a more experienced woman would accuse him of writing 'unconscious love letters': could the same be said of these? In his own *Memoirs* WBY recalled his father warning him that Tynan ('a very plain woman') might make herself very unhappy about him, and that it might be his duty to propose – a prospect he agonized over.[42] Far as she was from the dream-women of his imagination and his early poetry,

70

convention may have impelled him towards the idea – especially as he would spend nearly two months staying in her father's house that winter.

From London he had kept up with other members of the Dublin circle: Douglas Hyde was approached, not only for help with Irish translations and advice about folklore and Gaelic poetry, but even to provide suitable clothes for an Irish 'peasent' in a painting by a Bedford Park neighbour ('Do you know any old peasent who would sell his cloathes?'[43]) John O'Leary's sister Ellen, herself a poet, continued to take a motherly interest: 'among all her younger friends these latter days', O'Leary wrote to Hyde after her death in October 1889, 'you, after young Yeats, were altogether the most agreeable to her'.[44] (This cannot have endeared wby to Hyde, already irritated by his pretensions.) Irish literary life had continued active; the formation of the Pan-Celtic Society, 'national' and literary, on 1 March 1888 brought in many of wby's old circle,[45] and was exactly the kind of involvement he missed. His long visit to Ireland in late 1887 represented a determination, above all, to stay in touch.

On 9 August 1887 he set off from London via Liverpool by courtesy (as in his childhood) of the Sligo Steam Navigation Company. He arrived in the town on 11 August, and by September was staying out at Rosses Point: but here too he now felt displaced. 'This to me is the lonliest place in the world,' he wrote to Tynan. 'Going for a walk is a continual meeting with ghosts for Sligo for me has no flesh and blood attractions – only memories and sentimenttalities accumulated here as a child making it more dear than any other place.'[46] In August, before wby's arrival, his uncle George Pollexfen (saturnine as ever) had sent him a copy of a paranoid Unionist broadsheet, the *Union*, which denounced both the Gaelic Athletic Association and the *Gael* as seditious, specifically mentioning O'Leary's involvement; but they got on well, and wby spent his time between Pollexfen's summer house and 'Elsinore', the home of his cousin Henry Middleton. He found it easy to write there, and also collected some fairy stories 'for an article or two'. His poetic production included short lyrics and ballads, some inspired by Sligo history as retailed in the canonical books by O'Rorke and Wood-Martin;[47] but he also worked on portions of the developing narrative poem *The Wanderings of Oisin*, and a mythologically inspired story about a giant who loses his fairy love in a game of chess, 'dreamy and florid', as wby accurately described it in a letter to Sparling: it indicates that *Dhoya* was still in progress.[48] He also extended the first outline of *John Sherman*, reflecting his Sligo surroundings. 'Am as usual fighting that old snake – revery,' he wrote to Tynan, 'to get from him a few hours each day for my writing.'[49]

When the weather worsened he moved into Sligo town and stayed with his grandparents – since 1885 no longer at Merville, but occupying a smaller house overlooking the harbour. Here he worked on *The Wanderings of Oisin*

71

(referred to breezily as 'Oison'): by 18 November he thought it was finished, and set off on the 22nd to visit Dublin. The O'Learys had no room for him, though they were happy to feed him; so he remained based at the Tynans' until 24 January, bringing out friends from Dublin like Russell, an instant success, and the more stand-offish Hyde (who noted that the Tynans 'all have a frightful brogue'[50]). Here too WBY's intense correspondence with Katharine Tynan, and his own doubts about the expectations it aroused, may have produced some kind of indeterminate declaration. If there was one, it was easily rebuffed. Tynan's sister, Nora O'Mahony, sarcastically claimed long afterwards that

One night when a dear brother-in-law had come with his wife and baby to visit us, we were sitting playing cards in the old family parlour when the door to the grander apartments opened suddenly and to my surprise my darling Katharine came in. For I had left her listening with interest, as I thought, to the great W. B. Yeats, chanting 'The Lake Isle of Innisfree' or some other of his poems. Afterwards, she told me that the great WBY *had asked her to marry him*, saying 'would it not be a most lovely and suitable thing for two great poets to be united'. But though she liked him and was proud of her creation, she did not feel a bit like that! After a few minutes he followed her into the card room. And to make things worse, he began shaking his fingers at her playfully – which seemed the last straw.

'Oh' she cried at last, 'for heaven's sake, you go to the devil!' But being the best-tempered soul in creation he did no more than smile affectionately.[51]

This contradicts WBY's record that 'we were always very great friends and I have no reason to think she ever thought of me otherwise'.[52] But if he made a feeble and unconvincing overture, it may have been during the stay at Whitehall between 22 November 1887 and 25 January 1888. His next visits to Clondalkin were in the summer of 1891, by which time his romantic attention (and Tynan's) had finally found a focus elsewhere.[53] From 1887 to 1888 he was unconfident, sexually frustrated (by his own admission) and lonely for Ireland. Living in Bedford Park, he had met artists who talked easily of mistresses and *demi-mondaines*, and socialists who believed in sexual radicalism. All this alarmed him: at twenty-two, still dominated by his father, he felt unfinished. A diffident proposal to Tynan may have explored a career option as well as paid a social duty. From her side, however, there was at this stage little to recommend it – his personal attractiveness apart. By 1888 she was already interested in Henry Hinkson, another Dublin littérateur (though doomed to obscurity), whom she married in 1893; and, despite the heavy irony of her sister's retrospective account, WBY was very far from being 'great'. He would rapidly become so, and move quickly into literary (and social) circles far above Tynan's relentlessly productive drudgery. If he made a fumbling proposal in the winter of 1887/8, she may have later regretted turning it down:

all the more reason not to mention it in her memoirs, written with barely concealed resentment at his acquired grandeur and the company he kept, and determined to present the youthful WBY as something of an incubus, as well as an innocent figure of fun.

Other involvements in Dublin over that winter holiday were equally unsatisfactory. Russell, commencing a long period of withdrawal into spiritual study, was attempting to distance himself from poetic composition, partly because he did not want to be absorbed by WBY's dominant literary personality; he even burnt his manuscripts as a symbolic purification. The tension never relaxed throughout their long relationship. As Russell remarked to Tynan, it hardly mattered that he did not see his friend: he could supply the appropriate responses without actually hearing WBY speak, and pretend he was in astral communication. The suggested appropriate responses are noteworthy: 'Your poem is splendid.' 'Your paradoxes are getting more startling every day.' 'You should not say such hard things of your friends.'[54] Their approach to spiritual investigations continued to diverge: Russell, the mystic, stayed away from the disastrous seance attended by WBY that January, where the intrepid mage felt himself completely possessed by spirits, and was frightened away from mediums for the next ten years.[55]

His experience of Ireland on this first return home had been, in many respects, sobering. Tynan's country 'salon' and the determined self-promotion of her circle were already a subject for public satire: the Dublin *Evening Telegraph* of 14 January 1888 carried 'A Dublin Literary Coterie, Sketched by a Non-Pretentious Observer', written anonymously by Hannah Lynch, who had visited Whitehall in December. This mercilessly lampooned WBY as

Augustus Fitzgibbon, considered by himself and his friends to be a titanic power, who may accomplish great things and who may not, but whose boyish head is being in the meantime turned in the most delightful and most deplorable fashion by the circle which is fortunate enough to revolve round this elsewhere unappreciated star . . . They will tell you that he is too exquisite and ethereal to be understood or appreciated by the common British reviewer and hence his obscurity. All of this of course Fitzgibbon fondly believes and invites you to believe by the ingratiating sweetness with which he takes his spoiling. In his circle all are equally sincere in giving and returning flattery.

Russell found it hard to laugh at the portrait of his own stammering admiration of WBY until 'when I thought of what poor Willie Yeats would think, I began to scream with laughter and enjoyed it immensely'.[56] As for WBY, Ireland looked less attractive than from afar. While he could write there, and remained inspired by the notion of Celtic tradition, even Sligo had changed; Dublin was a smaller pond to swim in than London, and those who had known him as a tyro treated him less respectfully than new metropolitan acquaintances like Rhys. Whether he realized it consciously or not, a life lived between the two countries was the logical response. And he avoided Dublin for the next three and a half years.

IV

London provided a continuing education. Back in Bedford Park he read omnivorously: Stevenson's *Black Arrow*, Todhunter's legend-inspired Irish poems, George Meredith's poetry (though *Diana of the Crossways* 'made the reader think too much'), Tolstoy ('great and joyless').[57] But novels always took second place to poetry and philosophy. The psychology explored in WBY's own fiction remained obstinately philosophical – 'the antithesis that is the foundation of human nature being ever in my sight',[58] as he later put it. On another educational level, he signed up for the French classes offered to young socialists in the coach-house at the bottom of Morris's garden, but lost interest when his sisters joined and made made fun of him.

Willie's dramatic, intence way of saying his French with his voice raised to telling distinctness and every pronounciation wrong as usual, seemed to amuse Mr Sparling more than ever. He simply doubled up when Willie commenced. Willie of course divided it up into any amount of full stops when there weren't any, so Madame said 'Mr Yaytes you dont read poetry like that do you' 'Yes he does Yes he does' volunteered Mr Sparling, and in truth he [*sic*] was rather like his natural way of reading.[59]

He would periodically take up French lessons throughout his life but found himself constitutionally incapable of learning it, or any other language.[60]

More productively, in the summer of 1888 he contracted with Alfred Nutt to transcribe Caxton's version of Aesop's *Fables* from the folio in the Bodleian Library at Oxford, staying in York Powell's rooms in Meadow Buildings, Christ Church, during August. WBY despised Nutt's 'scientist' approach to folklore and would later get his own back by brutal digs in book reviews, but the surroundings nearly made up for it. 'I wonder any body does anything at Oxford but dream and remember the place is so beautiful. One almost expects the people to sing instead of speaking. It is all – the colleges I meen – like an Opera.'[61] He was eventually paid £5, but while there had to subsist on currant buns.[62] Afterwards, he recounted in his *Autobiographies*, he returned 'very pale to my troubled family', an assertion later stoutly denied by JBY. If he was tired, it was probably because he had delivered the manuscript of *Fairy and Folk Tales* just before leaving. Certainly from the late spring he was constantly near collapse with nervous exhaustion.[63] Though a further copying work assignment was forthcoming, it was uncongenial.[64] Moreover, he was beginning to make money under his own name, and in the process to make his reputation.

Over the five years from his arrival in London in early 1887, WBY contributed more than a hundred original items to newspapers – poems, reviews, articles and letters. There may have been other contributions to provincial papers, now untraceable.[65] This early journalism is distinguished by a notably different tone to that in his letters, and not only because accurate spelling and grammar have been supplied. The voice is authoritative, slightly grand, occasionally savage in a dismissal or attack. His London contacts had expanded the range of periodicals ready to print his articles: the fiery and charismatic W. E. Henley, whom WBY met in 1888, was just about to take over the *Scots Observer* (later *National Observer*) and filled the role of mentor and critic as well as publisher. Yet WBY often expressed a dislike of journalists, whom he saw conventionally as cynics, men about town, 'nothing in them but tittering jeering emptiness. They have all made what Dante calls the Great Refusal, that is they have ceased to be self centred have given up their individuality . . . especially the sucessful ones.'[66] There spoke his father's son.

Accused by Tynan of being obsessed with 'bookish things' to the exclusion of all else, he had rejoined, 'I bury my head in books as the ostridge does in the sand';[67] but 'bookish things' could be a battering-ram into the real world. Editorial work was one method of entry. By May 1887 the Dublin circle had begun to put together the collection eventually published in the spring of 1888 as *Poems and Ballads of Young Ireland*.[68] Though WBY was generally identified as the editor, it was a group effort; Tynan took a leading part, organizing proof circulation and choosing a cover. WBY's own priority was clear, declared in his determination to have advertisements printed at the end for other works by Tynan, Ellen O'Leary and himself: 'we want to let people know that there is a little school of us'.[69]

Accordingly, he put much thought into arranging the book's reception. Sparling was unreliable. Dowden was to be avoided as a reviewer, since 'the book is a nationalist book'. Lyster was 'too West British'. In fact, the book's nationalism was kept implicit; the epigraph, 'There are but two great parties in the end', seemed obscurely confrontational, but the division intended (by William Allingham, a Unionist) is simply between those who love Ireland, and the rest. Several critics noted the contributions by WBY, 'who ought to have a future before him',[70] and 'The Stolen Child' was singled out by several impartial reviewers – though log-rolling by friends was censured by O'Leary. 'The praises of you might in a sense pass, but laudation of Miss T. induces lows. Her things there have little or no merit; she only gave you her tenth best – or worst.'[71]

For WBY, the collection's importance – beside reprinting some of his own work – lay in advancing him another step into a literary career. The Bedford Park mafia (Todhunter, Ellis, York Powell) helped spread the word; reviewing commissions began to come from new sources, like William Stevens of *Leisure Hour*,[72] and a never-to-be completed project on Irish duellists and outlaws was floated by T. Fisher Unwin (WBY's reading for this would be recycled into journalism during 1891[73]). O'Leary referred cynically to *Poems and Ballads* later, in a private critique of Tynan to WBY. 'She's certainly no critic, and I am strongly of opinion that neither are you, save within very narrow limits, but then she's also a horrible word-monger which you mostly are not, at least now, for you were bad enough in that first book you edited.'[74] What mattered far more to WBY was the publication in September 1888, at the age of twenty-three, of his real 'first book', *Fairy and Folk Tales of the Irish Peasantry*.

This had finally been commissioned by his new friend Rhys in February 1888, to be delivered by the end of July. It was originally conceived as an edited version of Crofton Croker's *Fairy Legends*, the book WBY had brought to Rhys shortly after their meeting in May. In a letter to Tynan, WBY initially sounded unenthusiastic: he would prefer regular work, though it was 'better any way than writing articles about things that do not interest one – are not in ones line of developement – not that I am not very glad to do the Folklore book or any thing that comes to my hand'.[75] His response was, in the end, to fit the collection into his 'line of developement': like everything he would subsequently put his name to, it is very much his own. He used the project to arrange an interview with Lady Wilde, herself an authority on the subject, and paid her the first of several visits on 28 July 1888 (Lily, who accompanied him, noted the atmosphere of 'lowering twilight' and the two friendly Irish maids, who knew everyone). His correspondence shows the sources he plundered; and the eventual collection took in William Carleton, Hyde and poems of WBY's own like 'The Stolen Child' and 'The Priest of Coloony' (later 'The Ballad of Father O'Hart').

This was very far from any updated Crofton Croker, as WBY was determined to emphasize. 'Make plain to the mind of Scott [the publisher] that I have taken much trouble about [the] book,' he wrote menacingly to Rhys, 'and that there is *origonal matter of value which no one else could have got*, that is to say Douglas Hydes stories – one of them the finest thing in the book almost – and some gathering of my own besides in notes &c.'[76] Twelve years later, inscribing a copy for Augusta Gregory, he could afford to dismiss these notes as 'very amateur'. He was vague about 'something in the preface that roused the vehement denial of old Morris, but what it was I never heard'; however, Pollexfen-like, he remembered clearly that he was paid twelve guineas and the publisher forbade the editor ever to give anybody else as much again.[77]

The advantages were more than financial. In late September WBY was much exercised to see that the book received a favourable reception; he was particularly anxious to get a notice into the Sligo papers, and to his delight the *Sligo Independent* was the first critique he saw. Other reviews were friendly, and Todhunter loyally praised the volume in a public lecture of 27 November.[78] *Fairy and Folk Tales* established WBY as a reviewer of folklore collections; he was already a student of 'fairy' lore (preferring to spell it 'faery', which suggested occultism rather than archness). His approach was deliberately literal and 'unscientific'.[79] In his own writings on the subject, he created a taxonomy of the fairy world, using occultist distinctions regarding malignant spirits, and the findings of contemporary mythographers: but his preferred sources remained back numbers of the *Dublin University Magazine* (often transcribed for him by the faithful Russell) rather than the latest findings of the despised Nutt's *Folklore Journal*, which wanted tales to be 'full of little hooks, as it were, to hang theories on'.[80] While faithful to the integrity of the materials, he added artistic literary effects, injunctions about the decorum of dealing with the spirit world and a deliberately wide-eyed ingenuousness which qualified as fully 'Celtic'; this is the point of Max Beerbohm's celebrated cartoon 'Mr W. B. Yeats, Presenting Mr George Moore to the Queen of the Fairies'.

It was this literal approach, declaimed in the introduction to *Fairy and Folk Tales*, which probably incensed Morris. WBY remarked that readers might wonder why he had not rationalized a single hobgoblin. 'I seek for shelter to the words of Socrates [from Jowett's translation of the *Phaedrus*].' When asked if he believed the tale of Boreas carrying off Orithia from the banks of the Ilissus, Socrates's defence was: 'The wise are doubtful and I should not be singular if, like them, I also doubted . . . And, therefore, I say farewell to all this; the common opinion is enough for me. For, as I was saying, I want to know not about this but about myself.'

He continued to defend literal belief, writing to Hyde that the Theosophist Colonel Olcott 'is probably quite right about the real existence of these Irish goblins. At least I never could see any reason against their existence'[81] – an opinion he publicly repeated when reviewing Hyde's own *Irish Folk Tales*, where he railed against rationalism as 'that great sin against art.'[82] But ambivalence crept into his critique of David Rice McAnally's *Irish Wonders* in March 1889; and by 1896 his line on folklore had subtly changed. The original myths were deliberate artistic creations, rather than common beliefs. But this was the view of someone who no longer needed to advertise his Celticism so assiduously, and who was self-confessedly 'no democrat in intellectual things'.[83] Later he would modify this in order to stress the therapeutic function of supernatural belief as a refuge from the misery of life; and this too reflected his own predispositions and circumstances.

September 1888 was a low point in Blenheim Road. Lolly's diary records a financial crisis for the second half of the month, though social life continued. 'Dr and Mrs Todhunter came to tea the amusing thing about it was that Willie borrowed 3/– from them which they little knew was destined to purchase tea sugar butter and marmalade for their tea.'[84] WBY, exhausted by his copying work in Oxford and already tense about the impending publication of *Fairy and Folk Tales*,[85] was cast further into depression by the proofs of his own long-delayed collection of poems, *The Wanderings of Oisin*. He wrote in theatrical despair to Katharine Tynan:

I am not very hopeful about the book. Somewhat inarticulate have I been I fear. Some thing I had to say. Dont know that I have said it. All seems confused incoherent inarticulate. Yet this I know I am no idle poetaster. My life has been in my poems. To make them I have broken my life in a morter as it were. I have brayed in it youth and fellowship peace and worldly hopes. I have seen others enjoying while I stood alone with myself – commenting, commenting – a mere dead mirror on which things reflect themselves. I have buried my youth and raised over it a cairn – of clouds. Some day I shall be articulate perhaps. But this book I have no great hopes of – it is all sluggish incoherent. It may make a few friends perhaps among people of my own sort – that is the most.[86]

'Do what you can for it,' he added characteristically, sending on to her copies of the proofs. The letter may also be an implicit apology for the unsatisfactory passages between them the previous winter.

For the rest of the autumn he remained low-spirited, fighting off 'collapses' when he lost all energy,[87] wrestling with the latest draft of *John Sherman*, and periodically paying visits to the growing Blavatsky entourage in Holland Park. In December he joined her recently established Esoteric Section of the Theosophical Society. He continued to agonize about the directionless, cloudy, incoherent nature of his poetry; by December, the month before the publication of *The Wanderings of Oisin*, he was preaching the need to 'make poems on the familiar landscapes we love not the strange and rare and glittering scenes we wonder at – these latter are the landscape of Art, the rouge of nature.'[88] Privately, he had begun to criticize Tynan's poetry for its prosaic, pat quality: and with the last letter mentioned he enclosed the first draft of 'The Lake Isle of Innisfree'.

I will arise and go now and go to the island of Innis free
And live in a dwelling of wattles – of woven wattles and wood work made,
Nine been rows will I have there, a yellow hive for the honey bee
And this old care shall fade.

There from the dawn above me peace will come down dropping slow
Dropping from the veils of the morning to where the household cricket sings.
And noontide there be all a glimmer, midnight be a purple glow,
And evening full of the linnets wings.

This version lacks the dramatic, personal intervention which closes the poem as eventually published: 'While I stand on the roadway or on the pavements grey, / I hear it in the deep heart's core.' But in his *Autobiographies* wBY himself isolated the moment when he wrote 'Innisfree', in mid-December 1888, inspired by the same revelation he had described in *John Sherman*, when a Strand window-display suddenly transported him to the waters of Sligo. It was a key insight: the disproportionate emotion aroused by reading some banal verses about an 'emigrant's return', the power of association and memory which swept over him as he stared into a London shop, showed him that 'personal utterance' might be a way out of cloudy rhetoric. His excitement at the time was witnessed by Lily, who recalled it long afterwards:

In Bedford Park one evening, Helen Acosta [a Greek friend who also worked at Morris's] & Lolly painting & I there sewing – Willy bursting in having just written, or not even written down but just having brought forth 'Innisfree', he repeated it with all the fire of creation & his youth – he was I suppose about 24. I felt a thrill all through me and saw Sligo beauty, heard lake water lapping, when Helen broke in asking for a paint brush – she had not even pretended to listen. None of us knew what a great moment it was. Not that 'Innisfree' is one of his greatest, but it is beautiful & perhaps the best known.[89]

Altered and published in 1890, the poem would achieve immediate success – and still pursued him around the world, to his extreme irritation, forty years later.[90]

In 1888, however, it was an epiphany that would endure, showing him the way forward in a moment of despair. This came as the climax of two years' unremitting effort to establish himself as part of a 'little school'. Though he claimed this was in order to capture Rhys, whose 'mind runs in the direction of schools',[91] there was more to it than that. Todhunter, Tynan, wBY, Ellen O'Leary, Hyde supported each other indefatigably, checking each other's work, writing articles about each other, reviewing each other's books, and testing the claims of aspirant members (Evelyn Pyne, May Probyn) long since forgotten: accusations of log-rolling had begun early on. Their repertoire of sources and inspirations included not only Irish fairy lore and folk-tales, but also selective voices of early nineteenth-century Irish romanticism – notably the *poète maudit* James Clarence Mangan. Recruiting-grounds had been established, not only the Young Ireland Societies in Ireland but the Southwark Irish Literary Club. Here wBY gave a lecture on 13 June 1888, 'Folklore of the West of Ireland' – part of the recycling process whereby the work done for *Fairy and Folk Tales* cropped up in other places, such as a long article in the Theosophist magazine *Lucifer*, published 15 January 1889.[92] In his increasingly voluminous correspondence, wby was already handing out criticism to aspirant writers, a role he found congenial. The Irish circle was broadened, for him, by the milieu of Bedford Park, which opened contacts to the metropolitan literary world: not only Rhys, but also the more flamboyant Celtophile William Sharp. Though wby at first 'hated his red British face of flaccid contentement',[93] Sharp's writings (from 1893 in secret disguise as 'Fiona Macleod') would eventually help to broadcast Celticism to the world at large. From the summer of 1888 he had been visiting W. E. Henley on Sundays in nearby Chiswick: Henley's *National Observer* would be another important outlet. And by December 1888 he apparently knew the Wildes well enough to visit Oscar and Constance for Christmas dinner.[94]

He had first come face to face with the great aesthete at Henley's. Over the years since wby had heard him lecture in Dublin, Wilde had become formidable and utterly assured. At least one of his aphorisms sounded ringingly in wby's ear: 'I think a man should invent his own myth.' With marked kindness (and perhaps a speculative interest), Wilde invited this gauche and unknown young fellow-countryman to his Chelsea house; contrary to wby's later memory, he had not yet published his first book of poems. Wilde apparently believed he was alone in London; what the Yeats family thought of his defection is not recorded. The contrast between Tite Street and Bedford Park could not have been greater:

There was nothing mediaeval nor Pre-Raphaelite, no cupboard door with figures upon flat gold, no peacock-blue, no dark background. I remember vaguely a white drawing-room with Whistler etchings, 'let into' white panels, and a dining-room all white, chairs, walls, mantelpiece, carpet, except for a diamond-shaped piece of red cloth in the middle of the table under a terracotta statuette, and, I think, a red-shaded lamp hanging from the ceiling to a little above the statuette. It was perhaps too perfect in its unity, his past of a few years before had gone too completely, and I remember thinking that the perfect harmony of his life there, with his beautiful wife and his two young children, suggested some deliberate artistic composition.[95]

None the less, the guest asserted his own aesthetic independence:

When dinner was over he read to me from the proofs of *The Decay of Lying* and when he came to the sentence, 'Schopenhauer has analysed the pessimism that characterises modern thought, but Hamlet invented it. The world has become sad because a puppet was once melancholy', I said, 'Why do you change "sad" to "melancholy"?' He replied that he wanted a full sound at the close of his sentence, and I thought it no excuse and an example of the vague impressiveness that spoilt his writing for me. Only when he spoke, or when his writing was the mirror of his speech, or in some simple faery-tale, had he words exact enough to hold a subtle ear.

But the message of *The Decay of Lying* struck home: an audacious riposte to the positivist realism which WBY himself revolted against, and an assertion that 'truth' lay in imaginative creation. WBY had already written as much in the Epilogue to *The Island of Statues*, which was one of the few fragments of his very early verse which he preserved in his canon.

There were later visits, but WBY never quite overcame a sense of awkwardness; his would-be fashionable shoes were too yellow, his manner too intense, he unintentionally frightened one of Wilde's sons by telling him an unWildean fairy-story. Yet Wilde fascinated him: not only as another middle-class Irish Protestant who had remade himself, but as a conscious phrase-maker who 'always dismissed questions with epigrams . . . [one] was never quite sure whether or not he was boasting of uncommitted sins'.[96] He 'perpetually performed a play which was in all things the opposite of all that he had known in his childhood and youth'. But for all his delight in high life, WBY later stressed that Wilde was not a conventional snob; England was fairyland, the social ladder was a 'pantomime beanstalk' and the English aristocracy like 'the nobles of Baghdad'. This too struck a personal echo. As Magee perceptively noted, his schoolboy friend always 'liked exaggerated people – exaggerated. Dramatically – not colourless'.[97] Of the friends and mentors encountered in the late eighties, Morris, Sharp, Henley, Wilde and his mother, and Madame Blavatsky were all in this mould. The protest that 'London can give me nothing' was wearing thin.

V

WBY's two years of London apprenticeship were, appropriately, sealed by the production of his first volume of poems. He had been working on the long narrative *The Wanderings of Oisin* from early in 1887 (mentioning the tale in an article, 'Fin Mac Cumhail', for the *Gael* that April); his Sligo sojourn in the autumn was dominated by furious writing and rewriting. Even before a publisher was found, WBY had begun to drum up subscriptions for a volume featuring *Oisin* as title-poem; from January 1888 names began to mount up, including the established literary men Stephen Gwynn and Barry O'Brien. Others were dragooned by O'Leary, airily thanked by JBY on 20 March: '*We* ourselves have done very little. I have written to some people but not got answers from more than a few that I wrote to – in fact I do not think I have improved my position as a man of judgement and discretion with the few to whom I have written.'[98] Subscribers had promised 90 copies by late February 1888, rising to 110 in March. WBY already had a publisher in his sights – Kegan Paul, who had developed something of an Irish specialism with Tynan and Todhunter. Determinedly high-Victorian in his tastes, he was not unduly enthusiastic, and wby found him condescending and unhelpful. When he brought the first version of his manuscript to Kegan Paul on 12 March, the publisher required 200 subscriptions, necessitating redoubled efforts from O'Leary, Tynan, Father Mathew Russell, and other members of the 'little school': though Hyde was predictably unenthusiastic, alleging that he had failed to spread the light among the 'unliterary' of Roscommon.[99] In April wby's new acquaintances at the Southwark Irish Literary Club were pressed into service too. By the summer publication seemed assured, though there would be crises about the number of subscriptions, and the projected price of the volume, until the last minute. Kegan Paul waited until August before committing himself absolutely. This was the background to wby's demoralization when the proofs came in; but stray references in letters suggest that his spirits rose as he corrected them. By mid-December 500 copies were printed and 300 bound; though subscriptions had nominally exceeded the stipulated 200, Kegan Paul did not recover his full investment and public sales were low. But it would prove a historic volume, for wby himself and for literature at the *fin de siècle*.

While the book included a carefully arranged series of poems that had begun life in the mid-1880s (reorganized – and rewritten – in the 'Crossways' section of the eventual *Collected Poems*), the previously unpublished title-poem took most of wby's energies, and much of the reviewers' attention, not always favourable. The story of Oisin, son of the legendary Fianna chieftain Fionn MacCumhail, who travelled with a fairy love to the land of eternal youth, had been accessibly published by Bryan O'Looney (after Michael Comyn) in the *Transactions of the Oisianic Society* in 1859. In the winter of 1886 wby had proposed a poem on the subject for a projected volume, with A. P. Graves and Katharine Tynan, to be called 'Tales from Tara', but it was never written; he had probably come across it in P. W. Joyce's popularized prose version, appearing as 'Oisin in Tirnanogue' in *Old Celtic Romances* of 1879. The Laureate's 'Voyage of Maeldune' had appeared in 1880 and wby's 1889 publication was full of inescapably Tennysonian echoes: he would eradicate them in constant rewritings over the years. These began almost at once: changes were made at the most advanced proof-stage, and a number of first editions exist with his own changes added in; the eventual canonical version of the title-poem was different in practically every line. Over the years he reconstructed his poetic biography along with the poems themselves.[100]

Even if some of the influences behind the long poem which gave the book its name were familiar, arousing echoes as recent as Todhunter's *Children of Lir* as well as traditions of philosophic journeying in Eastern and Gaelic

literature, *The Wanderings of Oisin* displayed all the audacity which would
come to identify its author. The title, unpronounceable to English ears, is
one example (in a later version the hero would temporarily appear – more
helpfully – as 'Usheen'). The imagery, rhythm and diction of the opening
section, 'The Island of the Living', was equally arresting:

PATRICK

Oisin, tell me the famous story
Why thou outlivest, blind and hoary,
The bad old days. Thou wert, men sing,
Trapped of an amorous demon thing.

OISIN

'Tis sad remembering, sick with years,
The swift innumerable spears,
The long-haired warriors, the spread feast;
And love, in the hours when youth has ceased:
Yet will I make all plain for thee.
We rode in sorrow, with strong hounds three,
Bran, Sgeolan, and Lomair,
On a morning misty and mild and fair.
The mist-drops hung on the fragrant trees,
And in the blossoms hung the bees.
We rode in sadness above Lough Laen,
For our best were dead on Gavra's green.

This was unashamedly exotic to English ears. Along with familiar images of
bees hanging in blossom came obscure Gaelic names, striking repetitions, an
unremitting rhythm subtly varied as the poem proceeded through its three
sections. Similes were piled up in long lines to an incantatory climax, in true
Gaelic mode. When Oisin is led away across the 'oily sea' by the seductive
Niam (whom no English reader would have known to pronouce *Nee-av*), the
visions which pursue them are both exotic and presciently ominous; they
also assemble key images for the Yeatsian poetic lexicon.

On, on! and now a hornless deer
Passed by us, chased of a phantom hound
All pearly white, save one red ear;
And now a maid, on a swift brown steed
Whose hooves the tops of the surges grazed,
Hurried away, and over her raised
An apple of gold in her tossing hand;
And following her at a headlong speed
Was a beautiful youth from an unknown land.

But the poem was far more than an azure-and-gold tonal arrangement of islands, caverns, basaltic castles, painted birds, milky smoke and grass-blades hung with dewdrops (though all occur more than once). It is the 'ancient sadness of man' that drives Oisin on, as much as the temptations of Niam; the land of eternal youth is in fact never gained, though he samples islands of artificial pleasure, of inconclusive action (struggling with his own daemon), and finally of forgetfulness. And as WBY wrote in a cancelled commentary on the poem, after each island the hero 'longs for his old companions'. Oisin's song of human joy strikes the fairy world as unutterably sad; their king preaches liberation from 'sorrow with her osprey claw' and their songs re-iterate freedom from the laws and limitations of 'grievous Time on his old crutches', but he misses the real world. Strikingly, the story of journey and return is framed within a dialogue between St Patrick's Christian injunctions and Oisin's mounting realization that truth lies in the power and magic of his own lost 'pagan' past. Moreover, his final defiance, when he opts for risking hell with his dead companions, rouses an intentionally political echo: where Joyce had referred to Oisin's brotherhood as the 'Fena', WBY deliberately uses 'Fenians'.

PATRICK

On the red flaming stones without refuge the limbs of the Fenians are tost;
No live man goes thither, and no man may war with the strong spirits wage;
But weep thou, and wear thou the flags with thy knees, for thy soul that is lost,
For thy youth without peace, and thy years with the demons, and the godless fires
    of thine age.

OISIN

Ah me! to be old without succour, a show unto children, a stain,
Without laughter, a coughing, alone with remembrance and fear,
All emptied of purple hours as a beggar's cloak in the rain,
As a grass seed crushed by a pebble, as a wolf sucked under a weir.

I will pray no more with the smooth stones: when life in my body has ceased –
For lonely to move 'mong the soft eyes of best ones a sad thing were –
I will go to the house of the Fenians, be they in flames or at feast,
To Fin, Caolte, and Conan, and Bran, Sgeolan, Lomair.

In a famous 1867 sermon, the Catholic Bishop of Kerry had denounced O'Leary and the modern Fenians with the words that 'eternity is not long enough nor hell hot enough' to punish them; the assonance with Oisin's conclusion would have been clear to Irish readers. For WBY himself, the themes were both deeply personal and strongly predicted future preoccupations: conflicts with the self and the will, unattainable desires, and the attractions of conversing with the dead. To English readers, the pace, colour, varied rhythm and hard-edged clarity marked an important début. If the construction sometimes tottered, a unique diction still sounded through; themes like the impotency of old age and the flight of elusive beauty were enlivened by 'normal' similes (stars in the night sky are 'each one woven to his brother/ Like bubbles in a frozen pond'). Odd echoes prefigure later poetic effects ('as a fish in the water goes dumb as a stone', 'a moon waking white as a shell'[101]). The Gaelic theme and imagery, as well its superior quality and manipulation of metre, distinguished *Oisin* from WBY's other dramatic narratives reprinted in the collection (*Mosada, The Seeker, Time and the Witch Vivien*); yet, exotic and Gaelic though the title-poem was, WBY's Romantic education comes through. If Jeremiah Callanan and Ferguson are echoed, so are Shelley, Pre-Raphaelitism and William Morris.

And so is the 'sedative' effect which WBY himself gloomily discerned in his poetry as a whole: 'a flight into fairy land, from the real world, and a summons to that flight'.[102] Some of the poems looked back to his Theosophist induction of 1885 to 1886, using the language of Indian mysticism: Mohini Chatterjee's Vedantic teachings were reproduced in quatrains enjoining 'Long thou for nothing, neither sad nor gay', and 'Kanva on Himself', never republished in WBY's lifetime, turned Mohini's injunctions straight into poetic form. Others, like 'King Goll' (already published both in *Leisure Hour*, September 1887, and *Poems and Ballads of Young Ireland*), combined Shelleyan themes with an energetic attack which would become distinctively Yeatsian. Poems like 'A Lover's Quarrel Among the Fairies' were introduced with decisive stage directions ('A moonlit moor. Fairies leading a child'). The dramatic form dominated: dialogues, scenarios, playlets, enclosing philosophical exchanges punctuated by songs. This looked forward to his future development; so did the number and range of poetic voices and personae employed, with varying success. And despite the themes of withdrawal, feyness, depression and lassitude, at least one critic (in a private letter) pinpointed the poet's special quality: 'a gift of introducing the common-place with startling effect in his pictures'.[103]

Bound in plain dark blue and tightly printed, *The Wanderings of Oisin* was far less beautiful than any of WBY's future books; but in other ways it fully anticipated their impact. Copies were in hand by the end of the first week of January 1889, and the response vindicated WBY's relentless efforts to carve out a niche in the literary world. The volume was more than just an assembly of poems and constituted a fully conceived book in itself; the shape and the arrangement had preoccupied him for over a year. The poems were ordered thematically, not chronologically, and already he chose to exclude certain work already published, including dreamy sonnets and crudely political pieces. The tone was to be 'Celtic' rather than 'national': in other words, while using Irish modes and themes, it was to appeal to an audience beyond Ireland. But in Irish circles it caught a mood, provoking Todhunter to write to Dowden: 'I wish we had a Nationalist Dowden to direct the literary movement now on foot, which though genuine in its way is shallow & amateurish. I wish our Celtic literature, or at least the best portions of it, could be decently edited & translated. I don't agree with you in thinking that literature with a distinctly Irish note in it (even in the English language) must necessarily be bad & weak.'[104] Was WBY to be the nationalist Dowden? The quantity of critical response, preserved in WBY's own book of press cuttings, was exceptional for a first collection: reviews mounted up over the next six months.[105] It was recognized that Irish mythology as a poetic subject was not new: Aubrey de Vere, Todhunter, even Tynan had been there already. But Irish themes were still extremely fashionable: besides the strongly flowing Celtic tide, 1889 was the high point of the political 'Union of Hearts' between Liberal English society and Irish nationalism under the newly respectable Parnell. Coterie friends weighed in, not always quite as WBY wished. Henley in the *Scots Observer* gave an unqualified rave. Rolleston found the collection on the whole 'a missed opportunity': the poet needed 'a philosophy of life' and an 'interest in realities'. Todhunter's own feelings were mixed. Before publication he had been positive, encouraging Dowden to subscribe to their friend's son's book: 'He has genuine imagination, richness of diction & above all a power of writing easy musical verse quite remarkable in these days of Tennyson Rossetti & Swinburne & their followers. One has to go back to Coleridge & Keats to find the same kind of gift. In fact he has poetic genius. What will come of him & it heaven only knows.' Reviewing it, however, a reaction set in; he found 'flaws of execution – slovenly lines, awkward and uncouth constrictions, exuberances which are not beauteous, concentrations of expression which are crude and stiff rather than powerful'. Oscar Wilde, writing anonymously in the *Pall Mall Gazette*, 'recklessly' promised 'a fine future', mainly on the strength of WBY's poetic imagination; the *Spectator* mildly inferred plagiarism in a section of *Oisin*, which provoked a letter from WBY acknowledging the inspiration of O'Looney and Comyn but indignantly claiming the lines as his own.

In Ireland reactions were less enthusiastic. The *Irish Monthly* (February) thought WBY 'a true poet' but would not like to expose his poems to 'some of our worthy Philistine friends': the spectre of beautiful Edmund Russell hovered dangerously close. The *Freeman's Journal* was openly antagonistic: 'a jumble of confused ideas in a maze of verbiage'. The *Sligo Independent* appreciated the local references. The *Irish Times* was favourable if slightly condescending, and gratifyingly referred to the poet as an already established figure: 'Mr Yeats is more brilliantly imaginative, original and self-reliant than ever.'[106]

This was the word that was repeatedly used: imagination. The *Nation*, however, turned it against him: wby's imagination was 'indulged at the expense of his other faculties. And we think his imagination will never be brighter or more active in the future.' Tynan too looked to his probable future: while instructing her readers that wby 'has the Celtic heritage in no ordinary degree', she feared 'we can scarcely hope again for such fairy poetry as he has given us; the fascination of the human will draw him out, and in that direction his development will probably lie'. Thus she loyally publicized wby's manifestos in his letters to her the previous December. His own reaction, both to uneven reviews and slow sales, showed remarkable assurance. Enough critics forecast a distinguished future to compensate for sly digs from Dublin; and he was confident, he told Tynan, that 'I shall sell but not yet.' But what probably pleased him most was a London reaction: he was apprehended on Holborn Viaduct by William Morris and told, 'It is my kind of poetry.' Morris then promised to write about it, 'and would have said much more had he not caught sight of one of the decorated iron lamp-posts, then recently, I believe, set up [by] the Corporation and turned on it with frenzy, waving his umbrella'.[107]

Aesthetics as the bread of life, and personality as gesture: the lessons learnt at home and abroad were already being built into his art and his life. And in wby's great personal myth January 1889 was not only the month that saw the publication of *The Wanderings of Oisin*. On the 30th 'a hansom drove up to our door at Bedford Park with Miss Maud Gonne', and 'the troubling of my life began'.

'As I look backward,' he wrote long afterwards, 'it seems to me that she brought into my life in those days – for as yet I saw only what lay upon the surface – the middle of the tint, a sound as of a Burmese gong, an over-powering tumult that had yet many pleasant secondary notes.'[108] The 22-year-old English ex-débutante with a passion for Irish nationalism and romantic poetry invaded Bedford Park with an introduction to jby, but 'really to see Willy', as Lolly acidly pointed out. The Yeats girls 'hated her royal sort of smile' and noted that she was wearing slippers;[109] jby argued politics with her; the whole family was probably impressed by the fact that she extravagantly kept the cab waiting throughout. She told wby that 'she cried over "Island of Statues" fragment but altogether favoured the enchantress and hated Nachina'. Thus she cast herself precisely as the *fatale*, capricious beauty of whom the poet had dreamt.

He could not but succumb. Writing to Tynan in August 1887 (in response to a desperate appeal for ready-made ideas about the major poets' attitudes to women), he had tried to itemize poetic types of beauty. Swinburne's were 'passionate and gorgious animals', 'Tennisons . . . much more like actual every day people'; the neo-Romantics created 'essentially men's heroines with no seperate life of their own in this different from Brownings'.[110] Maud Gonne, by contrast, was majestic, unearthly, appealing all at once; and her classic beauty came straight out of epic poetry. Immensely tall, bronze-haired, with a strong profile and beautiful skin, she was a *fin de siècle* beauty in Valkyrie mode: both her appearance and her character represented tragic passion. But there was also a vulnerable side, shown to few, which struck an immediate chord with WBY. He at once saw her as a 'goddess', and remembered her standing luminous as 'apple-blossom through which the light falls . . . by a great heap of such blossoms in the window'.[111] In January the blossom must have been almond, not apple: but the image remained,[112] and the recognition. Implicitly, in his work, he had already cast a woman like this for a part in his life.

Yet at the same time there was something curiously self-conscious in his immediate idealization of her: it may have inspired a reflection twenty years later.

And when we love, if it be in the excitement of youth, do we not also, that the flood may find no stone to convulse, no wall to narrow it, exclude character or the signs of it by choosing that beauty which seems unearthly because the individual woman is lost amid the labyrinth of its lines as though life were trembling into stillness and silence, or at last folding itself away? Some little irrelevance of line, some promise of character to come, may indeed put us at our ease . . . But should it come, as we had dreamed in love's frenzy, to our dying for that woman's sake, we would find that the discord had its value from the tune.[113]

Even as he cast himself into thrall, like a Shelleyan hero, the writer in him was conscious of what he was doing.

Chapter 4: SECRET SOCIETIES
1889–1891

> You might make a strong point of the stir caused in Dublin by the Theosophical Society in the early 'nineties, and the impulse it gave to literature as seen in Yeats' early poems & in AE *passim* – how it pressed nationalism into its service in its campaign against materialism, & incidentally made spiritual heroes of the Anglo-Irish mob-leaders and gods of the 'fairies' etc. This would be a very interesting history if told with ironic judiciousness!

> W. K. Magee to Ernest Boyd, 2 July 1914

I

FROM 1889 until 1903, Richard Ellmann has suggested, following WBY's life in 'a strictly chronological account would give the impression of a man in a frenzy, beating on every door in the hotel in an attempt to find his own room'.[1] Tracing the young poet's different and apparently irreconcilable activities, working on several levels at once, Ellmann's organizing principle focused upon the divided self: WBY's (and his contemporaries') conception of the artist as embodying two men. Helpful as this is, it is not the full answer. Artificially separating out the several strands of WBY's experience in the early 1890s may seem an exercise in clarification, but it creates a false impression. The point is that his interests and involvements ricocheted off one another, driven by a number of consistent motivations. One was sexual frustration; another, professional ambition. These everyday impulses could – and did – drive him to produce unexpectedly exotic effects. Above all, he needed to belong to organizations and, once attached, to shape them into the image he desired.

Acutely conscious of being an outsider in Dublin and in London, lacerating himself for his apathy and indolence, WBY was spurred into never completed projects (a history of nineteenth-century Irish fiction, the long-running account of Irish duellists). Even when abandoned, they left useful residues to be thriftily transmuted into journalism.[2] He continued to educate himself frenetically through the resources of the British Museum, Dublin's new National Library (opened in 1890), John O'Leary's bookshelves, and the lucky-dip of reviewing: still capable of filling in gaps by implying knowledge which he did not possess (such as mastering texts in Irish, or, less difficult, reading Somerville and Ross's *The Real Charlotte*[3]). This could invite ridicule, but, as his reading broadened and his interests ramified, his control of material increased – notably in the occult and mystic writings of the sixteenth and seventeenth centuries, and in the neglected literature of early nineteenth-century Ireland.

This could make him something of a trial to other people. 'I had to roar at W. Yeats' long, long visit, and think that the tea must be of superior quality, and run in rivers,' wrote the Irish American poet, Louise Imogen Guiney, to a friend who had been exposed to a long harangue on Theosophy in September 1890. 'You poor old martyr!'[4] WBY's self-presentation was still a youthful mixture of art and artlessness: bearded, dark, intense, worried about his clothes, and deeply conscious of poetic models. His early nineteenth-century immersion in Irish patriotic literature supplied one particular inspiration: James Clarence Mangan, by whom WBY remained preoccupied. 'I know not whether I may not seem to have over-valued Clarence Mangan. No, I am not impartial – who is? Under even the most philosophical utterance is a good dose of personal bias . . . He never startles us by saying beautifully things we have long felt. He does not say look at yourself in this mirror; but rather, "Look at me – I am so strange, so exotic, so different." '[5] Of these early influences from the Young Ireland era, only Mangan would remain undimmed; ten years later WBY would electrify an Irish Literary Society meeting with an impromptu speech reiterating his early argument that Mangan's best work was 'as near perfection as anything that has ever been written', and that he helped create a new style. There may have been a further influence, in Mangan's idea that the artist of genius must wear a mask at will;[6] but the identification was more personal still. Not only did this romantic mystery-figure sustain an unhappy love-life and unrequited passion, but he too was an outsider, a victimized genius scrivening to support his family, who became the voice of his people.[7]

As for WBY, from the beginning of 1889 he was a poet with a widely reviewed book behind him, and a growing reputation in London as well as Dublin: even the attack from J. F. Taylor in the *Freeman's Journal* could eventually be accommodated, and praise repeated to him was retailed proudly in his correspondence throughout the spring of 1889. Sales of *Oisin* remained slow, but it made his reputation. Despite his complaints about being trapped in a groove of 'people who are like ones self – mystical, literary folk, and such like'[8] and missing the cross-section of Sligo society, he was forming a circle. His visits extended all over London, especially to literary women – taking in bluestocking teachers at North London Collegiate School, Lady Wilde's shaky salon in Chelsea, and currently fashionable writers like 'John Strange Winter' (Mrs Stannard) at Putney. From Bedford Park he launched a wide variety of missions, returning home to irritate his family by talking too much 'for effect'.[9] Even in London an Irish dimension remained; the Yeatses were visited by both Katharine Tynan and John O'Leary in the summer of 1889, and Ellen O'Leary's death in October sent shock-waves through their circle.

But WBY did not visit Ireland that year, though Jack remained in Sligo until October and his sisters made the annual pilgrimage. He planned to go in the spring of 1890, but was detained in London until the following autumn by publishing projects. While Sligo provided peace for writing poetry and 'romance', he was realistic enough to know that London contacts were necessary for bread and butter. 'The fact that I can study some things I like here better than elsewhere is the only redeaming fact,' he assured Tynan in October 1890. 'The mere presence of more cultivated people too is a gain of course but nothing in the world can make amends for the loss of green field & mountain slope & for the tranquil hours of ones own country side.'[10]

Yet from the beginning of 1889 there was another, intoxicating element which affected not only his preoccupations but his movements: the possibility of proximity to Maud Gonne. After the meeting on 30 January, they saw each other incessantly. WBY dined with Gonne, her sister Kathleen and her cousin May the very next day, where he was dazzled by the vehemence with which she baited a young military suitor of Kathleen, home on leave from India. WBY had dreamt of women like the girl in *The Revolt of Islam* – 'lawless women, without homes and without children'. He himself had conjured up dream-women of epic beauty, sadness and mystery: Gonne represented them all. Like the other women who would attract him, she was an independent spirit with a compelling, theatrical personality. And the fact that she saw him (or so he remembered) every evening for the next week could only be construed as encouragement.

Much of this, however, was misleading. Her mystery was yet to be plumbed; but though she was without a home, she would not long be without children. Gonne's background was dislocated, peripatetic and unstable. Losing first her mother and then her adored father, brought up between London, France and his military postings in Ireland, she had identified with that country as the one fixed point in her unhappy early life. She stressed her father's alleged Kerry ancestry, along with the much more questionable supposition that he nurtured Home Rule ambitions. Financially independent since her twenty-first birthday in 1887, she and her sister possessed £40,000 capital, around two million in today's terms, which guaranteed a large income; she was well-bred and beautiful; but she resolutely repudiated conventional 'society'. The Dublin establishment would come to view her with alternate alarm and derision ('a great red-haired yahoo of a woman', in the words of the timid Trinity don Louis Purser[11]); to them she exemplified a sort of *trahison des débutantes*, in which she was later joined by Constance Markievicz. This too appealed to WBY. From the start Gonne had sought out nationalists, who were initially suspicious of her: she moved from Oldham's Home Rule circle to demonstrations on behalf of evicted tenants in Gweedore,

County Donegal. Her identity with 'the people' of Ireland was based (as with many upper-class rebels) on memories of servants who had been kind to her: nationalism gave her restless and insecure spirit a conviction and a base, as well as a focus for her independent and feminist predilections. Her enormous capacity to inspire devotion, and a deep belief in self-sacrifice for public causes, would create for her a unique place in Irish public life. There was another reason also for her passionate interest in extreme politics. In the summer of 1887, at the French spa of Royat, she had met the much older Boulangist journalist and politician, Lucien Millevoye, already married, and begun her long liaison with him. In April 1889, less than three months after meeting WBY, she conceived Millevoye's child.

Her Irish suitor would not learn this for many years. But part of Gonne's attraction was her flouting of convention, and she never believed in marriage: when she eventually capitulated, it would only be as a sacrament (and a sacrifice) to the national cause. Partly, this may have been because sexual relations did not greatly appeal to her;[12] but she was also a New Woman,[13] and came from a family whose women believed they were foredoomed to unhappy marriages. (At an early age she had to cope not only with her own secret liaison, but with the existence of an illegitimate half-sister; Gonne sent the mother off to Russia as a governess and kept the child herself.[14]) Faced with WBY's relentless adoration, she took refuge in a return to her Paris house, where he could not – yet – follow her, and in admonishments that dedication to the national cause must transcend all selfish passion. But the strain of her private life and the unhappiness of her past gave her a heart-breaking vulnerability – hidden from most of her men friends, but eventually revealed to WBY. And this was a no less powerful part of her appeal.

The course of their relationship was quickly set. WBY much later recalled his obsessiveness, his neurosis, his sense of inadequacy, and his fear of making a fool of himself: all this was connected with an ideal of passionate asceticism, keeping his heart pure for love or hatred, like the mythical figure of Proud Costello. A hopeless love, in fact, freed him to work ('Our work after all is our true Soul,' he told Tynan in September 1890[15]). But WBY would also, as ever, turn adversity to advantage: and the work he adopted might go on to create the conditions for love's fulfilment. Thus within a year he was trying to present himself to Gonne as her *cicerone*, in occultism as well as in national revivalism: a year older, his need to dominate and his literary genius seemed to confer that advantage. Gonne, on the other hand, possessed only a talent for oratory (she had once planned to be an actress); she dabbled in art and wrote awkwardly. But it turned out he could not lead her: the force of her personality matched his own. Some contemporary photographs emphasize not so much her legendary beauty as a large and determined chin, and a mouth set hard at the corners. Much later, when he knew her full story, he could conclude, 'She was complete; I was not.'[16] It is a sexual reference, but also something more.

What he could do was help present her to the world, and he rapidly took on the task. In letters to Tynan he denied, rather defensively, that he was 'taken up' with Gonne, and admitted that she was sensationalist. 'I sympathise with her love of the national idia rather than any secondary land movement but care not much for the kind of red Indian feathers in which she has trapped out that idea.'[17] Embarrassedly, he claimed that Gonne had offered him help in staging a play he was working on, and that was all: 'As for the rest she had a borrowed interest, reminding me of Laura Armstrong without Laura's wild dash of half insane genius.' The awkwardness of the passage between himself and Tynan a year before still persisted. Unguardedly, however, he let slip in October that he would not have heard of Ellen O'Leary's death, 'only that on Monday I heard by chance that Miss Gone was in London and rushed off at once and saw her for about five minutes or less. She was just starting for Paris.'[18] This too forecast a pattern that would endure.

Meanwhile, he helped to create the cult of Gonne as 'the New Speranza' (Lady Wilde's youthful *nom de plume*, as the poetess of the *Nation*). He planted out articles in *United Ireland*, the *Boston Pilot* and elsewhere, describing Gonne's speaking-tours on behalf of the evicted Irish tenants, stressing her 'Irish nationality' and Celtic qualities of poetic insight, and describing aristocratic Parisian audiences reduced to tears.[19] At the same time he emphasized that she was not a revolutionary, and was 'no separatist under present conditions'. While he could follow her in cavalierly dismissing the importance of internecine murder among American Fenians ('a spy has no rights'[20]), their IRB sympathies were principally O'Learyite. Gonne, tutored in inept conspiracy among Millevoye's Boulangists, was more amenable to revolutionary politics than her Home Rule admirer, though she recalled long afterwards that he had taken the IRB oath before she met him.[21] Committed membership was embarked upon in the early 1890s, reflecting political polarization and dislocations among nationalists at the time; WBY may have taken the Fenian oath before leaving Dublin in 1887, but Gonne's sympathy for 'advanced nationalism' was at first echoed by him from a Home Rule standpoint. And until late 1891 the future seemed to belong to Home Rule.

II

Despite this bewitching eruption into his life, WBY's existence continued to be based at Blenheim Road. Here life carried on as before. Occasional entertainments were mounted (one on 20 February 1889 involved May Morris, her fiancé Sparling, John Power, and W. M. Crook). Mrs Alexander Sullivan, an American Fenian, was one exotic visitor in June 1889; the attractive but irreverent Imogen Guiney, in June 1890, another. JBY was painting portraits again, after a long period producing sketches only, but no more successful than before. Susan Yeats was unseen. Jack, when at home, was a cheerful presence; on 2 October 1889 he returned from his grandparents, shouting 'Sligo nonsense rhymes (he always comes home full of them) such as "You take the needle & I'll take the thread/And we'll sow the dogs tail to the Orange man's head."'[22] By May 1891 WBY was organizing a monthly Sunday or Monday evening 'At Home' to meet his literary friends.

But there was another side to it too. Yeats family life was convulsed by volatile irritations and upheavals. JBY, always ready to sparkle for the benefit of guests, was in private increasingly humiliated, aggressive and argumentative with his sons. The issues that separated them might be 'abstract and impersonal', but their resolution often came near violence.[23] The sons, for their part, shouted at their father in an unVictorian way: when, after one confrontation, Jack told his brother 'mind, not a word till he apologises', it represented a reversal of parent–child roles. WBY's professional success was not the only reason why his relationship to his siblings became increasingly distanced: a sense of survival drove him away.

But he could not afford to live elsewhere. His sister Lolly's diary monitors his earnings closely:

1889

		£	s.	d.
	Willie got			
	November 19	4	o	o
	December, Manchester Courier	o	3	6
[1890]	January 1st, Boston Pilot	3	o	o
	January 7th M Courier	o	10	o
	Feb 3rd M Courier	o	6	6
	Feb 20	2	o	o
	March 4th Boston Pilot	1	3	o
	April 3	o	8	6
	April 8 Scots Observer	2	2	o
	May 3rd Manchester Courier	o	2	6
	May 28 Scots Observer	1	1	o
	June 19 Boston Pilot	2	o	o
	July 14 Boston P	4	o	o
	Sep 20th Stephenson Fairy article	3	o	o
	Oct Scots Observer	2	o	o
	Nov 1st Weekly Review	1	o	2
	Nov 10/90 America	1	o	2

This vividly shows the range of his outlets, and the rates of his pay, at a time when a pound a week was a labourer's wage. He was justifiably proud of £7 earned for one article in *Leisure Hour*, and the pound per column offered by the *Scots Observer* and *Boston Pilot* was considered a good rate (though the *Observer* had to be dunned). Nor did such payments last long in Blenheim Road, being rapidly devoured by domestic debt ('the swally-whole', in family slang[24]). Not unnaturally, book sales preoccupied him. *The Wanderings of Oisin* had sold 174 copies by June: 146 already subscribed for, 28 on the open market. *Poems and Ballads of Young Ireland* was equally unspectacular; in late March 1889 he had to pay £0. 9s. 1d. as his share of the production costs, since it had sold only 275 copies at £0. 1s. 6d. each; WBY anxiously canvassed the chances of a cheap paperback.[25] By October he was hoping that the imprint of his Blenheim road next-door neighbour, Elkin Mathews, at the Bodley Head, might take over the unsold stock of *Oisin*; but in January it had still not covered its costs, and he had to ask O'Leary for help. The sum of £2. 3s. 10d. was owing to Kegan Paul, and legal action was threatened.[26] Helped by O'Leary, he succeeded in transferring the residue to T. Fisher Unwin, who rebound them and published a second issue in May 1892.

Therefore, publishing and reviewing contacts remained vital. WBY continued to see Rhys, and in late February or early March 1889 met the Parnellite MP T. P. Gill, later an influential patron in Dublin journalism. He doggedly provided anonymous paragraphs on London literary matters for the *Manchester Courier* from 1889 to 1890, as well as the 'Celt in London' column for the more munificent *Boston Pilot*: in both places he could 'trumpet' things about friends as well as make money (another example of the uses of adversity). Journalism, he told Tynan in October 1889, was 'good work for many people but no way, unless on Irish matters, good work for you and me, unless so far as it be really forced on us by crazy circumstance'.[27]

After the publication of *Oisin* he would place his offerings easily; some articles written in 1887 were finally accepted in 1889.[28] His American patrons, the *Providence Sunday Journal* and the *Boston Pilot*, continued to publish him until (respectively) late 1891 and 1892. In his 'Celt in London' column he reproduced, with apparent facility and occasional archness, the note of the middle-brow essayist, complete with 'insider' references.[29] He could also press the claims of friends like Hyde, Lady Wilde, and his poet colleagues, celebrate patrons like Ellen O'Leary, and puff the subscription list for John O'Leary's ever forthcoming memoir. Economical as ever, he shuffled themes, subjects and even phrases about between his journalistic productions, reflecting his current preoccupations (notably Blake[30]). His reviewing tone developed – more confident and swingeing, especially when attacking a trespasser on his own property such as McAnally's stagey *Irish Wonders*, which enabled him to assert 'real' 'Celtic' traditions of supernaturalism. The breadth of his reference became more and more striking: Dante, the *Mahabharata*, Ibsen, Edgar Quinet's *Génie des religions*, Swedenborg's *Spiritual Diary*. In July 1892 he had his first piece in the *Bookman*, a regular outlet from now on; another friend well established on the Irish literary circuit in London, Barry O'Brien, continued to send him books to review for the *Spectator* (the strangest, perhaps, being B. Douglas Howard's *Life with Trans-Siberian Savages*[31]).

Other forms of hack work still persisted in 1889, but were being shaken off. In June and July 1889 the *Girls' Own Paper* published two pieces of sentimental doggerel ('In Church' and 'A Summer Evening') commissioned by the Religious Tract Society (who also provided work for the agnostic JBY), but WBY was shamefaced in admitting as much to Tynan. 'I shall never do any more I think.'[32] Copying work was no longer necessary – the last stint was during August 1889 in Oxford – but Nutt too remained a useful contact, with WBY mediating between him and Hyde in the autumn of 1889. As a result, some of *Leabhar Sgéaluigheachta* was translated as *Beside the Fire* (1891). The Dublin group continued to help one another out. In October 1889 Tynan published a piece on WBY in the American *Magazine of Poetry*, romantically providing a childhood *à la* Chateaubriand by transmuting his uncle's Sandymount house into a castellated mansion within a dreamy park (WBY privately put her right about his parents' house and added 'the place that has really influenced my life most is Sligo'[33]). For his part, his advice to her became more and more pointed: to try long poems, to transcend the 'merely pretty', and (even in the biography of a nun, which she was writing) to get away from 'the white light of piety'. This was of a piece with the increasingly astringent note in his reviewing ('Alice Esmond' was told sharply that good poets, however much sadness they possessed, did not 'fondle it and pet it'[34]), and it hints at the widening gulf between himself and his early literary comrades.

Self-confidence was demonstrated in other ways too. In November 1889 he agonized about having shaved off his beard ('the symbol I knew myself by'). Lily recorded that he 'looks much better we all think; Jack got him to do it & when it was half off Willy nearly slaughtered him.'[35] Madame Blavatsky prophesied dire illness through losing 'the mesmeric force that collects in a beard' and in January 1890 he obligingly succumbed to the local epidemic of Russian influenza. He remained plagued by depressions, and in November 1890 told Tynan of a threat to his heart, 'but not of an important nature. The docter says that I have been wearing myself out & has directed me to live more deliberately & leasurely. By no means an easy thing for any one of my temprement.'[36]

The advice was hardly surprising, for, since his encounter with Maud

Gonne, he had been plunged into a ferment of writing. He had long intended to use a legend from *Fairy and Folk Tales* for a play: it concerned the Countess Kathleen O'Shea (WBY eventually spelt it 'Cathleen'), who sold her soul to save the country people in the west of Ireland from starving. His meeting with Gonne helped inspire the image of an aristocratic beauty sacrificing herself for love of the people – and (in a later development) turning her back on the devotion of her minstrel attendant. At this time he was reading William Carleton's *The Black Prophet* for another project, and it supplied the background of a Famine-ravaged land. 'The plot will be the best I have yet worked on – being both fantastic and human,' he wrote to a Dublin family friend, the antiquarian and archaeologist George Coffey, on 14 February; 'human enough to rouse peoples sympathies, fantastic enough to wake them from their conventional standards'.[37] In early March he was still absorbed in it, producing two prose versions before putting it into 'virse'[38] in *The Countess Kathleen*. On 6 May he read a scene to a new friend, the actress Florence Farr, for a theatrical opinion. It was not in proof until April 1892: a copyright performance took place at the Athenaeum Theatre on 6 May 1892, though it would not be acted publicly for many years (and then to an unanticipated reaction[39]). But the form and message – knowledge and power, and a poet's love sacrificed to a holy mission – were inspired by those electrically charged weeks following his first meeting with Gonne.

Other book projects cross-fertilized with his reviewing activity: notably an edition of the underrated mid-nineteenth-century Irish writer William Carleton for the Camelot series. From late April 1889 WBY was looking out for stories by him, and begging copies of his books; his editorial work was also recycled into an important review for the *Scots Observer*.[40] Carleton was a sensitive subject, because he had converted to Protestantism, been taken up by a distinctly Orange clique of literary entrepreneurs, and produced some proselytizing stories for an evangelical magazine. WBY defended him in the only terms possible for an Irish audience: 'his heart always remained Catholic, it seems to me'.[41] However, he took care to trace the original versions of Carleton's controversial work in the *Christian Examiner*, and assumed a certain authority in the area; when his *Stories from Carleton* was published on 23 August 1889 he received seven guineas from Walter Scott, but he had gained much more. 'When I want to read up a subject I get a book to do there on. I write to read & never merely read to write.'[42] He told the same correspondent, 'The introduction to Carleton you will hardly find of much interest, it was done in a great hurry to fill a gap and get Rhys out of a scrape.'[43] But it was important for two reasons. Reading Carleton at short notice and high speed gave him a sense of Irish dialogue, and of peasant life, which affected both his fiction and his ballads; and the reaction to such a controversial subject anticipated later battles with Irish public opinion. The *Nation* attacked Carleton's apostasy so violently that WBY wrote a long and passionate defence, arguing that 'Catholicism can well afford to be generous: no Catholic need show the bigotry of some poor sectary.' His view of authentic Irishness still stressed a peasant and Catholic identity; and his immersion in early nineteenth-century Catholic Irish fiction, together with his contemporary denunciation of the 'braggadocio' peddled for English audiences by the supposedly Anglo-Irish Charles Lever and Samuel Lover, helped dictate this view.

It found another expression in a volume of *Representative Irish Tales*, which WBY also began to edit in this *annus mirabilis* of creative energy; it eventually appeared in March 1891. His original ambition was to produce 'a kind of social history', with stories 'illustrative of some phase of Irish life', defending the 'square built power' of unfashionable Irish novelists like Gerald Griffin and the Banim brothers, who had written about the life of rural Catholic Ireland in the early nineteenth century.[44] This was prescient, but once again he had chosen a sensitive subject. In July 1891 the *Irish Monthly* would attack him for including tasteless and anti-Catholic material, and overly emphasizing 'the rollicking, savage and droll elements' of Irish life.[45] For WBY, however, his *Irish Tales* (taken together with *Carleton*) proposed a revaluation of early nineteenth-century Irish literature in English: he also projected (but never produced) a 'verse chronicle' of Ireland (derived from Davis's projected 'Ballad History'), a volume of 'Old Celtic romances' for Camelot, and a collection of Mangan's poems.[46] Yet another compilation, which did appear, was a collection of *Irish Fairy Tales* for Fisher Unwin's Children's Library, suggested in the summer of 1891 and published the following year with illustrations by Jack. In December 1889 he thought he might write a 'little history of "Irish Literature this Century" . . . I shall be systimatically political or national anyway, through out the thing.'[47] 'Political, or national anyway': national-mindedness was still seen as the better, and safer, part of politics. But in this too he was conscious of Maud Gonne's expectations as well as of his own hereditary insecurities.

He was about to embark upon another great project, which would take five years to bring to fruition. Since 1888 he had been close to his vague and depressive artist neighbour in Bedford Park, Edwin Ellis. Ellis was well established as a Yeats family friend. Although nearer to JBY's generation, having been part of his art school circle, he appealed to WBY as a fellow-poet (to whom WBY read his work, and whose own poems WBY pressed on Father Russell for the *Irish Monthly*). One of the bonds between WBY and Ellis (which may have distanced them accordingly from the elder Yeats) was a shared interest in mysticism: Ellis was committed to the Blakean idea of total art, fuelled by a mystic vision. Blake was a familiar presiding deity in Bedford Park;

Todhunter had a particular interest in him, and stressed that no one had yet mastered Blake's mystical language and myth.[48] The date of WBY's and Ellis's decision to produce a joint work on William Blake's prophetic writings is unknown, but the enterprise was fired by the galvanic energy released in WBY during early 1889. He announced the project to Tynan on 8 March, declaring his determination to confront Blake as a symbolist working in a magical context, rather than as an eccentric, and seeing this analysis of the poet as part of his own Theosophical researches. (He was further inspired by the erroneous belief that Blake was really an Irishman, in which he persisted through the early 1890s – though his new friend Arthur Symons, a Blakean since childhood, tried to put him right.) A large agenda had been mapped out by May 1889. 'The book must rouse a good deal of interest among literer[y] people & what will please me better influence for good the mystical societies throughout Europe . . . It has done my own mind a great deal of good – in liberating me from formulas & theories of several kinds.'[49] Already he was copying out the first edition of the *Book of Thel* in the Bodleian Library. By October 1889 he was sure he had found the key to the prophetic books, and was 'trying to unravel his symbolic way of using colour'. WBY's apprenticeship in Theosophy and his reading of the recently translated Cabbala now came into its own. Blake's doctrine of correspondence between 'Permanent Realities' and the 'vegetable glass of nature' fitted into this Neo-Platonist world. Moreover, WBY's own ideas of poetry as a reflection of 'immortal moods', or archetypal emotions, which he had derived from Shelley, were reinforced by Blake: a common inspiration apparently lay in Boehme's view of imagination as the vehicle of divine revelation. To clarify references, he read Boehme's mystic writings, and reread Swedenborg (first discovered by him in Dublin during the early 1880s). By 1893, when his work on Blake had finished, WBY had made the connection to the study of folklore as an affirmation of 'the ancient supremacy of imagination', which was 'God in the world of art': not only Blake but Homer, Aeschylus, Sophocles, Shakespeare, Dante, Goethe and Keats were 'little more than folklorists with musical tongues'.

This looks forward from the first flush of enthusiasm in 1889; but it illustrates a strength of WBY's synthesizing and autodidactic mind, which was to find assonances in all he read, bend them to his purposes, and create universal patterns by annexing writers and philosophies into his personal pantheon. Blake was a vital part of the process, referred to as 'my master'[50] and seen as someone whose inspiration, like WBY's own, was misunderstood by the everyday philosophy of a crudely materialist world. He was also becoming much influenced by the ideas in Arthur Hallam's *Essay on Tennyson* about the necessary impurity of popular art; his work on Blake crystallized lofty ideas about the dangers of fashionability, the role of an audience, and the public's hatred of the unusual.[51] It therefore became a personal mission for himself and Ellis to get back to the real Blake, not the 'dressed and brushed' version. They thought of producing a short biography as well as their ambitious edition. (And if this meant rediscovering an *Irish* Blake, all the better.)

In the process he also discovered the pleasures of scholarship – of a Yeatsian sort. His ideas may have been single-minded, his transcriptions imperfect, and his interpretations idiosyncratic – but in the course of their inquiries Ellis and wby made the important discovery of an unknown prophetic book, 'Vala, or the Four Zoas', in the possession of the Linnell family,[52] and worked directly from manuscripts owned by Lord Houghton and Charles Fairfax Murray. By December 1889 wby was staying at the Linnell house to copy out their manuscripts, plied with ancient port by the equally ancient Linnells, who thought he looked delicate (the lost beard and the oncoming influenza). By the end of August 1890 the bookseller and publisher Bernard Quaritch had agreed to publish their findings as *The Works of William Blake: Poetic, Symbolic and Critical*. No money was offered to wby (the contract was between Quaritch and Ellis), but prestige and a beautiful book were guaranteed. wby and Ellis were to be paid in copies, with an added honorarium for Ellis, who was expected to do most of the work. The whole question of collaboration and dual responsibility was a thorny one; wby enlarged upon it much later to Augusta Gregory. 'The actual interpretation of the philosophy . . . was made out absolutely to geather. His mind was far more minute than mine, but less synthetic. I had a tendency to make generalisations on imperfect foundations, & he to remain content with detached discoveries . . . With the exception of the part called "The Symbolic System" almost all of the actual writing is by Ellis.'[53] wby, however, had to warn Ellis off certain areas appropriated for himself; Ellis's 'wonderful industry' threatened to propel him into spheres where he was hampered by 'lack of mystical knowledge'.[54]

It is unlikely that wby accomplished this tactfully. Already, he was representing himself as a mage. Mrs Ellis, a neurotic German who was herself dreaded throughout Bedford Park, had banned him from the house by March 1891 because she thought he was casting spells on her husband ('the sight of me made her grow white with terror'[55]). In the end, the introduction to Volume I of the Ellis–Yeats *Blake* ('The System') remained wby's contribution; but their notes show he and Ellis collaborated intensely on each other's emendations. Ellis spelled out their agenda in a letter to John Lane:

Blake's system was of such richness that notwithstanding its simplicity it is more like the work of a period than of an individual, & in the absence of an intelligible account of it, has doomed its inventor to the position of a reputed madman. In conjunction with William Yeats – the author of 'The Wanderings of Oisin' – (a successful first volume of very picturesque, melodious & readable poetry for which even the Saturday

[*Review*] had none but good words,) – I am engaged in preparing a key to all Blake's myths, – & to show the value of W. Yeats's part of the work his chart of the personages of the great fable was laid beside Mr Quaritch's book [a copy of *Jerusalem*] for the Volumes [the Odde Volumes, a society of bibliophiles] to study. The name of 'Vala' as that of one of Blake's chief works is not generally known as it lay, an unsorted manuscript, for about a hundred years. It is now paged and explained & it will be issued by Mr Quaritch in his new complete edition of the poetic poems [*sic*]. The question of Blake's sanity will then be finally set at rest, for the works being brought together & the explanation printed along with them any competent family solicitor who is accustomed to arrange evidence will be able to see for himself whether the poet was a madman or not. The fact is that he adopted mysticism as a language & made it the vehicle of poetry, adding new terms & names as he chose, founding all on the Scriptures, & blending the Swedenborg, Boehmen, & Paracelsus modes of expression, & so dealing with the matter that whatever most readers find miserable & dry in their modes of expression, Blake by the infusion of his poetic vigour has left not only more philosophic, but even enjoyable.[56]

This was exactly what inspired wby. Blake had spoken to him; his mind spun with correspondences and connections. Blake's four Zoas, or mythological personages, corresponded to the four quarters of London – suddenly converted into a visionary territory which might be claimed, like Sligo. wby's notebooks of 1889 show that Blake had inspired him to play with fourfold divisions, based on the elements and the zodiac, related to Celtic as well as to Christian hierarchies of angels and gods.[57] His occult reading had fired him with notions of alchemy and its provision of metaphors for the imagination; Blake made him think in terms of the whole symbolic order of the cosmos. Most of all, Blake had been manipulated by wby into his own system of universal 'moods', accessible through visions to the man of genius. But this was wby's own contribution; and his approach to visions was essentially magical, not mystical. In the end Blake, like Russell, was a mystic, wrapped in obscurities; and wby was an apprentice mage, determined to penetrate beyond them.

III

In early 1889, as wby was drawn into the world of Maud Gonne, he was simultaneously proceeding with his ventures into occult experimentation. The two obsessions became closely associated in his mind, and would remain so. Throughout his life, episodes of sexual energy and confusion would be closely paralleled by periods of magical experimentation. Both the Theosophical Society and the Hermetic Order of the Golden Dawn (which he joined the year after Gonne's visit) acted as magnets for the frustrated as well as the credulous; both attracted a high proportion of unconventional woman acolytes; both were plagued by sexual scandals. Theosophist circles were convulsed in April 1889 by accusations levelled at the editor of their journal, *Lucifer*, the novelist Mabel Collins, who was alleged to have led two of the apprentice celibates astray (Blavatsky, as WBY remembered it later, 'could not permit her more than one'). The brethren were also shocked by reverberations from Chatterjee's dalliances. WBY visited Blavatsky's regularly in January and February 1889;[58] later in the year he brought O'Leary, who was brutally amused by the effete young men, slavish women and strong-minded old termagant dominating them all.[59]

WBY himself retained doubts about the implicit belief in Madame Blavatsky's Tibetan Masters that was required: her own cynicism and sharp tongue accounted for much of the attraction. He would later remember her as 'a sort of old Irish peasant woman with an air of humour and audacious power ... impressive, I think, to every man or woman who had themselves any richness'. Her astute and epigrammatical summaries dazzled him ('I used to wonder at and pity the people who sell their souls to the Devil, but now I only pity them. They do it to have somebody on their side').[60] He had less time for her followers, whose mystical credulity clashed with his own inclination towards magical experimentation and the verification of supernatural phenomena. For this reason he strongly backed the formation of an Esoteric Section of the Theosophical Society, devoted to such rituals; he joined it in December 1888, and renewed his pledges on 20 December 1889, along with the celebrated Annie Besant among others. During the spring of 1890, accompanied by Besant and Edwin Ellis, he dabbled in mesmerism and other magical experiments. However, he had from the beginning queried the conditions of absolute obedience to Blavatsky imposed on initiates; notes he kept in a contemporary esoteric diary show that she was prepared to allow him a certain latitude in order to keep him. For his part, he found no difficulty in describing his Blake studies as 'work on theosophy'. Renewing his pledges a year after joining raised some further doubts, though he dismissed any idea that Blavatsky's 'teachers' might be fraudulent as 'wholly unable to cover the facts'.[61]

His reflections on the Theosophists themselves, made in 1889, illustrate the attitude towards fellow-students of the occult which he would retain. This was combined realism (G. R. S. Mead had 'the intellect of a good sized whelk') and indulgence:

... they seem some intellectual, one or two cultured, the rest the usual amorphous material that gather round all new things. All, amorphous and clever alike, have much zeal, and here and there a few sparkles of fanaticism are visible. This section will not in any way, I believe, influence educated thought. For this as yet unattempted propaganda the society has so far neither men nor method. What effects it has produced upon it are wholly owing to the inherent weight of the philosophy.

However, he instructed himself to 'keep out of propaganda: not my work'. Instead, he proposed and forced through a scheme for organized occult research on a basis of empirical experiment (much as the Society for Psychical Research were doing, though the parallel was not mentioned). This initiative was finally too independent for Blavatsky's taste, and lay behind his severance from the Theosophical Society in October 1890 – ostensibly because of an article he wrote on *Lucifer* for the *Weekly Review*. He told O'Leary: 'I refused [to promise never to criticize the Society again] because I looked upon [the] request as undue claim to control right of individual to think as best pleased him. I may join them again later on'.[62]

This was truer than it seemed. What he objected to was an abstract and dogmatic religiosity, built around a personality cult. The eclectic Eastern flavour of Theosophy continued to attract him, and so did the sort of people he met there. In 1891 he was once again frequenting Theosophist circles, this time the Adelphi Lodge founded by William Wynn Westcott, Percy Bullock and John Watkins.[63] And at least two Adelphi members (Westcott and Bullock) were members of another occult order, which by then had won WBY's loyalty, the Hermetic Order of the Golden Dawn.[64] Its rival attractions had impelled Madame Blavatsky to sanction the formation of her Esoteric Section; many Golden Dawn initiates had passed through Theosophy, and retained Theosophical connections; many also lived in Bedford Park. For WBY (already since 1887 frequenting a Hermetic society of inquiry, with future Golden Dawn members), the path was an inevitable one. The Golden Dawn followed through the interest in ritual magic and study prescribed by Esoteric Theosophists, which was exactly what WBY had taken from the Blavatsky movement; and a central figure in its early formation exerted a considerable influence on his occult development. This was MacGregor Mathers.

Mathers had published *The Kabbalah Unveiled* in 1887, a commentary on ritual magic which provided the basis for much of the Golden Dawn's structure. He was already on the Theosophical circuit; acquainted with Blavatsky, he lectured to her devotees, though he refused to join the Society. It seems likely that he was already determined to build his own religion, with himself as prophet; he is closely associated with the foundation on 1 March 1888 of the Hermetic Order of the Golden Dawn, in the company of Westcott (a Freemason with Rosicrucian connections) and W. R. Woodman, Supreme Magus of the Rosicrucian Society in England. Allegedly, its rituals were 'revealed' in a cipher manuscript discovered on a bookstall by the Reverend A. F. A. Woodford (a Swedenborgian Mason who was safely dead by 1888). This seems analogous to the part played by Fräulein Sprengel, a Rosicrucian avatar invented by Westcott as his own creation-myth; it also parallels the function performed by Blavatsky's invisible Masters. The bookstall myth probably derives from Edward Bulwer-Lytton's occult novel *Zanoni*, and the cipher papers actually came from the estate of Kenneth Mackenzie, a fellow-Rosicrucian who had been close to Eliphas Lévi and founded other short-lived occult societies before his death in 1886.[65] Certainly, the invention of tradition was central to the process. Mathers helped write up rituals from the cipher manuscripts provided by Westcott; these were adapted from German Rosicrucianism, using language lifted from edited versions of papyri in the British Museum as well as from the writings of the Elizabethan alchemist and astrologer John Dee, and theories which owed much to numerology and the Tarot.[66] And inventing tradition came easily to wby, already predisposed towards Mathers's objectives: to ascend by stipulated 'paths' from the world of material consciousness to that of transcendent archetypes.

He probably met Mathers in the Reading Room of the British Museum after 1887 (wby got his ticket on 29 June of that year). In his novel *The Speckled Bird* he described Mathers in this milieu, and specified his age as thirty-six or thirty-seven, which suggests 1890 to 1891.[67] He could hardly have failed to notice him. Mathers, born Samuel Liddell Mathers, was an apprentice guru and self-created authority on ritual magic. He had not yet discovered his later identity as Scots Jacobite romantic ('the Comte de Glenstrae'), but was still a compelling and awesome figure, at least to people of wby's predilections. At this stage the Golden Dawn's organization was still dominated by Westcott, but Mathers's time would come.[68] To others, he probably seemed seedy as well as silly: but his dominance over the kind of people attracted to occultist circles, even in his later unstable period, was undeniable. By March 1890 Golden Dawn initiates included Moina (née Mina) Bergson, sister of the philosopher and later Mathers's wife, the Reverend W. A. Ayton, an alchemically inclined clergyman obsessed by Jesuit conspiracies, and Annie Horniman, Manchester Quaker, ex-art student and heiress, who provided Mathers with his income. (Constance Wilde had been a member, but had already left.) In the same month wby became the seventy-eighth name on the membership roll of the Isis-Urania Temple. His motto, and sobriquet, was 'Demon Est Deus Inversus': its recognition of the interdependence of opposites echoes not only Blavatsky but Blake.

He would, in turn, bring in figures from his own circle such as Florence Farr (July 1890), Maud Gonne (November 1891), John Todhunter (February 1892) and George Pollexfen (December 1893). In the manner of Freemasonry, the Golden Dawn spread by extending circles, like ripples in a pool. Conspiracy-theories abounded, even before the advent of the ultra-conspiratorial Aleister Crowley; the Reverend Ayton believed that 'the [pre-Reformation] Monasteries, under pretence of being Xtian Societies, were in reality Schools of Magic, and latterly almost entirely of Alchemy'.[69] By 1893 there would be

124 active members, with 170 initiated. Within the Order, antique precedents were stressed. Initiates saw themselves in a long tradition of priesthoods of inquiry, where hermetic adepts worked upwards through levels of magical study, emphasizing correspondences between colours, abstract qualities, mathematical numbers and various other aspects of life, according to cabbalistic subdivisions. A preoccupation with symbolism was in many ways a passport into the Order, and it was no coincidence that the Golden Dawn attracted aspiring artists and those of creative bent. Some of its rituals were closely connected with theatrical experiments. Outsiders saw the acolytes as bourgeois mediocrities, searching for a role: Maud Gonne, who soon left, winced at the way commonplace clothes showed under their robes. But Mathers's magnetic presence dominated, though even his acolytes admitted his manic 'delusions'.[70] After a visit to Paris, Mathers declared his 'Secret Chiefs' had authorized him to establish a Second, or Inner, Order, which would stress practical magic; this especially appealed to WBY, as did Mathers's supposed power to induce visions by means of symbols.[71]

'It was a club,' an ex-member remarked much later, 'like any other club, a place to pass the time in and meet one's friends'.[72] Like all clubs, it subsisted on gossip and internal crises. Briefly bankrolled by Annie Horniman as 'curator' of her father's ethnographical museum at Forest Hill, Mathers lost this position in 1891; the funds continued, however, and in May 1892 he decamped to Paris, where Horniman was paying for his wife to study art. In his absence Westcott deputized as leader until 1897, when Florence Farr took over. Mathers became more markedly eccentric; the sensitivities of members like Horniman could lead to sexual tensions; there was violent disagreement over the importation of dubious Egyptian rites. WBY himself unwillingly ran near the rocks of scandal when he had to evade the advances of Anna, 'Comtesse' de Bremont, briefly a member of the Order.[73] Still, he remained committed not only to the institution but, for a decade, to its bizarre presiding spirit.

His family, and some of his friends, found it hard to keep patient. 'Willie has been out of sorts lately,' wrote JBY to O'Leary in November 1890. 'He overworks himself – or rather over-fatigues himself seeing people & talking to people upon various paradoxical subjects in which he believes or persuades himself he is interested.'[74] But the Golden Dawn's magic was exerted in different ways. It was very much of its time: London in the 1880s pulsated with societies and fraternities for self-betterment, moral and spiritual, often with overlapping memberships. Through it, WBY could not only advance the search for magic which had preoccupied him since his art school days; he could (and did) meet people who interested him, who were attracted by him, and who (like Horniman) might play a useful role in the drama of his life. The fact that the Golden Dawn provided rich fishing-grounds for netting eccentrics would, like so much else in WBY's life, eventually be made to serve his art. In the meantime, it provided a dimension at once mysterious and glamorous, located in the unlikely purlieus of Fitzrovia, Camden Town and Shepherd's Bush. With its complicated, eclectic, but strictly defined grades, tests and examinations, the Golden Dawn approximated to a sort of university. It filled the need for self-education, and provided themes and motifs linked to the imagery of classical and folk myths: all of which appealed to WBY's fondness for self-referencing patterns. The language which Mathers created for initiates to approach their 'Higher Genius' implied the kind of transcendent powers for which WBY longed.[75] From 1892, the secrecy of the brotherhood was amplified by its retraction into the Second Order (Rosae Rubeae et Aureae Crucis, or R. R. et A. C.): Mathers's Rosicrucian inner circle, entered by complicated rituals, and devoted to magic. And when Mathers left for Paris, that city became a joint focus for the two intoxicating involvements which dominated WBY's life by 1890: the secret society of magical ritual, and the mysterious world of Maud Gonne. Finally, as 'Hiereus', or mentor, he would supervise her preparation for and initiation into the Golden Dawn and 'lead her in the Path that conducts from Darkness to Light'.[76]

The uses of occultism were manifold. Famously, in later life, he remembered that magic gave him metaphors for his poetry; this seems to have been a half-conscious motivation from early on. In his *Autobiographies* he took care to stress the importance of intellectual discipline, and the possibility of autosuggestion and telepathy. But from 1889 to 1890 there were other reasons too. The world of the Golden Dawn provided a compensation for the daily struggle in Bedford Park: a sign that, somewhere, a world might exist where reality could echo and confirm his magnificent imagination. This could prove a poetic tradition encompassing not only Blake but even Tennyson;[77] and, perhaps most importantly, an area of authority where he could assert himself over Maud Gonne. In a cancelled fragment of his unpublished novel a few years later he wrote of the 'intimacy which is only possible among lovers and among fellow mystics; they had shared with one another the long hidden secrets of their life, and their dream of [the] future was the same'.[78] Upheavals and tragedies in her own life made her deeply susceptible to the consolations of occult promises. WBY rapidly discovered this and used it. Here, at last, was a sphere where he was 'complete', and she was not.

Occult connections could fuse with nationalist activities in a way peculiarly attractive to Gonne; when WBY wrote a celebrated letter to O'Leary in July 1892, stating that the magical life was at the centre of all he did, the context was the proposed enlistment of Mathers (wearing his Jacobite revolutionary hat) for Fenian activities.[79] All in all, occultism had a particularly Irish relevance; in 1891 WBY was greatly excited by reading Dr Adam Clarke's memoirs, dealing with sorcery in eighteenth-century Dublin, and when millenarian hopes of nationalist revolution developed at the end of the decade, occult divination came into its own.[80] In some areas of nationalist activity WBY's position was ambiguous and his commitment suspect; occultism combined with Irishness, however, might not only confer political credibility but weave a lover's spell.

IV

Throughout 1890 WBY continued to build up other networks of association, often (like the Golden Dawn) operating through the fraternities of Bedford Park. His fascination with Florence Farr, a vague and unconventional beauty about to embark on an affair with Bernard Shaw, was sealed by a quintessential Bedford Park occasion: her performance in Todhunter's play *A Sicilian Idyll* at the local theatre on 5 May 1890. WBY had first heard the play read at home in Blenheim Road, but his ecstatic reviews for the *Boston Pilot* and the *Providence Sunday Journal* were prompted by more than duty. *A Sicilian Idyll*, which was essentially a tableau, reads now as derivative pastiche; but its contemporary production struck WBY as a revelation of anti-materialist art, and its subsequent West End *succès d'estime* suggested the wider possibilities of coterie culture. His fascination with the pose adopted by Todhunter, and the idea that an artistic movement or organization might claim critical attention by asserting itself against the dominant mode in poetry, helped to inspire him. It was no coincidence that May 1890 was also the month when he first mentions the group of writers, meeting regularly in the Cheshire Cheese pub off Fleet Street, who constituted themselves the 'Rhymers Club'.

The rudiments of such a circle were probably in existence in January 1890.[81] It was mainly 'Celtic', with a strong Irish predominance. Rhys, Rolleston and WBY were original moving spirits, joined off and on by Todhunter, Lionel Johnson, Ernest Dowson, Richard Le Gallienne, John Davidson and others. 'Celticism' could be very flexible; Victor Plarr claimed it on account of an Alsatian father, and Arthur Symons stressed his own Welsh and Cornish connections. Edgar Jepson maliciously claimed that the epicene Lionel Johnson demonstrated his Irish credentials by 'addressing me as "me dearr" '.[82] The Celtic element, in any case, became diluted with time. In the summer of 1891 WBY listed 'regular "Rhymers" who are now in London' as George Greene, Ernest Radford, Symons, Davidson, Le Gallienne, Johnson, Edward Garnett, Dowson, Todhunter and Edwin Ellis. That November, John Davidson described a meeting at Lionel Johnson's:

Low-ceiled rooms on third floor in Fitzroy Street, but plenty of space, walled with books and overpowering pictures by Simeon Solomon. Lionel moving about among them like a minnow, or an anatomical preparation – the Absin [the] you remember. George-a-Greene, the Pindar of Wakefield who translates Carducci was there; also Ernest Radford, forked radish that would fain be an eagle, and who begins his books 'As my friend Walter Pater said to me on Saturday – no it was Sunday afternoon'; W. B. Yeats the wild Irishman, who lives on water-cress and pemmican and gets drunk on the smell of whisky, and can distinguish and separate out as subtly as death each individual cell in any literary organism; Rolleston, once an Irish Adonis – now a consumptive father of four children; Dowson and Clough, two rosebud poets.[83]

Contemporaries outside the group saw it as an efficient machine for mutual admiration (if the word his admirers used most often about the early wby was 'imagination', the phrase which came most readily to his detractors was 'log-rolling'). For wby himself, the importance of the Rhymers was more complex. They filled his need for what Balzac called a *cénacle*, or a mutually supportive literary circle. They remain preserved in his *Autobiographies* (and a series of public lectures from about 1910) as 'the tragic generation', illustrating the theories he was evolving in his middle years: unfinished people, incapable of a religious instinct, mired in bohemia.[84] At the time, this was not so obvious. Some Rhymers were bohemian, notably Dowson, who was already celebrated for a youth dominated by hashish, drink and *belles de nuit*; but even he was, as early as 1896, wryly amused at the highly coloured way Symons presented this ethos to the general public.[85] Less generally emphasized was a strong homoerotic subculture. Charles Ricketts and Charles Shannon, whose high-camp ménage acted as a court of arbitration for aestheticism in painting, printing and *objets d'art*, were unofficial patrons. The tone was sustained by Lionel Johnson's poems of repressed desire, and the presence of John Gray (in some ways a Ricketts–Shannon creation), who lent his face and his name to the hero of Wilde's coded homosexual novel.[86] Wilde himself looked in and out. The formidably well-read Johnson was, at this stage, a powerful and decisive intellectual mentor for the 'incomplete' Yeats. One of the most striking bonds between members of the Rhymers Club was their joint influence as a reviewing mafia, exercising decisive influence on the *Star*, the *Pall Mall Gazette*, the *Speaker*, the *Daily Chronicle*, the *Bookman* and wby's American outlets. Moreover, one leading Rhymer, with whom wby rapidly formed a close friendship, had infiltrated literary London with even more precocious success than wby himself. This was Arthur Symons.

Symons was an exact contemporary of wby. He too was a poetry-struck provincial, still living with his parents and determined to make a literary career. Though his trail-blazing book on the Symbolist movement was nine years in the future, he was already a published poet and an influential critic. After early Browning-worship he had attached himself to Walter Pater as a mentor, and produced commentaries on Meredith, Michael Field, Vernon

Lee and other vogueish contemporaries; when he met WBY in 1890 he had just discovered literary Paris, whose English impresario he would become. Like WBY, he had cultivated Rhys and been rewarded by a commission to edit a Camelot selection (of Leigh Hunt, though the enterprising Symons had not previously read him). Boyishly handsome, Symons was good at 'collecting' eminent people, and they gave his first poetry collection a fair wind in the spring of 1888.

The Symons encountered in 1890 was not the sexually obsessed and mentally unstable ex-puritan of later years, whose image is so memorably fixed in WBY's *Autobiographies*. But he would introduce his Irish friend to several of his own preoccupations, including hashish and dance (it was probably with Symons that WBY saw Loie Fuller perform, bequeathing him an enduring image). Though WBY lacked a conventional musical ear, the Symbolist obsession with connections between music and literature appealed to him: the nuanced language of individual movements, the harmonies of atmosphere. How far Symons actually awakened this interest in Symbolism is another matter; WBY took good care to stress that his interest went back to reading Boehme, Blake and Swedenborg in the early 1880s.[87] But Symons read him Verlaine and Mallarmé, and preached the techniques of modern Symbolism. And it seems likely that through Symons WBY came to grips with Pater.

Paterian influences pervade the literary world of the 1880s and 1890s, and many of them echo WBY's own preoccupations: the idea of the poet as priest, the ascetic and hieratic dimensions of the artist's life, and the aphoristic lessons of Pater's essay 'Style'. A decade later WBY remembered 'sitting all day in a Dublin garden trying to persuade myself that Walter Pater was a bad writer, and for no better reason that that he perplexed me and made me doubtful of myself';[88] but his own prose would remain, in many respects, Paterian. In that stately language he would later memorialize the Rhymers' lack of centre, and their belief in the self-referencing nature of art. But they were much less consistent than that. They were riven with disagreements; Todhunter and Johnson specifically attacked the doctrine of 'art for art's sake'. They did subscribe to a certain cult of Wilde, particularly *Intentions* and *Dorian Gray* (both published in May 1891), shared by WBY. In Johnson's case at least, this carried overt homoerotic implications.[89] But the Rhymers' most passionate desire was for publication. WBY accordingly cultivated the publisher John Lane on the Rhymers' behalf; the first *Book of the Rhymers Club* appeared in February 1892, and WBY pressed on Tynan the suitability of the group as subject for a major article.[90] The *Book* included both 'Innisfree' (first published in the *National Observer* on 13 December 1890, and widely noticed) and 'The Man who Dreamed of Faeryland', which struck Symons as WBY's best poem yet. As far as he and Johnson were concerned, WBY's position in the Rhymers was as 'the one cygnet among the ducklings',[91] and reading their *Book* it is hard to disagree.

WBY knew how to make the most of this society, as of the others he formed and joined. But he was also aware that the Rhymers did not represent a single, coherent approach, though he grouped them together in a piece for the *Boston Pilot* in April 1892: 'The typical young poet of our day is an aesthete with a surfeit, searching sadly for his lost Philistinism, his heart full of an unsatisfied hunger for the commonplace. He is an Alastor tired of his woods and longing for beer and skittles.'[92] But this contemporary commentary on the future 'tragic generation' deliberately ended by singling out Todhunter for praise because of his Irishness. 'England is old and her poets must scrape up the crumbs of an almost finished banquet, but Ireland still has full tables.' This was a note calculated for Irish American ears, which it was safe to play across the Atlantic; his fellow-Rhymers, however 'Celtic' they thought themselves, would have felt more equivocal on the subject.

The company of the Rhymers, combined with life among the illuminati of the Golden Dawn, did much to create WBY's perceived image in the early 1890s: whether seen as compellingly attractive, grotesquely affected or (in Aleister Crowley's phrase) 'a lank dishevelled demonologist'. '*Such* a figure,' wrote Frances Wynne, a breezy and conventional Irish Protestant girl who wrote poetry. 'Hair a yard long and full of mysticism and magic.'[93] Symons advised him to wear black as 'elegant and inexpensive',[94] which added to the aura. In middle and old age he would talk endlessly about the Rhymers, generalizing from the dissolute lives and tragic fates of Dowson and Symons in order to present them as a generation doomed through their search for liberation: whereas he had found salvation by consecrating himself to the search for a cause.[95]

But the literary connections he was building into his life were not necessarily among doomed bohemians; and they were no less influential for that. In October 1890 Edward Garnett agreed to read *John Sherman* for Fisher Unwin; by March 1891 WBY reported he was 'quite enthusiastic'. It seemed that *The Countess Kathleen*, the Blake project and now *John Sherman* might all be published in 1891: 'I shall be well in evidence'.[96] The novel appeared in Fisher Unwin's 'Pseudonym Library' under the fairy-sobriquet 'Ganconagh', but WBY made no secret of his authorship. The appearance of a work so closely modelled on his Sligo background, and the continuing dilemmas of his personal life, led to some gloomy self-analysis – poured out to Tynan.

There is more of myself in it than in anything I have done. I dont imagine it will please many people but some few it may please with some kind of permiment pleasure . . . Except for the wish to make a little money I have no desire to get that kind of passing regard a book wins from the many. To please the folk of few books is ones great aim. By being Irish I think one has a better chance of it – over here there is so much to read & think about that the most a writer can usually hope for is that kind of un-prosperous prosperity that comes from writing books that lie amid a half dozen of others on a drawing room table for a week.[97]

For all the personal inspiration, however, and notwithstanding the Yeats/Pollexfen dichotomy which provided the theme of the book, his mother's family barely noticed its appearance. 'I don't think any of my Sligo relations – except possibly George Pollexfen – has ever read this Sligo story,' he wrote in Augusta Gregory's copy ten years later. 'One apologised to me every summer for not reading it, for several years. She used to say "I had a copy once but somebody borrowed it." I am sure that copy was given her. She would never have spent a 1/– on such a purpose.'[98]

In 1891 reactions closer to hand preoccupied him far more. 'Willie seems very well & is occupied in getting people to review his novel,' wrote JBY drily to O'Leary in November.[99] This was no more than the truth. 'When you review it,' WBY warned Tynan, 'you might perhaps, if you think it is so, say that Sherman is an Irish type. I have an ambition to be taken as an Irish novelist not as an English or cosmepolitan one chosing Ireland as a background.'[100] She obediently stressed the author's rootedness in Sligo, reinforcing the image of an Irish writer launched on the British market. The accompany-ing fantasy-tale *Dhoya* was calculated to a similar effect; it stimulated the *National Observer* to ask for more of the same, beginning the series of mystical stories which WBY would later gather together as *The Secret Rose*. Irishness and occultism, vitally connected, now constituted an essential part of his appeal.

The reviews of *John Sherman* and *Dhoya*, nearly all of which obligingly named the author, were uniformly respectful. The Pseudonym Library was intended for cheap holiday reading,[101] and Fisher Unwin's aggressive mar-keting produced respectable sales; 1,644 paper copies were printed, and 356 cloth. Even if all sold, WBY's half-profit contract meant he received nothing on the first thousand copies, but by early November this hurdle was cleared. JBY reported in December that 'Willie hears his novel is selling fairly well',[102] and by then he was expecting at least £30. The departure into conventional-ity pressed by his father had not brought a spectacular material reward. But, taken with *The Countess Kathleen* (now scheduled for 1892), and the poems he had published since *Oisin* in January 1889, WBY's achievement so far seemed to confirm what he would later state as a thesis: the Rhymers lacked a coher-ent centre, for all their immersion in Art, but Ireland could inspirationally make up the deficiency.[103] In pursuit of this theme, and in association with Maud Gonne, WBY had already embarked upon a campaign to prove the point. Simultaneously, he had to establish his own political credentials.

Chapter 5: THE BATTLES OF THE BOOKS
1891–1893

> I know that my work has been done in every detail with a delib-
> erate Irish aim, but it is hard for those who know it in fragments
> to know that, especially if the most that they know of me is about
> some contest with Irish opinion.
>
> WBY to J. M. Hone, 2 January 1916

I

IT is not easy to establish what formal links, if any, WBY had established to
the Irish Republican Brotherhood before the 1890s. Part of the reason lies in
the obscurity of the revolutionary movement itself, but there are also a num-
ber of conflicting testimonies. In old age he liked to say he was a Fenian 'of
the school of John O'Leary', and Maud Gonne (also in old age) denied that
she had been responsible for his politics:

Willie joined the IRB *before* I did, *possibly* before we met for the first time at John
O'Leary's tea party, but *more probably* I think, the following year [i.e. 1888], for it
was in London. He told me he was a member when he had gone to live by him-
self in Woburn Buildings. I was sworn in by Mark Ryan much later, I think about
1896 or 7.[1]

This implies some confusion about dates; it also contradicts WBY's own
statement that he 'never took any oath but regarded himself as one of the
party'.[2] But that denial comes from a period when he was anxious to dis-
tance himself from extreme republicanism, and the idea that WBY was
sworn in during the 1880s deserves some attention. The Young Ireland Society
of York Street in Dublin, which he had joined in October 1885, was seen by
the detectives of Dublin Castle as an IRB organization, and certainly took
a neo-Fenian stance; WBY may well have taken the oath during his membership.
But the Young Irelanders included many people whose republicanism was
purely verbal. WBY's *Autobiographies* and other evidence confirm that his real
commitment came when he joined the secessionist Irish National Alliance,
through Mark Ryan, originally formed in America in 1895; he was probably
a formal but inactive member of the main body before then. It is not un-
likely, given his predilection for oaths and societies, that he joined the IRB
under O'Leary's influence in the late 1880s – though Dublin Castle heard noth-
ing of it. More relevant is the almost complete dearth of 'advanced' political

sentiments in his correspondence up to the mid-1890s, and indeed the paucity of any political comments at all.[3]

The exception, inevitably, is the period of the Parnellite split. In December 1890 Parnell, his liaison with Mrs O'Shea exposed in the divorce court, had to fight to retain leadership of the Irish Parliamentary Party, eventually refusing to relinquish power. His minority of supporters were ranged against the majority, who preferred not to jeopardize the alliance with Gladstone's Liberals. Even without the vociferous anti-Parnellism which was rapidly mobilized among the Catholic clergy, the majority's dependence on an English alliance put O'Leary firmly and publicly in the Parnellite camp.[4] WBY took a similar line, writing that Parnell 'has driven up into dust & vacuum no end of insincerities'.[5] But he also implied that his support of Parnell arose from dislike of the combination of the priests and 'the Sullivan gang' (a Cork political mafia led by T. M. Healy); and he hoped the Liberals would now pass 'a good [Home Rule] measure if any measure at all'.[6] While he became a contributor to the Parnellite paper *United Ireland*, it did not stop him writing for the ultra-Tory *National Observer* (though he was put in a quandary when he had to review Ellen O'Leary's nationalist *Lays of Country, Home and Friends* in May 1891). When the issues of politically correct credentials arose, as with the tricky question of Rolleston's projected history of Fenianism, WBY's argument was consistent: such subjects should be tackled by 'good Irish men who can write', whether or not (by implication) they were republicans.

When he finally managed to get to Ireland in the summer of 1891, after constant postponements because of work on Blake, much had changed. Central members of his Dublin circle, like the poets Rose Kavanagh and Ellen O'Leary, had died; O'Leary was adrift and preoccupied; the nationalist movement was in chaotic disarray. Arriving in Dublin by 20 July, he visited the Tynans before moving on to stay with Charles Johnston at Ballykilbeg in County Down (leaving a litter of belongings behind him). He had delayed in Dublin because Maud Gonne's arrival was imminent: but her movements were elusive, and apparently dictated by political priorities. 'Miss Gonne said definitely in one of her notes that she *must* (if you please) be in Ireland on 31st July when Dillon & O'Brien [political prisoners] are released,' wrote Oldham to Sarah Purser. 'That is the only fixed date about her eccentricities (in mathematical terms) that I could coax out of her.'[7] She arrived on 22 July, and WBY called at her hotel, finding her exhausted, depressed, vulnerable. 'The old hard resonance had gone and she had become gentle and indolent. I was in love once more and no longer wished to fight against it.' None the less, he went to Ballykilbeg as arranged, though she summoned him back by 3 August. All this required small loans from O'Leary. Another sojourn with the Tynans followed, where Katharine, now engaged to Hinkson, was irritated by his self-absorption.[8]

He had good reason for distraction. Gonne had written to him an account of a dream, where they had been (in a past life) brother and sister, sold into slavery in Arabia. For WBY, this revelation of a spiritual association in another existence seemed to seal their love; but it was accompanied by a clear message from her about the platonic nature of their relationship. As he later remembered it, he went to her at once and asked her to marry him. 'No, she could not marry – there were reasons – she would never marry; but in words that had no conventional ring she asked for my friendship.' On 4 August they visited Howth together, a part of both their pasts; he felt more bound to her than ever. On 7 August he sent her the first of a series of love-poems, 'The White Birds'. Yet for six more years her letters continued to open: 'My dear Mr Yeats'. Her unattainability had been safely fixed.

From Whitehall, WBY moved to the very different surroundings of 3 Upper Ely Place. These rooms, taken in the name of a Theosophist civil servant called F. J. Dick, harboured a bohemian commune of occultists, and would provide him with a regular refuge over the next couple of years. (He even helped Russell paint a mural in one of the rooms, a collaboration he later strategically forgot.[9]) Here he wrote an essay on Russell, who had introduced him to this circle, as well as 'A Faery Song' – perhaps inspired by his efforts to collect fairy lore at Ballykilbeg. But his activities, especially after Gonne's return to France, focused more and more on the idea of a convention of literary societies, which eventually took place in the Rotunda on 15 September, under O'Leary's chairmanship. This was, effectively, the beginning of a long campaign in the cause of nationalist culture, which would dominate WBY's life for the next year.

His political commitments in the early 1890s relate closely to the vicissitudes of his private life; but the subject is inescapably coloured by how he viewed it long afterwards. In his *Autobiographies* he implies that he embraced extreme nationalism as a way of winning Maud Gonne. She was always irritated by the 'misconception that many people have, that Willie's real devotion to Ireland started with his love for me – it did not, he got that from his child days in Sligo and the influence of those mountains and lakes.'[10] But this misses the point: that his intellectual nationalism might have been radicalized into Fenian separatism in order to qualify himself as an appropriate suitor. His obsession, and her elusiveness, fuelled a sense of his own insufficiency – as a lover, as a nationalist, and even as an Irishman. Her decisive commitment to popular feeling, her passionate one-sidedness, filled him with admiration and foreboding; he would celebrate it all his life. But (like his father) he felt a certain suspicion about English conversions to passionate identification with Ireland. Gonne's holy mission cut directly across the more nuanced, ambiguous kind of Irishness which WBY inherited from his background, and which he was now trying to reconstruct. Literary Fenianism in general, and O'Leary's salon in particular, might provide a safe meeting ground, but a conflict of commitments always loomed.

The other point about WBY's nationalist activities is one that he repeated over and over again in later life: an early form appeared in the first draft of his *Autobiographies*. After the death of Parnell in October 1891, he states, 'I knew by a perception that seemed to come into my mind from without, so sudden it was, that the romance of Irish public life had gone and that the young, perhaps for many years to come, would seek some unpolitical form for national feeling.'[11] This begged the question that cultural revival, as we have seen, had begun several years before as a function of constitutional nationalism's success, not its failure. But it created the context for WBY's mission to create a national literature from 1891. The enterprise could be presented as politics continued by other means, side-stepping collisions between the various degrees of nationalist commitment across the spectrum, from literary Fenianism to hard-line separatism. If this was his intention, it was doomed: because where he and his colleagues were fated to disagree was precisely the question of politicizing literature.

In September 1891, a month before Parnell died, an attempt began among nationalist intellectuals to reorganize and bring together the literary Young Ireland Societies of the mid-1880s. WBY, probably prompted by O'Leary, published a manifesto in *United Ireland* on 3 October, following the inaugural meeting of what was called the 'Young Ireland League' on 15 September 1891.[12] In WBY's later, Olympian view, battle-lines were already being drawn up between the moderate 'pan-Celtic' cultural lobby and intellectual 'Fenians' (or fellow-travellers) like himself. Much of the preparation for this, in WBY's eyes at least, involved Maud Gonne. But her difficult private life had become racked with pain. After their emotional meeting in the summer of 1891 she returned to her secret family in France, promising to come back to Ireland. But she was kept from the inaugural meeting of the Young Ireland League by a tragedy: her little son Georges died in France of meningitis on 31 August. When she returned to Dublin on 10 October, WBY met her at Kingstown from the mailboat that carried Parnell's body. He had died suddenly at Brighton four days before. But Maud Gonne's mourning was not for him: her personal life had been shattered.

She told WBY she had adopted a child, who had died, but he was unprepared for the state he found her in.

I met her on the pier and went with her to her hotel, where we breakfasted. She was dressed in extravagantly deep mourning, for Parnell, people thought, thinking her very theatrical. We spoke of the child's death. She had built a memorial chapel, using some of her capital. 'What did money matter to her now?' From another I learned later on that she had the body embalmed. That day and on later days she went over again the details of the death – speech was a relief to her. She was plainly very ill. She had for the first days of her grief lost the power of speaking French, which she knew almost as well as English, and she had acquired the habit, unlearned afterwards with great difficulty, of taking chloroform in order to sleep. We were continually together; my spiritual philosophy was evidently a great comfort to her.[13]

The next ten days were charged with high voltage for both of them. All nationalist Ireland was in a state of shock at Parnell's death. WBY rapidly wrote a banal *pièce d'occasion* for *United Ireland* ('Mourn, and Then Onward!'), which would come back to haunt him in later life.[14] But he also wrote a poem which commemorated Gonne's overture to him in July, and reflected her secret sadness. It got as far as the proofs of his next collection, but he changed his mind and never published it. This decision was partly dictated by its uneven quality, but much more by the painful directness with which it reflected personal life.

CYCLES AGO

In memory of your dream one July night

The low crying curlew and peewit, the honey pale orb of the moon,
The dew covered grass in the valley, our mother the sea with her croon
The leaping green leaves in the woodland, the flame of the stars in the skies,
Are tossed in Love's robe for he passes, and mad with Love's feet for he flies.

You came and moved near me a little with pensive remembering grace
The sad rose colours of autumn with weariness mixed in your face,
My world was fallen and over, for your dark soft eyes on it shone;
A thousand years it had waited and now it is gone, it is gone.

'We were as if brother and sister of old in the desert land',
How softly you spake it, how softly 'I give but a friendly hand
They sold us in slavery together before this life had begun
But Love bides nobodies bidding being older than moon or sun.'

Ah cycles ago did I meet you and mingle my gaze with your gaze,
They mingled a moment and parted and weariness fell on our days,
And we went alone on our journeys and envied the grass covered dead
For Love had gone by us unheeding, a crown of stars on his head.[15]

Gonne remained in a highly wrought state. Near collapse, she endured endless seances and visions with WBY and Russell, asking if a child could be reincarnated and relying desperately on the uncertain expertise of the two young occultists. Russell reassured her, but WBY felt secret doubts. At a later session with Moina Mathers in London, she saw a vision of a 'grey lady' who had killed a child. WBY's idea that this represented a previous incarnation cannot have eased Gonne's sense of loss and guilt; nor did a later revelation that she had once been an Egyptian priestess whose corrupt lover, a priest, had 'given false oracles for money'. She was haunted by a dream 'of journeying on & on in a desert'.[16] The association with her French lover seemed a fated repetition of previous unhappiness. But her agony of autumn 1891, and Russell's consoling advice that a child could be reincarnated in the same family, would bring about a bizarre resolution. Two years later, still obsessed by her secret tragedy, she brought Millevoye to the memorial chapel at Samois where their son was interred, and in those strange surroundings they conceived a child.

However, during the traumatic mourning for Georges in October 1891, her resistance towards an alliance with WBY – forged in the pure light of hermetic inquiry – was lowered. For his part, the poetry she inspired in this state declared a need to protect her; drafts of 'The Sorrow of Love' and 'When You are Old' date from this time.[17] There is some evidence that he thought she had agreed to marry him at this stage: if so, it may date from these transfigured weeks, rather than from the interlude in August.[18] As a final claim on her, there was a shared possession: a notebook named 'The Flame of the Spirit', bound in white vellum, with a series of poems inscribed to Gonne. Pages were left blank for many more. WBY had been assembling it since July; he gave it to Gonne before she left Dublin, on 20 October. It contained love-poems like 'Cycles Ago', but also stern summons to occult service: 'No daughter of the Iron Times/The Holy Future summons you.' Another contemporary notebook, called 'The Rosy Cross Lyrics', is dominated by themes of suffering, denial and consecration.

> He who measured gain and loss
> When he gave to thee the Rose
> Gave to me alone, the cross.[19]

About a fortnight later, in London, she was initiated into the Golden Dawn. Magic seemed, at last, to be granting him what he wanted.

II

WBY had also returned to London (by 1 November), and found an 'alley' in Gonne's cousin May, who advised him to follow her to Paris. But he saw their future elsewhere. He had extracted a promise from Gonne to work for the new literary societies in Ireland over the winter: however, his real priorities appear in an injunction to Russell. 'Go & see her when she gets to Dublin &

keep her from forgetting me & Occultism.'[20] And he borrowed a pound from O'Leary to pay his share of cab-travel when she returned.

In early December this frantic excitement (compounded by the publication of *John Sherman* and *Dhoya* in October) produced its usual reaction – a black depression. Nor was he able to visit Dublin; though Rhys did, armed with introductions from WBY to Oldham and O'Leary as a way of meeting 'nationalist Ireland'. This mission shows that WBY's London circle was now co-operating in his Irish initiative. Late in 1891 it was decided to form an Irish Literary Society, arising from the established Southwark Irish Literary Club. On 28 December a planning meeting took place at Blenheim Road, principally organized by D. J. O'Donoghue and WBY, with Rolleston, Todhunter and others in attendance. WBY presented this as 'starting a London branch of the Young Ireland League',[21] a Fenian agenda which some of his associates would quickly try to short-circuit. From the beginning the relationship between Dublin and London activities provoked unease; and also from the beginning a problem loomed in the titular presence of Sir Charles Gavan Duffy as President of the new Irish Literary Society of London.

Gavan Duffy had spent a radical, nationalist youth as a Young Ireland firebrand in the 1840s, been transported to Australia after a failed rebellion, and ended up as Prime Minister of Victoria. WBY had met him through O'Leary in 1889, and corresponded with him about Mangan and the 'peasant poet' John Keegan: Gavan Duffy stood for nationalist literary culture in the heroic period. In the interim he had become an experienced politician, gentlemanly, resourceful and devious. Now living in respectable retirement at Nice, his name was thought to add cachet, and a 'national' pedigree; but his own approach to his involvement would be unexpectedly interventionist as well as politically moderate. Meanwhile, WBY went ahead with what to him was the most important aspect of the initiative: the plan for a series of books called the 'Library of Ireland', to be published by Fisher Unwin. Volumes would cost a shilling and appear every two months. Unsurprisingly, WBY was to be general editor – a condition insisted upon by Fisher Unwin, he hastily told O'Leary. He also assured O'Leary that, in such hands, there would be no danger of producing unreadable volumes by 'men of learning who cannot write', and that the series would preach 'sound national doctrine'. But Gavan Duffy had his own interests here: nearly a year before he had written to John T. Kelly of the Southwark Irish Literary Club, suggesting a programme of reprints and promising to raise the capital. He was not prepared to relinquish this project to WBY and his dangerously extremist associates. A conflict was inevitable.

WBY's agenda also involved Maud Gonne, who was detailed to begin a fundraising lecture-tour in France. Gonne first visited London in February

1892; one result was that WBY sent an early draft of 'When You are Old' with an accompanying piece 'When You are Sad', to Katharine Tynan on 2 March, for possible inclusion in a book of Irish love-songs. (Tynan included neither.) Simultaneously he was working up a celebratory article on Gonne for the *Boston Pilot*, and planting out in *United Ireland* the story that her French lecture-tour had inspired '2000 articles about her speaches – or rather the articles had reached this number a considerable time ago'.[22] On 9 April 1892 the Irish Literary Society held its first meeting: WBY toasted Ireland's intellectual life, 'when the pressure of political struggle is removed from the country'. This could have meant liberation from the Saxon oppressor, but was much more likely an anticipation of the Home Rule future still generally accepted. Rolleston was Secretary, and there was a strong Rhymer presence – Todhunter, Johnson, Plarr and Arthur Hillier. But if WBY thought that he could thereby manipulate the committee, he had much to learn. *United Ireland* noted sharply that he was 'irrepressible, but all at sea in matters of detail'. Its editor, Edmund Leamy, raised a contentious issue by declaring that the intellectual capital of Ireland must be in Dublin, given the dawning Home Rule future.[23]

This harked back to a controversy which had been rumbling since March: where should an Irish cultural initiative be located? By early May WBY realized he was becoming *persona non grata* in the cultural initiatives on both sides of the Irish Sea. His initial idea had been to extend the Young Ireland League to London, with its O'Learyite literary–Fenian principles; but his attempt to manipulate this through his Rhymers clique (and publishing contacts) were blocked by Rolleston and Gavan Duffy, while Dublin resentment at the London initiative was brewing ominously. Moreover, the Young Ireland League were not prepared to wait until the time came to continue the Yeatsian agenda; they wanted to start their own kind of Society, unimpressed by WBY's combination of neo-Fenian rhetoric and high literary art.

On 10 May WBY set off hurriedly to Dublin 'to do my best to found there a society of like purpose and nature' to the Irish Literary Society. The London initiative could not be successful 'unless we persuade Ireland to take part with us' in developments like the Library of Ireland (and a travelling theatre company, one of the many new ideas floated at this time[24]). In a letter to *United Ireland* on 14 May, he asserted the necessity to arrest denationalization: this was why 'we' had founded 'the Irish Literary Society, London', and not to 'do anything so absurd and impossible as to make London "the intellectual centre of Ireland"'.[25] He had effectively abandoned the London terrain to Rolleston, whether he recognized it or not, and was attempting to regain the initiative in Ireland. But the attempt to bring literary societies in Ireland together under the sagging Young Ireland League umbrella was fraught with difficulty: there was a rival in the field. On 21 May John T. Kelly, who had been involved in the Southwark Irish Literary Club but had now returned to Dublin, announced his intention to start a Dublin society 'similar to the one started in London, and entirely independent of it – a society which shall be thoroughly national, in the broad meaning of the word, and non-political'. WBY and O'Leary rapidly involved themselves, and took part in the meeting setting up the 'National Literary Society' on 9 June.[26] But the terms of Kelly's manifesto made it clear that aggressive Parnellism and neo-Fenianism were unwelcome. WBY was aboard, but at a cost.

Now he had to claim the initiative. On 2 June WBY sent a manifesto to the Conservative Dublin *Daily Express*. He gave hostages to fortune in his hastily compiled model for the Library of Ireland: Gavan Duffy's ballads, 'The Spirit of the Nation', John Mitchel's *O'Neill*. The idea of reissuing stand-ards from Young Ireland's heyday a half-century before was exactly what he would shortly denounce – but he himself initially proposed such a formula, while adding works 'ranging from Fenianism to the education question, from Oisin to Robert Emmet'. The objective was to make 'national and legendary heroes' known to a larger audience than scholars. The *Express* responded with a straightfaced leader stressing the literary talent to be found in the Trinity College Senior Common Room, which was hardly what WBY meant; in response he promptly wrote a rousing attack on the College's culture for *United Ireland*. The *Express* warned him that Irish political differences were potent enough to constitute 'a disqualification for the life in common of a social or literary club'.[27] The *Dublin Figaro* was more personal, producing a cari-cature and a snide column: 'I wonder how many Dublin folk are acquainted with the personality or the work of the moving spirit in the new Irish Literary Society?' Not for the last time, WBY was portrayed as someone who had managed to fool opinion outside Ireland, but who would be seen for what he was 'at home'.[28] But his private priority was to involve Gonne, and to com-bine cultural and separatist politics in a way that would cement their personal alliance. To O'Leary, currently in London, he trailed some ideas about the revolutionary potential of Mathers's murky connections in Paris; his own occult art, he unwisely added, prophesied that the time might be right for Gonne's 'plan'.[29] O'Leary's scoffing reply called forth WBY's celebrated defence of magic being at the centre of his life.

It is surely absurd to hold me 'week' or otherwise because I chose to persist in a study which I decided deliberately four or five years ago to make next to my poetry the most important pursuit of my life. Whether it be, or be not, bad for my health can only be decided by one who knows what magic is & not at all by any amateur. The prob-able explanation however of your somewhat testy post card is that you were out at Bedford Park & heard my father discoursing about my magical pursuits out of the immense depths of his ignorance as to everything that I am doing & thinking. If I had not made magic my constant study I could not have written my Blake book nor would 'The Countess Kathleen' have ever come to exist. The mystical life is the centre of all that I do & all that I think & all that I write.[30]

He certainly needed its consolations now. Despite Douglas Hyde's presidency, the National Literary Society gathered up hangers-on of organizations like the Pan-Celtic Society, establishment 'men of letters' and much of the Dublin milieu which WBY considered regressive, second-rate and collaborationist: one of its early projects was to be a concert during Horse Show week. By the end of July it was clear that the National Literary Society was far removed from the neo-Fenian Young Ireland League. Moreover, Gavan Duffy had no doubt which side he was on, and he was invited to chair the inaugural meeting in August.[31]

WBY's isolation was thrown into sharp relief when Gavan Duffy arrived in Dublin. In his *Autobiographies* (otherwise a very uncertain guide to this period) WBY recalled his own reaction with bitter humour:

He brought with him much manuscript, the private letters of a Young Ireland poetess, a dry but informing unpublished historical essay by Davis, and an unpublished novel by William Carleton, into the middle of which he had dropped a hot coal, so that nothing remained but the borders of every page. He hired a young man to read him, after dinner, Carlyle's *Heroes and Hero-Worship*, and before dinner was gracious to all our men of authority and especially to our Harps and Pepperpots. Taylor compared him to Odysseus returning to Ithaca, and every newspaper published his biography . . . One imagined his youth in some little gaunt Irish town, where no building or custom is revered for its antiquity; and there speaking a language where no word, even in solitude, is ever spoken slowly and carefully because of emotional implication; and of his manhood of practical politics, of the dirty piece of orange-peel in the corner of the stairs as one climbs up to some newspaper office; of public meetings where it would be treacherous amid so much geniality to speak or even to think of anything that might cause a moment's misunderstanding in one's own party. No argument of mine was intelligible to him.[32]

WBY's resort was to raise against Gavan Duffy the memory of heroic, Anglophobic extremism, by reminding him of the radical nationalism of his Young Ireland youth. The contents of the Library of Ireland were still at issue; WBY suggested starting with a study by Rolleston of Wolfe Tone, Lady Wilde on Patrick Sarsfield, and himself on 'ballad chronicles'. Gavan Duffy had adroitly put himself at the head of the National Publishing Company, set up to produce the books, and now claimed editorial powers as well. This effectively cut out WBY, who protested in letters to the press. Fighting his corner for a say in the Library's contents, he claimed 'a somewhat considerable experience of the editing of cheap books – I have edited five, some of which were sold in thousands';[33] he attempted to propose an alternative committee, which would include O'Leary and Hyde as well as 'safe' names like Sigerson. But the skills which had brought Gavan Duffy to the top of Victoria politics kept him smoothly obdurate. He could not publish works 'which would add to the causes of distraction already existing in the country'. Hiding behind the proposed National Publishing Company, he and his supporter, WBY's old enemy J. F. Taylor, were able to erect the wishes of the 'shareholders' against WBY's alleged desire to forward 'sectional' interests – a coded reference to extreme nationalism. WBY found himself not only tarred with the Fenian brush, but accused (as so often before) of manipulating the reputations of a self-serving literary coterie. 'It is not an edifying spectacle to see A reviewing B, and B in turn reviewing A, and both going into raptures of admiration.'[34]

Fisher Unwin's publication of *The Countess Kathleen and Various Legends and Lyrics*[35] at this very time handed weapons to the enemy, particularly in the carefully constructed poem which framed the collection, 'Apologia addressed to Ireland in the coming days'. This manifesto repeated the theme of his angry letter to O'Leary, fusing occultism and advanced nationalism in a manner calculated to appeal to Maud Gonne, and to irritate nearly everyone else. It was also the most powerful poetic rhetoric which he had yet written.

> *Know that I would accounted be*
> *True brother of that company*
> *Who sang to sweeten Ireland's wrong,*
> *Ballad and story, rann and song;*
> *Nor be I any less of them,*
> *Because the red rose bordered hem*
> *Of her whose history began*
> *Before God made the angelic clan*
> *Trails all about the written page,*
> *For in the world's first blossoming age*
> *The light fall of her flying feet*
> *Made Ireland's heart begin to beat,*
> *And still the starry candles flare*
> *To help her light foot here and there,*
> *And still the thoughts of Ireland brood,*
> *Upon her holy quietude.*
>
> *Nor may I less be counted one*
> *With Davis, Mangan, Ferguson*
> *Because to him who ponders well*
> *My rhymes more than their rhyming tell*

Of the dim wisdoms old and deep,
That God gives unto man in sleep.
For round about my table go
The magical powers to and fro.
In flood and fire and clay and wind,
They huddle from man's pondering mind,
Yet he who treads in austere ways
May surely meet their ancient gaze.
Man ever journeys on with them
After the red rose bordered hem.
Ah, fairies, dancing under the moon,
A druid land, a druid tune!

While still I may I write out true
The love I lived, the dream I knew.
From our birthday until we die
Is but the winking of an eye.
And we, our singing and our love,
The mariners of night above,
And all the wizard things that go
About my table to and fro,
Are passing on to where may be
In truth's consuming ecstasy
No place for love and dream at all,
For God goes by with white foot-fall.
I cast my heart into my rhymes,
That you in the dim coming times
May know how my heart went with them
After the red rose bordered hem.

Pace, inventiveness, rhythm and audacity struck the note already identified as uniquely Yeatsian; it also announced his arrival as a frankly political poet. But in practical terms he had lost. Even when Gavan Duffy's and Rolleston's National Publishing Company failed, they still outflanked WBY by swiftly approaching Fisher Unwin on their own accounts. His efforts to regain control were doomed, as Garnett's peace-making attempts did not disguise the fact that his own sympathies were with Rolleston in London.[36] O'Leary soothingly told him to stay out of it until Gonne returned to Dublin ('I know you cant be kept away then'[37]). WBY's final appeal came on 16 November, categorically threatening a split between the London initiative and the Dublin Society – which, he implied, supported him.

Our movement may split up on lines which the press will soon turn into one of Parnellite Dublin, & the Parnellite young men in the country parts, against what they will call 'West British' & 'Whiggish' Duffy & Rolleston. The most ardent of the youn[g] men are Parnellites & would be ready enough to raise such a cry against Duffy who is unpopular for Michellite reasons (his reasonable but not very readable defence never having made itself heard against the magnificent rhetoric of the 'Jail Journal').[38]

But this was unconvincing; he was now excluded, and even O'Leary censured him for trying to make unauthorized publishing deals on the Society's behalf.[39] Rolleston put it succinctly: WBY had

chosen to make himself the leader of a small clique of what are called 'advanced' men in Dublin who object to Sir C. Duffy on the score of his old quarrel with John Mitchel, & I think he cannot so far retrace his steps as to make it possible for Sir C. Duffy to work with him unless he is prepared to break with this clique altogether, which he certainly will not do.[40]

Garnett's attempts to mollify WBY were less realistic: 'I know you well enough to know that *you* don't want the credit & honour & glory – you want the eternal things . . . Let Duffy be the English Monarch, & you & Rolleston the joint Prime Ministers.'[41]

WBY had lost all along the line. The Library of Ireland did provide a few books, including Thomas Davis's *The Patriot Parliament* and O'Grady's *Bog of Stars*. When its productions fell into WBY's clutches as a reviewer, he showed little mercy. But that was the only consolation left to him. The London Irish Literary Society remained under Rolleston's control until 1893, when he returned to Dublin; while it provided a field for people like Lionel Johnson to discover their roots, it never greatly appealed to WBY. The Dublin National Literary Society was set on a path where it became more and more pious and provincial. In June 1893 WBY's high-handed and disorganized conduct of the Library subcommittee would be reprimanded by the Council (superbly remembered in WBY's *Autobiographies* as 'half a dozen young men who having nothing to do attended every meeting'). WBY himself occasionally turned up at its meetings to make a defence, strike an attitude or publicize a specific cause. By the early 1900s, even when the Society deigned to listen to 'a weird and very melancholy and despairing composition' by WBY, they swiftly revived their spirits by reading 'capital' or 'thrilling' pieces with titles like 'Young Tim Clancy' and 'The Dead Hand'.[42] Ironically, by that point WBY had separated from literary Fenianism as well. Accordingly, his *Autobiographies* would claim that the struggle against Gavan Duffy was a battle between his commitment to literary quality and the old Young Irelander's wish for nationalist banalities. But this interpretation reflected his position since the early 1900s, not his beliefs a decade earlier – when his plan had been to capture the National Literary Society and its Library for the Fenian interest, against the safe, all-embracing platitudes located in the middle of the nationalist road.

III

At the climax of the battle in October 1892 he had published an article in *United Ireland*, 'Hopes and Fears for Irish Literature', which clearly argued for an Irish literature of conviction, against the art-for-art's-sake approach of English contemporaries. At the end he loftily claimed that the true necessity for the artist was work and solitude. This reflected his own circumstances. He had been living in the Ely Place commune, not altogether happily: in a passage dropped from his *Autobiographies*, he remarked that his companions there never spoke of politics, idealized the peasantry as an abstraction, and completely failed to understand his love-poetry.[43] 'Desperately hard up', he had retired to Sligo, brought there by the death of his grandmother Elizabeth Pollexfen on 2 October 1892. Here he consoled himself with the reviews of *The Countess Kathleen*, including two ecstatic pieces by Le Gallienne and Johnson. Le Galliene was highly influential, and gave WBY 'the best lift I have yet had', but it was Johnson's judgement which brought criticism of his work to a new level: awarding WBY the distinction of treating 'Celtic notes of style and imagination, in a classical manner . . . and his art is full of reason'.[44] Though other reactions were more uncertain, and the middle-brow William Watson attacked him with gratifying fury in the *Illustrated London News*, WBY's reputation was further advanced – notably with his publisher. He returned to his project on duellists, now retitled 'Irish Adventurers', but it was destined never to appear. Between firing off his last salvoes to Rolleston and Garnett, he investigated local fairy lore with his uncle George Pollexfen and his cousin Lucy Middleton, 'the only witch in the family'.[45] He was also writing fiction: 'The Devil's Book', an early version of 'The Book of the Great Dhoul and Hanrahan the Red', was produced at this time and appeared in the *National Observer* on 26 November, one of WBY's last essays in the stagey Irish conversational idiom which he would soon denounce.[46]

But the real world kept breaking in. By now his grandfather was also seriously ill, and he too died on 12 November: calling impatiently at the end for his dead wife and saying with relief, just as he died, 'Ah, there she is.'[47] His estate was surprisingly small: Susan Yeats's share came to £116. 11s. 11d., and his son-in-law Arthur Jackson took over the firm. The great figures of his grandparents, who had towered over WBY's childhood summers (and would dominate his early autobiography twenty years later) were gone. 'With them went Sligo for us,' wrote Lily, '& all its charm and beauty, & our childhood seemed pushed back into space.'[48]

By the time he returned to the fray in Dublin in late November, WBY's mood was necessarily more sombre. The presidential address to the National Literary Society delivered by Douglas Hyde on 25 November gave him much to think about. Under the title 'The Necessity for De-Anglicizing Ireland', this rapidly achieved legendary status. It was credited with inspiring the foundation of the Gaelic League a year later, and became a canonical text of Irish cultural nationalism. But if the address is read in the context of its time, one can see Hyde stepping very carefully indeed between the fissures opened up in post-Parnell politics. While his basic argument was that Irish language, Irish pastimes and even Irish dress must be defined against English modes, he was careful to repeat that this message was essentially unpolitical: an agenda of cultural revival should be as attractive to Unionists as to nationalists and was above politics. A revival of language was the necessary pre-condition for any Irish identity at all; without it they might as well accept their fate and become a people purely imitative of English modes, 'the Japanese of Western Europe'.

Many of Hyde's audience besides WBY must have been waiting to see whose side the speaker would adopt: the comfortable collaborative culture of Sigerson and Gavan Duffy (both on the platform with him) or the more uncompromising ideals of WBY, and his own neo-Fenian youth. Hyde (not for the first or last time) neatly side-stepped the choice, and moved the argument on to a different plane. Moreover, this opened up a territory with disturbing implications for WBY. Hyde's address was Anglophobic enough to please him (and Gonne); but its central argument denied that there could be a distinctively Irish literature in the English language, and this contradicted everything WBY's own work stood for (as well as presenting him with an uneasy linguistic conundrum).

His answer appeared in *United Ireland* on 17 December 1892, and argued unequivocally that Irish literature could be written in English, but in a Gaelic mode: Hyde's own translations were adduced as proof, and the Irish language identified with 'the snows of yester year'. But this put him in awkward company (Dowden? Mahaffy?), so he simultaneously proved his credentials as a hammer of the Unionist establishment by a vituperative review of George Savage-Armstrong's collected works. As a professor of English literature, Armstrong 'cut himself off from the life of the nation', and therefore doomed himself to literary futility. The victim of this onslaught, an old friend of JBY, comforted himself with the thought that no 'person of brains & education is likely to be impressed by Willy Yeats's opinion on any subject'.[49]

Much later WBY saw Hyde's initiative as a deliberately political act: 'with more success . . . [bidding] for that forsaken leadership', and 'co-ordinating intellectual and political forces'[50] as he himself had failed to do. This was true, but Hyde was trying to bring it off by evading the kind of open political commitment with which WBY was uneasily identified. As for his own strategy, the final nail was put in the coffin by his failure in early January to commandeer (or at least infiltrate) the publication committee of the London Irish Literary Society. WBY's claim to be an associate editor was ruled out because of his intemperate attacks on Gavan Duffy, and (Rolleston added) because 'one must possess more scholarship (of the Dryasdust type if you like) than Y does'.[51] The future ignominious history of the National Publishing Company was not yet consolingly evident; WBY was forced to recognize how counter-productive his tactics had been, and how easily he made enemies.[52] He did not give up; a last vain attempt to trammel Gavan Duffy kept him in Ireland just when his and Ellis's *Blake* was being published. On 27 January 1893 Hyde witnessed 'a terrible row between Taylor and Yeats, between O'Leary and Sigerson' at a committee meeting ('I never saw anything like it, but I escaped without a blow, thank God'). On 2 February there was 'uproar again' between the same antagonists about the publication plans.[53] WBY was busily enlisting others to write for a projected journal (eventually the *Irish Home Reading Magazine*), into which he planned to infiltrate poetry and mysticism; he projected a provincial tour, disseminating improving books in the company of Maud Gonne; further consolation was provided by his initiation (with Florence Farr) into the 'Portal' grade of the Golden Dawn on 20 January.[54] But in Irish cultural politics the advanced men had lost this battle, and WBY knew it.

Most bitterly of all, he had been abandoned by Gonne. She cancelled her provincial engagements 'owing to illness' and returned to Paris after only two lectures.[55] On her next visit to Dublin in February they quarrelled, probably over her friendship with WBY's enemy J. F. Taylor; she became ill and put herself under Dr Sigerson's care. WBY was kept away from her; rumours circulated that she had become pregnant by him and had an abortion. The reality was that she had returned to Millevoye and, in December, would conceive her second child by him: the attempt to reincarnate Georges in a sacrificial act of intercourse by her dead son's tomb.

Gonne's life was spectacularly different from the fantasy WBY had incarnated in *The Countess Kathleen*, if no less surreal. For the moment he could feel close to her only through the work she inspired. He read from the *Countess* to the National Literary Society on 26 January and stayed in Dublin, continuing to associate himself with advanced nationalist opinion; at a National Club celebration of Robert Emmet's anniversary, he 'gave vent to the strong feelings of those present' by thrillingly quoting Emmet's speech from the dock.[56] This would have pleased Gonne, though her own appearances were mostly before French audiences. She lectured in Ireland during April, but by late May she was back in France, and WBY, after a Sligo visit, had returned to London.[57] There was, he recorded much later, 'a great breach' between them at this time, 'for reasons I knew nothing of'.[58] On 30 June he wrote 'Into the Twilight' – a poem suffused with Gonne's idea of Ireland as a mystical motherland, but also confronting the misery he had suffered through her, and through the politics so inextricably wound into their relationship. Thus, he later remembered, he 'called to myself courage once more'.[59]

> Outworn heart in a time outworn,
> Come clear off the nets of wrong and right;
> Laugh, heart, again in the grey twilight,
> Sigh, heart, again in the dew of the morn.
>
> Thy mother Eri is always young,
> Dew ever shining and twilight grey,
> Though hope fall from thee or love decay
> Burning in fires of a slanderous tongue,
>
> Come heart, where hill is heaped upon hill,
> For there live the mystic brotherhood
> Of the flood and flame, of the height and wood,
> And laugh out their whimsey and work out their will.
>
> And Time and the Word are ever in flight,
> And God stands winding his lonely horn,
> And love is less kind than the grey twilight,
> And hope is less dear than the dew of the morn.

He had written, less consciously and more ambiguously, about a similar relationship in 'The Devil's Book' the previous November. 'O'Sullivan the Red', insouciant peasant poet, summons through magic a fairy goddess Cleona. She appears as 'a tall woman, dressed in saffron like the women of ancient Ireland', with shining eyes and statuesque beauty. Dim at first, her image strengthens with each visitation, until she achieves a mortal beauty from 'the sorrowful dhrames o' the world' and offers herself to him. Faced with her reality, O'Sullivan panics and rejects her: preferring his enslavement to the phantom. This too would carry a prophetic charge.[60]

IV

For all his reverses, he had become a more public figure than before. His father wondered, only half ironically, if his eldest son nurtured ambitions to stand for the Irish Parliamentary Party, like Rolleston or Arthur Lynch. 'It would I think be a hindrance to Willie's proper work which is poetry and literature, but he would greatly like the new experience to say nothing of the glory & publicity.'[61] Thomas Stuart, a forgotten schoolfellow, wrote a paragraph about his schooldays in the *Dublin Figaro*, acknowledged by its subject with vague grandeur ('I remember your name very well & will I have no doubt remember your personality also, as soon as a meeting bring it to memory. It floats dimnly before me & may at any time take visable shape'[62]). The *Bookman*, for whom he had begun reviewing in late 1892, asked him as one of 'four distinguished poets' for an opinion on Tennyson's successor as Laureate: his response praised Swinburne and Tennyson, but saw the post as an anachronism. In Sligo, probably during November 1892, his growing fame had brought him into a new social orbit: he had met (and would later see in London) Constance and Eva Gore-Booth, daughters of Lissadell, one of the great Ascendancy houses glimpsed across demesne walls and tree-tops on his childhood walks.

What had brought him fame was not his political interventions but his books. Since May, Fisher Unwin had contracted to take over *The Wanderings of Oisin*, which conferred prestige if not money.[63] Even in its first 'meagre' form, *The Countess Kathleen* made a stir; his collections of fairy-tales were widely available; and at the end of January 1893 Quaritch brought out *Blake*. WBY, paid in copies, sold them on wherever he could; in Ireland he received reviews forwarded by Lily (Le Gallienne in the *Star*, Garnett in the *Speaker*, Johnson in the *Westminster Gazette*). Naturally, critics pitched upon the occultist emphasis – defended by WBY to Johnson as 'our resolve not to hide our debt to the men who have been fighting the battle'. Through the spring and summer of 1893 he spent a great deal of time at the headquarters of the Golden Dawn in Clipstone Street (twenty-nine visits between June and September), possibly making and consecrating the vital instruments for his initiation into the Second Order, but also seeking solace.[64] Not coincidentally, he was also writing occult stories. 'Out of the Rose' appeared in the *National Observer* on 27 May, ostentatiously Rosicrucian and chivalric, and dealing with contention between the illuminati few and the ignorant many. In other stories, such as 'The Heart of the Spring' (15 April) and 'The Curse of the Fires and Shadows' (5 August), Sligo settings and historical traditions were used specifically, in conjunction with fairy lore. Over and over again, a spiritual hero is misunderstood and rejected by the world, and triumphs only in death. And simultaneously, in much less awkward language, he was collecting and organizing the material which would be published by Lawrence & Bullen at the end of the year as *The Celtic Twilight*: not only an enterprise exploring the avenues opened up by Blake, but also an implicit commentary on Irish identity and literary culture.

Folklore and oral culture, as conceived by WBY and gathered in Sligo and elsewhere, was non-English, anti-materialist, anti-bourgeois, and connected to Theosophical and Rosicrucian symbolism, via Blake and Swedenborg. Through this identification, and his own painstaking presentation of it, he could fuse the lessons learnt from his father, his lost Sligo childhood, the Rhymers and, most recently, Maud Gonne. The stories retailed were often framed as told by an old man at Ballisodare, or by his uncle George's servant Mary Battle; but folklore could also contain archetypal stories, or 'moods', and those who investigated it must, like artists, 'dare to mix heaven, hell, purgatory and fairyland together'.[65] In this context 'twilight' meant the hour before dawn, when this world and the next were closest, the interpenetration of the spirit and the 'real' world recalling Swedenborg as well as Blake. The intellectual inspiration for *The Celtic Twilight* was eclectic. It included P. W. Joyce's books on Irish tradition, William Wilde's researches, Rhys's Hibbert Lecture on Celtic religion and (less identifiably) druidic lore. WBY may also have already encountered Henri d'Arbois de Jubainville's lecturers on Celtic mythology, stressing Greek parallels and doctrines of correspondence; the despised Alfred Nutt had reviewed them at length in the *Folklore Journal* for 1886, and Gonne would later translate some for the notes to *The Wind Among the Reeds*.[66] WBY had also noted David Fitzgerald's *Revue Celtique* articles in the early 1880s about themes of solar–lunar conflict as original elements of mythic confrontation.[67] As yet, folklore rather than mythology preoccupied him, though Gonne's mythic interests spurred him further.

Much of *The Celtic Twilight* had originally appeared in the *Scots Observer*, *Leisure Hour* or other journals (and Fisher Unwin had suggested a collection in the summer of 1891); but what mattered was the arrangement, and how it reflected WBY's preoccupations in 1893. Material was added, and accretions and bowdlerizations scraped off. Into the different genres (stories, poems, commentaries) he tried to infuse seriousness and, sometimes, tragedy. He was a more stringent editor than is often realized.[68] 'I have . . . written down accurately and candidly much that I have heard and seen, and, except by way of commentary, nothing that I have merely imagined,' he wrote in the preface, ending, emotionally, with a Blakean invocation: 'Hope and Memory have one daughter and her name is Art, and she has built her dwelling far from the desperate field where men hang out their garments upon forked boughs to be banners of battle. O beloved daughter of Hope and Memory, be with me for a little.' His own recent lost battles, and vanished childhood, were much in his mind.

In his work on *The Celtic Twilight* WBY can be seen recouping his powers and consoling himself through the arrangement of ideas into art: a gift which never abandoned him. In a Belfast lecture during late November he spoke of fairy lore as a consoling faith, 'sent by Providence' for those whose lives were starved and desires blighted. In connecting fairy belief with anthropological researches, he hinted at a scientific rationale; but more important, in his view, was its therapeutic function and literary inspiration. 'He did not think there was a great poet in the world who had not borrowed from folk lore.'[69] He was absorbing the lessons of his clash with Gavan Duffy and Rolleston, and the questions raised by Hyde. And he had to define a position regarding Irish literary revival and English cultural influence, in such a way that his own identities (Anglophone, Protestant, Blakean, occultist, London-resident) could be allowed for within an Irish nationalist framework. Building on his original answer to Hyde, he delivered a National Literary Society lecture in Molesworth Hall, Dublin, on 19 May 1893: its title was 'Nationality and Literature'.[70]

This came at a time when political disappointments, Dublin gossip, unhappy love and his own literary ambitions had brought him to a crossroads. He confided to an astrological notebook twenty years later that 'it was a year of great trouble' – a word which, with wby, usually carries a sexual implication.[71] His reaction was a Herculean attempt to redefine the whole vexed question of literature's relationship to the national effort – and, in the process, to claim a cosmopolitan identity for the Irish literary movement. Simultaneously he defended himself from the 'patriots' by stigmatizing English literature as irrelevant because decadent. (Would his friends in the Rhymers Club have agreed?) In the tradition of Matthew Arnold, he stressed the philosophical and anti-materialist side of 'Celticism'; but he also stated that the new Irish literature could learn from the Greeks and even the English. (This was, of course, exactly the achievement for which Lionel Johnson had lauded wby's own work a year before.)

In making the point, he advanced the theory that national literature developed from narrative epic, through drama, to lyric poetry.[72] The rather convoluted argument concluded that the full development of a nation's literature required a cosmopolitan frame of reference. Here he represented Rhymer thought, and also worked in some visionary hints about a forthcoming 'resurrection into unity' derived from his Blakean studies. The Irish achievement was still at the 'epic' stage of literature (though the lyricism of Mangan and Allingham gave him some difficulty here). Native drama and lyricism would develop. 'But we must not imitate the writers of any other country, we must study them constantly and learn from them the secret of their greatness.' It was permissible to read foreign writers; this was a necessary part of working at a national literature, rather than, in the Irish style, relying simply upon divine inspiration.

Alas, the inspiration of God, which is, indeed, the source of all which is greatest in the world, comes only to him who labours at rhythm and cadence, at form and style, until they have no secret hidden from him. This art we must learn from the old literatures of the world. We have hitherto been slovens . . . We must learn from the literatures of France and England for the supreme artists and then God will send to us supreme inspiration.

This synthesized the belief of the Rhymers and the Paterian notion of the artist as priest. It contradicted the implication of other Yeatsian dicta about 'thin-blooded cosmopolitanism';[73] but it represented the trend of his thought in the summer of 1893. By October he was considering publishing 'a collection of essays and lectures' dealing with Irish nationality under the title 'The Watchfire', but it never appeared, and the rousing Fenian poem he wrote for it remained unpublished: several of the ideas would later germinate in *Ideas of Good and Evil*.[74] He had come some distance from the 'Celt in London' column of four years before, when he had chastised Rolleston for his devotion to the 'poor bubble' of cosmopolitan literature, and ended nearly every article with a refrain preaching the necessarily 'national' basis of true art.[75]

Through the remaining summer of 1893 he stayed in London, immersed in preparation for his progress to the next stage of Golden Dawn initiation, the degree of 5 = 6 in the Second Order, which would bring him to the inner circle of the organization.[76] Stories which he wrote at this time reflect this involvement, as well as the company of Johnson and other Rhymers: the influence of Wilde and Pater joined the established inspirations of Shelley and Irish mythology. Few letters survive from this era. He was reviewing hard, reshaping *The Celtic Twilight*, and writing the uncharacteristic story 'Michael Clancy, The Great Dhoul, and Death', finished in September. By the time Tynan interviewed him for the *Sketch* in November, he was considering a volume of 'wierd stories of the middle ages in Ireland', which would eventually – in 1897 – appear as *The Secret Rose*.

As would often be the case, he was solaced by London literary companionship, and the consolations of occult study. But, acutely sensitive to Dublin's jeers about log-rolling, wby asked Tynan not to sign the *Sketch* interview. He made a gingerly return to that bruising environment in mid-September, accompanied by Lionel Johnson. They stayed with wby's friend Joseph Quinn, a medical student who had been imprisoned for Land League activities a decade before and was flamboyantly homosexual; he wore make-up and (allegedly) stays, and was besotted by a young Mayoman in the same lodgings. It cannot have been a comfortable ménage. Quinn had been involved in setting up the National Literary Society, and wby was asked to help with their projected magazine; he also helped launch Frederick Langbridge's periodical *The Old Country*, which appeared at the end of the year. wby suggested publishing a piece by Oldham on the Contemporary Club, and illustrating it with sketches done by jby in the mid-1880s. 'Such an article would be a most interesting record of the personal & social side of politics in this country for the last 8 years & should interest people quite apart from their political beliefs & offend no one.'[77] That innocent age of apprenticeship was already consigned to the past, and he was ready to act as impresario for his own history.

How WBY appeared in the present is captured in an interview with D. N. Dunlop for the *Irish Theosophist*, anxious for his memories of Madame Blavatsky, who had died in May 1891. The interviewer found him, probably in Ely Place, reading Homer and smoking a cigarette; the room 'indicated the style and taste peculiar to its presiding genius', decorated with 'designs by Blake and other less well-known symbolic artists'. Asked about Blavatsky's prophecies, WBY obligingly retailed her belief 'that the power of England would not outlive the century'.[78] But politics in the present remained a minefield. 'Gaelic' qualities were a priority, as he stressed in an ecstatic review of Hyde's *Love Songs of Connacht*: a *Bookman* piece which not only marks the high point of his admiration for Hyde, but also deliberately presents 'The Gael' to an English audience. For an Irish readership he was more combative, addressing two important letters to *United Ireland*[79] in defence of Richard Ashe King, who had attacked partisan politics as detrimental to 'Celtic' culture. But Alice Milligan, an uncompromising nationalist activist and editor, attacked WBY in turn for choosing 'some quiet paradise aspect' in which to develop his art, rather than linking it to the noisy field of battle in Irish politics.

This must have seemed to WBY ironic at best, and certainly unfair. Answering Milligan, he tried to have it both ways. A writer could pursue political commitments, but must 'endeavour to become a master of his craft, and be ever careful to keep rhetoric, or the tendency to think of his audience rather than of the Perfect and the True, out of his writing'.[80] A further letter of 30 December considered the position of 'oratory' in Irish life – partly inspired by Standish O'Grady's just published *The Story of Ireland*, which condemned this national addiction, and enshrined an early statement of the Parnell myth later adopted comprehensively by WBY. For the moment 'oratory' preoccupied him – a concept he did not yet distinguish from 'rhetoric', using both words to mean political invective. Against the show of passionate conviction and the ensuing loss of a sense of reality, WBY argued for tolerance and the recognition of half-tones; all this related to the Parnell split, as Irish politics continued to be dominated by recriminations over the lost leader. The Irish must realize that 'there is a truth and a beauty which, not being made by hands, are above all expediency, *above all nations*'.[81] One way to such a truth was to stop calling any critic of 'national dangers and weaknesses' a West Briton. This was heartfelt; it also articulated opinions which had to be suppressed when Maud Gonne was in the vicinity. Since their meeting in Ireland in the autumn of 1891, he had been thrown into personal and political turmoil: the need to prove himself to her remained constant, while the only spheres in which he could claim superior authority were occult study and artistic creation. And here too her influence was enduring.

The deep unhappiness which the setbacks of the early nineties brought was not always evident to his family. At the end of 1893 JBY considered his children and took, as ever, the cheerful view.

Someday Jack will be a substantial man with a cheerful kind hearted spouse & an open handed way of welcoming friends – something on the Merville pattern tho' on a smaller scale of course – & Willie will be famous & shed a bright light on us all & sometimes have a little money & sometimes *not*. Lolly will have a prosperous school & as I before remarked give away as prizes her eminent brother's volumes of poetry.[82]

WBY found it hard to be so sanguine. Long afterwards, when his 'Celt in London' pieces were reprinted as a book, he remembered his youthful self sitting in the National Library in Kildare Street, 'looking with scorn at those bowed heads and busy eyes, or in futile revery listening to my own mind as if to the sounds in a sea shell . . . I was arrogant, indolent, excitable.'[83] This spectacularly underrated his achievements at the age of twenty-eight. But he was still caught between competing gospels, and as yet unable to follow consistently the abstract truth he had preached to Alice Milligan. Looking back forty years later, he expressed this struggle in lapidary terms: 'I was a propagandist and hated being one. It seems to me that I remember almost the day and the hour when revising for some reprint my essay upon the Celtic movement [in *Ideas of Good and Evil*] I saw clearly the unrealities and half-truths propaganda had involved me in, and the way out. All one's life one struggles towards reality, finding always but new veils. It is the words, children of the occasion, that betray.'[84]

These were still the years of propaganda, though flashes of a keener perspective intervened. By late 1893 he was still bruised by those battles of the books where he had conspicuously failed to win his way. He returned to London at the end of the year; from then until 1896 he would spend almost no time at all in Dublin.

Chapter 6 : LANDS OF HEART'S DESIRE
1894–1896

> [*Axël*] seemed all the more profound, all the more beautiful,
> because I was never quite certain that I had understood. Indeed,
> I was quite certain of one thing only . . . I was not certain that
> Axel was a great masterpiece but I thought of it always as if it
> were a ceremony in some order or rite wherein I and my gen-
> eration had been initiated.
>
> manuscript draft for a preface to
Villiers de l'Isle-Adam's Axël

I

THE coolness between WBY and Maud Gonne in 1893, together with the dis-
illusionment and resentment arising from Dublin literary wars, shaped his
life for the next three years. He avoided the Irish capital; he looked elsewhere
for love; and consequently he made a determined attempt to build an inde-
pendent establishment in London. In July 1894 he was considering 'a volume
of Irish essays cheefly to be feirce mockery of most Irish men & things except
the men & things who are simple poor & imaginative and not I fear too many'.[1]
Resilient as ever, his reaction to adversity was combativeness. He also found
consolation in publicity. From 1893 his name was constantly in and out of news-
papers: he had become a news item, and events like Robert Louis Stevenson's
admiring letter about 'Innisfree' were rapidly broadcast to journalists.[2] This
was not without disadvantages; he was also an object of satire in Arthur
Lynch's *Our Poets* and the *New Ireland Review* (as 'William Blütiger Klein-
bier'[3]). And both he and Tynan had reached the point where they could
be plagiarized by the coming generation. WBY was noticeably less annoyed
about this than Tynan, partly because of the publicity value, partly because
his own early manner no longer pleased him.

There were also, as always, new projects and collaborations, such as his
attempt to help Frederick Langbridge turn his annual *The Old Country* into
a monthly magazine, and the perpetually postponed notion of an Irish
publishing house. WBY was also involved in the Irish Literary Society's quar-
terly, the *Irish Home Reading Magazine*, along with Barry O'Brien, Johnson,
Garnett and others. But these expedients did not meet his financial needs;
his correspondence for 1893 and 1894 shows him regularly borrowing small
sums. An urgently businesslike letter to O'Leary on 5 February 1894 cata-
logued his 'reasens' for inability to repay debts incurred over the previous year,

including 'a sudden crisis here at home, which swept away £4' ('please burn this letter').⁴ His heavyweight book-reviewing continued, but decreased in frequency; fiction seemed a more profitable avenue, with stories like 'Michael Clancy, The Great Dhoul, and Death' produced for the Christmas 1893 number of the *Old Country*.⁵

This publication was accompanied by wby's photograph ('Author of "The Countess Kathleen", etc.'). A soon to be familiar image was forming: shadowed face, dark clothes, misty gaze. There were good physical reasons for the latter: a conical cornea was diagnosed in April 1894, making the left eye 'practically useless'.⁶ But the air of detachment symbolized a drifting away from some of his old friends: his infrequent letters to Tynan were now addressed to 'Dear Mrs Hinkson', and even his recent collaborator Edwin Ellis cannot have been pleased by wby's perfunctory and satirical review of his visionary *Seen in Three Days*.⁷ The upheavals in Dublin had reinforced wby's single-mindedness, and determined him upon independence.

II

This meant a concentrated commitment to work, and the sowing of seeds which would germinate much later. By 24 August 1893 he had begun drafting poems in a small white notebook which would not achieve published form until *The Wind Among the Reeds* six years later; and an important article in the *Speaker* that same month defined his approach to folklore.⁸ It was, wby claimed, the necessary underpinning to mythology; Shelley lacked this substructure, which accounted for the cloudy quality of his poetry. Here, as in other occasional writings of 1893 to 1894, and in the discussions around the *Savoy* experiment two years later, he emphasized the need to derive inspiration from a basic energy, by knowing one's roots. This strength was sustaining wby himself through a difficult period of reassessment, finding passionate expression at this time in his review of Hyde's translations, *Love Songs of Connacht*.

As for me, I close the book with much sadness. Those poor peasants lived in a beautiful if somewhat inhospitable world, where little had changed since Adam delved and Eve span. Everything was so old that it was steeped in the heart, and every powerful emotion found at once noble types and symbols for its expression. But we – we live in a world of whirling change, where nothing becomes old and sacred, and our powerful emotions, unless we be highly-trained artists, express themselves in vulgar types and symbols. The soul then had but to stretch out its arms to fill them with beauty, but now all manner of heterogeneous ugliness has beset us. A peasant had then but to stand in his own door and think of his sweetheart and of his sorrow, and take from the scene about him and from the common events of his life types and symbols, and behold, if chance was a little kind, he had made a poem to humble generations of the proud. And we – we labour and labour, and spend days over a stanza or a paragraph, and at the end of it have made, likely as not, a mere bundle of phrases.[9]

Drafts of poetry and fiction were all infused with this belief, and so was his one-act play *The Land of Heart's Desire*. Drama possessed him at this time: he confessed in an anonymous review of July 1893 that he could 'read almost anything which is written in dramatic form'.[10] And this passion was closely associated with a Hammersmith neighbour, the actress Florence Farr.

Farr had long been on the Bedford Park circuit – doing embroidery with May Morris, and a frequent visitor to her sister Henrietta Paget next-door to the Todhunters. She had also joined the Golden Dawn with WBY, who was five years younger. A long acquaintanceship was ripening into something more. But her other admirer was Bernard Shaw (both suitors sat each other out for a gloomy evening at her Dalling Road lodgings on 13 July). Shaw wooed Farr through theatre: might WBY do the same? Oblique and independent, she sent out contradictory signals. Farr helped define the New Woman. Humorous, and sexy, she possessed a talent for friendship, and for exasperating people. According to Shaw 'an *aimable* woman, with semi-circular eyebrows', she could have been the great Shavian actress (Louka, Blanche) but never quite delivered; or the great Yeatsian muse, but could never keep her face quite straight. Sexually liberated and believing that intercourse once a day was a healthy habit, she enjoyed a brief marriage to Edward Emery, an unreliable fellow-actor, as well as an affair with Shaw in 1890, and an alleged fourteen lovers. Prepared to take the initiative, she none the less saw love-making (she said) as 'a stage performance'. WBY thought her torn between 'wit and paradox', 'tradition and passion' – and between himself and GBS. In the early nineties his admiration for her had not yet taken the form of direct courtship, and he would have to wait more than ten years to consummate the affair. But her 'tranquil beauty' became a touchstone for him, remembered every time he passed the statue of Demeter near the door of the British Museum Reading Room. And he could appeal to her occultist, stagey side, which Shaw ridiculed. For Farr, WBY provided a respite from the squalid scenes precipitated by Shaw's discarded lover, Jenny Patterson. Most of all, they could co-operate in theatre. Annie Horniman had offered Farr money to put on a theatrical season in the Avenue Theatre during 1893. According to family tradition, at the Pagets' Christmas party in 1893 Farr asked WBY to write a play which would create a part for her niece Dorothy. This became *The Land of Heart's Desire*.

For the moment, he wrestled from early 1894 with his verse play *The*

Shadowy Waters, conceived nearly ten years before as he talked to Russell on their rambles home from art school. But the influences on him were not, for the moment, Theosophical. Much of his time was now spent with Arthur Symons, for whom 1893 was the year when he imported Verlaine to lecture in London ('a dear old thing', in Beardsley's camp dismissal, while wby thought he resembled a permanently drunken Socrates[11]). And in that same month, November, Symons published 'The Decadent Movement in Literature'.[12] This popularized in English the French idea of *poètes maudits*, and would help suggest the views later expressed by wby in 'The Tragic Generation'. As he chased up literary contacts in Paris, and diligently pursued dancing-girls in London, Symons intuited the sense of an apocalypse and the perverse and intensely self-conscious style of a late civilization, corroborating wby's idea that English art was in its decadence while Ireland still possessed 'full tables'. Equally influential was Symons's presentation of France – Verlaine, Mallarmé, Huysmans's *A Rebours* and most of all Philippe-Auguste Villiers de l'Isle-Adam's huge Rosicrucian play *Axël*, recently published. This, in Symons's view, was 'the origin of the symbolistic drama . . . pure symbol'. For wby, just about to begin his own Symbolist play, it was a potent message: he was struck by Rémy de Gourmont's judgement that *Axël* 'has opened the doors of the unknown with a crash, and a generation has gone through them to the infinite'.[13] His visit to Paris, where *Axël* was to be staged, pressed it home.

On February 7 1894 wby left London on a journey he had planned for at least a month. It was his first visit to the Continent – made all the more momentous by the destination of Paris, to him a centre of occult studies and *émigré* Irish nationalism as well as Symbolist literature and experimental theatre. He had just finished *The Land of Heart's Desire*, and believed it had 'turned out one of my best things';[14] he stayed in the Mathers household at the Avenue Duquesne and re-established contact with Maud Gonne (now nearly four months pregnant, though he did not realize it). Once more he renewed his commitment to her: an unpublished poem written after this reunion directly reflects their recent estrangement, and her inspiration of his work.

> I will not in grey hours revoke
> The gift I gave in hours of light
> Before the breath of slander broke
> The thread my folly had drawn tight
>
> The little thread weak hope had made
> To bind two lonely hearts in one
> But loves of light must fade & fade
> Till all the dooms of men are spun,

The gift I gave once more I give
For you may come to winter time
But you white flower of beauty live
In a poor foolish book of rhyme.[15]

He also plunged into literary Paris, with Symons's advice as Baedeker. An introduction had been arranged, probably through York Powell, to Mallarmé; but the poet was in England (his wife had to mime this information to an uncomprehending WBY, who, despite the lessons in Morris's coach-house, never mastered oral French).[16] But his London contacts led him to Verlaine, who had stayed in Symons's Temple lodgings in November and given a reading at Oxford arranged by York Powell. WBY's visit to the presiding genius of decadence provided material for a *Savoy* article two years later, and a memorable passage of his *Autobiographies*.[17] Verlaine invited him to 'coffee and cigarettes plentifully' and fired off aphoristic judgements (famously on Tennyson's *In Memoriam*: 'he was too noble, too *anglais*, and when he should have been broken-hearted had many reminiscences'). For WBY, Verlaine was living proof that exposure to the ideal world of art dissolved conventional morality – and was closely linked to 'communion with spiritual ideas'. 'One . . . fancied as one listened to his vehement sentences that his temperament, his daimon, had been made uncontrollable that he might live the life needful for its perfect expression in art, and yet escape the bonfire.'[18]

A revelation of equal importance was provided by the performance of *Axël* staged at the end of his visit. (There were only two; each ran for five hours). Symons was in London, frantically translating Zola, but WBY went with Maud Gonne, appositely enough, since the play dealt with Rosicrucian wisdom and an esoteric love-alliance which finds peace only in death. Seeing it played, it is unlikely that WBY comprehended more than its atmosphere: but in the ensuing weeks he puzzled through the text in French, guided by Symons, and wrote a long critique for the *Bookman*. Here, WBY emerged as a didactic and arresting critic of drama, much as his rival Shaw had done with music. Realism, WBY argued, had only belatedly conquered the theatre; it was still strong there, and though the critical spirit had recognized Symbolist form in other areas, it had not affected drama. In France alone the achievement of Maeterlinck had prepared the way for *Axël*, in its uncompromising five hours of 'prose as elevated as poetry', where 'all the characters are symbols and all the events allegories'.

Unfortunately (if unsurprisingly) both audience and critical reception had been hostile: but this was irrelevant. WBY went on to quote Verlaine's supposed comment on Villiers's heroine Sara, which sounds far more like a judgement of his own: 'a mysterious woman, a queen of pride, who is mournful and fierce as the night when it still lingers though the dawn is beginning, with reflections of blood and of gold upon her soul and her beauty'.[19] The play's effect brought it near the 'hierarchy of recollections' which, in a rather Wordsworthian way, constituted wby's touchstone of beauty; it could thus take its place with 'a certain night scene long ago, when I heard the wind blowing in a bed of reeds by the border of a little lake, a Japanese picture of cranes flying through a blue sky, and a line or two out of Homer'.[20] It also gave him a favourite image of a lover 'veiled' with his mistress's hair ('where you will breathe the spirit of dead roses', Villiers added rather gratuitously). And one magnificent aphorism stayed with him for ever, expressing with a Wildean flair the vulgarity of quotidian existence and the attractions of the otherworld: 'As for living, our servants will do that for us.'

He would remain faithful to *Axël*, writing a preface for Thomas Sturge Moore's edition thirty years later; but even at the time he had to admit the play was impossibly extended and boring in theatrical terms. 'The imaginative drama must inevitably make many mistakes before it is in possession of the stage again, for it is so essentially different to the old melodrama and the new realism, that it must learn its powers and limitations for itself.' But even its mistakes were visionary. The public needed to be 'reminded very forcibly that the actor should be also a reverent reciter of majestic words'. wby returned to London the next day, fired with enthusiasm; his commitment to his own Symbolist drama, *The Shadowy Waters*, was now absolute. Maeterlinck's influence had provided what Ibsen lacked (though his drama disturbed and impressed wby since 1889). And this directly affected the theatrical experiment in which he was immediately engaged: the outcome of Annie Horniman's bequest to Florence Farr.

The Land of Heart's Desire had not been her only commission. Since November 1893 Shaw had been writing *Arms and the Man* for Farr; though Bedford Park rallied round, with Stepniak providing Bulgarian details for local colour, the play was not ready for the opening of the Avenue Theatre season. *The Land of Heart's Desire* therefore opened on 29 March 1894 with Todhunter's latest piece of laborious Arcadianism, *A Comedy of Sighs*. The programme ran, disastrously, for a fortnight, attracting general opprobrium and much jeering from an audience who had come prepared for the Avenue's usual music-hall fare. wby's play passed off with less attention: but it was not without interest. Behind the folkloric story of an unhappy young wife stolen away by the fairies lay the theme of a woman's escape from a confining house and family, possibly borrowed from *A Doll's House*, though in subsequent versions the influence of *Axël* predominated over the faint echo of Ibsen. Either way, it was a muted note; and this was drowned altogether when it reopened a week after the first run, as the curtain-raiser to Shaw's postponed (and hastily rehearsed) bombshell.

The success of *Arms and the Man* may have owed something to a brilliantly 'packed' audience. George Moore, celebrated for his scandalous realistic novels, carefully positioned himself to observe his fellow-Irishman. Not yet an admirer of WBY, he sarcastically noted the poet surveying the assembled literati, 'a long black cloak dropping from his shoulders, a soft black sombrero on his head, a voluminous black silk tie flowing from his collar, loose black trousers dragging untidily over his long heavy feet . . . an Irish parody of the poetry that I had seen all my life strutting its rhythmic way in the alleys of the Luxembourg Gardens'.[21] And the night belonged to Shaw, not Yeats. His detonating parody took on romance, melodrama and heroism, skewing the audience's perceptions and keeping the drama one sardonic jump ahead; the play's own vigour delivered a theatrical *coup*. WBY's reaction was, inevitably, resentful. His later recollection analysed this, while avoiding the subject of their rivalry over Farr (demoted, in this production, from playing Raina to Louka).

And from that moment Bernard Shaw became the most formidable man in modern letters, and even the most drunken of medical students knew it . . . though I came mainly to see how my own play went, and for the first fortnight to vex my most patient actors with new lines, I listened to *Arms and the Man* with admiration and hatred. It seemed to me inorganic, logical straightness and not the crooked road of life, yet I stood aghast before its energy as to-day before that of the *Stone Drill* by Mr Epstein or of some design by Mr Wyndham Lewis. Shaw was right to claim Samuel Butler for his master, for Butler was the first Englishman to make the discovery that it is possible to write with great effect without music, without style, either good or bad, to eliminate from the mind all emotional implication and to prefer plain water to every vintage, so much metropolitan lead and solder to any tendril of the vine. Presently I had a nightmare that I was haunted by a sewing-machine, that clicked and shone, but the incredible thing was that the machine smiled, smiled perpetually.[22]

Still Shaw, he went on to say, 'could hit my enemies and the enemies of all I loved, as I could never hit'. And 'hitting enemies' was now a vital part of WBY's approach to theatre.

Axël had shown him that the new Symbolist theatre need not be popular; Shaw's success forced WBY to console himself with the thought that he did not *want* to be popular. This feeling was reinforced by Farr. Her prejudice against the single-mindedness that brings success was strengthened by the Avenue Theatre experience: Shaw had not only relegated her to a smaller part, but was increasingly besotted by Janet Achurch. Like Todhunter, who referred to his disastrous *Comedy of Sighs* as 'an experiment on the taste of the British public',[23] Farr and Yeats consoled themselves that Shavian success could only be won at the price of crude populism. And Farr was, after all, the impresario. 'She is desirous of doing my next play,' wby confided to O'Leary, 'as it is a wild mystical thing carefully arranged to be an insult to the regular theatre goer who is hated by both of us. All the plays she is arranging for are studied insults'.[24] The message of André Antoine's Théâtre Libre, so recently absorbed by wby in Paris, was to be preached in London.

As it happened, Todhunter's uncomprehending audience at the Avenue had not been outraged by the avant-garde, but simply annoyed at the theatre's switch from its usual pantomime programme. But this was not wby's view. 'The whole venture will be history any way for it is the first contest between the old commercial school of theatrical folk & the new artistic school'.[25] Farr's 1894 season took its place in the mythology of dramatic modernism, along with J. T. Grein's productions of Ibsen, and *Widowers' Houses* in 1892. Long afterwards, she wrote to GBS that with Annie Horniman's money she 'secured [Todhunter] you and Yeats & Beardsley's poster. And I'm afraid poor Todhunter is the only person connected with the affair that appears as a ridiculous failure!'[26]

At the time, however, Shaw's success left the others in the shade. Farr and wby continued to meet through the summer. On 30 July, in the company of Henrietta Paget and, according to jby, 'a mediumistic chemist's assistant', they consoled themselves with a seance at Dalling Road. Later, they would co-operate in further theatrical experiments. But in 1894 what mattered were wby's ideas about unpopular theatre. Further consolation was provided by the fact that Fisher Unwin's published version of *The Land of Heart's Desire* sold well, and was published in America. By the summer, his wounds healed, wby could be lofty about Dublin's provincialism: even the *Second Book of the Rhymers Club* was let down by the 'dreadful burden of the TCD tradition' (Rolleston and company), and Gavan Duffy's New Irish Library was eviscerated in private and public. By contrast, he hailed Russell's collection *Homeward, Songs by the Way* as a masterpiece.[27] This was a deliberate campaign, as wby confessed to O'Leary. As his autobiographically inclined review of Russell showed, the experiences of the 1880s were already being placed in a contrived perspective; and, while pressing the claims of the old coterie (O'Grady, Hyde, Todhunter, Tynan), his exposure to the avant-garde of Paris and London had carried him on to a new stage. In the process, his metropolitan reputation had been consolidated; when in September 1894 Ernest Radford wrote to Elkin Mathews about attacks on the Century Guild journal the *Hobby Horse*, he remarked, 'I take it for granted that Yeats will take his stand at your side, for [in] that case his name would bear weight.'[28] wby now knew the practical importance as well as the psychological compensations of building a reputation which would sustain a writer's life both in London and Ireland.

III

By the autumn of 1894 WBY was ready to venture to Ireland again. On 10 October he travelled to Dublin, staying at the North Circular Road lodgings for a fortnight. But his correspondence betrays a continuing sensitivity about mockery from enemies within the Gavan Duffy camp; he was aware that Dublin opinion was all too ready to accuse him of self-inflation.[29] He soon moved on to Thornhill, George Pollexfen's cheerless house, the only base left to him in Sligo. As usual, WBY brought with him an agenda of work: on this occasion, the project of revising his poems for a collected edition, and the never-ending struggle with *The Shadowy Waters*. On 5 November he wrote to JBY that its 'legendary details' kept conflicting with theatrical imperatives;[30] he was reading French 'every day', or so he claimed. The lessons learnt in Paris and at the Avenue Theatre were already being put into practice.

George Pollexfen's household provided other opportunities too. His housekeeper, Mary Battle, was an eloquent Mayo woman with second sight; Pollexfen himself, now an initiate of the Golden Dawn, was one of the few members of the family sympathetic to his nephew's occult interests and became an obsessive astrologer, much in demand. From the gloomy atmosphere of Thornhill, WBY and his uncle corresponded with 'sorores' and 'fratres' of the Golden Dawn about cabbalistic ritual ('with references to the Fire Wand enclosing a magnetized rod, our G. H. Frater Non Omnis Moriar, usually keeps a stock here, which he sells to members. At the present moment we are out of them, but some are on order. When they come in, I will send you one if you wish it, but if you prefer it, you can, of course, have one made yourself. The usual size is about six inches'[31]). With Mary Battle, WBY discussed the Tipperary atrocity which convulsed Ireland that winter: a woman had been burned alive by her husband and his friends, in the apparent belief that she was possessed by fairies. Some Irish newspapers had connected this 'diseased spirit' to the undiscriminating interest in folklore encouraged by WBY and Hyde. With a fine sense of discrimination, Mary Battle assured him that normal practice would simply have been to threaten the fairies out, and the tragedy occurred simply because 'they are so superstitious in Tipperary'.[32]

WBY spent some time writing occult stories for Henley, but there was little prospect of a literary income until his anthology, *A Book of Irish Verse*, appeared. Novel-writing continued to present the best financial possibilities; however, he already thought of *John Sherman* as 'youthful and languid', and felt that Irish fiction lacked the 'central fire' produced by the Carleton generation.[33] The idea of the novel that would become *The Speckled Bird* was already forming, but poverty loomed. At this point George Pollexfen may have offered his nephew an allowance of a pound a week,[34] but WBY, with his habitual sensitivity about financial obligations, did not mention it in any surviving correspondence. As winter came on, he stayed at Thornhill. He encouraged his cousin Lucy Middleton in psychic experiments; this Sligo sojourn provided, as ever, the consolations of childhood.[35] But he also ventured into local society. In late November, and again in mid-December, he stayed with the Gore-Booth family at Lissadell, their austere neo-classical mansion on the Raughley peninsula, lost among woods and avenues. This was a level of county society to which Pollexfens did not aspire; WBY had breached it through the power of art, and the Gore-Booth enthusiasm for the avant-garde. He found them 'a very pleasent kindly inflamable family . . . ever ready to take up new ideas and new things'.[36] Eva and Constance, both beguiling and imaginative, were excited by folklore, and the Irish books lent them by WBY; for his part, he saw their enthusiasm as representative of the 'nationalizing' of 'the more thoughtful Unionists'.[37] (But he shrewdly surmised that authority really resided with a cynical old aunt, Joanna Arabella Gore-Booth, who held the household in thrall from her bed upstairs.)

Far from Maud Gonne and Florence Farr, at a crossroads in his writing, and desperately wanting sympathy, WBY felt a brief affinity with Eva. He shared confidences about Gonne with her; it was becoming his usual way of forging friendships with sympathetic women, flattering the confidante while inhibiting the development of a full love-affair. As he later remembered it, WBY wondered about pressing his suit but decided 'this house would never accept so penniless a suitor'; when a Tarot reading delivered the Fool, he knew nothing would come of it.[38] It is hard to believe he felt much regret; he settled instead for directing Eva's reading-programme in Irish matters, and encouraging her poetic ambitions in emotionally charged language ('when ever the fealing is weightiest you are at your best'[39]). 'She needs however like all Irish literary people a proper respect for craftsmanship,' he unguardedly told his new friend Olivia Shakespear, '& that she must get in England'.[40] She did go to England, and found her *métier* there: but it took the form of feminism and female relationships, and she died in London thirty years later.

The Gore-Booth girls continued to feature in WBY's life through the long winter and cold spring: Lough Gill froze over, and at a skating-party in March they made coffee on the shore.[41] But while based in Sligo, he kept a weather eye on literary affairs in Dublin. Moreover, the months in the country allowed him to reassess his position in Irish cultural confrontations. Just before leaving London, he had written a significant letter to Alice Milligan:

My experience of Ireland, during the last three years, has changed my views very greatly, & now I feel that the work of an Irish man of letters must be not so much to awaken or quicken or preserve the national idea among the mass of the people but to convert the educated classes to it on the one hand to the best of his ability, & on the other – & this is the more important – to fight for moderation, dignity, & the rights of the intellect among his fellow nationalists. Ireland is terribly demoralized in all things – in her scholourship, in her criticism, in her politics, in her social life. She will never be greatly better until she govern herself but she will be greatly worse unless there arise protesting spirits.[42]

Settled into Sligo, he began to mount a campaign as a 'protesting spirit', sending letters about literary matters to *United Ireland*, stressing the need to work outside Ireland, rejecting the solipsistic attitude that 'Irish opinion' was all that mattered. His literary vendetta against Dowden continued, using the old benchmark of Samuel Ferguson's 'Irishness'.[43] Dowden had criticized the new Irish school as rhetorical and sentimental; in the ensuing exchange he caught WBY on a raw spot by insisting, 'I have never advertised myself, and I have never shrunk from being criticised.'[44] The implication that he was pushy and thin-skinned came close to home, though WBY riposted that the movement he represented was more often criticized for not being patriotic enough. Some consolation was provided by a debate at Trinity on 27 February 1895, where the motion 'that the Irish Literary revival is worthy of support' was overwhelmingly endorsed; and WBY then moved the public debate on a stage by instigating a controversy over a list of 'Best Irish Books'.

This was exactly the kind of involvement he liked best: *ex cathedra* judgements, categoric lists and the promulgation of aesthetic agendas. He prepared for it painstakingly by a letter to Standish O'Grady, guaranteeing that his letter to the *Express* would be printed ('We want to start a new contraversy, in continuation of a present one on "Prof Dowden & Irish Literature"'[45]) and promising the publisher Fisher Unwin that he would plug at least two of the works on his list. His first salvo was fired on 27 February 1895, listing his '30 best books'. This excluded 'every book in which there is strong political feeling' – a deliberate attempt to spike the guns of the Gavan Duffy camp, always ready to play the political card. (A later letter listed a few 'political' books he might have included – carefully balanced, from the Tory historian Richard Bagwell through the Liberal Unionist W. E. H. Lecky to the separatist voices of Tone and Mitchel.) For the moment he concentrated on works of 'imagination' – an odd catalogue, redolent of Sligo parlours. It included some short stories, Lever's *Charles O'Malley*, a good deal of Carleton, O'Grady, Hyde and others of his own company, as well as the plagiarizing Nora Hopper. The accompanying commentary betrayed a strong reason for airing the subject in the first place: it carried an unashamed puff for his own forthcoming anthology, *A Book of Irish Verse*.

Thus far, Dublin opinion saw the old game of self-advertisement; and it was not entirely wrong. WBY continued to write indefatigably to friends, commanding them to join in. But the list is interesting none the less. O'Grady's pastiche-Carlylean prose-poems continue to be over-estimated; d'Arbois de Jubainville is grandly enlisted (in misspelled French); romantic history in the Celtic mode predominates. When Dowden replied with his own list, WBY attacked the inclusion of unIrish writers like Swift and Berkeley – a piquant irony for the future, when they would become central to his inspiration. But this too represented an ulterior agenda, for it was timed to coincide with the much heralded publication of the *Book of Irish Verse*. After seeing a draft of WBY's introduction the previous August, Lionel Johnson had written to Tynan, 'He will certainly be massacred by a certain kind of Irish poet if ever he sets foot in Ireland again. And Moore's statue will certainly fall and crush him – or itself, which is vastly preferable!'[46] The text explains why WBY orchestrated a discussion in the Dublin press on Irish canons of literature for the month before publication.

That whole campaign had been calculated to prepare the ground for the arguments set out in WBY's introduction. Most eighteenth-century Irish writers were excluded (though Goldsmith just scraped in) and the 'imperfect' inheritance of bardic tradition was stressed. *Pace* Johnson, although Thomas Moore's 'artificial and mechanical' style was criticized, he was credited with playing a genuine Celtic note. Dowden was excluded, though he was allowed 'an odd moment' of inspiration, and Trinity's devotion to 'alien themes' attacked; Rolleston, another recent enemy, dismissed; Allingham and de Vere favoured; Tynan and Weekes received the traditional endorsement, though a careless subeditor dropped several verses from Tynan's 'Children of Lir'. Praise for Hyde, however, was oddly faint ('before all else, a translator and a scholar').

The real venom, however, was reserved for Young Ireland 'rhetoric'; only Mangan (episodically) escaped it. This was, of course, also a coded attack on Gavan Duffy and on J. F. Taylor, who was portrayed in all but name:

the Irishman of our times loves so deeply those arts which build up a gallant personality, rapid writing, ready talking, effective speaking to crowds, that he has no thought for the arts which consume the personality in solitude. He loves the mortal arts which have given him a lure to take the hearts of man, and shrinks from the immortal, which could but divide him from his fellows.

In his peroration WBY repeated the message of his review of Hyde's *Love Songs of Connacht* (and raised yet again the image which would provide the title of his 1899 collection of poems): 'the poor peasant of the eighteenth century could make his ballads by abandoning himself to the joy and sorrow of the moment, as the reeds abandon themselves to the wind which sighs through them, because he had about him a world where all was old enough to be steeped in emotion'.[47]

The introduction to *A Book of Irish Verse* was followed by four long articles which appeared in the *Bookman* from July 1895 (thrifty as ever, WBY intended to make a book of them[48]). Taken with his newspaper campaign and the anthology introduction, they show him still trying to define cultural nationalism, and assert a legitimate pedigree for it. In the process he raised the eternal question of Irish nationality, and the sense of national identity, a topic which he argued with Standish O'Grady, who saw 'nationalism' as a recent growth, irrelevant to Irish history in the medieval period. In August 1895 WBY wrote to O'Grady:

I should perhaps in my Bookman article have used the phrase 'the armed hand of race' instead of 'the armed hand of nationality'. I find it hard, knowing how jealous one country is of another, even to day, when people travel so much, to beleive that the Irish had no racial hatred (no matter how completely they lacked a racial policy *i.e.* nationality) for invaders who spoke a different tongue & had different customs & interests. Then too, one cannot forget a lot of gaelic poems like 'the battle song for the clans of Wicklow' (translated by Ferguson). It is [*recte* 'is it'] not possible that while the racial unity of England expressed itself in a method of government, the racial unity of Ireland expressed it self in things like the bardic order & in popular instincts & prejudices. That while the English nobles therefore expressed English racial purpose at its best, the Irish nobles, warped by their little princedoms & their precarious dynasties were more for themselves & less for Ireland, than the bards, & harpers & the masses of the people? You of course know & I do not. You speak from particular knowledge, I from general principles merely.[49]

The argument that the intellectuals and 'common people' shared a true sense of nationality, denied to venal politicians, had obvious contemporary relevance; and the *Bookman* articles contained a coded message. Propagandists like Davis and impatient hacks like Moore had lost their bearings by adopting English models: even Mitchel went similarly astray. The real achievement belonged to writers like J. J. Callanan, whose translations achieved the authentic Irish note, and Ferguson, Allingham and de Vere; not the 'interesting, unsatisfying, pathetic movement' that was Young Ireland. Carleton, moreover, was the 'true historian' of Ireland. Thus yet another salvo was fired at Gavan Duffy and his New Irish Library; while at the same time, he tried to establish a genuine Irish literary tradition in the English language, implicitly culminating in the efforts of WBY himself.

Thus these articles reflect his brooding in Sligo over the defeats of the previous year. But they also introduced (or at least presented in full) WBY's developing theory of 'Moods'. This notion of *Zeitgeist*, accessible through poetic insight, owes much to early nineteenth-century transcendentalism as well as to WBY's established distrust of positivism and rationalism. Historical and scientific analysis is impatiently rejected: O'Grady appears as the 'one historian who is anything of an artist', rising above 'dates and dialectics'.

In Ireland we are accustomed to histories with great parade of facts and dates, of wrongs and precedents, for use in the controversies of the hour; and here was a man who let some all-important Act of Parliament (say) go by without a mention, or with perhaps inaccurate mention, and for no better reason than because it did not interest him, and who recorded with careful vividness some moment of abrupt passion, some fragment of legendary beauty, and for no better reason than because it did interest him profoundly.[50]

For the rest, WBY's round-up of Lecky, Patrick Joyce, Hyde, Lady Wilde and others tended to be condescending, even towards writers he had reviewed enthusiastically in the past. Modern-day Irish poetry was a subject limited by his inability to discuss his own work; the endorsement of Tynan was notably lukewarm, and he took refuge in prophetic assertions about a coming 'age of imagination, of emotion, of moods, of revelation', which owed more to the notions of the Golden Dawn than to literary criticism at any level. This prepared the way for an assertion that Russell was the most beautiful poet of the day, paying unconvincing tribute to his technical ability as well as to his inspiration. By the last article, WBY had returned with a wolfish appetite to the 'best books' controversy, Dowden, and the 'vacant verses' of Trinity College men – thus contriving to insult Tynan's husband Henry Hinkson, who had recently compiled such an anthology. As an *envoi*, he loftily denied any intention of log-rolling before proceeding to list his *forty* 'best books'. This time he included the political rhetoric of Tone and Mitchel, and ended – on the disarming grounds that nothing better yet existed – with his own *Book of Irish Verse*. The whole campaign could be seen, from one point of view, as a breathtakingly egregious performance; but it also may be read as a manifesto on behalf of Irish writing in English, an attack on conventional Irish political pieties, and a demonstration that retirement to Sligo had enabled WBY to consider his critics and emerge unreconciled.

IV

The energy which he brought to this controversy might give the impression that his own poetry had been, for the moment, relegated to the background, but he was simultaneously preoccupied by how it should be presented to the public. At first he decided upon a new collection, to be called 'Under the Moon'. (The more obvious references to Blake and Shakespeare were Celticized by the additional 'fact' that the moon governed 'peasants, sailors, fishermen' – at least according to a publisher's blurb.[51]) Before leaving for Ireland in October 1894, WBY was discussing with Fisher Unwin 'a new and corrected edition' of his previously published poems; he was also negotiating provisional terms with Elkin Mathews. The correspondence continued from Dublin.

Fisher Unwin's seemed the more attractive firm, especially given WBY's estab-lished relationship with Edward Garnett; though Fisher Unwin himself was neurotic and authoritarian, and notoriously difficult to handle, which explains the insistent tone of WBY's letters.[52] But he also wrote with a new sense of professional confidence – and a clear expectation that he would be publish-ing other volumes before long, since he stipulated a specific size and format so that future works could resemble it. He named the printer to be used and asked for a say in choosing the artist, as well as 'a royalty from the first copy'. Subsequent letters (much drafted and redrafted) are preoccupied with bring-ing all his work together: the sense of a canon in the making is unmistakable. And he demanded that all rights should revert to him *unconditionally at the end of a term of years*. I partly insist on this because if ever a first rate publish-ing house arise in Ireland I must needs publish in part with them.'[53] That 'in part' is striking: the divided life was apparently to continue, whatever the suc-cess of the Irish renaissance.

For the moment he had two London publishers bidding for him, and could state his terms. The ex-art student remained severe about appearances ('not green & no shamrocks'[54]); his choice of Charles Shannon as an appro-priate illustrator showed a sharp eye for the current vogue. Fisher Unwin met most of his terms; and through the autumn and early winter at Thornhill WBY worked on *The Shadowy Waters* before dinner but devoted the evenings to revising the work of his youth. The title-poem of *The Wanderings of Oisin* (rechristened, temporarily, 'Usheen') was pared down and lost some (not all) of its romantic embellishment. (Some Maeterlinckian effects, like the quat-rain at the end of Book I, would be pruned in later editions.) *The Countess Kathleen* followed, shortened and made more dramatic. After *The Land of Heart's Desire* a selection of the shorter poems from his first collection were rearranged under the title 'Crossways' – proving that they represented what WBY now viewed as a period of experiment. Another group of lyrics, chiefly from *The Countess Kathleen*, were grouped together as 'The Rose'. Several of the poems would be further changed in later collections; Gaelic names re-mained inconsistent, while specifically classical allusions would eventually be grafted on to poems like 'The Sorrow of Love'. Certain ninetyish phrases still predominated; but the phrase 'wandering stars', for instance, was trans-formed into 'all dishevelled wandering stars', gaining at a stroke the resonance and rhythm already seen as Yeatsian.[55] And, with accessibility to an English audience firmly in mind, a glossary was provided for some names and local references.

The whole arrangement was carefully worked through; it owed nothing to the accidents of chronology. Archaic and recondite expressions were pruned: juvenilia from the 1880s like 'Miserrimus' disappeared. Read together, the three long dramatic pieces stressed a tension between old Irish beliefs and conventional religious piety – and between 'Fenians' and bishops. There was, therefore, a Parnellite message for those with an eye to such things. But overall the themes that emerged emphasized tradition, beauty and the Celtic essence, while politics and 'the world' were shunned. Thus the collected poems bore little indication of the man who had originally written them, while their arrangement owes much to the agenda which w b y had set himself during his Sligo retreat.

In mid-February 1895 w b y sent the final revisions off from Sligo: the preface is dated 'Sligo, March 24'. By the time it was in the press, he wrote to Tynan, reverting to their old manner:

All the old things are re-written. I wonder how they will receive it in Ireland. Patronize it I expect & give it faint praise & yet I feel it is good, that whether the coming generations in England accept me or reject me, the coming generations in Ireland cannot but value what I have done. I am writing at the end of the day & when I am tired, this endless war with Irish stupidity gets on my nerves. Either you or I could have more prosperous lives probably if we left Ireland alone, & went our own way on the high seas – certainly we could have more peacable lives. However if the sun shine in the morning I shall be full of delight of battle & ready to draw my bow against the dragon.[56]

The next month, May, he returned to London, after a rather unsuccessful fortnight with Hyde in Roscommon. w b y's ineptness with a fishing-rod amused his host (he hooked a visiting clergyman by the ear) and Hyde's sister Annette made, according to Hyde's diary, an *amadán* of the poet.[57] A few weeks later the *Bookman* carried an extremely equivocal review by w b y of Hyde's *Story of Early Gaelic Literature* (too 'historical', 'dry as dust'[58]). Their close association was definitely over.

On 21 August, in Bedford Park, he received his first copy of *Poems*, to be published in October. Lily noticed 'he can't part from it but sits not reading it but looking at the outside and turning it over and over'.[59] He had good reason to. For one thing, it was beautifully produced, though the cover was by H. G. Fell instead of Shannon; it showed St Michael destroying a serpent, and w b y came to dislike all the art-work. Some shamrocks had crept on to the spine, but the frontispiece, representing an angelic coronation, carried a suitable suggestion of the finale to *The Countess Kathleen*. More importantly, the contents were received with considerable respect. In an intelligent review (preserved by w b y) W. P. Ryan analysed this 'readdressed work', recognizing in the obsessive fine-tuning a visionary power and a quest for artistic perfection; he also noted that the 'alien' tone of the first poems, derived from deliberately exotic Gaelic imagery, had been replaced by the beauty of everyday

POEMS

BY · W · B · YEATS ·

LONDON : PVBLISHED BY T. FISHER VNWIN ·

Nº XI : PATERNOSTER BVILDINGS : MDCCCXCV ·

6. The frontispiece of *Poems* (1895) by H. C. Fell. WBY later came to despise Fell's art-work as weak and tired, but it does reflect the Christian-mystic and medievalist preoccupations evident in his writing at the time and suggests the apotheosis of *The Countess Cathleen*, which was included in the volume.

things.[60] Ryan understood that the plays and poetry, placed in careful apposition to each other, summed up a concrete and integrated achievement. But it would, more practically, prove a long and steady seller, revised fourteen times over the next three decades and creating a regular income. In 1929 WBY wrote: 'This book for about thirty years brought me twenty or thirty times as much money as any other book of mine – no twenty or thirty times as much as all my other books put together.'[61] As a record of his youth, evidence of the road since travelled, and provider of his middle years, *Poems* (1895) deserved WBY's gratitude. It also symbolized an important stage in the development of his public self.

V

The summer of 1895 opened a new era in his personal life too. Since the estrangement with Gonne in 1893, WBY had been attracted to other women, following his inclination towards the unconventional: not only the alarming Florence Farr but also the fey and slightly manic Irish artist Althea Gyles, and the Gore-Booth sisters, for whom he arranged fortune-telling sessions with Moina Mathers. Sentimental contact was established through the brokerage of occult interests, but things did not proceed further. Women like Gyles and Farr were drawn to more experienced and authoritative figures; his own social as well as personal inhibitions, as he had found in Sligo, kept him a certain distance from the Gore-Booths, while they in turn looked elsewhere. Constance found a dashing Polish art student, Casimir Markievicz, and Eva chose the suffragist Esther Roper. At a dinner for the *Yellow Book* on 16 April 1894, however, WBY had noticed the beauty and distinction of Lionel Johnson's cousin Olivia Shakespear. More decisively, she noticed his dramatic looks and saw to it that Johnson arranged a meeting. A note in her handwriting is appended coquettishly to Johnson's letter of 30 May: 'I shall be so glad to see you.'[62]

Shakespear had been to *The Land of Heart's Desire* and admired it, but that June she was also just about to publish her own first novel, *Love on a Mortal Lease*. The title, from *Modern Love*, is apposite; she resembled one of Meredith's astringent beauties, trammelled by the expectations of her class and background. Though involved, if rather tangentially, in London literary life, it was not her original milieu. Two years and three months older than WBY, she came from an upper-class military family; her mother was a sister of Johnson's father. Like Johnson, she followed intellectual fashion and felt oppressively isolated within her philistine family; he found her 'the only member of my family to whom I can really disclose myself'.[63] Her marriage in December 1885 to Henry Hope Shakespear, a solicitor from a similar (but much less well-off) Anglo-Indian background, is hard to explain; it may have been a gesture of desperation. He was fourteen years older, and 'ceased to pay court to me from the day of our marriage'. One child, Dorothy, was born nine months later. Her fiction is dominated by the theme of a loveless marriage to an older man, and the frustration of intelligent women trying to live life on their own terms. Her cousin Lionel provided a lifeline, and by the 1890s she was entertaining his circle at her Kensington house. A sad and slightly detached manner hid a sharp brain and a mind of her own. Her future son-in-law Ezra Pound fantasized that Olivia had spent her previous life as a Byzantine: 'She has a nasty 3rd-century-Christian streak in her nature. That's why she hates Christ like the devil.'[64]

To WBY, struck by her 'distinction', she resembled Eva Gore-Booth; dark-haired and lovely, in photographs of the time she looks slightly like a more reflective Maud Gonne.[65] And she was soon told of WBY's hopeless attachment. By August 1894 he was writing chatty letters to her about her next novel (*Beauty's Hour*), which Symons would publish in the *Savoy* in 1896. WBY suggested she reconstruct a character as 'one of those vigerous fair haired . . . young men, who are very positive, & what is called manly, in external activities & energies & wholly passive & plastic in emotional & intellectual things'.[66] Implicitly, he was declaring that he was the very opposite: no wonder she later accused him of writing 'unconscious love letters'. In November she sent her new novel, *The Journey of High Honour*, to Sligo, and WBY returned enthusiastic critiques, while pointing out the wooden quality of her male characters, 'refined, destinguished, sympathetic . . . because your own character & ideals are mirrored in them'.[67] By April he was writing to her of his regret at having to stay on in Sligo, and expressing impatience to meet again.

Their friendship was cemented by occult interests and literature. He explained to her his plan of writing stories that would not be 'mere phantasies but the signatures – to use a medieval term – of things invisable & ideal',[68] and analysed her visions as well as her novels. 'I no more complain of your writing of love, than I would complain of a portrait painter keeping to portraits. I would complain however if his backgrounds were too slightly imagined for the scheme of his art. I have never come upon any new work so full of a kind of tremulous delicasy, so full of a kind of fragile beauty as these books of yours however.'[69] This was calculated flattery – he does not praise Shakespear's work to other correspondents at the time. After his return to London in May, she was apparently determined to put these 'unconscious' declarations into concrete form. Perhaps it was inevitable that in WBY's first love-affair the woman would take the initiative; he presented himself in his *Memoirs* as naïve, hesitant, almost girlish, and when Shakespear made a declaration WBY assumed not only that she (like Johnson) 'loathed her life' but that she (unlike him) 'had had many lovers'. He hesitated in a maidenly way for a fortnight and then agreed to pursue matters, subsequently caught unaware by the passion of her first kiss (on the train to Kent, visiting her friend and ally Valentine Fox).[70]

This was mid-July 1895. She clarified the conditions of her marriage and told WBY he would be her first extra-marital affair. Consummation now seemed an even more difficult matter. According to WBY's recollection they decided to wait and elope when her mother died. This would certainly have made more financial sense – though under the law of the day she would not have been able to divorce Shakespear and would inevitably have lost custody of Dorothy. They decided to take advice from experienced female friends: WBY probably choosing Florence Farr, and Shakespear confiding in her friend Valentine Fox, to whose house she had brought WBY on 11 July. WBY thought they sustained this chaperoned existence 'for nearly a year', possibly from June 1895 until his move into Woburn Buildings the following spring.

That summer the literary and artistic circles frequented by WBY were preoccupied with sex. On 5 April 1895, while he was still in Sligo, Oscar Wilde had been arrested; the trial began shortly after WBY's return to London. On 19 May, the day before it began, he called at Lady Wilde's to express sympathy and relay support from 'some of our Dublin literary men'; a letter to Dowden, asking him to write sympathetically to Wilde, survives. Dowden, unsurprisingly, refused. WBY's unequivocal support is admirable: compounded of gratitude to someone who had helped him, solidarity with an avant-garde Irish writer, and a cosmopolitan determination not to be shocked (after all, he was aware of the leanings of friends like Lionel Johnson, and had shared lodgings with Joseph Quinn). Others in the Rhymers circle were less certain, and more compromised: Wilde had been their patron, and several were implicated in the homosexual underworld. Symons had a further reason for sensitivity. He had been trying to place his third volume of poems, *London Nights*, which pursued themes of sexual passion and prostitutes too enthusiastically for Lane's Bodley Head or William Heinemann; it ended up with Leonard Smithers, ex-solicitor, art dealer, bookseller and pornographer ('I'll publish anything that the others are afraid of'[71]). It appeared in June, hot on Wilde's conviction, and was unsurprisingly panned for its immorality. One review was headed, succinctly, 'Pah!' WBY, just preparing to venture into his own version of sexual excess, wrote that Symons deserved congratulation 'upon having written a book which, though it will arouse against him much prejudice, is the best he has done'.[72] He went on to stress that this was because of Symons's sexual honesty rather than his poetic technique. Within a year he would be casually referring to Max Nordau's work on 'degeneration' as related to artistic genius. It was all a long way from Sligo.

Nor was he the only literary entrepreneur who decided it was a good time to tackle conventional morality head-on. Smithers, in the wake of the Wilde débâcle, approached Symons about editing a new magazine to rival the *Yellow Book*. Beardsley, already fired from the latter, was brought aboard, though his sly obscenities were (with some difficulty) restricted to an illustration in the prospectus. And the new magazine chose as its title the *Savoy*, seen by many as a daring reference to the hotel where, the world now knew, Wilde had taken his rent-boys. During the late summer of 1895 the *Savoy* venture took shape; and wby, whose friendship with Symons was strengthening as Johnson disintegrated into alcoholism, was brought in at an early stage. Symons, wby found, had 'the sympathetic intelligence of a woman'; his pose of sexual obsession masked a nature 'incapable of excess . . . [he] lived the temperate life Pater had commended'. (Symons's much recorded contemporary *affaire maudite* with an amoral dancer called Lydia, though it did happen, does indeed sometimes read like an elaborate fantasy.) In the post-Wilde fall-out, wby's move into the *Savoy* circle shocked Dublin acquaintances like Russell and Rolleston ('I think you should clear out of Arthur Symons's vicinity, and come over here. It will be much better for you morally'[73]).

But he was determined on independence in more ways than one. Blenheim Road was gloomier than ever. Susan Yeats was bedridden, and jby making very little from illustrative work. Jack had moved out after his marriage to a fellow art student Mary Cottenham White ('Cottie') in August 1894. Lily had left the Morris embroidery workshop, so money was especially short. Though Lolly was receiving an income from her book on brushwork painting techniques, she was increasingly neurotic and edgy. Lily's diary for the summer of 1895 records the comings and goings at Bedford Park: visits from Olivia Shakespear ('Willy's latest admiration, very pretty, young and nice'), uncle John Pollexfen, who was suspected of carrying mumps into the household ('Think of a poet with mumps'), and a traumatic interlude when Susan Pollexfen's sister Agnes arrived in a deluded state of manic psychosis, having escaped from a mental home: 'no sleep and unceasing talking'. After five shillings spent on telegrams, she eventually departed in the custody of two nurses and her distraught husband.[74] wby felt guilty at consigning her once more to the asylum. (Writing his memoirs twenty years later, he agonized over the point but his sisters made him omit the incident to save family feelings.) Finally, in August jby himself succumbed to mysterious stomach pains and severe depression.

It was at this point that Symons suggested wby temporarily share his rooms in the Temple, at Fountain Court; he had lived there since February

1891, having found his lodgings through George Moore, already a Temple inhabitant.[75] The apartment was actually leased by Havelock Ellis (physician, savant and sexologist), who sublet to Symons and kept some space for himself; but he was away, and his room was free. WBY needed little persuading; the Symons version in later years was that he 'begged for a winter's home' when he was homeless.[76] He had left Bedford Park by 26 September, when York Powell wrote to Katharine Tynan:

Mr Yeats is not yet well. We are all anxious about him. He has not yet got out of his sadness and illness of weeks ago. I wanted him to come down here [Oxford] but he says he cannot get away from home. He is very pleased with Lily's letters [from Sligo] and I think he will get used to Willy's being away, if it gets Willy into regular work.[77]

The family attitude towards WBY's defection was sceptical. Lily, for one, was so closely bound to home that a quarter-century later she could still vividly remember the security and joy of Easter 1894, spent with her brother and father. JBY sketched his son while she read *The Prisoner of Zenda*. 'I sat one side of the fire in Blenheim Road, Papa the other, and Willy between us. The talk was pleasant. We all had a holiday feeling and Papa did this beautiful sketch of Willy . . . I would be glad to have a copy in memory of that day of spring and holiday and youth.'[78] For her, such moments eclipsed all the insecurity and frustration of Bedford Park life; but her brother felt differently. After he left, she missed him and remained uncertain how anyone could make the break. 'What is the "poet" up to?' she asked JBY the next month. 'Is he paying his way? – And what is his book doing?' Paying his way remained a difficulty; he hoped to manage on ten shillings a week, and a small account-book in his handwriting records loans and debts to Symons. He periodically returned to Blenheim Road, sometimes because Symons had borrowed all his money; he told Lily his new style of life 'tended to economy'. She noticed (with implicit surprise) that he 'visibly and unmistakably enjoyed himself' and was pleased to see them all. But to the others, by and large, his departure was a relief. Describing a later return visit, JBY confided to Lily, 'He has the greatest wish to be friendly and peaceable, but he can't manage it, and though I was very sorry to see him go, for he is in good humour, both attractive and affectionate, still wherever he is there is a constant strain and uneasiness.'[79] For his part, removal from Blenheim Road took him away from an environment where he was gently but mercilessly satirized ('WB is reading an article which he has written on Standish O'Grady in the "Book-man" to Mr O'Leary, who says it is no more like him than the man in the moon'[80]). This was a loss as well as a relief.

But his new rooms suited him. The set occupied the top storey, with a stone balcony looking down on a wide courtyard and a fountain; WBY's apartment, connected to Symons's by a corridor, provided privacy when he needed it. The *rus in urbe* of the Temple, with its collegiate serenity just off the Strand, appealed to him: as it turned out, Blake too had lived in Fountain Court in old age, and in the 1890s the Inns of Court housed many literary birds of passage (John Gray, Edward Martyn, Ernest Dowson, George Moore). Most of all, he could follow through the commitment to Olivia Shakespear. However, this would not happen just yet.

At this very point, Maud Gonne returned to his life. Unknown to WBY, she had had a second child, Iseult, by Millevoye in August 1894; but their relationship was foundering and she wrote to WBY from Dublin in November 1895, asking him if she had been appearing to him in spiritual visions.[81] For her part, she was convinced she had met him astrally; they had even re-visited Howth together. This bombshell coincided with a disastrous visit from Shakespear, when WBY went out to buy cakes for tea and succeeded in locking himself out of his rooms. The omens were hardly good.[82] And on 13 November Gonne herself materialized in London; they dined together. Four days later she returned to Paris (and Iseult); but she was back in his life. Their correspondence continued through the winter, with Gonne encouraging Irish nationalist links to Mathers's shadowy 'Highlander' organizations, and promising to write about WBY's work for French magazines. (Hardly a literary critic, or even a proficient writer, her piece was eventually cut down to a brief biography.) By January 1896 WBY was apparently thinking that some day he might go to live and work in France.

All this, coinciding with the early stages of his affair with Shakespear, cannot have been easy. But her (and literary London's) claims on him were reinforced by the great event of 11 January 1896, when the first number of the *Savoy* was published in London. Symons's editorial denied that they subscribed to any movement, including 'Decadence': 'for us, all art is good which is good art'. This was dangerously close to Wilde's defence of his love-poetry in court, six months before. But the contents were Pre-Raphaelite rather than Decadent. Realism and psychological exploration were represented by Havelock Ellis's critique of major European figures; iconoclastic autobiography by Shaw's 'On Going to Church'; discursive gossip by the first of a series of 'Causeries', an idea lifted from the *Speaker*. Most striking was WBY's prominence. The first number included two love-poems, 'The Shadowy Horses' (later known as 'He bids his Beloved be at Peace') and 'The Travail of Passion', appositely Pre-Raphaelite in tone, and a short story, 'The Binding of the Hair'. This provided the setting for another poem, later separately published as 'He gives his Beloved certain Rhymes'; all three were probably addressed to Shakespear, particularly the last. It is sung to a young, wise, dark-haired queen, married to an old, somnolent foolish husband; the singer is a love-sick bard, whose passion transcends his death.

By then, they were all but lovers; full consummation probably waited until WBY moved into an independent flat in Woburn Buildings in February. As he recalled it in his *Memoirs*, embarrassment and inexperience continued to dominate the episode. Choosing a bed together in a Tottenham Court Road shop, where 'every inch increased the expense', was an agony, and he was at first 'impotent from nervous excitement'. Shakespear's sympathetic and tolerant approach eased matters. She met him the next day (for study in the British Museum) in her usual manner, to his surprise; and it was all right in the end. His sexual insecurity, fears and longings may be reflected in the very poems and story so prominently displayed in the *Savoy*: consummation and death are inevitably linked, along with images of drowning, smothering and absorption.[83] If WBY's autobiographical recollection really matches his mood at the time, there is a strong implication of reluctance and ambiguity as well as inexperience and uncertainty. And Shakespear's rather world-weary and sarcastic persona of later years – a Balzacian rather than Meredithian heroine[84] – may owe something to the uneven course of her first extra-marital entanglement.

From her lover's point of view, the beginning of 1896 had established him anew: equipped with independent living-quarters and a beautiful married mistress, he was also the star of a scandalous new journal. In that role he was observed by Max Beerbohm at a dinner to launch the *Savoy* in the New Lyric Club on 22 January, attended by the contributors to the first number. (The menu-card survives: *Bisque d'écrivisses, Filet de sole au vin blanc, Noisettes de mouton tomates farcies, Faisan roti et salade, Bombe glacé à la Vénitienne, Champignons sur croûtes*.) To Beerbohm, the principal revelation was the pornographer–publisher Smithers's wife, 'brought out from some far suburb for this occasion only', and trying gallantly to cope.

Perhaps, if I had not been so preoccupied by the pity of her, I would have been more susceptible to Yeats's magic. I wished that I, not he, had been placed next to her at the table. I could have helped her more than he. The walls of the little room in which we supped were lined with bamboo instead of wall paper. 'Quite original, is it not?' she said to Yeats. But Yeats had no reply ready for that; only a courteous, lugubrious murmur. He had been staying in Paris, and was much engrossed in the cult of Diabolism, or Devil-worship, which appeared to have a vogue there. He had made a profound study of it: and he evidently guessed that Beardsley, whom he met now for the first time, was a confirmed worshipper in that line. So to Beardsley he talked, in deep vibrant tones across the table, of the lore and rites of Diabolism – 'Dyahbolism' he called it, thereby making it sound the more fearful. I daresay that Beardsley, who always seemed to know by instinctive erudition all about everything, knew all about Dyahbolism. Anyhow, I could see that he with that stony commonsense which always came upmost when anyone canvassed the fantastic in him, thought Dyahbolism rather silly. He was too polite not to go on saying at intervals, in his hard, quick voice, 'Oh really? How perfectly entrancing!' and 'Oh really? How perfectly sweet!' But, had I been Yeats, I would have dropped the subject sooner than he did.

At the other end of the table, Arthur Symons was talking of some foreign city, carrying in his waistcoat-pocket, as it were, the *genius loci*, anon to be embalmed in Pateresque prose. I forget whether this time it was Rome or Seville or Moscow or what; but I remember that the hostess said she had never been there. I liked Symons feigning some surprise at this, and for saying that she really ought to go. Presently I heard him saying he thought the nomadic life was the best of all lives for an artist. Yeats, in a pause of his own music, heard this too, and seemed a little pained by it. Shaking back the lock from his brow, he turned to Symons and declared that an artist worked best among his own folk and in the land of his fathers. Symons seemed rather daunted, but he stuck to his point. He argued that new sights and sounds and odours braced the whole intelligence of a man and quickened his powers of creation. Yeats, gently but firmly, would have none of this. His own arguments may not have been better than Symons's; but, in voice and manner and countenance, Symons was no match for him at all. And it was with an humane impulse that the hostess interposed. 'Mr Symons', she said, 'is like myself. He likes a little change.' This bathos was so sharp that it was like an actual and visible chasm: one could have sworn to a glimpse of Symons' heels, a faint cry, a thud. Yeats stood for an instant on the brink, stroking his chin enigmatically, and then turned to resume the dropped thread of Dyahbolism. I could not help wishing that he, not poor Symons, had been the victim. He would somehow have fallen on his feet: and his voice, issuing uninterruptedly from the depth of the chasm, would have been as impressive as ever.[85]

VI

The *Savoy*, like Florence Farr's idea of the theatre, found self-validation in unpopularity with 'the public'; Symons's editorial in the second number on 25 April judged the initial reception 'flattering because it has been for the most part unfavourable'. This appealed to WBY; so, perhaps, did Havelock Ellis's major essays on Nietzsche, the first of which now appeared, stressing his parallels with Blake, his attacks on perceived morality, and discussing the Greeks' pursuit of unity in style as a hallmark of culture. All these ideas would be taken up by WBY. His own work was represented by a short story, 'Rosa Alchemica', summing up the theme of 'Moods' which dominates his work at this time. He was putting the finishing touches to the collection which would appear the next year as *The Secret Rose*; his fiction was becoming more integrated and coherent, centred around occultism and folklore, using *alter egos*, recurrent themes and even names.[86] To his delight, in late February Henry Davray, a friend of several Rhymers, had approached him about translation into

French.[87] Already a secondary literature was appearing about the Celtic Revival; in 1894 W. P. Ryan had published (independently in Dulwich) *The Irish Literary Revival: Its History, Pioneers and Possibilities*, attempting to detach the movement from the Yeatsian bandwagon, reassert its origins in the Southwark Irish Literary Club, and restore a political angle. But through the *Savoy* and his *Bookman* reviews, as well as the success of *Poems*, WBY effortlessly possessed the ear of literary London, and could put his own stamp on the past. In May 1896, reviewing Lady Ferguson's biography of Sir Samuel, he was able to look back 'twelve years ago' to his youthful response to Ferguson; and he stressed that though a Unionist, Ferguson had been accounted by John O'Leary 'a better patriot than himself' because his writing was rooted in Irish character and Irish history. Thus Ferguson transcended his background, that of establishment Dublin, which resembled 'that fabled stony city of Arabia'.[88] The parallel with WBY himself was clearly implied.

At thirty he was at last coming in to his own. A year before, he had carefully explained to Tynan the point at which a writer's reputation attracted satirical attack, and the way it could transcend such adversity through reaching a general public. Around the same time he confided to Fisher Unwin that he had reached the stage where having his work selected for anthologies was no longer a help.[89] He was about to negotiate a substantial advance for his fiction. His plan, he told Joseph Quinn, was 'to return to Ireland to live in about two years, as that time will about see the end of my present mass of work'. This sense of viewing his work as a developing whole is borne out by a letter to Davray in March. While lofty about his biography ('I never keep articles about myself'), he recommended several review articles on his poetry and plays – particularly John McGrath in *United Ireland*,

the most important Irish article on my work . . . he says that my criticism & speaches have made 'a revolution in Irish literary taste' – I think this is his phrase. You must excuse the egotism of this quotation; but the article pleased me, because I have worked in Ireland for a long time to check the rhetorical writing which our political necessities have developed & to persuade our own not very well educated Irish public to accept literature as literature, & not as partly disguised politics.[90]

Meanwhile, he was moving from Ireland: sending to Dublin for the few belongings he had kept there and searching for cheap furniture in London. The destination was a set of rooms on one floor of 18 Woburn Buildings, an atmospheric but dingy court near Euston Station and the British Museum, now called Woburn Walk. WBY found it through Symons's charlady, the resourceful Mrs Old, who came in to work for him from Islington and whose husband held the lease. He paid Symons £3 for the basic necessities which accompanied him: a bedstead, mattress, bolster and pillow, a table, seven

PLATE I

Above, left: John Butler Yeats just before his marriage, 1863 – still a student of law.

Above, right: Susan Pollexfen Yeats as a young married woman, *c.* 1873.

Left: WBY as a baby, drawn by his father. 'I think your birth was the first great event in my life . . . I was for the first time – I suppose – pure animal. I never felt like that afterwards at the birth of the others.'

PLATE 2

Above: WBY as a child, Sligo, *c*. 1873.

Facing, above: The older Yeats generation at Sandymount Castle, Robert Corbet's house in the Dublin suburbs, *c*. 1860. From left to right: JBY's sisters Grace Yeats, Mary Wise (born Yeats), and Jenny Yeats; Robert Wise and Michael (the man-servant), in doorway; Uncle Robert Corbet, sitting to right of door; a Beatty cousin, standing; another sister, Ellen Yeats, sitting beside Corbet; JBY's brother, Isaac Yeats, on the ground. The flag on the turret was flown when Corbet was in residence.

Facing, below: The Pollexfen house, Merville, as it was when the Yeats children stayed there. This contemporary photograph conceals the basement level, and the extensive outbuildings behind, but it was not grand: in Lily's words, 'a solid house, big rooms – about 14 bedrooms, stone kitchen offices & a glorious laundry smelling of soap full of white steam & a clean coke fire with rows of irons heating at it . . . 60 acres of land round it – a very fine view of Ben Bulben.'

PLATE 4

PLATE 5

ve, left: JBY, *c.* 1875, when he had embraced the
of an insecure artist.

ve, right: George Pollexfen, *c.* 1906

ing, above: Sligo Harbour in the later nineteenth
tury; the Pollexfen fortunes were based on
mers like the one surrounded by older rigged
s.

ing, below: The Middleton & Pollexfen mills on
river at Ballisodare, outside Sligo.

PLATE 6

Above: Sketches made by the Yeats children at Branscombe, Devon, on a rare family holiday in the summer of 1879: WBY's is on the right. The children had begged for black paint but JBY disapproved of it on artistic grounds.

Left: WBY about nine years old, sketched by his father.

PLATE 7

Above, left: WBY about twenty, still bearded and not yet in his poet's 'uniform'.

Above, right: Jack Yeats, *c.* 1900.

Left: George Russell ('AE') in 1890, about five years after he first met WBY.

PLATE 8

PLATE 9

Above: Lily and Lolly in the early 1890s.

Right: WBY painted as the mad 'King Goll' by his father, reproduced in the *Leisure Hour*, September 1887. In later years WBY regarded this picture as 'a pathetic memory of a really dreadful time'.

Left: 3 Blenheim Road, the Yeats home in Bedford Park.

PLATE 10

Above: Maud Gonne aged twenty-three in 1889, the year WBY met her.

Left: Gonne, *c.* 1890–92, perhaps after the death of her first child in August 1891.

Facing: WBY in the early 1890s, probably with John Todhunter at the Irish Literary Society (London). By now the characteristic sartorial style has been assumed: black velvet coat, exaggerated tie, cigarette, beribboned pince-nez.

PLATE II

PLATE 12

Above: WBY in 1894, probably in the garden at Blenheim Road.

Left: Samuel Liddell MacGreg Mathers, self-proclaimed Com de Glenstrae.

Facing, above: Farr's niece Dorc Paget in *The Land of Heart's Desire*, from the *Sketch*, 25 Apri 1894.

Facing, below: Florence Farr, around the time of her success *A Sicilian Idyll* and *Arms and th Man*.

PLATE 13

PLATE 14

Above: The sisters Constance (later Markievicz) and Eva Gore-Booth in the early 1890s, at the time WBY first met them.

Left: Arthur Symons in 1896, around the time WBY shared rooms with him in the Temple.

PLATE 15

Above: WBY in his study, as in the *Tatler*, 29 June 1904: conclusive evidence of how fashionable Irish things had become. *Where There is Nothing* had just been played in London, and an important exhibition by Irish painters had opened at the Guildhall. Identifiable objects in the room include a death-mask of Dante, Blake engravings, and books on mysticism and magic.

Right: Woburn Buildings, drawn by R. Schurabe. WBY's study was the room with the large window directly above the cobbler's shop.

PLATE 16

Olivia Shakespear in the *Literary Yearbook*
(1897), at the time her affair with WBY was
coming to an end. It was accompanied by a
profile (she had recently published her novel
Beauty's Hour). WBY was given similar treat-
ment in the same issue.

pieces of tapestry canvas, two pieces of plushette, and two blankets.[91] There cannot have been room for much more. He was in possession of a large, low sitting-room 'looking on a raised flagged pavement where no traffic can come – & the bedroom, very small & draughty, looks out on St Pancras Church with its caryatids & trees'.[92] Dorothy Richardson, who moved in across the court eight years later, thought the narrow houses 'retained something of an ancient dignity, and, with the faded painted ceilings of their main rooms, a touch of a former splendour';[93] but they had come down in the world. Like the Temple, Woburn Buildings provided an off-beat style at minimum cost: but the social atmosphere was very different. The attic room above, which wby would later take over, was inhabited by a pedlar; below him was an aged cobbler; opposite, a stonemason. A blind beggar was on permanent station outside, selling matches and bootlaces. All that was missing, as wby remarked, was a pawnshop.

Richardson used to watch his long daily conversations with the cobbler on his way out of the house: 'the two stood obviously in an equality of communication, discussing, agreeing, disagreeing, never at a loss and frequently amused, usually parting in laughter'. Appropriately, wby brought to the Buildings a certain Irish sociability. In late February he wrote to Rhys, 'henceforth I mean to be at-home on Monday evening. Please help me to start by coming next Monday with Mrs Rhys – Any time after 8 – I am asking Symons & one or two others. Tea & whisky & no dress.'[94] His account-books indicate that Benedictine soon replaced the whiskey, but otherwise it continued as intended. Richardson used to watch these gatherings from her opposite window, 'shadowy forms seated in high-backed antique chairs or standing clear in the window-space . . . chiefly being talked to by the tall presiding figure, visible now here, now there, always in speech'. This habit of a regular 'evening', like Mallarmé's Tuesdays or Dowden's Sundays, had begun in Bedford Park; in Woburn Buildings, however, he could entertain on his own terms, if not elegantly. Years later, he was still offending the fastidious aesthetes Ricketts and Shannon by the plebeian style of his table: 'the plates of soup plumped down – the chops with a knife and fork plumped down, potatoes in the middle of the table, then pastry, and then a portion of cheese all set down like an inventory before the guests'.[95] But to be able to entertain at all, to live alone on his precarious income, to have gained an independent purchase in literary London, represented a symbolic victory. Its extent – and cost – remained known to few.

Chapter 7 : WAITING FOR THE MILLENNIUM
1896–1898

> People should be asked to support the Irish Literary Theatre
> on patriotic grounds, but they should first be made to feal that
> there is an actual school of Irish spiritual thought in literature
> & that their patriotism will support this. Ireland is leading the
> way in a war on materialism, decadence, triviality as well as
> affirming her own individuality. That is our case.
>
> WBY to T. P. Gill, 13 November [1898]

I

THE interrogative tone of WBY's poetry has often been noted; less obvious, but more biographically illuminating, is the way he used fiction to ask questions about his own personality and life. This was most marked from 1896 to 1897, when he embarked upon a long novel and published a collection of short stories, both reflecting his own recent experience. And, like many of his contemporaries, he constructed literary *alter egos* to express different facets of his personality. From his fiction of the 1890s emerge the outlines of two basic characters, Michael Robartes and Owen Aherne. The names, which themselves took some time to evolve, are neither English nor completely Gaelic, but suggest 'Old English' – the term used for descendants of the Norman settlements, who had often intermarried with Gaelic stock and retained the Catholic faith. 'Irish' credentials, and the people's religion, were combined with gentle descent. 'Hearne' (a name with nationalist as well as occult associations) would come to have a special resonance for WBY, eventually attaching to the hero of his autobiographical novel.[1] A third *doppelgänger*, the poet Red Hanrahan, was more unequivocally Gaelic (and more specifically based on the eighteenth-century poet Eoghan Rua Ó Súilleabháin), but Robartes and Aherne expressed aspects of WBY's own ambiguous tradition and preoccupations. Robartes, inspired by both Mathers and Russell,[2] appears in WBY's stories as a fanatical searcher after occult truth. Aherne, more cautious and undecided, represented another kind of seeker for supernatural wisdom, probably based on Lionel Johnson. And from 1896 to 1897, the idea that such a quest was near its goal was much in WBY's mind.

The concept of millennialism was widely prevalent in his circle. Blavatsky had prophesied that the world would pass from a cycle of materialism into a cycle of spiritual growth some time in 1897. Russell was fervently attached to this idea, as were the Matherses, and WBY was affected by it too. Paris as well as London was full of tiny occult societies, arguing frantically about the advent of a New Age. From the early 1890s he had been preoccupied by prophecy, partly as a way of anticipating his future with Maud Gonne, whom he apostrophized as an avatar of the coming spiritual era.[3] Forty years later, he would put *The Celtic Twilight* firmly in this context: 'a bit of ornamental trivial needlework sewn on a prophetic fury got by Blake and Boeheme'.[4] If one note dominates his work in the later 1890s, it is apocalypse: the stars disrupted in their courses. And from early 1896 Russell was bombarding him with calls to immerse himself in the world of Celtic supernaturalism (and reconstruct the old hermetic fellowship of himself, Russell, Johnston and Weekes): Ireland's special idealism must be forged into a new world order for the dawning century.[5]

In London WBY could retain a certain distance, though at this time (March 1896) he began his long occult correspondence with the illustrator W. T. Horton. Horton, edgy and manic, was nervously attracted to the Golden Dawn and to WBY; he made desperate sorties up from Brighton to discuss invocations and rituals before bolting away from commitment to the Order. He also attempted to interest WBY in Thomas Lake Harris's Brotherhood of the New Life, a sexually obsessed group of Utopians. Horton continued to receive instructions from WBY at his most hieratic ('the intellect must do its utmost before inspiration is possible. It clears the rubbish from the mouth of the sybils cave but it is not the sybil'), and obligingly sent WBY accounts of visions which indicate how the poet appeared to his more dazzled English acquaintances ('I know you'll take it in the right spirit'):

It is night.

Yeats – naked and gaunt, with long black dishevelled hair falling partly over the face of a deathly whiteness, with eyes that flame yet have within them depths of unutterable sadness.

He is wearily going on his way following many lights that dance in front and at side of him.

Behind follows with outstretched arms a lovely girl in long trailing white garments, weeping.

Within Yeats a knocking is heard & a voice 'My son, my son, open thou unto me & I will give thee Light.'[6]

Horton constantly attempted to lure him down to Brighton, but WBY was ruthlessly prolific with excuses; and though he obtained a 'not very good' horoscope from George Pollexfen for Horton,[7] he was used by WBY as a butt for his more sceptical friends ('a mad artist . . . [who] comes from time to time & I talk to him like a father . . . a kind of turbid Russell only he sees nightmares instead of Gods').[8] None the less, he wrote an introduction for Horton's mystical *Book of Images*, published in 1898.

London occultism represented a different world from Russell's increasingly frenetic campaign for the return of the Gods to Ireland, but there were connections. Dorothea Hunter, a Golden Dawn initiate who had arrived there by the same route as WBY (Bedford Park and Theosophy), corresponded closely with him about rituals; her Irish background made her a suitable sounding-board for his developing ideas about a specifically Celtic form of occult inquiry. From her side there was more to it, since she was secretly in love with him, but their relationship remained mediated through magic alone.[9] His occult notebooks show that by December 1897, Golden Dawn members were attempting Celtic invocations, conducted by WBY. London life, Olivia Shakespear, contacts with publishers, Monday evenings at Woburn Buildings[10] provided a necessary detachment. Yet, through the spring of 1896, Russell's summonses became more and more impatient. 'What am I to understand? Am I to tell my men to go ahead? . . . Are your fixtures definite enough for that?' Visiting London to galvanize his dilatory friend, Russell was taken to tea at Olivia Shakespear's and decided her drawing-room in Porchester Square was infested with yellow devils. He was by now at a point of manic excitement where he had become convinced of the birth of an avatar for the New Age: he wrote excitedly to WBY, declaring categorically that 'the Gods have returned to Eri'. Schools must be set up to study the old beliefs, and a priesthood prepared to assume spiritual authority.

The mage of Woburn Buildings was more restrained, for good reasons. The affair with Shakespear provided one, though it would run its course by the following spring. His own contribution to the millennium currently lay in writing short fictions about the pursuit of old beliefs; from this point he was able to refuse commissions to write poems for the *Sketch* or produce short-order poetic biographies.[11] His rate by 1898 was £2 per thousand words. A series of articles on Blake for the *Savoy* enabled him to write to O'Leary repaying 'the money I have owed you for so long' (£6).[12] Most importantly, by the end of the year the publishers Lawrence & Bullen would purchase an unwritten novel for £105 – half to be paid in weekly instalments of £2 over six months, and half on publication.[13]

This project was well advanced by June 1896, when WBY told O'Leary, 'I shall pass through Dublin some time in August I beleive on my way to Tory Island where I go for local colour for a new story.' What took him to Ireland in the end was not Russell's blandishments, but his own conscious garnering of experience to turn into profitable fiction. Moreover, this would be a different kind of visit from previous sojourns, spent in obscure lodgings on Dublin's north side or living off sceptical Pollexfen relations at Sligo. For one thing, he was travelling with Arthur Symons, who was determined to be impressed by Celtic glamour. For another, their first destination after

Dublin was Tillyra (or Tullira) Castle in Galway, the home of Edward Martyn, where they arrived on 27 July. The castle was surprising enough: an exercise in Gothic medievalism grafted over the previous decade on to a medieval keep. Turrets, gargoyles, mullioned windows, stained glass and coats of arms were all brand-new; WBY's artistic eye flinched at the 'mechanical ornament'. However, the scale and vision of it all were undeniably impressive, especially since the owner lived monastically in an austere chamber, using the great hall only to play the organ.

Edward Martyn was himself a surprising combination of aesthete and ascetic. Though Irish, he was a contact of Symons rather than WBY: he had had rooms in the Temple in the 1880s, and was known in London salons. He was an old friend of George Moore (bound to each other, WBY later judged, 'by mutual contempt'), who probably sent Symons and WBY his way, and joined them at Tillyra on 5 August. But Martyn was also an early enthusiast for the Gaelic League, and WBY could have already met him through Hyde. The condescension of WBY's *Autobiographies*, and the inspired ridicule of George Moore, have guyed Martyn for posterity: moon-faced, obese, epicene, frantically Catholic, from an Old English family intermarried (according to WBY) with local peasant stock. In excised passages of his *Autobiographies*, WBY recorded that Martyn 'had learned from some priest that almost all lost souls were lost through sex', and speculated that his father's lechery emerged in Martyn as 'an always resisted homosexuality'.[14] Martyn's obsession with Palestrina's music and Gothic architecture, his violent aversion to the presence of women, his hair-splitting religious conscience, and his mother-dominated life immured in his cut-stone fortress lent themselves to malicious caricature. But he was also a talented minor playwright, who not only possessed financial means and enthusiasm, but was prepared to put them behind Irish cultural revival.

This connection would make WBY's visit memorable, though his preoccupations were determinedly other-worldly. Already excited by recent immersion in rituals and invocations, he threw himself at Tillyra into cabbalistic experiments and shared visions. *Faux*-medieval surroundings, millennial intuitions, recent reading, and Symons's expectant presence all combined to induce spectacular manifestations. Lunar invocations produced two separate visions, a centaur with a bow and the goddess Diana; these were conflated into the image of a marvellously beautiful woman archer shooting at a star. It was checked with Dr Westcott of the Golden Dawn, who provided an appropriate symbolic explanation. WBY believed it also echoed a short story of William Sharp's, 'The Archer', simultaneously written for the *Savoy*: but Sharp had taken the idea from a letter of WBY's describing the vision, hastily ran off a story, and announced it as a joint revelation.[15]

This kind of subterfuge was inseparable from Sharp's daily existence, which now began to intertwine with WBY's. In June he had written excitedly to Sharp about the need to further 'the mutual understanding and sympathy of the Scotch Welsh and Irish Celts'; this seemed about to happen. And Sharp's creative energies were now released by becoming a mouthpiece for the mysterious and invisible Celtic-visionary writer called 'Fiona Macleod', who struck a resonant chord with the current vogue for spiritual Celticism. Fiona, permanently *en route* to Hebridean islands or mountain crofts, communicated through Sharp in soulful letters as well as unearthly stories and essays. By August she was in close contact with WBY. Thus it was important to assure him that his 'Archer' vision was parallel to her own. 'In a vague way I realise that something of tremendous moment is being matured just now. We are on the verge of vitally important developments. And all the heart, all the brain of the Celtic races shall be stirred.'[16]

Installed in a castle, surrounded by admiring company, fired by the sense of a dawning age where his supernatural questions would be answered: WBY's sensibilities were honed to a fine edge by 5 August, when he and Symons set off with Martyn and Moore on an expedition to the Aran Islands. This was a great inspiration to Symons, who described it in one of his gushing

EDWARD MARTYN

"HAVING A WEEK OF IT" IN PARIS.

GRACE PLUNKETT

7. Grace Plunkett's cartoon caricaturing Edward Martyn's misogyny, aestheticism and figure; though published in 1920, it preserves the image he had already acquired when WBY met him in 1896.

'causeries' for the *Savoy*, and told Rhys that they were determined to return and spend a week ('I am getting a vast deal of all kinds of literary material'[17]). As they sailed out to Aran, wby read Fiona Macleod's *The Washer of the Ford*: 'and when I laid down the book, talked with an Arran [*sic*] fisherman of the very beliefs and legends that were its warp and woof'. On his return wby wrote excitedly to Sharp about fairy manifestations on Aran, and the 'new-old celtic mysticism'. Plans to return were obstructed by the weather, and he went on to Sligo instead. But the islands occupied a special place in his imagination, and in that of his generation. Like those of Greece or the southern Mediterranean in later years, they provided glimpses of a society and way of life whose rhythms and dignity suggested classical parallels to literary-minded visitors. (And, as with those later resorts, the *cognoscenti* who 'discovered' them resented later popularizers; the novelist Violet Martin, of Somerville and Ross fame, was annoyed when Symons revealed Aran's beauties to *Savoy* readers, and was relieved that the article was not illustrated.[18]) One particular exchange with an old islander held a long-lasting echo for wby: he was assured that if anyone came to the community for sanctuary, having killed a man, they would hide him. 'Which one – you or Symons – do you think they took for the murderer?' John Quinn asked straightfacedly in later years. 'Symons seemed a very mild-mannered man – they must have meant you.'[19]

Tillyra was not merely the base for romantic expeditions to Aran. Martyn's friends included exotic part-time Galway residents like the Duras-based Comte Florimond de Basterot (recluse, aesthete and disciple of the racial theorist Gobineau), as well as other local notables such as the Morris family at Spiddal – the acerbic Irish lawyer Lord Killanin and his lively children. The literary visitors made quite a stir. Martin Morris passed on his impressions of wby to Violet Martin, whose report to Edith Somerville economically conveys various layers of Ascendancy snobbery:

He is mad about his old legends and spirits, and if someone said 'Thims fine lobsters' or anything, he would begin 'There's a very curious tradition about lobsters' and then he was off. He is thinner than a lath – wears paltry little clothes wisped round his bones, and the prodigious and affected greenish tie. He is a little affected and knows it – He has a sense of humour and is a gentleman – hardly by birth I fancy – but by genius. Arthur Symons, who was here with him, was not much liked I think – just a smart little practical man of letters who knows how and has no genius at all.[20]

It was a new world to wby, and judging by his recollections decades later (in *Dramatis Personae*) his reaction to his host was rather ungracious. By then, he and Martyn had been sundered by an ancient disagreement; but there were other difficulties too. Oliver Gogarty put it robustly: 'Yeats hated Edward Martyn because he was a R. C. There was in Yeats, derived doubtless from his parson grandfather, a bigotry that probably could not have been discovered in the grand-parent but which brooded in Yeats. This, and of course the jealousy of the "household of continuance".'[21] This last point may have owed more to WBY's latter preoccupations that to his youthful self; *Dramatis Personae* would be written in order to associate WBY's ancestral stock with Irish gentry in a way that Moore and his friends could not aspire to. At the time of his visit, he described Martyn as the product of long descent from Crusader stock; but even in 1896 a certain condescension towards the Catholic family in their rebuilt Big House is discernible. Though Martyn later dropped out of WBY's life, he would continue to remain a butt in his correspondence – especially in his letters to another Galway notable, who was equally dismissive of her Tillyra neighbour, for much the same reasons.[22] She was Augusta Gregory, the widow of Martyn's neighbour, friend and patron Sir William Gregory of Coole. And her friendship with WBY would be much the most lasting and important result of that visionary Celtic summer.

II

In 1896 Augusta Gregory was forty-four, and had been widowed for four years. Born into a Galway county family, the Persses, she had married the much older William Gregory at the age of twenty-eight. From being 'on the shelf' in the philistine, horsy and hard-line Protestant world of Roxborough, she had moved to the Gregory milieu of retired colonial governors and liberal Tory politicians in London and 'abroad', with only temporary returns to his estate at Coole, buried amid plantations near Gort. Plain, decisive and masterful, she never lost a certain air of the evangelically minded county lady; but this was only one side of a complex personality. After her death an old Galway acquaintance, who as a young girl had known her well, wrote:

She was the most complicated woman I can think of . . . Loving – cold. Womanly – cold. Patriotic – cold. Very calculating, dutiful, courageous, purposeful, and all built upon a bedrock sense of humour and love of fun and a bitter sarcasm with a vein of simple coarseness of thought and simple inherited Protestantism.[23]

From childhood she had nurtured a romantic literary ambition, as well as an attraction towards romantic nationalism; as a young bride from 1881 to 1882 she had taken up the cause of the Egyptian rebels, defending Arabi Bey in a long pamphlet; and the prevalent tendency to describe her even in the 1890s as resembling Queen Victoria should be discounted. While her husband was still alive, she had had a passionate affair with the professional philanderer Wilfrid Scawen Blunt; local rumours persisted about the parentage of her only son, Robert, who arrived when Sir William was sixty-four.[24] By the time she met wby and Symons in 1896, she had already begun to write. After her husband's death in 1892 she had written to de Basterot:

As for myself, each day seems more sad and empty & I dare not look forward to the lonely years before me. I have Robert, but only his holidays and I shall miss more & more that bright many-sided compassionateness I appreciated so much. I have no plans. I am trying to get rid of my homes, but have no inclination towards any new one. I must sell this [London] house & if I can let Coole (where I cd not live alone except in summer) it wd be a relief to my income which I must make the most of for Robert's sake.[25]

But widowhood liberated her too. She had subsequently discovered, like many others, an interest in 'Celtic' folklore; when wby met her at Tillyra, she had begun to learn Irish. Within a year she would begin to publish articles on fairy traditions, folk-tales and language revival in the *Spectator*, *Nineteenth Century* and *Westminster Budget*, as well as in Irish outlets like the *Kilkenny Moderator* and Dublin *Daily Express*. Her rapid friendship with wby created suspicion among her old imperialist friends like Enid Layard; and her political views would (with characteristic independence) change throughout her life, tending more and more to separatist nationalism – a process eventually crystallized by the Black and Tan campaign of 1920 to 1921. In the 1880s she had opposed Home Rule, and as late as November 1898 she could privately confess her doubts about joining 'ruffians' like Michael Davitt, William O'Brien and Archbishop Walsh on the council of the Gaelic League; but, like wby, she had chafed under the dead hand of conservative Irish Protestant society and was conscious that change was afoot. As she later remarked, 'we are all born bigots in Ireland & want a great deal of grace to get us out of bondage'.[26] In an article for the *Cornhill*, May 1900, she finally (and cautiously) 'came out' as an Irish nationalist. She had found her role.

For wby, she provided access to local Galway tradition, through the Irish language but from a Big House perspective; it was a heady combination. Though mutually impatient with the constraints of their Unionist backgrounds, they shared a certain Irish Protestant solidarity, in cultural if not devotional terms (he never accompanied her to the local Church of Ireland at Gort, though other members of his family did[27]). Their meeting in August 1896, which she recorded in a retrospective diary entry a year later, was a landmark for them both.[28] They had actually met already, on 14 April 1894, at the London house of the Morrises; but from 1896 a long friendship was sealed. Arthur Symons, who did not like her, claimed to have spotted it from the start:

'La Strega' put her 'terrible eye' on WBY and he was lost to lyric poetry. He really meant that WBY was lost to Symons himself. An invitation was issued to Coole. Though the two poets did not stay there, travelling on to Sligo, staying with George Pollexfen at Rosses Point and then in a Glencar cottage where Symons poured out sub-Yeatsian poems during early September,[29] a vital connection had been made. WBY continued to commission horoscopes from Pollexfen, and organize collaborative visions with Golden Dawn members through the penny post. But friendship with Gregory would provide an Irish base to replace Sligo, and a mentor who would in many ways replace his family.

As with nearly all the women who meant something to him, their friendship quickly coalesced around an idea for collaborative work, in this case a large-scale survey of folklore and fairy-tale. It was initially conceived as a book but eventually took the form of six long essays by WBY, published between 1897 and 1902: Gregory provided much of the basic material and placed the second essay in the *Nineteenth Century*, a new outlet for WBY. The final instalment would be *Visions and Beliefs in the West of Ireland*, published by Gregory in 1920.[30] (As far as she was concerned, the substance of the earlier articles was as much hers as WBY's.[31]) As with his other collaborators, their mutual log-rolling became notorious.[32] Moreover, in exploring the mythological origins of folklore, WBY showed himself less and less chary of offending Catholic sensibilities. 'The Tribes of Danu', published in November 1897, aroused clerical criticism by dismissing the philistine aspects of modern Catholicism, and comparing the doctrine of transubstantiation with sighting fairies; a year later his generalizations about pagan beliefs among the Irish peasantry would be considered equally offensive. Remembering these experiences in old age, he recalled:

My object was to find actual experience of the supernatural, for I did not believe, nor do I now, that it is possible to discover in the text-books of the schools, in the manuals sold by religious booksellers, even in the subtle reverie of saints, the most violent force in history . . . when we passed the door of some peasant's cottage, we passed out of Europe as that word is understood. 'I have longed', she said once, 'to turn Catholic, that I might be nearer to the people, but you have taught me that paganism brings me nearer still.'[33]

But he learned from her as well. These long essays, offered around to publishers as they were written, derived from the local lore and idioms of the Gort area, and combined the folklore collected by Gregory and WBY with the insights of Max Müller, James Frazer and other writers on ancient religion. Many of the beliefs recorded were rationalizations of quotidian tragedies (infant mortality, mental disturbance), though this aspect was resolutely ignored by Gregory and WBY.[34] Her ability to talk to people was essential; language apart, he found it difficult to understand the local accent, and his stylish black clothes meant he was mistaken for a proselytizing clergyman.[35] She appealed to him, however, as far more than a collaborator, or a 'county' benefactor. Rather than a replacement or surrogate for his *distraite* mother or improvident father, she provided a satisfactory version of George Pollexfen. She flattered him with a shared language of caste (though occupying a higher niche in the Ascendancy structure than he did): 'the old battle between those who use a toothbrush and those who don't'.[36] With her knowledge of the world, Jamesian *aperçus*, and tendency to artistic lion-hunting, she provided a sophisticated sounding-board for analysing his complicated relationships with interesting people. While he encouraged her work, he may not have rated it as highly as he implied; certainly by the 1920s, when dividing his acquaintances into astrologically derived 'phases', he could put her under Phase 24 in the undemanding company of Queen Victoria and John Galsworthy. 'There is great humility – "she died every day she lived" – and pride as great, pride in the code's acceptance, an impersonal pride, as though one were to sign "servant of servants". There is no philosophic capacity, no intellectual curiosity.'[37]

How he appeared to her at the outset of their long relationship is more conjectural. His humour appealed: and WBY presented himself to her, through letters and anecdotes, in a feline and amusing way. His genius and charisma were electrifying. And so were his good looks. In his relationship with Gregory, as with many others (men as well as women), WBY used his gift for fascination to 'loan himself out'. He slipped easily into the fantasies of people as diverse as Horton, George Moore and Annie Horniman, rather like one of the succubi he read about in treatises on magic. But Gregory's firm grasp on reality meant that their friendship, unlike many others, never soured – though it may at the outset have rested on some unfulfilled hopes. Their relationship quickly stabilized into mentor and artist: while she addressed him as 'Willie', his letters to her remain to 'Lady Gregory'. The adherence to formality is surprising even for the time: yet they rapidly became each other's closest friend and confidant, and remained so – with only an occasional slight passage of annoyance – until her death nearly forty years later. Over that period, while she sustained him in many ways, he helped her to emerge as one of the most prominent Irish writers of the day. In identifying her so deliberately by her title rather than by her Christian name, he not only defined their relationship, he helped create the image and the name by which she would live, write and become famous.

Yet at first, in the later 1890s, her letters to him carried a certain tentative air of gaiety and romance. Given Gregory's capacity for affairs with younger men, Maud Gonne's malicious belief that she was in love with WBY may not have been far off the mark. For his part, he quickly confided in her about Gonne: possibly as a tactful form of warning. 'And then there is his love for Miss Gonne preying on him,' she recorded in her diary in November 1897. 'He fell in love with her ten years ago, & for 2 or 3 years it "broke up his life" he did nothing but write to her & see her & think of her – '[38] When she arranged that the *Nineteenth Century* take their second folklore article, she later resented that the money thus earned by WBY was squandered responding to a summons sent from Gonne in Belfast. 'There I had let him take my article to make the fifteen pounds to keep him in change, and he had gone off and spent it and "no purpose served, no object to be gained, no work to do".'[39] This was an inaccurate memory (and is all the more piquant as it was made to her own lover at the time), but the resentment is palpable. When Gregory finally met Gonne in December 1898, her reaction was revealing: 'a shock to me for instead of beauty I saw a death's head & what it says to him I know not'.[40] She rapidly assumed a proprietorial role in his life, with an accompanying right to disapprove, and he accepted it.

For the moment, in the summer of 1896, the contact had been made. And that winter would bring another influential friendship. Back in London by 13 October, WBY resumed the threads of his metropolitan life. He continued to work on his verse play *The Shadowy Waters*; and he also started to plan a visit to Paris. This was partly to gather material for his projected novel, whose advance payment helped to finance the journey; partly to follow up supernatural Celticism with Mathers; and partly to pursue Maud Gonne, who was planning Young Ireland Societies in the French capital. Olivia Shakespear, distracted by her father's death, was not much in London; WBY's thoughts were already elsewhere. By 30 November he was in Paris, staying first at the Hôtel Corneille opposite the Odéon Théâtre: a bohemian resort with Balzacian associations, favoured by O'Leary in exile (and Little Billee in *Trilby*[41]). Here he met a saturnine young fellow-Irishman, John Millington Synge.

Synge, like WBY, was a middle-class Irish Protestant (though his forebears were bishops rather than rectors, and the family retained some money and land); like WBY, he was an apprentice bohemian, setting out on a life as an artist, though at this stage music appealed to him as much as literature. Six years younger than WBY, he was in some ways more confident (a Trinity background, fluent French); their very similarity raised a prickle of mutual suspicion, never quite dispelled throughout the friendship. Synge was immune to WBY's variety of occultism, and suspicious of the extreme-nationalist cabals of Parisian Irish which WBY patronized in Gonne's wake. But during this French sojourn WBY and Gonne began to discuss the idea of putting on 'Celtic' plays, by the inevitable Fiona Macleod among others, to whom WBY wrote setting out his ideas about Symbolic drama. Synge was in the background throughout. As WBY remembered it later, he also instructed his fellow-Irishman to seek inspiration in the Aran Islands rather than in continental journeyings. Though Synge already knew about the islands from family connections there, WBY referred to him proprietorially as 'a new man – a TCD graduate – I have started in folklore'.[42] But Synge soon showed that he would go his own way.

However dependent Synge may or may not have been on WBY's advice, they became friends and stayed in touch. Meanwhile, WBY's own *cicerone* Symons arrived, and they attended the Théâtre de l'Œuvre's first production of Alfred Jarry's *Ubu Roi*: an anti-realist satire which none the less parodied Symbolist techniques as well. It was greeted with riots, and left WBY as disorientated as the rest of the audience; Symons's shrewd review concluded that *Ubu Roi* 'is the brutality out of which we have achieved civilisation'. WBY stayed on in Paris over Christmas, consulting Mathers about 'what might become a celtic magic',[43] but there were more mundane schemes afoot as well. In January he helped Gonne to found a Paris branch of the Young Ireland Societies (L'Association Irlandaise). A journal followed, *L'Irlande Libre*; so did the gossip, resentments and backstairs organization inseparable from *émigré* political intrigues. WBY's notion that the Paris Young Irelanders could form an advance-guard of the Celtic theatre movement came to nothing. But the involvement provided an overture to the turmoil of nationalist politicking into which she would draw him over the next year.

In all this activity, his affair with Shakespear had necessarily dropped into the background. Since July 1896 they had coincided in London for a mere six weeks (mid-October until late November); and after he returned from Paris in the second week of January 1897, Gonne followed in February. As his *Memoirs* recall, he was forced to admit his continuing obsession. At a tryst with Shakespear, 'instead of reading much love poetry, as my way was to bring the right mood round, I wrote letters. My friend found my mood did not answer hers and burst into tears. "There is some one else in your heart," she said. It was the breaking between us for many years.'[44] It is a painful passage, revealing more about the low voltage of WBY's sexual feeling for Shakespear than he had perhaps intended. As always, he viewed himself more clearly through the filtering lens of poetry. A year later he published 'Aodh to Dectora', later titled more revealingly 'The Lover mourns for the Loss of Love'.

> Pale brow, still hands, and dim hair,
> I had a beautiful friend,
> And dreamed that the old despair
> Might fade in love in the end:

> She looked in my heart one day,
> And saw your image was there,
> She has gone weeping away.

Shakespear's view may be reflected in a vision she described to WBY a few years later. He appeared as a Greek prisoner-poet teaching Platonic philosophy to his Persian captors. Otherwise, his main activity was to offer incense at the marble tomb of a beautiful woman

> & to lie long in trance communing with her who [was] buried there & my longing had almost made for her a living body . . . At last the Persian queen, who loved that man who was myself, became angry because of the woman in the tomb & because he . . . would have no living love & because he said that no living beauty was like that marble beauty, & she had him thrust into the tomb & fastened the door upon him for ever.[45]

Their separation marked the beginning of a protracted period of misery for WBY. Guilt at the failure of his affair with Shakespear, at his own sexual inadequacy, and possibly at his implicit relief that the liaison was over was compounded by despair at the unattainability of Gonne. Meanwhile, the turmoil of occult expectations did not decrease, and political intrigue festered in Dublin. He had two refuges. One was the attentive ear of his new friend from Coole, whom he saw frequently in London during that February. The other was the expression of his confusion in supernatural fiction.

III

In December 1896 WBY wrote to O'Leary: 'next week the novel begins'. It would not be abandoned until May 1903: 'an impossible novel . . . a novel that I could neither write nor cease to write'.[46] By February 1897 it had acquired a quintessentially ninetyish title, 'The Benizons of the Fixed Stars', changed the following year to 'The Lilies of the Lord'; *The Speckled Bird* emerged as a title only in 1902. He embarked upon it when his other eternal work-in-progress, *The Shadowy Waters*, was running into difficulties. Both projects closely reflected continuing themes in his life, notably the attempt to reconcile spiritual search and actual existence. From the first draft *The Speckled Bird* bore the marks of WBY's life in 1896. Its structure followed the axis from Paris to Aran which WBY prescribed to Synge; architectural detail was supplied by Tillyra (and eventually Corcomroe Abbey in Clare); the characters seek revelation through occult training, building a secret Order through trance and ritual, while the protagonist, Michael, caught in an impossible love, learns to abandon his old hope 'that one would be wisest when happiest'. Its theme was later described by WBY as 'the antagonism between the poet and the magician'; it tried to outline a reconciliation between religion, art and sexual love. As fiction (certainly as readable fiction) it was handicapped by WBY's firm belief that art was not a criticism of life but a revelation of the realities behind life.[47] But its theme was that embarked upon by Proust and Joyce in the same era: the boy set apart, by sensibility and experience, to be an artist. And the message was one familiar to those prospectors too. The artist should give up searching for 'happiness'; that was for ordinary people. *Axël*'s injunction to let one's servants do one's living resounded in the background.

The boy in WBY's planned novel is reared feudally in the far west of Ireland, and obsessed by the world of fairy; like John Sherman, he is an only child brought up by one parent (in this case his father). He progresses to an interest in occult ritual and invocation, and the pursuit of an inspirational love-object whose character is partly Maud Gonne's, but whose marital situation is Olivia Shakespear's. In the version written after 1901, the hero's experiences among London occultists are described satirically, in the tone WBY developed for his entertaining letters to Augusta Gregory; much later he would define his failed novel as an attempt to explore the various and confusing paths open to him at the *fin de siècle* ('the way of the chameleon'). The outline and first draft of 1896 to 1897 were less coherent. As originally conceived, it began in the Aran Islands; the draft written from 1897 to 1898 shifted to western Connacht. A still later version would incorporate elements from Golden Dawn controversies and Maud Gonne's secret life. But even in its first draft the transpositions from WBY's own experiences were obvious. The hero's eccentric father was called John, like WBY's; the son was called Michael, the name he would give to both Robartes and his own son; the mother was dead. (The Sligo name 'Bruen' also occurs.[48]) 'Michael' (first De Burgh, then Leroy, finally Hearne) is marked for special destiny by family background, eccentric education, mystical vision and genius.

The draft outline of 1896 is revealing about his creator's view of his own life. 'He takes a mistress. She soon begins to weary him. Hitherto he has known, with increasing intensity, the persecution of sex, but its satisfaction ends the glamour as well as the satisfaction for a time.' If this derives from his experience with Shakespear, 'Margaret' indicates WBY's vision of Gonne. She possesses a legendary, 'lonely' type of beauty, inaccessible to the common taste; 'a face that could only have been moulded out of a passionate ancestry', but a nature marked by kindness and self-sacrifice rather than passion; she is a 'pilgrim' (brought up, like Gonne, peripatetically) who transcends common love. No attempt was made to capture Gonne's romantic and powerful personality; Margaret remains a vision without a character. In both early versions she is introduced as a child, a persona WBY would often associate with Gonne. In the second version she is also the hero's first cousin. Physically, she and Shakespear provided the template for Michael's and WBY's idealized and legendary women: 'Grania with her fair hair and her grey eyes and her flesh like an apple blossom, and Deirdre with heavy and dark hair and pale ivory skin and eyes full of compassion.'[49] In the draft of 1897 to 1898, called 'The Lilies of the Lord', she is linked to the Virgin: this includes passages of hectic and fervent Mariolatry, marking the high point of WBY's rejection of his Protestant background and wish to identify with 'the people'. The drafts of 1896 to 1898 included nothing beyond Michael's childhood; but a cancelled passage indicates that (again like Proust and Joyce) WBY believed that an artist's childhood profoundly predicted his later life. 'Children live a fantastic life, in which there is everything except human love and human pity and human regret. They weep, like geniuses, tears upon tears for some dead Orpheus of whom they have dreamt and pass with wondering indifference, like geniuses, among the sorrows of their own household.'[50]

WBY's life during these years was also transmuted into fiction (though more alchemically) in the occult stories which he published in the *National Observer* and elsewhere from the early 1890s and which came together as *The Secret Rose* in 1897. Some dated back to the weeks when he had shared O'Leary's North Circular Road lodgings; later stories, like 'Rosa Alchemica', were written (so he said) 'when I had left Dublin in despondency'.[51] The variation in literary achievement is considerable, though he tried to remove some of the more laborious and stilted effects in a frenzy of last-minute proof corrections. The themes are more consistent. Using frameworks derived from his reviewing and reading during the 1890s (notably the collections of Lady Wilde, Jeremiah Curtin, William Larminie and Hyde), he pursued the old theme of the 'war of the spiritual with the natural order'; 'all the history of various quests for the ideal & very phantastic', he told Davray.[52] Much of the *mise-en-scène* seems inspired by the Parisian prophetic and millennialist fringe culture which so affected Huysmans, Mallarmé and Villiers. WBY (who had read his Golden Dawn friend A. E. Waite's work on Luciferianism in France) wanted to parade 'all the modern visionary sects' before the reader, like the temptations of Saint Anthony.[53] He was already determined to historicize his own era for posterity. The symbolic cover by Althea Gyles and dedication to AE stressed their old alliance in mystic quests, but the stories also used the interest in folktale images which his friendship with Gregory had revived. The scale of his revisions constantly delayed publication (and rewriting would continue through many new editions). He was attempting to unite so many different occult preoccupations that his priorities shifted constantly between one secret tradition and another.

Accordingly, indecision dogged the collection. A. H. Bullen, the publisher, rejected two stories ('The Tables of the Law' and 'The Adoration of the Magi'), then changed his mind and printed them separately; but not before the original pattern of the volume had been spoiled. WBY had wanted to end with 'The Adoration of the Magi', whose theme of a religious annunci-ation relayed through a dying prostitute in a Paris brothel was too blasphemous, as well as too Decadent, for Bullen's nerve. The story used what would become one of WBY's favourite quotations, Mallarmé's remark that his generation saw the trembling of the veil of the temple; it brings together millennialism, sexual decadence and the search for wisdom in a quintessentially Yeatsian way. As *The Secret Rose* was published, however, the final story was just as emblematic. The opening passage of 'Rosa Alchemica' raises the question of how far a 'sympathy' for the occult is 'but the sympathy of the artist, which is half pity, for everything which has moved men's hearts in any age'. Michael Robartes's frantic search for occult knowledge is observed by the detached, studious, essentially impotent figure of Owen Aherne, who has tried the priest-hood, political revolution, alchemy, and found all wanting. Finally convinced to follow Robartes into an occult Order, Aherne journeys with him to an ancient house on the west coast of Ireland (like de Basterot's): amid symbolic peacocks, starry heavens and spears, visions are induced through 'incense' and dancing. The would-be illuminati finally awake to angry attacks from the outraged local fisher-folk. Aherne escapes and takes refuge in a devout and unthinking Catholicism (or, looked at another way, in doctrines of transfer-ence and supererogation).

This and other stories echoed Huysmans's preoccupation with the close relationship between 'the supernatural of evil and the supernatural of good', transposed to Ireland – and even to Irish history. WBY had read Ernest Renan on the connection between Celticism and the New Age: in the chronology of *The Secret Rose*, medieval searchers give way to Elizabethan wood-kerne, and then eighteenth-century poets ('Red Hanrahan') before ending with 'Rosa Alchemica', which deals with (vaguely) contemporary times. Aherne represents WBY's inclination to choose religious authority, but also his attrac-tion to the heresy attributed to the twelfth-century prophet Joachim of Fiore. Taught by Symons, Pater, Lionel Johnson and Renan (in translation), WBY knew that Joachim prophesied a New Age, or Third Reign of Heaven on Earth. Through Aherne, WBY adapted Joachim's ideas to claim the existence of 'Children of the Holy Spirit', whose work is 'to reveal that hidden substance of God which is colour and music'. This chimed with Blake's vision: the 'Children of the Holy Spirit' may stand for poets at large, for whom – in the antinomian tradition of the visionary sects – divine inspiration enables a self-made morality. Here, as elsewhere at this time, an echo of Nietzsche sounds through, probably derived from Havelock Ellis's *Savoy* articles. And an important group of stories in *The Secret Rose* (later comprehensively rewritten from 1902 to 1903 and published separately) concerns Red Hanrahan, a passionate poet, lover and seer. Hanrahan, besides supplying another *alter ego* for WBY, was inspired by actual eighteenth-century Gaelic poets like Eoghan Rua Ó Súilleabháin, who had achieved legendary reputations. WBY was effectively creating his own folklore.[54]

For all their emphasis on religious heresy and illuminati traditions, the stories deal with the choices of the artist. Aherne echoes Lionel Johnson's refuge in erudition and Catholicism; Robartes follows Russell's and WBY's search for enlightenment through vision. The terrain – Dublin, Paris, the west of Ireland – is that traversed by WBY himself in these years; the influences – Luciferianism, the apocalypse, the Cabbala, Rosicrucianism – echo writers like Huysmans whom he had encountered through Symons. Moreover, Blake had taught him that 'all art is a labour to bring again the golden age'.[55] Revelation is sought, in a milieu dominated by symbols and innocent of humour. Art is seen as spiritual transmutation, achieved through visions with a strong application of Celticist top-dressing (a formula rapidly and efficiently plagiarized by Fiona Macleod). In later revisions the peasantry become progressively less idealized.[56] And it is possible to place these stories in the distinctive Irish Protestant supernatural tradition of Maturin and Le Fanu, where uneasy Anglo-Irish inheritors are caught between the threatening superstructure of Catholicism, and recourse to more demonic forces still, against a wild landscape which they have never fully possessed.

The Secret Rose reflects another arcane subculture too: it was no accident that the language was by turns narcotic and hallucinogenic. WBY had learnt to take hashish with the shady followers of the mystic Louis Claude de Saint-Martin in Paris, and with Davray and Symons the previous December.[57] In April 1897 he experimented with mescal, supplied by Havelock Ellis, who recorded that 'while an excellent subject for visions, and very familiar with various vision-producing drugs and processes', WBY found the effect on his breathing unpleasant; 'he much prefers haschish', which he continued to take in tablets, a particularly potent form of ingestion.[58] The stories in *The Secret Rose* grow out of the underworld of the *Savoy* as well as the disciplines of supernatural study.

Reactions to the collection were ambivalent; drug-taking apart, WBY's conjunction of Irish 'paganism', occultism and spirituality was not universally popular.[59] He wrote defensively to O'Leary: 'The book has on the whole been very well received . . . It is at any rate an honest attempt towards that aristocratic esetoric Irish literature, which has been my chief ambition. We have a literature for the people but nothing yet for the few.'[60] The question of an elite audience would preoccupy him more and more; in the end, he would find it not through fiction but poetry, and most of all drama.

IV

Theatrical enterprise would dominate his ideas by the summer; already in the spring of 1897 his frequent conversations with Gregory took up this theme, and she recorded in February his idea for a school of 'romantic drama' presenting work by O'Grady, Macleod and himself. Her diary indicates that he was becoming increasingly reliant on her. His income had dropped back after the 1896 injections from the *Savoy* and his novel advances, and he recorded in his *Autobiographies* that she began early on to lend him money so that he need not rely on a journalistic income. She wintered in London and he dined repeatedly with her at Queen Anne's Mansions, where she proudly showed off 'my young countryman' to her literary acquaintances.[61] She also listened to his troubles about Gonne, now back in his life since her February visit: he appears not to have confided about Shakespear, perhaps because that collapsing affair showed him in a more ignominious (and adulterous) light. His presentation of Gonne to Gregory unleashed a certain frustration and irritation, which may have been the obverse of idealization (as when he remarked that Gonne could be 'locked up as mad' if the true extent of her visionary faith were known). From the beginning of their relationship, the politics he supported in Gregory's company differed from those he embraced while with Gonne. On 21 March 1897, dining with Gregory, Barry O'Brien and the co-operativist and social reformer Horace Plunkett (who was still a Unionist), he pressed the latter to emerge as Parnell's successor, by endorsing a strong measure of local government.[62] This represented the language and expectations of moderate Home Rule and establishment politics. Yet when Gonne summoned him he could adapt to different company. At this very time she had drawn him back into the circles of extreme Dublin nationalism; this was, he told his new friend and admirer, the poet Robert Bridges, 'an absurd crusade among absurd people'.[63] He would always emend his presentation of Irish politics depending on the sympathy of his audience (and Bridges had no interest at all). WBY would none the less emerge not only as President of the 1898 Centennial Association of Great Britain and France, but of the Wolfe Tone Memorial Association. Both organizations were inspired by the memory of the 1798 Rising, and carried coded references to revolution in the present: initiating, among other developments, the cult of Tone and the practice of commemorative visits to his grave at Bodenstown.

In April WBY helped Gonne overcome nationalist suspicion and arrange a fundraising tour in America. This precipitated the kind of intrigues and enmities inseparable from Clan na Gael (the American Fenian organization), as well as a struggle between the Dublin Centenary Committee and the body chaired by WBY in London.[64] From this point he supported the idea of turning the Centenary movement into a permanent 'Convention', set up as a sort of alternative parliament and controlling delegations to Westminster. This was at once a neo-Fenian attempt to hijack the Irish Parliamentary Party and a revival of the 'withdrawal' technique urged on Parnell in the early 1880s. The millennium was apparently expected in political as in spiritual affairs. Later, WBY remembered that he adopted this idea in order to cut out 'some wild Fenian movement'; at the time it looked like wild Fenianism, though not quite wild enough for Gonne. But his position in political organization, part time and ambivalent, could not be decisively influential. For his part, he exercised more direct power over her through his developing idea of a mystical Celtic Order. As often before, misery in his personal life was combated by asserting his authority in an organization which he could dominate. The materials for a Celtic Order were ready to hand: not only Russell's permanently primed spiritual fervour, boosted by the apocalyptic poems written by WBY in 1897,[65] but the influence of Fiona Macleod. Sharp himself still aroused feelings of ambivalence; later that year WBY vetoed his chairmanship of an Irish Literary Society meeting, as it 'would bring ridicule on the whole movement'.[66] But Fiona was different. WBY had compared her to the French Symbolists for the *Bookman*, and praised her in Gonne's *L'Irlande Libre*; Sharp/Macleod wrote about WBY for the *North American Review* and corresponded excitedly about psychic experimentation. The pressure of this frenetic ventriloquism propelled Sharp into a nervous collapse later in 1897, but WBY moved implacably on. After the publication of *The Secret Rose* he escaped to Ireland. He visited Standish O'Grady in Dublin, encouraging him to return to the story of Cuchulain and market it as effectively as Fiona Macleod; by mid-May he was at Rosses Point with George Pollexfen, whose inflexible bachelor routines ironed out irregularities 'as a mangle does clothes'.[67] WBY set himself to working on occult symbols in Celtic mythology and firmly refused to become involved in public speaking, telling Alice Milligan, 'I have managed to reduce my life into perfect order & am getting a little work done . . . if I speak on politics anywhere I will introduce a stream of alien ideas into my mind which will spoil my work.'[68]

But Gonne's involvement in counter-demonstrations against the royal Jubilee dragged him to Dublin: here, she had temporarily joined forces with James Connolly's Irish Socialist Republican Party, probably not realizing that its socialist identification (at this stage) outweighed its republicanism. The charismatic and brilliant Connolly had emerged from the slums of Irish Edinburgh to bring the Marxist gospel to the Irish labour movement; a gifted writer and polemicist, he had already become a key figure in the radicalization of Irish labour politics. Gonne joined his tiny party in January 1897; in June she took a leading part in its preparations to mount anti-Jubilee demonstrations. Anti-socialist though she was, she addressed her first Dublin public meeting under Connolly's auspices on 21 June, attacking the 'Irish mercenaries, prison cells and hangmen' who made the British imperial system possible; she called for a mass demonstration against the royal Jubilee the next evening. On 22 June she and Connolly duly headed a protest procession headed by a black hearse. This provoked accompanying riots, window-smashing and stone-throwing: finally there was a police baton charge, after which 200 people were treated for injuries and one woman subsequently died.[69] WBY was at Gonne's side. He later remembered being torn between admiration for her and fears for her safety; he insisted they remain in the National Club during the police charge, to her fury. His account to Sharp a week later conveys his defensiveness and uncertainty:

I got a letter from Miss Gonne saying that she wanted me to help her in some political negociations in Dublin & I had to start off in a hurry & when there got envolved in the processions & riots which have been going on there. It was fortunate that I went as I was able by main force to keep Miss Gonne out of a riot in which one woman was killed. Miss Gonne had organised the processions & felt responsible & thought that she should be among the people when the police attacked them. She was very indignant at my interference. I refused to let her leave the National Club. She showed a magnificent courage through the whole thing. I dislike riots, & knew that a riot was inevitable, & went into the matter simply to try & keep her out of harms way. She is now the idol of the mob & deserves to be.[70]

He also wrote to Gonne, and her reply, while affirming their friendship, accused him of making her do 'the most cowardly thing I have ever done in my life'. Even more painfully, she told him their destinies were different; he should not involve himself in 'the *outer* side of politics', while she was 'born to be in the midst of a crowd'. 'It is therefore impossible for us ever to do any work together where there is likely to be excitement or physical danger.'[71] More bitter still, all her admiration after the event was for Connolly, who was 'the only man who had the courage' to 'save Dublin from the humiliation of an English jubilee without a public meeting of protestation'.[72] She then retired to Aix-les-Bains to recuperate.

WBY fled in a different direction: to Tillyra, where Gregory found him 'white, haggard, voiceless', longing for peace to 'think & write & forget brawls'. By the end of the month he was 'getting an odd lyric written', thus delaying his projected new collection (*The Wind Among the Reeds*) yet further. But, troubled by his eyesight and obsessed by this apparent inadequacy in anything to do with Gonne, he was at a low point when, after a week or so back in Rosses Point, he and Russell arrived on 27 July to stay with Gregory at Coole.

WBY had visited briefly the year before, but the summer of 1897 was his first real immersion in what would become the centre of his Irish life. 'I found at

last what I had been seeking always, a life of order and of labour.'[73] Driving
to the small Georgian mansion up its long avenue past woods and lakes, he
felt he had found sanctuary: he would tell John Masefield that it was to him
'the most beautiful place in the world',[74] thus displacing Sligo. Paths through
woods led down to a mysterious lake; a great walled garden was set with clas-
sical statuary and rare trees. He had always believed that a 'change of sur-
roundings is necessary to give new ideas';[75] the less dramatic, more 'civil'
landscape of Coole would henceforth provide (as Sligo once did) the place
where he could write poetry. On his first visit, he later recalled, he did little
work – and then discovered that this was a disappointment to his hostess.[76]
By the following summer, when he was again at Coole, a routine had been
established and Russell could write to Gregory: 'he ought to be locked in
his room with a certain amount of work to be done or he ought not to get
dinner until he has produced a specified number of lines every day'.[77] This
reflected Russell's own facility (by no means an unmixed blessing). But WBY's
standard rate at this time was about half a dozen lines a day, produced with
racking effort. The point was, as he put it more than once, to treat the cre-
ation of those five or six lines as hard labour, redrafting them until he could
bear no more; the process passionately outlined in his poem 'Adam's Curse'[78]
seems to have been an accurate representation. The appearance of the drafts
themselves suggests – in the varyingly legible handwriting, the heavy black
strokes through unsatisfactory words, the jagged scribbles to excise a line –
something of the effort with which he confronted a blank page. Even with
a prose draft worked out already, a lyric was carved, reshaped and adapted;
the process continued even after it had reached its first printed form. Russell
found it hard to forgive his friend's refusal to leave his work alone, and WBY's
approach could not have been more different from Russell's relentless pro-
ductivity. But the fact that one of the 'odd lyrics' written during this summer
was 'The Song of Wandering Aengus' illustrates exactly what WBY was cap-
able of, and Russell was not.

Coole may have been a refuge, but even the chance of uninterrupted work
did not make him happy in the summer of 1897, which was (he claimed in a
cancelled passage of his *Memoirs*) 'the most miserable time of my life'. 'I was
tortured by sexual desire and disappointed love. Often as I walked in the woods
at Coole it would have been a relief to have screamed aloud. When desire
became an unendurable torture, I would masturbate, and that, no matter how
moderate I was, would make me ill.' Guilt was thus implicit in his sexual frus-
tration and his attempts to relieve it.[79] His self-laceration was connected to
his failure with Shakespear as well as to his longing for Gonne, though he
did not tell Gregory as much. A good deal of time was spent in a dejected
daze, probably not helped by the supply of drugs from Paris. But, miserable

though he was, the long withdrawal to Coole and the company of Gregory produced more than poetry. Gregory's memory of his three months' stay was intriguingly different. For all his private unhappiness, he produced 'brilliant conversation' in the evenings, 'pouring out his ideas in rapid succession – hair-splitting, fanciful – full of wit & poetry, deep & subtle thought – his stories of his London friends wd make us laugh till we cried'.[80] Possibly these swings of mood were accentuated by drugs, but what he brought to Coole was not illusory. His friends, like Synge and Russell, became regular visitors too; their conversation and interests illuminated Gregory's life. That wet

8. George Russell sketching at Coole: a quick self-portrait which the 'hairy fairy' did in one of Gregory's scrapbooks during the late 1890s.

summer, she and WBY began collaboration on the folk-tale collections which generated his series of long articles from November. And one afternoon in August (not in 1898, as Gregory later remembered it), visiting de Basterot with Martyn, the conversation 'revived an old project for an Irish theatre'.[81]

The idea derived from WBY's acquaintance with avant-garde French theatre, a literary enterprise, expressing the ascendancy of the playwright rather than the actor-manager *à l'anglais*, like Beerbohm Tree and his 'vulgar pantomime'. The early ideas he shared with Florence Farr were still influential; the newly conceived Irish theatre was intended to begin with a production of *The Shadowy Waters*, in which she would star. The choice of this play is important. For the purposes of Coole, and the current preoccupation of WBY and Russell, the new project would be 'Celtic', a concept WBY had already

183

floated to the Young Ireland Societies in January. The original version of their manifesto, signed by WBY, makes this clear: it is reproduced here as drawn up in WBY's handwriting, with many excisions and afterthoughts.

THE CELTIC THEATRE

We propose to have performed in Dublin in the spring of every year certain Celtic and Irish plays, which whatever be their degree of excellence, will be written with a high ambition; <we pro> and to make a beginning next spring, with two plays, a play of modern Ireland and in prose by Mr Edward Martyn & a play of legendary Ireland & in verse by Mr W B Yeats. <Plays> We expect to follow them <by> with plays by Mr George Moore, Mr Standish O'Grady, Miss Fiona MacCleod [*sic*] & others, in other years; & <to> so to to [*sic*] build up a Celtic & Irish dramatic school. Dramatic journalism has had full possession of the stage in England for a century, & it is perhaps impossible for audiences, who are delighted by dramatic journalism, however brilliant, to delight in the simplicity & naivety of literature unless it is old enough to be a superstition We hope to find in Ireland an uncorrupted & imaginative audience trained to listen by its passion for oratory, & believe that our desire to bring upon the stage the deeper thoughts & <passions> emotions of Ireland will ensure for us a tolerant welcome, & that freedom to experiment <without which no man no longer> which <exists no longer in modern England> is not found in the theatres of England, & without which no new movement in art <is> or literature can succeed. <We> We will show that Ireland is not the <locus natura> home of buffoonery and of easy sentiment, as it has been represented, but the home of an ancient idealism, and we are confident of the support of all Irish people, who are weary of misrepresentation, in carrying out a work <which> that is <above> outside all the political questions that divide us

We have asked for a guarantee fund of £300 <for our first perform I> for our first attempt, & <of> about half of this has been guaranteed already. <Any> The profit <that may be made>, if any, will go <towards a fund> to make a fund for the production of plays in succeeding years.

Signed for provisional committee by
W B Yeats
<Coole Park, summer of 97>[82]

By the end of July ideas were far enough advanced for WBY to ask Alice Milligan if the Gaelic League *feis* could be postponed until 1899 so it would not clash with the 'Celtic' plays he planned (with Gregory and Martyn) for the next year. In the same month he airily told Ashe King that 'the money has been practically all subscribed for a start'. Subscriptions came in readily, if rather vaguely (T. M. Healy found WBY's writing illegible, but gamely added, 'I gather you ask my support to some Irish project, & as I am sure you are not connected with anything that is not meant for the elevation of the country put me down for any sum you think reasonable'[83]). But there were unforeseen bureaucratic difficulties ahead.

The 'Celtic' theatre would be renamed the 'Irish Literary Theatre' in October, as WBY, Russell and Martyn thought this 'less dangerous'; partly a political decision, partly because WBY had recently discovered that 'Celticism' was a highly problematic concept in historical or cultural terms.[84] But its original name and inspiration reflected the constellations whirling around WBY and Russell at Coole in late July. If WBY was depressed, Russell was in a dangerous state of elation. Since Sligo he had embarked on a psychic binge, and at Coole he began firing off drawings of supernatural visitations, shown to any locals reputed to possess second sight, who dutifully corroborated their accuracy. WBY always thought of Coole as a particularly haunted place; in its damp and misty atmosphere fairy manifestations appeared as 'strange visions after walking in [the] woods', of 'immortal, mild, proud, shadows'.[85] Russell was less restrained; his manic energy was inseparable from the project begun at Coole. When WBY returned to London in October he may have felt some need to distance himself.

Established once more in Woburn Buildings, he bombarded Russell with questions about Celtic rituals; but he also tried to direct his energy into less supernatural channels. At Gregory's London dinner-table WBY had met the pioneer of Irish agricultural co-operation, Sir Horace Plunkett; Plunkett, after further meetings at Coole, persuaded WBY to address the third annual Irish Agricultural Organization Society's (IAOS) conference in November 1897. There, he discovered Plunkett was searching for an organizer to set up an agricultural banking network for the Society. WBY suggested the unlikely figure of Russell,[86] sending the candidate firmly encouraging letters. Russell was currently employed as an accounts clerk in Pims' drapery store; the suggested new career sounded nearly as mundane, but the effort to make it 'harmonius' with his artistic soul would engage his powers, and teach him concentration, much as WBY's own work for the Jubilee and 1798 Centenary Committees had done. 'When I began speaking on politics first my mind used to be absorbed for days before & very anxious, & now I hardly think of what I am to say until I get to the meeting & when it is over it goes straight out of my mind.'[87] Declarations that Russell's recent literary work was immortal were accompanied by inconsistent assurances that it did not matter if he were currently unable to write. WBY's campaign to press Russell into Plunkett's service was reinforced by telling Gregory to write him similar letters and producing a *Sketch* article on the visionary's work. In the end, bludgeoned by so much attention and effort, Russell agreed.

It would be a long and successful career, in its way; and WBY's influence had decisively brought it about. He told Gregory that he wanted to save Russell from American Theosophists, with whom he was much taken up:[88] he had been invited to their latest dubious venture at Point Loma, California. WBY may also have wanted to save him from the sentimental English Theosophist Violet North, whom Russell would none the less marry the following June, to WBY's enduring disapproval.[89] It is also likely that the religious mania gripping his friend had begun to worry him: besides a habit of attacking priests, and a declared intention to walk through Ireland preaching the return of the native gods, there was a strong suicidal element in many of his visions at this time.[90] WBY must have known that the effect on Russell's writing would be deleterious; but already he was accusing him of using 'horrible' Theosophical phraseology in his poems, and later he would decide that Russell was creatively sterile, dissipating his talents in undiscriminating visions. It is possible also that WBY wanted to make sure that the dominant figure in the planned Celtic Theatre would be himself.

But he needed Russell for the accompanying project: the Celtic Order. Partly planned to capture Gonne, it also involved George Pollexfen, Sharp/Macleod, Dorothea and Edmund Hunter, Mathers and Annie Horniman. Edmund Hunter produced an impressive Celtic Tree of Life; later on, detailed rituals would be worked out for ascent through orders of adeptship. For the moment, Celtic images were summoned through visionary experiments, in which WBY was a leading spirit.[91] Notebooks were filled with evocations and correspondences. The holiness of Irish landscape, in keeping with the old bardic doctrine of *dinnseanchas*, was stressed. The notion of a holy island with a Temple of the Heroes had been particularly noted by WBY in a book by Nora Hopper years before; he thought he had seen the mythic site when he visited Lough Key with Hyde in April 1895.[92] Irish gods and heroes were investigated and evoked, including Deirdre, Cuchulain, Conchobar, Fergus and Lugh (under whose special guardianship Gonne put herself). Aengus, Irish god of love, was identified by apple blossoms brought by supplicant girls. Celtic mythology, WBY explained to Russell, 'will give me an orderly background to work upon. I felt the need of this badly when writing "The Shadowy Waters".' More immediately, he was preparing for the coming Celtic millennium, and provided a piece for the *Irish Homestead* in December declaring that, in an impending annunciation, Celtic spirituality would redeem the world; the international brotherhood of Celts took in Renan, Lamennais, Chateaubriand and Villiers.[93] In all this, he was making his own elaborate claim on Irishness.

Exciting though this was, Russell could (like WBY himself) adopt a sceptical tone when writing to Gregory;[94] they both had a highly developed sense of humour, and the expectations and pretensions of the Celtic movement made irony irresistible. This was permissible among true believers, but others were more brutal. When WBY gave a talk, 'The Celtic Movement', at the London Irish Literary Society on 4 December, *United Ireland* could not restrain itself.

His romantic theme was the enduring revelation of the Primitive Pastoral Pagans of Ancient Ireland who sat watching Golden Sunsets on Primeval Evenings, communing with Nature in a seerlike trance of inspiration till Daisies seemed to develop into white-limbed Damosels with eyes like the fairy flax, and the soft effulgence of the Omnipresent bathed their souls in the Melancholy Fatalism which is the fundamental reason why Mr Healy disagrees with Mr Dillon.[95]

The lecture was a straightforward polemic about the necessity of being Irish in Ireland: Hyde dressed up with references to Renan. It later formed the basis for an important essay, 'The Celtic Element in Literature'. As delivered in London, it emphasized the natural magic which Celts associated with their land and their devotion to the heroic ideal, which meant that love might be conceived 'not for the real woman, but . . . for the divinity of one's real imagination'. Here, as in his contemporary fiction, an autobiographical resonance is not difficult to hear.

WBY's own life, however, had changed since the summer. Gregory had by now moved centrally into his world, and into that of his family: she was commissioning sketches of the poet by JBY, who evasively remarked 'with him I have never succeeded – some uncertainty of *intention* always hangs over my pencil'.[96] She plotted to arrange an exhibition for JBY. She bought Jack's early work, organizing a successful Dublin show during February 1900, and trying to send him to Paris to perfect his style.[97] In 1900 she may have purchased Jack's poignant water-colour of Rosses Point, *Memory Harbour*, and presented it to WBY for Woburn Buildings.[98] She measured his rooms for furniture and curtains, which he worried about ('I wish I saw clearly in the matter'[99]). Fascinated by his combination of independence and hopeless ineffectuality, she noted WBY's routines (the breakfast cooked by himself but not cleared away, the fire economically raked out whenever he left the room). When he was ill she turned up morning and evening to care for him. She provided items like an enormous leather easy-chair; she helped turn his rooms into something like the stylistic triumph desired by their inhabitant (dim blues, tall white paschal candles, walls hung with brown paper, painted furniture, mystic hangings, prints and engravings by Blake, Rossetti, Beardsley[100]). In November she sent him Bovril, port, pies and champagne: on a later occasion, when a bottle blew up, the redoubtable Mrs Old remarked that she would more readily have sacrificed the neighbouring St Pancras Church.[101] Travelling in Connemara, she ordered him suits from the local tweed. From London he reported diligently about his health – digestion, eyes, teeth.

Dr Lang says that the eye which has been so bad for years that it has been useless is worse but that the other is exactly as it was. His words were 'the eye is going on very well'. The weakness lately seems to be a matter of general health. I must not try them too much, & I am to wash them in some borax mixture. He asked me what use I was making of them. Was I reading too much MSS etc. He tried me with all sorts of glasses & said that my glasses were all right.[102]

Before long, friends who worried about his eyesight (and the financial stringency that exacerbated it) knew to approach her: 'you have more influence over him than anyone'.[103] She found JBY exasperating, and at first gulped hard at his description of 'the British Empire and the Church of Christ' as 'shams',[104] but she made it clear to him that she was building up WBY's strength, feeding him, eventually keeping him. JBY gracefully assented. 'I am so glad you think Willie looking well & that you hope to make him look better. I feel great confidence in the strawberry & cream regimen.'[105] She traced folk-remedies for his eyes (dog-violet, boiled in milk: it did not work[106]). And she wrote to him in tones of familial intimacy and firmness. 'How bad of you to get ill just when I am not there to look after you. Do take care of yourself now, & feed yourself properly – & with any threatening of rheumatism you should look to your underwear.'[107]

She also introduced him to a new level of London society; he was soon lunching with celebrated (if aged) lion-hunters like Lady Dorothy Nevill. From his side, he provided artistic stimulation: dining constantly in Gregory's London flat at Queen Anne's Mansions, introducing her to interesting friends like Lionel Johnson ('he is quite safe at dinner. He does his drinking mostly in his own rooms'[108]) and inviting her to Monday evenings in Woburn Buildings. And the Theatre project developed, uniting them further. A great correspondence about money-raising and searching for premises accumulated from November 1897: influential Dublin supporters like Plunkett and Gill were sounded out; letters were sent to Irish notables (Lecky, Healy, Redmond, Dillon) about the monopoly exerted by Dublin's few large theatres. A licensing problem intervened: plays could not be produced outside the three Patent Theatres. The answer seemed to be a temporary licence, in conjunction with a relaxation in the law, through amending the Local Government Bill currently under discussion. Merciless pressure was brought to bear on the Irish Parliamentary Party (normally the butts of WBY's neo-Fenian rhetoric). Eventually, thanks to his, Gregory's and Martyn's persistence, Timothy Harrington's amendment was carried whereby the Lord-Lieutenant was given powers to license performances 'provided the profits go to some artistic or literary object', by application to the Privy Council. A blow had been struck for experimental drama, and against the commercial monopoly of the Dublin stage.

By the autumn of 1898 the way lay open. It had been cleared by politicking at establishment level in London and Dublin, carried out with Gregory's implacable persistence and invincible authority. The lobbying about the theatre from 1897 to 1898 came at a time when political *rapprochement* was in the Irish air. A joint campaign to revise Ireland's financial contribution to the British exchequer had brought Unionists and nationalists together; Lord Castletown briefly appeared as a possible national leader, followed even more improbably by Plunkett. The chimera passed, but Gregory seized the moment. In her friendship with WBY and his circle, she had found her *métier*, and Coole would soon be written up as a 'salon'. 'Lady Gregory is a talented lady,' gushed the *Independent*,

who takes a keen interest in matters literary and artistic, in particular those which are distinctively Irish. Coole is a rendezvous for the members of the rising Irish school. To those acquainted with the rollicking tradition of the neighbourhood in the old days, when duels and elopements, hunts and dances, were the chief joy of existence, it seems almost incongruous to picture 'the feast of reason and the flow of soul' in those parts.[109]

WBY had been central in this transformation; but Gregory required adaptation on his part too. The weapons, and the terrain, were markedly different from those demanded by Gonne. The contradictions between the two sides of his life were about to be sharply brought home.

V

Almost as soon as WBY had returned from Coole, Gonne had summoned him to the north of England for a gruelling series of Irish nationalist meetings about commemorating the 1798 Rising in its approaching centenary year. She had evidently decided they could work together politically after all. 'I find the infinite triviality of politics more trying than ever,' he assured Gregory. 'We tare each others character in peices for things that don't matter to anybody'.[110] But this understated his commitment. Since March 1897 the 'Central Centenary Committee of Great Britain' had become a battleground between factions of the Irish Parliamentary Party, the neo-Fenian rump of Parnellites, the IRB and the Irish National Alliance (INA). WBY was already identified privately with the last (the 'Wolfe Tone Memorial Committee' was pure Fenian-speak): in a cancelled passage of autobiographical reminiscence, he stated that the INA 'made me President of the '98' behind the scenes.[111] This came practically *ex officio* through his presidency of the Young Ireland Society in London. In early March he was paired as a delegate with someone who (rhetorically at least) represented the extremist line: Frank Hugh O'Donnell.[112] O'Donnell was, however, an ageing eccentric who had adopted many causes and claimed even more: his autobiography, characteristically concealed under the title *A History of the Irish Parliamentary Party*, asserted that he had more or less invented Home Rule, and inspired and controlled the career of Parnell. Himself a Castle Catholic of independent means, he had by the late 1890s come to specialize in vituperative and Anglophobic chauvinism, and to advocate a holy war of extermination against the foreigner (Jews as well as Saxons); he already had access both to Boer funds and to influential members of the French Foreign Office. However, his over-compensating vehemence did not convince everybody, and O'Donnell was more than once accused of being in the pay of the Castle which he so virtuously denounced.

It is more likely that he was a genuine eccentric, addicted to public rows and prepared to foment them under a number of guises: in his perverseness, facility and barefaced cheek there are echoes of George Moore and, as with Moore, wby was initially fascinated by him. Unfortunately for wby, one of O'Donnell's strategies in March 1897 was to send letters to the nationalist press under the pseudonym 'Fuath na Gall' ('Hatred of Foreigners'), claiming to represent a revolutionary party with an Irish executive in Great Britain, and cutting across the Central Centenary Committee which he and wby officially represented as well as challenging the constitutionalist Irish Parliamentary Party.[113] wby's desperate arguments that the Committee was comprehensively representative, 'believing that the memory of the men of '98 is a National and not a party memory', did not prevent an inevitable split developing. Much as with the literary societies, a Dublin committee and a London committee emerged, and an uneasy relationship between them. The fact that O'Leary was Chairman of the Dublin group, and wby of the London committee, did not mend matters: Dublin Castle noted that overall control rested with the IRB and Fred Allan, who had effectively sidelined the INA. At a Dublin meeting of the Centenary Committee, O'Donnell violently accused the local representatives (including O'Leary) of treachery against the Londoners; O'Leary refused to hear wby's explanation, and their long friendship was from that point clouded.

O'Donnell became an increasing liability. The following year he embarked on a series of scurrilous pamphlets libelling not only Michael Davitt but his INA associates in London, and he stirred up gossip about Gonne in *émigré* circles at Paris. Along with other difficulties, wby had to write to the 'Sons of St Patrick' in France, denouncing Charles MacCarthy Teeling for spreading rumours that she was an English spy. wby's final view of O'Donnell, long afterwards, was that he was 'half-genius, half sewer-rat':

The last picture of him that rises before my mind is seeing him look a little drunk and very old in a crowded bus, where he was repeating aloud a speech which he had just delivered at the Irish Literary Society: I do not remember what it was, but his good speeches were all much alike, English crime and Irish virtue – that virtue which he refused to admit in detail – 'They have oppressed us and ground us down yet we taught them their letters and held them over the baptismal font.' His imagination was travelling back to the seventh century.[114]

In 1897 O'Donnell's capacities for mischief were still undimmed. By the winter in London, WBY was fatalistically involved once more ('frightful moon and mars aspects . . . plunged me into three quarrells'[115]). Gonne departed for America on 17 October, where she attracted much opprobrium from Clan na Gael. In her absence WBY relapsed into London society, dining several times a week with Gregory and dazzling her friends.[116] When Gonne returned in January 1898, she had allegedly raised £500 for the Amnesty Association and £500 for the Wolfe Tone fund. (If so, it was practically all they got: by the end of 1898 only £561 had been raised towards the £14,000 needed.[117]) WBY advised her to bank the money rather than incur criticism through distributing it: perhaps they could meet in London or Dublin to discuss it? He scanned her letters anxiously to gauge the warmth of her addresses, and reported to Gregory when 'my dear friend' and 'affectionately your friend' took over. By late January Gonne's 'visions of a little temple of the heroes' had possessed him: he became obsessed once more with the castle on Lough Key. They planned to travel in the Irish countryside and commune with 'the forces of gods & spirits & too get sacred earth for our invocation' (if it could be done on a budget of thirty shillings a week).[118] Later on, a more expensive pilgrimage was projected to Bayreuth. 'She seems anxious to make me feel that she will give me a perfect friendship though nothing else.'[119]

But Russell, after Gregory his chief confidant, knew that WBY's golden hopes were dependent upon the political commitment enjoined by Gonne. By New Year 1898 it seemed to the new agricultural organizer that all the visionaries were being led astray. Having once 'knelt at the inner shrine', he was now slaving for Plunkett and the IAOS, explaining to hungry-looking farmers the advantages of buying pigs. O'Grady was editing the *Kilkenny Moderator*. And WBY was immersed in nationalist squabbles. 'I can never make out the ideas of the "98" enthusiasts,' Russell wrote to Gregory.

Perhaps it is sheer love of a row. I met Willie coming out of a '98' meeting last year and his face was shining over with delight. 'Its a jewel of a country! Its a jewel of a country! We have been fighting like hell for the last five hours and have fixed up nothing. oh it's a jewel of a country!' His face could not have expressed more delight if he had the Beatific Vision before him, or a vision of the Black Pig.[120]

This referred to an old folk-prophecy of an apocalyptic battle in the Valley of the Black Pig, which had inspired WBY's millennialist poem two years before;

roams through the Vast.

I praise Yeats and his
Black Pig in many a ballad
and tale of future Ireland and
many a wild vision :—
"Who is he that rides upon the storm?
who carrieth a black porker
and sheds shadowy terror and laughter.
It is William Mac Yeats
Bard of the Gael!

I envy these fellows in the
future who will have folk like
[...] and little to make
picturesque their romanzas.
Ah [...] why was I not born fifty
years on this. But I must

9. A letter from Russell to Gregory, dated 29 November 1897, satirizes WBY's preoccupation with the apocalyptic prophecy of the 'Black Pig'. 'He fondles it in his heart as a lover the sweetest glance of his girl. I believe in dreams he tucks this weird animal under his arm and roams through the Vast . . .' Yet simultaneously Russell was sending millennial summonses to WBY and eagerly awaiting the annunciation of a New Age. As with WBY himself, an ironic tone could be summoned or discarded at will, especially when writing to the sceptical Gregory.

and visions of war were still preoccupying the inner circles of the Fenian movement. However, by February 1898 the quarrels between the London and Dublin '98 Committees were complicated by resentment at constitutional nationalists getting in on the act (the National League of Great Britain under T. P. O'Connor). WBY, as President of the Centenary Committee grandiloquently representing 'Britain and France', issued a statement deprecating this and regretting that they had not joined individually in his organization.[121] Given its committee membership and public rhetoric (both strongly Fenian in tone), this was hardly likely. Through February intrigue deepened: Gonne issued summonses to Dublin, and then cancelled them. She was now preaching insurrection to audiences in the west. WBY privately confessed his disillusionment with it all to Gregory; when he finally departed to Dublin on 9 March she saw him off at Euston, and told him to stay out of trouble. As to 1798, she remarked that if it had worked as intended (instead of turning into 'a massacre of protestants'), 'we shd all now be celebrating it'. WBY acutely contradicted her. 'He says he wd not, he wd be against the existing Govt then!'[122]

Finally on 12 March the ''98 Convention' began, with an executive meeting at which constitutionalists were accommodated. The next day WBY spoke from the 'Connacht' platform in Phoenix Park, emphasizing that the moment 'must not be made subservient to any party purpose'. He also addressed a City Hall meeting in explicitly Fenian mode, eulogizing the 'high and holy cause' and attacking English oppression.[123] He then returned, exhausted but relieved, to London on 18 March. There he collapsed into illness, only forcibly dragged out by the necessity of entertaining the implacable George Pollexfen (and dealing with his uncle's robust hypochondria). But '98 continued to distract him. On 13 April he spoke at an 'Inaugural Banquet' for the '98 Centennial Association of Great Britain and France, preaching 'The Union of the Gael', attacking the Irish Parliamentary Party as 'the movement that has gone', and calling for a return to the guidance of Emmet, Tone, Davis and Mitchel (diluted by the conservative constitutionalists Burke and Grattan). A 'more intense national feeling' had arisen, and Ireland had learnt to hate English values, not only because they were English, but 'because we know they are evil'. For Ireland 'a day will come . . . though not, perhaps, in our day' when – as in the story of Manannán mac Lir, the sea-god – a foundering ship would be saved by 'a flaming hand laid suddenly on the tiller'.[124] This is the most Fenian of his public utterances; but it is counterpointed by the weariness of his private references.

Throughout 1898 WBY's existence was nearly as divided as that of Sharp/ Macleod. He was press-ganged into Gregory's campaign for a literary theatre, lobbying establishment figures like William Field, MP, Timothy Harrington and Adam Findlater, while at the same time tugged by Gonne around expatriate Irish cabals on the business of commemorating 1798 and inaugurating a new age of revolution. He made occasional tentative efforts to bring the two parts of his life together – suggesting for instance that the Theatre consider peasant plays written by priests whom he and Gonne encountered in their journeys around Ireland. But in February 1898 the tension had emerged into the open, when Gonne (supported, again, by James Connolly) took up the issue of alleged famine conditions in the west of Ireland. Her exhortations to provoke a confrontation by attacking the property of landlords were denounced to WBY by Russell and Gregory, whose diary records her appalled reactions.

I was aghast, & spoke very strongly, telling him first that the famine itself was problematic, that if it exists there are other ways of meeting it, that we who are above the people in means & education, ought were it a real famine, to be ready to share all we have with them, but that even supposing starvation was before them it wd be for us to teach them to die with courage [rather] than to live by robbery . . . He was very much struck & said he had only thought of the matter as it wd affect her [Gonne] – not as it would affect the people (which I fancy is her point of view also) but that now he saw how wrong such a line wd be & he would try to dissuade her from it.[125]

None the less, politics and occultism contrived to bind them together. In late April he travelled to Paris to study Celtic mythology with her, staying with Mathers at Auteuil. His old mentor and Gonne were 'at war over the management of "the Celtic mysteries" now well begun . . . both like true mystics pride themselves upon never having compromised anything in their lives'.[126] But they all worked on visions together and anxiously awaited the unlikely arrival of Fiona Macleod to finalize the ceremonies of initiation. Despite WBY's letters to Sharp professing profound supernatural communion, and hectic replies about Fiona's 'intense emotional crisis', she chose to join them on the astral plane only.

By 8 June he had been reunited with Gonne in Dublin, planning expeditions to the prehistoric passage-tombs at Newgrange 'to interview a god or two', as he jauntily told Gregory.[127] Russell described him as 'mysterious and magnificent' on the subject of the Celtic Order – a 'war' was brewing about it all.[128] More down-to-earth confrontations were already on the way. On her way to the unveiling of a plaque to the '98 hero Lord Edward Fitzgerald on 12 June, Gonne broke an arm falling from her carriage. WBY had not been present, having gone to sit for a sketch commissioned by Gregory from his father. He postponed his departure to Coole and joyfully took charge, reading George Moore's new novel *Evelyn Innes* (featuring a pen-portrait of himself) out loud to the invalid. This impelled her to recover enough to resume aggressive activities, incensing the Dublin '98 Committee by accusing them of financial extravagance. By the time the foundation stone for the Wolfe Tone Memorial was finally laid, she was at odds with most of her colleagues.

By 20 June wby had arrived at Coole and 'orderly life again'.[129] He discussed visions of fairies and 'Elizabethan' ghosts with local people; he began to work hard at the current draft of his novel; and he claimed to be 'getting on fairly well' with learning Irish, which his hostess tried to impart in the intervals between reading him *War and Peace*.[130] Gregory, with her prize regained, cast the net towards other members of the family; she had already asked jby for sketches of Hyde and Russell as well as wby, and Jack was now invited to Coole as well. But even at Coole, Gonne's presence remained potent: wby wrote asking her if she had visited him astrally. From 11 July he began to keep an occult diary devoted to dreams, visions and ideas about ritual, all directed towards Gonne. His confidants, currently Gregory and George Pollexfen, were apparently assured that the influences were tending towards a union.

In August he had to leave Coole to join Gonne for demonstrations and banquets in Dublin and London, where he was embarrassed by 'Tom fools' like an English fellow-traveller 'who recommended everybody to buy a breech-loader & prepare for the day of battle & wound up by singing a patriotic song apparently of his own making'.[131] But by 15 August he was cheered by the reception he and Gonne received on returning to Dublin to see John O'Leary lay the foundation stone for the Wolfe Tone Memorial – the high point of the Centennial celebrations, and the occasion which drew much the largest crowds. Once again wby provided a Fenian oration. But the event was conspicuously attended by several moderate MPs, and the sharp-eyed IRB doctor Mark Ryan noted that the Fenian founding father, James Stephens, was excluded from the platform; while Maud Gonne was welcomed less enthusiastically by the organizers than by the crowd.[132]

With the autumn, the commemorative frenzy calmed down; but the urbane tone in which wby presented it to Gregory, and the antics of Frank Hugh O'Donnell, concealed a serious underlying agenda. From the perspective of Arthur Griffith's *United Irishman* at least, the '98 Clubs intended to continue as nuclei of advanced nationalism and the focus of a new republican movement. They were the forerunners of the radical-Fenian 'Dungannon Clubs' which would emerge in Ulster and reconstruct the IRB from within. But the INA had declined to insignificance, and would shortly merge once again into the IRB. Though a delegate to the USA in 1899 boasted that the London cell included 'the brightest lights of the age, literary and professionally [*sic*]', its moment had passed with 1898; serious operators looked elsewhere.[133]

It is unlikely that wby understood this. From 1897 to 1898 the high temperature of extremist politics had been accompanied by feverish personal antipathies, with much slanderous gossip directed at Gonne; this would influence a number of WBY's otherwise gnomic poems in his next collection, *The Wind Among the Reeds* (such as those eventually titled 'He thinks of those Who Have Spoken Evil of his Beloved' and 'The Lover pleads with his Friend for Old Friends'). That memory stayed sharp; but the politics of extremist nationalism filled him with at least as much alarm as excitement, an alarm exacerbated by Gregory's disapproval. To him, the chief importance of the '98 movement (as Russell implied) lay outside politics: it brought him close to Gonne, currently riding on a wave of activity. By making Fenian speeches in March 1898, at a time when his private opinions were very different, he could atone for the Jubilee demonstration fiasco the previous summer. And if he could support her in politics, she would support him in his dream of a Celtic occult order. The first of September saw him at the Galway *feis*, an innovatory festival of Gaelic culture, and the Coole fraternity was once again joined by Russell. But WBY continued to correspond with Gonne about a pantheon of Irish heroes, and to keep his 'visions notebook'. Communication was attempted astrally and chemically (mescalin on 16 September, hashish four days later). Unsurprisingly, visions followed. Since the spring, he had been involving other Golden Dawn members in visionary experiments, conducted when geographically apart: the objective was to define Celtic ritual, but 'these messages at the worst are messages from ones deeper self'.[134]

As he headed for Dublin in late November, the Order of Celtic Mysteries was taking firm shape, and had – in his mind at least – bound Gonne more closely to him than ever before. 'His mysterious Celtic order is I believe being launched with a couple of members,' Russell reported to Gregory on 2 December. 'He is the most wonderful person. We never had anyone like him before.'[135] To a lover's self-delusion and an occultist's sense of power were added attempts at euphoria through hallucinogenic drugs. At last, he believed, he possessed the formula which would enchant Gonne and focus his own interests. The Order of Celtic Mysteries owed much to WBY's reading in Gaelic traditions, via Eugene O'Curry and others. From the myths and sagas researched in the National Library came figures like Gonne's sun-god Lugh and Tuatha De Danaan talismans, providing a four-cornered symbolism of Cauldron, Stone, Sword and Spear. Eventually they would be related, via the symbolism of tarot and ordinary playing-cards, to Pleasure, Power, Courage and Knowledge. Pan-Celticism, already aired by WBY in *L'Irlande Libre*, enabled him to claim Bretons, Scots and Welsh for his system. It also led him to the dangerous argument that Irishness was not necessarily defined by Catholicism. Celtic belief was far more atavistic. All this drew him closer to Fiona Macleod, the 'real voice of the Celt' (even if worked through ventriloquism):[136] and Macleod/Sharp obligingly produced an eloquent *Bookman* article in late 1898, pressing wby's claims. How much he knew of Fiona's identity at this stage is doubtful: in the spring of 1898 he had apparently taken at face value her excuses and evasions, putting off their meeting in Paris. But in late June he unguardedly told Sharp that a Fiona product (*Green Fire*) was not one of 'your' best stories, and by 1900 he and Russell were writing to each other ironically about 'MacSharp'.[137] Russell was by then engaged in full-blown controversy with the Celtic hybrid. Fiona's political opinions had come to look suspiciously like Sharp's Celtic Unionism, and her writing like plagiarism ('every time she bobs her head out of the Astral Light I will whack it, at least so long as it bobs up in connection with Irish things'[138]). In 1898, however, a curious complicity was still maintained. 'The one who shares my life and self is here,' wrote Fiona to wby, referring to Sharp. 'I will talk over your letter to *us* – for to *us* it is – though you send it to me.'[139] This admission of a shared self was carefully phrased. When queried about the nature of their collaboration, Fiona replied in the language of vision and allegory (matches, wind, a torch). wby must have had suspicions this early. But the concept of an invented *doppelgänger* is unlikely to have troubled him much, especially in his exalted mood of late 1898, when all things seemed possible.

VI

December 1898 was also to mark the culmination of another campaign: the Irish Literary Theatre was to be announced. In July they had the good news that the legal difficulties over a performing licence had been resolved. From August, wby was cultivating and flattering T. P. Gill at the *Express*, promising him articles and suggesting contributions; Plunkett's take-over of the paper seemed auspicious, encouraging wby to believe that Trinity College itself was being won by the Celtic enlightenment. While Gregory was relieved that their enterprise was to abandon the 'poor Sharp-ridden' identification of 'Celtic', the Pan-Celtic idea was still to be encouraged for purposes of bringing in respectable supporters.[140] In late 1898 wby launched himself into Dublin literary life more energetically than at any time since his battles with Gavan Duffy.

As had become usual, his tactic was to stage a public 'controversy' 'to keep people awake' until the announcement of the theatrical initiative. He had been limbering up for such an engagement since May, when he attacked his old adversary George Savage-Armstrong at the Irish Literary Society on the subject of 'the barrenness of the so-called intellect of Ireland'.[141] The next month his involvement in Rolleston's poetry anthology for Ward had started him thinking about a new edition of his own *Book of Irish Verse*, as a salvo in the campaign.[142] But the orchestrated discussion in the *Express* began on 18 September 1898 with an article by John Eglinton (W. K. Magee),

'What Should be the Subjects of a National Drama?' He accused the new school of misinterpreting and twisting ancient legends by taking them out of context. WBY replied, through the medium of reviewing Nora Hopper. Further exchanges accused him and his followers of escapism, while he argued for exaltation above utilitarianism. Poetry, he said – as so often – should be a revelation, not a criticism, of life (as Arnold claimed). Other combatants included Russell, whose article 'Literary Ideals in Ireland' supplied the title when the 'controversy' appeared as a book the following year.

WBY was currently in aggressive form, flexing his polemical muscles (and appalling George Pollexfen) by hissing a stage-Irish turn at a Sligo Masonic concert. Writing to his father on 1 November, he described his larger strategy: 'I have tried to provoke a contraversy, as Russell is going to join in, if "Eglington" takes the fly, & I want to excite general interest in Irish legends & in the Irish literary attitude in Dublin this month, as a preliminary to the publication of our dramatic project in December.'[143] But he had not originated the idea of a public discussion, which had long been in Russell's mind. Two years before he had suggested to WBY 'raising the standard of idealism in Ireland', against English materialism and imperialism. At that point, in 1896, he had visualized a book in which Magee, Lionel Johnson, O'Grady, Hyde, WBY and himself would declare their principles of heroism and renewal; Magee and O'Grady had already been instructed. 'I propose that you or Lionel Johnson shall take our Celtic wisdom, our distinct message to the world as Greece, Egypt, India had their message, and one or other of you could write about our future, or literature, or poetry, or life, or whatever subject you were most inspired by . . . You should of course be natural leader having the genius, glamour, etc.'[144] This reflected Russell's manic surge of cosmic enthusiasm in 1896; by early 1897 he decided public interest had waned. But the idea remained, and when the Magee–WBY debate opened, Russell firmly claimed responsibility. 'I am afraid,' he told Gregory, on 12 November,

I am the culprit with whom you must deal for the prolonged Yeats Eglington [*sic*] controversy. I thought and still think it a good thing to create public interest in such a discussion and I carefully fomented the dispute on both sides. I had a little private joy in this as I have long been battered by Yeats on one side and Eglington on the other for just those things they accuse each other of and so I have stood aside with much delight while they went for each other. However as you will see by this week's copy I have intervened, perhaps to make confusion worse confounded – for really they did not know exactly what they were arguing about – Willie thought the Celtic Renaissance was insulted and Magee did not understand Yeats.[145]

This summing-up was not unfair. Magee's horizons were self-consciously cosmopolitan, WBY's (for these purposes) jealously 'Celtic', though he used

Symons's tutorials to prove his point. 'His *theory* is right enough but he sweeps in illustrations in the most reckless way,' grumbled Russell to Gregory; 'men whom he has not read like Mallarmé, men who are only third rate like Gosse, Dowson and Lang are mentioned along with Dante, Shakespeare, Tennyson and Browning. Would you believe it he only knew two of Mallarmé's lyrics! Willie Magee who reads French like a native wonders at Yeats's applications of mysticism to such men. I wish Willie would always write poetry and stories and leave criticism alone.'[146] This was a vain hope. But, though wby invoked Wagner's creation of musical drama, and the French avant-garde, his message was the old one: local inspiration and national culture produced pure art, and would raise a new standard against the derivative crassness of popular Dublin theatre. In the campaign for a new Irish drama he had, as was becoming habitual, assumed the role of public spokesman.

Not all his Irish friends appreciated his Olympian pose, but he had now acquired an influential new admirer, the avant-garde novelist George Moore, whom he had met some time before at the Cheshire Cheese and through the Temple fraternity. Devious, uncontrollable, unable to resist the temptations of a demonic sense of humour, Moore was deeply mistrusted by all his acquaintance; but he was a close and influential observer of literary talent, and he saw wby's genius at once. 'I am your best advertiser,' Moore had assured him in October; 'inside the houses I frequent I cry: I am not the Lord, there is one greater than I, the latchet of whose shoe I am not worthy to tie.'[147] Moore assured wby that he would 'figure conspicuously' in his introduction to Martyn's plays, as well as featuring in Moore's own novel *Evelyn Innes*, where reviewers noted that the moody musician Ulick Deane was a close likeness: dishevelled good looks, romantic bohemian lodgings, unrequited adoration of the Wagnerian heroine, and even a certain passivity in the pursuit of love. This portrait marks the high point of Moore's infatuation. Flattered, wby even provided Moore (in circumstances of great secrecy) with the text for a letter from Deane printed in the second version of the novel.[148] The response of wby's intimates to this immortalization was equivocal. jby worried about Moore's '*version* of Willie – to me it will be a sort of complicated insult'. Katharine Tynan's reaction was no less characteristic. 'She remained thoughtful for a moment & then quietly remarked "What a splendid advertisement."'[149]

Moreover, Moore (an evangelist on behalf of the French avant-garde) was a devotee of Antoine's Théâtre Libre and a director of J. T. Grein's little Independent Theatre. wby was disposed to listen to the advice which his new friend showered upon him. 'To fully realise yourself you must produce more. The question arises can you produce more. I think you can. If you don't your genius will not perish, it will result in a small gem of great beauty, not a jewel of the first magnitude like Shelley, but equally pure in quality. I hope however that you will abandon politics as Wagner did and that you will realise as he did that his mission was not politics but art'.[150]

Later he would learn to fear Moore's professions of friendship ('he has what Talle[y]rand called "the terrible gift of familiarity"'[151]). But WBY's star seemed set on the ascendant as 1898 came to a close. Magical ritual, Celticism and the theatre were interconnected; the new drama, he would later insist, meant 'the preparation of a priesthood'.[152] Myth and ritual would be enacted which stemmed from 'an inherited subject matter known to the whole people'. And this assertion of hieratic authority would finally bring Gonne to him. He had led both Gregory and George Pollexfen to expect news after he joined her in Dublin in December, staying at the Crown Hotel. They read together in the National Library; he attended Pan-Celtic meetings and argued with people like Magee, Lady Fingall, Lord Castletown. His hopes of uniting all the elements of his enterprise, personal and artistic, had never been higher. The stars were indeed about to be thrown out of their courses; but not in the way he expected.

Chapter 8 : SHADOWY WATERS
  1898–1900

> To recover the desert I took refuge in the theatre.
>
> Chateaubriand, *Mémoires* (Book V), as quoted
> in Fiona Macleod, *The Winged Destiny*

I

IN early December 1898 WBY's Dublin life seemed a sea of tranquillity. On the 6th he wrote to Gregory, holidaying in Venice, from his eyrie in the National Library:

Miss Gonne is in Dublin & I see a good deal of her. She is rather deep in occult science just now – which pleases me. I should have written to you before but since I have been in Dublin I have been in a ceaseless whirl of activities – dinners, committees, old friends to look up & the like. My only time of leisure is when I come here where I am now writing & go to a table away among the private passages of the National Library. The librarian lets me go & read where I like & so I escape draughts & noise. I am reading Morris's 'Wood Beyond the World' a most beautiful dreamy book reminding one of forest glades & summer flowers . . .[1]

The chief interruptions were arguments with Magee; their controversy was still being carefully choreographed, with a view to the oncoming theatrical announcement. This idyll must have pleased Gregory, who sent him money from Venice, but it was the calm before a storm which would fundamentally alter WBY's landscape. His next letter, only two days later, records the stunned reaction of someone staring out at the wreckage. 'MG is here & I understand everything now. I cannot say more than that if I am sorry for my self I am far more sorry for her & that I have come to understand her & admire her as I could not have done before.'[2]

What had happened in the interim? His occult researches with Gonne, their close proximity, and an intensive and much discussed dream-life had peaked on 7 December. The previous night WBY dreamt of their spiritual and physical unity (and drew up a horoscope for the time when he had been vouchsafed this vision[3]). He knew that 7 December saw an exceptional astrological conjunction: for both their natal horoscopes, Venus and Mars were 'in close trine', mirroring each other and suggesting a conjunction of marriage.[4] When they met on that auspicious date Gonne had been more demonstrative than ever before, revealing that she too had astrally travelled to him, dressed in white, and been joined to him by the god Lugh. They kissed; a commitment had been made. But (he later told Gregory) she 'begged me to see her no more':[5] and when WBY none the less went to her on 8 December, he found her depressed. There, in her sitting-room at the Crown Hotel, she told him about her long liaison with Millevoye and the birth of her two children.

Why she did so is an interesting question. In his *Memoirs* WBY implies that the information was volunteered as a reason why she could not marry; but in a persuasive reading, Deirdre Toomey has suggested that Gonne might just as easily have told all in order to remove an impediment.[6] If she had broken with Millevoye three months before, this might indeed make sense. Certainly, in December she needed WBY's support. The 1798 Centennial had been a damp squib, Millevoye's political campaigns were running on to the rocks, she herself was an object of reproach and resentment, as well as admiration, in the circles she had chosen to frequent. She had drawn much criticism during the Wolfe Tone Memorial celebrations, and neither she nor WBY were involved in Mark Ryan's successor organization to the Centennial Association, the Irish National Club.[7] Whatever her reasons, she threw WBY into utter confusion. A highly charged seance which he attended at the Sigersons' on 12 December cannot have helped. The next day he began to keep a notebook of 'visions of old Irish mythologies', turning for solace to the iconography they had made their own.[8] The following day he evoked yet more visions with George Coffey and his wife. Though Gonne recovered first and set off to the west of Ireland on 13 December to survey evictions and attend secret meetings, WBY wrote brokenly to Gregory, 'my most true friend':

my letters must have greatly bewildered you with their so contrary nature. The truth is I shrank from putting on paper any but vague things but really there is no reason why I should not write a little of what I will tell you upon sunday. I wrote my first letter in despair because I was too unnerved to see things truely & unselfishly. The fact is that M G has told me with every circumstance of deep emotion that she has loved me for years that my love is the only beautful thing in her life, but that for certain reasons which I cannot tell you, reasons of a generous kind & of a tragic origin, she can never marry. She is full of remorse because she thinks that she has in the same breath bound me to her & taken away all hope of marriage. For years she kept 'a wall of glass between us' as she puts it & the very day before she gave way she begged me to see her no more. She has changed altogeather since she spoke of her love & is gentle & tender & I am now much happier than I have been for years for I am trying to see things more unselfishly & to live to make her life happier, content with just that manner of love which she will give me abundantly. Much more has happened than I can tell you here for one shrinks from writing many things, but it will be a great releif to talk to you about much that I cannot write. My nerves are still feeling the effects; & a restless night has given me a rather bad cold & a little asthma so that I feal like a very battered ship with the masts broken off at the stump. She has gone to Loughrea about some evicted tenants but returns I think to morrow. I want you to understand that I am at peace now about my self – for the first time for many dreadful years but very troubled about her. When I wrote my first letter my trouble was so great that I could not think coherently. After I went back to her after writing to you her goodness & her tenderness stilled all that was selfish in my trouble or so I think.[9]

Gregory was already on her way back from Venice; she hurried from London and met WBY in Dublin. She also interviewed Gonne, founding a life-long mutual dislike.[10] Her return galvanized him into mounting a publicity onslaught about the Irish Literary Theatre, working on Gill and Rolleston; as usual, work provided a refuge. But on Gonne's return from the west, the fever still ran high. As WBY recorded it, he once more proposed marriage on 18 December, after yet another shared astral experience, full of sexual connotation. But she again refused: 'I have a horror and terror of physical love.' The next day she departed. If she had at first unburdened herself to him with a view to facilitating a proposal, she rapidly retreated to declaring her inability to marry. It might be that neither of them knew what they really wanted. WBY certainly took refuge in vacillation, but, in a sense, they both backed off, and WBY's later interrogations of his behaviour return repeatedly to this theme.[11]

What emerged was an asexual commitment to each other, heavily reliant on the idea that they had been paired in a previous life as brother and sister: it was a return to the revelation of 1891. But from 8 December he had to re-fashion her image, whether as consecrated virgin, or lawless woman with no home or children. As with Olivia Shakespear, whom he had initially judged promiscuous and decadent, his first interpretation had to be radically reread. For many years he had been writing about the idealization of women; from December 1898 the work inspired by Gonne (notably *The Countess Kathleen* and *The Speckled Bird*) would have to be revised. But in the real world he remained indecisive. Despite the offer of financial help from Gregory, he did not pursue Gonne to France until six weeks later; irresolution in love remained his theme. If it had briefly crossed Gonne's mind that their relationship might be resolved by marriage, his uncertain and shocked reaction to her confidences confirmed her feeling that that their alliance would take no conventional form. She may have felt some reasonable disappointment.

Back in Paris from late December, she soothed herself with suggestive visions about Celtic Rites initiation ceremonies, relayed to WBY: these involved grasping spears, while 'fountains of fire' rose within her. Initiation 'purified' her and 'sealed her lips for the work'.[12] 'Work' was, once more, her consecration. She denied that she was lonely and stressed the mystical bond between them as a barely concealed substitute for sex ('I have had a partial initiation of the sword but feel it is not complete. This too we must try together'). But by Christmas her fellow-initiate had escaped to George Pollexfen and Mary Battle at Sligo. From there, in between therapeutic evocations of Aengus with George Pollexfen, helped by hashish pellets, he had continued to write confused and uncertain letters to Gregory. '. . . all I have gained through so many years is staked against all that I have ever hoped for; for certainly things cannot remain as they now are. My soul takes comfort in many excellent divinations but my mind doubts & fears. I feal too that her life is at stake. I used to think that just what has happened would make all the differance, would bring me content. As it is I find myself too restless for the quiet of Sligo . . .'[13] This too sits oddly with a scenario where Gonne had categorically refused marriage, but would fit an alternative situation, where she had given him some hope.

Nor was the story unknown to others. After Gonne's revelations, wBY moved briefly to the Rathmines lodgings used by Russell, and the latter wrote to Gregory on New Year's Eve:

The whole story of this passion of his I know from the beginning many years ago and it has the most pathetic and spiritual interest for me. It has wrought alternately on the noblest and least attractive sides of his character, but on the whole many most beautiful and human things in him are due to it and they outweigh the rest. Still I cannot say that I wish for him what he wishes for himself, nor do I not desire it for him.[14]

For her part, Gregory soothed wBY with a letter on New Year's Day 1899: 'I want you to have all you want, & I believe that suffering has done all it can do for your soul, & that peace & happiness will be best for both soul & body now.'[15] But still he postponed seeking them in Paris.

By 9 January he had turned up in Dublin 'in good spirits', according to Russell; 'he has a new theory about a Formorian king whose name pleased him ("Alathan" [actually Elathan]) and he is building a gorgeous intellectual structure on the strength of sundry visions'. Moreover, Mary Battle had told him 'if he was not married when he came next to Sligo he never would be, an oracular statement which fills him with hope'.[16] He had restored his spirits through Sligo and work. The publicity barrage for the Irish Literary Theatre had to be arranged via Gill; differences in the Pan-Celtic League were adjudicated; and on 22 December a project was mooted to Gregory, that she 'collaborate with me in the big book of folk lore'. (The suggested basis for collaboration was tightly restricted, and she initially refused.) There were also the diplomatic difficulties which arose when the Chief Secretary's wife, Lady Betty Balfour, decided to mount 'living pictures' from *The Countess Kathleen* in the Secretary's Lodge at Phoenix Park. The Irish Literary Theatre had to disassociate itself from the aura of Castle patronage, though wBY collaborated so far as to coach the beautiful Lady Fingall for the part. And even from Thornhill, wBY had been arranging social life for his return to London. By

mid-January he was back at Woburn Buildings, having announced the incep-
tion of the Irish Literary Theatre to the National Literary Society.[17]

Only at the end of January did he arrive in Paris. Gonne at first was unable
to see him, giving illness as a reason, though she may also have disapproved
of WBY visiting Mathers; she was now half-convinced that the self-styled
Comte de Glenstrae was an English spy. WBY saw his admirer and translator
Davray, and spent time with Synge, whose austerity and dedication impressed
him. Eventually, he and Gonne met and talked at length; but he found her
withdrawn and rather cold. She had apparently lapsed into depression after
the psychological catharsis of December, and she may have felt chagrin at his
irresolute response. But she had other worries too. Millevoye was deeply
implicated in planning Paul Déroulède's attempted *coup* at this very time, and
was subsequently arrested on 23 February; whatever the state of their personal
relationship, she was committed to her lover's political causes, and had learnt
much of her language from *La Patrie* and *La Croix*, which presented England
as a conspiracy run by Freemasons and Jews ('*l'ennemie séculaire*'[18]).

For the moment, however, the forces of evil seemed ascendant. WBY heard
more of her past ('I do not wonder that she shrinks from life,' he told Gregory[19])
and returned to London in mid-February after 'a depressing time'; there he
succumbed to the general influenza. A letter from George Pollexfen, accom-
panying a loan of £7, probably rubbed salt in the wound. 'I was in hopes you
would have required more and for another purpose but suppose affairs did
not culminate favourably. When I told Mary some time back that you had
gone to France she said you were in great form at present (i.e. then) but added
that something *you and I* had in mind would not come off this time. I made
no remark in reply to this, but wondered whether the prognostication might
refer to the Celtic Rites or to another matter more immediately to do with
your going to Paris.'[20] The Paris visit had left him determined not to see Gonne
until after the summer, or so he told Gregory. He now stayed in London, too
low in funds to do much but comforted by gifts of food and wine from Greg-
ory, dining out, and recommencing his Monday evenings. The visitors to
Woburn Buildings in late February and early March included Davray, Moore,
Farr, Rhys, Todhunter, Sarah Purser and – inevitably – Gregory. The partial
confidences of December had placed her even closer to the centre of his life.

II

By now, in any case, the theatre project had been announced; and this had
dominated WBY's public life since his return from Sligo in mid-January. The
public was addressed through a series of manifestos. First, at a meeting of the
National Literary Society on 9 January in Dublin, a 'fashionable' audience

sat through a lengthy amateur concert before listening to WBY explain that 'all literature and all art is national' (witness Ibsen and the Greeks), but that the concept of 'national' meant reconciling 'men of all creeds and parties in the service of Ireland'.[21] This was well gauged for a congregation of Castle Catholics and university luminaries, who were then told of the plan for an Irish Literary Theatre, 'to be conducted under the auspices of this society': the Antient Concert Rooms had been engaged (since December) for the second week of May. Gill's *Daily Express* gave this event a certain prominence, and was equally helpful in publishing WBY's letter and article of 12 and 14 January which made the new departure manifest.

From the beginning the Irish Literary Theatre trod a difficult path between its claims of 'national' politics, its avant-garde ambitions, and the patronage of the establishment. The guarantors included Lecky, the arch-conservative Professor J. P. Mahaffy of TCD (who hoped they would avoid any use of the Irish language), Plunkett, Lord Castletown, Lord Ardilaun, Lord Dufferin, the Duchess of St Albans, Dillon, Redmond and Healy; Gonne's name struck a lonely 'advanced' note on the roll-call.[22] WBY was acutely sensitive to embarrassments like the endorsement of Lady Betty Balfour's 'living pictures' ('Imagine Miss Gonne at the Chief Secretaries Lodge') or the Vicereine's attendance at a lecture to the National Literary Society by Margaret Stokes (there could be 'no special chairs'). The aid and comfort of the conservative *Daily Express* was a similarly mixed blessing.[23] With such calculations in mind, WBY made his manifesto for the Irish Literary Theatre an attack on the Irish establishment for cutting itself off from the life around it; hence the 'cold and conventional' imagination of the Protestant/Unionist world. His long-standing vehemence against Trinity College culture had been fuelled by the obstructionist stance taken by Trinity dons before the 1899 Commission investigating the use of Irish in primary schools. But it was also tactically important to distance the Irish Literary Theatre from the dead hand of establishment approval, and his brilliant manifesto to the *Daily Express*, 'The Academic Class and the Agrarian Revolution',[24] should be seen as part of this campaign. Attacking Robert Atkinson's disparaging remarks about Gaelic literature, WBY ringingly asserted that Trinity College's contempt for Irish culture stemmed from the class interests of those threatened by national revival and the agrarian movement. Yet it was this world which, chivvied by Gregory and WBY himself, had backed the new dramatic experiment; whereas scepticism was expressed by the new voice of advanced nationalism, Arthur Griffith's *United Irishman*. 'Mr Yeats's project', Griffith announced, was 'an attempt to produce a really high-class Anglo-Irish drama; but such plays as he meditates can never be popular. They are too far above the people's heads.'[25]

Rival theatrical innovation had already appeared in nationalist circles, and would continue to do so – including Alice Milligan's Irish-speaking drama at Aonach Tír Conaill (a Gaelic festival in Donegal) the previous November, and pageants mounted by Maud Gonne and her associates. This made WBY's publicity onslaught all the more important. He was justifiably proud of the newspaper coverage appearing from mid-January, sending cuttings to both Gregory and Gonne; after his return from Paris in February, he threw himself into the task of finding actors for the May programme. By March, after lengthy discussions with Florence Farr, he had decided upon professionals rather than amateurs. After listening to Farr and WBY at a Monday evening gathering, JBY sarcastically reported, 'If all one hears is true, London is crowded with beautiful & charming actresses & capable actors, the supply far exceeding the demand – so that if they only search they cannot fail to find suitable people.'[26] The journalist H. W. Nevinson met WBY for the first time on 16 March, on the search in Hampstead society, and left a vivid impression in his diary: 'tall, thin, rather stooping, with long, straight topped head quite black, narrow face, eyes rather close, & the left looking a little outwards: clean shaved, showing blue'. Most of all, WBY's energy, mannerisms, and self-absorption were impressive; he

talked incessantly, moving his hands a good deal, & sometimes falling into a chant: says 'D'y' see?' every sentence. Talked chiefly of himself, his spiritual experiences, trances, visions and apparitions: sometimes the spirit forbids him to say what was in his mind & his tongue becomes like a stone. Calls himself a Cabalist, but a sceptic too. Is as good a typical young poet as could come out of Ireland. Has laughter too, espec. in gossip about other men.[27]

He would shortly need this sense of humour: trouble arose before the end of March over Martyn's scruples about the blasphemous content of *The Countess Cathleen*, and it was only quashed with difficulty.[28] WBY and Farr went to Dublin for a week on 30 March, and returned on 7 April 'having completed his arrangements for the Celtic Theatre', while Russell was left struggling with posters representing 'really occult angels.'[29] Rehearsals and publicity were handled from London, where Nevinson would shortly enlist the *Daily Chronicle* in the cause of the poet's burgeoning reputation.

From mid-April WBY extended his theatrical message to the London public, with an important statement to the Irish Literary Society on 23 April.[30] The large audience included family, friends, literary collaborators like A. P. Graves and Dora Sigerson Shorter, and the antagonistic journalist D. P. Moran, who had already made WBY a target for his brilliant gibes and would soon found the *Leader*, devoted to the same project.[31] WBY announced a future programme of plays by Standish O'Grady and Fiona Macleod, and said that by playing in small halls, to discriminating audiences, they would target 'the exceptional man – he did not mean the man of any class or the man who read books, though he meant principally the man who reads and loves the old Irish legends'. Again, 'national' was interpreted as safely all-inclusive, by looking to ancient Greece and modern Norway. 'With the Gaelic language movement there might grow up every spring about the time of the old festival of Baltaine [*recte* Beltaine] a national, perhaps he should say a racial, festival.' He and Martyn 'in all humility' followed Ibsen, whose literary theatre was founded on conquering 'the opposition of a cosmopolitan and denationalized class'. But while praising *Ghosts* and *The Wild Duck*, WBY contrived to attack realism; his artistic priorities were clearly visible. 'If we were to restore drama to the stage – poetic drama, at any rate – our actors must become rhapsodists again, and keep the rhythm of the verse as the first of their endeavours.'

WBY's (and Farr's) essential plea was for hieratic, lofty drama where words mattered, not action: and this was a concept received sceptically by the Irish Literary Society. Todhunter, who must have felt rather embittered at his exclusion (given WBY's previous raptures about his plays), asked an awkwardly specific question. How could *The Countess Cathleen* be played, according to WBY's principles? Would the actors not have to be specially trained for a year? Norreys Connell was even tougher: 'he did not think that Mr Yeats' idea of the theatre could ever successfully appeal to the people for support, and as a modern imitation of the old theatre it seemed impossible (Applause)'. Others stressed the importance of popularity. Every speaker on record dissented. Most damagingly, Edmund Gosse contradicted WBY's entire interpretation of Ibsen's career: which was, at the outset, firmly based on commercial drama. But few of these criticisms seem to have taken hold, at least to judge by WBY's subsequent lecture in Dublin, 'Dramatic Ideals and the Irish Literary Theatre'.[32] By now the Irish Literary Theatre's publicity was accumulating fast, with their declared intention of putting on an original Irish play every spring ('Beltaine', the ancient Celtic summer festival) and a classic in the autumn ('Samhain'). For May 1899 the programme was to be WBY's *The Countess Cathleen* and Martyn's *The Heather Field*, played at the Antient Concert Rooms: described by a contemporary as 'a rather shabby tenement in Brunswick Street, about the size and proportions of a moderate Dissenting chapel', with rows of hard wooden benches and a skimpy gallery.[33]

The Countess Cathleen had been much revised since WBY's original conception of February 1889 – first for publication in 1892, then for republication with *Poems* in 1895. The version played in 1899 had been yet further changed (and 'Kathleen' had become 'Cathleen'), though a new publication would not appear until 1901.³⁴ Two further revisions would follow in 1912 and 1919. By 1899 the character Aleel had come into focus as hopeless poet–minstrel attached to a self-sacrificing goddess-figure – a pointer towards the increasingly subjective direction which the play would take. Other 1899 alterations had been dictated by Martyn's worries about the plot. In a famine-stricken Ireland, with demonic ghouls harvesting the souls of starving people by offering corrupt bargains, a beautiful countess offers her own soul in return for the salvation of her people. Though WBY would eventually classify it as an anti-politics play, his demon soul-merchants must, to a contemporary audience, have looked like Protestant proselytizers or English oppressors; and Famine Ireland was, to any reader of John Mitchel, an inescapably political *mise-en-scène*. But the play's controversial potential did not lie only in politics. Although the Countess's salvation is eventually guaranteed by her transcendent intentions, Martyn agonized over the religious implications; on 22 March WBY had written desperately entreating him not to back out and agreeing to refer any problematic passage to a 'competent and cultivated theologian'. Favourable reports notwithstanding, the issue simmered on, joyfully stirred by Moore. Just before the performance Martyn turned up at the hotel where WBY and Farr were staying, tried to change his mind once more, and had to be firmly talked round.³⁵

But the chief controversialist was an old acquaintance, probably drawn in by his obsessive hatred of Maud Gonne as well as by his previous passages with WBY: Frank Hugh O'Donnell. With the eclipse of the 1798 Centenary movement, O'Donnell had become increasingly extremist, at least for public consumption. 'It is time to seek anew the old path of courage and honour,' he announced in April 1899. 'Hurrah for the native tongue! Hurrah for native swords!'³⁶ He deluged the nationalist press with manifestos about everything from the Norman invasion to the Oath of Allegiance; the printed text of *The Countess Cathleen* provided a perfect cause, since it contained a scene in which an enraged peasant assaulted a religious image of the Virgin (excised from the acting version). First in a letter to the *Freeman's Journal* and then in pamphlets (circulated by late April), O'Donnell denounced the play as a blasphemous calumny on the Irish nation. WBY, 'a meandering decadent with a diseased mind', presented them 'just like a sordid tribe of black devil-worshippers on the Congo or the Niger'.

Going, going, gone! An Irish wife – an unchaste Irish wife – secured for hell for a hundred crowns! The Celtic Muse of W. B. Yeats is tireless in its flattering appreciations of the Irish nation. Its men, apostate cowards; its women – such as this; its priests, the prey of demon swine; its shrines, kicked to pieces by its Celtic peasantry; the awful majesty of the Christian God flouted and mocked by spirits from the pit!

What is the meaning of this rubbish? How is it to help the national cause? How is it to help any cause at all?[37]

'His object is to get up a row at the performance,' Russell assured Gregory.[38] But this was not perceived as disadvantageous. 'Dublin is improving all round. Art, music, literature, drama are becoming of more general interest. The next thing which will happen will be the fight with the priests and the reformation will reach Ireland in its last & most spiritual phase.' Russell added fuel to the flames by writing a skit of the *Countess* for the current issue of the *Irish Homestead*, the agrarian co-operative journal which was being transformed under his editorship. The *Daily Nation* joined in by vituperatively rejecting advertising copy for the play, and exhorting audiences to demonstrate 'that the people of the Catholic capital of Catholic Ireland cannot be subjected to affront with impunity.'[39]

Thus, when the play finally opened on 8 May, it carried a controversial advance reputation, as well as a history of tension behind the scenes. The ideas with which WBY approached rehearsals may be guessed from a long letter to the *Daily Chronicle* of 27 January, which outlined the dramatic principles to which he would, by and large, remain faithful: formalized chanting, simple scenery altered by light, and a powerful directorial presence stressing that the function of art was to invoke spiritual realities. Believing a commercial audience was the enemy of the ideal theatre, WBY had originally wanted the *Countess* acted in full hieratic Bedford Park style. But, pressed by Martyn and others, he rapidly gave in to populism and cast May Whitty instead of Dorothy Paget, who was consoled with the assurance that 'you act according to a quite new way, & according to a theory of acting which Mrs Emery & myself alone as yet have accepted'.[40] He also had to abandon his plans for a Bayreuth-style finale, though he continued to dream of a full operatic *Countess Cathleen* for years.[41] Having ended up with professional actors, he was anxious to dispel the belief that the Dublin opening would be an amateur affair: Gill was told emphatically that they were paying 'a great deal of money' in salaries.[42] It was, after all, competing not only with the imported dramas so often excoriated, but also with a tradition of patriotic melodrama alive and well at the Queen's Theatre.[43] This ambition did not come cheaply: WBY had stressed to Dorothy Paget that he was risking other people's money. Actually the backing principally came from Edward Martyn, so it was perhaps only fair that the popular success of the Irish Literary Theatre's first double bill was not *The Countess Cathleen* but *The Heather Field*.[44]

As to the *Countess*, JBY's reservations were probably shared by many. 'I hope Willie will go on writing dramas & that sometime he will prove he can write dramas which are to be *acted* as well as chanted. A lyric or any other out-pouring of musical passion is all the more penetrating if the personality uttering it is already familiar to you in story or drama. The Countess of [*sic*] Kathleen is itself such a drama and I cannot agree with Willie in all his ideas as to the rendering of it.'[45] But the audience reaction to both plays, taken together, was enthusiastic enough to drown out ambivalence; some hissing on the last night was countered by a cry from the gallery: 'Don't mind thim, Mr Yeats, they're only Tim Healy's curates.'[46] The week of theatrical performances was celebrated by garden parties, art exhibitions and public lectures, climaxing in a famous dinner given by the *Daily Express* at the Shelbourne Hotel, attended by (among others) WBY, Moore, Martyn, Hyde, Magee, O'Leary, O'Grady and a rather bemused Max Beerbohm. Moore's memory of it is preserved immortally in *Hail and Farewell*, beginning, 'I read an historic entertainment in the appearance of the waiters . . .'[47]

The dinner's *leitmotif* was celebration of controversy, and the coming together of various strains in the theatrical movement. Martyn was awarded extravagant praise, while WBY combatively rebutted criticism and stressed the symbolic construction and setting of the *Countess* – besides claiming that two Catholic priests approved of it. This was shrewd, but (as Frederick Ryan pointed out) ceded the argument of clerical interference in the first place.[48] The Irish Literary Theatre's mission, according to WBY, was 'to spiritualize the patriotism and the drama of this country'. According to Moore, in an embarrassing encomium on WBY, it was to introduce a native genius of Shakespearian proportions. But Arthur Griffith's recently established and IRB-influenced *United Irishman*, sharp for its purposes, decided that the imprimatur of Gill and Plunkett should be exposed as an attempt to broaden 'co-operation' from the agrarian into the cultural sphere, with obvious and sinister political intentions:

Mr George Moore preached to our salvation. Let the Irish Nation grasp the pen of Yeats for its sword and buckle on the churn of Plunkett and be saved! It is cheering to know that Mr Moore's artistic eye can catch the hint of the sun of art in Erin's sad, dun sky, and that his temperament now permits him to return to Ireland and play the critic of her politicians. His keen, logical mind detected an analogy between the Irish economic struggle of the recent past and the struggle for National existence of Greece, Italy, Holland and France. Poor Mr Yeats must have suffered agonising torture while Mr Moore slapdashed him with flattery with the heady vigour of an honest whitewasher slinging around his limewash. Mr Yeats replied to the critics of his play, and replied pertly. He was ready to admit, he said, that nobody was ever robbed in Ireland and that no woman was ever false to her husband. Tommy Dodd would have uttered a better quip. Dr Shaw revealed himself a Philistine and Mr J. F. Taylor, who had listened, horrorstruck and indignant, to his one guiding star being rudely criticised by Mr Moore, gently-savagely reviled that gentleman. Dr Sigerson,

Dr Tyrrell, Dr Bernard and Mr Max Beerbohm said nothing, in graceful speeches Mr Anderson puffed his business. Dr Hyde spoke in Irish, to the utter rout of the *Express* reporters, and Mr O'Grady hinted darkly of a military movement, causing one knight of commerce to murmur to heaven a prayer for his soul. Then Mr T. P. Gill blessed his guests – and all was over.

Will the union of Butter and Poesy endure? Will their conjugal embraces yield to the birth of a new Irish Nation? I fear not. Barrenness and incompatibility of temper, if nothing worse, will lead to a quarrelling and a separation. I prefer poetry unbuttered and sniff suspiciously at butter idealised. I do not want Mr Plunkett to wrap me up my pound of butter in the book of the 'Countess Cathleen'. I do not feel my heart thrilled as I gaze at the insignia on the invisible-green standard of symbolic patriotism which our poetic dairymen and practical poets have unfurled. I prefer the old flag with its harp to the new one with its churn. Also, I prefer my poetry without cream.[49]

This attack, like O'Donnell's, seized on a fundamental point: given WBY's recent Fenian profile, the language of 'patriotism' surrounding the theatrical initiative reasonably led people to expect a nationalist agenda. Yet this was clearly no part of the Irish Literary Theatre's brief. Tempers were further raised by a celebrated letter to the *Freeman*[50] from thirty National University students attacking WBY's representation of 'the Irish peasant as a crooning barbarian, crazed with morbid superstition', thus allowing England to deny the national claims of 'a loathsome brood of apostates'. WBY claimed this was a sectarian interposition, but once again it arose from baulked political expectations. The students had been expecting a celebration of national character and history, and believed them travestied instead. Politics had joined religion in a classic Irish *cause célèbre*. 'From the point of view of publicity,' as James Cousins put it, 'the occasion was a howling success.'[51]

The implications of the controversy so successfully orchestrated by WBY and Russell were far-reaching. Current ambiguities were mirrored in the reaction of the *United Irishman*. The paper was more or less republican, anti-Semitic (particularly over Dreyfus) and of advanced nationalist opinions: it despised Pan-Celticism as a middle-class dilution of pure Irish nationality.[52] Correspondents to its columns saw opposition to the *Countess* as reassuring evidence of nationalist 'zeal', too soon dissipated.[53] In initially opposing the play, the journal stressed the fact that it was so Wagnerian as to be 'un-Irish': WBY's 'Celtic-named puppets' were really 'Teutonic dolls'. None the less, the playwright had to be congratulated 'not as the artist, but as the standard-bearer of revolt'.[54] This reflected uncertainly on the part of Griffith (intuitively antipathetic to WBY, but anxious to remain friendly with Gonne) and his drama critic Frank Fay (longing for dramatic innovation but unimpressed by the production values of the Irish Literary Theatre). Long afterwards WBY claimed that Griffith, at that stage anti-clerical, had boasted of 'sending coal-porters into the gallery to cheer whenever they hear anything the church won't like'.[55] Accordingly, the paper shifted the ground to the question of the playwright's patriotism.

Mr Yeats has proved himself to be an artist; we know him to be patriotic; nevertheless he has exhibited a startling misconception of the character of his countrymen. This is a fault which he must correct if he desires enthusiasm to animate those who otherwise would uphold him only through a sense of duty. Beyond this, for the defects of Yeats the Artist, as Irish Nationalists, we little care. We shall watch with real anxiety how he will take his victory over the Ignoramus, the Bigot and the Philistine. If he takes the enthusiasm of Monday night solely as the artist's tribute he may be lost to Ireland; if he takes it primarily as the acclamation of the Patriot he may grave his name on his country's heart.

But this was not to say that the forces called up by O'Donnell had been vanquished, or that WBY had won the argument.

No less prophetically, the ideas which so incensed his antagonists were built into the framework of his spiritual and occultist life. *Beltaine*, the occasional journal of the Irish Literary Theatre which was published to coincide with their first season, preached drama as the 'preparation of a priesthood' and referred to theatre as liturgy, using mythic narratives. These ideas may have come to him via Blake or Frazer's *Golden Bough* but they also (in their references to the Greek theatre of Dionysius) hint at absorption of Nietzschean notions at least three years earlier than usually supposed.[56] The theatre would provide a common symbolism and a common meditation. Crucially, in WBY's personal quest the theatre would slowly replace the Celtic Rites on which he had worked with Gonne (he had originally asked her to play the Countess, and been refused). He continued to draft rituals until 1901, but more and more desultorily. The invocations, visionary effects and spiritual propaganda that had accumulated in his occult notebooks could now be transferred to another, more public forum; self-knowledge could come through the discipline and projection of a dramatic persona. And in the theatre, as in occult tutelage, he could demonstrate to Gonne a sphere of mastery. She attended the plays, but shunned the attendant publicity, removing herself to Mayo to unveil 1798 monuments and preach land agitation. Just as predictably, by 21 May WBY had disappeared to Coole, where he remained, on and off, until September. Gonne's letters to him, lamenting the collapse of the anti-Dreyfus case in France, the establishment of the Waldeck-Rousseau government, and the ascendancy of Jews and socialists, probably fell on deaf ears, and she soon reverted to their traditional preoccupations of mystic colours and Celtic rituals. But WBY knew he had had a great success in Dublin, and from the peace of Galway he continued to dictate publicly to Gill. 'The one thing I most wish to do is drama & it seems to be a way, the only way perhaps in which I can get into a direct relation with the Irish public.'[57]

III

Where did poetry fit into this programme? WBY's belief in drama reconciling the enterprise of art and the need to preach, and enabling him thereby to purchase a claim on Irishness, came just at a time when he had published a book of poems: but *The Wind Among the Reeds* signalled his last new collection for several years, and WBY himself saw it as something of a swan song. Though its appearance in April 1899 more or less coincided with the unveiling of the Irish Literary Theatre, it had been even longer in the making. From late 1897 WBY had been writing to Elkin Mathews about the design and appearance of a new volume. His correspondence through 1898 kept up the refrain, and in July JBY cynically remarked that he had been announcing it 'for nearly six years or thereabouts'.[58] Proofs had been sent to and from Thornhill in the autumn, followed by anxious inquiries about binding and complicated instructions about the notes accompanying the poems – 'really elaborate essays in the manner of "The Celtic Twilight"', as he told Davray, whom he was cultivating for a review in *Mercure de France*. 'They have given me a good deal of trouble & will probably make most of the critics spend half of every review in complaining that I have written very long notes about very short poems.' But he hoped to reap 'the forgiveness of the philistines'. A cover commissioned from the unreliable Althea Gyles was still under discussion in January 1899; WBY was simultaneously harassing Fisher Unwin about a new edition of *Poems* (with 'a very good sketch of myself as frontispiece'). His efforts paid off, and both books were on reviewers' desks by the end of April, just before the début of the Irish Literary Theatre.

The Wind Among the Reeds included several poems which existed in draft as early as 1892; and as finally arranged the volume carries a distinctly autobiographical implication.[59] This is evident in the deliberate use of named personae (Aedh, Hanrahan, Michael Robartes, Mongan), a gallery of characters through whom WBY expressed his moods. In later versions these names became abstractions ('The Poet', 'The Lover'); in 1899, as WBY made clear in a celebrated note, they represented specific feelings and qualities.

Hanrahan is the simplicity of an imagination too changeable to gather permanent possessions, or the adoration of the shepherds; and Michael Robartes is the pride of the imagination brooding upon the greatness of its possessions, or the adoration of the Magi; while Aedh is the myrrh and frankincense that the imagination offers continually before all that it loves.

Art-as-priesthood was spelt out, disguising the personal agenda of love-poetry and the private language of magical ritual – both themes that run through *The Wind Among the Reeds*. Love-poems predominated, in intensity if not quantity; and it is tempting to trace two themes, and even two groups, throughout. One group, usually featuring Robartes, inevitably suggests the doomed affair with Olivia Shakespear and conveys the regrets of a lover who cannot quite convince himself, nor lose himself in love: post-coital *tristesse* occurs in 'The Shadowy Horses', or 'Michael Robartes remembers Forgotten Beauty', while 'The Cap and Bells' presents the fulfilment of love as the loss of potency and of life itself. Another group of poems strikes a note of desperation, and the longing for total possession in death. These were inspired by 'Aedh's' commitment to Gonne, and include 'Aedh wishes his Beloved were Dead', 'Aedh hears the Cry of the Sedge' and 'Mongan thinks of his Past Greatness':

> I have drunk ale from the Country of the Young
> And weep because I know all things now:
> I have been a hazel tree and they hung
> The Pilot Star and the Crooked Plough
> Among my leaves in times out of mind:
> I became a rush that horses tread:
> I became a man, a hater of the wind,
> Knowing one, out of all things, alone, that his head
> Would not lie on the breast or his lips on the hair
> Of the woman that he loves, until he dies;
> Although the rushes and the fowl of the air
> Cry of his love with their pitiful cries.

If many poems suggest the conventional love-in-death trope of the *fin de siècle*, with passion defeated through self-immolation and exhaustion, they are redeemed by an audacious marriage of simplicity and elaborateness: the language of Mallarmé is linked to the energy of folk rhythms, as in 'Aedh tells of the Rose in his Heart'.

> All things uncomely and broken, all things worn out and old,
> The cry of a child by the roadway, the creak of a lumbering cart,
> The heavy steps of the ploughman, splashing the wintry mould,
> Are wronging your image that blossoms a rose in the deeps of my heart.

Much revised by this stage, the poems in this volume were rarely changed again. They reflected the circumstances of his life: political expectations, doomed love, mystical faith, the slings and arrows aimed at Gonne by an uncomprehending world. Another note struck by the collection stressed Celticism, visions of apocalypse, and what can only be described as flamboyant obscurantism. This quality is most obvious in poems that did not come quite right, like the much rewritten 'Aedh pleads with the Elemental Powers'. But it also pervades the hard, mysterious simplicity of 'The Song of Wandering Aengus', a near-perfect adaptation of the Gaelic *aisling* form, where a visionary woman appears to the dazzled poet – who in this case is also the god of love. The final arrangement had been sent off in late November 1898, when he was still expecting some kind of mystic apotheosis, and a final reconciliation with Gonne. This is expressed in what was probably the last poem written before publication, and destined for immortality: 'Aedh wishes for the Cloths of Heaven'.

> Had I the heavens' embroidered cloths,
> Enwrought with golden and silver light,
> The blue and the dim and the dark cloths
> Of night and light and the half light,
> I would spread the cloths under your feet:
> But I, being poor, have only my dreams;
> I have spread my dreams under your feet;
> Tread softly because you tread on my dreams.

Yet the book as a whole (and WBY conceived of it as an entity) strikes an indecisive note between despair and anticipation; both love-poems and visionary *aperçus* convey a sense of deferred climax, and return again and again to the themes of exhaustion and silence (subject of a famous 1897 essay by Maeterlinck, noted by both WBY and Symons). This throws into even sharper relief the occasional challenging grace-note, like the unaffectedly virtuoso little ballad 'The Fiddler of Dooney'. First published in 1892, the 1899 version was shorn of minor folksy archaisms, and it emerged as the kind of poem which WBY could by now handle to perfection. Verbal complexity is lent by place-names, a dance rhythm is manipulated masterfully, and a sardonic twist of language leaves a subversive message lingering at the end: finally affirming the priesthood of art above the pieties of convention.

> When I play on my fiddle in Dooney,
> Folk dance like a wave of the sea;
> My cousin is priest in Kilvarnet,
> My brother in Moharabuiee.
>
> I passed my brother and cousin:
> They read in their books of prayer;·

I read in my book of songs
I bought at the Sligo fair.

When we come at the end of time,
To Peter sitting in state,
He will smile on the three old spirits,
But call me first through the gate;

For the good are always the merry,
Save by an evil chance,
And the merry love the fiddle
And the merry love to dance:

And when the folk there spy me,
They will all come up to me,
With 'Here is the fiddler of Dooney!'
And dance like a wave of the sea.

This Mozartian touch mercilessly exposed the limitations of younger contemporaries already attempting the Yeatsian mode. Though WBY temporarily dropped it from his *Collected Works* in 1908, in 1909 it was not only readmitted to *The Wind Among the Reeds* but placed as the signature-poem which ended the collection.

Reactions to the volume were quizzical. In some quarters bewilderment was expressed at WBY's deliberate search for obscurity, particularly in his notes ('Why did he write them?', JBY querulously inquired of Gregory[60]). Elsewhere, *The Wind Among the Reeds* was inevitably used as ammunition in the battles around the Irish Literary Theatre. A front-page article in the *United Irishman* regretted WBY's mistiness and obscurantism, while an important long review by Francis Thompson in the *Academy* described him as a pure poet with an authentic but 'contracted' gift: a unique voice speaking across a narrow range. Above all, the new volume's reliance on elaborate magical symbols was worrying.

The only road out is the clumsy expedient of explanatory notes. This is not the true use of symbolism, and from a purely poetical standpoint is quite inartistic. It creates wanton difficulty. Mr Yeats should at any rate be clear to the few who understand the system of mythological imagery. But his arbitrary use of it often leaves even them in dark. 'I use this to signify so and so,' is the formula. But he should not 'use it to signify' anything. He should use it, if he needs it, for what it does signify; and if he is unsure what it signifies, he should not use it at all. It is wantonness to darken his poetry by employing recondite imagery, which he confesses elaborately he is doubtful about the meaning of. Frankly, there is more ingenuity than insight in much of it.[61]

WBY rather defensively claimed that George Moore, Edmund Gosse and York Powell considered *The Wind Among the Reeds* his best book. (He inaccurately thought that York Powell compared it to 'Sapho'.[62]) He put the usual effort into arranging reviews, advising Symons about his piece in the *Saturday Review*,[63] which duly stressed the technical virtuosity and accessibility of the new volume (and incidentally advertised the Irish Literary Theatre). Equally 'inspired' was Stephen MacKenna's long article in the *Gael*, 'The Personality of W. B. Yeats', which shows the close identification of WBY's public persona and the impact of his work ('strikingly handsome . . . he looks like his poems'). The poet had become, according to MacKenna, 'the first Irishman of the day', yet remained resolutely other-worldly. MacKenna wrote as an insider, revealing how WBY had arrived at his sartorial style by working through various affectations. The conclusion could hold true for his literary work as well. He was much exercised about his inability to learn the native language. He had now achieved 'infinite quiet dignity . . . absolute self-possession'. He was still picturesque, but no longer laughable. He projected a loveable quality, especially for women, and yet had developed a 'hard practical common sense' on committees and a good business head.

This last quality was much in evidence immediately after the appearance of the new volume and his revised and reprinted *Poems*. In May and June he relentlessly pressed Fisher Unwin for a new financial deal, 'a greatly increased royalty etc.', encouraged by experienced literary friends like Clement Shorter. This was essential. The two books signed off an era, containing 'all of his published poetry which he cares to preserve'.[64] He had ceased writing lyric poetry, and would not return to it for over a year. This meant practical as well as artistic deprivation. For a single poem he could now demand £5 (though he accepted less);[65] the £40 which arrived from the *North American Review* in August for his long article, 'The Intellectual Movement in Ireland', was a rare bonus, easing his 'desperate' financial state and enabling him to pay his debts and send £5 to JBY. His strategy in the summer of 1899 was to make sure as much of his work as possible was on sale to coincide with the Irish Literary Theatre campaign. *The Wind Among the Reeds* and the second edition of *Poems* were both in the shops, and in June he suggested reissuing his *Book of Irish Verse* (with twelve new pages) to cash in on his other sales.[66] He now told Lily that he would 'review no more books because, though it brings in money more quickly, it gets me into all kinds of difficulties & quarrels & wastes my time.'[67] Solicitations from magazine editors for short lyrics were firmly refused. His own view, at this juncture, was that his future lay in poetic drama.

By late May he was at Coole, sketching, painting in pastels[68] and burying himself in a rewrite of *The Shadowy Waters*. His theatrical baptism had taught him that any hope of an eventual production as play rather than dramatic poem depended upon radical reconstruction, and he cherished an ambition to see it in rehearsal by late autumn. Moore, staying near by with Martyn, offered copious advice. The original love-story, set in shadowy Irish prehistory, had taken an occult turn *à la* Villiers de l'Isle-Adam: Moore suggested excision, simplification and more sex, deeply offending Russell. The results would be published a year later in the *North American Review*, but the poem, like its hero Forgael, never reached a final destination. WBY wrote to Russell that he now conceived the play as a hymn to 'the ideal human marriage'.[69] Yet a central uncertainty remained: were the lovers to end apart or together? Equally suggestive of his own private life was the theme of Forgael's insufficient commitment to love: a passion which simply demanded a reflection, not a reciprocity. This Tristan and Isolde clung together through uncertainty rather than commitment. And Dectora's symbol, like Gonne's, was apple-blossom. This was closely connected with the visions of apocalypse and a New Age which still intermittently haunted him. A carefully recorded dream in early July, brought on by invoking apple-blossom, had WBY careering in a runaway þrake, through a city like Paris, flying by workmen preparing their tasks for the Last Day. He ended at a wide river, with descending parachutes advertising quack remedies, pushed by a charlatan, and awoke 'in great terror' of some unknown horror hiding in the dark. 'I had been writing during the day at the part of "The Shadowy Waters" where its hero curses all visible things because they shut out the invisible peace. It seemed to me, that this medicine man repeated the curse and that he was the world which shuts out nature. The apple blossoms are symbols of dawn and of the air and of the east and of resurrection in my system and in the poem.'[70]

The roots of WBY's inability to bring *The Shadowy Waters* to a conclusion lay deep in the inconclusive passages with Gonne six months before, but the play's theatrical potential was further limited by his desire for a poetic, ritual drama of atmosphere – markedly Maeterlinckian, though WBY elaborately denied the influence. Meanwhile, work on it stopped him writing anything else, owing, as he explained it, to his slowness in composition, producing at most 'five or six good lines a day'. By 19 August only 400 lines had been written. 'I dont think it will be a popular poem, but I think it may be a good deal noticed for it is very wild & passionate.'[71] Work continued through autumn and winter, complicated by Moore's advice (though Russell loyally offered to 'strangle him if necessary'[72]). Finally a version was dispatched to the *North American Review* in early January 1900; but this too was fated to a life of revisions.

Thus the composition of *The Shadowy Waters* involved considerable stress, psychological as well as financial. As so often, his health broke down in mid-June, and JBY wrote anxiously to Gregory about the danger of rheumatic fever ('you are to him as a mother, better than a mother'[73]). She took him to a shooting lodge in the hills to recuperate; they returned to Coole to be joined by Hyde and his German wife, a disastrous acquisition in WBY's view.

A dragon . . . never done abusing the Irish language & Ireland & everything that Hyde cares about. She is fairly pretty & probably a flirt & certainly a curious narrow peevish person who is yet always looking about for a sympathy, which she is always, unknown to herself, repelling. Hyde never shows any sign of temper, or of thinking her way of talking unusual, but everybody here has been amazed by it, including a priest who says he would 'die of it in a week'. Martyn points her out as another argument against women & marriage.[74]

At a public meeting in Gort, where the Kiltartan Gaelic League had recently been launched, Hyde and WBY spoke against Anglicization, and WBY launched a particularly passionate manifesto about language revival.

For good or for evil he had to write his own books in English, and to content himself with filling them with as much Irish thought and emotion as he could, for no man can get a literary mastery of two languages in one lifetime; but he foresaw without regret a time when what was the work of his life would be in a foreign language to a great part of the people of this country . . . The nationhood of Ireland had been committed to their care by the saints and martyrs of the generations that had gone before them, and the language of Ireland was necessary to its preservation . . . Irish nationhood was like some holy sacrificial fire, and where we stood watching O'Neill and Sarsfield and Emmett [sic] and Davis had watched before.[75]

This declaration of Fenian principles was not an isolated outburst to educate Mrs Hyde. It was a salvo in a battle opened by WBY with a speech in a Trinity College debate on 31 May, where the motion that an Irish literary movement would result in provincialism was unanimously rejected. WBY also used the occasion to reply to the journal of the Gaelic League, *An Claidheamh Soluis*, where Patrick Pearse had declared (in English) that the time had come to 'crush' the Irish Literary Theatre for daring to suggest a national culture could be expressed in any language other than Irish.[76] WBY defended this idea more unequivocally than ever before, while skilfully rejecting commercialism and materialism; and he prophetically endorsed the notion of artistic extravagance, 'far better than that apathy, or cynicism, which were deep-setting sins here in Dublin'. A bitter reference to the cold welcome afforded Irish writers in Dublin not only linked his work to Ferguson's, but proved that the gibes of the *United Irishman* had the power to hurt. However, the subsequent issue of Griffith's paper indicated that the editor was not impressed. ' "I believe the work of Ireland is to lift up its voice for spirituality, for ideality, for simplicity in the English-speaking world," said Mr Yeats. We believe nothing of the kind. The work of Ireland is to uplift itself, not to play the missionary nation.'[77] Not for the first or last time, WBY's artistic ambitions were accused of diluting authentic nationalism. For his part, Pearse went on to spend much of the summer exposing (in English) WBY's claims to be 'Irish' or 'national' since he could not speak the native tongue.[78] Given the background, WBY's endorsement of advanced nationalism at Gort was unsurprising. It shows a line being thrown to the *United Irishman* and *An Claidheamh*, a demonstration that the theatre movement was sound on the national question, a repudiation of Trinity College values, and a consciousness on WBY's own part that he had a rendezvous with Gonne two weeks later.

They met in Belfast in mid-September and travelled on to Dublin. WBY's letters show him disconsolately waiting at the Nassau Hotel and anticipating a meeting to protest against British policy in the Transvaal: 'irrelevant for me', but, he told Gregory, Gonne had to be supported as 'all kinds of intreagues' might leave her without speakers. 'A miserable Feniain, among the rest, is beleived to have destroyed the invitations to members of parliment which he was given to post, but whether by direction of his particular clique or not heaven knows.'[79] After attending a pro-Boer meeting at Beresford Place on 1 October, chaired by O'Leary, WBY returned to Coole. Here he became involved in Moore's recasting of Martyn's play 'The Tale of a Town' (to emerge as *The Bending of the Bough* in the Irish Literary Theatre's next season);[80] Moore recalled WBY's literary intelligence, 'as keen as a knife', cutting through the knots Martyn had tied into his play, while the agonized author sat mutely by. He emphasized WBY's abstracted but ruthless discounting of Martyn's feelings, spending days at Tillyra dismembering 'The Tale', while Gregory pursued Moore with letters about the poet's dietary and rest requirements.[81] The idea of Moore's and WBY's co-operation on a play about the legendary lovers of the Fianna cycle, Diarmuid and Grania, dates from this time – as does Gregory's strenuous advice against the project. But in mid-November WBY returned to Dublin, collecting Gonne, and they travelled to London together. She went on to Paris, after breaking the journey in Woburn Buildings. Thus they remained like the brother and sister they believed they once were: interdependent, travelling together, but chaste.

IV

The love-lives of his London friends were less tramelled. WBY returned to the news that his illustrator and friend, the fragile bohemian Althea Gyles, had taken up with the publisher Leonard Smithers, whom he severely banned from Monday nights at Woburn Buildings. 'This may, & probably will make her quarrell with me for which I shall be sorry as I imagine I am about the only person who belongs to the orderly world she is likely to meet from this out.'[82] Elsewhere, however, he implied that drunkenness rather than immorality made

Smithers socially intolerable;[83] and where sexual licence was concerned, he still resented the way Russell 'bemoralized' him about his London friends. 'He & I are the opposite of one another,' he told Gregory.

I think I understand people easily & easily sympathize with all kinds of characters & easily forgive all kinds of defects & vices. I have the defect of this quality. Apart from opinions, which I judge too sternly, I scarcely judge people at all & am altogether too lax in my attitude towards conduct. He understands nobody but himself & so must always be either condemning or worshiping. He is a good judge of right & wrong so long as they can be judged apart from people, so long as they are merely actions to be weighed by the moral sense . . . when he speaks of any action connected with a man like either Moore or Symons he is liable to be equally wrong because of his condem[n]ation of the man. His moral enthusiasm is with him an actual inspiration but it makes him understand ideas & not human nature. One pays a price for everything.[84]

A year later he would visit the ill and increasingly *distraite* Gyles, abandoned by Smithers and fallen under the ministrations of Annie Horniman, illustrating how the circles of WBY's apparently far-flung life overlapped. And Horniman was involved in another sphere where WBY's 'stern' judgement of opinions and 'easy' (or lax, or uninterested) attitude towards personalities came into sharp relief, and which reclaimed him during the winter of 1899/1900: the occult brethren of the Golden Dawn.

Trouble had been brewing in the Order since December 1896, when Mathers had quarrelled with Horniman. While WBY had stayed friendly with Mathers, he had become distanced from him by late 1899, and increasingly suspicious of the Comte de Glenstrae's obsession with Egyptological rites. From Coole, WBY had been sharing invocations and dreams with his correspondents; on his return to London he reread Swedenborg, attended Golden Dawn meetings, and helped found an irregular debating society called the 'Fellowship of the Three Kings', which combined literary exchanges with discussions of symbols and mysticism. But, as so often in these years, the private agenda of spiritual inquiry intended to capture Gonne was interrupted by events in the political world where she imperiously declared her own authority.

The long-fomented war against the recalcitrant Boers in South Africa began in October – seen by radicals and nationalists as naked imperial interference with a noble republic of independent-minded farmers. Gonne, much involved with ideologues of the French Right, took it as further evidence that the Jewish-financier conspiracy represented by Dreyfus stretched to Britain. In November she formed the 'Boer Franco-Irish Committee' with Arthur Lynch – currently a Fenian pro-Boer, but with a chequered future ahead of him. (Richard Best drily recalled her lecturing at Neuilly 'to an audience of six' about Britain's iniquity, accepting a bouquet of roses, and sweeping out on the arm of Lynch – who, when Best next met him, had accepted a commission in the British Army.[85]) Dublin meetings centred upon the rooms of the Celtic Literary Society and involved Connolly, Gonne, Griffith, O'Leary and the charismatic young Fenian William Rooney, but also constitutionalists like Davitt and William Redmond. Gonne pressed WBY to join in with a poem for the cause or articles in the *United Irishman*, which she was privately subsidizing with 25*s.* a week. 'Its circulation has *doubled* during the last month & it is really *very* good, but I don't suppose you ever see it.'[86]

By mid-December he had given Gonne a public letter of support for her Boer victory meeting[87] – though he cannot have been sorry to miss the meeting itself, since it ended in a riot and the arrest of James Connolly, charged with the unseditious crime of driving without a licence.[88] Gonne's anti-recruiting plans later developed further: she considered the bombing of British troop-ships and toured America with incendiary speeches. The bomb-scheme was to be financed by the Transvaal, but money was diverted into the pocket of the inevitable Frank Hugh O'Donnell. She further alleged that he betrayed a French agent sent to make contact with the IRB; though in actuality O'Donnell himself was acting for the Boers and relaying money to the IRB, who were determined to cut Gonne out. 'Her chatter and conceit could jeopardise the freedom and lives of many people'.[89] By the end of 1899 WBY was uneasily monitoring revolutionary activity in Gonne's circle; anticipating trouble in the Golden Dawn as Mathers moved towards denouncing more of the London brethren and claiming full powers; and planning the next season of the Irish Literary Theatre, to begin in February. But at this point family life intervened: on 3 January 1900 his mother died quietly at home in Bedford Park.

She had been away in a world of her own for some years; the bad-tempered outbursts recorded by her daughters had apparently been replaced by a slippage into silence and mental feebleness, precipitated by a series of strokes.[90] In a composed letter to Gregory the next day WBY remarked 'it has of course been inevitable for a long time; & it is long since my mother has been able to recognise any of us, except with difficulty. I think my sister Lilly & myself feal it most through our father.' This was true. A few months later Olivia Shakespear's own mother died, and he wrote to her, 'When a mother is near ones heart at all her loss must be the greatest of all losses.'[91] The tone is speculative rather than experienced, and he was honest enough not to compare his own loss to Shakespear's. But a link to Sligo and the powerful Pollexfen world was snapped; the ménage at Bedford Park was transformed; and WBY saw the future through his father's eyes, swiftly pointing out that with a less expensive household JBY could give up magazine illustrations and paint portraits for exhibitions.[92] None the less, at the end of the month he was once more irritating his father by treating him 'de haut en bas'.[93] By April 1900 the elder Yeats had paid his current debts and gone to Paris to view the Louvre. WBY's recourse was less glamorous: a violent bout of influenza at the end of January. Once recovered, he threw himself into political and occult activity with an energy galvanized – as so often before – by personal catharsis.

Chapter 9 : OCCULT POLITICS
1900–1901

> We who are seeking to sustain this great Order must never
> forget that whatever we build in the imagination will accom-
> plish itself in the circumstance of our lives.
>
> WBY, *Is the Order of R.R. et A.C.*
> *to remain a Magical Order?*

I

THE Irish Literary Theatre's second programme was announced in Janu-
ary 1900: Edward Martyn's *Maeve*, Alice Milligan's *The Last Feast of the
Fianna*, and *The Bending of the Bough*, whose authorship was politely disputed
behind the scenes. Martyn at last gave way resentfully to Moore, feeling it
was 'too ugly' to claim as his own.[1] Rehearsals took place in London, where
Gregory tried to keep the peace, noting that WBY implicitly believed every-
thing Moore said about his collaboration with Martyn: 'all very well, but he
doesn't believe him when he attacks Miss Gonne's morality'.[2] The season
opened on 20 February, this time in the Gaiety Theatre. Once again, enter-
tainment was organized by Dublin hostesses, an issue of *Beltaine* was pub-
lished, and a spice of controversy was added by the *drame à clef* aspect of *The
Bending of the Bough*. Its theme of local politics and national commitment was
variously interpreted as a satire on the recently reunited Irish Parliamentary
Party, and 'the rise, fall and extinction of Lord Castletown'. WBY crisply told
George Coffey, 'You can tell any body you like that O'Brien is not in the play
& that a great deal of patriotism is in it.'[3] Martyn's pique was fuelled when
Moore's appropriation of his original play eclipsed the lack-lustre *Maeve*
and fustian *Last Feast of the Fianna*. In January, when negotiations had looked
ominous, WBY was already calculating where to raise backing if Martyn
pulled out. The potential donor whom he had identified was his ally in the
Golden Dawn, Annie Horniman.[4]

   WBY travelled from London with Gregory and Moore.[5] As before, the
Theatre's season was marked on 22 February by an entertainment, this time
at the Gresham Hotel rather than at the Shelbourne. The backing of the *Express*
was no longer offered since Gill had been removed in a *coup* the previous
September, to WBY's chagrin ('a great blow to all our interests'[6]). No longer
useful, he was ruthlessly ignored. 'I think Gill feels a little hurt that he has
never heard anything from anybody about the arrangements for the Literary
Theatre this year,' wrote Russell to Gregory. 'Considering the part he took

last time both in the Express & getting up the dinner I think Yeats Martyn or Moore should have consulted him or let him know what was going on or if anything similar was to be attempted this time. Nobody here seems to bother about the Theatre because nobody knew what was to be done, or what the newspapers were to say & how they were to be worked.'[7] All in all, the occasion was a good deal more muted than in 1899. The *United Irishman* admitted 'that the audiences have been small, wretchedly small, only goes to show how low and how far our people have fallen from the appreciation of true art and sympathy with Irish thought, tradition and sentiment'.[8] At the Gresham lunch (menu in Irish and food in English, the *Express* tartly remarked) Moore, unreliable as ever, swerved into a manifesto on behalf of Gaelicization, unexpectedly committing the Irish Literary Theatre to a translation (by Hyde) of *The Land of Heart's Desire*. He had previously alarmed Gregory by his wish to have *The Shadowy Waters* translated: she feared '"Three Men in a Boat" talking gibberish'.[9] wby, in line with his speeches of the previous summer, called for educational reform to build the Irish language into the syllabus, and instructed the Irish Parliamentary Party to resist 'any denationalising system of education'.[10] This identified the patrons on whom the Theatre now relied. Martyn was kept mollified, and remained committed to meeting all their outstanding debts at the end of the third year.[11] But he had been eased out of the inner circle and would shortly transfer his energies and his money into a campaign to eradicate women from church choirs.

With the loss of the *Express* as well, support had to be ensured from more conventional nationalist quarters. *Maeve* was taken as a patriotic allegory, but Gregory was relieved that *The Bending of the Bough* 'hits so impartially all round that no-one is really offended'; when wby announced to the audience that the Theatre's future productions would be 'equally patriotic in intention', she privately resolved to 'keep politics out of plays in future'.[12] Meanwhile, indefatigably squaring journalists at tea parties, she put a brave face on it. But the programme attracted less attention than the previous year, and disagreements were nearing the surface. wby had only recently recovered from influenza; he had no play of his own on the stage; the excitement, barrage of publications and high exposure of the previous season had been dispersed. The year 1900 had dawned, with no sign of the expected millennial revelations. Moreover, since the previous autumn he had become involved in Gonne's and Griffith's pro-Boer movement. This commitment, allied to the anti-climax of the Theatre season, pressed wby into a forward political stance in the spring of 1900.

In the version recollected for his *Memoirs* many years later, he recalled drifting into fringe Fenianism through the '98 commemorations and the Wolfe Tone Memorial Association. 'I formed a grandiose plan without considering the men I had to work with, exactly as if [I] were writing something in a story.' Just like Frank Hugh O'Donnell, his active imagination constructed more exciting politics than those available from the materials to hand. The *Memoirs* then dissolve, strategically, into a series of undated vignettes: his idea of a secessionist parliament, the Jubilee riots (actually 1897), the Centennial celebrations. Some incidents are probably conflated, such as Gonne's and Connolly's performances in the anti-Chamberlain demonstration (December 1899) and the Jubilee riots of two years before;[13] the order of events becomes inescapably confused. In the WBY version, Fenian activity is improbably seen as the impetus behind the reunification of the Irish Parliamentary Party in 1900; the threat to its electoral machine posed by the mass mobilization of the United Irish League was a far more influential factor. Thus WBY's own tentative political involvements are placed at the centre of national events.

What can be established is that Gonne rapidly adopted the movement against the Boer War as a focus for her various political interests, and WBY cautiously followed her. They visited Mark Ryan, who had been a key figure in the shortlived INA, in search of Boer funds – an occasion mordantly relayed to the Boer agent in Brussels.

'Millevoye's young lady' came to our Chief's house, quite furious at not having received what she demanded. She was accompanied by one named Yeats who it is said is the latest successor to Millevoye, and before this young man she said all she had heard at your house and further ... She declared that you had claimed to be in communication with Irish revolutionaries 'through a person who did not belong to their organization'!!! Without doubt, within 24 hours all Dublin will know she has not had success because, and because, and because etc. etc.

If she is not a spy she is almost one and her bragging is more dangerous than treachery itself.[14]

Gonne was also involved in the revived land agitation, issuing manifestos encouraging the tenants to go to jail: 'What do they risk?' It would bring them 'honour' and 'relieve them of the maddening monotony of watching the land'.[15] Both WBY and Russell were associated with Gonne's Evicted Tenants Committee, but a year earlier Gregory had recorded her disquiet, and WBY's ambivalence, at Gonne's extremism.[16] Her campaign was more and more associated with the *United Irishman*'s other cult-figure, John ('Foxy Jack') MacBride, IRB man and hero of the South African struggle, whose parliamentary candidature for South Mayo at this time was presented by the paper as a contest of 'The Gold of the Jews against the Irish Brigade'.[17] WBY accordingly weighed in too. On 20 March 1900 he wrote to the *Freeman's Journal* with the idea of a protest against the Queen's forthcoming visit to Ireland. This was no more than the line taken by the Irish Parliamentary Party in the House of Commons, but WBY's powerful polemic indicted the Queen's advisers with 'hatred of our individual National life' and accused the monarch of doing the work of a recruiting sergeant. He called for a Rotunda meeting, choosing 2 April as the centenary of the introduction of the Act of Union into the British Parliament – a proposal swiftly put forward by Gregory, as it was less stridently anti-monarchist.[18] O'Leary would chair it, disassociating Ireland from any welcome offered to 'the official head of that empire in whose name liberty is being suppressed in South Africa as it was suppressed in Ireland a hundred years ago'.

This Fenian language, together with O'Leary's presence, sharpened WBY's challenge that 'all Irish members' should be on the platform. When they subsequently came aboard, he tried to make the Parnellite MP Timothy Harrington stand down in favour of MacBride. In his manifestos WBY aligned himself nearer separation, and what Pollexfens would have called 'disloyalty', than the acceptable (if fudging) language of Home Rule. It looked like a burning of boats; George Pollexfen allegedly cut off a subvention to his nephew because of it, and Lecky certainly resigned as a guarantor of the Irish Literary Theatre. WBY took care to point out to Gregory that 'he had nothing to resign as his guarantee had not been renewed'. But his own pro-Boer alignment in March 1900 exposed the implicit contradictions between the neo-Fenian rhetoric of his political life, and the polite pluralism of 'respectable' cultural revivalism represented by the backers of the Irish Literary Theatre.

Having alienated the Pollexfen world, he tried to explain himself to Gregory (safely in Italy).

I dont think we need be anxious about next years theatre. Moore talks confidently of finding the money, & I feal sure that our present politics will have done more good than harm. Clever unionists will take us on our merits & the rest would never like us at any time. I have found a greatly increased friendliness on the part of some of the young men here. In a battle, like Irelands, which is one of poverty against wealth, one must prove ones sincerity, by making oneself unpopular to wealth. One must accept the baptism of the gutter. Have not all teachers done the like?[19]

He would use this argument in his public defence too. But Gregory was not entirely convinced; certainly her opinion of Moore and his influence was not enhanced, and a month later she resolutely dissuaded WBY from embarking on a joint American lecture-tour with him to campaign against the war. Though he assured Gregory that he was relieved not to go, his early reaction had been enthusiastic: Moore's polemic against 'the vulgarity of a materialism whereon England founds her worst life & the whole life that she sends us' appealed to him, rather than the simple-minded Anglophobia and anti-Semitism expounded by 'our extremists'.[20] Arthur Griffith and D. P. Moran liked to fulminate about 'Irish soldiers sacrificed on the altar of the Hebrew Moloch' and 'the swarming Jews of Johannesburg';[21] Moore, more subtle and much more sympathetic, continued to fascinate him. WBY even suggested, later in the year, that his outrageous friend should enter Parliament 'if he had a definite offer of a seat without a contest'.[22] But their relationship remained clouded by Moore's uncontrollable propensity for saying scandalous things about Gonne, and WBY's uncontrollable propensity for repeating them to her.

The Boer War had aligned Irish nationalism along a broad front, and the Irish Literary Theatre fell into line. Both Martyn and Moore were prominent pro-Boers, or at least anti-imperialists, and WBY had identified himself with the most extreme wing. Though his further public letters attacking government censorship stressed protest within the law, he could no longer sit on the fence. Ripples from the splash of his letter about the Queen's visit rocked the Irish Literary Society in London, where WBY's election to the committee caused A. P. Graves to resign as Secretary, in protest against his political stance. Despite his lofty references to 'our extremists' in letters to Gregory, WBY was by now seen as their mouthpiece.

Publicity was, apparently, inescapable. Sensibilities were intensified by the royal visit; Gonne became the butt of attacks in a Dublin society magazine, the *Figaro*, which branded her a government spy. This led to a libel suit brought by Gonne and a public assault on its editor (Ramsay Colles) by Arthur Griffith. WBY offered tentatively to testify in the court case but was refused; once more, he watched others around her behave decisively while he remained irresolute in the world of action. Meanwhile the irrepressible Frank Hugh O'Donnell interposed once more. In May WBY confided excitedly to Gregory that their old enemy

has been busy 'Felon setting' as we call in Ireland making public the treasonable acts of others. I have a lot of documents & have accused him & am trying to get a court of investigation – all this is private of course. The person attacked is Maud Gonne & he has been driven on by an insane jelousey. I doubt if I shall get my court, as O Donnell has some people in his power I am afraid – or rather in his pay. It is a very unpleasant business and one of which I got first warning curiously enough by clairvoyance.[23]

The 'court' was evidently an internal Fenian investigation, to be arranged through Mark Ryan in London. This letter is one of the few concrete pieces of evidence that WBY was actively involved in the movement, but he was also lobbying constitutional politicians like Dillon and Davitt.[24] For much of the spring and early summer he was in London, displaying in struggles over the Golden Dawn the decisiveness which he felt he lacked in other involvements. But Gonne, beleaguered on several fronts, pressed him with inquiries about meetings on the astral plane. In late June they travelled to Dublin together: he *en route* to Coole, she to preside over her 'Patriotic Children's Treat' (a triumph of publicity) on 1 July.[25] He evidently pursued her romantically once more, and after they parted wrote her a letter of 'kind sweet things'. She replied on 7 July:

my dear Friend I do not want you to make up your mind to sacrifice yourself for me. I know that just now, perhaps, it is useless my saying to you 'love some other woman'. All I want of you is not to make up your mind *not* to, to put it before you as a duty, that would be wrong the gods do not want that, & it makes me very sad. As for me you are right in saying I will be always to you as a sister. I have chosen a life which to some might be hard, but which to me is the only one possible. I am not unhappy only supremely indifferent to all that is not my work or my friends. One cannot go through what I went through & have any personal human life left, what is quite natural & right for me is not natural or right for one who has still his natural life to live – All I want of you is not to build up an imaginary wall of duty or effort between you and life – for the rest the gods will arrange, for you are one of those they have chosen to do their work.[26]

This was what he wanted to hear: consecration for them both, and freedom to work on their separate paths. Their relationship probably inspired the new love scene between Aleel and the Countess in *The Countess Cathleen*, added later that year. The poet–musician offers himself along with his artistic homage, the Countess affirms her prior commitment to the people. Their exchanges closely echo his enduring dialogue with Gonne. Cathleen fantasizes briefly about the life they could have together, far away and at peace, and then admonishes herself.

> . . . Although I weep I do not weep
> Because that life would be most happy, and here
> I find no way, no end. Nor do I weep
> Because I had longed to look upon your face,
> But that a night of prayer has made me weary.

Aleel has been led astray by a vision of Aengus, pagan god of love; she steels herself against his power to waken 'the passionate, proud heart'.

> Do not hold out to me beseeching hands.
> This heart shall never waken on earth,

But when Aleel apologizes for his temerity, she tells him art confers true aristocracy – and implicitly deplores her own frigidity.

> God's procreant waters flowing about your mind
> Have made you more than kings or queens; and not you
> But I am the empty pitcher.

And when he has gone, she admits how he has stirred her 'imagination and heart'.[27] Here, if anywhere, is an echo of Gonne's alleged revulsion from physical love (at least where WBY was concerned), and the hopes he retained that her hidden vulnerability would bring her to him in the end. And in a parallel process of autobiographical transposition, the next drafts of *The Speckled Bird* reflected conflicts with colleagues in his search for occult wisdom.

II

Throughout the spring of 1900 WBY was simultaneously involved in a crisis concerning the politics of the Golden Dawn. By April Mathers's antagonism towards the London branch had become absolute. Quarrels about ultimate authority raised the complicated and dubious story of the Order's origin-myth, with Mathers revealing that the letters from the mysterious 'Anna Sprengel' had been forged by William Wynn Westcott, and claiming for himself the authorship of most of the rituals.[28] Largely true as this may have been, it was not what the fratres and sorores could afford to hear. In late March Florence Farr, now the rather unlikely Chief Adept, had consulted the brotherhood (including WBY) about Mathers's pretensions, and on 2 April he attempted to 'annul' resolutions which they had passed reflecting on his integrity and financial probity. An incidental effect of all this was to rehabilitate Annie Horniman in the Order. Since she had first clashed with Mathers over matters of money as well as spiritual authority, her judgement appeared vindicated. Her adoptive name and motto, 'Soror Fortiter et Recte', was carefully chosen; she knew she was right. While her obsessiveness, self-importance and energy continued to irritate the other adepts, WBY supported her firmly. He had, moreover, already measured her up as a prospective backer for his theatrical ventures.

On 17 April 1900 Mathers sent an envoy to break into the Isis-Urania Temple at 36 Blythe Road, Hammersmith, and take possession of the magical 'properties' there. The emissary was the 25-year old Aleister Crowley. As yet uninitiated in the Order, he had attached himself to Mathers and embarked on a career in occultism where both his fame and his fabulism (as 'the wickedest man in the world') would eventually eclipse those of his mentor. He was ejected when Farr called a police constable, but sent notices claiming the right to take over proceedings. Guard duty was taken over by Edmund Hunter, who appealed to WBY (a friend and ally through Celtic ritualism as well as membership of the Second Order); on 19 April they changed the locks and awaited Crowley's next assault. He arrived before midday, wearing full Highland dress plus the 'mask of Osiris'. The inhabitants of Hammersmith may have been more surprised than WBY, who believed he had been warned of this intervention by occult divination and astral communications ('a clear proof of the value of systematic training even in these subtle things', he pointedly told Russell[29]). Less subtly, Hunter was a proficient boxer and his reputation had gone before him, which may have been a more decisive factor in the ejection of Crowley. But the wickedest man in the world was also discomfited to encounter WBY, whom he had met the year before and cordially hated – an antipathy sealed by WBY's unenthusiastic response to Crowley's poems (their author put it down to 'bilious' jealousy). In the battle of Blythe Road, WBY's divinations and Hunter's fists saw off the satanic incursion. WBY stayed in the building guarding its contents until 25 April, and arranged legal proceedings against Crowley through the eminent barrister Charles Russell.

WBY had now broken finally with Mathers, his early mentor, and took the leading part in his suspension. At a meeting of the Order on 21 April he delivered an address repudiating Mathers's influence and fanaticism, and outlining ideas for the Order's reconstruction: his scheme amounted to a Reformation, replacing Mathers's pretensions to papal infallibility with the individual consciences of a committee of seven, along with the 'Scholar's' approach to occult matters advocated by Horniman and WBY. He himself emerged as 'Instructor in Mystical Philosophy'. On 23 April WBY heard that the legal case against Crowley had been won. But he remained intensely worried about unwelcome publicity, the effect of the farce and scandal on innocent devotees like George Pollexfen, and the danger that someone like Crowley ('a person of unspeakable life', already embroiled in homosexual scandal) should gain control.

In May the Order passed new by-laws which put WBY on an executive council with Farr and Horniman, now invited back as Scribe. But the threat of a Mathers–Crowley takeover was replaced by another kind of struggle. Horniman, returned to the circle of power, presented herself as the guardian of probity and began rooting out administrative inefficiency; she particularly rebuked Farr for intellectual sloppiness, and frivolous deviation into Egyptological studies such as *The Book of the Dead*. Relations became increasingly strained, and WBY was caught between his commitment to an old (and attractive) friend, and his cultivation of a potential patron. Once again he was put in the position of trying to please two women, often by appearing to each as she wanted him to be. But this was more feasible with Gonne and Gregory than with Farr and Horniman. He felt worried about breaking with Farr, and fragments of draft letters show the efforts he put into explaining. Interestingly, he connected their struggle back to the wars over the Irish Literary Society in 1893:

We can make a great movement & in more than magical things but I assure you that if (through week vitality, through forgetfulness or through any other cause) you make it difficult for us to reley upon one another perfectly you make everything impossible. I know through long experience that practical work is an endless worry, an endless waste of time, unless every body carries out their promises, in serious matters, with the most scrupulous care for letter & spirit alike. Years ago Rolleston failed me in the negociations over the 'New Irish Library', & he has made all work in common impossible. We are very good friends but we have never sat on a committee togeather since & I do not think we ever will. We agreed upon a *modus vivendi*, between two contrary projects & he abandoned it, while I was in Ireland, under the influence of Gavan Duffy flatteries & promises. In the arts, & in social life one can be tolerant, one can forgive, in public life once can seldom forgive without doing great mischief.[30]

His friendship with Farr survived; in December he introduced her to the Irish Literary Society, where she chanted 'Innisfree' to an appreciative audience.[31] But in occult commitments he had firmly opted for Horniman's side.

Some relief from the tension was afforded by fictionalizing it in *The Speckled Bird*, to which he returned at the end of April 1900. A slightly satirical note was introduced into his hero's adventures among the adepts, along with a more sceptical portrait of Mathers.[32] A Horniman-figure also appeared, dressed in 'a dark blue dress that was meant to resemble more closely than it did the dress of one of Rossetti's women, and there were some paint marks on the dress'; she trembles with intensity and whistles Wagner. The closeness of other portraits in this circle to Golden Dawn members made it all the more impossible for him to finish the novel, or to publish it; to the fratres and sorores, sworn to secrecy about their Order, it would have constituted an odious betrayal. By the 1902 version, his mockery would be still more overt.

But if the passages of *The Speckled Bird* inspired by the Golden Dawn in 1900 are ironical, those which record his and Gonne's pursuit of 'Celtic Mysteries' are not. Michael attempts to involve Margaret in a spiritual and mystic discipline devoted to finding the secret of the Grail, through a consecrated order of visionaries and the evolution of patterns of ritual. The letters where he pleads with her are probably modelled closely on those he sent to Gonne (now lost).

O my beloved is it not right that you who are so beautiful should become the first priestess of this last reconciliation, the first swallow of this new summer? What other priestess is there? The beautiful must preach a faith whose preaching shall at last be [?] but odours and sweet sounds and sudden emotions and the light among evening clouds and in drooping hair.[33]

But she shatters him by replying in a brief letter announcing her marriage. Michael goes for solace to his occult mentors and they fail him, the Mathers-figure by his lack of 'personal sympathy', the others by their obsessiveness.

Thus through the spring of 1900 WBY had been embattled on two fronts: anti-war politics and the defence of Gonne in Dublin, and the struggles over the Golden Dawn in London. In both arenas he struck a firm attitude, but his private allegiances were divided. He survived the tension, solaced by friendship as well as by the consolations of art; from about this time he began to see Olivia Shakespear again. They shared details about dreams and visions, and in the following year he would write for the *Kensington*, a magazine in which she had an interest. Her ironic, sophisticated sympathy became once more a constant resource for him in London, and remained consistent until her death. Nor did political and occult confrontations interfere with his writing life; he never forgot that his professional status depended upon the London marketplace. The shift from writing lyric poetry to plays, and his abandonment of reviewing, enforced careful consideration of his literary income. So did the increasingly inconvenient allocation of his various books between different publishers. Fisher Unwin still published his early poems, plays and novels. Lawrence & Bullen possessed his short stories, prose and the contract for *The Speckled Bird*. Elkin Mathews had published *The Wind Among the Reeds*, and Hodder & Stoughton had taken on *The Shadowy Waters*. WBY found Fisher Unwin too frugal (he paid an exceptionally low royalty), and Bullen erratic (he drank). In early May 1900 he was attracted by overtures from Macmillan about taking on all his work, but by 20 May, probably swayed by readers' reports emphasizing WBY's dangerous politics, they had withdrawn.[34] In any case, by mid-June WBY decided to put 'all arrangements about my books in the hands of [A. P.] Watt, the agent'. But Fisher Unwin tenaciously held on to the *Poems*, and WBY continued to deal with him directly ('Unwin & Watt are I beleive not on terms'[35]). Renegotiation was completed in December, while a long flirtation with Hodder & Stoughton for an inclusive arrangement came to nothing.[36] He was also warned by London publishers that his political reputation counted against him. In the case of the *Dome* WBY astutely suspected this was a stratagem to pay him less money, though it had certainly swayed Macmillan.[37] But he now knew he could command as much as £40 from American publishers for a long article. The move to an agent (with whom he stayed all his life) was a recognition of professional status, and of his own bargaining power, made at a time when he was decisively taking control in several other areas of his life as well.

Meanwhile, in a June heatwave, he longed to leave London and jingoist celebration of victories over the Boers, but lengthy dentistry (advised and possibly paid for by Gregory) delayed him with 'stoppings' and fittings for false teeth. Even when he escaped to Dublin, Gonne's difficulties with O'Donnell kept him from the west until the end of the month. Once at Coole, however, he fervently attacked his own work – and that of other people. A long and merciless letter went off to the unfortunate Horton about the 'monotony and arridity' of his recent sketches. Cultural enterprises continued to spark into life in Dublin, but wby, who was becoming worried at Gaelic League zealots causing trouble in literary organizations, preferred to stay at Coole.[38] A letter he sent to D. P. Moran's new journal the *Leader* on 26 August effectively argued against the pure Fenian line in cultural matters, and provided a self-defence against the continuing campaign waged against his 'West-Britonism' in the columns of *An Claidheamh Soluis*.[39] When he did venture to Dublin in October to preside at a Gaelic League concert in the Gresham Hotel, he trod very carefully indeed and obviously bore in mind the rancour aroused by Leaguers in the National Literary Society. After a programme that included Moore's *Melodies* as well as step-dancing, wby spoke in English on the Irish language. 'It was no use disguising from themselves that they had now going on in Ireland a war of civilisation, and upon that war not only did the issue of Irish Nationality hang, but the very greatest issues that a man could concern himself with.'[40] He moved on to attack English commercialism and vulgarity, and to call for a new Irish dramatic movement: short plays in Irish, without scenery, played all over Ireland 'in barns'. 'They should revive the old Irish drama' (an undefined concept). This manifesto suggests that theatre might be the arena which would reconcile the different messages he was constrained to broadcast. Ironically, it would prove the very opposite. Nevertheless, the Irish Literary Theatre inaugurated a twelve-year period when he would write a play a year, often revolving around themes which he had already investigated in his poetry – notably the rival claims of imagination and passive contemplation versus the world of action.

Thus from the summer of 1900 much of his poetic composition took the form of 'writing out in prose the substance of some lyrics' – though some tentative poems emerged, including 'Echtge of Streams' (later 'The Withering of the Boughs').[41] He could provide detailed critiques of his friends' art, brutally condemning Horton's drawings and counselling Russell to remember how 'all ancient vision was definite and precise': 'if you want to give ideas for their own sake write prose'.[42] But the theatre seemed able to supply a form of art that could be both didactic and beautiful. For the rest of the summer he lay low while debates about literature and nationality rumbled on in O'Grady's newly established *All Ireland Review*; though at the blessing of the cross erected by Gregory on the poet Raftery's grave in August, WBY spoke vehemently 'in support of the Irish language' on a platform with Douglas Hyde.[43] He resisted calls to protest meetings in Dublin, returned to *The Speckled Bird*, wrote up fairy lore in collaboration with Gregory, and sent manifesto letters to journals like the *All Ireland Review* and Moran's *Leader*, which — excelling in mordant satire — had adopted him as a prime target.[44] But apart from the novel, into which he poured the uncertainties and dissatisfaction of his recent passages with Gonne and the Golden Dawn, he devoted himself to collaboration with Moore on their joint play, *Diarmuid and Grania*.

The mythic Arthurian story concerned the wife of a legendary Irish king, who seduces and elopes with a young warrior; after her lover is apprehended and put to death, she returns to her husband. A scenario, and possibly a draft, had existed since late 1899. In October of that year WBY and Moore had worked on it at Tillyra, and WBY thought Grania 'a wonderful part for a great actress if she can be found'.[45] Moore's letters, however, record an extraordinary kaleidoscope of ideas which dazzled and bewildered WBY through the summer and autumn of 1900.[46] In keeping with Moore's infatuation with WBY, their reciprocity was perceived as a kind of marriage. Moore would write Grania's part ('the dramatic point is [a] woman offering to a man a set of sensuous temptations'), and WBY Diarmuid's; Moore would create the structure, WBY the style. Not the least extraordinary aspect of the collaboration is the fact that Moore's version of it in *Hail and Farewell* appears substantially accurate. But temperamental incompatibility, and WBY's ambivalence about Moore's literary effects, meant that they kept encroaching on each other's territory. WBY altered the structure, Moore invaded the dialogue; WBY wanted 'poetic words', Moore longed for the elemental shock of French Realism. None the less they persevered, and when the summer ended the play accompanied WBY and Moore to Dublin, where the third act rendered Gonne 'breathless with excitement', or so WBY told Gregory.[47] But they were on the search for that 'great actress' who could illuminate the part of Grania, and this brought the two playwrights to Mrs Patrick Campbell's dressing-room at the Royalty Theatre, where she was starring in *Mr and Mrs Daventry*, on 26 October 1900.

Beatrice 'Stella' Campbell was then, at thirty-five, in her full-blown prime; she had just played Maeterlinck and Rostand in Dublin (to a rather equivocal reaction), and she took to *Diarmuid and Grania*. She also took to WBY. It was the beginning of a long flirtation, conducted on several levels. She expressed a desire to play Grania in Dublin in six months' time, and indicated that she would do so in style; when Moore told her it could be done for £250 she replied superbly, 'I intend to spend more than that on the shields alone.'[48] The plan that evolved, however (at Moore's suggestion), was that the Benson Company mount the play in Dublin the following autumn, and Mrs Campbell introduce it to London at a later stage (having paid WBY and Moore £200, which would help finance the Dublin performance). This betrays uncertainty about whether it was actually ready, and by mid-November relations between the collaborators were strained. In part this arose from rivalry over Mrs Campbell, but it was mostly based on sound intellectual grounds. If Moore told WBY 'collaboration is mutual concession', WBY icily reminded Moore that while he himself had given way on questions of dramatic construction, Moore was committed to giving WBY his way in matters of style and vocabulary: 'remember that this is the original compact'. Symons was suggested as an arbitrator, but WBY, while agreeing, feared exactly the kind of surreal public confrontation which his collaborator loved ('who knows but I may have to write a whole number of "Beltaine" about Moore'[49]). By 25 November uneasy co-operation had begun again. By mid-December there were hopes that the end was in sight, apart from Martyn's objections on 'moral grounds'. Gregory was indispensable, appealed to by both men and enlisted by WBY to oversee the arrangements made with the Irish Literary Theatre for *Diarmuid and Grania*: he at once feared the play being 'injurious' to the Theatre, and hoped that it would be successful enough to play a simultaneous London performance.[50] And over all hung the fear of Martyn's sensitive moral conscience and the possible loss of his financial backing: a fear only allayed in December, when Annie Horniman offered a large guarantee 'if Argentine's securities do not fall more than they have done already'.[51] The fish that WBY had been patiently playing was now brought near the bank.

Meanwhile Moore had comprehensively invaded WBY's London life, inviting himself to dinner with the poet's friends and appearing regularly at his Monday evenings ('Mrs Emery may chant something'[52]). He also set off an explosion in the Irish Literary Society when WBY proposed him for membership, only to have the suggestion blackballed by 'respectable' elements, led by Barry O'Brien. This provoked agonies of introspection in WBY: would he seize it as a good resigning issue for himself?[53] The Society had become prey to bourgeois sensibilities; in the same month of December the Vice-President Richard Henn Collins resigned because of WBY's intervention in a discussion on Irish humour. (JBY also thought his son's vehemence on this occasion was 'touched by the revolutionary ardour of the time'.) Feelings were 'stormy' enough for WBY to wonder 'if the planet Mars is doing anything unusual', but Moore had created his own astrological weather. Only the Celtic Rites remained, as a private agenda, and though WBY marshalled and co-ordinated research across a wide front, ardour was cooling. Fiona Macleod was now *persona non grata*. Russell had pursued her in the *New Ireland Review* for unsound ideas and derivative pseudo-Celticism, while WBY and

Gregory had turned down her play *The Immortal Hour* for the unstated reason that it frankly plagiarized *The Shadowy Waters*.[54] As for Gonne, her invitation to join a 'club' setting up a retreat house 'in a Gaelic speaking part of the country with a peasant woman as caretaker & servant' evidently did not appeal to wBY as a method of escape: though it might have been the nearest they ever came to creating a Castle of the Heroes.

But she came to London at the end of December, and asked to spend New Year's Eve with him: she wanted him to read *The Shadowy Waters* to her. This may be the occasion which inspired a draft for a lyric, never completed. In its rough state it conveys the irresolution, self-pity and confusion induced by her presence, as well as isolating a moment in the journey from experience into art.

Subject for lyric

I

O my beloved you only are
    not moved by my <sorrows> songs
which you only understand

You only know that it is
    of you I sing when I tell
    of the swan on the water
    or the eagle in the heavens
    or the faun in the wood
Others weep but your eyes
    are dry.

II

O my beloved. How happy
I was that day when you
Came here from the
railway, & set your hair
aright in my looking glass
& then sat with me at
my table, & <then> lay resting
in my big chair. I am
like the children, O my
beloved & I play at
<life &> marriage. I play
<at> with images of the life
you will not give to me O
my cruel one.

III

I put away all the romances.
how could I read of queens
& of noble women, whose
very dust is full of sorrow.
Are they not all but my
beloved whispering to me.

I went into the woods. I
heard the cry of the birds
& the <cry> of the deers, <?& I>
& I heard the winds among the
reeds, but I put my hands
over my ears for were not
they my beloved whispering to
me. O my beloved, why do
you whisper to me of sorrow
always.

IIII

O my beloved what wer verses to me
If you <are> were not there to
               listen
& yet all my verses a little t you.
Your eyes set upon far
               magnificence
upon impossible heroism
have made you blind and have
            made you deaf
you gave your country a flame
<I fear> you hav no thing bu
the s verses, that ar but like
<?rushes> & leaves in the
middle of
    a wood.
Other eyes fill with tears but
          yours are dry[55]

That New Year's Eve which saw out 1900 – once anticipated as a mil-
lenarian year – was a time for reassessment. 'The war has made the air elec-
trical just now,' WBY remarked.[56] A year before, Gregory had written in the
Spectator about country prophecies of war in the Valley of the Black Pig, and
related them to what was happening in South Africa.[57] As it happened, the
war did not carry apocalypse in its wake, but it revived nationalist politics,
invigorated fringe journalism, and brought George Moore back to Dublin.

A new mood had been asserted by the first issue of Moran's *Leader* in September, with its scorching attack on pinchbeck Anglicization and its celebrated call for an Irish Ireland – implicitly challenging WBY's endorsement of an Irish literature in English. The post-war dispensation had also reasserted nationalist–Unionist polarities. Horace Plunkett, only a year before seen as a possible reconciliator between the two traditions, alienated any potential nationalist constituency through supporting the war (as Gonne sharply told WBY) and lost his bid to get returned as MP for Dublin in October 1900.[58] The anti-war movement had not only inspired Gonne's friend and collaborator Arthur Griffith to form the 'Transvaal Committee', later to become Cumann na nGaedheal, and later still Sinn Féin: she herself became President of the new radical organization for Irishwomen, 'Inghinidhe na hÉireann' ('Daughters of Ireland'). And through her involvement in the movement she met the nationalist hero John MacBride, who asked her to join him on an American tour in February 1901.

As for WBY, he had been forced into a stance which had alienated Unionist Ireland and London publishers. His own impatience with 'respectable' nationalist Ireland was evident. Simultaneously his polemics in English journals had begun to irritate Standish O'Grady, who complained at figuring 'among the other interesting barbarians whom you are exhibiting to the Philistines'.[59] The press enthusiastically covered WBY's presence at a Transvaal Committee meeting which voted to give President Kruger the freedom of the city of Dublin. But how far he would be comfortable with the believers of advanced nationalism remained to be seen. Hyde made Moran promise not to make a practice of attacking WBY, but Russell wrote worriedly to Gregory at Christmas after a particularly virulent series of onslaughts:

The Leader is getting too absurd in its remarks about Anglo Irish writers. They are written by Ryan but Moran ought to stop it. The last review of Rolleston's anthology was too absurd. I am afraid Moran is a 'priest's boy'. The book does not 'appeal to the heart of the Irish Papist'. The Irish people 'don't know anything about art' 'don't want it'. Yeats 'never wrote a line to touch an Irish heart'. If Moran does not mend his ways I will set the United Irishman on him. I prefer the 'United Irishman' any day to the Leader. It is better written, more ideal [*sic*] there are good poems and real thought in it and I am sorely tempted to write for it.[60]

WBY wrote dismissively of Ryan's animus in a letter to Gregory. 'It is wonderful the skill with which these people play on subtle hints of heresy when they review AE or myself; & after all they are right from their point of view. It is as much their very respectable instinct for heresy, as rage against something they cannot understand, that keeps them ever harping on symbols.' Gregory came to view the persistent attacks in robustly Catholic-versus-Protestant terms, and was shortly giving him the kind of advice he was ready to hear:

It is certainly rather depressing this set being made against you & especially not having it a fight in the open. If the priests honestly think you a danger they ought to say so & not shelter behind Moran and Gill. And if your writings are a danger, why are you so abused for writing in a way hard to understand? There is a sort of stupid cowardice about it all, for it is this heartbreak in Ireland, the priests are throttling the people, & yet we are obliged to use them in any effort to get at the people.

Clearly, just now your work is not directly with the masses – which would be the most directly interesting work – but that matters less as the Gaelic movement has taken up their education, & any of the beautiful work you do, besides having a direct influence on the best minds, is there ready for the time when your own countrymen will dare to praise it . . . it really seems as if in a short time Edward [Martyn] will be the only recognised man of letters in Ireland![61]

By late January, a small volume containing their manifestos was in print, under the title *Ideals in Ireland*. Though the *Leader* was guardedly favourable, WBY still felt his own work would never be accepted by Moran as properly Irish: he would always be the target of the bigotry of 'self taught men', mystified by unfamiliar intellectual standards and unable to rise above utilitarianism or piety.[62] Significantly, in the controversy over Moore's rejection by the Irish Literary Society WBY declared 'my first duty is to ideas & . . . toleration is among the first of these'. The controversies of 1901 reaffirmed this belief, which would only harden with time.

III

Tolerance of heterodoxy was, however, much less desirable in Golden Dawn affairs, which preoccupied WBY through January and February 1901. While he held his Monday evenings, dined out (forging a lasting friendship with Thomas Sturge Moore) and lived his usual London life, he was simultaneously locked in struggles with his fellow-occultists. Much as the study-programme of the Order supplied his need for an academic structure, the squabbles among the adepts resembled controversies within a university department: dealing with hierarchies of authority, curricula, workloads and methods of examination. WBY's disagreement with Farr revolved around her desire to admit members at a low level of achievement to the Council. Elitist as ever, he tried to bring her into line by threatening to withdraw his support from her theatrical projects, which he had been encouraging throughout December. He also held out 'in strict confidence' the prospect of 'a theatre of art', which had been suggested to him by 'a group of writers & artists'.[63] A copy was sent to Horniman, proving that they were now firm allies; and on 1 February 1901 the conflict climaxed at a Council meeting. WBY took Horniman's side in attacking notions of 'freedom' and individual conscience; they emphasized authoritative forms of election, and the importance of not splintering into 'groups'. Horniman was not merely the 'Scribe'; she footed the secretarial costs, and many members apparently suspected her of harbouring ambitions towards a Mathers-style dictatorship. She left a long (and sometimes incoherent) record of these struggles stressing her alliance with WBY against the unholy.[64] 'The Demon [WBY] made a speech which by its beauty enforced silence but it fell on the ears of an audience who were on a different plane of thought'; Farr 'energetically enquired from the Demon "who and what are *you* in the Order" or words to that effect'.[65] In the end WBY and Horniman fell together, voting in a minority of two against regularizing 'groups' and allowing free development. Apparently, all the other Council members were energetically engaged in 'group' activity already.

The next day (2 February 1901) WBY produced the first in a series of open letters which attempted to salvage the position by taking a high line.[66] 'It would ill become my dignity to continue longer than my duty towards the Order requires, an elected member of a Council where party feeling has run to such extravagance.' While he would be happy to go on teaching magical philosophy, the 'ignobility' of the Council's behaviour in sacred surroundings revealed the corruption of 'well bred and friendly people'. Three further letters followed, for circulation before the next meeting of all members of the Second Order on 26 February. But, disappointingly, he elicited only indirect responses. His arguments condemned Farr's inexperienced and slapdash approach, and approved Horniman's zealous, even pedantic commitment. This endorsement was genuine. While he needed Horniman's support and resources, he believed in her carefully constructed and hierarchical approach: all the more so as the by-laws of the Second Order in May 1900, which were now being questioned, embodied his beliefs.[67] He was convinced that group activity produced a composite 'magical personality', abandoning integrity and provoking disruption. Suspicion, distrust and corruption could only follow. 'We who are seeking to sustain this great Order must never forget that whatever we build in the imagination will accomplish itself in the circumstance of our lives.'[68]

WBY's third letter, drafted on 21 February, stressed that the dangers of untramelled group activity would lead to Black Magic, and the 'enchantment of sensual passion'. The ethos of the Order was to facilitate a religious quest, and indeed to reconcile 'Paganism and Christianity'. The tone is that of *The Secret Rose*:

Sometimes the sphere of an individual man is broken, and a form comes into the broken place and offers him knowledge and power if he will but give it of his life.

If he give it of his life it will form a swirl there and draw other forms about it, and his sphere will be broken more and more, and his will subdued by alien wills. It seems to me that such a swirl has been formed in the sphere of this Order by powers, that though not evil in themselves are evil in relation to this Order.[69]

On 25 February Robert Palmer Thomas ('Lucem Spero') circulated a counter-statement, carefully analysed by WBY and Horniman. It accused Horniman of 'persecuting' group members for supposed 'heresy', retreating into neurotic obsessiveness, and nurturing a particular animus against Farr. (The copy in WBY's papers is furiously annotated by the subject of these criticisms.) Thomas's accusations against WBY indicate (as George Mills Harper has put it) 'the kind of mingled dislike and respect he commanded':

This frater did you all great service during the Revolution [against Mathers] as you know from your printed documents. Since then he has attended the council meeting at intervals and we all bear him witness that he has talked at greater length than all the other members put together. His position among us is due to his long connection with the Order, the originality of his news on Occult subjects and the ability with which he expresses them rather than the thoroughness of his knowledge of Order work and methods which is somewhat scant. He is however a shining example of the help we may get from Members who have no special talent for passing Examinations.[70]

But his opposition to the Council's decision on groups was 'a flagrant piece of audacity before which the little tyrannies of our late Parisian Chief pale'. WBY briefly annotated the suggestions of his opponents: 'Chaos'. But after the general meeting on 26 February he, Horniman and J. W. Brodie-Innes (who had attempted a compromise amendment) resigned their positions on the Council. There was a general agreement that the rules of the Golden Dawn needed revision, but not by him. It was a severance from old comrades, such as Dorothea Hunter, with whom he had planned the Celtic Rituals, and whom he had known since his youth. But to WBY the larger issue was what mattered: the fragmentation of an organization which could have formed a powerful 'personality', calling up inspiration for ritual and research purposes. He decided to remain a member, but not an officer, and began to write his general apologia. This appeared as a private pamphlet under the title *Is the Order of R.R. et A.C. to remain a Magical Order?* in March 1901.

Thus he adopted a strategy he had learnt in his struggles over the Irish Literary Society, and would often embrace in the future: after a political setback, he attempted to regain authority through a powerful written statement. He produced an argument for exclusivity, hierarchies and a compulsory oath – written in the hope that constitutional revisions might enable him to regroup his forces, fight the battle through written manifestos, and win in

243

the end.[71] *Is the Order of R.R. et A.C.*, however, went beyond the immediate necessities, developing into a wide-ranging consideration of the position of magic in the cosmic order. It holds, therefore, an important place in WBY's canon; but it was written for adepts, probably with the conscious intention of asserting the Christian, Cabbalistic and Rosicrucian traditions of the Golden Dawn against the Egyptological deviations of Farr and her friends.[72] WBY argued that symbols and evocations could work only in the Order's traditional system of carefully observed degrees (just as he was secretly planning for the Order of Celtic Mysteries). Diversity could be blended into unity only through symbolic ritual, constructed around an image of ascension (like the Cabbala's Tree of Life). By following the route advocated by Farr, the 'Organic being' of the Golden Dawn would be fractured; its 'ancient units' would succumb to 'anarchic diversity'. As so often, he presented a Blakean (or Neo-Platonic) view of the 'real' world as merely a symbolic image of the invisible order; there are several references to Plotinus, whose translator Stephen MacKenna he was seeing at the time. To his antagonists, this seemed like mysticism. But (following his early Vedantic influences) WBY also preached the actual results of spiritual concentration. Almost in the same words as his letter to the adepti, he stressed that the 'Magic of Power' could bring about real changes in the circumstances of everyday life, if formulated strongly enough in the imagination. This was the belief that had sustained him through the struggles of his own life. And his spiritual communion with Gonne was certainly in his mind when he mentioned 'lovers or friends' using similar meditations to intensify their affection. Above all, he reiterated a strong argument against supposed 'freedom'. 'In our day every idler, every trifler, every bungler cries out for his freedom'. The only meaningful freedom is 'the right to choose the bonds that have made them faithful guardians of the law'. Many of these beliefs lie behind the play he was to write in the very near future: *Where There is Nothing*.

Farr's strong disagreement with this pamphlet prompted a 'postscript', written on 4 May 1901. But by now the reorganization of the Order had been commandeered by others, though WBY managed by dint of sheer energy to impose his influence on some of the revised by-laws.[73] His conflict with Farr did not, after all, prevent them collaborating on simultaneous enterprises, like her verse-chanting performances,[74] and several of his opponents themselves resigned from the Council a year later. By then the Order had been plagued by Frank and Edith Jackson, or 'Mr and Madame Horos', two shady American opportunists. They pulled off the remarkable achievement of hoodwinking Mathers, who at one stage believed that Madame Horos might be Anna Sprengel herself, or – just as likely – a reincarnation of Blavatsky: she explained her large figure by the revelation that she had absorbed Blavatsky's astral self. The couple infiltrated Golden Dawn circles in London but were exposed as frauds, and worse was to come: in December 1901 they were convicted of raping a sixteen-year-old girl at a spurious Golden Dawn initiation ceremony. Unjustified as it was, the Order suffered irredeemably bad publicity and had to change its name (to the Hermetic Society of the Morgenröthe).[75] Splits, persecution-complexes and mutual recriminations vindicated many of WBY's prophecies, and his satiric darts in the 1902 version of *The Speckled Bird* owe much to these events. The Golden Dawn, however, survived – after a further split in 1903, which produced the Order of the Stella Matutina. WBY continued his association with this branch at a remove, acting as an authority on ritual, and corresponding with members. But his ambition to dominate its administrative councils was over.[76]

He managed to reap, as so often, a literary profit. The previous October he had begun his long essay entitled simply 'Magic'.[77] It was substantially in existence by 4 May, when he delivered it as a lecture to the Fellowship of the Three Kings in London. H. W. Nevinson, whom WBY as usual mistook for someone else, sourly described the audience as 'many dull, patient women, letting words pour over them, hopefully as only patient women can'.[78] WBY told them of a 'great mind', into which all minds flowed, with a memory which could be evoked (or triggered) by symbols; this owes something to the notion of the Golden Dawn as a composite 'magical personality'. In 'Magic' he allows visions (of, for instance, past lives) not to be literally true, but to be 'symbolical shadows of the impulses that have made them'. In other words, psychological representations of the unconscious mind. It was an interpretation he had previously applied to fairy lore, and would in future use in relation to psychical research. The creative imagination is related to a spiritual communion lost to most of the materialist, post-industrial world. Blake is an obvious inspiration here, but WBY also stresses the secrecy of the subject, and a central uncertainty. Frater D. E. D. I. may have become detached from the inner circle of the Golden Dawn, but the approach he had preached to his erring brethren permeated the thoughts which he shared with the world at large. And upheavals in the Golden Dawn impelled him back to the long-planned Order of Celtic Mysteries. In his determination to produce a 'whole fabric' he had produced a hierarchy of colours, symbols and grades of degree, finalized by the end of May.[79] This, he believed, would shape his work for the foreseeable future. 'I have hesitated for a long time about throwing myself into it, as I knew it would turn fealing against me,' he told Fiona. 'But the growing Catholic party in this country is already so suspicious of me, that I will lose nothing by saying all I have to say. I will indeed rather gain.'[80]

IV

His expectations were not far off the mark. Visionary articles like 'Magic', bad publicity for occult societies and unbridled Celticism in general laid him open to snide attacks from journalists in alleged 'interviews' during the early summer of 1901; he complained continually of misrepresentation in the papers.[81] First of all an interlude at Stratford for Shakespeare's 'history' plays, and then an escape to Sligo provided relief. But on his way through Dublin he was told by Bullen, who had been trying to place WBY's books with booksellers, that there was a strong clerical prejudice against him, affecting even Gill (who may also have been smarting at being 'dropped' by the Irish Literary Theatre). George Pollexfen also made clear that Sligo conservative opinion was antipathetic to his nephew since his stance against the royal visit; WBY wrote to Gregory from Thornhill that he was 'in rather low spirits about my Irish work'.[82] Even when they managed to enjoy a series of joint visions of a 'tall fair beautiful Queen-like figure', George had to be dissuaded from asking her questions about his health.[83] His uncle's selfishness and miserliness depressed him, with his refusal to make the Rosses Point house comfortable in case the rent was raised. But WBY stayed on, finishing two long essays, 'Ireland and the Arts' and 'What is "Popular Poetry"?'[84] and working on his increasingly autobiographical novel (currently called 'Michael'). In late June he went to Dublin, and pursued his autobiographical theme by making a sentimental return to Sandymount Castle, once the home of his disgraced uncle. He was moved by the experience, and wrote about it to Lily. On the way out the owner showed him 'a house where he said the neighbours said I had been born'.[85] It was confirmation that he had become famous: as was the fact that a lost copy of the first pamphlet edition of *Mosada* was valued, for the purposes of a lawsuit, at £5.[86] His early life was now incorporated into a public reputation.

Coole held him for most of the summer of 1901; the guests included Synge, Russell, Hyde and Violet Martin, who as usual reported back to her cousin in Cork.

Yeats looks just what I expected. A cross between a Dominie Sampson and a starved R.C. curate – in seedy black clothes – with a large black bow at the root of his long naked throat. He is egregiously the poet – mutters ends of verse to himself with a wild eye, bows over your hand in dark silence – but poet he *is* – and very interesting indeed – and somehow sympathetic to talk to – I liked him – in spite of various things – and I got on well with him, so far . . . It is strange to talk of 'deep subjects of life and death' without any selfconsciousness, and I must say he induces that, and does it himself. He is not at all without a sense of humour, which surprised me. He thinks The Real Charlotte very big in the only parts he has read, which are merely quotations in reviews . . . But he doesn't approve of humour for humour's sake – (here Miss Martin said beautiful things about humour being a high art) . . . Today Augusta made me add my initials to a tree already decorated by Douglas Hyde, AE and more of the literary crowd. It was most touching. WBY did the carving, I smoked, and high literary conversation raged and the cigarette went out and I couldn't make the matches light, and he held the little dingy lappets of his coat out and I lighted the match in his bosom. No one was there, and I trust no one saw, as it must have looked very funny.[87]

For all the attractions of Coole he travelled to Dublin to see Alice Milligan's plays in August and spoke at the rather genteel Pan-Celtic Congress, choosing an appropriate tone to stir things up. 'Mr W. B. Yeats, referring to the language movement, said it had created a revolution, the whole thought of the nation had been changed by the movement; and if it went on as it had been doing it would be shaking governments.' His line was deliberately nationalist: 'throughout the entire British Empire there were not at the present day ten thousand persons whose opinion was worth anything in any art . . . Not even the healthy and happy had the art; they had the Horse Show.'[88] But this did not convince everybody. At the same gathering, Russell asked Moran of the *Leader* why he attacked WBY when he was doing good work for Ireland; 'he put it on religious grounds'.[89] The object of criticism enjoyed himself greatly amid Druidic ceremonial, 'traditional chanting' and arguments about the Celtic credentials of Cornwall. He enthusiastically entered into the debate on 'a national costume', advocating an authentically Irish evening-dress as well as day-wear. 'If some two or three people in Dublin who were accustomed to entertain a little among their propagandist people were to institute a custom, urging them to come to periodical entertainments in national costume, they would find this number of nine people [allegedly already appearing in Celtic costume at Dublin parties] would soon increase rapidly.'[90] He admitted they would have to face the ridicule of 'the small boy'; since saffron kilts were in question, Violet Martin would probably have had something to write about too. Nor is it difficult to see why the scholarly Celtophiles and their Ascendancy patrons were looked at askance by Gaelic Leaguers, who boycotted the proceedings.[91] But WBY was now privately determined to begin initiations into his own Celtic Order that autumn, as the first round in the coming battle 'between the Church and the mystics'.[92] All could be incorporated: joint visions with Russell, symbolic colours sketched by Gonne, Gregory's forthcoming work on sagas. A great system would emerge to transcend all petty politics, provide protection against enemies, and herald a new era.

These expectations sustained him through the saga of *Diarmuid and Grania*, which continued at Coole. Moore wrote suggesting that music be

10. WBY, Synge and Russell fishing on Coole Lake, sketched by Harold Oakley, an art school friend of Robert Gregory, perhaps in September 1901.

introduced at the end of the play, an idea that bore fruit. But he had also realized by now that his 'psychological explanation of the legend' by means of Grania's character was incompatible with WBY's vision:[93] 'a play written by one man and corrected by another would not be better in the end than a carefully corrected Latin essay, a repainted picture or a stuffed animal'. None the less, the summer of 1901 at Coole was remarkable for another collaboration. Gregory had been assiduously turning her folklore collections into a book; WBY had guided her to the John O'Daly translation of the Cuchulain legend in the Royal Irish Academy, and provided much help in what was to become *Cuchulain of Muirthemne*.[94] She was now well embarked on a career as a creative writer, and during the summer she worked with WBY on a short drama – almost a morality play – which arose directly from the disappointing '98 Centennial movement. The original inspiration was allegedly a dream of WBY's in which an old woman entered a cottage where a marriage was in preparation; the play's development revealed that she represented Ireland (as in a traditional Gaelic *aisling*) and led away the bridegroom to fight with the French invasion force in 1798. The symbolism, however, was anticipated by Martyn's *Maeve*; and the nationalist moral was a response to a direct challenge. On 4 May 1901 Frank Fay of the *United Irishman* had attacked *The Countess Cathleen* and *The Land of Heart's Desire* in highly specific terms:

They do not inspire; they do not send men away filled with the desire for deeds . . . before he will be even on the road to achieving greatness as a dramatic poet, Mr Yeats must tackle some theme of a great, lasting and living interest. In Ireland we are at present only too anxious to shun reality. Our drama ought to teach us to face it. Let Mr Yeats give us a play in verse or prose that will rouse this sleeping land. There is a herd of Saxon and other swine fattening on us. They must be swept into the sea along with the pestilent crowd of West-Britons with which we are troubled, or they will sweep us there. This land is ours, but we have ceased to realise the fact. We want a drama that will make us realise it. We have closed our ears to the piercing wail that rises from the past; we want a drama that will open them, and in no uncertain words point out the reason for our failure in the past and the road to success in the future.

Within the month an answer would come from Coole but not, perhaps, from the corner expected. Textual evidence suggests that Gregory wrote most of the play; her own diaries, and contemporary rumour, bear this out.[95] WBY always gave her due credit for providing the language, but implied that plot and construction were his. This annoyed her in later life but at the time she accepted that his was the name that would sell. Later that year she would write to him, with a certain impatience, 'I cannot think of anything but "the Daughter of Houlihan" for the play, I am sure anything is better than "Cathleen".'[96]

Cathleen ni Houlihan, as it became none the less, bears the hallmark of the other plays Gregory came to write. It is straightforward, rather heavy-handed, reliant on predictable dramatic by-play, and – for all its mechanical construction – dramatically very powerful. It is also directly propagandist, on the lines of the article 'Felons of Our Land', which she had published in the *Cornhill* the year before. It would be played to maximum political effect the next year,[97] but by 1904 WBY expressed a distinct discomfort with this aspect.

It may be said that it is a political play of a propagandist kind. This I deny. I took a piece of human life, thoughts that men had felt, hopes they had died for, and I put this into what I believe to be a sincere dramatic form. I have never written a play to advocate any kind of opinion and I think that such a play would be necessarily bad art, or at any rate a very humble kind of art. At the same time I feel that I have no right to exclude, for myself and for others, any of the passionate material of drama.[98]

This suggests unease, as well as collaboration. But in 1901 the 'message' of *Cathleen* was compatible with his preoccupations: the peasant family is preoccupied by material gain, until the spirit of Ireland redeems their son by promising him a glorious death. A critique of money-grubbing and utilitarianism is thus combined with the Fenian ethic.

In 1901 WBY and Gregory also collaborated on a short play, *The Pot of Broth*, which, like Hyde's *Casadh an tSúgáin*, relies on one extended (and ancient) joke; here again Gregory provided local colour, and WBY some lyrics. Other poetry written in the summer included much of 'Baile and Aillinn', which was his first essay at a poem about 'the Irish heroic age' since *The Wanderings of Oisin*. This was part of a projected series or cycle in lyrical and narrative verse, which, he told Bridges, 'I have always ment to be the chief work of my life – The giving life not to a single story but to a whole world of little stories, some not endeed very little, to a romantic region, a sort of enchanted wood.'[99] The enchanted woods of Coole had concentrated his mind. Gregory's translations suggested a weaving together of tradition, place and story, in the manner of 'the old Irish poets', but with the vigour and vitality of Balzac's *Comédie Humaine*. He wrote to several correspondents about the greatness of her projected book, and the way it had liberated ideas and techniques which he had wanted to tackle 'since I was twenty'.

But drama remained in the ascendant. 'I know that to almost every artist & poet too, perhaps to almost every craftsman, there comes a time when he grows weary of his own craft & longs for some thing else,' he wrote to Horton that summer.[100] 'Then comes the deceiving voices & he is lost if he obey them.' To many, WBY himself seemed to be obeying a deceiving voice as he plunged further into drama and away from lyric. Despite their occult differences he pressed the claims of Florence Farr's poetry-chanting performances, accompanied by a twelve-stringed 'psaltery' made specially for her by Arnold Dolmetsch, and during the summer wrote excitedly of their efforts to strip poetic expression back to its vocal elements. Gregory's work inspired his own short play about Cuchulain, begun at Coole and finished in the autumn. The success of an American production of *The Land of Heart's Desire* encouraged him further, though it brought no money. He told Thomas Sturge Moore that it proved 'if one writes actable little plays now, without too many characters they will find there way on to some stage'.[101] By mid-July he was thinking of another collaboration with George Moore, who had taken up residence in Dublin and thrown himself into local controversies in a 'religeous spirit of impartial hate';[102] they thought of 'a religeous Don Quixote'.[103] This would become *Where There is Nothing*, and create yet another controversy between them.

For the moment, though, they looked to the first public performance of their current collaboration. This marked the Irish Literary Theatre's last, rather subdued season, which opened in the autumn. There were few accompanying celebrations, apart from an exhibition of 'sketches of life in the west of Ireland' by Jack Yeats, resolutely publicized by Gregory. An attempt to lure Shaw over 'to stir things up' failed. After a summer of rewriting, the current version of *Diarmuid and Grania* was performed on 21 October 1901 in the Gaiety Theatre.[104] During the summer WBY had cast a horoscope which showed there would be a 'row' on that date, but was cheered by the fact that the auguries were much better than for *The Countess Cathleen*. He was wrong on both counts. There was no row, but the play was a disaster.

This was not for want of effort. In March WBY had been transfixed by a Gordon Craig production of *Dido and Aeneas* for the Purcell Society, played before a backdrop illuminated by coloured light-projections: 'It was like watching people wavering on the edge of infinity, somewhere at the Worlds End.'[105] This was how he envisaged *The Shadowy Waters* as well as *Diarmuid and Grania*, and he turned excitedly to the possibilities inherent in avant-garde production. Shortly afterwards the Benson Shakespeare cycle at Stratford had provoked an ecstatic article from WBY, arguing against the half-round theatre and in favour of Wagner's 'half-closed fan'.[106] But for *Diarmuid and Grania* in Dublin that autumn, a more old-fashioned approach obtained. The costumes, allegedly researched from illuminated manuscripts, were impressively dreadful. Even Elgar's music for the death of Diarmuid, and his song for the nurse Laban, failed to raise the tone. The audience indulged in some cruel mockery and an unfortunate line of Diarmuid's to Grania, 'The fools are laughing at us', brought down the house. Critical reaction was no more favourable; a famous quip had it that in the first act the players fell asleep and in the last, the audience did. O'Grady roundly refused to go near it, and his *All Ireland Review* rejected it as 'a coarse English society play in fancy dress . . . a heartless piece of vandalism on a great Irish story'.[107] The *Leader* objected to the concentration on 'degenerate and unwholesome sex problems',[108] and the modernity of Grania's conception was generally condemned ('Mrs Tanqueray B.C.'). This was a direct result of Moore's input. Whatever form the play had eventually taken, the audience expected Frenchified smut from the notorious novelist; the theatre management had at one stage tried to conceal the authorship of Moore and WBY for fear of scaring away a 'respectable' audience.[109] Violet Martin, sufficiently intrigued by her recent exposure to the Irish literary renaissance to attend on 25 October, sent the inevitable report to Somerville in Cork. She found the play 'a strange mix of saga and modern French situations' – the latter being Moore's responsibility, while WBY had presumably contributed 'beautiful writing here and there' as well as 'the peculiar simplicities that arose'. Her résumé of the plot illuminates why so many people found it offensive.

In the first act [Grania] is on the verge of an enforced marriage to Finn; she states without any contemptible subterfuge her reasons for objecting to this, and finally deludes Finn's friend Diarmid into falling in love with her and taking her away from the marriage feast a la young Lochinvar. He only yields after much lovering on her part – then curtain. The next act is sometime afterwards, and the really novel position is that she has become tired of Diarmid. I give George Moore some credit for that. Never was anything like her ecstacies of love for him in the first act. She then falls in love with Finn, which she might have done in the beginning and saved the writing of the play – and the curtain is Diarmid's discovery of them in howlts [embracing], and his resolve to go and hunt an enchanted boar, which a family witch (a stout lady in a grey teagown and conversational English accent) has prophesied out of her spinning wheel is to be the death of him. The last act is Grania's noble endeavours to dissuade him from the hunt, amid much thunder and lightning out of the woods. He makes one or two as backhairy [dubious] remarks to her on her conduct as George Moore could wish and retires to hunt the boar. After interludes there is a banging and roaring at the back, and Diarmid is carried in to make dying speeches to Finn and Grania and to be carried off to a funeral march, with Grania striking attitudes all round the place. Finally the court humourist, alone on the stage, says 'grand will be the burning of Diarmid, but grander will be Grania's welcome to Finn'. If this is the lofty purity of the Irish drama I am indeed mystified.[110]

But the play's hostile reception was provoked by more than its contents. Unionist Dublin still resented WBY's objections to the late Queen's visit – as the Chief Secretary George Wyndham warned him through Moore.[111] And in nationalist circles the use of an English troupe – the Benson Company – was bitterly resented. They had been engaged with a view to creating a box-office draw, faced with the withdrawal of Martyn's subsidy, but the strategy backfired. The Bensons had objected to the suggestion that they play Hyde's *Casadh an tSúgáin* as well, though threatened by Moore with popular disapproval (caught 'between the Gaelic League & Alexandra College', as WBY caustically put it[112]); this had probably got out. How they would have managed the Irish-language dialogue is not revealed. In the event it was acted by Hyde himself, with some Gaelic Leaguers coached by William Fay, who had already collaborated on tableaux mounted by Maud Gonne and Inghinidhe na hÉireann. Audiences had been small, reviews restrained, and the general effect gloomy ('Can't one be cheerful and Irish at the same time?' grumbled Holloway[113]); but Fay's capacities as producer were impressive.

Moreover, his brother was the influential drama critic of the *United Irishman*, Frank Fay, both a Gaelic enthusiast and an ambitious actor, who had intelligently criticized both *The Countess Cathleen* and *The Land of Heart's Desire*. WBY had discussed collaboration with both Fays in the summer, but felt unable to guarantee the level of political sympathy they demanded.[114] From every point of view, Frank Fay was determined to castigate *Diarmuid and Grania*, and he was not short of easy targets. The use of a vulgar English company was 'intolerable'. 'That Mr Benson should bring a lamb, or a kid, or whatever the animal was, on the stage did not astonish me (nothing that he could do would astonish me), but I think that the authors might at the rehearsals have insisted on his not doing so.'[115] In a curtain speech after the single performance, WBY tried to reclaim the moral high ground by saying that they were trying to get away from the 'vulgarity' of English commercial theatre, and implicitly apologizing for the Bensons, but this succeeded only in infuriating them as well (Mrs Benson was doubly insulted since she happened to be three parts Irish). 'She volubly protested that we were an English company,' recalled her husband, 'that at his invitation we had crossed the stormy St George's Channel, and had done our best, according to our capacity, for his play. We could not possibly allow him to step forward on our stage and insult us and our nation.'[116]

Diarmuid and Grania gave Dublin much innocent and malicious pleasure. WBY retained a certain affection for it, suggesting its revival as a dance play to Frederick Ashton as late as 1930.[117] But the disaster of October 1901 precipitated the end of his collaboration with Moore, as well as other enterprises. By November Moore was giving astounding tongue-in-cheek interviews calling for clerical censorship and announcing that the Irish Literary Theatre was looking out for plays by priests;[118] WBY could only disassociate himself. 'I suppose we would both be more popular if I could stop from saying what I think & he from saying what he does not think,' he remarked wearily to Gregory.[119]

A young National University student, James Joyce, reacted more decisively: in a superb polemic, 'The Day of the Rabblement', he announced that offensive parochialism had taken over the Irish Literary Theatre.

But WBY had anticipated him. Even before the production of *Diarmuid and Grania* he had declared that the Theatre had run its course.[120] This was announced in *Samhain*, the Irish Literary Theatre's magazine published to coincide with the performance. Moore, Martyn and Gregory also contributed. WBY cast his eye back over the Irish Literary Theatre, welcomed the controversy aroused, and took credit for the fact that experiments in Irish theatre were happening in other quarters. Moore analysed the faults of the *Countess Cathleen* production – the wrong kind of scenery, insufficiently trained actors, WBY's insistence on chanted verse. The attitude to *Diarmuid and Grania* (not yet played when *Samhain* was written) remained evasive. But the editorial message was clear: the experimental Irish theatre must be European rather than provincial or English-derived, and subsidies from bodies like Dublin Corporation were essential. This did not appeal to Frank Fay and the *United Irishman*. 'People who present addresses to the rulers of England would certainly not permit our money which unfortunately they control to be devoted to an institution whose principal object would be to act plays holding up to opprobrium England and her methods.'[121]

Whatever WBY's aesthetic intentions, politics were inseparable from Irish theatre. In *Samhain* he returned to the idea of a cultural 'war between an Irish Ireland and an English Ireland', and William Fay's idea of a touring company devoted to Irish works, but he concealed his own stance. 'I am not going to say what I think . . . I want to get back to primary ideas. I want to put old stories into verse, and if I put them into dramatic verse it will matter less to me henceforward who plays them than what they play, and how they play it.'[122] For him, political confrontation meant reacting against the dead hand of the Irish establishment. In *Samhain* he quoted his father (not by name) on how 'petty commerce and puritanism' had brought about English decline. WBY then moved on to denouncing Pollexfen values among 'the Irish upper classes', who 'put everything into a money measure'.

The poor Irish clerk or shop boy, who writes verses or articles in his brief leisure, writes for the glory of God and of his country; and because his motive is high, there is not one vulgar thought in the countless little ballad books . . . All Irish writers have to choose whether they will write as the upper classes have done, not to express but to exploit this country; or join the intellectual movement which has raised the cry that was heard in Russia in the 'seventies, the cry, 'To the people'.

Moses was little good to his people until he had killed an Egyptian; and for the most part a writer or public man of the upper classes is useless to this country till he has done something that separates him from his class. We wish to grow peaceful crops, but we must dig our furrows with the sword.[123]

His considered views had been assembled over the summer in the two important essays 'Ireland and the Arts'[124] and 'What is "Popular Poetry"?'[125] Yet again he preached the message of the artist as priest, and the ancient connection of art to religion, through ceremony. Modernity had brought a loss of integument, a disruption, which must be repaired. William Morris had tried to restore it by bringing art into the objects of everyday life; in Ireland, artists could use the national passions, 'love of the Unseen Life and love of country'. A strong autobiographical theme runs through 'Ireland and the Arts', published in the *United Irishman* and therefore necessarily carrying the tone of an apologia. WBY looked back to his art school apprenticeship, and his early writing 'some sixteen years ago' in 1885, when he had believed 'that art is tribeless, nationless, a blossom gathered in No Man's Land'. Now he believed that Irish art, like Greek art, must stem from the people – the whole people. 'I would have Ireland recreate the ancient arts, the arts as they were understood in Judaea, in India, in Scandinavia, in Greece and Rome, in every ancient land; as they were understood when they moved a whole people and not a few people who have grown up in a leisured class and made this understanding their business.' Tentatively, he suggested that the sculptor John

Hughes should create Aengus and Etain rather than Orpheus and Eurydice, and academics should look to local history and traditions instead of continental literature or classical history. Thus far, his *United Irishman* readers could agree. But, he went on to argue, this did not mean trying to make one's work popular: the prime duty was to please oneself. The artist 'must comfort himself, when others cry out against what he has seen, by remembering that no two men are alike, and that there is no "excellent beauty without strangeness". In this matter he must be without humility.'

This too was autobiographical. At this very time he was careful to contradict the report of an interview in which he allegedly claimed to be 'acquiring my native tongue by degrees [in] hope that I may live to see Irish become the language of the artistic and intellectual world in Anglo-Saxondom'.[126] His actual argument was both more honest and more realistic. 'I could not now write of any other country but Ireland, for my style has been shaped by the subjects I have worked on. . . . now I think my style is myself. I might have found more of Ireland if I had written in Irish, but I have found a little, and I have found all myself.' In both these essays he surveyed his beginnings, his movement from cosmopolitan to local inspiration, and the tension between patriotism and artistic imperatives.[127] And he interrogated his own relation to 'popularity'. Popular taste, in the sense of accessibility and conventionality, must not be indulged; true 'popularity' meant striking a chord which reverberated in the unconscious memory of the people. Gregory's translations and Fiona Macleod's versions of Gaelic provided his examples, but the argument implied a defence of his own 'unpopular' art, and a hardening elitism. 'Indeed, it is certain that before the counting-house had created a new class and a new art without breeding and without ancestry, and set this art and this class between the hut and the castle, and between the hut and the cloister, the art of the people was as closely mingled with the art of the coteries as was the speech of the people that delighted in rhythmical animation, in idiom, in images, in words full of far-off suggestion, with the unchanging speech of the poets.'[128]

His own style deliberately strove for these last qualities, and he would search for them with the readiness for experiment, and toleration of deviance, which he had (in true nineties style) adopted on his masthead. 'A society that was a court of morals,' he had told the Irish Literary Society in March,

would be of necessity governed by the average thought, the thought which exhibits itself in the newspapers, and it would not be able to do its proper work, which is to find occasions when thought that is too sincere, too personal, too original for general acceptance, can express itself courageously and candidly . . . Good writers are in their work, and often in their lives, discoverers and experimentalists and for this a large freedom is essential.[129]

The contemptible 'new class', as well as suggesting the materialism of decadent English values, could also stand for Irish philistinism. He had argued the same case in the *All Ireland Review* a year before, disingenuously describing Moran's concept of a 'Battle of Two Civilizations' as 'a quarrel of two traditions of life, one old and noble, one new and ignoble': the intellectual Irish tradition versus the ill-educated bourgeoisie. This was not what Moran had meant; WBY had carefully refined the journalist's crude polarization of Irish civilization versus English. The revision allowed WBY himself to appear on the side of the angels, as long as he emphasized his own enmity to the Protestant middle classes from whence he sprang.[130] Russell complained to Gregory that 'Willie by his theories has lain upon men burdens grievous to be borne and departs from them himself whenever it is convenient',[131] but this missed the point. By late 1901 WBY had identified his approach to the next phase of cultural enterprise – through drama – in Ireland; he had also intuited its potential enemies.

Chapter 10 : NATIONAL DRAMAS
1901–1902

> Everything he does seems to stir up some rancour, and he is
> nearly always doing things.
>
> *Southern Cross*, 16 January 1903

I

JUST before Christmas 1901, a detective shadowing Maud Gonne recorded that she was seen off at Euston Station 'by a man of theatrical appearance and glasses, presumably W. B. Yeats of London'.[1] The description is unintentionally apt. From late 1901 a new phase of theatrical activity began for WBY, but it was not restricted to Dublin alone. *Samhain* 1901 sounded an *envoi* to the Irish Literary Theatre, and WBY accordingly transferred some energy to the London arena. After his return from Ireland he revived his contacts with a group of like-minded artists and littérateurs from Bedford Park and Hampstead with a view to creating a 'Theatre of Beauty'. Since early in the year they had been absorbing WBY's theories of musical speech and dramatic purpose, through meetings of the Fellowship of the Three Kings. They would eventually call themselves the 'Masquers'.[2] This initiative involved Farr, Gordon Craig's sister Edith, Laurence Binyon, Thomas Sturge Moore, Pamela ('Pixie') Colman Smith and others; an important late arrival was the artist Charles Ricketts, just converted to WBY's theatrical qualities.

In November he was seeing much of Farr and planning joint performances with Arnold Dolmetsch's newly constructed psaltery. This was a musical instrument derived from a single-string lute. WBY first heard Farr use it in her Egyptian play on 16 November and he instantly contacted Dolmetsch, whom he probably knew through Moore; the Dolmetsch ménage at 'Dowlands', Dulwich, provided the musical background for *Evelyn Innes*. Shaw thought it created 'a nerve-destroying crooning like the maunderings of an idiot-banshee',[3] but for WBY the sound of the psaltery seemed a perfect accompaniment to the way poetry should be intoned on stage, and he devoted himself to publicizing the fact. This campaign brought him into strange company, such as the super-imperialist poet Henry Newbolt. WBY, scourge of the Empire and the 'Famine Queen', discovered an admiration for Newbolt's 'patriotism' and placed a rapidly written essay, 'Speaking to the Psaltery', in Newbolt's *Monthly Review* the following March.[4] By mid-December 1901 he was 'working every day with Dolmetsch at the chanting' and engaged upon magic experiments at Woburn Buildings, described in the usual deprecating way to Gregory. (If an alchemist friend succeeded in experimenting on rabbits with a new recipe for the elixir of life, 'we are all to drink a noggin full – at least those of us whose longevity he feals he could honestly encourage'.[5]) He was also using his publishing contacts to further the publication of Gregory's *Cuchulain of Muirthemne*, writing a preface for her and studying Gaelic mythology in the British Museum for an expanded version of *The Celtic Twilight*. A. P. Watt was now negotiating for him, trading in the long-standing novel contract for a book of essays which would become *Ideas of Good and Evil* and arranging for a new edition of *The Secret Rose*, with the Hanrahan stories rewritten in Gregory mode. WBY described his mood as cheerful, despite constant eye trouble and a financial crisis; he warned Gregory he might need £3 or £4 down for the commissioned preface to her forthcoming volume of Cuchulain stories, and £10 obligingly arrived.

When in London, none the less, the circles of ninetyish aestheticism continued to engross him: an artists' freemasonry preoccupied with the revival of poetic drama, contributing to the *Dial*, the *Pageant*, the Vale Press, Laurence Binyon's Artists' Library, and shortly to possess their own house journal in Pixie Colman Smith's art magazine the *Greensheaf*.[6] Thus WBY's cultural enterprise was still centred on London as well as Dublin, and theatrical reform was in the avant-garde air in both cities. But the Dublin dramatic movement would, in the end, predominate. Its organization was already in place; audiences were prepared; journalistic coverage was guaranteed; and Gregory's attentions were firmly concentrated on that side of the Irish Sea (she had always disapproved of WBY's dissipation of theatrical energies into the London scene). There was also the question of funding. WBY had targeted Annie Horniman (who was probably sending him money privately[7]) as a potential Maecenas; not that he was alone in this. Gregory caustically compared her to a shilling lying at the bottom of a tub of electrified water, with everyone trying to scoop it out. While the London Masquers may have intended to try their luck in this game, the Dublin enterprise promised more immediate returns. And in late November WBY was discussing with Gregory the plays which the Fays' company might put on in the spring – 'the Irish play' and 'The Poor Old Woman' (a working title for *Cathleen ni Houlihan*). He was, moreover, clear about the importance of publicizing it as 'the first attempt at a permanent Irish company'.[8] This did not rule out bringing both Farr and Gordon Craig to Dublin. He also planned to persuade the drunken Bullen to set up in Dublin and specialize in Irish writers; and in March he visited Stratford again, to absorb ideas from the Shakespeare cycle. Still energetic, he confided a new plan to Gregory:

I am going to surprize you by an idea that has been in my head lately. I never until yesterday spoke of it to anybody. I have an idea of going on the stage in small parts next autumn for a few months that I may master the stage for purposes of poetical drama. I find I could get on quite easily, & that with the exception of rehersal times it would only take my evenings. Does the idea seem to you very wild? I should make about £2 a week, & learn my business, or at any rate never have to blame myself for not having tried to learn it. I would not of course go on in my own name & I would tell people exactly why I did the thing at all. I beleive that I construct all right – with wild confusions which I get out of – but I have a very little sense of acting.[9]

In the event, she dissuaded him. But it proves how stage-struck he had become; nor was he the only one. Olivia Shakespear, now firmly back in his inner circle, was co-operating with Florence Farr in writing 'Egyptian' plays: *The Shrine of the Golden Hawk* was put on with *The Beloved of Hathor* on 20 January, faithfully reviewed by WBY. Both plays were written by two women central to his life. Though he had referred to *The Beloved of Hathor* as 'very amateurish' on its first peformance the previous November, his review stressed the 'unearthly' quality of the drama, and its originality. 'One understood that something interesting was being done – not very well done, indeed – but something one had never seen before and might never see again.'[10] This summed up the attractions of the avant-garde, for others as well as himself. Monday evenings at Woburn Buildings in January and February were dominated by chanting, and by WBY's developing theories, reverently recorded in the diaries of his admirer Nevinson.[11] On 24 February the company included Lady Margaret Sackville, a 21-year-old poet who would begin editing the *Celt* a year later; to the delight of the surrounding tenements, she left the family carriage, complete with liveried footman, standing at the door of Woburn Buildings for the duration.[12]

Meanwhile, by the spring of 1902, fringe theatrical activity was rife in Dublin: much of it revolved around the Fay brothers and their amateur 'Ormond Dramatic Company'. The previous August WBY had seen them direct and act in Alice Milligan's *The Harp That Once*, *The Deliverance of Red Hugh* and *Eilís agus an Bhean Dhéirce* at the Pan-Celtic Congress. The brothers, five and seven years younger than WBY, were passionately committed to the theatre. William Fay, expansive and a 'character', was a comedian with professional experience; Frank, more agonized and intellectual, was an actor and critic who knew the European theatrical scene and had a special interest in 'dramatic recitation'. Their collaboration with Inghinidhe na hÉireann meant that an amateur company lay to hand which was emphatically not English (though they were still rehearsing cross-channel comedy farces with titles like *His Last Legs*). A difficulty was posed by Frank Fay's Griffithite nationalism, but

WBY and Gregory had, after all, written *Cathleen ni Houlihan* in response to his challenge, and theatrical ambition would prove more potent than political rectitude. In June 1901 WBY, James Cousins and Sarah Purser had discussed plans for a national theatre company, without the Fays, but by November an alliance was on the cards, pressed forward by publicists like Frederick Ryan, asking (as 'Irial' in the *United Irishman*) 'Has the Irish National Theatre Failed?' The Irish Literary Theatre had been too ambitious, recondite, elitist; the obvious solution lay to hand. Russell was already committed to the Fays and had offered his *Deirdre* to them, working with actors from Inghinidhe na hÉireann. WBY turned up at rehearsals and tried unsuccessfully to interfere with Fay's direction.[13] By the end of the month, as has been seen, WBY and Gregory were discussing what plays they could perform with the new combination.

It would never be an easy collaboration. In later years the Fays claimed that they had been written out of Irish theatrical history by the determination of WBY and Gregory to annex the movement for themselves; a union of equals was misrepresented as the Irish Literary Theatre taking the Fays on board and giving them a chance.[14] Russell would not have disagreed. In 1914, reading Gregory's memoir of these years, he wrote:

She centralises herself a great deal too much, and I think she gives too little credit to the Fays. Yeats Martyn and Moore started the romantic movement so far as the writing of plays is concerned in modern Ireland, but the two Fays are entitled entirely to the credit of starting an Irish school of acting. Without them it could not have been done. They trained the actors, they established the tradition, and they worked at it for years without aid from Yeats or Lady Gregory. It was with a good deal of difficulty I induced Yeats to give them *Kathleen* [sic] *ni Houlihan* . . . It was at their suggestion, not Yeats or Lady Gregory's, that the National Theatre was formed.[15]

Russell admitted that without the backing and plays of WBY, Gregory and Synge, the Fays and their theatrical energies would have remained obscure and unsung. They had, however, more to offer than Gregory or WBY allowed in later years.[16] The performance which launched them into real prominence was Gregory's and WBY's *Cathleen ni Houlihan*, the 1798 *aisling* play they wrote together at Coole, in which an old woman summons a young man to fight for Ireland (in the guise of herself) instead of getting married. Russell recalled, 'Maud Gonne got it out of him by promising to play Kathleen herself.'[17] But this arrangement owed as much to Willie Fay's connection with her Inghinidhe na hÉireann (as their producer and stage-manager) as to her friendship with WBY.

On 13 January 1902 Gonne and WBY met in London, and she committed herself to appearing in his play, though she had categorically refused, on principle, to act *The Countess Cathleen* three years before.[18] Her advent as a star of the production filled Willie Fay with forebodings, which he afterwards felt were justified.[19] From Dublin she wrote imperiously to WBY about plans for the production. Her movements between Paris, London and Dublin complicated attendance at rehearsals, though she was able to alter the plot by insisting on a more decisive and committed nationalist gesture at the end.[20] (George Moore's attempt to highjack the direction of rehearsals was firmly repulsed.) The programme also included Russell's *Deirdre*, which had been privately performed at the Coffeys' on 2 and 3 January. WBY resentfully found it thin and faint, like 'wall decoration'; he would shortly afterwards embark upon his own version which, Moore-like, attempted to reintroduce primitivity and sex. But, creaky as it was, Russell's play was a favourite with the company, perhaps because it allowed for a wide range of acting input. By contrast, it rapidly became clear that *Cathleen ni Houlihan* – called for this production 'Kathleen' – was a vehicle for Gonne.

Both plays were performed in St Teresa's Hall, Clarendon Street, from 2 to 4 April 1902, under the auspices of the Fays' 'Irish National Dramatic Society'; Inghinidhe na hÉireann's banner hung by the little stage. It was a modest enterprise. Frank Fay recalled six years later, 'The company by which these two plays were acted consisted of my brother, myself, Mr Digges, Mrs Digges, Mr P. J. Kelly, and some others, principally young poets and writers. Both plays were rehearsed by my brother, W. G. Fay; the scenery was painted by him and by AE, and the dresses were designed for *Deirdre* by AE and made in Dublin by lady friends of his.' The contribution of WBY and Gregory was played down, and before the production they seem to have remained deliberately in the background. Gregory attended a rehearsal, but slipped away to Venice well before the first night on 2 April. WBY remained in London until late March, turning up in time to give an interview in the *United Irishman*, stressing that 'my subject is Ireland and its struggle for independence'. Apparently, neither of them anticipated the response to their joint production.

Each night 300 people crowded into the inadequate hall, packed to standing room; and it was not Russell's attempted evocation of other-worldly beauty that galvanized them but the propaganda of Gregory and WBY, and the fame – or notoriety – of Gonne. At thirty-six she was no longer the great beauty of ten years before; Violet Martin, seeing her at *Diarmuid and Grania* the previous October, had found her looks terrifying ('the features still handsome the nose salient and short but the badness of the expression was startling. A huge mop of curled yellow hair crowned her big fat body. One look at her would be enough for anyone to form an opinion'[21]). But her stage presence and her fiery reputation elevated the part of Cathleen from polemic to dramatic grandeur. The resonance of certain lines struck echoes from the pure Fenian tradition: 'They shall be remembered for ever, They shall be alive for ever, They shall be speaking for ever, The people shall hear them for ever.' The *All Ireland Review* saw it as a political meeting rather than as a play, 'Maud Gonne, the well-known Nationalist agitator, addressing not the actors, as is usual in the drama, but the audience'. Stephen Gwynn's reaction is more often quoted, and probably more typical of the audience: 'I went home asking myself if such plays should be produced unless one was prepared for people to go out to shoot and be shot.'[22]

As for wby himself, he rapidly joined in with an article for the *United Irishman* a week later, stressing aesthetics rather than politics, and deliberately bidding for long-term collaboration. 'Perhaps I was stirred so deeply because my imagination ignored, half-unconsciously, errors of execution, and saw this art of decorative acting as it will be when long experience may have changed a method into a tradition, and made Mr Fay's company, in very truth, a National company, a chief expression of Irish imagination.'[23] Immediately after the performances, on 5 April, discussions opened with the Fays. There seemed to be enough common ground to overcome political differences, since their style, like wby's, stressed control of dramatic effect through voice rather than movement, and a 'method' approach to living the part. By 21 April, from London, wby was holding out the promise of backing from 'a wealthy friend'. But in the first place he suggested that a year be spent gaining more theatrical experience, and then broadcasting an appeal to backers. 'I think we must work in some such way, getting all the good plays we can from [James] Cousins and Russell and anybody else, but carrying out our theories of the stage as rigorously as possible . . . I will do my best to do a good deal of strong dramatic work in the immediate future.' He had already assured Fay, 'I see no serious difficulty before you but the getting of good plays in sufficient quantity at the start. In the autumn I had better write a new Samhain, you had better start formally with a proper blast of trumpets.'[24]

The phrase 'our theories' implied a collaboration. However, the expectation that he would not only provide plays but produce a publicity journal which would be a direct successor to that of the Irish Literary Theatre showed a certain assumption of control as well as continuity.[25] The Fays, moreover, needed careful handling; in the view of Joseph Holloway, a Dublin architect with a passion for the stage, 'it is mighty hard to pull with them, their tempers are vile and they treat those under them like dogs'.[26] Frank was especially spiky, and simmered with suppressed rage. Though there would eventually be plenty of difficulties between wby and the brothers, these did not initially arise in the anticipated arena of political propriety: the Fays rapidly adopted WBY's attitude, placing artistic independence and experiment above the expectations of nationalist audiences. There was still a degree of friction between them. WBY liked to think of the Fays (especially in retrospect) as enthusiastic amateurs in the mystery-play tradition, while they thought of themselves as professionals, and disliked the intellectualism, theories and mistiness inseparable from WBY's idea of the theatre. Only a year before their collaboration at St Teresa's Hall, Frank Fay had been deriding WBY's 'oratorical statues' in favour of 'things of flesh and blood'; he had also called on WBY to write in Irish, and inveighed against 'Saxonism' as furiously as D. P. Moran himself. In many ways Hyde rather than WBY would have been his ideal Director of a National Theatre.[27]

By the spring of 1902 WBY's ideas of theatrical production were firmly fixed, owing much more to avant-garde circles in London and ideas derived from Wagner and Maeterlinck than to the strictures of the *United Irishman*. From May his London lectures with Farr and Dolmetsch made this clear ('Recording the Music of Speech', 'Poetry and the Living Voice', 'Speaking to Musical Notes'[28]). His lecture series 'Speaking to the Psaltery', with demonstrations from Dolmetsch, Farr and others at Clifford's Inn on 15 May and 10 June, attracted every prominent theatre critic and theorist in London. William Archer produced a lengthy and favourable review in the *Morning Leader*, which was followed by other respectful notices, though Shaw derided the whole enterprise explosively, in public and private. This was unsurprising; besides his irritation at Farr's defection into 'nonsense', WBY's dramatic theory was the opposite of Shaw's. It revolved around the expression of ideals, not the discussion of ideology, stressing formal personalized gesture, and the delineation of character through action, often in a heroic mode. Hence his dislike of bourgeois realism on the stage; the theatre should reflect the unities of life, not its surface manifestations. Indeed, his much worked upon essay 'Magic' provided a key: tragedy as the expression of unity. This approach conceived of theatre as a religious experience, with the audience as a congregation. It is no coincidence that WBY's immersion in this aspect of drama followed closely upon his setbacks in the Golden Dawn.

Little of this was original: the theory of 'total' theatre, integrating song, dance, mime and acting, owed much to Symons's mediation of European ideas.[29] Also, by early 1902 WBY was deeply affected by the stagecraft of Gordon Craig, dreaming of importing him to Ireland (would Martyn pay?). And WBY shared Maeterlinck's commitment to indefinite settings, and reliance on the music of the voice. Though he usually disclaimed the Belgian's influence, he joined a campaign in June 1902 to protest against the banning of *Monna Vanna*. Here too there was common ground with Frank Fay, who admired Maeterlinck: his 1902 staging of Russell's *Deirdre* was influenced by

Aurélien-François Lugné-Poë's 1895 production of *Pelléas* at the Opéra-Comique, and WBY rather to his surprise was impressed by it.

The success of the performance at St Teresa's Hall had sent him back to London full of energy, despite continuous eye trouble. He even returned to his novel, finding to his delight that he could dictate at high speed to a typist.[30] This concentrated burst of activity was brought to an end by a bout of influenza in early May, when his eyes were also diagnosed as suffering from 'muscular strain'.[31] But he continued to work through dictation; significantly, the amanuensis for many of his letters was now Annie Horniman. And he continued to spread the message of the new theatre, travelling to Oxford to address about thirty students 'in some Don's room' (actually the St John's College Essay Society) on 18 May. Robert Gregory, now at New College, reported that 'his visit and lecture were I think a great success, though a large part of the audience at the latter were rather unappreciative, and the dons who asked questions were terrors'; WBY agreed.[32]

That same month of May 1902 saw Gregory's own apotheosis: her *Cuchulain of Muirthemne* had appeared at the end of April to a gratifying reception, helped by WBY's hard work among the review editors. Quibbles would later arise about the high claims made for stories essentially derived from the work of others,[33] and Gregory's excruciatingly arch dedication to 'The People of Kiltartan', describing herself as 'a woman of her house, that has to be minding the place, and listening to complaints, and dividing her share of the food', may have raised a few eyebrows. Above all, WBY's hyperbolic preface, privately commissioned by Gregory 'on business terms', certainly alienated some readers.[34] Its sonorous (and self-absorbed) first sentence was much repeated: 'I think this book is the best that has come out of Ireland in my time.' The *Leader* was provoked to a hilarious piece, 'Kiltartan, Mr Yeats, and Cuchulain',[35] and the *Freeman* weighed in by accusing him of blasphemy in his remarks about Ireland as a 'Holy Land'. The sarcasms of Irish reviewers drove him to draft a long letter to the *United Irishman*, defending his view of *Cuchulain* as 'a book of the National Stories of Ireland, a book meant for everybody, the Iliad of a people'. Unlike his own deliberately esoteric writing, Gregory's work represented an accessible national literature which would 'restore the spirit of the eleventh and of the twelfth centuries which were also the centuries of perfect learning'. His peroration returned firmly to the twentieth century, with a bitter attack on Irish reviewers – 'common hacks', dependent on popular prejudice. 'Too craven to praise but in conventional meaningless sentences, they come into their courage when ignorance cries them on.' This may have been fair comment, but it was unwise to compare them to English literary journalists, 'men who have made some study of literature, who have given some proof of good taste'.[36] He sent the draft to Gregory; it may have been intended to console her rather than for publication, and in any case he took her advice not to publish it. 'They [the Dublin reviewers] are only untaught children.'[37]

But in June his name was suggested as a director of the *United Irishman*: a dividend from the success of *Cathleen ni Houlihan*. He refused, 'as I considered I could not make myself responsible for their attitude towards the Irish members [of Parliament]. To my surprise my name was put forward as one that would be satisfactory to the extreme element. They would have found me anything but satisfactory but I am pleased at the compliment.'[38] The nationalist credibility gained over the last two years was carefully guarded; he concurrently refused to donate some work to a publication under royal patronage because he could not 'mix myself up with English royalties . . . considering that I am nothing of an imperialist and very much of an Irish "extremist"'. So he was, when approached by this kind of enterprise, and to English friends he was proud and proprietorial about incidents such as Maire Quinn's assault on a Unionist with a soda-water bottle, during Gonne's anti-loyalist demonstration against Edward VII's visit in July 1903.[39] However, the audience on each side of St George's Channel required different descriptions, and, as his own fame increased and his social circle widened, the ambiguities multiplied. Thus the next year, writing to the *Freeman's Journal* to protest against the King's visit, he implied that he himself was 'a Nationalist who considers what is called the "link of the Crown" inevitable',[40] and his reaction to the *United Irishman*'s invitation shows that he felt a residual commitment to the Irish Parliamentary Party. On 22 March 1902 Nevinson was surprised by his sympathy for the parliamentarians. 'Much talk about Irish politics and the gap of 10 years when young men turned to letters and the old men cut themselves off. He regrets all this, which surprised me.'[41] But faced with a dinner-table of complacent English imperialists, a tougher line was necessary, as he described to Gregory in May 1903:

I dined with the Lawrences (Indian Lawrences) last night, & [it] seemed to me that our Irish movement has for a chief privilege that it has all the platitudes against it. Somebody said 'what does Ireland want. Why does she not tell us what we are to do. She cries out & yet though we are anxious to do what ever is right she does not tell us.' I said 'nothing simpler, clear out'. The conversation languished after that for a little until somebody began saying how bad politics were for a country & so on. Then somebody spoke of the poverty of the Irish people being caused by their large payments to the priest. I said that the land laws & over taxation had something to do with it but the speaker, who was Lady Lawrence stuck to the priest because she had once known a butler who came in for £300 & she concluded he gave it to the priest 'because nobody ever found out what he did with it'. I behaved well but would not have been able to do so much longer.[42]

II

By the early summer of 1902 WBY was no stranger to grand houses, but his connections there were firmly artistic – as with the glamorous Wilfrid Scawen Blunt, aristocrat, poet, friend to Irish and Egyptian nationalism, and ex-lover of Gregory (twenty years before). In June 1902 WBY spent a weekend at Newbuildings with Blunt, who wanted to write 'a Cuchullin play' for the Irish theatre; fellow-guests included Lord Alfred Douglas and the influential printer Sydney Cockerell, whom WBY rapidly adopted as an arbiter for book design. But he was impatient to get to Ireland and Coole, and from late May was making preparations, asking Russell to find him lodgings in Rathgar. 'He brings over two psalteries,' the latter gloomily warned Gregory,

and is going, he says, to start the new art in Ireland if he can. I am sorry I ever turned his mind on the subject for I foresee he looks upon me as the proper person to use the psaltery in Ireland. I am like Willie in not knowing one note from another, and I am less adventurous and dread going out of my depth in strange arts. He has been worrying me to send him over 'chants'.[43]

To WBY himself, Russell wrote (rather unfairly), 'speaking in unison is done [in] every church, and is no discovery. I do not suppose you, or any of your audience, ever were in church, but it is done there constantly to a fixed notation, and is very impressive as a mere piece of sound.'[44]

WBY, however, remained enthusiastic about spreading the word; he had realized, he told William Archer, that his early 'folk' poems conformed to 'actual little tunes'.[45] The prospect of Coole, where he could write lyrics and talk about cantillating, excited him, but he told Gregory that he was delayed by sheer poverty. 'I am sorry to say I am desperately hard up. I have paid my rent & everything up to date except type writing, but unless Elkin Matthews to whom I have written owes me something I shall get away with difficulty.'[46] Whether or not financial help was directly forthcoming from Coole, Gregory provided the useful idea of subletting Woburn Buildings during his absences, and Sturge Moore's sister took the rooms for the summer. There was subsequently some trouble with bed bugs, but WBY had got safely away on 21 June, armed with the dreaded psalteries for Fay and Russell, and a working-model theatre constructed for him by Gordon Craig.

He did not delay in Dublin, merely spending a few days at George Moore's – though long enough to join with Moore, Hyde and Griffith in a protest about excavations at the Hill of Tara, a particular cause of Gonne's in which she involved many exotic foreign aristocrats.[47] By 27 June he was at Coole; within a month he was sending drafts of plays to Willie Fay,[48] as well as writing some lyrics. At the *feis* of traditional music held locally he heard singing of a kind which seemed to him unique. He pursued Hyde obsessively for information about it: the possibilities of the psaltery remained fixed in his mind.[49] The workshop atmosphere of Coole generated further collaborations too. The revised and extended new edition of *The Celtic Twilight*, finished in the spring and published later that year, embodied much of what Gregory had taught him. And this summer also saw a venture which both consummated his writing-relationship with Gregory and decisively ended that with Moore.

wby's notion for a play about religious iconoclasm may have originated the previous November, when he had seen Bjørnson's *Beyond Human Power*, then playing with Mrs Patrick Campbell. wby was struck by it as 'an unbeleivers account of beleif', and criticized the unconvincing portrayal of a visionary clergyman.[50] This may have reacted with another, more concrete inspiration: a transcendentalist friend of Russell, Philip Francis Little. Beside him, Russell appeared an earthbound rationalist. From the sea-wall at Bray, Little harangued the passing bourgeoisie about vision and reality, attacking the assumptions of respectable life; he wanted to live, Diogenes-like, in an overturned truck at Kingstown. The subject of Little and his mission to save the world had occurred to both Russell and wby as a good literary theme – probably to be handled in fiction.[51] The title was ready-made, first used by wby in a short story of 1896, 'Where There is Nothing, There is God'. It is probable that he and Moore (to whom such a subversive theme was instantly attractive) discussed the idea in April 1902 and also when wby stayed in Ely Place during June. Moore wanted another collaboration, and wby was apparently meditating a play about a young man who rejects respectability and tries to turn the world upside-down. On 3 July 1902, however, Moore produced a draft scenario about a young intellectual who adopts the life of a tinker, spurns civilization as barbaric, attempts to found his own religion, endures many vicissitudes (including an attempt to revolutionize a monastery) and is eventually killed by outraged villagers.[52] On 31 August he met wby at the Galway *feis*. The idea of a Little play came up, and wby (who had been elected President of the Fays' Irish National Dramatic Society on 9 August) told Moore he could no longer collaborate with him, as he was committed to the Society. In early September Moore allegedly wired wby that he was now writing a novel on the theme, and 'will get an injunction if you use it'. wby frantically set to writing, and by 26 September had completed the play, *Where There is Nothing*. It is the story of Paul Ruttledge, a landowner who becomes a tinker, subverts the accepted norms of life, enters a monastery, preaches disorder, and is eventually killed by villagers. Throughout, eccentricity and drunkenness stand for spiritual vision and 'the irresponsibility of the saints'. There are echoes here of the Joachimite antinomianism in his own *Secret Rose*

267

stories, and further aspects of his anarchist hero were inspired (and developed) by London acquaintances like Stepniak and Prince Kropotkin; but the family resemblance to Moore's July scenario is undeniably close. (Strangely, the name of Moore's land agent was Tom Ruttledge.) Gregory's input was considerable, as WBY always admitted: the dialogue used the inversions and painstaking constructions which were coming to be called 'Kiltartan' ('Oh! Paul, Paul, is it to leave you we must? And you never once struck a kick or a blow on me this time. Not even and you in pain with the rheumatism').[53]

Moore accordingly felt peeved and continued to issue legal threats. Russell wrote rather doubtfully to Gregory that Moore would not carry them out unless the plot and idea were actually his own: in which case WBY should of course 'invent something else, and put the idea in another shape . . . I don't know what part each took in shaping the thing. Willie I dare say knows his own inventions.'[54] Whatever about this, he was determined to stake his claim to the plot, enlisting his new American friend John Quinn to copyright the play in New York and arranging publication in the United Irishman. Moreover, at least in the first flush, WBY thought he had written a good play. 'I have enlarged and enriched it in the last couple of weeks,' he wrote to Quinn on 22 October. 'And I will probably make a few more alterations before it comes out in its final form here. It was written in a fortnight and a day, and I will not know what it is really like till I have talked it over with my friends. At any rate it will serve one good purpose, it will give our little theatrical company in Dublin the long play they are beginning to feel a necessity.'

Ten days later it was published in the United Irishman, with a rather disingenuous introductory note.

Where There is Nothing is founded upon a subject which I suggested to George Moore when there seemed to be a sudden need of a play for the Irish Literary Theatre; we talked of collaboration, but this did not go beyond some rambling talks. Then the need went past, and I gradually put so much of myself into the fable that I felt I must write on it alone, and took it back into my own hands with his consent. Should he publish a story upon it some day, I shall rejoice that the excellent old custom of two writers taking the one fable has been revived in a new form. If he does I cannot think that my play and his story will resemble each other. I have used nothing of his, and if he uses anything of mine he will have so changed it, doubtless, as to have made it his own.[55]

Whoever owned the original inspiration. WBY's accompanying article, 'The Freedom of the Theatre', showed how preoccupied he had become by the subject of controversial themes to do with law, the Church, the state, sobriety and custom. Thus early, he was anticipating the kind of troubles which Synge's plays would bring a year later. It was not the business of Art, he argued, to set good examples: 'the reign of the moralist is the reign of the mob, or of some Jack-in-office'. Strikingly, he admitted the personal relevance of his anarchistic play.

We are interested in religion and in private morals and personal emotion, and so it is precisely out of the rushing journey of the soul through these things that Ibsen and Wagner get the tumult that is drama. Doubtless, the character must always have something of the dramatist when it is a character that is pictured from within . . . Ireland is, I suppose, more religious than any other European country, and perhaps that is the reason why I, who have been bred and born here, can hardly write at all unless I write about religious ideas.[56]

Thus he cleverly used *Where There is Nothing*, which would inevitably be accused of godless cosmopolitanism, to stress his own Irishness. 'I only know that I want to upset everything about me,' Paul tells his friend the friar. 'Have you not noticed that it is a complaint many of us have in this country? and whether it comes from love or hate I don't know, they are so mixed together here.'[57] The play written hastily at Coole in the autumn of 1902 carries an autobiographical message, reflecting his experiences with the Golden Dawn and Parisian occultists, and his recent reading of Spenser (Paul struggles with allegorical Beasts) as well as Blake and Tolstoy. Nietzsche's part is less clear. Gregory wrote to Quinn on 9 October, 'I am glad Yeats had finished it before your Niedsche [*sic*] (for which he is very grateful) came, for it is the more original', but WBY had at least a second-hand knowledge of the philosopher already.[58] The play's hero – dominating, eccentric, magnetic – is a true Yeatsian *alter ego*; A. B. Walkley saw Paul as 'a poet wanting to live poetry'.[59] Like the hero of *The Speckled Bird*, he gives himself to a spiritual idea, and when the play was rewritten five years later, Paul's name was changed to that of the autobiographical novel's hero, 'Hearne'.

The play's subtext is revealing, but opinions were divided as to whether it was any good. Russell hated it as 'merely clever' and utterly disagreeable.[60] Nevinson, who helped Farr with the copyright reading in London on 20 October, thought it 'too Fabian or anarchist in doctrine, too preachy, much too undramatic and obvious. Some of the satire excellent, some too obvious & common, as of a man who approaches social questions for the first time.'[61] John Quinn extravagantly approved of it – as well he might, since it reflected many of the ideas he had discussed with WBY that summer. WBY himself continued to revise and reshape it in his mind after its precipitate publication; on 18 November, for instance, he told Gregory that he had reformulated his hero as a Pan-like figure, persuading people to live in the moment (a Blakean resonance, as so often).[62] It had already been much reconstructed when he rejected it for his *Collected Works* six years later, in favour of the version called *The Unicorn from the Stars*. His comments cast some light on its inception:

No I can't have 'Where There is Nothing' in the edition. Though 'The Unicorn' is almost altogether Lady Gregory's writing it has far more of my spirit in it than 'Where There Is Nothing' which she an [*sic*] I and Douglas Hyde wrote in a fortnight to keep George Moore from stealing the plot. Hyde forbid me to mention his name for fear of consequences and you must not mention it even now and for the same reason I did not mention Lady Gregory except in that old Preface which you know. There is certainly much more of my own actual writing in 'Where There Is Nothing' but I feel that this new play belongs to my world and that it does not.[63]

But in the conditions of 1902 the play as written reflects the arguments of WBY, Hyde and Gregory for being 'king and priest in one's own house',[64] against ruling Catholic pieties – a fight shortly to be waged by Synge. Copyrighted by a small New York printing arranged by Quinn,[65] it could now be played, but it was not very dramatizable. The avant-garde Stage Society in London expressed interest, and WBY devoted much effort to ideas for its production,[66] but it did not come off until June 1904; an enterprising devotee wanted to put it on in Ballyhaunis, County Mayo, but got no further than an inquiry; and the Fays stayed clear. For the moment, in 1902, it created an utter rift between WBY and Moore. When they next met, at Symons's house two years later, Moore refused to shake hands and left without a word. As for Russell, who probably provided the original spark, he had written resignedly to Gregory in August:

I am not going to touch Little. I leave him with a protest to W. B. Y. and Moore. I am sure when they have both written no-one will recognise any similarity between their work or will trace the fantastic original. I think I will try this young man looking for a Messiah, who is quite as good a man as Little. The play might end by his discovery of himself.[67]

As it happened, the young man was James Joyce, embarking on an odyssey which would echo in many ways Paul Ruttledge's determination to tear down the veil of the temple.

III

The summer of 1902 introduced new players to the cast of WBY's life, and rang down the curtain on some long-established scenes. The friendship of John Quinn did more than midwife *Where There is Nothing*; it helped transform life for the whole Yeats family. Quinn was a 32-year-old Irish American lawyer, enormously talented and energetic, about to start his own Manhattan firm specializing in financial and corporate law and already making money. He was closely involved in Tammany Hall politics, and, though a determined bachelor, pursued an active and colourful love-life. None of this was

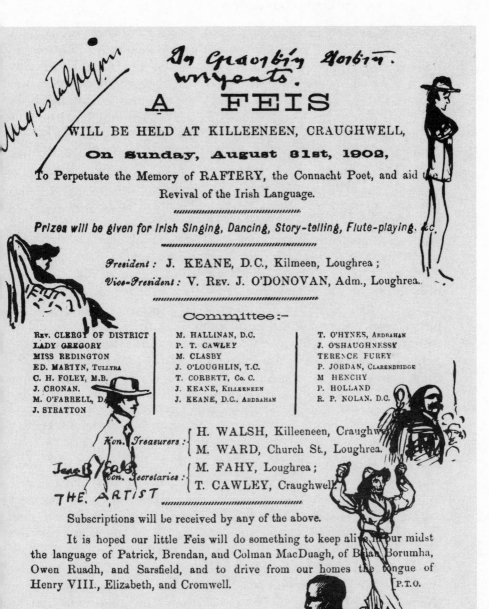

A FEIS

WILL BE HELD AT KILLEENEEN, CRAUGHWELL,

On Sunday, August 31st, 1902,

To Perpetuate the Memory of RAFTERY, the Connacht Poet, and aid the Revival of the Irish Language.

Prizes will be given for Irish Singing, Dancing, Story-telling, Flute-playing, &c.

President : J. KEANE, D.C., Kilmeen, Loughrea ;
Vice-President : V. Rev. J. O'DONOVAN, Adm., Loughrea.

Committee :—

Rev. CLERGY OF DISTRICT	M. HALLINAN, D.C.	T. O'HYNES, Ardrahan
LADY GREGORY	P. T. CAWLEY	J. O'SHAUGHNESSY
MISS REDINGTON	M. CLASBY	TERENCE FUREY
ED. MARTYN, Tullyra	J. O'LOUGHLIN, T.C.	P. JORDAN, Clarenbridge
C. H. FOLEY, M.B.	T. CORBETT, Co. C.	M HENCHY
J. CRONAN.	J. KEANE, Killeeneen	P. HOLLAND
M. O'FARRELL, D.	J. KEANE, D.C., Ardrahan	R. P. NOLAN. D.C.
J. STRATTON		

Hon. Treasurers : { H. WALSH, Killeeneen, Craughwell
M. WARD, Church St., Loughrea.

Hon. Secretaries : { M. FAHY, Loughrea ;
T. CAWLEY, Craughwell.

Subscriptions will be received by any of the above.

It is hoped our little Feis will do something to keep alive in our midst the language of Patrick, Brendan, and Colman MacDuagh, of Brian Borumha, Owen Ruadh, and Sarsfield, and to drive from our homes the tongue of Henry VIII., Elizabeth, and Cromwell. [P.T.O.]

---

11. John Quinn's copy of the programme for the Killeeneen *feis*, held in homage to Raftery. He attended from Coole with Gregory, Hyde, Jack Yeats and WBY, who all appear in Jack's sketches: himself as 'The Artist', Gregory in a wicker chair, WBY with arms folded, Hyde heavily moustached, and Quinn at the bottom below an unidentified Irish dancer.

271

unusual; what was remarkable was the way he employed his resources. Quinn possessed an uncanny eye for avant-garde art, and would buy an astonishing number of Post-Impressionist masterpieces at a very early age. He was also fascinated by the new wave of Irish literary culture gathering around WBY. Ripples had reached New York, though Quinn's first contacts had been through his interest in the paintings of JBY and Jack. By the end of 1901 WBY was corresponding with him, thanking him for sending William James's *Human Immortality*. When Quinn came to Ireland for the first of three consecutive annual trips in August 1902, he made his way to Coole, and was present on 31 August at the Killeeneen *feis* organized to commemorate the poet Raftery. His companions there included Jack Yeats, Hyde and Gregory, but the focus of his interest was WBY. WBY, like his father and brother, realized he had met a patron of apparently infinite resources and goodwill; Quinn, with his eye for the first-rate, knew that he had encountered a genius.

Many of Quinn's attitudes echoed WBY's own. Impatient with the pieties of Irish life, he was notably anti-clerical and fiercely individualistic; he satirized Arthur Griffith and Irish American 'patriots', believing in the ultimate sanctification of the artistic conscience. At his worst he could be a wordy, didactic bore; but his quick intelligence and enormous energy were put at the disposal of the Yeats circle. He quickly took responsibility for copyrighting WBY's plays in America, and dealing with Macmillan in New York on the poet's behalf. And he pursued a still closer intellectual relationship. Famously, he is supposed to have introduced WBY to Nietzsche, sending him *Thus Spake Zarathustra* shortly after he returned to New York, and subsequently other volumes. WBY himself gave Quinn the credit, writing to him a year later that he had been 'the first to introduce me' – though when acknowledging the arrival of *Zarathustra*, he remarked, 'I have long desired to have it', having bought an abridged version in London.[68] Certainly from 1902 to 1903 he read the German philosopher intensively for the first time. But in letters about his new passion, WBY makes the connection between Nietzsche and Blake which had been specifically stated by Havelock Ellis nine years before in the second number of the *Savoy*: a journal dominated by WBY's own work and certainly read by him.[69] Symons had written an essay, 'Nietzsche and Tragedy',[70] and WBY's own theorizing about drama, and the phases of ancient Greek culture, used Nietzsche's formulations before he met Quinn. These were probably acquired second-hand through Symons and others. Quinn thought he introduced WBY to Nietzsche, and WBY flattered him by confirming the diagnosis. But oddly, years later, Oliver Gogarty believed that he had been the first to introduce WBY to Nietzsche as well.[71]

In any case, if Quinn was going to assume a proprietorial role, nobody felt like contradicting him. From 1902 he devoted his considerable (and increasing) resources to Irish art: commissioning Russell to paint WBY 'with the creatures of his imagination round about him',[72] subsidizing an ambitious series of Irish portraits from the astonished JBY, subsidizing the Irish National Dramatic Society with an annual subvention (£25, later raised to £50[73]). And from the autumn of 1902 there was a new repository for his munificence, focused on the Yeats family and located in Dublin.

The gathering pace of cultural excitement in Dublin impelled *émigré* intellectuals to return. Moore had already set up house in Ely Place; 'Everyone is so anxious to get you to come & live in Dublin,' Gonne told WBY in May.[74] But his own ambitions remained divided between the two countries, and in the end it was his family who returned instead. JBY had continued to gather little moss, but a Dublin exhibition of his work arranged by Sarah Purser in October 1901 marked the beginning of a new phase.[75] It amounted to a retro-spective of his paintings over two decades, and suddenly the dramatic, impres-sionist quality of his portraiture looked self-willed and confident instead of raw and unfinished. The show was a considerable success; it re-established JBY in Dublin's eyes, and began the long connection with John Quinn. Local commissions, however, were less forthcoming. JBY confided to his eldest son, 'We Yeatses have such bad characters the people who live in good society and have their feet on the rock of ages and order their portraits disapprove of us, so that I am likely to starve for my sins.'[76] Quinn and Gregory both com-missioned portraits, but others did not follow; through the summer of 1902 JBY was borrowing small sums from his children, as well as pressing them to drum up commissions. Russell had been similarly employed, lobbying to get JBY a job at the School of Art. In June 1902 Russell confided to Gregory:

I really think, between ourselves, that Willie and Jack between them should come to some arrangement to provide their father now growing old with a home. I think Willie wastes endless time and he has a duty to his father which no sophistries about genius can get over. I continually hear comments on his heartlessness in allowing his sister Lolly to support his father and other sister Lily who cannot owing to her asthma do very much. Mr J. B. Yeats borrows endlessly until some of his best friends simply had to pull him up very sharply. Now Willie could very easily send his father one pound a week. It is preposterous nonsense to say he could not. He could very well afford to give less time to the G. D. and similar matters. If he only did three hours work every day he could earn about three hundred a year. He may object to doing ephemeral work but he still could do all the poetry he does at present, and if the work he occupies his time with at present is not 'ephemeral' work I don't know what is . . . 'The good man is merciful to his biographer' and I think if Willie heard some of the comments made by people who have known the Yeats's for years he would get red all over. And frankly, again, though I do not talk of these things myself, I have little or nothing to urge on the other side . . . It is hardly a pleasant matter but I think this flight from the disagreeable is taking a good deal of the moral character out of Willie's work which really loses by his isolation.[77]

He had overstepped the mark. A scorching letter came back from Coole, accusing Russell of listening too much to Sarah Purser; its tone may be surmised from Russell's cowed rejoinder. 'I think it is better not to discuss Willie. I am sorry I wrote about it at all. It is really no business of mine to discuss his relations to his family. I knew all you said already and a good deal more on both sides as well.'[78]

Help, however, was indirectly on the way. Since early 1902 Lily and Lolly had been negotiating with Evelyn Gleeson, a well-off woman of Irish extraction who wanted 'to find work for Irish hands in the making of beautiful things'. This took the form of a manufacturing and retailing centre for fabrics, rugs, embroidery and, eventually, printing. With a Dublin friend, Augustine Henry, finance was arranged: too vaguely, as it turned out. But Lily's training at William Morris's, and Lolly's enterprise with brushwork and graphic design, had found an outlet at last. By July arrangements had been made to set up 'Dun Emer Industries' in Dublin. Lily would take responsibility for embroidery work, and Lolly for printing, with firm encouragement from JBY. 'You have every bit as much intellect as Willie,' he told Lolly, 'only you have not his serene self-confidence. And [not] having this you have not his patience. Lily and Willie both have a talent for making phrases – but Lily has not your power of reasoning, power of intellect. You are here quite as strong as Willie, only you don't exercise it.'[79]

These very likenesses would bring Lolly and WBY into conflict over many aspects of the Dun Emer business – which he would subsidize in its future incarnation as the Cuala Press, just as Russell wanted him to bankroll his father. The undertaking appealed to him, especially in its printing enterprise, which he discussed with Cockerell as early as May:[80] the very opposite of Gavan Duffy's old Library of Ireland, it would produce expensive and beautiful limited editions not only of WBY's work but of his favourites (Lionel Johnson, just dead,[81] and Allingham) and his circle (Russell, Hyde). By the autumn the Yeatses had left Blenheim Road, with its shabby, sunny rooms, painted bedroom ceilings, sunflowers in the garden: the backdrop to their youthful memories of material deprivation and artistic ambition. Back in Ireland at last, Lily felt restored to a culture which spoke her language. Even the bricklayer mending the hearth in her new house remarked, when he 'made a big hole . . . "that would do for Mr Yeats's play 'Where there is nothing'"'.[82] But the values of Bedford Park were exported to the house in Dundrum where the 'industries' were begun, and the Yeatsian domestic atmosphere – sociable, volatile, relentlessly self-analysing – was transposed to 'Gurteen Dhas', the Churchtown bungalow where JBY and his daughters set up house on 1 October 1902.

From the beginning WBY was involved – slightly to the consternation of those backing the venture. 'He is a genius,' Augustine Henry warned Gleeson, 'and his ways in society are to be excused *completely* – and you must not blame him, he is probably in the clouds. Of course he is much spoiled by admiration of women.'[83] These women did not include his younger sister. JBY entreated him to make his peace with Lolly, though in Lily's view (years afterwards) the fault was not on his side. 'WB was also working very hard for very little and had all the troubles over the theatre, such bitter disappointments, and the infernal Maud through it all.'[84]

For all the disagreements, the business was under way by October. Long before, WBY had stipulated 'if ever a first rate publishing house arise in Ireland I must needs publish in part with them'.[85] With the majority of his books he kept his word, giving his sisters the first publication in a limited edition, followed by a commercial press edition a few months later. In November he refused John Lane the rights to his next book of verse, which Lane wanted as a condition for publishing *Where There is Nothing*: his poems were 'already promised' to his sisters.[86] Though he had been writing very few lyrics during these years of theatrical excitement, by December Lolly was printing trial proofs of *In the Seven Woods*, her brother's first collection since 1899 (bulked out by the play *On Baile's Strand*). Working at Dun Emer became a way-station, almost a rite of passage, for many young women involved in nationalist cultural enterprises: future writers, painters, Sinn Féin activists and Abbey actresses served their time there. '100 years ago [Lolly and Lily] would have wanted to make them loyal & Protestant,' JBY remarked ironically to Elkin Mathews, 'now they only seek to make them happy & rational & healthy, sleeping with their windows open & not knuckling down to brothers or anybody else or anything else – this marks the "Progress of the Ages".'[87] Dun Emer was one proof of cultural self-confidence taking root in the cynical world of the Irish metropolis by 1902. Another was provided by the brief irruption into WBY's circle of the man who would immortalize that metropolis, in that era: the youthful James Joyce.

In August Russell had written excitedly to WBY about 'an extremely clever boy who belongs to your class more than to mine and still more to himself. But he has all the intellectual equipment, culture and education which all our other friends lack.' He wrote even more ecstatically to Gregory; Joyce had presented himself at the Russells' house (haranguing him about avatars, a sure way to Russell's heart), and they had spent a hectic summer night of talk.[88] Russell was now well known for his undiscriminating adoption of young hopefuls, and WBY had learnt to be wary about swans who invariably turned out to be geese. But both he and Gregory rapidly saw that this was something different, and the attention they paid the twenty-year-old student was remarkable. So, in its way, was the lack of attention he paid them.

Joyce had already made his mark with a clear-sighted attack on the Irish Literary Theatre in 'The Day of the Rabblement', but he passionately admired WBY's literary achievement: he could recite 'The Adoration of the Magi' off by heart and the mesmeric beauty of certain poems (notably 'Who Goes with Fergus?' from *The Countess Cathleen*) remained canonical for him.[89] After a glamorous but slightly scandalous career at the Royal University, he was following a haphazard course as a medical student. In October Russell told him that WBY would be in Dublin the following month and would like to meet him (he had already dined at the Nassau Hotel on 4 November with Gregory and JBY). There was accordingly a rendezvous outside the National Library, followed by an awkward encounter in an O'Connell Street café. It was an intense occasion, much recapitulated and mythologized; Ellmann has compared it to the meeting between Goethe and Heine, a symbolic conjunction in the history of world literature. More immediately apparent was the mutual suspicion between an established Irish Protestant aesthete and a Jesuit-educated Catholic Dubliner with a preternaturally mordant eye for social pretensions. Soon afterwards WBY wrote (but never published) a slightly fictionalized account of their meeting. 'He asked me "Why did I make speeches? Why did I concern myself with politics? Why had I given certain of my stories and poems a historical setting?" . . . all these things were a sign that the iron was getting cold.' Joyce's own affiliations and energies were strange to him; WBY realized that he was dealing with a new force, something that could not be predicted. His version betrays the wistful tone of a man nearing forty, confronted by the ruthlessness of youthful genius. 'Presently he got up to go, and, as he was going out, he said, "I am twenty. How old are you?" I told him, but I am afraid I said I was a year younger than I am. He said with a sigh, "I thought as much. I have met you too late. You are too old."' Joyce in later years denied this, but at a stage of life when good manners meant more to him than they did in 1902.[90] Their disagreement was inevitable. One of the points WBY recalled making to Joyce involved a defence of folklore against the 'sterility' of urban culture, Great Memory against individual consciousness. Joyce's lofty and laconic reply rankled enough for WBY to repeat it more than once. 'Generalizations aren't made by poets; they are made by men of letters. They are no use.'[91]

Still, he showed WBY some of his 'Epiphanies' and verses, which intrigued the older poet. After their meeting WBY sent Joyce an important letter from London: in it he subtly reproved Joyce for condemning WBY's 'treacherous instinct for adaptability' in his critique of the Irish Literary Theatre, asserted his own authority as an established literary figure with a base in England, and hinted at his autobiography.

Remember what Dr Johnson said about somebody 'let us wait until we find out whether he is a fountain or a cistern.' The work which you have actually done is very remarkable for a man of your age who has lived away from the vital intellectual centres. Your technique in verse is very much better than the technique of any young Dublin man I have met during my time. It might have been the work of a young man who had lived in an Oxford literary set. However men have started with as good promise as yours and have failed & men have started with less and have succeeded. The qualities that make a man succeed do not shew in his work, often for quite a long time They are much less qualities of talent than qualities of character – faith (of this you have probably enough), patience, adaptability, (without this one learns nothing), and a gift for growing by experience & this is perhaps rarest of all.

I will do anything for you I can but I am afraid that it will not be a great deal. The chief use I can be, though probably you will not believe this, will be by introducing you to some other writers who are starting like yourself, one always learns one's business from one's fellow-workers, especially from those who are near enough one's own age to understand one's own difficulties.[92]

WBY lived up to this; Joyce was not the only apprentice writer who received thoughtful letters of advice from him at this time.[93] Nor did his help stop there. On 2 December, forewarned by Gregory, he met Joyce off the Irish Mail at six in the morning, gave him breakfast, brought him to the review editors of the *Academy* and the *Speaker*, and finally to Arthur Symons's flat.[94] Joyce went on to Paris that evening, to stay at WBY's old haunt the Hôtel Corneille, armed with the address of Maud Gonne (which he did not follow up, a loss to literary history). WBY sent him several long letters, showing that he milked what contacts he could on Joyce's behalf, and entertained the young man again *en route* back to Dublin on 23 December. But Joyce's failure to approach Gonne was emblematic. His interests, his paths, his art would all diverge from WBY's, despite his half-resentful admiration of the early poetry. At the end of his life Joyce admitted that he lacked 'pure imagination', which WBY pre-eminently possessed: 'no surrealist poet can equal it'.[95] But in 1902 he was, as he would famously put it, flying by the nets of an enveloping national culture, just as WBY was trying to fashion such a phenomenon. Proof that WBY was jolted by the opinions of this merciless young prodigy lies in the preface he wrote for his essays *Ideas of Good and Evil*, but suppressed. He related his initial worries about the 'reckless opinions' of the essays, and his anticipation of being thought a 'disturber who carries in his hand the irresponsible torch of vain youth'. And then he met Joyce, whose relentless questioning 'exasperated and puzzled him', who told him his work was 'deteriorating', and that he was, in the end, 'too old'. Approaching forty, this rang like a knell.

A year later, reissuing his stories *The Tables of the Law*, he added a note to the preface. 'I do not think I should have reprinted them had I not met a young man in Ireland the other day who liked them very much and nothing else at all that I have written.'[96]

IV

By the time wby and Joyce sat down suspiciously together in the O'Connell Street café, the Irish National Dramatic Society had performed its first season in its new incarnation, with wby as President. It had emerged during the summer from the chrysalis of the old Fay company (whose name appeared for the last time at the October 1902 season), but it was not an easy conception. Of the old Irish Literary Theatre connection, Martyn had become alienated through the cavalier treatment he had received; Moore had fallen out over *Where There is Nothing* (and was *persona non grata* with nationalists because of squibs like *Parnell and His Island*). Gregory and wby alone survived. From the Fay–Inghinidhe side, Maud Gonne came uneasily aboard, but firmly allied herself with the guardians of nationalist rectitude; in September she vetoed rehearsals of Gregory's first solo effort, *Twenty-five*, because it presented an optimistic view of emigration, advancing instead Padraic Colum's anti-recruiting play *The Saxon Shillin'*. Politics were heavily involved in the choice of plays, but so was straightforward dramatic competition. Willie Fay, for instance, withdrew wby's *The Hour-Glass* from Inghinidhe na hÉireann in September, because he wanted it for the Irish National Dramatic Company; from early on Gonne made it clear to wby that the constituency attracted by the connection with Inghinidhe and Cumann na nGaedheal was far more 'national' than the elite tendency of the redefined Fay company. By midsummer 1902 the *United Irishman* was in deep financial trouble, totally dependent on IRB subventions arranged through John MacBride to keep going, and therefore tied to a hard separatist line.[97] But both the Fays knew where their artistic future lay, and abandoned the nationalist societies with relief. Gonne's eventual severance was inevitable. Her own view of this history was given in an angry letter to wby a year later:

You forget the existence of the National Theatre Society [formed from the Irish National Dramatic Society in January 1903[98]] was originally due to Inginide na hEireann & Cumann na Gaedhal. If these Societies had not taken Fay up he would still be contentedly playing vulgar English farces in the Union Jack Coffee Palace. It was after Inginide na hEireann passed a resolution forbidding any of their members to act for Fay in his English farces & for the Coffee Palace that he came to me & said he would rather act for Nationalists if he could get National pieces & we introduced him to Russell who gave him or rather gave us his 'Deirdre' to act. Have you forgotten how both Russell & I urged you to let us have your 'Kathleen' how you said Lady Gregory thought you should not – & how at last to make things smooth I consented to act Kathleen. It was Inginide na hEireann & Cumann na Gaedhal who financed each of Fay's first attempts at National performances. On each occasion we not only gave him the dresses & scenery we had paid for, but also gave him more than the fair share of profits & even when there was a loss made up something for Fay, not for himself naturally but with the idea of helping the formation of a National Theatre Co – Members of Cumann na Gaedhal personally gave money & collected money for the Company & all this because we wanted a NATIONAL Theatre Co to help us combat the influence of the low English theatres & music halls.

It is absurd for you to say you did not know all this from the beginning though I will believe you have forgotten it now & have grown to think that it is you & Lady Gregory & her friends who started the National Theatre Co.[99]

For the moment, the nationalist societies continued to co-operate. When 'W. G. Fay's Irish National Dramatic Company' presented a 'Samhain' season at the Antient Concert Rooms it was organized (according to Fay) 'by Cumann na nGaeheal [*sic*], a Dublin political body'[100] and hailed on the front page of the *United Irishman* as the birth of a potential Irish national theatre, 'a powerful agent in the building up of a nation'. None the less, the opening reception was attended by several prominent Unionists – O'Grady, a Bourke of Clanricarde, Captain John Shawe-Taylor. Even the ironic nationalist journalist William Bulfin thought it symbolized a new spirit of cultural co-operation.[101] The plays ran from 28 October to 1 November and included Russell's *Deirdre*, *Cathleen ni Houlihan* (with Gonne), James Cousins's *Connla* and *The Racing Lug*, Fred Ryan's *The Laying of the Foundations*, WBY's (and Gregory's) *Pot of Broth*, and P. T. MacGinley's *Eilís agus an Bhean Dhéirce*. At the second night James Cousins felt an ominous 'twinge' at WBY's attitude 'that we were contributors to him and not he to us'.[102]

Further performances followed in early December and January. Though WBY's plays were not over-represented, his presence was dominant, notably in editing a new issue of *Samhain*. This stressed the patronage of Cumann na nGaedheal, and reviewed the dramatic activity of the past year, criticizing Hyde's 'carelessness' and elevating 'personality' above propaganda in literature. He also published *Where There is Nothing* in the *United Irishman* on 30 October, and gave the lecture (before a matinée audience) 'Speaking to Musical Notes', with Florence Farr and the inevitable psaltery. Frank Fay produced a noticeably grudging review, mentioning that he himself had 'been reading and thinking about rhythmical recitation for years'. He condemned Farr's performance and WBY's emphasis, while other Irish critics were even more dismissive.[103] But WBY was inevitably prominent, as was noted by Bulfin at the opening reception on 24 October:

[Mr Yeats] pervades the hall. He wanders about like a troubled soul in spiritland or elsewhere. He is not dressed like anyone else, nor does he look like anyone else. And if he were dressed like anyone else he could simply be grotesque, for he was not meant for ordinary clothes. He is an original character. He has many enemies and many friends. Everything he does seems to stir up some rancour, and he is nearly always doing things. I have done my best to find out from my conversations with him whether he unconsciously goes around driving poles into beehives or whether he does it purposely, simply for the sake of notoriety. I have not been able to convict him of doing it purposely. He wanders in the realms of the mind, just as he does in the physical world – taking little note of where his steps are leading him. He just goes on and on, treading on corns, and hitting up against prejudices, and cannoning against scruples, and wondering greatly why there is anything in the Universe but himself. He is intellectually proud, possibly without knowing it. He is a man whom you cannot judge by any conventionality, or any ordinary standard. He evades analysis. You may think you have him proved beyond yea or nay to be a great original thinker, when he will gravely and gracefully deliver himself of some oracular absurdity, which causes you to reconsider his case. He will then proceed to blow soap bubbles of fancy into the air until the sky is paved with them, and he will sportively pursue one bubble after another until he is tired of the sport. Then when you are on the point of convicting him of being a tuneful trifler and a melodious ninny-hammer, he will suddenly change his mind and talk with amazing brilliance and force on the most elevated themes – talk with intense earnestness and sustained eloquence, with correct and accurate fluency and with measured poise of thought which cannot be art, and must be something higher. Take not the book by the cover or by the dog-eared leaves. Judge not a man by his neck-ties or by his way of brushing his back hair. And furthermore if you are looking at the merits of any person, place or thing through a mist of irritation, wait until it gets off your nerves.[104]

His great talent for managing publicity now had a new focus, and he had learnt how to manipulate the collusive antagonisms of Dublin life. According to a later recollection, 'if they had a play coming on which was likely to prove controversial he could call round to *The Leader* office, tell D. P. Moran the editor and [his] ostensible enemy about it, and ask that, if the play had to be attacked it should be on some, to W. B., unimportant ground, rather than the one that might prove damaging to the theatre effort as a whole. Always D. P. would see what he could do about it and no harm would be done.'[105] On another level he cultivated London theatrical contacts like Edith Craig and gleaned much about staging techniques, lighting and costumes – 'more than [Gordon] Craig likes', he reported gleefully to Gregory.[106] He was a highly active President of the Irish National Dramatic Society. The publication of *Where There is Nothing*, together with his public pronouncements on artistic freedom, struck his thoughtful critic Thomas Kettle as a deliberately nihilist and amoral stance: WBY's 'rationalistic whimsies' prevented him from understanding 'the sanctity and compulsion with which the Catholic religion has established itself in the imagination of Ireland'.[107] It was debatable whether or not wby realized his offensiveness; Paul Ruttledge-like, he made enemies unintentionally.

By early December, for instance, wby was telling Frank Fay that the sooner they had James Cousins as an adversary, the better. Yet Cousins had provided two plays for the company's first season; he had introduced the Fays to Russell; he saw himself as a founding father. Nor was he a hostile Griffithite, being a moderate nationalist, a Theosophist, and an intimate of Russell's. This may have been part of the problem, since wby was currently furious with his old friend for reprinting some early Yeats poems, now despised by their author, in the *Irish Homestead*. Faced by wby's outspoken condemnation of his new plays *Sold* and *The Sword of Dermot*, Cousins left. Another new playwright stayed longer in favour – the gauche but talented Padraic Colum, who had visited wby and read him his Ibsenite play about the United Irish League the previous April. But from the Society's inception, the choice of plays presented problems. When Colum's *The Saxon Shillin'*, recipient of a Cumann na nGaedheal prize, went into rehearsal in December, Fay wanted revisions; Gonne and Griffith, on behalf of the nationalist societies, objected. Griffith (whose paper had been sniping at wby through November) eventually resigned and Russell was brought in as peacemaker, suggesting new procedures for choosing plays. But the evaluation of appropriate material remained an electric issue. wby's own one-act play, *The Hour-Glass*, was probably constructed with this in mind: supernaturalism was expressed in language of conventional religiosity, stressing the power of mystical belief over the arrogance of free thought.[108] When the idea first occurred to wby the previous April, he had written to Gregory: 'It cannot offend anybody & may propitiate Holy Church.'[109] The wrangles of November and December 1902, however, demonstrated that no detail was too small to escape Cumann na nGaedheal's hawk-like eye for national impieties. By late December wby was privately preaching apostasy in the form of non-Irish plays. The Fays, he told Gregory, should 'play foreign masterpieces. I find I can get through Miss Horniman a translation of a fine play of the heroic age of Sudermans.'[110] A clause in the Society's constitution had allowed for the playing of such 'dramatic works of foreign authors as would tend to educate and interest the public', but to Gonne this would be an unforgivable breach of the principles upon which the various elements had united to form the Irish National Dramatic Society. By now, however, her own personal drama was embarked on a course which, to wby, would constitute a worse betrayal by far.

Chapter II : THE TASTE OF SALT
1902–1903

> As long as ten years ago I said to myself 'I must not commit
> the mistake of the political revolutionists, which, as far as I
> can see, every theatrical reformer is ready to commit. The
> political revolutionist always thinks "The people are uncor-
> rupt, and noble, it is only the Governments that are corrupt."
> He stakes his life upon that belief, and loses it. On the con-
> trary, the people are no wiser than their education. Let us have
> no faith in the people. The people have to be converted very
> slowly; they have to be taught their A.B.C. painfully. Let us
> believe in ideas and our friends.'
>
> WBY to Gordon Craig, 16 November 1911

I

WHEN WBY returned to London in November 1902, he was blissfully un-
aware that Gonne was preparing yet another shock to rock his life to its
foundations. 'I am in the best of good spirits,' he wrote to Gregory on 18
November. 'Last year I began the winter in black gloom.' His good humour
enabled him to savour the resentments aroused among 'all my psaltery
people' by Farr's indolent, gossipy ways, and to mock the 'grateful and happy'
Horniman, lashing out money for 'six new psalteries'. In November he
received a proof of his new poem 'Adam's Curse' from the *Monthly Review*
– a lyrical but sharp-edged evocation of his conversation with Gonne and
her sister the previous May, lounging in a Kensington drawing-room as the
moon rose. It would be the central poem of his next collection, and stands at
the balancing-point between the romance, mistiness and elevated 'beauty'
of his nineties poetry, and the new, toughened diction which he had con-
sciously begun to seek. The poem itself hinges on the contrast between the
two voices:

> We sat together at one summer's end
> That beautiful mild woman your close friend,
> And you and I, and talked of poetry.
>
> I said 'a line will take us hours maybe
> Yet if it does not seem a moment's thought
> Our stitching and unstitching has been naught.
> Better go down upon your marrow bones
> And scrub a kitchen pavement or break stones
> Like an old pauper in all kinds of weather;

For to articulate sweet sounds together
Is to work harder than all these and yet
Be thought an idler by the noisy set
Of bankers, schoolmasters, and clergymen
The martyrs call the world.'

                    That woman then
Murmured with her young voice for whose mild sake
There's many a one shall find out all heartache
In finding that it's young and mild and low.
'There is one thing that all we women know
Although we never heard of it of it at school
That we must labour to be beautiful.'

I said, 'It's certain there is no fine thing
Since Adam's fall but needs much labouring.
There have been lovers who thought love should be
So much compounded of high courtesy
That they would sigh and quote with learned looks
Precedents out of beautiful old books;
Yet now it seems an idle trade enough.'

We sat grown quiet at the name of love.
We saw the last embers of daylight die
And in the trembling blue-green of the sky
A moon – moon-worn as if it had been a shell
Washed by time's waters as they rose and fell
About the starn and broke in days and years.

I had a thought for no one but your ears;
That you were beautiful and that I strove
To love you in the old high way of love;
That it had all seemed happy and yet we'd grown
As weary hearted as that hollow moon.

It was written, and published, at the very time when the relationship it invoked was to take a traumatic new direction. While he was cheerfully settling down to a winter in London, reviving his interest in spiritualist experiments at Woburn Buildings and negotiating about the arrival of 'a gass oven', she was in Paris with the IRB man and Boer War hero John MacBride. 'You are so good writing to me even when I am silent,' she told WBY on 28 December. 'Thank you, you are a kind friend always.'

By then, her mind was made up. At thirty-five, MacBride was a year younger than Gonne, and from a dramatically different background (small Catholic shopkeepers in County Mayo). Like her, he had joined the INA split in the mid-1890s, and they were brought together in the anti-war campaign of 1900. Red-haired, heavy-drinking, physically brave, rather inarticulate and utterly unmystical, he incarnated the authentic and uncompromising Irish nationalism to which she had dedicated her life. More than a year before, in America during the spring of 1901, he had asked her to marry him; though it was against her feminist principles, she eventually consented. Her own position after the break with Millevoye had become more and more difficult, and MacBride was now based in Paris, scraping a living as secretary to an American journalist.[1] 'Marriage I always consider abominable but for the sake of Iseult, I make that sacrifice to convention,' she wrote to Kathleen.[2] In June 1902 she told her disapproving sister: '1st I am to become Catholic, 2nd I am to get married to Major MacBride, this last is not public yet.' She added, more defensively, that she was 'getting old and oh so tired and I have found a man who has a stronger will than myself and who at the same time is thoroughly honourable and who I trust . . . As for Willie Yeats I love him dearly as a friend but I could not for one minute imagine marrying him.'[3] None the less, she may have worried about his reaction. From this time, hints can be discerned in her letters to him – about her inclination to Catholicism, her meetings with MacBride's family in Mayo, her own increasing 'decrepitude' and rheumatism.[4] And through these very months of late 1902, she was also becoming more and more estranged from him on theatrical matters, perhaps a reflection of her deliberate desire to make a break.

But nothing could prepare him for this. Since December 1898 his great powers of rationalization had been directed towards convincing himself that their 'spiritual' relationship was the better part of passion. Time and time again his folklore stories concern a countryman (sometimes a 'poet') who is offered knowledge or pleasure by a fairy queen. When he chooses pleasure and becomes her lover, he is left bereft, making mournful songs until he dies.[5] Renunciation brought the reward of artistic achievement and continuing inspiration. Gonne was, however, about to shatter the understanding on which this compact was based.

Her alienation from WBY over theatre matters proceeded in step with this. In January 1903 she was in Dublin, complaining during rehearsals of the changes to Colum's play; 'Griffith declares it is spoiled from an artistic point of view & all openly say it is because Fay fears to vex the *respectable*.'[6] But Fay by this point had lost all patience with the 'absolutely fossilized' approach of the nationalists.[7] She and WBY were on different sides in the dispute, though he remained in London. It was there he heard about her engagement, in early February. His later recollection of receiving a telegram just before addressing a public meeting probably refers to his lecture 'The Future of Irish Drama', given in London on 7 February.[8] It was, for him, not only a private trauma but a public humiliation; his poems had solemnized their relationship before his reading public as well as his friends. Ricketts's reaction was probably fairly typical. 'Have you heard the news that Maud Gonne has gone and left Yeats and the future of Ireland for matrimony and comfortable Catholicism? Yeats is unconsolable in sonnets of the Oh thou! type to various little lilts and tunes.'⁹

The first three letters he sent her have been lost, but the fourth survived, a passionate plea to her to remain the inviolate self he had so often celebrated. 'In the name of 14 years of friendship', he implored her to think again. For all his anguish, his arguments were coherent and compelling. First, their ancient bond: he quoted from his diary of 12 December 1898, recalling their spiritual marriage in a dream and implicitly accusing her of a bigamous betrayal. 'I claim that this gives me the right to speak.' But his subsequent arguments stressed the danger of debasement – religious and social. Marriage with MacBride would make her 'fall into a lower order & do great injury to the religeon of free souls that is growing up in Ireland, it may be to enlighten the whole world.' 'The priests will exult over us.' 'You possess your influence in Ireland very largely because you come to the people from above. You represent a superior class, a class whose people are more independent, have a more beautiful life, a more refined life.' Above all, 'thrust down . . . to a lower order of faith' and society, she would destroy the *persona* she had created for herself. 'It was our work to teach a few strong aristocratic spirits that to believe the soul was immortal & that one prospered hereafter *if one laid upon oneself* an heroic discipline in living & [? to] send them to uplift the nation. You & I were chosen to begin this work & <just> just when <you> I come to understand it fully you go from me & seek to thrust the people <down> further into weakness further from self reliance.' She must not betray her pride, her solitude, her inspiration. He stressed the unworthiness of Catholicism rather than of MacBride himself – the priests had truckled under to the government over the Act of Union and had betrayed the Fenians. 'When the day of great hazard has come', they would tell the people, 'Be quiet, be good cristians, do not shed blood.'¹⁰

Thus he tried to show that revolution and mysticism, both essential to Gonne's being, were threatened by this *mésalliance*. What is not stated is the question: why him, and not me? His own position as lover (and MacBride's) went unmentioned, though it may have been expatiated upon in the earlier letters. Possibly it was too bitter an issue to be articulated, though it would powerfully affect WBY's self-image from now on. His hard-won confidence was jolted. As recently as December he had confided to Edith Craig, 'I seldom get credit for an absurd amount of timidity and shyness, which has a way, when I meet any body for the first time or practically for the first time, of hiding embarrasment under a brazen manner.'¹¹ In the aftermath of Gonne's bombshell the brazen manner was shaken, but then adopted all the more resolutely.

In any case, she was unmoved. She had retired to a French convent for instruction; from there she replied soothingly that their friendship need not change. As to Catholicism, '<my>our nation looks at God or truth through one prism, The Catholic Religion'. In other words, to be Irish required being Catholic, the very conclusion WBY had devoted years of concentrated activity to disproving. And as for social superiority: 'You say I leave the few to mix myself with the crowd while Willie I have always told you I am the voice, the soul of the *crowd*.'[12] This indeed was the kernel of the ancient difference between them. It was now exacerbated by her adoption of Catholicism. Farr's version to Nevinson put it tersely: '[Gonne] hates marriage & all sex. They had a sort of understanding to be together in old age. Now he contemplates an onslaught on the Church.'[13]

On 21 February Gonne married MacBride at the Church of St-Honoré-d'Eylau in Paris, attended by nationalist delegates from Ireland (one of whom read a long poem in Irish) and old comrades from South Africa. Like her stage performances, the ceremony was transmuted into a new form of political theatre.[14] She assured WBY three days later that when called on to abjure all heresies, 'I said I hated nothing in the world but the British Empire which I looked on as the outward symbol of Satan in the world . . . in this form I made my solemn Abjuration of Anglicism & declaration of hatred of England.'[15] The marriage of the two 'irreconcilables' was viewed by their friends with grave misgivings. Arthur Griffith, Violet Russell, Ella Young all feared the worst, partly because of MacBride's conventionality (though he had his own illegitimate family in South Africa). Those who were principally interested in WBY, however, thought it might be a turning-point. Gregory sent 'a most kind & thoughtful letter' to Gonne, advising her to keep her own money by marrying under English law;[16] Annie Horniman, who had moved firmly into his life as amanuensis, and wanted more, sent him flirtatious accounts of Tarot divinations which were scantily veiled summonses to a partnership ('work for love brings Divine Wisdom'[17]).

Their hopes were quelled by the disastrous course of the Gonne–MacBride marriage. As early as the honeymoon (in southern Spain, allegedly reconnoitring assassination arrangements for an impending royal visit to Gibraltar), the couple's incompatibility and MacBride's drunkenness were spectacularly evident. Gonne returned to Paris alone, and significantly headed for London, where WBY met her, as so often before, at Euston.[18] Though a son (Seaghan, later Seán) was born the next year, there was little hope for the union; and by a terrible irony, the precipitating cause for its dissolution would be MacBride's molestation of his step-daughter Iseult, for whose protection

Gonne had sought refuge in marriage. As for her attitude to WBY, they continued to quarrel about the theatre, to collaborate on Celtic rituals, and to disagree about religious philosophy ('*Neiche* [*sic*] *is not Celtic*,' she admonished him). She shrewdly chided him for manipulating the Celtic Rites to express his repugnance at her conversion to Catholicism, finding no difficulty in adapting their old symbols of spear, cauldron, stone and sword to Christian archetypes. 'Why Willie it was you yourself who taught me these things.' By early May, less than three months after the wedding ceremony, she was confessing that she had made a terrible mistake. As for him, his distant princess was now unattainable in a different way: a Catholic wife and mother of two children.

II

These upheavals had accompanied a period of equally frantic literary and theatrical activity. In December 1902 the Irish National Dramatic Company had revived *Cathleen ni Houlihan*; chanting performances had continued, in WBY's absence schooled by Sturge Moore, though Farr was becoming ominously restive in her role and turned in a mutinously inadequate performance on 5 January for WBY's theatrical friends ('there are times when she makes me despair of the whole thing'). But his London associates, currently calling themselves the Literary Theatre Club, planned an ambitious Craig production of *The Countess Cathleen*, financed by Ricketts – 'a much bigger thing than I had foreseen', WBY told Gregory, '[which] will enormously strengthen my position'. And his new book of lyrics and plays, *In the Seven Woods*, was planned by Dun Emer as 'a specially beautiful and expensive first edition of some of my best things', followed by a cheaper Bullen edition.

In the process WBY informed Gregory that he was 'full of new thoughts for verse though all thoughts quite unlike the old ones. My work has got far more masculine. It has more salt in it.'[19] This growing taste for salt was important; it presaged a new theatrical departure, which would shape the nascent Irish National Theatre Society irrevocably. On 21 December 1902 WBY had written to Synge (last seen in Coole the previous October, *en route* to Aran) that they would meet in London '& I will get you to show me your play'. On 20 January Synge read *Riders to the Sea* to some of WBY's and Gregory's London acquaintances at her London flat in Queen Anne's Mansions.

By early February the play had been read three times, the audiences including Gonne, Chesterton and Arthur Symons; on 3 March, Synge's far more controversial *In the Shadow of the Glen* was read at Gregory's flat to Masefield, Farr, Symons and WBY.[20] It was clear that a new voice had been raised, using Irish idiom in an uncompromisingly poetic but earthy way, with

a real sense of dramatic language and pace. Through 1902 WBY had been dir-
ecting Synge towards reviewing opportunities, and giving him advice. But
with his earliest plays Synge achieved what WBY knew his own drama lacked:
unstagey heroics, real passion, the expression of combative individuality.
'Saltiness' was here in full measure. As with Joyce (and, later, Pound), WBY
at once recognized a special voice, and he knew too that this would take the
Irish National Dramatic Company in a new direction. 'Foreign masterpieces'
were no longer necessary. By mid-March he was pursuing his plans with Greg-
ory at Coole. Their relationship had become even closer. From mid-December
1902 he addressed her as 'Dear Friend' ('I need not tell you that I am always
wishing for the time to pass swiftly until we are together again'[21]). With Gonne's
defection, he turned to Coole more than ever. Gregory had already adopted
Synge into her *cénacle* (though he always maintained a certain detachment);
he was now to become part of the inner circle who would direct the Irish
National Dramatic Society the way they wanted it to go.

Simultaneously, the Society was reorganized following the disagreements
over production, and dwindling audiences during December. Russell helped
draft the constitution in late January 1903, and it was formally adopted in early
February, with Fay's Irish National Dramatic Society giving way to the 'Irish
National Theatre Society' (INTS). WBY was President, with Gonne, Russell
and Hyde Vice-Presidents; William Fay Stage-Manager and Fred Ryan
Secretary. His presidency was not a foregone conclusion. Russell was first un-
animously elected, but declined and (as he later remembered it) 'had great
difficulty in getting the members to elect Yeats'.[22] All members had voting
rights; plays were nominated by the executive, and a vote of 75 per cent in favour
determined their ratification. Crucially, a Reading Committee was consti-
tuted, of WBY, Russell, Gregory, Ryan, Colum, Griffith and Gonne.[23] All this
was hammered out when WBY was in London, but he testily denied that he
was annoyed or had ever desired a veto, though he 'certainly disapproved of
a democracy in artistic matters'.

This would shortly become all too plain. And already he had confided to
English friends like Gordon Craig ideas about the theatre and its audience
which might not have appealed to all his Irish associates.

Our movement too is a real movement of the people. We don't play for the merely
curious or for people who want to digest their dinners in peace, but for zealous brick-
layers and clerks and an odd corner boy or two. That is to say we have a thorough-
going unruly Elizabethan audience. The poor parts of the house are always full.[24]

Craig annotated the letter 'does the bricklayer go in for indigestion?', but the
point was clear. Padraic Colum noted acidly that Reading Committee meet-
ings were held in Gregory's sitting-room at the Nassau Hotel because WBY

suggested it would be warmer; the centre of decision-making thus shifted to her sphere. In moving from the Royal Hibernian Hotel to the Nassau (a gloomy set of apartments on the corner of South Frederick Street) she not only turned her back on Anglo-Ireland, but invaded the territory of Gonne, who lodged there too. And the Reading Committee was the arena where battle over the theatre's directions was waged. WBY used it to block Cousins's *Sold* once and for all, to get *The Saxon Shillin'* temporarily withdrawn, and to restore Gregory's *Twenty-five*.[25] This, with WBY's own *Hour-Glass*, constituted the INTS programme at Molesworth Hall, Molesworth Street, Dublin, on 14 March. Robert Gregory, now an art student at the Slade, provided the set designs for his mother's play and costumes for *The Hour-Glass* (with sets by Sturge Moore). A small profit was made, paid into a general fund; the actors were still unsalaried. *The Hour-Glass*, written as a prose play, was melodramatically acted, and not much liked; WBY would later rewrite it in verse, with a subtler ending.[26] But the season was, all in all, a success. For WBY it marked his return to the public forum after Gonne's marriage. He gave a lecture, 'The Reform of the Theatre', and explained Craig's theories in the intervals, though Russell was amused to notice that he forgot to produce the model stage 'entrusted to me as a sacred charge'.[27]

The prominence of the WBY–Gregory axis did not go unnoticed, and his ambitious ideas about lighting effects and dramatic staging gave ample fuel to Dublin wits (not least the stage-manager William Fay and his long-suffering assistant Shaun Barlow). But he was pleased with *The Hour-Glass*. 'It proved itself indeed as I always foresaw the strongest of the little plays,' he wrote to Quinn.

It is the first play in the production of which my ideas were carried out completely. The actors were dressed in purple with little bits of green here & there, & the back ground was made of green sacking. The effect was even more telling than I had expected. Everything seemed remote, naïve spiritual, & the attention, liberated from irrelevant distractions, was occupied as it cannot be on an ordinary stage with what was said & done.[28]

The INTS subsequently performed on Easter Monday at Loughrea, County Galway, where Father Jeremiah O'Donovan was building a church that would be a memorial to Irish arts and crafts; near by at Coole, WBY began to plan rehearsals (at last) for *The Shadowy Waters*. He was back in Dublin in late April, attending the Contemporary Club, talking theatre, staying up late. A prospectus was produced for the INTS, stressing the need for 'a permanent home'; the usual venues (Antient Concert Rooms, Molesworth Hall, St Teresa's Hall) were only episodically available and none was really suitable. Currently, rehearsals went on in a room behind a Camden Street butcher's, rented for ten shillings a week and partly sublet to the Gaelic League. The INTS's early account-books show the tiny scale of payments, cost of props and general outlay (including complimentary tickets for the Yeats family).[29] WBY, as President, had his sights fixed higher.

Resourceful as ever, he had recovered strikingly well from the blow dealt him by Gonne two months before, though this may have owed something to determined bravado. He now chose to publish the vision of four years before, when her symbol of apple-blossom brought on a dream of the World's End (set in her city, Paris), with visions of wickedness, unworthiness and cant; his fear when he awoke, that an armed thief was hidden in his bedroom, must have seemed like a rueful prescience of MacBride.[30] However, on Gonne's marriage day WBY had written cheerfully to Russell that he had just had 'rather a good time' lecturing at Cardiff, mentioning her quite casually. And, despite the new constitutional arrangements, Gonne and he were set on a collision course over the INTS; resignations were threatened by those actors suspicious of WBY's intentions, and by late April he suspected (approvingly) that Fay 'would like to abolish the democrisy'.[31]

Meanwhile he kept his London options open. His 'Theatre of Beauty' associates were evolving into a short-lived 'Masquers Society' involving Symons, Walter Crane, Edith Craig, Sturge Moore and other aesthetes. WBY was the first signatory to a circular issued on 17 March 1903, proposing 'a society for the production of plays, masques, ballets and ceremonies, which convey a sentiment of beauty'.[32] Plans for a production of *The Countess Cathleen* were still in the air, though in the end they would come to nothing. WBY's correspondence with Gilbert Murray of the Stage Society proves that he took this enterprise very seriously; much as with the Literary Societies ten years before, he visualized a dual movement, with one arm in London and another in Dublin. His speaking-tours with Farr and the psaltery in the spring and early summer of 1903 were intended to popularize 'the New Art' in London as well as the new theatre in Dublin. G. K. Chesterton, in a piece entitled 'Mr Yeats and Popularity', expressed disingenuous surprise that the two evangelists for Beauty did not take their psaltery message to 'third-class carriages and respectable public-houses . . . and combine ecstasy with emolument'.[33]

Undaunted, WBY and Farr kept up their close association, travelling to provincial venues together. It seems likely that this is when their relationship at last became more intimate. Farr told Nevinson that WBY was 'not personally attractive to her, not as a lover, nor she thinks to other women',[34] but this may have been strategic, since Nevinson admired her too. What evidence there is suggests the affair was 'very brief' and happened after Gonne's marriage. Both were lonely and unattached; WBY 'decided to read sensual literature to her to see what would happen'. The liaison ended in equally hard-headed fashion, with Farr – true to form – saying, 'I can do this for myself.'[35]

Like the love-affair, the Masquers never quite took off, though WBY was anxious they should touch Charles Ricketts for the £150 which he had earmarked for 'a dramatic experiment'.[36] Subscriptions were disappointing and several committee members uncooperative; WBY returned to London for an inaugural meeting on 6 July, where Gordon Craig's defection was the final blow. By late July, though WBY was drafting 'The Opening Ceremony for the Masquers' for the new Society, he was simultaneously warning Murray that his own interest must be concentrated elsewhere (leaving his correspondent, as Gregory remarked, in the position of someone asked to hold a baby and seeing its mother vanish in the crowd). 'The only thing I see quite clear in the business is that the £150 ought not to be allowed to go adrift.'[37] This was pure Pollexfen, right down to the metaphor, but by November the Masquers had run irredeemably aground.[38]

The involvement serves as a reminder, however, that WBY remained wary about Dublin opinion. The ridicule of local journalists still rankled, and in April he asked Bullen not to send the reissued *Celtic Twilight* or (still more) his essays *Ideas of Good and Evil* to the Dublin papers. '[They] sell no copies & I don't see why I should give them the opportunity of attacking me.' As ever, his London circle proved more appreciative, particularly his Golden Dawn associate Annie Horniman. She was now writing many of his letters, and would soon start trying to usurp Gregory in the domestic arrangements at Woburn Buildings. And he commissioned her to design costumes for his new play *The King's Threshold*, initially for a planned Masquers' production in London. It was a year since WBY had dangled 'his wealthy friend' and her possibilities before Fay. This was beginning to take concrete form and would culminate in a solid offer in October 1903 – after WBY had abandoned his London theatrical ambitions.

But the Dublin enterprise would remain bedevilled by political proprieties, spearheaded by the new Mrs MacBride, and WBY was determined to set his face against this. Asked by the Chicago *Daily News* to define 'what Ireland needs' in March 1903, he produced a deliberately anti-propagandist manifesto:

The greatest need is more love for thoughts for their own sake. We want a vigorous movement of ideas. We have now plenty of propaganda and I would not see less. For now the agrarian movement seems coming to a close the national movement must learn to found itself, like the national movement of Norway, upon language and history. But if we are to have an able nation, a nation that will be able to take up to itself the best thoughts of the world, we must have more love of beauty simply because it is beauty, of truth merely because it is truth. At present if a man make us a song, or tell us a story, or give us a thought, we do not ask 'is it a good song, or a good story, or a true thought?' but 'will it help this or that propaganda?'[39]

This did not mean political apathy. In the summer he could poke fun at the Maynooth seminarians welcoming Edward VII by hanging out his racing colours, and the Unionist assumptions of establishment Dublin continued to incense him.[40] But at the same time he repeated to Quinn the need for artistic free thought. 'One must be able to express oneself freely, and that is precisely what no party of Irishmen Nationalist or Unionist, Protestant or Catholic, is anxious to permit one . . . I am often driven to speak about things that I would keep silent on were it not that it is necessary in a country like Ireland to be continually asserting one's freedom if one is not to lose it altogether.'[41]

Quarrels with his theatrical colleagues were, therefore, inevitably coming to a head. In the early summer of 1903, however, WBY was able to assert his authority still further within the company, by using his influence to make their first English season a dazzling success. The critical arrangements, as Frank Fay was careful to recall, were really made by Stephen Gwynn, who prepared the way with a *Fortnightly* article, 'An Uncommercial Theatre', and set up a series of matinées through the London Irish Literary Society. But WBY's name and Gregory's contacts drew in reviewers like William Archer and Max Beerbohm, and a fashionable audience (Lord Monteagle, Wilfrid Blunt, Anne Thackeray Ritchie, 'Michael Field', Henry James, J. M. Barrie – and Annie Horniman), who flocked to a performance of *The Hour-Glass* at Queen's Gate Hall, South Kensington, on 2 May 1903. (WBY noted acidly that the ILS members themselves did not turn out to support their fellow-countrymen.[42]) The company were still amateurs with day jobs ('typists, electricians, book-keepers, shop assistants', according to Fay) who had snatched time away from their employment; they were excited and over-strained, and resignation threats began to multiply. None the less, they scored a great success. Reviewers like William Archer in the *Morning Leader*, A. B. Walkley in *The Times*, and the faithful Nevinson hailed their naturalness, gravity and containment (Archer singled out William Fay for especial praise). The *Daily News* said all WBY would have wished about 'the expression of the aspirations, the emotions, the essential spirit and movement of the people'. Lady Aberdeen (once and future Vicereine of Ireland and indefatigable do-gooder for all things Irish) suggested that the company play for six months at the St Louis exhibition the following year, as part of the 'Irish Industry' presentation.[43] As WBY saw at once, professionalization loomed, and his idea of a dramatic movement that would bridge both London and Dublin seemed a step nearer. He tactfully wrote to the press ceding all credit to

Willie Fay as 'founder of the Society', and to Frank as the expert in dramatic speech;[44] but public attention was inevitably concentrated upon himself.

He had further reasons for satisfaction. During their time in London, Gonne spent two hours with him confessing that she had 'married in a sudden impulse of anger' against Millevoye, and was now regretting it. To Gregory, he affected a certain detachment. 'I feel somehow that the Maud Gonne I have known so long has passed away; I had the feeling that a time of bitterness & perhaps of self-distrust & of fading life had begun for her.' For him, on the other hand, life was exceptionally full: receiving compliments on the Theatre Society's success, looking after George Pollexfen (in London for an operation), and delivering another series of lectures, this time on heroic and folk poetry, accompanied by Farr. These were timed to coincide with the publication of *Ideas of Good and Evil*, also in May. It contained a number of trumpet-blasts on behalf of the new drama, as well as the texts of important recent essays, introductions and lectures since the late 1890s – 'What is "Popular Poetry"?', 'Magic', the Blake essays, 'The Moods' and 'The Celtic Element in Literature'. This last included, as a coda, a blatant puff for Gregory's *Cuchulain*; but not all his friends were so favoured. All references to Horton's work were dropped from 'Symbolism in Painting', though it had originated as an introduction to his *Book of Images*; Horton's sense of grievance became permanent, unassuaged by WBY's tactless explanation that his work was not 'mature' enough to be mentioned.[45] Despite the familiarity of some of the pieces, reviewers treated the book as a unity: it was seen as a manifesto for WBY's idiosyncratically spiritual idea of poetry's function. Nevinson, well briefed, discerned a Blakean theme throughout and stressed WBY's commitment to passionate utterance. English criticism was reserved for his airy citation of writers with whom he was not closely familiar, and his chancy quotations ('Mr Yeats shares with Coleridge a memory of unfailing and often enlightening inaccuracy'[46]). The Irish reception was, as he had anticipated, unfriendly. The *Irish Times* emphasized his insincerity and affectation, while Magee in the *United Irishman* questioned WBY's contemptuous repudiation of the common man.[47] The *Leader*, as usual, struck a rebarbative note, denouncing WBY as 'a prosperous charlatan':

What after all is Mr Yeats? He is one of the most complex personalities we have. There is a touch of the real poet in him, and a spice of the amateur (but not insincere) politician. Added to these, he is a sort of quaintly-comic man, who confuses matters for us by letting on to let on that he takes himself seriously. Added to this again, he is as handy a man as any under the sun at successfully 'planting' his literary wares: 'no flies on him' *there*! As to the spook business and the seeing of visions, probably nobody but Mr Yeats himself could tell how far he is in earnest. Indeed, he has been so long posing in that peculiar spiritual line now, that probably not even he himself could tell if he really sees anything – and in any case it doesn't matter.

Stephen Gwynn took up the cudgels on the mystic's behalf, but 'Imaal' responded vigorously. 'Twice is too much to read any of Mr Yeats's prose writings; once is too often to read most of them, I should say. Mr Yeats is at home in *The Dome*; he should abide there, "and all such men as he".'[48] This argument would be heard again: WBY's decadent qualities belonged in decadent England, and there he should stay.

Combative in public, WBY felt some private doubts about *Ideas of Good and Evil*. While he still held by the opinions in it, he wrote both to Russell and Quinn that the book no longer reflected his current mood. It was lyrical, yearning, remote, but he wanted to express himself 'by that sort of thought that leads straight to action, straight to some sort of craft'.[49] In Nietzschean terms, Apollo was to replace Dionysius. But once again he had brought off an accomplished coup, synchronizing performances, lectures and book. He would retire to Ireland for the summer and reap the benefits – spending a few days with Hyde and then visiting George Pollexfen at Rosses Point before settling at Coole in late June. (Here at long last he caught his first trout, which was ceremoniously cooked for his breakfast; but JBY was staying there too and, true to form, managed to eat it by mistake.[50]) He could also plan the next phase of theatrical experiment, which would revolve around the plays unexpectedly produced by Synge.

III

Back in Dublin, Gregory took the plunge and read *In the Shadow of the Glen* to members of the INTS in her Nassau Hotel rooms. The long-threatened split was precipitated by Synge's portrait of a heroine who deceives her old husband and then abandons her mercenary lover to take to the roads with a tramp. The fact that her name was Nora served to confirm that 'Ibsenity' had finally arrived in Dublin. There were murmurs about an 'insult to Irish womanhood'; ominously, Gonne decided it sounded 'horrid' before she read it.[51] This was followed by a crisis on the Reading Committee, when Cousins's play *Sold* resurfaced. Russell and Colum wanted it (Cousins had, after all, provided them with two successes); WBY, who had already blocked it the previous December, was implacably opposed ('rubbish, and vulgar rubbish'[52]), and told Russell that if it was accepted he would resign from the Society. The Fays supported him, to the fury of the Inghinidhe connection. Inevitably, Cousins went instead. His plays went too, to the Cumann na nGaedheal Theatre Company – which, like Martyn's 'Players' Club' at the

Queen's Theatre, was offering a refuge to the growing number of those unable to co-operate with WBY and the Fays.

Russell stayed, but unhappily – all the more so as he felt *In the Shadow of the Glen* had been adopted through an irregular procedure of private readings, rather than through evaluation by the Reading Committee.[53] The fundamental difficulty lay in WBY's implacable determination that the Society should choose plays according to his own priority: a literary theatre. Gregory loyally supported him, but more and more equivocally as her own facility for writing simple dramas increased. Twenty years later she would tell the founders of the Chicago Little Theater that the Irish mistake was 'to confuse theatric with literary values . . . poetry must serve the theatre before it can again rule there'.[54] But this was a lesson which she would take time to learn.

WBY's own theatrical (and political) ideas were demonstrated in the play he wrote at Coole during these difficulties: still called 'Seanchan' (pronounced 'Shanahan') after its poet hero, but later *The King's Threshold*. Derived from a story in Lady Wilde's *Ancient Legends*, it was set in medieval Ireland and concerned a bard who elected to go on a near-fatal hunger-strike in order to assert the priority of cultural over political authority. WBY thought it at the time 'the best thing I have ever done', and promised Fay that the part of Seanchan would give him 'the highest opportunities' and 'establish all our fame'. Thus the Fays were to be bound ever more tightly to him. Russell was originally asked to speak a prologue, representing the thoughts of the hero's sceptical old uncle. Gregory's hand is apparent in the Kiltartan dialogue of this addition, and a fragment of the draft is in her handwriting.[55] Russell was, however, reluctant, and WBY wooed Fay for this part too ('I hope you won't mind being your own uncle. I have an uncle but I cannot sacrifice him, as he is my only wealthy relation, and may be in the theatre besides, nor is he so unlike my old man that he mightn't find himself in it'[56]). But the prologue, unperformed though it remained, stressed the central theme: the necessity for temporal authority (king and mayor) to recognize the poet's power. This – as Max Beerbohm mischievously pointed out when the play reached London a year later – was directly applicable to WBY himself. In Beerbohm's sparkling analysis, WBY had recognized he was 'not taken seriously enough', and, being Irish, demanded his due in a play rather than through writing letters to the papers or pompous articles (as William Watson had just ineffably done). Dublin reached the same conclusion, the *Leader* construing 'Plays With Meanings' to represent 'Mr Yeats's creed of revolutionary sentiment ministered to by poetic imaginings'.[57]

From August, the rift within the Society became irreparable. *The Shadow of the Glen* provided the issue for Gonne, Hyde and some actors to leave the

INTS over its abandonment of 'National and propagandist work'.[58] In the same month Griffith founded an organization called Sinn Féin ('Ourselves Alone'), a strongly Anglophobic grouping which subordinated all criteria to the Irish-Ireland ideal. The new issue of *Samhain* in early September carried (as well as the text of Synge's *Riders to the Sea*) a reprint of WBY's 'The Reform of the Theatre', which directly challenged the Griffithites by inveighing against 'mere propaganda', defended the Society's English tour, and prepared the ground for the announcement of subsidy from an Englishwoman.[59]

WBY was ready for a fight. He had, after all, supported Gonne's campaign against the royal visit that summer, through letters to the *Freeman's Journal* (concocted with Gregory at Coole).[60] And he had Frank Fay, Griffith's erstwhile drama critic and chief anti-Saxonist arbiter, firmly on his side. Fay wrote to him, that there could be no question of a 'friendly' split with the secessionists. 'Our society has been blackguarded up and down Dublin ever since we refused "The Saxon Shilling" and the blackguarding has been done by one of our own people [Cousins].' Fay further argued that they must play anything well written (so long as it did not 'uphold the Unionist idea'), and not hide in 'the shelter of the church'. WBY could not have put it better himself. And Rule 64 of the reconstructed INTS stressed that 'no sectarian discussion shall be raised, nor shall any resolution which deals with irrelevant and contentious subjects be proposed at a General Meeting of the Society'.

Unsurprisingly, to Gonne and Cumann na nGaedheal, Fay appeared a turncoat, having sold out to 'anti-national' interests and 'select' audiences; and WBY was tainted with Unionism. She told him this in furious letters, berating him and Gregory for their ruthless takeover of the Society and the theatre movement; she was fiercely determined to retain the performing rights to *Cathleen ni Houlihan* for 'the National Societies', only lending back the vital wig for the name-part with extreme reluctance.[61] But, in possession of the Fays, Gregory, most of the actors, all the public *réclame* and the prospect of Horniman's money, the INTS could ignore all secessionists. From 7 October 1903, at the Molesworth Hall, they presented their most electric season yet, starting with *The King's Threshold*, followed on 10 October by *In the Shadow of the Glen*. The controversial costumes for the former were designed and made by Annie Horniman. 'Do you realise that you have given me the right to call myself "artist"?' she wrote to WBY. 'How I do thank you!'[62] That 'right' would not be cheaply bought.

For the moment, all attention was directed on Synge's play. The malcontents had done their work, which created great publicity; even before it was played, an article denouncing it had appeared in the *Independent*, which articulated middle-class Catholic respectability, and WBY had implicitly defended it in his open letter to the *United Irishman*. That defence was reiterated in his speech to the audience after the curtain on 10 October: 'his usual thumpty-thigh, monotonous, preachy style', according to the jaundiced Holloway,[63] but delivering an important message. He defended the artist's right to 'show life, instead of the desire which every political party would substitute for life'. It has been claimed that he was trying to ingratiate himself with Horniman's non-political strictures,[64] but this is to anticipate the con-

With a bad cold alas.

Miss Horniman

12. Annie Horniman 'with a bad cold alas', sketched by JBY at the Abbey, probably in 1905.

ditions of 1906 to 1907; it is consistent with all his arguments in 1903, and was more likely aimed at Griffith, Sinn Féin and Gonne. At any rate, Horniman made her offer of a theatre that night.

From this point too *United Irishman* denounced the INTS on antinational grounds. Even their successful English tour betokened Ibsenite corruption: 'Some of our friends, I fear, now tour Connemara and see – Scandinavia.'[65] 'Cosmopolitanism never produced a great artist nor a good man yet and never will.' The paper also attacked *The King's Threshold* for good measure, affecting to believe that the audience's sympathies were on the side of the sensible king and his faithful soldiers, and would have approved the execution of the tedious, sulky, self-important poet hero. This kind of pointed gibe at the author was inevitable, given WBY's prologue. Though the theatre audience was spared it, it was printed in the *United Irishman* on 9 September and made clear the identification of Seanchan with his progenitor.

The controversy over Synge's play, however, attracted far more attention. His story of marital infidelity amd financial calculation presented a view of Irish rural life which was too much even for the *Irish Times*. Enormous public interest had been generated. On 17 October, George Wyndham, the aesthetically inclined Chief Secretary, took six seats – one of them a red armchair, which gave an unwelcome air of Castle patronage. This was all the nationalist critics would have expected. Griffith began a lengthy campaign, accusing Synge of lifting the old story of the Widow of Ephesus and using it to slander Irish womanhood. This formalized his separation from the Society. The *United Irishman* carried, in succession, Gonne's manifesto 'A National Theatre', JBY's defence of Synge and the principle of self-examination, and WBY's 'An Irish National Theatre', which would be reprinted in the 1904 *Samhain* and laid out the principles upon which Horniman parted with her money. Thus the controversies of October helped define the terms on which the INTS would go forward.

That stormy season also pushed the nationalist societies out to the fringe again, where they continued to play politically uplifting dramas to tiny audiences.[66] The issue of *Samhain*, published to coincide with the performances, once again included the texts of some plays, and WBY's random thoughts about the year's dramatic activity. Those who read between the lines could see that Hyde was now out of favour, and the INTS was being deliberately distanced from Cumann na nGaedheal 'propaganda'; here WBY struck on a ringing phrase, 'the pure joy that only comes out of things that have never been indentured to any cause'. Russell, while not a Sinn Féiner and still attached to the INTS, was increasingly unhappy about the split, especially when WBY brought pressure on him to retract his offer of *Deirdre* to the secessionists. WBY himself, to judge by a private memorandum, would have liked to keep the Gaelicist element at least within the INTS; he feared the power of the language lobby as an alternative focus, and the splits in the literary societies of the 1890s provided an ominous precedent.[67] But once the breach was made, he was unswerving. Much that happened in the autumn of 1903 presaged later confrontations; the Synge issue distilled all the difficulties WBY had already experienced with the ideologues. The self-assertive tone of *Samhain* was sharply attacked by Thomas Kettle in *New Ireland*. 'Can it be that these petulant sayings, this fashion of pitting himself against "the mob", spring from the consciousness that the ideas which underlie and direct his art are essentially antagonistic to the ideas which underlie and direct the lives of the great majority of his countrymen?' Kettle meant, apparently, Catholicism as much as pious nationalism, and his warning was all the more clear because it came from someone usually construed as intellectually sympathetic, if conservative. 'A philosophy, like an animal, can maintain itself only as long as it abides in harmony with its environment. Mr Yeats will no doubt follow the path of his intellectual development whithersoever it leads him. But there is this danger: that his reading of life may diverge so widely from ours that all his fine artistry will not save his work from automatic extinction – in Ireland at least.'[68]

Gonne weighed in too, less subtly, with the old accusation of cosmopolitan corruption. 'The best and truest writings of our greatest living poet, W. B. Yeats, are understood and appreciated by the people; the poems and essays they do not understand are those touched by foreign influence from which Mr Yeats has not altogether escaped, having lived long out of Ireland ... Mr Yeats asks for freedom for the theatre, freedom even from patriotic captivity. I would ask for freedom for it from one thing more deadly than all else – freedom from the insidious and destructive tyranny of foreign influence.'[69] But with financial backing assured, and liberated by Gonne's defection and (in his eyes) diminishment, wby stuck firm. As usual, he summed up the situation (from his side) in a series of manifestos: three combative articles for the *United Irishman*.

The final piece, appearing in the same issue as Gonne's attack, bore the challenging title 'The National Theatre and Three Sorts of Ignorance'. Ostensibly, this was his answer to the sustained abuse of Synge in the *Independent*, but he flung down a gauntlet to the *United Irishman* itself as well. 'Extreme politics in Ireland were once the politics of intellectual freedom also, but now, under the influence of a violent contemporary paper, and under other influences more difficult to follow, even extreme politics seem about to unite themselves to hatred of ideas.' Anglophobia would inhibit 'the imagination of highly-cultivated men, who have begun that experimental digging in the deep pit of themselves, which can alone produce great literature'. This must be taken to refer to the author of *The King's Threshold* as well as that of *The Shadow of the Glen*. He then listed the 'Three Sorts of Ignorance'. There was that of 'the more ignorant sort of Gaelic propagandist', condemning anything not written in 'country Gaelic' (including Plato). Then there was 'the more ignorant sort of priest, who, forgetful of the great traditions of his Church, would deny all ideas that might perplex a parish of farmers or artisans or half-educated shopkeepers'. And finally the ignorance of 'the politicians, and not always of the more ignorant sort, who would reject every idea which is not of immediate service to his cause'. Irish nationalism must allow 'ideas, and beauty, and knowledge' as an 'Ark of the Covenant more valuable even than victory'.

He had rarely put it more clearly, and never with such hauteur: the battles of 1902 to 1903, his self-discovery as a playwright, his enthusiasm for Nietzsche and the fellowship of Coole lent his polemic an unequivocal edge, while his quarrel with Gonne and Griffith at last allowed him to identify the enemy. For a liberal Protestant to refer to Catholicism this way in public broke one of the taboos which sustained the uneasy collusions of Irish life; if to some his stance seemed self-regarding and amoral, to others his language smacked of the Protestant Ascendancy at its most contemptuous.[70] And for the *United Irishman* these arguments always implied closet Unionism. 'Obviously, if politics are dropped, Ireland's connection with England will not be endangered.'[71] WBY's conscience was clear on this point: he had lent his name to enough anti-royalist demonstrations, argued at enough dinner parties, addressed enough nationalist societies, kept enough Fenian company. Only the previous May he had been instrumental in founding the 'National Council', or 'People's Protection Committee', to protest against the manipulation of the King's visit by the Irish authorities.[72] But in the furore over Synge's play, and the associated argument about the direction of the INTS, he was sure where he stood; and the fact that he confronted Maud Gonne MacBride was – now – no inducement to shift his ground.

IV

Confidence had also been imparted by the publication (in August) of *In the Seven Woods*, a short collection of poems bound with the play *On Baile's Strand*. It was Dun Emer's first book, and WBY's first collection for four years. Lolly's press had worked on it since February, with WBY as dictatorial as ever. To judge by surviving pulls of preliminary pages, he wanted to change everything from the wording of the publisher's name to his sister's choice of press-mark ('impossible') and dictated 'no title page & all information at end'. He was also importunate about the colour of the endpapers and cover – evidently demanding blue or grey, though this was not mastered until later volumes. 'Surely all you have to do would be to put paper in solution of indigo. I know nothing about paper dyes, but I thought the process simple. They die cloth at Lady Gregory's gate house.'[73] In some desperation, Lolly protested to a correspondent, 'I have done the whole printing of it myself with the help of two young village girls whom I have had to teach (as well as learn myself).'[74]

Despite imperfections, it was a credit to her. She printed 325 copies;

booksellers were rather chary, but subscription copies brought in £135, taken up by an eclectic range of family (George Pollexfen, Isabella Varley), old friends (Tynan, York Powell, Willie Wilde) and recent followers (Gogarty, Ella Young, Father O'Donovan).[75] It rapidly sold out. Quinn arranged a copyright edition in America, interceding energetically with Macmillan.[76] WBY had thought the collection, subtitled 'Being Poems chiefly of the Irish Heroic Age', was 'much more likely to please Irish people than any I have done'.[77] The medievalism of *Baile and Aillinn*, 'The Old Age of Queen Maeve' and *On Baile's Strand* carried through the promise of the title; 'The Withering of the Boughs' echoed a ninetyish dreaminess; and the collection also included the near-final version of 'The Song of Red Hanrahan', a paean of sacrificial nationalism which would remain Gonne's favourite of all his poems. But the volume marks, rather uneasily, a transition. The title-poem, written the previous August, celebrated the peace of Coole and the restoration of a sense of proportion in escape from public agitation, with the threat of apocalypse introduced ironically at the end.

> I have heard the pigeons of the Seven Woods
> Make their faint thunder, and the garden bees
> Hum in the lime tree flowers; and put away
> The unavailing outcries and the old bitterness
> That empty the heart. I have forgot awhile
> Tara uprooted, and new commonness
> Upon the throne and crying about the streets
> And hanging its paper flowers from post to post,
> Because it is alone of all things happy.
> I am contented for I know that Quiet
> Wanders laughing and eating her wild heart
> Among pigeons and bees, while that Great Archer,
> Who but awaits His hour to shoot, still hangs
> A cloudy quiver over Parc-na-Lee.

Three poems about Gonne struck a new note, not simply because they dealt with ageing and imperfection. In 'The Arrow' he was pierced by the memory of her

> . . . when newly grown to be a woman,
> Blossom pale, she pulled down the pale blossom
> At the moth hour and hid it in her bosom.

But in 'The Folly of Being Comforted' he described the decay of her physical beauty. He had originally written of 'crowsfeet' around her eyes, but she objected on the disingenuous grounds that readers would assume he meant Gregory ('It was the first time that I realised that she was human'[78]). All the same, the ageing of the siren meant no release; as so often, he saw her as a phoenix, forever re-created to trouble his peace.

> But heart, there is no comfort, not a grain
> Time can but make her beauty over again
> Because of that great nobleness of hers;
> The fire that stirs about her, when she stirs
> Burns but more clearly; O she had not these ways,
> When all the wild summer was in her gaze.
> O heart O heart if she'd but turn her head,
> You'd know the folly of being comforted.

Here, and most of all in 'Adam's Curse', the direct, personal colloquialism struck home. He would shortly write to Russell that he had been fighting an 'exaggeration of sentiment and sentimental beauty' in his early work: 'I have been fighting the prevailing decadence for years & have just got it under foot in my own heart – it is sentiment and sentimental sadness, a womanish introspection.'[79] The newer poems of *In the Seven Woods* were introspective in their own way, but the autobiographical note, diffused and distant in his early lyrics, sounded here with a new confidence, expressed in a harder diction. More than half the book was taken up by the play *On Baile's Strand*; an introductory note stressed that its much rewritten form foreshadowed 'a change that may bring a less dream-burdenend will into my verse'. Thus his poetry was beginning – if unevenly – to reflect his achieved personality. He was growing into his life.

He was also about to embark on another new departure. In the spring Quinn had negotiated with Macmillan in New York about taking over WBY's poems and plays in the USA,[80] and since the early summer he had been planning a lecture-tour of America. This had long been pressed by the indefatigable Quinn, who had founded a short-lived New York branch of the Irish Literary Society.[81] Its President, oddly, was WBY's old High School friend Charles Johnston; three of WBY's plays (*Cathleen ni Houlihan, The Pot of Broth* and *The Land of Heart's Desire*) had been played at the Lyceum Theater under their auspices from 4 to 5 June (with JBY's portrait of his son, bought by Quinn, displayed in the lobby). When WBY was proposed as honorary Vice-President of the New York Society, however, the Catholic Archbishop Farley quietly resigned from the committee on undefined grounds of 'propriety'. *The Countess Cathleen* cast a long shadow. But the Lyceum plays were a success, and Quinn believed that American audiences were ready to hear WBY in person. From the poet's point of view, the performance of his work by the Irish abroad was a landmark. He wrote emotionally to Quinn, 'I suppose it was some thought of this kind that made Keats's lines telling how Homer left great verses to a little clan seemed [*sic*] to my imagination when I was a boy a description of the happiest fate that could come to a poet.'[82] Quinn, possessive as ever, had made all the arrangements: on 4 November WBY sailed on the *Oceanic* from Liverpool. In the last year he had found a theatre company, lost Gonne, met Joyce and presented Synge to the Irish public, and he was discovering a new, assertive voice in drama and poetry. For all the grumbling, his fame was firmly established in Dublin and London. He was ready and able for a new world.

Chapter 12 : FROM AMERICA TO ABBEY STREET 1903–1904

> 20 May 1904. Yeats and Rothenstein to grub . . . Character
> and personality in art were discussed. They were both rather
> struck by the obvious fact that great natural talents and ability,
> or natural gifts, are fairly common: what constitutes the super-
> iority of the really talented man is his own sense of the impor-
> tance of his gifts; that he persists in them, husbands them, and
> is never discouraged. He survives almost by persistency.
>
> Charles Ricketts, *Self-Portrait*

I

'MR YEATS seems to be making frantic efforts to interest the American
public in himself, in advance of his lecture season here,' wrote a sarcastic
reader at Macmillan in New York, in the course of turning down *The King's
Threshold*.[1] John Quinn must have fumed, but he privately admitted to Russell
that from the summer of 1903 enterprises like the New York Irish Literary
Society looked like a design 'to boom the works of Yeats'. This, Quinn in-
sisted, was not the case: 'a Yeats "boom" . . . is precisely what should be
avoided, if possible. Kipling was killed by Doubleday, McClure and com-
pany and by a few alleged friends. Yeats needs no boom and wants no boom
and a boom is of all things the thing that is most to be feared.'[2]

None the less, Quinn spent the weeks before WBY's arrival in a storm of
preparations. Antagonistic 'Gaelic Society' members had to be dealt with,
demanding 'whether you spoke Irish or not and why you were selected to speak
on the Irish revival'; unsuitable would-be critics of WBY's work were merci-
lessly choked off; most of all, a strenuous schedule had to be arranged with
itineraries, fees and a photographic portfolio ('the less retouched the better').[3]
Arrangements had been set in train the previous May, and were firmly in place
by July.[4] The tour was to cover the East, Mid-West and California; lectures
were to be given largely to educational institutions, for a fee of $75 each or
$240 for four. Quinn arranged the rates and saw off colleges who tried to
bargain it down or wanted to charge at the door, though $50 might be enter-
tained from very small institutions. Complications arose. Princeton claimed
poverty (alleging that Hyde had paid *them* in order to lecture there); Columbia
wanted sole rights to WBY in New York (Quinn had to threaten them with the
trustees); Californian colleges had to be charged $125 to cover the high costs
of travel; and some disingenuous strokes were pulled.[5] But in the end an

intensive programme was agreed, and Quinn deluged editors with promotional material which sold the Irish poet as 'comparable only to Maeterlinck'. Private contacts were assured 'he is not a boy, as some people imagine, but is a man of mature age – 38 or 39 years – and is as sincere and courageous an Irishman as lives and one of the most charming men I have ever met'.[6]

The lecturer arrived on 11 November 1903, armed with four basic pieces, typed out by Gregory: 'The Intellectual Revival in Ireland', 'Heroic Literature of Ireland', 'The Theatre and What it Might Be', 'Poetry in the Old Time and in the New'.[7] However, he was also prepared to deliver occasional *causeries*, and to change material employed in the lectures (he was still amending them at Christmas). 'I trust to the inspiration of the moment when speaking to a college,' he explained to Lily, 'but I have to elaborate everything for a great audience.'[8] The effect of his own performances, he discovered, varied from place to place.

And there were many places.* At first he spent a few days in a hotel but then moved into Quinn's lavishly equipped apartment, hung with paintings by Russell and both Yeatses; he also had the run of his host's office facilities. Introductions from O'Leary brought him to Irish American nationalist leaders like John Devoy and William Carroll, but he also contacted the more moderate William Bourke Cockran (a Sligo man), and a circle of New York journalists whom he had known in his youth – Frederick Gregg, Charles Johnston and Charles Fitzgerald. Johnston (Protestant and Theosophist that he was) wished to direct Irish Americans towards Irish culture rather than 'shallow American society';[9] but hostile echoes from advanced nationalism had already been picked up by Quinn, and WBY expected trouble from people like Father Peter Yorke in San Francisco (a cousin of John MacBride). Carefully set-up pieces like a long article in the *New York Morning Sun* by James

---

* There is a copy of some of the planned itinerary in NLI MS 30, 539. As it worked out, it was: 16 Nov., Yale; 17 Nov., New Haven Literary Society; 18 Nov., Smith; 19 Nov., Amherst; 20 Nov., Trinity College, Hartford; 23 Nov., Philadelphia (with Ezra Pound in the audience); 25 Nov., CCNY; 28–30 Nov., Wellesley; 1 Dec., Harvard; 3 Dec., Bryn Mawr; 4 Dec., Vassar; 5 Dec., Brooklyn; 7 Dec., Bryn Mawr (again); 8 Dec., Philadelphia (again); 16 Dec., Science and Art Club, Germantown, Pa.; 17 Dec., McGill University, Montreal; 19 Dec., Twentieth Century Club, Brooklyn; 20 Dec., Sligo Men's Association Dinner, New York, with Bourke Cockran; 27 Dec., Washington; 28 Dec., lunch with Roosevelt at the White House; 29 Dec., Press Club Reception, New York; 30 Dec., Arts Club, New York; 31 Dec., at *Parsifal*, then Authors' Club reception, New York; 3 Jan. 1904, Carnegie Hall lecture; 4 Jan., leaves New York for the West; 5–8 Jan., at St Louis; 9 Jan., Indianapolis; 11 Jan., Purdue, Lafayette; 13 Jan., Twentieth Century Club, Chicago; 14 Jan., Women's Club, Chicago; 15–17 Jan., Notre Dame; 18 Jan., Indiana University, Bloomington, Indiana; 20 Jan., St Paul; 27 Jan., San Francisco, Berkeley, and a Celtic evening at the Alhambra Theater; 29 Jan., Stanford; 30 Jan., Alhambra Theater (again); 31 Jan.–3 Feb., visits, dinners, clubs; 7 Feb., Chicago (again); 8 Feb., Hull House, Chicago; 9 Feb., University of Wisconsin; 10 Feb., Beloit College; 11 Feb., Chicago (third visit); 12 Feb., Toronto, Queen's University; 13 Feb., University of Toronto; 14 Feb., Niagara Falls; 15 Feb., New York; 16 Feb., Baltimore; 18 Feb., Brooklyn (again); 19 Feb., Wells College; 21 Feb., CUA, Washington (again); 24 Feb., Newark, NJ; 25 Feb., Bridgeport, Conn.; 26 Feb., Paterson, NJ; 28 Feb., Emmet Lecture at Academy of Music, New York.

Gibbon Huneker anticipated criticism and tried to head it off[10] ('There is no pose about Mr Yeats. He does not come to make money or to assume superior attitudes'). Huneker was later lined up by Quinn to defend WBY against charges of 'decadence'.[11] Another journalist announced that WBY had come to America 'to escape the surveillance of the English police'.[12] This controversial reputation ensured heavy press coverage and necessitated painful judiciousness on WBY's part – as he found when he idly gave one journalist the impression that he would be glad to see Kipling dead.[13]

But he learnt fast, smoothly telling interviewers, 'I love Ireland first of all things, but I dislike to be interviewed on the subject', the Irish being passionate and therefore 'quick to misunderstand'.[14] Once they had overcome their preconceptions about fairies, interviewers were surprised by his energy and humour. He talked indefatigably about the theatre, publicizing the work of the Fays, recalling Gonne's effect as Cathleen ni Houlihan, describing the new playwright Padraic Colum inaccurately as 'the not very lettered son of an unlettered farmer'. But he had to provide opinions on issues of the day, such as feminism – producing an endorsement of women's education so long as it did not 'masculinise' them, which would mean an end to art and civilization.[15]

By and large, during his first weeks in New York he made a favourable impression. Socially, not everyone appreciated his oracular remarks about fairies or his congenital inability to remember names;[16] non-Irish audiences, like the New York Arts Club, were less impressed than Irish America. But the emigrant Irish, basking in the reflected glory of his fame, suspended their reservations about the depth of his nationalism. Arriving at a time when they wanted respectability above all, WBY's sophisticated Celticism, and high claims for Irish culture above English materialism, struck a satisfying chord. The Catholic backlash, which Quinn had feared from the 'Protestant-heresy-hunting' elements of the New York Irish Literary Society, never transpired, partly because of Quinn's own assiduous cultivation of Clan na Gael contacts as well as his determination to explain WBY to 'the thinking people'.[17] His agenda was clearly stated in a letter to T. J. Shahan of the Catholic University in Washington: 'No-one is better fitted than Yeats to place before the young Irishman of today an ennobling idea of the ancient dignity and ideals of Ireland, in place of the truculence and servility that is too often seen among our people in Ireland and this country.' To upwardly mobile Irish Americans this carried weight, even if some disappointed locals wanted to make him more authentically Irish by 'putting cuffs on him and sprinkling him with holy water'.[18]

For WBY himself, the American tour coincided with the emergence of his differences with advanced nationalism in Ireland; he was determined to avoid politics by stressing the roots of Irish intellectual revival in the ancient saga literature. Outside the college circuit, his audiences were diverse: drama clubs and literary societies, as well as Irish American groups. But much of what he said was directed at the last. To Aran Islanders, he told them, America was nearer than England. He spoke passionately against the dilution of Irishness and the importance of locale to audiences who probably never realized he lived in London. The structure of his lectures stayed much the same (they would be recycled for the next five years). Local sensitivities were observed, and targets he had attacked in *Samhain* were praised in his lectures. Oratorical flourishes grew as he gained confidence. He often ended his 'Intellectual Revival' lecture by comparing the different roles of different nations to so many stops on the organ of the world: at Carnegie Hall he gave it an extempore brio by pointing to an actual organ that happened to be on stage.[19] Gaelic legends, heroic traditions and the role of a national theatre in reviving them provided the general theme. 'The Intellectual Revival in Ireland' stressed the roll of heroes and martyrs in Irish history (including Parnell, 'that astute and lonely spirit'), but generally he avoided politics for literature. According to WBY's thesis, Parnell's political unifying of Ireland was injurious to intellectual individualism, which burst out afterwards – a theory he would later develop into a central thread in the interpretation of his own life. The Gaelic League, the theatre, the revival of language and literature were all located in the post-1891 period, and presented in a kaleidoscopic whirl which also took in Russell's mysticism, agricultural co-operation, O'Leary's inspiration, the stained-glass industry and the excavations at Tara. It was, in a way, an essay in precocious autobiography.

But everything revolved around the theatre, which, he claimed, supplied a national language to those who, like himself, had lost Gaelic. They could erect on the stage a civilization to combat that of England. In a rather idealized picture, he told American audiences about country theatre groups invading Dublin from all over Ireland, preaching Gaelic League values like the wearing of Irish clothes. His lecture 'Poetry in the Old Time and in the New' carried through the theme of the battle of two civilizations – in this case, implicitly arguing for an elite culture based on a Morrisite rejection of modern debasement in applied arts, and a return to the essential aristocracy of folk tradition. Medieval 'serfdom of the body' was less degrading than modern 'serfdom of the soul'. 'Out of the written book has come our decadence, our literature, which puts the secondary things first. It is because of the written book, in which we speak always to strangers and never with a living voice to friends, that we have lost personal utterance.'[20] 'Thank God,' he remarked in an unguarded moment, 'in my country no-one reads books.' WBY's account of the search for an uncorrupted culture in Connacht relied on the resonance of personal reflection: 'When one comes upon something that a man has said straight out of the mind in a moment of frenzy, one finds that among these country people there was [*sic*] an almost incredible refinement.' Throughout, tradition was set against imitation. The idea of an integrated culture led, unsurprisingly, to the illustration of music and poetry combined in his and Farr's performances with the psaltery. His lecture 'Heroic Literature of Ireland' allowed an opportunity to press the claims of Gregory's work, while 'The Theatre and What it Might Be' described WBY and his associates 'training the shop-girls and shop-boys' of Fay's company back to the assumptions of an age where 'culture came to a man without effort; it came to a peasant bending over the scythe or to the wife rocking the cradle'.[21]

Thus the content of WBY's lectures repeated the preoccupations of his essays and reviews over the past two years or so, but the far-flung schedule arranged by Quinn enabled him to extend the crusade to provincial American aesthetes, clerical students, New York clubwomen and the children of the Irish diaspora. All had their own reasons for welcoming his message, and most warmed to the force, charm and other-worldliness of his persona. WBY began his lecture tour in the Eastern colleges – starting at Yale, and taking in Harvard, Trinity College Hartford, Williams, Amherst, Wellesley, Mount Holyoke, Smith, Vassar and Bryn Mawr. By 27 November he had given nine lectures in as many days and was tiring, but he told Russell doggedly that 'a couple of weeks will make me a really good lecturer'. He was particularly successful at women's colleges like Bryn Mawr and Wellesley, where a certain cult developed around his looks;[22] for his part, he delighted in the admiration of unargumentative women, as he privately admitted to Gregory. At Harvard he met William James and made a particularly successful trip south to Philadelphia, where he had a long-standing admirer in Cornelius Weygandt. In mid-December he ventured north to Canada, where the *Montreal Daily Star* hailed him with a classic torrent of Ossianic gush: 'The man, who has won for himself a unique place in the literary world is a true type of the old Keltic bard, tall, thin, flashing deep-set eyes, sensitive mouth and masses of black hair, it takes but a little stretch of the imagination to picture him wandering from castle to hut, singing the songs of old Ireland.'[23]

After Christmas in New York, the wandering bard set off to Washington, where a lunch on 28 December with Roosevelt had been arranged by Quinn. The President was already a firm supporter of the Irish literary movement, and a particular admirer of Gregory's work. A fellow-guest's assertion that WBY astounded his host by discoursing on 'the little people' is probably *ben trovato*,[24] but Quinn evidently felt some nervousness about the encounter. 'If he invites you to go horseback riding, decline,' he unnecessarily instructed his protégé, 'because he is a rather vigorous rider and a jumper.'[25] WBY made contacts among the Catholic establishment of the city, returning later to lecture at the Catholic University; the clerical audience appreciated his 'unique idea of accomplishing national independence, not by force of arms nor radical politics but by the gradual weaning of Irishmen from English custom and the English tongue.' Despite Quinn's efforts to protect him from 'irrelevant lectures and dinners',[26] he spent the final days of 1903 being lionized at the Press Club and Authors' Club, and speaking to the Arts Club, though he apparently did not (as on later visits) try to meet American fellow-poets. On 3 January he gave a much heralded lecture at Carnegie Hall, before departing to the West.

Here he delivered 'The Intellectual Revival in Ireland', chaired by Bourke Cockran; in an excited letter to Gregory he described practising in the deserted auditorium, with his histrionic final flourish (the organ again) applauded by the Irish caretaker. Quinn had 600 flysheets pasted up and sent out 2,000 circulars, though in the event a freezing night kept the audience below 600. Those who came, however, were not disappointed. WBY was well rehearsed by now and Quinn had impressed on him the importance of this particular audience. The speech stressed a Moranite line on the Irish–English conflict as 'a war between two civilisations', and Devoy shepherded an admiring Clan na Gael deputation to signify full approval afterwards. Privately, Quinn was rather put out by the disappointing attendance, and the lecture did not break even financially. He kept this quiet, fulminating only to close friends about the opposition from priests and 'bullet-headed Firbolgs' and redoubling his efforts to get profitable college bookings.[27] None the less, by this point WBY had been won over to America at its elegant best, even considering that the architecture 'in what they call here their "old colonial style" would have been a delight to Morris'.[28] The cultivated, unshowy side of American society appealed to him; and, most important of all, his self-confidence soared. 'Good news still comes from Willie,' JBY told Gregory on 7 January, 'a popular success and money in his pocket. It will be interesting to see him on his return, but the critics will remind him that he is mortal.'[29]

For the moment the traveller was ready to embark on further conquests. On 4 January he left New York for six weeks to take in the Mid-West, the West Coast and Canada. Though he told Gregory he had begun to be homesick, he was determined to give twenty more lectures, calculated to bring in £400 to £500. He was closely instructed by Quinn to pace himself, conserve his energy and refuse dinners. Further details were given of people to avoid, excuses to make, even where to sit on the train. In Quinn he had found a temporary substitute for Gregory: someone who could deliver unstinting admiration, close affection and peremptory instruction about changing his clothes and not bolting his food. In this, as in other needs, the effects left by his unconventional upbringing continued to reverberate through his adult life.

On 5 January he arrived in St Louis, and stayed there till the 8th, discussing arrangements for the Irish pavilion at the World's Fair; he then moved on to Indianapolis and Purdue (an unsuccessful performance for engineering students, whose reaction was 'like wet sand') before addressing the Twentieth Century Club at Chicago on 13 January. There, to Quinn's fury, a pretty girl persuaded him to give an impromptu lecture at the University of Chicago,

This is Willy lecturing on Speaking to the Psaltery in the wild and woolly West—

13. WBY in America, as seen by Jack Yeats in a letter to Quinn, 15 December 1903. 'This is Willy lecturing on Speaking to the Psaltery in the wild and woolly West.'

where the Dramatic Club was performing *The Land of Heart's Desire*. Here too a journalist claimed that he spoke unguardedly about the ignorant and materialist aspects of American life, corrupted by 'the degradation of industry' common to all modern countries. 'But I want to repeat,' he allegedly added, 'that America is great, great even in its ugliness. As your aristocracy grows the passion for beautiful things will grow. In the growth of that aristocracy lies your hope.' WBY assured Quinn that this was an invention, but he certainly gave some hostages to fortune. Here, and later in San Francisco, he let slip ideas which anticipated later, more considered reflections – as when he hypothesized that England's literary greatness was due to its Norman–French component; only after Saxonism gained the ascendant under Cromwell, he claimed, did race-hatred between England and Ireland develop. As he moved on from Chicago through Notre Dame, Bloomington and St Paul, his fame grew. An evening with Irish priests at Notre Dame, like 'big children & all over six feet', was particularly treasured and entered his canonical store of memories. Here WBY could talk about Ireland as he knew it and exchange fairy and folklore stories; he remained deeply impressed by the Notre Dame clerics' lack of bigotry, and the way that, when Irishmen encountered each other abroad, common Irishness cancelled out religious prejudice. He was now turning down invitations to Pasadena and Oregon, as the travelling was too expensive. On 27 January he arrived in San Francisco to full-page press coverage. Quinn had a useful contact in the Irish American ex-mayor, James Phelan, and a Celtic evening was arranged at the Alhambra Theater for the benefit of the League of the Cross; even Father Peter Yorke, John MacBride's fire-breathing cousin, was favourably disposed, to Quinn's secret disappointment. Instead of the anticipated fireworks, Yorke benignly remarked that 'in one week [WBY] has done more for the Irish name and the Irish cause in the centers of culture than could be done in years'.[30] Even in this quarter, the *cachet* lent by WBY's glamour to Irish identity far outweighed the questionable propriety of his political opinions.

WBY stayed in San Francisco until 3 February, speaking at Berkeley and Stanford, and disobeying Quinn by accepting invitations to dinners, visits and clubs: a long newspaper interview captured him at the top of his form.* He made one lasting friendship with a local writer named Agnes Tobin, whose translations of Petrarch he would help edit, and loyally praise. Slightly older than WBY, she was well-off, intense and determined to enter the European artistic milieu. Like Quinn, she used contacts made through WBY to become a regular fixture in the lives of writers she 'took up' across the Atlantic. She may have wanted more from the poet himself, but they remained (as he later put it with relief) 'best of friends & likely to remain so & at that only'.[31] Though one newspaper recorded his reading of a poem called 'The Lake Idol of Innisfree',[32] he was by now a well-known and established lion. This caused some resentment, particularly among representatives of Plunkett's Irish Agricultural Organization Society, also attempting to raise money in the USA but with far less success; sniping by Father Tom Finlay and others was repeated back to him, and the ensuing resentment cannot have helped relationships back in Dublin.[33]

By 7 February he had returned to Chicago, where he lectured at Hull House and made forays to the University of Wisconsin and Beloit College. He was starting to flag and his distrait manner offended at least one hostess, who declared 'she would not again expose herself to "being bruised by Willie

* See Appendix.

Yeats"'.[34] On 12 February he was in Toronto, where he expressed the essence of his message. 'Americans', he said, 'knew something of the public, passionate life of the island in its struggle for self-aggrandisement; of its inner, subtle, picturesque, intellectual life they knew but little. Yet this latter aspect of the Irish life was infinitely more important and the basis on which depended the future of Irish national life.'[35] This was deliberately echoed in his admonition at Washington a week later, against armed force and radical politics, and in favour of cultural self-assertion. On both counts, he was using American audiences to present his arguments against advanced nationalists at home. But, like every Irish celebrity on tour in the USA, he tailored his message to his audience, and this would become plain when he returned in triumph to New York.

He arrived back there (via Niagara Falls) on 15 February, having stayed away longer than intended. There were engagements at Baltimore, Bridgeport, Brooklyn, Newark, and a return visit to Washington; but he was, unsurprisingly, tired, ready for a break and feeling homesick. He was also beginning to speak less carefully. His speech at the Catholic University on 21 February endorsed language revival in hard-line Gaelic League terms, forecasting 'a complete recreation of the land of Erin', with 'the hills and the valleys echoing once more with the sweet music of the gaelic tongue . . . the time is coming when the English tongue will have been expurgated'.[36] Even considering the University's recently founded Chair in Celtic Languages, this was strangely at odds with his remarks on this sensitive subject at home. But he was tired, and perhaps careless. Quinn had to woo him intensively to accept these late engagements; and when he proposed that WBY give a major speech to mark the centenary of Robert Emmet's death, at the invitation of Devoy and Daniel Cohalan, WBY at first refused. Exhaustion was one reason; but he was equally concerned by the political implications. Quinn's opening argument, that it would be 'the same place [the Academy of Music] and the same sort of audience that Maud Gonne and MacBride first spoke to when they came here together', was at best an ambiguous inducement. Quinn tried further arguments: it would scotch rumours that WBY had criticized the United States in his Western speeches, besides making him $200, or £70. But WBY refused. The money no longer seemed so vital ('what's £70 now that I am feeling so rich') and he longed to return and see the INTS productions of *On Baile's Strand* and *Riders to the Sea*. And the theme was disquieting. Emmet, executed leader of a doomed uprising against the British government in 1803, was a sacred icon of advanced nationalism; as it happened, the actors who had resigned from the INTS from political scruples had put on a specially written centenary play about him, with *Cathleen ni Houlihan*, at the Molesworth Hall just before WBY departed to the USA.[37] 'My mind is not

full on politics,' he told Quinn; he preferred to stress 'general national prin-
ciples' rather than nationalist rhetoric about the destiny of the Irish race.[38]
But Quinn, seeing a chance to redeem the disappointment of Carnegie Hall
a month before, insisted. The fee was raised to $250; the date was brought
back to 28 February; and even WBY's misgivings about the subject were over-
come. At the same time he was preoccupied with Gonne's attack on him in
the *United Irishman* and had written to her defending his stance on intellec-
tual freedom *vis-à-vis* nationalist conventions. As he got down to work on
his speech, he confided to Gregory: 'I had no idea until I started on it of how
completely I have thought myself out of the whole stream of traditional Irish
feeling on such subjects.'[39]

Clan na Gael, he thought, would 'ask for Irish-Ireland thoughts rather
than politics'. This, as the event would prove, was very far from the case.
However, WBY used the basic framework of his 'Irish Revival' speech, and
grafted on to it an account of Emmet's career. A Leckyean view of the late
eighteenth century stressed the iniquity of the Act of Union 'destroying the
nation'; Emmet emerged, like William Tell, as a 'saint of nationality', imbued
with the 'ecstasy of self-sacrifice'. His revolutionary gesture was compared
favourably to the constitutional evasions of O'Connell, and even of Parnell;
this led into the 'Irish Revival' thesis, and gave him an opportunity to revile
the creation of 'bribes' like the Irish legal establishment, created to 'draw away
the Irish intellect to other purposes than Irish ones'. As far as WBY was con-
cerned, the emphasis fell on cultural independence rather than on advanced
politics; his 4,000-odd listeners (by the *Gaelic American*'s computation) may
not have heard it that way, especially when he called for a nation 'like a great
tree [to] lift up its boughs towards the cold moon of noble hate no less than
the sun of love'. In support of preparation for 'the necessary battle' he read a
poem that 'went through Ireland like a fire' during the Boer War – twenty
quatrains cursing England.[40] As in Washington, he was giving an audience
what he assumed it wanted, in terms that bear little relation to his private
opinions as recorded at this time. For this reason, the Emmet speech was
certainly the success Quinn hoped for; it was the great climax of WBY's Amer-
ican tour, and when he died thirty-five years later the front page of Devoy's
paper was devoted to recollections of the address as – implicitly – WBY's
greatest achievement.[41] To the Clan na Gael mind, this may well have been
so. But in 1904 the occasion had an importance for Devoy and Cohalan
which had little or nothing to do with Irish intellectual revival, or even with
the Emmet centenary. The event in the Academy of Music was planned, and
used, as a great opportunity to make a public statement against Washington's
pro-British foreign policy, and to demonstrate support for Russian aims in
Asia. The *Gaelic American*'s headline said it all: 'Emmet the Apostle of Irish

Liberty: Memorable and Significant Meeting. Irishmen Sound the Tocsin against English Alliance and Proclaim Friendship for Russia'. A Russian flag hung on the platform behind WBY; 'a delegation of noted Russian ecclesiastics – something before unheard of at an Irish meeting – occupied conspicuous places on the platform'; and resolutions were passed supporting Russia and denouncing the State Department's proposed Arbitration Treaty with England. For Clan na Gael, WBY's peroration served as the curtain-raiser for a high-profile Irish American demonstration against the foreign policy of Roosevelt and Secretary Hay.

This instructive involvement showed that WBY's own priorities could be hijacked for the purposes of local politics. He devoted his remaining days to social occasions, receiving glad-handing and unwanted free drinks from Irish American hoteliers[42] and a final reception from the New York Irish Literary Society on 6 March, described in detail by Francis Hackett. The affectations of fame, in Hackett's opinion, were becoming evident; but 'the poet of the Irish race' was an inspirational figure, offering apostolic benedictions and invoking a national ideal 'more enduring than those of Brunnhilde, Siegfried, Parsifal: the spiritual destiny of the Celt'.[43] This, at least, was familiar territory, far more congenial than confounding the Asian strategies of Secretary Hay. 'I am setting a good many people reading our Celtic books,' he had written to the Duchess of Sutherland, '& it was for that I came here – & our Celtic books mean to me not in the end books but in the end a more passionate kind of life.'[44]

He arrived back in London on St Patrick's Day, after 'a beautiful passage' (much of it spent in discussions with William Strang, the Scottish painter, who had done an etching of him the previous year). He had good cause to be satisfied, and not only because Americans had been introduced to 'Celtic books'. Quinn's boast to Gregory that no Irishman since Parnell had made such an impression in the United States was probably true, despite 'the coldness and studied neglect of many of our Catholic papers'.[45] He had spoken to sixty-four gatherings, possibly to 25,000 to 35,000 people; he had earned $3,230.40.[46] The spectacular difference this made to his usual financial state may be gauged from the fact that in the subsequent two months he brought in exactly £2. 13s. 0d. By June 1904 the total income made by *The Celtic Twilight* and *Ideas of Good and Evil* was less than £100, swallowed by advances; similarly, his plays had not yet earned out the meagre £34-odd which WBY owed on advances. Only the faithful *Poems* produced an unencumbered £31. 15s. 1d., and this was over three years.[47] Suddenly, he seemed rich. Tentatively, he decided to invest £400: 'I have never had a penny to invest before.'[48] This brought its problems too; by October the income tax authorities were trying to assess him on estimated earnings of £500 per annum, largely due to his public prominence, and he had to prove his penury to an inquiry.

But the dividends reaped in America were more than financial. 'What has pleased me so much,' he had written to Gregory from Bryn Mawr, 'is getting this big audience by my own effort.'[49] Hearing him both at the beginning and at the end of his tour, Cornelius Weygandt thought he had transformed his mastery of the art of public speaking.[50] His success emboldened him for public debate with Griffith and other opponents, and for 'vehement' exchanges with Gonne. He had become an orator; the articulacy and energy of utterance, which he had only intermittently discovered before, had been liberated. Alone on a new continent, admired by strangers, he had been able to reflect upon his personality, public and private, while constant attention made him assess himself anew. He was cheerful, decisive, engaged.[51] Quinn reported proudly to Gregory:

He was always on time and made the entire Western trip alone and never missed a train and did it all just as planned very successfully – Mrs Jack [Yeats] to the contrary notwithstanding. She 'felt he must have been so helpless' and was 'so sure he could not have got on unless everything had been planned' whereas I took care to assure her that he gave a good account of himself, was always on time, and was eager and alert to do the correct and right thing always. His self-helpfulness was really remarkable. The person who says he cannot always be relied on to do and say the right thing and is not keen and alert to the facts of a situation, simply does not know Yeats.[52]

Physically too there were changes. He was on the edge of forty: his black hair was slightly silvered; he had put on a little weight. He wore a long chinchilla fur coat, purchased for the Mid-Western winter and much mocked by George Moore.[53] Age was becoming a preoccupation; his description of Cuchulain to Frank Fay for *On Baile's Strand* carries a strong autobiographical implication.

I have also to make the refusal of the sons affection tragic by suggesting in Cuchullains character a shadow of something a little proud, barren & restless as if out of shere strength of heart or from accident he had put affection away. He lives among young men but has himself outlived the illusions of youth. He is probably about 40, not less than 35 or 36 & not more that 45 or 46, certainly not an old man, & one understands from his talk about women that he does not love like a young man. Probably his very strength of character made him put off illusions & dreams (that make young men a womans servant) & made him become quite early in life a deliberate lover, a man of pleasure who can never really surrender himself. He is a little hard, & leaves the people about him a little repelled – perhaps this young mans affection is what he had most need of. Without this thought the play had not had any deep tragedy. I write of him with difficulty for when one creates a character one does it out of instinct & may be wrong when one analyses the instinct afterwards. It is as though the character embodied itself. The less one reasons the more living the character. I felt for instance that his boasting was necessary, & yet I did not reason it out. The touch of something hard, repellent yet alluring, self assertive yet self immolating is not all but it must be there.[54]

Above all, in America the lyric gift began to return to him, if not with particularly distinguished results. He began the poem 'Old Memory' at Bryn Mawr in early December, finishing it on the train from Canada ten days later, and wrote 'Never Give all the Heart' while staying with Quinn in Manhattan. His new-found confidence enabled him to take a high line with his American publishers, Macmillan; in January he firmly requested a new royalty arrangement and demanded speedy US publications of *The Countess Cathleen* and *The King's Threshold*.[55] By March he was emphasizing the new market created in the wake of his American success, and the need for a regular future arrangement leading towards a collected edition. He was also able to use a counter-offer from Scribner against them. On his return to London, he got the deal he wanted: Macmillan had first refusal on all his books in America, and remained his publishers there for life.

wby knew he owed America much, but his feelings about the country stayed ambivalent. The criticisms he had allowed himself on his first Chicago visit hinted at a real reservation. Like most of the impressions he formed, his reactions combined uncanny prescience with predetermined ideas derived from his imagination; irrelevant intrusions, like the Russian ecclesiastics who shared the stage with him in New York, apparently left no impression. The article 'America and the Arts', written after his return, preserved some of his thoughts. He liked the vividness and immediacy of American life, but deplored a certain crudeness. He ostentatiously praised American women, in public and private,[56] and Jack Yeats's wife heard that college girls had developed crushes on him *en masse*; she fantasized that he might come home married.[57] He thought that education was 'a national passion' and college teaching exemplary in its imaginativeness (though he was probably comparing it to his father's idea of Trinity College, Dublin, a distinctly limited standard). In 'half-Latin' California 'one could almost hear the footsteps of the Muses'. But America needed an aristocracy, to build on the elegance and culture he intermittently glimpsed in certain houses and institutions. His own predispositions towards authority and tradition, setting more and more firmly, made him happy to be back in Europe.

All his friends noticed the increased self-confidence, along with the fur coat and the slight paunch, while his family noted with relief the increased bank-balance. Already in early February, Lily was asking him to put money urgently into the embroidery enterprise at Dun Emer – which he saw as a riskier venture than Lolly's printing, sending back a short but much re-written letter. 'I have forseen this moment all the while but it is anoying,' he confided to Gregory. 'If I give much it will go without effect (for it will not be enough) & if I give little I shall be blamed always. I dont know whether it is selfish of one, but my sisters have for so many years written me so many complaints.'[58] As it happened, the crisis at Dun Emer passed – but not for long. And there was an even more predictable request on the way. Though claiming merrily he 'hardly had courage to write' the words, JBY rapidly required one of his 'loans': £20, marking a new level of ambition. WBY was home with a vengeance.

II

Throughout his absence he had remained preoccupied with what he re-peatedly referred to as 'my little theatre'. In America he had perfected the version of recent Irish theatrical history which would later infuriate the Fays. The origins of the Irish National Theatre Society lay in the Irish Literary Theatre begun by Gregory, Martyn and himself. They then, in WBY's version,

realised that we must take some of our own countrymen and educate them for the stage. This at first seemed impossible, because in Ireland there are extremely few who have the leisure for such an experiment. After all, our project at that time was only an experiment. 'Let us go to the clerks and the shop girls,' one of us said, 'and train them for the stage after their work hours. Let us try.' We found the task far easier than we expected. It was only another evidence of the spirit of intellectual interest which pervaded all classes. We formed a company and rehearsed at night.[59]

The contributions of Fay's training and Inghinidhe na hÉireann's enterprise were sublimely ignored. And much as WBY claimed the history of the Irish theatre for himself, he asserted control over the dramatic present. When Colum's *Broken Soil* had a success in December, he wrote to Lily:

Columb's success has overjoyed me. I was more nervous about that play than any-thing else, for my position would have been impossible if I had had to snuff out the work of young men belonging to the company. It would have always seemed that I did so from jealousy or some motive of that sort. Now, however, one can push on Columb and keep one's snuffers for the next. One man that we did snuff out, Cousins, has been avenging himself on Columb in the United Irishman.[60]

While he had to accept the Reading Committee's decisions taken in his absence (such as their rejection of his and Gregory's justifiably forgotten *Heads or Harps*[61]), he kept an eye on the theatre's development and tried to influence the choice of plays. The Irish National Theatre Society was now

317

an established presence in Irish life, its position cemented all the more firmly by the *United Irishman*'s opposition; Dublin Castle attempted to woo them into giving a performance before the King on his next visit (offering portrait commissions to JBY as an extra blandishment). But WBY's direct contribution to the repertoire was disastrous. The latest version of *The Shadowy Waters* was played in January: reviewers found it vapoury and incoherent, and patrons stayed away (or came to laugh). At a late stage Frank Fay was still desperately seeking guidance as to what the play was about, and it showed.[62] Synge thought it 'the most DISTRESSING failure the mind can imagine, – a half empty room, with growling men and tittering females'.[63] Tiny audiences were now a serious problem. And by early February WBY was more and more worried about the choice of plays for the theatre ('of which I am the head') and was determined to hurry back to take control.

He arrived in time for the INTS's London season which, arranged by Stephen Gwynn,[64] began on 26 March 1904; WBY's *Plays for an Irish Theatre*, containing *The Hour-Glass*, *Cathleen ni Houlihan* and *The Pot of Broth*, was published simultaneously by Bullen. The programme included WBY's own *King's Threshold* and Synge's *Riders to the Sea*. Horniman enthusiastically intervened wherever she could, selling tickets to friends, firing off letters about costumes and props, and chivvying others for not pulling their weight.[65] Once again critical opinion had been well prepared, and a fashionable audience poured in, including many Liberal politicians. The simplicity and intensity of the INTS's acting style was hugely effective. John Masefield reported to Jack Yeats that Synge's play had the house in tears (enough handkerchiefs 'to make a topsail'), while WBY got 'a great call' and had to make a curtain-speech.[66] *The King's Threshold* was received with some reservations, but Walkley in the *TLS*, Beerbohm in the *Saturday Review* and most of all Archer in the *World* blew resounding trumpets. Beerbohm astutely noted that the Irish used 'simplicity' as a form of exoticism:

One could not object to them as to the ordinary amateur. They were not floundering in the effort to do something beyond their powers. With perfect simplicity, perfect dignity and composure, they were just themselves, speaking a task that they had well by heart. Just themselves; and how could such Irish selves not be irresistible? Several of our metropolitan players are Irish, and even they, however thickly coated with Saxonism, have a charm for us beyond their Saxon-blooded fellows. The Irish people, unspoiled, in their own island – who can resist them? But footlights heighten every effect; and behind them unspoiled Irish people win us quicklier and more absolutely than ever. And behind London footlights! There they have not merely their own charm, but that charm also which belongs to all exotics. Many people went many times, lately, to 'In Dahomey', fascinated by the sight of a strange and remote race expressing through our own language things most strange to us and remote from us. Well, we are as far removed from the Irish people as from the negroes, and our spiritual distance seems all the greater by reason of our nearness in actual mileage. I admit that it was, in a way, more pleasant to see those negroes than to see these Irish folk. When we contemplate negroes, one clear impression comes through our dim bewilderment: we are assuredly in the presence of an inferior race. Whereas he must be a particularly dull Saxon who does not discern and confess (at any rate to himself), that the Keltic race is, spiritually and intellectually, a race much finer, and also much more attractive, than that to which he has the honour to belong.[67]

The Times warned the Irish players about becoming *too* fashionable; Shaw, won over at last to this kind of avant-garde, offered to write them a play. WBY, still buoyed up by American confidence, seemed to some of his acquaintances too full of himself;[68] but he deeply impressed a stage-struck young Australian, Louis Esson, who attended an evening gathering at Gregory's London flat. WBY urged him to forgo cosmopolitanism, make an Australian theatre, 'keep within your borders' and create a tradition. This was the voice of authority, and Esson never forgot it.

It was a heady return to the Old World. After the London triumph, WBY went to Coole in early April and spent a peaceful fortnight there, fishing for pike (an enduring craze). He then inspected theatrical preparations in Dublin before travelling on to London, where he attended an Irish Literary Society meeting to hear Stephen Gwynn talk about the poetry of Tom Moore, whose early nineteenth-century combination of Irish soulfulness and English Romanticism provided an easy target for uncompromising nationalists. WBY's response was to call for an oral culture rather than Moore's drawing-room ballads, in tones which echoed his new self-assertiveness. 'He thought he was the first man who had stood up to the printed book and had told it what he thought of it.'[69] Events in America since his departure had stiffened his backbone still further. At Coole he had heard the repercussions of the visit by the seceding Irish actors to the St Louis exhibition, led by Dudley Digges and Maire Quinn. They wanted to play *Cathleen ni Houlihan*, *The Land of Heart's Desire* and *Diarmuid and Grania*: WBY had refused permission, and expected Russell to withhold his *Deirdre* as well. But Russell, who thought the INTS took too high a line about permissions, gave them the right to perform his play and, when WBY remonstrated, offered to resign from the INTS.[70] Meanwhile, the Digges troupe spread confusion by appearing in America as 'National' players, profiting by the original company's recent London publicity; John Quinn sent violent exhortations to Coole about the St Louis 'fakirs', blaming John MacBride for supporting them.[71] Others too were seen as enemies on this issue. T. P. Gill had fallen from favour, P. J. Kelly was formally expelled from the INTS for agreeing to accompany Digges to St Louis, and WBY threatened legal action if they pirated his plays.[72]

Above all, his relationship with Russell, increasingly uneasy, shifted further into antagonism.

But there were more positive developments afoot too. After the London triumph, Horniman's offer to provide a theatre premises materialized decisively. On 8 April WBY sent Horniman's proposal to Russell (as Vice-President); on 9 April he saw the Under-Secretary, Sir Antony MacDonnell, about the question of a patent, before other theatrical interests tried to block them; on 10 April the Dublin theatre-fanatic and architect Joseph Holloway was approached about adapting a theatre.[73] For a premises had been found: the hall of the Mechanics' Institution, just north of the Liffey, which had had a previous existence as the 'Prince's Theatre', specializing in variety entertainment. Horniman obtained it, along with some adjacent buildings (including, to the pleasure of Dublin's wits, a defunct morgue). It was to be adapted and let rent-free to the INTS, under several conditions (notably, that seat-prices be kept up, and *hoi polloi* kept out). It was, in other words, to be a high-class venture.

Horniman herself was in Dublin during April, excitedly overseeing the preliminary arrangements, and taking WBY to see the future theatre on 11 April – where they had to retreat before the abusive outgoing manager ('May you and your morgue have luck!'[74]). WBY continued to move between Dublin and London; a reaction to recent excitements was beginning to set in, and he blamed a lowering of his spirits on the horoscope. But there were more tangible reasons. The patent hearings for the new theatre dragged on into the summer, sarcasms about Gregory's new book irritated him, and rival theatrical ventures continued to threaten. The nascent Ulster Literary Theatre put on *Cathleen ni Houlihan* without permission, encouraged, to WBY's especial annoyance, by Gonne; he formally withdrew her right to license performances of a play she believed she owned. And Russell, yet again, annoyed him by allowing the Ulster group to perform *Deirdre* – 'some nice boys who wanted to constitute themselves the Belfast branch of the society', Russell complained to Gregory, 'and who never realised the lofty skyreaching dignity of the Theatre Society until they got an indignant letter from [the Society's Secretary, George] Roberts putting them in their "proper place"'.[75]

Writing at length to Roberts on 18 May, WBY revealed his worries about the growing resentment of the INTS directorate in nationalist circles – and his acute sense that their choice of plays for the coming winter would be crucial. Shaw still promised a play, but tortured WBY with hints about its scandalous contents. 'That it will be amusing is certain, but whether it will be possible or not I don't know. It probably will for Mrs Shaw is doing her best to keep him off dangerous subjects.' More immediately, WBY was passionately committed to Synge's *The Well of the Saints*: 'a really astonishing play', he told Quinn, 'one of the masterpieces of our time as I think'. Posterity might not agree, and nor would much contemporary critical opinion, but WBY prepared the way by writing about it indefatigably, especially to correspondents with newspaper connections.

There remained the question of his own dramatic output. From 26 to 28 June the Stage Society put on *Where There is Nothing*, to an uncertain critical response – though some reviews were surprisingly good. WBY's rather Meredithian curtain-speech about the 'spirit of mischief' did not clarify matters, and privately he agreed with the hostile critics, telling Quinn that it now seemed 'a patchwork, not an organism'.[76] However, it attracted a fashionable audience (in marked contrast to the Stage Society's regular clientele), one of whom, the Countess of Cromartie, subsequently asked WBY to tea. Here he bumped into Queen Alexandra at a children's party, an encounter drolly recounted to Quinn: 'The whole scene was very unexpected and curious and seemed to me not unlike a scene on the stage. I never saw so many beautiful people together.' His friends Ricketts and Shannon found the meeting of this equally unworldly pair hilarious: 'out of innocence he disregarded all the conventions and spoke to her in the Yeats way. She knew nothing of course of Yeats's disloyal manifestos when royalty was in Ireland, knew his poems, and wished to hear when next he gave one of his plays.'[77] He declared his impatience to shock Maud Gonne with this intelligence as soon as he could; and this London visit enabled them to meet again, and attend the Guildhall exhibition of Irish art together. These various attractions held him in London until mid-July, when he returned to Coole, the pike in the lake, and the affairs of the new theatre.

Once there he threw himself not into lyric poetry but dramatic construction: reworking the unsatisfactory *Where There is Nothing*, and beginning a play on the theme of the tragic Irish heroine Deirdre, which preoccupied him throughout the summer. The subject was resonant: already treated by Russell and Rolleston, WBY was apparently anxious to put his mark on the story of 'Ireland's Helen' (or, as Dublin would have it, 'The Second Mrs Conchobar').[78] Given that *On Baile's Strand* had been his most successful play so far, he had also decided that myth and saga were more dramatically effective for him than the medieval allegory of *The King's Threshold* or the Nietzschean modernity of *Where There is Nothing*. And here, as ever, Gregory's influence was vital. WBY spent all summer and much of autumn 1904 at Coole; their collaboration became even closer. His eyes were especially troublesome, and she typed most of his letters; her own voice sounds through them, in the archness of language and modulation of tone for different correspondents (high-flown and arty to Quinn, but self-consciously 'country' to Synge, with much about saving the hay). As for his own family, the instructions from Coole about their several careers were peremptory enough to annoy even Lily, who instructed JBY:

I don't like your writing to Jack. You say too much. He is all right and knows what he is doing. He never drifts. Willy and Lady Gregory are both too ready to critize [sic] and direct. They forget Jack is at the beginning and is *seven years* younger than Willy. What of Willy's technique seven years ago. They all forget this and from their pedestal direct and order others a great deal too much. Willy was full of 'Do this, you must do that, etc.' A press man is absolutely necessary and so on to us this time last year. He even threatened us and bullied generally. But Lolly and I are hardened and know him and stood our ground. Jack does not show fight. He is only wounded. Jack knows what he is doing and doing well.

Why Willy looks upon himself as an authority upon needlework and a kind of design necessary in particular, I was not to get designs from either Jack or Cottie but go to his pets, young Maclagan, Mrs Traquair and Mr Gethin. The first send [sic] me a ridiculous design, the second promised me one a year and a half ago. It has not come yet. And the last send [sic] me one, quite commonplace and the wrong size. He is such a great man I must not say anything. In reality no one ever heard of him but Willy and his mother. Don't worry Jack. He wants encouragement and his work is beautiful and his own. When we are all dead and gone great prices will be given for them. I know they will.[79]

In the matters that most closely concerned them, the artist's children all knew their own minds: this was their inheritance.

One of WBY's involvements with Dun Emer this summer concerned a selection of Lionel Johnson's poems. His choice drastically under-represented the Fenian mode which distinguished Johnson's 'Irish' verse, and he had his reasons. WBY was not only deliberately distancing himself from advanced nationalist propaganda but also simultaneously working on a long memorandum for Horace Plunkett to use in the battle for the new theatre's patent, which would stress the non-political nature of the venture. The very name chosen was carefully neutral: 'The Abbey Theatre'. The memorandum, completed in July 1904, is an absorbing document: it gives a Yeatsian description of each play produced since the days of the Irish Literary Theatre, emphasizes the Irish, artistic and uncommercial nature of the enterprise, modestly deprecates his own plays, and administers some sharp digs in the ribs ('[Russell's] *Deirdre* is by a dear friend and a charming writer, but I do not consider it a good play'). *Cathleen ni Houlihan* is interpreted in as unpolitical a fashion as possible. Throughout, he projects a sense of continuum:

I claim that, leaving aside my own work, we have done a great deal for the intellect of this country – discovering and training into articulateness J. M. Synge, whom I believe to be a great writer, the beginning it may be of a European figure . . . We have caused a great deal of intellectual discussion, and we have done all this without playing to any party. We have pleased and affronted all in succession.

The manifesto reflects an intense concentration on the new theatre in July; Synge and Russell were also at Coole, followed by a spectacularly unsuccessful visit from Horniman, at her most edgy and obtrusive, in August. On WBY's trips to Dublin witnesses were dragooned for the patent hearings, and the importunate George Moore was mercilessly squeezed ever further to the sidelines. In retaliation Moore circulated an article denouncing the Fay style of production and direction, but WBY was by now a veteran of these skirmishes. He sent Fay a masterpiece of advice, which also hints at how closely he identified Synge's developing style with the Society's dramatic ethos.

If I were you I would make your article an attack on realistic stage management. The position of attack is far stronger than the position of defence. Put Moore on the defensive and you will win. Be just to Antoine's genius, but show the defects of his movement. Art is art because it is not nature, and he tried to make it nature. A realist, he cared nothing for poetry, which is founded on convention. He despised it and did something to drive it from the stage. He broke up convention, we have to re-create it . . . We must grope our way towards a new yet ancient perfection . . . We desire an extravagant, if you will unreal, rhetorical romantic art, allied in literature to the art on the one hand of Racine and [on] the other hand of Cervantes. We can no more learn from Antoine than a writer of verse or a writer of extravagant comedy could learn from a realistsic novelist. Moore once said to an interviewer 'nobody will ever write a realistic novel again. We are all gone now, Zola is dead Huyssmans is in a monastery, and I am in Dublin.' Moore knows that his kind of novel is obsolete, but because he is an amateur in plays and stage management, he does not understand that his kind of play and his kind of stage management is equally obsolete. Our movements are clumsy for we are children, but we are a devil of a long way farther from our coffins.[80]

The patent hearings were an unqualified success; all the opposing counsel could do was allege that WBY's drama was immoral, without being able to remember the names of any of his plays.

The new theatre was safe. This was just as well: workmen had been on the site all summer, furniture ordered, and stained glass commissioned from Sarah Purser's workshop, though Horniman had been intensely worried about the dangers of symbolism, settling in the end for safely non-committal Celtic nut trees, symbolizing knowledge. Queen Maeve and her wolfhound were already featuring on the notepaper. The longed-for permanent home of the INTS was in the making. Those excluded were accordingly resentful, but they had lost the contest: while the *Leader* fulminated against the 'intolerable air of superiority in mind and culture' projected by WBY's 'set', Maud Gonne was driven to recycling Gregory's work into articles on 'Emer' for the

United Irishman and producing – in *Dawn* – a play uncannily reminiscent of *Cathleen ni Houlihan*.

III

Meanwhile the inspiration of all this envy, based at Coole, was still trying to define the nature of his own theatrical ambition. Writing to Ricketts that summer, he described the hallmark of his plays as 'a cry for a more abundant and a more intense life'; the notion of 'tragic exultation' was lodged firmly in his mind, perhaps best expressed in the poem that became the Musician's song in *Deirdre*, proudly sent both to Quinn and Farr in late September. Echoes of Nietzschean philosophy chimed with resentment at the attacks of Dublin quidnuncs and reservations about the power of industrial big business to vulgarize culture, as seen in America. His correspondence during the summer reverted to the topic of 'plebeianising', and a mordant note to Russell about the *Leader*'s attacks spoke for Gregory as well: 'Neither your character nor the character of any of us need defence. We should not discuss such things with any but our equals.'[81] WBY's increased consciousness of class difference at this time also reflected the social nature of the acting profession, still regarded in many circles as 'unsuitable'. In constant contact with people he described as 'clerks' and 'shop-girls', his supposed hauteur may often have been absent-mindedness (or myopia); but it was not moderated by the influence of Coole, and it was resented. And there was a definite sense of difference, reflected oddly in his comment to Synge that women of Maire Garvey's or Maire Walker's 'class' did not 'have sensitive bodies', however high their ideals, and that this made the dramatic transmission of intense emotion problematic.[82] The thought was expressed with such uncharacteristic awkwardness that he himself may not have been comfortable with it. But it indicated a firmly held sense of difference, unremarkable for the age but, in the Irish context, reinforcing resentments and divisions which reached below the crust of social class, down into the lava of religious and political tensions.

Meanwhile the rehearsal season drew on, and WBY was thinking hard about the procedure for choosing plays by committee; the terms of the patent now provided a useful rationale for insisting on an airtight procedure ('I have had a long experience of societies, and I have never known a society that was lax about its rules without getting into trouble sooner or later'). Arrangements about a quorum, proxy voting and Chairman's casting vote were closely argued; this bore fruit a month later, when by-laws for the Reading Committee were adopted.[83] Not all the directors were happy. Synge anticipated trouble about choosing plays, convinced that the ex-Griffithite Frank Fay represented a 'neopatriotic-Catholic clique . . . which might be serious'. He was mistaken: Fay had long ago attached himself to the WBY bandwagon and attacked the continual sniping at the poet ('What did we Irish do that the gods put so much bitterness & jealousy into our hearts?'[84]). This was a course he would later regret. But the question of plays for the new theatre was highly sensitive. And it was about to be inflamed by one of Shaw's most unerring darts.

By mid-September *John Bull's Other Island* had arrived at Coole. As long ago as March 1900 he had agreed to write a play for the Irish Literary Theatre, but by the time he delivered it circumstances had changed and, as Shaw himself remarked, 'like most people who have asked me to write plays, Mr Yeats got rather more than he bargained for'. Long out of Ireland and utterly opposed to returning, Shaw had none the less built up a reservoir of exasperated reflection. Now it burst. Reading the sprawling, inventive, sarcastic text, WBY must have wondered at once what Dublin would make of it. All stereotypes were reversed, the Irish characters being hard-headed and calculating, the English woolly and sentimental. 'Standing here between you the Englishman, so clever in your foolishness, and the Irishman, so foolish in your cleverness,' remarked Shaw's protagonist, 'I cannot in my ignorance be sure which of you is the more deeply damned.' The Gaelic League was heartlessly mocked (the only genuine Gaelicist was a romantically minded English developer). Public pretensions and religious pieties were exposed. There was a sharp Moranite dig that 'calling the unfortunate island Kathleen ni Hoolihan . . . saves thinking'.[85] The brilliant 'Preface for Politicians', which makes the play a key text in understanding Anglo-Irish relations, was yet to come; in dramatic terms it was wildly over-long; but even in first draft *John Bull's Other Island* raised serious questions. Could the new theatre open with such a sustained blast of iconoclasm?

In a letter which was obviously a joint concoction with Gregory, WBY told Shaw: 'You have said things in this play which are entirely true about Ireland, things which nobody has ever said before . . . It astonishes me that you should have been so long in London and yet have remembered so much.'[86] He added, disingenuously, that he thought it would not be 'dangerous'; there would be indignation, but they could survive it. Privately, its great length gave an excuse to stall, though Synge, predictably, wanted to press on with it, after cuts. There were also technical difficulties; a motor accident, for one thing, had to be represented on stage. GBS wrote straightfacedly to WBY on 31 August, asking about modern machinery: 'It occurs to me that as you will deal in fairy plays you may have involved yourself with hydraulic bridges.'[87] Fay was worried about casting it, but WBY held his counsel. Shaw cannily kept his options for an English production open throughout, and when WBY returned to London he was able to see it done experimentally by J. E. Vedrenne and Granville-Barker at the Court Theatre. He admitted to Gregory that he disliked it. Even though it acted 'very much better than we cd have foreseen', it was 'fundamentally ugly and shapeless'. He never found Shaw easy.[88] Old rivalries persisted, and in nearly every way *John Bull's Other Island* was the antithesis of a WBY play. The difficulty of casting an English actor to play Broadbent was made much of; the length was considered intractable; by 1 May 1905 WBY, with relief, allowed Shaw to give 'that green elephant' to Calvert for an English production.[89]

Meanwhile, the company prepared for their first season at the Abbey Theatre. WBY was in Dublin when rehearsals began on 31 October, along with John Quinn, who was fitting in a brief and much postponed visit – in the course of which he also met WBY's London circle and tried to persuade Charles Shannon to paint a portrait of the poet.[90] For his host, however, the theatre subsumed all. The new locale seemed to provide an opportunity to express his theories about abstract sets, and he conceived the idea that Jack should paint backdrops of Synge's play: 'Jack will mass colour and form and treat the whole thing decoratively.' Many of his colleagues had reservations but WBY, recently horrified by Beerbohm Tree's pantomimic *Tempest* in London, was inexorably anti-commercial. 'Even if an artist's work prove to be less effective than the ordinary stage scene to ordinary eyes, it will soon grow even to ordinary eyes much more effective, as the artist learns his business, and from the first it will show an individual mind.'[91] Other ideas for visual innovation at the Abbey included bringing in Robert Gregory; looking at the work of 'Madam Macrovitch' (his old friend Con Gore-Booth, now married to the dilettante Polish artist Casimir Markievicz, who had taken all too readily to Dublin's bohemia); and searching for inspiration among the Japanese prints in the British Museum. 'One must have a complete asthetisism,' he told Synge, 'when one is dealing with a synthetic art like that of the stage.'

Not everyone agreed. His old friend, artist and Masquer Pamela Colman Smith, 'alone seems to understand what I want to make a design', and Jack's ideas were regretfully rejected. But WBY remained at the centre, convinced of his own indispensability ('the moment I am gone the old business will begin again'[92]). And there were ominous portents: a long struggle had commenced with Horniman over the seat prices, pegged at a shilling in the Abbey but sixpence at other Dublin theatres. Relations with his benefactor were further threatened by public disagreements over the 'archaeologically correct' costumes which she designed for *On Baile's Strand*. And Dublin's cultural life was further enlivened (or envenomed) that autumn by the first engagement in the long-running campaign by Hugh Lane, Gregory's connoisseur nephew, to bring a permanent collection of modern painting to the city. Hostilities were declared when the Royal Hibernian Academy crassly terminated Lane's show of Modern French art from the Staats-Forbes collection in order to prepare for the Decorators' Guild exhibition. This was aimed as a body-blow against Lane's and Gregory's campaign to found a gallery, based on the purchase of the pictures at the Academy. Lane, who could be both outrageous and ruthless, occupied a sensitive position. It was sharply remarked that he was a notably successful art dealer who turned famous profits; but he had already bought a number of the paintings himself and was prepared to donate them. WBY, who had visited the show 'almost every day', played a leading part in the campaign, writing to influential friends and lobbying journalists. Both the *Freeman's Journal* and the *Irish Times* opened subscription lists, and by January 1905 enough money had been raised to buy 160 of the Staats-Forbes paintings for £160,000.

Given Gregory's involvement, WBY's commitment was inevitable. He even appeared on the same platform as George Moore at the latter's lecture promoting the paintings.[93] But the issue of Lane's gallery held a broader importance for him, since the scheme's opponents were exactly the elements in whom he discerned his own enemies. On the one hand, Lane was assailed by the bourgeois Dublin establishment, who thought the pictures worthless and wrote to the papers saying so; and on the other, by the *United Irishman*, which harped on Lane's own art dealing and insinuated he was lining his pockets. WBY eventually forced an apology from Griffith (their 'first serious quarrel', he told Quinn). On both wings, the philistines were massing: 'the political question is giving a lot of trouble', he told Shorter.[94] He brought to the battle his post-American confidence, his heightened consciousness of class and tradition, and his long history of struggling with Dublin opinion. For all its inspired malice and free-wheeling chronology, George Moore's recollection of his former friend's public intervention indicates as much:

As soon as the applause died away Yeats, who had lately returned to us from the States with a paunch, a huge stride, and an immense fur overcoat, rose to speak. We were surprised at the change in his appearance, and could hardly believe our ears when, instead of talking to us as he used to do about the old stories coming down from generation to generation, he began to thunder like Ben Tillett himself against the middle classes, stamping his feet, working himself into a great passion, and all because the middle classes did not dip their hands into their pockets and give Lane the money he wanted for his exhibition. It is impossible to imagine the hatred which came into his voice when he spoke the words 'the middle classes'; one would have thought that he was speaking against a personal foe; but there are millions in the middle classes! And we looked round asking each other with our eyes where on earth our Willie Yeats had picked up such extraordinary ideas. He could hardly have gathered in the United States the ridiculous idea that none but titled and carriage-folk can appreciate pictures. And we asked ourselves why Willie Yeats should feel himself called upon to denounce the class to which he himself belonged essentially: on one side excellent mercantile millers and shipowners, and on the other a portrait painter of rare talent . . . We were led to understand that by virtue of our subscriptions we should cease to belong to the middle classes, and having held out this hope to us he retired to his chair and fell back overcome into the middle of the great fur coat, and remained silent until the end of the debate.[95]

When the Abbey opened on 27 December 1904, wby had spent months of intrigue in Irish cultural wars; and he received a victor's reward. Not only the luxurious little theatre, but the programme and the publicity were identified as his and Gregory's enterprise. The lobby was hung with jby's portraits; the season was dominated by their plays *On Baile's Strand, Spreading the News* and *Cathleen ni Houlihan* (with Maire nic Shiubhlaigh [Walker], thought by some to be better in the part than Gonne). Synge's *Shadow of the Glen* completed the list. Publicity had been carefully arranged; Masefield attended and wrote a rave notice for the *Manchester Guardian*. Gregory was kept in Coole, ill with influenza, which directed the spotlight solely on wby. He gave endless interviews, showed journalists over the theatre, and announced forthcoming productions (Gregory's *Kincora*, Synge's *Well of the Saints*, his own *Deirdre*, Gregory's versions of Molière). His persistence about stage-effects paid off: *On Baile's Strand* featured a curtain of untreated jute, flooded with golden light, while Cuchulain's son stood revealed in silhouette against brilliant blue backlighting. Even Willie Fay admitted the effect 'could never be obtained by paint'.[96] Horniman's idea of an Irish Bayreuth seemed near achievement, though wby had humiliated her during rehearsals by telling the company that her costumes made them look like Father Christmases and fire extinguishers.[97] And on the evening of 27 December he was able to telegraph to Gregory: 'Your play immense success. All plays successfully packed house.'

He had had a triumph, but there were clouds on the horizon. Audiences, apart from the first nights, stayed very small. And, considered as the climax of Irish theatrical experiments since 1899, the Abbey opening was as remarkable for other absences too. Actors like Dudley Digges and Maire Quinn, playwrights like Moore and Martyn, were no longer in the picture, while Maire nic Shiubhlaigh, Russell and others still aboard were feeling increasingly mutinous. People like the Walkers had come into the theatre for political self-realization as much as for stage-struck dazzlement. The old *esprit de corps* of Inghinidhe na hÉireann or Sinn Féin lent them 'the solidarity and intensity of a sect, and the high spirits of a social club.'[98] But the Fays were professionals who wanted to build a solid enterprise; other recruits, like the Allgood sisters, were out for a career and a good time; and wby saw himself as a dictator in the cause of art, ready to dominate, divide and rule. Those who worked for the Abbey directors would see the old ideas of a political co-operative increasingly threatened; their memoirs in later years would try vainly to stress that the theatrical movement which entered its apotheosis in the newly opened Abbey on 27 December 1904 was the product of more than one man's genius.[99] But as far as posterity was concerned, they were irretrievably swept aside into subordinate roles by WBY's increasingly powerful sense of his own history.

Chapter 13 : DELIGHTING IN ENEMIES
1905–1906

> Mr Yeats had done more than anybody else to create an Irish
> Theatre, and he had also done more than anybody else to pre-
> vent anybody going there [laughter].
>
> Tom Kettle at the Irish Literary Society, 5 February 1906

I

DURING the summer and autumn of theatrical preparations and cultural pro-
paganda in 1904, WBY's emotional life remained quiescent; he had reason to
cultivate detachment, since the nature of Horniman's obsession with him was
more and more obvious. She showered him with unwanted gifts from con-
tinental watering-places, and wrote of her desire to take him travelling with
her. In June she even presented an indirect proposal via JBY, assuring the poet's
father of a prophecy 'that she wd marry a man from overseas, tall, dark and
very thin, with some foreign decorations'; the reason (perfectly calculated
to appeal to her prospective father-in-law) was 'to make him a comfortable
home'.[1] While WBY had no intention of fulfilling this fate, he knew how much
he owed his benefactor. Accepting the jaunty tone of her frequent letters (often
a jarring combination of flirtation and threat) was a small price to pay, but
he had become a pastmaster at witholding himself. Dublin opinion watched
it all with pleasure, and Joyce's friend Gogarty produced a limerick:

> What a pity it is that Miss Horniman
> When she wants to secure or suborn a man
> Should choose Willie Yeats
> Who still masturbates
> And at any rate isn't a horny man.[2]

However, almost from the very moment that Horniman's theatre came
into being, WBY's emotions were suddenly magnetized elsewhere. In January
1905 the insecurely stitched-together MacBride marriage finally began to
unravel in public. Gonne, told by a London solicitor to discuss her position
with 'some friend' who could offer advice, asked her cousin May to contact
WBY. He wrote to her, and she replied gratefully. As always, in adversity she
needed him; as always, he responded to her twitch upon the thread.

He had long been hearing rumours about the marriage – some true
(MacBride's drunkenness), some not (their baby Seán's epilepsy). But the truth

was spectacularly shocking. On 9 January, having had an interview with May Bertie-Clay, WBY wrote to Gregory. He was still reeling at the catalogue of MacBride's crimes: violence, sexual abuse, threats to the children. Two days later he wrote in even greater shock, having heard details about MacBride's seduction of the seventeen-year-old Eileen Wilson (Gonne's half-sister[3]) and his molestation of the eleven-year-old Iseult, 'the blackest thing you can imagine'. WBY felt accordingly bitter at the refusal of nationalist politicians to support Gonne: Barry O'Brien earned his particular contempt for attempting to hush it up. 'For the sake of the country . . . the MacBride legend must keep its lustre.' Fortunately for herself, Gonne had retained control of her fortune;[4] she had already offered a separation settlement to MacBride, but both May Bertie-Clay and WBY wanted her to withdraw it. A divorce must be sought, even at the risk of the Millevoye liaison coming out. WBY was conscious that his own relationship with Gonne would also be dragged into public view. MacBride frequently complained of the friendship, and had already removed WBY's books from Gonne's Paris house (their 'presence had always annoyed him considerably'[5]). He had even threatened to shoot him 'some while back' – 'the only cheerful piece of news I have had in days', WBY told Gregory; 'it gives one a sense of heightened life'.[6] His hands were tied, as he was implicated in the counter-charges threatened by MacBride – though the latter was mollifyingly told by Barry O'Brien 'that kind of thing never seemed to interest Yeats'.[7]

Just as with her revelations about the Millevoye liaison in December 1898, Gonne had completely thrown WBY off course; and as before he attempted to carry on a normal life, organizing his Monday evenings, consoled by astrology, and sustained by confessional outpourings to Gregory, still ill at Coole. There was also the support of Nietzschean philosophy. 'The whole thing has made me very wretched,' he told Gregory, 'but has awakened nothing of the old feeling – a little to my surprise – no feeling but pity and anger . . . I feel, as I always feel about these things – that strength shapes the world about itself, & that weakness is shaped about the world – & that the compromise is weakness.' He also set himself to help where he could: Quinn was immediately told the outlines of the case, emphasizing MacBride's 'erotomania from drink', and was eventually asked to find supporting evidence from the hero's activities in the USA. From January, Gonne's correspondence with WBY returned to its former frequency. Her tone was dependent, appreciative and gentle. 'Of men friends', she told him, 'I have found few who cared or troubled & I have asked help of none.' In February proceedings were entered for a French divorce, at hearings attended by an alternately tearful and aggressive MacBride. Given the nature of the evidence, Gonne's religious advisers did not oppose the idea. In February WBY was in Dublin, waiting to hear how matters went in Paris, and his letters to Gregory suggest an obsession getting out of hand:

I cannot bear the burden of this terrible case alone – I know nothing about lawyers & so on. I see that I shall have to do a great deal – I have had a letter today from Mrs MacBride, which shows that she is utterly broken down at one moment she asks me about lawyers, at another she begs me 'to keep out of this horrible affair' she 'brought this trouble on herself' she should 'fight it alone' & so on. Her cousin, who is a very charming woman, does not seem to know what to do. You alone can help us all, I think. It will probably be legal seperation but that is for the lawyer to say – Mrs Clay is anxious that it should be divorce as she thinks MacBride will be on the watch, for any imprudence of Mrs MacBrides to trump up a case against her – she thinks she will never have any any security, especially, I dare say, because of her habitual imprudence. Mrs MacBride seems indifferent as to whether it is seperation or divorce. There is another reason why it may be necessary to prepare a case of divorce – MacBride may be got to leave the country & let a seperation suit go by default if threatened with the whole scandal. I think Mrs MacBride should proffess a readiness to go into the whole case then the whole case would involve him ultimately in a criminal prosecution. I have, what is perhaps a wild project, for the getting of MacBride out of the country & about this I rather want to see you, *in Dublin*. When you know the story you will feel that if she were the uttermost stranger, if ones bitterest enemy one would have none the less, even to the putting aside of all else, to help her. You will be a protection to me, though I need hardly say I am not thinking of that.[8]

In early March he returned to London, continuing to try to marshal evidence against MacBride from Quinn in New York (against Clan na Gael's implacable opposition) and from old United Irish League enemies in Mayo. 'I do not think much of ordinary morals,' he told Quinn, 'but this man has been a drunken cad from the first.'[9] Even Horniman offered to help – a mixed blessing at best. But legal wrangles and MacBride's procrastination kept matters in limbo. By winning a libel case he had brought against the *Independent*, MacBride hoped to keep reports of any trial proceedings out of the English and Irish papers, and nationalist opinion supported him rather than his wife. 'The trouble with these men,' WBY complained to Gregory, 'is that in their eyes a woman has no rights. I could see that he [Dixon] thinks that Mrs MacBride's objection to drunkenness a morbid peculiarity. I feel at every turn that by turning Catholic she put herself in their hands – she accepted their code and that is for women a code of ignoble submission.' JBY, revelling in the gossip, wondered if feminism would claim her: 'if Miss Gonne, when this is over, raises the standard of revolt among the ladies here, Dublin is ripe for a revolt'.[10] But Gonne remained withdrawn in Paris, immersed in painting, coming to terms with her disastrous mistake. By the end of June WBY confided to Quinn his own hopes, which echoed his father's:

She seems to be quite easy in her mind and to have recovered her old serene courage. I imagine that this case will break up the old United Irishman group and I cannot say I am sorry. I am hoping that by the mere force of circumstances she will be put into the centre of some little radical movement for personal freedom. The women's question is in a worse state in Dublin than in any place I know, and she seems naturally chosen out by events to stir up rebellion in what will be for her a new way . . . of course I dont know in the least what she is thinking in this matter.[11]

Gregory, realistic as ever, threw cold water on the notion of Gonne leading the women of Ireland to liberation. 'I hope she, & every woman with a drunken husband, may succeed in getting free. Where I don't quite agree with you is the probability of her being able to do any more work in Ireland. I think that is over for her.'[12] But wbn felt that she was ready for action again, and that this cause might divert her from sterile politics; he had heard from Fay about conditions in working-class Dublin, where a woman would be enslaved by religion to keep bearing children to a drunken husband 'who hands his besottedness on in the blood'. His own preoccupation with descent, breeding and aristocracy was taking firm root, and the MacBride case helped to fix it.[13]

Gonne was not, in the event, going to give up her political faith; by now she was consoling herself that 'English agents' were to blame for MacBride's intransigence. None the less, wbn's commitment to her cause moved her deeply. 'I have given up thanking you,' she told him. 'I have *always counted* on your friendship, ever since I knew you & it has never failed me. In the terrible time I have been through it was a great comfort & a great support to me, it helped me in a wonderful way – one does not thank for help of this kind, only one can never forget it.'[14] It took her back to the black days after the death of her baby son: her affection for wbn had been forged in that time of desolation, and now it returned in another. As for wbn, he wrote to Quinn that his feeling for her was 'affection of the most lasting kind . . . I do not say that it is any kind of passion, but it is the feeling one has for some near and dear relative.'[15]

When the divorce suit was heard in Paris on 26 July, Russell's fears that 'it will end in a bad scandal and everything will be public' proved right. Much, though not all, of the squalid detail was reported.[16] Gonne reserved most of her annoyance for the 'allegation' that she was English, not Irish. MacBride continued to receive the support of O'Leary and others. Finally, in order to acquire a status recognized in Ireland, Gonne settled for a judicial separation under Irish law administered by French judges, rather than an outright French divorce. The case would not be settled until the summer of 1906; in the process MacBride was allowed to return to live in Ireland, despite his interlude fighting for the Boers. Gonne would therefore maintain her family based in France, for the children's protection. She kept wby informed about her efforts to keep Iseult's name out of court, and the allegations mounted against her by MacBride's friends, ranging from promiscuity to morphine addiction. By now she was arguing against her old friend with her accustomed vigour: 'there is more good than you admit in the unconscious thought of the masses of the people'.[17] But the separation brought about by their quarrel over advanced nationalist politics versus the demands of individual art had been healed.

II

That same quarrel, however, continued to simmer in the new theatre. The Irish renaissance was now a well-established phenomenon: the *Bookman* of January 1905 devoted itself to 'The New Irish School', with a brooding portrait of wby on the cover and a reverent lead article by Annie Macdonnell, 'a Scottish Gael' who had been favourably reviewing him for years. She followed his own prescription in dating the movement back to 'the break-up of the Nationalist Party and the death of Parnell [which] let loose forces which had hitherto been absorbed by politics'. wby, 'Irish of the Irish', was 'yet the most fastidious artist, the most undoubted and the most magical poet among English writers today', speaking in many voices, mediated through a gallery of characters (Oisin, Cuchulain, Hanrahan, Ruttledge). From the point of view of the shape-changer himself, the time was ripe for the Abbey to branch out: writing to commission a translation of *Oedipus Rex*, he told Gilbert Murray 'the country is in its first plastic state and takes the mark of every strong finger . . . I believe we are going to make a great dramatic school here'.[18] And this mould was not necessarily going to bear the stamp of nationalist propriety. At this very time wby was revising *The King's Threshold* to make it more of a political satire, portraying the Mayor as a United Irish League politician muttering about grazing land, and making the poet express still more clearly the voice of individual artistic conscience.

However, when the theatre put on Synge's *Well of the Saints* in early February, the reaction was disappointing. According to Moore's recollection, it 'very nearly emptied the Abbey Theatre. We were but twenty in the stalls: the Yeats family, Sarah Purser, William Bailey, John Eglinton, AE, Longworth and dear Edward [Martyn], who supported the Abbey Theatre, though he was averse to peasant plays. All this sneering at Catholic practices is utterly distasteful to me, he said to me. I can hear the whining voice of the proselytiser through it all.'[19] wby admitted the audiences were thin, but claimed Moore was a champion of the play;[20] he subsequently defended Synge in a lecture to the Catholic College, where he was warmly applauded, and took a forward part in the discussions of national drama which galvanized Dublin's literary circles that spring.[21] The reaction of his old adversary Dowden to the new season was interesting. 'As far as the Gaelic movement cultivates a taste for what is good in Irish literature,' he wrote to Tynan,

it will surely help towards an appreciation of what is good in *all* literatures. As far as it is illiberal & inhospitable of [*sic*] what is good in other literatures, it is acting injuriously also towards Irish literature. The Irish National Theatre seems to me rather cosmopolitan in spirit. It might, for instance, deal with an Irish subject, but under the influence of Ibsen or Maeterlinck. But I think its influence at present is very limited.[22]

Ironically, WBY would probably have agreed.

On 25 March Gregory's *Kincora* opened – a historical play with 'decorative' sets which was well reviewed. Though audiences were well below capacity, it made a profit of £50. Gregory presided over a rather bizarre tea-party on the stage afterwards, enlivened by what Violet Martin described as WBY's '*very* high-class conversation'.[23] The Abbey was starting to generate its own traditions, shaped by Yeatsian theory and the relentless paternalism of Coole. Accordingly, it diverged more and more from the original ideals of those who wanted a co-operative nationalist society. Brigit O'Dempsey, who joined the company at this time aged eighteen, arrived at her audition in a star-struck state: to her WBY was 'a god', and his initial appearance impressed her deeply. However, as she remembered it, his constant 'posing' became an irritation – 'striding up & down a room, or in the stalls of a theatre, with an eye on the incoming audience, tossing back his dark forelock and handling a flapping butterfly tie, wearing his unconventional black jacket. All this nonsense was swift to destroy any admiration I may have had for the man, while my appreciation of his work increased.'[24] More particularly, she was struck by how his patience with neophytes alternated with 'insufferable rudeness' to actors who failed to understand his wishes: one of the gentlest members of the company was driven to saying, 'Mr Yeats if you speak *once* again like that, I'll knock you into the footlights.' O'Dempsey thought that if this had happened, no one would have pulled him out. 'However the knock-out blow did not occur for W. B. drifted off the stage moaning for Lady Gregory who waddled along and led him by the hand to have a cup of coffee.'[25]

Other enterprises were in train too. WBY was much involved in the negotiations between George Roberts, Joseph Hone and James Starkey which would finally produce an Irish publishing house: Maunsel & Co. His publisher Bullen was wooed as a backer, since WBY foresaw the importance of his own work having an Irish imprint: 'the one reproach against me in Ireland is – that

I write for the English market'. At the same time he wanted to eliminate Russell (he 'would get all the bad poems in Dublin printed'[26]), and replace Starkey with Stephen Gwynn. He succeeded in this; but Maunsel & Co. remained a small outfit, and wby's next major book (*Poems 1899–1905*) was published in England, while Dun Emer brought out the revised *Stories of Red Hanrahan* in mid-May (bravely printing 500 copies, though subscriptions were unenthusiastic). Russell felt accordingly ill-treated: 'I should trust my own judgement about the kind of books which would sell in Ireland more than Gwynn's and W.B.Y.'s.'[27] Meanwhile, the Abbey had a success with William Boyle's *The Building Fund* and Colum's *The Land* in April and June 1905, though wby felt that (like *Kincora*) these productions lacked the transforming genius of Synge's drama.[28] By early June he was able to look back on a season of twelve plays that had aroused considerable public interest and created a following (though in true Dublin style the *Irish Times* tended to review them without entering the theatre, since their drama critic confessed 'plays depress my spirits'[29]).

It remained true that wby's own work apparently consisted of rewritings and revisions. He returned to *On Baile's Strand*, refining the characters of Cuchulain and Conchobar, and pointing up the tension between heroic public style and private, personal fulfilment.[30] Defending himself to Holloway, he claimed that a new work could take a year to write, and that 'he was gaining new knowledge each day' in dramatic craft so could put the old works right in a few weeks. Though he felt his lyric capacities were now accomplished enough for his recent poetry to need no alteration, Dublin opinion speculated freely that his poetic inspiration had reached its end.[31] His reading, eclectic as ever, looked towards the cosmopolitanism advocated by Dowden: in May he bought forty volumes of Balzac from Bullen (a taste formed by his father's recounting stories like *La Peau de Chagrin* thirty years before), continued to preach Nietzsche, and discovered Ben Jonson's plays with delight. Most significantly of all, for his fortieth birthday in June, Gregory organized a present from a group of friends: William Morris's Kelmscott edition of Chaucer, costing £40. wby would spend the summer reading it at Coole and extolling its qualities of vitality, flexibility and 'masculinity'.

Perhaps because of this, he turned yet again to the eternally unsatisfactory *Shadowy Waters*. Its production, as he remarked to Quinn, was 'hardly suitable for more than about fifty people who know my work well':[32] but the Theosophical Society wanted to perform it during their London convention from 8 to 9 July, starring Florence Farr as Dectora. wby affected detachment, but he was separately involved in negotiations with Farr about playing Emer in Wilfrid Scawen Blunt's *Fand* (a poetic play which proved even more unactable than *The Shadowy Waters*). Farr's prompt-copy shows that he advised her closely, as well as providing programme notes for the performances.[33] When he returned to London in mid-June for rehearsals, their relationship took on a heightened intimacy; his letters to her at this point begin 'Dear Friend', and there was much anxious comparison of horoscopes, always a sign of erotic intensity. By the end of the production, however, his dictated letters were briskly addressed to 'Dear Mrs Emery'. Uncontrollable as ever, she may have responded to him romantically but resisted his staging-ideas, and his attempts to smuggle in Robert Gregory for the sets. And for WBY the whole enterprise was sabotaged by Robert Farquharson's epicene playing of Forgael – 'the most despicable object I ever set eyes on – effeminate, constantly emphatic . . . ridiculous with a kind of feeble feminine beauty. The very sign and image of everything I have grown to dispise in modern English character, and on the English stage. He is fitted for nothing but playing the heroine in Stephen Phillips' plays, a sort of wild excited earth-worm of a man, turning and twisting out of sheer weakness of character'.[34] To Symons, he railed further against Farquharson's effeminacy: 'for the first time in my life I shuddered as I suppose the ordinary man shudders at everybody & everything that is called decadent'.[35]

This extreme revulsion may be connected with his determination to pursue 'masculinity' in his reading, and in his own work; more prosaically, it was also a reaction of jealousy against Farr's leading man, with whom she sustained one of her ironic flirtations. Either way, it helped propel him into yet another bout of rewriting. When he returned to Coole the summer of 1905 was devoted to *The Shadowy Waters*, largely reconstructed by mid-September. While the original impetus came from his interest in stagecraft, in the process he had learnt much about poetry: he now saw it had to 'come out of the fundamental action', not from some vague notion of beauty.[36] By late October Gregory was inviting actors to attend a reading,[37] and the rewritten play would be put on in the Abbey in December.

The summer at Coole was energetic, with even Gregory worn out by self-invited guests such as WBY's aristocratic admirers, the Countess of Cromartie and Lady Margaret Sackville, and left speechless by Horniman's demanding visit. And while he worked on *The Shadowy Waters* WBY was simultaneously preparing a *coup* in the theatre itself. As early as May he had confided to Blunt 'we believe that the company very shortly will have to become a regular paid company, and this will give us much more time for rehearsal'.[38] To Synge and other intimates, he pressed the argument that the whole future of the theatre (especially looking to English tours) depended upon professionalization. His letters to Gregory aggressively advocated this course as the only way to eradicate the malcontents, and assert the directors' full authority. On 12 June Horniman was primed to send him a formal letter offering to guarantee salaries: thus her continuing power was assured.[39] The strategy was described in terms of 'freeing' the actors to commit themselves to the theatre full time: but it was inevitable that some of them would see it as instituting a form of servitude rather than liberation.

The matter was doubly sensitive because the arrangements whereby the co-operative society would become a salaried company were handed over to Russell, who had resigned from the INTS in April 1904; and during 1905 he had become still further estranged from WBY. There had been the matter of Maunsel & Co., where WBY had argued against his involvement. There was the controversy over Lane's projected gallery, where Russell believed that WBY's influence had been thrown against his nomination as curator. And there was the MacBride separation case, where WBY had conflicted with Russell and Ella Young over their desire to arrange arbitration between the warring couple.[40] When Gregory and WBY asked Russell to draft a new constitution for the Abbey, he obeyed: under the new arrangement the Irish National Theatre Society would be comprised of authors and other nominees; the actors would cease to be Society members and give up their votes; and there would be a paid secretary and book-keeper. Crucially, real power would be vested in an executive committee of three, to be kept separate from the Reading Committee. As WBY later wrote to Quinn, it was putting 'an end to democracy in the theatre'.

Although Russell drafted the form of the new arrangement, he was determined to sever all links with the Abbey when it was completed. 'Remember', he told WBY, 'that this dramatic society started among these people who came together & invited you in as President and you will see the thing in their point of view.'[41] He himself, punch-drunk from years of conflict with WBY, became increasingly disenchanted as he worked on the new rules throughout August; even the tone of his letters to Gregory changed. He was tired of 'continual rows & appeals to me to intervene'. For his own part, WBY was acutely conscious of the need to keep up ecumenical appearances, retaining vital token Catholics and nationalists like Colum: 'I dont want good taste to be suspected of a theological origin.'[42] Russell stressed that the business and acting sides of the theatre should be kept apart; Fay's tyrannical propensities should be restricted to the sphere of stage-management; absentees should have Society membership revoked. WBY must be on the three-person executive committee, 'not because you are a good business man but you would act on it as conveying to the other two the general policy & they would keep you to hard facts about money & business'.[43] Inevitably, the triumvirate that emerged was Gregory, Synge and WBY.

Accordingly, the actors' independent status was gradually whittled away. Russell had wanted those who did not accept salaries to remain full members of the Society, but WBY argued against it: he worried about uncommitted and uneducated people filling up vacancies, and argued for candidates like Robert Gregory instead. As for the business committee, despite Russell's views about his friend's commercial inability, WBY wanted to be a member of a small group: Starkey, Gwynn, Keohler and himself. By mid-September Russell was at the end of his tether. 'I dont care,' he wrote to WBY at Coole. 'I am only suggesting rules for the future work of a society I shall have no further part in and it is for you to consider whether you want the rules to be practical or not . . . Why the devil do you talk of the new rules as a compromise? What do you want. If you want anything else why don't you say so at once . . . Who on earth is there to oppose you? Can the general members carry on the Society without you or Synge or Lady Gregory?'[44] In their final exchanges, bitterness was unconcealed.

By now WBY had his head, but Gregory was less certain. She worried that the new arrangements would tie them into a framework inherited from the old Society, making the triumvirate committee responsible for aspects they could not control. More covertly, she worried about the continuing importance of Horniman, whom she now loathed. But a meeting at Coole from 16 to 17 September with Synge committed her to the plan; and on 20 September the idea of a limited liability company publicly emerged. On 22 September the momentous general meeting 'ending democracy' took place. WBY's speech denied they had become a commercial company, praised the devoted service of the actors, and detailed the personal investment in the company made by Quinn, Gregory and himself:[45] had the 'present directors' really adopted a commercial approach, he claimed, there would be a huge deficit because of paying them commensurately. The money earned by the old Irish National Dramatic Society had sustained the Fays' efforts, and been returned many times over. What was not stressed publicly was the backing from Horniman which made the new step possible. As WBY told Gregory privately, she had offered 'enough money to run the company & give us full power . . . her money will be given as a personal matter which will she says free her from the responsability for our acts which she would feel, if she was herself a shareholder.'[46] As to joining the directors herself, she rather pathetically told WBY, 'You have had experience of me on one society is not that enough.' She had played along with his strategy and enabled him to emerge holding all the cards he needed. He tried to convince Gregory that Horniman had been 'angelic' ('I think she must have been ill at Coole'), and deserved to be humoured ('her nerves seem to be all right, she is merely weak, but one never knows').[47] He allowed her to draft the programme for forthcoming London performances, which caused predictable difficulties. For public purposes, however, Horniman's contribution was played down, and WBY's own assertion of authority correspondingly emphasized. In the long run Gregory's misgivings about Horniman's behaviour would prove better founded than WBY's reassurances.

All this infuriated Russell, who later recorded his view of the theatre's history in a letter to Gregory:

The facts are the society was not started by Yeats but by the actors, that I drew up the rules and that I had considerable difficulty in inducing the members to elect him as president. These members subscribed a certain sum every week for some time towards the use of a hall. No doubt Yeats was the best known member but the plays produced by Colum, Ryan myself & others and contributions made by persons like Miss Purser and other friends were entitled to be considered when deciding whether the sum belonging to the society at the time about £90 I think should be allocated altogether to those who remained with Yeats as being solely created by them. The members opposed to Yeats were as you may remember in a majority and it was important to him to get them to resign and as I recognised his right to control the theatre which Miss Horniman gave him I took a great deal of trouble in arguing & persuading those members opposed to Yeats to go. They felt aggrieved that a society for which they worked hard & which they conceived would be run best on democratic lines should be captured by one person but I induced them to promise to resign on terms which if not absolutely just were at least reasonable considering everything . . . It is very unfortunate that Yeats should arouse such savage enmities among people who long ago had every inclination to serve him and it would do him no good to have this matter made public.[48]

But he had long accepted that he had been out-manoeuvred, and was by now completely alienated from WBY. 'He would wreck anything he is concerned with,' he told Gregory,

by his utter incompetence to understand the feelings or character of anybody he is dealing with. With you or Synge *anyone* might arrange a compromise but if W.B.Y. is to act as diplomatist then I see nothing for it but a row & publicity of the whole business – and it will certainly do neither W.B.Y. or the drama any good. Pack W.B.Y. off to London, Coole or America & settle the matter yourself or let Synge do it if you cannot stay on. Every time I meet W.B.Y. I feel inclined to throw him out of the window when he talks business. He has no talent for anything but writing and literature or literary discussions. Outside that he should be fined every time he opens his mouth. If I was autocrat of Ireland, I would give him twenty thousand a year if at the end of a year he had written two hundred lines of poetry – if he opened his mind [*sic*; for 'mouth'] on business or tried to run any society I would have him locked up as dangerous to public peace.[49]

From late October WBY was safely 'packed off' to London, but he left festering discontent behind him, and continued to take the high line which Russell and his friends found so offensive. 'I simply don't know what your friends want,'

he wrote to Colum in November. 'I made an offer to them at a general meet-
ing which might have been a basis for discussion. They said nothing at all.
I asked if they had anything to suggest. Dead silence. I asked if they had any
complaints. Dead silence. Life cannot stand still & we have gone on with
our work.'[50]

He was in particularly ebullient form; John Masefield, dining at Woburn
Buildings, found his host 'very well and merry & wore a black velvet coat
that must have cost pounds'.[51] (He also straightfacedly advised Masefield to
abandon poetry in favour of singing ballads in music-halls.) Furthermore, what
had brought WBY back to Britain was a very successful Abbey tour to London,
Oxford and Cambridge at the end of November, accompanied by a series of
lectures given by WBY himself on Irish drama. Though there was some resent-
ment among the players at the prices charged for the distinctly up-market
venues, and at Horniman's increasingly assertive role, the glamour of an
English tour, which would make a clear profit of £150,[52] helped sweeten the
bitter pill swallowed in September.

But the realities of the *coup* were more and more obvious. Horniman, less
angelic by the day, now wanted voting powers commensurate with her invest-
ment. And the position of a limited liability company under the Friendly
and Industrial Societies Act gave WBY, Gregory and Synge a hundred shares
each, while the actors each possessed only one. More and more, the malcon-
tents felt fettered rather than 'freed'. Politics simmered below the surface.
WBY's dislike of the IRB Dungannon Clubs distanced him further from the
more Fenian-minded members of the company. He was also suspicious of
the Gaelic League, which was moving away from the non-partisan, unpolit-
ical stance advocated by Hyde; certain branches were becoming, in effect,
IRB recruiting cells. However, he remained acutely conscious of the need to
keep some kind of nationalist profile. The composer Herbert Hughes began
'drifting into violent politics of the United Irishman sort', through his mem-
bership of the Dungannon Clubs; WBY, who early on identified 'the clubs'
as inimical to his kind of theatre, saw at once that such associations 'would
be rather a help to us than otherwise' so long as the music was right.[53] He
also remained preoccupied by Colum's importance for the Abbey's credib-
ility, encouraging Horniman to write him soothing letters. But by Decem-
ber 1905, when WBY returned to Dublin, resentment boiled over. Maire nic
Shiubhlaigh caused a crisis by endlessly procrastinating about signing the
new contract, and arguing about her salary. WBY's strategy of offering her the
additional post of wardrobe-mistress backfired badly at Christmas, with nic
Shiubhlaigh furiously rejecting it as a menial task. He lost his temper with
her; she fled to sanctuary with Lily and Lolly at Churchtown; Gregory sent
long letters to Lolly, 'taking no notice at all of the attacks on you [WBY] but

trying to show her what a perfect idiot Maire has been';[54] WBY sent 'a deliberately bloodcurdling letter to my sisters, in hopes that it may get round'.[55] JBY, who took the actors' side, gleefully reported everything to Rosa Butt. According to him, Lolly 'always sees Willie's meddling behind Lady Gregory', and Lolly stoutly said as much to Gregory herself:

[nic Shiubhlaigh] finds just as Lily and I (and even Papa feels) that it is quite useless trying to talk reason to Willie, who can never see any side of anything but his own & who if at all opposed at once becomes overbearing and rude. I know – we all know – this from our own experience . . . I wish you had been in Dublin & then I don't really think there would have been all this upset for everyone. I do not think it was so much what Maire was asked to agree to, as all the various offensive things said. I know Willie came out here & wasted his & my & Maire's afternoon to no purpose. His manner was sneery & offensive & Maire would discuss nothing. Willie kept on telling her that she was 'a beginner' & had much to learn & so on, & at the same time spoke the whole time of Mr Fay & Miss Allgood & the others as if they were finished actors & actresses . . . I know what harm he would have done here if he could have baulked us in our own work. He does not understand practical life. Since he was a small boy he was always too easily led to make a good leader himself & instead of learning to control a naturally disagreeable temper, of late years he has indulged himself in fits of temper. I have indeed heard Miss Horniman speak of his bad temper as if it were a feather in his cap. Just as stupid people would speak of a child of two, showing self will by kicking & screaming for what he wanted.[56]

But 'bad temper' was by now an inseparable part of WBY's managerial armoury. He continually told Gregory and Synge that one of the directors, at least, must be seen to 'have an awful temper' ('I shall have to be very delicately managed, you understand'[57]). Driven by a rather artificially sustained outrage, he continued to plan strategy for seizing control of the business committee and to proclaim his intention to sue nic Shiubhlaigh (often in letters dictated to Horniman). He backed down only when Gregory and Synge categorically refused to support him, and finally admitted privately to Gregory that he had been too hasty.[58] 'I am rather tired of acting as drag on his impetuosity,' wrote Gregory to Synge, 'but am comforted by the thought that it means vigorous health.'[59]

None the less, the upheavals of New Year 1906 did much to cement together the three directors. The solidarity of class as well as aesthetic priorities was implicit in many of WBY's arguments, and Gregory at least was not deaf to it. This helped precipitate a general walk-out in early January, when several key players deserted the company. They included George Roberts, Maire Garvey, James Starkey, Helen Laird and Frank Walker; Gregory heard they 'had struck because we were "not national enough, did not have six-penny seats or [?] longer plays by Irish authors"'.[60] On 5 January Willie Fay reported 'from the front' to WBY in London, telling him that the seceders were secretly rehearsing Colum's play *The Land*, intending to perform it as 'The Irish National Theatre Society'. Colum was also being seduced; Fay was already wondering about legal action.[61] From London WBY used Horniman to try and win back Colum; from Scotland (after discovering the weakness of the directors' position under the terms of the patent) he wrote mollifying letters on his own account, assuring Colum that he had 'in a spirit of perfect aimability been playing at tiger', but he lost the argument. The seceders were eventually compensated with £50 and some costumes, and left – in the course of time to start a theatre company of their own.

Horniman was once more enlisted to send a supportive letter to WBY, Synge and Gregory as directors of the new limited liability company. 'I highly approve of this, for I have spent so much time and money on my side I consider it to be fair that every precaution should be taken by the members towards carrying out the objects as announced by you.' The gift of the theatre was, momentously, transferred to the limited liability company. 'Those members who have not followed you have completely ignored me & so I have no reason to believe that they wish for any further help in any way. They have never formally protested to me against your new plans & so under whichever name they may choose to call themselves, I can have nothing to do with them.'[62] The seceders' tactic of trying to capture the name of 'Irish National Theatre Society' thus misfired: Gregory wrote to Synge on 12 January 'if we could bribe them to resign & start a new soc. – it wd be best – & I think not impossible'. This is essentially what happened.

But the Fays, crucially, stayed with the Abbey. Frank Fay was now a fully committed Yeatsian. In mid-January he sarcastically relayed to WBY Colum's criticism that the company ignored the popular voice of the country ('I asked him if he was ever introduced to the Popular Voice or would know him if he met him. No reply'[63]), and appealed to Gregory: 'I fear if some of the Directors don't come to my rescue I shall be found some morning knocking loudly on the door of the Richmond Asylum asking, What is Nationality? What is a Nationalist? And do two Nationalists make one Nationality? It's the straight road to lunacy trying to talk to these people.'[64] Colum, now fully alienated, wrote angrily to WBY disputing Gregory's statement that ' "the theatre was given to Mr Yeats to carry out his dramatic projects". This is disclaiming the notion that the Abbey Theatre is the theatre of a society aiming at the creation of a national drama. It is altogether a personal adventure.' This meant he had to resign in order to keep faith with 'the aims of the society to which we first belonged'.[65]

While WBY lectured in Scotland and visited Lady Cromartie, the Abbey rehearsed Boyle's *The Eloquent Dempsey*, which was put on later in January despite wby's hatred of its 'vulgarity' and Horniman's preference for Molière. Compromises evidently still had to be made, and he was prepared to woo Moran by telling him it was 'a *Leader* play'. Horniman (who calculatedly let wby know she had a further £25,000 earmarked for artistic purposes) had to be humoured: her antipathy to Irish nationalism was by now explicit, and vociferously articulated on every possible occasion. But in essential matters he had lost Russell, driven out the nationalist malcontents, kept the Fays, and retained executive power in the hands of the directorate. The *United Irishman* broadcast the cause of the disaffected. wby had 'absorbed for his own personal ends the disinterested work of a large number of people given on the undertaking that they were aiding in a work which was devoted primarily to the development of the highest interests of nationality in the country'.[66] Tempers had run high, and old antipathies resurfaced along with yet deeper tribal attitudes. Discussing Martyn's scruples, Gregory wrote to wby, 'Edward is a joy – and will give you new notes for your diary. These RC's haven't the courage of a mouse, and then wonder how it is we go ahead'.[67] Finally, at the annual general meeting in May, wby marshalled all forces (including his sisters) to vote out the dissidents. They included some of the best actors, such as nic Shiubhlaigh and Maire Garvey, the latter a particular *bête noire* of the Gregorys ('Robert thinks it was worth the whole row to have got rid of Miss G and that she embodies all that is most odious in Irish life'[68]). The seceders, forced into the position of Dudley Digges and Maire Quinn before them, formed the 'Theatre of Ireland', an explicitly nationalist company; nor would they be the last to leave. From January 1906 the Abbey was set on a different path, controlled by its triumvirate. Gregory reminded wby of a country saying: three yew trees planted in a row 'will wear out the world from its beginning to its latter end'.

III

The path had been cleared by wby's determination to assert himself. His comments to Russell are revealing, for their self-consciousness as much as for their actual content.

I desire the love of a very few people, my equals or my superiors. The love of the rest would be a bond and an intrusion. These others will in time come to know that I am fairly strong & a capable man & that I have gathered the strong & capable about me, and all who love work better than idle talk will support me. It is a long fight but that is the sport of it. The antagonism which is sometimes between you & me comes from the fact that though you are strong & capable yourself you gather the weak & not too capable about you, & that I feel they are a danger to all good work. It is I think because you desire love. Besides you have the religious genius to which all souls are equal. In all work except that of salvation that spirit is a hindrance.[69]

The ideas of 'masculinity' generated by his American triumph, his reading of Nietzsche, and the cataclysmic change in Gonne's circumstances dictated a new view of himself. Throughout the crisis in the theatre he had determinedly stressed his own belief in autonomy, his 'dangerous' qualities, his 'intolerable tongue', his 'delight in enemies': he pointedly told Gonne that he 'revelled in his unpopularity'.[70] His sense of self-presentation had always been acutely developed, but since America it had taken a new and more aggressive form. In early December 1905 he was already considering another American tour, involving performances from Farr and the Abbey players.[71] He remained secretly less certain than he claimed, admitting to Gregory that he often did not know why he acted decisively, and that he found it hard to recapitulate afterwards the circumstances which made him do so.[72] But his old, uncertain self would become more and more deeply buried beneath the armour of the quarrelsome, self-proclaiming public man.

His older friends fell back into the past as well. Despite their differences, the death of William Sharp in December came as a wrench; though he hardly mentioned the event in his correspondence, he wrote a moving letter to Sharp's widow.[73] 'Thousands will feal his loss with a curious personal regret.' He himself sensed that he had lost someone who, for all his ridiculousness, could communicate with a rare intimacy: 'a strange mystery & also a dear friend. To talk with him was to feal the presence of that mystery, he was very near always to the world where he now is & often seemed to me to deliver its messages. He often spoke to me of things of my personal life that were unknown to him by the common channels of sense.' Carefully choosing his words, he told Mrs Sharp 'that one, who was so often at [*recte* as] it seemed out of the body which he had, cannot have undergone any unrecognizable change or gone very far away'. Indeed, Sharp bequeathed him a posthumous message – 'I, and I only, am the author – in the *literal* and literary sense – of all written under the name of Fiona Macleod.' wby had known this for years, but he hardly cared. Their correspondence about symbolic colours, mystic correspondences, and the voices of fairies seems to have petered out after 1902. The immediate affairs of the theatre had claimed him, though a few years later he would write to Elizabeth Sharp regretting his inability to 'return to what are still to me the supreme interests'.[74] Dreamy Celticism was dissolving behind him. Not coincidentally, his reading through the summer of 1906 concentrated on Elizabethan drama. He had finished his selection from Spenser (an old love) and written an important introductory essay; now he immersed himself in Dekker and Jonson.[75] The taste for salt, and the idea of himself as a violent and combative leader of men, had taken over.

This new approach necessarily affected his volume *Poems 1899–1905*. Completing the draft introduction at Coole in July, he wrote of his dissatisfaction with the imitation of 'trivial and conventional' nationalist models in his early poems. 'Perhaps,' he concluded, 'one can explain in plays where one has so much more room than in songs & ballads, even those elaborate emotions that are oneself.'[76] Accordingly, he held up the *Poems* while he rewrote large sections of *On Baile's Strand* – to be mounted and restaged with full Yeatsian colour effects by Robert Gregory, at the Abbey on 16 April. He was also preparing a short lecture-tour to Liverpool and Leeds, aided and abetted by Farr, and living an ever-grander weekend-life at houses like Lady Cunard's, Lord Howard de Walden's, and the Horners' at Mells – though his own finances had returned to a perilous state, and by late March he was borrowing from Gregory again.[77] Further delays were imposed by his efforts to wrest back *The Wind Among the Reeds* from Elkin Mathews, since WBY was now possessed by the wish to bring all his works together under Bullen's imprint.[78] *Poems 1899–1905* eventually appeared in October 1906: by the end of the year they would sell 800 copies, 'the quickest sale I have had'.[79] As to the summer at Coole, he prepared himself for yet another bout of rewriting. Probably with an eye to directing his energies elsewhere, Gregory suggested he return to the becalmed craft of *The Speckled Bird*, refloating it as 'a sort of framework for opinions, a setting for ideas, sermons and conversations' like *Marius the Epicurean* or *Wilhelm Meister*.[80] WBY dubiously assented, but thought it more likely that he would complete it as planned, publish it as a novel about 'Michael's mystical life, and then start another book about his literary life; it will become a kind of spiritual autobiography'.[81] But the world reflected in his unfinished novel belonged to his youth, and it stayed behind him. None the less, Gregory's idea of a prose setting for brief 'sermons' appealed, and probably inspired his idea of 'getting rid of my opinions by every afternoon for half an hour (say) dictating to you a certain number of detached paragraphs if you can make time – I have a great many odds and ends to say.' The literary form of connected *pensées* would prove particularly well suited to his eclectic intelligence, forever preoccupied with the pattern of things. By late June he had accumulated about 12,000 words for a 'Book of Impressions', offered to Bullen but not, in the event, published as such. Bullen saw the potential of these concentrated reflections, and serialized them in the *Gentleman's Magazine*, which he edited; later they would appear from Cuala under the title *Discoveries*.

WBY was in Dublin for the revised *On Baile's Strand* at the Abbey in mid-April; later performances in Irish provincial towns were planned but came to little. Undaunted, he thought the performance of his play and Gregory's adaptation of Molière's *Médecin malgré lui* 'have shown our people at their very best'. At last his verse plays seemed to be receiving the handling they deserved.[82] Meanwhile, the Abbey players prepared for British performances in Manchester, Liverpool and Leeds in late April, where their success led to a long tour in the north of England and Scotland from late May to mid-July. Claiming her reward for backing WBY's recent *coup*, Horniman acted as promoter, using contacts in Theosophical and society circles. The company made a particular impression in Leeds, where Golden Dawn contacts may have clinched the booking, and the free-thinking circle around Alfred Orage and the Leeds Arts Club also prepared the ground. Farr was much involved, writing for the *New Age* and giving psaltery recitals. Audiences were small and they lost £50, but the inspiration of the drama helped confirm Orage in his Nietzschean mission; he launched himself on the London world as a result.[83] The Irish avant-garde seemed to be conquering provincial England.

For all the dynamic effect of his players, WBY struck one observer in Leeds as 'a ghostly wraith' who avoided contact with people. He had good reason. He was distracted by Gonne's affairs, with the MacBride libel hearing fixed for early June and the divorce case coming on in July: he suggested visiting her in Paris during April, encouraged by Gregory (who sent him £10 for the purpose[84]). But he threw himself instead into rehearsing the players, often to their incomprehension ('Well, Mr Yeats says I've got it: what it is I've got, I couldn't for the life of me tell you; but I hope to God I don't lose it'[85]). Another actor, complimented by WBY on the emotional intensity with which he declaimed the names of old Irish heroes, replied, 'Sure I thought they were mountains.'[86] There were always minor problems to do with the theatre (a draughty skylight, wigs to be collected in London, disobedient smoking backstage), and Horniman's determination to design 'artistic' costumes remained a sore trial. But after the late April performances in England, WBY was convinced they were on the right track. 'Deliberate effort' and professional commitment were creating a great acting school. 'If we can get enough of an audience here to keep our players and our playrights busy with the expression of Irish life,' he told Quinn, 'we shall make a great movement in the end even if it turn out that we get out best welcome in your country or in England.'[87] As this implicitly admitted, audiences were still a problem. On first nights WBY could be seen looking through the curtain and counting the audience, under the impression he was invisible.[88] The withdrawal of Colum and his friends 'has set the little gossipy barren group who look upon themselves as the official supporters of everything Irish of an intellectual sort, mewing after us'.[89] Still, he had by now committed himself fully to the Irish theatrical enterprise. 'I have made a general rule by confining work

to Ireland for the present & also of never making myself nominally respons-
ible when I cannot give the time to work at a thing properly,' he told Sturge
Moore. 'My Irish work gets every day more exciting.'[90] An out-of-town
engagement in Dundalk on 15 May was only fairly successful; WBY breezily
told Synge, 'The country towns in Ireland are mainly animal, but can some-
times be intoxicated into a state of humanity by some religious or polit-
ical propagandist body, the only kind of intellectual excitement they have got
used to.'[91]

Further extending its ambitions, the company launched itself on Scot-
land for its major tour from 26 May. WBY's ideas for the programme had
been eclectic: 'comedy must make the ship sail, but the ship must have other
things in the cargo'. They played, therefore, *Riders to the Sea*, *Cathleen ni
Houlihan*, *The Pot of Broth*, *The Shadow of the Glen*, *Hyacinth Halvey*, *Spread-
ing the News* and Boyle's *The Building Fund*, the last being the only play not
written by one of the directors. The programme stressed the authenticity of
style and sets, with 'unique fac-similes' of original properties taken from
Aran cottages: a young islander had been imported to check all dress details.
Reviews ranged from respectful to highly favourable; the *Manchester Guardian*
(already a patron of Synge's work) hailed *Riders to the Sea* as a classic in the
making.[92] As they progressed into Scotland, they were met with unqualified
praise. Frank Fay thought that the Irish avant-garde 'appealed to the Scottish
brains', and WBY's contacts like Lady Cromartie and the artist Phoebe Anna
Traquair provided strong support.

But within the company trouble was yet again brewing. Horniman had
seen much of WBY in London during the spring, and her mood was swing-
ing towards manic excitement. More and more determined to take an active
part, she decided to travel with the players, and their uninhibited behavi-
our jarred with her every preconception and preoccupation. Away from
Dublin the company felt liberated. They were young, and they were fêted.
They came from a class which the socially conscious Horniman viewed with
ill-concealed suspicion. And, released from everyday work, romance was
blooming; on this tour Willie Fay's relationship with the much younger
Brigit O'Dempsey (whom he later married) became evident, as did Synge's
love for another girlish actress, Molly Allgood.

All of this was anathema to Horniman. Any question of sexual impro-
priety upset her; the social differences which she conceived to exist between
herself and the players became an obsession. Synge reported to Gregory
about Horniman's interference, over-sensitivity and obtuseness, while
Horniman logged obsessive complaints about Fay's book-keeping, in-
efficiency and 'vulgarity'.[93] Her letters descended on WBY in an avalanche,
alternately angry, cajoling and bitterly flirtatious ('you really might at any rate

pretend that my return to London would be convenient to you'⁹⁴). The fact that the tour, while a critical success, actually lost money (just under £200) was thus a doubly sensitive point. WBY was summoned to Edinburgh to settle arguments. He ended by taking Horniman's side, writing to Gregory in defence of her attack on the company's indiscipline, while implicitly admitting that his support was part of the Faustian bargain upon which the theatre's fortunes rested.⁹⁵

Mephistopheles-like, even before the tour ended, Horniman was implacably trying to renegotiate the financial provisions once more. On 4 July she offered a subsidy of £60 a year and gave the directors the right to fix prices of seats – and thus the freedom to open the theatre to a broader audience, as Gregory had long wanted. But WBY was uncertain about lessening Horniman's commitment to the Abbey. The £25,000 still glittered, and even if Horniman was reserving it (as she hinted) for an English National Theatre, he wanted such a theatre to 'grow out of our work and take its tradition from us'.⁹⁶ As the provincial tours showed, cultural imperialism could be reversed with a vengeance. However, their benefactor also wanted to impose limitations on the Abbey about touring. She had decided the management as it stood was not competent, telling WBY that in six months she had spent £1,070, nearly half her annual income, and stressing that Fay must be stripped of his business role.⁹⁷ By early August, at her insistence, a business manager was engaged: W. A. Henderson from the National Literary Society, 'a nervous, quiet creature' still shocked by *The Countess Cathleen*, according to Synge, while WBY remarked that he 'sucked up vulgarity like a sponge'.⁹⁸ His evasions about agreeing terms were masterfully dealt with by WBY, and the company was still more tightly brought under the directors' control. They now possessed, according to Horniman, 'Home Rule and a subsidy'.

More ominously, Willie Fay was given cause for resentment. Furious with Fay's happy-go-lucky attitude and obsessed with the belief that George Moore had spread scurrilous allegations about her, Horniman thought she had now handed all powers over to the directors and taken a back seat. 'You have often blamed me for taking things to heart & being too much in earnest – being middle-class in fact,' she wrote sadly to WBY.

But if I had been otherwise I could never have held out for so long. Everything was made as hard & unpleasant as possible in ways that to you seemed to be of no importance & I am *thankful* to feel that it is over. I hope that it will be a long, long time before I am obliged to go to Dublin again, to be snubbed & affronted by snarlers and sulkers & always feeling the insult of being forced into George Moore's presence. You imaginative people are like mirrors, all passes away from you happily, you don't take any permanent impressions like the unemotional people who care & feel seriously. I'm not writing at all crossly, but you must believe me.⁹⁹

By the summer of 1906 WBY was involved in other controversies as well, including the by now annual row with his sisters and Dun Emer, this time over a projected second volume of Russell's poems. Lolly knew it would be a commercial success in Ireland but WBY vetoed it, taking his usual high line. An exchange of bruising letters aligned him against Jack and Lily as well as Lolly and JBY.[100] In mid-August he actually resigned as their literary adviser, and had to negotiate his way back by briefing Katharine Tynan to ask for him as editor of her own proposed volume. He played on their ancient friendship, confiding that his dream of an Irish theatre might have originated in the days when he visited her father's farmhouse, and took shape in the early 1890s. 'You will remember my old battles in Dublin,' he reminded her, 'and you will understand that this is vital to me, vital to keep a series that is associated with my name, if it were nothing else, from drifting into the amateurish Dublin way.'[101] Tynan, for all her dislike of the Abbey and resentment of the Gregory circle, agreed. But while her brother was still estranged, Lolly poured out her rage against WBY in a long letter to Bullen.

He felt himself of immense importance before and your letter made him worse . . . My father and brother Jack (who has just come from Coole) are also very anxious for me not to agree at once (if at all) to Willie's proposals – as they say that the only result would be I would be bound to do everything he liked, but he would not be bound at all. The whole thing began by his quarrell [sic] with AE so he writes these kind of brow beating letters at intervals to me. I have had much more disagreeable letters from him than this one – but the others annoyed me so much that I burnt them . . . He has quarrelled with all his friends in Ireland (but Lady Gregory and the little mutual admiration society down there).

She added bitterly that in financial terms 'he does nothing at all *for his family & never has*', while demanding excessive royalties for his work and forcing Robert Gregory's designs on them ('he thinks or thinks that he thinks so much of them that he speaks as if he was in a Cathedral when he speaks of them').[102] Her suspicions would have been confirmed if she had seen Gregory's careful presentation of WBY's case to Quinn. 'It is a real grief to him, he took a pride in the Press and would have made a great success of it . . . But his sisters think Russell popular and prefer trusting to him.' Gregory privately hoped that the press would fail altogether and be taken over by 'some capitalist'; Lily and Lolly 'have taken the Dublin craze for inefficiency as opposed to efficiency and it makes their brother fight the harder'.[103]

By mid-November he had indeed fought his way back on board, though the press was determined to limit his authority ('don't have WB on top whatever you do', Lily warned her sister, comparing his attitude to that of the British government during the Boer War[104]). Lolly, asking Quinn to look at the terms of the agreement, insisted on keeping some control 'over my own press. I don't want Robert Gregory's masterpieces. And I do want the editor to have the books ready for me at the time I fix.' In the end Russell, the inevitable broker, drew up brief terms, binding WBY to work as editor within designated schedules, and leaving the choice of authors to mutual agreement. WBY 'signed it like a lamb' and went on to edit Tynan's book with a dictatorial hand, in one case taking the first and last verses of a poem only.[105] Gratitude for her tactical help was not allowed to interfere with editorial ruthlessness.

SARSFIELD STAFFOLD
GORTSHOW·Sept 25th 1906

14. Robert Gregory performing epic feats on 'Sarsfield' at the Gort Show, 25 September 1906, sketched by Jack Yeats – an episode which entered local mythology and would be built by WBY into his elegy many years later.

By December 1906 he was at loggerheads with Lolly once more, over her reluctance to pay sufficient royalties – a traditional difficulty for author–publisher relations.[106] But he was equally determined to keep the standards up, and to prevent Dun Emer from sinking to 'the sort of thing you may see coming out in the Tower Press and read in the *Celtic Christmas*' (in other words, the work of Russell's derivative disciples). He saw the disagreement over the Dun Emer list as part of a general struggle against Russell-style amateurism, low standards and uncommitted work, affecting the theatre too.[107] For all JBY's pleading, this mattered more than keeping the family peace. And WBY's relationship with his family, as with the world in general, had settled into a new mould since America and the Abbey wars. His father now wrote carefully constructed and rather respectful letters to him, and even his sisters, for all their resentment, recognized his inevitable dominance. Only Jack, secure in his emotional and artistic resources, went his own way unaffected.

IV

Not even the Abbey directorate were exempt from the tension inseparable from WBY's relationships. Both Synge and Gregory were extending their range as playwrights and promising new developments in comedy and drama for the theatre; meanwhile WBY struggled with *Deirdre* and endlessly redrafted *On Baile's Strand* and *The Shadowy Waters*. But no verse plays had been included in the 1906 tour, and by mid-August WBY was writing to Synge in terms of ill-concealed threat.

You and Lady Gregory and Boyle can look forward to good performances of your plays from the present Company and from people who will join it in the natural course of things. I am getting them, of course, for my prose plays. But I am essentially not a prose writer. At this moment in spite of Frank Fay's exquisite speaking I could get a much better performance in England of a play like *Deirdre* . . . With a proportion of say one romantic or verse play to every three peasant plays, and that one play passionately played, we shall sweep the country and make enough money to make ourselves independent of Miss Horniman. We have also to think of playing several weeks in London each year. The alternative to this is the giving of my plays to English companies, for if I am to be any use ever in Ireland I must get good performances. Till I get that I shall be looked on as an amateur.[108]

This was part of his campaign to make a big splash with *Deirdre* by putting a celebrated tragedienne in the role. Mrs Patrick Campbell would star in London and Florence Laetitia Darragh in Dublin; the latter would have to be brought over from England. WBY always claimed Darragh as Irish, and 'a great tragic actress' to boot: she had performed Wilde's *Salome* with Farr, and was an established figure on the London stage. Though Ricketts admired her, Darragh's personality was problematic. Even Ricketts admitted frankly that his own liking for her might be no recommendation, since he generally 'disliked all women'.[109] But she had aspired to run a theatrical company of her own, she was a friend of Horniman's, and she would, WBY calculated, play a part in linking the Abbey to a nascent English National Theatre and to Horniman's £25,000.[110] She also kept WBY informed about Horniman's fluctuating moods, and the state of the weather regarding future financial support for the theatre.[111]

But in Gregory's view Darragh had designs on the Abbey and wanted to infiltrate it with her friends from the English theatrical world. Her style filled Gregory with foreboding; Willie Fay resented dictation about casting;

PLATE 17

Augusta Gregory, *c.* 1912.

PLATE 18

PLATE 19

Above: George Moore leaves Coole, probably
5 October 1902, while WBY, rather proprietorially,
stays on.

Facing, above: Edward Martyn's house, Tillyra
Castle, recently built when WBY stayed there in 1896
but undeniably impressive for all its brand-new
castellation and 'mechanical decoration'.

Facing, below: Lady Gregory's Coole Park around
the same time – a total contrast. Its Georgian plain-
ness was relieved only by the Diocletian window in
the façade (and two Victorian bows added to the
garden front), but the great glory of the demesne
lay in the rare trees, walled garden, and ancient
surrounding woods.

PLATE 20

PLATE 21

ve: Maud Gonne's entrance
Cathleen ni Houlihan, 1902.

ht: Riders to the Sea, 1906,
acme of naturalistic Abbey
e (but still preserving the
h Literary Theatre stare').
m left to right: Honor
elle (Helen Laird), Sara
good and Emma Vernon
ra Esposito).

ng, clockwise from top left:

ert Gregory, June 1902, the
before he left Oxford and
t to study art at the Slade.

garet Gregory in 1909, two
s after their marriage, with
hard.

lie Fay.

k Fay as Cuchulain in *On
e's Strand*, 1904.

PLATE 22

Above: Annie Horniman's costumes for *The King's Threshold*, 1903. She thanked WBY for giving her the right to call herself 'artist', but he said they made the cast look like 'Father Christmases and fire extinguishers'.

Right: Charles Ricketts's designs for a 1914 revival of the same play could not have been more different, and were far closer to WBY's imagination; as were the Ricketts costumes for the Blind Man and the Fool in *On Baile's Strand*, 1915, illustrated here.

PLATE 23

Above: The foyer of the Abbey Theatre, drawn by Raymond McGrath.

Left: The Abbey stage.

PLATE 24

Above: The Abbey Theatre in an embroidery by Lily Yeats, much as she described it to JBY in a letter of 30 October 1910: 'Motors carriages and cabs in a string outside – Willy has won his fight – a hard fight.'

Facing, above: Maud Gonne MacBride, John MacBride, their son Seaghan (later Seán), and assorted firearms, featured in the *Tatler*, February 1904, as 'Three Irish Irreconcilables in Paris'.

PLATE 25

Above: John Quinn at the time WBY first knew him.

Left: WBY arrives in New York, 11 November 1903.

PLATE 26

Printing at Dun Emer, 1903. From left to right: Esther Ryan correcting proofs; Beatrice Cassidy at the ink-roller; Lolly Yeats at the press.

PLATE 27

Above: JBY in the St. Stephen's Green studio, 1906.

Left: WBY as seen by Augustus John, 1907. 'One looks a gypsy, grown old in wickedness and hardship.'

PLATE 28

Above: Ruth Pollexfen's wedding, St Columba's College Chapel, 20 July 1911: Jack Yeats, 'Cottie' Yeats and wby, while Sara Allgood kneels in homage to the poet (and his new clothes, designed by Hugh Lane).

Facing, above left: Ezra Pound, probably at Stone Cottage, *c.* 1913.

Facing, above right: George Hyde-Lees, *c.* 1910, aged about eighteen. Dorothy Shakespear told Pound in 1911 'Georgie's face is square: but she is very handsome, I think, as well. She is awfully intelligent.'

Facing, below: A postcard photograph of Stone Cottage sent by wby to Pound.

PLATE 29

PLATE 30

PLATE 31

Above, left: A spirit photograph of wby, perhaps taken at Mme Juliette Bisson's; she specialized in these, but they were discovered to be faked from illustrations in *Le Miroir*.

Above, right: 'Julia's Bureau', the psychic communications centre set up by W. K. Stead at Cambridge House, Wimbledon.

Right: Etta Wriedt, the celebrated American medium often consulted by wby, through whom 'Leo Africanus' announced himself.

Facing: Rabindranath Tagore.

PLATE 32

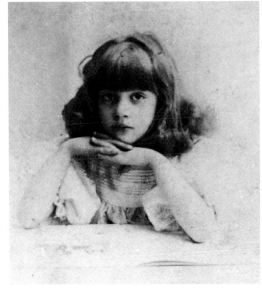

Above: Iseult Gonne photographed by Reutlinger of Paris, *c.* 1906. *Right*: Maud Gonne photographed by Reutlinger at the same time.

Below: WBY photographed by Lena Connell, *c.* 1910.

and Frank Fay reacted violently to WBY's idea of her replacing Sara Allgood as Dectora in *The Shadowy Waters*. Through the summer of 1906 WBY continued to argue that while the company could handle 'peasant work' perfectly well, they needed larger, tragic pieces, with acting on a commensurate scale. Drafting the contents of a new occasional magazine on *Samhain* lines, to be called the *Arrow*, gave him a forum for these ideas[112] and an announcement made at an Abbey 'At Home' and concert on 13 October was aimed at a wider audience than those present. He stated 'they had decided deliberately to take up, first, Irish legendary and historical plays, just as our national theatre had to do ... In a few years they hoped to place upon the stage plays that would represent a higher phase of life, in which may be found something truly characteristic of Ireland'; but the winter would be devoted to training actors for historical and romantic work. Thus the public was prepared for Gregory's *The Canavans* and his own *Deirdre*.[113]

As he juggled the programme for the 1906/7 season (which would prove a turning-point for WBY's theatre), preoccupied by the need for special lighting effects in *The Shadowy Waters* and arguing for the place of verse drama, the company were rehearsing for the winter season. Horniman, fresh from Bayreuth and laden with gifts for WBY, continued to deluge her Irish client with letters: 'I'll try and find you a cigarette-case in Prague or Dresden worth losing ... I'm a scratchy sort of cat, but that's good for your sort sometimes.'[114] Darragh condescendingly came to Dublin to star in WBY's *Deirdre* and *The Shadowy Waters* and the playwright haunted the rehearsals, at his most intense.[115] *Deirdre* had been written with great difficulty (the manuscript amounts to a thousand pages) and it showed. He had begun working on it two years before, as part of a planned heroic cycle; by 1906 it had been refined (in line with his own changing priorities) to an emblematic story of passionate love subverting the codes of medieval courtly society. Darragh fitted his idea of an Irish Isolde, but her performance on 24 November displeased the Dublin critics (and everybody else except WBY). Within the highly charged atmosphere of the company, her propensity for repeating unpleasant remarks and her Duse-like airs of grandeur created furious resentment. Frank Fay believed her ascendancy was the result of WBY's ignorance about acting, which meant he judged performances according to some arcane idea of 'distinction'; Gregory, more concretely, decided to force his eyes open by telling him that Darragh had boasted he was infatuated with her. But during this stormy autumn his feelings were fully engaged elsewhere. For Gonne chose this time to reappear in Dublin life. When she visited the Abbey on 20 October, accompanied by WBY, some of MacBride's supporters in the audience hissed her. She paused deliberately and glared back at them with a fine contempt, but it was a painful moment. This, as nothing else could, helped crystallize his antagonism to the narrow-minded nationalism of 'the clubs'; it also put him in the public position of Gonne's escort and protector.

The frenzy of rehearsal, argument and rewriting over, WBY might have been able to collect his thoughts but for a constant stream of complaints and threats from Horniman. Still seething from the effects of the summer tour and obsessed by enmity to Willie Fay, she was now incensed by Gonne's return to centre-stage. Driven beyond endurance, she unwisely told WBY that 'Mrs MacBride deserved what she got' when she visited the theatre. But for the moment he had to accept even this scourging. The reasons appear in WBY's long memorandum to the Irish National Theatre Society, dictated to an increasingly doubtful Gregory on 2 December 1906 and not, for the moment, widely circulated.[116] It was inspired by the mixed success of his verse drama, Darragh's failure in Dublin and the prospects for popular theatre at the Abbey; over all hung the prospect of the end of Horniman's subsidy in four years' time. WBY's strategy was thus aimed at ensuring further investment from Horniman, even at the price of alienating the Fays. According to WBY's argument, Boyle and Gregory alone drew audiences. The theatre 'could not run indefinitely on peasant comedy'. The actors it had lost through secessions had – he now admitted – been among the best. The Abbey must widen its capacities by performing 'foreign masterpieces' and importing foreign stars 'as opportunity offers'. The theatre, as he had dreamt of it, 'must if it is to do the educational work of a National Theatre be prepared to perform even if others can perform them better representative plays of all great schools', and be eventually supported in this by a national endowment.[117] WBY argued therefore that new capital must be sought, to buy in 'efficient teachers' who would broaden the Abbey's range while preserving and protecting their specialities of Irish comedy and Yeatsian verse plays. Thus he explicitly criticized Willie Fay's limitations, called for a new star who could handle 'romance and tragedy', and a new post of 'paid managing Director to correlate all [the Theatre's] activities'.

But at the same time he admitted that Horniman would probably not pay for all this. ('I can see William Fay's face as he reads this sentence. It will brighten like the face of a certain old Fenian when Mrs MacBride's Italian revolutionist [Cipriani] wound up a detailed project for a rising in Connacht with the sentence "I see no chance of success before this course."') What should be done immediately was to restrict Willie Fay's role to acting and producing comedy: 'the business side of the theatre and the non-artistic side of the stage work must be put into other hands'. Behind this lay WBY's conviction that his own verse plays were not served well by the Fays, that Farr should be brought over from London to teach elocution, and that an actress like Darragh must be enlisted to play tragedy. As if this were not enough, the memorandum criticized Frank Fay's lack of passion in speaking, claiming that his performance were actually disimproving. Moreover, 'from the first day of the Theatre I have known that it is almost impossible for us to find a passionate woman actress in Catholic Ireland . . . I must therefore have the right to bring in a player or players from without when I can do so without burdening the finances of the Company more than my work is worth. To do this it will be necessary that he or she sometimes play in other work than mine.'

This could only be read as an attack on Willie Fay's authority, with Horniman behind it. The manifesto loftily ignored the thoughtful arguments about the theatre's direction addressed to him by Frank Fay since the summer, and it clearly presented WBY's wish to impose Darragh on the company. Here, he stood alone because Gregory found her style particularly repellent. Where WBY interpreted 'passion', Gregory saw 'something mean, ignoble & sensual, something never seen in any play of yours over here'.[118] On 29 December she wrote him a long and worried letter from Coole, unhappy at the prospect of Fay's humiliation, arguing against importing either Darragh or Farr, and 'fretting at ever having to go against you'. She sent him money to buy a new travelling-rug at the Army & Navy Stores ('I haven't given you anything "worthwhile" for a long time except annoyance, obstinacy, exasperation & thin skin') and ended with a moving tribute: 'I was thinking last night how much you have done for me. Without you I shd be a useful helper of Agricultural Organizations, a writer of the rank of Stephen Gwynn (at best). You gave me faith in myself (following faith in you) and you have done much (very much) towards making these years past very full & very happy ones.'[119] The elegiac note reflected more than a sense of the year's ending: WBY's proposals had precipitated a serious crisis. As so often, he was caught between strong-minded women. Though his benefactress objected to the idea of involving Farr because of her 'carelessness' (not to mention her enduring attractiveness to WBY), Horniman was aware of WBY's controversial proposals which in essence repeated a brief memorandum of her own.[120] From the outset she, after all, would guarantee the new Managing Director's salary, and she insisted Fay give up executive authority and all control over the 'international masterpieces' which she longed for the Abbey to produce: thus Dublin would rival Bayreuth. Though Synge pointed out to Gregory that Fay had 'in reality built up the company', this was accepted neither by Horniman nor by WBY.[121] Through late December he worked on Synge and Gregory to agree; Horniman, it now transpired, was prepared to pay the large sum of £500 a year for 'a thoroughly good man',[122] but she continually evoked 'the principles of *Samhain* 1904' – in WBY's words – like 'the books of the Early Fathers'.[123] To WBY it was all unpleasantly like the Golden Dawn struggles precipitated by Farr, whose careless temperament and Fay's were 'very similar'.[124] As before, he was in the position of mediating between the benefactor's stipulations and his colleagues' doubts, assuring them that he had done his best to protect Fay's interests against Horniman's opposition. 'When I am talking to you and to Lady Gregory I put Fay's limitations (when I have a point to carry),' he told Synge, 'but I assure you I put even more strongly his genius when talking to Miss Horniman.'[125] By early January, however, his letters about Fay were almost as extreme as Horniman's. As a final blandishment, a non-acting Executive Manager would liberate all the directors from time-consuming organization and correspondence: 'Many and many a time we have had to go to the typewriter the first thing after breakfast with the result that our imaginations were exhausted before we got to our play-writing.'

In the end, after much cliff-hanging and many threats of resignation the other directors tentatively agreed to consider the proposals. They continually passed back and forth to each other the unpalatable task of telling Fay, who reacted with predictable anger. Relations within the company were set for another storm. Gregory's agonized explanation of her position to Synge did little to help relations:

I would not for a moment think of accepting this 'fancy man' but that I think Yeats wants a new excitement, a new impetus, or will tire of the theatre, and I feel myself very much bound to him, besides personal friendship, because we are the only survivors of the beginning of the movement. I think his work more important than any other (you must not be offended at this) and I think it our chief distinction. I think on the other hand it will suffer rather than gain by the new element, but he must have experiments, and it would be a very great pity if he had to go to England for them ... I dont think any compromise is possible with Miss Horniman but that wouldnt matter if we could arrive at an understanding with Yeats.[126]

Synge's relationship with WBY was soured not only by Gregory's tactless comment, but also by Synge's stout defence of Fay (who excelled at his plays) against WBY (who resented Fay's inability to handle Yeatsian themes). 'I am annoyed with Synge's assumption that I am doing all this for the sake of my own plays,' WBY told Gregory – adding waspishly 'he judges us by himself'.[127]

From London in early January 1907 WBY fired off angry letters to Gregory, snowed in at Coole, and to Horniman, sunning herself at Tunis; but a thunderbolt struck when Gregory learnt that WBY had promised Horniman the rights to his plays after the current patent expired in 1910.[128] Gregory felt that the whole structure was cracking around her. Their joint authorship, and the suppressed emotion in her own feelings towards WBY, lie behind an outburst in early January:

You will have given Miss Horniman one of our strongest possessions or weapons. She can take your plays from Ireland altogether or force you to put them into some movement opposd [*sic*] to your views. You will have betrayed those who have been working for you. You will yourself be in a humiliating position, seeing your friends and comrades dictated to and not being able to [to] take their side.

Synge and I have a right to protest because we were never told of this supposed bargain at the same time we accepted the subsidy. I certainly should not have done so at that price ... I am taking it to heart very much – Those plays were our own children, I was so proud of them, & loved them, & now I cannot think of them without the greatest pain ... If you agree with me you might perhaps send a line, for I am wretched.[129]

Gonne had once referred to his love-poems as their joint children; but Gregory's sense of possession was even more heartfelt. In WBY's complicated and highly charged friendships with women, his genius for collaborative work created bonds of union which replaced more conventional kinds of attachment, which is why Gregory's plea comes nearer to a declaration of love than any other letter in their vast correspondence. It also served a tactical purpose: WBY hastily clarified that no 'promise' of his plays had ever been given to Horniman, whose own recollection was that she had asked to be allowed produce the plays if the INTS collapsed. On 11 January Gregory, Synge and Fay finally agreed to appoint a new Managing Director, with certain conditions (and a salary rise of £100 for Fay).[130] The arrangement so uneasily put in place would last only six months.

Once again the company had come through a potentially bitter struggle, and WBY had imposed his will on his colleagues. To compensate, he even admitted Darragh's shortcomings to Gregory, and amity seemed restored. (He also confronted the actress with her reported comments about him, receiving, unsurprisingly, 'passionate denials'[131]). But the desire for 'new excitement' discerned by Gregory was about to be met from a different quarter. The impetus came from Synge at his most saturnine. He firmly opposed WBY's wish to import any 'foreign masterpieces' other than those few which illuminated the Abbey's own work, and, though 'nearly in distraction' with the play he had been gestating for months, by 13 November it had been read (by Fay) to Synge's fellow-directors.[132] By the time of the directors' arguments over theatrical policy during Christmas 1906, it was well advanced in rehearsal. *The Playboy of the Western World* forcibly altered WBY's view of the Abbey Theatre's needs. Both his artistic judgement and his intellectual honesty left him in no doubt that this was not only Synge's masterpiece, but a masterpiece of a new sort. While perfectly adapted to the Abbey style of acting, it far transcended 'peasant plays', providing exactly the kind of wild poetry which WBY's own verse drama strove for, and which the Abbey desired above all to produce. In a circular of 'advice to playwrights who are sending plays to the Abbey', wby had laid down that

a play to be suitable for performance at the Abbey should contain some criticism of life founded on the experience or personal observation of the writer, or some vision of life, of Irish life by preference, important from its beauty or from some excellence of style; and this intellectual quality is not more necessary to tragedy than to the gayest comedy. We do not desire propagandist plays, nor plays written mainly to serve some obvious moral purpose: for art seldom concerns itself with those interests or opinions that can be defended by argument, but with realities of emotion and character that become self-evident when made vivid to the imagination.[133]

Synge's tale of a pretend parricide and the passions he arouses among the women of a sardonically observed Western village was mocking, eloquent and heroic, turn by bewildering turn. wby saw that this kind of play could answer the needs of the theatre; it could also answer the critics who thought the Abbey, having lost Colum and his associates, was already growing stunted. At the height of the row over secession, in a National Literary Society debate about 'The Irish Peasantry and the Stage', Tom Kettle had put the case against wby's drama more subtly than most of his opponents:

He was afraid Mr W. B. Yeats had constructed his own views of Irish life. Mr Yeats had done more than anybody else to create an Irish Theatre, and he had also done more than anybody else to prevent anybody going there [laughter]. He thought the fundamental mistake into which Mr Yeats had fallen was that he had mistaken life for literature. Inside the seas of Ireland there were roughly two millions of Irish peasants; and amongst these they would find every virtue and every vice. And if any-body called up a type to which everybody must conform under pain of blasphemy against the national idea then he (Mr Kettle) did not think anybody could profess to understand him.[134]

Through the brilliant kaleidoscope of the *Playboy*, the Abbey Theatre would confront this criticism, and present Irish life at its most authentic when at its strangest. wby was ready to seize the tide. His own plays had on many levels been less than satisfactory. But by 1907 he had learnt much. The confidence discovered in America had been put to good purpose in dealing with Gonne's marriage crisis, in reorganizing the Abbey, and in construct-ing his latest canon for *Poems 1899–1905*. He had discovered too that both poetic and dramatic inspiration could be rooted in the fundamental realities of life expressed through 'common idiom'.[135] And Synge's play would now give him this very issue to defend in public, with the combative powers he was learning to wield so well.

Chapter 14 : SYNGE AND THE IRELAND OF HIS TIME 1907–1909

> We are beginning once again to ask what a man is, and to be
> content to wait a little before we go on to that further question:
> what is a good Irishman?
>
> WBY at the *Playboy* debate, 4 February 1907

I

BY the beginning of 1907 the Abbey Theatre was in the throes of recon-struction. WBY was in search of a new Managing Director with a business mind rather than an artistic temperament. Englishmen were allowed to apply, and J. E. Vedrenne of the Court duly found them the youthful Ben Iden Payne ('a vegetarian . . . Bernard Shaw says that vegetables are wonderful for the temper'[1]). Gregory remained worried about the experiment, and want-ed Willie Fay placated by a less arrogant approach: 'I feel sure you should talk to him as you would to me (only with more of the harp-strings in your voice)'.[2] WBY's relations with Synge, while less high-handed, remained slight-ly uneasy: Synge begged him not to bring the new man over until the *Playboy* had been got through, and WBY resented the implication that Payne had been imposed for the sake of Yeatsian verse drama.[3] But it was true that he expect-ed the new Managing Director to extend the range to 'classical and roman-tic work', with Fay restricted to Irish dialect plays, and his letter to Payne made this absolutely clear.[4] Moreover, Horniman had convinced WBY by telling him the new man would 'help his plays to worthy representation': it was 'an effort made by me on your behalf and that of your work'.[5] Gregory was no less anxious to protect WBY's drama, arguing strongly that *The Pot of Broth* should not appear as a curtain-raiser for the *Playboy*, since that would be 'an injustice to Yeats'. 'I know you don't consider your own plays enough,' she chided him, 'and you have never looked like a tiger with its cub as Synge did last night with the Playboy.'[6]

Thus by mid-January the reception of Synge's forthcoming play was already an issue. Should 'objectionable sentences' be excised? Should the directors 'make a sort of a compact with *The Peasant*' in advance? Nervous as they were, the directors hung on grimly, but embarked on some judicious pre-production censorship. The violence of Pegeen, the frustrated heroine, was toned down, though she never became the 'decent likeable country girl' Fay begged for. Though they ignored pleas to remove the threatening torture scene in the last act, Gregory and WBY cut out some of the 'bad language'.[7] Almost fortuitously, the *Playboy* arrived at the climax of WBY's campaign of baiting pious nationalism represented by Griffith's new organization Sinn Féin; and, immediately following Horniman's attempted seduction, it also provided the ideal opportunity to reassure Gregory of his real commitment to the Dublin theatre. He seized the chance with both hands. When the play opened the puritanical Holloway (who had been excluded from rehearsals and smelt a rat) set the tone by denouncing 'Synge the evil genius of the Abbey Theatre and Yeats his able lieutenant'.[8]

The play opened on Saturday, 26 January, with gallery and pit well filled but the stalls sparsely attended. The first two acts were received quietly, but (according to contemporary notes scrawled by Sara Allgood) catcalls began when the hero attacked his father – well before the celebrated uproar at Christy Mahon's invocation of Mayo girls arrayed in their 'shifts'. Cries of 'God save Ireland' alternated with 'Where is the author? Bring him out and we will deal with him' and – significantly – 'Sinn Féin for ever'.[9] WBY was in Scotland at the time, trying to improve his precarious finances with a lecture-tour. His dazzled host in Aberdeen, Professor Herbert Grierson, remembered his arrival much as Hazlitt recalled Coleridge's – 'he began to talk and so far as I know has continued to do so ever since' – and was struck by the fact that his visitor launched straight into the importance of Sinn Féin, the need for a coming fight with the Church, and the power of Synge's new play. Thus it cannot have been entirely unexpected when, after a triumphant lecture, the Grierson household was woken in the small hours by Gregory's famous telegram telling WBY of the riot and summoning him to the scene: 'Audience broke up in disorder at the word shift.'[10]

Arriving back in time for the second night, on Monday, 28 January, he noted that 'about forty men who sat in the middle of the pit succeeded in making the play completely inaudible': he rapidly identified them as Griffithites. On 29 January he gave the first of many controversial interviews. Sitting beside a more or less silent Synge, he cited the tradition of exaggeration in art and remarked that 'so far as he could see the people who formed the opposition had no books in their houses'. The commonplace and ignorant were attempting to exercise a dictatorship.[11] 'With the coming of Yeats,' W. P. Ryan remarked gloomily to Henderson, 'I knew that the trouble would be aggravated.'[12]

Already newspapers were calling for the play to be withdrawn. WBY was determined to run it for the intended seven nights, and for longer if it did not receive a hearing. On 29 January the police were summoned to the theatre. This was partly to deal with 'a Trinity College *claque*' led by a nephew of Gregory's, who drunkenly sang 'God Save the King' and was subsequently arrested for assaulting a policeman. Hugh Lane was also present, 'pointing out to the police members of the audience for ejection'. All was blamed on WBY, though he had little to do with either initiative, since Fay summoned the police in the first instance on the Monday night; none the less the *Independent* delightedly described WBY 'making his appearance at the head of a force of policemen'.[13] Disturbances continued throughout the week, reported at gleeful length in all the Irish papers. On several occasions WBY harangued the audience from the stage. There were several arrests and fines. By the end of the week he believed 'opinion had turned in our favour'; on 4 February he celebrated with a public debate in the theatre – an idea he had announced, to Synge's evident surprise, as soon as he returned.[14] This, together with his readiness to give newspaper interviews, proved his appetite for public confrontation. Gregory's line was that people who came to the theatre 'must take what is provided for them'; Synge's, equally characteristic, that he 'didn't care a rap'.[15] But for WBY the issue was one of artistic freedom and liberation from a censorship, not imposed by the Church but by dictatorial 'societies, clubs and leagues'[16] – in other words, by Griffith's Sinn Féiners.

Sinn Féin was the movement arising out of Cumann na nGaedheal, advancing from 1905 a nationalist programme stressing self-reliance in

15. Synge raptly watching a late rehearsal of the *Playboy* on 15 January 1907, caught by JBY: Gregory described him as looking 'like a tiger with its cub'.

The Amateur Chucker-Out.

16. *The Abbey Row*, a
speedily produced
Dublin pamphlet, im-
mortalized the actions
of the principals in the
Playboy controversy.
The elegant connois-
seur Hugh Lane, who
had allegedly 'pointed
out to the police mem-
bers of the audience for
ejection', appears as an
unlikely bouncer; WBY
is caught addressing
the audience from the
stage, in regulation
pince-nez and artistic
bow-tie; while Synge is
identified by his con-
temptuous dismissal of
public opinion.

"I Don't Care a Rap."

The Poet addressed the Audience.

culture, economics and politics, and preaching a robust line in Anglophobia without endorsing violent separatism; it bore strong similarities to contemporary continental right-wing nationalist organizations. Griffith, at the outset friendly towards both WBY and the theatre movement, had hardened into enmity since *The Shadow of the Glen* – an antipathy exacerbated by his support of MacBride in Gonne's separation case. To WBY and his friends, Sinn Féin's overtones of Catholic confessionalism and cultural chauvinism were ominous (even Quinn was reduced to incoherent rage by their 'vaporings'[17]). For the Sinn Féiners the *Playboy* came at exactly the point when the movement was organizing various groups into a 'League' on the basis of their 1905 programme. From their point of view the enterprise of Synge, WBY and Gregory represented the corruption and decadence of modern Ireland. The way the political issue was seized upon by Coole is reflected in a letter from Robert Gregory:

We have won a complete victory over the organised disturbers – Sinn Fein men to a great extent. It was quite necessary that someone should show fight and we are the only people who have done it. Judge Ross said to my mother last night 'You have earned the gratitude of the whole community – you are the only people who have had the pluck to stand up against this organised intimidation in Dublin.'[18]

This helps explain why feelings ran so high: the opposition was interpreted far more politically than in the days of Frank Hugh O'Donnell's and Cardinal Logue's attacks on *The Countess Cathleen*. The support of the Dublin Metropolitan Police was unfortunate, especially when they targeted people like Padraic Colum's innocent father as well as the zealot Piaras Béaslaí: and WBY was universally castigated for their intervention (as well as for not speaking Irish, and bearing 'a Saxon name').[19] But with the Church staying out of it, he could wrong-foot Sinn Féin by appropriating their language ('the country that condescends either to bully or to let itself be bullied soon ceases to have any fine qualities'[20]). Griffith's journal, which had for some time been booming the Theatre of Ireland at the Abbey's expense, contemptuously attacked the play as 'a vile and inhuman story told in the foulest language we have ever listened to from a public platform . . . the production of a moral degenerate, who has dishonoured the women of Ireland before all Europe'.[21] Other opponents included unexpected figures like Dr Sigerson and Alice Milligan, who attacked WBY for courting censorship in the interests of self-advertisement. Stephen Gwynn, while recognizing the play was not a 'social document', worried that it would effectively justify anti-Irish stereotypes.[22] Russell also abandoned them, publishing a satire on WBY and Synge in *Sinn Féin* and refusing to chair the public meeting of 4 February, choosing to appear

in the gallery instead. There was, however, a good deal of public support, espe-
cially in letters to the papers.[23]

The meeting of 4 February, considered unwise by Synge and 'dreadful' by
Gregory,[24] provided wby with his apotheosis. Majority feeling was clearly
against the play. Even those temperamentally sympathetic, like Francis
Sheehy-Skeffington and Francis Cruise-O'Brien, opposed the theatre man-
agement for having called in the police. Few defences of Synge were offered.
One came from a Kerry medical student (and friend of Joyce's), Daniel
Sheehan, who announced that the play was about 'sexual melancholia' and
spoke so frankly about rural frustrations that several ladies hurriedly left.
'Mr Synge had drawn attention to a particular form of marriage law which,
though not confined to Ireland, was very common in Ireland. It was with a
fine woman like Pegeen Mike and a túbercule Koch's disease man like Shaun
Keogh – and the point of view was not the murder at all, but when the artist
appears in Ireland who was not afraid of his life and his nature, the women
of Ireland would receive him.'[25] jby was at his most mischievous. After
announcing that 'in this country people cannot live or die behind curtains of
deceit', he guyed the notion of an isle of saints and scholars by slyly adding
'plaster saints' – a line readily seen as anti-Catholic, and featured in headlines
as 'Mr J. B. Yeats's Sneer'. ('Kill your father!' wby was advised by the audi-
ence.) Synge stayed away, ill at home, and determined to sustain the Olympian
stance he had taken since *In the Shadow of the Glen*. 'On the French stage you
get sex without its balancing elements: on [the] Irish stage you [get] the other
elements without sex. I restored sex and the people were so surprised they saw
the sex only.'[26] Gregory withdrew from public engagement too, probably influ-
enced by their recent disagreements over theatre management. Thus the
spotlight rested on wby, occupying the Abbey stage in evening dress.

He was determined to be confrontational, reminding the audience that
he had called in the police during *The Countess Cathleen* as well, but also
proclaiming his nationalist past. At that time, he remarked, he was 'Pres-
ident of the Wolfe Tone Commemoration Committee of Great Britain'
(laughter and applause); he also presented himself as 'the author of *Cathleen
ni Houlihan*'. This was rapidly immortalized. *Sinn Féin* responded with a
parody whose refrain ran 'They will be respectable for ever, The police will
protect them for ever', and the *Leader* raised this boast against wby for the
rest of its life. Moran described the riots as a reasonable response on behalf
of 'Ireland' for being libelled by wby and Synge – who then invoked the
police 'with a cry of "freedom of judgment"'. As it happened, constabulary
were always in attendance at the big Patent Theatres; but the ethos (and
supposed politics) of the Abbey made it different.[27] Gregory gave a jaundiced
version of the evening ('we had hardly anyone to speak on our side at all but

it didn't much matter for the disturbances were so great they wouldn't even let their own speakers be well heard'). But wBY's speech, carefully reprinted in the *Arrow*, crystallized his feelings about a confrontation which he welcomed in every way. The attack on the play was 'an annihilation of civil rights'; he contemptuously instanced a Liverpool priest who had withdrawn a play when the audience objected and – apparently speaking for the Abbey's Protestant directorate – added 'we have not such pliant bones, and did not learn in the houses that bred us a so suppliant knee'. ('"Oh", groans and hisses.') His peroration, addressed to the 'gentlemen of the little clubs and societies', threw down a challenge on behalf of the new generation, who 'wish again for individual sincerity, the eternal quest of truth, all that has been given up for so long that all might crouch upon the one roost and quack or cry in the one flock'.[28] Finally, even though he had not been the first to summon the police, he deliberately took the responsibility for this controversial action: it was 'right and manly to go to the full length' and charge people like Béaslaí. 'No-one would say he flinched from his fight.' And as an *envoi* he described – as Synge's alleged inspiration – that incident ten years ago, when he himself and Symons had stepped ashore at Inishmaan and been told that a man had killed his father and been sheltered by the community. This may have been irresistible, but it sabotaged the argument that the play's force depended on metaphor and exaggeration[29] (Irish country people did, apparently, admire murderers after all). He had never been so deliberately offensive to a Dublin audience.

wBY emerged from the confrontation convinced that the directors had won; the other side were quiescent, and his own curtain-call after *Cathleen ni Houlihan* on 9 February was taken as vindication. Audiences had increased; all that worried him was the threat to the Abbey's country tours and his own Irish American lecturing.[30] To Quinn, who had warned him about the outraged reaction from Devoy and other Clan na Gael stalwarts in the USA, he wrote, 'It has been for some time inevitable that the intellectual element here in Dublin should fall out with the more brainless patriotic force, and come into existence as a conscious Force by doing so.'[31] 'The mob' or 'the conventional public' constituted the enemy; and they were now identified with the Sinn Féin brand of nationalism, 'obscure members of the Gaelic League', inflamed by Griffith himself. To Farr, he speculated that Griffith's inveterate hostility arose from 'some fancied wrong in connection with Maud Gonne'.[32] But there were more than adequate ideological reasons as well.

From this point on wBY was preoccupied with 'opinion' and its disastrous effect upon art. The theme was addressed in a passage suppressed from *Discoveries*, and dominated the *Samhain* published in December 1908. It is unlikely that he yet saw matters with the bitter clarity recorded in his later

essay 'Synge and the Ireland of his Time': 'I stood there watching [the pro-
testers], knowing well that I saw the dissolution of a school of patriotism that
held sway over my youth.' But the fall-out of the explosion reached rural dis-
trict councils, who passed resolutions against the theatre, and led to formal
condemnations of Gregory from old enemies on the Board of Guardians at
Gort.[33] From other quarters too the controversy ignited long-standing resent-
ments: William Boyle, who had not seen the *Playboy*, none the less took the
occasion to vent an old animus against Horniman and WBY by withdrawing
his plays from the Abbey. Gregory was glad to see him go, but WBY correct-
ly anticipated that he would return in contrition.[34]

In some ways life apparently returned to normal with surprising ease. By
early February WBY was immured at Coole, once more revising *On Baile's
Strand*; within a month he felt capable of writing lyrics again, though there
would not be much evidence of this for another eighteen months.[35] He was
also excited by a new play, *The Piper*, submitted by Norreys Connell (Conal
O'Riordan) – grotesque and 'pretty dangerous'.[36] Back in Dublin, Synge
continued to nurture resentment against his fellow-directors for favouring
their own work; the advent of the new manager, Payne, did not improve his
humour, with the production of Blunt's troublesome *Fand* appearing 'a bas-
tard literary pantomime, put on with many of the usual tricks of the English
stage'. Invoking the 'Samhain principles', he threatened to walk out.[37] At this
dangerous point, the *Playboy* became controversial once more, this time in
connection with the company's English tour, planned for mid-May. Synge,
though he deliberately stayed out of all public controversy, bitterly resented
WBY's removal of his masterpiece from the programme for Glasgow and
Birmingham, for reasons of possible objections from 'slum Irish' as much as
from the Lord Chamberlain;[38] it certainly contradicted his public boasts
about the Abbey's readiness to confront censorship.[39] But it was pragmatic.
The players themselves were reluctant to put on the play in London, though
it eventually scored a considerable success.[40] And WBY continued to worry
about endangering the chances of an American tour, now a financial necess-
ity, as Horniman threatened to end her subsidy. He was meditating a
special introduction for the American edition of the *Playboy*, 'explaining
that the Play means that if Ireland goes on, loosing [*sic*] her strong men by
emigration at the present rate, and submitting her will to every kind of
political and religious dominion the young men will grow so tame that the
young girls will prefer any man of spirit, even though he has killed his father,
to any one of them'.[41]

Though the *Playboy* row ebbed away, it left behind an immovable deposit:
WBY's determination to separate art from political content, reiterated in pub-
lic over the next years with increasing frequency. He 'did not write Kathleen

ni Houlihan to make rebels'; 'in our theatre we have nothing to do with politics: they would only make our art insincere'; 'a literature freed from political objects is a Muse escaped from the pots and pans'.[42] 'Opinion' had joined 'rhetoric' in his personal devil's dictionary. If the Synge fracas had separated him from Russell's circle, it had also aligned him further than ever from the Griffithites – a process made easier by their espousal of John MacBride's case against Maud Gonne's. Symbolically, at this very point – mid-March 1907 – John O'Leary died. WBY, though in Ireland, did not attend his funeral: in Irish society, a notable and deliberate gesture. Later, he would explain this as a reflection of his contempt for the hangers-on who tried to associate themselves with the old man's nobility:

I shrank from seeing about his grave so many whose Nationalism was different from anything he had taught or that I could share. He belonged, as did his friend John F. Taylor, to the romantic conception of Irish Nationality on which Lionel Johnson and myself founded, so far as it was founded on anything but literature, our Art and our Irish criticism. Perhaps his spirit, if it can care for or see old friends now, will accept this apology for an absence that has troubled me.

But his own links with O'Leary had loosened, particularly since O'Leary's determined support of MacBride against Gonne; and WBY's invocation of Johnson is striking, because in both cases their actual friendship had lapsed well before death ended the connection, though it would later be brilliantly resuscitated for the purposes of autobiography.

II

Perhaps just as emblematic as his refusal to attend O'Leary's funeral was his decision to join Gregory and her son in Italy three weeks later: 'They've made Ireland too hot to hold them for the moment,' remarked Farr irreverently.[43] Oddly, little record is left of his first visit to a country, and a culture, which would inspire his imagination from this time on. WBY told his Scots friend, Grierson, that it was the latter's recommendation to read Edmund Gardner's work on Ferrara that sent him to Italy,[44] and Gregory concurred that he had 'set his heart' on seeing it. However, she was the impresario; she visited Venice every year, and seems to have made all the arrangements.

Gogarty later remarked that seeing Italy with her must have been like seeing it from inside a Black Maria;[45] a certain constraint may explain the lack of evidence about the expedition itself, or about WBY's immediate reactions. On 10 April he left London to join Gregory and her son for the journey south. They drove over the Appenines to Urbino, then down to Ravenna, Ferrara and eventually Venice, where she brought him to the Piazza San Marco and left him 'entranced by the rich colouring, the strange beauty of the joyous Venetian night'.[46] By 2 May he was at the Palace Hotel, Florence, still fretting about the low turn-out at the theatre, sending copy back for the *Arrow*, and receiving ranting letters from Horniman about arrangements for the Abbey's tour of England. After the initial aesthetic impact, it was not an entirely successful visit. WBY was struck down by colds and rheumatism, and spent his days sightseeing (the Baptistry, the Duomo), disapprovingly reading novels by D'Annunzio, and writing yearningly to an unreceptive Farr. Deprived of romantic responses, he attempted to woo her pragmatically: since his collected edition would retail at four guineas and large orders were coming in, 'you see I am worth being nice to, even to the extent of occasionally being written to'.[47] The party went on to Rimini, and then returned again via Ferrara to Ca Capello, San Paolo (Lady Layard's house), in Venice. WBY complained that 'I cannot be certain of anything, in this hurried life – going from place to place.'[48] Though they left prematurely on 22 May, summoned by the crisis over licensing the *Playboy* for performance in England, he does not seem to have been sorry.

But he had stored up a great treasure-trove of visual memories from the galleries, churches and towns of northern Italy. Not only would the architecture of Venice inspire suggestions for Abbey stage-sets; more profoundly, he formed his ideas about the reflection of civilization's development through painting, supplying images that resound through *Discoveries*. The artist's son began to react against the 1890s symbolism which had held him for so long. The progress of culture and ideas of beauty, from Titian (long familiar, but now for him the supreme master) down to the confusion of Post-Impressionism, would preoccupy him for years.[49] Just after his return he added a passage to *The Tables of the Law* recording 'Owen Aherne's' devotion to Sienese painting:

The pictures that I knew best, for they had hung there longest, whether reproductions or originals, were of the Sienese school, which he had studied for a long time, claiming that it alone of the schools of the world pictured not the world but what is revealed to saints in their dreams and visions. The Sienese alone among Italians, he would say, could not or would not represent the pride of life, the pleasure in swift movement or sustaining strength, or voluptuous flesh. They were so little interested in these things that there often seemed to be no human body at all under the robe of the saint, but they could represent by a bowed head, or uplifted face, man's reverence before Eternity as no others could, and they were at their happiest when mankind had dwindled to a little group silhouetted upon a golden abyss, as if they saw the world habitually from far off.[50]

Here too began his interest in Byzantine art, notably after visiting Ravenna. And above all his Italian journey conferred the inspirational notion of a great culture which had been sustained with patronage – an ideal of Renaissance courts, where the life of the mind was cultivated in miniature city-states on windy hills. One image of a poet's perfect life came to him outside Urbino, when the sight of a medieval tower reared up against a stormy sunset summoned up the vision of Ariosto's life dedicated to artistic perfection: the notion of the poet in his tower, long ago suggested by Milton and painted by Samuel Palmer, now took on a vibrant reality. Like much else about Italy, it would feed into the personalized imagery of his overwhelming imagination. Castiglione, the 'grammar school of courtesies', a life of artistic order and labour became central to his ideal. But the idea of artistic dedication usurping even adeptship, and a small, intensely cultivated audience replacing the wider world, had already been sown in the battles over the theatre just before the Italian journey. Both experiences predisposed him all the more to accepting Gregory's pronouncements *de haut en bas*. 'I have an open mind myself, & not the timidity created by logic,' she told him. 'Taste, like every other attribute of aristocracy, requires daring.'[51] This too was a lesson he would derive from his idea of Italy.

The journey there, however, had not restored him, and he returned to various crises sparked off by the Abbey's English tour. In the following weeks he reported 'a slight breakdown from overwork', and a month after their return he told Gregory, 'I feel that I have lost myself – my centre as it were, has shifted from its natural interests and that it will take me a long time finding myself again.'[52] While he was determined to shrug off external pressures and commitments, he was involved in yet another confrontation with Horniman. Angry at being left – as she saw it – to handle the Abbey's English tour, and annoyed at WBY's lengthy absence, she decided to transfer her energies and her money to a theatrical enterprise in Manchester, and to take Payne, the new Abbey manager, with her. WBY's last-ditch suggestion of starting a second company in Dublin, to play the kind of drama close to his heart and hers, was not enough to stop her.[53] But this was not all. Once again she asked WBY to allow his plays to be assigned to the new venture. Now, strengthened and counselled by Gregory, he refused outright, in a statement that was both honest and eloquent: it is, in its way, one of the best letters he ever wrote.

I have thought carefully over your proposal of yesterday and have decided that it is impossible as far as I am concerned. I am not young enough to change my nationality – it would really amount to that. Though I wish for a universal audience, in play-writing there is always an immediate audience also. If I am to try and find the immediate audience in England I would fail through lack of understanding on my part, perhaps through lack of sympathy. I understand my own race and in all my work, lyric or dramatic, I have thought of it. If the theatre fails I may or may not write plays – but I shall write for my own people – whether in love or hate of them matters little – probably I shall not know which it is. Nor can I make any permanent allocation of my plays while the Irish theatre may at any moment need my help. At any moment I may have to ask friends for funds with the whole mass of plays for a bait.[54]

From this point, knowing she had lost her prize, Horniman was finally disillusioned with the Abbey directors. She condemned Gregory, Synge and WBY not only as victims of the 'vampire Kathleen ni Houlihan', but as grasping and exploitative (thanks to an ill-received suggestion that she hand over the outstanding subsidy as a lump sum). Without her support, a financial crisis loomed. During the remaining two and a half years of the subsidy, the donor imposed more and more conditions, particularly regarding issues which she deemed 'political'. She also withdrew the extra salary granted to Willie Fay six months previously, which required painstaking explanations from WBY.[55] But Payne, after his brief administrative reign, had gone; he declared that as an Englishman his position had inevitably been a difficult one, though WBY added privately to Gregory that Fay had driven him away by persuading the other actors not to speak to him.[56] Henderson was given notice, and in the end Fay had to return as manager, to WBY's chagrin. 'I am the one who will suffer, as his little evasions and bits of temper exasperate me more than the rest of you,' he told Synge. 'I tried every kind of device in my imagination but none seemed possible.' They were, inevitably, headed for another crisis. 'The theatre is now a desperate enterprise, and we must take desperate measures.'[57]

His own work, as ever, provided both a resource and a refuge. Consolingly, Mrs Patrick Campbell was again expressing interest in producing *Deirdre* (though she wanted backing from Horniman)[58] and once settled at Coole in July WBY began to recast his plays for Bullen's projected collected edition. The changes he made reflected the difficulties of the past months: he took the 'conventional religiousness' out of *The Hour-Glass*,[59] and with Gregory reshaped *Where There is Nothing* into a new version, eventually called *The Unicorn from the Stars*. The hero's name was changed to 'Hearne', a literary descendant of the autobiographical protagonist in *The Speckled Bird*; the bizarre title concealed a reference from the Order of the Golden Dawn; while the setting was specifically eighteenth-century and dealt with millenarian ideas of rebellion against Britain. But even more strikingly, the theme of a visionary who owes his temporary status to the misapprehensions of a local community bore a marked resemblance to the *Playboy*.[60]

Staying on into the autumn, with occasional departures to Dublin and London,[61] Coole provided distractions too. Robert Gregory and his new fiancée, a fellow art student Margaret Parry, were 'fighting for mastery', and wby enjoyed the spectacle. 'Pretty, very clever, and with beautiful manners', Margaret at first impressed him: but she would with time become a committed enemy, absorbing and exacerbating her husband's resentment of his mother's semi-permanent guest. The autumn of 1907 at Coole was also enlivened by Augustus John, summoned by Gregory to produce a portrait of wby as a frontispiece for the planned collected edition of his works. John, not yet thirty, was already notorious: his vivid, innocent, libidinous bohemianism fascinated wby, though he had deep reservations about the sketches ('one looks a gipsy, grown old in wickedness and hardship'[62]). Much later he would decide John had divined 'an outlawed solitude' in him. John himself was equally amused by wby. 'He has a natural and sentimental prejudice in favour of the W. B. Yeats he and other people have been accustomed to see and imagine for so many years. He is now 44 [actually 42] and a robust, virile and humorous personality (while still the poet of course). I cannot see in him any definite resemblance to the youthful Shelley in a lace collar. To my mind he is far more interesting as he is.'[63] Everybody hated the sketches of wby, for different reasons: both wby and John knew that it was because they jarred with a public image that had fast become fixed into an icon.

Behind all this activity – the rewriting, the sitting to portraits, the frenzied communications to and from Bullen at Stratford through 1907 and 1908 – lay the project of the *Collected Works*. Since January 1907 discussions had been under way. As always with Bullen, expense was originally a difficulty, but money was eventually guaranteed by, of all people, Annie Horniman, an arrangement which made wby slightly uncomfortable.[64] Even as she detached herself from the theatre, she bound him to her by another golden thread. By February the project was clearly going ahead, and wby was wondering how to reclaim *The Wind Among the Reeds* from Elkin Mathews and *Poems 1899–1905* from Fisher Unwin; the latter brought in £35 a year, and the popular demand was for the kind of lyrics included in the former.[65]

Money was obviously a priority. wby's taxable earnings for 1907 were computed at £161. 2s. 13d., compared to £181. 19s. 10d. the previous year (and £207. 12s. 11d. in 1908). Though he still had some stocks from his American windfall, he was privately borrowing money from Horniman.[66] But what else led him to such a precocious step? He was certainly impelled by a developing sense of pattern and form in his work. Around this time he began to file rough papers, and to keep the drafts of a particular poem in the same manuscript book, so work can often be followed through from the first prose draft. He was also starting to accumulate *pensées* in large notebooks, some for publication. And he was possessed by the idea of correcting and revising the texts of his plays, probably to bring them into line with the priorities of the post-*Playboy* aesthetic, moving away from elaboration towards clarity of personal utterance.

The near daily letters fired off to Bullen through the summer preserve the intensity of his vision. 'I withdrew from active work in the Abbey Theatre with the purpose of devoting myself for a year to making a final text of all my works. But for this I would never have consented to a collected edition at this moment, as I believe that an edition containing so much that is immature or inexperienced as there is in my already published works would do me a very great injury.'[67] But here was the chance to repossess and reformulate his *œuvre* – to provide variant versions of *The Shadowy Waters*, to rewrite *Where There is Nothing*, to eliminate *The Pot of Broth* (Gregory's input into his dramatic work, vindictively revealed by Horniman to Bullen, had become a sensitive issue[68]), to print music with the plays ('it gets its meaning from the method of speaking and is a necessary record of that method. It is important to me that people whom I cannot personally teach and who may produce my work shall know my intention'[69]). He was particularly anxious that the popular early work should not eclipse his later experiments, recalling grimly how he had repositioned *The Wanderings of Oisin* at the end of his last collection to stop people saying 'it was such a pity Mr Yeats had fallen off so after writing it'.[70] *Deirdre* and *The King's Threshold* were emphatically defined as 'my most mature work' and therefore of especial importance in the canon.[71]

But Bullen, nightmarishly disorganized, had to be kept in order – sometimes by invoking Watt, more often by direct and reproachful letters. As far as the publisher was concerned, WBY was to get the order of poems right, to revise his texts, and if possible to extend the schedule in order to accommodate new work (two new plays and two new stories were envisaged during that creative summer at Coole). The complexity and variety of his early output left room for endless confusion. Bullen failed to understand why WBY rejected his own early criticism (such as the articles for the *Bookman*), and believed that 'practically nothing' of his prose before *Ideas of Good and Evil* was worth including, except the reflections on *Axël*.[72] For reasons not entirely aesthetic, WBY was also worried about the jumbling of material from *Samhain* into a projected section called – resonantly – 'Friends and Enemies'; he complained about 'fragments of letters reprinted from the United Irishman (just where mistakes are most likely & mistakes that might be very injurious to me for I have quarrelled with the paper & its party)'.[73] The collected edition was intended to declare a stage in his life when he had broken with several of the identifications and alliances which had marked his youth.

By the end of September copy had been sent for four suggested volumes – *The Celtic Twilight* and *Red Hanrahan*, *Ideas of Good and Evil*, *Poems* and *Verse Plays*. At least three further volumes were projected. The proof-stage would be an educational process for WBY, sparring with Bullen, who acidly pinpointed anomalies and, for instance, condescendingly advised the author to read Aristotle and Plato on 'magnificence' before generalizing about that quality in Spenser. (WBY snapped back: 'I know what Aristotle says & what is in the Decameron on that subject, but not Plato. I will look it up.'[74]) The question of self-presentation in frontispiece portraits was less easily resolved, and throughout the summer it was discussed, mediated and argued about by the women and patrons in his life. The Augustus John etching, completed in mid-December, seemed to WBY 'a translation of me into tinker language'; perhaps bearing Paul Ruttledge in mind, he rather admired it, but it was disliked by Gregory and utterly condemned by Horniman (which, given her financial input, effectively ruled it out[75]). WBY's idea had been to have 'Augustus John's melancholy desperado conducted by some four or five quite respectable persons' – in other words, for each volume to contain a different portrait, 'ballancing' John's image.[76] The old project of a Charles Shannon portrait was revived, while Gregory, resourceful as ever, lined up Sargent for a charcoal drawing, hoping Quinn would purchase it. (The finances were becoming complex: Bullen paid John £18 for the undesirable etching; Gregory paid Sargent £42 for a charcoal drawing, hoping to recoup from Quinn; Shannon agreed to do an oil for £100, one third of his normal rate, again expecting Quinn to buy the original[77].) WBY wrote a philosophical description of the odyssey to Quinn in January 1908:

I have had strange adventures in trying to get a suitable portrait. My father always sees me through a mist of domestic emotion, or so I think, and Mancini who has filled me with joy, has turned me into a sort of Italian bandit, or half bandit – half cafe king, certainly a joyous Latin, impudent, immoral, and reckless. Augustus John who has made a very fine thing of me has made me sheer tinker, drunken, unpleasant and disreputable, but full of wisdom, a melancholy English Bohemian, capable of everything, except of living joyously on the surface. I am going to put the lot one after the other, my father's emaciated portrait that was frontispiece for the 'tables of the law' beside Mancini's brazen image and Augustus John's tinker, to pluck the nose of Shannon's idealist, nobody will believe they are the same man, and I shall write an essay upon them and describe them as all the different personages that I have dreamt of being, but have never had the time for. I shall head it with this quotation; from the conversation of Wordsworth: – 'No, that is not Mr Wordsworth, the poet, that is Mr Wordsworth, the Chancellor of the Exchequer.'[78]

III

The autumn of 1907, however, was not entirely devoted to revision and organization of his work, for the Abbey was still in a critical state. Unwillingly, WBY found the company had to rely on the popular success of plays like George Fitzmaurice's *The Country Dressmaker*, a 'harsh, strong, ugly comedy' which he personally disliked. Financial pressure meant that there was little alternative, but WBY's own priorities were expressed in a rather high-flown letter to Florence Darragh – still kept waiting in the wings. The post-*Playboy* theatre, he wrote, must 'turn knowledge into instinct, and both alike into personality. I am feeling the same difficulty in my own work. I have got to the point now of having knowledge but if I cannot find an audience and players it must remain knowledge, and perhaps help others, by criticism, to more popular forms of creation. We can make something of ourselves always, but it is our age that decides whether it is to be our best or not.'[79] On the same day he wrote a more depressed letter to Sturge Moore about the lack of appreciation for his verse drama, but insisting on 'the dramatic poet's right to educate his audience as a musical composer does his'.[80] His sense of insecurity was well founded. Synge was simultaneously writing privately to Frank Fay that a WBY–Gregory theatre would be of no use to anybody, nervously adding that he should tear up the letter.[81]

In late October, however, WBY's faith was rewarded by a hugely encouraging bouquet. Mrs Patrick Campbell swept into Dublin, was honoured by a special matinée performance at the Abbey on 25 October, and announced from the stage that she would return a year later and perform *Deirdre* by 'my dear friend and your great poet'. WBY acidly noted that Dublin newspaper reports omitted the word 'great'; Horniman, demented by jealousy, warned him 'she admires your poetical powers & very likely she has taken a fancy to you too although you are much too old for a woman of forty who might well go in for someone young'.[82] (Though WBY and Mrs Campbell were exactly the same age, Horniman was proved right; she subsequently married George Cornwallis-West, ten years her junior.) At a late-night supper-party in Mrs Campbell's honour an unpleasant altercation developed with Casimir Markievicz over the terms on which the Theatre of Ireland had seceded.[83] But even these snide reactions could not mar the golden prospect. At last he would achieve popular acclaim with one of his verse plays – and broaden the theatre's reputation by presenting a major international star. The old mirage of attracting both a 'respectable' and a popular audience with one of his own plays came alluringly into view. Thus fortified, he could withstand even the utter flop of *The Unicorn from the Stars*. When it opened on 21 November, Frank Fay actually fell asleep on stage, and newspapers like the *Mail* could barely contain themselves. '"Where There Is Nothing, there is" – Mr Yeats. The whole thing is an essay, a sermon, a preaching, as someone said to me, "the gospel of lunacy" . . . The comments one heard and overheard were all in one key . . . A few days of it would kill the Abbey Theatre, and naturally.'[84] Buoyed up by Mrs Campbell, WBY took everything in his stride. 'You who love London will not understand me,' he wrote to Farr, 'but it is this narrow imbittered in many ways stupid town that touches my imagination. Elsewhere we become like other people, here perhaps because other people are rather disagreeable we remain ourselves.'[85]

Accordingly, he was becoming interested in the traditions of the caste and family background which he had been elaborately repudiating for twenty years. In early December he took Gregory to visit his Yeats aunts in Morehampton Road. JBY triumphantly reported the occasion:

Apparently they were both greatly impressed, finding something very satisfactory in a salon of old-world courtesy. Isaac was there, and two other Aunts. Willie, though he remembered their faces, did not know their names. This visit will perhaps soften their hearts as regards Willie. It is curious, but I find Willie with all his faults more lovable than Jack. The latter was too long in Sligo and so is full of ill will towards all his fellow creatures and suspicion and contempt. It is the way with commercial people. Willie thinks well of his fellow creatures except when he is fighting them, at any rate has a high opinion of human nature and believes it has a noble destiny. Jack of course sticks manfully to duty which makes him an admirable fellow citizen, but then it makes him a little cold and a little self complacent.[86]

Even the high-minded Yeatses, however, were realistic about their black-sheep brother. WBY subsequently told Gregory that Morehampton Road had not produced its greatest treasure, a silver cup presented to an ancestor in 1515. 'It should have been my father's but they were afraid he might pawn it.'[87]

But Dublin continued to send slings and arrows his way. The *Leader* in November attacked him for allegedly attending a 'God Save the King' dinner at the Corinthian Club, sitting between W. M. Murphy and a Castle ADC; Casimir Markievicz joyfully weighed in, gossiping widely about WBY's 'delight' at being asked to meet viceroyalty. Since Yeats family lore held that the Markievicz radicalism stemmed from the Count's being banned from Castle functions for 'rowdyism', WBY sent him an accordingly contemptuous rebuke,[88] while the *Leader* received a dignified letter explaining that he had attended under a misapprehension. He added carefully: 'I have long ceased to be an active politician, but that makes me the more anxious to follow with all loyalty the general principles defined by Mr Parnell and never renounced by any Nationalist party' – to ignore crown representatives 'until a sufficient National independence had made possible a new treaty'.[89]

Politics also lay behind rehearsals for the Abbey's next production, Norreys Connell's new allegorical play, *The Piper*. Fay hated it, and said so; Annie Horniman obligingly told Connell; WBY had to excuse Fay to Connell as 'really an excitable, hot-tempered, grown-up child, whose moods change with the weather, with the receipts of the last performance, with whatever other trivial accident moves him at the moment'.[90] On 4 December the directors convened a meeting about Fay, and decided to refuse him the right to re-engage players on his own authority; they further insisted on improved discipline and required 'that it be explained to the Company that this Theatre must go on as a theatre for intellectual drama, whatever unpopularity that may involve'. This was a clear victory for WBY, who was also infuriated at the new Managing Director, Ernest Vaughan, for choosing a touring programme without consultation. He succeeded in bringing up yet again his commitment to putting on more 'foreign' work – though his position was not helped by tactless encouragement from Horniman, declaring that the theatre was 'in the public eye an Irish toy'.

The company went off on tour to Scotland in early December, but a confrontation was obviously on the way. By 18 December WBY was writing tentatively to Gregory that Fay must be faced down. This was sensitive, since, as WBY knew, she depended on Fay for the successful playing of her own work. She turned against Fay only when he put on her Fenian play *The Gaol Gate* for performance in Galway without asking her – thus overbalancing the delicate equilibrium she sustained between her position as local great lady and nationalist playwright. Finally, she came out, sadly confiding to WBY that 'class distinctions' and 'Romanism' made even-handed dealings with Fay impossible.[91] Synge also fell in behind WBY for his own reasons, as Fay was pursuing a vendetta against Synge's fiancée, the young actress Molly Allgood. With actors like Allgood and J. M. Kerrigan up in arms against Fay, the directors could pose as arbiters rather than open enemies – much to WBY's relief. By Christmas Eve, he could outline his strategy to Gregory: 'I want the company & not the directors to shove him out if he is to go.'[92] Working through Synge, WBY painstakingly orchestrated the chorus of complaints emanating from the actors;[93] his long letters, anticipating difficulties and preparing positions, show that he had learnt much in the long-ago struggles over the Golden Dawn. The case was broadened out to influential people: Quinn was told that the recent poor season was the fault of Fay's insistence on more popular work, the players being 'all scared out of their wits by the "Playboy"', and consoled by the success of 'two rather unintellectual plays'. The brothers were clearly marked for the axe.

Throughout, a political agenda lurked in the wings. Horniman's dislike of Fay was certainly influential, but his ousting should be seen against the background of Gregory's worries about a nationalist programme in Galway, the enmity of Sinn Féin, the *Leader*'s attacks on WBY, and his own growing inclination towards the values of a cultural elite in Ireland. Synge, indeed, interpreted the struggle in terms of an Ascendancy problem of governance, warning his dictatorial colleague that 'coercion has never been a success in Ireland'.[94] Matters were also complicated by the worsening relationship with Horniman, to whom WBY had to pay a soothing visit in London in mid-

December. On 13 January 1908 Fay resigned, bringing with him his brother Frank, already discontented, and his wife, Brigit O'Dempsey.[95]

The directors evidently felt that the Fays had something of a case. A year before Synge had told WBY that Fay must be accommodated to a certain degree, 'as he has in reality built up the company'.[96] Public statements stressed that the parting was amicable. WBY lent them his rooms at Woburn Buildings when they left Dublin to seek their fortunes, and they were allowed to take *The Rising of the Moon* and *The Pot of Broth* for a projected season in the USA. Fay wrote to WBY in a friendly tone about these arrangements, offering whatever royalty was appropriate.[97] When the Fays took refuge with William Boyle in Camberwell, he gathered 'the quarrel was more between the other members of the Abbey Co. and Fay, than between the latter and the directors'.[98] This was just how WBY had wanted it to seem. But Fay's letters to Boyle and others made clear the extent of their bitterness. They were now *persona non grata* with the Yeats circle – an enmity that was compounded when the Fays, playing in New York later that spring, were billed as the 'National Theatre Company' (they were still members of the Irish National Theatre Society). They were thus seen as emissaries of the Abbey; the New York press even alleged that WBY was accompanying them. From this point it was open warfare, waged on the spot by John Quinn, while WBY implacably pursued the Fays and their promoter Charles Frohman, accusing them of bad faith and worse. He was only persuaded to withhold his most violent letters because of an unpropitious horoscope. 'I have never advertised myself in my life,' he told Quinn inaccurately, 'but I am always ready to advertise my cause, especially if one can do it by attacking where attack is a pure pleasure.'[99] In early March Frank Fay wrote bitterly to a friend:

We wanted plays that would bring the public in & free us from the ignominy of having to live always out of Miss Horniman's pocket, & we did not care whether such plays had parts that suited us or not. Had we consulted our ideas of what suited us or not, we would have appeared in very few of the Abbey plays. We aimed at & succeeded in getting ensemble. Both of us played many a rotten part. If the Abbey directors would engage a professional company, they'd hear the truth about many of their plays & that truth would surprise them.[100]

He claimed that only WBY and Gregory were allowed to veto plays. As for the American row, neither he nor his brother had wanted to be advertised as the Irish National Theatre Company, preferring to be known as 'The Irish Players', but had given in to Frohman's insistence. None the less, the Fays bore the brunt of the directors' wrath. On 13 March 'all 3 Fays' were suspended from the Irish National Theatre Society.

It was a sad ending to an association which had formed the basis of the great theatrical experiment. Without WBY, there would have been no Abbey, but without the Fays there would have been no Irish National Theatre Society. Both brothers blamed WBY for the rupture. Frank wrote bitterly that he was 'an impossible creature to head a theatre; his complete ignorance of acting is in itself sufficient to incapacitate him & his impish faculty for making mischief in a small place like Dublin is another reason'.[101] This was to forget the enthusiasm with which Fay had abandoned Griffith and enlisted behind WBY's banner of pure art – and to ignore the impetus of avant-garde production which WBY had brought to the theatre movement. But when Fay claimed that he 'helped put Yeats in the saddle', he had a point. Without WBY, in any case, the Fays' future was bleak; they inevitably joined up for a time with the earlier secessionist exiles Dudley Digges and Maire Quinn, but American tours did not follow, and they returned to comparative obscurity in Britain. Frank Fay, after small parts in touring companies, eventually went back to voice coaching. He remained savagely angry with WBY, Gregory and Synge, and reverted to attacking them on the Griffithite basis of their 'alien creed'.[102] What he really resented, however, was the way they monopolized the programme with their own plays, and the insensitivity with which they treated the lower ranks. By 1910 he was sounding out the Abbey about returning, but to no avail. There was no real contact for nearly twenty years, when WBY's remarks at Stockholm about the Fays' part in the early Abbey Theatre drew an angry response.[103] But by then, history belonged to him.

In January 1908 the immediate effect of vanquishing the Fays was a great boost to WBY's morale. He heard in the recently founded United Arts Club that 'Yeats-baiting' would now stop;[104] he faced down public criticism of the Abbey's choice of plays, issuing a foolhardy public challenge that he would put on any rejected play which was subsequently recommended by 'three Dublin men of letters';[105] he appointed Kerrigan in charge of voice production and handed over stage-management to Sara Allgood (with mixed results), while he declared his intention to handle 'all romantic and tragic work'.[106] He even began once more to think of putting on Sudermann's *Teja*. The next play that was produced, however, was Connell's controversial *The Piper*, which opened on 13 February. A hostile reaction from the pit necessitated a speech from the stage by WBY on 15 February, explaining it as a Parnellite allegory, which attacked those who failed Robert Emmet and celebrated 'the ceaseless heroic aspirations of the Irish people'. Though the playwright nervously disagreed, WBY considered this a great triumph, reminiscent of the *Playboy* debate; according to newspaper reports, 'The play was given a respectful hearing although there were some occasional expressions of disapproval; at its conclusion there was a great outburst of applause and loud cries of "Author".'[107] He felt more and more in control and began to plan a Craig-like production of *The Well of the Saints* (though Robert Gregory, dilatory as ever, let him down over the scenery and he engaged Ricketts instead[108]).

This excitement took its toll. WBY's exhaustion may be measured by a celebrated incident on 10 February, when he joined some acquaintances at dinner in the United Arts Club. 'Presently they got up to go & I was startled to see a clean glass & port & no plate before me. I appealed to the attendant to know whether I had eaten my dinner or not. One said yes & one no. Presently they came to me & said they had both come to the conclusion I had not. I then eat [*sic*] my dinner & was rather late at rehearsal – I am not yet certain on the point however.'[109] He was further distracted by the financial implications of Horniman's alienation. The position was summed up by JBY in early December:

Miss Horniman is losing money as fast as she can over a theatre venture of her own in Manchester, scanty and scantier audiences, and her expenses over £100 a week. Willie has consulted the stars and sent her the results, which are all disastrous. And still she goes on obstinately, although she knows all about the stars and accepts them.

Willie has just *crushed her* in a letter war they have been waging, and for that reason he is making every effort to get to London that he may see her and make some arrangements now while she is *humble*. He is the only one belonging to the Theatre with whom she has not quarrelled. She has of course long ago quarrelled with all her own friends.[110]

But she continued impossible. In February WBY found himself giving a signed copy of his *Poems* from the collected edition to Helena Molony of Inghinidhe na hÉireann in order 'to buy off a possible libel action against Miss Horniman', who had sent them an insulting letter.[111] Nor was she his only difficulty. Intrigue buzzed around him; friends of the Fay connection like Helen Laird placed letters in the Dublin press about their quarrel, audiences fluctuated worryingly, his own pace of work was racked up to breakneck speed ('every moment of my time marked out'[112]).

Through the spring he immersed himself in all aspects of theatre business, desperately conscious of the need to make money in preparation for Horniman's defection and to remedy the deficiencies left by the Fays. Only his feline humour, and his ability to see social relations in terms of a *comédie humaine*, sustained him. 'Peace in the Abbey,' he later reminisced, 'varied with the size of Sara Allgood's waist. When she did herself well, this increased, and it was no longer necessary to cast her for all the young heroine parts: instead she would readily play the old peasant women for whom she had especial genius. But whenever she was ill, and returned with a waist reduced, immediately there was turmoil and confusion.'[113] There was, however, a price to be paid. *The Piper* survived, and brought the best three days' takings ever. But after

379

his speech on 15 February wby collapsed with influenza, unable to move or even write letters for nearly a fortnight. 'He is really working himself to death,' Gregory told Quinn, 'and is of course not able to write a line, and I hope he will soon get away and leave things to Synge, who was really responsible for the break-up, and is now not at all inclined to take his share.'[114] By 27 February he was shakily back at rehearsals; by early March he was again working eight-hour days in the theatre, despite hopes that management would eventually be handed over to Norreys Connell.[115] Gregory continued to complain about the dissipation of his energies. 'His creative work is worth a good deal more to us all than the settling of a dispute between Miss Allgood & Miss O'Donoghue or the extinguishing of the stage carpenter's pipe, but he really enjoys this administrative work for a while. I am keeping outside, to be able to come in at the next split.'[116]

Despite his recovery, his letters to Gregory in March are long, frantic rambles. The Fays' sharp practice in New York obsessed him, since it seemed to spoil the chance of a lucrative Abbey tour before the subsidy ran out; this quarrel seemed one more landmark struggle in the drama of his life, with Willie Fay playing the part of MacGregor Mathers, and the Abbey's integrity representing the ark of the Order of the Golden Dawn. He pursued them as inexorably as those deviant mages who had opted for 'groups' in 1901. And as ever, the struggles of his life were reflected in his work. Amid all the frenetic theatre business, he was impatient to write: since early in 1907 he had wanted to settle down to a year's composition of lyrics. There were also the attractions of Mrs Campbell, who had gratifyingly announced to journalists that wby was 'an Irishman of truly cultured taste' compared to Shaw, 'who has no taste'.[117] In November her offer had inspired him to begin an appropriately passionate play for her ('when I saw her in the Modern Plays she was doing here I told her that she was a volcano cooking eggs'[118]). This would become *The Player Queen*, fated to be nearly as long in gestation as *The Shadowy Waters*. For all these reasons, he longed through the spring of 1908 for a summer of writing at Coole.

Meanwhile, the idiosyncratic *pensées*, which had appeared in the *Gentleman's Magazine* and elsewhere, had been gathered into *Discoveries*, the last Dun Emer Press book before his sisters split from Evelyn Gleeson to form the Cuala Press (a move fraught with even worse financial insecurity[119]). Published in mid-December 1907, it was essentially a series of musings about communication – beginning with a memory of bringing the players to Loughrea at Easter 1903 and seeing Father O'Donovan's arts-and-crafts church: 'the worst of the old & the best of the new side by side without any sign of transition'. His ill-humour had been compounded by the players' insincerity, the audience's reaction to the play, the crudeness of provincial life, the obscenities scrawled in the visitors' book of the hotel. Finally all his impressions coalesced into 'a single thought':

If we poets are to move the people, we must reintegrate the human spirit in our imagination. The English have driven away the kings, and turned the prophets into demagogues and you cannot have health among a people if you have not prophet, priest and king.

This key insight marks the whole collection: the integrity of national art depends upon the intensity of the artist's personal vision. Taken with the pattern of references to Villon, it is clear that Synge and the *Playboy* lie behind these allusive, concentrated reflections. Equally significant is the way that so many of them are cast in the direct tone of personal experience, even autobiography, ranging from his hashish experiments in 1890s Paris to his recent visit to Italy. He was also prepared to declare frankly his reservations about work like Russell's *Deirdre*.[120] Remembering his youthful visit to Verlaine, he wrote:

It was not till after his death that I understood the meaning his words should have had for me, for while he lived I was interested in nothing but states of mind, lyrical moments, intellectual essences. I would not then have been as delighted as I am now by that banjo-player, or as shocked as I am now by that girl whose movements have grown abrupt, and whose voice has grown harsh by the neglect of all but external activities. I had not learned what sweetness, what rhythmic movement, there is in those who have become the joy that is themselves. Without knowing it I had come to care for nothing but impersonal beauty. I had set out on life with the thought of putting my very self into poetry, and had understood this as a representation of my own visions and an attempt to cut away the non-essential, but as I imagined that vision outside myself my imagination became full of decorative landscape and of still life. I thought of myself as something unmoving and silent living in the middle of my own mind and body, a grain of sand in Bloomsbury or in Connacht that Satan's watch fiends cannot find. Then one day I understood quite suddenly, as the way is, that I was seeking something unchanging and unmixed and always outside myself, a Stone or an Elixir that was always out of reach, and that I myself was the fleeting thing that held out its hand. The more I tried to make my art deliberately beautiful, the more did I follow the opposite of myself, for deliberate beauty is like a woman always desiring man's desire. Presently I found that I entered into myself and pictured myself and not some essence when I was not seeking beauty at all, but merely to lighten the mind of some burden of love or bitterness thrown upon it by the events of life.

IV

Yet he continued to struggle against the waves: for all the ill-feeling in the theatre, it is hard to believe he ever intended to carry out his many threats of resignation. Now, at last, there seemed a chance of using the Abbey to project his own ideas of drama. The Fays were gone and his own control asserted. But the theatre had less than two years left of Horniman's subsidy, and time was running out. The programme that opened on 19 March reflected these ideas rather awkwardly: his own *The Golden Helmet*, Fitzmaurice's *The Pie Dish*, and a Kiltartanized *Teja*. The reviews were mixed. He pinned his hopes on Norreys Connell's management, on Mrs Campbell's promise, on the plays of his own yet to be written; his vision of the Abbey's future involved extending the company's range so they could play a wider repertoire in other countries. 'It is this ambition that really keeps me at work here,' he told Connell. 'So far as I am personally concerned, I would do much better elsewhere. I have the greatest longing to write lyric before all my fires are gone as well as one more play at any rate. And that play when I write it will be beyond the capacities of this company.'[121]

Unsurprisingly, considering this bleak view and his own combativeness, he was lonely in Dublin. *Discoveries* gave old enemies a point of attack: 'the trivial tattle of a soul, so self-absorbed as to think the meanest of its thought-impulses worthy of record', wrote Seamus Ó Conghaile in the *United Irishman*. His sisters' house at Dundrum, Gurteen Dhas, provided no refuge: it was a kind of rival court to Gregory's headquarters at the Nassau Hotel, and those resentful of the Abbey directorate tended to congregate there. Moreover, there had been a family upheaval. JBY's hopes of commercial success in Dublin had receded again, since the final payment on the Thomastown lands had come through – £411 – and been swallowed by debts. Undaunted, he embarked on yet another experiment in living. In August 1907 Hugh Lane had organized a fund among JBY's well-off friends (Jamesons, Pursers) to send him to Italy. The object of this munificence accepted, hesitated, prevaricated and then plunged off in another direction altogether. For at the same time Lily was planning to visit an Irish exhibition in New York, if only to stop herself being driven mad by her sister (she announced that she now remained undecided only 'whether it would be melancholy or violent madness').[122] JBY swiftly determined to spend the Italian money on going with her. He was not encouraged. WBY refused to help him by casting a horoscope, Sarah Purser objected to the misapplication of the testimonial fund, and John Quinn (correctly foreseeing a long period of importunacy) desperately tried to dissuade him. But JBY was implacable: armed with introductions from the Jameson family, he expected to get commissions and, like his eldest son, return temporarily rich. He and Lily arrived in New York on 29 December 1907.

He did not become rich, but he did not return. 'To leave New York,' he wrote insouciantly, 'is to leave a huge fair where at any moment I might meet with some huge bit of luck.' In a less optimistic mood he remarked, 'Why do birds migrate? Looking for food – that's why I'm here.' But by and large he loved America, which seemed an Elysium where 'the women have no affectation and can talk seriously, and the men have no pretension, and people meet together to talk'.[123] Relying on Quinn, well-off friends and his own merciless charm, he worked out a bohemian life which suited him – sketching, painting, talking and calling in favours. And his relationship with his elder son entered a new phase. Linked by long, discursive curiously abstract letters, they now reversed the usual balance of father and son: JBY looking for approval, complaining that WBY denigrated his ideas, sending him drafts for short stories and setting up theories to be shot down. 'No I do not understand your dramatic ideas,' wrote WBY a year after his father's departure, 'any more than you understand the ideas of my generation, more than I shall understand in a few years' time the generation now at school. Even Shaw, as I know, begins to find the young unintelligible. Here and there I already meet a young man who represents something which I recognise as new, and which is not of my time – he is very often a sort of Catholic by the by.'[124]

This betrays a certain alienation from his theatrical colleagues. Rather than discuss matters with them, he sat in his hotel room consulting horoscopes about the next row.[125] He spent his time between the Nassau Hotel and the Abbey, 'where I have no friends only business associates – for Synge is always faint & far off.'[126] He also joined the United Arts Club, recently founded by Lane's friend Ellen Duncan, located in Lincoln Place behind Trinity (and from 1910 on Stephen's Green). The club was to be one of the bridgeheads for Lane's infiltration of Post-Impressionism into Dublin through a celebrated exhibition in 1911; but it was primarily a meeting-place for the city's respectable bohemians (Russell, the Markieviczes, Rolleston and Dermod O'Brien were all founder members).[127] Living in Dublin more consistently than at any time since his youth, WBY made some new acquaintances – including Horace Plunkett's cousin Lord Dunsany, who wrote fantasy-tales from his appropriately fairy-tale castle outside Dublin. He also stayed with the enlightened (and plutocratic) Lord Dunraven at Adare.[128] Fences were mended too with some old adversaries. He accepted a play from the Sinn Féiner Thomas MacDonagh, and agreed to lend the Abbey to the Theatre of Ireland. And it was at this time too that he became friendly with a stage-struck but well-connected young woman called Mabel Dickinson.

A sense of loneliness had persisted since the excitements of the spring: he had written Farr from Italy in May 1907 using the tones of a wistful lover ('do you know I find it very hard to find out how to write to you. I want you too [sic] understand that I am sorry you are away & I am afraid to say, because you get cross if one says such things & yet after all I shall be very glad when you return'[129]). At the end of the year Quinn had congratulated him on the forthcoming collected edition but warned him 'successes of that sort don't make all of life. One wants affection and friendship and some-times love too. If one doesn't care for a legal wife he should be entitled to a "visiting wife".[130] Though W B Y remarked in March 1908 that he was keep-ing 'tolerably virtuous' in 'virtuous Ireland', it was from about this time that Dickinson moved into the position of 'visiting wife'. Like W B Y she was a mem-ber of the United Arts Club, and occasionally acted at the Abbey, where she also gave exercise classes. Born in 1875, she was thirty-three when they met. She came from a level of Dublin society akin to W B Y's own, rather than that of the Allgoods or the Fays. Her father (who died in May 1905) had been the much loved vicar of St Ann's, Dawson Street, and Dean of the Chapel Royal at Dublin Castle, as well as Professor of Pastoral Theology at Trinity;[131] her brother, Page Dickinson, was a neurotically snobbish Dublin architect and aesthete (and a pioneer in the appreciation of Dublin's Georgian heritage). Family connections included the Lytteltons, and Irish-Indian families like the Lawrences. When W B Y knew her first, she was living with her widowed mother on Marlborough Road, but in 1908 she conveniently moved to rooms on Nassau Street, where she practised as a 'medical gymnast and masseuse'. By April he was scribbling her brief notes, with assignations appended:

Last night I said 'you were very nice' as I thought that was quite the most unre-vealing remark I could make and then hurried to the United Arts to say what I did think; and found there Madame Markiewicz and argued with that steam whistle for an hour expecting you to arrive at every moment with a sort of Comus rout of amateur players.

You can act. You have dignity without stiffness and emotion without insincerity and movement without artifice – and deserve a better part.

Your ever
W B Yeats

4 to-morrow (Monday)
or 4.15[132]

Her acting interests meant he could write to her as an 'artist'; her social back-ground meant she would be presented to Gregory as someone who might run bazaars and drum up support for the Abbey among the ladies of Dublin. But she also provided a more elemental form of release to W B Y, and by the sum-mer he was writing to her as 'yours always'. On subsequent visits to Paris he wrote meaningful letters about the effect that the great neo-classical nude studies in the Louvre had on him, since he had known her. However, her sta-tus would remain 'visiting'. She insisted he burn her letters, and the affair, 'purely amorous', was unknown even to his best friends.[133] Unremembered by contemporaries, it is impossible to analyse her appeal for him. But sexual fulfilment and a sympathetic ear were not enough to meet his ideal – an ideal

which now owed something to ideas of class as well as aesthetics. 'I some-
times think that the combination of joyous youthfulness with the simplicity
and conscious dignity that makes up what we call the great lady is the most
beautiful thing in the world,' he had told Quinn the previous October.

Many a high born woman has it not, though most have something of it. The form
at any rate without the substance. Maud Gonne had it, especially in her young days
before she grew tired out with many fools, and the little Countess of Cromartie has
it more than anyone I have ever known.[134]

Measured against this exalted company, a statuesque young physiotherap-
ist from the upper middle classes of Protestant Dublin would inevitably be
found wanting.

In April he had returned to London, in order to be painted by Shannon
and sculpted by Kathleen Bruce. Ricketts had to be seen about Abbey stage-
sets, and he shuttled back and forth to Stratford – not only to check Bullen's
progress with the collected edition, but to see Sara Allgood triumphing in
William Poel's production of *Measure for Measure*. But on 5 May he was sum-
moned back to Dublin by the ominous news that Synge was ill once more.
The recurring trouble was in fact Hodgkin's disease, producing lymphomas
that were no longer operable. While this was not yet generally known, and
Synge would live on for months, WBY now expected the worst. '[The thought
of] Synge's illness has for the first time in my life made death a reality to me,'
he told Mabel Dickinson (forgetting for the moment Dowson, Wilde,
Johnson and O'Leary). 'My mother was so long ill, so long fading out of life
that the last fading of all made no noticeable change in our lives. But Synge's
illness, & the almost inevitable stopping of a mind I have been so near to, is
almost unbelievable. I am fond of Synge, but not a little to my wonder (con-
sidering how intimate we have been) it was the death of his imagination that
set me sorrowing. Will you take this as proof that I have no heart?'[135]

After picking up the pieces at the Abbey he returned to London in early
June to see a new play by Masefield and to have an audience with Mrs
Campbell at her most dazzling. She had, it turned out, her own ideas about
speeding up the gestation of *The Player Queen*, pressing money and two
dozen bottles of wine on him 'to write it on'. Knowing the value of withhold-
ing himself from importunate women, and conscious that more strings
were attached to these gifts than to Gregory's Bovril, WBY refused. 'I wish I
liked Mrs Campbell as much as I admire her,' he told his father. 'She is kind,
generous & a great artist, but she leaves one exhausted after a few minutes
conversation. She is always at some height of intensity, or rather jumping
from height to height. One follows gasping.'[136] He had other reasons too for
evading Mrs Campbell's blandishments: since March he had been planning

to go to Paris, and to Gonne. He spent a week there, clearing his mind to begin *The Player Queen* and writing letters to Mabel Dickinson. It was as if his interest in a new woman required exposure once more to the flame of the spirit, which Gonne would always represent, and against which he still measured all romantic experience. This set the tone for 'a strange summer full of surprises and bewilderment'.[137]

From the beginning of that year, 1908, WBY's thoughts had been preoccupied by Gonne. Their correspondence had stayed friendly throughout 1907, with even the *Playboy* issue not dividing them as much as might be expected. Gonne was firmly on the side of its critics ('it would be a misfortune if the crowd began worrying over subtleties for it would be an end of action'[138]), but since the very same people had supported MacBride against her, she did not play a prominent part. In late September, however, she told him 'for years I wore blinkers so as to never cease working for the cause & only see the one end & object. Now I have taken them off & find so much to look at.' It was what he had hoped to hear for nearly twenty years. Their mystical interests remained a bond: they shared visions by post; in the autumn he worked hard on her horoscope, ostensibly to forecast the outcome of her latest legal imbroglio with MacBride, but probably with some private hopes of his own. He wrote to her confidante Ella Young that Gonne's horoscope revealed 'a climacteric period about every 14 years – this period is due at opening of next year',[139] and a French astrologer was consulted about Gonne's prospects for 1908, responding in encouraging terms. 'Two unions are clearly indicated by your stars: the second seems to me likely to be rather *libre* que legale. It can take place this very year (I mean to say from the 21 December next to the 20 December 1909). The year 1908 will be for you, dear friend, a period of struggles and triumph.'[140] In November 1907 they had been briefly reunited in Dublin. As with Shakespear years before, as soon as WBY turned towards another woman he found himself interrogating his feelings towards Gonne: he wrote in his diary a year later that she unconsciously made his other love-affairs 'but as the phoenix nest, where she is reborn in all her power to torture and delight'. Meanwhile she poured out letters describing visions of him, and astral communications, implicitly laying the claim which only she could impose. Even as his involvement with Dickinson got under way in April 1908, he had been planning to visit Gonne, with financial help from Gregory.[141]

From 19 June he was there at last, established opposite her house in the Grand Hôtel de Passy. He visited art galleries – 'thanks to Hugh Lane I now find all kinds of pictures delightful that I once could understand nothing of' – and rediscovered Paris.[142] Moves were even made, through an intermediary, for a reconciliation with MacGregor Mathers (who superbly demanded total repudiation of all WBY's statements made at the time of their quarrel[143]).

He found Gonne oddly subdued, tentative, taken up with her painting and her children. She was educating her four-year-old son Seán to know only French and Irish, since this would 'set the barrier of language between him and his father', who could speak nothing but English – a 'patriotic' irony relished by WBY. An authentic note of Dublin was briefly introduced when the vinegary Sarah Purser came to lunch, shuddered at the caged birds' racket, and finished 'by looking steadily at little Seaghan Mac Bride and saying to his mother "Aren't you afraid he'll grow up to be a murderer?" '[144] Seán's half-sister Iseult was now a charming and precocious fourteen-year-old, appealing particularly to WBY through her passion for the classics (notably the 'Ilead'): 'she all but set the house on fire by making a burnt offering on the mantlepiece to Artemis a few days ago'. The atmosphere of Gonne's Parisian retreat, with its sunshine, floor-length mirrors, Russian embroideries, oriental rugs, singing birds and charming, fey children, sealed their *rapprochement*. The day after he arrived, she 'said something that blotted away the recent past & brought all back to the spiritual marriage of 1898'.[145]

By the time he left on 25 June, their relationship had come nearer to a conventional resolution than ever before. He wrote in a notebook she gave him that though her new-found Catholicism prevented her remarrying, and 'the old dread of phisical love has awakened in her', she 'seems to love more than of old'.[146] She wrote to him with deep affection after he had gone, though telling him not to give up his London life or to immerse himself too completely in the theatre, which 'has made you take up old class prejudices which are unworthy of you, & makes you say cruel things which *sound* ungenerous'.[147] But mystically she felt they were attuned to each other once more, and so did he. It was demonstrated to him as powerfully as possible. He dreamt of her every night, and on 25 July, he recorded in his notebook, he tried to evoke a union with her. On the 26th she wrote him an ecstatic letter about a dream experienced the night before, when (he recorded) he had 'made evocation & sought union' with her. Her response could not have been more vivid:

You had taken the form I think of a great serpent, but I am not quite sure. I only saw your face distinctly & as I looked into your eyes (as I did the day in Paris you asked me what I was thinking of) & your lips touched mine. We melted into one another till we formed only *one being, a being greater than ourselves* who felt all & knew all with double intensity – the clock striking 11 broke the spell & as we separated it felt as if life was being drawn away from me through my chest with almost physical pain. I went again twice, each time it was the same – each time I was brought back by some slight noise in the house. Then I went upstairs to bed & I dreamed of you confused dreams of ordinary life. We were in Italy together (I think this was from some word in your letter which I had read again before sleeping). We were quite happy, & we talked of this wonderful spiritual vision I have described – you said it would tend to increase physical desire – This troubles me a little – for there was nothing physical in that union – Material union is but a pale shadow compared to it – write to me quickly & tell me if you know anything of this & what you think of it – & if I may come to you again like this.[148]

Farr, always sharp for her purposes, noted how silent WBY had fallen since going to Paris: 'I imagine that the long years of fidelity have been rewarded at last.'[149] In August or September he wrote 'Reconciliation', which, as published in *The Green Helmet*, read:

> Some may have blamed you that you took away
> The verses that they cared for on the day
> When, the ears being deafened, the sight of the eyes blind
> With lightning you went from me, and I could find
> Nothing to make a song about but kings,
> Helmets, and swords, and half-forgotten things
> That were like memories of you – but now
> We'll out for the world lives as long ago;
> And while we're in our laughing, weeping fit,
> Hurl helmets, crowns and swords into the pit.
> But, dear, cling close to me; since you were gone,
> My barren thoughts have chilled me to the bone.

An original version stated more explicitly

> but now
> That you have come me again I'll throw
> Helmet and sword and crown in a pit

and celebrated the way that the lovers had 'remade the world'.[150] It seems clear that their reconciliation went beyond the spiritual. Yet throughout he wrote love-letters to Dickinson: he had reproached her for not accompanying him to London ('my big settle looks cross & harder than usual because it has of a sudden remembered that you have never sat on it'). He told her that his romantic feelings for Gonne were over: 'she will not make another attempt to get rid of her husband (as she can in three years) unless he makes more trouble. She is content and I think happy. We have talked over the old things sadly perhaps but always as old things that have drifted away.' Even more pointedly, he insisted that Dickinson had made Dublin 'pleasant to me', and stressed how he had changed since his youthful visits to Paris, when he had worshipped Moreau and the Decadents.

. . . now I am all for David and above all Ingres whose Perseus is all classic romance – the poetry of running feat & clear far sighted eyes – of a world where you would be perfectly happy & have innumerable pupils. Ten years ago when I was last in Paris I loved all that was mysterious and gothic & hated all that was classic & severe. I doubt if I should have liked you then – I wanted a twilight of religeous mystery in everybodies eyes.[151]

By 4 July he was at Coole, after calling on his sisters who found him 'very nice, brotherly and affectionate & not at all "the great man"'.[152] Here he settled to writing lyrics and working on *The Player Queen*, though he continued to cast horoscopes about Gonne[153] and enjoy passionate visions where they were crowned together with emeralds and rubies, symbolizing day and night; he also had (for the first time) straightforwardly erotic dreams about her which left him 'wretched all day – wishing to be with her'. He was still weakly, and Gregory's solicitude was noted (and mocked) by Ian Hamilton, staying there at the time. Her familiar regimen accomplished more than Mrs Campbell's money and wine, and a prose version of his play was completed by 29 August. In the meantime, there had been plenty of distractions: his imagination was stirred by a visit to the Burren, that unique tract of limestone country in Clare, where the Gregorys took up residence from 11 July. Here WBY worked on a second series of *Discoveries*, redrafted *The Player Queen*, and wrote to Dickinson describing – in distinctly unidyllic terms – the primitive conditions of the people. Visitors included Jack Yeats, who surprised his brother by revealing a matter-of-fact belief in visions, and Evans Wentz, an American folklorist, who had pursued WBY from California, and would eventually produce a huge book (*The Fairy Faith in Celtic Countries*) dedicated to WBY in gratitude for bringing 'the first message from fairyland' to America's West Coast.[154] Wentz (a friend and pupil of William James) was a euphoric true believer in irrationalism: Neo-Platonist philosophy, psychical research and theories of the daemon figure largely in his book, deeply influenced by *The Celtic Twilight*. Both WBY and Russell were required to produce sightings and fairy lore during the summer of 1908: an exhausting business, from which WBY escaped to Dublin, where Poel had been brought over to rehearse the players in Calderón's *Life is a Dream*. This latest attempt to put on a 'foreign masterpiece' was fated to be as unsuccessful as the rest.

Nor was this the Abbey's only difficulty, since Horniman had not relaxed in her determination to cut them off. She remained obsessed by WBY, letting herself into Woburn Buildings during his absences, and haranguing him about dust on his books and moths in his underwear drawers. But with a codicil to her will she now revoked a legacy of money and property originally designed to ensure the Abbey's continuance. WBY hoped for money from a London tour, but Norreys Connell tactfully disassociated himself from managing such a venture. A Galway programme was also planned, to coincide with an industrial exhibition. The Abbey's money problems were mirrored by his own ('I am poorer than I ever was in my life,' he wrote to Dickinson from the Burren. 'I was plunged in misery the other night by dreaming I had spent 3/6 on strawberry ices – only my collected edition can lift me into opulent air again.'[155]) But despite the impending financial crisis, WBY was grimly determined to impose his own dramatic vision. He took the opportunity of a visit from the British Association in early September to make this clear in a public speech:

> When we wish to give a remote poetical effect we throw away realism altogether, and are content with suggestion: this is the idea of the Japanese in their dramatic art: they believe that artificial objects, the interior let us say of some modern house, should be perfectly copied, because a perfect copy is possible: but that once you get to sea and sky you should only suggest.[156]

He had stayed in touch with Gordon Craig, to whom he complained about theatrical difficulties over the summer, while the 'respectable' stayed away from the Abbey stalls: 'we have recreated the world-old alliance which made the arts flourish in past times between the peerage and the gutter'. The September performance of *The Hour-Glass* was, thankfully, a considerable success, and at the first night 'Willy spoke well and was very well received', Lily reported to her father.[157] But the theatre, like his own poetic work, had reached a crossroads.

Since the early summer he had been keeping notebooks recording his reaction to theatrical productions like Poel's: the notions of 'abstract musical energy' and 'passion and energy', flowing unchecked to create their own rhythm, suggest the trend of his poetry at this time, as he searched for a dramatic pulse. In his revision of *The Tables of the Law* he made Owen Aherne express a key insight: 'I know nothing certain as yet but this – I am to become completely alive, that is, completely passionate, for beauty is only another name for perfect passion. I shall create a world where the whole lives of men shall be articulated and simplified as if seventy years were but one moment, or as they were the leaping of a fire or the opening of a flower.'[158] Other autobiographical jottings stress the inadequacy of the 'vague immensities' which his art school generation had imbibed from second-hand Indian philosophy twenty years before.[159] And by mid-September he had recovered enough of his own creative impetus to write poetry. That summer at Coole produced not only the meditative lyric 'At Galway Races', but a short cry from the heart about the distractions he had suffered over the past months: the first draft, sent to Craig on 15 September as 'a poem I wrote this morning', spoke in the direct, personal tone which he had quarried out of daily experience.

> All things can tempt me from this craft of verse
> One time it was a woman's face, or worse

> The seeming needs of my fool-driven land;
> Now nothing but comes readier to the hand
> Than this accustomed toil. When I was young
> I had not given a penny for a song
> Did not the poet carry it with an air
> As though to say 'It is the sword elsewhere'!
> I would be now, could I but have my wish,
> Colder and dumber and deafer than a fish.[160]

On 5 October he left his 'fool-driven land' to meet Gonne in London. Taking the first tentative steps from her self-imposed French exile, she seemed 'sad & gentle' as if after a religious conversion, and told him of her gratitude to Gregory for the advice to marry under English law, which had enabled her to keep her property out of MacBride's clutches. Best of all, she spoke 'of her old politics of hate with horror'.[161] He confided to Gregory: 'I think she wants to marry me, but she has practically no chance of divorce & as that seems impossible she wants merely friendship, she cried while she was telling me these things. I think she is probably lonely. I am trying to hit on a more tranquil occupation I could help her in.' This suggests a certain evasion, reminiscent of their passages in 1898. She was never more attractive to him than in these transient moods of affectionate submissiveness. However, she continued to argue for a union in a world 'where desire is unthinkable' and (on 20 October) she wrote in his notebook a message which connected this abstinence directly with his creative energy, and made her identification with the Countess Cathleen absolute:

I saw Aleels love for me lighting the years like a lamp of extraordinary holiness & voices said 'You did not understand so we took it from you & kept it safe in the heart of the hills for it belongs to Ireland. When you were purified by suffering so you could understand we gave it back to you. See that you guard it safely for poems of great beauty may be born.'

His own sense of vulnerability was suddenly brought home by the news of Arthur Symons's collapse into a manic psychosis which would last for years, and from which his creative talent would never quite recover. Everyone assumed (as it turned out, inaccurately) that it was the stage of syphilis known as general paralysis of the insane: WBY thought overwork precipitated the breakdown and bitterly blamed Symons's demanding wife Rhoda (who was independently wealthy but refused to use her own money). His friend's collapse struck a final death-knell for the nineties generation of Rhymers, and helped confirm his view of them as doomed by their own excesses. 'He was the only man I think with whom I have had an entirely intimate and understanding friendship. With Lionel Johnson even there was always a slight veil. He had the subtle understanding of a woman & his thought flowed through life with my own, for many years, almost as if he had been one of the two or three woman friends who are everything to me,' he wrote to Gregory.[162] He visited Symons, and corresponded for a while with Rhoda about the worthless verses which the deluded poet was producing in reams; but, as she sarcastically noted, WBY's inquiries soon lapsed, and Symons, like Johnson and Dowson, was consigned to the ranks of those who had lost their souls through a lack of artistic coherence. As it happened, Symons, like Tiny Tim, did *not* die: his therapy took the idosyncratic but effective form of drunken binges in the Café Royal, organized by his new object of adoration, Augustus John, and accompanied by WBY's other admirer, the rich Californian Agnes Tobin. Symons eventually recovered, though Tobin (less accustomed to the pace, and liable to collapse when exposed to Wagner) eventually succumbed to nervous exhaustion herself.

For the moment WBY was hard hit; but he was consoled by the fact that Gonne travelled back to Dublin with him on 14 October. A police report recorded sourly: 'During her stay there she was not observed to associate with any suspects here but was much in the company of Mr W. B. Yeates [*sic*] of the Abbey Theatre.'[163] They saw MacDonagh's play (which he thought a failure),[164] and he escorted her to the mailboat on 27 October, where George Roberts noticed him standing with his head uncovered among giggling girls and huckster shop-women, as the boat drew out: 'he can carry off any scene with dignity'.[165] He needed all his sang-froid for a brief visit to Mrs Campbell at Liverpool, where she was playing *Electra* with Florence Farr. ('Are you afraid of me?' she demanded. 'Not in the very least,' he replied, 'you merely fill me with alarm.'[166]) She was still preparing herself to play *Deirdre*, and, though according to Lily her brother 'felt as if a fiery serpent had invited herself to tea',[167] he was determined to go ahead with it. Her extravagant bravura would be misapplied to a role he had created with the more restrained Darragh in mind, but that was a secondary consideration. The point was that she would make a great impact, and tempt the elusive 'respectables' to the Abbey stalls.

He was not disappointed. On 9 November Mrs Campbell delivered a triumph in Dublin: even the grudging Douglas Hyde thought her *Deirdre* the greatest tragic acting he had seen. She fitted in surprisingly well with the Abbey company and promptly bought the English and American rights to the play. 'I am now accepted as a dramatist in Dublin,' WBY told Quinn;[168] and the Abbey had at last turned the financial corner and begun paying its way. The December 1908 issue of *Samhain* proudly trumpeted these successes. As well as giving the Abbey side of the Fay imbroglio, and superbly dismissing the efforts of other theatrical societies, WBY also took up the theme of opinions in art, and daringly suggested that 'that pleasure in the finer culture of England, that displeasure in Irish disunions and disorders which are the root of reasoned unionism, are as certainly high and natural thoughts, as the self-denying enthusiasm that led Michel Gillane [in *Cathleen ni Houlihan*] to probable death or exile'. By 22 November the company were rehearsing *Deirdre* in London and prepared to scale new heights. Entering Mrs Campbell's glamorous circle turned even the indolent Sara Allgood into a fashion plate, recalling to WBY the transformation of Balzac's provincials when they hit Paris. When the play opened on 27 November, there were curtain-calls for WBY – though the audiences liked it more than the critics.

As for the author, he was back where adulation came easier than in Dublin: and he established himself once more in Woburn Buildings. A dazzled admirer, who visited him unannounced on a Saturday evening in early December, found 'a room in darkness save for a low fire which threw a fitful light upon books in great disorder, papers tumbled anyhow upon the floor, a crystal gazing-glass, two tall green candle-sticks, some Beardsleys, a Rossetti and the poet's pastels of Coole Park'.[169] WBY explained the darkness because 'I have a dread of going blind', and showed him some favourite books – including an 1827 Ballantyne Club edition of Gavin Douglas's *Palice of Honour* (1553), whose definition of poetry as 'pleasaunce and half wonder' he thought best of all. Warming up, he told stories of de Nerval and Baudelaire, and recited lyrics from *The Countess Cathleen* following the musical notes as printed for the play – subsequently producing the manuscript, along with tarot cards and astrological calculations.[170] He was back in the world which he had made.

There were other victories too. Maud Gonne had come to London to see *Deirdre*: and he followed her back to Paris, where he stayed a month, writing *The Player Queen*, reading Balzac (in English), taking French lessons. He was from time to time infuriated by Gonne's adoring hangers-on, notably his *bête noire* Ella Young, who 'talks elementary text books all day, when she is let, with an air of personal inspiration'.[171] But it was pleasant to be out of Dublin, to be once again in Gonne's magical presence, to be able to reverse his relationship with Gregory by sending a box of exotic Algerian fruit to Coole for Christmas. And from the tone of his correspondence with Gonne (as well as evidence given by WBY's widow long afterwards and hints in his astrological calculations), it seems that now they finally became lovers.[172] If poetic inference is admissible, the lines in 'A Man Young and Old' nearly twenty years later might also be invoked; using the Homeric imagery always associated with Gonne WBY would proclaim

> My arms are like the twisted thorn
> And yet there beauty lay;

> The first of all the tribe lay there
> And did such pleasure take –
> She who had brought great Hector down
> And put all Troy to wreck –
> That she cried into this ear
> Strike me if I shriek.

Pleasurable or not, final consummation does not seem to have heralded a new phase in their relationship; instead, it confirmed Gonne in her belief that their love must take the form she had decreed. The day after they parted she wrote something more like a conventional love-letter than anything else in their vast correspondence. 'Dearest – it was hard leaving you yesterday, but I knew it would be just as hard today if I had waited. Life is so good when we are together & we are together so little – !' She then told him she had gone to him astrally the night before ('I think you knew'). But the conclusion of the letter indicates that, while a physical consummation had been reached, she felt it could not continue:

> You asked me yesterday if I am not a little sad that things are as they are between us – I am sorry & I am glad. It is hard being away from each other so much there are moments when I am dreadfully lonely & long to be with you, – one of these moments is on me now – but beloved I am glad & proud beyond measure of your love, & that it is strong enough & high enough to accept the spiritual love & union I offer –
>
> I have prayed so hard to have all earthly desire taken from my love for you & dearest, loving you as I do, I have prayed & I am praying still that the bodily desire for me may be taken from you too. I know how hard & rare a thing it is for a man to hold spiritual love when the bodily desire is gone & I have not made these prayers without a terrible struggle a struggle that shook my life though I do not speak much of it & generally manage to laugh.
>
> That struggle is over & I have found peace. I think today I could let you marry another without losing it – for I know the spiritual union between us will outlive this life, even if we never see each other in this world again.
>
> Write to me soon.
>
> Yours
>
> Maud[173].

By mid-January she was sending him bracing letters about the advantage conferred on artists who abstained from sex. For WBY, however, inspiration had returned through Gonne, and out of their union in December grew a series of poems, originally grouped under the (mistaken) names of a medieval alchemist and his wife. For all this elaboration, they are direct, interrogative and employ deliberately plain diction. They included 'Words' (first titled 'The Consolation'), written on 22 and 23 January 1909.

I had this thought awhile ago,
My darling cannot understand
What I have done, or what would do
In this blind bitter land;

And I grew weary of the sun
Until my thoughts cleared up again,
Remembering that the best I have done
Was done to make it plain;

That every year I cried at length
My darling understands it all,
Because I have come into my strength,
And words obey my call;

That had she done so who can say
What would have shaken from the sieve?
I might have thrown poor words away
And been content to live.

Here, he immortalized the idea that her inability to understand him was irrelevant, since that very failure was what galvanized him to produce his best work. And 'No Second Troy' fiercely celebrated her uncompromising politics, probably recalling that Jubilee riot eleven years before when she accused him of failing her.

Why should I blame her that she filled my days
With misery, or that she would of late
Have taught to ignorant men most violent ways,
Or hurled the little streets upon the great,
Had they but courage equal to desire?
What could have made her peaceful with a mind
That nobleness made simple as a fire,
With beauty like a tightened bow, a kind
That is not natural in an age like this,
Being high and solitary and most stern?
Why, what could she have done being what she is?
Was there another Troy for her to burn?

As for Gonne, after a torrent of letters in January she became more evasive again; in May she would reiterate her renunciation of physical love. In December 1909 he wrote 'King and No King', which – placed in the same alchemical-marriage group – takes as its trope the consummation of a love previously forbidden by fear of incest. Their old brother–sister reincarnation fantasy must lie behind this, and the poem comes back to his recurrent wish for the consolations of a more conventional relationship:

> ... Whereas we that had thought
> To have lit upon as clean and sweet a tale
> Have been defeated by that pledge you gave
> In momentary anger long ago;
> And I that have not your faith, how shall I know
> That in the blinding light beyond the grave
> We'll find so good a thing as that we have lost?
> The hourly kindness, the day's common speech,
> The habitual content of each with each
> When neither soul nor body has been crossed.

But this was no longer on offer; they would remain separated geographically but united astrally. From WBY's point of view this certainly left room for Mabel Dickinson's ministrations. But how much Dickinson knew of this, let alone understood, is not recorded.

V

Thus December 1908 set a milestone in WBY's life, and it was not the only one. At this point too Bullen finally reported to Watt that the collected edition was now complete (adding an ominous proposal that WBY should take a lump sum rather than royalties[174]). Financially, it was not a great success; over the next four years only half of the thousand sets printed were sold. Macmillan declined to take it for America, while Chapman & Hall proved inefficient distributors at home. There was also the competition of much cheaper and readily available Yeats works from Fisher Unwin, whose *Poems* was still in demand; over the year 1909/10 it sold 447 copies, earning £28. 10s. 2d.[175] But the *Collected Works* meant something different to its author. WBY felt able to tell Farr, 'I think nobody of our time has had so fine an edition – I believe it will greatly strengthen my position – for my work is far stronger when put all together. I have been myself surprised by the unity of it all & by its general elevation of style, as I think.'[176] Volumes had been appearing since the summer, and reviews had been mounting up: the attention was uniformly respectful, though it was generally noted that the enterprise was a daring one. As Lytton Strachey put it, a collected edition 'implied a claim to a recognised and permanent place in the literature of a nation'.[177] The nation in question was, by inference, England rather than Ireland, and the tradition that of romantic introspection. WBY's claim was seen to rest soundly on his early poetry, with his prose given less than its already considerable due. An exception was a review by Bullen's influential assistant, Edith Lister, writing pseudonymously in the *Fortnightly*: emphasizing the new preface to *John Sherman*, she judged its conclusion 'with its story of the homecoming of the awakened man is more beautiful, because it is more true, than the ending of any other book I know'. Her special knowledge extended not only to the edition which she had seen through the press, but to WBY himself, whom she held in deep affection.[178] As for the author himself, he was determined that such juvenilia be labelled 'early work', and no sooner was his achievement immobilized in canonical form than the old dissatisfaction crept in. On 12 January 1909 he secretly confided to Quinn that he was already filing away ideas for rewriting sections that did not quite please him.

For WBY, the publication of his collected edition fixed him into the history of his time. Noting that English art was developing into two camps, with the followers of Augustus John challenging the romanticism of Ricketts and Shannon, he felt his instinct and intellect both went with Ricketts: that was, he might have said, his generation. The deaths of Johnson and O'Leary, Symons's collapse, his *rapprochement* with Gonne, sharpened his preternatural sense of the pattern of personal experience. He was conscious that George Moore was already working on a memoir, 'a novel with real people in it', and obtaining advice from libel lawyers.[179] In Paris he had met a student doing a thesis on his own work (which meant, he was told, that people in the Sorbonne must think he was dead). Critical appreciation of his poetry and plays was accumulating, often advancing interpretations from which he cautiously disassociated himself.[180] Allan Wade's bibliography of his writings, assembled for the *Collected Works* in 1908, astonished him by its completeness. At the same time he was rediscovering his family history. He was struck by the Pollexfen likeness in Shannon's portrait of him; he became interested in the 'ancestor-book' kept by Lily; and in March he would investigate the family's alleged coat of arms.[181] The year 1909 would mark a vital stage in the public construction of that literary personality which he had been developing since the publication of *The Wanderings of Oisin* exactly twenty years before.

With New Year of 1909, he set off from Paris for Dublin. In London *en route* he saw Farr and Agnes Tobin, and then, when passing through Manchester, had the misfortune to be afflicted with rheumatism and nursed by Horniman at her most rapacious. Not fully recovered, he was back in Dublin by 4 January and immersed in theatre crises. Sara Allgood's stage-management was erratic; Henderson, back in employment, wanted more money, and further annoyed him by bowdlerizing an article about Allgood carefully planted out in the *Freeman* by WBY;[182] mornings had to be spent dictating letters and supervising rehearsals instead of writing. Overall, money problems loomed. The theatre's reserve fund contained just over £600, but to be able to continue when the patent expired the following year they had to count on at least £1,100 in hand. Though WBY carried on doggedly with his French lessons, his life was being taken over once more by everyday Dublin matters. And his health suffered. His smoking habit (adopted on and off through his life) had produced headaches and palpitations. Synge was back in hospital; wby begged Gregory to come from Coole and help out. But surprise at her silence was replaced by severe chagrin and genuine consternation when Robert Gregory wrote on 4 February, telling him that she had herself been at death's door, having suffered a cerebral haemorrhage and – as she put it in a pencilled note – 'nearly slipped away'. Robert's letter carried an implied rebuke about the 'excitement and worry' his mother had been subjected to, and told wby that he and others would have to manage the theatre as best they could. The crisis further soured relations between them. (None the less, filial solicitude did not stop Robert and Margaret abandoning their new baby at Coole as soon as his grandmother was convalescent, and removing themselves to an artistic life in Paris – much as Robert himself had been left for a year as a baby while his parents had travelled abroad.)

For wby the shock of Gregory's critical illness was intense, bringing on a wave of chronic insecurity and fear ('like a conflagration in the rafters'). Without her, the structure of his life would collapse. All the confusions of his recent experience were put into proportion, and he expressed it in a poem sent to her 'with love' two days later.

> Sickness brought me this
> Thought, in that scale of his:
> Why should I be dismayed
> Though flame had burned the whole
> World, as it were a coal,
> Now I have seen it weighed
> Against a soul?[183]

For her part, she told him she was 'glad of the illness that brought you nearer to me'.[184] A week later he was himself at Coole: still feeling too fragile to write *The Player Queen* but keeping a notebook of aphorisms and reflections, many too deliberately controversial to print. Some thoughts were inspired by his father's letters from New York ('Genius vanishes at the first breath of ambition'), others by his current reading – especially the crash course in Balzac to which he had remained committed.[185] But all, like his published *Discoveries* a year before, revolved around the expressed need to base his work on real life.

His own private life continued complex. In late February he had planned to join Gonne in London, though she was detained in Paris; but he was still seeing Mabel Dickinson, dining with her in early March, reading her parts of his diary, and considering her for a part in *The King's Threshold*.[186] His own combative feelings towards Dublin adversaries stayed strong. In early March he wrote a note comparing 'Griffith & his like to the eunics in Rickett's picture watching Don Juan riding through hell',[187] which would find its way – like many of his jottings – into poetry. Unashamed sexual desire was associated with creative power; 'Those that hated *The Playboy*' were impotent in every way, staring at the legendary lover on his stallion, 'maddened by that sinewy thigh'.

Politics on stage continued to release highly charged feelings. When Sara Allgood agreed to act in an entertainment where 'God Save the King' was to be played, Lady Lyttelton had to meet WBY secretly and warn him, so a diplomatic illness could be planned. Possibly influenced once more by Gonne, he was also taking care not to alienate the new generation of nationalists whom he had described to his father. When P. S. O'Hegarty asked him in December to speak to a Sinn Féin group in London, he was careful to agree, choosing the title 'Ireland and the Arts', though the crisis over Gregory's illness meant the occasion was continually postponed.[188] When it took place on 13 June 1909, Gregory noted the opposition to the *Playboy* had died away, and the audience approved of their commitment to it. He remained on cautiously friendly terms with Thomas MacDonagh, writing a testimonial when he applied for a job at the National University.[189] He persuaded Horniman to allow the Theatre of Ireland to put on performances in the Abbey. And he supported theatrical initiatives at Patrick Pearse's experimental nationalist school St Enda's, 'one of the few places where we have friends'. Perhaps this was easier because he was conscious of 'a sinking of national feeling': both political and artistic movements seemed at a low ebb. After attending a performance of O'Grady's *The Coming of Finn* put on by the boys at St Enda's, he wrote to Gregory, 'the waiting old men of the defeated clan seemed so like ourselves'.[190] The impression must have been made all the more poignant because he and Gregory were themselves waiting for a death: and it came only two days later.

Synge's passing was no less traumatic for being so long anticipated. Months before WBY had written to Dickinson about the effect on him of that expected event; though the word 'cancer' was avoided, a full year before Synge died Gregory had realistically noted that there was little hope.[191] The previous May Synge had entrusted WBY with the disposal of his writings in case of his death, forbidding the publication of his early prentice work.[192] In November 1908 WBY had worked closely with him over a book of poems in preparation for Cuala.[193] Through February and March 1909 WBY visited the gloomy nursing-home off St Stephen's Green, closely observing the unique, laconic, uncompromising personality as his strength faded. Synge too knew exactly what was happening: on 23 March he sent a message through

Molly Allgood that he wanted to see WBY and 'make arrangements'. But he died the very next day, and WBY's 'arrangements' involved closing the Abbey, organizing newspaper notices, and giving an address in Synge's memory at the United Arts Club – where, to his surprise, Markievicz 'spoke like a gentleman' about all WBY had done for the dead playwright. The same note was struck by Gregory. Emotionally closer than ever to WBY since her own illness, she told him in a characteristic letter what would console him most.

You did more than any for him, you gave him his means of expression – You have given me mine, but I wld have found something else to do, tho not anything coming near this, but I dont think Synge would have done anything but drift but for you & the theatre – I helped him far less – just feeding him when he was badly fed, & working for the staging of his plays and in other little ways – & I am glad to think of it for he got very little help from any other except you & myself – I wonder if he was ever offered a meal in Dublin except at the Nassau?[194]

The great triumvirate of Synge, Gregory and WBY was broken. At the funeral WBY's wreath was inscribed 'In memory of his gentleness and courage', with a quotation from Plotinus: 'The lonely return to loneliness, the divine to divinity.'[195] More prosaically, as he walked from the grave in Mount Jerome Cemetery he remembered Synge's remarking he could never look at a daffodil after enduring Annie Horniman's hectoring letters on yellow notepaper: unconsciously maladroit to the end, she had sent in his memory a large wreath of daffodils.[196]

The emblematic meaning of Synge's death would haunt WBY for the rest of his life, inspiring a continual elegy in prose and verse. After the deaths of O'Leary and Johnson, the collapse of Symons, the emigration of his father, and the publication of his own *Collected Works*, Synge's death fell as the final curtain on an era. But since Synge had also stood for the freedom of the artistic imagination against the middle class of (largely Catholic) nationalist Ireland, his loss was enormous. It was easy, in retrospect, to see Synge as the victim of Dublin philistinism rather than of Hodgkin's disease. Moreover, these struggles would continue. Not only was there Synge's own unfinished *Deirdre* to produce, 'a magnificent sketch of what would have been his greatest work',[197] but WBY rapidly came into conflict with the family and the publisher (George Roberts of Maunsel & Co.) about including his early journalism in a posthumous edition. And his personal bereavement would be distilled over and over again, in prose as well as poetry.[198]

And yet the loss was, in some ways, curiously abstract. Synge was vital to WBY's sense of himself; his genius had marshalled the lines of battle and driven the enemy out into the open. But his detachment, his solipsism, his unclubbability, his certain sense of self had always sustained a gulf between him and his fellow-directors. Discussing WBY's projected essay, Gregory (who had never liked the *Playboy*) honestly articulated the reservations they both felt.

As to writing about Synge, I should not like to do it – I have nothing to say that you are not saying. We knew him together so much. Indeed, I wd like you to give some impression of that, of the theatre years in Dublin when none of us saw anyone from outside, we just moved from the Abbey to the Nassau & back again, we three always, & the Fays or Colum or 2 or 3 others sometimes. I like to think that he stayed here also, I suppose the only country house in Ireland he came to.

Also, we don't want a series of panegyrics, & we cant say, & don't want to say what was true, he was ungracious to his fellow-workers, authors & actors, ready in accepting praise, grudging in giving it – I wonder if he ever felt a moment's gratitude for all we went through fighting his battle over the Playboy? On tour he thought of his own plays only, gave no help to ours – if he repeated compliments they were to his own. I sometimes wondered if all my liking for him came from his being an appreciative listener.[199]

Paradoxically, Synge possessed a certain saturnine self-centredness reminiscent of George Pollexfen: WBY would later render it as 'a furious impartiality, an indifferent turbulent sorrow'.[200] With Synge gone, the friends of WBY's youth dissipated, and his own career apparently entering on mid-passage, these were the qualities which he would cultivate in his own solitude: a solitude which he would more and more locate in a sense of Anglo-Irishness.

Chapter 15 : SEVERANCES
1909–1910

> Mr Yeats reserves his fiercest attacks for politics. The nation-
> alist movement, he tells us – and we suppose that he would
> include the Unionist movement – is destroying the national
> imagination. The process began with the Young Ireland group,
> and has been going on ever since. A political party connotes the
> agreement of a large number of people in one conception, and
> 'when a group of people are organised about a conception, the
> result must be commonplace' . . . Mr Yeats says, truly enough,
> that most of our political conceptions are based on hatred,
> whereas literature and all other good things are only created
> out of love. At this point we begin to hope that Mr Yeats has
> thought out a practical and national policy of love – but he has
> done nothing of the sort.
>
> *Irish Times*, 5 March 1910, leading article on WBY's
> lecture 'The Theatre and Ireland'

I

BEREFT of Synge, WBY haunted Dublin through March 1909. Lily was
struck by his telling her he 'had no near friend left', and their father com-
miserated ('people say Willie is not human but these people have not had
a tete-a-tete with him'[1]). His own position as unofficial literary executor
quickly led to arguments with the Synge family and Maunsel.[2] Therapy was
provided by escaping to London for a week, seeing Ricketts, Shannon and
Mrs Campbell, but with Gregory convalescing in Venice, he had to bear the
brunt of Abbey organization. Synge's directoral chair was filled by the play-
wright Norreys Connell, employed on a salary. WBY dreamt of relinquishing
control to him and and returning to *The Player Queen*, but Connell required
advice about everything from production technique to costumes ('Remember
new clothes are the company's passion. There is no crime they are not cap-
able of to get them'[3]). Poverty also kept him in Dublin, though Gregory tried
to tempt him to Venice, writing elegiacally from the Layard palazzo 'it often
seems as if the last 10 years had been a dream & Cuchulainn & the theatre
had never existed'.[4]

WBY's mind was turning the same way. 'He is very anxious to get free of
the theatre,' Lily reported,

& to get to his own work. The theatre, he says, doubles his expenses & takes his
writing & thinking power. It, the theatre, is really fairly started now, but the papers
here are so dishonest. They seem to have no honour, any vulgar musical comedy

from London they give glowing notices to, while original work at the Abbey they mock at or do not notice at all. I see the reporters here on the first nights – a set of whiskey-sodden half-sirs, full of jealousy and ignorance.[5]

These reactions were reflected in the essays on Synge's work already pre-occupying him, and exacerbated by sickness and constant headaches. With Gregory away, and Dublin unfriendly, WBY took refuge at Dunsany Castle. Its owner, now thoroughly stage-struck, was described by WBY as 'a man of genius . . . [with] a very fine style . . . a handsome young man with a beauti-ful house full of pictures'. More defensively, and more realistically, he summed up Dunsany's work to Gregory as 'very nearly very good'.[6] In London, Dunsany was launched on Ricketts and Shannon, and introduced to the glamorous Mabel Beardsley. Finally, WBY would 'claim him for Ireland' by publishing Dunsany on the Cuala list.[7] For his part, Dunsany became a generous bene-factor to the Abbey appeal. But this new swan was not entirely perfect: intense and fidgety, he could occasionally drive WBY 'to distraction'. In unguarded moments WBY admitted that he himself provided Dunsany with the scenario for his play *The Glittering Gate*,[8] and a more restrained estimate of his talent was eventually given to Gordon Craig:

He is a man in whose genius I believe, though I am very doubtful whether it will ever come to anything. He is one of the few English speaking men today, who have a gift for style, style like that of Baudelaire in the Prose Poems. I am trying to make a dramat-ist of him. But he doesn't know how to revise his work, and he has little patience. He is splendid for a scene and then all goes to pieces. But what is good in his work is nearly as good as it can be. It is all worked out of time and out of space. Impossible cities and impossible wildernesses, and people with wonderful names, invented by himself, but alas! it is a great misfortune to be born in the Peerage, life is to[o] pleasant for him. Fifty pounds a year and a drunken mistress would be the making of him.[9]

And even Dunsany's motor-car and castle could not exorcize Synge's ghost – nor the idea that he had, as JBY put it in a memoir, died of Ireland.[10] He had left a lively inheritance. Productions of *The Well of the Saints* and the *Play-boy* (now the Abbey's most valuable possession) were planned for spring and summer; his unfinished *Deirdre* was pieced together, with a production scheduled for January 1910; negotiations with the recalcitrant Synge family took a long time to establish who owned the copyright. When the *Playboy* reopened at the Abbey on 27 May, it was received respectfully. Even George Moore's repeated visits, and his declaration that it was the greatest play written for two centuries, failed to arouse controversy.[11] A London produc-tion was planned for June, along with performances of WBY's own *Deirdre*; judging Connell over-sensitive and too lenient with the actors, WBY continued to involve himself with every facet of theatre management, though plagued by headaches. Even in London, irritations pursued him, such as the irrepressible Aleister Crowley's threat to publicize the rituals of the Golden Dawn (which WBY tried to circumvent by establishing a copyright through publication in Latin[12]). And when the ex-Abbey actress Maire nic Shiubhlaigh had a success in the rival Theatre of Ireland with Seamas O'Kelly's play *The Shuiler's Child*, *Sinn Féin* celebrated by publishing a front-page attack on WBY's drama – all the more hurtful as it was written by an old family friend, Susan Mitchell.

Oh Yeats, Yeats! with your broken-kneed heroes and barging heroines, even your drawing-room Deirdre, tender, appealing, complex as she was, did not save you, who, with all your talk of tradition, have only succeeded in producing on [*sic*] Kiltartan French and pigeon English some few passably competent comic actors and actresses. I feel very sad for you and for your loss in the possibilities that your futile dictatorship flung away, certainties now, and you have lost them . . . Give us no heroics any more: your heroic actors haven't in any case a leg to stand on! Cultivate Lord Dunsany if you will. I will foresee something big in the empty bottles and the picklock at the door of heaven, but get him an audience, man, get him an audience. The 'Glittering Gate' is no farce, and the empty bottle deserves more than an empty laugh. Pull yourself together, Man of Genius, save your theatre. There is yet a little time.[13]

This was part of a general campaign on behalf of those who had seceded from the Abbey – particularly actors who had gravitated to Casimir and Constance Markievicz and the Theatre of Ireland, currently drawing large audiences. Gregory's *Kincora* had already been similarly condemned 'for hopelessly flat acting and deplorable stage management . . . the thing beat all Abbey records. The degeneracy of the Abbey Theatre is painful.'[14] For this onslaught, the Yeats circle blamed Russell, who angrily denied the imputation in a letter to John Quinn –incidentally confirming WBY's loneliness in the Dublin of 1909.

I have never at any time in my life depreciated Yeats genius either publicly or privately. I have never at any time been in opposition either publicly or privately to the Abbey Theatre . . . W.B.Y. has made a great many enemies among the younger writers in Dublin and there are many, all members of the rival theatre Seamus O Sullivan, Colvin, Stephens, Keohler & others. These are all friends of mine and every Sunday evening they come to see me. I know they feel bitterly to W.B.Y. but for this I am not responsible . . . None of my friends George Moore John Eglinton Colum O Sullivan Stephens are on what could be called friendly terms with W.B.Y. I am not myself but I can assert truly I have nothing to reproach myself with in my relations to him.[15]

WBY's refusal to conceal his contempt for Russell's acolytes, combined with the struggle for control of the Theatre Society, had driven a deep wedge between the two friends. Also, though Russell's politics remained those of moderate nationalism, many of his protégés were more 'advanced'. It was no accident that *Sinn Féin* so readily published attacks on WBY; the spectrum that took in Griffith and advanced nationalism, the IRB Dungannon Clubs, the Theatre of Ireland and Constance Markievicz, with her recently formed boy-scout militia 'Fianna na hÉireann', represented a political culture from which he was deliberately distancing himself. Over the next five years the soul of Irish nationalist politics would be contested between these small groups and the more 'establishment' Home Rule agenda of the Irish Parliamentary Party, whose star rose as the Liberal government was driven to rely more and more on their support at Westminster. WBY's political instincts were moving to this side – and proportionately further from the Fenian commitments of ten years before.

It was thus all the more ironic – and infuriating – that at this very point Horniman chose to precipitate another row on the grounds of 'politics'. With the Abbey company playing the Court Theatre in London during the summer, their stars were much in demand, and Sara Allgood was engaged by the society hostess Edith Lyttelton to entertain what WBY described as 'a Unionist suffrage meeting' at her house in late June.[16] To general astonishment, Horniman seized this as an issue to break on, declaring her intention to withdraw her subsidy from a company which took up political stances, against the express terms of their contract. Ominously, she had already become restive about continuing her subsidy until the end of 1910, and had recently suggested that the directors buy her out.[17]

Through early July a series of increasingly manic letters from Horniman fired thunderbolts in all directions – notably to Mrs Campbell, who had engaged the sublimely apolitical Allgood for the occasion. Mrs Campbell's bemused reply provoked Horniman to exceptional heights of invective, revealing the abiding resentment of WBY which lay beneath. 'You are most generous, a woman in your position to defend a mere amateur dramatist, and it was very brave of Mr Yeats to risk annoying you, a *really* important person . . . I have always intended to stop all help, if ever politics was dragged in, in an undeniable way.'[18] The storm broke on WBY's head as he was journeying to Coole, and he was unable to stop Norreys Connell from resigning with alacrity on 2 July.[19] Gregory's reaction was to welcome the chance of a break, a course in which she thought WBY concurred. But this strategy was short-circuited by a rather bewildered apology to Horniman from Edith Lyttelton on 7 July; WBY extracted an angrier response from Allgood, who none the less agreed 'for the good of the theatre' not to take on recitation engagements 'without permission of the directors'.[20] The day after Lyttelton's apology Horniman wrote to her 'Dear Demon' more revealingly than ever before:

But the root of all this is deeper – I know that you hold the Nietschian doctrine that you have no duties towards those who have neither Genius, Beauty, Rank (race or family) nor Distinction, that there are 'Slaves' & that I am one of them & that no arrangement nor pact with me is of any importance. On my side I firmly hold that what I truly *am* is not affected by your opinion, & that you have as good a right to hold it as I have to resist it. If you can get people to take my place with whom you can feel on terms of Nietschian equality the position would be much simpler. They would have no delicacy (such as I feel) in insisting upon what they might think fit. On my side I should aid in every way the arrangements to buy me out & I should only take a sum of money on the clear understanding by all concerned that it should be made public that I had been got rid of completely so as to rid you of what seems to be an incubus & a stigma.

You know quite well how I have tried my best to serve Art in your country & other people say that I have been very patient. Perhaps you will see some good points in the despised 'slave' when you look back on the last six years when you are an old man. That remark you may label as 'sentimental', but that does not affect the fact to label anything does not alter its nature in reality.

If you get those guarantors together & they object to paying me £500 for freeholds costing £1,500, I'll take less; even a 'slave' can avoid being greedy, but something must be paid so as to impress the 'Sinn Fein' and 'The Leader'.

It is very sad that it should have come to this between us (another bit of 'slave' sentiment;) but you have chosen your own course & I *accept* fully that you have a full right to it, in contradistinction to your contention that we poor 'slaves' should *bow* to everything said by a superman.

May be you may still in the 'back of your mind' (my dear friend) come to value me a little in the 'future'.[21]

In the end, the tone of imperious offensiveness faltered; this is, like so many of her communications, a love-letter by other means. And as always, his reply to her was implacable: asserting that the theatre had done all it had promised, in creating a disciplined company and 'a remarkable body of plays of a new kind'; yet again, the promise was held out of 'foreign work well played'.[22] In any case, pushed by Gregory, he would use Horniman's more submissive mood to negotiate their way to freedom. By the end of August the issue was narrowed to the £800 subsidy outstanding, and a sum of £200 for upkeep; Gregory and wby calculated they needed at least this £1,000 plus £500 to keep going. The story was not over. Money wrangles would continue throughout, and there would be further crises at the Abbey before the Horniman subsidy and the old patent expired in December 1910. But the terms for their liberation had been set. All that was needed was money.

II

There was one obvious reason for WBY's distraction, and for Horniman's resentment and volatility, during the summer of 1909. Maud Gonne came to London in May and stayed on, visiting Symons, making friends with Agnes Tobin, and seeing much of WBY. When she left, Florence Farr reported sardonically to Quinn: 'He is very apt to go to Paris to see M. Gonne & they are thinking of Italy with the cousin Mrs Clay as chaperone. But I know he will go to Coole now in a fortnight because he has to write "The Player Queen" for Mrs Campbell.'[23] She was right. As to WBY's relationship with Gonne, it now seemed clear that she was determined not to pursue their physical affair. He recorded in his diary that she had told him in May this must be so: 'we are divided by her religious ideas, a Catholicism which has grown on her', as well as by what he believed to be her aversion to sex. On 21 June he wrote:

What end will it all have – I fear for her & for myself – she has all myself. I was never more deeply in love, but my desires, always strong, must go elsewhere if I would escape their poison. I am in constant terror of some entanglement parting us, & all the while I know that she made me & I her. She is my innocence & I her wisdom. Of old she was a phoenix & I feared her, but she is my child more than my sweetheart . . . Always since I was a boy I have questioned dreams for her sake & she herself always a dream of deceiving hope, has all unknown to herself made other loves but as the phoenix nest, where she is reborn in all her power to torture and delight, to waste & to enoble. She would be cruel if she were not a child, who can always say 'you will not suffer because I will pray'.[24]

By now, he believed her repressed desire was diverted into extreme politics, and her Catholicism provided a self-justifying rationale for both.

Other sexual tensions too emerged from his visits to Paris the previous year. John Quinn's mistress Dorothy Coates had also been holidaying there in June 1908: a pretty, intelligent Virginian (with a Native American grandfather and an Ulster mother) but neurotic and, as time would show, litigious. Under her influence, JBY ruefully remarked, Quinn 'becomes a tiger and gives you the life of a dog, and if you say anything resenting such treatment he does not hesitate to remind you of what he has done & of your dependent position.'[25] Meeting WBY at Gonne's, Coates spoke freely to him and possibly over-interpreted his response. 'It was she herself who told Willie that she had been Quinn's mistress,' according to JBY. 'She herself told me that she was a bachelor girl, which is an American institution, and means a woman leading the kind of existence that is led sexually by the bachelor man.'[26] In Coates's case it would lead to a lengthy claim against Quinn's estate, and in older age – it was alleged – to a career as a Mayfair consultant for those afflicted by sexual problems. From references in letters, it is evident that WBY subsequently spoke about her round Dublin with his habitual indiscretion; she responded (or retaliated) by telling Quinn that he had attempted to seduce her. Quinn took her word for it, and despite a Dublin meeting with WBY in mid-August 1909 where they 'had the whole thing out', there was no communication between them for several years.

Thus one more name was added to the growing list of estranged friends – and one who had helped WBY to combat the financial exigencies of a writer's life. In the summer of 1909, however, a new possibility came into view. After decades of negotiation, a National University of Ireland had just been founded, embracing the provincial Queen's Colleges and the Catholic University in Dublin; the latter institution, reborn as University College, Dublin, would become the powerhouse and forcing-ground of a new Catholic elite. It would also sustain a powerful clerical influence. Possibly in an attempt to circumvent this, some of the younger intellectuals associated with it (notably Thomas MacDonagh) mounted a campaign to appoint distinguished outsiders to well-paid teaching-posts (lectureships worth £400 a year). The suggested candidates included the German philologist and Celtic scholar Kuno Meyer, Douglas Hyde and WBY.[27]

This carried radical implications, as MacDonagh fully recognized. He was a talented poet, an astute critic and an apprentice playwright, but his relationship with WBY remained edgy. In 1903 he had dedicated a book of poems to the older poet, who had advised him about publishing strategy, and the next year he submitted a play to the Abbey. But though they maintained a mutual intellectual respect, MacDonagh's politics were Sinn Féin, and his cultural affinities lay with Russell's circle and the Theatre of Ireland rather than with WBY. The forthcoming revival of the *Playboy* on 27 May had swiftly raised exactly the kind of problem implied by WBY's appointment, as both men saw. 'I cannot withdraw the Play Boy,' wrote WBY tersely to MacDonagh, 'though I see of course quite well the effect it may have on my chances of that Chair. No, if they wont give it to me because I am myself I shall be well out of it.'[28] Privately he confided he 'should much sooner accept an invitation I got some time ago from Gordon Craig to join his "circle" of ne'er do wells and Bohemians in Florence'.[29] By 7 May it emerged that the bandwagon had been set rolling too late, and another appointment had been made. WBY expressed his relief; to Gregory he added that 'ancient incompetence' would rule in the new University as in the old College. He rapidly convinced himself that it was his own decision not to go forward, and Dublin was in any case 'an unendurable place to live in'.[30] Meanwhile he joined the Gregorys at Coole and took refuge in *The Player Queen* and his episodic diary of reflections. But he was not done with controversy yet.

While WBY was being sounded out about academic posts in Dublin, his old rival George Bernard Shaw was battling English censorship. In May his new play *The Shewing-Up of Blanco Posnet* (a morality-farce set in a peculiarly Shavian Wild West) was refused a licence by the Lord Chamberlain. Simultaneously, the evidence Shaw gave to the Joint Select Committee on Censorship was suppressed. He was looking for a row. He had unfinished business with the Abbey ever since *John Bull's Other Island*, and was building a friendship with Gregory, who daringly but unsuccessfully suggested that he take Synge's place as an Abbey director. When he offered *Blanco* to the Abbey in July 1909, it was an unmistakable challenge. Although WBY was cautious (as in all matters to do with Shaw), Gregory instantly seized on its potential. She privately thought the play 'a little sentimental & not very good' but since the censor had banned it in London, a golden opportunity was presented for an Abbey *coup*. The point was that English censorship law did not run in Dublin; letters patent for Irish drama derived from monarchical authority, so any gagging would have to be specifically ordered by the Viceroy, Lord Aberdeen (a passionate Home Ruler). And even a brief reading of the play showed that it contained nothing to offend Irish nationalist opinion, and hardly anything inimical to the Church: Shaw's forensic skills were played over a fairly straightforward story of the operation of providential grace, and the humbling of an atheistical cowboy. It was the perfect issue on which to flaunt the theatre's independence of official Ireland, and allay the suspicions of Sinn Féin.[31]

The Irish administration walked into the trap. Once the play was accepted, official disapproval was conveyed through the Under-Secretary at Dublin Castle, ironically a Liberal, Home Ruler and Abbey supporter, James (later Sir James) Dougherty. As he expressed it, the issue involved misuse of the Abbey's patent, which forbade (among other things) 'profanity or impropriety of language' and 'misrepresentation of sacred characters which may in any degree tend to expose religion or bring it into contempt'. (This legalistic line rapidly collapsed into the much vaguer claim that *Blanco* was not the kind of play which the Abbey was supposed to present, since the only Irish thing about it was its author.) Gregory, as patentee, was summoned by Dougherty on 12 August and took the main part; but WBY travelled up from Coole with her for three further visits to the Castle on 13 and 14 August, and one to the Viceregal Lodge on 20 August. As Gregory described her 'fight with the Castle' in great detail a few years later, the theatre directors faced down royal authority; Dougherty and Aberdeen, fundamentally sympathetic, had been put in a corner by the low-brow English censor (an ex-bank manager, as Dougherty apologetically explained) and the equally uncultivated King. (WBY thought the monarch was taking a leading part, inspired by hatred of

Shaw.) In point of law, the Castle could not ban the play; all it could do was rely on persuasion and, failing that, revoke the patent. The Abbey, in fact, held all the cards – so long as the play provoked no public unrest. This involved squaring Sinn Féin, and behind the scenes WBY and Gregory prepared Irish journalists before releasing to an entranced public the Castle's warning letter. The day before this appeared, Russell wrote to Gregory that, acting on WBY's instructions, he had 'got at' Griffith to prevent any demonstration against the play.[32]

The worst Griffith did was to make snide remarks about the Abbey currying cheap favour with anti-Castle elements;[33] this referred to WBY's letter to the press on 22 August, which took the deliberately nationalist line of defending an Irish playwright against the English censor. He was, at the same time, genuinely concerned. The issue of censorship would preoccupy him more and more. He saw it as the chief target to be aimed at by the new Academic Committee of English Letters, which he would shortly join, and he first thought of staging *Oedipus Rex* in Dublin to demonstrate how much 'we are better off so far as the law is concerned than we would be in England'.[34] To oppose censorship on nationalist grounds killed two birds with one stone. Even habitual opponents like Patrick Pearse in *An Claidheamh Soluis* got the point: while discounting the Anglicized Shaw as one of 'the legion of the lost ones, the cohort of the damned', he hailed WBY and Gregory for 'making a fight for Irish freedom from an English censorship'.[35]

To Dublin, it was an extra spectator sport in Horse Show Week. During August, Shaw, the unlikely nationalist martyr, stayed immured in a Kerry luxury hotel, but Lily observed her brother running around Dublin 'in great spirits, snorting fight' accompanied by Gregory 'in quite a becoming hat'.[36] Rehearsals continued, under Gregory (her son felt that WBY only joined this bandwagon at the last minute, and scooped undeserved credit[37]). Small changes were made to the text, though not those required by the censor. Shaw was annoyed, as he wanted the message rammed down the audience's throats.[38] But just before opening night, on 25 August, WBY issued a classic and prophetic statement:

To-morrow night *Blanco Posnet* will have a triumph. The audience will look at one another in amazement, asking what on earth did the English Censor discover objectionable. They will understand instantly. The root of the whole difference between us and England in such matters is that though there might be some truth in the old charge that we are not truthful to one another here in Ireland, we are certainly always truthful to ourselves. In England they have learned from commerce to be truthful to one another, but they are great liars when alone. The English Censor exists to keep them from finding out the fact. He gives them incomplete arguments, sentimental half-truths, and above all he keeps dramatists from giving them anything in sudden phrases that would startle them into the perception of reality.[39]

His sister's reactions bore this out. With Jack and his wife she sat in the audience 'and waited to be shocked and no shock came . . . God and the invisible powers are spoken of and to in strong terms and even *criticised*. This we don't mind over here as we do it every day and are not afraid or struck down. In England they keep things invisible for wet Sunday evenings, a sort of bogeyman.' It was none the less a great first night, jammed with 'Horse Show people hoping to see something improper'.[40] Ticket sales realized £100, all seats were sold, and fifty people turned away; even Lord Dunsany only managed to get in because an aunt of Shaw's was too intoxicated to claim her place. The British press were there in force and the Trieste *Piccolo della Sera* was represented by James Joyce, as bewildered by the play's 'flimsiness' as everybody else. WBY's predictions came exactly true: he reported to Farr that 'Shaw's play went enormously & [Chief Secretary Augustine] Birrell swore & stamped & said Lord Aberdeen had made the whole Irish government ridiculous.'[41] By an adroit stroke, *Cathleen ni Houlihan* was played in the supporting bill (much as it had been wheeled out in the wake of the *Playboy*), making their nationalist credentials all the more obvious. WBY received a warm letter from Gonne in Paris, congratulating him on rediscovering his principles. As for Shaw, he had enjoyed yet another *succès de scandale* (and one far beyond the play's merits). From now on he was a firm friend to the Abbey and to Gregory, advising her about matters such as the right proportion of takings to pay to authors,[42] while waiving all charges to himself for *Blanco*. And Castle dignitaries continued to attend the theatre; a certain discreet collaboration may be hinted at by the attendance of Dougherty's wife and daughter at Gregory's 'At Home' entertainments a year later.[43]

She stayed on in Dublin, supervising theatrical affairs, while he went to Coole, where he struggled with *The Player Queen* and his perennial summer task of reading Balzac. To WBY, Gregory's authority, integrity and style had been demonstrated at their best. He felt, therefore, all the more incensed when several Coole tenants applied to the Land Court to have their rents reduced, at a time when landlords were already complaining of the new impositions laid on them by recent financial legislation. On 7 August he drafted the idea for a poem which took 'personal utterance' into unashamedly controversial politics:

Subject for poem. 'A Shaken House'. How should the world gain if this house failed, even though a hundred little houses were the better for it, for here power [has] gone forth or lingered, giving energy, precision; it gave to a far people beneficient rule, and still under its roof living intellect is sweetened by old memories of its descent from far off? How should the world be better if the wren's nest flourish and the eagle's house is scattered?[44]

The resulting poem was eventually printed at the end of the following year ('To a Certain Country House in Time of Change', later 'Upon a House shaken by the Land Agitation'). The original idea was not softened nor made more palatable; not only Gregory's plays and *Cuchulain of Muirthemne*, but even her husband's imperialist career were celebrated and exalted as admirable attributes of aristocracy and 'Big Houses', while the idea that such privilege might be redistributed was scouted as pointless. It was true – as WBY knew – that Coole was a poor estate, run on the margin, and that Gregory had spent twenty years in retrenchment trying to pay off debts; but this was not the public perception of landlords and colonial governors in the Ireland of 1909 and 1910. The poem necessarily read like a deliberate challenge to conventional nationalists, and symbolized how much he had distanced himself from their opinions since the death of Synge.

WBY knew about Ascendancy penury at first hand; he stayed on into October partly because he had hardly any money left. Relief did not come until Fisher Unwin sent £32 for a year's sale of *Poems*.[45] *The Player Queen* remained recalcitrant; by 10 October, reading it to Robert and Margaret Gregory, he knew that his summer's work had been wasted, and he bought a loose-leaf file in order to start again (a prospect that gave him a sleepless night from excitement[46]). In mid-October he could afford to return to Dublin and take lodgings in an old house at Glasnevin where Swift had stayed, which provided peace and a writing-table in his bedroom for fifteen shillings a week.[47] But his move from Coole had been dictated by a traditional summons. In late October Gonne appeared at the Abbey on WBY's arm, 'fine and majestic in black, walking in a cloud of heavy perfume'.[48] Only a forthcoming Abbey tour to Manchester (engaged by Payne for Horniman's theatre on a half-profits basis) brought him unwillingly back to England in November.

Once again he was enmeshed in the complications of the players' love-lives, the calculation of percentages, the exigencies of Mrs Campbell over the eternal *Player Queen*. In London his social life continued to burgeon. Though constantly worried about the state of his dress clothes, he dined with the Prime Minister at Edmund Gosse's, on 29 November. He sat beside Asquith, and their host was grateful that WBY 'kept things going' – though in a typically Yeatsian way. Lloyd George's epoch-making budget was just about to be thrown out by the Lords, precipitating constitutional crisis, and WBY was warned not to talk politics. He tried, therefore, to reassure Lord Cromer by telling him, ' "I look upon English politics as a child does at a race-course, taking sides by the colour of the jockies' coats, and I often change sides in the middle of a race." This rather chilled the conversation & somebody said to me presently "Lord Cromer is interested in nothing but politics." [49]

But he continued to feel frustrated by theatrical work, and alienated from life in general. Before leaving Dublin he had been greatly struck by John Martin Harvey's *Hamlet*, and wrote to him in terms which hint at emotional identification:

A performance of Hamlet is always to me what High Mass is to a good Catholic. It is my supreme religious event. I see in it a soul jarred & broken away from the life of its world, – a passionate preparation of sanctity. I feel that the play should seem to one, not so much deep as full of lyric loftiness & I feel this all the more because I am getting tired of our modern delight in the Abyss. [50]

III

In early January 1910 he was back in Dublin for the first night of Synge's *Deirdre*, intending to spend six weeks there; Lily thought him 'well, cheerful and hard up, and full of plans and hope'. [51] The critical and popular success of Synge's last play vindicated his optimism, and made him feel that there was hope for avant-garde work, since much of his recent demoralization had been due to the theatre's reliance on the popular realism of Casey and Boyle. His energies galvanized once more, he dreamt of performing *Oedipus Rex* 'against a great purple curtain' – and committing the Abbey to a new obsession, Gordon Graig's experimental all-purpose columnar screens, designed to create geometric illusions of depth and shade by abstract effects. To his delight, a working model arrived in Dublin in January. As usual, however, success brought its problems. Much of the effect of *Deirdre* had been due to Molly Allgood's haunting performance in the part written for her by her dead lover. (She was much improved, in WBY's opinion, by Mabel Dickinson's instruction in Swedish drill. [52]) One result was the enduring jealousy of her sister Sara Allgood. Another was an embarrassing overture from Frank Fay, who wanted to return to the company. And, in the wake of the Abbey's recent success, the directors' plans to buy out Horniman led to long and embittered negotiations.

By mid-December Gregory was firmly convinced that they must mount an 'appeal' to purchase the theatre from Horniman, writing to WBY that 'it would be a fine dramatic thing for someone to do'. [53] The very same day WBY began to calculate what kind of an offer might be acceptable, and by 21 December an audit of the accounts convinced him they were in a position to move forward. South African magnates were wooed to Abbey performances; WBY considered selling the Canadian Pacific stock in which he had invested his American earnings; and, above all, the sum needed to buy out Horniman had to be agreed. Pollexfen-like, while admitting that she had spent about £5,000 on the buildings, WBY had no intention of offering so much. Not only was there the question of the subsidy due until December 1910, which would be deducted, and the cost of replacing the electric lights, but in mid-January he got the buildings valued at the advantageously low sum of £2,000–£2,300.[54] After deductions, he decided to drop their offer to £1,000 from the £1,500 originally envisaged. Lily gleefully told JBY, 'Willy had it valued by an expert . . . His valuation was some hundreds under Miss Horniman's own valuation. Bernard Shaw says he always thought there was a Jewish droop about Willy's nose. Willy says "Shaw has no sense and no knowledge of life and this is seen in all his plays." '[55]

Shaw had offered to act as broker with his old friend and patron, but in the end it was Gregory who had to face Horniman alone, telling her she and WBY wanted to form a limited liability company and offering her less than the £1,428 minimum she demanded. At a terrible meeting in London all their latent antipathy flared up, with Horniman accusing the directors of fraudulence and threatening jail. Still shaken, Gregory wrote to WBY afterwards:

I had no quarrel with her – wolf and lamb! – but I will never if I can help it see her again and hear her insane accusations against my friends, dead and living.

I am glad now I went through that dreadful visit, for I am pretty sure it would have been a mistake letting her have that proposal to show against us. She got into Shaw's mind that we (or you, as he said) were beating her down . . . I was so thankful I kept even good humour with Miss H – of course if she was sane one would have turned on her, but it was the performance of a raving lunatic. I could not keep her to the point.

I was not even angry, it was like looking at some malignant growth. One wondered how she came to be there, and felt a desire to be away and clear of it.[56]

Relations were not helped by Shaw telling Horniman that she was giving them a bargain (which was true). As usual with Horniman, WBY was in a sensitive position; Gregory later claimed that she had to force him to write an angry remonstrance to Horniman by threatening that otherwise she would close Coole to him. He did so, reluctantly, but she released him from sending it.[57] But by 18 February WBY could report to Gregory that Horniman had agreed to take the £1,000: the agreement for sale dated two days later committed Horniman to paying the two final subsidies in June and September 1910 (£400 in toto) and receiving £1,000 from the directors. To the patron herself WBY wrote, 'do not think that I am not grateful for all you have done – yes I am even when you write to Maunsell accusing me by implication of bad faith. I conclude you do not mean it & remind myself of other days.'[58] They still had the rest of 1910 to get through, with Horniman angrier than ever; but the arrangements for a succession were in place.

Throughout, wby's creative energies were as remarkably engaged as ever: designing sets for Gregory's Goldoni adaptation *Mirandolina*, terrifying the actors at rehearsal by imposing fines for late attendance, and completing his own short verse play *The Green Helmet*. He was, however, relieved in March of some theatrical duties by a new manager, Lennox Robinson, first encountered as a playwright in April 1908. His controversial one-act drama *The Clancy Name* was played that October, and others rapidly followed. Robinson, a lanky young Protestant nationalist from Cork, appealed greatly to wby: 'he is a serious intellect and may grow to be a great dramatist'. In February 1910, to fill the gap left by Connell, wby sent Robinson off to learn the production business from Shaw and Granville-Barker in London – comparing himself to the man who took Ibsen from behind the chemist's counter in Bergen. Robinson spent six weeks staying in Woburn Buildings. He did not follow through Gregory's idea that he learn boxing from Robert in order to eject troublemakers from the theatre, but he duly took over management of the Abbey and stayed there, on and off, for most of his life.

Gregory had her reservations, especially about Robinson's taste for Cork realism rather than verse drama: from her perch backstage she sent wby beady-eyed progress reports on his protégé's development. Despite this, wby left more and more to Robinson, and the Abbey programme reflected this change ('a strange ending to the poetic playhouse Yeats wanted', Russell remarked to Quinn[59]). Receipts accordingly increased threefold by June 1910. As for Robinson, unworldly, absent-minded and eventually alcoholic, the stress of dealing with the players nearly reduced him to a nervous breakdown at the end of his first season; by September 1911 wby wanted him to run the business side, and produce only the plays he was interested in. None the less, he wanted to retain his young acolyte, 'the only person we have ever found who could keep order in the company'.[60] And Gregory probably thought the price worth paying, if it released wby for his own work. On 11 February 1910 he sent her his draft of the last (and best) lines in *The Green Helmet*:

> And I choose the laughing lip
> That shall not turn from laughing, whatever rise or fall,
> The heart that grows no bitterer although betrayed by all,
> The hand that loves to scatter, the life like a gambler's throw;
> And these things I make prosper, till a day come that I know
> When heart & mind shall darken that the weak may end & the strong,
> And the long remembering harpers have matter for a song.[61]

The ruthless tone reflects his own life, spent between the Abbey and his secluded writing-room at Glasnevin. He no longer saw sundered friends like Russell[62] and newer acquaintances like MacDonagh never became intimates, though he advised them as generously as ever about their work. His irritation with Dublin cliques remained unabated; Gregory, always alert to threats and distractions, worried that he was becoming too interested in Gertrude Kingston's attempt to set up a London art-theatre, which reassembled many of the old troupe (Sturge Moore, Ricketts, Masefield, Craig). But his energies were monopolized in February by planning lectures for the Abbey's fundraising drive, and in the course of this he would clarify much about his own life.[63]

He had outlined a lecture-series in January, 'The Fall of Romance', according to Lily – 'but since then he says he is in better spirits so he is going to call it "the rise of romance"'.[64] As the lectures emerged and were delivered to fashionable London audiences in March 1910, however, they synthesized literary commentary with autobiography. A dry run at the United Arts Club on 8 February showed him that he had to know exactly what he meant to say. He delved back into the books of the Rhymers Club for material, and by mid-February he had decided to concentrate in his poetry lecture upon Dowson, Johnson and the connection between poetry and personality – an odd reversion to some of the ideas preached by JBY, as his son acknowledged in a graceful letter.

I have just finished dictating a first sketch of my lecture in London, it is on the dialect drama with Synge as the principal figure. All three lectures have worked themselves out as a plea for uniting literature once more to personality, the personality of the writer in lyric poetry or with imaginative personalities in drama. The only ground on which I differ from you is that I look upon character and personality as different things or perhaps different forms of the same thing. Juliet has personality, her nurse has character, I look upon personality as the individual form of our passions (Dowson's in his poetry or Byron in 'Manfred' or Forbes Robertson in a romantic part have all personality but we do not necessarily know much about their characters). Character belongs I think to Comedy, but all that's rather a long story and is connected with a whole mass of definitions.

I probably get the distinction from the stage, where we say a man is a 'character actor' meaning that he builds up a part out of observation, or we say that he is 'an emotional actor' meaning that he builds it up out of himself, and in this last case – we always add, if he is not commonplace – that he has personality. Of course Shakespeare has both because he is always a tragic comedian.

In the process of writing my third lecture I found it led up to the thought of your letter which I am going to quote at the end. It has made me realise with some surprise how fully my philosophy of life has been inherited from you in all but its details and applications.[65]

He had been meditating on definitions of personality in art and relating them to his Rhymer colleagues since the previous summer. As always, a general argument was inferred from personal experience – not always to his audience's liking. The youthful William Carlos Williams, who attended WBY's lecture at the Adelphi, was appalled when Gosse as Chairman cut the speaker short – in Williams's view, because WBY defended the decadent lives of 1890s figures like Dowson and Johnson and condemned contemporary England for denying them an audience.[66] Shaw, chairing the final lecture, tried to sabotage his old sparring-partner in his summing up, warning the audience not to get the impression that they had to be Irish in order to be artists. 'I am so anxious that the peculiar impression Mr Yeats makes in coming from a strange land and a strange people should not discourage you.'[67] But what mattered was the fact that WBY was placing the companions of his youth firmly in a past which he had left behind him, while defending the 'reckless courage' of any artist ready (like many of the Rhymers) to 'enter into the abyss of himself'. And the conflict between the lessons of art and the necessities of everyday Irish politics was spelt out clearly by a Dublin lecture to the Gaelic League on 3 March, ostensibly on 'Ireland and the Theatre'. To an eclectic audience (including MacDonagh, Colum, Dunsany and Patrick Pearse) WBY spoke passionately about art, propaganda and the writer's personality. Irish literature must seek the uncompromising, vigorous simplicity of personal utterance, not the second-hand pieties which the Young Ireland movement had to peddle in order to create national consciousness half a century before. His current attitude was reflected by an evident determination not to trim his sails to the Gaelic League's sensitivities. 'Mr Yeats fears that Ireland is going to be de-Irishised by English Victorian commonplace being translated into Irish and spread through Ireland at secondhand,' wrote one disgruntled reviewer. 'Early in the night he acknowledged that he did not know Irish. So he was not himself in a position to judge.'[68]

The *Irish Times* noted that WBY, 'always interesting because he is so splendidly impatient of what we common people regard as the realities of life', was interrogating the growth of a new spirit of national co-operation in Ireland. 'We are all trying to discover where we agree with one another rather than to accentuate the points on which we differ', but WBY had decided to highlight disagreements and to reject practicalities.[69] He had his reasons. This lecture, with its attack on the 'perpetual apologetics' of the long nationalist argument founded on hatred of England, its denunciation of hack journalism, and its celebration of Synge as the uncompromising voice of the real Ireland closely reflected the long essay he was gestating in March and April 1910, which would be published in July of the following year as 'J. M. Synge and the Ireland of his Time'.

Thus throughout the spring WBY's thoughts were running on autobiography, as well as on the raw wound of Synge's death. Working up his fundraising lectures for the Abbey appeal, 'Synge and the dialect drama' were much on his mind, and the necessity to produce a long introduction to Synge's *Collected Works* concentrated his attention. Gregory supplied him with letters and other material from Coole; he also canvassed friends like Masefield, who astonished him by telling him how much Synge had revered WBY's own writing.[70] He retired to Dunsany Castle at weekends, where he found – as at Coole – his lyric gift could return. In mid-March he turned aside from the Synge essay to draft a brief and lapidary poem about creative work, 'The Fascination of What's Difficult',[71] blaming his obsession with 'theatre business, management of men' for harnessing the winged horse of creative imagination. The tone bears out his advice to MacDonagh at this time: 'I often ask myself when I have written a poem, could I have said this or that more simply in prose, and if I could I alter the poem.'[72] But his great effort went into the prose of the Synge essay, which he was writing 'rather elaborately and certainly very slowly'. Gregory received progress reports ('I am at present attacking Young Ireland'), and in May he could tell her that 'some of [it] seems to be as good as any prose I have written . . . an elaborate peice of work which will however enfuriate the anti-Play Boy people. I begin with the row & then go on to account for it.'[73]

As so often, he was a good critic of his own work: 'J. M. Synge and the Ireland of his Time' is not only a crystallization of WBY's thoughts on art and nationalism in 1910, but a powerful implicit statement of autobiography. It charts the development of his own mind, starting with deceptive simplicity at the point when he was called back from Aberdeen to the riotous opening of Synge's play, and realized that he was set on a different path from the original inspiration which had guided his early work. 'I stood there watching, knowing well that I saw the dissolution of a school of patriotism that held sway over my youth' – a sentence drafted over and over again, in what is usually a fluent manuscript.[74] It had not happened as instantly as that, since the *Playboy* riots came as the climactic battle of a war which had been raging since at least 1903, when WBY opened hostilities with 'The National Theatre and Three Sorts of Ignorance'.[75] WBY had already isolated '[Synge's] bitter misunderstanding with the wreckage of Young Irelandism', as early as January 1909 – before the playwright's death.[76] But by 1910 he was able to connect this process into his already complex autobiography, recapitulating upon the lessons taught by O'Leary, the arguments with J. F. Taylor and Arthur Griffith, and the inadequacy of Young Ireland's approach to national identity. The final version reached a level of compression, allusiveness and subtlety which he had not achieved before.

Thomas Davis, whose life had the moral simplicity which can give to actions the lasting influence that style alone can give to words, had understood that a country which has no national institutions must show its young men images for the affections, although they be but diagrams of what it should or may be. He and his school imagined the Soldier, the Orator, the Patriot, the Poet, the Chieftain and above all the Peasant; and these, as celebrated in essay and songs and stories, possessed so many virtues that no matter how England, who as Mitchel said, 'had the ear of the world', might slander us, Ireland, even though she could not come to the world's other ear, might go her way unabashed. But ideas and images which have to be understood and loved by large numbers of people, must appeal to no rich personal experience, no patience of study, no delicacy of sense; and if at rare moments some Memory of the Dead can take its strength from one, at all other moments manner and matter will be rhetorical, conventional sentimental; and language, because it is carried beyond life perpetually, will be as wasted as the thought, with unmeaning pedantries and silences, and a dread of all that has salt and savour. After a while, in a land that has given itself to agitation over-much, abstract thoughts are raised up between men's minds and Nature, who never does the same thing twice, or makes one man like another, till minds, whose patriotism is perhaps great enough to carry them to the scaffold, cry down natural impulse with the morbid persistence of minds unsettled by some fixed idea. They are preoccupied with the nation's future, with heroes, poets, soldiers, painters, armies, fleets, but only as these things are understood by a child in a national school, while a secret feeling that what is so unreal needs continual defence makes them bitter and restless . . .

Even if what one defends be true, an attitude of defence, a continual apology, whatever the cause, makes the mind barren because it kills intellectual innocence; that delight in what is unforeseen, and in the mere spectacle of the world, the mere drifting hither and thither that must come before all true thought and emotion. A zealous Irishman, especially if he lives much out of Ireland, spends his time in a never-ending argument about Oliver Cromwell, the Danes, the penal laws, the rebellion of 1798, the famine, the Irish peasant, and ends by substituting a traditional casuistry for a country; and if he be a Catholic yet another casuistry that has professors, schoolmasters, letter-writing priests and the authors of manuals to make the meshes fine, comes between him and English literature, substituting arguments and hesitations for the excitement at the first reading of the great poets which should be a sort of violent imaginative puberty . . .

How can one, if one's mind be full of abstractions and images created not for their own sake but for the sake of party, even if there were still the need, make pictures for the mind's eye and sounds that delight the ear, or discover thoughts that tighten the muscles, or quiver and tingle in the flesh, and so stand like St Michael with the trumpet that calls the body to resurrection?

The reception of Synge's play had become an epiphany, expressing WBY's essential recognition of himself; the essay delivered a sweep of prophetic vision which forecast much of his own art and life for the next three decades. This stressed brutal and astringent truths, the need for Irish literature to admit some English models (notably the Elizabethans), and the denial that Irish history was

419

a parade of pasteboard heroes. Synge (described with deliberate inaccuracy as 'by nature unfitted to think a political thought') was recruited to the cause, defiantly rejecting reassuring pieties and the platitudes of journalists. 'A mind that generalises rapidly, continually prevents the experience that would have made it feel and see deeply, just as a man whose character is too complete in youth seldom grows into any energy of moral beauty.'

Here, if anywhere, was pure autobiography: he was to say of his own youth, compared to Gonne's, 'she was complete, I was not'. And the uncompleted essay travelled with him to France in the early summer, where he stayed in Gonne's seaside house. 'It has been a great help to the Synge essay my coming here,' he wrote to Gregory. 'I have talked out all the political part & partly by differing from Maud Gonne & partly by agreeing with her have revised it all in my mind. I have made it double the force it was. I think it will be the most elaborate thing I have written.'[77] It must have been at Colleville that he wrote a passage about 'the morbid persistence of minds unsettled by some fixed idea . . . They no longer love, for only life is loved, and at last, a generation is like a hysterical woman who will make unmeasured accusations and believe impossible things, because of some logical deduction from a solitary thought which has turned a portion of her mind to stone.'

It is true that he also referred (a year later) to Annie Horniman's obsessed mind as 'a piece of stone'; but he had written in his journal of March 1909 that 'the soul of Ireland has become a vapour and her body a stone',[78] and in this image he conflated – yet again – Gonne and her adopted country. In 1916, in a much more famous work also written in Gonne's house, he found once more the image of a heart turned by fanaticism to stone, fixed in the fluvial stream of life. As so often, when he wrote about individual freedom versus nationalist commitment, he thought of her.[79]

The publishing history of 'J. M. Synge and the Ireland of his Time' was as complex as its gestation. Intended as an introduction to Synge's *Collected Works*, it was completed in mid-September 1910. Only at this point did WBY discover that George Roberts at Maunsel had already printed the *Manchester Guardian* essays and other unapproved material, slipped in at a late stage after being left off the proof contents-page. Complaints to the Synge family were unavailing; 'Roberts has deliberately deceived us both.'[80] Maunsel defied Edward Synge and WBY on the strength of a clause in the contract with the executors which could be interpreted as allowing them to include journalism. WBY's efforts to mobilize Maunsel's financial backers, and to invoke Synge's own deathbed wishes, came to nothing, though he pursued Roberts mercilessly and persuaded Gregory to withdraw her works from him too.[81] This quarrel helped estrange him from yet more of his Dublin acquaintances.[82] In July 1911 Cuala published the essay as one of their beautiful – and expensive – little books: it was out of print by September, but resurfaced in *The Cutting of an Agate*, a collection initially produced for the American market (and to protect his Cuala copyrights there) in 1912.

It remains one of the most revealing of WBY's early autobiographical ventures, though reviewers were bemused by its 'lack of orderly sequence . . . a kind of diary, as though its author had unpacked his ideas concerning much that had engaged his thoughts in the literary history that Ireland is now achieving for herself . . . with only a secondary interest in Synge himself. Often it reads as though the thought of Synge suddenly crossed his mind, with the result that he penned down some sentences concerning Synge that are startling in their illumination.'[83] The composition of the essay shows that this apparent randomness was artful in the extreme: but the critic was astute in defining it as an instalment of WBY's own literary and political testament.

IV

For WBY, the summer of 1910 began with an idyll. In late April he suddenly decided to join Gonne and her family at their house on the Normandy coast – using this departure as an excuse not to escort Gregory's grandson and his nurse from Victoria to Euston (besides, 'I rather doubt my recognising either Richard or his nurse in a crowd at a railway station'[84]). Instead, on 30 April he took the ferry to Cherbourg, on a calm sea and under sunny skies; after a rail journey through Calvados, Gonne swept into Le Molay station yard on a cart and drove him to Colleville, 'a big ugly house on the sea beach' near Vierville.[85] There was 'no-one to speak to, even if one did know French'; but May Gonne was present as chaperone and they were soon joined by Iseult, now sixteen, 'tall and very pretty'. Gonne was in tranquil rural mood, ostentatiously pious, continually saying masses for those 'who died for Ireland' to release them from purgatory. In this frame of mind she brought WBY to the neighbouring Mont-Saint-Michel on 11 May. The combination of austerity and magnificence astonished him, as well as an atmosphere of sanctity and romance in a sea-girt fortress which must have recalled his own *Speckled Bird*. As usual, he and Gonne found something to disagree about – in this case, her insistence that priestly control created a high and severe art. But the visit helped to release poetic energies, already finding a voice after his long silence. He not only refined the political arguments in his Synge essay; lyrics came easily, including some of the poems to Gonne which would appear in *The Green Helmet* at the end of the year.

At this distance, and in this company, the news of the death of Edward VII on 6 May must have made very little interruption. However, it would precipitate the last great battle with Horniman. With WBY in France and Gregory at Coole, Lennox Robinson was left to decide whether the Abbey should be closed as a mark of respect. He wired to Gort for advice; the telegram did not reach Gregory in time, so the Abbey, alone of Dublin's theatres, remained open, despite Gregory's eventual advice to close for courtesy's sake. Horniman, already embittered by the negotiations apparently concluded in February, took violent umbrage and demanded a full public apology for what she interpreted – yet again – as a deliberately political act. Gregory's rather offhand statement simply regretted that the theatre had stayed open 'owing to accident' (which pleased neither Horniman nor Sinn Féin). wby refused to sack Robinson; Horniman withheld the subsidy due in June; the directors for their part refused to pay her the £1,000 agreed in February. All was back at an impasse, while the issue about a 'political' gesture eventually went to arbitration.

wby and Gregory, however, were by now in a strong position. They had been fundraising assiduously since the beginning of the year, helped by an initial £300 from Dunsany, and the goodwill of Dublin's elite; the campaign now moved into top gear. Gregory, in particular, felt it would be worth sacrificing Horniman's £400 subsidy in order to be free of her, and resented having to make even a half-hearted apology. 'I know the greeting in London will be – "so Miss Horniman made you apologise!" I want to change it to "so you have thrown over Miss Horniman." I believe that we shall get more than the £400 for showing independence.'[86]

wby publicized the Abbey's position in a letter to *The Times*, placed to coincide with the company's season at the Court Theatre. They were taking three times the amount of last year; unlike the Moscow Arts Theatre, they could soon be solvent; £2,000 was already subscribed (from luminaries like Barrie, Birrell, Hutcheson-Poe, Lord Pirrie, Lord Iveagh, Blunt, Dunsany, the Duke of Leinster and the Duchess of Sutherland – several of them staunch Unionists, but none put off by 'politics').[87] The target of £5,000 remained elusive, but money continued to come in. In September wby was still looking for a rich patron to take over the lease, and trying to control his annoyance at Martyn's convoluted reasons for not coming to their aid.[88] On 21 September, however, he was able to make an encouraging statement to the players.

. . . [I] told them how much money we had got as the result of our appeal, described the finance Committee, said we might be able to arrange a system of profit sharing but did not make a definite promise. I then urged them all to remain with us and pointed out how very nearly the Theatre was paying, described to them the advantage for an artist even though he got less money in the year of not having to be anxious about it or to give much thought to it. I then showed them the Craig design which you sent on to me, I think his beautiful design for 'The Hour Glass' excited them. Then I went up into the office to receive the complainants.[89]

So he and Gregory had worked out a new arrangement, based on a limited liability company composed of themselves, with no public share subscription and no published accounts.[90] Subscribers would be donors, not shareholders. The remains of the Irish National Theatre Society were to be dissolved, though WBY worried that the Fays might materialize, Lazarus-like, and block it. Players' contracts would henceforth include a commitment to sign an attendance-book. The last vestiges of the old, uncommercial co-operative were gone. With all this in place, a reversal of the old patent was applied for on 19 November 1910; the new patent was granted a week later. The sum of £2,139 had been raised. Gregory was still convening highly social 'At Homes' at the theatre, where the Dublin plutocracy and their well-dressed wives (including the famously philistine W. M. Murphy of the *Independent*) were appealed to for money by WBY.[91] A final symbol of victory was provided by the return to the company of the independent-minded Maire nic Shiubhlaigh, duly warned by Gregory that she would have to put up with a lot from the Allgood sisters, which turned out to be no less than the truth. While nic Shiubhlaigh's chief duties were to be with the second Abbey company and acting school planned for the new year, the theatre rapidly mounted a production of her great success, *The Shuiler's Child*, in November. Thus Susan Mitchell's criticisms of the year before were, eventually, taken to heart: the 'broken-kneed heroes and barging heroines' of verse drama were to be leavened by injections of popular realism.

The disagreement with Horniman over the purchase terms went to arbitration with C. P. Scott of the *Manchester Guardian*, who in May 1911 decided in the directors' favour. WBY had already decided to be magnanimous, and release Horniman from the terms if she felt they were unfair.[92] He promptly sent her a generous letter, much redrafted, implicitly apologizing for 'giving her pain' in defending himself and his fellow-workers, and regretting their estrangement: 'let us restore our old friendship by remembering the thousand other things that we agree upon'.[93] But her only reply was a long and violent telegram. The old friendship was finally over. Soror Fortiter et Recte did not meet her Dear Demon again until twenty-eight years later, shortly before her own death. Socially obsessed to the end, she wrote bitterly to Joseph Holloway: 'My initial mistake was simple – it took me a long time to learn that there was no room for an educated middle-class woman who loves the arts in Dublin. Commercial Manchester is a very different city.'[94] But her emotional investment had run far deeper than that.

Either way, WBY had won all along the line. The theatre had survived, aided by the support of such unlikely bedfellows as Lady Ardilaun and T. M. Healy, and audiences were flocking in. 'The Abbey would cheer you up to see it,' Lily wrote to JBY.

Motors carriages and cabs in a string outside – Willy has won his fight – a hard fight. I asked him the other night how the company was getting on together. 'The usual quarrelling,' he said. 'But then,' said he, 'the founder of the Christian religion had the same trouble with his Company and had to invent the parables to keep them in good humour.'[95]

V

The theatre may have been solvent, but WBY's own finances remained perilously uncertain. In 1909 and 1910 his annual income hovered around £180. His Cuala books brought in very little – less than £30 for *The Green Helmet* in 1910; though American sales were steadily increasing, the low dollar rate worked against him. *Poems 1899–1905* had been replaced in March by *Poems: Second Series*, which sold 650 copies over the next two years, bringing a royalty of just over £30.[96] Poems were appearing irregularly and his lecturing earnings had been donated to the Abbey appeal. In the summer of 1910 he was rescued from penury only by an offer of £100 from Chappells for the rights to *The Countess Cathleen*, which Franco Leoni wanted to adapt into an opera. WBY agreed, with the inevitable condition that Craig do the staging. His commitment to Craig also appears in a scorching letter of resignation from the Council of the Shakespeare Memorial Theatre, which he condemned for appointing only respectable 'excellent persons' who 'would neither do nor allow to be done anything I could take pleasure in'; he demanded they elect to supreme authority an artist like Craig, or some European innovator. 'I have always thought that men who love the arts in England – unlike those in Latin countries – are poor spirited and I wish that your committee had done something to give them more Continental minds.'[97] But, ironically, he was about to join the ranks of the respectable himself.

During the spring and summer of 1910 a number of steps were taken to bring him into the paths of the literary establishment, where rewards might accompany influence. In April he was elected to the Academic Committee of English Letters, an organization dominated by Edmund Gosse and consisting entirely of 'excellent persons'. It was developed by a subcommittee of the Royal Society of Literature, which it was expected to supersede – playing for literature the part that the Royal Society played for science, the Royal Academy for art and the British Academy for scholarship. As it turned out, it did not; its business tended to concentrate on matters like excluding Mrs Humphry Ward. Henry James described the committee as 'a *pleasant* and a plastic, elastic, aspiring thing'; putting it another way, the ruthless younger generation saw it as 'a terrible and solid phalanx of A. C. Bensonism', while Arnold Bennett and H. G. Wells shunned it as 'grotesque'.[98]

Other members included Arthur Balfour, Charles Lyell, John Scott Haldane, Laurence Binyon, Conrad, Hardy and Kipling. But for WBY it served a purpose, which Gregory spotted with her usual perspicacity:

It is just what will be of service to you in two ways, one with the stupid public who only recognise names they are officially ordered to accept, and one, the placing of you in terms of equality in a distinguished body . . . even if they dont meet often, you will take your proper place there.[99]

WBY disapproved of omissions from the membership, but he thought it might do some good in the current battles against censorship. So he dutifully returned to London for meetings, lobbying assiduously about elections. Just as importantly, Gosse made it clear that this recognition might help towards another, more concrete advantage for WBY. This was currently taking the specific form of a Civil List pension – which could provide a modest guaranteed income for life.[100]

The idea had been floated since late 1909, with Gosse playing a leading part, and support offered by the nationalist MP and littérateur Justin McCarthy. Membership of the Academic Committee, Gosse told Gregory, 'gives him a claim which cannot be put by'; he issued further advice about the letter she should send to the literary-minded Chief Secretary (and Abbey supporter), Augustine Birrell. Asquith, who had met WBY at Gosse's house, was already prepared; supporting signatures might include Ian Hamilton, George Wyndham, Lord Crewe, S. H. Butcher, Austin Dobson, Lord Cromer, and Gosse himself.

This was the Establishment in full force. The campaign reflected the changes in WBY's social life, moving from bohemian Mondays at Woburn Buildings to weekends with Lady Katharine Somerset and her Cabinet Minister guests.[101] But in terms of Irish politics, taking a pension in the royal gift immediately raised awkward questions. When first sounded out by Gosse, through Agnes Tobin, WBY told him 'if the French land in the West of Ireland I won't undertake not to join them when if [sic] they want me so there will be no deceit in the matter'.[102] Now that things had moved on a stage, Gregory put the position clearly.

About the Civil List, it is very important, for that sum would make a great difference for all your life, & help you to arrange it. I have never been under the impression that it was impossible for a Nationalist, but I have never gone into the matter. I think you should, if Gosse speaks of it, get the lists & see what revolutionaries, if any have had it in the past. Standish O'Grady is the only one I know of who has it now. And he cd tell also whether your freedom wd be in any way bound by it, whether for instance it cd be taken away if you shouted against a royal visit or tore up any more carpets. If there is any honourable obligation as to abstaining from these things, of course you could not take it.[103]

But, reassured on this point, they went ahead. Gosse wrote to Gregory at Coole on 23 July, sending a draft petition and asking her to show it to Birrell: 'I feel that, if we do anything, we ought to make use of his important sympathy.' Gregory replied by return, in a letter now lost. As later recounted to Birrell himself, she asked Gosse to collect some signatures for a draft petition of her own, which he resented, 'especially the allusion to the Academic Committee wh he takes the credit for'.[104] Possibly she also felt Gosse's changes to the petition emphasized WBY's loyalty too effusively and told him so: he had already stressed that 'Yeats's genius as a poet and the disinterested character of his work ought to be the two prominent points, I think.'[105] Gosse was famously touchy, and responded with an astonishingly offensive letter: 'I am lost in wonder at what can have induced you to interfere in an affair when your opinion was not asked, and when you seem to intend neither to give any help nor take any trouble.'[106] This letter apparently refers to the official petition to the King, which Gosse had been handling. He was proprietorial about WBY, whom he had been cultivating since the mid-nineties – not only entertaining him constantly but (like Gregory) lending him money.[107] Gregory's own campaign was aimed at her friend Birrell in Dublin Castle, and perhaps Gosse mistook this point, believing that she was trying to dictate to him how to go about the kind of elevated string-pulling which was, to him, the very breath of life. Later, she told Quinn that she took the initiative by writing to the Chief Secretary and 'arranged Yeats's pension with Birrell in a box at the Court Theatre in fifteen minutes'; whereas Gosse claimed that it 'was settled by the Prime Minister in an immediate reply to my letter to him'.[108] In any case, as Gregory saw the matter, once Gosse rejected her co-operation she had to continue the campaign to pressurize Birrell alone. Through early August she collected signatures from luminaries such as Hamilton, Lord Dunraven, Lord Lytton and Thomas Hardy.[109] By then, in any case, Gosse's petition had gone to the King, with a fair wind from the Prime Minister.

Gosse's letter created storms at Coole. As far as Gregory and her son were concerned, she had been insulted: what was WBY going to do? He should, of course, take up the cudgels on behalf of his old and devoted friend, and Robert apparently made this clear. As WBY recorded in his intermittent diary, he drafted a stinging letter to Gosse, breaking off the friendship between them; but it was not sent, and Gregory did not press the point. She later told Quinn that this was a second draft; at first she 'told Yeats that she expected him to reply', and when she saw his first draft, 'a milk and water thing', 'said that if he hadn't any sense of dignity or self-respect he should remember that he was her guest, and she insisted on a stronger reply'. He produced one, but was miserable and unhappy about it; she kept it for a fortnight and returned it to him. The whole affair consumed pages of his diary. In accounting for his own behaviour, he tried to rationalize it as the result of his efforts since his youth to 'destroy in myself, by analysis, instinctive indignation' – which meant giving in to 'vanity'. In a letter drafted to Robert Gregory, but really 'trying to put myself right with myself', he explained:

As I look back, I see occasion after occasion on which I have been prevented from doing what was a natural and sometimes the right thing either because analysis of the emotion or action of another, or self-distrustful analysis of my own emotion destroyed impulse. I cannot conceive the impulse, unless it was so sudden that I had to act at once, that could urge me into action at all if it affected personal life. All last week the moment that my impulse told me I should demand with indignation an apology from Gosse, my analysis said, 'You think that from vanity. You want to do a passionate thing because it stirs your pride.' . . . In impersonal and public things, because there this distrust of myself does not come in, I have impulse. I would have explained it by saying that it is the world I have been brought up in – you have always lived among defined social relations and I only among defined ideas – but then my family seemed to me to have more than enough of the usual impulses. I even do my writing by self-distrusting reasons. I thought to write this note in the same way as I write the others.[110]

The address to Robert Gregory is a fiction; there is no evidence that this or other explanatory missives were ever sent, and (appearing as they do in his diary) they resemble his dialogues with an imaginary *alter ego* like Leo Africanus or Owen Aherne more than anything else. And however high-flown his reasoning, in other entries he lacerated himself. His abstract reasoning about 'impulse' and 'passion' is inconsistent with the 'personal' criteria which he admitted existed (Gosse's kindness to Symons, his own indebtedness to Gregory, and above all – though barely mentioned – the risk of endangering the pension). He knew he had behaved inadequately.

As I look back on the whole thing, I come to see that Lady Gregory and Robert expected me to act at once, on a code. Instead of asking 'Why has Gosse done this?' instead of being, what is worse really, interested in his character and motives, I should have been in a very simple state of mind. I should have spoken of him with contempt, or written to him with contempt – there was nothing else to do . . . Since I was fifteen and began to think, I have mocked at that way of looking at the world, as if it was a court of law where all wrong actions were judged according to their legal penalties. All my life I have, like every artist, been proud of belonging to a nobler world, of having chosen the slow, dangerous, laborious path of moral judgment. And yet the moment the code appears before me in the personality of two friends, I am shaken, I doubt myself. I doubted because I talked. In silence I could have thought the whole thing out, kept my vacillation to myself. I could have appealed to what is best in Gosse, perhaps reconciled those who will be enemies, or at any rate I could have recalled him to his better self. My father would have done this because he would have been himself. I neither dealt with the matter like an artist, nor as a man of the world.[111]

In the end he deduced – as he always did – a lesson for himself. 'Why do I write all this? I suppose that I may learn at last to keep to my own in every situation in life; to discover and create in myself as I grow old that thing which is to life what style is to letters: moral radiance, a personal quality of universal meaning in action and in thought.'

But none of this interrogation was passed on to Gosse. As often before, he had been able to separate internal agonizing from public action. Gosse wrote a friendly note to him on 29 July, to say the petition had gone to the King; on 5 August the Prime Minister's letter was sent to Coole, awarding WBY the annual pension of £150 available through the death of John Davidson. As WBY wrote to Birrell, this set him 'free' from anxiety and from the need of doing less than the best I can'; Birrell gracefully replied that the Prime Minister had been 'at least as eager as I was', and compared the award to Dr Johnson's – 'the money best spent in England during the whole of my beloved eighteenth century'.[112] WBY wrote into his journal a stern letter which he records was sent to Gosse on 6 August, rebuking him for his inadequate apology; but there is no indication that it was sent, either in Gosse's correspondence or in the tone of their subsequent exchanges. (This is probably the second letter which Gregory told Quinn she made him write, and then witheld from the post.) It is easy to condemn WBY for pusillanimous behaviour, but, as Gregory herself realized, a great deal was at stake. With the pension, his annual income was nearly doubled. Gregory, mollified, set herself to persuading him that his next act should be to join a London club. Regarding the pension, she had warned him, 'some screechers may screech, but that needn't trouble you'.[113]

This proved all too true. Those who had become alienated from him took the news sourly. Quinn thought it would be 'pathetic' to see WBY become 'a prop of throne and constitution', while Russell replied loftily, 'All radical youth ends in Toryism in the [sic] old age and he would gradually like Wordsworth have become a prop of throne and constitution before he died.'[114] More vituperatively, the Leader and Sinn Féin journalists took to pillorying 'Pensioner Yeats' as a lackey of the British government, and continued the assault until he died. 'The Pensioner is, of course, a pure-souled patriot; in payment for his patriotism Emmet got the rope but Pollexfen Yeats, the author of "Cathleen ni Houlihan", gets three pounds a week from the British Government.'[115] WBY believed the price worth paying. He had seen – as he thought – Symons driven mad, and Masefield into mediocrity, by writing for money in order to meet their wives' expectations. Long ago, in Blenheim Road, he had decided that the same would not happen to him. (This may have influenced his own inclination towards independent or unattainable free spirits, such as Farr and Gonne.) While he accused himself of cowardly behaviour over the Gosse–Gregory affair, she forgave him, and on the matter of artistic conscience, his mind was clear. Whatever lay beneath the surface, Coole in August still exerted its charm. Shaw came to stay, and WBY felt their old antipathy begin to moderate; each thought he was beginning to know the other at last. He resumed relations with Dickinson, visiting her on Dublin trips, writing to her once more as 'My Friend', and telling her she had inspired a lyric ('The Mask') for *The Player Queen*.

And there was always the theatre, Sara Allgood's threats to leave, and the excitement of Craig's new ideas for a shifting proscenium. At this time he completed his essay 'The Tragic Theatre', published in Craig's journal, which summed up theories of dramatic art in terms of his own developing taste. In the process he coined some of his most ringing aphorisms about the theatre: 'tragedy must always be a drowning and breaking of the dykes that separate man from man, and it is upon these dykes comedy keeps house'. The distinction between 'character' (the foundation of comedy) and 'passion' (the basis of tragedy) seemed to him symbolized by the difference brought into modern art by Manet's style of portraiture (character incarnate). This replaced the debased models of nineteenth-century academicism, but also signalled how far modern consciousness had departed from the passion expressed by Titian. The argument for abstract scenery, using light rather than paint, develops from this distinction: drama, like modern painting, must liberate itself into 'a noble, capricious, extravagant, resonant, fantastic art'. These were key words, and much in this essay reflects his own artistic development. Tragic pleasure is defined as the 'intensity of trance' which he felt watching his own plays, constantly reinterpreted (and rewritten), dependent on the most fragile illusions. He identified this state as 'reverie' – the word he would eventually choose for his autobiography.

Another delicate negotiation was also getting under way, with the object of providing an income – and from almost as unlikely a source as the largesse of the English crown. WBY's old adversary Dowden had been stricken by ill-health, and Trinity College was sounding out possible successors to the Chair of English Literature. The prospect was not as strange as it would once have appeared. WBY was mellowing towards Trinity (though he remained resolutely opposed to recruiting actors from its ranks). On 15 March he had spoken there, and been praised by the redoubtably reactionary Vice-Provost Mahaffy – now equally famous in Dublin as a wit and a snob, and a central figure in the Unionist pantheon which WBY had spent his youth reviling. In the summer, as Dowden showed no sign of recovery, Robert Tyrrell approached wby, who wrote to Mahaffy (misspelling 'professorship'). Mahaffy, possibly for mischief's sake, was surprisingly encouraging. By September Gogarty could tell Gregory that all but two Senior Fellows were favourable towards wby, though jby warned him 'they are a very astute people – like the Vatican, their ideas are ignoble, but they make no mistakes in carrying them out'.[116] wby's nationalism was no disadvantage, 'rather in his favour', in view of the existence of the rival new university. The Civil List pension (not yet public knowledge) made him appear all the more desirable; if it created difficulties about the salary, it could be temporarily assigned elsewhere.

As for wby, the thought of Dowden's rooms ('very lofty and large – Georgian') and his £600 a year was irresistible. At the same time he 'feared the effect on my imagination of any regular critical work', one day telling Gogarty that he would press for it, and changing his mind the next.[117] A couple of months spent lecturing for agencies in England might be a less distracting way of supplementing his income. But rumours began to circulate. Gregory assiduously cultivated Mahaffy, telling him to read wby's Spenser and Shakespeare essays,[118] while Dunsany brought his influence to bear with Lord Iveagh, Trinity's Chancellor. In December wby himself saw Mahaffy, an encounter described by Lily. 'Willy spoke of his own bad sight and hoped it would not come in the way of the work. "Oh" said Mahaffy, "that is all right. There is no work to do. Dowden never did any." How mad the Dowdens would be.'[119]

Indeed, Dowden's opinion was the one variable left out of the calculations, and, as Ezra Pound put it, he 'rose from the grave' to prevent this bizarre succession, living on until 1913.[120] In a silky dismissal a year later, he told the importunate jby that his son might be 'a very inspiring Professor of Poetry, such as they have in Oxford, who may choose his own themes, and give a few annual lectures', but he was no scholar. For wby's own sake it would be a calamity if he had to undergo the labour of teaching through the year. Besides, 'the process of appointment is usually to become first an assistant to some Professor & teach Anglo-Saxon, to publish some piece of scholarship, & show one's capacity in scientific research, & then to climb to a Professorship. One must accumulate a vast quantity of knowledge, & keep abreast with German, French & American publications.' This obvious snub was followed by a bland denial that there was any thought of canvassing for a replacement in any case, which – when the day came – must be done through official channels.[121] A quiet but decisive revenge was exerted for wby's fierce assaults in the 1890s.

As the prospect receded, wby felt some relief, though he did ask Sydney Cockerell to find out about the Oxford Chair of Poetry. He confided that the idea of having to live in Dublin for much of the year dismayed him and eventually concluded that his 'wandering life' was probably best. 'I long for a life without dates and without any settled abode. If I could find that I could write lyrics again.'[122] But his life was more peripatetic than most people's, and had evolved into a pattern where certain kinds of writing were creatively associated with particular locales. A set of Trinity rooms and an annual lecture-schedule would have changed all this, probably not for the better. And in his inimitable Pollexfen way, an unsuccessful project was turned to profit. In November 1910, when still feeling favourably disposed to the idea, he began to think about his lectures. He fixed on 'Chaucer and his Age', bought some books, persuaded Farr and Dickinson to read aloud to him, and became 'excited by the change of method that came when poets wrote to be read out not to be sung'.[123] The new rhythms and colloquial diction of his work from this point may owe something to his thrifty preparation for a job which he never actually got, and which he could never have found fulfilling.

Nevertheless, the fact that he would have considered entering an institution which he had for so long attacked as the musty abode of intellectual death indicates some kind of reconciliation with the Irish Protestant world. The end of September 1910 saw another kind of reckoning, which, like much else this year, brought him sharply up against the forces and influences that had shaped him. George Pollexfen died slowly from stomach cancer. As WBY noted, in the face of real calamity the great hypochondriac was heroically uncomplaining. Lily nursed him throughout in his uncomfortable Sligo house, surrounded by racing mementoes, Masonic regalia and astrological diagrams. On 1 September WBY wrote worriedly to her: should he come? Would he be any help? Would George simply fear that his advent, after so long, could only mean the worst? In the end, he stayed away. News of the imminent end reached him as he wrote the last words of his Synge essay. On 26 September George died, heralded by a banshee shriek outside the window, heard by both Lily and the nurse. With him went – for the Yeatses – the last vestige of Pollexfen Sligo.

WBY arrived in the town the next day, for the great funeral. Hundreds of Middleton & Pollexfen workers lined the streets for the procession, eighty Masons marched in full regalia (the two Prince Masons threw white roses into the grave, the rest acacia leaves), a wreath arrived from Jack in the old racing colours of primrose and violet, and Catholics were admitted into the Protestant church for the first time. Such strange people turned up that it was 'like the dredging of a pond', WBY remarked to Lily.[124] From the Imperial Hotel he sent an emotional letter to Gregory, building up a picture of George as the paternalist, class-free gentleman employer, knowing everyone in the firm personally, preferring to travel by public transport because he 'liked talking to the old women on the car & helping them up & down'. Under the inheritor Arthur Jackson 'it will be a harder rule now – Belfast rule'.[125] 'How strangely the death of those we have known in childhood moves us,' he reflected. 'They seem in the first shock of loss the stronger part of ourselves.'[126] The idealization of George was prompted by this reaction. The real George was expressed in his very carefully drawn will: an estate of £50,000 left in equal divisions to his siblings or their heirs. Of Susan's share Lily and Lolly got one third each, Jack and WBY one sixth – about £920. JBY, to his consternation and fury, got nothing.

To WBY it seemed 'characteristic and just': the girls needed more. 'I have my pension, & Jack has Cottie & the comic papers.'[127] JBY's resentment took the form of peremptorily requiring 'loans' from his children and WBY wondered whether his father should be summoned back from his penurious exile. 'But Jack wont have him back,' he told Gregory.

He says Lily wants him back just as a mother always wants her worst child to be brought home . . . that he is so 'wilful' Lily would be worn out & so on. So I have sent the 'loan' – £5 & Jack has done the same. I thought Jack was really alarmed at the idea of my father's return. I wanted him to write to Quinn & arrange it, he & I to pay. He says he always fought with my father after a week.[128]

For WBY too his father was better at a distance. Their relationship, conducted by letter, had already become more reciprocally appreciative.[129] *Rapprochement* with JBY was further eased by the loss of George Pollexfen, one of the vital surrogate parents WBY had adopted in his troubled youth. Essentially, he inherited more than the £920; more even than George's astonishingly large collection of occult materials – Tarot divinations, horoscopes, clairvoyance records, Golden Dawn rituals – not, in the event, returned as directed to 'Sapere Aude' (W. W. Westcott) in the Camden Road. 'How much of the past has broken from me in these last three years,' he wrote to Lily in 1911.[130] Synge's death had already made him confront the conflict between art and nationalism. After George's funeral WBY embarked on his own pond-dredging: the re-evaluation and recovery of his past, and all that had made him what he was.

Chapter 16 : TRUE AND FALSE IRELANDS
1910–1911

I have been driven into public life – how can I avoid rhetoric?

WBY, speech at *Poetry* banquet, Chicago,
1 March 1914

I

AFTER his sad return to Sligo, WBY moved between Coole, Dublin and London – a pattern made possible by the precious refuge of Woburn Buildings and all it stood for. If the death of Synge, the loss of Pollexfen Sligo, and the sniping about his pension combined to turn him away from Ireland, his London life always lay alongside: a parallel but invisible existence (like that of Swedenborg's ghosts) into which he could slip with ease. And as always, he retreated from personal dislocation into work. He found distraction through supervising the Craig designs for a revival of *The Hour-Glass*, where the use of masks and dominoes, along with the first use of the famous screens, excited him greatly. Renegotiating the Abbey patent also required attention, but he still found time to interview a new Belfast playwright, St John Ervine, whose devotion to Northern dialect appealed to him, and to consider how Molly Allgood's engagement to the *Manchester Guardian* journalist G. H. Mair might help their publicity. Farr's wedding-present to them was a characteristic piece of advice – 'only to meet now & again like sensible people: that is the only endurable kind of marriage'.[1] For Molly, seen in Abbey circles as something of a good-time girl, the suggestion was probably not uncongenial.

Resentments, alarms and excursions continued to bedevil the company, and by the end of the year WBY was wondering about a new three-tier salary structure, marking the manager Henderson for the axe and engaging in bruising encounters with Sara Allgood over her contract. There were also negotiations with Farr, who was to play in *Deirdre* in the New Year: WBY offered her expenses only, but she trumped him by straightfacedly demanding a special payment 'because of the watchfulness she will have to keep up at Euston & Holyhead to keep the porters from breaking the psaltery'.[2] However, at least the trivia of theatre business no longer involved Horniman. Life became easier on other fronts too. An English lecture-tour during November, where large audiences were treated to disquisitions on theatrical theory and JBY-style generalizations about writers, brought him £120.[3] *The Green Helmet* had been bought by the *English Review* for their September issue, at a price of £20. He could firmly resist his father's suggestion that he make money by writing for *Harper's Weekly*. And when WBY received his five-year horoscope from Charles Dumas late in 1910, it showed a generally favourable aspect for early 1911, even if his inquiries about moral struggles, spirituality and marriage were answered by the advice to avoid women with too intense a psychic nature.[4]

In December *The Green Helmet and Other Poems* appeared, containing the verse play and a distillation of the lyrics written over the difficult last three years. WBY expected a hostile response to these poems, and admitted they might be thought obscure – except for 'His Dream', which, he claimed, was 'merely the exact record of a dream'.[5] Reviewers were uncertainly attuned to the new voice breaking through. Some noted his ability to be both 'modern' and 'wild': the perceptive Ulster writer Robert Lynd appreciated the power with which he expressed anger.[6] All the *leitmotifs* which appear in his next major collection, and are often attributed to the influence of Ezra Pound, were there to be read in 1910. Pound himself noted the transition from '*dolce stile*' to '*stile grande*', and proudly identified their aims as the same. But the sharp new edge had been honed for some time, and so had the tone of undisguised autobiography. The collection featured a group of poems celebrating Gonne, which delineated her in all but name, though reviewers fought shy of making the identification: her Homeric beauty, her betrayal of him, the effects of age, the achievement of peace. No one, however, could know that 'Against Unworthy Praise' might be read in the light of the consummation of their affair in 1908.

> Oh, heart, be at peace, because
> Nor knave nor dolt can break
> What's not for their applause,
> Being for a woman's sake.
> Enough if the work has seemed,
> So did she your strength renew,
> A dream that a lion had dreamed
> Till the wilderness cried aloud,
> A secret between you two,
> Between the proud and the proud.
>
> What, still, you would have their praise!
> But here's a haughtier text,
> The labyrinth of her days
> That her own strangeness perplexed.
> And how what her dreaming gave
> Earned slander ingratitude
> From self-same dolt and knave;

> Ay, and worse wrong than these.
> Yet she, singing upon her road,
> Half lion, half child, is at peace.[7]

Dickinson was there too, but represented in the slightness of 'A Drinking Song' and 'The Mask' rather than in the ringing grandeur of the poems inspired by Gonne.[8] Shafts were fired at Russell and certain Dublin enemies. And, strikingly, two poems celebrated the side of Irish life which afforded him escape from that world, and declared an unashamed elitism. 'Upon a House shaken by the Land Agitation' argued for the superior values of Coole; 'At Galway Races' celebrated a unity of culture 'Before the merchant and the clerk/Breathed on the world with timid breath'. WBY's covert sympathy with an Ascendancy Ireland now irretrievably in decline was sharply noted by Russell in a letter to Quinn:

Some of the verses to Maud Gonne were beautiful, 'Another Troy' [*sic*] especially. I laughed over the 'Threatened House'. W. B. Y.'s affection for the aristocracy increases & he will slip into the reputation of Professor Mahaffy who never speaks without reference to 'his friend' the king, princess, duchess, duke, lord or whoever the rank may be. I think even the Peers would be amused over Yeats 'Threatened House'. W. B. Y. believes he is the Duke of Ormond. He told me he was once but his ancestors so far back as can be traced were good tradesmen just as mine were good farmers. The basis of this family tradition I believe is the fact that a great great grand aunt was called Butler & got a pension from the Lord Lieutenant.[9]

None of this would have surprised WBY, who in the New Year of 1911 found Dublin increasingly tedious. Gregory's new play *The Deliverer* was put on with the revived *Hour-Glass* on 12 January 1911, and caused an immediate coolness with Dunsany, who was convinced she had plagiarized his own *King Argimenes and the Unknown Warrior*, which opened a fortnight later (a first night not attended by WBY or Gregory). Though the Dunsanys principally blamed the 'Bad Old Woman In Black', their relationship with WBY never really recovered.[10] When Gregory's next play *Full Moon* was generally condemned, WBY reflected, 'it is melancholy the way the Dublin press & Dublin leaders generally dislike all that is strange or distinguished. They talk the others round . . . I am planning a lecture on the Irish democrasy & its love of coarse logic.'[11] To Dickinson, who provided refuge from the Arts Club, he confided untactfully, 'I find less and less in Dublin to give me pleasure,' adding, 'Dublin seems always the same except that it seems always a little further away from one's thought. It seems to sink slowly as if into dim water, as one grows older. It has not changed in twenty years – I mean the Dublin one dines with or could dine with if one would. The other Dublin has events enough.'[12]

The London he dined with was very different. At Reigate Priory for the weekend with Lady Katharine Somerset, he met Winston Churchill: 'I liked what little I saw of him. He seemed to me a mixture of ungraciousness and geniality . . . very obviously the most able man there' – and, he later added, 'much the worst bred'. With Lady Desborough he encountered Balfour, 'gentle & modest', very far from the 'Bloody Balfour' of nationalist demonology. Before their rupture the Dunsanys had entertained him with the millionaire Lord Howard de Walden (who 'said that one should never lose an opportunity of listening to Yeats though one should forget what he said'[13]). He was now invited to dine at Downing Street, and seated beside Margot Asquith. Meanwhile, his own entertainments at Woburn Buildings were still limited by his cutlery (which at least enabled him to turn away Masefield's wife, whom he cordially loathed[14]). But he had become a prize lion in the Edwardian social safari. His cachet in London was heightened by a brilliant Abbey season there in February 1911; his plans to bring Nugent Monck over and set up an acting school were further encouraged by seeing Monck's production of *The Countess Cathleen* at Norwich, done 'like a page of a missal'.[15]

Social life came easily to him but, as always, serious friendship was central to his existence, especially friendship with women. And his disillusionment with Dublin was compounded in March by a rumour that Gonne was to be blackballed at the Arts Club; wby wrote forcefully to Constance Markievicz calling for a mass resignation of Gonne's friends in support. Political opposition might be explicable, but this was personal, 'most cruel as well as most unjust'.[16] The commitments of friendship inspired a 'little set of very personal poems' which he worked upon through January 1911, centred around a lyric celebrating the three women who had made him what he was – Shakespear, Gregory and Gonne. He wrote to Gregory that these first-draft lines referred to her:

> . . . her hand
> Showed me how I could unbind
> The weight that none can understand
> Youth's bitter burden, & would give
> Every good gift that may be
> Could I copy her & live
> In a laborious reverie.[17]

The language seems so implicitly sexual that the passage (as it finally appeared) has not unreasonably been taken to refer to Shakespear; but, even as adapted in 'Friends', its theme of the restorative power of work must refer to Gregory's gift. Meanwhile, the power of his imagination could still transform reality. The day he finished this poem, which took three exhausting weeks, he allowed himself a walk on Hampstead Heath. 'I saw an old man flying a kite which was lost to view in the mist. One thought of some eastern magician as one watched the string vanish in the sky.'[18]

Thus WBY spent early 1911 alienated from Dublin and deeply preoccupied by the pattern of his life and relationships; casting horoscopes involved detailed 'rectification', playing back crises and traumas in his past in order to relate them to astrological movements. As always, involvement with the supernatural encouraged psychological self-exploration. His own past presented itself in other ways too. He was now firmly installed once more in the orbit of Olivia Shakespear, and through her he discovered a new circle of acquaintances. Sundered as lovers, it is possible that a sexual relationship had been restored at some point; in any case, they were now firmly reunited as friends.[19] Shakespear was still beautiful, still impatiently married to her unsatisfactory husband, still presented an alluring blend of sarcasm and sympathy; her literary interests and occultist dabblings brought congenial company to her Kensington house in Brunswick Gardens. Here WBY met Eva Fowler, a German-American married to a Leeds businessman; she organized seances and WBY took to visiting her country retreat, Daisy Meadow near Brasted in Kent, where he found it easy to write. And here too he met Shakespear's friend Edith Ellen ('Nelly') Hyde-Lees, who married Olivia's brother Harry on 1 February 1911.

She was a pretty, vivacious woman in her early forties, with two children and an unsatisfactory marriage behind her. Born Ellen Woodmass, she had married Gilbert Hyde-Lees in 1889 but left him shortly thereafter. Having been adopted by a well-off uncle, he had presumably been able to keep his estranged family in a certain style. Nelly and her children lived the peripatetic life of the rentier classes, taking houses in pleasant parts of the Home Counties and travelling on the Continent. The background on both the Woodmass and Hyde-Lees side was that of upper-middle-class county families, well-off and independent, with an inclination to the bohemian and slightly rackety: Nelly's position had for long been the uncertain one of a married woman without a husband.[20] When WBY became friendly with her in 1911, after 'knowing her vaguely for years',[21] she was about to enter a more settled phase of her life, as Mrs Tucker. Gilbert Hyde-Lees had died in 1909, and when she married Shakespear's art-collecting brother they moved into 16 Montpelier Square, Knightsbridge, not far from Olivia's Kensington home. Her children by Hyde-Lees were now nearly grown up: Harold was twenty and his sister George, whom he called 'Dobbs', eighteen.[22]

Before 1911 George had not met her mother's famous poet friend: she had been away at school (seven different establishments in all), and he had in any case been estranged from Shakespear and her circle until about two years before. Probably on 8 December 1911 George was introduced to WBY in Shakespear's drawing-room: she had noticed him in the British Museum that very morning. The encounter was inevitable. Even before they became linked by marriage, Olivia's daughter, Dorothy, was inseparable from George Hyde-Lees, and they lived in and out of each other's houses. The girls had much in common, being intelligent and independent-minded, artistically ambitious, and resentful of their worldly mothers. Though Dorothy was older by six years, George was well up to her; 'awfully intelligent' and 'alarmingly intuitive', as Dorothy put it.[23] Her unsettled upbringing had made her a good linguist, and she was an omnivorous reader with a taste for the unconventional and risky (Lombroso at seventeen; all George Moore before then). Tall, sun-tanned, with a face described by Dorothy as 'square' but very handsome, she knew her own mind: her breadth of reading and sharpness of intellect would continue to strike all who met her, along with a mocking and iconoclastic sense of humour.[24] Like the fey and beautiful Dorothy, she was impatient with convention, and her mother's plans for her; but George also shared the Shakespear–Tucker circle's interest in occult and psychic phenomena, joining the Order of the Golden Dawn in 1914 as well as attending seances and lectures at the Society for Psychical Research.[25] Moreover, for anyone of literary tastes Olivia's salon possessed compelling advantages. It was the matrix which brought together not only WBY and George Hyde-Lees, but introduced into the circle the extraordinary young American poet and literary entrepreneur Ezra Pound, with whom Dorothy fell quickly and irretrievably in love.

Pound had arrived in England in 1908, aged twenty-two, fresh from an abruptly terminated teaching career in Wabash College, Indiana. He was fizzing with manic genius, hungry for experience, and single-mindedly determined to meet writers. In April 1909 Elkin Mathews published his well-received collection *Personae*. His pretensions, extremism and overweening arrogance alienated many, but he had quickly found his way to Shakespear, and through her to WBY – for Pound 'the only living man whose work has more than temporary interest'. This homage was carried through in Pound's own poetry of this period, as well as in his adoption of a Yeatsian poet's uniform – brimmed hat, pince-nez, even an earring donated by Agnes Tobin. Determined to meet the Irish poet, he had laid siege almost since his arrival: sending WBY his first book, spotting him at theatres, and cultivating the circle around Elkin Mathews's bookshop. An acquaintance with Eva Fowler and a friendship with Olivia Shakespear did the trick. By the summer of 1909 he was frequenting Woburn Buildings, to the irritation of some Monday-night regulars: no one could be further from the ideals of literary good behaviour as prescribed by Edmund Gosse. But for WBY 'this queer creature', as he described Pound to Gregory, came along at exactly the right time, and he seems to have picked him out at once. WBY was conscious of encroaching middle age, and the admiration of the young people in the Shakespear circle was a tonic. Pound possessed that air of demonic charlatanry which always attracted WBY, but there was substance beneath. His friendship with the young American – bumptious, enthusiastic, but gifted with an uncanny editorial sense and a useful knowledge of European literary tradition – came when WBY had already determined to colloquialize his language, to strip away redundant prettiness, to strive for the uncompromising effects achieved by Synge. And beneath his affectations, Pound too was in search of tautness, precision, the elimination of redundant archaism, the rediscovery of a classical hardness.

In January 1910 WBY had privately reflected that 'the strange thing is that the literary imagination has become dramatic in our time, while the stage has refused its opportunity to learn'. From about this time he began to channel dramatic effects into his poetry, and to turn aside from the concentration on play-writing which had taken so much of his energies since the turn of the century. In the same letter he added, 'I always try for the most natural order possible, largely to make thought which being poetical always is difficult to modern people as plain as I can.'[26] Pound similarly declared that poetry should have the virtues of good prose – '*nothing* that you couldn't in some circumstance, in the stress of some emotion, *actually say*'.[27] Their collaboration was yet to come; but Pound's company already provided a vital counteracting influence to the respectable literary world of Gosse, the Academic Committee, the pension, the sounding-out for university chairs. Olivia Shakespear, who had brought WBY so much, was the unintentional conduit for this new influence as well.

Shakespear herself probably had mixed feelings about it. She disapproved of her daughter's obsessive love-affair with an obscure and erratic young American, who had initially paid court to herself, and tried to dissuade them. Her strictures convey very clearly the assumptions and tone of the world she now inhabited ('she has modelled her social life quietly on mine – but she has not the sense to see that what is suitable for a worn out woman of my age, & a girl of hers, is very different'; 'if her father died . . . I should probably marry again, & she wd be very much de trop – raison de plus for her marrying'[28]). But Pound was not to be put off. By May 1911 he was back in Europe, and his friendship with WBY was cemented by daily meetings when they were both staying in Paris that month. Gregory was also there, working with WBY on what he described as 'the big book on Fairy Belief that we have been doing for years. My part is to show that what we call Fairy Belief is exactly the same thing as English and American spiritism except that fairy belief is very much more charming.'[29] For WBY this synthesis of psychical research and fairy lore was now firmly established, and fused the interests of the Tucker circle with those of his most constant collaborator: the result, *Visions and Beliefs in the West of Ireland*, would appear in 1920, but preoccupied him for years before.

Stimulated by Pound and disciplined by Gregory, WBY devoted the summer of 1911 to a last, sustained burst of dramatic activity – as if he were reorganizing and revising the theatrical *œuvre* which had meant far more to him than to his public, before launching himself into other waters. His revised and extended volume of *Plays for an Irish Theatre*, to be published by Bullen and illustrated by Craig's stage-settings, was being put into final shape; he stressed to Bullen that the volume must include the stage version of *The Shadowy Waters* to 'show that I understand my trade as a practical dramatist'.[30] The introduction, written in Paris, summed up the evolution of WBY's ideas over the past decade, and the whole production was intended to stand as a testament. It would include *Deirdre, The Green Helmet, On Baile's Strand, The King's Threshold, The Shadowy Waters, The Hour-Glass* and *Cathleen ni Houlihan*. He also returned to *The Countess Cathleen*, adapting it for Leoni's operatic project and adding new lyrics (such as 'Lift the White Knee' in the second scene, which he proudly told Gregory took him only twenty minutes to write[31]). In Paris he met Leoni himself, who now wanted to take over the opera from Chappells and stage it at Covent Garden with Clara Butt. This rather nonplussed WBY, who gathered that Butt had a wonderful voice but no artistic standing. Still, he authorized Leoni to see Craig about the production, which remained in the realm of enthralling might-have-beens.[32]

Theatrical production continued to obsess him, as his enthusiastic correspondence with Craig shows; even Craig began to wilt under the barrage (affecting at one point not to know who WBY meant by 'Dunsaney', and to assume that he was the stage-carpenter). In June a long newspaper interview was planted out, in which WBY declared that he would never stage any of his verse dramas in the future without using Craig's revolutionary screens. At the same time he emphasized that the Abbey was now comfortably in profit, attracting large audiences, and presenting realist drama by Robinson, T. C. Murray and George Fitzmaurice.[33] With the arbitration about the Horniman affair decided in his favour, firm control established over actors' salaries and organization, and financial insecurity receding, he was beginning to sense the end of a chapter. *The Player Queen* would remain, rivalling *The Shadowy Waters* as a permanent work in progress. But he knew that the theatre's future could not be built on his own verse drama; accordingly, he felt an inclination to leave that form and return to lyric. In this way the reordering of a decade's dramatic work and the final break with Horniman chimed with the stimulus of Pound's admiration and the discovery of a younger generation. By the summer of 1911, with his uncanny sense of an impending change in the wind, WBY was pulling up his anchor.

II

As so often, a change of creative orientation was paralleled by reconsiderations in his personal life. Later, he would describe his feelings towards the Dublin world, and Irish life in general at this time, as 'estrangement'. The loss of Pollexfen Sligo, the resolution of the theatre's affairs, the everyday spite of Dublin life, all conspired to keep him distant. Personal links could not be broken, and when his cousin Ruth Pollexfen was married from Lily's house in July, WBY was proud to be asked to give her away. (She had been brought up by Lily, since virtual abandonment by her parents; her father Alfred's only contribution to the bridal pair was an abusive telegram, luckily intercepted.) On 20 July WBY was in Dublin for Ruth's wedding, splendidly dressed in a new suit which he had saved for the occasion (thus wearing old clothes for a previous engagement with the Asquiths and the Duchess of Sutherland). He made a brief speech, pleased everybody, and received an accolade from Sara Allgood, who was photographed kneeling in playful homage to him at the reception. But he saw it as his 'one civic act'[34] that summer and kept clear of other commitments – lying low at Coole or Dunsany Castle, only occasionally tempted out by admirers like Gogarty, who entertained him to expensive meals and good champagne, which made him feel uncomfortably like Molly Allgood.[35] His reputation for stand-offishness, and over-fondness for grand company, was by now firmly established in certain sections of Dublin opinion, and he was not bothered to combat it.

But if he had entered high society, and acquired a taste for country-house life, he had never prostituted his art in order to do so. Nor, in his own view, had he compromised his politics. He explained clearly to his father why he even refused to chair a dinner in Craig's honour that July, when he discovered it would mean proposing the King's health:

Lady Gregory and I have only held our movement together by insisting that nobody in England even thinks of proposing such a toast at a gathering which has an exclusively artistic object. At last we have got all parties to accept this and Unionist and Nationalist are quite peaceful with each other, and various viceroys have very good-humouredly accepted the fact that there was no God Save The King at the Abbey. We both, for Lady Gregory was even more urgent about it than I was, felt that it would be impossible to go back to Ireland having admitted the contrary. If the fact gets into the papers I am quite certain to have no chance for the Trinity professorship, but I am not sure that I want it.[36]

Given the political conditions of 1911, this statement carries great weight. The battles of the previous decade had proved that eternal vigilance was needed if he were to keep one step ahead of condemnation from Arthur Griffith and other guardians of advanced nationalist purity. Through the collusion behind the public row over *Blanco Posnet*, and the repudiation of Young Ireland simplicities in 'J. M. Synge and the Ireland of his Time', WBY's political antennae had been tuned towards a change in the pitch of Irish politics, as Home Rule inexorably moved on to the immediate agenda. Since the Liberal landslide victory of 1906, Conservative strategy had used the House of Lords veto to block legislation. Lloyd George's daring budget of 1909, the peers' ill-starred resistance and the two general elections of 1910 had brought matters to a crisis. By the summer of 1911 the Parliament Act had removed the Lords' veto – and with it, the last apparent bulwark against Home Rule legislation for Ireland. The Liberals were formally committed to it, and since 1910 their majority depended upon the votes of Redmond's Irish Parliamentary Party at Westminster. Even in Dublin Castle, Home Rule opinions had long been held by officials like MacDonnell and Dougherty. A Home Rule bill was promised for 1912. Expectations of an agreed, autonomous Irish future were expressed even by leader-writers in the *Irish Times*. Such beliefs were also subscribed to by enlightened landowning gentry like Lord Dunraven, John Shawe-Taylor and Colonel Hutcheson-Poë: supporters of the Abbey and Hugh Lane's projected modern art gallery, believers in tenants' land-purchase schemes, acquiescent to the imperially minded nationalism represented by Redmond now that Arthur Griffith and Sinn Féin were articulating the strident alternative. More and more, these were the kind of people with whom WBY spent his time in Ireland: apart from the bohemian cliques of the United Arts Club, who – if their politics can be defined at all – represented an equally moderate nationalism. Convergence seemed the order of the day, and Home Rule the inevitable future.

Events from 1912 would show that the political agenda might be dictated by a different drum, beaten from the North, and the easy expectations of WBY's new Liberal acquaintances, like Asquith and Haldane, would waver and dissolve in the face of such intransigence. At the same time advanced nationalism would move into the vacuum and rediscover a radical voice. In 1910 and 1911, however, this was not evident. WBY's occasional diary makes it clear that he shared the general supposition of impending Home Rule, and felt that the opposing shibboleths of old-style polarities had served their purpose. His essays and lectures repeated the message, preaching that independent nationality would depend on artistic radicalism, since the days of oppositional politics had gone by. The implicit elitism of this approach was exacerbated by his growing distaste for the strident tones of new journalism and new money in Edwardian Ireland. But Home Rule remained the desideratum, even if the price was accepting Catholic triumphalism, and an elite educated by Clongowes Wood College and the National University. He had set himself against the household gods of Trinity College and know-nothing Unionism, when they had been in the ascendant; twenty years on he was prepared to scourge the Catholic Establishment which was apparently succeeding to their place. He was clear in his mind that their institutions represented the faith and assumptions of the majority of the country, and therefore enjoyed a legitimacy not possessed by their predecessors, but he was equally convinced that – for all the rhetoric of nationalist rectitude – they shared many values founded on the debased intellectual currency of Victorian materialism, and its denial of ancient tradition. Moran, Griffith and others saw WBY's opinions as the simple product of galloping snobbery and the original sin of Protestant descent. His social life, and his developing preoccupation with his own family background in these years, helped to lend substance to this view. But snobbery is never simple, being founded on an insecurity that can be psychological as much as social; and preoccupation with family is a natural response to entering one's late forties childless, with the landmark figures of the last generation crumbling away.

WBY's powerful sense of personal history, which never deserted him, was especially strong in these years, when he consulted astrologers to establish patterns past and future, and watched his country enter a new phase in its own history. Though the politics of Westminster divisions and national elections are rarely discussed in his correspondence, he moved socially in London among people for whom they were the breath of life; and his political astuteness is reflected in a suggestion to Gregory in September 1911 that they should include in their programme *Falsely True*, a play by John Redmond's daughter Joanna. Not only would its conventionality balance the *Playboy* for their projected American tour; it would 'show that we are accepted by the recognised authorities of nationalism and that we have no particular bias. Redmond got a great reception I am told when he came in [to the House of Commons] last night, I don't think that we have perhaps realised the value that has been given to his name by recent events.'[37] Through necessity, he had developed a finely tuned sense of the way politics conditioned his complex public life – dictating the tone of a letter to the papers, the avoidance of giving a toast at a dinner, the choice of a play at the Abbey. And politics would affect the decision he took in the summer of 1911: to undertake a major tour of the Abbey Company through America, playing the controversial *Playboy* as 'the completion of our work'.[38]

443

III

For WBY this tour would mark not only the culmination of their project, but his own gradual disengagement. He was determined not to commit himself to touring with the Abbey, simply travelling out for the advance publicity, spending a month at most, and leaving the players to complete the tour until the following spring. The company were in good heart, after a successful summer tour to Stratford, and elsewhere, ending up at the Court Theatre; Nugent Monck's second company would fill the gap in Dublin during their absence and train a new generation of actors, though Gregory had severe reservations about it.[39] When the overture came from the theatrical agents Lieber & Co. via James Roche, an ex-nationalist MP, WBY was advised to ask for a lot of money, take the *Playboy* to Irish America, 'fight it out & win that fight again'.[40] Lieber not only insisted on the *Playboy* as a condition of the engagement, but offered good terms (all expenses and 35 per cent of the profits).

True to form, the company was racked by last-minute crises, rows and threatened defections. Molly Allgood was behaving as *prima donna assoluta* and WBY decided privately that Maire nic Shiubhlaigh, returned to the fold, was unfortunately no longer able to act. The young actress Cathleen Nesbitt was recruited for the American tour, and was struck by WBY's 'great weariness and remoteness'; she was also bewildered by the company's assumption that she was a spy ' "put in by the management", as they called Lady Gregory and Yeats'. WBY disliked her acting style, and she did not last. But as she became accepted by her fellow-actors she noted how Gregory and WBY tried to preserve the illusion that the actors were simple peasants: 'pretending they caught us all wild off the trees like monkeys', as Kerrigan whispered to her at a party.[41] Relationships were tense and backstage crises continued to erupt. None the less, on 8 September WBY was able to come before the curtain at the conclusion of his *Deirdre* and make an announcement in the inimitable style which Dublin loved to mock:

We feel that we must seem to many of you to be neglecting our principal work by going so far from Dublin and for so long a time, for on Wednesday next we leave Queenstown for America. From the very start of our theatre we have desired to take our plays to Irish America. Some seven years ago I lectured to a great school of Irish boys in a religious house in California. As I went to that house I passed under palms and all kinds of semi-tropical vegetation, and yet these boys were thinking almost the same thoughts that young Catholic boys would have thought in Dublin. The Irish imagination keeps certain of its qualities wherever it is, and if we are to give it, as we hope, a new voice and a new memory we shall have to make many journeys.[42]

Nugent Monck's newly established drama school at the Abbey was offered as consolation. As for WBY, he embarked with the players on the *Zeeland* at

Queenstown on 13 September (having booked a stateroom to himself, though he had to share it at the last minute with Robinson).

He needed his comforts. He knew he was heading into storms; JBY forecast that there would be a fight ahead – and that it might make his fortune. News of his pension had reached Irish America, and been much criticized, while the Abbey's reputation with the expatriate political organization Clan na Gael was distinctly 'anti-national'. Moreover, the part played by John Quinn in the MacBride marriage separation had alienated John Devoy, Joseph Garrity and other leaders of Irish American nationalism, and Quinn was closely identified with the Abbey. A contest was inevitable, and WBY was determined to dictate the terms. In late July he had suggested putting together a book of essays for the American market, to capitalize on the tour (and protect the copyright of his Cuala material in the USA): the material would include *Discoveries*, the Spenser introduction and – significantly – 'J. M. Synge and the Ireland of his Time'.[43] Although it came out (as *The Cutting of an Agate*) a year after the American visit, it shows his readiness to draw up battle lines and declare his position. Above all, his priority was to clarify how the Abbey stood in Ireland: one disgruntled observer noted, 'I had never seen a visitor to America more oblivious to the country he was visiting.'[44]

This is borne out by his pronouncements from the moment he arrived in Boston. His public lectures were less painstakingly prepared than in 1903; no typescripts survive, and his addresses owed much to the autobiographical pieces delivered in March 1910, and to the Synge essay not yet published in America. But some off-the-cuff interpositions can be gleaned from newspaper reports. In a discussion at the Poetry Society of America he sharply denied that the supposed dreaminess of Irish poetry had anything to do with national characteristics,[45] and the emphasis of his lectures fell on Synge and his uncompromising importance for an independent Irish culture. He also took care to assert the Abbey's political credentials. On arrival in Boston he publicized a story about their actresses refusing to stand for 'God Save the King' ('which in Ireland resolves society into its original elements') on board ship, though nic Shiubhlaigh denied such an incident ever took place. He stated further that the theatre movement, unlike Young Ireland, did not feel it could advance Irish independence, 'but we can prepare for the day after it has been obtained'.[46] His expectation of a consensual Home Rule future was reaffirmed in his statement that the Gaelic revival had led to the unity of various elements in Irish life. Most of all, though, he stressed the Abbey's pride in unpopularity, their commitment to presenting the 'kernel of reality', their achievement in making drama rather than song the vehicle of the Irish spirit. He was carefully preparing for the inevitable controversy when the *Playboy* opened three weeks later: thus he presented the *Blanco Posnet* affair as 'a national question, the defending of Irish freedom from English authority', when Dublin's 'streets [were] crowded with people waiting to see whether England or Ireland would win the battle'.[47]

The Boston streets may not have been crowded when the company opened their American season at the new Plymouth Theater on 23 September, but the auditorium was. Deliberately, the opening programme did not include the *Playboy*, scheduled for 16 October; it was cautiously composed of *The Shadow of the Glen*, *Birthright* and *Hyacinth Halvey*. Before the performance, WBY lectured on the history of the theatre movement, elaborately providing pointers towards interpreting what was to come. The audience was led to expect close observation of local accents, folkcraft and – in Synge's play – an approach once considered controversial but now (they were assured) completely acceptable. The Boston audiences were not fully convinced (when *Riders to the Sea* was played, it drew contemptuous laughter from the gallery). But, by and large, the company was received attentively by audiences and rapturously by the critics, even though a campaign was mounted against it in the local Irish American press.

WBY's effort to educate American audiences was best expressed in a speech to the Drama League, later released to the newspapers. He stressed the transformative effect of good modern theatre (Galsworthy was approvingly instanced) but asserted Ireland's unique access to a more ancient dramatic strength: a Homeric note which England could not conquer. This assertion, well calculated for Irish American ears, was swiftly followed by an emphasis upon the Abbey's avoidance of patriotic politics, and its commitment to challenging conventional Irish ideas. The sensitive question of portraying Irish 'types' was related to the *Punch* cartoons of fifty years before, and he explained how O'Connellite nationalism had provided a compensating image of 'national glorification'. This, according to WBY, was no longer needed, and his subsequent argument was derived closely from his Synge essay:

Every kind of enthusiast, political, religious, social, had endowed some section of Irishmen with the virtues he most admired, and national song and national novel – we used the word constantly – was [*sic*] expected to show Ireland in the best possible light. We were not a people curious about life, looking at it with disinterested contemplation, but a kind of army organized for offence and defence. We understood nothing but propaganda.[48]

Synge's work exploded the unreality of Irish life, through the theatre of exaggeration. Like the work of Cervantes, the *Playboy* was now a national treasure. Other Abbey characteristics were explained: Gregory's work was briefly (and rather condescendingly) outlined, the new school of Robinson, Murray and Ervine was explained as a reaction 'against us older writers', and Craig's symbolic scenery described – a theme returned to in WBY's Harvard lecture, 'The Theatre of Beauty', on 5 October. Here the meretricious nature of realistic scenery was condemned, the use of light rather than paint extolled, Japanese-style symbolic effects invoked, 'the shock of new material' apostrophized. He talked knowledgeably of experimental stagings by Kermendy, Reinhardt, Fortuny, and the Moscow Arts Theatre's plans for *Hamlet*. The lecture as reported in newspapers differed considerably from the later, printed version;[49] he related theatrical experimentation to a change in Irish mentality after the Boer War, 'when all thought of a general revolution [in Ireland] had vanished from the minds of the people, the interest in Irish history and romance which it had sustained also flagged'. Here, he was returning to his own autobiography, remembering the disillusionments of the millennium that never came. Synge, with his explorations of 'the distinctive and bizarre', had shown a new path instead.

By the time Gregory arrived on 29 September, WBY had painstakingly opened the way and could slacken his efforts; he celebrated his liberation by a visit to an impressive Boston medium, probably Mrs Chernoweth.[50] But in some quarters opposition was implacable. The Catholic weekly *America* attacked the players every Saturday for 'Gallic decadence', 'Ibsenism' and paganism. By 4 October Irish American political organizations were denouncing *Hyacinth Halvey* as anti-nationalist. The case was summed up by Dr T. J. Gallagher of Boston:

Nothing but a hell-inspired ingenuity and satanic hatred of the Irish people and their religion could suggest, construct and influence the production of such plays . . . I first thought Mr Yeats was playing a grim joke on Boston audiences. Next I thought him insane. But there is a method in his madness. Through every play one purpose runs, and that is to show that the Irish people are too savage, too crude and unreliable to be trusted with Home Rule; in fact unfit for anything but fettered slavery. Secondly, to show their boasted morals and religion are a myth, for contempt of both is expressed many times in every play I witnessed Saturday night.[51]

WBY's reply was deliberately mild, concentrating on the issue of 'paganism' and explaining Synge yet again. However, in an interview with the *Boston Pilot* (a patron of his own work twenty-five years before) he was sharper. 'It is not asking too much that what Irish Dublin accepts ought not to be rejected by Irish America without too much thought, nor is it, perhaps, saying too much to suggest that Dublin might know its Ireland better than those for whom Ireland is but a memory or a tradition.'[52] And from this point his arguments became more aggressive: it was part of the theatre's business to admit the evil that existed in the Irish as in all people. A speech on 6 October to the John Boyle O'Reilly Club (named after the patriotic editor who had published his own early work) praised the *Pilot* and struck some appropriately nationalist notes, but continued the exploration of his own past which marked his lectures since 1910. The fall of Parnell in 1890 initiated a cultural revolution: 'everything became individual'. This meant recognizing the distinctive harshness as well as graciousness of Irish artistic individuality – related, daringly, to 'the spirit of Goldsmith and the spirit of Swift' rather than to more conventional Irish models. Ireland's salvation must lie in 'a passion for truth' that would enable them to build on the basis of reality, not sentimentality.[53] The message, yet again, was that of the Synge essay: the clarity of artistic vision must replace the pasteboard pieties of Young Ireland traditionalism.

In a parallel argument, this could be translated into an appeal for the reconciling vision of Home Rule. Not only did WBY make much of the theatre's support from Redmond, Gwynn and other nationalist MPs; at the Twentieth Century Club a day later he spoke about the bringing together of Protestant and Catholic Ireland, and gave the cultural movement the credit. 'We had to bring out of these really warring elements a national consciousness.' Catholics had to be educated mentally, and Protestants emotionally (a frequent refrain of his father's). In this too Synge played his part; and yet again WBY compared him to Swift. These speeches helped turn the tide in the players' favour, eliciting declarations of support from Massachusetts Gaelic League branches and John Boyle O'Reilly's sister. But WBY's patience with Irish Americans was becoming strained, and in New York he finally accused them of being thirty years behind what was really happening in the country they still spoke of as home. 'It is far more honour to Ireland to have produced a dramatist like Synge than to fill every theatre in the world with a thousand green-coated clog-dancers.' This raised the question of the place of Protestants in the broad church of cultural nationality, a nettle he was ready to grasp. Asked to define an Irish play, he said it was as hard as defining a nation, but 'a play that is written today by an Irishman who has grown up past the formative period under Irish influences might be a definition'.[54] The Abbey's great victory, he asserted, lay in attracting people (including priests) who came to see what they liked, even if it meant also sitting through what they hated 'with our fierce Irish hatred'.

By now, he was making overt connections with the politics of the day. He stressed his own work for Home Rule, and the improved conditions in Ireland since the settlement of the land question. (The opinions in his poem about the Coole tenants were suppressed for American audiences.) The national spirit had not lessened; but a Home Rule bill was on the way, if not, as he expected, from the Liberals in this Parliament, then from the Tories in the next. In a long interview published in the *New York Times* after his departure, he spoke of the breadth of culture and tolerance in modern Ireland; England had taught the Irish to hate and the lesson been learnt too well, but with self-government his fellow-countrymen would achieve self-discipline. The Irish future must turn away from materialism and industrial values. The next great need was not revolution but education.[55]

Thus his American speeches not only reflected and refined opinions about culture and politics arrived at in the aftermath of Synge's death, but expressed WBY's belief in an impending Home Rule future. During his brief stay in New York, he did not meet Quinn but dined at the Petitpas boarding-house to meet his father's friends (and froze out one of them who asked him to give his father money); he was back in Boston for the *Playboy*'s long-awaited opening on 16 October.[56] Devoy's *Gaelic American* was campaigning hard against the play, and the Central Council of Irish County Associations of Boston condemned it as 'the foulest libel that has ever been perpetrated on the Irish character', but WBY's series of pre-emptive propaganda strikes paid off. The Boston papers by and large obediently reproduced the Yeatsian version of the play's history, and its importance; the legendary Mayor Fitzgerald endorsed it; the audience allowed itself some mild hissing, but that was all. WBY departed on the *Lusitania* two days later, still giving interviews that stressed Synge's and Gregory's connection with real Irish people, unlike the deluded views of Irish American expatriates, embalmed in a Boucicault version of Ireland fifty years out of date.

He left Gregory behind, and she bore the brunt of future difficulties until the tour ended the following March – exasperated by Robinson's vagueness, infuriated by American press reports that she held permanent court at the Petitpas restaurant ('Quinn wants me to contradict it as it is not a very respectable place'[57]) and finally facing the wrath of incensed Irish America during the New York run of the *Playboy*, when the audience rushed the stage and – Yeats-style – she harangued them before the curtain.[58] Her conduct was all the more admirable, since her heart was not really in it. She later admitted to WBY:

I dont think you will like it, but I want to put down even if I dont publish what I feel in touring Playboy round. I have grown to detest it, I have so much that is painful associated with it, and I shall some day get the more credit for this. If I was fighting for Countess Cathleen it would be another thing. And though it is not the fault of the play, I do feel rather indignant at the Synges never saying one word of thanks or acknowledgement, but writing to Curtis Brown to demand an increased Royalty![59]

Her great spirit saw her through, and the American tour was in several ways her liberation – even setting the seal on a brief and secret love-affair with Quinn that Christmas, which would have astonished those who persistently likened her to Queen Victoria. Quinn was still disenchanted with wby, though she did her best to reconcile them, and made some headway.[60] But she defended him from accusations that he had run away before the fight got going ('it doesn't take a man to fight a few priests and potatoes, a woman is good enough for that').[61] A delegation of 'prominent Catholic' women ('the stupidest set I ever met') drove her beyond endurance – 'to the extent of telling them that the Box Office has got a collection of "stink pots" and *rosaries* lost in the fight!'[62] Abusive anonymous letters followed ('I seen ye where [*sic*] got slated in New York. How is the Pensioner? Yours, Mike'[63]). Worse was to come after Christmas. At Philadelphia the Clan na Gael politician Joseph Garrity co-ordinated full-scale opposition to the performance on 18 January, the police and the District Attorney supported him, and the players were actually arrested for sacrilegious and immoral behaviour. The finale was provided by Quinn's triumphant defence in their celebrated court appearance.

From Dublin wby watched closely. He was delighted with the controversy (and the profits), dreaming of future American tours with his own verse dramas acted before Craig screens, and telling the *Irish Times* that the American opposition was composed of 'half-educated men' and mendacious priests.[64] For Quinn's part, the affair made him more anti-'pathriot' than ever. His cultural entrepreneurship was redirected from Ireland to French Post-Impressionist painting, with his organization of the historic Armoury show, featuring his own Cézanne, Gauguin and Van Gogh. But wby felt vindicated, and repeated the argument presented over and over again in his American speeches: the Abbey, represented by himself, Gregory and Synge, for all their Protestant background and avant-garde culture was more Irish than the transplanted Irish American reactionaries who opposed it. 'We are the true Ireland fighting the false.'[65]

IV

By this point he needed reassurance. The news from America coincided with his reactions to the first appearance of George Moore's memoirs, in the shape of an extract from *Ave* which appeared in October. The Irish renaissance of the 1890s was already being built into literary history, and all the principals were beginning to look to their autobiographies. wby's lectures of 1910 had sketched out some of his own territory, and in May 1911 he had encouraged Gregory to put down her own version (which became *Our Irish Theatre*): 'the more you make it a personal narrative the better'.[66] Moore followed the same advice, and – being Moore – took it beyond the limits.

Hail and Farewell, as the completed trilogy became, is its author's masterpiece: a fantastical autobiography which reverses the story of St Patrick, portraying the author as a missionary called to Ireland to deliver it from Christianity by means of high culture. Its great strength, and beauty, is the re-creation of the seductive atmosphere of a certain place and time: Irish light and shade, the alternate sublimity and seediness of Dublin, the lurches from grandiose gesture to sarcastic sneer. Much of this is conveyed through recollected conversation, necessarily inaccurate, but the voices which echoed down from the summer of 1899 were instantly recognizable and horribly funny. Hyde, Gregory, Plunkett, Gill and most of all Edward Martyn achieved instant and merciless immortality. Most of those betrayed, like Gill, were deeply hurt. Gregory thought Moore's treatment of his love-affair with 'Stella' (the painter Clara Christian) was inexcusable, and that 'no-one ought ever to speak to him again, though I suppose we shall all do so'. As for Coole and herself, she bravely found 'some charm in it' and 'shook with laughter' over the portrait of Martyn. 'I resent his description of Hyde most.'[67] Russell took a generous line: 'Yeats, Hyde, myself and other literary folk will never get so vivid an account of ourselves and our follies written by some more sympathetic critic.'[68]

wby bitterly remarked that Russell could afford to be indulgent, since Moore presented him as 'a mixture of Shakespeare and Mohammed'.[69] His own portrait was very different. Moore's revenge for the débâcle of *Diarmuid and Grania*, and the march wby stole over *Where There is Nothing*, had been a long time coming, but here it was at last. The admiration and attraction Moore had felt towards the young wby was lightly sketched in, but quickly overshadowed by the hilarious picture of the sage of Coole, relentlessly fussed over by Gregory – vain, vague but preternaturally sharp to seize his own advantage. Above all, the snobbery which many of wby's enemies had come to see as his Achilles heel was delineated to deadly effect. The portrait was all too superficially recognizable; but, written without affection, it misses the uncertainty beneath wby's affectations, the dazzling charm of manner, the humour, the loyalty to his friends, for which so many forgave him so much. And it did much less than justice to a literary genius which was still developing untold powers. Reading this portrait of himself in late 1911, all wby's hard-won achievements and solidly established fame provided scant comfort. 'At first I was relieved to find it no worse,' he confided to Gregory, 'but when I have taken it up since it has always seemed to me a dreadful thing, ill bred & often spiteful & yet he is trying to be just. Fifty years hence it will be one of those indispensable distracted [?] books that go to the making of the history of every epoch that has vigour.'[70] On the same day Lily visited him, bringing some copies of family portraits he had requested, and subsequently wrote to their father: 'I think he naturally resents Moore's book. He laughed about it but when I was standing up to go away he said, looking at the copy of Uncle Pat's portrait and the General "After all they are finer than Moore's squireens and their low gate lodge loves." [71]

This reflection is significant, and so are the portraits. He was already collecting inspiration for his own autobiography, which would consummate the efforts made in these years to understand pattern, purpose and origins in his life. His feelings about Synge's importance, the continuing battle with the inheritors of Young Ireland nationalism, the apparent imminence of a Home Rule Ireland dominated by the Catholic middle class were all clarified by the publication of Moore's skewed history. The process led him back to the lost domain of his youth and his family. His journal for 1909 had continually reverted to the parallels between the artist and the aristocrat, and the vital need to resist 'ill-breeding', but this was a private reflection. Now that the Ascendancy world was going, he would more and more unashamedly proclaim his fellowship with people who, like George Pollexfen, knew how to behave. His identification with the Gregory ethos was soldered through the sense of a disappearing past, acquiring as it receded the enhanced and idealized allure of nostalgia.

Chapter 17 : GHOSTS
1911–1913

> I have begun to feel that I belong to a romantic age that is
> passed away. I am becoming mythical even to myself.
>
> WBY to Edwin Ellis, n.d., but probably 2 August 1912

I

FROM the late autumn of 1911, alone in Dublin, WBY confronted his history. The shock of seeing himself through the silky veil of Moore's malice brought home the realization of middle age and the recognition of a change in his own work. He had long been a compulsive rewriter, but now he redrafted more comprehensively than ever, particularly his early plays. He was also inspired to remember old friends, and to seek supernatural guidance. From that point can be traced the long gestation of his *Autobiographies*. More and more frequently, the poet's ruthless search for a theme ended in himself.

Meanwhile, he was immersed in day to day Abbey business, while Gregory stayed with the players in America. Independence had not eliminated all their problems. Horniman continued to haunt them from a distance, since her influence in the Manchester Gaiety Theatre was cast implacably against the Abbey, and forced them to give up their practice of playing a lucrative season there. At home, Nugent Monck's 'school' caused resentment among the actors left behind; nor, perhaps, did they relish the prospect of a programme made up almost entirely of Gregory's plays. For her part, Gregory did not share WBY's high opinion of Monck, or her fellow-director's roseate expectations of the 'second company'.[1] And Monck's instability and carelessness would cause considerable problems before he, like so many other managers, abruptly left.

None the less, WBY retained his old skill at handling publicity: he spent Christmas and New Year manipulating journalists on the Abbey's behalf, and trying to frighten off a flattering *Times Literary Supplement* profile of the rival Theatre of Ireland by telling the journalist about Constance Markievicz's ominous military boy-scout movement.[2] The Abbey was costing £100 a week, leaving no leeway for salary rises. But WBY's enthusiasm overrode all, particularly where the new Abbey 'school' was concerned. Out of sixty original applicants, 'a second company' of seventeen had emerged, several of them, in WBY's view, able to understudy or even supplant the established stars. Fascinated by the process of seeing actors taught, he decided that this clarified the distinction between those who acted from 'experience' and emotion (Molly Allgood) and those who created character from observation (her sister Sara).[3] 'All good art is experience,' he had written in his 1910 diary, 'all popular bad art generalization.' Theatrical form and style provided a language for interpreting the importance of 'personality' in artistic expression – a preoccupation reaching back to his father's table-talk decades before. The path of connection was becoming clear between the artist he had become and the long apprenticeship of his youth.

In the frantic present there were the usual problems with those actors (like Arthur Sinclair) popular enough to be tempted by music-hall engagements, and with playwrights whose work was exposed to WBY's inimitable critiques. (Seamus O'Kelly, author of *The Shuiler's Child*, must have chafed when his subsequent play was returned with the comment that the next season must be 'devoted to two very important plays, which have taken precedence, a work of mine as well as a work of Lady Gregory's'.[4]) All this was retailed in long letters to Gregory through the winter and spring of 1911/12, along with light relief such as an application from an unsuspected transvestite to join the school ('he or she as a young woman would have been perfectly charming'[5]). During January the vicissitudes of the company in America necessitated firm action on WBY's part in Dublin too – all the more so as his own early return had left Gregory to bear the brunt of the transatlantic *Playboy* controversies. The first he heard of it was when journalists descended on the theatre looking for quotes: WBY issued a series of statements breathing defiance, deriding the time-warp inhabited by Irish Americans, accusing Catholic societies of spreading lies and slanders, and superbly dismissing the opinions of 'half-educated publicans in Phildelphia'.[6] The fact that the staunchly conservative and Unionist *Irish Times* editorial agreed warmly with his analysis may have given him pause for thought; but he carefully related the *Playboy* to the existence of 'an educated patriotic Ireland . . . insisting upon its standards being recognised, and upon having life put as freely at the service of the artist as it is in all other countries'.

But this represented WBY's own agenda rather than any recognizable Irish reality, as was neatly demonstrated by a series of attacks on the Abbey emanating from 'educated patriotic Ireland' itself. Patrick McCartan in *Irish Freedom* denounced Gregory, WBY and Synge for their ignorance of 'the genuine peasant';[7] the *Irish Catholic* and the *Leader* revived their campaigns against the dead playwright (with the embellishment of an allegation that he had died not of cancer but venereal disease[8]); the general attack on the Abbey's drama was echoed in England, with a violent onslaught in the *New Age*. Here, a dismissal of WBY's 'vague, pale, gaping drama' became a full-scale condemnation of his influence at large. 'The future critic, searching for the causes of English literary impotence, will probably be inclined to rest upon the works of Mr Yeats. He is one of the many revenges Ireland has taken upon us.' (Intriguingly, Ezra Pound was reviewing anonymously for the *New Age*; at this time he was quite capable of mounting an attack on WBY's plays, and the style is suggestive.⁹) To WBY's pleasure, this was rebuffed by the rising poet and fantastical novelist, James Stephens, and he could now be philosophical about twenty years of attacks from journalists. 'We are free men & they bound,' he reminded Stephens. He also affected not to mind a steady stream of anonymous letters ('the Leader being pious is read by women who are much given to them that I suppose is the reason'¹⁰). Later in the year he confronted the Abbey's unpopularity in verse, publishing 'At the Abbey Theatre' in the *Irish Review*: a direct challenge to Hyde to explain why the theatre could put on nothing that pleased the Dublin audience (and implying that Hyde himself knew how to manipulate popularity).

> You've dandled them and fed them from the book
> And know them to the bone; impart to us
> We'll keep the secret – a new trick to please.
> Is there a bridle for this Proteus
> That turns and changes like his draughty seas?
> Or is there none, most popular of men,
> But, when they mock us that we mock again?

There was an edge to this, since Hyde had infuriated Gregory and WBY by publicly disassociating the Gaelic League from the Abbey during the *Playboy* troubles in America.¹¹ 'An Craoibhín Aoibhinn', adroit as ever, replied smoothly in verses which claimed that he thought as one with the Irish people, while WBY 'bewildered' them:

> A narrower cult but broader art is mine,
> Your wizard fingers strike a hundred strings
> Bewildering with multitudinous things,
> Whilst all our offerings are at one shrine.
> Therefore we step together. Small the art
> To keep one pace where men are one at heart.¹²

But taken with Ernest Boyd's denunciation of the Abbey's decline in the same paper, and the letters to the *New Age* supporting the attack on WBY, the controversy was bad for business. A series of mystery plays adapted by Colum and put on from January were surprisingly contentious, and Gregory's work attracted small houses. Something new was required.

WBY devoted himself in January 1912 to meeting this need by adapting the Jebb version of *Oedipus*: 'making it very simple' and putting the chorus into 'rough unrhymed verse'. It was a doubly attractive project, since the play had been censored in England, and WBY wanted to build on the *Blanco Posnet* precedent by performing a version at the Abbey. This meant rather cavalier cuts, inflicted without going back to the original Greek (unless a convenient helper managed to be around). WBY remained very critical of existing translations, which 'won't speak', but his own free-style approach would equally appal others.[13] However, when the English ban was lifted, he lost interest in the project; it would not be revived for fifteen years. His routine through January allowed him to work at poetry in the mornings, then to go to the theatre and dictate letters to Raven Byrne; he pursued his own writing after business. On occasion he journeyed to London to keep up with involvements like Gosse's Academic Committee, though he now accepted that 'it will be 10 or 20 years before [it] matters so far as anyone's public position is concerned, the one advantage of it is that one gets to know writers and to find out one's friends and enemies'.[14] Principally, though, his effort went into rewriting his plays. Not only did the Abbey need new material (and since 1910 playwrights received a royalty); the revision process represented an attempt to review and reconstruct his own artistic autobiography.

This went right back to *The Land of Heart's Desire*, which he found dislikeable and wanted to change radically – 'it is as though another man wrote it'.[15] As with *The Hour-Glass* (rewritten partly in verse to embody far more complex philosophical ideas) and *The Countess Cathleen*, he set to pruning sentimental and flowery effects; his return to these particular early plays echoed other explorations into his past at this time. They also lent themselves to the analysis of folklore and the supernatural which he had embarked upon with Gregory. Most of all, they adapted well to the new stagecraft of Gordon Craig and Max Reinhardt.[16] Craig had shown him the eloquence of light, colour and abstract sets, while Reinhardt demonstrated the dramatic use of sound, now worked into *The Hour-Glass* by having the strokes of a bell counterpoint the Wise Man's dying speech. 'I conceive of a play as a ritual,' WBY told Craig. 'It need not give all to the first hearing any more than the Latin ritual of the church does so long as the ultimate goal is the people.'[17] One of his criticisms of Seamus O'Kelly's play had been its propagandist bias, lacking 'the disinterested curiosity about human life out of which good plays are made'. The latest version of *The Countess Cathleen* embodied this approach, and when it opened (first on 14 December 1911, and again in February) it not only made money but impressed even the Markieviczes.[18] It was performed in a Nugent Monck production, pageant-style, with Monck himself playing Aleel; WBY supervised the lighting cues from the balcony, while Craig's screens came briefly into their own. Both plot and characterization were more intensely personalized: Cathleen and Aleel became legendary lovers doomed to part, the poet offering retreat from the public world, the Countess dedicating herself to her destiny and making her house, like Gonne's, 'a refuge/That the old and ailing, and all weak of heart/May escape from beak and claw.' The opera project had apparently subsided, but there was new interest in an Italian translation of the play – mediated through James Joyce, who reappeared in WBY's life that July, bringing his little son to visit him in Woburn Buildings ('for a wonder he was polite: gave me tea and Georgie fruit'[19]).

Translations, however, like collected editions, kept coming up against the obstacle of WBY's determination to revise his work until it stood all of a piece, conforming to the latest standards which he had set. In 1912 this meant not only simplicity but a deliberate denial of consciously 'poetic' diction. Writing about Masefield's new poems that year, he commented, 'I feel that the very reality of their contents, the superficial resemblance to prose, requires great precision in the style, research in the epithet.'[20] This was an implicit instruction to himself. Both his poems and early plays were to be subjected to this process; Bullen's *Collected Works*, in WBY's view, already needed revision after only four years, and he plagued his publisher with demands for addenda or – better still – revision of the sheets which were not yet bound. At the same time he was as conscious as ever of his markets. At Fisher Unwin's suggestion the new-look plays were to be published two by two in a series of short volumes and sold for a shilling through the theatre, which would augment his exiguous royalty income. Though the Fisher Unwin *Poems* brought in £36 in 1911 (compared to the £20–£25 of previous years), he was happy to sell manuscripts to commercial dealers when necessary: £30 thus acquired went to carpets, curtains and a newly papered ceiling at Woburn Buildings in the summer of 1912.[21]

II

For all the time WBY spent in Dublin, his London retreat and his English life were never far from his mind. And by 1912 the question of the connection between Ireland and England monopolized public debate. The Liberal government had faced down opposition in the House of Lords, and since 1911 the new Parliament Act was law; there was now, apparently, no insuperable constitutional obstacle to the introduction of a Home Rule bill for Ireland. The legislation that was brought forward in April showed very little advance on the abortive bills of 1886 and 1893, being in some ways less radical, but the important thing was that, unlike previous efforts, it would pass the Commons and could not be thrown out by the Lords. Since it was actually viable, even Griffith welcomed it as a step forward, while mainstream nationalist opinion was wildly enthusiastic. And this concentrated the mind of Protestant Ireland.

457

In the north-east, during the spring and summer of 1912, concentration took the form of dogged Protestant resolutions against anticipated rule from Dublin by Roman Catholic bishops and fire-breathing Fenians, asserting that Asquith and Lloyd George were exceeding their powers and manipulating an unrepresentative Parliament in order to betray loyal Ireland. This analysis was readily seized upon by an opposition Conservative Party already committed to the idea that the Liberals were acting *ultra vires,* and traditionally prepared to encourage Ulster Unionist intransigence. Unionist and Protestant reactions elsewhere in the island were less extreme, but even among Dublin intellectuals with an inclination towards cultural nationalism, a certain unease was evident. This reflected not so much fear at the onset of Catholic ascendancy, as scepticism about the tolerant credentials of advanced nationalism. For since the foundation of Sinn Féin, and the activity of the IRB Dungannon Clubs commandeered by advanced men like John MacBride, the prospect of Home Rule threw into sharp relief the *Kulturkampf* symbolized by the conflict between Arthur Griffith's or D. P. Moran's exclusivist rhetoric and the pluralist arguments of Magee, Russell or WBY himself. The notions aired thirteen years before in the Dublin *Daily Express* and *Literary Ideals in Ireland* gained new relevance now that the Home Rule future was apparently at hand, and by 1912 several voices from the liberal Protestant tradition were questioning the probable form of cultural nationalism in the new Jerusalem. WBY's old sparring-partner W. K. Magee wrote bleakly to JBY:

You ask me why I dislike the Irish language movement so much . . . & on the whole I have to acknowledge that I do. It is an instinct, and though I might struggle with it as with a besetting sin, and endeavour to root it out, I see no reason for doing so, as the fact of my having this instinct, in common with probably the majority of the more rational (forgive me) of my fellow-countrymen, is its sufficient and unanswerable vindication. The claim for the Irish language seems to me only a new form of the old impossible claim of one race and tradition to extirpate its rival in this country. So far from meaning any real national distinction, the victory of the Irish language (which by the way is inconceivable – a sufficient argument in itself!) would remain always or indefinitely what it is, only *more so,* and this prospect would be by no means pleasing to my imagination. It represents the stick-in-the-mud element in Irish life, not that which I (and you too!) would prefer to see prevailing – initiative, and a general aspiration of social and individual development as human beings . . . Whether, however, it is the Protestant or the bigot in me (I suspect it is both) I do object to the sentiment underlying the language movement as illiberal as well as insincere, for really Irishmen have no intention of learning the language. If the choice is between vulgarity and intellectual squalor on the whole I choose vulgarity. But there – I am at it again!²²

wby was formally committed to the language movement, but many of Magee's reservations would have struck a ringing chord. By now distinctly ex-Fenian, his nationalism was of a more conventional stamp. He was closely interested in the progress of the Home Rule legislation mooted from early 1912, passing on political gossip to Gregory, relaying the plan for temporary exclusion of some Ulster counties, and hearing from journalist friends that Home Rule might incorporate a 'senate' in which he himself, along with Russell, Hyde and Dermod O'Brien, would be asked to serve as representatives of arts and letters.[23] He was responsive to the emphasis on common Irishness, and on 'a change in the mind of the country' declared in the first number of MacDonagh's and Colum's *Irish Review*.[24] But in January 1912 he told Gregory that the chief danger to Home Rule came from extreme-Catholic claims to control legislation in any Home Rule parliament, encouraged by cabals at Rome and aggressive papal pronouncements: Cardinal Logue was thought to be conspiring against Home Rule, at least until Catholic control of education was assured. 'The hands that struck Parnell at work again.'[25]

Thus wby was not immune to Protestant fears about Catholic ambitions to control free thought in an independent Ireland. He was none the less well aware that this could be manipulated for purely political ends, and in April he put his name to a public letter from Irish Protestants who supported Home Rule and contradicted the claims of Unionist politicians that they feared for their future in an independent Ireland.[26] The signatories were not, in general, members of any nationalist associations: their names were drawn from Dublin's professional middle class. Although wby signed along with them, his private comments do not indicate an implicit faith in Catholic tolerance. His contemporaneous campaign against the censorship bill in Britain, for instance, stressed that in Ireland the Catholic Church would use it to keep out of the newspapers everything they considered anathema – not only Divorce Court reports but the socialism of *Reynold's News* and the anarchist opinions of the fringe radical press. 'It is an attack on opinion pretending to be an attack on morals.'[27] And by the end of 1912 he would no longer find it possible to give automatic assent to public statements avowing Protestant trust in the liberality of Catholic opinions. When Stephen Gwynn invited him to attend a Protestant Home Rule meeting convened in London, and propose a motion affirming faith in the tolerance of the Catholic Church, he received (significantly, from Coole) a distinctly dusty answer:

I cannot abide the circular of the Protestant Home Rulers. It is ungenerous in feeling and untrue in fact, I have no desire to protest against 'efforts in North-east Ulster to drag religion into political controversy'. I would gladly take part in any meeting that might help to lighten their fears and to show them that if danger to their freedom

459

came, others would confront the danger at their side. Nor can I go to a meeting that is to prove 'that there is no shadow of foundation for the charges of intolerance which have been hurled against our brothers of the Roman Catholic Church'. There is intolerance in Ireland, it is the shadow of belief everywhere and no priesthood of any church has lacked it. I would have gladly have had my part in any declaration that the great majority of Irish Catholics are tolerant and easy, and that intolerance can be fought and crushed after Home Rule as it cannot be now, or in any declaration that the danger to religious freedom is not in the granting of Home Rule but in its continued refusal; but how can I who have been denounced by Cardinal Logue for a romance, and seen lying leaflets based on material sent from Dublin distributed at chapel doors in America during the tour of the Abbey Players, or how can any man who has read the 'Irish Catholic' and can take the pains to know the meaning of his words, affirm that there is not both shadow and substance? I daresay that politics will not in our time escape from statements that have but temporary value, but I believe that a man of letters should have no part with them, for his life if it has meaning at all is the discovery of reality.[28]

He promised his support on any occasion 'not against my conscience', and was as good as his word. At the meeting on 6 December he lent his name to a resolution 'that this meeting – whilst sympathising with those in N.E. Ulster who apprehend that they may suffer in consequence of the bestowal upon Ireland of self-government, is convinced that their fears are groundless'. And at a further meeting in Dublin he proposed a motion 'that the responsibilities of self-government and the growth of political freedom are the most powerful solvents for sectarian animosities'.[29] But by then, the promised land of Home Rule was receding like the Gaelic otherworld of Hy Brasil: Ulster intransigence and Liberal pusillanimity had interacted to exacerbate nationalist impatience in the South.

At this meeting WBY produced a testament. Looking back to his youthful nationalism, he affirmed the need for a national legislature in order to release the nation's potential and draw the best of its energies back from England. Strikingly, he returned to the theme of bigotry:

I often see the life of Ireland today (so full it seems to me of prejudices and ignorances in all matters of science, politics and literature) under the image of a stagnant stream where there drifts among the duck-weed, pieces of rotting wood, a dead dog or two, various rusty cans, and many old boots. Now, among the old boots drifting along there are a very objectionable pair, Catholic and Protestant bigotry. Some Irishmen object to one or other of those boots so much that they can think of nothing else, and yet we have merely to make the stream move again to sweep them out of sight.

But he admitted (as in his letter to Gwynn) intolerance *did* exist in Ireland; Ulster Protestant fears were genuine, and therefore 'it is their duty' to protest.

Those who think as I do differ from them – not because we deny the bigotry (we have had the stench of that stagnant stream too long under our nostrils for that) – but because we believe that the danger to religious freedom is not in the giving but in the refusing of Home Rule.

A country divided into two polarized parties, in permanent postures of defence and attack respectively, had no choice but to be bigoted. But this must evaporate with independence. WBY's subsequent argument would not have pleased all Home Rulers, attractive as it might have been to his Irish Protestant audience:

I know many Catholic young men who believe upon the contrary that almost the first event of a self-governing Ireland will be the rise of a most powerful anti-clerical party and of much continental irreligion. I should be sorry to believe this, to believe that we can but exchange one form of intolerance for another. No, the best minds of Ireland have been tolerant from the beginning, priest and layman alike – It is the worst minds and the mediocre minds that make up that stagnant stream.

In a peroration he recalled (yet again) the kindness he had received in America from the seminarians at Notre Dame, at a time when Catholic authorities were denouncing him as a pagan mystic; common Irishness, encountered in exile, transcended religious division. Perhaps more realistically, he remarked in conclusion that if Irish Protestants could not 'fight for our own land through any form of persecution known to modern times, and win, we are poor creatures, and the country will be well rid of us'.

This hit the mark with his audience, as WBY reported to Gregory. 'I had a great success last night . . . everybody congratulated me. The meeting had followed Hyde's lead & insisted on Catholic tolerance until the audience had become a little uneasy. I therefore rather strengthened the insistence on intolerance in my speech.'[30] By then (January 1913) his patience with delicate susceptibilities was running low: he had become involved, as will be seen, in campaigning which had aligned him against 'respectable' Irish opinion over the question of Hugh Lane's modern art gallery. But he had long before established his refusal to follow what Moore (writing of Hyde) called the 'Catholic Protestant line' – insisting (through over-compensation and wishful thinking) that Catholic social and political teaching presented no threat to Protestant consciences. WBY was a veteran of too many Irish struggles to subscribe to that. His commitment to Home Rule was unquestioned, but its apparent advent coincided with WBY's own rediscovery of family tradition, his burying the hatchet with the Trinity College culture, his friendships in great houses from Adare Manor to Dunsany Castle, and his assumption into a kind of artistic establishment in England. This could not but affect his response, and his identifications. On his holiday with Maud Gonne in France during the Home Rule summer of 1912, WBY read Whitley Stokes's redoubtably Protestant study of the Celtic church, and drily noted how it marshalled an anti-Catholic argument for Irish identity.

Even more notably, through the Home Rule upheavals of 1912 he refined his view of Parnell. Mosaic prophet, son of the Ascendancy, dissident against conventional sexual morality, cast out by the people at the behest of their priests, the Uncrowned King's downfall inspired, in WBY's epical construction, the cultural revival led by himself and his generation. Gregory also spread this interpretation, probably inspired by WBY.[31] In the introduction to a Cuala volume of Dunsany's writings which WBY wrote at Colleville during that summer of 1912, Parnell emerges as 'that lonely and haughty person below whose tragic shadow we of modern Ireland began to write'.[32] In this introduction WBY repeated his assertion that for twenty years the Irish imagination had been 'entangled in a dream', following the popular culture of Davis and Young Ireland, enshrined in badly printed books of 'emerald green'. These were symbolically set against the elegant dove-grey productions of Cuala, with their font of eighteenth-century type (Caslon Old Face, by now traditional for fine printing): books 'intended for few people & written by men and women with that ideal condemned by "Mary of the Nation" who wished she said to make no elaborate beauty but to write so as a peasant could understand'. By contrast, this new 'library of Ireland' was dedicated to the few. Dunsany was aligned with Synge and Gregory, and a resounding claim was made on the Georgian tradition of 'our grandfathers'. WBY's assertion of Protestant civil rights and his unashamed claim on the Ascendancy contribution to Irish life is usually related to his speeches on divorce legislation in 1926; but all the elements are articulated in his pronouncements on Home Rule fourteen years before.

III

In other ways too WBY was reverting during 1911 and 1912 to past connections and preoccupations. Supernatural studies were always with him: despite his unhappy experiences in Dublin in the mid-1880s he from time to time frequented seances, mediums and the murky waters laboriously charted by the Society for Psychical Research. But from 1909 he had begun to experiment consistently in this area, encouraged by his friendship with Everard Feilding, an Honorary Secretary of the Society (which WBY himself joined as an associate member in 1913).[33] At first, while he used the language of 'scientific' investigation favoured by the SPR, his inclination was towards the more 'spiritist' school, believing in supernatural survival rather than looking for psychological explanation. Later he moved towards a more questioning approach, in line with SPR orthodoxy. But the years just before the First World War saw a fashionable craze for mediums, despite a series of exposures and the irritation of rationalist intellectuals like Samuel Butler (who threatened 'if ever a spirit form takes to coming near me, I shall not be content with trying to grasp it, but, in the interest of science, *I will shoot it*[34]). WBY's joint studies with Gregory into the connections between folklore and spiritualism impelled him to seances in 1909; his friendship with Eva Fowler, Nelly Tucker and others in Olivia Shakespear's circle brought him into a mediumistic ambience; and his September 1911 visit to the celebrated Mrs Chernoweth (a trance medium specializing in dead poets) led him further along the path. System-builder that he was, he determined upon a general theory. The connections between folklore, psychic communion and a generalized anthropological approach had long been debated by writers well-known to WBY.[35] The non-mystical language of the SPR, testing detail and accumulating evidence, appealed to him, but he was prepared to speculate and – where necessary – to suspend disbelief. Reviewing his own occult experiences, and his long-established habit of analysing dreams, WBY moved towards a synthetic idea.

For years the *Journal of the Society for Psychical Research* had been publishing material on dreams and the subconscious; several of Freud's commentaries appeared there, and his work was exhaustively discussed. By 1916 at the latest WBY was familiar with the reputation of both his work and Jung's.[36] Speaking to the British Association on 4 September 1908, he had described *The Hour-Glass* as 'a parable of the conscious and the subconscious life', invoking Frederic Myers's work, but through his Neo-Platonist training he had long ago come to believe that abstract reasoning was of limited value compared to intuitive visions and mystical union. WBY was familiar with current ideas about the unconscious – a concept explored by many of his intellectual guides, including Boehme, Nietzsche and Plotinus (whose doctrine of the soul had recently been popularized by Bergson, as well as by MacKenna's translations).[37] The notion that geniuses, especially writers, had a special connection to their subliminal stream of consciousness had long been with him. More recently, he was impressed by the recent work of Theodor Flournoy and Myers on evidence of existence beyond the grave; it brought him back to the ideas of Swedenborg, another name familiar to the SPR, frequently cited by spiritualist writers like James Hyslop.[38] On 12 January 1912 he gave the lecture 'A New Theory of Apparitions' to the United Arts Club, summed up rather ironically by the *Irish Times*:

The burden of the flesh alone keeps men from dreaming. Dreams come when death's twin brother sleep has released us from the body. Disembodied souls, wandering about the universe, and thirsting for incarnation, find us in the semi-freedom of sleep. They rush into our dreams, and there find a temporary incarnation. People under the influence of hypnotism are in the receptive state of dream, and so become *media* for the incarnation of the wandering ghosts. Dreams are irresponsible things and the medium is, therefore, an irresponsible person. Strange promptings to wickedness invade him. He is capable of devilish deceits. Mr Yeats's theory, it would seem, explains the notorious fact that much of the history of modern spiritualism is a record of trickery, deception and even uglier things.[39]

More suggestively, the reporter inferred that spiritualist mediums and everyday dreamers were 'in the same state as ghosts . . . in a state in which the passions of life reproduce themselves in dream'. This lecture was a dry run for subsequent addresses to the SPR on 25 January (an audience of 'lady novelists and psychical researchers', he told Gregory[40]) and to the Quest Society a week later. And these ideas would by 1914 coalesce in the commentary on Gregory's *Visions and Beliefs in the West of Ireland* and in his long essay 'Swedenborg, Mediums, and the Desolate Places' – bringing together his early occultist reading, the search for ancient wisdom in folklore, and his current quests up Soho staircases for voices from 'the other side'.

By the end of January 1912 he could write to Gregory, 'I am deep in my ghost theory . . . I have now found a neoplatonic statement of practically the same theory. The spirit-body is formalist in itself but takes many forms or only keeps the form of the physical body "as ice keeps the shape of the bowl after the bowl is broken" (that is the metaphor though not quite the phrase).'[41] From 1912 he read widely about supernatural happenings, pursued his acquaintanceship among the SPR and consulted mediums 'controlled' by familiars. Eva Fowler's cottage, where he stayed for a week from 24 May 1912, became a frequent resort. Always the autodidact, WBY set himself an agenda of intensive research through his rediscovery of spiritualism, with its accompanying cloud of self-referencing witnesses.

With Gregory's return from America in March 1912, he was released from the Abbey's bondage, and returned to London. Here, however, he was afflicted by acute digestive illness and severe rheumatism, which meant days fasting in bed, restricted to a milk diet. He was already, therefore, in an enervated and edgy condition during May and June when he was exposed to a series of unsettling experiences at seances in London. The first occurrence was on 9 May, when he went to W. T. Stead's psychic centre at Wimbledon, Cambridge House, for a sitting with the famous American medium Etta Wriedt.[42] The occasion was recorded not only by WBY himself but by Stead's secretary Edith Harper. Mrs Wriedt identified her spirit controls by reading out names 'written up' in the dark: 'when a name was recognised the voice was immediately heard from the trumpet'. Here, WBY was convinced, a spirit made itself powerfully evident, calling for 'Mr Gates' in a strong Irish accent, and introducing himself as WBY's appointed guide 'Leo'. From other hints ('you will find me in the encyclopaedia') his identity was pieced together as 'Leo Africanus' (more properly Al Hassan Ibn-Mohammed al-Wezar Al-Fasi), a Spanish Arab explorer, historian and poet from the sixteenth century whose image would provide WBY with an imaginary *alter ego* for years.[43]

'When you first came to me,' wrote WBY some time later, 'I had to the best of my belief never heard of you or your work.' Actually, at an earlier seance on 3 May 1909 a supposed 'Leo' had materialized, offering obscure hints ('African name . . . a Pope') and been interrogated; and 'Leo', like most disembodied souls who turn up at seances, was not only an exotic foreigner but also a distinguished and well-attested figure. His work had come back into circulation over the previous fifteen years or so, and would have been familiar to, among others, WBY's friend in the Golden Dawn, R. W. Felkin, who was both an Arabist and an authority on African anthropology.[44] His entry in *Chambers's Biographical Dictionary*, first port of call for mediums and their researchers, immediately precedes that of Leonardo da Vinci and was familiar to WBY, since he owned the volume. His story also raised a resonant echo from the long-ago fantasy of reincarnation dreamt by Gonne to account for her affinity with WBY (and keep him at brotherly length): for Leo had been sold into slavery in the desert, ending up in the Rome of Pope Leo X.[45] Much of this suggests a certain subliminal preparedness. But even in his account of the happenings of 9 May, WBY still wondered whether his disembodied visitor might be a symbolic being – the constellation Leo, perhaps. He also decided Leo represented a 'solar' influence (oddly, since he would come to see his own astrological influences as lunar). But the inspiration of an exotic guide, who had himself written poetry, travelled afar and investigated the witches, cabbalists and astrologers of Fez, was sustaining. And at further seances with Etta Wriedt, on 5 and 18 June, Leo came through again, minus the Irish accent, giving further details and obligingly revealing a full understanding of (modern) Italian, which for WBY seemed proof positive.[46] WBY's revelation to the seance that in early 1899 Charles Williams had materialized a form who was his guide, called 'Leonora', gave Mrs Wriedt some further help.[47] Still, the seance of June was all the more potent: because through Mrs Wriedt's trumpet, to WBY's shock, came a voice which (he later recorded privately) was that of Maud Gonne. 'She used phrases which I have heard her use at a moment of great emotion & with the intonations of this moment.'

While telling himself that it all might be 'a dream fabrication of the subliminal consciousness of myself & the medium', this was deeply unsettling: it seems to have been a specific reminder of their brief sexual affair.[48] There was, further, a materialization, as a bunch of violets was seized and pressed into his hands ('apporting' flowers was a speciality of Mrs Wriedt's). wby later asked Olivia Shakespear to use her powers of divination and – as he put it – 'psychoanalyse' them: her reading of their aura, delivered by automatic writing, survives in disjointed notes dated 6 June 1912. Possibly suspecting why they meant so much to wby, Shakespear (who had old scores to settle with Gonne's astral influence) decided they came 'from some dead person' and carried 'some fundamental insincerity'.[49]

But wby slowly convinced himself that Leo was sincere, 'sent to give you confidence and solitude'. He only 'adopted' him fully in 1915, writing both sides of an exchange of letters to actualize his guide, and inventing a personality for him which would, by contraries, define his own. It owes a good deal to Robert Brown's introduction to his edition of Leo's *Description of Africa*, which contains a long section on the author's character, and the dialectical construction had long been a favourite form of his.[50] But it also carried wby back to the invented personae of Robartes and Aherne, through whom he had discovered a voice to write occult fiction. Essentially, the 'Leo Africanus' script closely resembles the stories written for *The Secret Rose*. In this 'letter' he would write:

You wish me to [tell] you what leaves me incredulous, or unconvinced. I do not doubt any more than you did when [among] the alchemists of Fez the existence of God, & I follow tradition stated for the last time explicitly in Swedenborg & in Blake, that his influence descends to us through hierarchies of mediational shades & angels. I doubt however, though not always, that the shades who speak to us through mediums are the shades they profess [to] be. That doubt is growing more faint but still it returns again & again. I have continually to remind myself of some piece of evidence written out & examined & put under its letter in my file. How can I feel certain of your identity, when there has been so much to arouse my suspicion.[51]

wby analysed the reasons for scepticism, the case for auto-suggestion, for Leo's being a 'secondary personality' of his own, the suspicious alacrity with which the medium picked up some clues and discarded others. Yet he accepted 'proofs' of the medium's veracity with a certain credulity.[52] wby's records of seances, inscribed at vast length and carefully kept, indicate a struggle between the spirit of inquiry enjoined by the SPR and a powerful emotional wish to believe. But, if only as a strategy of intellectual discipline, the appearance of Leo was a potent inspiration. At a time when wby was ill, uncertain and alone, he had summoned up a voice from the void. Synge and George Pollexfen might be dead, but not gone; all the rituals and self-exploration of his long occultist apprenticeship might have been leading in the end to this. Since childhood, he recalled,

I have always been conscious of some being near to me, & once when I was a child I heard its voice, as though someone was speaking in the room, but something in your

[Leo's] tone, which was a little commanding [and] boisterous, always prevented me from recalling that faint voice.

Yet recall it he did; and the unsettling seances of the summer of 1912 brought him back to the visions of his Sligo youth, his sense of a mission, his mystic bond with Gonne, the world he had tried to re-create in *The Speckled Bird*. Most potently, these keys helped unlock his lyric energies. On 2 August he departed to Gonne's Normandy house, exhausted by excitement and illness but determined to work on what he already conceived as 'a new volume of verse'.[53]

His fortnight there was spent in an intense frenzy of writing. The weather was unseasonably cold, wet and blowy. He was still convalescing from his stomach troubles. They were visited, to WBY's discomfiture, by James Cousins and his wife, old Dublin opponents whom he always found ineffably tedious. But he could play with the children's menagerie, observe the disturbing Iseult (now eighteen), fly kites with Seaghan, and visit Bayeux. He worked on prefaces for collections by Dunsany and Tagore, but principally he wrote lyrics; Cousins heard him rhythmically murmuring for three hours on end. By 8 August he had written a poem about Father Rosicrucius in his tomb and one 'on a child dancing, one of the best I have written'.[54] By 13 August he had added 'Love and the Bird' (later called 'A Memory of Youth') – a coda to 'Adam's Curse', where his attempt to distance himself from his love for Gonne was in the end confounded by her power to mesmerize and enchant.[55]

> The moments passed as at a play,
> I had the wisdom love can bring,
> I had my share of mother wit;
> And yet for all that I could say,
> And though I had her praise for it,
> And she seemed happy as a king,
> Love's moon was withering away.
>
> Believing every word I said
> I praised her body and her mind,
> Till pride had made her eyes grow bright,
> And pleasure made her cheeks grow red,
> And vanity her footfall light;
> Yet we, for all that praise, could find
> Nothing but darkness overhead.
>
> I sat as silent as a stone
> And knew, though she'd not said a word,
> That even the best of love must die,

And had been savagely undone
Were it not that love, upon the cry
Of a most ridiculous little bird,
Threw up in the air his marvellous moon.

One result of this concentrated burst of creativity was that he collapsed again with illness when he returned to London on 16 August; but by the 23rd he was at Coole, where he described his routine to Edwin Ellis. 'I read from 10 to 11. I write from 11 till 2, then after lunch I read till 3.30. Then I go out into the woods or fish in the lake till 5. Then I write letters or work a little till 7 when I go out for an hour before dinner.'[56] He was working on the long narrative poem which eventually became 'The Grey Rock', as well as shorter lyrics. To his excitement, his creative energy showed no sign of abating. He returned to London in October to meet Gordon Craig, visit the Tuckers (and George Hyde-Lees) at Lynton in north Devon, and stay with Eva Fowler, 'partly drawn by an automatic writer who was there from whom I am getting wonderful material' for the essay which became 'Swedenborg, Mediums, and the Desolate Places'.[57] And back in Dublin between 26 and 30 October he sat for four seances at the Cousins' house with the medium Alfred Vont Peters, one of which was also attended by Gonne. Peters generally dealt in oracular psychological generalizations about his sitter; still, for WBY he managed to bring in not only a sulky Leo Africanus but also Blake, Synge and Parnell. As to the latter, 'the people he had worked for had not been known as a people, they were a crowd, that is all. He had worked for the country people, their traditions and their rights,' but been brought down by 'the white dog' of religious hypocrisy.[58] Here, looking forward to 'Parnell's Funeral', is proof that what was heard at seances might be echoed later in WBY's art.[59]

These sessions (carefully recorded by WBY) prove that his mediumistic obsession had taken firm hold. But he returned to Coole until late November, far longer than was usually the case – not a cause of unmitigated pleasure to the younger Gregorys, but necessitated by his constant stomach trouble, now ominously resembling severe ulcers. He was helping to plan an exhibition of Craig's work, arranged by Ellie Duncan of the United Arts Club, and working on a new set for *The Countess Cathleen* with designs by Jack and an appliqué backdrop by Lily. And he required the peace of Coole, since his poetic inspiration continued unchecked. By mid-November he had completed a long poem which he described as 'an epic for me', probably 'The Grey Rock'.[60] His own reading helped concentrate his activity: immersed in his friend Grierson's edition of Donne, he recorded that now at last he understood how 'the more precise & learned the thought the greater the beauty, the passion'.[61] But at the same time the voices in his head, the presences around the medium's table, the memories of his youth, were being forged into a poetic statement which, if often obscure, spoke in a new voice. In this process two further influences were brought to bear in 1912: one from America and one from India.

IV

In June 1910, irritated at the prevalent condescension and ignorance where Indian culture was concerned, WBY's artist friend William Rothenstein had founded the India Society, along with several of WBY's acquaintances, including Rolleston. January 1911 found Rothenstein in Calcutta, where he visited the wealthy and sophisticated Tagore family. This was a level of Indian society different from that of WBY's early guru Mohini Chatterjee; the Tagore ancestors included the 'Oriental Croesus' who was entertained by Queen Victoria and fascinated Dickens,[62] and the current generation numbered a leader of the Brahmo Samaj movement for religious reform and a translator of Molière and Maupassant. The member of the family who made least impression on Rothenstein was a handsome, silent man of fifty, Rabindranath Tagore, who was by then a well-established literary figure in Bengal. But it was Rabindranath who came to England in the summer of 1912, arriving in London in mid-June. Rothenstein found him lodgings in Hampstead, and launched him on the literary world. On 27 June he introduced the Indian visitor to WBY.

WBY was immediately struck by Tagore's distinction and charm, and still more by the translations he had made of his own lyric poetry. On 7 July there was a gathering in Tagore's honour at Rothenstein's house, where WBY gave a reading, and the Indian poet was introduced to Pound, Rhys, Nevinson, May Sinclair, Alice Meynell, Charles Trevelyan and others; he had already met H. H. Fox-Strangeways of the India Society and the *Times*, as well as Sturge Moore. Others were enlisted at a distance, like WBY's friend and translator Davray of the *Mercure*. This influential circle presented Tagore to the world at large. Both Sinclair and Pound wrote him up for the *North American Review* and the *Fortnightly* respectively.[63] Three days later there was a Trocadero dinner sponsored by the India Society and the *Nation*, with WBY as host. Now completely devoted to Tagore's work, he described the Indian poet's advent as 'one of the great events of my artistic life . . . I know of no man in my time who has done anything in the English language to equal these lyrics', and compared him to the medieval troubadour poets, and Thomas à Kempis, whose love was redirected towards invisible nature.[64] To connoisseurs of WBY's enthusiasms, the note was familiar, but it was more extreme than anything since his endorsement of Gregory's *Cuchulain*.

Why did Tagore's work and personality inspire this reaction? Sturge Moore produced a maliciously detached account for his friend R. C. Trevelyan:

Yeats and Rothenstein had a Bengalee poet on view during the last days I was in London. I was first privileged to see him in Yeats rooms and then to hear a translation of his poems made by himself read by Yeats in Rothenstein's drawing-room. His unique subject is 'the love of God'. When I told Yeats that I found his poetry preposterously optimistic he said 'Ah, you see, he is absorbed in God.' The Poet himself is a sweet creature beautiful to the eye in a silk turban, he likes Keats & Wordsworth best of English poets, has read everything including my work. It is a pleasure merely to sit beside him, he reposes the mind & the body. Speaks very little, but looks beneficent and intelligent. The poems read were little pieces. Dealing each one with some image in a narrative biographical way.

(To his wife, Sturge Moore added that 'Yeats read them abominably as usual so that it was very difficult to hear the last word of each retch of his parson's kaw.'[65])

Tagore's impact is slightly reminiscent of Mohini Chatterjee's on Dublin followers a quarter-century before, but his philosophy had little connection with the Vedantic beliefs preached by his predecessor. As Sturge Moore ironically indicated, his poems were lyrics in the Vaishnav tradition, expressing the yearnings of the heart towards Vishnu and his incarnations, leading eventually to a rather woolly doctrine of universalism. (Sturge Moore, again: 'God appears under the image of King, Friend, or Thou, whose big feet are on the footstool of the world, and the rest somewhere else, unspecified. The Soul was I.'[66]) In the original they were intricately rhymed; in translation they appeared as gnomic prose-poetry, and appealed to the popular taste that had already made Nietzsche's *Zarathustra* a cult book (and would later deify Khalil Gibran). They also struck a chord with the kind of late Romantics who venerated Asian wisdom, oddly coinciding in their taste for the exotic with apprentice modernists and veteran Theosophists. For wby, Tagore's poetry not only reminded him of the Indian aesthetic fusion of sensuous and spiritual love, so influential in his own early work; it seemed linked, like Synge's art, to a noble and ancient tradition binding together aristocrat, peasant and poet. Unity of being arose from unity of culture. Even more relevant was Tagore's relationship with Indian nationalism. The Bengali poet was culturally self-confident, and told wby of his ambition to restore 'India's faith in herself' after 'insults at the hands of the west';[67] India, like Ireland, would reconquer the conqueror by force of spiritual power. But, coming from an influential family and living on the cusp of the Bengali and the English worlds, Tagore disliked nationalist chauvinism, would later oppose Gandhi, and remained unpopular with more vehement Indian anti-imperialists. To wby, the parallels with his own position were obvious. As he later put it to Rothenstein, he was biased in favour of Tagore's work (in this case his autobiography) because it 'pointed a moral that would be valuable to me in Ireland'.[68]

Published in 1913 as *Gitanjali* ('song-offerings'), Tagore's poems achieved great success. Though their author would later prove rather sensitive on the subject, much of this was due to WBY's support and help. The process vividly illustrates just how influential he had become. Richard Aldington and others observed the efficiency of the Yeatsian publicity-machine working at full stretch; the young American Robert Frost noted that Tagore was led to WBY as the undisputed First Poet of the day. 'How slowly but surely Yeats has eclipsed Kipling.'[69] For the fifteen months of Tagore's stay, WBY relentlessly pressed his case in the circles where he wielded influence. The inevitable Florence Farr was produced, to chant Tagore poems in Yeatsian fashion – much to Tagore's dismay.[70] By late November WBY was pressing Gosse about electing Tagore to the Academic Committee (though Gosse succeeded in excluding him through 'malice', which WBY did not forget[71]). With Pound enlisted, and for the moment equally enthusiastic, six Tagore poems were placed in the December issue of *Poetry*, with a commentary by Pound that compared Tagore's importance to the rediscovery of Greek literature by the Renaissance. Richard Aldington saw the whole Tagore boom as an exercise in 'snob appeal . . . worked with consummate skill'.[72] Together, Sturge Moore and WBY emphasized to Tagore the importance of carefully timing his publications, in order to build a long-term reputation.[73] But when Tagore won the Nobel Prize in November 1913, it seemed the apotheosis of a lightning campaign in which WBY had been a decisive and Napoleonic general.

How much did the English version of Tagore's poems owe to WBY's intervention? Along with Sturge Moore, he certainly adapted the poet's own translations, cutting out archaisms, inversions and Edwardian gentility.[74] When Fox-Strangeways of the India Society had the temerity to make further changes, WBY blisteringly asserted to Rothenstein his proprietorial interest:

I have had an interminable letter from a man called Strangways suggesting alterations in Tagores translation. He is the sort of man societies like the India Society fatten. He is a manifest goose. I want [you] to get the society to understand that I am to edit this book & that they are [to] send me proofs as any other publisher would. I cannot argue with a man who thinks that 'the ripples are rampant in the river' should be changed because 'rampant' suggests to his goose brains 'opposition to something'. I am very busy – I work like a clerk – and I cannot carry on a correspondence with this man. I have replied politely saying I would go carefully through the text in proof but do please see that he goes back to his pond.[75]

As this letter hints, WBY had from the beginning opposed Rothenstein's wish to see Tagore's poems published by the India Society. He wanted a commercial publisher and a wide distribution. 'Properly managed the book might have a very large sale, as the Theosophical Society have educated a large religious public into Indian interests.'[76] As so often, his business acumen was proved right: the Society issued *Gitanjali* in 750 copies, at the high price of 10s. 6d. each, in November 1912; WBY contributed an introduction and Rothenstein a frontispiece. Sturge Moore grumbled at the 'abominable price', second-rate poems, and the fact that WBY's closing remark was an unacknowledged quotation from Sturge Moore himself.[77] But when Macmillan took it over the following March, they ran up twenty reprints over two years. Two other volumes of poems shortly followed, *The Gardener* and *The Crescent Moon*, and Cuala would publish the most successful of Tagore's many plays, *The Post Office*, which WBY privately and publicly hailed as a 'masterpiece'.[78] The cult rapidly became a craze.

Tagore's response to this powerful advocacy was understandably appreciative, but increasingly ambivalent. He was at first overwhelmed with gratitude, writing a breathless article on WBY for the Calcutta press: 'a fountain showering gentle beneficence all around, every time I have met him in private I have felt with increased intensity the potency of his physical, intellectual and imaginative fullness'.[79] He went on to make some comments which suggest that, if WBY had interpreted Tagore in the way that suited him, the process was symbiotic: according to the Indian, the Irishman was engaged in a war against 'modernism' which was 'not a new thing . . . [but] threadbare, played out'. WBY himself apprehended the world through his 'soul', not his intellect, 'recognising the perennial presence of a playful Providence'. Privately, Tagore became unhappy and nervous about WBY's slowness of pace and strange inaccuracies when adapting his post-*Gitanjali* volumes.[80] For WBY, however, the intricacies of literal translation (with Tagore as with Sophocles) must give way to creative enthusiasm. And this could be shared with new initiates. At Colleville in August, where he was working on the introduction to *Gitanjali*, Iseult became enthused by Tagore's poems, and WBY saw no reason why she should not purchase a Bengali grammar and, thus armed, translate into French the poems in *The Crescent Moon*. Though this project foundered, he brought Iseult to meet Tagore in London the following summer.[81]

Further, he determined that the message should be spread to Ireland. *The Post Office* joined the Abbey's repertoire, complete with Craig screens, and on 23 March 1913 WBY delivered a markedly autobiographical lecture on Tagore in Dublin.[82] Though as a boy, he said, he had saturated himself in Indian influences, he had ignored them since he was twenty;[83] but from the summer of 1912 he had been 'intoxicated' by Tagore, often too moved by his work to read it in public. What appealed was the Indian's spontaneity, his identification of poetry with sanctity, and the way his lyrics lent themselves to being sung (Tagore's low opinion of Farr had evidently not reached him). Tagore's inspiration derived from his refusal to deal with politics, and to save himself and his artistic soul for higher things: thus wby inferred from Tagore's situation both a parallel for his own position and a vindication of it.

Like all feverish infatuations, the Tagore passion ran its course. Pound's enthusiasm had always been dependent on his master's. 'I'm fed up with Tagore,' he told Dorothy from Italy in May 1912. 'I wish he'd get thru' lecturing before I get back. I don't want to be any more evangelized than I am already – which is too dam' much. And I much prefer the eagle's gods to any oriental beetle with 46 arms.'[84] Quite soon, wby himself began to worry about the failure of communication with Tagore. A month after his Dublin speech he confided to Rothenstein that the 'organised intelligence' and garden-city culture of Europe, which men like themselves found second-rate and tedious, was exactly what impressed Indian visitors – who accordingly undervalued the dignity and solitude of their own tradition.[85] As for Tagore, by February 1914 he had become rather resentful of the way people assumed wby had more or less written *Gitanjali*. A year later he summed up their relations more fairly:

There are people who suspect that I owe in a large measure to [C. F.] Andrews' help for my literary success, which is so false that I can afford to laugh at it. But it is different about Yeats. I think Yeats was sparing in his suggestions – moreover I was with him during the revisions. But one is apt to delude himself, and it is very easy for me to gradually forget the share Yeats had in making my things passable. Though you have the first draft of my translation with you I have allowed the revised typed pages to get lost in which Yeats pencilled his corrections. Of course, at that time I could never imagine that anything I could write would find its place in your literature. But the situation is changed now. And if it be true that Yeats' touches have made it possible for Gitanjali to occupy the place it does then that must be confessed.[86]

For wby's part, he would come to see Tagore as a strayed artistic soul who, like Hyde, was misled by 'the folk mind' into not knowing whether he was writing sense or nonsense. Eventually wby found Indian poetry unsatisfying because of its absence of tragedy. But Sturge Moore had hit the essential point long before when he remarked that wby's introduction to *Gitanjali* 'treats the book too much as if it represented a life's work which it does not'.[87] In 1912 Tagore still had a long artistic odyssey before him; and so had wby.

V

wby was not alone in his determination to make Tagore's Western reputation during 1912 and 1913; an important lieutenant in the campaign was his new American admirer Ezra Pound. From 1912 Pound became more and more closely integrated into the emerging world of literary modernism in

London. In his early London days he had cultivated those of the last generation, who would bring him to WBY (Binyon, Plarr, Rhys, Elkin Mathews, the Shakespears); when this had been achieved, his affinities shifted to 'les jeunes' who would become known as 'Imagists'. This group eventually extended to Richard Aldington, Ford Madox Ford, F. S. Flint, Pound's sometime fiancée Hilda Doolittle, T. E. Hulme, and some of the circle round Harold Monro's *Poetry Review*. Pound was their inventor and impresario, defining them against what he denounced as the conventional fatuity of the 'Georgian' school. In 1912 he suddenly pinned the label 'Imagist' on the contemporaries he published in *Poetry* magazine, to their own surprise ('a group of ardent Hellenists who are pursuing interesting experiments in vers libre'). Privately, he put it more sharply: 'laconic speech . . . Objective – no slither; direct – no excessive use of adjectives, no metaphors that won't permit examination. It's straight talk, straight as the Greek!'[88] This assertion was an interim judgement, and he would keep trying out new definitions on the wing. To many of Pound's circle, WBY seemed by contrast a voice defined by the past ('a gargoyle', according to Ford[89]). But Pound's homage to the Irish poet's hieratic authority remained profound if not unquestioning. James Longenbach has pointed out that his definitions of Imagism (however elastic) owed much to WBY's ideas published more than a decade before in 'The Symbolism of Poetry',[90] and the American's early verses bore an embarrassing debt to *The Wind Among the Reeds*. As 'the Eagle', WBY hovers over Pound's early correspondence with Dorothy Shakespear: magnificent, unworldly, very slightly ridiculous, but – as Pound would have put it – unquestionably the real thing. WBY was, for the younger generation, a link to what was already the mythologized world of the 1890s. His readings could summon up that aura, as in one occasion at the Poetry Bookshop about this time:

The dark curtains were drawn across the windows and the room was in darkness except for the golden light shed on the reader's table from the two slender oak candlesticks. From the workshop next door came the muffled beat of the gold-beaters' mallets. A ripple of expectation ran through the packed audience, then a deep expectant hush as the poet stood silent for a moment framed in the candlelight against the dark curtain, a tall dark romantic figure with a dreamy, inward look on his pale face. He began softly, almost chanting, 'The Hosting of the Sidhe', his silvery voice gradually swelling up to the final solemn finale.[91]

WBY invoked magic; while for him, his reverent London disciples offered an uncritical appreciation which was not available in Dublin. There were other compensations too. By the summer of 1912 he – like several others of the artistic avant-garde, notably Augustus John – had enjoyed a casual affair with the beautiful but insipid Alick Schepeler, sending her letters of roguish sexual innuendo from Coole.[92] He also met Pound's friend the musician Walter Rummel, and discussed collaboration on yet another version of *The Countess Kathleen*. And Pound slipped more and more into the role of unofficial secretary, reader, amanuensis. His manners remained deliberately farouche (he unapologetically broke chairs, and at dinner with Eva Fowler chose to eat all the table-decorations before the meal began[93]). His aggressive partisanship had its disadvantages. A casual complaint from WBY about the India Society's meanness with complimentary copies of Tagore's book led to such a violent assault by Pound on Rothenstein that WBY had to step in.

I assumed that he had done it in the way that is customary among the faint energies of our dying European civilisation . . . He is a headlong ragged nature, is always hurting people's feeling, but he has I think some genius and great good will . . . Hercules cannot help seeming a little more than life size in our European Garden of the Hesperides. His voice is too loud, his stride too resounding.[94]

'Hercules' suggests a formidable dispatcher of tasks and assailant of monsters. And while their relationship remained that of master to disciple, WBY admired Pound's scholarship, patchy as it was, and his easy authority about medieval Romance literature. Though this involved a fair amount of 'high-hatting' (in Aldington's phrase), it lent substance to his slangy, avant-garde literary manners.[95] WBY himself knew something about high-hatting. And remarkably, from 1912 he began to accept small emendations suggested by Pound to his own work.

This was observed by others in the circle, such as George Hyde-Lees. Long afterwards, an interviewer quoted her recollections. ' "Well, I was young at the time, but even I knew that certain words W. B. used no longer had the same meaning. Ezra did this" – she wrote, as it were, across a manuscript. "He went through the poems and W. B. accepted his suggestions." '[96] It did not, however, happen quite so smoothly as that. The first poems whose final shape was influenced by Pound were five sent to Harriet Monroe for publication in her new Chicago magazine *Poetry* in December 1912: 'The Realists', 'The Mountain Tomb', 'To a Child Dancing in the Wind', 'A Memory of Youth' and 'Fallen Majesty' – a distinguished group, created in the onset of lyrical energy after WBY's summer of seances.[97] WBY gave the poems to Pound, self-appointed overseas editor of the magazine, who with astonishing insouciance amended them. In 'Fallen Majesty' and 'To a Child Dancing' small but decisive changes were made – all the more sensitive since they affected references to Gonne and Synge.[98] WBY initially saw them as 'misprints'; when he realized what Pound had actually done, he threatened 'in a fury' to withdraw the poems. But he forgave his disciple.[99] From this point, November 1912, Pound exercised a variable degree of influence on the final versions of WBY's poems. WBY himself described the process to Gregory in early January, after Pound had helped him remove 'Miltonic generalisations' from a draft of 'The Two Kings'.

He is full of the middle ages and helps me get back to the definite and the concrete away from modern abstractions. To talk over a poem with him is like getting you to put a sentence into dialect. All becomes clear and natural. Yet in his own work he is very uncertain, often very bad though very interesting sometimes. He spoils himself by too many experiments and has more sound principles than taste.[100]

The results are probably to be found in his next contribution to *Poetry*, the major poem 'The Grey Rock', which he was working on in the late autumn.[101] Originally called 'Aoife's Love', it ambitiously combined a reworking of Celtic legend with a contrapuntal voice recalling his own poetic apprenticeship among the Rhymers twenty years before; their personal dissoluteness was praised as a concomitant of artistic integrity. It preached the same moral lesson as his 1910 lecture 'Friends of my Youth'. Not all the surviving Rhymers appreciated being fixed into the heroic frieze of WBY's life, and he had to issue some hurried disclaimers. The deeply respectable Rhys was mortified by the speed at which their history was being written, and wrote pointing out that many of them were still alive and flourishing. 'Neither you nor Rolleston came into my head at the moment,' WBY assured him. 'One begins to think of "the rhymers" as those who sang of wine & women – I no more than you am typical.'[102]

More importantly, new influences were making him review his own poetic development. As far as WBY was concerned the commitment of Pound and his friends to a 'free' rhythm, based on musical phrases, was suspect. But Pound's influence would encourage what became one of WBY's controversial hallmarks – the disquieting expression of earthy, crude images in traditional and dignified verse forms. One of the key words whose sense changed under Pound's influence was 'reality': from this point WBY began to use it to mean not only Platonic perfection but uncompromising actuality. At the seance on 18 June 1912 'Leo' had told WBY that in 1914 his work would change, would 'swim by itself'. By the end of 1912 the change was taking place. In a notebook given to him by Gonne that Christmas, WBY inscribed an opening statement which reflected his (and Pound's) priorities:

First Principles

Not to find ones art by the analysis of language or amid the circumstances of dreams but to live a passionate life, & to express the emotions that find one thus in simple rhythmical language [deleted: which never shows the obviously studied vocabulary]. The words should be the swift natural words that suggest the circumstances out of which they rose [deleted: of real life]. One must be both dramatist and actor & yet be in great earnest.[103]

He was ending the year in a state of exhaustion and introspection. His dyspeptic illness was not yet shaken off; his specialist Avery suspected appendix trouble and ordered him to lose a stone, on a drastic diet which cut out salt, sweets, milk, green vegetables, potatoes and spirits. But his intellectual enterprise persisted. His trafficking with Leo Africanus, his discovery of Tagore, the admiration of the younger generation in London, all encouraged reassessment: and at this point he began urging his father to write his autobiography, revisiting the Dublin of his youth and defining the credo of his artistic generation. In late November WBY returned to Coole, feeling melancholic; Gregory was preparing to depart once again with the players for America. Leaving, he was filled with thoughts of death and age and – in one of his moments of superb tactlessness – sent her this poem:

> If you, that have grown old, are the first dead
> Neither catalpa tree, nor scented lime
> Should hear my living feet, nor would I tread
> Where we wrought that shall break the teeth of time.
> Let the new faces play what tricks they will –
> Your ghost & mine for all they do or say
> Shall walk the stairs and garden gravil still
> The living seem more shadowy than they.[104]

For Gregory, just sixty years old and about to rejoin her quondam lover John Quinn in New York, this hardly struck a welcome note. She replied cautiously: 'The lines are very touching. I have often thought our ghosts will haunt that path and our talk hang in the air – It is good to have a meeting place anyhow, in this place where so many children of our minds were born – You won't publish it just now will you? I think not.'[105] He took the hint and kept it private until *Seven Poems and a Fragment* ten years later.[106] But for WBY in December 1912, it crystallized the self-image which summed up the year's experiences: a ghost haunting his own life.

In this mood, back in London, he was interviewed by the *Daily News*.[107] He colluded with the journalist in presenting himself as a survivor of the 1890s, standing out against the modern world ('the whole of ancient life cultivated man. It was an organised pageantry. How different it is today!'). Further, he denounced poets who wrote about contemporary politics instead of the essence of beauty; this meant playing to an audience, an 'entirely destructive' process. It is ironic, not to say contradictory, that a week later he would publish his highly political – and highly contemporary – poem 'The Gift' (later 'To a Wealthy Man who promised a Second Subscription to the Dublin

Municipal Gallery if it were proved the People wanted Pictures') and thus take his place in the violent public controversy over the question of a new art gallery for Dublin.

This was a long-standing issue. Fifteen years before, when campaigning for the first loan exhibition of modern French art in Dublin, Russell had urged on WBY the need to supplement their literary enterprise with 'a new art movement', stimulated by 'the force of good examples never seen here'; he had, moreover, denounced 'the apathetic wealthy classes who have not the civic patriotism of second rate English towns where there are municipal galleries'.[108] WBY had responded with a public letter of support. Over the intervening period Gregory's nephew, the connoisseur and dealer Hugh Lane, had carried on this torch, declaring his intention in 1903 and following it through when he tried to raise money to buy the Staats-Forbes collection in 1904/5. Following a large number of private donations, the Dublin Corporation had been committed from March 1905 to allotting £500 a year to maintain 'a Municipal Gallery of Modern Art . . . for the reception of the valuable pictures which had been presented to the State'. That year, Lane began his self-education in modern French painting, adding Manet and Renoir to El Greco and Corot; but, though he quarrelled with the Royal Hibernian Academy, he kept up his campaign for a permanent Dublin gallery. In June 1906 the Corporation agreed to maintain 'temporary premises', which from late 1907 were fixed in Clonmell House, Harcourt Street. It turned out that a special Act of Parliament had to be passed for the Corporation to exercise the powers which they had assumed. This was done in 1911, and in the meantime Lane accepted financial responsibility.

In the subsequent years Lane was knighted, received the Freedom of the City of Dublin, set up a showpiece home in Cheyne Walk, Chelsea, turned huge profits by dealing for South African diamond millionaires, and became even richer – none of which endeared him to Dublin opinion. But he continued to lavish attention, and pictures, on the gallery-in-waiting. His bargaining-point was the thirty-nine pictures he had provisionally given to the gallery, on the condition of a permanent home; they ranged from Courbets and Corots to works by Degas, Manet, Monet, Pissarro and Renoir.[109] After much lobbying, the Dublin Corporation had accepted the principle of a Municipal Gallery of Modern Art, but for Lane, who had begun already to canvass architects and designers, this was insufficient. In November 1912 he threatened to withdraw the bulk of his bequest (now worth £60,000) unless a proper building was raised. Following a Mansion House meeting on 29 November 1912, a large public subscription was declared to be necessary, and got under way, organized by a Citizens' Provisional Committee. At this point opposition began to be voiced: and, since Gregory and

Lane were closely linked (his house in Cheyne Walk was now her base in London), this affected the Abbey. The same people whose resources were cultivated in their own fundraising drive of 1910 were now approached once more, not entirely to their pleasure. Notably, the Guinness magnate Lord Ardilaun showed a distinct lack of enthusiasm, partly because one of the sites canvassed for the gallery was St Stephen's Green park, donated to Dublin by his family, and incensed the Lane–Gregory camp by remarking that there was little evidence of a public demand for a modern art gallery. Tempers mounted, and the issue was exacerbated by the insecurities and sensitivities arising over the advent of Home Rule.

Probably during his stay at Coole in late November and early December, WBY worked on a poem as a contribution to the campaign; back in London, he spent some time in the British Museum checking references to Italian history, since the poem was constructed round the idea of Renaissance culture to which the Gregorys had introduced him.[110] The first version was headed 'To a friend who promises a bigger subscription than his first to the Dublin Municipal Gallery if the amount collected proves that there is a considerable "popular demand" for the pictures'. On 1 January, after an evening with Pound going through it 'line by line', he sent it to Lane with an explanatory note, suggesting publication in the *Irish Times*. Lane, who liked controversy, was enthusiastic. A few days later WBY had dinner with the journalist Joseph Hone, who promised an accompanying leading article. A Corporation debate on the subject was imminent; on 20 January they would actually vote an annual £2,000 grant for the gallery.[111] With these auguries, WBY advised Lane to bank on that support instead of throwing down the gauntlet to the capitalist classes. 'He replied that he hated Dublin,' wrote WBY ruefully to Gregory. 'I said so do we.'[112] The die was cast, and on 11 January 'The Gift' was published, with Hone's accompanying article. This was poetry as political manifesto, and its echoes reached further than Dublin Corporation and the gallery question. The timing of its publication was aggressive, and actually counter-productive; but the content of the poem was even more offensive. A fantasy of Renaissance Italy and noble patronage was set against Ardilaun's frugality; the tone of aristocratic disdain was compounded by the Olympian references to 'Paudeen' and 'Biddy' – symbolizing, through diminutives of the patron saints Patrick and Bridget, the Irish 'people'. The poem's moral might be taken as a counsel to the elite to ignore the popular will, and as such, it was bound to arouse anger. Although WBY made it clear privately that the poem was written against the Ardilauns, the person most outraged by it was William Martin Murphy – the millionaire newspaper proprietor and transport magnate who had taken a leading part in the anti-Parnellite movement and who had come to symbolize (not always fairly) the

17. 'The Gift' (later 'To a Wealthy Man who promised a Second Subscription to the Dublin Municipal Gallery if it were proved the People wanted Pictures') as first printed in the *Irish Times*. Embedded amid news items reporting the gathering Home Rule crisis, unrest in the Balkans, and the latest meeting of the Municipal Art Gallery Building Fund Committee, it appears as a deliberate political intervention.

essence of bourgeois Dublin philistinism. Murphy wrote to the press 'from Paudeen's point of view', asserting the right of ratepayers to say where their money went and declaring he 'would rather see in the City of Dublin one block of sanitary houses at low rents replacing a reeking slum than all the pictures Corot and Degas ever painted'.[113] 'I am told that various people answered Murphy very effectively,' wby told Gregory on 24 January. 'He merely showed himself up by the ill-manners of his letters, as my sister says "They always do". Unfortunately he is not likely now to listen to any protest against the tone of the criticism in the Independent. I've a couple more poems in my head, to be written if the Gallery falls through.'[114] As the tone of this letter indicates, the conflict had taken a very traditional configuration indeed, highlighting wby's developing affinities with Ascendancy values and Protestant traditions. At this very moment, as has been seen, he decided to take a public line on the dangers of anti-Protestant bigotry in a Home Rule Ireland;[115] the campaign over Lane's gallery, and the direction it took, must be seen in conjunction with his simultaneous political statements of December 1912 and January 1913, publicizing his feelings about Catholic intolerance.

Although the fundraising issue continued to simmer, attention now shifted to the positioning of the future gallery itself. Lane, whose taste ran to the spectacular, had become committed to the idea of a dramatic new gallery spanning the River Liffey, rather like an enclosed Venetian bridge; his friend Lutyens was working on a design. Though other sites were canvassed (on the Green, beside Dublin Castle, or on Earlsfort Terrace by the new National University), a public meeting in February seemed to conclude that agreement was reached on a Liffey site replacing the metal 'Halfpenny' footbridge (then considered an eyesore, now a much loved landmark). Lane believed he had the support of the Corporation, the *Irish Times* and the *Freeman's Journal*; but he needed £20,000, since building the bridge foundation alone would cost £11,000.[116] The Citizens' Provisional Committee elected to raise the money, but wby quailed a little at Lane's remorseless ambition, confiding to Gregory his own preference for the Earlsfort Terrace site. A whispering campaign began to denigrate Lane's motives, and to attack Lutyens as un-Irish. Lane, the bit between his teeth, now began to issue threats. He had been offered, he said, 'a fine new London Gallery for French art & himself as curator if he would give [his] pictures to London'. He had recently bought a Degas for a fabulous £4,500; he would withhold it, and the rest, unless the bridge site, and Lutyens's plan, was accepted. But by the autumn of 1913, £5,000 was still needed; and this too affected the Abbey, since Gregory and (less willingly) wby had guaranteed a proportion of their American tour income for the gallery fund.[117] Thus personal, political and professional reasons implicated wby more and more closely in Lane's cliff-hanging campaign to give the Dublin public what he thought good for them.

It is clear that this was much in his mind through the spring of 1913, even from chance remarks made in the course of interviews about the Gordon Craig exhibition organized by the United Arts Club ('the modern painter leaves out what everyone can see, that he may emphasise the more what he alone can see'[118]). On St Patrick's Day WBY sent a powerful letter to the *Irish Times* advocating the bridge site, though he regretted not building a gallery adjacent to the new university, where students could wander amid great art between lectures (again, an echo of an idealized Italian city-state). A Corporation debate on the issue was due on 19 March, and on the 18th he delivered a public lecture, 'The Theatre of Beauty', to publicize the Craig exhibition. Here, and in accompanying newspaper interviews, he made a deliberate connection between Craig's aesthetic, his celebrated Russian productions, and the need to accept the new non-representational art ('the only real art, judged by better eyes; it selects the permanent, the important, and it touches the emotions'). But this required a sophisticated understanding – as, paradoxically, did the aesthetic of genuine folk art. Vulgarity was 'modern' in another sense; a history of the concept would show that in ancient times only the educated few understood how to guide the artistic productions which would elevate the many. To achieve immediate popularity, modern art must necessarily be insincere.

Many of these arguments had been advanced at least five years before, in lectures such as 'The Immoral Irish Bourgeoisie'.[119] But now, though supposedly referring to Craig's theatre, he was really reiterating the argument in his *Irish Times* poem about Lane's gallery. Murphy may, indeed, have been in WBY's sights when he called for a study of the history and psychology of vulgarity. 'He thought the psychology of it was the tendency all over the world to educate men whether they liked it or not, and when they had educated a man against his will he revenged himself by liking all the worst things.'[120] While much of the lecture specifically referred to avant-garde theatrical production, his statements were obviously fashioned as weapons in the simultaneous controversies which preoccupied him. Reporting on the exhibition to Craig, he wrote:

In Ireland we have a most ignorant press & a priest created terror of culture. Lady Gregory & I have lit our little lanthorn & kept the wick a light by solid determination. We would have found a better public elsewhere but we could not have found in ourselves & others this determination which exists for the same reason that our stupid public exists. Ireland is being made & this gives the few who have clear sight the determination to shape it.[121]

Less than a week after his Dublin lecture about the theatre came his address (probably to many of the same people) on Tagore. And here too he declared his stance against the debasement of modern politics, and the lowering of artistic standards for a general audience. Praising Tagore for his determination to adhere to higher things, wby added:

Do not think I am condemning politics. They are necessary for Ireland, and I have no doubt they are necessary for India; but my meaning is – different men for different tasks. For those whose business it is to express the soul in art, religion or philosophy, they must have no other preoccupation. I saw all this years ago, at the beginning of this movement, and I wrote the 'Countess Cathleen' to express it. I saw people selling their souls that they might save the souls of others.[122]

The analogy was strained, to say the least, but he succeeded in reminding his audience of his long and contentious engagement with Irish opinion over questions of artistic freedom. Though the Countess had succeeded in what she set out to do, he concluded, contemporary soul-sellers did not. Thus Tagore's poetry, Lane's gallery, Craig's screens were all drawn together in his mind during March 1913, in a series of public statements intended to dictate priorities to an Ireland 'being made', and to declare independence from the shibboleths of the Catholic bourgeoisie. He wrote to Gregory, in the course of advising her how to deal with opposition on the current American tour:

I always feel in the end one gains from keeping ones attitude towards ones art & the world so simple that one can use all ones thought & not a selection. It gives one more enemies but it increases ones power in a greater proportion . . . I should not perhaps be so anxious to free myself from all diplomacies if I had not suffered so much from a series of false positions in the past. My last lecture here – that on Tagore – was to some extent an attempt to free myself from the need of religious diplomacy.[123]

In this at least, he succeeded; by now the *Leader* was attacking the Abbey for its donation of £1,000 to Lane's gallery fund, identified by Moran with the avant-garde pretensions of a self-designated elite.

VI

Ironically, at this stage the question arose – for the last time – of a university post for wby in Dublin. In early April Dowden at last died. wby sent a graceful note to his daughter (whom he knew in another persona, as the celebrated medium Hester Travers-Smith), recalling Dowden's kindness to him in his youth, but what preoccupied him was the immediate future. Gregory counselled postponing his mooted American lecture-tour and

18. A *Leader* cartoon of 5 April 1913, responding to the offer of £1,000 from the Abbey to the gallery fund. The editor, D. P. Moran, was a temperance advocate who hated the powerful brewing interests ('Mr Bung'), and the profit-making Theatre is seen as a public house, as in the opening scene of the *Playboy*. Gregory is Pegeen behind the bar, the lead Abbey actor Arthur Sinclair represents her loy-carrying customer, while 'Pensioner Yeats' acts as floor-sweeper and potboy.

awaiting overtures from the Fellows of Trinity: 'you cd hardly refuse I think at this Home Rule moment'.[124] By early May he had conferred with Louis Purser, who dangled the prospect of a Chair of Poetry specifically tailored for wby, involving seven or eight lectures and £120 a year. wby wrote to Vice-Provost Mahaffy on 14 May that he would gladly be considered a candidate for such a post, but would be more cautious about a teaching chair in literature. An attractive mirage emerged: Magee would be appointed 'prof. of literature with the examinations to do', while wby gave lectures in poetry. But it was dissipated by the candidature of Wilberforce Trench, whom wby considered a Protestant bigot with reactionary teaching ideas. In any case, he resented the way that academic politicking interfered with his writing, especially as he had just produced 'one of the most passionate things I have ever done', a long lyric and, he thought, potentially a great one. 'I have been writing for six hours without stopping & I wish Dowden had lived another year.'[125]

He also resented returning to Dublin from London; as so often, he was keeping a dual career in view. Already he had lent his name to a London-based group called 'The Society of the Theatre', involving Augustus John, William

Poel, Pound, Stanislavski and others, committed to advancing Craig's ideas of 'theatrical drama'.[126] By the spring of 1913 he was cautiously in touch with his old acquaintance Florence Darragh, who held out the promise of large-scale financial backing for a London-based repertory theatre specializing in Craig scenery and WBY's plays: there were plans for an opening programme of *On Baile's Strand*, a Dunsany play and Craig's old triumph, *The Masque of Love*. 'It would mean a mass of magnificent designs & the connection of my work (whether it succeeded or failed in the ultimate London performance) with the history of the stage,' he wrote unguardedly to Gregory.[127] She must have flinched, but he was by now canny enough to know that beginnings must be cautious, and he warned Darragh that her grandiose plans might mean truckling to debased public taste. ('I am not talking merely out of my Dublin experience now, but from my original theory founded on my whole experience of life.'[128]) They relied in any case for finance on Darragh's influence with 'rich young Jews who spend £500 a year a peice at the hoziers'; and these potential angels rapidly dematerialized. WBY kept the project at arm's length, offering literary advice only. But initially he had been enthused by the idea: it seemed to offer not only a showcase for his plays, still underestimated in Dublin, but a purchase on the world of English high culture where so much of his reputation had been made.

Other forces drew him back to London in the spring of 1913; and one of the most magnetic had to do with those memories of the 1890s which had come to dominate his personal myth, and act as reminders of mortality. One central figure in his life moved off-stage; in September 1912 Florence Farr, after a brief period trying to make a living in the casinos of the French Riviera, set off to spend the rest of her life in Ceylon, where she improbably took on the headship of a girls' school. She would, as she jauntily put it, 'end my days in the "society of the wise" as the Vedanta books say one should'.[129] The end would come sooner than expected, since she developed cancer four years later. And just before Christmas 1912, WBY had heard that one of his old acquaintances from the 1890s, Mabel Beardsley, had been diagnosed with the same disease.

As Aubrey's sister, Mabel inherited a certain mystique: WBY remembered a tongue-tied young musician, introduced to her at a Woburn Buildings Monday evening, saying that it was 'like meeting King Arthur'.[130] Others recalled her as jolly, strapping and unshockable. 'Being Aubrey's sister little that is hidden to most young girls was unknown to Mabel,' wrote Rothenstein rather primly, '& there was nothing that cd not be discussed.'[131] WBY had more or less lost touch with her, but wrote a sympathetic letter ('I have never seen as much of you as I would'). From January 1913 he began visiting her mother's Hampstead house on Sundays. At first he met other visitors there, as the old

1890s circle regrouped by her bedside; stories and jokes were passed around, along with memories of outrageous behaviour twenty years before. 'How her life, her speech would horrify the pious Dublin people & yet how base & dark they seem in contrast,'[132] WBY wrote to Gregory. Ricketts, another regular visitor, made her a series of dolls (a fashionable aesthetic preoccupation of the time[133]), fantastically dressed: WBY found her with their faces turned to the wall when she had Mass said on 13 January. The esoteric and sophisticated Beardsley circle, discussing sexual inversion and the Russian ballet, appealed to him as an escape from Dublin spite and intrigue (he was currently weathering attacks in the press from Russell's followers and was incensed by meeting the co-operativist sage himself, 'fat and confident', at Asquith's on 17 January[134]). As her strength slowly declined, Mabel kept Sunday afternoons for WBY alone; the invalid's 'passion for reality' and the gaiety with which she approached death inspired him to a sequence of short poems, 'On a Dying Lady'. Seven were completed by early April. These poems, he told Farr, were 'among my best & very unlike anything I have written before'; combining simplicity and exoticism, they struck echoes of the courtly-love tradition which influenced Pound (WBY told Beardsley jokingly that he disliked his ridiculous Christian name and would like to have been called 'Florimond'). Pound's criticism helped refine the poems, whose original rhyming scheme he found trite, despite WBY's defence that it was Elizabethan. 'Elizibeefan . . . its just moulting eagle.' But WBY thought highly enough of the series to consider holding up his next collection until they could be published. Good taste apparently dictated suppressing them until Mabel had died, though it did not prevent him sending drafts to the subject herself, who indomitably lived on until 1916.[135]

Through the spring of 1913, while he observed and participated in Irish political campaigns and kept a close eye on Abbey affairs, he maintained his very different London existence: lunching at the Asquiths', befriending Rupert Brooke, manoeuvring on the Academic Committee for Tagore's election, arranging for the Royal Society of Literature to give the Edmond de Polignac Prize to his protégé James Stephens.[136] His health slowly returned to normal, though the various regimens had caused a severe weight loss; his creative energy continued, and by 5 March he had completed 'The Three Hermits'. As ever, he was restlessly rewriting early work and urging Bullen (who now owed him £400 on sales) to incorporate changes into the *Collected Works*: it must be 'a collection precisely [of] those things I wish to be my permanent self'.[137] He was conscious of a distinct change, a new note, in his recent poetry. But his public stayed a step behind. In 1913 his *Poems*, steadily reprinting, were selling more than ever (over a thousand copies, and 880 the following year), figures matched by the cheap editions of *The Countess Cathleen* and

The Land of Heart's Desire.[138] But there was less demand for his recent work. Anthologies proved that he was still best known for the poems written before he was thirty.

And he was still searching for guidance. In early April he was seeking clairvoyant advice and attending seances in Dublin, at the Cousins' Sandymount house, with a non-professional medium called Mrs Mitchell – requiring information, among other things, about the prospects of the Darragh–Craig theatrical venture.[139] On 1 May he told Gregory that he had to be back in London for seances with Mrs Wriedt on 12 and 13 May, 'the only vacancies I could get . . . I want to try a very important experiment.'[140] But far more important to him was his exposure to the automatic-writing talents of a girl called Elizabeth Radcliffe, to whom he had been introduced by the resourceful Eva Fowler.[141]

Bessie Radcliffe's background was described by a family friend as 'good, solid stock, very English, intelligent but not imaginative, decidedly conventional in all their ways'; she herself was 'an attractive, well-educated creature, of rather downright speech and with a few remnants of the schoolroom's uncertain manner'. Her upper-middle-class background, unusual for a medium, meant that her disapproving family tried to discountenance all publicity.[142] At seventeen or eighteen she became known in the family circle for attracting supernatural experiences, visits from the dead, and poltergeists; but, like Stainton Moses, Kate Wingfield and other predecessors, her speciality became automatic writing in foreign or ancient languages not formally known to Radcliffe herself (though on at least one occasion they were quotations from schoolbooks kept in her parents' house[143]). By the middle of May WBY wrote excitedly to Gregory (from Lady Desborough's house at Taplow, where he was staying) describing Radcliffe at work. He was ready to be convinced – especially when authorities at the British Museum (rather guardedly) attested to the correctness of the various languages reproduced in her script. Several encounters with Radcliffe followed, and a long correspondence in which WBY desperately tried to divine messages from the material poured out by her 'controls'. A more sceptical observer described one of the first encounters in Fowler's London flat, with WBY looking 'like a gross exaggeration of the Idea of a Poet, as laid up in heaven'. The 'control' produced furious scribblings which were deciphered as violent abuse of Radcliffe herself, with threats to harm her.

Yeats at once took charge. 'Leave this spirit to me,' he said; 'I will exorcise him.' He then rose to his great height, and taking a stick – or was it the poker? – he drew a complicated pattern on the carpet ('Would you mind moving the tea-table a trifle? Thank you') while muttering incantations.

487

'There,' he said; 'that will settle him. He cannot harm you now.' [Radcliffe] took up her pencil and wrote: 'Ha! ha! if you think that folly can stop me, you will find you are badly mistaken.' The deflation of Yeats was complete. His long, angular body subsided into an arm-chair. He had the beaten look of a defeated boxer in his corner.[144]

This particular 'control' was identified as the seventeenth-century classicist Thomas Creech, easily traced in the *Dictionary of National Biography*, and wBY remained uncertain of the extent to which unconscious memory was supplying the information. Still, he persevered and by May 1913 had a more specific claim on Radcliffe, for he was agonizedly anxious to solve a sudden crisis in his private life. He had continued to see Mabel Dickinson, in Dublin and London; they collaborated on spiritualist experiments at the end of March. And in late May – now aged thirty-eight, and probably becoming impatient – she wrote to him telling him she was pregnant.[145]

He was, as he privately recorded in a notebook, 'horror struck; there seemed no possibility of doubting it'. Yet something must have made him feel he had cause to wonder. He told Gregory of the crisis, and she emphasized that if Dickinson was pregnant he had to marry her.[146] But he looked for occult guidance too. 'In the first week of June' he consulted Radcliffe's controls, and decided they gave him reason for delay. On 6 June he met Dickinson in London; there was a violent quarrel, which suggests he expressed scepticism, and then a truce. On 8 June he pressed Radcliffe to 'interpret the Greek which you sent me . . . it is very obscure. I doubt if the spirits got all their message through . . . The matter I asked about is of great importance.'[147] Phrases which translated as 'cruel, cruel, cruel' and 'the torch of splendour' were not much help; in a series of letters wBY searched for alternative meanings ('the matter is of tragic importance'; 'I am living under much strain & anxiety'[148]). Finally, as he recorded in his notebook, 'they said I was deceived & that I should not take the action I had all but decided on. "Deception, deception, deception, you have said; you are right – *Refrain, Refrain, Refrain*" were their words.' This suggests that he presented rather a leading question, though he recorded that he kept the form of his written inquiry to the controls out of Radcliffe's sight, and had left out all names and facts – which might account for her slowness in producing the answer he wanted. By the time of his unpublished essay on Radcliffe, written in October, he was referring to these responses as 'the most precise and circumstantial answers'. He was at last convinced, and he must have received a corroborating admission from Dickinson at the end of June. She was apparently not pregnant at all, if she ever had been.[149] Though he continued to see Dickinson in July, at a session in Eva Fowler's cottage Radcliffe's control obligingly gave 'a warning (not produced by a question) against seeing [Dickinson] which caused "strain and hesitating debate". They spoke exactly as a wise friend would have spoken, but in the first instance they knew what no friend could have known.'[150]

His wise friend at Coole was more outspoken:

Thank God you are free! It has been a terrible time – I dont think you felt it more than I did – perhaps not so much – An ugly undignified forced marriage instead of a sacred & reverent sacrament – You have been saved 'but so as by fire' – I cant say I am surprised. I had such a strong conviction at times of the 'deception, deception, deception' – & more than that I had especially in waking up at night, a certainty the whole thing was a myth, but one mistrusts a judgement that goes with one's wishes.[151]

Later she wrote that 'this unpleasant business . . . has troubled my thoughts of you. From beginning to the present it has not been worthy of you.' WBY felt much the same, and was accordingly thankful for his deliverance. Dickinson disappeared from his life, and went on to an English marriage and a respectable old age.[152] His faith in the investigations with Elizabeth Radcliffe had been, in his eyes, vindicated, and the scepticism which he had tried to cultivate about the materialization of Leo Africanus was dissipated. 'Spirit identity' had been proved, and the existence of ghosts who could guide him. Later that summer he wrote in his notebook:

I have the sensation of beings of independent existence, & of much practical wisdom who draw constantly on modern editions of the Classics (I hope yet to know what editions) & on modern ideas & use them in the service of their own independent thought . . . I get the presence of living, independent minds gathering together a language of thought & symbol out of the books and thoughts of those in association with the medium & the medium herself, & drawing about them earth bound spirits who follow certain obscure tracks of affinity.

They 'plunge into our world like seabirds that plunge under water & fish'; and 'these great beings do not become secondary personalities or create such in the mind of the medium but in the subconscious mind of an epoch, a family, a phase of a race & express themselves through their general thought'.[153] Their influence lay behind the known world, affecting it like unseen magnets drawing iron filings into patterns on a sheet of paper.[154] Later he would develop some of these ideas into the system of influential archetypes which lies behind *A Vision*. For the moment he was still speculating and – to his own satisfaction – confirming the information relayed through mediums and automatic-writing, as well as grappling with theories of telepathy. The misheard, disjointed quality of mediumistic communication was, he believed, due to long-dead spirits fastening on to the residual conciousness of more recent ghosts. On 8 October he finished a long essay on Radcliffe's script, written for his own reference and updated and revised over the next years,[155] though he never published it, and progressively watered down its conclusions. But at the time of writing it echoed the conviction of contemporary commentaries like Theodor Flournoy's *Spiritism and Psychology* and James Hyslop's *Psychical Research and Survival*; mediums like Radcliffe had actually proved that the spirit lived on.[156] By the time he lectured to the Dublin Society for Psychical Research on 31 October, he was prepared publicly to state his conviction: 'he had the strongest reasons to believe that the soul survived death, very little changed'. Speaking in detail about the state of the soul after death, he likened it to the state of sleep, with 'the dissolution of personality and the moral sense' that accompanied dreams.[157]

He believed that everything done by the dead could be done by the living, if only the living soul got detached from the body. The soul was suggestable to itself . . . when the soul died it went over the most passionate moments of its life. When these passions exhausted themselves it passed into a state of lucidity, which corresponded to the state one entered at rare moments in dreams.

The reaction of the general Dublin public may be imagined. When he sent a letter to the *Irish Times* protesting against a heavily ironic report ('we feel we must congratulate both him and his friends, the spirits, upon their linguistic accomplishments'[158]), the editor riposted: 'we agree with Mr Yeats that life is too short for explanations of his psychical adventures'. Certainly what is most striking is his need to believe, and his determination to present leading questions and suggest likely interpretations, until a pattern or a 'message' shaped itself.

Equally impressive is the dividend paid in creative work. The seances of 1912 and 1913 not only lie behind the essay completed in 1914, 'Swedenborg, Mediums, and the Desolate Places'; they helped inspire his most sustained burst of poetic activity for many years, and the collection of poems called *Responsibilities* stands as their testament. Under the elliptical, pared-down, colloquial style (encouraged but not, for all his claims, inspired by Pound) ran a stream of obscure reference not only to WBY's personal history but to his supernatural investigations. The confluence was not always successful; but at certain points the combination of personal testament and ideas such as those put forward in his lecture 'Ghosts and Dreams' produced a sort of controlled poetic explosion. There is no record of the exact date of composition of 'The Cold Heaven', first published in 1912, but it concentrates the influences of these years. Staring at a winter sky, desperately looking back at where his life had gone, the lacerating memory of his failure with Gonne and his theories of death, ghosts and dreams come together in a passionate fusion.

Suddenly I saw the cold and rook-delighting Heaven
That seemed as though ice burned and was but the more ice,
And thereupon imagination and heart were driven
So wild, that every casual thought of that and this
Vanished, and left but memories, that should be out of season
With the hot blood of youth, of love crossed long ago;
And I took all the blame out of all sense and reason,
Until I cried and trembled and rocked to and fro,
Riddled with light. Ah! When the ghost begins to quicken,
Confusion of the death-bed over, is it sent
Out naked on the roads, as the books say, and stricken
By the injustice of the skies for punishment?[159]

Chapter 18 : MEMORY HARBOUR
1913–1914

> We watch him in these controversial poems of his building up
> a legend around himself; a stirring legend that will, I believe,
> hit the fancy of the young men of Ireland as the Celtic Twilight
> never did.
>
> J. M. Hone's review of *Responsibilities*,
> *New Statesman*, 24 April 1915

I

'IF one can judge by the influence in my youth of Duffy's "Young Ireland",'
remarked WBY to Gregory in the autumn of 1913, 'the power of our epoch on
Ireland in the next generation will greatly depend upon the way its person-
al history is written.'[1] He made the same observation, using the same
analogy, to Tynan a month later; he felt part of a historic generation now,
like Tynan, publishing precocious autobiographies. A resentful admiration
for the way his old adversary Gavan Duffy had put his stamp on history con-
firmed his desire to create an autobiographical art which would assert the
place of his own tradition in Ireland, as the country moved towards appar-
ent independence. One campaign began with the carefully orchestrated
publication of 'A Gift' in January 1913 – a public poem about public opinion
– and climaxed in the October publication of his *Poems Written in Discour-
agement*, dealing with the struggles of the enlightened against Blind Men and
Fools. Another strategy was to present a personal, intimate history that made
its own claim on the national life. This is the background to the poems pub-
lished in *Responsibilities* in 1914, many written the previous year: and, still more,
to his own first volume of autobiography, completed at the end of 1914. That
disingenuous masterpiece called down the curtain on a phase in his own life:
it tells us as much about WBY in 1914 as about the childhood of a poet in
Victorian Ireland.

It also reflects his renewed interest in his father's ideas on style, person-
ality and art, which can be traced through their letters (both writing with a
future public in mind). This process was clarified by the publication of
Dowden's correspondence, which showed the young JBY issuing the same
insouciant assertions that still flowed from his pen in the Petitpas boarding-
house half a century later. The idea of JBY writing his autobiography continued
to preoccupy his son, but – possibly remembering the endlessly unfinished
portraits, scraped down again at the moment of completion – by the summer

of 1913 WBY was suggesting a book 'of criticism & philosophy extracted from your letters & lectures': talk continued by other means. A sense of personal history had brought the realization of how much the conversation at Bedford Park and the York Street studio had formed his own mind – if only by reaction.

Thus the intersection between personal history and public life lies behind many of WBY's pronouncements in 1913 and 1914 – even on so anodyne an occasion as the presentation of the Royal Society of Literature's Edmond de Polignac Prize (a hefty £100) to James Stephens in November, for *The Crock of Gold*. As the cynical Richard Aldington observed it, WBY 'spoke in his beautiful voice; he expressed Celtic lore with his more beautiful face: he elevated and waved his yet more beautiful hands. He blessed us with his presence. He spoke of spirits and phantasmagoria. He spoke of finding two boots in the middle of a field and the owner of the boots listening for the earth-spirits under a bush. He praised Mr Stevens' [*sic*] Crock of Gold. He read one of Mr Stevens' poems, which was admirable as he read it.'[2] But Aldington did not note WBY's key remark, that Stephens's book 'had given him more pleasure . . . than it could give to another man, wise and beautiful though it was, because it was a proof that his own native city of Dublin had vigour and lived with a deeper life'. The idea that Ireland, on the brink of Home Rule, might at last produce an original and unpietistic creative literature seemed to him the vindication of what his generation had tried to do. Synge in his different mode had shown the way, and Joyce's astonishingly accomplished short stories (which WBY was soon to read) would give further evidence still.

And yet the old limitations persisted, and the old enemies – concentrated by the summer of 1913 into the question of Lane and his art gallery. The Abbey was now firmly identified by its directors with the campaign to raise funds; its donation of money from the 1912/13 tour was described by the Mansion House Committee as all that prevented the project's collapse. At a special Abbey performance in aid of the fund on 9 May, WBY stressed that in the current era they were playing to an enormous audience of the unborn: the future denizens of a Home Rule Ireland, nurtured on a cultural nationality 'more lasting and penetrating than any that Young Ireland could give'. He described the present moment as 'the generation in which the Irish people became a modern people'. By using 'modern' in an untypically positive sense, he was identifying the gallery campaign with Ireland's artistic and political maturity. At the same meeting Lord Mayor Sherlock rashly declared that Lutyens's bridge site was as good as agreed upon.[3] However, over the next month a reaction set in which – in WBY's view at least – proved that Irish development was arrested. The Lord Mayor, a supporter of the Lutyens plan, went to the

493

United States for the summer, and in June the opponents of the bridge site rallied. By 14 July the question was once again in doubt when only fourteen members turned up to the vital meeting of the Dublin Corporation, less than the quorum necessary to pass the plan.

WBY took up the cudgels, speaking before a benefit performance of *Blanco Posnet* at the Court Theatre in London, and thus confounding the theatre movement, once again, with Lane's enterprise. Outlining the history of the projected gallery, he stressed that in order to secure pictures worth £70,000, Ireland needed to raise a further £10,000 (of which £1,000 had been guaranteed by the theatre). But he moved on to wider issues, reminding the Irish aristocracy that they had left the intellectuals and artists to struggle alone, and reverting to his theme of independence in the making. But that independence was now threatened.

There is a moment in the history of every nation when it is plastic, when it is like wax, when it is ready to hold for generations the shape that is given to it. Ireland is now plastic, and will be for a few years to come. The intellectual workers in Ireland see gathering against them all the bigotries – the bigotries of Dublin that have succeeded in keeping 'the Golden Treasury' out of the schools, the bigotries of Belfast that have turned Nietzsche out of the public libraries. If Hugh Lane is defeated, hundreds of young men and women all over the country will be discouraged – will choose a poorer idea of what might be . . . if the intellectual movement is defeated Ireland will for many years become a little huckstering nation, groping for halfpence in a greasy till. It is that, or the fulfilment of her better dreams. The choice is yours and ours.[4]

He would repeat these phrases and images in his autobiography and poetry for years: they show his belief that the old enemies still waited at the gate. Though he tactfully omitted the phrase 'by the light of a holy candle' after 'groping in a greasy till' (reserving it for a private letter to Gregory), his target was Catholic piety as much as commercial vulgarity. It cannot have helped to defuse sensitivities in Dublin, but Lane in any case had the bit between his teeth. After the abortive meeting Lane told the Lord Mayor, 'I feel that the Dublin Corporation has killed the goose that lays the golden egg without yet securing the egg.' He immediately ceded one (comparatively unimportant) painting to the Scottish National Gallery, and threatened to dispose of the rest to other galleries 'if the next meeting of the Corporation is not satisfactory'. This ill-concealed dictation did not help matters, and nor did his remark that the beauty of Lutyens's bridge gallery 'would set a standard for Irish architects to look up to'. Gregory, always more judicious than either her nephew or her fellow-director, felt he had gone too far: 'the ungraciousness of Hugh and the vulgarity of the opposition and the contempt shown towards art makes one ashamed as one so often is of Dublin'.[5] Still, she added, 'I don't see that he can withdraw [the pictures], and from his own letters I think it was only the ones he has in London the Gallery would lose.'

But this was too sanguine. By mid-August she was 'at my wit's end' about the gallery. The Dublin Chamber of Commerce had now come out against the bridge site, but Lane refused to consider any other. The Ardilauns would not countenance building in the Green, but Merrion Square remained a good compromise. Gregory felt Lane's withdrawal of the pictures would destroy his reputation, vitiate his original promise and 'discredit all of us workers'. Interestingly (in view of what was to happen), she was nearly as critical of Lane's behaviour as Gonne was – though Gonne put it rather differently, telling W B Y that Lane was a swindling social climber, 'acting as after all one expects a jew picture dealer to do – he has lived & made his money in that world, so I suppose he has adopted their habits of mind & conduct'.[6] Gregory summed up to Quinn, revealing her own traditional antipathies and exasperations:

As to the Gallery I dont know what will happen. There is a sort of materialistic recrudescence in Dublin, 'something useful' wanted though no money or energy is to be spent except on convents and churches. The Lord Mayor is being bullied by a vulgar man called Murphy and I am really afraid that after all we may lose the pictures . . . I dont mind Americans being materialistic because they work with a sort of fiery energy for what they want. But these Dubliners dont work hard or get up early or take the trouble even to keep themselves clean, and yet, cry out against any who look from things visible to things in [vi] sible.[7]

And in the same letter she enclosed a poem W B Y had 'just written' in response to Murphy's letters. Though he would eventually call it 'September 1913', he had been meditating it since early July and it was drafted by 9 August, on a visit to Somerset to investigate a medium. The title was probably chosen to commemorate the date when the Corporation finally rejected the paintings on 19 September.[8] By late August, however, he had heard reports that the Corporation would throw out the gallery plan because the architect was English. He pointed out to Gregory that this, though lamentable, was a better ground (from their point of view) than Lane's stubbornness over the bridge site – since it put the blame clearly on local chauvinism. Here he echoed a thought from 'Synge and the Ireland of his Time' (and anticipated his poem 'Easter 1916'): 'Ireland like a hysterical woman is principle mad & is ready to give up reality for a phantom like the dog in the fable.'[9]

The poem he drafted in Somerset used the shopkeeping image from his London speech. And he decided, as with 'The Gift', to place it as publicly as possible. Once again he arranged publication in the *Irish Times* through J. M. Hone, and there it appeared on 8 September, awkwardly titled 'Romance in Ireland (On reading much of the correspondence against the Art Gallery)':

What need you, being come to sense,
But fumble in a greasy till
And add the ha'pence to the pence
And prayer to shivering prayer, until
You have dried the marrow from the bone,
For men were born to pray and save?
Romantic Ireland's dead and gone –
It's with O'Leary in the grave.

Yet they were of a different kind,
The names that stilled your childish play;
They have gone about the world like wind.
But little time had they to pray
For whom the hangman's rope was spun;
And what, God help us, could they save?
Romantic Ireland's dead and gone –
It's with O'Leary in the grave.

Was it for this the wild geese spread
The grey wing upon every tide?
For this that all that blood was shed?
For this Edward Fitzgerald died?
And Robert Emmet and Wolfe Tone,
All that delirium of the brave?
Romantic Ireland's dead and gone –
It's with O'Leary in the grave.

Yet could we turn the years again,
And call those exiles as they were,
In all their loneliness and pain,
You'd cry – 'Some woman's yellow hair
Has maddened every mother's son' –
They weighed so lightly what they gave.
But let them be, they're dead and gone:
They're with O'Leary in the grave.

All WBY's recent public pronouncements on Irish history and modern personality find a voice in this major poem, published in Dublin's Unionist paper. O'Leary's grave (which WBY had not attended for his funeral) now seemed the repository of noble nationalism. The structure, rhythm and language of the poem deliberately recalled – and even parodied – Thomas Davis's 'The Green above the Red'.[10] This sharpened the point that for WBY the self-less romance of nationality was represented not by any Young Irelanders, but by three eighteenth-century Irish Protestants, whose *sprezzatura* recalled the Italian noblemen of 'The Gift': a careless grandeur which would be dismissed by modern Paudeens as deluded sexual passion. Theme and subject enabled him to combine lofty thought and bitter reality, in the manner Pound encouraged: flavoured, at least in his critics' eyes, with the prejudices derived from Gregory. A note made in WBY's notebook about this time is relevant:

Great art, great political drama is the utmost of nobility and the utmost of reality compatible with it. The persons of a drama fall into two groups commonly, the group where nobility predominates and the group where reality predominates. If there is too much of the first, all becomes sentimental, too much of the second, all becomes sordid. Nobility struggles with reality, the eagle and the snake.[11]

By striking this balance, and in its resonance, attack and clarity, 'September 1913' stands with the great polemics of literature. Stephen Gwynn was not mistaken when he sensed 'a touch of the middle-aged Milton' about it.[12] Perhaps more than any of his poems since 'Innisfree', it gave phrases to the language ('delirium of the brave', 'Romantic Ireland's dead and gone'). And it set the tone for *Poems Written in Discouragement*, which Cuala published the following month in a limited-edition booklet. It also seemed to place a seal on the Lane controversy, confirmed by the Corporation vote on 19 September. The arguments advanced in public debate accused Lane of log-rolling, described the paintings as voguish humbug, and called for public energies to be diverted elsewhere. Lane promptly removed his pictures from the Harcourt Street premises, sending some to Belfast and some to London. If matters stayed as they seemed, the situation was clear: through the Corporation's pusillanimity, Murphy's enmity and Lane's arrogance, the pictures were lost to Dublin.

But it was not quite as it seemed, and the situation continued to change behind the scenes, setting the terms for endless future controversy. Gregory and WBY were deeply involved in the débâcle: not least because the money raised for the aborted gallery would, technically, have to be returned to the subscribers. This presented considerable trouble for the Abbey, where many of the company had resented making over their profits in the first place. It had been a bad year, with very low returns on their London season. In early November some players began agitating to repossess the 'Guarantee Fund', which contained American tour profits held in trust for the gallery appeal. Rather than open this Pandora's box, WBY wanted to retain the money, pending the arts policy of an independent Irish parliament. Gregory felt even more vehemently about not returning it; the Dublin rumour-mill thought she had 'a shady scheme . . . to snatch the money subscribed and take it for the Abbey', but she really wanted to keep it safe for the next phase of Lane's campaign.[13] The players, led by Arthur Sinclair, actually reached the point of threatening to sue her for return of the money, and she agreed to WBY's proposal of legal arbitration (which had worked so well in the final Horniman imbroglio). However, when the Irish Attorney-General J. F. Moriarty gave a preliminary opinion favouring the players' side, and WBY was prepared to abide by it, she was furious.[14] Here as elsewhere, the Lane affair released feelings of great bitterness.

But if there were any chance of a gallery being built, the directors wanted to seize it. And in early November WBY explained Lane's strategy to Gregory: as with so much else, it anticipated the Home Rule future. Lane wanted to postpone things until he would be dealing with an Irish parliament rather than city councillors, meanwhile founding a 'really great' international gallery in London, built round his French pictures. Then, armed with unassailable prestige as 'a lever to work the Irish parliament with', he would make Dublin an offer it could not refuse on the basis of 'a completely new collection . . . he says he is tired of the old one, and knows much more now'. Finally, and – as it would turn out – crucially, 'He has remade his will. He has left everything to the modern gallery, but has now left his money to the Irish national gallery, and his pictures to England.'[15] (Belfast would get nothing; they had objected to one of the paintings as it showed a mother with no apparent wedding-ring.) Lane was a young man, and the world was not at war; the terms of his will represented a strategic flourish, to be changed with different circumstances. But it stored up trouble in a way that nobody could anticipate in the autumn of 1913.

That autumn was further shadowed by ominous developments in Irish politics. In October the Home Rule bill was preparing for its third passage through the Commons. The paramilitary Ulster Volunteer Force had come into existence, threatening armed resistance against its implementation, and in September Edward Carson declared that such a measure would be met by a provisional government in Ulster. In November a nationalist volunteer organization was founded in Dublin, involving some political extremists but rapidly taken under the wing of Redmond's Irish Parliamentary Party. Unsurprisingly, when WBY tried to interest the Irish leader in the gallery question, he had other things on his mind. But the local Irish crisis in the autumn of 1913 was ignited by the politics of Labour, as Gwynn indicated to WBY when telling him that Redmond felt it politically impossible to bring pressure to bear on the Corporation.

. . . the important point from his view is that there is no use – in fact, it would be lunacy at the present moment – to discuss in public the spending of money on a gallery in Dublin, with the falling-down of tenement-houses and the general starvation. He thinks that the public, however unreasonably, would be simply furious at the idea. Unluckily, he does not know or care anything about paintings, and he has been prejudiced by the line that Lane has taken . . . It is rather heart-breaking to think that we could have bought that space near the University and had the whole thing launched long ago . . . I hope to God that Murphy and the Ardilauns may be damned to an eternity of the Dublin Corporation.[16]

For by September 1913 Murphy was locked into another kind of struggle – with his workforce, whom he had forbidden to join James Larkin's Irish Transport & General Workers' Union. The crisis was provoked not by the original strike of the tram-workers but by the owners locking them out of work – threatening to push large numbers of them over the edge of subsistence as winter came on, in a city whose social conditions were belatedly being recognized as worse than in any other European capital. This confrontation, against the background of the decaying slum Dublin described to WBY by Gwynn, mobilized many of WBY's old friends and enemies. On one side Gonne revived the unlikely socialist comradeships of her anti-Boer War days, and Shaw provided support from the stage of the Albert Hall; on the other, Murphy, the Dublin establishment and the Catholic episcopacy refused arbitration and closed ranks. The political beliefs of those who supported the workers were not WBY's; perhaps their most prominent champions among Dublin's intelligentsia were Constance Markievicz and Russell, from whom he was by now estranged. Russell's great letter 'To the Masters of Dublin' appeared in the *Irish Times* on 7 October and was reprinted as a broadsheet: it accused 'an oligarchy of four hundred masters [of] deciding openly upon starving one hundred thousand people'. WBY would not have approved of Russell's analogy between an arrogant bourgeoisie and the Irish landed aristocracy, 'already becoming a memory', but the manifesto made the connection between the Corporation's lack of cultivation and the capitalists' oppression (and Larkin had spoken out in favour of Lane's gallery). Slum Dublin was unknown to WBY, except perhaps through his protégé James Stephens's luminous little novel *The Charwoman's Daughter*. But though his poem against Murphy was written weeks before the lock-out, it was published just after the employers' decision, and exploded as a salvo in that battle too. At any rate, the enemy was the same, and as early as 18 September, lying awake at night, WBY had 'got the idea for the letter called "Challenge to William Murphy"'.[17] What finally provoked his anger into a public statement was, predictably, clerical interference.

As the locked-out workers' living-standards declined drastically, British sympathizers organized by the *Daily Herald* and led by the left-wing philanthropist Dora Montefiore offered temporary refuge to their children. Catholic organizations such as the Ancient Order of Hibernians were mobilized to prevent them leaving, leading to confrontations at the boat-train on 22 and 23 October. It was claimed that socialist agitators were abducting children to godless England; Protestant proselytism was also alleged, and priests were well to the fore, raiding the public baths where the children were being prepared for the journey, and interrogating parents at railway stations. They were aided by Catholic notables like Countess Plunkett and Maud Gonne, who supported the strikers but opposed the removal of children, declaring her fears of the white slave trade.[18] At a peace meeting on 27 October, WBY appeared alongside the Protestant Archbishop, the Warden of Trinity Hall and other prominent Dubliners. While he spoke powerfully about the conditions of the city's working classes, he avoided endorsing Larkin's case; impartiality was needed, and the intricacy of the situation must be recognized. The real target of his speech was an attack on the press – easily identified as Murphy. However, the Lord Mayor (chairing the meeting) adroitly cut him short, telling him he would find opportunity elsewhere to 'express contempt for anyone he liked'.[19] The notes WBY made for his speech survive:

I do not wish to complain of Dublin's capacity for fanaticism, you cannot have sincere religious feeling in a not very well educated community without that capacity. It is the shadow of enthusiasm everywhere. I do not even complain of the poor devil of a Hibernian who goes to a railway station to prevent a father from buying a ticket for his own child . . . I do not even complain of the priest who shepherds him, being very certain that the general run of the clergy of all denominations are just as intolerant as their congregations permit. When I think, however, of the press of Dublin which is owned by one of the parties to this dispute, and remember how the nationalist press has printed open incitements, publishing the names of working men and their wives for purposes of intimidation, and that the Unionist Press – with the exception of one article in the *Irish Times* – has been disgracefully silent, I find no words to express my contempt. The press of Dublin with the plain connivance of the Castle and the Castle police, has deliberately incited, with the object of breaking up the organisation of the working-class, an attack on the elementary rights of the citizen, whose like has not been seen in any city of Western Europe during living memory.[20]

Prevented from delivering this thunderbolt from the platform in the Mansion House, he turned it into a letter to a surprising recipient: the *Irish Worker*, organ of Larkin's Transport & General Workers' Union. Published on 1 November, WBY's unexpected manifesto indicted the Catholic Church and Murphy's control of the press, and drew a warm response from Russell: 'I have differed from you in many things but I felt all my old friendship and affection surging up as I read what you said. It falls on us to make a fight for social and intellectual freedom.'[21] Their *rapprochement* did not mean complete sympathy; WBY remarked to Gregory a week later that Russell was a bad controversialist, since he was 'only strong in a frenzy', while their own 'spirits rise for battles we have not chosen'.[22] Still, he was on the side where he belonged and his speech and letter were not isolated gestures: he pressed for the Abbey to put on a polemical play about drunken policemen, 'while the strike is on'. The old enemy had shown himself once more, hoof and horns: he told Gregory, with ill-concealed relish, 'sooner or later we'll have to face the Catholics on the question of sex'.[23]

His mind, as so often, was going back to Synge and the *Playboy*; and when WBY sat down that autumn to write an explanatory comment for his *Poems Written in Discouragement*, he traced, in his systematic way, a pattern which linked together three great public upheavals in Irish life, and mapped his own intellectual development against them.[24] The draft, written with many excisions, reflects a thought in the process of crystallization:

During the <twenty or> thirty years I have been reading Irish newspapers there have been three <events which stirred my imagination profoundly> public controversies which <have> stirred my imagination <profoundly>. One was the fall of Parnell. There were sound reasons upon one side or the other to justify a man in joining either party, but there were none to justify lying accusation forgetful of past service, in frenzy of detraction. And another was the dispute over the Play Boy <& there again there were sound reasons for one or other side>. There were <natural reasons> sound reasons for opposing, or for supporting, that violent laughing thing but none for the lies, the unscrupulous rhetoric spread against it in Ireland & from Ireland to America. The third was the Corporation's refusal of the <great> building for Sir Hugh Lane's famous collection of pictures. One could respect the argument that Dublin with its poverty & its slums could not offord the twenty thousand pounds the building would have cost the city <but here again the ignoble thing was not the argument> but not the minds that made use of it. <One saw the public mind in decomposition & wondered if it would ever again be a living thing.>

The conclusion of this commentary, constantly rewritten, indicted 'religious Ireland' for keeping 'devine things' as 'a round of duties seperate from life': a crossed-out passage asserted, 'It may well be that Ireland will have to become irreligious or unpolitical even, before she can change her habits.' The only bulwark against middle-class vulgarity was reared up by 'a few educated men & the remnants of an old traditional culture among the poor': he first wrote, and then excised, 'we who are trying to educate Ireland'. But he left in the scathing conclusion, that the Parnellite split first revealed publicly 'how base at moments of excitement are minds without culture'. This was retained in all the editions of his poems about Lane's gallery. It stands as the record of his disillusionment with Irish public attitudes, and his readiness – by 1913 – to confront them from the vantage of unashamed elitism.

II

That view, moreover, was reflected in his artistic and esoteric life as well. In July 1913 he had decided to reorganize his English winters: to leave London and find a base in the country, where he could work uninterruptedly, helped by Ezra Pound as his secretary.[25] The plan was inspired by weekends spent with the Tuckers and Eva Fowler; his original idea was to borrow her Kent cottage, Daisy Meadow. Here he spent much of July, pursuing supernatural investigations with Elizabeth Radcliffe. Dedicated to her voices since the Dickinson imbroglio, he was determined to prove their authenticity. The key proof could be a message from someone so obscure as to leave no record that could have been absorbed by the medium through everyday channels. WBY was excited to receive details of one John Mirehouse, whose motto, family mansion and wife's maiden name could be checked independently; further 'proof' was provided by the ghost of a nun from Gort who had been in the Crimea with Florence Nightingale. But the nun's life turned out to be fully covered in a book published in 1897, and the Mirehouse details were traceable in directories. Only Thomas Emerson, a policeman who committed suicide in 1850, seemed a genuine discovery. WBY ruthlessly used his contacts in the Asquithean social world (Edith Lyttelton, Eddie Marsh, the Reginald McKennas) to extract information from Scotland Yard records, and spent much of July and August making pilgrimages to follow up clues. Long letters to Gonne, his father and Gregory triumphantly asserted the genuineness of this phantom, and much of September and October at Coole was spent writing his long essay on Radcliffe.[26]

He remained preoccupied by her for years: wearying his friends with her feats, sending her anxious notes requiring guidance, defending her to a sceptical investigator,[27] summoning her to Daisy Meadow or Eva Fowler's London flat. Radcliffe, like many mediums, would give up her powers when she married; unlike Mrs Wriedt or Mrs Piper, she was not in it for financial reasons, and was determined to avoid publicity. WBY had to write a contrite letter when he mentioned her gifts, though not her name, in a Dublin speech that November. Since she had provided 'the most important evidence I know on the most important problem in the world . . . I felt that I wanted to explain to that gathering of people some of whom I have known all my life that there was a reason for an added fervour in my manner of speech.'[28]

Radcliffe was not alone in being embarrassed by that 'added fervour'. After prolonged exposure to WBY's addiction, Pound complained that when 'some question of ghosts or occultism comes up, then he is subject to a curious excitement, twists everything to his theory, usual quality of mind goes', and George Yeats recalled in later years that his single-mindedness on the issue became a worrying obsession.[29] It may have contributed to a slight estrangement from Gregory at this time. In March, staying with Quinn in New York, she had poured out accumulated resentments about WBY – his cowardice about the Gosse affair, his 'disgraceful subservience' to Horniman, his use of her own work. After the Lane débâcle, they disagreed about how to handle the actors' claim on the guarantee fund. She reminded him, to his discomfiture, that he by now owed her £500. Worst of all, a certain constraint developed over his visits to Coole.

Robert Gregory was technically master of the estate and house since his majority in 1902; his father's will was clear on the point, and his mother had often represented herself as keeping it together for him until he came of age. But she continued in charge as before. In part, this suited her son and his wife, who liked to spend a good deal of time abroad; and the house had now become an inextricable part of his mother's life as a summer *salonnière*, an identity which she was understandably reluctant to jeopardize. Nor had Robert shown any marked taste for estate management. But the fact that she continued to throw Coole open to WBY for months on end raised problems. The younger Gregorys had not wanted him there during the latter stages of Margaret's pregnancies; and before his visit in the autumn of 1913 Gregory had to ask him, rather awkwardly, if he would mind providing his own wine, '& perhaps a special decanter'.[30] Resentment from Robert and his wife had long been building up, and Margaret Gregory had given her side of things to a surprised Lady Dunsany three years before:

Apparently Coole was left to Mr Robert Gregory but Lady Gregory continued to live there and run it and Mrs G accepted the position when she married and now I think regrets it but is too fond of Lady G. to protest. But Lady G. did say when she married that Yeats would cease to live there most of the year and he has not ceased and until now has even had the Master of the House's room. That at last she has struck at, but of course their living a good deal in Paris to paint at first must have made it impossible for her now to alter the position. I know there is no reason why a great mind should mean a great soul but she related one or two petty meannesses of his which I should have thought beneath him . . . Mrs G. says that he does not mind what Lady G's opinion of him is as he knows she will forgive him anything in the end, and that he knows the young Gregorys, the real owners, hate his presence and has no shame about staying on.[31]

It is unlikely that relations were improved by his attempt to press Gregory to seances with a Mrs Charlotte Herbine, whose card he kept, appropriately, in his copy of Ennemoser's *History of Magic*. By contrast, the Shakespear–Tucker–Fowler circle were deeply sympathetic to these investigations, and it was while staying with Nelly Tucker at a rented weekend house called 'The Prelude', Coleman's Hatch, in Sussex, that WBY found a vacant cottage near by. He took Olivia Shakespear to vet it, which must have reminded them both of choosing a bed for their trysting-place twenty years before. (A year later, a local expedition together to see a Burne-Jones window at Rottingdean reduced her to tears: 'it has carried me back twenty years', she told him, to the year they met.[32]) At Stone Cottage, he could work up his lectures for the forthcoming American tour. Woburn Buildings could be redecorated (its staircase painted dramatically in red and black), though Coleman's Hatch was near enough London for him to keep up his Monday evenings. With his pension, he could afford it; and in any case during 1913 and 1914 his writing income averaged an exceptional £400.[33] Pound as amanuensis would save his eyes, which were giving chronic trouble: one was so inflamed as to be useless. And he could, implicitly, declare a certain independence from Coole. Gregory saw this at once, writing regretfully that he and his companion could have come to Coole to work. By then it was too late: he had been annexed by Pound.

In a celebrated letter Pound loftily told his mother the arrangement would 'not be in the least profitable . . . Yeats will amuse me part of the time and bore me to death with psychical lectures the rest. I regard the visit as a duty to posterity.'[34] But he had achieved the dream which brought him to England. Though still uneasy about Pound's 'desire personally to insult the world', the Eagle had been domesticated into Uncle William, later one-half of 'Billyum & Ez'. Their close connection was solemnized by the £40 prize which *Poetry* awarded WBY for 'The Grey Rock' in early November 1913, and which he gracefully returned (except for £10 to order a book-plate), suggesting that it be given to a struggling younger poet, and nominating Pound. The three winters they spent in Stone Cottage, and indeed Pound's whole London sojourn, would haunt and sustain the American through the nightmare of his later life. In the *Cantos*, written after his incarceration for Fascist collaboration nearly forty years later, a radiant flash of memory amid the psychotic shadows preserves Stone Cottage for ever by conjuring up WBY's incantatory voice:

> so that I recalled the noise in the chimney
> as it were the wind in the chimney
> but was in reality Uncle William
> downstairs composing.
> that had made a great Peeeeacock
> in the proide ov his oiye
> had made a great peeeeeeecock in the . . .
> made a great peacock
> in the proide of his oyyee
>
> proide ov his oy-ee
> as indeed he had, and perdurable

They moved in during the second week of November. Pound read to WBY, helped with correspondence (and posting), took dictation; WBY's letters sent from Stone Cottage acquired something of the disciple's didactic staccato. They went for walks, and in the evenings Pound even tried to teach the older man how to fence ('I encourage myself with the belief that I am growing thin,' WBY told Mabel Beardsley). It was not a total retreat from the world. Woburn Buildings still celebrated its Mondays, and Radcliffe was firmly told that her spirits wanted them to meet once a week '& if we cannot get writing to meditate together'.[35] And the old preoccupations possessed him. Still working on the essays and notes to accompany Gregory's survey of Irish supernatural beliefs, WBY reread Ennemoser's *History of Magic* and Cornelius Agrippa's *Occult Philosophy*; the latter especially provided much about Neo-Platonic correspondences with the celestial world, solar and lunar spheres of influence, and divination, as well as the occult power of poetry, the enchantment of harmonies and the potency of incantation.[36] Pound introduced him to *De Daemonialitate* (supposedly by the seventeenth-century Franciscan 'Lodovico Maria Sinistrari', but really yet another invented text), which supplied potent imagery of incubi and succubi. They also read together a seventeenth-century French Rosicrucian romance by the Abbé de Montfaucon de Villars, *The Comte de Gabalis*, subsequently translated by Shakespear. From this first winter, as James Longenbach has shown, the two poets followed a 'curriculum'. The winter months resembled a prolonged reading-party: later they would proceed to Landor, Rennaissance Neo-Platonists, Homer. And from Pound's side, WBY's occult explorations and Gregory's folktales coincided with his own interest in Japanese literature, particularly ghost stories and plays, which in turn cross-fertilized WBY's search for a new sort of theatre, discovered in the disciplines of Noh drama. For all his belief in the sharp shocks of reality, Pound was also a devotee of WBY's *Ideas of Good and Evil*, and echoed the call for an esoteric symbolism that addressed an initiated elite, trained to understand. In November and December 1913 they worked their way through a supernatural syllabus, whose results would be codified next year in WBY's essay 'Swedenborg, Mediums, and the Desolate Places'.

But worldly matters could not be left outside the door of the lonely cottage 'by the waste moor (or whatever)'.[37] Eternal Abbey problems resurfaced. Lennox Robinson wanted to give up most of his production and management duties, with WBY's blessing and to Gregory's relief – but not before he was responsible for disastrous losses of at least £300 on the winter tour of 1913/14.[38] Sara Allgood was as usual threatening to leave for a better salary, while Frank Fay was once more trying to negotiate a return. There were even renewed rows about disturbances over the *Playboy* in Liverpool at the end of November: to WBY's fury, Andrew Wilson, currently Stage-Manager at the

Abbey, colluded in withdrawing the play ('he should have remembered that we faught the Castle in Dublin').[39] And WBY continued to read and criticize work submitted to the theatre as decisively as ever. The directors had been expecting great things of the new play from the Ulster 'realist' St John Ervine, but WBY dismissed it in a masterly letter accusing Ervine of seduction by Shaw.

Shaw has a very unique mind a mind that is part of a logical process going on all over Europe but which has found in him alone its efficient expression in English. He has no vision of life. He is a figure of international argument. There is an old saying, 'No angel can carry two messages.' You have the greater gift of seeing life itself.

Ervine (while privately thinking it odd that WBY could communicate with ghosts, but not with GBS) valued the advice more than the abandoned play – especially since WBY came up from Stone Cottage to discuss it.[40] This was WBY at his most percipient. His help was at this time extended once more to a much greater writer: at his prompting, Pound approached James Joyce, who had become immersed in publication difficulties, first with *Dubliners*, then *A Portrait of the Artist as a Young Man*. Pound now had patronage to bestow, through the *Egoist* magazine as well as *Poetry*, and he also possessed an almost unerring eye for genius. The *Portrait* began serial publication in the *Egoist* in February, and WBY was not alone in recognizing a masterpiece.

After the Irish disillusionments of the summer and autumn, the retreat to the New Forest restored his confidence. This was infectious: at a seance on 11 December with Charlotte Herbine a spirit told him 'that I should marry, that I was better than when he saw me last'. WBY confessed his nervousness about the impending astrological conjunction but the spirit told him briskly that his horoscope was incomplete. 'He said nothing would harm me for the next seven or ten years when my life would be at its height, or some such phrase. I had only begun to find myself in 1910 I had not yet done my best work, in plays or any thing. He besought me to get rid of "mystery" and symbolism, all was quite simple.'[41]

It could have been Pound speaking, and perhaps, in a sense, it was. Life in Stone Cottage had provided all WBY needed – or nearly all. In a fragment dated 28 December, he wrote

> I'd have enough if Heaven would send
> Peace in my body and my own thought
> And one intimate friend
> For the rest is naught.

Since Dickinson no intimate friend had emerged; his chief consolation was probably the continuing closeness to Olivia Shakespear. But by the time he left for America in January he could sum up the last months as 'the best winter I have had in years – the only winter in which my evenings have not been a problem & the only winter in which my creative power has been a conscious pleasure'.[42]

However, the exit from Paradise had been marred by a serpent, in the predictable form of George Moore. The January and February 1914 issues of the *English Review* carried extracts from *Vale*, the final volume of *Hail and Farewell*. They were ominously titled 'Yeats, Lady Gregory and Synge', and dealt with those figures as they appeared to Moore's elaborately astonished eye ten years before. He repeated private conversations, retailed gossip, and was apparently determined to out-do his own impressive record of offensiveness. The first extract, with tremendous panache, plunged straight into WBY's materialization at Lane's fundraising meeting in 1904, fresh from America, endowed with 'a paunch and a huge stride' and upholstered in a fur coat. Most wounding of all was Moore's innocent amazement at WBY's contempt for 'the middle classes', considering his bourgeois origins.[43] This came at a sensitive time, when WBY was in the process of rediscovering his family traditions. And there was more: a picture of WBY reclining at Coole, fed strawberries by adoring ladies, while reciting 'Adam's Curse' about the back-breaking work of poetry. There was an unforgiveable report of a railway-journey conversation where Moore asked WBY if he had ever consummated his love for the unnamed but unmistakable Maud Gonne ('the golden-haired Isolde whom, perhaps, the poet missed or found in Brittany or Passy'). WBY was recorded as saying, 'I was very young at the time and was satisfied with . . .' – but Moore, in a touch of genius, affected to forget exactly what had satisfied him. Finally, a backbiting evening of Dublin conversation was recalled, devoted to the subject of 'why Yeats had ceased to write poetry'. Moore created the portrait of an exhausted talent, who had redirected his brilliance into becoming the impresario of others: forcing Synge to ruin his health by returning to rural Ireland, and masterminding Gregory's unlikely début.

Breathtaking as Moore's tastelessness was, WBY saw it would be folly for him to engage in a public duel; he contented himself by allowing Pound to write a pseudonymous piece in the *Egoist*, which repeated the points made by WBY in private letters. But Gregory's position was different. She had felt a certain fondness for the earlier volume, which described her solicitude for the young WBY; but Moore had only been sharpening his claws. In the extract from *Vale* he managed to infer not only a murky side to her marriage, but a bigoted girlhood spent trying to convert Catholics.

Augusta abandoned missionary work when she married, and we like to think of Sir William saying to his bride, as he brought her home in the carriage to Coole, 'Augusta, if you have made no converts, you have at least shaken the faith of thousands. The ground at Roxborough has been cleared for the sowing, but Kiltartan can wait.' And the bride may have agreed to accept her husband's authority for had she not promised to love, honour and obey? However this may be, the Gospels were not read by Lady Gregory round Kiltartan. I should like to fill in a page or two about her married life, but though we know our neighbours very well in one direction, in another there is nothing we know less than our neighbours, and Lady Gregory has never been for me a very real person.

This unreality was extended to her writing, subtly deprecated as a patchwork plagiarism from scholars like Kuno Meyer, masterminded by WBY. But the real danger lay in the charge of proselytizing. Gregory's mother had indeed been a violent Protestant, who had attempted to wean local Catholics from their faith. Though her daughter's diary makes her own abhorrence of this quite clear,[44] Moore's allegations gave potent ammunition to those Dublin circles where the Abbey was already an object of suspicion. Her initial reaction was that 'there is no answering such things, they must be endured'.[45] But WBY sharply disagreed, realizing the danger to the theatre's reputation if Gregory were to be identified as an evangelizing Protestant – a charge already circulating privately in Dublin, as he reminded her. Quinn also cabled advice to act aggressively. However, Gregory's first remonstration with the publisher was both timid and naïve, admitting that her mother and sister ardently spread the Protestant word, but that she 'shrank from any effort to shake or change the faith of others'. Moore smoothly claimed that he meant no harm by his 'banter'. 'Of course, proselytising is to me a virtue. I am a fervid proselytiser, as you will see in *Vale*, if you read the book.' Further:

I cannot allow it to be thought that I look upon the preaching of the Gospel as a shameful act . . . I only said that you had done what Christ enjoins us to do. In your letter to Heinemann you say that though your mother and sisters read the Bible in cottages, you confined yourself to practical help. This would be interpreted by Moran and his like 'that while your mother & sisters read the Bible you distributed tea and sugar'. The least said on this matter the better.[46]

However, pressed by WBY (who suggested finding a top-class lawyer through his well-connected friend Clara Huth Jackson[47]), Gregory got the offending passage withdrawn from the published book after threats of legal action. Lane, portrayed as an eccentric and affected transvestite, similarly forced withdrawal of statements about his picture-dealing. Moore never forgave either of them.[48] Seeking bigger game, he departed grandly to Palestine to research a scandalous novel about the life of Christ. WBY meditated 'a serious attack', but held it over.[49] Instead, like his adversary, he took to creative memoir, writing the poem which would appear as a dedicatory epistle to *Responsibilities*. Addressed to his ancestors, it invoked past Yeatses and Pollexfens, relying (not always accurately) on Lily's records, and finally apologizing for not carrying on their line:

Pardon that for a barren passion's sake,
Although I have come close on forty-nine,
I have no child, I have nothing but a book,
Nothing but that to prove your blood and mine.

In less dignified mode, he added another poem to close this new collection, which indicted Moore as a 'passing dog' relieving himself on 'all my priceless things'.[50] But 'Pardon, Old Fathers', as he told Mabel Beardsley and Gregory, provided immediate therapy, and concentrated his mind on matters which Moore could not defile: WBY's family gods, and the incorruptible world of memory, mother of the muses.

Long in the future, taking his own refuge in memory, Pound would apostrophize his companion as 'William who dreamed of nobility'. That dream of an artistic aristocracy, derived from Ferrara and Coole, was central to both the poets at Stone Cottage, and Moore's attack coincided with a deliberately symbolic demonstration of homage to the ideal, which provided another kind of therapy. In late November Pound had suggested giving a dinner for the ageing Wilfrid Scawen Blunt, who represented poetic aristocracy incarnate. It was originally to be in London, but 'escaping the usual air of Hampstead & of literary men's wives';[51] eventually it was fixed as Sunday lunch in Blunt's own country house, Newbuildings Place, on 18 January 1914 in celebration of his seventy-fourth birthday. Thus it provided another forum for WBY to affirm commitment to an artistic freemasonry; and those who travelled to pay homage to Blunt, in a motor-car hired for £5, comprised a delegation of former Rhymers and aesthetes (WBY, Plarr, Sturge Moore) and young Imagists (Pound, Frederic Manning, F. S. Flint, Richard Aldington). There were, evidently by intention, no Georgians.

It was a freezing day, but a certain state was maintained. The meal included a roast peacock, allegedly at WBY's request.[52] Pound's address praising Blunt's espousal of radical causes mixed up Mazzini and Arabi, and the container for their poems of homage, a stone casket carved with a recumbent figure by Gaudier-Brzeska, looked rather odd; Plarr, the ex-Rhymer who had made an unfortunate marriage, rapidly became *de trop* and was sent to Coventry by the others on the way home for his pushy behaviour.[53] But it was considered a success, worth advertising, and an account was planted out in *The Times* some months later.[54] Blunt, who drily recalled difficulties with the Abbey over his play *Fand* a decade before, responded to his lionization with a slightly crusty amusement. He claimed he had never really been a poet, had only written verse 'when I was rather down on my luck and made mistakes either in love or politics or some branch of active life', and preferred to be celebrated as a horse-breeder. He appreciated their verses of homage, 'if they were verses . . . I waited for a rhyme that did not seem to come'. After some barbed remarks about WBY's addiction to blank-verse plays, he toasted the company – 'Mr Yeats especially, as I have said the most disagreeable things to him.' In reply, WBY spent little time on rebutting Blunt's charges (though he instanced his own use of rhyme in *The Green Helmet*). Principally, he took the opportunity to identify himself with Pound and the younger generation ('we represent, I should say a school, he at one end of the stocking and I at the other, a very remote antithesis') and to praise Blunt for declaring in his early work a poetry of personal utterance, against the prevalent abstraction, 'the result of the unreal culture of Victorian romance'. As with so many other statements of WBY's at this time, this evolved into autobiography:

If I take up today some of the things that interested me in the past, I find that I can no longer use them. They bore me. Every year some part of my poetical machinery suddenly becomes of no use. As the tide of romance recedes I am driven back simply on myself and my thoughts in actual life, and my work becomes more and more like your earlier work, which seems fascinating and wonderful to me.[55]

Thus WBY and Pound had made their point. It was this ritual homage which Pound would seize upon in his later poetry of expiation: the moment when he 'gathered from the air a live tradition' remained as a positive act of artistic integrity.[56] For WBY it meant even more. The visit was a demonstration of his own place in a 'live tradition' – back to the Rhymers, and forward to the new generation, both paying homage to a radical aristocrat from the Gregory world. It was a bonus to be told by Mrs Fowler that a Foreign Office friend had said he would 'never speak to any of those poets again' for honouring the old anti-imperialist;[57] but the intended audience was the literary world of 'A. C. Bensonism', the malicious Moore, and the philistines of Dublin (where Moore's attack had been joyfully taken up and widely reprinted). Fortified by all this, WBY set off across the Irish Sea. The last week of January was spent dealing decisively with the revolt among the players about the money they had raised for Lane's defunct gallery, led by Arthur Sinclair. For all Gregory's protests, a compromise was arrived at, and peace restored on the basis of the Solicitor-General's opinion, which backed the players.[58] On 31 January WBY sailed for the United States.

III

This venture had been planned long before: arrangements had been completed with James Pond's Lyceum agency in early August 1912. Unlike the last tour, it was not intended to coincide with the Abbey season in America; though the players were there at the same time, WBY had come to make money on his own account. Pond had quoted $200 per three-day engagement, and WBY originally hoped to make £1,000,[59] later, more realistically, whittled down to clearing £500. There was a specific reason for this. He had found out from Gregory that the money she had discreetly lent him over the years now added up to that sum, and – connected as this was with their recent coolness – he felt it incumbent upon him to pay her back.

WBY spent an intensive two months lecturing in the East and Mid-West.* Still estranged from Quinn, he gloomily anticipated a cheap New York hotel (though he longed to return to the Plaza after his tour 'if Pond lets me'). He found JBY cheerful but needy as ever: the old man owed $537 to the Petitpas boarding-house, where WBY 'spent three evenings & was taught dancing by several ladies'. The Petitpas debt at once swallowed up $200 of his son's profits (followed by £50 the next year).[60] His repertoire of speeches derived from those he had given in 1910 to raise money for the Abbey, but were extensively reworked: they were given under the titles 'John M. Synge and the Ireland of his Time', 'Contemporary Lyric Poets' and 'The Theatre of Beauty'. To his surprise, the last (rewritten at Stone Cottage in November and practised on two occasions in London) proved most in demand, though he remained dissatisfied with it, and apparently varied its content from place to place. As WBY told his father, many of JBY's ideas came into it – notably on the way personal content defined great poetry. But its chief object was to categorize the two main types of drama, poetic and realistic, and to relate the technical innovations of Craig and Reinhardt to the return of the poetic play. This was fairly standard, but the influence of recent events (and the company of Pound) may be traced in his comment that while 'realism was readily grasped by the uncultured mind' of democracy, 'the reaction against democracy was creating an aristocracy of good taste'. Maeterlinck and D'Annunzio were cited as playwrights who would dramatize 'the inner being'; the expression of beauty was related to a dialectical struggle, quoting Ibsen's dictum that 'all

---

* He arrived on 6 Feb. and stayed at the National Arts Club until 11 Feb., speaking at the University Club of Brooklyn on the 9th, the Poetry Society on the 10th, the League for Political Education on the 11th. On 12 Feb. he lectured in Montreal, moving on to Toronto for a Gaelic League occasion. On 15 Feb. he was in St Catherine's, Ontario, on 16 Feb. he spoke at Buffalo, on the 17th at Wells College; on the 18th he attended a seance at Mr and Mrs Roland Crangle's, and on 19 Feb. he spoke at Detroit. On 20 Feb. he was at Cleveland, on 21 Feb. at Kenyon College, Gambier, Ohio; he was in Chicago from 23 Feb. to 2 Mar. Here his engagements were: 23 Feb., Twentieth Century Club; 24 Feb., University Lecture Association (with an address to a small group of Irish Americans in the afternoon or evening); 26 Feb., Fortnightly Club and Book and Play Club; 28 Feb., Teachers' Association and Northwestern University. The *Poetry* Banquet was on 1 Mar. On 3 Mar. he was in Memphis, 5 Mar., Cincinnati (the Women's Club, and a Drama League dinner for 200), 6–7 Mar., at Pittsburgh, 9 Mar., Washington DC, 10 Mar., New York, 12 Mar., Washington, Conn., 13–16 Mar., Amherst, 17 Mar., Yale, 18 Mar., Stanford, Conn., 19 Mar., Amherst again, 20 Mar., Montcler, 21 Mar., Orange, NJ, 22 Mar.–2 Apr., New York. He spoke on 23 Mar. to the Drama League, 24 Mar. at Philadelphia, 25 Mar. at Brockley, 26 Mar. at the University of Pennsylvania. He spent the last few days at his own devices, sailing on 2 Apr.

art is a battle with the phantoms of the mind'. Thus Mrs Campbell, 'in ordinary life . . . like a pirate in a cave, always enforcing her authority', excelled in playing selfless parts; Gregory, who lived her own life 'in heroic obedience to a self-created iron law', wrote of even wicked characters 'with infinite indulgence'; Synge 'tasted all the bitterness of dying that he could reach out and find new beauty'. 'Great art comes not from thought, but from ecstasy. And ecstasy always co-exists with pain.'[61] The artist must confront reality, avoiding sentimentality and emotionalism. This could be done by a great realist like Flaubert, but not by a Galsworthy; and his audiences were left in little doubt that the 'poetical' dramatist came nearer the essence of things than either.

On previous tours WBY's lectures had been promotional, explaining the function and history of the Irish literary movement. In 1914 he provided some of this material, fighting the *Playboy* war over again and describing the Irish playwrights' discovery of traditional speech. But he was chiefly concerned with presenting a personal testament. It was part autobiography – the friends of his youth, yet again. 'If poetry is to be a personal utterance, there must be personality, and personality needs a disturbed life for its development, for, as Goethe says, "by action, not by thought, we know ourselves".' The Rhymers found 'action' in dissolute lives; he 'attributed his own salvation to the excitement of Irish politics'. Nor did 'personality' stop there:

If I need the most complete external exposition of any man's life I cannot give him a greater memory than is in that life . . . But if I give an exposition of my own mind, I am the spectator of the ages. The Tale of Troy is quite near to me, probably much nearer than anything I read in this morning's paper . . . [Poetic language expresses] a vast symbolism, a phantasmagoria going back to the beginning of the world, and always the Tale of Troy, of Judea, will be nearer to me than my own garden, because I am not limited by time. I am as old as mankind. Out of all that rises the inner art of poetry, the language of music and the arts, which is not the natural language.[62]

This recalled Wilde's *Decay of Lying*, and his celebrated comment that one of the greatest tragedies of his life was the death of a character in Balzac; it struck an echo back to the lessons of the nineties. This was not an altogether welcome resonance in the America of 1914. Unsurprisingly, some audiences were reported as finding him difficult to understand. The private reaction of an undergraduate at Amherst may have been broadly representative:

One side of me was embarrassed, made uncomfortable, perhaps even offended by the stance, the pose, the theatrical quality – us Anglo-Saxons weren't supposed to do things that way – and another, I hope more sensitive side, was mightily impressed, awed, fascinated by the intonations of the music, the risings and fallings, pauses and resumptions beyond anything we could be told by spelling and punctuation marks.[63]

Though WBY was treated with great respect and *gravitas*, press coverage was much scantier than in 1903/4, or 1911. But he was expressing ideas which would dominate in his work over the next decade.

He was also responding to current events. Before leaving, he had defined his objective as reaching 'my own countrymen' in the United States, implying that he would carry the controversies of recent months into Irish American terrain. As it happened his lectures avoided these issues, and his audiences were in the main university students and literary societies, not emigrant associations – even though Pond's brochure was printed in green and bedecked with harps and shamrocks. The question of censorship arose both in his lectures and in interviews (Maeterlinck had just been placed on the Index); in a New York interview he praised the ancient Greek attitude to sex ('the most healthy of all peoples') and remarked 'the man who is sex-mad is hateful to me, but he was created by the moralists'. And in Detroit on 19 February he gave an interview on the Irish political situation, guardedly optimistic. 'It will be fortunate for Ireland if a compromise can be arranged by which Ulster will remain, under home rule; for this Ireland will have two parties, of fairly equal strength, in its political affairs, and a much better administration can be expected under that condition.' He later remarked that the Unionist leader Carson (as MP for Trinity College) had no right to advocate Ulster's cause at Westminster, and in the event of Home Rule would be in the position of a traitor; he must even now be looking for a convenient exit from an 'excessively awkward position'. The expectation of Home Rule had changed the nature of nationalism.

There was a time when every young man in Ireland asked himself if he were not willing to die for his country. Ireland was his sweetheart, his mistress, the love of his life, for whom he faced death triumphantly. That is the theme of my 'Kathleen ni Houlihan'. And it is not over-drawn, as those who know Ireland may attest. But Ireland has changed. The patriotism of the Irish is the same, but the expression of it is different. The boy who used to want to die for Ireland now goes into a rage because the dispensary doctor in County Clare has been elected by a fraud. Ireland is no longer a sweetheart but a house to be set in order.

Just before he left he told a New York reporter that the Ulster crisis would actually be conducive to a settlement, 'because the reaction from the display of militarism would advance the common sympathies of English and Irish democracy'. Democracy could not afford to be halted by military force, he declared, and would vindicate its supremacy over armies and aristocracy. (It should be noted that, though he had earlier condemned 'democracy' in artistic terms, as encouraging shoddiness and sentimentality, he clearly saw it as a political good.) But he favoured the recent proposal to allow Ulster to vote herself out of a Home Rule parliament after ten years, because he thought that by then the province would be reconciled. 'He favoured Home Rule as a step, although he said he was a Nationalist.'[64]

His opinions were also solicited on current trends in poetry, and he took the opportunity, without naming names, to deliver a pronouncement on Pound and his circle:

My contemporaries lived wild lives with the manner of bishops. Nowadays I see about me young men of twenty-four or twenty-five who live lives of comparative propriety in the manner of bandits. On[e] friend wears the cloak of an Italian student, Two have given up wearing hats because they say they have never found headgear to suit them. Poetry is once more full of passion and audacity. Yet these young men have not yet classified themselves. It will be a full ten years before we shall be able to measure them.[65]

Later, referring specifically to Pound, he remarked 'the very keenness of his intellect will make his apprenticeship a long one' – a quintessentially Yeatsian compliment. He also revealed an admiration for Conrad ('a great novelist') and, less expectedly, for Arnold Bennett's *Old Wives' Tale* ('a masterpiece in a perfectly different art'). But he was dismissive about American drama, and the transatlantic literary scene in general. 'I would say that in America you have no self-conscious literary class whose members write for the appreciation of one another, such as existed once in New England. Such a class tends to produce excellence in literature, but I do not find it here.' More than once he told them they suffered through being distant from Paris, the origin of 'nearly all great influences in art and literature'.[66]

This tactlessness hints at a certain dissatisfaction, and he was often tired, bored and lonely. The Moore controversy followed him; though his replies to reporters were dignified ('he hinted that jealousy was the motive of the attack but did not attempt an answer'), he spoke bitterly about it to William Phelps at Yale, and fell out with his father over the latter's indulgent attitude on the subject.[67] As the exhausting tour wore on, several observers noticed his withdrawal into abstraction, shaking himself out of a trance in order to perform. (At Amherst, probably bored beyond endurance, he told his hosts that he was accompanied by a spirit being in the form of an invisible 'little green elephant'.[68]) There were few refuges, though a particularly successful seance in Buffalo provided much needed respite. He was happiest in Chicago, staying for a week with Harriet Monroe and enjoying a great success. Hundreds came to hear him speak at Northwestern University (and hundreds were turned away). He gave six lectures around the city, attended an Abbey performance of *The King's Threshold*, and was generally lionized; here alone there was widespread newspaper coverage, and he had to evade a posse of reporters when he went to visit a medium in Edgewater. He lectured on 'magic and mysticism' and declared his commitment to 'Christian mysticism'.[69] He also spoke to a small group of a dozen influential Irish Americans, explaining the importance of not boycotting the *Playboy*. Finally, on 1 March, *Poetry* gave a banquet for more than a hundred people in his honour, including some visiting Abbey people like Lennox Robinson and young American poets such as Carl Sandburg and Vachel Lindsay, whom WBY singled out for praise in his speech. Lindsay treasured this as 'the literary transformation scene of my life'.[70] WBY also spoke of Pound, once again forecasting a long apprenticeship but citing 'The Return' as the most beautiful poem written in free verse. His speech hinted that Pound's values had joined those of Synge in his own aesthetic message:

If your American poetry is ever to be great it must be humble and simple. Your poets must use the fervour of their lives in the work, must breathe into their verses. The poet must give his nature as it is – the evil with the good. Try to get rid of poetic diction and all that is artificial. Let the readers encourage their poets to be simple and not to try to preach and deal in the abstract.[71]

None the less the intelligence and energy of the Chicago literary world pleased him, and only there did he seem to rediscover his pleasure in America. Moving on to Memphis, Cincinnati and Pittsburgh was a disappointment and Ernest Boyd, meeting him at a Washington reception, noted yet again his abstraction. 'He had taken flight from his ignominy in a species of trance, leaving the shell of himself to pay the penalty of greatness.'[72]

'Greatness', by now, clearly hung about him. His Montreal audience included an old Bedford Park neighbour, Georgina Sime, who had known him as a vague and (she thought) somewhat pathetic youth a quarter-century before. When he took the platform, she was astonished. 'It was not Willie Yeats but William Butler Yeats who confronted me . . . a man in middle life, a man calm, self-possessed, with an ample dignity of his own, whose tailor was clearly of the highest rank in his profession.' She was struck by how little attempt he made to impress his audience, standing apart and expecting adulation, which he received in full measure.[73] Francis Hackett, sharing a railway journey to Philadelphia with him, equally remarked his self-presentation even in private: hieratically pronouncing opinions, moving his hands, staring raptly ahead. 'When I talked he suspended his animation, like a singer waiting for the accompanist to run down.'[74] (He did, however, express great interest when Hackett told him about Jung's theory of England's national superiority complex.) Hackett was mesmerized by WBY's monologue; he talked brilliantly of John Mitchel, approving his denial of the dubious Victorian god of 'progress', and believing (incorrectly) that this anticipated Carlyle.

Yet his nationalism seemed moderate and constitutionalist: he liked Asquith, and thought Home Rule inevitable, with the aid of British public opinion. As for the United States, his prejudice came through again: in America, culture was seen as a possession of the prosperous. But his interest was caught by everything, down to the lack of billboards at the Pennsylvania Station, and his aphorisms ranged from the insistence of Chicago plutocrats on tangible art to the kind of women who marry artists. Hackett emerged from the railway carriage dazzled, but feeling he had never quite connected. 'The Yeats I met did not meet me.'

His friends saw a different side, and one of them now re-entered his circle. When he returned to New York on 10 March, a letter was waiting from John Quinn: at the urging of Dorothy Coates (currently ill with tuberculosis), he wanted to make up their quarrel. 'I have always felt that apart from intellect you were always generous in your sympathies and full of humanity and that your heart was in the right place.' WBY answered at once. Though he was about to leave yet again for Amherst and Yale, on his return to Manhattan they were reunited and WBY moved into the familiar apartment (now hung with astonishing Post-Impressionist paintings) for the last ten days of his stay. He and Quinn were more or less inseparable for this time, 'like brothers together', JBY reported to Lily. For Quinn's part, he found WBY 'as boyish and as good a companion as ever': 'that droop of the head and apparent abstraction' were simply a defence against boring strangers. And Quinn exerted himself to make WBY's last week entertaining: dinners, enjoyable louche company at Petitpas, a luncheon given by the Bourke Cockrans at the St Regis, and finally a great dinner thrown by Quinn at Delmonico's. The thirty-eight guests included JBY, the Bourke Cockrans, the Theodore Roosevelts, James Huneker, Judge Cohalan, Charles Dana Gibson, the expatriate Rhymer Richard Le Gallienne, and WBY's old school friends Johnston and Gregg. Guests received a privately printed pamphlet of nine WBY poems, with a studio portrait by Arnold Genthe. Here, WBY gave his last speech (scandalizing Judge Keogh: 'why John, he must be a regular pagan!').[75] The next day he boarded the *Adriatic* for home. JBY saw him off; at the last moment, 'with five minutes to spare', his son suddenly begged him to return too, 'he paying all the expenses. When I resisted he suddenly said "I wish you would write me a series of letters out of which I could make a book."'[76] WBY had been pressing the idea on him for months, but the sudden appeal on the dockside was what stuck in the old man's mind. As WBY left America, he was preoccupied with how to sustain his eternally improvident father. And he and Quinn began to work out the principle of an arrangement which would last until JBY's death: WBY would send the great collector a steady stream of manuscripts, for which Quinn would pay money into a trust fund, and out of that fund subsidize JBY – whose money problems loomed over WBY's departure from New York, just as they had dominated his arrival.[77]

There was another financial arrangement to be made, but a more gratifying one; after his return he was able to repay Gregory her £500. She replied in one of her best letters, at once graceful and magnificent, in the manner of a Henry James heroine. But as in James, there was a subtle aftertaste of moral blackmail:

As to that money, I am rather sad. I was much happier in giving it than I shall be in getting it back. Remember no-one knows a word about [it] & never wd have known – so you are giving it of your own free will, and I am all the more touched by this because you have worked so hard for it & for me. I dont pretend that it is not of importance to me, it will straighten out some difficulties, & more than this, it was money I should in all likelihood have invested for my children had I not thought it a better investment.[78]

Once again she subtly indicated that, for her, supporting his work was like rearing a family. The old bond was reaffirmed between them, after the constraint of 1913 and 1914, and this made all the miseries of his American tour worth while. But he was completely exhausted, and felt he could never face another lecture: a mood which, at the same time, he ruefully knew would pass.[79]

IV

Back in London WBY picked up the threads of his life, returning to the Shakespear circle, where Pound's long-awaited but perilous marriage to Olivia's daughter at last took place on 20 April. The hunger for mediums was unappeased; while in Canada he had managed to attend seances, notably with Mrs Wriedt on 14 February. (She provided good value, bringing in Synge with messages for Gregory; a sceptic might note that WBY had just lectured on the Irish Theatre, and that Gregory's memoir *Our Irish Theatre* was currently in the bookshops.) In London Eva Fowler introduced him to a priest with access to a ghost immune to threats of exorcism, relics of the true cross, and (Samuel Butler-style) a revolver.[80] In less ironic mood, his friend R. W. Felkin identified one of Radcliffe's voices for him as Anna Luise Karsch, who – he was told – initiated Goethe into Rosicrucianism: George Hyde-Lees was set to looking up details about her, and Radcliffe promptly asked for a reading-list on Rosicrucianism, which WBY ingenuously helped to provide. And a month after his return, on 8 May 1914, he went to Paris with Everard Feilding of the Society for Psychical Research.

They attended seances with the famous Mme Juliette Bisson, who specialized

in theatrical effects (cabinets, ectoplasm, spirit photographs, nude mater-
ializations), but whose collaborations with a shady colleague ('Eva C') had
recently been exposed as fakes.[81] Unsurprisingly, WBY and Feilding found their
experiences with her 'entire failures'. They were, however, merely awaiting
Gonne's return from Colleville in order to travel on 11 May to the village of
Mirebeau, near Poitiers, where Feilding had been authorized by the Vatican
to investigate a supposed miracle. Religious pictures in the sacristy of the
local church had been producing drops of liquid blood, the roof of the church
dripped with gore at the elevation of the Host, and miracles had taken place
at a Calvary which the Abbé was building on a neighbouring hill.[82] The cir-
cumstances were classic: an introverted rural community, a priest at odds with
his bishop, a cult of the Sacred Heart, scenes of mass excitement, and a
supernatural call to build 'a great church' – a basilica of thirty-three domes,
one for each year of Christ's life. And the blood, when later analysed, was not
human; even at the time of the investigation, WBY was considering ways in
which the Abbé Vachère could have faked the manifestation, or deceived him-
self, though he thought 'a sceptical explanation difficult'.

But the importance he placed on the adventure is shown by a long report
which he dictated when they returned to Paris. Undertaking a spiritual quest
in Gonne's company was a matter of great personal significance to him,
underlined by a gnomic message from the priest: as they left Father Vachère
told him urgently to 'learn some French and come again, for I am too old to
learn English and I wish to talk to you'. The whole episode was reminiscent
of the atmosphere presciently evoked in *The Speckled Bird*. Father Vachère
informed Gonne that he had been told by a miraculous voice that she would
come and live by his church in Mirebeau some day; as for WBY, he reported
to Gregory, 'I am it seems intended for a mystic apostolate the voice used this
strange sentence "if he does not give his intelligence to me, I will take his
intelligence away & leave him at the mercy of his heart".'[83] (Gregory sharply
replied, 'That sentence is the long cry of the church's – give us your intellect,
to save your soul.'[84]) As Gonne recorded it, the Abbé (who had been told his
visitor was a great Irish writer) 'said, pointing to Mr Yeats, "Tell him our Lord
says he must write for Him. He must become an Apostle of the Sacred Heart.
He will have special help for doing this" ' – a message repeated in various ways.
'Then pointing to me, he said, "elle a le coeur", and to Mr Yeats, "il a l'intel-
ligence".'[85] This echoed their mystic marriage of long before. For WBY, the
images of sanctity and the messages from God reminded him that 'a few
days before [I] had schemed out a poem, praying that somewhere upon some
seashore or upon some mountain I should meet face to face with the divine
image of myself. I tried to understand what it would be if the heart of that
image lived completely within my heart, and the poetry full of instinct full

of tenderness for all life it would enable me to write.' Back in Paris, the 'scheme' was entered into his occult notebook:

Subject of poem. Now I know what it is I have sought in the dark lanes of the wood, always thinking to find it at every new corner: what I have sought on the smooth sand of little bays of the sea, places delightful under the feet; what I have sought behind every new hillock as I climbed the shoulder of the mountain I have sought that only I can see the being that bears my likeness but is without weariness or trivial desires that looks upon far off things, bearing its burden in peace

It would become the conclusion of 'Ego Dominus Tuus', a philosophical dialogue about art and personality not finished until December 1915.

> I call to the mysterious one who yet
> Shall walk the wet sands by the edge of the stream
> And look most like me, being indeed my double,
> And prove of all imaginable things
> The most unlike, being my anti-self,
> And standing by these characters disclose
> All that I seek; and whisper it as though
> He were afraid the birds, who cry aloud
> Their momentary cries before it is dawn,
> Would carry it away to blasphemous men.[86]

Thus the messages from Mirebeau were related to guidance from Leo Africanus, now worked closely into his continuing argument with himself (in America he had told Hackett his lectures would not be turned into essays but dialogues, 'of a man wandering through the antique city of Fez'[87]). His link with Gonne had been strengthened too; staying with her in Paris after the Mirebeau adventure, he was impressed by Iseult's literary gift, and offered to edit a book of her prose poems. As often before, sexual and supernatural excitements coincided, maintained by no less than six seances with Juliette Bisson, which produced 'extraordinary' effects: ectoplasm materialized in great quantities, with agonized convulsions on the medium's part, and spirit photographs were taken.[88] He returned to London at the end of May, with much to think about – particularly in view of his essay 'Swedenborg, Mediums, and the Desolate Places', to which he would devote the summer. On 6 June he was once again trying to find guidance from Leo Africanus via Mrs Wriedt at Cambridge House.

There was also a London production of *The King's Threshold* to oversee, with marvellous costumes by Ricketts: visiting the painter just after his return from Paris, WBY impressed him by the lucidity with which he discussed British public morality, the hypocrisy of the mob over Parnell and Wilde, the hypnotic effect of a popular catch-cry (complicated in the Wilde case by 'the

Britisher's jealousy of art and artist, which is generally dormant but called into activity when the artist has got outside his field into publicity of an undesirable kind'[89]). This probably reflected his reading of Mrs O'Shea's recent book about her life with Parnell, but it also refined the ideas in his notes to his new collection of poems, *Responsibilities*. Cuala produced this in May 1914;[90] Macmillan would eventually publish a fuller version incorporating *The Green Helmet* poems and the rewritten *Hour-Glass* in 1916.

The volume was carefully constructed. Its title was derived from the first, anonymous epigraph: 'In dreams begins responsibility.' Allegedly from an 'Old Play', it echoes the assertion in his 1912 lecture 'Apparitions': 'Dreams are irresponsible things and the medium is, therefore, an irresponsible person.'[91] The second epigraph, from Confucius via Pound, also referred to the reality of a dream-world. But the contents of the book were relentlessly personal, and even formally autobiographical. Right up to proof-stage in April WBY had been altering the order of poems and reframing the whole collection between his dedicatory poem to his ancestors, and the *envoi* against Moore. Nor was the collection dedicated only to Yeatses and Pollexfens: the first poem, 'The Grey Rock', was both an attack on 'the loud host' of the Griffithites in Ireland and a memorial to the Rhymers (or to what WBY had decided they represented).[92] Here too he was casting himself as the survivor of a tradition. His adaptation of different poetic modes was seen in several poems (like 'The Two Kings', 'The Three Beggars', 'The Hour before Dawn') combining a narrative form reminiscent of Ferguson with a pared-down modern language suggesting Pound's editorial pencil. Although Pound himself, infuriatingly, chose to dismiss 'The Two Kings' as uselessly Tennysonian when reviewing the volume, it was carefully balanced in apposition to 'The Grey Rock'.[93] Obscure as the result sometimes was, a powerful personal voice expressed itself through laceratingly direct imagery. There was also a group of poems for and about Gonne – and, strikingly, Iseult ('To a Child Dancing in the Wind', 'A Memory of Youth', 'Fallen Majesty', 'Friends'), while supernatural visions were indicated in 'The Mountain Tomb' and 'The Magi'.

But the collection centred on the public poems provoked by the gallery dispute. For WBY, Lane carried on the essential tradition of nobility in patronage, as Parnell represented nobility in politics; and the two were directly connected in 'To a Shade', again deliberately located in September 1913. And the formal repudiation of mean lives and bourgeois values was echoed in the images of beggars, wildness, sexual freedom. 'Running to Paradise' (also written in the miraculous month of September 1913) expressed this with a rhythm and diction reminiscent of much simpler poems in his first collections, and 'The Witch' delivered the same message with radical compression:

> Toil and grow rich,
> What's that but to lie
> With a foul witch
> And after, drained dry,
> To be brought
> To the chamber where
> Lies one long sought
> With despair.

Revising it for republication by Macmillan in 1916, WBY substituted 'some stale bitch' for 'a foul witch'; this was objected to by an editor, and to Pound's annoyance WBY agreed ('much as I desire to see the vocabulary of the seventeenth century restored I prefer to leave martyrdom to the young who desire it').[94] But the impulse proves his determination to rid himself of the late-Victorian 'embroidery', now debased by imitators. 'A Coat', intended to end the collection before he added the closing lines about Moore, declared his intention as clearly as possible:

> Song, let them take it
> For there's more enterprise
> In walking naked.

Responsibilities, especially taken with the *Green Helmet* poems, is a strikingly autobiographical collection, full of addresses, recollections, manifestos. It is also extraordinarily rich and dense in texture: if less coherent than *The Wind Among the Reeds*, it announced a savage energy as well as phenomenal recent creativity. Moore's allegation that WBY's poetic days were over could have received no more ringing contradiction. But it inevitably divided the critics. Clement Shorter in the *Sphere* saw it as 'a painful example of W. B. Yeats's decay as a poet'. Ford Madox Hueffer grudgingly admired the harshness and modernity of this new voice.[95] Pound, of course, hailed it (with some lofty reservations) in *Poetry*. Robert Lynd in the *Manchester Guardian* understood it as a new departure, verse laboured 'with a deliberateness like that of Flaubert in writing prose'; like several other reviewers, he noted the importance of family influences and JBY's ideas. But the most perceptive commentary came from Joseph Hone, who had helped arrange the original publication of 'The Gift' and 'September 1913' and was himself working on a book about WBY's poetic development. Hone asserted that the *Collected Works* of 1908 had ended a chapter; the importance of that publication was not that WBY had said all he had to say, but that what he said would now be said differently. This had been hinted in *The Green Helmet* and 'Synge and the Ireland of his Time'; it was proved by *Responsibilities*. WBY's search for a public had produced not only a new political viewpoint but an 'individual protesting voice'.

It may be that Synge saved Mr Yeats for Ireland when he suggested that poets should use the whole of their personal life for material if again they would be read by strong men and thieves and deacons, and not by little cliques only. Mr Yeats may not have found an Irish audience; but he is more than ever preoccupied with the thought of one, or he would not be writing these typical poems in which all his personal experience is bound up with Irish events.[96]

'The whole of his personal life' is indeed there: Gonne, Gregory, Lane, politics, the occult, and the struggle to achieve artistic clarity out of it all through a new language. That autumn, as he completed his essay on Swedenborg and mediums, he told Farr it was the last project which would require research: 'henceforth I shall make all out of myself'.[97] Towards the end of his life, in a famous late poem, he would declare the need to search back into his own experience and emotions, 'where all the ladders start': but the process had taken shape a quarter-century before, in this landmark collection of 1914.

As reviewers puzzled over it in the summer, he was preparing for Coole, but Ireland was not a peaceful refuge. With Home Rule on the statute book, events proceeded to crisis: gun-running for paramilitaries in North and South climaxed in the terrible events of 26 July, when a company of the King's Own Scottish Borderers fired on a crowd of demonstrators, leaving three dead and dozens wounded. This was a Rubicon: its tragic effect is preserved in Jack Yeats's powerfully elegiac painting *Bachelor's Walk, In Memory*. Nationalist feeling in Ireland ran dangerously high. But as a last-ditch conference met in London to arrive at a compromise over Ulster's intransigence, Europe descended into international war. The day after its declaration, on 5 August, WBY wrote to Robinson, 'I wonder how the war will effect the minds of what audience it leaves to us. Neitsze was fond of foretelling wars for the possession of the earth that were to restore the tragic mind, & banish the mass mind which he hated . . . In Ireland we want both war & peace, a war to unite us all.'[98] The idea of war uniting all the Irish was Redmond's strategy too: he declared the whole-hearted commitment of nationalist Ireland to the war effort, hoping to defuse Ulster's hostility to Home Rule and to profit by any post-war settlement. For the moment, the legislation was postponed and the deadlock remained.

WBY's own reactions were personal. He worried at once about Gonne, thankful to hear she was safe in the Pyrenees, and then apprehensive once more when she returned to northern France to nurse the wounded. He also feared the results for the Abbey, with English tours stopped and audiences diminished; in a letter to the *Irish Times* he appealed for support from local patrons. He retired, as intended, to Coole in late August, where he walked in the woods and counted the swans on the lake, but further travel plans (Austria and even India) had to be cancelled. A journalist, engaging him on the subject of war in October, found him vague – but not too vague to refuse to sign a protest to Germany from 'men of letters' (probably the Royal Society of Literature).[99] This detached approach persisted. He avoided invitations to subscribe to war-effort publications, and when the Abbey was asked to put on charity performances 'for the Belgians' he drew up a careful policy of requiring the usual fee and then making a 'voluntary' donation from the company itself. As to the larger issues, he saw the conflict as a battle between the ideas of the New and Old Testament (Germany representing the latter) and, more concretely, was struck early on by the incompetence and 'useless heroism' of British officers. 'England is paying the price for having despized intellect,' he told the no doubt sympathetic JBY. 'The war will end I suppose in a draw & everybody too poor to fight for another hundred years though not too poor to spend what is left of their substance preparing for it.'[100] But so far it affected him only slightly. Back in London, he happened to be in the Bank of Ireland during the first Zeppelin raids, and was invited to take refuge with the directors, but his chief reaction was to note the modesty of their lunch. He also approved of the appearance of the blacked-out streets: 'not one lighted advertisement of Bovril'.[101] But he was surprised by the preoccupation with the war in every conversation – unlike the talk in the Stephen's Green Club in Dublin, where it seemed extremely far away. He himself sustained this approach in Woburn Buildings and Stone Cottage (where he and Pound planned their second winter). In late 1914 the war still seemed to him a strange interlude where people endlessly told each other untrue stories.

But this would change, as the carnage lasted longer than anyone expected, and attitudes altered with it – especially in Ireland. The Volunteer movement soon split over Redmond's endorsement of the war, with the minority Irish Volunteers taking an advanced IRB line. An early warning of polarized feelings came in November. WBY had come back to Ireland to speak at the Thomas Davis centenary meeting of the Trinity College Gaelic Society on 17 November. One of the other speakers was to be Patrick Pearse. Pearse's revolutionary opinions had moved from culture and education to politics: he was now in IRB councils, and known for emotional Fenian speeches – and for his opposition to the war effort. Mahaffy had just been elected Provost and, at his most offensively reactionary, forbade the students to have 'a man called Pearse' at their meeting on the grounds that he was 'a declared supporter of the anti-recruiting agitation, as it appeared in the "Irish Volunteer"'.[102] The Society stuck firm, refusing to alter their platform, and regretting that 'the teaching of Thomas Davis, which at least represented the gospel of free speech and liberty of conscience, should have borne no fruit in Trinity College'.[103]

The whole matter put WBY in a difficult position. He realized the sensitivity of the situation; after a long history of attacking Trinity and its ethos he had very recently mended his fences with the Fellows, including Mahaffy himself. He wired the students that if they insisted on Pearse, he should be chaired by Canon Hannay (the novelist 'George A. Birmingham', who was both a Gaelic enthusiast and a playful sceptic about advanced nationalism). This would 'keep them out of further trouble with the college'.[104] But it was not enough. The event was forced to move outside the walls to the Antient Concert Rooms, and WBY had to fulfil his commitment, delivering a 'Tribute to Thomas Davis' and by his presence implicitly endorsing Pearse.[105] However, he took great care to steer this support away from politics. He praised Pearse for 'doing much for Irish literature', and emphasized Mahaffy's contribution too; but the Provost had forgotten a vital principle, by 'refusing to listen to a scholar on his own subject, even though they greatly objected to his politics'. Pearse's alleged anti-English and anti-recruiting views were mentioned; if true, 'he was as vehemently opposed to the Unionism of Dr Mahaffy as he was to the politics of Mr Pearse, but he would like to hear Mr Pearse on Davis'.[106] WBY went on, rather surprisingly, to attack the 'evil influence' of O'Connell, but also to condemn Mitchel for preaching hate of England instead of love of Ireland. 'Hatred of England soon became hatred of their own countrymen as when they learned to hate one man, perhaps for a good reason, they hated probably twenty men for bad reasons.' Replying, Pearse reversed this message: Mitchel's *Jail Journal*, he said, was 'one of the holy books of Ireland: the last gospel of the New Testament of Irish nationality, as Wolfe Tone's *Autobiography* is the first'. This was prophetic, as was the rough reception awarded Tom Kettle, who had joined the British army to fight in France.

Holloway noted WBY's unconcealed boredom during Pearse's 'deadly monotonous' speech. As his own words proved, his views of advanced nationalists had hardened; he saw Griffith as 'a mischievous personality, better out of the country',[107] and his dislike of Pearse was probably exacerbated by Gonne's admiration for him. But he disapproved of censorship and did not identify with the war effort. According to Lily, 'He could not get out of it. He says he hates Pearse's politics. The government he says want the Military authorities to put down certain papers. The Military want the government to do it.'[108] WBY's own account to Gregory shows how determined he was to hold the ring for 'respectable' opinion, as well as his scepticism (at this point shared by many) about Pearse's politics.

All went well and was quite unimportant. Russell wrote a long eloquent letter which the chairman (Gwynn's son [Denis]) refused to read as the Society he is president of consists of students of the National University and he did not think it right to critise T.C.D. I made him get Kettle as Kettle is now in the army and you may have seen in the Irish Times the noisy reception he got. I have been very anxious as I have to think of our Abbey stalls. I got in a great many home truths not in the final draft of my speech and amused myself by making them cheer for Nietsche [*sic*]. They applauded wildly when the chairman said (he was thinking of Pearse) a lot of Irishmen seemed to be possessed with the idea of dying for their country (he meant it was an hysterical emotion). I got him to ask all those who wanted to die for their country to hold their hands up. One man did amidst laughter, Pearse made a long mono-tonous speech about Emmet and Wolfe Tone. I hear that he once said to his school 'I dreamed last night that I saw one of my boys going to be hanged. He looked very happy.'[109]

This brush with Dublin politics hinted at antipathies and confrontations which were hardening beneath the surface, but WBY was as yet unconscious of them. He returned to England with relief. There was more decoration to be done to Woburn Buildings, and he spent several days at Brighton with the Tuckers before removing himself to Stone Cottage, with both the Pounds. His supernatural investigations since 1909 had brought him back into Golden Dawn circles, probably through Felkin, who now presided over the Stella Matutina division.[110] In mid-October WBY studied new rituals to advance to a higher degree; and he had been joined in this involvement by George Hyde-Lees, whose induction into the Order that year (as 'Nemo') began under his sponsorship.

Also in October, at Coole, he had finally finished his long essay 'Swedenborg, Mediums, and the Desolate Places', though it would not be published until Gregory's *Visions and Beliefs in the West of Ireland* was ready in 1920. It stands as a record of his preoccupations in these years, and his reading in modern spiritualists (Hyslop, Myers, Lodge, Flournoy) as well as ancient occultists. Above all, he was determined to present folk-stories as 'an ancient system of belief', echoing the implications of anthropologists like E. B. Tylor and Frazer as well as devotees like Evans Wentz, and echoing a controversy between Edward Clodd and Andrew Lang twenty years before.[111] Like Lang, WBY argued that psychical researchers and anthropologists were confronting the same reality. And he felt it equally important to assert the seriousness of spiritualist inquiry; for all the seedy deceptions practised in Holloway and Soho, there remained – as in folktales – the 'gravity and simplicity' of the idea that the dead are all around us, and that there are spirits who can guide us.

Thus he made connections back to his earliest passions: Blake, 'who grows always more exciting with every year of life', Boehme, the Neo-Platonists, Paracelsus, and finally Swedenborg, who was, in his turn, related to the American medium, Andrew Jackson Davis. There are echoes too of the Stone Cottage curriculum ('a Japanese poet' is invoked, along with Pound's translations) and of Freudian speculations on dreams and the unconscious, absorbed through the *Journal of the Society for Psychical Research*. Swedenborg,

WBY points out, defined the unconscious mind, 'a discovery we had thought peculiar to the last generation'. The core of the essay, however, relates Irish fairy belief to the themes and theories of spiritualist investigation – not very satisfactorily. Manifestations at seances, like the stories of second-sighted countrymen, were relayed with a deliberate lack of analysis and scepticism; the tone was very different from his contemporary unpublished essays on Elizabeth Radcliffe and the Mirebeau 'miracle', which employed the pseudo-scientific sobriety of the SPR style. None the less, the essay is an impressive personal synthesis, not least for the beauty of its language and the powerful evocation of a dimension in which 'we are all in a sense mediums' and may appeal to guiding spirits. And his own life is firmly placed in the frame, from the opening sentence. 'Some fifteen years ago I was in bad health and could not work, and Lady Gregory brought me from cottage to cottage while she began to collect stories . . .' Unlike the accompanying essay, 'Witches and Wizards and Irish Folk-lore', a rather scrappy compilation of *faits divers* from occult reading, the Swedenborg essay is a defiant instalment of autobiography. Accordingly, it not only echoes *Responsibilities*, published at this time; it also complements the work which had obsessed him since the summer, and which he moved to Stone Cottage to complete. This was an account of his childhood and youth.

V

When WBY sat down in London during the tense summer of 1914 and began to write about his childhood he was completing a long process of self-examination, concentrated since 1912 but going back at least to the aftermath of Synge's death. This helps explain the limpid flow of the prose, and the sharp edges of the framework. But it was also stimulated by the fact that Tynan and Gregory had recently published memoirs, the recent savaging from Moore, his long interrogations and analysis of ghosts and dreams, his disillusionment with modern Ireland, and his readings in Stone Cottage, including Joyce's *Portrait*, whose influence may be traced in the child's-eye impressionism of his opening passages.[112] From the beginning he was determined to write 'not autobiography in the ordinary sense, but reveries about the past'.[113] Above all, the book begun as 'Memory Harbour' is a meditation both on personal history and Irish history, as well as on the making of a mind: written at a time when he was firmly convinced that he and his friends 'would live as a generation'. As he reached the end, he wrote ruefully to JBY about modern artists 'who have overthrown my world by substituting sensation for sentiment. The generation of the mangel-worzel has followed that of the green carnation, & I am growing old.'[114]

Once he began writing, the book possessed him. A letter to Beardsley repeats what he wrote to many confidantes at this time:

I have been writing my 'Memories' – they will stop at my twentieth year for after that I could not write freely – I should have to be unkind or indiscreet. I have never written anything so exciting, for it runs in my head all day. It brings before [me] many little strange events from earliest childhood that have shown what I can only call supernatural interference.[115]

By 9 July he had written twenty-four pages, expecting to produce an essay about twice that length in all. But ten days later he had written fifty pages, 'vivid and strange', and was completely gripped by it. 'I have never written anything so exciting, for it is the history of my mind.'[116] Even an attack of neuralgia would not stop him; by the end of the month he thought the first draft all but finished. At Coole he turned aside from it to finish his Swedenborg essay, but he returned to it in mid-October, and continued to add to the text until the end of the year, when he dictated it to Pound at Stone Cottage.[117]

In writing it he was transported back to Sligo. From the first he was determined to call it 'Memory Harbour', and to illustrate it with Jack's painting of the same name – a central image of their Sligo childhood, painted just after their mother's death in 1900. 'That picture is my frontispeise & in a sense my text'.[118] 'It was the Rosses Point as Jack saw it as a child,' Lily remarked:

the sun shining, the thatch like gold, a ship coming to anchor, the pilot boat going out, the sea captain in his shore going clothes off to town on a car, the Island, the light-house, everything visible and everything happening at the same time and all at its best. The Rosses Point to us as children was paradise, & I think to us all when we look back is as Jack painted it.[119]

Unfortunately, the title had already been used, by Filson Young; though WBY tried to keep it, and Cuala initially announced it under that name, it was changed to 'A Revery on Childhood and Youth', and finally *Reveries*.[120] The book became a family enterprise, with illustrations by Jack and JBY (produced by Cuala in a separate folder), printed by Lolly, and reliant on anonymous contributions from Lily. WBY pursued his cousin Lucy Middleton for recollections of supernatural experiences in Sligo, but he was above all dependent on Lily for family lore as well as memories. 'He picked my brains,' she told Ruth Pollexfen. 'Most of the early part is my memory, not his, and I am very glad to have helped, and don't tell.'[121] He also relied on her judgement, and wanted her to see the finished draft. More reluctantly, he felt it should be read by Jack, but he was determined to keep its contents from Lolly until the typed copy arrived at her printing-press. As it was, changes were made even at proof-stage. He realized the delicacies involved, and did not want to offend their Sligo relations unnecessarily: Lily made him remove a description of their aunt Agnes Gorman's terrible visit to Bedford Park in a state of manic delusion, and WBY's guilt at informing her 'keeper' ('she had put her trust in us and we were going to betray her').[122] But he was determined to stand by what was 'essential to my picture'[123] – the artist's child to the end.

His own reaction to Tynan's autobiography a year before had alerted him to his contemporaries' reactions. While finding it 'careless & sometimes stupid', he had been moved by the portrait of himself in youth; in the letters she quoted he 'recognised the thought, but the personality seems to me someone else'.[124] His own account would chart the creation of that youthful personality, from the standpoint of the man he had become. At the same time he was very conscious of the readership he wished to reach. (When he began the next instalment he first thought publication would have to wait for his death, 'but found after writing some hundreds of pages that one does not write so well for so remote an audience'.[125]) He had no doubts about the importance of his autobiography: he had made his feelings clear in his lecture of 1910, when he announced that a poet's 'life is an experiment in living and those that come after have a right to know it'. In *Reveries* this echoes back to his early youth: 'I often said to myself how terrible it would be to go away and die where nobody would know my story.' This was no longer a danger. He had already been written into history by Tynan, Gregory and Moore, while books devoted to his work had appeared or were being written by Hone, Forrest Reid and the 'absurd' Horatio Krans.[126] And he had realized – and repeated over and over again – that his generation would stand out in history, as the Young Irelanders did, and not be 'detached figures'. As he completed *Reveries*, he confided to Gregory his determination to help fix this immortalization. 'I think it is partly with that motive I am trying for instance to improve my sister's embroidery and publish my father's letters. Your biography when it comes will complete the picture.'[127] The day after finishing his memoir, spending Christmas at Coole, he wrote to JBY:

I have brought them down to our return to London in 1886 or 1887. After that there would be too many living people to consider, & they would besides have to be written in a different way. While I was immature I was a different person & I can stand apart & judge. Later on I should always, I feel, write of other people. I dare say I shall return to the subject but only in fragments. Someone to whom I read the book said to me the other day 'if Gosse had not taken the title you could call it "Father & Son"' . . . You need not fear that I am not aimable.[128]

A long campaign lies behind the lovely little book which Cuala produced in 1915,[129] but it is artfully concealed. In Paterian fashion, the style competes for attention with the subject matter: it is tentative, almost languorous.

Impressions float into the child's mind: a noise, a colour, an outburst of tears. The effect of 'reverie' was carefully constructed by checking letters, interrogating Lily, and looking up genealogies; but in this, as so much else, WBY's artistic ambition was to apprehend 'reality' by going beyond the limits of 'reasoning' and achieving a passionate insight through lived experience. This is the rationale of his autobiography: since 1912 he had written over and over again that the history of the past era would be shaped by personal memoirs.

So even in the child's-eye view of Merville, expanding out to Rosses Point and the Sligo countryside, there is a sense of impending threat, explosions off-stage, dislocation to come. In the background the Pollexfen clan loom against the landscape, defining the world; at their centre is the old seafaring grandfather, preparing – like Pope Julius – his tomb. The mundane reality of Middleton & Pollexfen as property developers, town councillors and urban Protestant bourgeoisie is irrelevant. Though no false claims of aristocracy are made, they emerge as figures of archaic distinction and overwhelming personality. The Yeatses are also evoked impressionistically – old pieces of silver, clerical traditions, a family tree which someone used as a spill to light his pipe. In New York, still smarting at Moore's aspersions, he had persuaded his father to talk about family traditions, and to itemize the family treasures which disappeared when Sandymount Castle was broken up. 'Once he used the phrase "we had great family influence".'[130] The characterization (notably of George Pollexfen) is sharper than anything in his early fiction, proving that he had read Balzac to advantage. And his father strides negligently through it all, the tension between him and his wife's family openly admitted, along with his improvidence. His attitude to WBY, in whom he inspired 'admiration and alarm', was delineated in terms which would hurt JBY when the book was published. He 'terrified' his son 'by descriptions of my moral degradation and humiliated me by my likeness to disagreeable people'. The book begins with unhappiness and sustains the theme throughout: a misery 'not made by others, but a part of my own mind'. Hamlet is cited, not accidentally. And themes are traced which forecast the pattern of his later life, notably the presence of the supernatural: those voices heard from the air in his early childhood.

If one concern is to create personal identity through family background, another is to establish family identity by relation to Irishness. Here too the *Kulturkampf* developing in Irish life over the previous decade influenced WBY's intention. Working from Lily's annotations made on the back of family prints and engravings, he sketched the Yeats background of Marlborough generals, captains of yeomanry, hard-riding country clergy: all quintessential emblems of Protestant Ascendancy, even if Robert Emmet had been a family friend. 'I am delighted with all that joins my life to those who had

power in Ireland.' As well as evoking a Victorian boyhoood, *Reveries* celeb-
rates Ireland before Home Rule.

A knowledge of the status he had attained by 1914 is subtly assumed, and
indicated (he now dines with the kind of people in whose parks and woods
he used to trespass as a suburban naturalist). But no grand claims are made,
which might substantiate Moore's caricature. Though the relationship
with the declining Thomastown estate is slightly idealized, the poverty of
the Hammersmith period is directly confronted. A year before, it had been
brought vividly back by a profoundly depressing visit to his Blakean collab-
orator Edwin Ellis, who had suffered a severe stroke.[131] The awakening of
sex is dealt with metaphorically ('the bursting of a shell'); observations of
homosexuality in a pederast teacher, and two Sligo boys, are given in an off-
hand, man-of-the-world way. But overall, the story is of the growth of a poet's
mind. He is throughout taught to view the world as an artist's son. In that
sense at least, he is born into the elect. His reading is related to his own early
work; Scott gives way to Sligo county histories. Susan Yeats and Mary Battle
stand behind the stories in *The Celtic Twilight*. The passionate confusion of
his early education is relived: again, his father devastates received ideas with
his iconoclasm but puts nothing in their place. Their recent *rapprochement*,
and the ideas broadcast in JBY's letters from New York, helped inspire a long
passage about his father's attitude to personality, generalization and abstrac-
tion; while Dowden, though his early support and encouragement are grace-
fully acknowledged, is finally drawn as a portrait of artistic limitation and
bourgeois respectability.

Towards the end of the book, the public persona of the youthful poet has
emerged. WBY took the opportunity to present his own version of the figure
painted more superficially by Tynan: cadaverous, affected, unhappy. The
light-heartedness and enthusiasm which Tynan wistfully recalled (and which
she implied had subsequently been hidden under layers of Gregory-induced
grandeur) are not evident, though they can be verified from his youthful
letters. But his objective in *Reveries* is to re-create the early slights, the obses-
sions, the religious sense, the effort to discover self-possession, which lay behind
his early work; to explain the emergence of his genius, and with it his unpop-
ularity; and to give due weight to his search for supernatural guidance. At a
very late stage, with the rest of the book in galley-proof, he introduced a descrip-
tion of the traumatic Dublin seance in 1888.[132] Part of the reason was to refute
Tynan's cheery and deflationary account, but he was also inspired by going
to a medium who produced George Pollexfen's spirit, with the message that
their psychic work together had been of great importance to him.[133] Thus,
Reveries is about WBY in 1914, not between the ages of one and twenty.

With equal deliberation, and equally with an eye to contemporary politics,

Reveries leads up to the young WBY's meeting with O'Leary and his exposure to the ideas of Young Ireland: 'the poet in the presence of his theme'. J. F. Taylor, probably far more important in recollection than at the time, stands for all Dublin enmities. And as the country waits, in that favourite image culled from O'Grady, like 'soft wax' for shaping, the two monoliths of Catholic Ireland and Protestant Ireland still stand opposed. The youthful WBY's innocence about the innate strength of conservatism and piety is ruefully evoked: but (again reflecting 1914) it is the conservatism and piety of Catholic, not Protestant, ascendancy. Though the memoir ends in the 1880s, Synge is a haunting presence just off-stage.

When a commitment to personal utterance emerges towards the end, it reflects, like so much else, discoveries made much more recently than his twenties. But he knew he was making history, and that his own experience was essential for understanding that. More questionably, he thought history was firmly shaped in 1914; the creation of a Home Rule Ireland had been paralleled by the construction of the poet's self. In that new age, his generation would be identified as avatars. He was already determined to continue writing his autobiography. As with the *Collected Works* of six years before, the process seemed to reflect the close of an era. And as he ended the book at Coole that Christmas, he wrote as if most of his life had gone by, and there was little to anticipate. The irony is enormous. For, rich as his achievement had been, what lay ahead was more astonishing yet: perhaps his greatest poetry, political revolution, war, new loves, marriage, fatherhood, still more radical changes of creative direction, spectacular supernatural revelations, public controversy and acclaim beyond anything he had yet experienced. He knew nothing of this when he closed the book in diminuendo mood with 'the old thought' he had first hit upon in his 1909 diary (and would rediscover in his notes for a famous poem seven years later): a classically Yeatsian aphorism on the very idea of anticipation.

For some months now I have lived with my own youth and childhood, not always writing indeed but thinking of it almost every day, and I am sorrowful and disturbed. It is not that I have accomplished too few of my plans, for I am not ambitious; but when I think of all the books I have read, and of the wise words I have heard spoken, and of the anxiety I have given to parents and grandparents, and of the hopes that I have had, all life weighed in the scales of my own life seems to me a preparation for something that never happens.[134]

APPENDIX

'The Poet Yeats Talks Drama with Ashton Stevens'
San Francisco Examiner, 30 January 1904*

For two hours he had been talking to a thousand and more people from the stage of the Alhambra Theater on the subject of the Celtic Revival. In these circumstances, an ordinary man dealing with an ordinary subject would have been tired – not to mention the condition of his auditors. But Yeats, leader in her poetry, patriotism and drama, is essentially of Ireland – extraordinary and tireless. During the afternoon he had addressed the students of the University of California, in a rather 'measured' way, he feared; but the last two hours in San Francisco had warmed him up. He was now ready to talk a little.

We sat at a table in one of the Alhambra offices, the nearest available place. He lighted a friendly cigarette and buttoned a long chinchilla overcoat over his conventional evening clothes, for the night was cutting and the room without any warmth of its own. Even with the chinchilla there were many angles discernible in his lean lengths; and his face, as plastic to mood or emotion as an actor's, was angular too, and magnetism of a delicate nervous sort was in his face as well as in his words and the swift angular gestures that went with them. But he had none of the actor's self-consciousness. Always the subject was the thing, even when I ventured to say that the Celtic spirit, in the opinion of some, was important largely for the personalities of its re-creators.

He had spoken of Lady Wilde, and I had deplored the dearth of English drama from the time of the Irish Sheridan to the time of her Irish son.

'There, in Sheridan and Oscar Wilde, you have personalities,' he said, 'the personalities that made drama. After Sheridan and until Wilde, the English drama had machinery, good machinery, but no personality. I think a disturbed life, such as an Irishman's, makes for drama.'

'No conflict, no drama,' I quoted.

'Precisely,' said he. 'Conflict develops character in men as well as in plays; it develops personality, without which there is nothing strong nor lasting. The modern Englishman is not individually strong; he is strong only in the mass. He is skillful in the mechanism of the drama, but that is all; his drama is a machine, for it lacks personality. Turn from it to the drama of Wilde or Bernard Shaw and you will find not so much machine but real personality. These men have something to express; it is more than a manner and a form. Their dramatic construction is intuitive, instinctive, you may say; it expresses personality. Wilde's contempt for the modern British drama of Britons has been equalled only by Shaw's. Why, when Wilde was asked why he went to a London theatre where one of his plays was being acted, he said: "I go to see if the audience succeeds."

* See above, p. 311, and Chapter 12, n. 51, p. 590.

'The English stage is quite despicable,' added Yeats, in a tone of sorrow rather than of anger.

'Now, there's Pinero,' I offered, by way of specification.

'A fine technician, a master of stagecraft, I'll grant you that – but no personality,' he returned with vim. 'Pinero has not what Arnold calls the literary conscience.'

'You've seen many of his plays?'

'Some comedies, and I read, or rather I should say I failed to read his "Second Mrs Tanqueray." I had to give it up.'

So much for Pinero. I told Yeats that he should have seen Mrs Patrick Campbell play Paula Tanqueray, and he regarded me kindly through his gold-framed glasses, as much as to say, 'Drama, my dear boy, should be bigger than its mimes.' Then he did say this:

'You go to one of the first performances of a popular play, and possibly enjoy it. You go again, a few years later, when that play is revived, and you say, "It's so old-fashioned!" because the popular mode of construction has changed, and the play is not strong enough to survive the change.'

He looked to see if I followed, and when I nodded affirmatively, he clinched his argument with an epigram: 'Stage-craft is always changing; drama is eternal.'

'Up to Sheridan's time,' he went on, 'the audience sat on the stage. That was changed in Sheridan's time, and realism became possible, and – English drama died. It was the beginning of the age of scenery. Huge canvasses were spread and many lights introduced, and managers and audiences became accustomed to accepting in place of drama an inferior kind of excitement, which has found perhaps its lowest expression in the musical comedies and the popular-novel-like dramas of to-day.'

He paused for a new cigarette, and to myself I wondered how William Butler Yeats would like my job or that of any other paid play-taster, whose life, with the exception of rare intervals, is one long musical comedy or popular-novel-like drama. I put the question, but not in exactly those words. I asked him what he would do if he had not written dramas of his own, and should find himself a dramatic critic on an American newspaper. And in answer he compromised by telling me not what he would do, but rather what I myself might do in that distressful position.

'You might do like Mr Walkley, the London "Times" critic. Walkley has adopted a fair compromise by saying of certain typical productions, "If people like this sort of thing they will like this specimen of it." Your mission – at least your duty – is to tell the public whether the play will please the public, and why, or why not; and to tell so far as possible what you like or dislike, and why or why not. That is about all an honest critic can do. But I imagine American newspapers are not so unlike the English in that "sporting" and "dramatic" go hand in hand, or column by column.' He smiled grimly. 'The Track and the Stage!' he said with irony; 'I believe that is the proper combination.'

'But you may depart from it,' I suggested.

'And then one may get the sack,' he suggested back.

'Not invariably,' said I. 'My editor, for instance, puts a premium on independent opinions expressed in signed reviews. While he may not personally share in my

534

opinion that Ibsen's "Ghosts" is a great drama, he in no way interferes with the publication of that opinion. He is even sufficiently liberal-minded to permit me to scalp an occasional musical comedy.'

'In that case,' said the poet, cheerfully, 'you are fortunate – for you have a mission. By pegging away you can do some good, perhaps. Where you find intellect in a play you can prize it; for intellect is good, and illuminative of the conscience. The imaginative intellect is especially good. And you can expose for their full unworth the apparently "virtuous" plays that corrupt – plays that are written not with conviction but merely to profit big theatrical syndicates whose sole object is the making of money out of a corrupted public taste. Many a play with a so-called good ending is a despicable piece of rot.'

'For example, Mr Yeats?' said I; and he chose a play at random, from the recent London successes, not knowing, and I forgetting at the time, its authorship, for which our own American Madeline Lucette Ryley is responsible. However, the selection of an American play brought the moral that much nearer home. He said:

'Forbes Robertson – pretending to despise it – and Gertrude Elliott produced "Mice and Men" in London. It ran for five hundred performances. Its story will serve to illustrate what I have in mind. The hero is a brainless scapegrace – you will observe he is a character by whose presence the masculine portion of the audience is not made uncomfortable. The heroine is a hoyden; you know the type – none of the women are made uncomfortable by her presence. Well, the brainless hero is in love with another man's wife; and he goes away; and he returns in two years quite cured, and falls in love with the hoyden; and everybody is delighted, because they are about to marry. Then the brainless hero receives a letter from the other man's wife, and in virtuous scorn tosses it into a waste basket, where it is found by her husband.'

For an instant Yeats stopped and with an ironic gesture pictured the situation.

'For the sake of a virtuous pose, a gesture on the part of the actor, the author permits his hero to throw the married woman's note into a waste basket where it may be found by her husband. For such conduct a man of the world would be expelled from his clubs. But the curtain falls to the tune of joyous wedding bells. The author's eye is so firmly fixed on the moral law that he doesn't know that he has made his hero a cad. And the audience – well, the commercial stage is so consistently unreal that the audience doesn't know the difference.'

He struck a match, and while it flamed I asked Yeats how he would write such a play.

'I wouldn't,' said he.

'But supposing,' said I.

'Well, then, suppose a great writer should be forced to undertake the dramatic treatment of such a subject – say by order of a king, anything you like. He would, naturally, make us feel that the married woman had been wronged. And then – we should feel that we had been trapped into sympathizing with an immoral person, and obloquy would be heaped on the dramatist's head.' Yeats' tone was bitter.

'"Ghosts,"' he said, harking back to Ibsen with a gesture of detachment, 'has its place among the necessary plays. The dramatist should cast the light of his conscience into obscure corners.'

'And must he not, if he would make his message plain, have the architectural quality?'

'Yes, architecture is vital; you cannot have great drama without construction, "the art of preparation," as the French say.'

'And that means action?'

'Yes, always action – in this age. But a modern public will tolerate the stopping of the action for, say, wit. Wilde taught them that toleration. The public may be stopped for wit –'

'Or for poetry?'

Yeats laughed aloud at that query. 'This age will stop nothing for poetry,' he said. 'The play may pause for persiflage – for the modern audience has a feeling for wit, you must grant it that – but not for poetry.' And the poet said it with an Irishman's smile in his eyes.

It is on account of their esoteric and mistily poetical qualities that Yeats' dramas have by many English and American critics been deemed too fragile for 'the fire of the footlights.' It is James Huneker, music critic for many years before he was called to the dramatic desk of the New York 'Sun' to further the illusion that that newspaper is being published in the twentieth century, who says: 'I find Mr Yeats' plays full of the impalpable charm – he almost makes the invisible visible! – we catch in Chopin, Chopin in one of his evanescent secret moods. But place these shapes of beauty out from the dusk of dreams, place them before "the fire of the footlights," and they waver and evaporate.'

Not unmixed praise! but the same writer takes up the cudgel for Yeats – whose own, by the way, is as swift and stout a weapon as I want to know – when 'The Literary Digest' reprints several newspaper reviews of the solemn elderly school under the general heading of 'Is Mr Yeats a Decadent?' Why not 'Is Mr Yeats a Democrat?' – why not?

We talked of these things over our cigarettes, and I said, 'I suppose you are used to being called a decadent?'

'No,' he protested good-humoredly, 'and I don't want to be. The truth is, I am rather at a loss to know just what is meant by the common application of "decadence." Is it the absence of "action"? May not the man in a cell dream of his paradise? One cannot make the bearing of thought on action the question of decadency, else surely all the monks and most of the saints are decadents.'

'One of your critics ascribes your decadence to your insistence on the hair in describing women – "dim heavy hair" and such phrases.'

'I think I know the one you mean,' Yeats smiled. 'And he did describe a mood in my work that is passed, whether for good or evil – I sometimes think for evil; for I can no longer produce in myself that mood of pure contemplation of beauty; since I began writing for my little theatre in Dublin my work has been in the line of action, and even in what lyrics I have written lately there has been much of this activity and life. But the critic you mention was good enough to contrast my later work with what he believed to be my earlier, as proof positive of the decay that had set in. He selected a poem of mine as showing no symptoms of decadence, saying that it had the spirit of the primitive Irish epic – and this poem, which he thought was one of my earliest, was one of my very last. Then he said that I had been influenced by the French, and unwittingly flattered again, for I'm a very poor French scholar. I think it all came about because I am a friend of Arthur Symons.'

Symons, I believe, does not mind being labeled 'decadent.' Neither should I if I could rewrite D'Annunzio in Symons' English. The mention of Arthur Symons ran us unerringly into D'Annunzio, about whose plays Yeats confessed himself puzzled.

'I can't make out "The Dead City,"' said he. 'It is supposed to be "real," and if "real" why should the characters talk in that unreal way. His "Francesca da Rimini" I can follow easily enough, for that is a flight of fancy, But as drama – Well, in the first act there is an admirable scene with the jester – which has nothing to do with the play. And later there are an astrologer and a peddler – and, as I remember, nothing to do with the play. But at present' – and he took off his glasses and wiped them and smiled a humorous judicial smile – 'I do not like to say that I do not like D'Annunzio's plays. Sometimes it takes a long time to understand an artist. I do see most lovely passages in his work, but it will take me perhaps a long time to understand him as an artist that has influenced the whole of Europe.'

'Give me the final test for the plays I see,' said I, still pursuing the light.

'Your theatre will not be doing good modern work,' he answered, 'till you can write after a performance, "It is as great as Tolstoy, it is as great as Balzac!" – not till then.'

And not till then did we remember that Yeats' friends were without waiting to take him to the feast, and the janitor waiting to lock up.

'If they weren't waiting I'd be good for a couple of hours more,' said Yeats, and I believed him with all my heart and wished he had them to spare.

ABBREVIATIONS

THE following abbreviations have been adopted for frequently recurring names of publications, places and people. Otherwise, for printed sources the usual convention has been adopted of a full citation in the first instance, followed by a recognizable shortened form. Manuscripts are cited by location, and in the case of the NLI a call-number is given.

ABY	Collection of Anne Yeats
AG	Augusta, Lady Gregory
Au	W. B. Yeats, *Autobiographies* (London, 1955)
Berg	The Henry W. and Albert A. Berg Collection, New York Public Library
Berkeley	Bancroft Library, University of California at Berkeley
Bodleian	Bodleian Library, Oxford, MSS Eng. lett. c. 194–5, e. 87–8 [JBY–Rosa Butt letters]
Buffalo	Lockwood Memorial Library, State University of New York at Buffalo
Cave	Richard Cave (ed.), George Moore, *Hail and Farewell: Ave, Salve, Vale* (1933 edition, reprinted and annotated, Gerrards Cross, 1976)
CH	A. Norman Jeffares (ed.), *W. B. Yeats: The Critical Heritage* (London, 1977)
CL, i	John Kelly and Eric Domville (eds.), *The Collected Letters of W. B. Yeats. Volume 1: 1865–1895* (Oxford, 1986)
CL, ii	Warwick Gould, John Kelly and Deirdre Toomey (eds.), *The Collected Letters of W. B. Yeats. Volume 2: 1896–1900* (Oxford, 1996)
CL, iii	John Kelly and Ronald Schuchard, *The Collected Letters of W. B. Yeats. Volume 3: 1901–1904* (Oxford, 1994)
CLJMS, i and ii	Ann Saddlemyer (ed.), *The Collected Letters of John Millington Synge* (2 vols., Oxford, 1983–4)
CT	W. B. Yeats, *The Celtic Twilight* (London, 1893)
CUA	Archives, Catholic University of America, Washington DC
CW	W. B. Yeats, *Collected Works* (8 vols., Stratford-upon-Avon, 1908)
E & I	W. B. Yeats, *Essays and Introductions* (London, 1961)
ECY	Elizabeth Corbet ('Lolly') Yeats
Ellmann, *IY*	Richard Ellmann, *The Identity of Yeats* (2nd edition, London, 1964)
Ellmann, *M & M*	Richard Ellmann, *Yeats: The Man and the Masks* (2nd edition, Harmondsworth, 1979)
Emory	Robert W. Woodruff Library, Emory University, Atlanta, Georgia
Ex	W. B. Yeats, *Explorations* (London, 1962)
FFTIP	W. B. Yeats (ed.), *Fairy and Folk Tales of the Irish Peasantry* (London, 1888)
FJ	*Freeman's Journal*
FS	William M. Murphy, *Family Secrets: William Butler Yeats and His Relatives* (Dublin, 1995)
G–Y L	Anna MacBride White and A. Norman Jeffares (eds.), *The Gonne–Yeats Letters 1893–1938: Always Your Friend* (London, 1992)
Harvard	Houghton Library, Harvard University, Cambridge, Massachusetts
Hone	Joseph Hone, *W. B. Yeats 1865–1939* (London, 1942)
HRHRC	Harry Ransom Humanities Research Center, University of Texas at Austin

Huntington	Henry E. Huntington Library, San Marino, California
I & R, i and ii	E. H. Mikhail (ed.), *W. B. Yeats, Interviews and Recollections* (2 vols., London, 1977)
IGE	W. B. Yeats, *Ideas of Good and Evil* (London, 1903)
Illinois	University Library, University of Illinois at Urbana–Champaign
ILS	Irish Literary Society (London)
JMS	John Millington Synge
Kansas	Kenneth Spencer Research Library, University of Kansas Libraries, Lawrence, Kansas
KT	Katharine Tynan (later Hinkson)
L	Allan Wade (ed.), *The Letters of W. B. Yeats* (London, 1954)
Leeds	Brotherton Library, University of Leeds
LNI	W. B. Yeats, *Letters to the New Island*, first edited by Horace Reynolds in 1934; the edition used here is by George Bornstein and Hugh Witemayer for the *Collected Edition* (London, 1989)
LTWBY, i and ii	Richard R. Finneran, George Mills Harper and William M. Murphy (eds.), *Letters to W. B. Yeats* (2 vols., London, 1977)
MBY	Collection of Michael Yeats (all family correspondence not otherwise attributed in the notes was in this location at the time of writing)
Mem	Denis Donoghue (ed. and transcriber), W. B. Yeats, *Memoirs. Autobiography – First Draft, Journal* (London, 1972)
MG	Maud Gonne MacBride
NLI	National Library of Ireland, Dublin
NLS	National Library of Scotland, Edinburgh
Northwestern	McCormick Library of Special Collections, Northwestern University, Chicago
NYPL	New York Public Library
Pethica	James Pethica (ed.), *Lady Gregory's Diaries 1892–1902* (Gerrards Cross, 1996)
PF	William M. Murphy, *Prodigal Father: The Life of John Butler Yeats 1839–1922* (London, 1978)
R L-P	Ruth [Pollexfen] Lane-Poole
Reading	University of Reading Library
SIUC	Morris Library, Southern Illinois University at Carbondale
SB	W. B. Yeats, *The Speckled Bird*, with variant versions, annotated and edited by William H. O'Donnell (Toronto, 1976)
SMY	Susan Mary ('Lily') Yeats
SQ	Maud Gonne MacBride, *Servant of the Queen* (London, 1938)
TB	Ann Saddlemyer (ed.), *Theatre Business: The Correspondence of the First Abbey Theatre Directors: William Butler Yeats, Lady Gregory and J. M. Synge* (Gerrards Cross, 1982)
TCD	Trinity College, Dublin
Tulsa	Archives, Tulsa University, Oklahoma
UP, i and ii	John P. Frayne (ed.), *Uncollected Prose by W. B. Yeats. Volume 1* (London, 1970) and John P. Frayne and Colton Johnson (eds.), *Uncollected Prose by W. B. Yeats. Volume 2* (London, 1975)
'VN'	W. B. Yeats's 'Visions Notebook', begun 11 July 1898, in a private collection
VP	Peter Allt and Russell K. Alspach (eds.), *The Variorum Edition of the Poems of W. B. Yeats* (2nd edition, New York, 1966)

VPl	Russell K. Alspach, assisted by Catherine C. Alspach (eds.), *The Variorum Edition of the Plays of W. B. Yeats* (London, 1966)
VSR	Warwick Gould, Phillip L. Marcus and Michael J. Sidnell (eds.), *The Secret Rose. Stories by W. B. Yeats: A Variorum Edition* (London, 1992)
Wade, *Bibliography*	Allan Wade, *A Bibliography of the Writings of W. B. Yeats* (3rd edition, London, 1968)
WO	W. B. Yeats, *The Wanderings of Oisin and Other Poems* (London, 1889)
WTIN	W. B. Yeats, *Where There is Nothing,* first published 1903; the version used here is that edited by Katharine Worth, together with *The Unicorn from the Stars* (Gerrards Cross, 1987). It is also in *VPl* (1966).
YA	*Yeats Annual* (London, 1982–), followed by number and date. (Nos. 1 and 2 edited by Richard Finneran; from no. 3 (1985), edited by Warwick Gould
YAACTS	*Yeats: An Annual of Critical and Textual Studies* (1983–, various publishers), cited by number and date
Yale	Beinecke Rare Book and MS Library, Yale University
YO	George Mills Harper (ed.), *Yeats and the Occult* (London, 1976)
YT	Robert O'Driscoll and Lorna Reynolds (eds.), *Yeats and the Theatre* (London, 1975)

NOTES

INTRODUCTION

1. Russell to George Moore, quoted in John Eglinton (W. K. Magee), *A Memoir of AE* (London, 1937), 110–12. Cf. his review of *Reveries* in *New Ireland*, 16 Dec. 1916, 88–9, where he inveighs against WBY for denying his own past in the form of his early poetry.
2. To Ernest Boyd, 17 Aug. 1914, Healy Collection, Stanford.
3. *Literature, Science, Philosophy*, edited by Josue V. Harari and David F. Bell (Baltimore, 1982), 106: a reference I owe to Denis Donoghue.
4. *Is the Order of R. R. et A. C. to remain a Magical Order?* (1901), 26–7.
5. James Longenbach, *Stone Cottage: Pound, Yeats and Modernism* (Oxford, 1988), 184–5.
6. 'J. M. Synge and the Ireland of his Time', *E & I*, 314.
7. To Gordon Craig [28 May 1913], Arsenal, Paris.

Prologue : YEATSES AND POLLEXFENS

Epigraph: MBY.
1. Proudly repeated by WBY in *Au*, 23. Also see JBY, 'Memoirs', unpublished (p. 101 of TS transcript, courtesy of W. M. Murphy, to which later page references refer): 'One day while still a school boy he showed us some verses that delighted because of a wild and strange music. I remembered his mother's family and their puritan grimness and, turning to a friend, said "if the sea-cliffs had a tongue what a wild babbling there would be! I have given a tongue to the sea-cliffs." ' *FS*, 397–8, locates the earliest use of this image in a letter to Edward Dowden of 8 Jan. 1884.
2. See T. V. Sadleir, Registrar, Office of Arms, to WBY, 30 May 1925.
3. The elder Benjamin, who died in 1750, was the son of Jervis Yeats, a merchant of New Row. Jervis was enrolled freeman of the City of Dublin in 1700; his will is dated 1712. He had three sons, John, Benjamin and Samuel. Benjamin's son, the Benjamin who married Mary Butler, died on 17 Dec. 1795, according to *Wilson's Dublin Directory*.
4. See SMY to WBY, 31 Aug. 1933. The first Irish Voisin was Abraham, born 29 Oct. 1637 in New Orleans, naturalized in England in 1657, and married to Anne Heaton in Dublin on 29 Dec. 1668. His daughter Mary married Edmond Butler (probably son of Edmond Butler of Monkstown, d. 1705) in 1696 or 1697, and died in 1745 (?), being buried, by request, near Archbishop King, at St Mary's, Donnybrook. Their grandson, John, born in 1725, married Margaret Goddard on 27 May 1750. His daughter Mary Butler was born on 25 Feb. 1751 and married Benjamin Yeats (the younger) on 22 Aug. 1773; she died in 1834. This and much other information comes from SMY's records: her 'Odds and Ends' scrapbook (MBY) and notes she copied (6 Mar. 1906) from a record in an old prayer-book dated 1750, the property of Miss Jane Yeats of Bray. SMY also wrote a long letter to her father on 17 May 1909, giving details of Yeats wills she had looked up in the Custom House, which add some information.
5. William also had a large house at Dundrum: SMY to R L-P 23 Mar. 1937.
6. Daughter of William Corbet and Grace Armstrong of Hackwood, County Cavan, who had been married on 31 Mar. 1791. Jane, their youngest child, was born on 4 Oct. 1811. William Corbet was solicitor in Chancery and King's Exigenter in the King's Bench Exchequer; he died on 25 Apr. 1824, aged sixty-seven; his family came originally from Shropshire. (Information taken by SMY from the family Bible of the Corbets in 1913,

then owned by her uncle Isaac Yeats of 52 Morehampton Road). Grace Armstrong Corbet lived to be ninety-three, dying at Sandymount Castle in 1861.

7. He was an uncle by marriage of Jane (Corbet) Yeats, having married an Armstrong: SMY's notes at HRHRC.

8. An early letter to him from his brother (11 July 1845) commiserates about sickness; he was absent from the laying of the foundation stone for the new church at Tullylish in Mar. 1861, due to 'ill health' (*Belfast Newsletter*, 18 Mar. 1861). Also see E. A. Myles, 'Notes for a History of Tullylish, Diocese of Dromore' (1923), Representative Church Body Library, Dublin.

9. According to SMY, this was because they never spoke of the dead, but there may have been more to it. See *PF*, 550, n. 62, for some cautious speculation.

10. According to Lennox Robinson, the turrets were added to Sandymount Castle in a hurry by an early nineteenth-century owner who had unwisely invited an Italian acquaintance to stay in *his* castle, and had to make the boast good. TS notes for a biography, Lennox Robinson Papers, Emory. The Reverend Yeats's addresses (after Tullylish) were Madeley Terrace, Sandymount (1855–7) and The Cottage, Sandymount Green (1858–62). For WBY's return to Sandymount Castle in a later incarnation, see Chapter 9, p. 246, below.

11. Other children of the marriage were Mary Letitia (1841–95), who married Robert Blakely Wise; Ellen, who died unmarried in 1869; Robert Corbet, who died aged fifteen; Grace Jane (1846 to 8 Feb. 1935); Jane Grace ('Jenny') (1847 to 25 Sept. 1938); William Butler, who went to Brazil and died in 1899; Isaac (1847–1930); and Fanny, who married a Dr Gordon and lived at 26 Morehampton Road, dying on 6 Sept. 1944. Her birth date is not recorded, but she must have lived well into her eighties. Grace and Jenny, who lived to be over ninety, and Isaac, who died at eighty-three, lived at 52 Morehampton Road, Dublin.

12. JBY to Joseph Hone, 29 Dec. 1915, Kansas. This letter also records the Huguenot fantasy. 'Among my ancestors was a man called Voisin – must have been a French Huguenot. That's the man I'd like to have met. He dyed the whole family in a sort of well-mannered evangelicalism. At least I cannot otherwise account for it among a family so intelligent as were my father's family. Its being well mannered points to a French source.' Huguenots or not, a reference of SMY's to 'old cousin Ellie Yeats, the narrow pious Plym' is interesting (letter to WBY, 19 Jan. 1932); the strict faith of the Plymouth Brethren appealed to many mid-nineteenth-century Irish Protestant families, including that of Charles Stewart Parnell.

13. 'Things were so terrible that they never sat down to their very plain meals without drawing down the blinds as at any moment some starving person might press their face to the window.' (SMY to Joseph Hone, 7 May 1939, HRHRC).

14. JBY to WBY, Hone, 11.

15. JBY, 'Memoirs', 50.

16. See JBY, 'Memoirs', 5–6.

17. JBY to Rosa Butt, 16 Jan. 1908, Bodleian [for location, see Abbreviations list].

18. SMY to R L-P, *c.* Dec. 1913.

19. SMY to R L-P, 9 Oct. 1939.

20. SMY to R L-P, 3 May 1921. However, Grace Corbet was not one of the King's County Armstrongs, but from the less elevated Cavan branch.

21. According to SMY's notes in HRHRC, there had been Pollexfens in seventeenth-century Galway. A Pollexfen will of 1637 showed that John Pollexfen (husband of Susan, father of James) held land and tenements in Ireland as well as England (SMY to JBY, 17 May 1909). A more immediate Irish connection was WBY's great-grandmother Mary Stephens, from Wexford, the wife of Anthony Pollexfen (according to SMY's scrapbook; elsewhere she is called 'Anne', which may be a confusion). Another family tradition involved the Pollexfens' descent from Francis Drake, whose third wife was Elizabeth

Pollexfen of Woodbury; SMY wrote to WBY on 19 July 1938 that Drake's 'daughter' Ann Pollexfen married General Elliott, defender of Gibraltar. The Drake family tree shows at least three Pollexfen–Drake marriages in the seventeenth century, but all involve descendants of the Admiral's brother Thomas. The Anne Pollexfen Drake who married Elliott was a great-great-great-granddaughter of Thomas Drake. Gifford Lewis has pointed out that the status of the family in the eighteenth century was armigerous, and produces interesting Chancery Court material in 'The Pollexfen Ancestry of William Butler Yeats', unpublished TS (Sept. 1994). Jack Yeats visited the tomb of Anthony and Mary Pollexfen, his and WBY's great-grandparents, in Brixham.

22. For family background, see W. M. Murphy, *The Yeats Family and the Pollexfens of Sligo* (Dublin, 1971), extended in Chapter 1 of *FS*.

23. See Gifford Lewis, *The Yeats Sisters and the Cuala* (Dublin, 1994) for a useful corrective view of the Pollexfen background.

24. Elizabeth Pollexfen Middleton, cousin and eventually mother-in-law of the enterprising William Pollexfen, died in 1853. The firm was called Middleton & Pollexfen until 1882, when on Middleton's death it became Messrs W. & G. T. Pollexfen & Co.

25. The girls were Susan (1841–1900), who married JBY in 1863; Elizabeth (1843–1933), who married Reverend A. B. Orr in 1878; Isabella (1849–1938), who married John Varley, the painter, in 1878; Alice (1857–1932), who married Arthur Jackson, the eventual inheritor of the family firm; and Agnes (1855–1926), who married Robert Gorman. The boys were Charles William (1838–1923), of Liverpool; George Thomas (1839–1910); William (1844–1846); John Anthony (1845–1900), a sea-captain in Liverpool; William Middleton (1847–1913), an engineer who went insane; Frederick Henry (1852–1929), the black sheep; and Alfred Edward (1854–1916).

26. JBY to Rosa Butt, 'Aug. '07', Bodleian.

27. JBY to Rosa Butt, n.d., Bodleian.

28. The remark occurs in ibid., but also in JBY to SMY, 27 Jan. 1914.

29. See pp. 6–7, below.

30. 'No sleep and unceasing talking': a description quoted in *PF*, 183.

31. See interview with Thomas McGreevy, *I & R*, ii, 409.

32. SMY to Joseph Hone, 9 May 1939, HRHRC. William Pollexfen's mother is elsewhere 'Mary'.

33. See my essay 'Protestant Magic: W. B. Yeats and the Spell of Irish History', *Paddy and Mr Punch* (London, 1993).

Chapter 1 : THE ARTIST'S CHILDREN
SLIGO 1865–1881

Epigraph: *SB*, 127.

1. 'Memoirs', 38.

2. ibid., 7.

3. JBY to Rosa Butt, 31 Oct. 1910, Bodleian.

4. Same to same, n.d.

5. 'Memoirs', 114.

6. Though he never mentions Henry Thomas Buckle, many of his opinions seem to stem from that source too.

7. JBY to Rosa Butt, 18 Nov. 1910, Bodleian. He had just found out that George had left him nothing in his will; see p. 432, below.

8. Same to same, 18 Mar. 1921, Bodleian.

9. *Sligo Independent*, 12 Sept. 1963.
10. SMY to R L-P, 22 Oct. 1928.
11. JBY to Rosa Butt, 3 Oct. 1918, Bodleian.
12. Same to same, 20 May 1915; also 20 Oct. 1910.
13. 17 Apr. 1863, from South Hampton Terrace, NLI MS 31, 106. My thanks to Linda Satchwell for her transcription and drawing this letter to my attention.
14. JBY to Rosa Butt, 23 Nov. 1908, Bodleian.
15. Will registered 2 June 1863, Principal Probate Registry, Dublin. The date of death (24 Nov.) is according to Canon J. R. Leslie, 'Biographical Index of the Clergy of the Church of Ireland' (4 vols., unpublished, Representative Church Body Library, Dublin), and the Letters of Administration attached to the will.
16. e.g. Registry of Deeds 1854.9.209, whereby Reverend Yeats got £500 through charging his personal and ecclesiastical estate to Corbet's company, for half-yearly payments on the security. In 1861, £500 was raised on the lands for JBY (1861.4.13.2); at the same time the entail was broken by deed, so JBY could dispose of it as he pleased.
17. Registry of Deeds 1861.13.51, for the unpaid debt; 1862.2.86, 1866.1.202, 1868.12.37, 1873.7.95, 1875.37.148, for mortgages. The last deed details the charges on the land: jointure of £100 to JBY's mother, and four mortgages totalling £3,550 at interest rates varying from 4.5 to 6 per cent.
18. A deed of release of 18 Apr. 1752 shows William Humphrey of Holborn (Mary Butler's uncle) deeding Thomastown farm, thirty acres of bog at Ballyna, and a parcel of ground east of Dorset Street, Dublin, to John Butler. (The lands were to go to Mary Butler's brothers, but they died without issue, so the property passed to her son.) This deed was sent to WBY by T. V. Sadleir after a search at the Registry of Deeds, on 25 Aug. 1925. The lands were eventually sold in 1888 under the provisions of the Ashbourne Act.
19. As SMY pointed out, on the evidence of Trollope's clergymen: letter to R L-P, 25 Oct. 1937.
20. *PF*, 38–9.
21. His will was proved 23 Nov. 1870, with effects under £12,000; JBY's mother, Jane Grace Yeats, was the sole executrix (National Archives copy, grant of probate T5807). He had left Sandymount Castle two years before and was living at 17 Upper Mount Street. His partnership (with Armstrong) had been dissolved in the mid-1860s; but he was not, despite family lore, formally bankrupt at the time of his death. However, lengthy claims against his estate survive in MBY. Twenty-five creditors were allowed sums ranging from £911 to 10s. Jane Grace Yeats got £233. 14s. 0d.; JBY, £68. 7s. 4d.
22. SMY to R L-P, 25 Oct. 1937.
23. JBY to Rosa Butt, 18 Mar. 1921, Bodleian.
24. See for instance *Sligo Independent*, 21 Jan. 1860, and editorials in ibid., 11 Feb. 1860, 9 May 1863 and 25 July 1863. Middleton & Pollexfen possessed the only steam-tug in the port, a profitable monopoly which would be threatened by pilots' reforms. In the many salvage claims reported by the local press, Middleton & Pollexfen are invariably prominent.
25. *Au*, 9.
26. Editorial, 25 July 1863.
27. *Sligo Independent*, 10 May 1879.
28. *Sligo Champion*, 9 Sept. 1871; *Sligo Independent*, 26 May 1877.
29. Editorial in *Sligo Independent*, 22 July 1876.
30. ibid., 21 Nov. 1868, reporting Middleton's speech on the borough election.
31. Black-bound family album, MBY.
32. See *PF*, 52–3.
33. JBY to Rosa Butt, 21 July 1917, Bodleian.

34. SMY to R L-P, 17 Feb. 1935.
35. Interview with Mrs Henry Franklin of Sligo, 1 July 1946, Ellmann interview book, Tulsa.
36. JBY to Isaac Yeats, 10 July 1911, ABY.
37. Describing his difficult daughter ECY, he wrote: 'As a Pollexfen she has a tendency to be gloomy and pessimistic, with a desire to wound her best friends, to positively stab them to the heart, though only as words go. This *last characteristic she inherits* directly from her mother. The desire to be cruel only comes on her when she [is] tired or out of spirits. When the fit has passed, she does not remember having said anything that could hurt anyone's feelings. This also was a trait of her mother's.' (JBY to Rosa Butt, 9 July 1911, Bodleian).
38. Same to same, 3 Mar. 1903, Bodleian.
39. See same to same, 29 Nov. 1915, 20 Oct. 1910, Bodleian. 'There was another woman, but *of her you must never ask me.* It was many years ago and happened when I was very young.' Elsewhere he refers to it as 'nearly 40 years ago'.
40. Letters of 10 Nov. 1872, 6 Feb. 1873, NLI MS 2064 (copies by SMY).
41. 20 Feb. 1873, loc. cit.
42. See *PF*, 57ff.
43. JBY to WBY, 25 Apr. 1915; see Murphy, *The Yeats Family and the Pollexfens of Sligo*, 16.
44. JBY to WBY, 10 May 1914, quoted ibid., 87.
45. Six were born of the marriage but Robert Corbet Yeats, born 27 Mar. 1870, died on 3 Mar. 1873 of croup at Merville, and Jane Grace, born 29 Aug. 1875, died less than a year later of bronchial pneumonia.
46. n.d., but postmarked 3 Mar. 1903, Bodleian.
47. *Au*, 29. 'Sang jaune' was the view of the Comte de Basterot (an enthusiastic racial theorist) in 1896: my thanks to Deirdre Toomey for this reference.
48. SMY scrapbook, 33.
49. SMY to George Yeats, 28 Apr. 1939.
50. JBY to R L-P [1902].
51. JBY to WBY [1904]; WBY to Dorothy Wellesley, 7 Dec. 1937, Meisei University (Japan).
52. See for instance P. Colum, 'My Memory of John Butler Yeats', *Dublin Magazine*, 32, 4 (Oct.–Dec. 1957); also in 'Memoirs'. Sometimes 'looking' appears as 'spitting'.
53. SMY scrapbook, 16.
54. SMY to R L-P, 8 Dec. 1930.
55. SMY to R L-P, 3 Jan. 1938.
56. SMY, 'Odds and Ends', 28. ECY's diary records a visit from Martha Jowitt in 1888, having left 'seven years ago'.
57. SMY, 'Odds and Ends', 28.
58. SMY to R L-P, 5 May 1937.
59. To R. L-P, 23 Aug. 1938.
60. Fragment, MBY.
61. See A. N. Jeffares, 'Yeats's Birthplace', *YA* 3 (1985), 175–8.
62. SMY, 'Odds and Ends'.
63. JBY to WBY, 1 Mar. 1919, courtesy of W. M. Murphy.
64. 'Memoirs', 78.
65. Interview with George Yeats, 8 Oct. 1947, Ellmann interview book, Tulsa. The doctor was W. E. Carnegie Dickson. See also Agnes Gorman to WBY, n.d., in response to inquiries about childish illnesses he may have had: 'The Misses Davys, who lived next door in Union Place, said you got a bad fall from a nursegirl's arms, when a baby, and you were never the same after it. Another friend remembers a very serious illness you had when about 4 or 5 years old from which it was at one time thought you would never recover.' In blue paperback notebook, with horoscope notes, MBY.

66. JBY to Susan Mitchell, 6 Sept. 1913. Also JBY, 'Memoirs', 102: 'I think what characterizes genius is an infinite seriousness. My son as an infant was more serious than other infants. That was why his aunts said – "He was such a nice baby." '

67. JBY to Susan Yeats, 1 Nov. 1872, NLI MS 2064 (copy by SMY).

68. See for instance 75ff., 79ff., 90ff.

69. 'Memoirs', 100.

70. 'Magna est veritas et prevalebit' was one example: see Marguerite Wilkinson, 'A Talk with John Butler Yeats about His Son', *Touchstone* (New York), vi, 1 (Oct. 1919), 16–17.

71. Oliver Edwards, TS draft of unfinished biography of WBY (hereafter 'Oliver Edwards TS'), 21.

72. See SMY to JBY, 26 May 1917, NLI MS 31,112 where she recalls the Branscombe summer: JBY reading them *David Copperfield*, Potter walking the girls into the village to their lodgings, teaching them chess moves in the dust of the road; the children begging for black paint, disapproved of by JBY on artistic grounds. Once acquired, Jack painted horses. They also made big stones into dolls, with faces painted by Jack. 'Willy and the Ford boys had a smugglers' cave.'

73. Anne Yeats, 'Memories of My Father and My Uncle', a paper read to the Irish Literary Society in London, 26 Nov. 1991; KT, interview with WBY, *Sketch*, 29 Nov. 1893.

74. See SMY's annotations to *Reveries*, ABY.

75. WBY to Louis Purser, 20 Mar. 1911, private collection. Other references from SMY to R L-P, 22 Mar. 1931, and interview with Mrs Henry Franklin of Sligo, 1 July 1946, Ellmann interview book, Tulsa.

76. SMY to R L-P, 5 July 1927. Ellie Connolly's lessons are mentioned in JBY to Susan Yeats, 18 Dec. 1872, NLI MS 2064 (copy by SMY).

77. J. B. Yeats, *Ah Well: A Romance in Perpetuity* (1942; repr. London, 1974), 12–13.

78. SMY, 'Odds and Ends', 15 [9 May 1941].

79. JBY to John Todhunter, 24 Apr. 1870, Reading.

80. SMY to Joseph Hone, 21 June 1942, HRHRC. Elsewhere she calculated that WBY 'lived entirely in Sligo from his fourth to his tenth year' (SMY to R L-P, 21 May 1939). In fact, he was continuously there from the age of seven years and one month to nine years and five months (*PF*, 59).

81. Often on board the *Sligo*, for which Middleton & Pollexfen were the agents; they advertised it as 'quite new, very fast, and has proved an excellent Sea Boat for conveyance of Passengers, Livestock and Merchandise' to Liverpool. (*Sligo Champion*, 28 Jan. 1860).

82. SMY to Joseph Hone, 19 May 1939, HRHRC. WBY adds memories of cabinets with relics of distant journeys.

83. SMY, scrapbook, 6 (under heading 'Elizabeth Pollexfen').

84. *Au*, 52.

85. For Elizabeth Pollexfen's education, see SMY's scrapbook. Mrs Middleton and Mrs Pollexfen are recorded as supporting the Parish Clothing Funds for regular Sunday School attendance (*Sligo Independent*, 21 Jan. 1863) and William Middleton and William Pollexfen subscribed to the Coal Fund and the Infant School (ibid., 7 Mar. 1863).

86. *Sligo Independent*, 13 and 27 Aug. 1864. The issue concerned invitations to the annual RAS ball, and once again the committee was dominated by Wynnes, Tottenhams and Gore-Booths.

87. JBY to Rosa Butt, 31 Oct. 1910, Bodleian.

88. See advertisements in *Sligo Independent*, 22 and 30 Nov. 1867, Lower Rosses, Upper Rosses and Creggy Connell. 'There are magnificent sites for Villa residences and Bathing Lodges on this estate. It is situated within 3½ miles of the town of Sligo. There is a valuable oyster bed connected with Lower Rosses . . . The purchaser can have immediate possession. Each townland has a right to Sea Manure, and all are well watered, and opened

up by roads maintained at the expense of the barony.' Middleton bought Lower Rosses in two lots: one for £6,250 (492 statute acres, with a net yearly profit rent of £261. 1s. 1d.); and one for £2,700 (275 statute acres, rented at £167. 7s. 7d.).

89. *Sligo Independent*, 21 June 1879.

90. *Mem.*, 77, 102.

91. Diary/sketchbook for 1888. On a rare occasion when the Wynne children visited Uncle Matthew Yeats at Fort Louis, the Yeats children violently attacked them with pails of water: SMY's scrapbook, 4–6.

92. *Au*, 14.

93. SMY, scrapbook, 4.

94. ibid., 13.

95. *Au*, 12–13, 15ff., 76ff.

96. SMY to R L-P, 23 Feb. 1926; see also 11 Oct. 1937. 'The present moment was so irritating he never spoke of the past or future.'

97. SMY to Joseph Hone, 21 June 1942, HRHRC.

98. SMY to R L-P, 2 Dec. 1935.

99. Same to same, 4 Apr. 1937. Their acquired Sligo accent was of particular interest to the scholar of phonetics Alexander Ellis when they lived in Bedford Park.

100. *Au*, 14–15.

101. SMY to R L-P, 4 Oct. 1937.

102. *Sligo Independent*, 4 Apr. 1868.

103. So a local bank manager remembered being told, when he tried to get out of church-going on account of bad weather. Note by SMY in family album.

104. *Mem*, 153–4; *Au*, 31; *LNI*, 72.

105. *UP*, i, 210.

106. SMY to R L-P, 23 June 1936. However R. M. Smyllie, recalling his own Sligo background in 1941, remarked that though Jack Yeats was a familiar figure in the town around 1900, he never saw WBY there; and 'The poet disappointed me greatly in later years when I discovered that he knew far less about Sligo than I expected him to know.' (*Sligo Champion Sesquicentenary 1836–1986* [a special commemorative album of the paper], 39).

107. *Au*, 27.

108. *CL*, i, 3–4.

109. School reports and timetables are preserved in MBY; also a letter from B. G. Tours to Joseph Hone, 13 Oct. 1943 (Tours was Chairman of the Old Boys' Association and provided some information from school records). Also see *Au*, 35, 49.

110. SMY to R L-P, 27 Oct. 1931.

111. Wilkinson, 'A Talk with John Butler Yeats about His Son'.

112. JBY to WBY, 22 Feb. 1881 (from 90 Lower Gardiner Street, Dublin).

113. Cancelled passage in NLI MS 30,790, 'How I Began to Write', 1 July 1938.

114. Interview with Richard Ellmann, 7 July 1947, Ellmann interview book, Tulsa.

115. *Au*, 35.

116. SMY to R L-P, 28 June 1937.

117. SMY, notes at HRHRC.

118. The certificate is in MBY.

119. *Au*, 30.

120. Or possibly after the spring term. B. G. Tours to Joseph Hone, 15 Oct. 1943 (MBY), affirms that he was definitely there that term.

121. This is stated in SMY's recollection in HRHRC, and it is the address given when she registered at the Art School in May 1882. The unflattering description is in her annotation of *Reveries*, ABY.

122. SMY to Joseph Hone, 25 Feb. 1842, HRHRC. For these parties, see my essay 'To the Northern Counties Station: Lord Randolph Churchill and the Orange Card', *Paddy and Mr Punch*, 241.
123. SMY's notes in HRHRC.
124. *Au*, II. JBY was particularly pained by allegations of bad temper and violence. 'None of my children have ever been slapped except once when I gave a single slap to Jack's bare arm.' (JBY to Rosa Butt, 20 Mar. 1920, Bodleian).
125. 'Memoirs', 85.
126. Interview with WBY by Horace Reynolds, 9 Dec. 1932, Harvard.
127. JBY to Rosa Butt, 6 Mar. 1908, Bodleian. Gregg eventually became editor of the *New York Evening Sun*; for a biography see *CL*, i, 7. Also see TS by Willard Conneely, 'A Talk with W. B. Yeats', HRHRC, which quotes WBY as saying that he began writing 'about 15'. SMY's memory is in her notes at HRHRC. See also Wilkinson, 'A Talk with John Butler Yeats about His Son'.
128. Wilkinson, 'A Talk with John Butler Yeats about His Son'.

Chapter 2 : EXPLORATIONS
DUBLIN 1881–1887

Epigraph: TCD MS 3986 D.
1. *Au*, 64–6.
2. See *PF*, 131.
3. 'Memoirs', 27.
4. *Au*, 61; also *UP*, i, 170, which describes Howth as a literally fairy-haunted place. 'Village Ghosts' was published in the *Scots Observer*, 11 May 1889, and reprinted in *CT*.
5. See below. Gerard Manley Hopkins thought Ferguson 'pushed' WBY's *Island of Statues* (letter referred to below, n. 55), but there is no direct evidence of this.
6. See WBY to Mrs Travers Smith (Dowden's daughter), 27 Apr. [1913], Harvard, after her father's death, saying,

    how deep a loss I feel your father's death to have been, and how much he once was to me.
    I have a very vivid and charming memory of certain Sunday mornings when my father brought me to see him & I think his encouragement was the first I had from a man of letters. One morning he read out some chapters of his then unpublished life of Shelley & those chapters & all they contained are clear in my memory today. When I was 17 or 18 I read his poetry a great deal too & how gracious he always was, a noble figure which seemed to represent the tradition of culture where it is one with courtesy.

    WBY was at this time, after many vicissitudes, hoping to succeed to Dowden's Chair; see p. 483, below.
7. SMY, 'Odds and Ends', as quoted in *PF*, 133.
8. In Apr. and May SMY and LCY were still entered as living at Island View, Howth, in the General Register of the Metropolitan School of Art. The first *Thom's Directory* entry for JBY at Ashfield Terrace is 1885, but this probably represents a time-lag.
9. 1 Mar. 1922, quoted in *CL*, i, 9. Also see *Au*, 83.
10. *PF*, 136–7.
11. 'Yeats in the Making', *Poet's Lore*, Philadelphia, 17, 2 (Summer 1906), 102–12 (*I & R*, i, 6–12).
12. SMY, 'Odds and Ends', 1–2.
13. *PF*, 572.
14. SMY, 'Odds and Ends', 13.

15. Magee repeatedly consigned his schoolday memories of WBY to paper: see the *Erasmian*, June 1939, the *Dial*, 72, 3 (Mar. 1922), *Dublin Magazine*, 28, 3 (July–Sept. 1953), 25.
16. *Dublin Magazine*, 35.
17. 'W. B. Yeats at School', *T.P.'s Weekly*, 7 June 1912 (*I & R*, i, 1–3).
18. Reverend F. R. Montgomery Hitchcock, quoted in Oliver Edwards TS, 25.
19. Johnston, 'Yeats in the Making'.
20. Letter from M. A. Christie to *TLS*, 20 May 1969, relaying the written reminiscences of his uncle, McNeill.
21. Oliver Edwards TS, 25.
22. *CL*, i, 8.
23. JBY to WBY, 12 Sept. 1917, courtesy of W. M. Murphy.
24. Her father was Serjeant Richard Armstrong, a Dublin barrister who had lost his wits. She married first Henry Morgan Byrne, a solicitor, and later – allegedly – 'a Welsh gardener', who fled from her eccentricities (*PF*, 560).
25. George Yeats to Allan Wade, 24 Aug. 1953.
26. *CL*, i, 154–5.
27. To Olivia Shakespear, 26 May 1924, *L*, 705.
28. WBY to Mary Cronin, *CL*, i, 6–7.
29. See JBY, 'Memoirs', 93, 98, and many references in SMY's letters.
30. 'Memoirs', and Wilkinson, 'A Talk with John Butler Yeats about His Son', 12.
31. 'Memoirs', 82.
32. 'Memoirs', 8.
33. Interview with George Yeats, 1 Mar. 1946, Ellmann interview book, Tulsa; also *Au*, 79–80.
34. 'Memoirs', 28–9. 'I find the Trinity College intellect noisy and monotonous, without ideas or any curiosity about ideas, and without any sense of mystery, everything sacrificed to mental efficiency. Trinity College is intellectually a sort of little Prussia.'
35. John Bennett to Joseph Hone, 2 June 1939, NLI MS 5919. See also General Register of the Metropolitan School of Art. Additions to the fee of £1. 1s. 6d. brought it up to a few pounds at most.
36. SMY to R L-P, 28 Aug. 1936.
37. *Au*, 81.
38. Lecture on 'My Own Poetry' reprinted in the *Irish Times*, 26 Jan. 1924.
39. 'The Tragic Theatre', *UP*, ii, 387.
40. Or so Ellmann thought, *M & M*, 32. On 30 May 1897 WBY wrote to Robert Farquharson Sharp: 'I think, 1886, must be correct for my giving up art. I have no way of finding out with certainty & it is made the more difficult by there being the usual period of drifting.' (*CL*, ii, 107).
41. *Report of the Committee of Enquiry into the Work Carried Out by the Royal Hibernian Academy and the Metropolitan School of Art* (HMSO, Dublin, 1906), 60–61.
42. Interview with KT, the *Sketch*, 29 Nov. 1892. Shelley's Prince Athanase supplies a leit-motif for WBY's youthful self-image:

> His soul had wedded wisdom, and her dower
> Is love and justice, clothed in which he sate
> Apart from men, as in a lonely tower,
> Pitying the tumult of their dark estate.

43. NLI MS 30,060. The most detailed treatment of this prentice work is in George Bornstein (ed.), *The Early Poetry. Volume 1: 'Mosada' and 'The Island of Statues', Manuscript Materials*

by W. B. Yeats (Ithaca and London, 1987) and *Volume 2: 'The Wanderings of Oisin' and Other Early Poems to 1895* (Ithaca and London, 1994).

44. See 'The Magpie', reprinted by Bornstein in *Early Poetry. Volume 2*, 403.

45. On this early work, see George Bornstein, 'The Making of Yeats's Spenser', *YAACTS* 2 (1984), 21–9.

46. A cancelled passage in NLI MS 30,790 – though he admitted that he had formed an interest in such people 'before I had been much humiliated'.

47. A notebook marked '10 Ashfield Terrace' includes 'The Blindness', which frequently mentions 'a crater of wild olives'. Russell's contemporary reference to 'The Equator of Olives' may represent a mishearing: see A. Denson, *Letters from AE* (London, 1961), 3. In 'How I Began to Write', NLI MS 30,790, WBY recalls one play being 'an imitation of Shelley, its scene a crater of the moon'.

48. TCD.

49. *PF*, 133.

50. 4 Apr. 1885, Reading.

51. *Au*, 92.

52. To Mary Cronin, as above.

53. 8 Jan. 1884, *PF*, 134. The *Island* was also sent to Dr William Frazer, a Dublin dermatologist with literary leanings; see *CL*, i, 75. Todhunter thought it 'not on the highest level' but liked it; to Dowden, 28 May 1885, TCD.

54. 23 July 1885 and 26 Aug. 1886, TCD.

55. To Coventry Patmore, 7 Nov. 1886, C. C. Abbott (ed.), *Further Letters of Gerard Manley Hopkins Including His Correspondence with Coventry Patmore* (Oxford 1971), 373–4. On 24 Dec. 1913 WBY correctly described it to Carlos Linati as 'a feeble early work, only valuable to collectors'.

56. NLI MS 30,790.

57. 'Memoirs', 30–31.

58. Dominic Daly, *The Young Douglas Hyde: The Dawn of the Irish Revolution and Renaissance 1874–1893* (Dublin, 1974), 87.

59. 'Memoirs', 57.

60. *Au*, 93.

61. Oldham to Sarah Purser, n.d., NLI MS 10,201.

62. H. W. Nevinson, quoted in Harry Nichols, 'The Contemporary Club', *Irish Times*, 20–21 Dec. 1961.

63. *Mem*, 52.

64. Daly, *Young Douglas Hyde*, 72.

65. Leon Ó Broin, *Revolutionary Underground: The Story of the Irish Republican Brotherhood 1858–1924* (Dublin, 1976), 88.

66. 10 Jan. 1888, NLI MS 5925.

67. C. H. Oldham, R. I. Lipmann, F. I. Gregg, John R. Eyre, W. Stockley, J. Stockley (Daly, *Young Douglas Hyde*, 202, n. ii). See *FJ*, 13 and 20 Feb. 1886, for a lively meeting where McCarthy Teeling was censured and expelled – attended by WBY.

68. See *I & R*, i, 11.

69. For a detailed consideration of WBY's work for the *Gael*, see John Kelly, 'Aesthete among the Athletes', *YAACTS* 2 (1984), 75–143.

70. *PF*, 144.

71. To Frederick Langbridge, 12 Oct. [1893], *CL*, i, 366–7.

72. Henry Summerfield, *That Myriad-minded Man: A Biography of G. W. Russell 'A. E.' 1867–1935* (Gerrards Cross, 1975), 16, says WBY's interest in Sinnett was 'Easter 1885'. Johnston recalled reading him at that time: see Johnston to Ernest Boyd, 12 July 1915, Healy

Collection, Stanford, adding that he interviewed Sinnett and Mohini Chatterjee (not Blavatsky) in Notting Hill. Magee definitely situates the 'craze' as beginning when Johnston was in his final year at the High School. The article stimulated by his London visit appeared in the *DUR*, July 1885, 66. In Aug. the *DUR* announced the possibility of a visit from Mohini Chatterjee 'towards the end of the year'; as it happened, he came in 1886 (see below, nn. 79, 81).

73. Magee, 'Portrait of Yeats', *Irish Literary Portraits* (London, 1935) (repr. *I & R*, i, 5–6).

74. *CL*, i, 99.

75. 'How I Began to Write', NLI MS 30,790.

76. Baron von Reichenbach (*Physio-physiological Researches on the Dynamics of Magnetism*, London, 1850) believed that the force of 'Od' resided in magnets, crystals and human hands or fingers; he related this to mesmerism and faith-healing.

77. 'The Poetry of AE', *Daily Express*, Dublin, 3 Sept. 1898 (*UP*, ii, 121–4).

78. Though the significance of the word 'Hermetic' indicated a resolution to study more than Theosophy: see Peter Kuch, *Yeats and AE: The Antagonism that Unites Dear Friends* (Gerrards Cross, 1986), 14. By Apr. 1886, however, the Society became the Dublin Theosophical Society, which WBY declined to join.

79. His article on Althea Gyles is also relevant: the *Dome*, Dec. 1898 (*UP*, i, 133). Johnston told Ernest Boyd there was a preliminary meeting in Apr. or May at Oldham's rooms (12 July 1915, as above).

80. This was encouraged by the work of Max Muller (notably his editions of *The Sacred Books of the East*, 1879–1910) and English versions of *The Buddhist Sutras* (1881), *The Bhagavad-Gita* (1882) and *The Upanishads* (1884). But it had been anticipated by Goethe, and Indian philosophy also influenced Emerson, Whitman and other writers devoured by WBY at this time. Andrew Lang's *Myth, Ritual and Religion* (2 vols., 1887) was the inescapable vade-mecum.

81. Purser MSS, NLI 10,201: an undated postcard, but postmarked Apr. 1886. The Charter members of the Society were L. A. M. Johnston, WBY, F. T. Gregg, H. M. Magee ('Eglinton's' elder brother), E. A. Seale, W. F. Smeeth, R. A. Potterton and Charles Johnston. The *Irish Theosophist* was started by D. N. Dunlop, a Scot resident in Dublin.

82. Peter Washington, *Madame Blavatsky's Baboon: Theosophy and the Emergence of the Western Guru* (London, 1993), 88–9.

83. See Russell to AG, postmarked 9 May 1900, Berg. For Chatterjee, see P. S. Sri, 'Yeats and Mohini Chatterjee', *YA* ii (1994), N. Guha, *W. B. Yeats: An Indian Approach* (Calcutta, 1968) and H. R. Bachchan, *W. B. Yeats and Occultism* (London, 1976), Chapter 2, especially 18ff. for biographical details. He translated Sankaracharya's *Viveka-Chudamani* in the *Theosophist*, vi–viii, and *The Bhagavad-Gita* in 1887.

84. Following WBY, it is generally thought that Chatterjee visited Dublin in 1885, but see n. 79 above; the fact that an article by him appeared in the *DUR* in May 1886 also augurs for the Apr. 1886 date. WBY's poetry from this point shows Chatterjee's influence. See the first version of 'The Indian upon God': 'From the Book of Kauri the Indian – Section V. On the Nature of God', *DUR*, Oct. 1886. This may be a fragment of a projected series. Also see P. S. Sri, 'Yeats and Mohini Chatterjee', *YA* ii (1994).

85. See the original version, 'The Way of Wisdom', the *Speaker*, 14 Apr. 1900: reprinted with a useful commentary by Vinod Sena in *Quest*, 69, 62 (July–Sept. 1969). It carried a favourite quotation from *Axël*: 'As for living, our servants will do that for us.' By the time he reprinted it as 'The Pathway' in *CW*, however, he would add, 'How many years it has taken me to awake out of that dream.'

86. Russell to Sean O'Faolain, wrongly annotated 23 Apr. 1939 (*recte* 1930?): transcript in Ellmann MSS, Tulsa. cf. Russell, *Song and Its Fountains* (London, 1932), 9–11.

87. *The Candle of Vision* (London, 1918), 5–6.

88. A recollection of Russell's recorded by Denson and quoted in Kuch, *Yeats and AE*, 27; he said these were the happiest days of his life.

89. Kuch, *Yeats and AE*, 52.

90. Deirdre Toomey points out that 'mentally vibrate' is a Golden Dawn phrase, which hints that this is post-1890.

91. *LTWBY*, ii, 573–4.

92. This is clarified in NLI MS 30,115, 'My Friend's Book', a TS of WBY's review of *Song and Its Fountains*, with much autobiographical reminiscence.

93. To Ernest Boyd, 12 Oct. 1914, Healy Collection, Stanford.

94. Kuch, *Yeats and AE*, 8, interestingly discusses WBY's conflicting later accounts of his reaction to Russell's visions. In *Au* he recorded that he came to believe in their supernatural origin when Russell's predictions were vindicated; but in his earlier review of *Song and Its Fountains* he claimed that he became convinced through verifying Russell's visionary representations by 'the obscure symbolism of alchemy'. Such knowledge was hardly available to him in 1884.

95. Lévi was translated into English in 1886. Cornelius Agrippa's *De Occulta Philosophia* [1531] had been available in English since the seventeenth century, but Henry Morley published his *Life* in 1871 and A. Prost's long commentary appeared in French in 1881–2.

96. Though Madame Blavatsky claimed to have been granted her insight and considerable spiritual power by an ancient Tibetan brotherhood of Masters; the description of their existence given in Sinnett's *The Occult World* is adapted in early WBY poems like 'Anashuya and Vijaya'.

97. See James Olney, 'W. B. Yeats's Daimonic Memory', *Sewanee Review*, 85 (1977), 587–603.

98. See KT, *The Middle Years* (London, 1916), 27–30, and *Twenty-five Years* (London, 1913), 208–9. These occasions may have taken place on WBY's visit from London to Dublin, Nov. 1887 to Jan. 1888; see Chapter 3, below.

99. *Au*, 103–5.

100. Denson, *Letters from AE*, 6–9, quoted by Kuch, *Yeats and AE*, 55, with commentary.

101. Russell to Carrie Rea, 1886, quoted by Kuch, *Yeats and AE*, 14.

102. Reprinted in *UP*, i, 88ff.

103. See *UP*, i, 84.

104. See his remarks quoted at the Ferguson centenary in Trinity. 'On one occasion, when he was dining with him, Ferguson expressed his desire to see Dublin a literary city. This was one of the great hopes of his life, and to some extent that hope was coming about.' (*Daily Express*, Dublin, 16 Mar. 1910).

105. *CL*, i, 8. In a notebook, probably from 1884, there are random jottings attacking Eliot for 'shouting the moral law'.

106. *UP*, i, 104.

107. *Twenty-five Years*, 141, for the Oldham connection. WBY thought they had been introduced by O'Leary and his sister, but KT records that she met O'Leary through the Yeats family when JBY was painting her portrait in the summer of 1886; also see the *Sketch*, 29 Nov. 1893.

108. To Mrs James Pritchard; Geoffrey Barrow, 'Katharine Tynan, Letters 1884–1885', *Apex One*, 1 (1973).

109. 7 Nov. 1886, 27 Jan. 1887, Abbott, *Further Letters of Gerard Manley Hopkins*, 273, 151.

110. See Chapter 3, p. 72, below.

111. The major effort was for the *Gael*, 28 May 1887; see Kelly, 'Aesthete among the Athletes'. Notes followed in *Irish Fireside*, 9 July 1887, and *Truth*, 4 Aug. 1887. See Carolyn Holdsworth, ' "Shelley Plain": Yeats and Katharine Tynan', *YA* 2 (1983), 59–92.

112. See especially an influential review of *WO* in the *Irish Times* and the *Magazine of Poetry* (Oct. 1889), as well as the interview quoted above.
113. 28 Aug. 1906, Harvard.
114. *Daily Express*, Dublin, 27 Aug. 1898 (*UP*, ii, 116–17).
115. 'The Younger Poets of Today', unattributed cutting in Ellmann MSS, possibly from *Magazine of Poetry* (Oct. 1889), 454.
116. Pamela Hinkson, 'The Friendship of Yeats and Katharine Tynan', *Fortnightly Review*, Oct. 1953, 174 (July–Dec.), 254. The phrase 'clearing away the rubbish' was strangely enough repeated by Ezra Pound in 1914: Omar Pound and A. Walton Litz (eds.), *Ezra Pound and Dorothy Shakespear: Their Letters 1909–1914* (New York, 1984), 325.
117. Published 6 Aug. 1887. See also p. 70, below.
118. See Kelly, 'Aesthete among the Athletes' for a discussion.
119. Russell to O'Faolain, as above.
120. 27 June 1947, Ellmann interview book, Tulsa; also *SQ*. She had met O'Leary and JBY the day before at the Contemporary Club. Also see MG to Joseph Hone, 20 Mar. 1939, NLI MS 5914: 'We met for the first time at John O'Leary's tea party.' This is not altogether to be trusted, as she was liable to false-memory syndrome; but the repeated circumstantial detail is telling.
121. She was, for instance, born neither in Kerry nor in Dublin, as she sometimes claimed, but in Tongham, Surrey, on 2 Dec. 1866. See Conrad Balliett, 'The Lives – and Lies – of Maud Gonne', *Éire-Ireland*, 144, 3 (Fall 1979), 17–44.
122. *Au*, 83.
123. *Mem*, 52.
124. *PF*, 135.
125. Daly, *Young Douglas Hyde*, 90.
126. NLI MS 3726A.

Chapter 3 : TWO YEARS: BEDFORD PARK
1887–1889

Epigraph: Reading.
1. JBY to O'Leary, 23 May 1887, NLI MS 5925.
2. Same to same, 16 Jan. 1888.
3. *CL*, i, 15.
4. Ian Fletcher, 'Some Aspects of Aestheticism', *W. B. Yeats and His Contemporaries* (Brighton, 1967), 20, quoting *The Queen*, 1880–81.
5. The word 'suburban' was used by James to mock aestheticism in *The Tragic Muse* (1889).
6. It is Saffron Park in *The Man Who Was Thursday*, and is also described in his *Autobiography*.
7. Geoffrey Paget to Josephine Johnson, 15 Jan. 1975; my thanks to Professor Johnson for this reference.
8. GBS shared the generally low opinion of Sparling, exacerbated by his own interest in May Morris. 'A tall slim immature man with a long thin neck on champagne bottle shoulders, and not athletic. He was brave, sincere and intellectual in his tastes and interests. Having apparently complete confidence in himself, he had a quite unconscious pretentiousness which led his audiences and new acquaintances to expect more from him than he was able to give them.' (Michael Holroyd, *Bernard Shaw. Volume 1, 1856–1898: The Search for Love*, London, 1988, 225). GBS's affair with May provided the inspiration for *Candida*.
9. *CL*, i, 56. It was the same as the Terenure house in Dublin.
10. For descriptions of the house, see ECY to William Rothenstein, 19 Oct. 1939, Harvard;

Ernest Rhys, 'W. B. Yeats: Early Recollections', *Fortnightly Review*, NS, 138 (July 1935), 52–7 (*I & R*, i, 35–6) KT, *Sketch*, 29 Nov. 1893.

11. 17 Sept. 1888.
12. 13 June 1940, Ellmann interview book, Tulsa.
13. Legge was a civil servant and literary critic, Crook a Sligo man who taught school in Clapham and lectured on Irish affairs; *CL*, i, 14, 26.
14. *CL*, i, 64.
15. Interview with George Yeats, 1 July 1946, Ellmann interview book, Tulsa.
16. As he himself recorded: *CL*, i, 92.
17. *CL*, i, 97.
18. *CL*, i, 101.
19. John Kelly deduces that this was probably his payment from Scott for *FFTIP*.
20. *CL*, i, 5.
21. Nevinson, Masefield, Symons, Horton and Sturge Moore all fit this mould.
22. Rhys, 'W. B. Yeats: Early Recollections'.
23. *CL*, i, 50. The meeting was at the Radfords', and GBS recorded in his Pitman pocket diary, 'An Irishman called Yeats talked about socialism a great deal.'
24. *Au*, 148–9.
25. Since *Ye Pleiades* of Feb. 1888 had a piece by ECY entitled 'Love Me Love My Dog', she cannot have been entirely ignorant on the subject.
26. To KT, *c.* 15 June 1888, *CL*, i, 71.
27. See below, p. 74.
28. *CL*, i, 50.
29. It seems loosely based on a tale in the *Book of the Dun Cow*, *Leabhar na hUidhri*, about the bewitching of King Eochaid by Edain; WBY used it again, in 'The Two Kings'. O'Curry had published it in his *Manners and Customs of the Ancient Irish* in 1873, and Lady Wilde in her *Ancient Legends* in 1887; but WBY does not seem to have used these repositories for material until after 1887, and the story also appears in O'Grady's canonical (to him) *History of Ireland* (1878). See Phillip Marcus, 'A Source for Dhoya', *Notes & Queries*, 216 (Oct. 1967), 383–4.
30. *CL*, i, 104.
31. See below, pp. 110–11.
32. *CL*, i, 55.
33. To Elizabeth White, 30 Jan. 1889, *CL*, i, 131.
34. cf. 'The Coolun' in *Lays of the Western Gael* (1888): 'With the dew of the meadow shining/On her milk-white twinkling feet.'
35. *CL*, i, 54–5.
36. *CL*, i, 98.
37. See below, pp. 296, 361–3. And Griffith would, accordingly, republish 'Ferencz Renyi' in his newspaper the *United Irishman* on 24 Dec. 1904.
38. 27 Apr. 1887, *CL*, i, 11.
39. 11 July 1887, *CL*, i, 26.
40. 12 Feb. 1888, *CL*, i, 48.
41. 6 Sept. 1888, *CL*, i, 93–4.
42. *Mem*, 32. His father is identified by a version of the story told by Russell to Monk Gibbon, *The Masterpiece and the Man: Yeats as I Knew Him* (London, 1959), 31.
43. *CL*, i, 112.
44. 2 Nov. 1889, Hyde MSS, TCD.
45. *CL*, i, 83.

46. *CL*, i, 41.
47. T. O'Rorke, *History, Antiquities and Present State of the Parishes of Ballysodare and Kilvarnet in the County of Sligo, with Notice of the O'Haras, the Coopers, the Percevals and Other Local Families* (Dublin, n.d.); W. G. Wood-Martin, *History of Sligo, County and Town.* [Volume 1] *From the Earliest Ages to the Close of the Reign of Queen Elizabeth* (Dublin, 1882); [Volume 2] *From the Accession of James I to the Revolution of 1688* (Dublin, 1889).
48. *CL*, i, 36.
49. *CL*, i, 38.
50. Daly, *Young Douglas Hyde*, 87.
51. Nora O'Mahony to Austin Clarke, *c.* 1930, Huntingdon. For speculation about the proposal see Carolyn Holdsworth, *YA* 2 (1983), and James McFadden, *YAACTS* 8 (1990).
52. *Mem*, 32.
53. See McFadden for a countering speculation.
54. Denson, *Letters from AE*, 6.
55. Possibly at the Sigerson house in Clare Street. See above, p. 51; Kuch, *Yeats and AE*, 54; KT, *Twenty-five Years*, 208–9; *Au*, 102–3.
56. Kuch, *Yeats and AE*, 28–9; Gibbon, *The Masterpiece and the Man*, 55. See Summerfield, *Myriad-minded Man*, for a full account.
57. *CL*, i, 108.
58. *Au*, 128.
59. ECY's diary, 18 Jan. 1889.
60. He finally admitted to AG on 7 Feb. 1913: 'I shall never speak it.' Berg.
61. *CL*, i, 93.
62. Pethica, 151.
63. *CL*, i, 62 ('I could only speak with considerable difficulty at first.')
64. 'The Strife of Love in a Dream', an Elizabethan version of the first book of Francesco Colonna's *Hypnerotomachia Poliphili* for Lang's new edition in Aug. 1889. This introduced him to a Renaissance decadent masterpiece which helped inspire 'Leda and the Swan' nearly forty years later, according to Giorgio Melchiori, *The Whole Mystery of Art: Pattern into Poetry in the Work of W. B. Yeats* (London, 1960).
65. See correspondence between Winifred T. Davis and Horace Reynolds, Harvard, for attempts to trace these in 1935. *UP*, i, 28, estimates the quantity of traceable work.
66. *CL*, i, 91.
67. *CL*, i, 72.
68. See JBY to O'Leary, 23 May 1887, NLI MS 5925, and WBY to KT, 25 June 1887, *CL*, i, 24.
69. To Hyde, 23 Aug. 1889, *CL*, i, 183.
70. *Graphic*, 9 June 1888.
71. *CL*, i, 69, n. 2.
72. *CL*, i, 65.
73. See *CL*, i, 58–9; *UP*, i, 198–202, 159, 185. There is a dubious report by Edward Garnett in Berg.
74. Verso of O'Leary autograph sent by WBY to Constance Gore-Booth, late 1890s, Harvard.
75. 12 Feb. 1888, *CL*, i, 48.
76. *CL*, i, 102.
77. Oct. 1901, in AG's copy. Berg. *Au*, 149; *Mem*, 32. The figure varies between 'some twelve pounds' and '£14', but twelve guineas seems right.
78. ECY's diary.
79. An important article in *Leisure Hour*, Oct. 1890 (*UP*, i, 175–82), may have been written in 1887.

80. *CL*, i, 89.
81. *CL*, i, 194.
82. *UP*, i, 189.
83. *UP*, i, 410.
84. 27 Sept. 1888.
85. It was published at the end of the month.
86. *CL*, i, 93.
87. *CL*, i, 118.
88. *CL*, i, 119; also see 97–8.
89. SMY to R L-P, 17 June 1930.
90. On 20 July 1901 he wrote to Robert Bridges (*CL*, iii, 90) that he had grown 'not a little jealous of the "Lake Isle" which has put the noses of all my other children out of joint'. Hugh Kingsmill saw him in Switzerland in 1924, 'reciting "Innisfree" with an air of suppressed loathing', while his female audience 'beamed ardently at him, as though ready at a word to fall in behind him and surge towards the bee-loud glade' (*I & R*, ii, 295–6). On another occasion it was sung in the open air by 2,000 boy-scouts (*I & R*, i, 152). WBY wrote to Edith Lister at Bullen's: 'Imagine "Innisfree" as a marching song – poor island.' (28 July? [from Coole], Harvard).
91. *CL*, i, 128.
92. *UP*, i, 130–37.
93. *CL*, i, 24.
94. So he claimed in *Au*, though some doubt is cast by his assertion that *WO* was already published – and it did not appear until the end of 1889. However, the detail that Wilde was working on the proofs of *The Decay of Lying* is strong circumstantial evidence for 1888; WBY may have confused two visits. On 25 July 1888 he first visited Lady Wilde; SMY records another visit on 16 Nov. 1889 (SMY to KT, Illinois).
95. *Au*, 134–5.
96. A reflection possibly prompted by WBY's later knowledge of Moore. See Conneely, 'A Talk with W. B. Yeats'; also Ralph Shirley to Arland Usher, 21 June 1939, HRHRC.
97. W. R. Rodgers, transcript of 'W. B. Yeats: A Dublin Portrait', HRHRC.
98. NLI MS 5925.
99. Hyde to Ellen O'Leary, 2 Feb. 1888.
100. See especially George Bornstein, 'Remaking Himself: Yeats's Revisions of His Early Canon', D. C. Creetham and W. Speed Hill (eds.), *Text: Transactions of the Society for Textual Scholarship* (1991).
101. cf. 'All Things can Tempt me' and 'Adam's Curse'.
102. *CL*, i, 54.
103. *CL*, i, 132.
104. 4 Feb. 1889, TCD.
105. See NLI MS 31,087, a collection of cuttings.
106. Reviews quoted in the text are as follows: 9 Mar. 1889; *Boston Pilot*, 4 May 1889; 5 June 1888, TCD; *Academy*, 30 Mar. 1889; 12 July 1889; 1 Feb. 1889; 16 Feb. 1889; 4 Mar. 1889; 25 May 1889; *Providence Sunday Journal*, 12 May 1889.
107. *Mem*, 21.
108. *Mem*, 40.
109. SMY notebook, ECY diary; see *CL*, i, 134, n. 3.
110. *CL*, i, 30.
111. *Au*, 123.
112. In a notebook entry of 13 July 1899, at Coole, he recorded his use of apple-blossom as an occult invocation, adding 'the apple blossoms are symbols of dawn and of the air and

of the earth and of resurrection in my system and in the poem [*Shadowy Waters*]'. See below, p. 219.

113. 'The Tragic Theatre' from *The Cutting of an Agate* (*E & I*, 243–4).

Chapter 4 : SECRET SOCIETIES
1889–1891

Epigraph: Healy Collection, Stanford.

1. Ellmann, *M & M*, 73.
2. *CL*, i, 256, for a round-up.
3. *CL*, i, 424.
4. *CL*, i, 240, n. 3.
5. *UP*, i, 118–19.
6. In 'An Extraordinary Adventure in the Shades', Mangan wrote of 'Mannerism' and genius. 'You shall tramp the earth in vain for a more pitiable object than a man of genius with nothing else to back it up . . . Transfuse into this man a due portion of mannerisms – the metamorphosis is marvellous . . . Mannerism! destitute of which we are, so to speak, walking humbugs; destitute of which the long odds are, that the very best individual among us, after a life spent in the treadmill system, dies dismally in a sack.' See David Lloyd, *Nationalism and Minor Literature: James Clarence Mangan and the Emergence of Irish Cultural Nationalism* (London, 1987), 197, and for further reflections on the 'mask', 206–7, 212–13.
7. Though WBY recurred more often to Mangan's chilling ode 'Siberia' than to the well-worn 'Dark Rosaleen', he characteristically interpreted it as referring to the inner land-scape of alienation – not as a metaphor for the famine conditions under which it was written.
8. To KT, 9 Mar. 1889, *CL*, i, 153.
9. *Au*, 155–6.
10. *CL*, i, 231.
11. My thanks to Deirdre Toomey for this reference.
12. Or so WBY alleged.
13. *G–YL*, 19, implies she attended her sister Kathleen's wedding when she was herself eight months pregnant, which shows a distinct lack of conventionality. The belief in cursed marriages is recorded in *SQ*, 333.
14. Margaret Wilson's subsequent life is described by Tania Alexander, *A Little of All of These: An Estonian Childhood* (London, 1987), Chapter 3. The half-sister, Eileen Wilson, lived with MG in Paris.
15. *CL*, i, 228.
16. *Mem*, 63.
17. *CL*, i, 154–5.
18. 23 Oct. 1889, *CL*, i, 192.
19. See *UP*, i, 213–15; *LNI*; and WBY's handwritten paragraph of hyperbole about MG destined for an unnamed newspaper, at Harvard.
20. *CL*, i, 167–8.
21. See below, p. 112.
22. To KT, 10 Oct. 1889, *CL*, i, 190.
23. *PF*, 161.
24. *CL*, i, 158, 223–4.
25. *CL*, i, 145, 156–7.
26. *CL*, i, 280.

27. *CL*, i, 191.
28. See *UP*, i, 146–62, though 'Irish Fairies' dates from later – cf. *CL*, i, 175–82.
29. e.g. the fact that Sir Charles Gavan Duffy was working on 'the last few chapters' of his life of Thomas Davis 'in a house near Park Lane' (*LNI*, 15).
30. A favourite phrase about the grass blade that carries the universe upon its point crops up regularly (e.g. *LNI*, 78).
31. Gamely reviewed by WBY on 7 Oct. 1893 but left unsigned.
32. *CL*, i, 182.
33. *CL*, i, 195. SMY wrote to KT that their maid Rose 'liked it so much that she said "I wish Miss Tynan would just walk into the kitchen so as I could tell her."' (17 Nov. 1889, Illinois).
34. *LNI*, 88–9.
35. SMY to KT, 17 Nov. 1889, Illinois.
36. *CL*, i, 235.
37. *CL*, i, 145.
38. *CL*, i, 153, 165.
39. See below, Chapter 8. Spelt 'Kathleen' in its early incarnation, WBY eventually settled for 'Cathleen'.
40. 14 Oct. 1889, *UP*, i, 142–6.
41. *CL*, i, 174.
42. 23 Aug. 1889, *CL*, i, 183.
43. 1 Sept. 1889, *CL*, i, 186.
44. *CL*, i, 199.
45. *CL*, i, 187, n. 4.
46. *CL*, i, 194, 170–71, 184.
47. *CL*, i, 201.
48. See Ian Fletcher, 'The Ellis–Yeats–Blake Manuscript Cluster', *Book Collector*, 21 (Spring 1972), 72–94.
49. *CL*, i, 218.
50. *UP*, i, 273.
51. See review of Housman's *Blake*, *UP*, i, 280.
52. Material at Reading records WBY's thoughts on the survival and dispersal of Blake MSS (for instance MS 991, an account in WBY's handwriting of Mrs Blake's dealings with her husband's literary estate, and also WBY to Geoffrey Keynes, 13 and 27 Feb. 1913, apologizing that he cannot remember or find out how he and Ellis discovered the 'Book of Ahania').
53. *CL*, i, 226, n. 4.
54. *CL*, i, 241.
55. *CL*, i, 244.
56. 5 Oct. 1890, Kansas.
57. NLI MSS 13,569, 13,570, 13,574. See M. C. Flannery, *Yeats and Magic: The Earlier Works* (Gerrards Cross, 1977).
58. 13 Jan. and 3 Feb. at least, from the evidence of ECY's diary.
59. *UP*, i, 298–302; *Au*, 281–2; *CL*, i, 185, n. 2.
60. *Au*, 173–5, 179. cf. Voltaire's dying words: asked to renounce the devil, he refused on the grounds that in the circumstances he needed all the allies he could find.
61. Occult notes and diary.
62. *CL*, i, 234–5.
63. *YO*, 328.

64. On its formation, see R. A. Gilbert, *The Golden Dawn and the Esoteric Section* (London, Theosophical History Centre, 1987).

65. See R. A. Gilbert, 'Provenance Unknown: A Tentative Solution to the Riddle of the Cipher Manuscript of the Golden Dawn' in Albrecht Gotz von Olenhausen (ed.) with the assistance of Nicholas Barker, Herbert Franke and Helmut Moller, *Wege und Abwege: Beiträge zur Europäischen Geistesgeschichte der Neuzeit: Festschrift für Ellic Howe zum 20 September 1990* (Freiburg, 1990), 79–89.

66. Mathers used a Swedenborgian masonic ritual document as his model. Despite its use of masonic structures, the Golden Dawn was Christian Cabbalist in its Outer Order, and Rosicrucian in its Inner Order. My thanks to Deirdre Toomey for guidance on this point.

67. See Ellic Howe, *The Magicians of the Golden Dawn: A Documentary History of a Magical Order 1887–1923* (London, 1972), 41–2, for other descriptions of Mathers in his British Museum days.

68. See Howe, 38, for conflicting claims regarding the Golden Dawn's foundation; for its organization, R. A. Gilbert, *The Golden Dawn Companion: A Guide to the History, Structure and Workings of the Hermetic Order of the Golden Dawn* (Wellingborough, 1986).

69. Howe, *The Magicians of the Golden Dawn*, 63.

70. Israel Regardie, *My Rosicrucian Adventure* (Chicago, 1936), 14.

71. Gerald Yorke's foreword in Howe, *The Magicians of the Golden Dawn*, ix–xix.

72. George Cecil Jones to John Symons, quoted in Howe, *The Magicians of the Golden Dawn*, 61.

73. Howe, *The Magicians of the Golden Dawn*, 50; see Pethica, 151, for WBY's account to AG. The Comtesse used to provide coffee for him at her flat near the British Museum.

74. 18 Nov. 1890, NLI MS 5925.

75. Dorothea Hunter told Ellmann, 'the Order was my university. In it were collected, classified and edited the great traditions of occultism and mysticism – from which we could deduce that of which we were capable.' See Warwick Gould's brief biography of her in *YA* 9 (1992) [*Yeats and Women*, ed. Deirdre Toomey], 142.

76. Howe, *The Magicians of the Golden Dawn*, 58.

77. *UP*, i, 253.

78. *SB*, 221.

79. See below, pp. 120–21.

80. See below, Chapter 7.

81. Rhys, 'W. B. Yeats: Early Recollections', dates it as the winter of 1889/90.

82. Karl Beckson, *Arthur Symons: A Life* (Oxford, 1987), 61.

83. To William Symington McCormick [November 1891], John Sloan (ed.), *Selected Poems and Prose of John Davidson* (Oxford, 1995), 175–6. George Arthur Greene was one of the organizers.

84. See especially his 1910 lecture 'Friends of my Youth', NLI MS 30,088; also his 1936 BBC broadcast 'Art and Ideas'; and *The Trembling of the Veil*.

85. See Dowson to Symons, 5 July 1896, in Desmond Flower and Henry Maas (eds.), *The Letters of Ernest Dowson* (London, 1967), 371–2 – a letter asking Symons to tone down a biographical article, assuring him that he has become 'the most pastoral of men'.

86. See Jerusha Hall McCormack, *John Gray: Poet, Dandy and Priest* (Brandeis, 1991), 21ff.

87. Ernest Boyd, *Ireland's Literary Renaissance* (Dublin, 1916), 139–44, 172–5, 184–9. On WBY's use of mysticism and symbolism, see also M. Bowra, *Memories* (London, 1966), 240–41.

88. *UP*, ii, 261.

89. Johnson's *Poems* (1895) are full of yearning towards men friends (including the 'beautiful sibilline lips' of Manmohan Ghose); many are addressed to people, including a poem to Lord Alfred Douglas about choirboys. (See also below, Chapter 6, n. 87, for his poem

to Davray.) Three poems printed posthumously in a 1928 pamphlet edited by Vincent Starett included a poem in Latin to Wilde thanking him for writing *Dorian Gray*: 'Hic sunt poma sodomarum/Hic sunt corda vitiorum/Et peccata dulcia.' There is a copy in WBY's library.

90. *CL*, i, 253.
91. Beckson, *Arthur Symons*, 81. See also Dowson to G. A. Greene, 27 Nov. 1893 in Flower and Maas, *The Letters of Ernest Dowson*.
92. 23 Apr. (*LNI*, 5–7ff.).
93. *CL*, i, 257, n. 7.
94. Interview with George Yeats, 1 June 1946, Ellmann interview book, Tulsa.
95. *UP*, ii, 257; also introduction to *Oxford Book of Modern Verse*; and see George Bornstein, 'Last Romantic or Last Victorian', *YA* i (1982), 117ff.
96. *CL*, i, 245.
97. *CL*, i, 246.
98. Now in Emory Special Collection.
99. 9 Nov. 1891, NLI MS 5925.
100. *CL*, i, 274–5.
101. The Pseudonym Library, founded in 1890, would be Fisher Unwin's greatest success. It was a popular imprint 'specifically suited by their brightness and originality' for holiday reading. Pocket-sized and cheap, they were sold on railway bookstalls and usually achieved several editions. See Warwick Gould, 'Journey without Maps', *YA* ii (1995), 229–31.
102. To O'Leary, 1 Dec. 1891, NLI MS 5925.
103. See *UP*, i, 245–50 for *United Ireland* article, 15 Oct. 1892.

Chapter 5: THE BATTLE OF THE BOOKS
1891–1893

Epigraph: *L*, 405.
1. MG to Hone, 23 Mar. 1939, NLI MS 5919.
2. In conversation with Patrick McCartan in 1937: see 'William Butler Yeats – the Fenian', *Ireland-American Review* (Nov. 1940), 45, and *Yeats and Patrick McCartan: A Fenian Friendship. Letters with a Commentary by John Unterecker and an Address on Yeats the Fenian by Patrick McCartan* (Dolmen Press Yeats Centenary Papers, No. x, Dublin, 1965).
3. There is, however, an intriguing transcription in WBY's handwriting in Huntingdon of a newspaper article from the mid-1860s, attacking 'pro-British' Irish bishops from a distinctly Fenian viewpoint. Its provenance is unknown.
4. See Ó Broin, *Revolutionary Underground*, Chapter 4.
5. *CL*, i, 237.
6. *CL*, i, 242.
7. 8 July 1891, NLI MS 10,201.
8. *CL*, i, 263, n. 2.
9. See James White, 'AE's Merrion Square Murals and Other Paintings', *Arts in Ireland*, 1, 3 (1973), 4–10.
10. MG to Ethel Mannin, 29 Oct. 1946, NLI MS 17,875.
11. *Mem*, 50.
12. Date according to *CL*, i, 269, n. 3. See *UP*, i, 206–8.
13. *Mem*, 47–8.
14. See WBY to AG, Aug. 1922, SIUC, for his horror at seeing it printed on a banner at an Irish American gathering; he first supposed it was a biblical quotation.

15. It is dated 'Dublin, October 1891' and written into the notebook called 'The Flame of the Spirit'; this is the version quoted here, reproduced in Bornstein, *Early Poetry: Volume 2*, 487. The slightly different version pulled from the proofs of *The Countess Kathleen and Various Legends and Lyrics* is in ibid., 488.

16. *CL*, i, 272.

17. *YA* 7 (1989), 190.

18. George Mills Harper (ed.), *Yeats's 'Vision' Papers. Volume 2: The Automatic Script 25 June 1918–29 March 1920*, Steve L. Adams, Barbara J. Frieling and Sandra L. Sprayberry (eds.) (London, 1992), 229.

19. See Bornstein, *Early Poetry: Volume 2*, 484. The 'Rosy Cross' notebook is NLI 30, 318; 'The Flame of the Spirit' was auctioned to an unknown buyer by Sotheby's on 23 July 1987.

20. 1 Nov. 1891, *CL*, i, 266.

21. *CL*, i, 277.

22. *CL*, i, 295.

23. *United Ireland*, 2 Apr. 1892. See Donald Pearce, 'Dublin's National Literary Society, 1892', *Notes & Queries*, 19, 6 (12 May 1951).

24. *Au*, 229: a significant anticipation of later priorities. The quotations come from a letter to Rolleston on 10 May, apologizing for not being able to attend an ILS meeting.

25. *CL*, i, 297.

26. At a meeting in the Wicklow Hotel on 24 May a Provisional Committee was appointed; on 31 May a public meeting was arranged for the Rotunda on 9 June, where WBY moved the foundation of the NLS, particularly stressing the Library project. See *CL*, i, 300.

27. 3 June 1892. 'There are Nationalists whose friendship no man need disdain but there are others with whom it would be difficult to cultivate even a distant acquaintance.'

28. 18 June 1892.

29. *CL*, i, 301.

30. *CL*, i, 303.

31. *CL*, i, 305, for WBY's doleful report to O'Leary. He put a brave face on it elsewhere by claiming that he had always intended the London ILS to be 'federated with a central body in Ireland', but this concealed the fact that the 'central body' was to have been the Young Ireland League, not the newly created and respectable National Literary Society.

32. *Au*, 224–5. See Daly, *Young Douglas Hyde*, 153, for Hyde's favourable reaction to Gavan Duffy and an ILS meeting on 30 July; Gavan Duffy impressed them by his practicality and business acumen in publishing matters. WBY is not listed as attending.

33. *CL*, i, 311.

34. *CL*, i, 313.

35. In a version very different from later revisions; see M. J. Sidnell, 'Yeats's First Work for the Stage: The Earliest Versions of *The Countess Cathleen*' in D. E. S. Maxwell and S. B. Bushrui (eds.), *W. B. Yeats 1865–1965: Centenary Essays on the Art of W. B. Yeats* (Ibadan, 1965).

36. *LTWBY*, i, 6.

37. 8 Nov. 1892.

38. *CL*, i, 333–4.

39. 12 Nov. 1892: 'You have no authority to make proposition to him as you have done.'

40. *CL*, i, 350, n. 5.

41. 18 Nov. 1892, *LTWBY*, i, 6–8.

42. This meeting in the early 1900s, where Sara Allgood's recitation of 'Moll Magee' was ill-received, is recorded in an unattributed cutting in Henderson's cuttings book, Kansas. For WBY's reprimand, see *Au*, 229–30. The motion recording that 'Count Plunkett be required to convey to the Library subcommittee the dissatisfaction of the Society regarding the manner in which the meetings of the subcommittee have been conducted, the

apparent absence of minute book or report of its proceedings' was put by Messrs McCaul and Curtis at a meeting of 29 June: NLS minute book, NLI MS 1465–6. The offending report, a very scrappy production, is in NLI MS 5918, reprinted in *CL*, i, 358.

43. See 'Yeats's First Draft', 134. 29, notes in Ellmann MSS, Tulsa.

44. *CH*, 78–82.

45. To AG, 25 May 1930; quoted in *CL*, ii, 127, n. 3.

46. See *VSR*, 185ff. for this original version.

47. A recollection of SMY: *PF*, 174.

48. To John Quinn, 19 Feb. 1915, NYPL.

49. *CL*, i, 304, n. 7.

50. *Mem*, 60.

51. *CL*, i, 245, quoting a long letter from Rolleston to Hyde. This correspondence varies between suspicion of WBY, uncertainty as to how far he actually represented the Dublin Society, and belief that he was being 'sensible and disinterested' (23 Jan.). Rolleston's letters also make clear that he was being ground between WBY's and Gavan Duffy's implacable contempt for each other. Both London and Dublin subcommittees were to draw up lists of books, but power remained with Gavan Duffy as editor-in-chief and Rolleston and Hyde as subeditors.

52. *CL*, i, 352.

53. Daly, *Young Douglas Hyde*, 154–5.

54. Howe, *The Magicians of the Golden Dawn*, 97, who claims he completed the 5=6 initiation the following day. cf. below, p. 129.

55. *CL*, i, 341, n. 4. WBY and Hyde themselves went to Cork on 23 Jan., where the meeting was chaired by the ex-Young Irelander Denny Lane, and the condescension of the Dubliners was not universally welcomed. See Daly, *Young Douglas Hyde*, 160, for a rather ingenuous report.

56. *United Ireland*, 11 Mar. 1893.

57. *United Ireland* for 22 Apr. and 6 May reports speeches at Loughrea, New Ross and Dublin. By 27 May she was once more speaking to 'L'Union de la Jeunesse Republicaine' in Paris. On 4 Apr., in Sligo, WBY completed the mournful nationalist 'Ballad of Earl Paul', not subsequently collected. WBY attended a GD Council of Adepts at Clipstone Street on 30 May, and was active in London literary circles in early June.

58. Astrological notes for 1893, MBY, probably compiled 1914–15: referring to Apr. 1893. 'It was a year of great trouble. A great breach with MG . . . Later on I went to Paris & saw her again. A real breach for reasons I knew nothing of had however taken place.'

59. *Mem*, 68. The poem here is as it appeared in *National Observer*, 29 July 1893.

60. See their exchanges in Dec. 1898: below, Chapter 8.

61. JBY to SMY, 10 June 1892 [1893?], courtesy of W. M. Murphy.

62. *CL*, i, 318.

63. Contract dated 25 May 1892, NLI 30, 654.

64. Howe, *The Magicians of the Golden Dawn*, 107.

65. *CT*. See also *UP*, i, 283–8, 'Causerie'.

66. MG to Hone, 23 Mar. 1939, NLI MS 5919.

67. *UP*, i, 187–8, 327.

68. Mary Helen Thuente, *W. B. Yeats and Irish Folklore* (Dublin, 1981), 104, puts this case convincingly.

69. *United Ireland*, 2 Dec. 1893. In Dublin on 31 Oct. he gave a more defiantly anti-rational and literal account of fairy life (*United Ireland*, 4 Nov. 1893), but he still described these beliefs as the expression of emotional and psychological needs.

70. *UP*, i, 266–75.

71. Astrological notes probably compiled 1914–15. See also n. 53, above.

72. He had anticipated this in his letter on Tennyson's death to the *Bookman*, Dec. 1892 (*UP*, i, 251).

73. See his piece on Allingham in *United Ireland*, 12 Dec. 1891 (*UP*, i, 212).

74. Until *Poetry*, Jan., 1980, 223–6, with an interesting commentary by Christina Hunt Mahony and Edward O'Shea. The poem stresses vigilance, and keeping the faith with past generations who had fought for 'Eri, our old/And long-weeping mother'.

75. *LNI*, 12, 30, etc. He continued, however, to attack 'Anglo-Irishness' much as the 'Celt in London' had done; the 'braggadocio and swagger' of debased eighteenth-century types was compared to the 'serious, reserved and suspicious' Irish peasant, as the true race type.

76. See his notebook signed 'D.E.D.I., 28 June 1893', *YO*, 3. He had been admitted to the Portal grade on 20 Jan. (Howe, *The Magicians of the Golden Dawn*, 97).

77. *CL*, i, 366–7. For Quinn, see Sally Warwick-Haller, *William O'Brien and the Irish Land War* (Dublin, 1990), 57–8.

78. 'Interview with Mr W. B. Yeats', *Irish Theosophist*, ii, 2 (15 Nov. 1893), 147–9 (*UP*, i, 298–302; and *I & R*, i, 19–23).

79. *CL*, i, 369–74.

80. *CL*, i, 371.

81. My italics.

82. JBY to SMY, Dec. 1893, courtesy of W. M. Murphy.

83. *LNI*, 4.

84. ibid., xviii.

Chapter 6 : LANDS OF HEART'S DESIRE
1894–1896

Epigraph: n.d., NLI MS 30,285.

1. *CL*, i, 395.

2. *CL*, i, 368–9.

3. *CL*, i, 401, 437.

4. *CL*, i, 377.

5. It had begun, according to WBY, as a version of a Reynard tale, and on its first outing was cast in a heavy-handed 'Oirish' dialect; see above, p. 125.

6. *CL*, i, 385.

7. *Bookman*, Feb. 1894 (*UP*, i, 317).

8. 19 Aug. 1893 (*UP*, i, 283ff.).

9. *Bookman*, Oct. 1893 (*UP*, i, 295).

10. *UP*, i, 274; even, in this case, an anonymous five-act play about Anne Boleyn written by a Catholic zealot.

11. Beckson, *Arthur Symons*, 98; *CL*, ii, 281, n. 1, quoting Clodd's diary.

12. Its first appearance was in *Harper's New Monthly Magazine*.

13. Draft preface, NLI MS 30,285.

14. *CL*, i, 379.

15. Dated 10 Mar. 1894; printed by Bornstein, with variants, in *Early Poetry: Volume 2*, 493. This version follows pencilled revisions; an alternative has 'retake' in the first line, with line 3 reading 'Before a slanderers breath could break'.

16. York Powell had arranged Mallarmé's English tour: Roger Pearson, 'A Change of Heir: Mallarmé at Oxford and Cambridge in 1894', *Oxford Magazine*, 103 (Fourth Week, Hilary term, 1994).

17. *Au*, 341–2.
18. *Savoy*, April 1896 (*UP*, i, 399).
19. *UP*, i, 323–4.
20. *UP*, i, 324. For his recurrent image of 'the wind among the reeds', see below, p. 146.
21. Richard Cave (ed.), *Hail and Farewell: Ave, Salve, Vale* (1933 ed., repr. and annotated, Gerrards Cross, 1976), 78–9. Max Beerbohm also recorded his appearance: 'a white streak of shirt-front and above that a white streak of face; and I was aware that what I had thought to be insubstantial murk was a dress-suit with the Author in it. And the streak of the Author's face was partly bisected by a lesser black streak, which was a lock of Author's raven hair . . . It was all very eerie and memorable.' (*I & R*, i, 28).
22. *Au*, 282–7. He was also consoled by Wilde turning up at the theatre and praising WBY's short story 'The Crucifixion of the Outcast' – further encouraging his inclination to side with 'decadence' rather than Shavianism.
23. Josephine Johnson, *Florence Farr: George Bernard Shaw's New Woman* (Gerrards Cross, 1973).
24. *CL*, i, 384.
25. *CL*, i, 386.
26. Johnson, *Florence Farr*, 63.
27. *Bookman*, Aug. 1894 (*UP*, i, 375–7).
28. 18 Sept. [1894], Reading.
29. See e.g. letter to Fisher Unwin, *CL*, i, 429.
30. *CL*, i, 407.
31. 'Shemeber' (Pamela Carden Bullock) to George Pollexfen, 3 Jan. 1895, *LTWBY*, i, 11–12 (where it is wrongly addressed to WBY).
32. *UP*, ii, 272; Genevieve Brennan, 'Yeats, Clodd, Scatological Rites, and the Clonmel Witch Burning', *YA* 4 (1986), 207–15; Hubert Butler, 'The Eggman and the Fairies', *Escape from the Anthill* (Mullingar, 1985), 63–74.
33. *CL*, i, 424–5.
34. *PF*, 176.
35. On 19 Aug. 1911 Lucy Middleton wrote to WBY in answer to a request for recollections of psychic phenomena explored by them both in Sligo; he was beginning to write his reminiscences. Her account (*MBY*) may refer to this time:

   That time at 'Avena' Ballisodare [the Middleton house by the mills], there was a *very* old mirror in the drawing-room. I sat on a sofa. The mirror was on the wall behind my head. You sat also on the sofa. Suddenly I heard knocking on the mirror. Then you asked if there was a spirit there and the answer was yes. Then you asked other questions. I do not remember what they were, but you got answers which rather upset you. Then suddenly I saw a most beautiful white light, over the lawn in front of the house, and I thought that was good. Then upstairs there were knocks everywhere. Henry also heard them there. (I think, as a very small child I saw beautiful lights & heard strange sounds in that house, but they all seemed to me so natural I never minded them much, not knowing anything about such things then.)

36. *CL*, i, 418.
37. *CL*, i, 455.
38. *Mem*, 78–9.
39. 26 Dec. [1898], *CL*, ii, 331.
40. *CL*, i, 463.
41. *CL*, i, 447.
42. 23 Sept. [1894], *CL*, i, 399.
43. *CL*, i, 430–31; *UP*, i, 347ff. and also above, pp. 52–3.
44. *Daily Express*, Dublin, 29 Jan. 1895; *CL*, i, 435, for WBY's reply.

45. *CL*, i, 438.

46. 18 Aug. 1894, Illinois.

47. See above, p. 140, for another reference to this image in his review of *Axël*; it also recurs in *LHD*: 'The reeds are dancing by Coolaney Lake', etc.

48. *UP*, i, 360ff.

49. *CL*, i, 472.

50. Also see his *Bookman* review of Todhunter's *Life of Patrick Sarsfield* (*UP*, i, 388–9) for reflections on the decadence of historical writing; he attacked 'conventional patriotism' for overthrowing 'honest research' and creating 'a mystery play of devils and angels'. Thus to attack 'conventional patriotism' he was prepared to shift his entire philosophical ground regarding the achievement of historical insights.

51. *Good Reading about Many Books, Mostly by Their Authors*, published by Fisher Unwin (1894), 197.

52. See John Kelly, 'Yeats's Relations with His Early Publishers', A. N. Jeffares (ed.) *Yeats, Sligo and Ireland* (Gerrards Cross, 1980), 11.

53. *CL*, i, 402.

54. *CL*, i, 434.

55. My thanks to Warwick Gould for this insight.

56. 7 Apr. 1895, *CL*, i, 457–8.

57. *Amadán* means 'fool' (Hyde's diary, as translated by Dominic Daly, private collection). Interestingly, on this visit WBY did manage to meet the influential newspaper editor Jasper Tully.

58. *UP*, i, 358–9. It was, significantly, a volume in the New Irish Library series, so considered by WBY as fair game.

59. *PF*, 182.

60. Since the current numbers of the *Irish Theosophist* were heavily freighted with endless serials about Cuchulain, Fand, Lugh Lamfada, the birds of Aengus and so on by 'AE and Aetan', WBY probably felt it was time to move on.

61. See Bornstein, *The Early Poetry: Volume 2*, 16–17.

62. See John Harwood's *Olivia Shakespear and W. B. Yeats: After Long Silence* (London, 1989), 37, a book which casts invaluable light on this important relationship and on Shakespear's own life.

63. *YA* 4 (1986), 70.

64. Pound and Litz, *Pound and Shakespear Letters*, 211.

65. See especially Mendelssohn's photograph, frontispiece, *YA* 4 (1986), which appeared with a profile in the *Literary Yearbook* for 1897.

66. *CL*, i, 396.

67. *CL*, i, 415.

68. *CL*, i, 459.

69. *CL*, i, 464.

70. See Harwood, *Shakespear and Yeats*, 46, n. 23 and 198–9; he dates this as 15 July 1895.

71. Beckson, *Arthur Symons*, 114.

72. *UP*, i, 373–5.

73. Denson, *Letters from AE*, 16.

74. *PF*, 182–3. See below, p. 528, for WBY's memory of this incident in 1914.

75. See Symons to Rhys, 7 Feb. 1891, Princeton, which establishes that he moved in on 5 Feb.

76. Beckson, *Arthur Symons*, 264.

77. Illinois.

78. SMY to John Quinn, 11 Apr. 1921, NYPL, quoted in W. M. Murphy, 'Home Life among the Yeatses', A. N. Jeffares, *Yeats, Sligo and Ireland*, 180–81.

79. *PF*, 195.
80. SMY diary, 11 Aug. 1895.
81. *G–YL*, i, 52–3.
82. In *Au*, WBY put this incident at the end rather than the beginning of their affair; but he situates it in the Temple, which means that it was at this stage of events. Harwood suggests very late 1895 or January 1896.
83. Harwood's treatment (63ff.) is necessarily speculative but highly perceptive.
84. Warwick Gould in *YA* 4 (1986), 276.
85. *I & R*, i, 28–9.
86. Such as 'Herne' or 'Hearn', and 'Bruin'.
87. Symons had told Davray as early as 1892 that WBY was 'much the best of our younger poets'; Beckson, *Arthur Symons*, 82. Lionel Johnson dedicated a poem, 'To Passions', to Davray in 1894, dealing characteristically with self-hatred, haunting thoughts, and struggles with temptation. 'I know thee, O mine own desire!/ I know not mine own self so well.'
88. *UP*, i, 405.
89. *CL*, i, 454, 461.
90. 19 Mar. 1896, *CL*, ii, 14. cf. a throwaway remark in a review of June 1896 (*UP*, i, 405). '[Ireland] is so busy with opinions that she cannot understand that imaginative literature wholly, and all literature in some degree, exists to reveal a more powerful and passionate, a more divine world than ours; and not to make our ploughing and sowing, our spinning and weaving, more easy or more pleasant, or even to give us a good opinion of ourselves, by glorifying our past or our future.'
91. Symons to WBY, 'Tuesday' [26 Sept. 1895], MBY. See *YA* 5 (1987), 59, and *CL*, ii, appendix.
92. Pethica, 160.
93. 'Yeats of Bloomsbury', *Life and Letters of Today*, 21, 20 (Apr. 1939), 60–66. See also John Masefield, *Some Memories of W. B. Yeats* (Dublin, 1940).
94. *CL*, ii, 8.
95. *YA* 4 (1986), 57.

Chapter 7 : WAITING FOR THE MILLENNIUM
1896–1898

Epigraph: TCD.
1. Captain John Aherne was a French-educated United Irishman revolutionary in 1798. The names Herne, Hearne or Ahearne recur in WBY's fiction from 1894; 'Michael Hearne' first turns up in an uncollected story of Oct. 1896, 'The Cradles of Gold'. Heron symbolism runs through WBY's dramatic work, culminating in *The Herne's Egg*. 'Hearne' was the name of a 'witch doctor' on the borders of Clare and Galway ('The Fool of Faery', *Kensington*, 1, 4, June 1901). From 1901 WBY knew the work of Lafcadio Hearn, the Greek–Irish interpreter of Japan, who also wrote ghost-stories; see my introduction to Paul Murray, *A Fantastic Journey: The Life and Literature of Lafcadio Hearn* (London, 1993). On the treatment of the name and its images, see Warwick Gould's essay in *YO*, especially 272–9.
2. Or so WBY told Russell: Kuch, *Yeats and AE*, 113.
3. See 'The Flame of the Spirit' notebook, described above, p. 117.
4. *Ex*, 333.
5. Kuch, *Yeats and AE*, 108–9.
6. *LTWBY*, i, 23–4.

7. Who was led astray by 'some memory of something I had told him about a certain Austrian count' (20 July 1896, *CL*, ii, 41–2). This indicates that Pollexfen's horoscopes relied upon more than astrological input.

8. To AG, 10 Dec. 1897, *CL*, ii, 155–6.

9. See Warwick Gould's reconstruction to this relationship in *YA* 9 (1992), 134–88.

10. Where on 22 June 1896 he entertained Havelock Ellis and Arthur Symons; on 3 Jan. 1898, Osman Edwards, Sarojini Chattopadhyay, Florence Farr, Arthur Symons and Dorothea Hunter.

11. See letter to Clement Shorter, 24 Mar. 1896, *CL*, ii, 16–17, and his refusal two years later to do a study of Tennyson for William Blackwood – who was told severely that it should be done 'by someone who has grown up among English people & English scenery', not among 'the lean kine of a Celtic country'. (11 Mar. 1898, *CL*, ii, 197).

12. 26 May 1896, *CL*, ii, 31.

13. And a 20 per cent royalty after 2,500 copies. See 'Agreement' in MBY dated 23 Dec. 1896; but negotiations had begun some time before. Gould and Toomey believe the contract postdates some or all of the payments in advance. The novel was being discussed by the Yeats family at least as early as Apr. 1896. These terms were inaccurately recapitulated by WBY in a letter to Fisher Unwin, 20 Dec. 1900, HRHRC. *IGE* eventually replaced the unfinished novel, to earn the outstanding £50.

14. Draft of *Dramatis Personae*, Harvard.

15. See *CL*, ii, 46–7.

16. n.d., but probably 1896, Yale.

17. Symons MSS, Princeton.

18. Gifford Lewis, *The Selected Letters of Somerville and Ross* (London, 1989), 240.

19. 23 Aug. 1907, Alan Himber (ed.), with the assistance of George Mills Harper, *The Letters of John Quinn to William Butler Yeats* (Ann Arbor, 1983), 84.

20. Lewis, *Letters of Somerville and Ross*, 240.

21. To Horace Reynolds, 15 June 1936, Harvard.

22. See a letter of *c.* 1906, Berg. 'Edward is a joy – and will give you new notes for your diary. These Papists haven't the courage of a mouse, and then wonder how it is we go ahead.' The 'diary' was probably a draft of *Discoveries*. See below, p. 346.

23. Joseph Hone, 'I Remember Lady Gregory', RTE radio talk, broadcast 14 Mar. 1956, Kansas. The authority was a niece of Aubrey de Vere, probably Annie Cole (for whom see Pethica 26, n. 9).

24. A long-lasting Gort legend had it that Robert was fathered, by arrangement, by the local blacksmith, who was later assisted to emigrate to America. The blacksmith, known as 'Seanín [Little John] Farrell', was – like Robert – of notably small stature.

25. 17 Mar. 1892, Gregory family MSS, Emory.

26. To WBY [Nov. 1898], from Venice, and fragment [Christmas 1900], Berg.

27. Arnold Harvey to Bishop Wyse Jackson, 15 Jan. 1964, recalling his life at Coole as Robert Gregory's tutor, Berg.

28. Pethica, 118. 'E. Martyn had also poets with him, Symonds [*sic*] and Yeats – the latter full of charm & interest & the Celtic revival – I have been collecting fairy lore since his visit –' Their first meeting is recorded in her diary, 14 Apr. 1894, Berg. 'At the Morrises I met Yates [*sic*] looking every inch a poet, though I think his prose "The Celtic Twilight" is the best thing he has done.'

29. See the poems in *Images of Good and Evil* (1899), written in Ireland. Symons also produced at Rosses Point the 'Preface' to the second edition of *London Nights*, which declares, 'I contend on behalf of the liberty of art, and I deny that morals have any right of jurisdiction over it.'

30. See Thuente, *Yeats and Irish Folklore*, 235ff. WBY's articles appeared in *New Review*, Nov.

1897; *Nineteenth Century*, Jan. 1898; *Fortnightly Review*, Sept. 1900 and Apr. 1902. *Visions and Beliefs* would include his 'Witches and Wizards and Irish Folklore' and 'Swedenborg, Mediums, and the Desolate Places', written in 1914. He was still referring to the project as 'a big book of folk lore' in a letter of 22 Dec. to AG.

31. *YA* 9 (1992), 7.

32. See *UP*, ii, 299, 327–8.

33. *Au*, 400.

34. cf. Russell's interesting letter to AG when *Visions and Beliefs* was finally published. '. . . not all dreams are explicable by material causes or are even traceable to suppressed desires as the psychologists would have them . . . I think it a great pity we have no sympathetic psychologist questioning these people. Wentz was not subtle enough, and W. B. Yeats who is subtle has not I think your way of being intimate with the folk you allure to confidence.' (9 Sept. 1920., Berg). See *UP*, ii, 221–2, for a good circumstantial account of how AG and WBY collected folklore, in 'Irish Witch Doctors', *Fortnightly Review*, Sept. 1900.

35. Elizabeth Coxhead, *Lady Gregory: A Literary Portrait* (rev. ed., London, 1966), 41.

36. *TB*, 14.

37. In George Mills Harper and W. K. Hood, *A Critical Edition of Yeats's 'A Vision' (1925)* (London, 1978) she appears anonymously in Phase 24 as 'a certain friend' and is profiled quite recognizably (103–4). In the 1937 version, published after her death, she is named. Also see his 'Modern Ireland: An Address to American Audiences 1932–3', edited by Curtis Bradford, in Robin Shelton and David R. Clark (eds.), *Irish Renaissance* (a special number of the *Massachusetts Review*, Dublin, 1965), 16, for a direct assertion that AG had 'no philosophical interests'.

38. Nov. 1897, Pethica, 151.

39. 'Statement by LG to JQ', Quinn papers, NYPL, recording a conversation in 1913. Also see *YA* 9 (1992), 71. In fact WBY went to Belfast in Sept. 1899 with money from the *North American Review*.

40. Pethica, 197.

41. See D. J. O'Donoghue, *Irish Independent*, 26 Mar. 1909.

42. To Sharp, 4 July [1898], *CL*, ii, 250. In *Au*, WBY puts this instruction in 1899, three years after their meeting. For a full consideration and further references, see my 'Good Behaviour: Yeats, Synge and Anglo-Irish Etiquette', *Paddy and Mr Punch*.

43. To Fiona Macleod, [?12] Jan. 1897, *CL*, ii, 75.

44. *Mem*, 89. See Harwood, *Shakespear and Yeats*, for a close deconstruction of this memory.

45. 'VN': my thanks to Warwick Gould and Deirdre Toomey for their transcription.

46. *Au*, 376–7.

47. The phrase comes from an important letter to Richard Ashe King, 5 Aug. 1897, *CL*, ii, 130. This belief is constantly expressed by him in different ways, even when at his most 'political' (see his letter about Ashe King's speech to the National Literary Society, *United Ireland*, 30 Dec. 1893, *CL*, i, 371–4).

48. See Symons's 'In Sligo', *Savoy*, 7 (Nov. 1896), for an account of a Rosses Point pilot called Redmond Bruen. Jack Yeats remembered 'all the Bruens', *YA* 11 (1994), 99.

49. *SB*, 120.

50. *SB*, 127.

51. 1925 Introduction; draft (in the form of a letter to Ashe King) is in NLI MS 30,372. 'Rosa Alchemica' was started in Fountain Court and completed in Woburn Buildings, which fixes it as late 1895 or early 1896.

52. 19 Mar. 1896, *CL*, ii, 15.

53. *Au*, 376. See also Marjorie Reeves and Warwick Gould, *Joachim of Fiore and the Myth of the Eternal Evangel in the Nineteenth Century* (Oxford, 1987), 236.

54. See Thuente, *Yeats and Irish Folklore*, 22–3, for an associated point.

55. *UP*, ii, 52; see also Reeves and Gould, *Joachim of Fiore*, 222–3.

56. Thuente, *Yeats and Irish Folklore*, 219–20.

57. The life of Saint-Martin (1743–1803) was written by A. E. Waite; the Martinist leader in the 1890s was Gerard Encausse, known as 'Papus'.

58. 'Mescal: A New Artificial Paradise', *Contemporary Review*, June 1898. Symons, who took a more spectacular trip, was another guinea-pig.

59. See WBY's letter to the *Speaker*, 18 May 1897.

60. 30 May 1897, *CL*, ii, 104.

61. The first instance was 14 Feb. 1897, Pethica, 125.

62. Pethica, 136. Plunkett's diary for 21 Mar. 1897 (Plunkett Foundation, Oxford) recorded that he 'met Yates [*sic*] the new Irish poet and Barry O'Brien & had a most interesting symposium on Ireland. My fellow guests told me they and many others like them had agreed that I was the only possible Irish leader.'

63. 16 Mar. 1897, *CL*, ii, 82.

64. See report of meeting of '98 Centenary Committee in London, *United Ireland*, 10 Apr. 1897. F. H. O'Donnell excoriated the unrepresentative (i.e. non-Fenian) committee in Dublin, and the London delegates (WBY, Ryan, O'Donnell) 'refused to surrender the right and authority of their central body to organise England, Scotland and France'. O'Donnell was simultaneously involved in a row over his review of O'Leary's *Recollections* in the *Athenaeum*, which may have begun WBY's estrangement from his old mentor.

65. Such as 'The Desire of Man and Woman' in the *Dome*, June 1897 (later 'He mourns for the change that has come upon him and his Beloved, and longs for the End of the World'); he was working on a proof in Sligo.

66. Pethica, 156. His letter to Sharp himself, 20 Nov. 1897, was masterly, asking him to give way to Martyn: 'Little things, like taking the Chair & so on, which mean nothing to you & me mean something to a man like him, a man who is not very young & not at all successful.' (*CL*, ii, 149).

67. To Robert Bridges, 6 June 1897, *CL*, ii, 110.

68. 25 May 1897, *CL*, ii, 101–2.

69. See *Irish Times*, 21–2 June 1897, which plays down the violence; but ensuing correspondence makes clear it was considerable.

70. From Tillyra, 30 June [1897], *CL*, ii, 117. See also Pethica, 148; meeting AG just afterwards, WBY said that 'by main force & lock & key' he kept MG inside. '– he himself disapproved of it – not because of disrespect for the Queen for he thinks it was right to make some protest against the unhappy misgovernment & misfortunes of Ireland during her reign – but that he thinks the impulse shd come from the <mob> people themselves, & not be thrust on them from above –'

71. *G–YL*, 72–3.

72. Margaret Ward, *Maud Gonne: Ireland's Joan of Arc* (London, 1990), 47.

73. *Mem*, 101. This conflates these impressions with his 1896 Tillyra visit, but certainly refers to 1897.

74. John Masefield, *Some Memories of W. B. Yeats* (New York, 1940), 21.

75. According to a letter from Russell to AG, 16 July 1898, Berg.

76. *Mem*, 102.

77. 16 July 1898, Berg. Also see a letter of 5 July 1901: 'Lock him up. Treat him as the [Balearics?] did their children. No work no breakfast.'

78. See below, pp. 282–3.

79. *Mem*, 72, 125.

80. Pethica, 149–50.

81. *Mem*, 117. Pethica, 152–3, recalls taking WBY into the estate office at Duras '& there we had tea & talked, & the idea came to us that if "Maeve" could be acted in Dublin, instead

of London as E. M. thought of – & with Yeats "Countess Kathleen" it would be a development of the literary movement & help to restore dignity to Ireland.'

82. This last clause was probably added by AG when filing the draft for her archives. It is now in Berg and must precede the version AG remembered typing out from dictation. The typed copy has additional signatories – Standish O'Grady, Edward Martyn, George Moore and Fiona Macleod. This is significant; in Jan. he had sounded out Macleod and O'Grady about Celtic plays for the Young Ireland Societies and shared the idea with AG in Feb.

83. 28 Apr. 1899, Berg.

84. See WBY to AG, 24 Oct. 1898, *CL*, ii, 277. WBY later realized that the concept of 'Celticism' was bogus through reading an article by Andrew Lang.

85. *I & R*, i, 15–19, quoting Cornelius Weygandt.

86. WBY to AG, 17 Nov. 1897, *CL*, ii, 144–5.

87. 22 Jan. 1898, *CL*, ii, 175.

88. 17 Nov. 1897, *CL*, ii, 144–5.

89. See his letters to AG, 13–14 June 1898, *CL*, ii, 236–8.

90. *Mem*, 131.

91. See Warwick Gould's article on Dorothea Hunter, *YA* 9 (1992), 132–88.

92. 'The Gifts of Aodh and Una' in *Ballads in Prose*, singled out by WBY in the *Bookman*, Aug. 1895, and *Daily Express*, Dublin, 24 Sept. 1898 (*UP*, i, 366; *UP*, ii, 126–7).

93. *UP*, ii, 70–71.

94. Letter accompanying 'Black Pig' sketch, n.d. [29 Nov. 1987], Emory, quoted by R. Schuchard in *YA* 3 (1985), 155; see below, p. 192.

95. *United Ireland*, 11 Dec. 1897: possibly by F. H. O'Donnell.

96. Letter of Dec. 1897, Berg.

97. AG to Lord Gough, 3 May 1898, Gregory family MSS, Emory. She was also the presiding genius behind a show of Jack's in May 1898.

98. WBY recollected that Jack gave it to him; but a letter dated 'Sat. 5th' from AG to WBY, Berg, remarks: 'I wrote to Hugh Lane about Memory Harbour & he went to Guildhall & asked it to be sent to Woburn Buildings.' The painting is reproduced on the front endpaper of this book.

99. 10 Dec. 1897, *CL*, ii, 155.

100. See 'A Poet at Home: A Pen Portrait of Mr Yeats', the *Gael*, 20, 1 (Jan. 1901), and Reginald Hine, 'Memories of W. B. Yeats', TS, HRHRC. The leather chair features in the draft poem to MG, below, pp. 238–9. Also see John Masefield, *Some Memories of W. B. Yeats*, and Richardson, as above, p. 161 – though she thought the art-serge curtains were dark green and the candles white.

101. 10 Apr. 1900, *CL*, ii, 511.

102. 11 Aug. 1898, *CL*, ii, 260.

103. See Russell to AG, 31 May 1902, Berg. York Powell had written worriedly to Russell.

104. Pethica, 217.

105. 'Thursday', probably 1898, Berg.

106. *UP*, ii, 219, for an account.

107. 'Monday', possibly 1901, Berg.

108. 25 Mar. 1898, *CL*, ii, 204.

109. 29 May 1898.

110. 3 Oct. 1897, *CL*, ii, 135.

111. NLI MS 30,502, quoted in *CL*, ii, appendix.

112. See letter to *FJ*, 5 Mar. 1897.

113. See e.g. *United Ireland*, 13 Mar. 1897.

114. NLI MS 30,502.

115. To Russell, 10 Dec. 1897, *CL*, ii, 153. The quarrels concerned the rivalries between the Centenary Committees; arguments over Sharp's chairing an ILS meeting; and a wrangle with Elkin Mathews over the American rights to *The Wind Among the Reeds*.

116. Pethica, 161.

117. Ó Broin, *Revolutionary Underground*, 91. The PRO records claim that Mark Ryan had got $10,000 (£2,000) from the INA in America in Jan. 1898 – probably an exaggeration of MG's collection.

118. To Russell, 22 Jan. 1898, *CL*, ii, 176.

119. To AG, 23 Jan. 1898, *CL*, ii, 178.

120. 7 Feb. 1898, Berg.

121. Of which Mark Ryan was Treasurer and G. Lavelle Secretary: *United Ireland*, 5 Jan. 1898.

122. Pethica, 177.

123. Mark Ryan, *Fenian Memories*, edited with an introduction by T. F. O'Sullivan (2nd ed., Dublin, 1946), 185–6. He incorrectly dates it as 20 Mar., but see *FJ*, 14 Mar. 1898, for a report.

124. *'98 Centennial Association of Great Britain and France: Report of Speeches Delivered at the Inaugural Banquet Held at the Holborn Restaurant, London, on Wednesday, 15 April 1898* (Dublin, 1898).

125. Pethica, 167.

126. To AG, 18 May 1898, *CL*, ii, 228. See also obsessive letters from the Matherses (28 Mar. 1898, 6 Apr. 1898, 31 Oct. 1898).

127. 8 June 1898, *CL*, ii, 234.

128. To AG, 8 July 1898, Berg.

129. To JMS, 21 June 1898, *CLJMS*, i, 26–7.

130. To SMY, 11 July 1898, *CL*, ii, 251–3. Pethica, 187.

131. To AG, 11–12 Aug. 1898, *CL*, ii, 259. This was the Reverend H. M. Kennedy, Vicar of Plumpton: see Ryan, *Fenian Memories*, 186–7, who locates this occasion at the Frascati Restaurant, Oxford Street, on 9 Aug. It is reported in *FJ*, 10 Aug. There were delegates from South Africa, France, America and Australia; the toast 'Ireland a Nation' was proposed by Lionel Johnson, 'The Men of 98' by J. F. Taylor. WBY chaired a meeting addressed by MG in St Martin's Hall the next day, assembling many of the same people. There were further demonstrations in Dublin on 13 and 15 Aug. AG had herself spoken at the celebration of 12 Mar. (see *Tuam Herald*, 12 Mar. 1898), recommending tree-planting as a safe form of commemorating revolutionary heroes.

132. WBY stressed the warmth of her reception to Sharp, 22 Aug. [1898], *CL*, ii, 264. For a report of his speech, see *FJ*, 16 Aug. 1898. England could not 'settle the Irish question with a handful of alms . . . this movement sprung [*sic*] from the hearth of the people like smoke from the inextinguishable fire of patriotism which burned within their hearts for ever.' For a full account, *CL*, ii, 261, n. 3.

133. Ó Broin, *Revolutionary Underground*, 94–5.

134. To Russell, 27 Mar. 1898, *CL*, ii, 205.

135. Berg.

136. See *Sketch*, 28 Apr. 1897, and 'Le Mouvement Celtique: Fiona Macleod', *Irlande Libre*, 1 Apr. 1898 (*UP*, ii, 108–10).

137. e.g. postmarked. 13 Jul. 1900, 8 Aug. 1900, Berg.

138. To AG, 5 Aug. 1900, Berg. By 1901 they were at each other's throats in the *All Ireland Review*.

139. 5 May 1898, Yale.

140. To WBY from Venice, n.d., but probably Dec. 1898, Berg.

141. See letter to AG, 1 June 1898, *CL*, ii, 230–32.
142. See Rolleston to WBY, 1 July 1898, Kansas, and letters in Berg, June–Aug. 1899.
143. See also a letter to Sharp, 1 Nov. 1898, *CL*, ii, 284–5, relating this 'controversy' to the preparation of public opinion for the theatre.
144. Russell to WBY, n.d., but 1896.
145. Berg. She reported this letter to WBY. Also see *CL*, ii, 289–90, 294–303.
146. n.d., Berg.
147. 13 Oct. 1898, misquoted in *LTWBY*, i, 41. Another contact was Edmund Gosse; they dined at his house on 9 Jan. 1898.
148. Letters of 28 Oct. 1898, 24 Nov. 1898. For the description of 'Ulick's' rooms, see *Evelyn Innes* (1898 version, pub. by Fisher Unwin), 300–303.
149. Both quotations from JBY to AG, 29 July 1898, W. M. Murphy (ed.), *Letters from Bedford Park: A Selection from the Correspondence (1890–1901) of John Butler Yeats* (Dublin, 1972), 41–2.
150. 24 Nov. 1898, *LTWBY*, i, 45.
151. To AG, 5 June 1900, *CL*, ii, 537. Actually it was Mirabeau.
152. *Beltaine*, 1899: a message also preached in his letter to Ashe King, 5 Aug. 1897, *CL*, ii, 129–30.

Chapter 8 : SHADOWY WATERS
1898–1900

Epigraph: *Winged Destiny* (London, 1910), 329.

1. 6 Dec. 1898, *CL*, ii, 312–13.
2. 8 Dec. 1898, *CL*, ii, 314.
3. See 'VN', 1.30 a.m., 7 Dec.
4. See Mary K. Greer, *Women of the Golden Dawn* (Rochester, 1995), 215.
5. 15 Dec. 1898, *CL*, ii, 320.
6. *YA* 9 (1992), 120–22.
7. Ryan, *Fenian Memories*, 192. MG later addressed it as an occasional lecturer, but in 1899 neither she nor WBY took any part.
8. See occult notebook, MBY. Druids, mountains, the cauldron, wands, the stone of the Dagda, Elathan, Lugh all feature.
9. Postmarked 16 Dec., *CL*, ii, 319–20.
10. She wrote to Enid Layard: 'I am afraid she is only playing with him, from selfishness and vanity . . . I don't wish her any harm, but God is unjust if she dies a quiet death.' (Mary-Lou Kohfeldt, *Lady Gregory: The Woman behind the Irish Renaissance*, London, 1985, 130).
11. Reflected in *The Tower* as well as in the material for *AV*.
12. *G–YL*, 99–100.
13. 26 Dec. 1898, *CL*, ii, 330.
14. *CL*, ii, 329, n. 5.
15. Berg.
16. Postmarked 10 Jan. 1899, Berg. For 'Elathan' see also *G–YL*, 102.
17. See below, pp. 206–8.
18. *La Croix*, 17 Apr. 1897.
19. 9 Feb. 1899.
20. 24 Feb. 1899, MBY, quoted in *LTWBY*, i, 46–7.
21. See *Daily Express*, Dublin, 10 Jan. 1899, reporting the ILS 'At Home' on 9 Jan.
22. WBY particularly wooed Lecky, hoping that he would agree to read Lionel Johnson's prologue to *The Countess Cathleen*.

23. On Gill, see Russell to AG, 10 Jan. 1899, Berg.
24. 11 Mar. (*UP*, ii, 148–52).
25. *United Irishman*, 11 Mar. 1899.
26. JBY to AG, 11 Apr. 1899, Berg.
27. *YA* 7 (1990), 91.
28. For a full contemporary account, see Pethica, 219–20.
29. Russell to AG, 7 Apr. 1899, Berg.
30. *Irish Literary Society Gazette*, i, 4 (June 1899); also *UP*, ii, 153–8.
31. For the earlier attacks, see 'The Future of the Irish Nation', *New Ireland Review*, Feb. 1899. 'A certain number of Irish literary men have "made a market" – just as stock-jobbers do in another commodity – in a certain vague thing, which is indistinctly known as "the Celtic note" in English literature, and they earn their fame and livelihood by supplying the demand which they have honourably and with much advertising created.' This is an attack on WBY's 'The Celtic Element in Literature'.
32. Given to the National Literary Society on 6 May and published on that date in *Literature* (*UP*, ii, 162–4), but also reported in *FJ* on 8 May.
33. *Recollections of Dublin Castle and Dublin Society, by a Native* (London, 1902), 3–4. It later became the Academy Cinema.
34. The changes are preserved in WBY's 1899 copy in the Huntingdon. Also see Colin Smythe, 'The Countess Cathleen: A Note', *YA* 3 (1985), 193–7, and details of revisions in *CL*, ii, 669–80.
35. He had seen a draft of Moore's 'Edward Martyn and his Soul', NLI MS 30,502.
36. *United Irishman*, 15 Apr. 1899.
37. *A Pseudo Celtic Drama in Dublin*: a copy is preserved in Henderson's cuttings book, NLI MS 1729. This and *Souls for Gold* appeared as separate letters in the *FJ* and were amalgamated as a pamphlet printed by the Nassau Press in London. *Souls for Gold* is conveniently reproduced as Appendix VIII in AG's *Our Irish Theatre: A Chapter of Autobiography* (Gerrards Cross, 1972 ed.), 261–70, and fully discussed in *CL*, ii, 669–80.
38. 1 May 1899, Berg.
39. Robert Hogan and James Kilroy, *The Irish Literary Theatre 1899–1901* (Dublin, 1975), 39.
40. *CL*, ii, 395.
41. In 1911 there were plans to turn it into an opera by means of a Franco Leoni score, designs by Gordon Craig, and the contralto of Clara Butt: see below, p. 440.
42. *c.* 1 May 1899, *CL*, ii, 406.
43. Recently produced work included *Wolfe Tone*, *The Irishman*, and much Boucicault.
44. Apart from some sour English critics: *The Times* thought 'it says a great deal for the acting that *The Heather Field* is endurable on the stage at all' (Hogan and Kilroy, *Irish Literary Theatre*, 48).
45. Berg.
46. *Daily Express*, Dublin, 15 May 1899.
47. Cave, *Hail and Farewell*, 128.
48. *United Irishman*, 20 May 1899; cf. James Joyce's later disapproval.
49. 'A Literary Dinner', by 'Cugaun' [Griffith], *United Irishman*, 20 May 1899.
50. 10 May 1899.
51. Hogan and Kilroy, *Irish Literary Theatre*, 39. For the student point of view, see C. P. Curran, *Under the Receding Wave* (Dublin, 1967), Chapter 6. James Joyce was, famously, a non-signatory.
52. See 1 Apr. 1899. For Ryan's critique of Griffith's anti-Semitism, see 26 Aug. 1899. The paper also nurtured an early cult of Wolfe Tone (1 July 1899, 5 July 1899, 12 Aug. 1899, 26 Aug. 1899) and advocated the cause of old Fenians in search of Corporation sinecures,

like Tom Clarke (who failed, despite the *United Irishman*'s vehement endorsement, to be elected Clerk of the Rathdrum Union (30 Sept. 1899) or Supervisor of the Abbatoir (16 Oct. 1900).

53. 'F.A.C.' to *United Irishman*, 19 Aug. 1899.

54. 13 May 1899.

55. Sketch for continuation of *Au*, NLI MS 30,502.

56. Possibly imbibed through John Gray as well as Havelock Ellis: see McCormack, *John Gray: Poet, Dandy and Priest*. But the major source was Ellis: see Reeves and Gould, *Joachim of Fiore*, 238–9.

57. 22 May 1899, *CL*, ii, 416.

58. 20 July 1898, Berg. He had mentioned the title in an 1893 interview; see also above, Chapter 6, n. 47. Also see Symons, 'In Sligo', *Savoy*, 7 (Nov. 1896): 'There is always a sighing of wind in the reeds, as of a very gentle and melancholy peace.'

59. Many were written in a bound MS book dated 29 Aug. 1893, discussed in detail by Curtis Bradford in *Yeats at Work* (Carbondale, 1965). A note of the title was recorded opposite a draft of 'The Host of the Air', now available in an edition by Carolyn Holdsworth, '*The Wind Among the Reeds': Manuscript Materials* (Ithaca and London, 1993).

60. Postmarked 22 Apr. 1899, Berg.

61. *CH*, 108.

62. To AG, 24 Apr. 1899, *CL*, ii, 400. Actually the comparison was to the less celebrated Egil Skalla-Grimson, a medieval Icelandic poet whom WBY himself had mentioned in *CT*.

63. 6 May 1899, *CH*, 109–13.

64. Preface to *Poems* (2nd ed.), dated 24 Feb. 1899.

65. Correspondence with Symons in MBY shows he accepted payments of £2 and these prices were not outstanding: John Davidson got £25 for a poem in 1896.

66. 11 June [1899], *CL*, ii, 422. Also see *United Irishman*, 17 Feb. 1900, and review on 10 July 1900.

67. 12 July 1899, *CL*, ii, 433.

68. Russell's letters to AG (Emory) contain many references to this.

69. 27 Aug. 1899, *CL*, ii, 443.

70. 'VN', as transcribed by Gould and Toomey.

71. To William D. Fitts, 19 Aug. 1899, *CL*, ii, 439.

72. To AG, 12 Oct. 1899, Berg.

73. 21 June 1899, Berg.

74. To JBY, 11 Aug. [1899]. Dunleavy and Dunleavy insist that Lucy Hyde's first visit to Coole came later, but WBY to Clodd, 27 July [1899], confirms Hyde's 1899 visit, and they were at a Gort meeting on the same date (reported *Daily Express*, Dublin, 31 July 1899).

75. *Daily Express*, Dublin, 31 July 1899, reporting a meeting of 27 July; also *An Claidheamh Soluis*, 29 July 1899. The Kiltartan Gaelic League was founded on 16 July.

76. Hyde later begged MacNeill not to let *An Claidheamh* attack the Irish Literary Theatre: 'They are not enemies to us. They are a half-way house.' (Janet Egelson Dunleavy and Gareth W. Dunleavy, *Douglas Hyde: A Maker of Modern Ireland* (Oxford, 1991), 207).

77. 3 June 1899.

78. See especially issues of 10 June 1899, and nearly every week thereafter. The leaders on 1 and 8 July were particularly violent attacks on Anglo-Ireland.

79. *c.* 30 Sept. 1899, *CL*, ii, 454.

80. See Moore to AG, 7 Nov. 1899, Berg.

81. Cave, *Hail and Farewell*, 212–13. See also Moore to AG, 'Monday night' [7 Nov. 1899], from the Shelbourne Hotel (Berg), for an indication of WBY's involvement: 'I beg you to save me from further emendations from our friend. I am sure that they will be excellent but my sanity must be considered. Today I sent him the fifth act and the first scene

of the second – this scene is intended to balance the first scene of the fifth act. I was a little disappointed that he did not like the fourth letter. It was impossible for me to write a new situation but I trust that by a judicious turn I kept what situation there was. The play no longer ends in the fourth act and the structure of the act is I think good . . . I hope that you will get him to write about the fifth act but no emendatering [*sic*]. I want him to write The Shadowy Waters. If he could only finish it. It would be finished by now if it had not been for Martyn's play.'

82. To AG, 28 Nov. 1899, *CL*, ii, 474.

83. To AG, 21–2 Dec. 1899, *CL*, ii, 480.

84. 2 June 1900, *CL*, ii, 534–5.

85. W. R. Rodgers, 'Notes for the Radio', MS notebook in HRHRC.

86. *G–YL*, 114.

87. *FJ*, 18 Dec. 1899. The meeting was precipitated by Trinity's award of an honorary degree to Joseph Chamberlain. It took place on 17 Dec. and was boycotted by nationalist MPs; there was a large police presence, defied by Connolly, who commandeered the demonstrators' vehicle and suggested storming Dublin Castle to MG (she uncharacteristically demurred).

88. *United Irishman*, 23 Dec. 1898.

89. See Donal McCracken, *The Irish Pro-Boers 1877–1902* (Johannesburg, 1989), 77, for reports to Leyds, probably from O'Donnell; these events climaxed in Mar. 1900.

90. See *PF*, 215–17, and Deirdre Toomey, 'Away', *YA* 10 (1993), 3–32: an exceptionally illuminating essay.

91. 20 May 1900, *CL*, ii, 530.

92. To AG, 4 Jan. 1900, *CL*, ii, 485–6.

93. JBY to Rosa Butt, postmarked 3 Feb. 1900, Bodleian: 'Yesterday I was much bothered over a speech I wanted to make last night. Two days before I had gone to see Willie and read him some notes of what I had meant to say, and he had rather treated me de haut en bas, irritating me muchly, so I was very anxious to make a good speech. *And I did*. No mistake about it. I said to myself: "I am a Papa struggling to maintain my position", so I threw away all false modesty and spoke out with all my might, saying what I thought.'

Chapter 9 : OCCULT POLITICS
1900–1901

Epigraph: *CL*, iii, 40

1. AG to WBY, [?25] Nov. 1899, Berg. He left Moore the rights to both plays in his will.

2. Pethica, 231.

3. 'Wednesday', n.d., HRHRC. For possible models in the play, see Pethica, 244.

4. WBY to AG, 31 Jan. 1900, *CL*, ii, 492–3.

5. A journey described in Cave, *Hail and Farewell*, 234–5, and Pethica, 240–41.

6. Cancelled phrase in WBY to AG, 30 Sept. 1899, Berg; see *CL*, ii, 455.

7. 18 Feb. 1900, Berg.

8. 24 Feb. 1900, written by Griffith, not Fay.

9. Pethica, 236.

10. *Daily Express*, Dublin, 23 Feb. 1900.

11. An agreement outlined in Martyn to WBY, 31 Mar. 1899, NLI MS 13,068.

12. Pethica, 246–7.

13. See *G–YL*, 116, for the 1899 incident.

14. Leyds Archives, quoted in McCracken, *Irish Pro-Boers*, 77; the correspondent may be O'Donnell, playing a deep game. The original, in French, reads:

La 'Demoiselle à Milllevoye' est venue chez notre directeur, toute furieuese de n'avoir pas reçu ce qu'elle demandait. Elle était accompagnée d'un nommé Yeats, qu'on dit d'être le dernier successeur de Millevoye, et *devant ce jeune homme, elle a dit tout ce qu'elle avait entendu chez vous*, et encore . . . Elle déclarait que vous aviez dit d'être en communication avec des révolutionnaires irlandais 'par l'entremise d'une personne qui n'appartenait à leur organisation'!!! Sans doute, avant 24 heures le Tout Dublin saura qu'elle n'a eu pas de succès parceque, et parceque, et parceque, etc. etc.

Si elle n'est pas espionne, elle l'est presque, et sa vantardise est plus dangereuse que la trahison même.

Excepté parmi le petit peuple, elle a la réputation la plus detestable. On met en circulation des histoires de 'trois enfants en nourrice a Paris', mais elle se montre partout dans nos Meetings, et nous sommes obligés de la souffrir. Mais on ne peut pas être trop prudent quand elle est près.

15. *United Irishman*, 9 Dec. 1899.
16. See above, pp. 179, 194.
17. *United Irishman*, 24 Mar. 1900: F. H. O'Donnell again. See also ibid., 3 Mar. 1900. The paper printed frequent interviews with MacBride as well as hand-outs of his portrait.
18. Pethica, 258.
19. 10 Apr. 1900. cf. article in *Samhain*, quoted below.
20. 5 June 1900, *CL*, ii, 537.
21. *United Irishman*, 15 July 1899, 23 Sept. 1899, 17 Feb. 1900; *Leader*, 23 Dec. 1899.
22. To T. P. Gill, *CL*, ii, 574.
23. 27 May 1900, *CL*, ii, 526–7. For the dealings with Boer agents and confusions about money, see above.
24. To AG, 28 June 1900, *CL*, ii, 549–50.
25. See *United Irishman*, 7 July 1900, 'What We Owe to the Children' by MG, and accompanying reports. MG's figure of 30,000 children attending her anti-loyalist picnic is generally accepted; but it was a mechanical calculation made by the faithful *United Irishman*. 35,000 children were attending school in Dublin; 5,000 were at institutions like the Masonic Schools, which supported the rival Queen's Breakfast; therefore 30,000 were supposed to attend the Patriotic Treat, which was reported accordingly.
26. *G–Y L*, 129–30. He was at Coole by 2 July.
27. See *VPl*, 81ff.; it begins Scene III.
28. He did, however, believe in the authenticity of the inspirational cipher MS, which had actually been drafted by Kenneth Mackenzie using a sixteenth-century cipher code, and subsequently appropriated by Westcott. See R. A. Gilbert in *YA* 13 (forthcoming); and 'Provenance Unknown: A Tentative Solution to the Riddle of the Cipher Manuscript of the Golden Dawn' in Albrecht Gotz von Olenhausen (ed.) with the assistance of Nicholas Barker, Herbert Francke and Helmut Moller, *Wege und Abwege: Beiträge zur Europäischen Geistesgeschichte der Neuzeit: Festschrift für Ellic Howe zum 20 September 1990* (Freiburg, 1990).
29. 2 May 1900, *CL*, ii, 524.
30. *CL*, iii, 26–7.
31. To AG, 9 Dec. 1900, *CL*, ii, 597.
32. As John Dunn. See *SB*, 192ff., especially 195.
33. *SB*, 200.
34. See Warwick Gould, 'Playing at Treason with Miss Maud Gonne', *Modernist Writers and the Marketplace* (London, 1996).
35. To W. J. Stanton Pyper, 22 Dec. 1900, *CL*, ii, 617; also see WBY to Fisher Unwin, 18 Nov. 1900, *CL*, ii, 591, demanding an increase in royalties and a fixed-term contract for three or four years at most.
36. WBY to Fisher Unwin, 20 Dec. 1900, *CL*, ii, 612–13, details the books which Bullen might part with – *SR*, *CT*, *The Tables of the Law*, and advance rights on *SB*. There were, he

admitted, many unsold copies of *SR* and possibly *CT*. On 7 May 1901 he told Gregory, 'I have arranged with Watt that henceforth he will take full responsibility as to who I publish with. I am to say "I have handed over all my affairs to him" & so escape the difficulty of [*sic*] caused by ones personal relations with publishers.' (*CL*, iii, 67).

37. To AG, 9 Dec. 1900, *CL*, ii, 597–8.

38. A worry originating a year before: see WBY to Rolleston, 6 Aug. 1899, *CL*, ii, 436.

39. By Moran. See 19 June 1900. The ostensible target was the ILS.

40. Report in *An Claidheamh Soluis*, 27 Oct. 1900.

41. To AG, 6 June 1900, *CL*, ii, 539. 'Echtge of Streams' was offered to John Lane on 13 Aug.; it used some of the images from the unpublished 'Cycles Ago': see above, p. 116.

42. 2 May 1900, *CL*, ii, 522.

43. *Independent*, 31 Aug. 1900. This was a pet cause of AG's: see her article in *An Claidheamh Soluis*, 14 Oct. 1899.

44. The letter to the *Leader* mentioned above (written 26 Aug., printed 1 Sept.) called for 'an intellectual and historical nationalism like that of Norway, with the language question as its lever', rather than 'purely political nationalism' – the straight Hyde line. Yet, as usual, WBY also argued for the validity of Irish national expression through the English language.

45. To SMY, 1 Nov. 1899, *CL*, ii, 461. See also Moore's letters to WBY in MBY.

46. The following quotations are taken from undated Moore letters in the Berg.

47. 13 Oct. 1900. In Aug. Moore had thought of taking WBY off to Moore Hall to finish it: Moore to AG, 11 Aug. 1900, Berg.

48. WBY to AG, 25 Dec. 1900, *CL*, ii, 619.

49. To Symons, 17 Nov. 1900, *CL*, ii, 588–9.

50. To AG, 2 and 25 Dec. 1900, *CL*, ii, 594–5, 618–21.

51. To AG, 25 Dec. 1900, *CL*, ii, 619.

52. WBY to John Masefield, 6 Dec. 1900, *CL*, ii, 596. Masefield first went to Woburn Buildings on 5 Nov., according to *Some Memories of W. B. Yeats*, 10. However, the untitled TS draft in HRHRC has 11 Nov., and Pethica, 287, fixed it as the 12th.

53. WBY to AG, 12 and 20 Dec. 1900, *CL*, ii, 603–4, 609–10; also typed copy of letter to Law, 16 Mar. 1901, MBY, which argues for the principle of tolerance and offers WBY's own resignation from the committee. In this letter he attacked the Society's patronage of Edward Carson and F. H. O'Donnell. It is an important statement.

54. See *CL*, ii, 457, n. 1, 552, n. 1.

55. Angle brackets indicate deletions. The original is in WBY's 1893 notebook of poems, 129–32, undated. I have followed Carolyn Holdsworth's transcription in '*The Wind Among the Reeds': Manuscript Materials*, except for the penultimate line, where I read 'wood' instead of 'crowd', as does Richard Ellmann, whose transcription of the original is in Tulsa.

56. To W. S. Pyper, 22 Dec. 1900, *CL*, ii, 617–18.

57. 'A Prophecy', 11 Nov. 1899; she later imported some of this material into *The Unicorn from the Stars*.

58. Though WBY believed some Fenians voted for him; see an interesting letter to AG, 13 Oct. 1900, *CL*, ii, 575–7.

59. *All Ireland Review*, 1 Dec. 1900 (*UP*, ii, 244).

60. Russell to AG, postmarked 27 Dec. 1900, Berg. The latest offence was a review of the *Treasury of Irish Poetry*, 30 Dec. 1900; protests followed on 5 and 12 Jan. 1901. Also see *Leader*, 3 Nov. 1900, for 'Mr Yeats's Jug', a caustic commentary on recent interviews with the poet in English papers (*UP*, ii, 243–4); and for WBY's analysis, a letter to AG, 8 Jan. 1901, *CL*, iii, 10–11.

61. Berg (incomplete). This could date from the 1899 *Countess Cathleen* controversy, but James Pethica convincingly attributes it to 24 May 1901.
62. To AG, 23 Jan. 1901, discussing the controversy over the Brooke–Rolleston anthology, *CL*, iii, 19.
63. 29 Jan. 1901. See also T. S. Moore to R. C. Trevelyan, n.d., but 1901, University of London, suggesting a visit to WBY to discuss a production of *The Shadowy Waters*. 'I hope my theatre is actually going to be, or at least to try to be. But please keep this fact a profound secret.'
64. For a close analysis, see George Mills Harper, *Yeats's Golden Dawn* (London, 1974), Chapter 6.
65. Quoted ibid., 43.
66. *CL*, iii, 30.
67. Harper, *Yeats's Golden Dawn*, 54. Harper guesses that WBY may have drafted them, but the style is uncharacteristic.
68. *CL*, iii, 40.
69. *CL*, iii, 44.
70. Harper, *Yeats's Golden Dawn*, 63–4. The last comment is bitchy: WBY did not proceed to a further degree until much later.
71. He might also have been the driving force behind a pamphlet by Brodie-Innes suggesting a new constitution: see ibid., 90–91.
72. They still had several preoccupations in common. WBY's library contains Volume VIII of *Collecteana Hermetica*, edited by William Wynn Westcott – *Egyptian Magic* by S.S.D.D. (i.e. Farr), published in London by the Theosophical Publishing Society in 1896. Some of its contents are suggestive, such as the explanation of the hawk with a human head as representing the Ka [Ego] of a King or Queen; while the emphasis on symbolism, chains of creation and reincarnation echo many of WBY's occult preoccupations. The chapter on Gnostic magic deals with initiation, disciplines, formulae, cycles of ascent and Neo-Platonic wisdom.
73. Or so Harper thinks: *Yeats's Golden Dawn*, 94–5.
74. There were two of these at the very height of the controversy, on 16 Feb. and 23 Mar.
75. See *CL*, iii, 14.
76. The opposing organization, from 1903, was Waite's 'Independent and Rectified Rite'. By 1914 WBY had become more active in the SM, probably becoming Imperator and instructor in 'ancient traditions'.
77. See WBY to AG, 13 Oct. 1900, *CL*, ii, 575. It was published in the *Monthly Review*, Sept. 1901, and reprinted in *IGE*.
78. *YA* 7 (1990), 98.
79. 1: Ordering sources of Celtic knowledge. 2: Symbolism and astrology. 3: Methods of divination, talismans, etc. 4: Mystical philosophy. 5; Clairvoyance. 6: Thaumaturgy. 7: White magic. On 4 Aug. he defined the initiation procedure, revolving round obligations symbolized by the cauldron, stone, sword and spear.
80. [?26] May 1901, forthcoming *CL*, iv, appendix.
81. *UP*, ii, 247, 253–4.
82. 25 May 1901, *CL*, iii, 74.
83. Notebook, MBY: 'Visions of old Irish mythologies, begun Dec. 13 1898. Less my own visions than the visions of others & of myself with others. My own are in diary.' This vision, the first in a series with 'F.L.' (George Pollexfen), was induced by incense and dated 17 July 1901.
84. See below, pp. 254–5.
85. 28 June 1901, *CL*, iii, 84. SMY replied on 1 July.
86. To AG, 22 Dec. 1901, *CL*, iii, 139.

87. Lewis, *Selected Letters of Somerville and Ross*, 252.
88. For a full report, *see Celtia*, Dublin, Sept. 1901, i/5, 145–6.
89. AG to WBY, n.d., but Aug. 1901, Berg.
90. *Celtia*, i/5, 141.
91. Hyde warned WBY about this in a letter from Enniscrone, July 1901, MBY, and in another on 1 Aug. 1901, *LTWBY*, i, 88–9.
92. To Sharp, 4 Aug. 1901 (private collection).
93. See an important letter of 'Friday', Berg.
94. See WBY to AG, 18 May 1901, *CL*, iii, 69–70.
95. See James Pethica, '"Our Kathleen": Yeats's Collaboration with Lady Gregory in the Writing of *Kathleen ni Houlihan*', *YA* 6 (1988), 3–31; also Pethica, 26 May 1925 ('Rather hard on me, not giving my name with Kathleen [*sic*] ni Houlihan that I wrote all but all of') and 26 July 1930. Also see Constant Huntingdon to Margaret Gough, 6 Dec. 1944, Gregory MSS, Emory, which mentions the 'bombshell' about *Cathleen ni Houlihan*; and John Campbell, 'The Rise of the Drama in Ireland', *New Liberal Reviw*, Apr. 1904. Undated fragments in the Berg collection refer to 'our Kathleen' and show that she changed the proofs for Bullen, to restore the ending 'as it is acted' – a significant intervention. The Berg MS is all in her hand – a first draft in notebooks and additional sheets. At the end of the notebook (where the Poor Old Woman enters) AG wrote, 'All this mine alone.' This is corroborated by W. Boyle to Holloway, 20 Feb. 1908: 'The odd thing is that Fay told me Lady Gregory wrote the whole of it except the part of "Kathleen".' (Private collection: my thanks to Dr Nicholas Boyle for this and other references).
96. 'Friday' [late 1901], Berg.
97. See below, pp. 261–2.
98. Statement during the Irish National Theatre's patent inquiry, 1904; Ellmann transcript, Tulsa.
99. 20 July 1901, *CL*, iii, 91.
100. 20 July 1901, *CL*, iii, 92.
101. 11 Aug. 1901, *CL*, iii, 105.
102. WBY to ECY, 25 July 1901, *CL*, iii, 94.
103. WBY to JBY, 12 July 1901, *CL*, iii, 87.
104. Text printed in *Dublin Magazine*, 26, 2 (Apr.–June 1951).
105. See WBY to AG, 3 Apr. 1901, *CL*, iii, 54–5. 'It was the only good scenery I have ever seen, a perfect fulfillment of the ideal I have always had. He got wonderful effects by purple robed figures against a purple back cloth.' The performance was on 26 Mar.
106. See the *Speaker*, 11 May 1901.
107. 19 Oct. 1901.
108. 24 Nov. 1901.
109. See WBY to F. J. Fay, 1 Aug. 1901, *CL*, iii, 97–8.
110. 28 Oct. 1901, Lewis, *Selected Letters of Somerville and Ross*, 254.
111. 14 Mar. 1901. He suggested that before putting on the play they should 'find some natural occasion for drawing a distinction between your political faith as nationalists & Home Rulers on the one hand, & your view of the Queen's visit on the other'.
112. To AG, 3 Mar. 1901.
113. 10 Apr. 1901, quoted in Hogan and Kilroy, *Irish Literary Theatre*, 90.
114. 'Griffith is I think strong on this point & influences the others': WBY to Russell, *c.* 9 Aug. 1901, *CL*, iii, 103.
115. Hogan and Kilroy, *Irish Literary Theatre*, 71. Actually in the end Benson simply carried a fleece; the kid had disgraced itself in rehearsals by 'eating the property ivy' (*Mem*, 123).
116. F. R. Benson, *My Memories* (London, 1930), 11.

117. The late Sir Frederick Ashton in conversation with RFF.
118. *FJ*, 13 Nov. 1901.
119. 19 Nov. 1901, *CL*, iii, 120.
120. AG had written to him about this decision in the spring (from Coole, 'Friday', Berg), and Moore's letters in the summer had also taken this decision as read.
121. Hogan and Kilroy, *Irish Literary Theatre*, 74–5. The idea of a Corporation subsidy had been suggested to WBY by Moore, 27 July 1901, Berg.
122. *Samhain*, 1, 6.
123. ibid., 9. He was thinking of Rolleston, whom he had told in Feb. 1900 to 'do something that will violently annoy the upper class to redeem his character' (Pethica, 241).
124. *United Irishman*, 31 Aug. 1901.
125. Practically written by June 1901 (WBY to AG, 6 June 1901, *CL*, iii, 79) and destined for the *Speaker*; eventually printed in the *Cornhill*, Mar. 1902. Both reprinted in *IGE*. See above, p. 246.
126. See *Daily Express*, Dublin, 5 Aug. 1901.
127. See especially 'What is "Popular Poetry"?', *E & I*, 3–4.
128. 'What is "Popular Poetry"?', *E & I*, 10–11.
129. WBY to Hugh Law (Assistant Secretary of the ILS), 16 Mar. 1901, *CL*, iii, 50–51.
130. *All Ireland Review*, 1 Dec. 1900. Also see *Samhain*, 1, above.
131. 2 Nov. 1901, Berg: after listening to WBY lecturing at a Merrion Row meeting to publicize the ILT.

Chapter 10 : NATIONAL DRAMAS
1901–1902

1. *G–Y L*, 146.
2. See R. Schuchard, 'W. B. Yeats and the London Theatre Societies 1901–1904', *Rev. Eng. Stud*, xxix, 116 (1978).
3. Holroyd, *Shaw*, i, 208.
4. WBY to Henry Newbolt, 5 Apr. 1902, *CL*, iii, 169. He had first met Newbolt at Robert Bridges' in Mar. 1897.
5. 20 Jan. 1902, *CL*, iii, 149.
6. From 1903; it published WBY's 'Dream of the World's End' (in no. 2), Russell's drawings and *Deirdre* (no. 7), and also embodied a strong Japanese theme, with several poems by Yone Noguchi in nos. 11–12.
7. *CL*, iii, 145.
8. 26 Nov. 1901, *CL*, iii, 126.
9. 22 Mar. 1902, *CL*, iii, 161.
10. *UP*, ii, 265–7; for the earlier reaction, *CL*, iii, 121.
11. R. Schuchard, '"An Attendant Lord": H. W. Nevinson's Friendship with W. B. Yeats', *YA* 7 (1990), 105.
12. *CL*, iii, 155.
13. Ella Young, *Flowering Dusk* (New York, 1945), 72–4.
14. This argument is advanced in Sean McCann, *The Story of the Abbey Theatre* (London, 1967), *The Splendid Years: Recollections of Maire nic Shiubhlaigh as told to Edward Kenny* (Dublin, 1955), Dawson Byrne, *The Story of Ireland's National Theatre: The Abbey Theatre, Dublin* (Dublin, 1929), as well as in Gerard Fay, *The Abbey Theatre: Cradle of Genius* (London, 1958), W. G. Fay and Catherine Carswell, *The Fays of the Abbey Theatre* (London, 1935) and T. G. K[eohler] in *Dublin Magazine*, 10, 4 (Oct.–Dec. 1935).

15. Denson, *Letters from AE*, 96–7. Also see Russell to Ernest Boyd, 14 Mar. 1914, Healy Collection, Stanford.
16. Also see P. Colum, 'Early Days of the Irish Theatre', *Dublin Magazine*, 24, 4 (Oct.–Dec. 1949) and 25, 1 (Jan.–Mar. 1950).
17. To Ernest Boyd, Healy Collection, Stanford.
18. See WBY to AG, 20 Jan. 1902, *CL*, iii, 149.
19. *CL*, iii, 305. Naturally, this does not appear in his recollections of 1935 (Fay and Carswell, *Fays of the Abbey Theatre*, 119).
20. *G–Y L*, 150. For full production details, see Antony Coleman, 'A Calendar for the Production and Reception of *Cathleen ni Houlihan*', *Modern Drama*, June 1977.
21. Lewis, *Selected Letters of Somerville and Ross*, 256.
22. *Irish Literature and Drama*, 158; also see *PF*, 245, for other reactions.
23. 'The Acting in St Teresa's Hall', *United Irishman*, 12 Apr. 1902 (*UP*, ii, 284–6).
24. *CL*, iii, 176, 173.
25. cf. McCann, *Story of the Abbey Theatre*, 101: 'The Irish Literary Theatre had given place to a company of Irish actors. Its committee saw them take up the work all the more gladly because it had not formed them or influenced them.'
26. 21 Sept. 1906, NLI MS 1804, 425–6.
27. See *United Irishman*, 18 May 1901.
28. 5 and 29 May 1902, 10 June 1902.
29. See Katharine Worth, *The Irish Drama of Europe from Yeats to Beckett* (London, 1978), 32. Formalism and chanting had distinguished French experimental theatre in the 1890s; Wagner and current ideas about ancient Greece fitted in too.
30. 2,000 words in an hour and ten minutes on 17 Apr.; see letter to AG, 18 Apr. 1902, *CL*, iii, 175.
31. WBY to AG, 23 May 1902, *CL*, iii, 184.
32. See WBY to AG, 23 May 1902, *CL*, iii, 185. Also Robert Gregory to AG in Gregory family papers, Emory. An Irish Club started by Samuel (later Dermott) Trench at Balliol tried to organize a dinner for WBY the following Mar. but could not get enough men: see Robert Gregory to AG 17 Nov. 1902, 14 Mar. 1903. WBY stayed with Eric Maclagan. Trench would become 'Haines' in *Ulysses*, though he was not English.
33. See Fiona Macleod in *Fortnightly Review*, Feb. 1903; *Leader*, 5 Mar. 1904, pointing out AG's reliance on Eleanor Hull; and *Athenaeum*, 26 Mar. 1904, on the debt to Standish Hayes O'Grady. For AG's careful preparation of reviews, see her letter to WBY, 'Saturday', probably 14 Mar. 1903, Berg, arranging a *TLS* discussion of *Poets and Dreamers* ('Symons inspired by you wd be best').
34. For its genesis, see fragment in Berg. WBY had already suggested a magazine article, but AG offered to pay him as much money for a preface putting the stories in context.
35. By W. P. Ryan, writing from a purist Irish-Ireland vantage on 5 July. He thought AG's work provided a temporary use but in twenty years would be of historical interest only as a specimen of the sort of artificial construction needed to revive Irish culture. Her style was 'a melancholy absurdity' and her project essentially a bastardizing one, working (albeit unintentionally) in English interests. WBY's claims for the book were resoundingly dismissed. It did, however, become a repository for Irish-Irelander lecturers short of a theme, especially those who could not read Irish: see MG's paper 'Emer' read to Inghinidhe, reprinted in *United Irishman*, 1 Nov. 1902, and self-confessedly lifted in entirety from *Cuchulain*.
36. Draft in Berg, dated 23 May 1902; also *CL*, iii, 187–9.
37. AG to WBY, 25 May 1902, *CL*, iii, 167, n. 1.
38. To AG, 16 June 1902, *CL*, iii, 203.
39. *CL*, iii, 417.

40. The draft in the Berg is more equivocal still.
41. Schuchard, '"Attendant Lord"', *YA* 7 (1989), 107.
42. 6 May 1903, *CL*, iii, 358–9. Sir Henry Lawrence (of Lucknow) was his host; Lady Lawrence, a sister of Mrs Coffey, had been brought up in Ireland.
43. 1 June 1902, Berg.
44. 16 June 1902, Berg.
45. 18 June 1902, *CL*, iii, 204.
46. *CL*, iii, 202.
47. See letter to *The Times*, 24 June 1902; and Hubert Butler, 'The British Israelites at Tara' in R. F. Foster (ed.), *The Sub-Prefect Should Have Held His Tongue* (London, 1990). MG brought in d'Arbois de Jubainville, the Duke of Tetuan, and many other 'names'; Hyde, Griffith, Moore and WBY visited the site to remonstrate with the owner, an occasion described in Griffith, 'Mr Rolleston, His Friend, and Tara', *United Irishman*, 15 Nov. 1902.
48. *The Hour-Glass* and *The Pot of Broth*.
49. The journalist William Bulfin recorded this occasion. He found WBY's manner

    nervous, uneasy, pins-and-needles – [it] made you anxious about him in spite of yourself . . . He is unsettled in his ways. He had just heard some singing which appeared new to him, and he wanted explanations about it from Dr Hyde. And he was particularly anxious that Dr Hyde should look it up and remember about it and take a note of it; and on no account to forget it, and occupy himself with it, and generally speaking to get it, whatever in the world it was, upon his nerves and mind, just as it had planted itself on the nerves and mind of Mr Yeats himself. It is a serious thing to be a poet like Mr Yeats, who dreams dreams and gets things on his nerves . . . (repr. from the *Southern Cross* in the *Gael*, Dec. 1902).

    Moore described the singer (Cave, *Hail and Farewell*, 330–31): 'a vague drift of sound, rising and falling, unmeasured as the wind soughing among the trees, or the lament of the waves on the shore, something that might go on all day long'.
50. *CL*, iii, 120, 128. Ricketts and Shannon, who saw it on 20 Nov. 1901, were equally struck, noting Campbell's 'magnetic force and emotional depth': Charles Ricketts, *Self-Portrait, Taken from the Letters and Journals of Charles Ricketts, Collected and Compiled by T. Sturge Moore and Edited by C. S. Lewis* (London, 1939), 70–71.
51. W. K. Magee, *Memoir of AE*, 107; Kuch, *Yeats and AE*, 204ff.
52. NLI MS 8777; see *CL*, iii, 228, n. 2.
53. See Daniel J. Murphy, 'Lady Gregory, Co-author and Sometimes Author of the Plays of W. B. Yeats', in R. J. Porter and J. D. Brody (eds.), *Modern Irish Literature: Essays in honour of William York Tindall* (New Rochelle, 1972), 43–52. AG probably provided touches of verisimilitude: 'Ward', for instance, is a generic traveller name in Ireland.
54. Sept.–Oct. 1902, Berg.
55. The version Quinn retailed to John Lane on 24 Oct. 1902 (letter book, no. 1, NYPL) is worth recording.

    In the Spring Mr Yeats and George Moore together with Mr George Russell ('A.E.') were discussing new plays and Russell told Yeats and Moore a story about a member of a well-connected family who had joined the tinkers in Ireland, and had related various of his experiences. Yeats remarked that the story as told to Moore and himself by Russell would make a good play, and thereupon Moore and Yeats began to sketch up the scenario. Subsequently Moore and Yeats had one or two talks about how the acts should run but no actual writing was ever done. Later Moore got tired of the matter and said that he did not care to go on with the play then and told Yeats that he might write the play if he cared to, Moore remarking that he might use the idea some time for a story.

    According to Quinn, WBY then went to the west; when Moore, visiting Martyn, heard that WBY was working on the play at Coole he threatened an injunction, claiming that they had begun a collaboration and WBY had treacherously gone on alone. 'Yeats asserts that there is not an idea or a scene of Moore in the play as written by him. Russell corroborates Yeats and is willing to testify as to the origins of the story.' AG similarly convinced Quinn that Moore had no case. 'Yeats has great confidence in the play and feels it is one of the best things he has ever done.' Hyde and AG agreed, according to Quinn; their own part in its inception was not mentioned by him to Lane. Quinn's own enthusiasm was real; on 1 Nov. 1902 he told AG that he hoped Lane would publish it and distribute it widely in the USA, which would make WBY's reputation there. Publishers did not agree, however, and he ended by paying Knickerbocker $72.09 for a copyright edition (letter of 1 Apr. 1903).

56. *UP*, iii, 298.
57. cf. 'General Introduction to my Work', in which he would write that as an Irishman saturated in English culture, 'My hatred tortures me with love, my love with hate.' (Edward Callan, ed., *Yeats on Yeats: The Last Introductions and the Dublin Edition*, Dublin, 1981, 63).
58. Berg, and see Reeves and Gould, *Joachim of Fiore*, 250–52.
59. *TLS*, 26 June 1903.
60. To AG, 25 Nov. 1902, Berg.
61. Schuchard, ' "Attendant Lord" ', 102.
62. For changes, see Katharine Worth's introduction to the Irish Dramatic Texts edition published by CUA and Colin Smythe (1987).
63. WBY to Bullen, 12 Feb. 1908, Kansas (also *L*, 503). There was a diverting controversy over a real-life tinker who claimed the play libelled him and was enterprisingly interviewed by the *United Irishman*: described by WBY in a fragment, NLI 30,343. Also see James Woods, *The Annals of Westmeath* (Dublin, 1907), 182–3.
64. *WTIN*, 1987 edition, 94: a Blake reference, also used in *IGE*.
65. Fifteen copyright copies only, at the Knickerbocker Press, with some changes, plus thirty of a large paper edition: see Wade, *Bibliography*, 60–61 (items 42–3). Also see Quinn to S. J. Richardson, 22 Oct. 1902, and to Harold Paget, 24 Oct. 1902, NYPL, for terms.
66. See especially a long letter to AG, 4 Dec. 1902, *CL*, iii, 266–9.
67. n.d., Emory.
68. *CL*, iii, 238. On 27 May 1902 Quinn ordered *Zarathustra* from a book dealer (letter book, no. 1, NYPL); on 15 Nov. 1902 he sent on *The Case of Wagner*, *Genealogy of Morals*, and poems; a letter of 3 Feb. 1903 shows him asking Elkin Mathews to send WBY Volume 8 of Wagner's prose works, translated by Ellis, and also Nietzsche's *The Crown of Bay*.
69. See above, Chapter 6, p. 159. WBY wrote to AG on 26 Dec. 1902 about his immersion in Nietzsche, who 'completes Blake & has the same roots – I have not read anything with so much excitement since I got to love Morris's stories which have the same curious astringent joy.' (*CL*, iii, 284). Also see WBY to Quinn, 6 Feb. 1903, *CL*, iii, 312–13.
70. An essay reprinted in *Plays, Acting and Music* (1903).
71. To Horace Reynolds, 19 Aug. 1941, Harvard.
72. Russell to AG, postmarked 30 Mar. 1903, Berg.
73. Quinn to AG, 15 May 1903, Berg.
74. *G–YL*, 155.
75. *PF*, 231–7.
76. ibid., 238.
77. Postmarked 10 June 1902, Berg.
78. 16 June 1902, Berg. Russell had already offended both WBY and AG by his moralizing letters about his friend's slow rate of work; see above, p. 182.
79. *PF*, 241.
80. *CL*, iii, 192.

81. On 4 Oct., in a state of drunken dissolution. WBY did not react very noticeably, apart from telling York Powell he might write in memory of him; they had become distanced from each other, and Johnson was only later incorporated into his personal myth.
82. *CL*, iii, 254–5.
83. 7 Nov. 1902: my thanks to W. M. Murphy.
84. To R L–P, 18 Apr. 1943. This is one of the very few references to MG in the vast corpus of Yeats family correspondence.
85. See above, p. 149.
86. *CL*, iii, 243.
87. 17 May 1906, HRHRC.
88. Preserved, like everything else, in a *Ulysses* reference: J. J. O'Molloy to Stephen, p. 140 of NY 1961 edition.
89. See A. Walton Litz, ' "Love's Bitter Mystery": Joyce and Yeats', *YA* 7 (1990), 81–9.
90. This comes from the later version as in Ellmann, *IY*, 86–8; the earlier quotation from WBY's TS 'The Younger Generation'. For Joyce's *envoi*, see W. R. Rodgers, 'Notes for the Radio'. 'John McCormick once repeated the story to Dulanty, the Irish ambassador in London, and Dulanty asked if it were true. Joyce was very cross about it, cross with Gogarty. "Why," said Joyce to Dulanty, "even if I'd *thought* it I wouldn't have *said* it to Yeats. It would have been unmannerly.'
91. Ellmann, *IY*, 86–91. He also remarked to an American interviewer a year later, 'It is useless to discuss philosophy with a man more than 27' – another echo of Joyce (*New York Morning Sun*, 15 Nov. 1903).
92. *CL*, iii, 249–50.
93. Others included Thomas MacDonagh and Henry G. O'Brien: see *CL*, iii, 246–7, 251.
94. On the strength of this one meeting Symons became an ardent admirer, and wrote to Elkin Mathews powerfully pressing the claims of Joyce's poems on 9 Oct. 1906. 'He is not in the Celtic movement; and though Yeats admires his ability he is rather against him because Joyce has attacked the movement.' (Symons papers, Princeton). This became *Chamber Music*; Symons kept up the pressure, reviewing the volume the following May.
95. Richard Ellmann, *James Joyce* (2nd ed., Oxford, 1982), 660–61, fn.
96. *CL*, iii, 456. It is also significant that WBY took to advocating the plays of Sudermann for the Irish theatre – advice first tendered by Joyce in 'The Day of the Rabblement'.
97. W. O'Brien and D. Ryan (eds.), *Devoy's Post Bag 1871–1928* (Dublin, 1953), ii, 347–8.
98. See below, p. 288.
99. *G–Y L*, 176.
100. *United Irishman*, 8 Nov. 1902.
101. Writing as 'Che Buono' in the *Southern Cross*, Argentine, 16 Jan. 1903.
102. *We Two Together* (Madras, 1950), 76.
103. See *United Irishman*, 8 and 15 Nov. 1902. 'To anyone who had not come within the glamour of Mr Yeat's personality, both speech and song bordered perilously on the ludicrous.'
104. ibid. (a cutting is in Gregory's scrapbook, no. 2, Emory).
105. Thomas McGreevy in *I & R*, ii, 410.
106. 26 Dec. 1902, *CL*, iii, 285.
107. 'Mr Yeats and the Freedom of the Theatre', *United Irishman*, 15 Nov. 1902; M. C. Joy wrote defending WBY on 29 Nov.
108. To an extent that eventually embarrassed WBY; see Adrian Frazier, *Behind the Scenes: Yeats, Horniman and the Struggle for the Abbey Theatre* (London, 1990), 59–60, for subsequent changes.
109. It was finished by the summer; see a letter of 13 June 1902, *CL*, iii, 201.
110. 26 Dec. 1902, *CL*, iii, 285. See also n. 96 above.

Chapter 11 : The Taste of Salt
1902–1903

Epigraph: Arsenal, Paris.

1. His own articles about the war in the *FJ*, 1906–7, provoked many complaints and contradictions.
2. Balliett, 'The Lives – and Lies – of Maud Gonne', 31.
3. *G–YL*, 154.
4. e.g., ibid., 156.
5. See *UP*, ii, 265, 269, and many other places.
6. *G–YL*, 162.
7. To WBY, 9 Feb. 1903, Reading.
8. To 'Na Geadna Fiadhaine' ('The Wild Geese') at the Bijou Theatre, Bedford Street; AG was present. Farr told Nevinson that MG 'had not even told him about the engagement until the day before it became public' (Schuchard, ' "Attendant Lord" ', 104), which fits the dates: it was first published in Ireland in the *FJ* on 9 Feb.
9. J. G. P. Delaney, ' "Heirs of the Great Generation": Yeats's Friendship with Charles Ricketts and Charles Shannon', *YA* 4 (1986), 58 (letter to the Fields).
10. *G–YL*, 164–6; *CL*, iii, 315–17.
11. 18 Dec. 1902, *CL*, iii, 281.
12. *G–YL*, 166.
13. Schuchard, ' "Attendant Lord" ', 104.
14. See report in *United Irishman*, 28 Feb. 1903.
15. *G–YL*, 167.
16. ibid., 108. See WBY to AG, 13 Oct. 1908, Berg. MG 'says that but for a letter of yours, or a message from you, I forget which, her husband would have been able to take half her fortune. It was owing to you that she got married according to English laws.'
17. 1 Mar. 1903, Tulsa; NLI MS 18,312.
18. Interview with MG, 27 June 1947, Ellmann interview book, Tulsa. See also below, p. 592, n. 16.
19. *CL*, iii, 303.
20. AG told M. Bourgeois (30 July 1913, Healy Collection, Stanford), giving circumstantial detail, that she read it out loud.
21. 16 Dec. 1902, *CL*, iii, 279.
22. To Quinn, 4 June 1909, Diakoff Collection, NYPL; my thanks to W. M. Murphy for this reference.
23. Some of their reports are preserved in the George Roberts Collection, NLI MS 5651.
24. 20 Nov. 1902, *CL*, iii, 258.
25. Made politically acceptable by reducing the amount earned in America by the emigrant hero. For the Nassau, see *SQ*, 332; also J. H. Pollock, *William Butler Yeats* (London, 1935), 33–4. When it closed in 1912, WBY recalled 'I have had so many meetings there with O'Leary, Taylor and the like.' (To AG, 3 Nov. 1912, Berg).
26. See Catherine Phillips (ed.), *'The Hour-Glass': Manuscript Materials* (Ithaca and London, 1994).
27. Russell to AG, 24 Mar. 1903, Berg. The idea may have owed something to Jack's penchant for working models: see JBY to Rosa Butt, Nov. 1900, Bodleian. 'Jack at work either on picture or a great undertaking which occupies all his evenings, a circus, with puppets of horses and men, a most laughable thing. Jack explains, a country circus tries to imitate life ancient or modern. He imitates the circus.'

28. 20 Mar. 1903, *CL*, iii, 333.
29. NLI MS 7267.
30. See *Greensheaf*, 2 (1903), 6–7, and above, p. 219.
31. *CL*, iii, 351.
32. Copy in Reading.
33. *Daily News*, 16 May 1903. Chesterton must have relished the conceit; he knew them both from Bedford Park days. My thanks to Owen Dudley Edwards for this reference.
34. Schuchard, ' "Attendant Lord" ', 104.
35. Interviews with George Yeats, 17 June 1946 and 8 Dec. 1947, Ellmann interview book, Tulsa.
36. Originally this was expected to be £600; it was derived from the earnings of the Vale Press *Faustus*.
37. *CL*, iii, 402.
38. WBY's feelings may be intuited by a fragment from AG to him (Berg), written while he was in the USA: 'I looked in at Mrs Emery's "Dancers" as I wanted to see her about music for Shadowy Waters. She had a good many people, and if she keeps them together it may be quite a useful society. Walter Crane dancing the Sarabande was a fine sight, his face wooden all the time. He is rather disgusted at the collapse of the Masquers. Mr Elliott who I met at the Sesame was sorry for your sake, you would be so disappointed! but I told him you would not take it to heart.'
39. 16 Mar. 1903.
40. See latter to *United Irishman*, 1 Aug. 1903, and a debate on 24 Oct. with Father Maloney at the London Irish Literary Society, where some priests walked out.
41. 14 July 1903, *CL*, iii, 398–9.
42. To AG, 8 May 1903, *CL*, iii, 363.
43. WBY told AG of this in a letter of 4 May. The company's subsequent visit in Mar. 1904 was probably in order to be vetted by the Exhibition Committee, who were to pay expenses. In the event, the company did not go, but several ex-members did, causing much annoyance and confusion when they described themselves as 'The Irish National Theatre Society'; see below, Chapter 12, p. 319.
44. *Academy*, 16 May 1903.
45. *CL*, iii, 400.
46. *Athenaeum*, 27 June 1903 (*CH*, 137).
47. *CL*, iii, 342.
48. See *Leader*, 26 Sept., 10 and 17 Oct. 1903. 'Imaal' was J. J. O'Toole. However, in *New Ireland* on 10 Oct. a piece was carried arguing that the Irish failed to appreciate WBY.
49. To Quinn, 15 May 1903, *CL*, iii, 372.
50. SMY to Quinn, 22 Sept. 1903, NYPL. 'When Willy appeared Papa drew his attention to the beautiful pink colour of the little bits of fish remaining . . .'
51. *G–YL*, 174.
52. For his reiterated condemnation in June 1903, see *CL*, iii, 385–7.
53. *G–YL*, 174.
54. Gabriel Fallon in *I & R*, i, 180–81.
55. Berg. Also see TS at Harvard, with prologue and additions. At Coole in late Aug. JBY was struck by how much work WBY and AG did 'jointly' (to Rosa Butt, 1 Sept. 1903, Bodleian).
56. 31 Aug. 1903. The prologue, though published in the *United Irishman*, was wisely never performed.
57. 17 Oct. 1903, an uncompromising piece by 'Chanel' [Arthur Clery]. 'This abnegation Mr Yeats preaches is the virtue which makes men martyrs and apostles, but which, if indiscriminately inculcated in the case of ordinary men, may easily be carried too far.' Chanel also thought *The Shadow of the Glen* 'one of the nastiest little plays I have ever seen'.

58. Principally Maire Quinn and Dudley Digges, later followed by P. J. Kelly. MG's decision was made final in late Sept., according to a letter to Roberts.

59. The same message was preached in an important open letter to the *United Irishman*, 10 Oct. 1903, *CL*, iii, 439–41.

60. 13 July 1903 and 1 Aug. 1903; a TS of the first is in AG's papers, with corrections by her (Berg).

61. *G–YL*, 132, 174, 177, 179.

62. *PF*, 258. See also a peremptory letter of hers to W. G. Fay, 21 Aug. 1903, Harvard.

63. Robert Hogan and Michael J. O'Neill, *Joseph Holloway's Abbey Theatre: A Selection from His Unpublished Journal 'Impressions of a Dublin Playgoer'* (London, 1967), 27.

64. Frazier, *Behind the Scenes*, 75–9.

65. McCann, *The Story of the Abbey Theatre*, 131.

66. On 31 Oct. and 2–3 Nov. the Cumann na nGaedheal Theatre Company presented *Cathleen ni Houlihan* and Connell's *Emmet*, as well as plays by Hyde, Cousins and Ryan. Patriotic dramas were turned out for the *United Irishman* week after week: see Frazier.

67. Memo, 'Reasons for and against the Establishment of the Gaelic Company', Berg.

68. *New Ireland*, 17 Oct. 1903.

69. *United Irishman*, 24 Oct. 1903.

70. See Tom Kettle, 'Mr Yeats and the Freedom of the Theatre', *United Irishman*, 15 Nov. 1902.

71. 18 Apr. 1903.

72. *CL*, iii, 377–8.

73. Page proofs and prelims of *In the Seven Woods*, with annotations, Harvard.

74. To Shelby, 11 Aug. 1903, Kansas.

75. See Cuala Archives, TCD; also ECY to Quinn, 7 Oct. 1903, HRHRC.

76. See Quinn to AG, 24 Mar. 1903, Berg.

77. To ECY, 25 July 1901, *CL*, iii, 94.

78. So Maurice Joy reported to Nevinson: Schuchard, '"Attendant Lord"', 110–11.

79. Apr. 1904, *CL*, iii, 577.

80. See Quinn to AG, 24 Mar. 1903, Berg.

81. Later, WBY remembered Quinn as having suggested the tour the day after they met at the Galway *feis*, 1 Sept. 1902 (*CL*, iii, 140); and see Quinn to AG, 15 May 1903 (Berg): 'one of the aims that I have for the [Irish Literary] Society is to have Yeats over here some time next year and also Hyde. I will have it arranged that Yeats will lecture at Harvard and Columbia Universities and before other Irish Societies and the same way with Hyde. You will remember that I mentioned this when I was at Coole.'

82. 28 June 1903, *CL*, iii, 389. The high-souled tone of the letter may owe something to its having been dictated to AG.

Chapter 12 : FROM AMERICA TO ABBEY STREET
1903–1904

Epigraph: Self-Portrait, Taken from the Letters and Journals of Charles Ricketts, Collected and Compiled by T. Sturge Moore and Edited by C. S. Lewis (London, 1939), 106.

1. George Brett to Quinn, NYPL.

2. To Russell, 3 July 1903, and to Horatio S. Krans, 20 Nov. 1903, rudely (but unsuccessfully) discouraging the latter from writing a book about WBY, Quinn letter book, no. 1, NYPL (the source of all subsequent Quinn letters unless otherwise stated).

3. See letter to Krans, above; to WBY; to George J. Bryan, 21 Nov. 1903.
4. Quinn to AG, Berg.
5. Quinn told a Californian correspondent that Colonel Higginson would be introducing WBY at Harvard, and then wrote to Higginson to tell him about the lecture and invite him to do so.
6. Quinn to James Phelan, 22 Oct. 1902, letter book, no. 1, NYPL.
7. See Richard Londraville's reconstruction of the texts of three of these in *YA* 8 (1991), 78–122.
8. *CL*, iii, 511.
9. Quinn to AG, 15 May 1903, Berg.
10. 22 Nov. 1903.
11. Paul Elmore Moore in the *New York Independent* and the *Evening Post* accused WBY of morbidity, sensuality and sickliness, instancing as proof the number of references to hair in *The Wind Among the Reeds*; with unconscious irony he contrasted WBY with the 'wholesome' Lionel Johnson. Huneker loyally pointed out that WBY's recent work was all against this tendency. See pp. 536–7, below.
12. *CL*, iii, 473.
13. ibid., 467.
14. See Karin Strand, 'W. B. Yeats's American Lecture Tours', unpublished Ph.D. thesis (Northwestern University, 1978), 15–17, for details of interviews.
15. *New York Morning Sun*, 15 Nov. 1903. A recurrent theme in his letters was the attractiveness of educated American women compared to argumentative English bluestockings.
16. See *CL*, iii, 490.
17. Such as Brisbane of the *New York Evening Journal*; see also his letter to Daniel Coholan, 16 Dec. 1903.
18. Quinn to Dr T. J. Shahan, 10 Feb. 1904, CUA Archives; also 'M' (probably M. F. Egan) to same, 28 Dec. 1903.
19. He used the organ-stop metaphor at a Co-operative Conference seven years before (*Irish Homestead*, 6 Nov. 1897) and two years later in a speech at Trinity (*Daily Express*, Dublin, 1 June 1899).
20. *YA* 8 (1991), 91.
21. Quoted in Strand, 'American Lecture Tours', 77.
22. ibid., 22.
23. 19 Dec. 1903.
24. *CL*, iii, 500.
25. 7 Jan. 1904, NLI MS 18,566.
26. Quinn to Mrs Byrne, 1 Feb. 1904.
27. Letters to James Byrne and Patrick Ford, 7 Jan. 1904.
28. *CL*, iii, 497.
29. *Massachusetts Review*, 5, 2. He was referring to a piece in the *Standard*, 5 Jan. 1904, about WBY's allegedly congenital blemish of 'self-consciousness'.
30. *CL*, iii, 538.
31. To AG, n.d., but after seeing Tobin in Paris, possibly 1910–11, Berg.
32. Strand, 'American Lecture Tours', 38.
33. Though Russell himself had turned against Finlay: see his letter to Quinn, Jan. 1904 (Denson TS), where he attributed Finlay's dislike of WBY to a fear that mysticism would destroy Jesuit education. My thanks to Warwick Gould for this reference.
34. Strand, 'American Lecture Tours', 344.
35. 'Renaissance of Irish Literature', a full report in *Mail and Empire*, Toronto, 15 Feb. 1904.
36. See Robert Mahony, 'Yeats and the Irish Language Revival: An Unpublished Lecture', *Irish University Review*, 19, 2 (Autumn 1989), 220–26.

37. By Harry Connell, on 31 Oct. 1903. Dudley Digges played Emmet, and Maire Quinn, Sarah Curran.
38. *CL*, iii, 537–8.
39. *CL*, iii, 551–2.
40. Not in version of speech printed in *UP*, ii, 310–27. See Berg TS, where WBY calls it 'The Song of Hatred', but it must be 'The Curse of the Boers on England', subsequently published by AG in *Poets and Dreamers*.
41. *Gaelic American*, 4 Feb. 1939.
42. See John Masefield to Jack Yeats, 27 Mar. 1904, Harvard.
43. Hackett's description is in a TS preserved at Yale.
44. *CL*, iii, 494–5.
45. See Sheridan to Patrick Ford, quoted by Quinn to WBY, 7 Jan. 1904, NLI MS 18,566.
46. According to George Yeats, in 1964.
47. See NLI 30,654. *CT* and *IGE* had earned £97. 2*s*. 7*d*. since publication, against advances of £109. 1*s*. 9*d*., while the plays had earned only £21. 18*s*. 11*d*. against their advance of £31. 10*s*. (increased to £34. 4*s*. 2*d*. 1/2 by copies which WBY had taken in lieu). A multiple of fifty would give something like the 1997 equivalent.
48. *CL*, iii, 593–4.
49. *CL*, iii, 482.
50. *Tuesdays at Ten* (Philadelphia, 1928), 147.
51. One newspaper interview in particular, with Ashton Stevens in the *San Francisco Examiner*, 30 Jan. 1904, gives a very vivid impression, and is an antidote to George Moore's famous description in *Vale*. It shows WBY at his liveliest and least pretentious, as well as revealing the considerable extent of his theatrical knowledge. See Appendix.
52. Jan. 1904, Berg.
53. See *San Francisco Chronicle*, 30 Jan. 1904; and below, p. 327.
54. *CL*, iii, 527.
55. *CL*, iii, 504–5.
56. Holloway diary, NLI MS 1802, 169.
57. 'Cottie' Yeats to Elkin Mathews, 16 Dec. 1903, HRHRC.
58. *CL*, iii, 548.
59. *New York Daily Tribune*, 15 Nov. 1903. cf. *Inter-Ocean*, Chicago, 17 Jan. 1904: 'We have a national theater, of which I am the head, which is making actors, and good ones too, of young Irish working people.'
60. *CL*, iii, 496.
61. See *CL*, iii, 462, and Volume 4 of AG's *Collected Plays* (Coole ed., Gerrards Cross). On a surviving TS AG wrote 'chiefly WBY's'; it does neither of them much credit.
62. Hogan and O'Neill, *Holloway's Abbey Theatre*, 33, and *LTWBY*, i, 122.
63. *CLJMS*, i, 76.
64. See Stephen Gwynn to W. G. Fay, 13 Dec. 1903, Harvard. Rather nervously, Gwynn suggested a cut of at least 20 per cent to the players, rather than a straight partnership.
65. See letters to George Roberts, Mar. 1904, in Harvard.
66. 27 Mar. 1904, Harvard.
67. *CH*, 44.
68. *CL*, iii, 563.
69. Cutting in Henderson scrapbook, Kansas, 43.
70. This correspondence is in the Theatre Collection, Harvard.
71. 11 June 1904, Harvard.
72. AG 'deplored' Kelly's expulsion; see an undated letter to WBY, Berg. In the same letter

she remarked that Russell 'must have an uneasy conscience to be so out of temper' and offered some gentle suggestions about improving *The King's Threshold*.

73. Hogan and O'Neill, *Holloway's Abbey Theatre*, 38.

74. ibid., 39.

75. n.d., but April 1904, Berg.

76. *CL*, iii, 615. Sturge Moore agreed, writing to R. C. Trevelyan (late June 1904, University of London): 'it was miserably acted there are lots of good things in it and first rate situations but there is no unity of impression or culmination of interest or focus of sympathy, and it is very long here and there boring one altogether'.

77. Delaney, '"Heirs of the Great Generation"', *YA* 4 (1986), 57.

78. Rolleston's poem had been published by Gill in Dublin in 1897, printed by Patrick Geddes at Edinburgh and illustrated by Althea Gyles.

79. SMY to JBY, 27 July 1904, from Frankfort, NLI MS 31,112. As this book goes to press, Jack Yeats's 1929 painting *Farewell to Mayo* has just been auctioned for £804,000.

80. *CL*, iii, 642ff. WBY made it clear that he expected Fay to reproduce sections of this very carefully constructed letter (which is really an article by other means) in any written riposte he made to Moore.

81. *CL*, iii, 658.

82. *TB*, 188.

83. On all this, see *CL*, iii, 654–5.

84. To Maire Garvey, 1 Sept. 1904, NLI MS 8320.

85. cf. Moran's own dislike of *Cathleen ni Houlihan* when he saw it in 1905. 'The "poor old woman" has gained admittance to the scented drawing-room where they take a little green sentimentality with their coffee and gossip. "Kathleen ni Houlihanism" makes Irish patriotism quite harmless.'

86. *CL*, iii, 660–63.

87. Michael Holroyd, *Bernard Shaw. Volume 2, 1898–1918: The Pursuit of Power* (London, 1989), 83.

88. He refused to provide a quote about GBS in Mar. 1915 'unless at considerable length, & after weighing my words; he is a very brilliant man & my friend' (UNC, Chapel Hill). Henderson's cuttings book, NLI MS 1730, 254, contains an unattributed interview with WBY, explaining that the play cannot be put on because of its length and casting difficulties, not because of the content: 'the story is badly told, but the situations are an astonishment, and the characters the life of the situations'.

89. WBY to Shaw, postmarked 1 May 1905, HRHRC. 'Green elephant' has a particular resonance: WBY was well known for having seen a vision of a green elephant following a man in Piccadilly, and Shaw used the phrase to denote the affectation he disliked in WBY ('he saw no green elephants at Coole', Michael Holroyd, *Bernard Shaw. Volume 3, 1918–1950: The Lure of Fantasy* (London, 1991), 195).

90. There was a difficulty about the price, but the idea came off four years later and the picture now hangs in the Houghton Library at Harvard.

91. To Frank Fay, *CL*, iii, 668.

92. *CL*, iii, 678.

93. At the Royal Hibernian Academy: see Hogan and O'Neill, *Holloway's Abbey Theatre*, 47–8; the date was 8 Dec. 1904. This was probably the incident described by Moore in *Vale* (see below).

94. *CL*, iii, 685.

95. For the sake of vividness, this is quoted not from the 1933 revised edition used by Cave, but from the original 1914 edition of *Vale* (164–7). See below, Chapter 18, n. 43, for WBY's belief that Moore was conflating two occasions.

96. James W. Flannery, *W. B. Yeats and the Idea of a Theatre: The Early Abbey Theatre in Theory and Practice* (London, 1976), 253.
97. Hogan and O'Neill, *Holloway's Abbey Theatre*, 49.
98. Frazier, *Behind the Scenes*, 112.
99. S. O.'Sullivan, *The Rose and the Bottle* (1946); Fay and Carswell, *The Fays of the Abbey Theatre*; nic Shiubhlaigh, *The Splendid Years*.

Chapter 13 : DELIGHTING IN ENEMIES
1905–1906

Epigraph: 5 Feb. 1906, Henderson scrapbook on National Literary Society, Kansas.

1. *PF*, 271.
2. Interview with Niall Montgomery, Ellmann interview book, Tulsa.
3. Subsequently married off to MacBride's brother Joseph, summoned from Westport for the purpose.
4. An Irishwoman wrote complaining that MG's separation contradicted advice she had previously given; MG replied that a woman with no income had to stay with the bread-winner, whereas she had 'the power of turning the drunkard out'.
5. *G–YL*, 208.
6. Feb. 1905, NLI MS 18,702 (copy).
7. WBY to AG, postmarked 12 Jan. 1905, Berg.
8. Feb. 1905, Berg.
9. 11 Mar. 1905, NYPL.
10. To Rosa Butt, 19 May 1905, Bodleian.
11. 29 June 1905, NYPL.
12. 'Sunday', n.d., but probably 14 May 1905, Berg.
13. This strikingly anticipates the theme of *Purgatory* more than thirty years later.
14. *G–YL*, 206.
15. Postmarked 11 Mar. 1905, NYPL.
16. MG thought the *Evening Mail* account was 'fairly just' (30 Sept. 1905); the *Independent*, though according to her pro-MacBride, was sued by him for libel after reporting some of the speech by MG's counsel. MacBride's version is preserved in a testimonial he wrote for Fred Allan (NLI MS 29,818). He stressed MG's 'impure life', her 'indelicacy', and her 'trying to force her ex-lovers on me'. A particular grievance originated in her contact with WBY immediately after their honeymoon. See above, p. 286.
17. Nov.–Dec. 1905, *G–YL*, 221.
18. This anticipates the later account in *Ireland after Parnell* of the country being 'like soft wax for years to come' (a phrase first encountered in Standish O'Grady's *Story of Ireland*); much as the MacDonnell article predicts the analysis of political energy being diverted into culture after 1891.
19. Cave, *Hail and Farewell*, 550; see also Hogan and O'Neill, *Holloway's Abbey Theatre*, 53–4.
20. To Quinn, 15 Feb. 1905, *L*, 446.
21. The lecture to the Catholic College was delivered in mid-Apr.; see *An Claidheamh Soluis*, 22 Apr. 1905, for a leader. Also *FJ*, 2 Feb. 1905, for a meeting at the 'Calarosa Club' attended by AG and WBY, who stoutly defended their choice of plays.
22. 18 Feb. 1905, Illinois.
23. Kohfeldt, *Lady Gregory*, 177.
24. To Gerard Fay, 'May 1952', NLI MS 10,954.
25. This view of WBY's interference is borne out by *Holloway's Abbey Theatre*, 45, and is

preserved in the tone of a letter from WBY to Roberts, 24 Oct. 1905, dropping him as Concobar for the English tour of *On Baile's Strand*. 'Please come round tomorow (Tuesday) about one. I have something important to say – I may as well tell you the truth – I don't like your Concobar & I must make a change. I think I should tell you that both the Fays are against my taking you out of the part but I am afraid it must be done.' (Harvard). Holloway thought this was why Roberts left the company the following Jan. (*Holloway's Abbey Theatre*, 67).

26. To Bullen, 15 May 1905, Kansas.
27. Cancelled passage in letter to AG, Berg.
28. His condescension towards Boyle is indicated in *Holloway's Abbey Theatre*, 59. He told him to keep to the *Building Fund* style, ' "for", added Yeats, "it is scarcely likely that one could be supreme in more than one thing." Yeats nearly had a fit when Boyle told him he wrote poetry, but recovered somewhat when Boyle said it was only comic poetry.'
29. WBY to Farr, 11 June 1905, HRHRC.
30. Perhaps reflecting the connection he now made between the characters of Cuchulain and Parnell: Hogan and O'Neill, *Holloway's Abbey Theatre*, 58.
31. Cave, *Hail and Farewell*, 541–3; Hogan and O'Neill, *Holloway's Abbey Theatre*, 61.
32. [29] May 1905, NYPL.
33. See Johnson, *Florence Farr*, 117–18, and *Inis Fáil*, Aug. 1905.
34. *TB*, 71.
35. 3 Aug. 1905, *L*, 458–9.
36. ibid.
37. See AG to Maire Garvey, 28 Oct. 1905, Harvard.
38. 7 May 1905, HRHRC.
39. A letter from Portman Square, in Harvard.

Dear Mr Yeats, It is a matter which gratifies me intensely, that the Society should be now able to free certain of its members so that their whole strength and energy should be given to the Theatre & its needs, practical as well as artistic. We must all have a little patience with the public and in time the Theatre will become part of the natural life of the community. If a time of difficulty should arise and there should be anxiety as to continuing these payments, I will now try to minimise this anxiety by offering myself as security. I will undertake to make up the salaries to the sums agreed on, when any deficiency occurs; but when more people are freed I must be informed first so as to know the extent of the liability.

For another concocted letter, and general speculation about WBY's strategy, see Frazier, *Behind the Scenes*, 119–20.
40. See a series of undated letters in Berg.
41. An interesting letter from Russell to Quinn, 4 June 1909, NYPL, repeated this analysis, discussing at length the enmities WBY had created in Dublin and stressing the difficulty Russell had in persuading the original National Theatre Society to elect WBY as President, he himself having refused. I owe this reference to W. M. Murphy.
42. To JMS, *TB*, 74.
43. n.d., probably Sept. 1905, Berg. See also Russell to WBY, Denson, *Letters from AE*, 52–4, which is 13 Sept. 1905 (not Apr. 1904, as printed).
44. n.d., Berg, but WBY's answer is 19 Sept. Also see *LTWBY*, i, 151–5; Kuch, *Yeats and AE*, 224–5; and the letter to Quinn mentioned in n. 41, above.
45. TS in Berg.
46. WBY to AG, *c.* 21 Sept. 1905, Berg.
47. n.d., but late Sept., and 6 Nov. 1905, Berg.
48. n.d., but probably Nov. 1907, Berg.
49. n.d., Berg.
50. n.d., but *c.* 15 Jan. 1906, Berg. He added an important postscript:

Even if Lady Gregory & myself leave old Society your friends will not be near a working majority. The Fays, Wright & Miss Allgood are alone enough to stop that. Furthermore there is in the long run no worthwhile way to be popular except good plays. At the same time I am ready to consider anything you suggest provided it does not weaken discipline or delay the work in any way. Remember it is we who are in the strong position. We are quite ready for any reasonable concessions but cannot concede anything that will make the work commoner or the discipline weak. My dear Colum in the long run popular support is not got by concession to it but by strength in the quiet doing of our work. Of demagogues Ireland has enough. By the by I never advocated a 'free gallery' & the popular theatre I want must be one for all classes – peer & peasant if that is possible but certainly not one class, like the theatre of the National Players.

51. Masefield to Jack Yeats, n.d., Harvard.
52. SMY to Quinn, 25 Dec. 1905, NYPL.
53. See WBY to AG, 11 Nov. 1905, Berg.
54. Berg.
55. To AG, late Dec., Berg.
56. 8 Jan. 1906, Berg.
57. 2 Jan. 1906, *TB*, 88. See also ibid., 89–90.
58. 5 Jan. 1906, Berg. While in Scotland in mid-Jan., he discovered the weakness of his legal position.
59. *TB*, 94. Also see *PF*, 306–7, for further letters about this imbroglio.
60. Draft from AG to JBY, Berg; also see AG to Colum, 9 Jan. [1906], Synge MSS, TCD.
61. Fragment in Berg, misdated 5 Jan. 1905.
62. 6 Jan. 1906, original in Kansas.
63. *LTWBY*, i, 160.
64. 16 Jan. 1906, Kohfeldt, *Lady Gregory*, 181.
65. 18 Feb. 1906, Berg. His actual resignation letter was dated 24 Apr. 1906, ibid. Also see Berg for AG's rebuttal of Colum's accusation that they were 'becoming less and less a theatre of the people'; she instanced their accessible plays and her own commitment to a sixpenny pit, and stoutly defended Willie Fay. WBY wrote savagely about Colum to Quinn on 4 Apr. 1906 (NYPL): 'He has the horoscope of the kind of pretty woman who never grows up. I know an old lady of title, who at an immense age keeps all the little mincing ways of what has been charming, and in her case, slightly scandalous five and twenty. I am sure that the stars had in all things except the scandal a like record at her birth as at Colum's. I have had wonderful letters from him, and so has Lady Gregory. He is turning in every direction, always trying to butter somebody's parsnips anew, and will not have a friend left in about six months.' Thus early, he was grouping unlikely people by horoscope-type, as he would do in *A Vision* twenty years later.
66. 10 Mar. 1906.
67. TL fragment, Berg. A later reference to WBY gleaning 'notes for his diary' suggests it belongs to this period, when WBY was drafting *Discoveries*.
68. AG to WBY, Berg.
69. 6 Jan. 1906, HRHRC, quoted in Kuch, *Yeats and AE*, 227–8.
70. *G–YL*, 224.
71. To Quinn, 5 Dec. 1905, NYPL.
72. 6 Jan. 1906, Berg.
73. 6 Jan. 1906, private collection.
74. 20 July 1909, private collection.
75. See an important letter to Bullen, 21 Sept. 1906, Kansas.
76. NLI MS 30,313.
77. WBY to AG, 27 Mar. 1906, Berg; he had only £3 left in his bank account.
78. Mathews would agree only to *The Wind Among the Reeds* being reprinted in a book

costing at least 8*s*. 6*d*. Eventually WBY had to leave it out of the first edition of Oct. 1906, though it was included in the revised edition from Apr. 1907.

79. To AG, 20 Dec. 1906, Berg. He hoped for a new edition at Easter 1907 when Mathews's rights over *The Wind Among the Reeds* and Fisher Unwin's over *Poems* would expire; but sales slowed, the book was not reprinted, and *CW* gained priority over it.

80. Berg, misdated 1905.

81. 30 May 1906, Berg.

82. To Holbrook Jackson, 19 Apr. 1906, Colgate University Library (Hamilton, NY).

83. See Tom Steele, *Alfred Orage and the Leeds Arts Club* (Aldershot, 1990), 128–32.

84. 17 Apr. [no year], Berg. 'If you don't [go] you must send it back – & you mustn't cash it till you are actually going to take your ticket – it will just get you there & back & give you a week or so – & if you stay longer, you can't be spending more than at Woburn Buildings or the Nassau.'

85. Arthur Sinclair, as recorded by Gabriel Fallon in *I &R*, i, 176; also see Hogan and O'Neill, *Holloway's Abbey Theatre*, 160. Sinclair, who joined the company in 1904, played Fergus in *Deirdre* (1906) and Thomas Hearn in *The Unicorn from the Stars* (1907).

86. Brigit O'Dempsey to Gerard Fay, as above.

87. 1 May 1906, NYPL.

88. SMY to Marie Freudenthal, 7 Mar. 1906, private collection.

89. WBY to Quinn, 1 May 1906, NYPL.

90. 7 May 1906, HRHRC.

91. *TB*, 124.

92. See reviews in Henderson's cuttings book, NLI MS 1730.

93. Frazier, *Behind the Scenes*, 176–7.

94. 19 June 1906, NLI MS 13,068.

95. 3 July 1906, Berg: an important letter, written from London after a weekend at Mells.

> Miss Horniman seems to me very reasonable – she is in good health and quite unlike her old self but she has made up her mind not to go in any business relation with Fay. At the same time she had made it perfectly plain that she looked upon the English work of this theatre as supplying her with what she called a career. I never had this in so many words but have always suspected that the finding of work for her was a condition of wholehearted support. She is prepared to treat us very generously under any circumstances but if we cannot restore her relation to some part of the work however circumscribed we will probably find either that she may break with us altogether on some unforeseen issue or that all her means may be taken up with some other project just at the moment when our theatre is in want of fresh capital.

96. To AG, 25 June 1906, Berg.

97. *TB*, 134.

98. ibid., 146–8; WBY to Nugent Monck, 10 Sept. 1911, private collection.

99. 30 Aug. 1906, NLI MS 13,068. She believed that Moore's article 'Stage Management in the Irish National Theatre', written as 'Paul Ruttledge' in *Dana* (Sept. 1904), hinted that she handed over the theatre for sexual rather than artistic reasons.

100. *PF*, 304ff.

101. 28 Aug. 1906. Part of this letter is in MBY, and part in Harvard.

102. 4 Oct. 1906, Kansas. The letter she mentions is a TS copy from WBY at Coole, dated 1 Oct. 1906, demanding a legal agreement to make him sole editor, paid a retainer through Watt, which he would pay back to her 'so long as the agreement holds good'. The orginal is in the Yeats collection at Bucknell, sent on by ECY to Emery Walker with a frantic plea for advice. WBY's letter is not a friendly document.

103. 12 Oct. [1906], NYPL.

104. See ECY to Emery Walker, 3 Oct. 1906, Bucknell: a letter specifically blaming the

influence of Coole, and revealing that Jack had advised them to try and dispense with WBY altogether.

105. ECY to Quinn, 29 Oct. 1906, 25 Nov. 1906, NYPL. Quinn's suggestions, dated 16 Nov. 1906, closely resembled Russell's terms, according to ECY.

106. She told Bullen that he demanded 20 per cent for *In the Seven Woods* and the same for *Hanrahan*, which she had not paid yet since the book had not sold well.

107. See WBY to KT, 28 Aug. 1906, Harvard. A long and grateful letter to her on 1 Sept. (Harvard) became a sustained critique of Russell's indiscriminate enthusiasm and reliance on 'inspirationism'. WBY specifically connected Russell, Starkie and nic Shiubhlaigh with the Dun Emer struggle: 'it is all one dispute'.

108. 13 Aug. 1906, *TB*, 139.

109. WBY to AG, 19 Jan. 1907, Berg.

110. To AG, 25 June 1906, Berg. In an interesting letter to JBY from Coole, 21 July 1906 (*L*, 474–6), WBY compared Darragh to Mrs Campbell as Deirdre, finding that Darragh came much nearer to the 'distinguished, solitary, proud' style of the new acting school, whereas Mrs Pat was 'trained in plays like Mrs Tanquery, where everything is done by a kind of magnificent hysteria (one understands that when one hears her hunting her monkey and her servant with an impartial fury about the house) . . . the problem with me just now is whether, as I am rather inclined to, to leap at the advertisement of a performance by Mrs Pat or to keep to my own people and my own generation till they have brought their art to perfection.' The idea of 'something to perfection brought' would stay with him. (In fact, when Mrs Campbell did play *Deirdre*, Dublin wits referred to it as 'The Second Mrs Concobar'.)

111. See e.g. a letter of 22 Sept. 1906, NLI MS 10,952.

112. It appeared on 20 Oct. and 24 Nov. 1906.

113. *Daily Express*, Dublin, 15 Oct. 1906.

114. Aug. 1906, NLI MS 13,068.

115. Hogan and O'Neill, *Holloway's Abbey Theatre*, 74–6.

116. A copy is in the Synge papers, TCD.

117. Curiously, on 10 Dec. at the National Literary Society, he stoutly defended the policy of limiting their programme to Irish plays: see Hogan and O'Neill, *Holloway's Abbey Theatre*, 78–9.

118. 'Friday', n.d., Berg.

119. NLI MS 18,680, where it is misfiled under 1923; not in *TB*.

120. See a detached note in her hand, in NLI MS 13,068.

I have come to the conclusion that the only way to preserve the authors' time so that they may do their own work is to engage a highly paid Managing Director who would be capable of stage management & general direction. The authors, when desirous to do so, to produce their own works. Other works (except peasant plays, which may be left to Fay) to be produced either by artists, directors, or the Managing Director. This new man to be responsible for them being kept up to the level of their production. If the other Directors agree & a suitable man can be found, Mr Yeats will accept my offer.

See also a letter of 16 July 1906: 'The careful arrangements you may make in December will *not* be carried out in January.'

121. *TB*, 186. Interestingly, Brigit O'Dempsey claimed that W. G. Fay respected Horniman and 'was always indignant at WB's and that old Trout's attitude to her': to Gerard Fay, 24 Nov. 1907, NLI MS 10,954.

122. WBY to AG, 27 Dec. 1906, Berg, and to JMS, 28 Dec. 1906, *TB*, 187–8.

123. WBY to AG, 3 Jan. 1907, Berg.

124. ibid.

125. 28 Dec. 1906, *TB*, 188.

126. 5 Jan. 1907, *TB*, 197.
127. 11 Jan. 1907, Berg.
128. Apparently in a long letter from WBY, 8 Jan. 1907.
129. Probably 10 Jan. 1907, *TB*, 202. Original in Berg.
130. *TB*, 203–4. They could withdraw their plays after six months if they wished, and Fay was to be guaranteed control of 'dialect work'.
131. 'She probably talked in the reckless sort of way the majority of us talk among our equals and forgot that it was quite a different thing to talk that way before people like Mac and the Allgoods, who have, more or less, to look up to us if w are to keep any kind of discipline.' (to AG, 17 Jan. 1907, Berg).
132. *TB*, 160.
133. Printed circular of 1906, signed 'WBY'.
134. 5 Feb. 1906, Henderson scrapbook on National Literary Society, Kansas. Kettle had founded the *Nationist* in late 1905 – and (so WBY told Quinn, 6 Dec. 1905, NYPL) had been expelled from it for 'some purely historical articles on liberal Catholicism in France and a mild article asking for lay control of the University College, Stephens Green'. WBY blamed Father Finlay (an enemy since their conflicting American tours of 1903/4); he added that Kenny had been similarly driven from the *Irish Peasant* by 'the umbrella of a parish priest'.
135. To Quinn, 16 Sept. 1905, NYPL.

Chapter 14 : SYNGE AND THE IRELAND OF HIS TIME
1907–1909

Epigraph: Arrow, i, 3, 23 Feb. 1907.
  1. WBY to AG, 14 Jan. 1907, Berg. Horniman guaranteed his salary in a letter of 17 Dec. 1906.
  2. Fragment, n.d., Berg.
  3. 9 Jan. 1907.
  4. 16 Jan. 1907, Margaret McKim Maloney Collection, NYPL. Payne confirmed this in his letter of resignation, 27 June 1907, Berg.
  5. See Horniman to AG, 26 Dec. 1906, NLI 5380, and to WBY, 31 Dec. 1906, NLI MS 13,068.
  6. 12 Jan. 1907, *TB*, 205, n. 1.
  7. See Fay and Carswell, *The Fays of the Abbey Theatre*, 212.
  8. 26 Jan. 1907, NLI MS 1805, 63.
  9. Berg.
 10. It is also significant that he had left her his address, evidently half expecting trouble. See Grierson's TS memorandum in NLS. The Aberdeen lecture was given gratis, while for an Edinburgh engagement he received '£5 with difficulty' (AG to Hyde, n.d., Hyde MSS, TCD). WBY blamed his financial crisis on ECY's refusal to pay him a proper royalty.
 11. *Evening Telegraph*, 29 Jan. 1907.
 12. 30 Jan. 1907, Henderson scrapbook, NLI 1730, 94–5.
 13. 30 Jan. 1907. For the calling in of the police on Monday night by Willie Fay, see *Evening Telegraph*, 29 Jan.; it is doubtful if WBY could have returned in time to arrange it. Also see AG to WBY, n.d., Berg, referring to a hostile *Weekly Freeman* article: 'He does not mention that it was Henderson who worked him [JMS] up that night, & Molly also, so that I found Synge intimidated & had to give my own orders to the police. I wish I had dismissed him there & then.'
 14. See *Arrow*, i, 3, 23 Feb. 1907, and Henderson scrapbook, NLI MS 1730, 96–7.
 15. *Irish Times*, 29 Jan. 1907; *Evening Mail*, 28 Jan. 1907.
 16. *Irish Times*, 31 Feb. 1907.

17. See an incensed letter to WBY, 23 Aug. 1907, Himber, *Letters of Quinn to Yeats*, 83–90.
18. To Hugh Viscount Gough, 3 Feb. 1907, Berg.
19. Béaslaí and Colum, arrested on 29 Jan., were both fined forty shillings after detention and prosecution. 'I cannot believe that Mr Yeats imagined my father could be a member of an organisation,' the younger Colum complained to Robert Gregory. 'Of course he is not.' (1 Feb. 1907, Gregory MSS, Emory). WBY gave evidence in court that Béaslaí ' "had addressed some words to me in Irish." "Were they complimentary or the reverse?" "I am sorry to say, I understand no Irish." ' (*Evening Telegraph*, 30 Jan. 1907). 'What an instance of National topsey-turveydom in the picture of this Irish dramatist, this authority on the ways and speech of the Western peasant, standing sick, silent and ashamed when addressed in Irish,' remarked a contributor to the paper.
20. *PF*, 315.
21. *Sinn Féin*, 2 Feb. 1907.
22. Richard M. Kain, 'The Playboy Riots' in S. B. Bushrui (ed.), *Sunshine and the Moon's Delight: A Centenary Tribute to John Millington Synge* (Gerrards Cross, 1972), 181.
23. *FJ*, 2 Feb. 1907. For Milligan, see *Evening Telegraph*, 4 Feb. 1907; for Sigerson, National Literary Society address reported on 25 Feb. 1907.
24. In a letter to Robert, duplicated to JMS, now at Emory: see *TB*, 210–14.
25. *FJ*, 5 Feb. 1907. For Joyce's interest see Richard Ellmann (ed.), *The Letters of James Joyce. Volume 2* (London, 1966), 211.
26. *PF*, 316.
27. See *Leader*, 9 Feb. 1907, and for the general theatrical scene, Seamus de Burca, *The Queen's Theatre Dublin 1829–1969* (Dublin, 1983).
28. *Ex*, 226–8, and *FJ*, *Irish Times*, 5 Feb. 1907.
29. *Sinn Féin*, 9 Feb. 1907, followed up the story and triumphantly established that the Aran parricide had killed his father by accident and 'the people did not glorify him for being the cause of his father's death, but pitied him in his sorrow'. The man's name was O'Malley. WBY had heard that story in Aran in 1896 (see above). But when JMS was there in 1898, all the nationalist papers reported a grisly murder of a father by his son – with a spade (*FJ*, 23 June 1898). JMS conflated both incidents.
30. As he wrote to Rosamund Langbridge (early Feb. 1907, private collection), and also Grierson (11 Feb. 1907, NLS).
31. 18 Feb. 1907, *PF*, 317–18.
32. n.d., from Florence, Foster–Murphy Collection, NYPL.
33. *TB*, 217, etc.
34. To Grierson, 11 Feb. 1907, NLS. Boyle admitted in a letter to D. J. O'Donoghue (13 Feb. 1907) that he had merely used the issue to withdraw: 'I have been boiling for some time.' (private collection).
35. To AG, 6 Mar. 1907, Berg. See below, pp. 388–9.
36. To same, 9 Mar. 1907.
37. *TB*, 222ff.
38. D. H. Greene and E. M. Stephens, *J. M. Synge, 1871–1909* (London, 1959), 269.
39. As in his speech to the British Association (*UP*, ii, 366–70).
40. See a letter from Stephen Gwynn, 23 Aug. 1907, Berg.
41. To Quinn, 18 Feb. 1907, NYPL.
42. 'The Immoral Irish Bourgeoisie', *Irish Times*, 11 Feb. 1908; interview with Robert Lynd, *Daily News*, 6 June 1910 (also *I & R*, i, 64–8); *Observer*, 19 June 1910. Also see lecture to Gaelic League, 'The Theatre and Ireland', *Evening Telegraph*, 4 Mar. 1910, and lecture 'The Living Voice', RDS, 13 Feb. 1907, *Evening Telegraph*, 14 Feb. 1907.
43. To Quinn, Apr. 1907, NYPL.
44. 28 June 1907, NLS. The book in question was Edmund Garratt Gardner's *Dukes and Poets*

in Ferrara (1904). WBY may also have been influenced by his study of Ariosto, *The King of Court Poets* (1906).

45. Horace Reynolds diary, Harvard, recording a letter of 6 July 1927.
46. Pethica, 315.
47. NYPL. He claimed that one shop had ordered 200 sets which seems unlikely, given the early stage of proceedings. Bullen may have been spinning him an encouraging line.
48. To Joseph Hone, 4 May 1907, HRHRC.
49. See R. Schuchard, 'Yeats, Titian and the New French Painting' in A. N. Jeffares (ed.), *Yeats the European* (Gerrards Cross, 1984), 142–59.
50. *VSR*, 152. This passage then goes on to describe Aherne's shifting his allegiance to modern Symbolist painters, to the narrator's resentment. My thanks to Warwick Gould for suggesting this point.
51. n.d., but *c.* 1909, Berg.
52. 27 June 1907, Berg. They had reached London on 26 May.
53. See letter in NLI MS 13,068, wrongly attributed to July 1906 (*recte* 1907).
54. 18 June 1907, misdated in *L*, 500–501. *TB*, 223–6, gives the background, and AG to JMS, 20 June 1907, shows that she was involved at every stage. Horniman's response is in NLI MS 30,596: 'But what are my arguments against the wooing of the vampire Kathleen ni Houlihan . . . I will not waste my time on a lost cause. This should be a great relief to your mind, to know that you need never fear any more interference from me.'
55. e.g. letter of 21 June 1907, NLI.
56. 27 Feb. 1908, Berg.
57. Letters of 25 June and 15 Aug. 1907, *TB*, 227–8, 236.
58. WBY to AG, 22 June 1907.
59. To Quinn, 7 Jan. 1908, NYPL.
60. As did AG's *The Canavans*, written while she was reading drafts of the *Playboy*: my thanks to Ben Levitas for this suggestion.
61. Masefield saw him at Binyon's *Attila* in London on 3 Sept., where he met Farr (Masefield to Jack Yeats, 4 Sept. 1907, Harvard); and Philip Moeller met him in the train at Athenry on 7 Sept., returning to Coole.
62. To Quinn, 4 Oct. 1907, *L*, 496.
63. Michael Holroyd, *Augustus John: A Biography* (rev. ed., Harmondsworth, 1976), 311.
64. See Ellmann MSS at Tulsa, which include a transcript of Horniman to Bullen, 3 July 1907; Horniman to Bullen, 11 Mar. 1907, MBY, shows that Bullen asked for £1,500 surety, claiming he would sell 750 copies at a subscribed price of four guineas; even with a cheaper Irish price and free review copies, she would recoup her money. She would then receive one third of the profits, and Bullen two thirds, after a 'reasonable royalty' for WBY. Also see WBY to Edith Lister a year later ('Sunday', 19 Apr. 1908, Kansas): 'I do not want to get his business with her & my business with her mixed up together.'
65. Mathews retained it, and brought out another printing in 1907; but it was eventually included in *CW*.
66. MBY A27 records a loan of £70 in 1908, and a letter in NLI MS 13,068 of 26 Mar. 1908 shows WBY repaying that amount to Horniman.
67. 8 July 1907, Harvard.
68. See Horniman to WBY, 7 July 1907, NLI 13,068. 'I hope that you are going to make it quite clear in the library edition that Lady Gregory has given you certain help in the peasant dialogue. I felt it only fair to tell Bullen what you told me some time ago, that she considers that she has a certain claim on your disposal of your work, because of the help she has given you.' Thus she took her revenge for his refusal to move his plays to Manchester.
69. n.d., but 1907, Harvard.
70. To Bullen, 30 Sept. 1907, Kansas.

71. To Lister, 14 Sept. 1907, Kansas.
72. To Bullen, early Mar. 1908, Kansas.
73. 27 Mar. 1908, 8 May 1908, Harvard.
74. Marginal note on proof of Spenser essay, *c.* May 1908, Kansas.
75. WBY to AG, 18 Dec. 1907, Berg. For reactions, see William H. O'Donnell, 'Portraits of W. B. Yeats: This Picture in the Mind's Eye', *YA* 3 (1985), 90–93.
76. WBY to Lister, Harvard, and to Farr, 'Tuesday', n.d., HRHRC.
77. See Sargent to AG, 17 May 1908, Emory, and AG to Quinn, 28 Mar. 1908, Berg.
78. 17 Jan. 1908, NYPL (*L*, 502).
79. 4 Oct. 1907, NYPL.
80. HRHRC.
81. Fay repeated this in letters of 26 and 29 Apr. 1908 to Patrick Hoey and Niall Montgomery, Huntingdon.
82. 3 Nov. 1907, NLI MS 30,586.
83. WBY allegedly referred to them as 'thieves and blackmailers' who 'stole £50 of my own and Lady Gregory's money', according to Casimir Markievicz. See TS copy of WBY to T. G. Keohler, 18 Nov. 1907, Berg, and JBY to Rosa Butt, postmarked 25 Oct. 1907, Bodleian.
84. 22 Nov. 1907, by 'F.M.A.'.
85. 29 Oct. 1907, HRHRC.
86. To Rosa Butt, postmarked 4 Dec. 1907, Bodleian. cf. same to same, 3 Jan. 1908: 'The ser-iousness of America at once delights me and puzzles me and alarms me. I find Jack was a great success with them. I believe that is because Jack was brought up by his grand-parents, who had this kind of seriousness, not having lived in what calls itself grand soci-ety and so not being practised in persiflage and levity. Jack's jokes are always serious.'
87. n.d., but Dec. 1907, Berg.
88. See SMY to JBY, 6 Sept. 1908, courtesy of W. M. Murphy: 'So he and Madame now pooh-pooh the Castle and are all for Sinn Fein Theatre of Ireland etc.'
89. 21 [*recte* 23] Nov. 1907, *UP*, ii, 356.
90. 10 Dec. 1907, Morris Library, SIUC.
91. 3 Jan. 1908, Berg. Galway was currently riven by agrarian unrest, and she wanted to attract 'the classes' to this local performance in early Jan. 1908: see correspondence in Berg, espe-cially a letter postmarked 26 Dec. 1907. Worries about 'no getting over class distinctions in the way of friendship' may be found in AG, n.d., but early Mar. 1908, Berg, and on Sat., 21 Mar., she wrote, 'They are all very much to blame, but not so much as Ireland & Romanism & the general feeling in the country that nothing means anything.' (Berg).
92. He blamed Fay's 'whole flawed generation' for the breakdown.
93. See especially 30 Dec. 1907, *TB*, 264–7.
94. 12 Jan. 1908, *TB*, 271.
95. Frank's discontent was partly due to his hopeless love for Maire Garvey, who eventu-ally married Roberts; when he died in 1931 SMY described him to R L-P as 'one of those people who got on with no-one, nursed grievances, and had a struggle to live'. But W. G. Fay's version of the break is significant.

> From the first Frank and I had seen in the National Theatre movement the possibility of a real art theatre, and we had been led to believe that the Abbey Directors shared our enthusiasm . . . Unfortunately the lavish encomiums of the English press had been too heady for our friends Yeats, Synge and Lady Gregory. They imagined we had arrived, when we had no more than started. We had a company that could do peasant plays with an accomplishment and a finish that had never been rivalled, much less excelled. But we should have to show much more than that before we could claim to be a real art theatre. (quoted in McCann, *Story of the Abbey Theatre*, 134).

96. 24 Dec. 1906, *TB*, 186.
97. Letter from Camberwell, early 1908, Berg.
98. Boyle to Holloway, 5 Feb. 1908, private collection.
99. See letters to Quinn, 3 Mar. 1908, NYPL, and to AG, 7 Mar. 1908, NLI MS 18,708 (copy).
100. To Patrick Hoey, postmarked 3 Mar. 1908, Huntingdon.
101. 'But as I helped put him in the saddle, I'd better say no more.' To Maire Garvey, 26 Apr. 1909, NLI MS 8320. He also attacked the way AG's plays were 'praised & praised with insincerity, by people who have their own fish to fry' (6 Mar. 1909, ibid.). Fay's correspondence in the Huntingdon repeats these views ad infinitum.
102. To Patrick Hoey, 24 Mar. 1909, Huntingdon. JMS's 'alien creed . . . prevented him from understanding those brought up in another creed . . . The pessimism that clings like a mist around Riders to the Sea is foreign to the Catholic nature.'
103. See W. G. Fay's letter book, NLI MS 2652, letters of 23 Dec. 1923 and 13 Mar. 1933.
104. WBY to AG, 9 Feb. 1908, NLI MS 18,708 (copy).
105. Later withdrawn when Guinan tried to take it up.
106. To Quinn, 3 Mar. 1908, NYPL.
107. *Daily Express*, Dublin, 17 Feb. 1908, has a full report. Norreys Connell faintly disputed this reading in his memoirs. WBY tried out his ideas on Holloway the day before, but Holloway still saw the play as an anti-Irish caricature. For *The Piper*, see Richard F. Peterson and Gary Phillips, 'W. B. Yeats and Norreys Connell', *YA* 2 (1983); also McCann, *Story of the Abbey Theatre*, 140–41.
108. *TB*, 272–9.
109. To AG, 11 Jan. 1908, Berg.
110. To Rosa Butt, postmarked 4 Dec. 1907, Bodleian. Drafts of WBY's letters to Horniman in the Berg show him threatening resignation from the Theatre. He was in London on 5 Dec. and Masefield spotted him there on the 19th, as he wrote to Jack (Harvard).
111. See WBY to Bullen, 12 Feb. 1908, Kansas: 'She has written . . . a most violent letter on the supposition that it is quite a different body and has excused herself by saying she couldn't possibly know what society it was as it gave its name in Irish . . . They, poor people, had simply written to hire the Theatre . . . I don't know what their intentions were but our Secretary who is a law student took a very serious view of the situation. She is always doing this sort of thing.'
112. To Lister, 18 Mar. 1908, Harvard (also see *L*, 505–6). On 21 May he wrote to the *Evening Mail*, giving the reasons for Fay's departure and denying that the Abbey discouraged the work of young writers, strategically citing as their one rejection a scandalous piece about an immoral priest.
113. WBY to L. A. G. Strong, 1920–22, *I & R*, i, 152.
114. 26 Feb. 1908, Berg. cf. her remark to WBY, 19 Apr. 1908: 'We must keep on our dignity, & not be spiteful. I thought Synge spiteful, & concluded it is because he is timid & had never, as you & I did, spoken up to the Fays face to face.'
115. WBY to Quinn, 3 Mar. 1908, NYPL.
116. To Quinn, 28 Mar. 1908, Berg.
117. *Telegraph*, New York, 9 Nov. 1907.
118. To Quinn, 29 Oct. 1907, Foster–Murphy Collection, NYPL.
119. See WBY to AG, 21 Jan. 1907, Berg, for a long-running row with ECY about the sums she paid her writers. Also see financial statement, Cuala Archive, Box 1, no. 34, statement 1906–10, TCD. Purchases and royalties built up nearly threefold over the period, while salaries and other expenses stayed low; but incomes from shows and exhibitions fluctuated wildly. The income from printing and embroidery increased, but they still traded at a loss and at the end of the first five years barely broke even.

120. A review in the *Bookman*, Feb. 1908, noted that WBY was 'coming out of the land of dreams into the intensity of personal life' – a phrase also used by the *Manchester Guardian*, 20 Jan. 1908.

121. 4 Mar. 1908, Conal O'Riordan (Norreys Connell) correspondence, SIUC.

122. JBY to Rosa Butt, postmarked 14 Sept. 1907, Bodleian.

123. *FS*, 350–51; and JBY to Ruth Hart, 21 Nov. 1913, TCD.

124. Examples would be Thomas MacDonagh and P. S. O'Hegarty.

125. As described in 'The Return of the Stars', NLI MS 30,535.

126. To AG [9 Mar. 1908], NLI MS 18,708 (copy).

127. See Patricia Boylan, 'Mrs Duncan's Vocation', *Irish Arts Review*, 12 (1996), and *All Cultivated People: A History of the United Arts Club, Dublin* (Gerrards Cross, 1988).

128. In Sept. 1907: ECY to Quinn, 22 Sept. 1907, NYPL.

129. Foster–Murphy Collection, NYPL. He had also continued to be jealous of the actor Robert Farquharson, as a 'young admirer' of Farr's: see Horniman to WBY, 27 Sept. 1907, NLI MS 13,068.

130. 8 Dec. 1907, Himber, *Letters of Quinn to Yeats*, 95.

131. Died 17 May 1905; son of a Bishop of Meath; Vicar of St Ann's and Precentor of St Patrick's, 1855–1902; Dean of Chapel Royal, 1869–1902; Professor of Pastoral Theology at TCD, 1894–1902; a supporter of temperance and the higher education of women.

132. 'Sunday' [April 1908], Berkeley.

133. So George Yeats told Ellmann: 17 June 1946, interview book, Tulsa.

134. 4 Oct. 1907, NYPL.

135. 11 May 1908, Berkeley.

136. Probably written from Paris in June; Yale.

137. To Dickinson, 30 Aug. 1908, Berkeley.

138. *G-YL*, 241.

139. n.d., but probably Sept.–Oct. 1907, Library of Congress.

140. Dr Ely Starr, for an unnamed subject born 21 Dec. 1866. WBY used this prediction when surveying the astrological history of their relationship, particularly their separation in 1893 and the spiritual marriage of 1895.

141. See Chapter 13, n. 84, for her offer the previous year.

142. Particularly Manet and Renoir, to judge by comments in his notebook: NLI MS 30,535.

143. The letter, evidently to MG, survives in MBY: obviously sent to WBY to gauge his reaction.

144. WBY to JBY, 17 July 1908, Boston, from Burren, partly quoted by Wade and misdated to 1909 in *L*, 532–3.

145. 'P.I.A.L. diary', 1909, MBY. MG's house is described in Young, *Flowering Dusk*, 101. For Iseult's votive offerings, see WBY to AG, n.d. [28 June 1908], NLI MS 18, 709 (copy).

146. The 'P.I.A.L. diary' records that their *rapprochement* began then. Curtis Bradford wrote in Ellmann's copy of 'Yeats and Maud Gonne' (University of Texas *Studies in Literature and Language*, iii, 4, Winter 1962): 'Not the full story, but as much of it as GY will let me tell.'

147. *G-YL*, 250.

148. *G-YL*, 257.

149. To Quinn, 13 Aug. 1908, NYPL.

150. *Mem*, 172–4. The poem was written down in Feb. 1909 but composed 'about six months ago'.

151. n.d. [11 June 1908], n.d. [20 June 1908], Berkeley.

152. SMY to Quinn, 5 July 1908, NYPL.

153. NLI MS 30,535 consists of notes made on 12 July, expecting some kind of resolution on the 14th; in fact, he received a letter on the 15th.
154. Originally presented as a doctorate at Rennes and published by Oxford in 1911. The dedication also extends to Russell, in even more flowery terms. One of Wentz's interviewees, Owen Conway of Rosses Point, 'said that Mr W. B. Yeats and other men famous in Irish literature had visited him to hear about the fairies, and though he knew very little about the fairies he nevertheless always liked to talk to them.' *Fairy Faith* contains much about Rosicrucianism, Theosophy, Neo-Platonism, and specifically instances Freud's interpretation of dreams; regeneration among the aged is also a preoccupation. (See 464, 467–8, 511.) WBY's influence is writ large throughout.
155. 26 July [1908], Berkeley.
156. 4 Sept. 1908, *UP*, ii, 367.
157. 6 Sept. 1908.
158. *VSR*, 158.
159. See NLI MS 30,535, a notebook of short essays begun 24 May 1908.
160. Arsenal, Paris. Both poems were printed in the *English Review* in late Sept.
161. To AG, 13 Oct. 1908, NLI MS 18,709 (copy).
162. ibid.
163. PRO, CO 904/10: my thanks to Warwick Gould and Deirdre Toomey.
164. Hyde called for the Author at the end, but only – he explained – 'to see what he looked like': WBY to AG, 17 Oct. 1908, NLI MS 18,709 (copy).
165. Roberts to Garvey, 17 Oct. 1908, NLI MS 8320. The police report recorded that on this date 'she left by express boat from North Wall for Holyhead'.
166. Recounted to JBY, 30 Oct. 1908, Boston. The Liverpool visit was 19–21 October.
167. To R L-P, 6 Sept. 1909.
168. 15 Nov. 1908, *L*, 512.
169. Reginald Hine, 'Memories of W. B. Yeats', TS in HRHRC. Masefield adds *Memory Harbour*, some Blake engravings and prints, a portrait of WBY by JBY, a Cecil French drawing of a woman with a rose between her lips. One of the Beardsleys was the famous poster from Farr's production of *The Land of Heart's Desire*.
170. Hine says *Cathleen ni Houlihan*, but it must have been *The Countess Cathleen*.
171. To AG [27 Dec. 1908], Berg: he finally terrified her into silence. Young's version is in *Flowering Dusk*, 101–2.
172. As Ellmann was told both by Edith Shackleton Heald and George Yeats: 8 Dec. 1947, interview book, Tulsa. George Yeats was sworn to secrecy by her husband. I am grateful to Elizabeth Heine, whose forthcoming work on WBY and astrology confirms Dec. 1908 as the date they became lovers.
173. *G–YL*, 258–9.
174. 29 Dec. 1908, Kansas.
175. NLI MS 30,654.
176. 'Tuesday', n.d., HRHRC.
177. *CH*, 164.
178. See Warwick Gould, 'Journey without Maps', *YA* 11 (1994), 239.
179. To Quinn, 27 Apr. 1908, NYPL.
180. Writing to Henry Meade Bland in response to an essay by the latter, he remarked: 'I don't think I meant anything so definite as old age by "the star hung low in the rim of the sky" but I wrote that long ago & know nothing of it but what the verses tell me or anybody. I have forgotten the mood I wrote it in.' (2 May 1908, Mills College Library, Oakland, Calif.).
181. See a letter to SMY, 'Sunday', n.d., MBY: he had been investigating the family arms, as

AG wanted to give him a bookplate incorporating it. (In fact, this eventually awaited his prize for 'The Grey Rock' in 1913.) However, a crest for Mary Yeates of Lifford had been found, with a goat's head and gates which recurred in family emblems. 'He [James Duncan] says the coronet means that at some time our ancestors held their land not direct from the King but from some great lord. It is a very old coat of arms so we need not fear to light upon an ancestor who paid honest money for it.' He was also excited by the prospect of quartering the Butler arms – as their ancestress was an heiress it was a 'heraldic necessity'. See *Mem*, 196, for a journal entry.

182. See WBY to AG, 20 Mar. 1908, Berg.

183. In a letter of 6 Feb. 1909, telling her he wrote it on 3 Feb., Berg.

184. n.d., Berg.

185. Thirty or forty volumes by then, he thought. See also Warwick Gould, 'A Crowded Theatre: Yeats and Balzac' in Jeffares, *Yeats the European*.

186. WBY to AG, 7 Mar. 1909; he dined with Dickinson on 9 Mar.

187. *L*, 525; *Mem*, 176, 244.

188. WBY to O'Hegarty, 23 Dec. 1908, Kansas.

189. 'He would create a taste for reading & for reading the best literature & that is the one thing that matters.' (26 Jan. 1909, HRHRC).

190. To AG, 22 Mar. 1909, Berg.

191. AG to Quinn, 28 Mar. 1908, Berg.

192. See TS memo about his will in Gregory papers, Berg.

193. JMS himself emphasized WBY's input in a letter to ECY, 24 Nov. 1908, Berg.

194. 'Wednesday', 24 Mar. 1909, Berg, and *TB*, 298.

195. Also used by Lionel Johnson in the conclusion to 'The Dark Angel'. WBY would re-employ it for the epigraph to JMS's *Poems and Translations*. The original source is *Enneads*, VI, 9, 11. In Taylor's translation, 'This, therefore, is the life of the Gods, and of divine and happy men, a liberation from all terrene concerns, a life unaccompanied with human pleasures, and a flight of the alone to the Alone.'

196. MS notes by SMY, HRHRC.

197. WBY to Farr, 25 Apr. 1909, HRHRC.

198. See below, Chapter 15, pp. 417–21. For the literary testament, see TS memo in Berg. According to WBY to Joseph Hone, 3 Oct. 1910 (copy, HRHRC), Roberts tricked Edward Stephens into agreeing to publish the *Manchester Guardian* articles.

199. Fragment, n.d., Berg.

200. *Au*, 520.

Chapter 15 : SEVERANCES
1909–1910

1. *PF*, 345, 348.

2. SMY to Quinn, 9 May 1909, NYPL: 'Aunt Augusta' had rubbed them up the wrong way, '& Willy sees eye to eye with her when he is actually *with* her'.

3. [?8] Apr. 1909, Conal O'Riordan (Norreys Connell) correspondence, SIUC.

4. 17 May 1905, Berg.

5. To Quinn, 12 Mar. 1909, NYPL.

6. To JBY, 29 Apr. 1909, *L*, 528–9; to AG, late Aug. 1911, Berg.

7. WBY to Dunsany, 19 Sept. 1911, Berg.

8. *Mem*, 210.

9. 8 May 1911, Arsenal, Paris.

10. *New York Evening Sun*, 2 Apr. 1909.

11. See WBY to AG, reporting ECY, 1 June 1909, Berg.

12. WBY to Felkin, 11 June 1909, and solicitors' letters in Berg. This failed; Crowley published the rituals in *Equinox*, and won in an appeal against an injunction launched by MacGregor Mathers.

13. *Sinn Féin*, 8 May 1909.

14. ibid., 20 Feb. 1909.

15. 4 June 1909, NYPL.

16. See WBY's TS 'Why the Abbey Theatre Remained Open', 3 Feb. 1911, Berg.

17. See letters of 19 and 20 June 1910, NLI MS 30,596. The plan was that she return the subsidy and the cost of running the theatre, taking a 'nominal sum' for the buildings and contents: 'I want to treat them well and also to avoid any misconception.' (to 'Mr Whelan', 19 June 1909, copied to WBY, 20 June 1909). Shaw was involved as a broker, suggesting a new limited company.

18. This correspondence is in Berg.

19. Connell was already wearied by the unprofessional behaviour of the actors: see R. F. Peterson and Gary Phillips, 'W. B. Yeats and Norreys Connell', *YA* 2 (1983), 46ff. He advised WBY to bring back the Fays.

20. Berg.

21. 8 July 1909, Berg.

22. Draft copy NLI MS 13,068.

23. n.d., NYPL.

24. 21 June 1909, 'P.I.A.L. diary', MBY. Through a misreading (and its placing in the MS) this has often been attributed to the beginning of the year, but it is certainly dated June.

25. To Rosa Butt, 16 Aug. 1908, Bodleian.

26. To Rosa Butt, 24 July 1918, Bodleian.

27. SMY to JBY, 26 May 1909, gives some of the background and mentions that Meyer supported WBY's appointment.

28. 5 May 1909, NLI MS 18,474.

29. To Quinn, 5 May 1909, NYPL.

30. To AG, 1 June 1909, Berg; to Grierson, 12 Oct. 1909, NLS; to Quinn, 5 May 1909, NYPL.

31. The best account is Lucy McDiarmid, 'Augusta Gregory, Bernard Shaw and the Shewing-Up of Dublin Castle', *PMLA*, 109, 1 (Jan. 1994).

32. An important letter.

   Will you tell Yeats if he is at Coole that I got at Griffiths [*sic*] over the Blanco Posnett [*sic*] performance. He did what was required this week but another correspondent had sent in an article with a different point of view and Griffith's comment is a blend of my advice & the other correspondent. Anyhow he sets his face against any row in the theatre & that is what Yeats told me he wanted. I could not get at Ryan of the Nation but anyhow I don't think he has much influence in these matters & Sinn Feinn [*sic*] will do what is necessary. (postmarked 19 Aug. 1909, Berg).

33. *Sinn Féin*, 21 Aug. 1909.

34. *Samhain*, 1904.

35. 28 Aug. 1909.

36. To JBY, 21 Aug. 1909, NLI MS 31,112.

37. Lady Dunsany's diary, 20 Oct. 1910 (private collection) records Margaret Gregory's view. 'Lady G. stage managed Blanco Posnet entirely last year and made it the success it was. Y. never saw it acted until the last dress rehearsal. Then, realising that all the English and foreign critics had collected and that there was a stir, he asked her to let him take the rehearsal, saying he wished the reporters to think he had stage managed it, and she is so used to giving way to him that she agreed.'

38. Dan H. Laurence (ed.), *Bernard Shaw: Collected Letters 1898–1910* (London, 1972), 860–61.
39. *The Times*, 25 Aug. 1909.
40. To JBY, 21 (reporting dress rehearsal) and 26 Aug. 1909, NLI MS 31, 112.
41. Farr to Quinn, n.d., NYPL.
42. A guinea a performance for one-act plays; on three-act plays, 5 per cent of takings up to £50, 7.5 per cent up to £100, 10 per cent thereafter.
43. *Irish Times*, 23 Nov. 1910.
44. *Mem*, 225–6.
45. To AG, 7 Oct. 1909, Berg.
46. To AG, 10 Oct. 1909, Berg. She collaborated on the new version, as a letter of 28 Nov. 1909 shows.
47. 'Fairfield', Botanic Road, near Dr Delaney's 'Delville', where Swift had been a frequent visitor. *Thom's Directory* describes it as 'vacant' in 1909, but the Gogarty family owned it and let out rooms in it. SMY described it to JBY, 19 Oct. 1909, NLI MS 31,112: 'There is writing of his [Swift's] on a pane of glass. Lady Gregory suggested to the landlady that she would add to the value of the house if she got Willy to write on another pane. "I will", said Willy, "if she provides the diamond."'
48. SMY to JBY, 2 Nov. 1909, NLI MS 31,112. On the following Sunday they were at Russell's, where he and George Moore were 'very friendly together'.
49. To JBY, 29 Nov. 1909, *L*, 540.
50. 25 Oct. 1909, University of Delaware. (On 6 Mar. 1900 he went to Benson's uncut *Hamlet* with AG, perhaps the beginning of this obsession.)
51. To JBY, 18 and 29 Jan. 1910, NLI MS 31,112.
52. To Dickinson, 16 Jan. 1910, Berkeley.
53. 17 Dec. 1909, Berg. WBY had canvassed the idea of an appeal two days before.
54. See WBY to Horniman, 22 Jan. 1910, NLI MS 13,068.
55. 18 Jan. 1910, 13 May 1910, NLI MS 31,112.
56. TL copy fragment, AG to WBY [Jan. 1910], Berg.
57. 'Statement by L. G. to J. Q.', NYPL.
58. 'Friday' [Feb.–Mar. 1910], NLI.
59. 25 Nov. 1910, NYPL.
60. To AG, 3 Sept. 1911, Berg: not an interpretation shared by many others. AG's feelings are shown by an undated letter from this period (Berg), where she stated that despite the good audiences they were producing 'too much Boyle & Co. I shall think every week lost till we get on some verse . . . I think we shall have to pray for a slump to show that we have kept to our ideas.'
61. Enclosed with letter of 11 Feb. 1910, Berg.
62. Who told Quinn he only saw WBY about once every six months, and then by chance: 21 Aug. 1910, NYPL.
63. See Robert O'Driscoll, 'Yeats on Personality: Three Unpublished Lectures', *YT*, 4–59.
64. To JBY, 18 Jan. 1910, NLI MS 31,112. Pound lectured at the Polytechnic in Regent Street on 'The Spirit of Romance' in 1909, and published a book of that title in 1910.
65. 23 Feb. 1910, *L*, 548–9.
66. *The Autobiography of William Carlos Williams* (New York, 1948), 115–16.
67. O'Driscoll, 'Yeats on Personality', 58.
68. *Irish Nation*, 12 Mar. 1910.
69. Leader of 5 Mar. 1910.
70. The gushing Masefield told him that JMS 'thought of him almost as God' (WBY to AG, 26 Apr. 1910, Berg). WBY was sceptical.

71. To AG, 20 Mar. 1910: see *Mem*, 242–3, for drafts, and 229 for the original inspiration in Sept. 1909.
72. 1 Apr. 1910, NLI MS 10,854.
73. To Cornelius Weygandt, 25 Apr. 1910, A. Weygandt Collection; to AG, 22 Mar., 1 and 4 May 1910, Berg.
74. Now in Berg.
75. See above, pp. 299–300.
76. *Mem*, 154–5, 211.
77. 5 May 1910, Berg.
78. *Mem*, 178.
79. See also *Mem*, 191–2, where he refers to women giving themselves to an opinion as to a 'terrible stone doll'.
80. To AG, 22 and 25 Sept. 1910.
81. WBY to Masefield, 12 July 1910, University of Vermont.
82. See a scorching letter from Maire Garvey, 15 Oct. 1910, NLI MS 8320, to 'A cailín na rúne'.

> I suppose you heard of all this pother about Yeats' Introduction – he has treated Roberts in what I can only call a scandalous manner. I don't mind anything a man would do in fighting with another so long as he confines himself to the rules of the game – but to run round behind backs & do all he could to injure the other man by trying to prejudice other people against him is nothing but meanness – of course the outside people being mostly sensible merely laughed. Yeats can go round the world & enjoy himself without troubling to do the work wh. he now says was his to do & when he has put other people to expense by his carelessness he can try to get out of it by bluff & impertinence. I know one thing that if Roberts depended on him or anyone under his influence for help in his work he'd be in a bad way – However Yeats's spite may embitter some of his own drink one of these days & then we'll hear a grumble.

83. *Academy*, Dec. 1910.
84. 25 Apr. 1910, Berg.
85. Later the scene of D-Day landings, and renamed Omaha Beach.
86. 6 Jun. 1910, Berg. Also an important letter of 22 May 1910, giving AG's version: 'I have never treated her as an equal without regretting it.'
87. *The Times*, 14 June 1910. WBY made this point in his TS 'Why the Abbey Theatre Remained Open', dated 3 Feb. 1911, Berg. Also see drafts of 1909 *Samhain* in Berg.
88. It turned out he objected to *Blanco*, not the *Playboy*. AG's solicitor, David Moore, finally took over the lease.
89. To AG, 21 Sept. 1910, Berg.
90. See WBY to Moore, draft, 27 Sept. 1910, with AG's MS additions, dated 2 Oct. 1910, Berg.
91. As reported in the *Irish Times*, 22 Nov. 1910.
92. To AG, 16 Feb. 1911. The final arbitration, dated 29 Apr. 1911, is in Berg; the decision was that Horniman was clearly not justified in witholding the subsidy.
93. 'Thursday', n.d., draft in NLI MS 30,908. AG, still furious at Horniman's accusations of fraudulence, opposed the idea of arbitration (to WBY, 7 Jan. 1911, Berg).
94. Diary, 1 Dec. 1910.
95. 30 Oct. 1910, NLI MS 31,112. Sara Allgood was a chief offender, deeply jealous of her sister and constantly threatening to leave. Since she was a key actress for the *Playboy*, this endangered the Company's most precious possession.
96. For annual income (£185. 3s. 9d. and £181. 15s. 4d.) see MBY A27; for royalties NLI 30,654.
97. 4 Feb. 1910.
98. For James, Bennett, Wells, see *Letters: The Journal of the Royal Society of Literature*, 6 (Summer 1995); for the younger generation, Dorothy Shakespear to Ezra Pound, 29 Nov. 1913, in Pound and Litz, *Pound and Shakespear Letters*, 280.

99. 'Tuesday', Berg.

100. See WBY to AG, 18 Apr. 1910.

101. He had already met Lady Ottoline Morrell on 9 May 1909 at a London tea-party with AG: see her diary, Berg.

102. To AG, 17 Dec. 1905. He was using, ironically, the metaphor Horniman employed to express her apolitical stance six years before: 'If the French were to land at the west of Ireland it would make no difference to me except that I would buy two evening papers instead of one.' It went back to a joke made by Gill in Nov. 1898, retailed in *Au*, 421.

103. Fragment [from Coole], Berg.

104. Draft, 29 July 1910, Berg.

105. 22 July 1910, Berg.

106. Original in Berg; also see *Mem*, 289–90.

107. WBY first attended an 'At Home' of Gosse's on 8 Dec. 1895; Gosse recorded eighteen subsequent visits to receptions, lunches and dinners. Book of Gosse, Cambridge University Library: my thanks to Adrian Frazier. There may well have been more. The loan is recorded in WBY's 1899 diary.

108. 13 Aug. 1910, Berg.

109. Letters in Berg. A (third) draft of the petition indicates how carefully AG was treading:

> We wish to draw the attention of HM's Government to the claims of Mr W. B. Yeats to a pension from the Civil List.
>
> Mr Yeats is everywhere acknowledged as being in the first rank of living poets. His prose writings, both critical and imaginative, are also in the first rank, as is his dramatic work, in verse & prose. He was chosen as one of the original members of the Academy Committee.
>
> He was the founder and is the managing director of the National Theatre Society of Ireland which is perhaps the most intellectual and vigorous of the repertory theatres of the British Isles, and which has been publicly recognised by the Chief Commissioner of Education in Ireland as a most valuable educational influence.
>
> Mr Yeats has for many years given lectures on literature in young men's societies in Ireland without any payment, nor has he taken payment for his plays performed by the Abbey Theatre Company, or for his constant and personal work there, which has taken up a great deal of the time and energy he might otherwise have put into his creative and more financially profitable work.

110. *Mem*, 252.

111. ibid., 256–8.

112. MBY. WBY to Birrell, 9 Aug. [1910], and Gosse to WBY, 27 July, are in the University Library, Liverpool.

113. [?24] Aug. 1910 and [?end of Dec.] 1909, Berg.

114. Quinn to Russell, 5 Mar. 1911, 2 June 1911, and Russell to Quinn, 20 Mar. 1911, NYPL.

115. *Leader*, 25 Nov. 1911: one of many such comments.

116. *PF*, 378. The Fellows opposed were the famously conservative Thomas Thompson Gray and the equally ferocious George Lambert Cathcart, both devoted to resisting change in any manifestation.

117. 7 Sept. 1910, Berg.

118. AG to WBY, 'Tuesday', n.d., Berg.

119. To JBY, 5 Dec. 1910, NLI MS 31,112. On 6 Mar. 1911 WBY retailed this conversation to Cockerell; it obviously went the rounds.

120. Allen Upward, *Some Personalities* (London, 1921), 26, records Pound's remark.

121. Letters of 2 and 11 Oct. 1911.

122. To Sydney Cockerell, 6 Mar. 1911, 22 Sept. 1910, *L*, 556, 550–51.

123. To AG, 11 Nov., 16 and 19 Dec. 1910, Berg.

124. SMY's notes for Joseph Hone, HRHRC.

125. Jack's judgement and, in the end, unfair: WBY to AG, 28 Oct. 1910. For another view of Jackson, see *FS*, 397, n. 70. However, from this time the *Leader* attacked the firm for not employing Catholics, using this as a stick to beat WBY. See a sketch of 9 Dec. 1911, where WBY speaks of the Abbey in the guise (inevitably) of a policeman. 'Now the Pollexfens of Sligo showed a woeful want of Art in excluding Popery from their official cast, and by doing so gave the whole show away. I did the thing differently, and that is where the divine afflatus comes in. Pollexfen adopted the crude and clumsy principle of no Papists need apply, but in my establishment it was – none but Papists need apply, especially Papists of very bad characters. Now, of course, we are both found out; but, oh, what a difference was in the Art.'

126. To AG, Jan. 1911, Berg.

127. To SMY, from Coole, n.d., Boston College.

128. To AG, 28 Jan. 1911, Berg.

129. See *PF*, 379; Ellmann, *M & M*, 210–11.

130. 15 Sept. 1911.

Chapter 16 : True and False Irelands
1910–1911

Epigraph: *Inter-Ocean*, 2 Mar. 1914.

1. 'But then,' WBY added, 'Mrs Emery is not of a domestic temperament.' To AG, Oct. 1910, Berg.

2. WBY to AG, 21 Jan. 1911, Berg, and to Dickinson, 28 Jan. 1911, Berkeley.

3. WBY to AG, 14 Nov. 1910, Berg.

4. Astrological notebook, MBY.

5. To Charles Rowley, 14 Jan. 1911, SIUC. It is a vision of death aboard a theatrical ship, hailed by a crowd on the shore, and may owe something to a dream of SMY's the night JMS died: see *Mem*, 200.

6. *Sphere*, 14 Jan. 1911; *Daily News*, 23 Jan. 1911.

7. Drafted in May 1910; see *Mem*, 246. Originally 'Raymond Lully and his wife Pernella'.

8. 'A Drinking Song' is a free translation of Goldoni's 'Vive Bacco, e Vive Amore' from *La Locandiera*, for AG's adaptation *Mirandolina*. 'The Mask' was in *The Player Queen*. See *Mem*, 258, 260.

9. 20 Mar. 1911, NYPL.

10. See Lady Dunsany's diary, 27 Jan. 1911, private collection. 'He read it to her a year ago and she loved it and wrote to me some days later mentioning that "the play of slaves and kings is much in my mind". It was, for, leaving her harmless, characteristic and sometimes really funny Irish comedies, she suddenly wrote The Deliverer with an Oriental background, slaves, an overseer and even ending in the last act with a remark about "the King's cats" – Eddie's ending with "the King's dog".' She believed that AG and WBY tried to short-circuit the London production of *Argimenes* in June.

11. WBY to AG [late Jan. 1911], postscript, Berg.

12. 28 Jan., 27 Feb. 1911, Berg.

13. Lady Dunsany's diary, 15 June 1910, private collection.

14. For these reflections, see letters to AG, 6, 25 and 13 Mar. 1911, Berg.

15. To Lister, 23 Mar. 1911, Kansas.

16. 19 Mar. 1911, Harvard.

17. 1 Jan. 1911; see Harwood, *Shakespear and Yeats*, 136, for a reading which connects this stanza to Shakespear. It is true that the MS draft shows him cancelling lines which

would identify the first 'friend' as Shakespear ('<Though we would part in tears> <It parted us in>' and the second friend as AG ('<taught> <shown> me how to live'); he may have wanted to introduce some ambivalence. But I think the order of women in the poem is Shakespear, AG, MG: the reference to 'fifteen years' (written at the end of 1910) and 'heart and delighted heart' seems clearly to invoke Shakespear (their love-affair began in 1895), and the change of 'youth's bitter burden' to 'youth's dreamy load' may still refer to the way AG's influence concentrated his mind and helped him release his frustrations in work. Also see Deirdre Toomey in *YA* 6 (1988), 224–5.

18. To AG, 22 Jan. 1911, Berg.

19. George Yeats thought there had been a second affair, but dated it as 1903, which is unlikely; Hone also thought so. The queries in the automatic script preserved after WBY's marriage in 1917, and the casting of horoscopes, suggest that he and Shakespear were close in 1910, which would relate interestingly to the recent resolution of his relationship with MG. But all this must remain speculative.

20. The Lees, according to Nelly, were county gentry who 'followed strange gods' in religious matters and had a tendency to be spendthrift, but every now and then 'saved the ship' by throwing up a commercial genius; George's great-uncle Harold made money on early railways, for instance. On the Woodmass side, Nelly's grandfather married the eighth daughter of the second Baron Erskine (of the 1806 re-creation) who was descended from the Earls of Buchan. See her letter to WBY, 29 Oct., n.y., MBY.

21. In Nov. 1911, staying with the Tuckers at Margate, WBY wrote to AG: 'She was a Mrs Hyde-Lees whom I have known vaguely for years.' (Berg).

22. Harold was born on 24 Nov. 1890 at Brighton. According to George's birth certificate, she was born on 17 Oct. 1892 at Fleet, Hants, but her horoscope book (in MBY) records her birth date as 8.25 a.m. on 16 Oct.

23. To Pound, 14 Sept. 1911, Pound and Litz, *Pound and Shakespear Letters*, 58.

24. These qualities are well caught in Curtis Bradford, 'George Yeats: Poet's Wife', *Sewanee Review*, 77, 3 (July–Sept. 1969), 385–404. Also see Grace Jaffé, *YA* 5 (1987), 139–53; Anne Saddlemyer, 'Georgie Yeats: More than a Poet's Wife', Jeffares, *Yeats the European*, 191–200.

25. Bergson's Presidential Address for 1911 is copied out on the versos of her brother's French vocabulary book, MBY.

26. To Gordon Bottomley, 8 Jan. 1910.

27. Richard Ellmann, *Eminent Domain: Yeats among Wilde, Joyce, Pound, Eliot and Auden* (Oxford, 1967), 66–7.

28. Quoted in Harwood, *Shakespear and Yeats*, 142, 147.

29. To JBY, 9 May 1911, Boston.

30. To Lister, 15 Aug. 1911, Buffalo; it was printed as an appendix.

31. Postmarked 30 May 1911, Berg. See *VPl*, 57–9. Sturge Moore said that 'the unique cadence of this lyric so perfectly sustains the meaning of these forty-five words, which convey so central an epitome of life in such a novel perspective, that even today [late 1920s–early 1930s] tears of admiration moisten my eyes as I read' ('Do We or Do We Not Know It?', *YA* 4, 1986, 147).

32. Interestingly, Eva Fowler knew Leoni, and WBY worked on *The Countess Cathleen* at Daisy Meadow in June. Leoni was also recommended by WBY's musical typist, Miss Anderson.

33. *Pall Mall Gazette*, 9 June 1911.

34. 'and I have been full of pride ever since': to Agnes Tobin, 30 July 1911, private collection.

35. To AG, 26 Aug. 1911, Berg.

36. 17 July 1911, Boston.

37. To AG, 5 Sept. 1911, Berg; Redmond himself was bringing pressure to bear on them through Bailey.

38. To AG, 28 May 1911.
39. To WBY, 7 Sept. [1911], Berg. Worried that WBY wanted to widen their range to Elizabethan work, she reminded him that they were not trying to out-do Tree in Shakespearean drama. 'I thought we had decided, or you had consented, that your verse plays should be our object outside folk drama.'
40. To AG, 28 Apr. 1911, Berg. The idea had long been mooted; see AG to WBY, 'Sunday 22', probably Dec. 1907, Berg. This shows Lieber was already under consideration; later she decided such a venture would be impossible without the Fays.
41. Cathleen Nesbitt, *A Little Love and Good Company* (London, 1975), 52, 56.
42. *Irish Times*, 9 Sept. 1911.
43. To Lister, 28 July 1911, Harvard.
44. Montrose J. Moses in *I & R*, i, 126.
45. See Jessie D. Rittenhouse [Secretary of the Poetry Society], *My House of Life: An Autobiography* (Boston and New York, 1934), 231–2.
46. Strand, 'American Lecture Tours', 91.
47. ibid., 93.
48. Quoted in Strand, 'American Lecture Tours', 101. See also the Boston *Sunday Post* interview, *I & R*, i, 73–5.
49. See *Harper's Weekly*, 11 Nov. 1911, and *UP*, ii, 397–401. Strand quotes the *Boston Evening Transcript* and the *Harvard Crimson*.
50. Otherwise Mrs Minnie Meserve Sproule; not Mrs Crandon, as asserted by Hone. See Strand, 'American Lecture Tours', 104.
51. Quoted in Strand, 'American Lecture Tours', 107.
52. Quoted in ibid., 109.
53. Quoted in ibid., 115. However, in a later New York interview he criticized Goldsmith for emigrating and writing for an English market.
54. Quoted in ibid., 120.
55. Quoted in ibid., 125.
56. WBY was at a reception in Roxbury on the 15th. The play had in fact been presented once already in the USA, at Chicago the previous May; see Himber, *Letters of Quinn to Yeats*, 135.
57. 12 Nov. 1911, Berg.
58. 27 Nov. 1911.
59. Friday 13th [?Dec., 1912], Berg: she was writing *Our Irish Theatre* at the time.
60. She wrote to WBY on Christmas Day from the Algonquin Hotel:

    One or two evenings ago I said to Quinn 'Will you ever be quite friends with Yeats again?' He said 'I don't know, I don't think about it, I feel no bitterness towards him.' I said 'I know you cannot or you cd not write so nicely of him as you do. It is not a thing I want to talk about, but Yeats said the other day "It is a strange thing that Quinn who knows me so well and I have lived with so much should think me capable of what he does."' He said 'When women get mixed up with things there are always quarrels' and changed the topic. I feel sure it is all right and that when you meet him again you can just talk as if nothing had happened. (Berg).

61. 'Tuesday 17' [Dec. 1911], Berg.
62. To WBY, n.d., Berg.
63. To WBY, 'Saturday', n.d., Berg.
64. Quoted in Strand, 'American Lecture Tours', 127.
65. To AG, 12 Nov. 1911. Shaw also encouraged this line: see Dan H. Laurence and Nicholas Grene, *Shaw, Lady Gregory and the Abbey: A Correspondence and a Record* (Gerrards Cross, 1993), 67–8.
66. 26 May 1911, Berg.

67. To WBY, n.d., Berg.
68. To Quinn, 7 Dec. 1911, NYPL.
69. To AG, 18 Nov. 1911, Berg.
70. 12 Nov. 1911, Berg.
71. 12 Nov. 1911, NLI MS 31,112. 'Uncle Pat' was great-uncle Patrick Corbet, son of William Corbet and Grace Armstrong; born in 1793, he served in the Burmese war, led a siege at Rangoon, became Governor of Penang, and died in 1840. 'The general' was John Armstrong (FRS 1723), son of Robert Armstrong and Lydia Harward, born in 1674, ADC to Marlborough at Malplaquet and Oudenarde, made Chief Engineer in 1714. He died in 1742, and was buried within the churchyard of the Tower of London.

Chapter 17 : GHOSTS
1911–1913

Epigraph: Reading.

1. For a list of AG's plays, see WBY to AG, 11 Jan. 1912, Berg. The 'second company' was paid, according to WBY, out of a special fund given to himself and AG 'to use as we please for the furtherance of the dramatic movement in Ireland' (to A. D. Wilson, 29 Apr. 1914, Berg); he does not say where this originated. For Monck in America, and his mental instability, see AG to WBY [Feb. 1913], Berg.
2. To AG, 2 Jan. 1912, Berg.
3. Same to same, 11 Feb. 1912, Berg.
4. 14 Apr. 1912, private collection; probably *The White Cockade* and the revised *Hour-Glass*.
5. 21 Jan. 1912, Berg.
6. See *Irish Times*, 20 Jan. 1912.
7. McCartan was an IRB member who would become much involved with revolutionary politics in the USA from 1917, and later still would organize a Testimonial Committee for WBY: see *Yeats and Patrick McCartan: A Fenian Friendship. Letters with a Commentary by John Unterecker and an Address on Yeats the Fenian by Patrick McCartan* (Dolmen Press Yeats Centenary Papers, No. X, Dublin, 1965).
8. WBY to AG, 11 Jan. 1912, Berg.
9. Dr Tom Steele suggests that this attack may have come from Pound, but believes the author is more likely Beatrice Hastings (letter to RFF, 2 Oct. 1995).
10. To AG, 9 Apr. 1912, Berg. His remark to Stephens is in a letter of 19 May; his defence of WBY was in the *New Age* on 9 May, following the attack on 2 May. A further attack appeared on 16 May.
11. See AG to Hyde, 7 Dec. 1911: 'Oh Craoibhin what are these wounds, with which we are wounded in the house of our friends? . . . We are fighting your battle if you did but know it, and the battle of all who want to live and breathe.' Hyde cravenly blamed the pressure put on him by Gaelic League fundraisers in the USA. See G. W. Dunleavy, 'The Pattern of Three Threads: The Hyde–Gregory Friendship' in Ann Saddlemyer and Colin Smythe (eds.), *Lady Gregory Fifty Years After* (Gerrards Cross, 1987), 140–1.
12. *Irish Review*, Dec. 1912 and Jan. 1913; for Boyd's subsequent attack, see ibid., Feb. 1913.
13. He did receive some help from Dr Rynd of the Norwich Cathedral Chapter: for this and other comments, see WBY to AG, 7 Jan. 1912, Berg. For a critique, see Bernard M. W. Knox (trans.), *Oedipus the King* (New York, 1959), vii.

Yeats, for reasons he did not see fit to explain, cut the play in the same highhanded way he edited Wilde's *Ballad of Reading Gaol* ('My work gave me that privilege'); what the result is in the case of Wilde I leave others to judge, but in the case of Sophocles it is close to disastrous. In the last scene of the play, for example, he has omitted ninety of the 226 lines Sophocles wrote, and he has moved part of speeches as much as a hundred lines away from their true position, not to mention the fact that at one point he has taken two lines from Oedipus, given them to the chorus, and slapped them into the middle of one of Oedipus's long speeches at a point where an interruption destroys the power of the speech. As if this were not enough, he has, in an earlier scene, omitted Jocasta's famous lines on chance, without which the play loses a great deal of its meaning.

David R. Clark and James B. McGuire agree that WBY sacrifices much irony and subtlety: see *The Writing of 'Sophocles' King Oedipus': Manuscripts of W. B. Yeats*, transcribed, edited and with a commentary by David R. Clark and James B. McGuire (Philadelphia, the American Philosophical Society, 1989).

14. To AG [18 Jan. 1912], *L*, 565.

15. To Stephens, 19 May 1912, private collection.

16. See Karen Dorn, 'Dialogue into Movement: W. B. Yeats's Theatre Collaboration with Gordon Craig', *YT*, 109–36.

17. 23 May 1912, Arsenal, Paris.

18. See James Flannery, 'W. B. Yeats, Gordon Craig and the Visual Arts of the Theatre', *YT*, 103–4, for its initial performance.

19. Ellmann, *Letters of James Joyce. Volume 2*, 298. Davray was simultaneously vetting French translations for him.

20. 12 July 1912, University of Vermont.

21. The royalty figure (£36. 4s. 9d.) probably included something from profits on anthologies, etc.; for detailed accounts from Fisher Unwin, see NLI MS 30,564. Plays brought in very little: *LHD*, £4. 10s. 7d. in 1912–13, *CC*, £4. 7s. 2d. In 1912 *Poems* made £64. 2s. 0d. For redecoration, see WBY to AG, 7 Apr. 1912, Berg: 'my rooms look very nice with their new green carpet & the blue green corduroy curtains. Mrs Old says "I wish her ladyship could see it."'

22. 6 Oct. 1911.

23. He heard this from Mair of the *Manchester Guardian*, Molly Allgood's husband, in May 1912. Other candidates included Dunraven, Lord Dudley, Horace Plunkett and 'Lord O'Donnell' (*recte* MacDonnell). This is an interestingly early anticipation of the Free State Senate established in 1922.

24. Mar. 1911.

25. 2 Jan. 1912, Berg. On 6 Jan. he commended Stephen Gwynn for condemning the new papal decree.

26. *Irish Times*, 11 Apr. 1912. 'It seems to us absurd to suppose that a difference in religious belief involves conflicting interests between ourselves and our fellow-countrymen. Should, however, any such conflicting interest develop, we are confident in our ability to give due prominence and effect to our views under an Irish parliament. Having enjoyed in a predominantly Catholic community the fullest tolerance and friendly relationship with the majority of our countrymen, we feel bound in honour in the present crisis to assert our confidence in the continuance and future development of such relationships.'

27. To Gosse, 25 Feb. 1912, Leeds.

28. 30 Nov. 1912, HRHRC. 'Chapel doors in America' refers to an American Jesuit, Father Kenny, who had led attacks on the Irish players in 1911; the *Leader* relayed his onslaughts for an Irish readership. WBY replied to him in *FJ*, 21 Nov. 1911.

29. 24 Jan. 1913, TS of speech, NLI 30,095.

30. 24 Jan. 1913, Northwestern.

31. See her interview in New York, 3 Dec. 1911. 'When did the new Irish literary movement begin? The moment Parnell died. That moment, according to Lady Gregory, was the sharply defined begining of a new era for Ireland. Usually it is rather hard to tell the exact moment when a movement in art or politics had its origin, but this is an exception.' E. H. Mikhail, *Lady Gregory: Interviews and Recollections* (London, 1977), 54.

32. Draft, NLI 30,272.
33. An envelope in MBY records seances with Mrs Feilding, 3 May 1909, Mrs Mitchell, 17 and 24 May 1909 (at the Cousins' house in Sandymount). A record of a seance dated 14 Aug. 1900 in MBY details an historically verifiable materialization (Joseph Damer, a Cromwellian diplomat); but it is unclear if WBY attended (he was based in Coole at this time). The circumstantial details are checked in a long TS dated Sept. 1900.
34. Quoted in Ruth Brandon, *The Spiritualists: The Passion for the Occult in the Nineteenth and Twentieth Centuries* (London, 1983), 91. cf. William Volckman, who grabbed 'Katie King', a spirit produced by Florence Cook, as she danced around the room in veils, shouting, 'I feel stays.'
35. Andrew Lang had argued for psychic folklore in the 1890s; he and Edward Clodd debated the matter in the Folk Lore Society and its journal (March–Sept. 1895). Warwick Gould points out that Lang's edition of Robert Kirk's *The Secret Commonwealth of Elves, Fauns and Fairies* (London, 1893) anticipates the methods of 'Swedenborg, Mediums, and the Desolate Places'. WBY knew both Lang and Clodd.
36. cf. James Olney, *The Rhizome and the Flower* (Berkeley, 1980). See H. W. Nevinson, *Last Changes, Last Chances* (London, 1928), recording a conversation with WBY on 30 Oct. 1916. 'He talked of Freud and Jung and the subconscious self, applying the doctrine to art. He said the great thing is to reduce the conscious self to humility, as by the imitation of some ancient master, so leaving the Unconscious Self free to work.' There is a note of Freud's and Jung's works with titles in German and the name of M. D. Eder, their future translator, in WBY's 1913 notebook, but in another hand. See Chapter 17, n. 157, below.
37. See *Journal of the Society for Psychical Research*, xiv (July 1910), for a long account of Ernest Jones's pioneering essay on Freud, and xxv (Nov. 1912), for Freud's own 'Note on the Unconscious in Psychoanalysis'. For long-standing theories of the unconscious, see Erich von Hartmann, *Philosophy of the Unconscious* (1868), a bestseller of its day, translated into English in 1884; and L. L. Whyte, *The Unconscious before Freud* (London, 1978).
38. See below, pp. 525–6. Theodor Flournoy, whom WBY read, discussed Freud's theory of dreams as disguised realizations of suppressed wishes, citing *Die Traumdeutung* (1900): see Hereward Carrington (trans.), *Spiritism and Psychology* (1911), 86. Myers, in *Human Personality and Its Survival of Bodily Death* (1903), redefined the subconscious as the 'subliminal', and devoted much discussion to personality and the self. The work of Hyslop closest to WBY's interests was *Psychical Research and Survival* (London, 1913): see especially 39 and 45.
39. There is an odd prediction here of 'In dreams begins responsibility'. See *Irish Times*, 13 Jan. 1912.
40. 26 Jan. 1912, Berg.
41. 31 Jan. 1912, Berg. The reference here is to the Cambridge Platonist Henry More, but the image comes originally from the 5th–6th C. AD Alexandrine John Philoponus' *De Aeternitate Mundi*: see Peter Kuch, '"Laying the Ghosts": W. B. Yeats's Lecture on Ghosts and Dreams', *YA* 5 (1987), 119, 135.
42. This was Wriedt's second visit. In 1911 she had been invited by 'Julia's Bureau', then in its final phase, but still providing detailed procedures for opening up communications with the dead; forms, records and stenographers were laid on. Mrs Wriedt charged a dollar per person and specialized in luminous forms, voices from a trumpet and 'apported' flowers, magically conveyed to the hands of the participants. See N. Fodor, *Encyclopaedia of Psychic Science* (London, 1933) for a long entry.
43. Harper's and WBY's accounts were preserved in an occult notebook, MBY, and in Curtis Bradford's transcription, NLI 30,499; WBY's subsequent long essay, and the antecedent communications, are discussed in Steve L. Adams and George Mills Harper (eds.), 'The Manuscript of Leo Africanus', *YA* 1 (1982), 3–47. There is an entry on Leo in the contemporary edition of the *Encyclopaedia Britannica* (xxiv, 453) as well as *Chambers's Biographical Dictionary*.

44. A French edition of Leo's *Description de l'Afrique* was published from 1894 to 1896. The English translation by John Pory, 'A Geographical Historie of Africa' (1600), was edited by Robert Brown and E. Denison Ross for the Hakluyt Society in 1896 and subsequently found by WBY (who, however, preferred to refer to the 1600 version). Accounts like Leo's lie behind surveys such as Andrew Lang's *Myth, Ritual and Religion* and E. B. Tylor's *Primitive Culture*, not to mention R. W. Felkin's article on Africa in *Proc. Royal Soc. of Edinburgh*, xiii, and his *Uganda and the Egyptian Sudan* (1882). Pory was widely circulated; Leo also turns up in the introduction to Ben Jonson's *Masque of Blackness* (1605), which WBY may well have read, and he was much used by Olfert Dapper for his *Description de l'Afrique* (Amsterdam, 1686), a major source for the final version of Frazer's *Golden Bough* (1911–15).

45. See above, p. 114. There is also an echo of the translation of Verhaeren's 'Les Moines', which WBY would have read in the *Irish Review* of May 1912. The 'moine epique' closely resembles WBY's version of Leo: he comes out of the desert, familiar with lions, into the Roman world. 'One has seen him walk along by the sounding deep . . .'

46. Ellen Anker asked him some simple questions in Italian, which for WBY seemed proof positive (notebook, MBY).

47. Williams, who lived near Woburn Buildings, had been exposed as a cheat in 1878: he regularly conjured up John King the Pirate, but a search revealed the piratical beard in his pocket.

48. cf. the references to 'shrieking' during love-making in 'A Man Young and Old'.

49. MBY. Harwood discusses this record in *Shakespear and Yeats*, 137–8, but without relating the violets to their origin at the Leo seance.

50. It was also probably influenced by W. S. Landor's *Imaginary Conversations*, a fashionable book at this time.

51. MBY; see Adams and Harper, 'The Manuscript of Leo Africanus'.

52. When told by 'Leo' to sit up straight in his chair, for instance, he believed that this could not be an observation of Mrs Wriedt's own, since the lights were turned out. On a summer evening at 6.30 p.m., this is hardly convincing – except for someone as myopic as WBY.

53. To Edwin Ellis, n.d., but probably 2 Aug. 1912, Reading.

54. To AG, 8 Aug. 1912, Major Gregory Collection. The poem was eventually published in the *Quest*, a spiritualist magazine.

55. I assume that this is the lyric of twenty-one lines mentioned in a letter of 13 Aug. to AG, Berg: and the poem which Cousins heard him intoning on 15 Aug., when he told MG he had finished it. The visit is described in J. H. and M. Cousins, *We Two Together* (Madras, 1950), 158–62.

56. 8 Sept. 1912, Reading.

57. To AG, 16 Oct. 1912, Berg: this was Elizabeth Radcliffe. See below, pp. 487–8.

58. MBY. There was a great deal more about Parnell, with the usual description of his 'burning eyes' and circumstantial details about Pigott. Peters had evidently read Barry O'Brien.

59. cf. 'Parnell's Funeral': 'Their school a crowd, his master solitude'.

60. To Ford Madox Ford, 14 Nov. 1912, Berg: it could have been 'The Two Kings'. Neither is '120 lines' but this was presumably a first draft.

61. 14 Nov. 1912, Bodleian.

62. See *All the Year Round*, 5 Apr. 1842, 80; he died in 1846.

63. *North American Review*, cxcvii (1913); *Fortnightly*, xciii (1913).

64. See *The Times*, 13 July 1912.

65. n.d., but July 1912, Sturge Moore MSS, University of London.

66. ibid.

67. Tagore to WBY, 13 May 1913, HRHRC.

68. n.d., Harvard.

69. To Sidney Cox, 2 May 1913; L. Thomson (ed.), *Selected Letters of Robert Frost* (New York, 1964), 72. Later Frost would decide that WBY missed greatness through affectation. WBY himself had seen Swinburne, not Kipling, as the monarch to dethrone; on 12 Apr. 1909, the day after Swinburne's death, he said to SMY, 'Now I am king of the cats.' This is a reference to an Irish folktale where an old couple talk before their fire of the death of a famous cat and his burial – whereat their own cat leaps up, shouts, 'I'm king of the cats now,' and vanishes up the chimney. It is, therefore, a more ironic remark than it may seem.

70. Sturge Moore to his wife, 14 Oct. 1912, University of London: 'in the matter of recitation etc. we seem to agree perfectly. He doesn't like Miss Farr at all, & can't understand Yeats recommending her.'

71. See same to same, loc. cit., and WBY to AG, 14 Nov. 1913, Berg: 'I am delighted at Tagore getting the Nobel Prize. It is a blow at Gosse, which amuses me.'

72. Quoted in Longenbach, *Stone Cottage*, 25.

73. WBY to Macmillan & Co., 19 Apr. 1914, British Library. But Tagore did not listen. 'When Mr Tagore was in England both I & Sturge Moore urged upon him a considerable lapse of time between the publication of his books here as we thought that many books soon after each other (though it would mean a larger temporary sale) would cause a reaction and be bad for his reputation in the end. It has been this understanding which has made me hold back the new volume of which I have the MSS.'

74. See the amended volume of *The Crescent Moon* in Rothenstein MSS, Harvard.

75. 7 Sept. [1912], but probably 17 Sept., Harvard.

76. To Rothenstein, 10 Aug. 1912, Harvard.

77. To his wife, 24–5 Nov. 1912, University of London. For all his grumbling he designed the cover of *The Crescent Moon* and accepted its dedication to himself.

78. In a speech in Dublin, 23 Mar. 1913 (see below, p. 483) and in a letter to Rothenstein, 1 Dec. 1912, Harvard.

79. The article appeared in *Prakashi*, and was translated in the *American Review of Reviews*, 49 (Jan.–June 1914).

80. See Sturge Moore to wife, 28 July 1913, late July 1913, University of London. Also 1 Aug. 1913: 'He is rather frightened about Yeats & my corrections. They are going over them together now. I shall be very curious to know how Tagore manages. It will require great tact. It really is not at all my fault if Yeats is vexed because I never even suggested doing anything till I was asked, but I may get into hot water with Yeats all the same if Tagore is a little cowardly.' Also see M. M. Lago (ed.), *Imperfect Encounter: Letters of William Rothenstein and Rabindranath Tagore 1911–1941* (Cambridge, Mass., 1972).

81. See WBY to Rothenstein, 19 Aug. 1912, Harvard. In 1913 Sturge Moore described meeting Iseult at WBY's, 'very lovely to look at and quite nice', though her real relationship to MG was not to be mentioned. Pound was there too. By Sept. 1914 Iseult had indeed collaborated with Tagore's nephew Devabrata Mukherjee in translating *The Gardener* into French, and WBY wrote to Tagore on 12 Sept. 1914, suggesting delicately that they be given publication rights; however, the collaboration foundered when Mukherjee fell in love with Iseult (*G–Y L*, 339–50).

82. Reported in *Irish Times* and *FJ*, 24 Mar. 1913; see below, p. 483.

83. This was to ignore the important essay 'The Way of Wisdom' (later 'The Pathway'), written in 1900; see above, p. 552, n. 85.

84. Quoted in Longenbach, *Stone Cottage*, 26.

85. 23 Apr. [1913], Harvard.

86. Tagore to Rothenstein, 4 Sept. 1915, Harvard; Lago, *Imperfect Encounter*, 195.

87. To his wife, 25 Nov. 1912, University of London.

88. Humphrey Carpenter, *A Serious Character: The Life of Ezra Pound* (London, 1988), 186–7, 196ff.
89. Ellmann, *Eminent Domain*, 62.
90. Longenbach, *Stone Cottage*, 81.
91. Joy Grant, *Harold Monro and the Poetry Bookshop* (London, 1962), quoting a 1959 broadcast by Arundel del Re.
92. 'Last night I dreamed that I was paying devoted but anxious & rather distant attention to an entire stranger – my dread being that she might be on the edge of that infirmity which we spoke of & my fear, which you attributed to the vanity of man. Then just as I discovered that she was not at all liable to it I awoke, and to my irreperable loss.' ([Sept. 1912], Huntingdon).
93. WBY to AG, 21 April [1914], Berg.
94. 14 Nov. 1912, Harvard.
95. For 'high-hatting', and Pound's scholarship, see Carpenter, *A Serious Character*, 42–3, 55, 91.
96. Patricia Hutchins, 'Yeats and Pound in England', *Texas Quarterly*, 4, 3 (Autumn 1961), 214.
97. On 15 Aug. Monroe had written to WBY reminding him they had met in Chicago and asking for poems.
98. For details see Ellmann, *Eminent Domain*, 64–5. The TS of the poems at Chicago University preserves Pound's emendations.
99. The imbroglio is outlined in the letter to Rothenstein quoted above – as an explanation why Pound was being so zealous in the Tagore affair.
100. 3 Jan. 1913, Ellmann, *Eminent Domain*, 66.
101. A Berg holograph is dated 21 Oct. 1912, but it was not published until the following Apr.
102. 17 Nov. [?], from Coole, according to Rhys, *Letters from Limbo* (London, 1936), 158–9; actually 13 Nov. 1912, British Library. It apparently refers to a letter WBY sent to G. A. Greene, which was passed on to Rhys.
103. Notebook, MBY.
104. [7 Dec. 1912], Berg. An alternative ending was provided, which is closer to *CP*:

> Let the new faces play what tricks they will
> In the old rooms – for all they do or say
> Our shades will walk the gravel still
> The living seem more shadowy than they

105. Quoted by Wayne Chapman, *YA* 6 (1988).
106. Though he considered it for the reprint of *Responsibilities* in 1917, going so far as to write it in on a proof.
107. 3 Jan. 1913.
108. Postmarked 10 Sept. 1898, Berg.
109. See Thomas Bodkin, *Hugh Lane and His Pictures* (2nd ed., Dublin, 1934), 30–32.
110. See WBY to AG, 13 Dec. 1912, Berg. Two MSS drafts of the whole poem exist, dated 24 and 25 Dec. 1912.
111. 20 Jan. 1913. £22,000, dependent upon the Committee presenting a site, plus £3,000.
112. 8 Jan. 1913, Berg.
113. *Irish Independent*, 17 Jan. 1913. For WBY's target, see his letter to Lane, 1 Jan. 1913: 'I have tried to meet the argument of Lady Ardilaun's letter to somebody, her objection to giving because of Home Rule & Lloyd George, & still more to meet the general argument of people like Ardilaun that they should not give unless there is a public demand.' (*L*, 573.)

114. 24 Jan. 1913, Northwestern.
115. See above, pp. 459–61.
116. Lane to WBY [Feb. 1913], Berg.
117. See AG to WBY, n.d., Berg, and 8 Nov. 1913, Berg.
118. *Irish Times*, 8 Mar. 1913.
119. *Irish Times*, 11 Feb. 1908.
120. *Irish Times*, 19 Mar. 1913.
121. [28 May 1913], Arsenal, Paris.
122. *Irish Times*, 24 Mar. 1913; there is a fuller report in *FJ*, same day.
123. 12 Apr. 1913, Northwestern.
124. 15 Apr. 1913, Berg.
125. To AG, 7 May 1913. The poem may have been 'Running to Paradise'.
126. Possibly by establishing a School for the Art of the Theatre: see Dorn in *YT*, 135–6. Other founding members were John Martin Harvey, Tomasso Salvini, Cecil Sharp and Craig himself, who probably wrote the prospectus.
127. 8 Mar. 1913, Berg.
128. 28 Mar. 1913.
129. To Quinn, 18 June 1912, NYPL.
130. WBY to Mabel Beardsley, 23 Dec. [1912], HRHRC.
131. To Joseph Hone, 22 Nov. 1939.
132. 14 Jan. 1913, Northwestern.
133. He may have been influenced by Lotte Pritzel's doll-sculptures – figures of wire and wax in decadent dance postures, reminding many of Aubrey Beardsley's work. There was a celebrated exhibition in Munich in 1913, inspiring a famous essay by Rainer Maria Rilke.
134. To AG, 18 Jan. 1913, Northwestern. 'He is probably the only person we know who has never doubted himself or judged himself, which is I dare say the same thing.'
135. See WBY to Farr, 18 Feb. 1913, private collection; to Mabel Beardsley, 24 Nov. 1913, HRHRC ('Florimond' was the Comte de Basterot's name. WBY cancelled 'Michael' before it – the name he gave the hero of *SB*, and his own son); Pound as quoted in Longenbach, *Stone Cottage*, 158; WBY to Bullen, 22 Feb. 1913, Buffalo. Beardsley eventually sent, or left, her own copies of the poems to Andre Raffalovich: see TS at Reading. For a commentary see Elizabeth Ingli James, 'The University of Reading Collection', *YA* 3 (1985), 170.
136. See WBY to 'Mr Ames', 3 Apr. 1913, RSL Archives: which contradicts Longenbach's assumption (*Stone Cottage*, 62) that WBY disapproved of the choice.
137. 22 Feb. 1913, Buffalo. Chapman & Hall were remaindering 125 copies; there were 500 left, most of them unbound.
138. See NLI MS 30,654. In 1913 and 1914 *CC* and *LHD* were down from 1,009 and 1,035 to 595 and 590 respectively, though *Poems* only dropped from 1,047 to 880.
139. See notebooks, MBY. He saw Brailey on 4 Apr. and Mrs Mitchell on 8 Apr. (he had previously visited her on 17 and 24 May 1909).
140. In the event, he saw a Mrs Webster instead, on 12 and 13 May: see WBY to AG, 10 May 1913, Northwestern.
141. In the spring of 1912, according to George Mills Harper and John Kelly, 'Preliminary Examination of the Script of E [lizabeth] R [adcliffe]', *YO*, 145. He certainly was meeting her at Daisy Meadow by Oct. 1912. Her parents lived in Kensington Square, near Mrs Fowler.
142. See L. E. Jones, *I Forgot to Tell You* (London, 1959), 37; St John Ervine, *Some Impressions of My Elders* (London, 1928), 252. Ervine recounts an incident similar to one in Jones's book, of a small object miraculously materializing in Radcliffe's clenched fist.
143. Jones, *I Forgot to Tell You*, 41–2. For other automatic writers, see A. Gauld, *The Founders*

of Psychical Research (London, 1968). Moses similarly convinced Myers by writing messages from people who could not be traced in biographical dictionaries, even though he reproduced mistakes that appeared in their newspaper obituaries.

144. Jones, *I Forgot to Tell You*, 44.

145. WBY recorded this in a small leather-bound notebook, with 'from Maud Gonne Xmas 1912' written in front, MBY. For the spiritualist experiments see 'Notes on Two Clairvoyant Descriptions by Brailey' made on 3 Apr. 1913, describing an experiment 'last week'.

146. So George Yeats told Ellmann in an interview of 17 June 1940, interview book, Tulsa.

147. 8 June 1913, private collection.

148. 11 and 17 June 1913, private collection.

149. See date of AG's letter to him, below. On 3 July (Berg) he wrote to her 'the releif of that other matter being over is immense'.

150. Notebook, MBY.

151. n.d., but probably 2 July 1913, Berg.

152. AG to WBY, 'Tuesday', Berg. Dickinson married Arthur Beresford Lane (1864–1939), a barrister resident in London, as his second wife in 1927. He was himself Irish, and his first wife had been a granddaughter of the Young Irelander William Smith O'Brien. Educated at Charterhouse and Trinity College, Cambridge, Lane was Secretary of the Railway Companies Association, and also involved in the Control Board (Liquor Traffic). Mabel subsequently retired to Devon and died in 1962, aged 87.

153. Small leather-bound notebook, with 'from Maud Gonne Xmas 1912' written in front, recording 'evidence' of seances, MBY.

154. An image he would use more than once, and which Pound borrowed both for his 1915 essay 'Affirmations II: Vorticism' and to epitomize his own work in the *Pisan Cantos* (74/449).

155. See *YO*, 7, 130–71. Some of his conclusions use very special pleading; for instance, the fact that mediums very often reproduced quotations from Greek and Latin grammars is put down to the spirit minds going back to their schooldays. And Radcliffe's sketches of blobs and lines were very readily seen as occult symbols of scarab and bullrush.

156. In Hereward Carrington's 1911 translation of Flournoy there is much that is echoed by WBY about 'usurpation', 'deceiving spirits' and automatic-writing. The tone is markedly similar, showing an ostensibly scientific desire for empirical proof (or disproof), but an extraordinary readiness to believe. His account of Mrs Piper's absorption of the incomplete memories of the dead (235) with a composite memory is very Yeatsian. James T. Hyslop's *Psychical Research and Survival* (London, 1913, in Mead's *Quest* series) is also echoed in the Radcliffe essay. Interestingly, Hyslop remarks 'daydreams and poetry in our normal lives are the best analogies' of the spirit state. WBY was also influenced by Rama Prasad's *Nature's Finer Forces* (1890), which postulates that evil or destructive acts done in one lifetime are enacted in reverse in the next. cf. also William James's suggestion, quoted in Wentz, *Fairy Faith*, 479: if 'there were in the universe a lot of diffuse soul-stuff, unable of itself to get into consistent personal form, or to take permanent possession of an organism, yet always craving to do so, it might get its head into the air, parasitically, so to speak, by profiting by weak spots in the armour of human minds, and slipping in and stirring up there the sleeping tendencies to personate'.

157. See *Irish Times*, 1 Nov. 1913. cf. William James, above. In WBY's 1913 notebook a pencilled note in another hand gives references to 'Dr Sigmund Freud, University of Vienna – "Traumdeutung", Dr Carl G. Jung, Univ. of Zurich, – Wandlungen und Symbol der Libido to be translated by Dr Eder (London, 2 Charlotte Street) Jahrbuch für psychoanalysischen und psychopathische Forschungen (Franzpanische Vienna).' M. D. Eder's translation of Freud's *On Dreams* was published in London in 1914 (A. A. Brill's translation of *The Interpretation of Dreams* appeared in 1913).

158. *Irish Times*, 3 Nov. 1913.

159. cf. *Visions and Beliefs*, 350. 'Did Cornelius Agrippa identify soul with memory when, after quoting Ovid to prove that the flesh cleaves to earth, the ghost hovers over the grave, the soul sinks to Oxos, and the spirit rises to the stars, he explains that if the soul has done well it rejoices with the almost faultless spirit, but if it has done ill, the spirit judges it and leaves it for the devil's prey and "the sad soul wanders about hell without a spirit and like an image"?' There are also cross-references to Rama Prasad's ideas about punishment in further existences (see above, n. 155). WBY's letter to Clodd, 6 Nov. 1898, about ghosts and revisiting, is also relevant (*CL*, ii, 290–93).

Chapter 18 : MEMORY HARBOUR
1913–1914

1. 14 Nov. 1913.
2. Quoted in Pound and Litz, *Pound and Shakespear Letters*, 282. On 18 Oct. 1913 WBY loyally told Stephens, 'The Academic Committee is the English substitute for the French Academy, and contains almost every English man of letters of eminence, so the prize is a real distinction.' (private collection).
3. *Irish Times*, 10 May 1913.
4. *Manchester Guardian*, 15 July 1913. Ireland as wax waiting for an impress is an image from Standish O'Grady's *Story of Ireland*. The shopkeeping image, which would be recycled in 'September 1913', may have been suggested by a poem of Thomas MacDonagh's in the *Irish Review* of June 1911: a vision of an Irish village where the people were bent double, hoarding 'pence in a till in their little shops'.
5. To WBY, 23 July 1913, Berg. She also worried about the vagueness of the bridge estimate. For Lane's comment about Irish architects, see *Irish Times*, 19 July 1913.
6. See AG to WBY, 16 Aug. [1913], Berg; MG to WBY, 5 Sept. 1913, *G-Y L*, 324.
7. 12 Aug. [1913], Berg.
8. See WBY to AG, 9 Aug. 1913, Berg. On 1 July he asked her to send an *Irish Times* with an account of the Corporation debates: 'it may move me to another poem'.
9. To AG, *c.* 26 Aug. 1913 (from 'The Prelude', though on Woburn Buildings paper), Northwestern. Aesop 118 (S. Handford, trans., *Fables of Aesop*, Harmondsworth, 1954, 122) tells of a dog crossing a river with a bone in her mouth, who loses it in the river when she snatches at the shadow bone mirrored in her reflection.
10.   Sure 'twas for this Lord Edward died, and Wolf [*sic*] Tone sunk serene –
       Because they could not bear to leave the Red above the Green;
       And 'twas for this that Owen fought, and Sarsfield nobly bled –
       Because their eyes were hot to see the Green above the Red.

    The full poem is in T[homas] W[allis] (ed.), *National and Historical Ballads, Songs and Poems by Thomas Davis, MRIA* (Dublin, 1876), 190–91. See Colin Meir, *The Ballads and Songs of W. B. Yeats: The Anglo-Irish Heritage in Substance and Style* (London, 1974), 92–3. There is a TS draft of 'September 1913' in NLI MS 21,873 with emendations in what looks like Pound's hand. This includes the variation: 'For this that Bond and Emmett [*sic*] died'. Oliver Bond was a 1798 United Irishman, evidently rejected as too obscure.

11. Brown leather notebook, MBY.
12. To WBY, 8 Oct. 1913, Berg.
13. See Lady Dunsany's diary (quoting Gogarty), 18 Jan. 1914, private collection.
14. For background, see letters from AG to WBY (8 Nov. 1913, Berg), and his reply (14 Nov. 1913): also copies of documents in Quinn collection, NYPL. The situation peaked in Jan. 1914: see below. 'They are children, very good when they are good children,' WBY told her. 'I do not think we should judge them as we would judge people accustomed to

money. They are all a first generation people just getting above a very precarious life. Money appears to them as a first necessity, it means a different social world & greater refinement.' See also AG to Quinn, 2 Feb. 1914, NYPL. Jonathan Pim, the Solicitor-General, concurred with Moriarty's opinion on 31 Jan.: the money should be returned to the players, less $200 and costs.

15. WBY to AG, 5 Nov. 1913, Berg.

16. 8 Oct. 1913, Berg.

17. Brown leather notebook, MBY.

18. *Irish Times*, 23 and 24 Oct. 1913. There is a letter from MG in the 23 Oct. issue, and an account by Montefiore of an interview with MG on 28 Oct.

19. *Irish Times*, 28 Oct. 1913.

20. NLI MS 30,615: cf. letter to *Irish Worker* as in *UP*, ii, 406–7.

21. 5 Nov. 1913, Denson, *Letters from AE*, 91.

22. 14 Nov. 1913, Berg.

23. WBY to AG, 10 Nov. 1913, Berg; the previous quotations come from letters of 15 and 5 Nov., NYPL.

24. Full MS in NLI MS 30,314; published version in the Cuala edition of *Responsibilities*, and a portion retained in *CP*. See *VP*, 818–20, for all the versions.

25. The plan was outlined to AG in a letter of 7 July 1913.

26. For the Radcliffe material, see Harper's and Kelly's discussion in *YO*, 131–71.

27. Professor Harold Hartley of Oxford.

28. 26 Nov. 1913, private collection.

29. See Longenbach, *Stone Cottage*, 249, and Ellmann interview book, Tulsa.

30. 'Sunday', summer 1913, Berg; two or three dozen bottles of sherry were suggested. Catherine Gregory was born on 21 Aug., after a difficult pregnancy.

31. Lady Dunsany's diary, 20 Oct. 1910, private collection, quoted (with some differences) in Mark Amory, *Lord Dunsany: A Biography* (London, 1972), 73–4. She added: 'Even allowing for much bias on her part there is a sordidness and pettiness shown by him which surprises one – and I must say that I had never detected anything of the kind – I never thought he had the straightforward simplicity and generous appreciation of other writers that A. E. shows, but I never thought him mean.'

32. Virginia Moore, *The Unicorn: William Butler Yeats's Search for Reality* (London, 1952), 253.

33. £382 and £413. 1s. 2d., MBY A27.

34. Carpenter, *A Serious Character*, 220.

35. 2 Dec. 1913, private collection; as with MG, he wanted to induce simultaneous meditation over the same symbol.

36. See 1897 edition. Agrippa was a supposed Rosicrucian; Henry Morley's commentary identifies him as a Platonic revivalist.

37. Canto 83.

38. See AG to WBY, 15 May [1914], Berg, for an account of his shortcomings.

39. To AG, 3 Dec. 1913. Also see WBY's letter to *The Times*, 4 Dec. 1913.

40. Dec. 1913. Incident and letter are given in Ervine's *Some Impressions of My Elders* (London, 1923), 251.

41. The astrological conjunction was Sun progressed in conjunction with natal Mars. See brown leather notebook, MBY.

42. To AG, 'Friday', early 1914, Berg.

43. See above, pp. 327–8. *Mem*, 269–70, records WBY's belief that Moore was confusing his speech after the RHA lecture with an address to the National Literary Society about the same time. At the former, he had called on the aristocracy to support Lane's gallery; at the latter, he had attacked the Irish bourgeoisie.

44. Pethica, 111–12.
45. To Quinn, 1 Jan 1914, Berg.
46. 9 Jan. 1914, Berg. AG's modest disclaimer is in a letter to S. Pawlins of Heinemann, 5 Jan. 1914, Berg.
47. Wife of a banking magnate and daughter of Sir Mountstewart Elphinstone Grant Duff, she was an old friend of AG's: see Pethica 70, n. 24.
48. On 27 May 1920 AG was innocent enough to ask Moore for a contribution to a memoir of Lane. After remarking that he was 'an extraordinarily clever picture dealer, apt at buying and equally apt at selling, works of art', Moore said that 'there is really nothing more to say, except perhaps that if he had lived he would have died a millionaire'. He then reminded AG that both Lane and she had put pressure on Heinemann 'to withdraw or mutilate' passages in *Hail and Farewell*; as a final stroke he offered to let her reprint his original passage about Lane for the memoir (Berg). It was brutal, but she should not have expected otherwise.
49. So AG told her sister, 15 Mar. 1914, Berg.
50. AG to Quinn, 20 Jan. 1914, NYPL, makes clear that by then WBY had written both poems: she quotes the last lines of the closing poem.
51. WBY to AG, 24 Nov. 1913, Berg.
52. See V. Meynell (ed.), *Friends of a Lifetime: Letters to Sydney Carlyle Cockerell* (London, 1940), 185–6; his wife later claimed it came as a surprise to him.
53. WBY to AG, 31 Jan. 1914, Berg, furnishes a description.
54. *UP*, ii, 410ff.: included there because Hone thought WBY wrote it, but it has more recently been assumed that Aldington was the author. This seems more likely on stylistic and other grounds. Also see *The Egoist*, I, i.
55. See account in HRHRC (Flint, F. S., Misc.).
56. See Canto 81.
57. To AG, 31 Jan. 1914, Berg. This letter shows he joined the boat at Liverpool, coming by train from Euston.
58. See AG to WBY, 22 Jan. 1914, Berg, for a letter dissenting from his advice to accept Moriarty's opinion. She would have supported full legal arbitration, but by short-circuiting it 'you propose for the sake of putting them [the players] in good humour to accept a decision which will leave us open to the charge of illegally paying the company money that doesn't belong to us'. Rather than accept such a 'shady proceeding', she wanted to take Quinn's opinion. On 28 Jan. she triumphantly wrote again, having found a letter of WBY's which had originally made the same point (Berg); but he was determined that the Company should depart to America in good humour. On 2 Feb. she was still complaining to Quinn about the Solicitor-General's opinion: see Quinn collection, NYPL, box 15, folder 3, which also has copies of the relevant documents.
59. To AG, 3 Aug. 1912, Berg.
60. '*I had not asked for it* or even hinted it,' JBY told Rosa Butt. 'It was a pleasant surprise, and money can't be abundant with him, but he lives always in the most thrifty way, never wanting to spend money on himself, in that like his mother.' (5 Nov. 1915, Bodleian). A gloomier version of finances is given in SMY to Quinn, 5 Apr. 1915, NYPL, emphasizing their own poverty (and dependence on a pound a month from Jack). Quinn had suggested JBY returning to Dundrum, bringing them a guaranteed £70 p.a. from WBY: SMY approved, but feared the old man would swiftly demand a studio in town. The earlier donation is recorded in JBY to Rosa Butt, 21 Feb. 1914, and the dancing evening in WBY to AG, 13 Jan. 1914, Berg.
61. The identification of Campbell and AG is my own, but seems unmistakable.
62. Quoted by Strand, 'American Lecture Tours', 159, 166.
63. A letter quoted in TS of Professor Humphries's address 'Yeats at Amherst, 1914' [14 June 1964], Amherst College Archives.

64. These quotations are given by Strand, 135, 137, 140, 149.

65. ibid., 123.

66. ibid., 138.

67. ibid., 140, 144, 147. Phelps wrote that WBY 'expressed hatred of George Moore, and said a great many "events" that Moore described in his book, conversations with Yeats, etc., never happened'.

68. Humphries's address, as above. In WBY's cuttings file in NLI there is a scrap of May 1900 (attribution illegible) which recounts: 'one is never safe in Mr Yeats's company. It is on record that he once talked to a noted theosophist with the appalling result that when the man got up he was followed over the carpet by a "little green elephant".'

69. Marie Chambers, 'Personal Glimpses: William Butler Yeats', HRHRC. This is consistent with his reading of Joachim, Swedenborg and Boehme.

70. See E. Ruggles, *The West-Going Heart: A Life of Vachel Lindsay* (New York, 1969); and, for the banquet, *Poetry* magazine MSS 1912–1976, Chicago University.

71. *Inter-Ocean*, 2 Mar. 1914.

72. Quoted in Strand, 'American Lecture Tours', 146.

73. G. Sime and F. Nicholson, *Brave Spirits* (London, n.d.).

74. F. Hackett, *The Invisible Censor* (New York, 1918), 114–18; a version was also published in the *New Republic*.

75. B. L. Reid, *The Man from New York: John Quinn and His Friends* (New York, 1968), 177–8.

76. JBY to Mrs Buss, 1 June 1917, HRHRC.

77. Quinn first suggested an annual retainer (28 Apr. 1914, Himber, *Letters of Quinn to Yeats*, 141); but by July the arrangement was made of payment per item.

78. 'Wednesday 8th' [?April] 1914, Berg.

79. To R L-P, 5 Apr. 1914 (written on board ship).

80. To AG, 1 May 1914, Berg.

81. See Brandon, *The Spiritualists*, 150–57; in Jan. her spirit photographs were shown to be based on pictures in *Le Miroir*.

82. See George Mills Harper, ' "A Subject of Investigation": Miracle at Mirebeau', *YO*, 172–89. Feilding later wrote a long report published in T. Bestermann (ed.), *Transactions of the Fourth International Congress for Psychical Research* (London, 1930).

83. 13 May 1914, Berg.

84. 15 May [1914], Berg.

85. Brown leather notebook, MBY.

86. A holograph in the Berg collection is thus dated. It also oddly echoes the translation of Verhaeren's 'Les Moines' printed in the *Irish Review*; see above, p. 615, n. 45.

87. Strand, 'American Lecture Tours', 149. This eventually became 'The Poet and the Actress', first reprinted in *YA* 8 (1991), with a commentary by David R. Clark.

88. See WBY to Radcliffe, 21 May 1914, private collection.

89. *Self-Portrait*, entry for 29 May 1914.

90. SMY to Quinn, 13 May 1914, NYPL, says 'our new book of his new poems will be out tomorrow'. Wade's *Bibliography* gives 25 May, but subscribers' copies would have been released before publication day.

91. See above, pp. 463–4. As WBY would have known, Walter Scott used 'Old Play' to signify that an epigraph was invented.

92. See *Mem*, 241, for its original inspiration.

93. See *LTWBY*, i, 289–90, for JBY's reaction. The grouping of the poems is considered in Warwick Gould, 'An Empty Theatre? Yeats as Minstrel in *Responsibilities*', J. Genet, *Studies in W. B. Yeats* (Caen, 1989).

94. [July 1916], BL. Pound annotated his copy 'emended by WBY to "some stale bitch" & then castrated by the greasy Macmillan'. George Yeats noted in her copy of *CP* that 'The Witch' was written to Olivia Shakespear.

95. *Outlook*, June 1914.

96. *New Statesman*, 24 Apr. 1915.

97. Oct. 1914, private collection.

98. Aug. 1914, private collection.

99. Barrett H. Clark, 'In London with William Butler Yeats', *New York Morning Sun*, 25 Aug. 1918.

100. 12 Sept. 1914, Boston. The theory about the Old and New Testament values is in Clark, as in n. 87, above.

101. SMY to R L-P, 18 Mar. 1939; WBY to AG, 8 Oct. 1914, Berg.

102. 10 Nov. 1914, TCD.

103. Charles Power to Mahaffy, 12 Nov. 1914, TCD.

104. WBY to AG, 17 Nov. 1914, Berg.

105. TS dated 20 Nov. 1914 in Ellmann MSS, Tulsa.

106. *Irish Times*, 21 Nov. 1914. Holloway reported it as 'pro-Germanism of Mr Pearse'; see Ruth Dudley Edwards, *Patrick Pearse: The Triumph of Failure* (London, 1977), 226.

107. To AG, 2 May 1911, Berg.

108. To R L-P, 20 Nov. 1914.

109. TS copy of WBY to AG, 21 Nov. 1914, Berg.

110. Gilbert, *Golden Dawn Companion*, 167–9, clarifies that WBY was 'active' at least after 1910, and Imperator and instructor in 'ancient traditions' in 1914.

111. See p. 614, n. 35, above.

112. Warwick Gould points out another possible influence in the fragment of autobiography published with William Allingham's *Diaries*.

113. To SMY, 28 July 1914, Boston.

114. 31 Oct. 1914, NYPL.

115. 'Wednesday', n.d., from Royal Societies Club, HRHRC.

116. See letters to Quinn, 9 July 1914, NYPL, and to AG, 14 July 1914, Berg.

117. See TS at NLI and Harvard. The MS is at Colby College.

118. To G. B. Thring, 16 Oct. 1914, quoted in Warwick Gould, 'Singular Pluralities: Titles of Yeats's *Autobiographies*', *YA* II (1994), 208.

119. To Quinn, 30 July 1914, NYPL.

120. ECY to Grant Richards, 9 Nov. 1914, HRHRC. The Quinn TS at Harvard is 'A Revery'. See also Gould, 'Singular Pluralities'.

121. To R L-P, 26 Sept. 1923. SMY later annotated her copy in great detail, identifying the anonymous (ABY).

122. See above, p. 155, for this incident. My thanks to Linda Satchwell, who has generously shared with me her analysis of the MS and its changes.

123. To SMY, 11 Nov. 1914.

124. To AG, 11 Nov. 1913, Berg.

125. Inscription in AG's copy of *The Trembling of the Veil*, Emory Special Collections.

126. WBY to Carlos Linati, 24 Dec. 1913, Pierpont Morgan Library. One might add critical commentaries by Weygandt and Gwynn, and Maurice Bourgeois's *Synge*.

127. 25 Nov. 1914; see *Rev. Eng. Lit.*, iv, 3 (July 1962). As to the embroidery, he wrote a remarkably long and careful letter to R L-P on 2 Sept. 1914 (MBY) about a plan to get Henry Lamb to design patterns for SMY to work, thus launching her into esoteric and fashionable artistic circles; he would pay for the experiment. He wished her to create art: 'I

want to make an attempt to lift their work into a world where people pay great prices and where workers aim at making their work the best of its kind in the world.'

128. *L*, 589.

129. It was supposed to be issued at Christmas 1915, but was held up by an American copyright difficulty; it went on sale on 29 Mar. 1916. It was revised when reissued with *The Trembling of the Veil* as *Autobiographies* in 1926.

130. To AG, 4 Mar. 1913, Berg.

131. His ancient enemy Mrs Ellis filled him with tales of the decline and decrepitude of his childhood friends and mentors. In a letter of 17 July 1911 to JBY (Boston) WBY describes the end of their friendship: 'Some twelve years ago I went to see him in Paris and realised with a shock how intolerable his wife was. Sometimes when one has not seen a person for years one goes back to them and realises that there is some burden there which one can never take up again though it did not seem too heavy once. I think he felt my hostility to her.'

132. See above, p. 51.

133. My thanks to Linda Satchwell for pointing this out. He was also much involved in verifying a vision of SMY's during the summer he wrote *Reveries*: see *FS*, 381–3.

134. The last word of the MS was 'comes', changed in the TS to 'happens'; otherwise, this concluding section was written as directly and fluently as nearly all the rest.

INDEX

THE abbreviations used are as in the notes. Writings by WBY (including *Samhain* and *Arrow*, which were largely his own work) are gathered in his composite entry. The journals and newspapers listed are those which recur in the text, or which were particularly important to WBY. The notes are also indexed when they contain substantial additional information rather than a short or passing reference. Pseudonyms are indexed, but not fictional personages (such as Michael Hearn or Michael Robartes) – with the exception of 'Fiona Macleod', who falls somewhere in between.

Abbey Theatre: finances, 225, 237, 258, 291, 296, 320, 337–9, 344, 349, 352, 389–90, 397, 406, 413–14, 421–4, 505, 605 (n. 17); premises, 320, 323; patent for, 322–3, 328–9; opening, 328–9; early seasons, 334–44, 373–4, 381–2; professionalization of the company, 337–43; tours in Britain, 341, 347–9, 369; change in direction (late 1906), 352–8, 596 (n. 120); reorganization into limited company (1910), 422–3; in USA, 443–50, 453–4, 460, 510, 514, 611 (n. 40); acting school, 453–4; and the Lane gallery appeal, 481, 483, 493, 497–8, 510, 620–21 (n. 14), 622 (n. 58)
   see also Horniman, Annie; Irish National Theatre Society; Yeats, William Butler
Aberdeen, Ishbel Maria Gordon, Countess of, 292
Aberdeen, John Campbell Gordon, seventh Earl of, 409, 411
Achurch, Janet, 141
Acosta, Helen, 79
'AE', *see* Russell, George William
Aeschylus, 99
Agrippa, Cornelius, 50, 505
Aldington, Richard, 471, 474–5, 493, 509, 622 (n. 54)
Alexandra, Queen, 321
Ali, Mir Alaud, 47
Allgood, Molly ('Maire O'Neill'), 328, 348, 376, 384, 399–400, 413, 423, 433, 441, 444, 454
Allgood, Sara, 328, 342, 353, 360, 378, 380, 384–5, 393, 397, 399, 405–6, 413, 423, 429, 441, 454, 505, 607 (n. 95)
Allingham, William, 24, 75, 131, 146–7, 274, 624 (n. 112)
All Ireland Review, 235–6, 251, 256, 262
Andrews, C. F., 473
Antoine, André, 142, 199, 323
Arabi, Colonel Ahmed, 168, 509
Archer, William, 263, 266, 292, 318
Ardilaun, Arthur Edward Guinness, first Baron, 206, 479, 495, 499, 617 (n. 113)
Ardilaun, Olivia Charlotte Guinness, Baroness, 423, 495, 499, 617 (n. 113)
Armstrong, Eliza, 17
Armstrong, General John, 612 (n. 71)
Armstrong, Laura, 34, 68, 93, 550 (n. 24)
Arnold, Matthew, 32, 53, 131, 198, 534
Ashton, Sir Frederick, 253
Asquith, Herbert Henry, 412, 425–6, 428, 436, 441–2, 458, 486, 516
Asquith, Margot, 436, 441
Association Irlandaise, *see* Young Ireland Societies
Atkinson, Robert, 206
Ayton, Reverend William Alexander, 104

Bagwell, Richard, 145
Bailey, William Frederick, 334
Balfour, Arthur James, 425, 436
Balfour, Lady Betty, 204, 206
Balzac, Honoré de, xxvii, 17, 108, 158, 172, 250, 336, 393, 398, 411, 512, 537
Banim, Charles, 98
Banim, John, 98
Barlow, Shaun, 289
Barrie, J. M., 292, 422
Basterot, Comte Florimond de, 167, 169, 177, 183, 546 (n. 47)
Battle, Mary, 130, 143, 204–5, 530
Beardsley, Aubrey, 138, 142, 155, 158–9, 187
Beardsley, Mabel, 403, 485–6, 505, 509, 527, 618 (n. 135)
Béaslaí, Piaras, 363, 365
Beatty, Dr Thomas, 15
Beatty, Reverend Dr, 2
Bedford Park, 26, 59–61, 65, 74–5, 80, 103, 107, 137, 140, 155–6, 158–9, 164, 257, 274
Beerbohm, Max, 211–12, 292, 295; cartoon of WBY and Moore, 77; records *Savoy* dinner, 158–9; on the Abbey players as exotics, 318–19
Bennett, Arnold, 424, 514
Benson, A. C., 424, 510
Benson, Constance, 253
Benson, Francis Robert, 253
Benson Company, 237, 251–3
Berkeley, George, 48, 146
Bernard, Dr John Henry, 212
Besant, Annie, 102
Best, Richard, 223
Binyon, Laurence, 257–8, 425, 474
'Birmingham, George', *see* Hannay, Canon James Owen
Birrell, Augustine, 411, 422, 425–6, 428
Bisson, Juliette, 517–19
Blake, William, 48, 95, 98–101, 102, 104, 109, 113, 129–30, 133, 148, 157, 159, 163–4, 177–8, 187, 213, 245, 269, 272, 466, 468, 525, 559 (n. 52)
Blavatsky, Helena Petrovna, 46–7, 50, 52, 62–3, 78, 81, 102–4, 133, 162
Bloggs, Frances, 60
Blunt, Wilfrid Scawen, 169, 266, 292, 336–7, 366, 422, 509–10
Boehme, Jacob, 99, 101, 109, 163, 463, 525
Boer War, xxviii, 221–3, 235, 239–40, 283–4, 313, 350, 447
Bookman, 96, 108, 129, 133, 139, 146–7, 180, 196–7, 334, 372
Boston Pilot, 44, 56, 70, 93–5, 107, 110, 119, 150, 160, 447–8

Bowen, Elizabeth, 50
Boyd, Ernest, 89, 455, 515
Boyle, William, 336, 343–4, 348, 352, 354, 366, 377, 413, 593 (n. 28), 598 (n. 34), 606 (n. 60)
Bradley, Katherine Harris, 63
Brémont, 'Comtesse' Anna de, 105
Bridges, Robert, 179, 250
Brodie-Innes, J. W., 243
Brooke, Rupert, 486
Brown, Robert, 466
Browning, Robert, 56, 88, 108, 199
Bruce, Kathleen, 385
Bulfin, William, 279–80
Bullen, Arthur Henry, 176, 234, 246, 258, 336, 346, 350, 370–73, 385, 396, 440, 457, 486
Bullock, Percy, 103
Bulwer-Lytton, Edward, 104
Burke, Edmund, 193
Butcher, S. H., 425
Butler, Mary, 2, 542 (n. 3), 545 (n. 18)
Butler, Samuel, 463
Butler family, 1, 435
Butt, Clara, 440
Butt, Isaac, xxviii, 2–3, 28, 30–31, 39, 41
Butt, Rosa, 3, 8, 11, 13, 342
Byrne, Raven, 456

Callanan, Jeremiah, 15, 147
Calvert, Louis, 326
Campbell, Beatrice Stella (Mrs Patrick), 267, 352, 382, 389, 392–3, 402, 407, 412, 534, 583 (n. 50), 596 (n. 110); likes *Diarmuid and Grania*, 236–7; interested in *Deirdre*, 370, 374, and plays it, 392; WBY sees her as a volcano cooking eggs, 380, and a pirate in a cave, 512; she sees him as more cultured than Shaw, 380; wants to give him wine to write on, 385–6; assailed by Horniman, 405
Carleton, William, 76, 97–8, 121, 145, 147
Carroll, William, 305
Carson, Edward, 498, 513
Casey, W. F., 413
Castletown, Bernard Edward Fitz-Patrick, second Baron, 189, 200, 206, 225
Cathcart, George Lambert, 608 (n. 116)
Catholic University of America, 305 (n.), 306, 309, 312
Chateaubriand, François Auguste René de, 96, 186, 201
Chatterjee, Mohini, xxx, 47–8, 85, 102, 469–70, 551–2 (n. 72)
Chaucer, Geoffrey, 336, 431
Chernoweth, Mrs (medium), 447, 463
Chesterton, Gilbert Keith, 60, 287, 290
Christian, Clara, 451
Churchill, Lord Randolph, 27
Churchill, Winston, 436
Cipriani, Amilcare, 354
Claidheamh Soluis, An, 220–21, 235, 410
Clan na Gael, 179, 191, 306, 309, 313–14, 332, 365, 445, 450
Clarke, Dr Adam, 106–7
Clodd, Edward, 525, 614 (n. 35)
Coates, Dorothy, 407–8, 516
Cockerell, Sydney, 266, 430
Cockran, William Bourke, 305, 516
Coffey, George, 97, 202, 261
Cohalan, Daniel, 312–13, 516

Coleridge, Samuel Taylor, 86, 293, 360
Colles, Ramsay, 229
Collins, Mabel, 102
Collins, Richard Henn, 237
Colum, Padraic, 278, 281, 284, 288–9, 306, 317, 336, 338, 340–41, 343, 347, 358, 363, 401, 404, 417, 455, 459, 594 (n. 65)
Comte, Auguste, 7
Comyn, Michael, 82, 86
Connell, Norreys (Conal O'Riordan), 208, 366, 375, 378, 380, 382, 402, 404, 405, 415, 601 (n. 107)
Connolly, Ellie, 17, 21
Connolly, James, 180–81, 194, 223
Conrad, Joseph, 425, 514
Contemporary Club, 39–45, 53, 64, 132–3, 289
Coole Park, *see* WBY; AG
Cooper, Edith, 63
Corbet, Patrick, 612 (n. 71)
Corbet, Robert, 2, 9, 62, 545 (n. 21)
Corbet, William, 542 (n. 6)
Cornwallis-West, George, 374
Cousins, James, 212, 260, 262, 279, 281, 289, 294, 296, 317, 467–8, 487
Craig, Edith, 257, 280, 285, 290
Craig, Edward Gordon, 257–8, 280, 282, 287–8, 291, 378, 390, 403, 416, 424, 440, 447, 468, 485, 487, 511; produces *Dido and Aeneas*, 251; WBY wants to bring him to Ireland, 263; invites WBY to join his bohemians in Florence, 408; his screens, 413, 456, 472; and *The Hour-Glass*, 422, 433; exhibition in Dublin (1913), 482–3
Crane, Walter, 290
Crewe, Robert Offley Ashburton Crewe-Milnes, first Marquess of, 425
Croker, Thomas Crofton, 63, 76
Cromartie, Sibell Lilian Blunt-Mackenzie, Countess of, 321, 337, 343, 348, 385
Cromer, Evelyn Baring, first Earl, 412–13, 425
Crook, W. M., 62, 93, 555 (n. 13)
Crowley, Aleister, 104, 110, 231–3, 404, 605 (n. 12)
Cruise O'Brien, Francis, 364
Cuala industries, 274, 380, 399, 403, 421, 445, 462, 472, 497, 520, 527, 601 (n. 119)
see also Yeats, Elizabeth Corbet; Yeats, Susan Mary
Cumann na nGaedheal, 240, 278–9, 281, 294, 296, 298, 361
Cunard, Maud Alice, Lady, 346
Curtin, Jeremiah, 176

Daily Express (Dublin), 120, 145, 169, 197–8, 206, 211, 225–6, 458
D'Annunzio, Gabriele, 368, 511, 537
Dante Alighieri, 96, 99, 199
Darragh, Florence Laetitia (Dallas), 352–5, 357, 374, 485, 487
Davidson, John, 107–8, 428, 577 (n. 65)
Davis, Andrew Jackson, 525
Davis, Thomas, 44, 53, 56, 98, 121–2, 124, 147, 193, 220, 418–19, 462, 496, 523–4
Davitt, Michael, 41–2, 169, 190, 223, 229
Davray, Henry, 159–60, 176, 178, 205, 214, 469, 567 (n. 87)
Dee, John, 104
Déroulède, Paul, 205
Desborough, Ethel (Etty) Grenfell, Baroness, 436, 487

de Valera, Eamon, 5
de Vere, Aubrey, 86, 146–7
Devoy, John, 305, 309, 312–13, 365, 445, 449
Dick, F. J., 114
Dickinson, Mabel, 388–90, 396, 398–9, 429, 431, 502, 506; background, 383–4, 602 (n. 131); begins affair with WBY, 383–5; coaches Molly Allgood, 413; pregnancy scare, 488–9; subsequent life, 618 (n. 152)
Dickinson, Page, 384
Digges, Dudley, 261, 319, 328, 344, 378
Dillon, John, 113, 187–8, 206, 229
Dixon, Henry, 332
Dobson, Austin, 425
Dolmetsch, Arnold, 250, 257–8, 263
Donne, John, 468
Doolittle, Hilda (H. D.), 474
Doran, John, 18
Dougherty, James, 409–11, 442
Douglas, Lord Alfred, 266
Dowden, Edward, 18, 26, 49, 57, 75, 86, 126, 146–8, 161, 549 (n. 6); Yeats family's view of, 29–30, 57; interest in the young WBY, 37–9, 44–5; WBY's attacks on, 52, 145; refuses to support Wilde, 154; advocates cosmopolitanism rather than nationalism in literature, 335–6; obstructs WBY's succession to his chair, 429–31; death, and WBY's second attempt, 483–4; in *Reveries*, 530
Dowden, John, 18
Dowson, Ernest, 107–8, 110, 157, 199, 385, 392, 416–17
Dublin Castle, 112, 190, 318, 409–11, 426, 442, 500
Dublin Hermetic Society, 46–7
Dublin University Magazine, 28, 39, 53, 77
Dublin University Review, 37, 39, 41, 52
Dufferin, Frederick Temple Hamilton-Temple-Blackwood, first Marquess of Dufferin and Ava, 206
Duffy, Charles Gavan, 118–24, 126–7, 131, 142–3, 145–6, 197, 233, 274, 492
Dumas, Charles, 434
Duncan, Ellen, 383, 468
Dun Emer industries, 274–5, 287, 300–301, 316–17, 336, 380
'Dungannon Clubs', 195, 341, 405, 458
Dunlop, D. N., 133
Dunraven, Windham Thomas Wyndham-Quin, fourth Earl of, 383, 426, 442
Dunsany, Beatrice, Baroness, 435–6, 503, 621 (n. 31)
Dunsany, Edward John Moreton Drax Plunkett, eighteenth Baron, 411, 417, 430, 467, 485; befriends WBY, 383; needs 'fifty pounds a year and a drunken mistress', 403–4; subscribes to Abbey, 422; thinks AG plagiarizes him, 435–6; Craig mistakes him for stage-carpenter, 440; published by Cuala, 462

Edward VII, King, 265, 292, 300, 318, 409–10, 421–2
'Eglinton, John', *see* Magee, W. K.
Elgar, Edward, 251
Eliot, George, 53, 553 (n. 105)
Elliott, Gertrude, 535
Ellmann, Richard, xxvi–xxvii, 89, 276
Ellis, Edwin, 12, 75, 98–102, 107, 127, 136, 453, 468, 530, 625 (n. 131)
Ellis, Henry Havelock, 156–7, 159, 177–8, 272
Ellis, Phillipa (Mrs Edwin Ellis), 100, 625 (n. 131)
Emerson, Thomas, 502

Emery, Edward, 137
Emery, Florence Farr, *see* Farr, Florence
Emmet, Robert, 120, 127, 193, 220, 312, 378, 428, 496, 525, 529; WBY's speech on (1904), 312–14
Ervine, St John Greer, 433, 446, 506
'Esmond, Alice', 96
Esson, Louis, 319

Fagan, Charles, 53
Farley, Archbishop John Murphy, 302
Farquharson, Robert, 337
Farr, Florence, 144, 152, 154, 159, 183, 205, 269, 286–7, 324, 345, 365, 374–5, 392, 396–7, 407, 429, 431, 522; hears *Countess Cathleen*, 97; and Golden Dawn, 104–5, 137, 231–2, 241–5, 355–6; acts in *A Sicilian Idyll*, 107; character, 137; collaborates with WBY in 1894, 137–8; and the Irish theatre movement, 207–8; and chanting, 250, 257–8, 263, 279, 287, 290, 308, 471; writes plays with Olivia Shakespear, 259; love-affair with WBY, 290–91, 337, 367–8; acts in *The Shadowy Waters*, 336–7; in *Deirdre*, 433; protects the psaltery from railway porters, 433; advice on marriage, 433; dismays Tagore, 471; moves to Ceylon, 485; on Egyptian magic, 579 (n. 72)
Fay, Frank, 292, 315, 318, 348, 355, 401, 423, 600 (n. 95), 601 (nn. 101, 102); as theatre critic for *United Irishman*, 212; challenges WBY to write a rousing nationalist play, 248–9; attacks *Diarmuid and Grania*, 252–3; theatrical work before INTS, 259–61; collaboration with WBY, 262–3, 278–81; as Seanchan, 295; abandons Griffithism, 296, 324–5, 343; advised by WBY how to reply to Moore, 323; opposes Darragh, 352–3; falls asleep during *Unicorn*, 374; split with Abbey, 377–80; tries to return, 413, 505
Fay, William, 284, 289, 308, 328, 342–3, 358–9, 370, 375, 401, 423; theatrical background, 252–4, 259; collaboration with WBY, 260–63, 278–81; success on English tour, 292; WBY ignores his contribution to training actors, 317; tells WBY about working-class Dublin, 333; criticized as stage-manager, 338, 375–6; and Brigit O'Dempsey, 348; Horniman's enmity to him, 348–9, and his respect for her, 600 (n. 95); opposes Darragh, 352; Horniman's campaign against him, 354–7; split from Abbey, 376–80
Feilding, Everard, 462, 517–18
Felkin, Robert W., 465, 517, 525
Fell, H. C., 150–51
Fellowship of the Three Kings, 222, 245, 257
Fenianism, xxviii, 21, 31, 41–4, 53, 84, 93, 106, 112–15, 119–20, 124, 132, 179–80, 189, 193, 220, 262, 285, 300, 322, 341, 405
Ferguson, Sir Samuel, 28–9, 41, 44, 52, 56, 69, 85, 122, 145, 147, 160, 220, 520, 549 (n. 5)
Fianna na hÉireann, 405
'Field, Michael', 108, 292
    see also Bradley, Katherine Harris; Cooper, Edith
Field, William, 193, 226–9
Figaro, Dublin, 120, 128, 229
Findlater, Adam, 193
Fingall, Elizabeth (Daisy) Plunkett, Countess of, 200, 204
Finlay, Father Tom, 311
First World War, xxix, 522–3

Fitzgerald, Charles, 305
Fitzgerald, David, 130
Fitzgerald, Lord Edward, 194, 496
Fitzgerald, John Francis, Mayor of Boston, 449
FitzGibbon, Gerald, Lord Justice, 27
Fitzmaurice, George, 373, 382, 440
Flint, F. S., 474, 509
Flournoy, Theodor, 463, 490, 525
Forbes-Robertson, Johnston, 535
Ford, Ford Madox (Hueffer), 474, 521
Fortuny, Mario, 447
Fowler, Eva, 437–8, 463–4, 468, 475, 487–8, 502, 510, 517
Fox, Valentine, 154
Fox-Strangeways, H. H., 469, 471
Frazer, James, 170, 213, 525
Freeman's Journal, 86, 90, 209, 212, 227, 264, 265, 296, 327, 397
Freemasonry, 104, 198, 205, 431
Freud, Sigmund, 463, 525, 614 (nn. 36, 37), 619 (n. 157)
Frohman, Charles, 377
Frost, Robert, 471
Fuller, Loie, 109

Gael, 44, 53, 56, 71, 218
Gaelic Athletic Association, 44, 71
Gaelic League, 126, 165, 169, 184, 220, 235, 252, 290, 307, 312, 325, 341, 365, 417, 455
Gallagher, T. J., 447
Galsworthy, John, 171, 446, 512
Garnett, Edward, 107, 110, 123–5, 129, 135, 149
Garrity, Joseph, 445, 450
Garvey, Maire, 324, 342, 344, 607 (n. 82)
Gaudier-Brzeska, Henri, 509
Genthe, Arnold, 516
Gibson, Charles Dana, 516
Giles, William, 59
Gill, Thomas Patrick, 95, 162, 188, 197, 203–4, 206, 210–12, 225–6, 241, 246, 319, 451
Gillmor, Alexander, 10
Gladstone, W. E., xxviii, 30, 113
Gleeson, Evelyn, 274–5, 380
Godwin, Ernest, 60–61
Goethe, Johann Wolfgang von, 99, 276, 346, 512
Gogarty, Oliver St John, 168, 272, 301, 330, 430, 441
Golden Dawn, Hermetic Order of, 101, 103–7, 110, 129, 132, 137, 143, 148, 163, 165, 222, 230–34, 241–5, 269, 347, 376, 380, 560 (nn. 66, 75), 577 (n. 26)
Goldsmith, Oliver, 146, 448
Gonne, Iseult, 127, 157, 286–7, 331, 334, 387, 421, 467, 472, 519, 616 (n. 81)
Gonne, Kathleen (later Pilcher), 91, 282, 284
Gonne, Maud, 5, 44, 122, 144, 163, 175, 212, 252, 257, 277, 385, 412, 429, 461, 468, 475–6, 499; birth and background, 57, 91–2, 118–19, 554 (n. 121); meets WBY, xxx, 57, 87–8, 554 (n. 120); character, 91; politics, 91–2, 114, 179–81, 189–95, 205, 213, 221, 313, 321, 333, 354, 386, 411, 420, 570 (n. 70), 576 (n. 87), 577 (n. 25); and Millevoye, 92–3; inspires WBY's work, 97, 203, 219, 230–31, 238–9, 284, 301–2, 388, 391, 393–6, 420, 434–6, 456–7, 467–8, 520, 522; political influence on him, 98, 114–15, 193–4, 196, 313, 399, 420; occult researches with him, 101, 106, 518–19; and the Golden Dawn, 104–6, 117; spiritual association with WBY, 114, 157, 195–6, 201–3, 285, 386–8, 391, 394–5, 465–6,
518–19; death of son Georges, 115–16; conception of Iseult, 117, 127; estrangement from WBY in 1893, 127–8, and reconciliation, 157; their political disagreements, 133–4, 194; and AG, 172, 179; anti-Jubilee demonstration (1897), 180–81, 227, 395; reveals her secret life to WBY, 201–5; and the theatre movement, 206, 278–81, 287–90, 295–300, 323–4; campaign against Boer War, 222–3, 326–30, 576–7 (n. 14); performance as *Cathleen ni Houlihan*, 260–62, 279, 306, 320, 328; marriage to and separation from MacBride, 282–7, 290, 293, 330–34, 347, 363, 445, 592 (nn. 4, 16); hissed at Abbey, 353–4; consummation of affair with WBY (1908–9), 386–9, 391–6, 407, 434–5, 465, 602 (n. 146), 603 (n. 172); entertains him at Colleville, 421, 461–2, 467–8; threatened with blackballing at the Arts Club, 436; and Lane gallery campaign, 495; and Dublin lock-out, 499–500; investigates 'miracle' at Mirebeau, 518–19; and First World War, 522
Gonne, May (later Bertie-Clay), 91, 117, 330–32, 407
Gore-Booth, Constance, *see* Markievicz, Constance
Gore-Booth, Eva, 129, 144, 152–3
Gore-Booth, Joanna, 144
Gore-Booth, Sir Robert, 23
Gorman, Agnes Pollexfen, 4, 16, 21, 24, 155, 528
Gorman, Elma, 4
Gosse, Edmund, 199, 208, 417, 438, 456, 528, 608 (n. 107); admires *Wind Among the Reeds*, 217; introduces WBY to Asquith, 412; and Academic Committee, 424–5; and Civil List pension, 425–8; excludes Tagore, 471
Gourmont, Rémy de, 138
Granville-Barker, Harley, 326, 415
Graves, Alfred Percival, 82, 207, 229
Gray, John, 108, 157, 575 (n. 56)
Gray, Thomas Thompson, 608 (n. 116)
Greene, George, 107–8
Gregg, Frederick, 27, 33, 35, 37, 48, 53, 305, 516
Gregory, Augusta, Lady, 30, 76, 100, 111, 175, 181, 185, 198–9, 217, 300, 301, 308, 345, 375, 384, 512; personality, 169–70; her politics, 169, 196, 227–8, 441; meets WBY, 169–70, 568 (n. 28); their relationship, xxix, 169–72, 357; collaboration on folklore, 170–71, 183, 204, 505, 569 (n. 34); and MG, 172, 179, 194, 201–5, 227, 232, 286, 333, 391, 573 (n. 10), 586 (n. 16); collaboration on theatre plans, 179, 183, 188–9; entertains him at Coole, 181–3, 189, 195, 218–19, 246–9, 288, 321–2, 503–4; and in London, 187, 191, 477; solicitousness, 187–8, 219–21, 309–10, 346, 380, 389, 503, 511, 595 (n. 84); and Irish Literary Theatre, 225–6, 237, 570 (n. 81); defends WBY against 'the priests', 240–41; collaboration on play-writing, 248–50, 268–70, 295, 356–7, 372, 580 (n. 95), 599 (n. 68); WBY supports her work, 250, 258, 264–5, 293, 308, 469, 507, 582 (nn. 33, 34, 35); her interest in Joyce, 276–7; and Irish National Theatre Society/Abbey Theatre, 287–9, 294–6, 317, 325–6, 328, 335, 339–44, 352–8, 376, 402, 405–6, 413–16, 421–3, 444, 449–50, 453, 455, 606 (n. 60), 611 (n. 39); influences WBY's views, 324, 344, 346, 369, 411–12; and Lane, 326–7, 478–83, 494–8; antipathy to Annie Horniman, 337, 339–40, 405–6, 414, 421–2, 503, 596 (n. 121), 607 (n. 86); and *Playboy*, 360–65, 449–50; brings WBY to Italy, 367–69; and Catholicism, 376, 507–8, 518, 568 (n. 22), 600

Gregory, Augusta, Lady (*cont.*):
(n. 91); illness (1907), 398; relationship with
Synge, 399–401, 449; and *Blanco Posnet*, 409–11,
605 (n. 37); coolnesses between her and WBY,
414, 426–9, 503–4, 511; and Civil List pension,
425–9, 503, 608 (n. 109); WBY's tributes to her,
436; tours with Abbey in USA (1911–12), 449–50,
453–4; love-affair with John Quinn, 449–50;
satirized by George Moore in *Hail and Farewell*,
451, 507–9, 622 (n. 48); advises about Mabel
Dickinson, 488–9; WBY repays her money, 517
WORKS
The Canavans, 599 (n. 60); *Cuchulain of Muir-
themne*, 248, 258, 264–5, 412, 469, 582 (nn. 33, 34,
35); *The Deliverer*, 435, 609 (n. 10); *Full Moon*, 435;
The Gaol Gate, 376; *Hyacinth Halvey*, 348; *Kincora*,
328, 335–6, 404; *Mirandolina*, 415; Molière
translations, 328, 347; *Our Irish Theatre*, 450, 517,
526, 528; *The Rising of the Moon*, 377; *Spreading the
News*, 328, 348; *Twenty-five*, 278, 289; *Visions and
Beliefs in the West of Ireland*, 170, 439–40, 464, 525;
(with WBY), *Cathleen ni Houlihan*, 248–9, 580
(n. 95); *The Pot of Broth*, 249, 279, 348, 359, 372,
377
Gregory, Margaret (formerly Parry), 370–71, 398,
412, 468, 503
Gregory, Richard, 421
Gregory, Robert, 169, 363, 367, 412, 415, 468, 568
(n. 24); on WBY at Oxford, 264; set-designs, 289,
326, 379; WBY presses him on Dun Emer, 350–51;
anti-Sinn Féin, 363; marriage, 370–71, 398; soured
relations with WBY, 398, 503; and AG's quarrel
with Gosse, 426–8
Gregory, Sir William, 168, 248, 412, 507–8
Grein, J. T., 142, 199
Grierson, Herbert, 360, 367, 468
Griffin, Gerald, 98
Griffith, Arthur, 195, 220, 266, 272, 281, 284, 288,
297–8, 315, 378, 418, 442–3, 524, 574–5 (n. 52);
founds Sinn Féin, 70, 286, 296; criticizes Irish
Literary Theatre, 206, 211–13; campaigns against
Boer War, 223, 229, 240; and MacBride marriage,
286; 'first serious quarrel' with WBY, 327; and
Playboy, 360, 363, 365, 399; growing enmity to
WBY, 405, 457–8
Guiney, Louise Imogen, 90, 94
Gwynn, Denis, 524
Gwynn, Stephen, 44, 81, 262, 292, 294, 318–19, 336,
339, 355, 363, 448, 459–60, 497–9
Gyles, Althea, 152, 176, 214, 221–2

Hackett, Francis, 314, 515–16, 519
Haldane, John Scott, 425, 442
Hallam, Arthur, 99
Hamilton, General Sir Ian, 389, 425–6
Hannay, Canon James Owen ('George
Birmingham'), 524
Hardy, Thomas, 425–6
Harper, Edith, 464
Harper, George Mills, 243
Harrington, Timothy, 188, 193, 228
Harris, Thomas Lake, 163
Harris, W. G., 25
Harvey, John Martin, 413
Hastings, Beatrice, 612 (n. 9)
Healy, Father James, 27
Healy, Johnny, 21

Healy, Timothy Michael, 54, 61, 113, 184–5, 187, 188,
206, 211, 423
Heaney, Seamus, xxviii
Heine, Heinrich, 276
Heinemann, William, 154, 508
Henderson, W. A., 349, 360, 370, 397
Henley, William Ernest, 75, 80, 81, 86, 143
Henry, Augustine, 274–5
Herbine, Charlotte, 503, 506
Hillier, Arthur, 119
Hinkson, Henry, 72, 114, 148
Hitchcock, F. R. Montgomery, 32–3
Hodder & Stoughton, 234
Hodgkin, Rose, 48
Holloway, Joseph, 252, 262, 297, 320, 360, 423, 524
Homer, 99, 133, 302–3, 505
Home Rule, 29–30, 41, 44, 62, 91, 93, 113, 119, 169,
179, 190, 228, 405, 442–3, 445, 448–9, 452, 457–61,
479, 481, 493, 498, 513–14, 516, 522, 530–31; Ulster's
resistance to, 442, 457–61, 513–14, 522
Hone, Joseph, xxvi, 112, 335, 479, 492, 495, 521–2, 528
Hood, Tom, 11
Hopkins, Gerard Manley, 39, 54
Hopper, Nora, 145, 186, 198
Horniman, Annie Elizabeth Frederika: supports
Mathers, 104–5; sponsors Farr's Avenue Theatre
season, 137, 140; fascinated by WBY, 171, 286, 291,
330, 348–9, 355, 374, 389, 397, 405–6; in Golden
Dawn, 222, 231–3, 241–7; provides financial
backing for theatre movement, 225, 237, 258,
291, 296, 320, 337–9, 344, 349, 352, 389–90,
405–6, 413–14, 593 (n. 39), 595 (n. 95); WBY's
amanuensis, 264, 286, 291; her own theatrical
interests and ambitions, 281, 318, 328, 339–41, 347,
368–9, 379; and AG, 323, 339–40; troubled
relations with Abbey, 326, 328, 347–9, 354–9,
369–70, 376–7, 400, 405–6, 420–23, 433, 453, 599
(n. 54), 601 (n. 111), 605 (n. 17); guarantees WBY's
CW, 371, 373, 599 (n. 64)
Horton, W. T., 163, 171, 235, 250
Howard, B. Douglas, 96
Howard de Walden, Thomas Evelyn Ellis, eighth
Baron, 346, 436
Hughes, Herbert, 341
Hughes, John, 254–5
Hulme, Thomas Ernest, 474
Huneker, James Gibbon, 306, 516, 536
Hunt, Leigh, 109
Hunter, Dorothea, 164, 186, 243
Hunter, Edmund, 186, 231–2
Hutcheson-Poë, Colonel William, 422, 442
Huysmans, Joris Karl, 138, 176–8, 323
Huxley, Thomas, 25, 35
Hyde, Annette, 150
Hyde, Douglas, 42–3, 45, 71–2, 76, 77, 82, 95, 131,
142–3, 145, 148, 165, 176, 187, 195, 198, 211–12, 226,
240, 247, 250, 263, 264–5, 294, 392, 408, 451, 459;
political opinions, 43, 341, 461; relations with
WBY, 57, 71, 455; WBY reviews *Love Songs of
Connacht*, 133, 136–7; delivers 'Necessity for De-
Anglicizing Ireland', 125–6; WBY criticizes other
works by Hyde, 146, 150; WBY stays at Ratra, 150,
186; Hyde's marriage, 220; at Coole, 220, 271–3;
Hyde helps with *Where There is Nothing*, 270;
leaves INTS, 295–6; replies to WBY's 'At the
Abbey Theatre', 455; reproached by AG for
attacks on Abbey, 612 (n. 11)

Hyde, Lucy, 220
Hyde-Lees, Edith Ellen, *see* Tucker, Edith Ellen ('Nelly')
Hyde-Lees, George (later Yeats), 437–8, 468, 475, 517, 525
Hyde-Lees, Gilbert, 437
Hyde-Lees, Harold, 437
Hyslop, James, 463, 490, 525, 614 (n. 38), 619 (n. 156)

Ibsen, Henrik, 96, 140, 142, 206, 208, 269, 294, 297, 335, 415, 447, 511–12, 535
Inghinidhe na hÉireann, 240, 252, 259–61, 278–9, 294, 317, 328, 379
Irish Agricultural Organization Society (IAOS), 185–6, 191, 311
Irish Daily Independent, 332, 361, 481
Irish Fireside, 52, 56
Irish Home Reading Magazine, 127, 135
Irish Homestead, 186, 210, 280–81
Irish Literary Society (London), 90, 118–19, 124, 126–7, 135, 180, 187, 207–8, 229, 233, 237, 241, 243, 255, 292, 319, 578 (n. 53)
    see also National Literary Society (Dublin)
Irish Literary Society (New York), 302, 304, 306
Irish Literary Theatre, 162, 183–5, 197, 203–14, 217–18, 220, 223, 225–6, 229, 235, 250–54, 260, 262, 268, 276, 278, 317, 570 (n. 81), 571 (n. 82), 575 (n. 76)
Irish Monthly, 56, 86, 98
Irish National Alliance, 112, 189–90, 195, 227, 283
    see also Fenianism
Irish National Dramatic Society (and Company), 261, 267, 273, 278–81, 287–8, 339
Irish National Theatre Society (INTS), 278, 287–300, 317–21, 323–6, 334–44, 354–8, 377–8, 405, 423, 587 (n. 43), 590 (n. 64), 593–4 (nn. 50, 65)
Irish Parliamentary Party, xxviii, 113, 180, 188–90, 225–8, 265, 405, 442, 498, 523
Irish Republican Brotherhood (IRB), 112–13, 189–90, 195, 223, 278, 283, 341, 405, 523
    see also Fenianism
Irish Socialist Republican Party, 180–81
Irish Times, 86, 298, 327, 336, 402, 417, 442, 450, 454, 463–4, 482, 490, 495, 499, 500, 522
Irlande Libre, 173, 180, 196
Iveagh, Edward Cecil Guinness, first Viscount, 422, 430

Jackson, Alice Pollexfen, 9, 31
Jackson, Arthur, 9, 31, 125, 432, 609 (n. 125)
Jackson, Clara Huth, 508
Jackson, Frank and Edith ('Mr and Madame Horos'), 244–5
James, Henry, 292, 424
James, William, 272, 308, 389, 619 (n. 156)
Jameson family, 27, 382
Jarry, Alfred, 173
Jepson, Edgar, 107
Joachim of Fiore, 177
John, Augustus, 371, 373, 392, 397, 474, 484
Johnson, Lionel, 109, 119, 124–5, 129, 131, 135, 146, 152–5, 162, 198, 367, 385, 391–2, 397, 400, 560 (n. 89), 585 (n. 81), 589 (n. 11); discovers his Irishness, 107; hosts a Rhymers meeting, 107–8; in Dublin with WBY, 132; influence behind *Secret Rose*, 177–8; drinks 'in his own rooms', 188; death, 274; WBY selects his poems for Dun Emer, 322;

memorializes him after death, 416–17; poem to Davray, 567 (n. 87)
Johnson, Samuel, 428
Johnston, Charles, 30, 32, 35, 44–8, 53, 62–3, 113, 163, 302, 305, 516
Johnston, William ('of Ballykilbeg'), 46
Jonson, Ben, 336, 345
Jowitt, Martha, 14
Joyce, James, 29, 175–6, 270, 288, 303, 330, 364, 585 (nn. 91, 94); critique of Irish Literary Theatre, 253; meets WBY and is helped by him, 275–8, 585 (n. 90); fails to visit MG, 277; admires WBY's imagination, 277; reviews *Blanco Posnet*, 411; entertained in Woburn Buildings with his son, 457; and *Dubliners*, 493; helped by Pound, 506; possible influence on style of *Reveries*, 526
Joyce, Patrick Weston, 82, 130, 148
Jubainville, Henri d'Arbois de, 130, 146
Jung, Carl Gustav, 463, 515, 614 (nn. 36, 37), 619 (n. 157)

Karsch, Anna Luise, 517
Kavanagh, Rose, 113
Keats, John, 86, 99, 302–3, 470
Keegan, John, 118
Kegan Paul, *see* Paul, Charles Kegan
Kelly, John T., 118, 120
Kelly, P. J., 261, 319
Kensington, 234
Keogh, Judge Martin Jerome, 516
Keohler, Thomas Goodwin (later Keller), 339, 404
Kermendy, Lazlo, 447
Kerrigan, J. M., 376, 378, 444
Kettle, Thomas, 280–81, 298–9, 330, 358, 524, 597 (n. 134)
Killanin, Michael Morris, first Baron, 167, 169
King, Richard Ashe, 133, 184
Kipling, Rudyard, 304, 306, 425, 471
Krans, Horatio, 528
Kropotkin, Prince Pyotr, 268
Kuch, Peter, 49

Labouchère, Henry, 54
Laird, Helen, 342, 379
Lamennais, Félicité Robert de, 186
Landor, Walter Savage, 505
Land War (1879–82), xxviii, 24, 30–31, 132
Lane, Arthur Beresford, 619 (n. 152)
Lane, Sir Hugh, 326–8, 338, 360–62, 383, 386, 442, 461, 478–83, 493–8, 501, 507–8, 520, 622 (n. 48)
Lane, John, 100, 109, 154, 275
Lane-Poole, Ruth (formerly Pollexfen), 441
Lang, Andrew, 199, 525, 614 (n. 35)
Langbridge, Frederick, 132, 135
Larkin, James, 499–501
Larminie, William, 176
Lawrence, Emily, Lady, 265, 384, 583 (n. 42)
Lawrence, Sir Henry, 265, 384, 583 (n. 42)
Lawrence & Bullen, 129, 164, 234
Layard, Enid, Lady, 169, 368
Leader, 207, 235–6, 240–41, 247, 251, 264, 280, 293–5, 323–4, 344, 364, 375, 376, 406, 428, 454–5, 483
Leamy, Edmund, 119
Lecky, William Edward Hartpole, 145, 148, 188, 206, 228
Lee, Vernon, 109
Le Fanu, Joseph Sheridan, 50, 178

Le Gallienne, Richard, 107, 125, 129, 516
Legge, J. G., 62, 555 (n. 13)
Leinster, Maurice FitzGerald, sixth Duke of, 422
Leisure Hour, 130
Leo Africanus, 427, 464–6, 476, 477, 489, 519, 614–15 (nn. 43, 44, 45)
Leoni, Franco, 424, 440
Lever, Charles, 98, 145
Lévi, Eliphas, 50
Library of Ireland (later 'New Irish Library'), 118–21, 124, 233, 274
Lindsay, Vachel, 515
Linnell family, 100
Lissadell, 20, 23, 129, 144
Lister, Edith, 396
Little, Philip Francis, 267, 270
Lloyd George, David, 412, 442, 458
Lodge, Sir Oliver, 525
Logue, Cardinal Michael, 363, 459–60
Longenbach, James, 474, 505
Lover, Samuel, 98
Lucifer, 51, 80, 102, 103
Lugné-Poë, Aurélien-François, 264
Lutyens, Edwin, 481–2, 493–4
Lyell, Charles, 425
Lynch, Arthur, 128, 135, 222–3
Lynch, Hannah, 73
Lynd, Robert, 434, 521
Lyster, Thomas W., 38, 75
Lyttelton, Edith, 405–6, 502
Lyttelton, Katharine, Lady, 399
Lytton, Victor Alexander George Robert Lytton, second Earl of, 426

McAnally, David Rice, 77, 96
Macaulay, Thomas Babington, 17
MacBride, John, 227–8, 240, 278, 283–7, 290, 305, 311–12, 319, 330–34, 338, 367, 386, 391, 458, 592 (n. 16)
MacBride, Maud Gonne, *see* Gonne, Maud
MacBride, Seán (Seaghan), 286, 330, 387, 467
McCartan, Patrick, 454, 612 (n. 7)
McCarthy, Justin, 54, 425
McCarthy, Justin Huntly, 41
MacDonagh, Thomas, 383, 392, 399, 408, 415–18, 459
Macdonnell, Annie, 334
MacDonnell, Sir Antony, 320, 442
MacGinley, P. T., 279
McGrath, John, 160
McKenna, Reginald, 502
MacKenna, Stephen, 218, 244, 463
Mackenzie, Kenneth, 104
Maclagan, Eric, 322
'Macleod, Fiona', *see* Sharp, William
Macmillan (publishers), 234, 272, 301–2, 304, 316, 396, 472, 520
McNeill, John, 32–3
Maeterlinck, Maurice, 139, 149, 216, 219, 236, 263–4, 305, 335, 511, 513
Magee, W. K. ('John Eglinton'), 31–2, 47–8, 81, 89, 197–200, 211, 293, 334, 404, 458–9, 484
Mahaffy, John Pentland, 126, 206, 429–30, 435, 484, 523–4
Mair, G. H., 433
Mallarmé, Stéphane, 109, 138–9, 161, 176–7, 215
Mancini, Antonio, 373
Manet, Edouard, 36, 429, 478

Mangan, James Clarence, 79, 90, 98, 118, 122, 131, 146, 558 (n. 6)
Manning, Frederic, 509
Markievicz, Casimir, Count, 152, 326, 374–5, 383, 400, 404, 456
Markievicz, Constance, Countess, 5, 91, 456; friendship with WBY, 129, 144; marriage, 152; theatrical involvements, 326, 404; at the Arts Club, 383, 436; WBY considers her a 'steam whistle', 384; founds Fianna na hÉireann, 405, 453; supports workers in 1913 lock-out, 499
Marsh, Edward Howard ('Eddie'), 502
Martin, Violet ('Martin Ross'), 89, 167, 246–7, 251–2, 261, 335
Martyn, Edward, 13, 157, 211, 220, 317, 328; background and personality, 165; entertains WBY (1896), 165–7; WBY's attitude towards him, 168; and Irish Literary Theatre, 183–4, 188, 207, 252–3; scruples about *Countess Cathleen*, 207; *The Heather Field*, 208, 210; *The Bending of the Bough*, 221, 225–6; AG's view of him, 241, 344; *Maeve*, 248; alienated from WBY, 278, 334, 422; later theatrical involvements, 294–5; in *Hail and Farewell*, 451
Marx, Karl, xxvii
Masefield, Constance (Mrs John Masefield), 428, 436
Masefield, John, 187, 287, 318, 341, 385, 416, 418, 428, 436, 457
Masquers, the (formerly 'Theatre of Beauty'), 257–8, 290–91, 587 (n. 38)
Mathers, MacGregor (formerly Samuel Liddell Mathers), background in occult organizations, 103–4; meets WBY, 104; influence in Golden Dawn, 104–6; involvements in Paris, 120, 157; entertains WBY there (1894) 138, (1898) 194, (1899) 205; in WBY's fiction, 162, 233–4; and Celtic millennialism, 172–3, 186, 194; quarrels with WBY and Golden Dawn, 222–3, 231–2, 242–4, 380; abortive moves towards reconciliation, 386
Mathers, Moina (formerly Mina Bergson), 104, 117, 152, 162
Mathews, Charles Elkin, 59, 61, 95, 142, 148, 214, 234, 266, 275, 346, 371, 438, 474
Maturin, Charles, 50, 56, 178
Maunsel & Co., 335–6, 338, 400, 402, 414, 420
Mazzini, Giuseppe, 509
Mead, G. R. S., 102
Meredith, George, 74, 108, 152, 158, 321
Merrick, Esther, 17
Meyer, Kuno, 408, 508
Meynell, Alice, 469
Meynell, Wilfrid, 54
Middleton, Alexander, 62
Middleton, Elizabeth, 4
Middleton, Henry, 20, 68, 71
Middleton, Lucy, 21, 125, 144
Middleton, Mary, 20
Middleton, William, 7, 9–10, 20, 23, 31, 547–8 (n. 88)
Middleton & Pollexfen, 4, 9–10, 19–20, 23, 31, 431–2, 529, 545 (n. 24), 547 (n. 81), 609 (n. 125)
Mill, J. S., 72
Millevoye, Lucien, 92–3, 117, 127, 157, 202, 205, 227, 284, 293, 331
Milligan, Alice, 133–4, 144–5, 180, 184, 207, 225, 147, 259, 363
Mirehouse, John, 502

Mitchel, John, 44, 120, 124, 145, 147, 148, 193, 209, 419, 515, 524
Mitchell, Mrs (medium), 487
Mitchell, Susan, 404, 423
Molony, Helena, 379
Monck, Nugent, 436, 444, 453, 456, 475
Monro, Harold, 474
Monroe, Harriet, xxvii, 514
Monteagle, Thomas Spring Rice, second Baron, 292
Montefiore, Dora, 499
Montfaucon de Villars, Abbé de, 505
Moore, George, 36, 77, 141, 156–7, 190, 205, 217, 222, 239, 273, 403, 438, 461, 510; relationship with Edward Martyn, 165; relationship with WBY, xxv–xxvi, 171, 507–9; and the Irish Literary Theatre, 184, 211, 225–6; growth of friendship, 199–200, 228–9; advises WBY on his work, 219; collaboration on *Diarmuid and Grania*, 221, 236–7, 250–53, 575–6 (n. 81); on *Where There is Nothing*, 250, 267–70, 278, 583–4 (n. 55); and the Irish National Theatre Society, 261, 323, 334; quarrel with WBY, 270; satirizes WBY in *Hail and Farewell*, 315, 327–8, 450–52, 453, 507–9, 514, 526, 528, 530, 621 (n. 43); WBY's ripostes, 508–9, 520–21; hated by Annie Horniman, 349, 595 (n. 99); suggests corporation subsidy, 581 (n. 121); suggested obituary for Hugh Lane, 622 (n. 48)
    WORKS
    Diarmuid and Grania (with WBY), 250–53; *Evelyn Innes*, 194, 199, 257; *Hail and Farewell*, 211, 236, 397, 507–9
    see also Gregory, Augusta, Lady
Moore, Thomas ('Tom'), 146–7, 235, 319
Moore, Thomas Sturge, 140, 241, 250, 257, 266, 287, 290, 348, 374, 416, 469–73, 509
Moran, David Patrick, 207, 229, 235–6, 240–41, 247, 256, 263, 280, 325, 344, 364, 443, 458, 508
Moriarty, J. F., 498
Morris, May, 65, 93, 137
Morris, William, 59–60, 63–5, 76–7, 81, 85, 87, 139, 201, 254, 274, 307, 309, 336
Morris family (Killanin), 167, 169
Moses, Stainton, 487, 618–19 (n. 143)
Mukherjee, Devabrata, 616 (n. 81)
Muller, Max, 170
Murphy, William Martin, 375, 423, 479–83, 495, 497, 499–501
Murphy, William Michael, xxv
Murray, Gilbert, 290–91, 334
Murray, T. C., 440, 446
Myers, Frederic, 463, 525, 614 (n. 38)

Nation, 87, 93, 98
National Library of Ireland, 29, 45, 89, 134, 200–201
National Literary Society (Dublin), xxx, 120–27, 131–2, 205–6, 235, 358
National Observer (formerly *Scots Observer*), 75, 80, 86, 94–5, 97, 111, 113, 125, 129, 130, 176
National Publishing Company, 121–3
National University of Ireland, *see* University College
Nesbitt, Cathleen, 444
Nettleship, John Trivett, 12
Nevill, Lady Dorothy, 188
Nevinson, Henry Woodd, 207, 245, 259, 269, 286, 290, 292–3, 469
New Age, 347

Newbolt, Sir Henry John, 257
New Irish Library, *see* Library of Ireland
Nietzsche, Friedrich, 159, 177, 213, 269, 272, 287, 294, 324, 331, 336, 345, 406, 463, 470, 494, 522, 525, 584 (nn. 68, 69)
Nineteenth Century, 169–70, 172
Nordau, Max, 155
North, Violet, *see* Russell, Violet
Nutt, Alfred, 65, 74, 77, 96, 130

Oakley, Harold, 248
O'Brien, Dermod, 383, 459
O'Brien, Kate, 21
O'Brien, R. Barry, 81, 96, 135, 149, 237, 331
O'Brien, William, 113, 169, 225
Ó Conghaile, Seamus, 382
O'Connell, Daniel, 313, 446, 524
O'Connor, T. P., 193
O'Curry, Eugene, 196
O'Dempsey, Brigit, 335, 348, 377
O'Donnell, Frank Hugh, 189–91, 195, 209–10, 212–13, 223, 227, 229, 235, 363, 570 (n. 64), 576–7 (n. 14), 578 (n. 53)
O'Donoghue, D. J., 118
O'Donovan, Father Jeremiah, 289, 301, 380
O'Grady, Standish James, 41, 68, 124, 133, 142, 145–8, 156, 179, 180, 184, 191, 198, 207, 211–12, 235–6, 240, 251, 279, 399, 425, 531
O'Hegarty, P. S., 399
O'Kelly, Seamus, 404, 454, 456
Old, Sarah Martha, 160, 187
Oldham, Charles Hubert, 39, 41, 45, 47, 53, 91, 113, 118, 132–3
O'Leary, Ellen, 44, 71–2, 75, 79, 90, 93, 95, 113
O'Leary, John, 46, 57, 59, 71–2, 90, 95, 103, 118, 174, 176, 178, 211, 221, 223, 228, 305, 307; as prototype of old republican hero, 42, 84; influence on the young WBY, 42–4, 53, 57, 112–13, 418; judgement on WBY's work, 44, 69, 75–6, 156; lends him money, 65, 113, 135–6, 164; helps *WO*, 81, 95; low opinion of WBY's magical researches, 102, 106, 120–21; supports Parnell, 113; and NLS campaign, 114, 119–24, 127; and 1798 Centennial Committee, 190, 195; supports MacBride against MG, 333, 367; death, 367, 385, 397, 400, 496; as portrayed in *Reveries*, 531
O'Looney, Bryan, 82, 86
O'Mahony, Nora, 72
Orage, Alfred, 347
O'Reilly, John Boyle, 447–8
Orr, Elizabeth (formerly Pollexfen), 4, 16, 61
Orr, Geraldine, 21
O'Shea, Katharine, 113, 520
Ó Súilleabháin, Eoghan Rua, 162, 178
O'Sullivan, Seamus, 404

Paget, Dorothy, 137, 210
Paget, Henrietta, 137, 142
Paget, Henry, 66
Pall Mall Gazette, 61, 64, 86, 108
Pan-Celtic Society and League, 71, 121, 197, 200, 204, 212, 247, 259
Paracelsus, 525
Parnell, Charles Stewart, xxviii, 2, 5, 30, 31, 41, 44, 55, 59, 86, 113, 115–16, 126, 133, 150, 180, 190, 307, 313–14, 334, 375, 448, 459, 462, 468, 501, 519–20, 543 (n. 12), 613 (n. 31)

Pater, Walter, 48, 108–9, 132, 155, 177, 346
Paul, Charles Kegan, 82, 95
Payne, Ben Iden, 359, 366, 369, 412
Pearse, Patrick, 5, 220–21, 399, 410, 417, 523–5
Peters, Alfred Vont, 468
Phelan, James, 311
Phelps, William, 514
Pinero, Arthur, 534
Pirrie, William James Pirrie, first Baron, 422
Plarr, Victor, 107, 119, 474, 509
Plotinus, 50, 244, 400, 463
Plunkett, Grace, 166
Plunkett, Horace, 179, 185, 188, 189, 191, 197, 206, 211–12, 240, 311, 322, 383, 451, 570 (n. 62)
Plunkett, Josephine, Countess, 500
Poel, William, 385, 389, 484–5
Poetry magazine (Chicago), 433, 471, 474–5, 504, 506, 511 (n.), 515, 521
Pollexfen, Alfred, 9, 441
Pollexfen, Alice, *see* Jackson, Alice Pollexfen
Pollexfen, Anthony, 3
Pollexfen, Elizabeth (aunt of WBY), *see* Orr, Elizabeth
Pollexfen, Elizabeth Middleton (grandmother of WBY), 4, 19, 125
Pollexfen, George, 4, 5–9, 19, 23, 71, 111, 130, 142, 143, 171, 180, 186, 193, 198, 294, 300, 452, 466; character, 6–7, 246, 401; relations with WBY, 71, 431–2, 530; and Golden Dawn, 104, 143, 170, 232, 432; investigates fairy lore, 125, 246; casts horoscopes, 163, 170, 568 (n. 7); WBY confides in about MG, 200, 204–5; angry at WBY's attack on Queen, 228, 246; death, 431–2; portrayed in *Reveries*, 529
Pollexfen, John, 155
Pollexfen, Ruth, *see* Lane-Poole, Ruth
Pollexfen, William (grandfather of WBY), 3–4, 9–10, 19, 21, 125, 529, 548 (n. 96)
Pollexfen, William Middleton, 5
Pond, James, 510–11, 513
Pound, Dorothy, *see* Shakespear, Dorothy
Pound, Ezra, 305 (n.), 430, 485, 497, 520, 525; relationship with Olivia Shakespear, 153, 438–9; WBY's view of his work, 288, 514–15; influence on WBY's work, 434, 439, 475–6, 486, 490, 511, 520, 525; arrival and career in London, 438, 473–4; view of WBY, xxvii, 438; and Dorothy Shakespear, 438–9, 517; possibly attacks WBY's plays in *New Age*, 455, 612 (n. 9); and Tagore, 469, 471, 473; and Imagism, 474; with WBY at Stone Cottage, 502–7, 523, 525–7; publishes Joyce, 506; defends WBY against Moore, 507; honours Blunt, 509–10
Powell, Frederick York, 60, 65, 74–5, 139, 156, 217–18, 301, 564 (n. 16)
Power, John, 93
Prasad, Rama, 619 (n. 156)
Pre-Raphaelitism, 26, 70, 80, 85, 157
Pritzel, Lotte, 618 (n. 133)
Probyn, May, 79
Proust, Marcel, 175–6
Providence Sunday Journal, 44, 95, 107
Psychical Research, Society for, 103, 438, 462–4, 466, 517, 526
Purser, Louis, 91, 484
Purser, Sarah, 35, 41, 47, 113, 205, 260, 274, 323, 334, 340, 382, 387
Pyne, Evelyn, 79

Quaritch, Bernard, 100–101, 129
Quinn, John, 167, 292, 294, 319, 321, 324, 383–4, 407, 426, 495, 508; collects WBY's MSS, 40, 516–17, 623 (n. 77); and *Where There is Nothing*, 268–9; befriends WBY, 270–73; at Coole, 271–2, 326; sends him Nietzsche, 272; as art-collector, 272, 450; patron of JBY, 272–3, 302, 382–3, 516–17; intercedes with American publishers, 301–2; organizes WBY's USA tour (1903–4), 302–6, 308–15; and MacBride separation, 331–2; helps Abbey in USA, 377, 445, 458; quarrels with WBY, 407–8, 428, 449–50, 511, 611 (n. 60); AG complains of WBY to him, 426, 503; affair with AG, 449–50, 477; reconciliation with WBY, 516–17
Quinn, Joseph, 132, 154, 160

Radcliffe, Elizabeth ('Bessie'), 487–90, 502, 505, 517, 526, 618 (nn. 141, 142)
Radford, Ernest, 107–8, 142
Raftery, Anthony, 236, 271
Redmond, Joanna, 443
Redmond, John, 188, 206, 442–3, 448, 498, 522–3
Redmond, William, 223
Reid, Forrest, 528
Reinhardt, Max, 447, 456, 511
Renan, Ernest, 177, 186–7
Rhymers Club, 107–11, 130–31, 142, 154, 416–17, 476, 509–10, 512, 520
Rhys, Ernest, 63, 74, 76, 79–80, 95, 97, 107, 109, 118, 161, 167, 205, 469, 474, 476
Richardson, Dorothy, 161
Ricketts, Charles, 108, 161, 257, 285, 291, 304, 321, 324, 352, 379, 385, 397, 399, 402–3, 416, 486, 519–20
Rising of 1798, 44; Centennial Association (1898), 179–81, 185, 189–95, 202, 209, 248, 570 (n. 64), 572 (nn. 115, 131)
Ritchie, Anne Thackeray, 292
Roberts, George, 320, 335, 342, 392, 400, 420, 607 (n. 82)
Robinson, Lennox, 415, 422, 440, 445–6, 505, 515, 522
Roche, James, 444
Rolleston, Thomas William, 39, 42–3, 86, 107–8, 113, 118–19, 121–4, 127, 128, 131–2, 142, 146, 155, 197, 203, 233, 321, 383, 469, 476, 581 (n. 123)
Rooney, William, 223
Roosevelt, Theodore, 305 (n.), 308–9, 314, 516
Roper, Esther, 152
Rosicrucianism, 103–4, 106, 129, 139, 178, 244, 517
Rossetti, Dante Gabriel, 86, 187
Rothenstein, William, 304, 469–72, 475, 485
Rummel, Walter, 475
Russell, Edmund, 62, 86
Russell, Father Matthew, 82, 98
Russell, George William ('AE'), xxvii, xxx, 47, 53, 56, 114, 116, 118, 138, 162, 194, 219, 227, 232, 235, 308, 322–4, 383, 458–9; early friendship, 42, 48–52, 72; disagreements over spiritual quest, 49, 51–2, 101; relationship with WBY, xxv, 73, 155, 178, 222, 336, 344–5, 542 (n. 1); WBY praises his work, 142, 148, and condemns it, 350–51, 381, 596 (n. 107); Russell's millennial beliefs, 162–4, 185–6, 191–2; WBY dedicates *The Secret Rose* to, 176; work-patterns, 182; at Coole, 183, 196, 246, 248; and Irish Literary Theatre, 185, 207, 210, 225–6; and IAOS, 185–6, 191; marriage, 186; wants to whack Fiona Macleod, 197, 237; and *Literary Ideals in Ireland* controversy, 198–9; discusses WBY with AG, 204;

annoyed at *Leader*'s attacks on WBY, 240;
complains about him, 256, 266, 273–4, 340;
conflicts over INTS, 260, 278–9, 288, 295–6, 298,
319–20, 328, 338–41; his *Deirdre*, 261, 320–22; and
Where There is Nothing, 267–70; and Joyce, 275–6;
disagrees with WBY about publishing, 336, 338;
opposes *Playboy*, 363–4; estrangement from
WBY, 404–5, 415, 428, 435, 486; intercedes with
Griffith over *Blanco Posnet*, 410, 605 (n. 32); in
Hail and Farewell, 451; and modern art in Dublin,
478; and 1913 lock-out, 499–50; reconciliation
with WBY, 500–501
Russell, Violet, 186, 286
Ryley, Madeline Lucette, 535
Ryan, Fred, 211, 260, 279, 288, 340
Ryan, Mark, 112, 195, 202, 227, 229
Ryan, William Patrick, 150–51, 160, 240, 360

Sackville, Lady Margaret, 259, 337
St Albans, Grace, Duchess of, 206
Saint-Martin, Louis Claude de, 178
Sandburg, Carl, 516
Sargent, John Singer, 373
Sarsfield, Patrick, 220
Savage-Armstrong, George Francis, 126, 197
Savoy, 136, 139, 153, 155, 157–9, 160, 164, 167, 177–8, 179
Schepeler, Alick, 474–5
Scott, Charles Prestwich, 423
Scott, Sir Walter, 17, 530
Scott, Walter (publisher), 63, 66, 97
Serres, Michel, xxvi
Shahan, T. J., 306
Shakespear, Dorothy (later Pound), 153, 438–9,
473–4, 525
Shakespear, Henry Hope, 152–4, 437
Shakespear, Olivia, 144, 155, 164, 175, 203, 223, 386,
474, 506, 517, 609–10 (n. 17); background and
personality, 152–3, 437; writings, 152–3, 259; starts
affair with WBY, 153–4; occult interests, 153, 463,
466; WBY's poems to, 157–8, 215–16, 436, 624
(n. 94); consummates affair with WBY, 158;
slackens off, 172–4, 175, 179, 182; revival of
relationship (1900), 234; introduces WBY to
Pound, and to Hyde-Lees family, 437; possible
second affair (1910), 437–8, 610 (n. 19); and Stone
Cottage, 503–4
Shakespeare, William, 99, 148, 199, 258, 413, 416
Shakespeare Memorial Theatre, 424
Shannon, Charles, 108, 149–50, 161, 321, 326, 373, 385,
397, 402–3
Sharp, Elizabeth, 345
Sharp, William ('Fiona Macleod'), 80, 81, 181, 193,
255; meets WBY, 80; communicates through
Fiona Macleod, 165–6, 180; dramatic ambitions,
173, 179, 184, 207, 237–8; plagiarizes WBY's work,
178; and Celtic Order, 180, 186, 194, 196–7, 245;
WBY's attitude to Fiona Macleod, 196–7; falls
out with Russell, AG and WBY, 197, 237–8;
WBY's reaction to his death, 345
Shaw, George Bernard, 107, 157, 250, 319–20, 359,
383, 414–15, 429, 506, 533, 591 (n. 89); meets WBY
at Morris's, 64; rivals for Florence Farr, 137; *Arms
and the Man*, 139–42; hatred for the psaltery, 257,
263; *John Bull's Other Island*, 325–6; Mrs Campbell
finds him less cultured than WBY, 380; *Blanco
Posnet*, 409–11; chairs WBY's Adelphi lecture,
417; WBY's judgement of him, 506, 591 (n. 88)

Shaw, Dr George Ferdinand, 212
Shaw, Norman, 60–61
Shawe-Taylor, John, 279, 442
Sheehan, Daniel T., 364
Sheehy-Skeffington, Francis, 364
Shelley, Percy Bysshe, 29, 37, 49, 57, 85, 88, 132, 200,
371, 550 (n. 42)
Sheppard, Oliver, 36
Sheridan, Richard Brinsley, 533–4
Sherlock, Thomas (Lord Mayor of Dublin), 493–4
Shiubhlaigh, Maire nic ('Maire Walker'), 324, 328,
341–2, 344, 404, 423, 444–5
Shorter, Clement, 218, 327, 521
Shorter, Dora Sigerson, 36, 207
Sickert, Walter, xxv
Sigerson, Dora, *see* Shorter, Dora Sigerson
Sigerson, George, 42, 122, 126–7, 202, 212, 363
Sigerson, Hester, 44, 202
Sime, Georgina, 515
Sinclair, Arthur, 454, 497, 510
Sinclair, May, 469
Sinnett, A. P., 45, 47, 551 (n. 72)
Sinn Féin (movement), 70, 240, 275, 296–7, 328,
360–65, 376, 383, 399, 408–10, 422, 428, 442, 458
Sinn Féin (journal), 363–4, 404–6
Sligo (town and county), 9–10, 14, 18–21, 23, 69–71,
79, 90, 101, 110, 125, 129–30, 143–4, 170, 182, 223
Sligo Independent, 10, 77, 86
Smith, Pamela Colman ('Pixie'), 257–8, 326
Smithers, Leonard, 154, 158–9, 221–2
Solomon, Simeon, 107
Somerset, Lady Katharine, 425, 435–6
Somerville, Edith Œnone, 89, 167, 251
Sophocles, 99, 42
Southwark Irish Literary Club, 63, 79, 118, 120, 160
Sparling, Henry Halliday, 61, 74–5, 95, 554 (n. 8)
Speaker, 136, 157, 277
Spencer, Herbert, 32
Spenser, Edmund, 38, 269, 345, 373–4
Stanislavski, Konstantin, 485
Stannard, Henrietta, *see* 'Winter, John Strange'
Starkey, James, 335, 339, 342
Stead, W. T., 464
Stephens, Edward, 604 (n. 198)
Stephens, James (Fenian), 195
Stephens, James (writer), 404, 455, 486, 493, 499
Stephens, Mary, 3, 5 (as 'Ann'), 543 (n. 21)
Stepniak, Sergius, 60, 140, 268
Stevens, William, 76
Stevenson, Robert Louis, 74, 135
Stoker, Bram, 50
Strachey, Lytton, 396
Strang, William, 54, 314
Stuart, Thomas, 128
Sudermann, Hermann, 281, 378, 382
Sullivan, Margaret (Mrs Alexander), 54, 93–4
Sutherland, Millicent, Duchess of, 314, 422, 441
Swedenborg, Emanuel, 49–50, 96, 99, 101, 109,
129–30, 222, 433, 463, 466, 522, 525–6
Swift, Jonathan, 146, 412, 448, 606 (n. 47)
Swinburne, Algernon, 86, 88, 129, 616 (n. 69)
Symons, Arthur, 138–9, 153–4, 177–8, 199, 216, 218,
222, 237, 270, 277, 287, 290, 337, 397, 400, 407,
427–8, 567 (n. 87), 570 (n. 58), 585 (n. 94);
influence on WBY, 99, 109, 263, 272 (regarding
Nietzsche), 537; early friendship, 107–10; and
French literature, 138–9, 173; as 'decadent', 154–6,

Symons, Arthur (*cont.*):
568 (n. 29); they share rooms, 155–7; and the
Savoy, 156–8; in Ireland, 164–8, 365; not liked by
Violet Martin, 167; breakdown, 391–2; takes
drugs, 570 (n. 58); helps Joyce, 585 (n. 94)
Symons, Rhoda, 392
Synge, Edward, 420
Synge, John Millington, 205, 260, 268, 303, 466, 468,
470, 493, 507, 512; meets WBY, 172–3; mutual
suspicion, 172, 356, 359, 383, 400–401; visits Aran,
173–4; visits Coole, 183, 246, 323; and Irish public
opinion, 270, 296–300; and INTS, 287–8,
294–300, 324, 338–43, 348, 352–8; relationship with
AG, xxix, 288; opinion of WBY's plays, 318, 366,
374; love-affair with Molly Allgood, 348; tensions
with other Abbey directors, 366, 374, 380; illness
and death, 385, 398, 399–401; literary estate,
399–400, 402, 420–21, 604 (n. 198), 607 (n. 82);
admiration for WBY's work in general, 418
WORKS
Deirdre, 400, 403, 413; *Playboy of the Western
World*, 357–67, 376, 399, 403, 408, 411, 418–20,
443–50, 454, 501, 505–6, 512, 515, 597 (n. 13), 598
(n. 29); *Riders to the Sea*, 287, 296, 312, 348, 446;
In the Shadow of the Glen, 287–8, 294–300, 348,
363–4, 446; *Well of the Saints*, 320–21, 334–5, 378–9,
403

Tagore, Rabindranath, 467, 469–73, 477, 483,
616 (nn. 73, 80, 81)
Taylor, Jane, 2
Taylor, J. F., 42–4, 90, 121–2, 127, 146, 211, 367, 418,
531
Taylor, John, 2
Taylor, Thomas, 50
Teeling, Charles MacCarthy, 190
Tennyson, Alfred, 82, 86, 88, 99, 129, 139, 199
Theatre of Ireland, 344, 363, 374, 383, 399, 404–5, 408,
600 (n. 83)
Theosophy (and Theosophical Society), 45–8, 50,
78, 85, 90, 99, 101–3, 133, 164, 306–7, 347, 470
see also Blavatsky, Helena Petrovna
Thomas, Robert Palmer, 243
Thomastown, estate at, 2, 9, 18, 24, 30, 57, 63, 382, 530
Thompson, Francis, 217
Tobin, Agnes, 311, 392, 397, 407, 425, 438
Todhunter, John, 12, 18, 37, 60, 69, 74–5, 77, 79, 82,
86, 99, 104, 107, 109–10, 118–19, 140–42, 205, 208
Tolstoy, Leo Nikolayevich, 74, 269, 537
Tone, Theobald Wolfe, 121, 145, 148, 179, 193, 496,
524–5; Wolfe Tone Memorial Committee (1898),
179, 189, 191, 195, 202, 226, 364, 572 (nn. 117, 132)
Toomey, Deirdre, 202
Traquair, Phoebe Anna, 322, 348
Travers-Smith, Hester, 483
Tree, Herbert Beerbohm, 183, 326
Trench, Wilberforce, 484
Trevelyan, Charles, 469
Trevelyan, R. C., 470
Trinity College, Dublin, 6, 7, 28–9, 33, 35, 39–40, 43,
120, 145–6, 148, 206, 220, 316, 360, 429–31, 443, 461,
483–4, 523–5, 608 (n. 116)
Tucker, Edith Ellen ('Nelly'; formerly Hyde-Lees),
437–8, 463, 468, 502–3, 525
Tucker, Harry, 437, 468, 502, 525
Tully, Jasper, 566 (n. 57)
Tylor, E. B., 525

Tynan, Katharine, 43, 39, 51, 53–6, 59, 63, 65, 68–70,
75–6, 87, 90, 92, 95–6, 99, 142, 146, 156, 160, 199,
301, 335, 492; log-rolls for WBY, 39, 54–5, 73, 79,
87, 96, 109, 111; meets WBY, 53, 553 (n. 107);
literary works, 53–4, 70, 72, 75, 82, 86, 135;
relationship with WBY, 54–5, 68, 70–71, 78;
possible proposal, 55, 72–3; her marriage, 72;
irritated by WBY, 114; loses touch, 119, 136, 148;
interview for *Sketch*, 132; enlisted by WBY in row
with Dun Emer, 350; her memoirs, 492, 526, 528,
530
Tyrell, Dr Robert, 212, 430

Ulster Literary Theatre, 320
United Arts Club, 378–9, 383–4, 400, 416, 435–6,
442, 463–4, 468, 482
United Ireland, 69, 93, 113, 115, 116, 119, 120, 125, 126,
133, 145, 160, 187
United Irish League, 227, 281, 332, 334
United Irishman, 195, 206, 211–13, 217, 220–21, 223,
226–7, 240, 248–9, 252–5, 260–65, 268, 278–9, 293,
296–300, 318, 327, 332, 341, 344, 574–5 (n. 52)
University College, Dublin (of the National
University; previously the Catholic College), 334,
399, 408, 443, 481–2
Unwin, Thomas Fisher, 76, 95, 98, 110–11, 118, 122–3,
129, 130, 142, 148–9, 160, 214, 218, 234, 371, 396, 412,
457, 561 (n. 101)

Vachère, Abbé, 518
Varley, Isabella (formerly Pollexfen), 45, 301
Vaughan, Ernest, 376
Veasey, Charles Cyril, 26
Vedrenne, J. E., 325–6, 359
Vegetarian, 65–7
Verlaine, Paul, 109, 138–9, 381
Victoria, Queen, 168, 171, 227–8, 252, 469
Villiers de l'Isle-Adam, Philippe-Auguste, 135,
138–40, 176, 186, 219; *Axël*, 139–41, 175, 372
Voisin, Abraham, 542 (n. 4), 543 (n. 12)
Voisin, Mary, 542 (n. 4)

Wade, Allan, 397
Wagner, Richard, 199–200, 212, 233, 251, 263, 269, 392
Waite, A. E., 176
Walker, Frank, 342
'Walker, Maire', *see* Shiubhlaigh, Maire nic
Walkley, A. B., 269, 292, 318, 534
Walsh, Archbishop William, 169
Ward, Mrs Humphry, 424
Watkins, John, 103
Watson, William, 125, 295
Watt, A. P., 234, 258, 372, 396
Webb, Alfred, 42
Weekes, Charles, 47, 146, 163
Wells, H. G., 424
Wentz, William Evans, 389, 525, 603 (n. 154)
Westcott, William Wynn, 103–5, 165, 231, 431
Weygandt, Cornelius, 308, 315
Whitman, Walt, 42
Whitty, May, 210
Wilde, Constance, 80, 104
Wilde, Jane Francesca, Lady, 76, 90, 93, 95, 121, 155,
176, 295, 533, 557 (n. 94)
Wilde, Oscar, 132, 352, 385, 533; lectures in Dublin,
35; WBY visits at Christmas (1888), 80–81, 557
(n. 94); reviews *WO*, 86; at Rhymers, 108–9;

scandal, 154–5, 519–20; WBY echoes 'Decay of Lying' (1914), 512; Wilde praises 'Crucifixion of the Outcast', 565 (n. 22)
Wilde, Sir William, 130
Wilde, Willie, 301
Wilkins, George, 35
Wilkins, William, 32–3, 45
Williams, Charles, 465
Williams, William Carlos, 417
Wilson, Eileen, 92, 331, 558 (n. 14), 592 (n. 3)
Wilson, Margaret, 558 (n. 14)
Wingfield, Kate, 487
'Winter, John Strange' (Henrietta Stannard), 90
Woodford, A. F. A., 103
Woodman, W. R., 103
Wood-Martin, W. G., 69, 71
Wriedt, Etta, 464–6, 487, 502, 517, 519, 614 (n. 42)
Wright, Claude Falls, 47
Wyndham, George, 252, 298, 425
Wynne, Frances, 110

Yeats, Benjamin, 1, 542 (n. 3)
Yeats, Benjamin William, 1, 542 (n. 3)
Yeats, Elizabeth Corbet ('Lolly'), 13–14, 31, 36, 59, 61, 91, 94, 274–5, 300, 341–2, 350–51; character, 14, 546 (n. 37); relationship with WBY, 14; records life in Bedford Park, 61–3, 78; printing and artwork, 65, 134, 155, 274, 317, 350; sets up Dun Emer, 274–5; prints *In the Seven Woods*, 300–301; disagreements with WBY, 341–2, 350–51, 595–6 (nn. 102, 104); sets up Cuala, 380, 601 (n. 119); prints *Reveries*, 527
Yeats, George, *see* Hyde-Lees, George
Yeats, Isaac, 375
Yeats, Jack, 12–14, 18, 20, 91, 134, 318, 431–2; character, 14, 322, 600 (n. 86); and Sligo, 14, 18; cheers up Blenheim Road, 14, 61, 94; early commercial work, 65–7, 98; relationship with JBY, 94, 322, 375, 432; with WBY, 96, 322, 350–52; AG tries to patronize him, 187, 195, 250; at Coole, 271–3; drawings, 271, 310, 351; SMY's faith in him, 322; and the Abbey, 326, 468; and visions, 389; and circuses, 586 (n. 27)
  PAINTINGS
  Bachelor's Walk, In Memory, 522; *Farewell to Mayo*, 591 (n. 79); *Memory Harbour*, 19, 87, 527
Yeats, Jane Grace (formerly Corbet; WBY's grandmother), 2, 13, 17
Yeats, Jane Grace (short-lived sister of WBY), 13
Yeats, Jervis, 542 (n. 3)
Yeats, John, Reverend, 2, 7
Yeats, John Butler, xxv, 1–2, 14, 25, 35, 37, 45, 70, 81, 96, 105, 126–7, 199, 207, 214, 330, 332, 379, 414, 526; attitude to England and Englishness, 3, 39–40; to America, 3, 382–3; and Pollexfens, 4, 8–9, 12–13; character, 6, 529; sociability, 6, 8, 11–12, 27, 60–61, 383; early career, 6, 10–12; marriage, 6–8; and money, 7, 9, 18, 26, 57, 61, 65–6, 273, 317, 432, 511, 622 (n. 60); to Trinity College, 7, 29, 35, 316, 430, 550 (n. 34); portrait-painting, 12, 26–7, 40, 42, 45, 54, 57, 64, 94, 132, 187, 195, 273, 328; relationship with WBY, 15–17, 27–8, 58, 94, 383, 432, 528–9, 576 (n. 93); influence on WBY's views, 28, 58, 68, 75, 416, 448, 454, 492–3, 511, 521, 530; Dublin life in 1880s, 28–31, 43; and Irish politics, xxix, 31; move back to London (1886), 57; and his children, 94, 134, 156, 375, 549 (n. 124); views on *Countess*

Cathleen, 210–11; on *Wind Among the Reeds*, 217; and his wife's death, 223–4; relationship with John Quinn, 272–3, 382–3, 407–8, 516–17; return to Dublin (1902), 273–4; correspondence with WBY, 351–2; at *Playboy* debate, 364; reports on WBY and AG at Morehampton Road, 375; moves to New York, 382–3; WBY wants him to write his autobiography, 477, 492–3, 516; his life in New York, 511, 622 (n. 60)
Yeats, Mary ('Mickey'), 23
Yeats, Mary Cottenham ('Cottie'; Mrs Jack Yeats), 155, 315–16, 322, 411
Yeats, Matthew, 30–31, 35, 57
Yeats, Robert Corbet, 13, 16, 21–2
Yeats, Susan (formerly Pollexfen), 4, 20–22, 27–8, 94, 125, 155, 432, 530; marriage, 1, 6–8, 11; character, 11, 546 (n. 37); depression, 21, 30–31; in Dublin (1880s), 30–31; strokes and ill-health, 61–2, 155; death, 233–4
Yeats, Susan Mary ('Lily'), 3, 5, 10, 13–14, 18, 22, 28, 31, 34, 36, 59, 61, 76, 91, 96, 125, 129, 150, 155, 223, 246, 341, 392, 413, 524; relationship with WBY, 13, 156; interest in ghosts, 50; embroidery-work, 65, 155, 322, 468, 528, 601 (n. 119), 624 (n. 127); hears 'Innisfree', 79; happy at Blenheim Road, 156; returns to Dublin, 274–5; and Dun Emer, 274–5, 316–17, 332; defends Jack's work to JBY, 322; and Cuala, 380; visits New York, 382; and George Pollexfen's death, 431–2; on *Blanco Posnet*, 410–11; on the fortunes of the Abbey, 414, 423–4; and Ruth Pollexfen (Lane-Poole), 441; helps WBY with his autobiography, 451–2, 508–9, 527–9; as family historian, 542 (n. 4)
Yeats, Thomas, 7
Yeats, William Butler, Reverend, 2, 9, 23, 28, 168, 411, 543 (n. 8), 545 (n. 16)

YEATS, WILLIAM BUTLER

BACKGROUND: birth, 13, 15; childhood, 13–17, 24–5, 27, 527–31, 546 (n. 65), 547 (nn. 66, 72, 80); education (London) 16–17, 24–7 (Dublin) 31–3 (art school) 36, 254, 530; reading and spelling difficulties, 17; attempts to learn French, 74, 139, 143, 395; self-education, 89–90
CHARACTER: vagueness, 16, 55–6, 60, 379; liking for gossip, xxvii, 32, 171; sense of humour, 32, 171, 183, 451; intellectual name-dropping, 32; dominating personality, 49, 376; combativeness, 55, 135, 341–2, 344–6; diligence, 58, 89–90; resilience, 148, 150, 243–4; shyness, 285, 437–8, 451; self-doubt, 426–8
FAMILY: relationship with sisters, 13–14, 156, 350–52; with JBY, 15–16, 27, 28, 58, 94, 156, 351–2, 432, 528–9; interest in family background, 375, 397, 507–9, 526–31, 603–4 (n. 181); autobiographical explorations, 416, 418–21, 432, 451–2, 477, 492–3, 510, 512, 521–2, 526–31
HEALTH: possible infantile tuberculosis, 16, 546 (n. 65); influenza, 96, 264; depression, 96, 118; teeth, 125; smoking, 133, 398; eyesight, 136, 188, 258, 264, 321; sick headaches, stress, exhaustion, 219–20, 403; digestive illness and rheumatism, 464, 468, 477, 486
LITERARY INVOLVEMENTS: early literary interests and writings, 27, 29, 37–8, 55, 542 (n. 1), 551 (n. 47); first publications and journalism, 37, 44, 59–60, 63–8, 74–7, 89–90, 94–6, 254; work-processes, 52, 182, 219, 371, 390, 421, 430–31, 468, 475–6, 526–31;

YEATS, WILLIAM BUTLER (*cont.*):
LITERARY INVOLVEMENTS (*cont.*):
earnings, 63, 94–5, 111, 164, 234, 266, 309, 312, 314–15, 371, 396, 412, 424, 433–4, 457, 486–7, 504, 511, 568 (n. 13), 575 (n. 65), 577 (n. 35), 590 (n. 47), 597 (n. 10), 607 (n. 96), 613 (n. 21); and publishers, 76, 81–2, 95, 111, 148–50, 275, 300, 316, 335–6, 346, 371, 577–8 (n. 36), 594–5 (nn. 78, 79); revisions, 82, 182, 397, 456–7, 486; interest in chanting, 257–8, 263, 266–7; and James Joyce, 275–8, 585 (nn. 90, 91, 96); change in style *c.* 1902, 302; and university jobs, 408, 429–31, 441, 483–4; and Academic Committee of English Letters, 424–6, 439, 456, 471, 486, 620 (n. 2); and Civil List pension, 425–9, 430; at Stone Cottage with Pound, 502–7

LOVE-LIFE: attractiveness to women, 34, 54–5, 171, 218, 308, 316; sexual tensions, 33–4, 72, 89, 158, 173–4, 182–3; love-affair with Laura Armstrong, 34, 68; Olivia Shakespear, 70, 152–4, 164, 173–6, 437, 567 (n. 82); Florence Farr, 137, 290–91, 368, 383; and MG, 87–8, 92–3, 113–14, 127–8, 138–9, 153, 157, 175–6, 179, 201–5, 230–31, 333, 386–9, 391–6, 407; reaction to her marriage and separation, 284–7, 330–34, 586 (n. 8); and Mabel Dickinson, 383–5, 488–9
see also individual entries

OCCULT AND SPIRITUAL INTERESTS: and fairy lore, 21, 77–8, 130–33, 389, 439–40, 526, 563 (n. 69); Theosophy, 46–8, 101–4 (*see also* separate entry); magical studies, xxv, 48–52, 505, 515, 553 (n. 94); seances and spiritualist investigations, 51, 73, 202, 447, 462–9, 487–91, 502–3, 514, 517–19, 525–6, 530, 614 (nn. 33, 34, 35) (*see also* Leo Africanus); and religion in general, 64, 84–5, 169, 268–9, 501; and folklore, 74, 76, 79–80, 129–30, 136–7, 170–71, 456, 463–4, 526; and Golden Dawn, 101, 103–7, 129, 132, 231–4, 241–5, 355–6, 525, 579 (nn. 67, 70, 76); millennial expectations, 162–6; Celtic Rituals and Order, 164, 180, 186–7, 191, 196–7, 203, 213, 233–4, 237–8, 243–5, 247, 287, 579 (n. 79); and astrology, xxx, xxxi, 201, 237, 251, 320, 331, 357, 383, 386, 389, 393, 434, 437, 506, 602 (n. 140)

POLITICS AND NATIONALISM: xxviii–xxix, 43–4, 55, 62, 106–7, 113–15, 126–7, 131–2, 179–81, 189–95, 212–13, 226–30, 265, 300, 362–7, 375, 399, 405, 412, 418–21, 441–3, 447–9, 457–62, 470–71, 523–5, 565 (n. 3); and Catholicism, 35, 98, 168, 176–8, 209–10, 240–41, 280–81, 286–7, 298–300 (visit to Notre Dame seminary, 311, 444, 461), 338, 443, 448, 458–62, 481–2, 494, 500–501, 531, 566 (n. 50), 597 (n. 134)

PUBLIC LIFE: relationship with Irish opinion, 38, 44–5, 73–4, 119–24, 143, 264–5, 280–81, 291–2, 299–300, 326, 435, 441, 479–83, 507, 574 (n. 31); reputation, xxv, 58, 109–10, 128–9, 135–6, 142, 160, 218, 371, 396–7, 454–5, 474, 485, 512–13, 515, 589 (n. 11); and NLS (Dublin), xxx, 114–15, 117–25, 562–3 (nn. 26, 31, 42, 51); and 'Best Irish Books' controversy, 145–8; and the Irish language, 220, 235–6, 255, 263, 298, 304, 312, 363, 417, 458–9, 578 (n. 44), 598 (n. 19); and Dun Emer/Cuala, 275, 300–301, 316–17, 322, 350–52, 595–6 (nn. 102, 104), 624–5 (n. 127); American tours, (1903–4) 302–17, 345, 533–7, 588 (n. 81), (1911) 444–50, (1913) 510–17; as a public speaker, 305, 307, 309 (Carnegie Hall

lecture, 1903), 312–13 (Emmet speech, 1904), 315, 460–61 (on Home Rule) 494 (Lane's gallery), 500 (1913 lock-out), 511–12; and Hugh Lane's campaign, 327–8, 477–83, 493–8, 501

THOUGHT AND INFLUENCES: views on painting, 36, 482; Indian philosophic interests, 47–8, 244, 470, 472–3, 552 (nn. 80, 84); and Neo-Platonism, 50, 244, 463, 505, 525–6; adoption of 'mask', 58, 90; and 'Celticism', 63, 71, 73, 77, 86, 107, 110, 131–2, 177–8, 183–5, 196–7, 246–7, 566 (n. 60); and Symbolism, 109, 139, 474; theory of 'Moods', 147, 159; use of *alter egos* in his work, 162, 427, 465–7; and 'popularity', 255–6, 282, 285–6; and philistinism, 256, 327–8, 400, 479–83; and elitism, 324, 333, 369, 385, 411–12, 434–5, 441–3, 450, 452, 461–2, 479–83, 501, 529–30; importance of Synge's work to him, 358–67, 381, 400–401, 416–21, 432, 493, 501, 515, 522, 526, 531; effect of Italian art and culture on, 367–9; and French art, 388–9; Japanese influences, 390, 505, 525; visits Mont-Saint-Michel, 421
see also Johnson, Lionel; Symons, Arthur

SOCIAL LIFE AND MOVEMENTS: in London, xxvii, xxx, 63, 80–81, 90, 94, 161, 237; drug-taking, 109, 178, 182–3, 196, 204; visits to Paris, 138–40, 172–3, 194, 205, 207, 384, 386–9, 393–4, 439–40, 517–19 (*see also* Gonne, Maud); and Woburn Buildings, 154, 158, 160–61, 187, 221–2, 393, 433, 613 (n. 21); life in Temple, 155–7; to Aran, 166–7; at Coole, 181–3, 189, 195, 218–19, 235–6, 246–9, 266–70, 288, 294, 319, 321–2, 324, 337, 346, 370–71, 389–91, 408, 468, 507; to Italy, 367–9, 381
see also Gregory, Augusta, Lady

THEATRE: xxix, 137, 139–42, 179, 183–5, 188–9, 197, 200, 205–14, 221, 225–6, 235, 250–54, Chapter 10 *passim*, 317–29, 334–44, 346–9, 352–8, 369–70, 373–82, 402–6, 413–17, 421–4, 429, 439–40, 446–7, 453–7, 484–5, 505–6, 511–12, 533–7, 592–3 (nn. 25, 39); 'Theatre of Beauty', 257–8; 'Society of the Theatre', 484–5
see also Abbey; Craig, Gordon; Masquers

WORKS

POETRY COLLECTIONS (in order of publication):
Poems and Ballads of Young Ireland (ed.), 75, 85, 95; *A Book of Irish Verse* (ed.), 143, 145–8, 197, 218; *WO*, 78, 81–7, 90, 95, 100, 111, 129, 149, 250, 397; *The Countess Kathleen and Various Legends and Lyrics*, 122; *Poems* (1895), 148–52, 160, 208, 214, 218, 234, 314, 396, 486; *The Wind Among the Reeds*, 130, 492, 508–9, 520–22, 526; *In the Seven Woods*, 275, 287, 300–302; *Poems 1899–1905*, 336, 346, 358, 371, 412, 424, 457; *Collected Works in Verse and Prose*, 269, 370–73, 396–7, 400, 457, 486, 521, 531, 599 (n. 47); *Poems: Second Series*, 424; *The Green Helmet and Other Poems*, 388, 424, 434–5, 520–21; *Poems Written in Discouragement*, 422, 497, 501; *Responsibilities*, 490, 492, 508–9, 520–22, 526; *Seven Poems and a Fragment*, 477; *Collected Poems*, 82
unpublished: 'The Flame of the Spirit', 117; 'The Rosy Cross Lyrics', 117

INDIVIDUAL POEMS (by *VP* title; if not in *VP*, by the title under which they appear in the text): Adam's Curse, xxx, 182, 282–3, 302, 507; Against Unworthy Praise, 434–5; All Things can Tempt me, 390; The Arrow, 301; At Galway Races, 390, 435; At the Abbey Theatre, 455; Baile and Aillinn, 250, 301; The Ballad of Father O'Hart, 76; The Ballad of Moll Magee, 69; The Cap and Bells, 215; A Coat, 520; The Cold Heaven, xxx, 490–91; Cycles Ago, 116–17; A Dawn-Song, 56; Down by the Salley Gardens, 69; A Drinking Song, 435, 609 (n. 8); Easter 1916, 495; Ego Dominus Tuus, 518–19; A Faery Song, 114; Fallen Majesty, 475, 520; The Fascination of What's Difficult, 418; The Fiddler of Dooney, 216–17; The Folly of Being Comforted, 301; A Friend's Illness, 398; Friends, 436, 520, 609–10 (n. 17); The Grey Rock, 468, 476, 504, 520; He bids his Beloved be at Peace, 157; He gives his Beloved certain Rhymes, 157; He hears the Cry of the Sedge, 215; He remembers Forgotten Beauty, 215; He thinks of his Past Greatness when a Part of the Constellations of Heaven, 215; He thinks of those who have Spoken Evil of his Beloved, 196; He wishes for the Cloths of Heaven, 216; He wishes his Beloved were Dead, 215; His Dream, 434, 609 (n. 5); The Hosting of the Sidhe, 474; The Hour before Dawn, 520; How Ferencz Renyi Kept Silent, 56, 70; In Church, 96; In the Seven Woods, 301; Into the Twilight, 128; Kanva on Himself, 85; King and No King, 395–6; King Goll, 85; The Lake Isle of Innisfree, 72, 78–9, 109, 135, 233, 311, 497, 557 (n. 90); Leda and the Swan, 556 (n. 64); A Legend, 66–7; Lift the White Knee, 610 (n. 31); Love and Death, 37; The Lover mourns for the Loss of Love, 173–4, 215; The Lover pleads with his Friend for Old Friends, 196; The Lover tells of the Rose in his Heart, 215; A Lovers' Quarrel among the Fairies, 85; Lug na Gall, 69; The Magi, 520; The Man who Dreamed of Faeryland, 109; A Man Young and Old, 393–4; The Mask, 429, 435; A Memory of Youth, 467–8, 475, 520; Miserrimus, 149; The Mountain Tomb, 467, 475, 520; Mourn – and Then Onward!, 116; Never Give all the Heart, 316; The New Faces, 477, 617 (n. 104); No Second Troy, 395, 435; The Old Age of Queen Maeve, 301; Old Memory, 316; On those that hated 'The Playboy of the Western World', 1907, 399; Pardon, old Fathers, 508–9; Parnell's Funeral, 468; The Poet pleads with the Elemental Powers, 216; The Priest and the Fairy, 35; Reconciliation, 388; The Realists, 475; Red Hanrahan's Song about Ireland, 301; Running to Paradise, 520; The Seeker, 85; September 1913, xxx, 494–7, 521, 620 (n. 10); Song of the Faeries, 37; The Song of Wandering Aengus, 182, 216; The Sorrow of Love, 117, 149; The Stolen Child, 56, 75–6; A Summer Evening, 96; The Three Beggars, 520; The Three Hermits, 486; To a Child Dancing in the Wind, 467, 475, 520; To a Shade, 520; To a Wealthy Man who promised a Second Subscription to the Dublin Municipal Gallery if it were proved the People wanted Pictures, 477–81, 492, 496, 521, 620 (n. 4); To Ireland in the Coming Times, xxx, 122–3; The Travail of Passion, 159; The Two Kings, 476, 520, 615 (n. 60); The Two Titans, 39; Upon a Dying Lady, 486; Upon a House Shaken by the Land Agitation, 411–12, 435; Voices, 37; The Wanderings of Oisin, 56, 71–2, 78, 81–5, 372;

When You are Old, 117, 119; When You are Sad, 119; The White Birds, 114; The Witch, 520–21; The Withering of the Boughs, 235, 301; Words, 394–5

unpublished: 'I will not in grey hours revoke', 138–9; 'Subject for Lyric', 238–9

PLAYS AND DRAMATIC POETRY: *Cathleen ni Houlihan*, 248–9, 258, 260–62, 279, 287, 302, 312, 318–19, 320, 322, 324, 328, 348, 364–5, 393, 411, 428, 440, 513, 580 (n. 95), 591 (n. 85); *The Countess Kathleen*, 97, 110–11, 121, 125, 129, 149–51, 203–4, 207–14, 230–31, 248, 251, 252–3, 260–61, 276, 287, 290, 302, 316, 349, 363, 393–4, 424, 436, 449, 456–7, 468, 475, 483, 486; *Deirdre*, 321, 328, 352–3, 370, 372, 374, 392–3, 403, 440, 444; *Diarmuid and Grania*, 221, 236–7, 250–53, 319, 451, 575–6 (n. 81); *The Golden Helmet*, 382; *The Green Helmet*, 425, 433–4, 440, 510; *The Hour-Glass*, 278, 281, 289, 292, 318, 370, 390, 422, 433, 435, 440, 456, 463, 520; *The Island of Statues*, 34, 37–8, 81, 87; *The King's Threshold*, 291, 295–300, 304, 316, 318, 321, 334, 372, 398, 440, 514, 519; *The Land of Heart's Desire*, 137–8, 140–42, 145, 152, 226, 248, 250, 252, 302, 310, 319, 456, 487; *Mosada*, 37–40, 52, 55, 85, 246, 551 (n. 55); (adaptation of) *Oedipus Rex*, 334, 410, 413, 455–6, 612–13 (n. 13); *On Baile's Strand*, 275, 300, 302, 312, 315–16, 321, 326, 328, 336, 346, 352, 366, 440, 485; *The Player Queen*, 380, 385, 389, 393, 398, 402, 411–12, 429, 440; *Plays for an Irish Theatre*, 440; *The Pot of Broth*, 250, 279, 302, 318, 348, 359, 372, 377; *The Shadowy Waters*, 56–7, 137–8, 140, 143, 149, 172, 174, 183, 186, 218–19, 226, 234, 238, 251, 289, 318, 336–7, 352–3, 372, 380, 424, 440, 591 (n. 76); *Time and the Witch Vivien*, 37, 85; *The Unicorn from the Stars*, 269–70, 370, 374; *Where There is Nothing*, 244, 250, 267–70, 274–5, 279, 321, 372, 451, 583–4 (n. 55), 584 (n. 63)

CRITICAL AND POLEMICAL ARTICLES, ESSAYS AND JOURNALISM: 'The Academic Class and the Agrarian Revolution', 206; 'America and the Arts', 316; the *Arrow*, 353, 365, 368; 'The Celtic Element in Literature', 187, 293; 'The Freedom of the Theatre', 268–9; 'Ireland and the Arts', 246, 254; 'An Irish National Theatre', 298; 'The National Theatre and Three Sorts of Ignorance', 299–300, 418; 'Nationality and Literature', 131–2; 'The Reform of the Theatre', 296; *Samhain*, 253–4, 257, 262, 279, 298, 353, 365–6, 372, 392; 'Speaking to the Psaltery', 257; 'The Tragic Theatre', 429; 'Symbolism in Painting', 293; 'What is "Popular Poetry"?', 246, 254, 293

EDITED AND CRITICAL COLLECTIONS: *The Cutting of an Agate*, 421, 445; *Fairy and Folk Tales of the Irish Peasantry*, 64–5, 74, 76–8, 97; *Literary Ideals in Ireland*, 241; *Representative Irish Tales*, 98; *The Works of William Blake*, 98–101, 110, 127, 129

FICTION: 'The Adoration of the Magi', 176–7, 176; 'The Binding of the Hair', 157; 'The Book of the Great Dhoul and Hanrahan the Red', 125, 128; 'The Crucifixion of the Outcast', 565 (n. 22); 'The Curse of the Fires and Shadows', 129; *Dhoya*, 55, 68–71, 111, 118, 555 (n. 29); 'The Heart of the Spring', 129; 'Out of the Rose', 129; *John Sherman*, 34, 68–71, 78–9, 110–11, 118, 143, 175, 201, 396–7; 'Michael Clancy, the Great Dhoul, and Death', 132, 136, 564 (n. 5); 'Rosa Alchemica', 159, 176–7,

YEATS, WILLIAM BUTLER (*cont.*):
FICTION (*cont.*):
    569 (n. 51); *The Secret Rose*, 111, 132, 159, 176–8, 180,
    242, 258, 267–8, 466; *The Speckled Bird*, 6, 106, 143,
    164, 174–6, 203, 231, 233–4, 236, 245, 269, 346, 370,
    421, 466, 548, 568 (n. 13); *Stories of Red Hanrahan*,
    336; 'The Tables of the Law', 176–7, 278, 368, 390
FOLKLORE AND THE OCCULT: *The Celtic Twilight*,
    129–31, 132, 163, 214, 267, 291, 314, 389, 530; *Is the
    Order of R.R. et A.C. to remain a Magical Order?*,
    243–4; 'Magic', 245, 263, 293; 'Swedenborg,
    Mediums, and the Desolate Places', 464, 468, 490,
    505, 519, 522, 525–7; 'The Tribes of Danu', 170;
    A Vision, 489, 594 (n. 65); 'Witches and Wizards
    and Irish Folklore', 526
MEMOIRS: *Autobiographies*, xxvii, xxix, 10, 24, 32, 59,
    62, 74, 79, 106, 108, 109, 112, 114–15; *Dramatis
    Personae*, 167–8; 'J. M. Synge and the Ireland of
    his Time', 365–6, 417–21, 442, 445, 495; *Memoirs*,
    70, 153–4, 158, 173, 182, 226–7; *Reveries over
    Childhood and Youth*, xxv–xxvi, 492, 526–31; 'The
    Tragic Generation', 138
PHILOSOPHICAL REFLECTIONS: *Discoveries*, 346,
    365, 368, 380–82, 389, 398, 445, 594 (n. 67); *Ideas of
    Good and Evil*, 132, 134, 258, 277, 291, 293–4, 314,
    372, 505; 'The Moods', 293

Yorke, Father Peter, 305, 311
Young, Ella, 286, 301, 338, 386, 393
Young Ireland (1830s–1840s), 44, 90, 120–21, 146,
    402, 417–19, 442, 445, 452, 462, 493, 496, 528
Young Ireland League, 115, 118–19, 121
Young Ireland Societies (in Dublin, founded 1885),
    39, 41, 43, 45, 53, 64, 79, 112, 115, 184, 189, 551 (n. 67);
    (in Paris, founded 1896 as 'L'Association
    Irlandaise'), 172–3